THE AUTOBIOGRAPHY

OR

HISTORY

OF THE

LIFE OF JOHN BOWES.

"YET I BEAR NO OTHER NAME THAN THAT OF CHRIST, WHOSE SOLDIER I AM, AND WHO ALONE IS MY HEAD."—*Zwingle*.

GLASGOW: G. GALLIE & SON, BUCHANAN STREET.
DUNDEE: M'GREGOR & WISE, TALLY STREET;
BOWES BROTHERS, 16 FENTON STREET, AND WESTFIELD HOUSE.
AND ALL BOOKSELLERS.

1872.

PREFACE.

The following was issued some years ago, when I was not near so healthy as at present:—"Prospectus of the Autobiography, or history, of the Life of John Bowes.—Having recently read the Lives of several distinguished men, and been struck with the superiority of what they wrote themselves to the productions of their Biographers; and being aware that at my decease, should the Lord delay his coming, a biography may be expected, I judge that my knowledge of letters, events, and persons with whom I have associated during my whole life, will enable me to supply useful facts which would otherwise fall into oblivion. For between twenty and thirty years 'The Christian Magazines,' Annual Reports, the 'Truth Promoter,' etc., have given extracts from my Journal; but even these have been curtailed. At the moment of publication, reasons existed for keeping back what may now be published with advantage. More than one-half of my life is but little known to hundreds of my present friends. This volume is intended to supply the needed information. The part I have taken on religious, temperance, peace, and other questions; the Public Discussions that I have held, and the blessing of God on my Travels in the three kingdoms, will furnish an amount of information and incident which will be interesting to hundreds of my contemporaries. Let the Christian reader join me in asking the Lord's blessing on this production. Should any of my friends know any facts, or have any letters of mine which are important, they would oblige me by forwarding them to this address as early as possible, to be returned if required. The volume will make about 600 pages, octavo. It will be bound in cloth; printed on excellent paper; and I have consented to have my portrait in it."

I hereby thank my friends for sending many valuable letters. They will perceive that several which deserved a place in this volume have not appeared for want of space; had I inserted all the articles and letters which I intended, we should have had another volume as large as this, and as I had promised only one volume, I have kept to my original proposal. The vast amount of interesting matter not inserted will be preserved, and, should the Lord delay his coming, either during my life, or afterwards, it may some day see the light. I have inserted all during the first years of my life and ministry that I wish, and as to the last years, the Annual Reports and the recent volumes of the "Truth Promoter" will supply this defect. Some of the greatest trials of my life have been passed over without my saying all that might have been said, and perhaps some will expect more than they will find. For this omission I give the following reasons:—1st. Some of the evils occurred in Christ's assemblies, where, as in a family, the rule should be to cover rather than display defects. 2nd. Some of them have been most fully confessed to me and others, and, therefore, are as fully forgiven, and buried to know no resurrection on my part. 3rd. Some of the persons are alive, and to publish facts might impair their usefulness, without any corresponding benefit. 4th. I have not had room for more than appears of either good or evil, and for the same reason I have not given an Index beyond the subjects indicated in the several chapters, and as the Journal includes many incidents not mentioned in the headings, the book must be read through to ascertain its contents. I have aimed to honor Christ and instruct my readers, and to Him and them the book is cheerfully committed. It will be seen that I have honestly given, early views which I don't now hold. For the last quarter of a century and more, my thoughts of Christ's assembly have been generally unmoved. Throughout it has been my life that has been delineated, as I have endeavored to follow no men or churches any further than they followed Christ, as I have drawn my views from the Scriptures alone, for I am not aware that all the influence of my relations or Christian associates has induced me to adopt a single opinion, or resort to a single practice which I could not find in holy Scripture. I have endeavored to be myself and not another; to please God, not man, and whatever good may have resulted from my life and varied labors, thus far, to Him only be all the glory.

WESTFIELD HOUSE,
DUNDEE, 1mo. 1st., 1872.

AUTOBIOGRAPHY

OR

LIFE OF JOHN BOWES.

CHAPTER I.

BIRTH—MY FATHER'S STATE—INFANCY—SCHOOL DAYS—FATHER'S CONVERSION—THREATEN TO GO TO THE SEA—MY CONVERSION—OFFENDED—ACCIDENT—RESIDENCE WITH EDWARD DAWSON—A DREAM—CALL TO PREACH—QUICK TEMPER—GO TO A BREWER—JOIN THE PRIMITIVE METHODISTS—PREACHING IN VILLAGES—TRAVEL IN BROMPTON CIRCUIT.

I WAS born at Swineside, in Coverdale, parish of Coverham, Yorkshire, June 12th, 1804. At this time my father, also named John Bowes, was a very worldly man, addicted to swearing, card-playing, and even sometimes to night-poaching; but I never saw him intoxicated. His father's example of drunkenness, and the sufferings of the family through it, had set him firmly against it. He gave up swearing by a remarkable incident. He was out among the sheep under his care with an excellent dog, which would have done almost anything for him. But he got angry, swore terribly at the dog, which stood still, as if amazed, and would not run in any direction. This turned off my father's attention from the confounded animal to himself, and as he discovered that his swearing had alarmed the very dog, he resolved to abandon it, and from that time kept his resolution, although in other respects, unchanged.

The measles left me so restless, that I asked to be carried to a neighbor's farm house in my mother's arms. And as I could eat very little at home, I was offered something, which I accepted, remarking, "Our cheese is all crust, and our bacon all sward."

My first knowledge of an umbrella, was acquired from a playmate who could not articulate well, nor for a long time convey to my understanding what he meant by a *numb-a-neng*.

In 1810, we removed to Melmerby, two miles distant.

I went to an old teacher here who almost killed me with the sickness which followed his putting tobacco into my mouth. This he did for sport, which was almost death to me.

While here I visited an old neighbor named Binks, at Carlton. A tall, ill-looking young woman, as I judged, would kiss me, so she said. I determined otherwise, and fled into a stable. She followed. I climbed a ladder into the hay-loft above the horses. She was ascending the ladder, when I uttered a note of defiance, and jumped from the window to the street. Happily, I alighted on the dunghill, but with my tongue between my teeth, cut through in one part, and bleeding so profusely as to hazard life. For long I had to take only liquid, and years after could hardly articulate plainly, and to this day that all but fatal leap has left its lasting impression on the tongue. Had Satan something to do with this? Was he foiled in totally silencing a tongue that has been used of God against his kingdom?

When about 6 years of age, I was put to school, being then the only child my parents had left, having buried two daughters; one before I was born, and another a few years after, younger than myself. Here I was corrected for swearing: why I never knew. If I did swear, it must have been from hearing other children, and not knowing the meaning of an oath. However, I had the conviction that I did not swear. On the other hand, my father said he heard me. As several children were together, it is possible he might have mistaken some other voice for mine. Parents should be very careful not to correct their children without good reason, such as a child can easily comprehend. When guilt is not felt, chastisement is regarded as an injury.

In 1811, we removed to Carlton, where we lived several years, on a small farm under my father's uncle, John Dawson, who said to me some years after this: "Thy father got thy fortune;" from which I concluded that he either let the land to my father at a cheap rate, or in some other way, which I never knew, assisted him. But I had a fortune in my father's example and instruction worth more to me and to society than all his uncle John's wealth. At that time we kept horses, and drove meal and flour to Kettlewell, over a mountainous and hilly road. Often I went with the horses. Sometimes they were restive and refused the hills, and sometimes they tired. One mare wrought excellently in winter, even if she laid out; but in the stable, often tired in the journey, as she never laid down. These were trying times. I have known this mare so tired that she could not take home the empty cart. But my father gradually got into a better class of horses. Often I have known him go this journey, reach home at preaching time, and hungry as he was, feed his mind with the word of God, while his hungry body had to wait till after the service. This was a grand instance of self-denial. Like the Saviour at the well of Samaria, he had bread to eat which the world knew not of. After this we removed to some land and a larger house at the low end of the village. Here we resided when I found the pearl of great price.

About this time my father was brought to an alarming sense of his danger. The manner of his being convinced was extraordinary. He was standing with some of his neighbors, very likely talking about the world, or engaged in some game, one Lord's day morning, while a Methodist local preacher and class-leader, named Thomas Scarr, returned from his class. As soon as he came up to them he stood still, and began to enquire, since a well-known person had dropped down dead that day, if the Lord should call them away suddenly into eternity, if they were prepared? They answered him not; but what he said was a word in season to my father. He came home convinced of sin, abandoned his old companions, and began from that time to live for another and better state. He joined the Wesleyan Methodist Society. After this, I was kept from running to that excess of youthful folly into which my companions fell. I once got into a sad scrape when hardly 12 years of age, at a cricket match, near Cover Bridge. A farmer's son, named Coates, in years and strength above me, wished to play the tyrant over me. Unwilling to brook his insolence, a fight took place, when I gained applause for my courage and success, but only to fear that I should meet a more formidable antagonist at home, as it would unquestionably reach my father's ears before me. It did; but whether the report carried had pleased him, or he had thought I had been punished enough in my combat with so big a boy, this time I escaped chastisement.

My father used to take me with him to hear the gospel proclaimed, or insisted on my going at almost every opportunity; and I can remember being convinced of sin when about 9 or 10 years of age; but I did not yield myself to follow truth at that time. Sometimes when I had been playing at different games, from Lord's day morning till evening, when about to retire to bed, I was convinced of my lost state, and afraid of being cut down before morning. I continued to sin, thinking I should find more pleasure in sin than in holiness, and that at some future period I would turn to the Lord. As I advanced in years, I felt a growing attachment to the pleasures of the world, and a growing dislike to prayer and preaching, and found no pleasure in any part of the service, except the benediction, which set the unwilling prisoner at liberty. And as I got more attached to sin, and out of love with the worship and service of God, I began to be greatly dissatisfied with home, and the control of a pious father, and I promised myself more happiness in the world when I got from under his guardianship, as I earnestly desired my own way.

While at William Watson's school, the whole assembly of scholars was delighted daily, for some time, with a rencounter which took place between a new scholar, Christopher Walls, the son of William Walls, innkeeper, and the teacher. He used to visit at this house, and his familiarity with the family was removed into the school. He had played with the boy and excited him evidently for sport. He did the same at school, until the boy, when he teased him with his cane, called him all sorts of names, some of which I remember, as "a great beast," "a great bull beast," etc. The master used the cane; the boy laughed, scolded, and wept, by turns. I was very sorry when the master tamed him, and made him like the rest of the scholars. It was amusement to us, but suffering to young Walls, and a course not to be recommended. I continued at school till I was about 13 years of age, and made great progress in arithmetic, in which I delighted, but nothing else pleased me.

About this time I thought of leaving home, but my intention was unknown to my parents for some time; but being very young, I did not know what way would be the best to provide for myself. At length I determined to go to the sea. In order to effect this, I prevailed upon my father to let me go as a private pupil to our parish minister, Mr. Law, to learn navigation. When I had got near learning it, I told my parents I was determined to go to the sea. For some time my father thought that my talking about it would be all, and that I should not possess a sufficiency of courage for such a line of life.

He neither encouraged me to go nor stay, till things came to a crisis. I was going to send a letter to a person near Hull, to get me into a ship. My mother seemed always much grieved when I talked on the subject; and when she saw me in earnest and determined to go, her anxiety augmented. My father was a very prudent man, and said little on the subject; but whenever mother heard of any disasters at sea, she told them most pathetically, and asked, what if I had been there? When I had opened my plan to father at length, telling him that he had been at a great expense with my education, and it behoved me to do something for myself,—that I might rise from a cabin boy to a captain, he said: "Well, John, if thou hast a mind to go to sea, I will never hinder thee, only know this, *it will break thy mother's heart.*" He said no more. His weighty words sank into my heart. Such reflections as these followed: "I know she loves me dearly;—if I break her heart I shall never be happy again;—should the vessel glide smoothly over the ocean, I shall think, but my mother is in her grave;—should the winds blow a hurricane, and whistle wildly in the shrouds, while the waves lash the foaming ocean into greater fury, ready to swallow up the ship, I shall think—I am the Jonah, that Providence will cast into a watery grave for having rashly hastened the death of a dear mother." But such was my love of amusement that, should I not get more liberty, I determined to threaten going to the sea, although I seriously intended it no longer.

Many an earnest prayer was put up by my father on my account. One Lord's day morning, a Methodist local preacher, named Anthony Bearpark, had to preach at Carlton, in Walls' long room, and my father insisted on my being there. To this I felt an aversion so great that I went out into the garden and wept bitterly, but did not dare to absent myself; for I knew the danger of disobedience. The head of the house would be obeyed. It was well; for had I not dreaded the consequences of disobedience, I should not have made one of the congregation. The text was Prov. i. 24, "I have called and ye refused." I had not been long there before I was brought to an alarming sense of my sin and danger, and felt deeply sorrowful on account of having so often grieved a tender parent, and above all for having offended a good God. I began to weep profusely, but with reluctance before the congregation, lest they would observe me; but I could not refrain. As soon as the service concluded, I went a distance into one of my father's barns, to pray; and there I wept, and prayed in earnest, "God be merciful to me a sinner," "Lord save or I perish." I felt a degree of hope that the Lord would have mercy upon me, and I went home. But who can tell, but those that have been in similar circumstances, what gratitude and joy was manifested in my father's countenance, when he beheld the flagrant rebel repenting! When I saw him walking about so happy that he could not be long in one posture, again I burst into a flood of tears at the recollection of the grief that I had caused him. His sorrow over me ended that memorable morning in the year 1817. He lived 36 years after that, and I know not that he had an hour's trouble on my account afterwards. But if any one had asked him before that morning, "Who among all the parents in the neighborhood would be likely to have the most trouble with their son?" he would have answered, "I shall; for my son's love of play, and games, and sport, seems to swallow him up, and to absorb all other thoughts." God did more in one hour than all other agencies had ever effected before. I have abundant cause to bless God for such a parent. He that had often prayed for me, and frequently warned me of my danger, now exhorted me to trust in the Lord. That very morning he had urged me to go and hear the gospel by all the weight of his authority. Had he not done this, I should not have gone, and thus I might have remained in my sins to the present moment, or might have been cut off in rebellion.

Here is a lesson for parents not to allow their thoughtless children to neglect the means of salvation. When my son Robert Aitken was about 15 years of age, I desired him to attend an open-air discourse, which I delivered in Manchester, before one of my journeys to Scotland. He had an errand to go for his master, and hoped it might take him so long as to hinder his attendance; but it did not. He came; the word took hold of his heart, and from that night he gave himself to the God of his fathers, and could sing—

"And thou shalt be our chosen God,
And portion evermore."

These two instances of God's great blessing on the exercise of parental authority, should encourage parents to command their children to hear the gospel.

"Praise the Lord, O my soul! for He hath dealt bountifully with thee." It was about July, 1817, when I was thus convinced. I gave up my old companions, and joined the Wesleyan Methodist Society. The Lord blessed me many a time in secret prayer, and at the class-meeting and prayer meeting. Sometimes I could almost believe that my sins were pardoned; and at other times I had doubts of my acceptance with God. This caused me to mourn and weep at times, when I might have been rejoicing. Sometimes I have kneeled down to pray, and I have thought of wrestling and pleading with the Lord till he spoke peace to my soul. I have prayed this way for some time, and then have risen from my knees without any consciousness of the blessing; thinking, the Lord will set my soul at perfect liberty in his own due time: not seeing his love wished to save "Now." Here I lost my way; for I used to think after I had risen up, that if I had only continued a little longer waiting upon the Lord, and pleading the sacrificial atonement made by his Son, I should have got the blessing. I continued in this state for some months. One day I was meditating upon my condition, and thinking, "If death should remove me into another world, I don't know whether I shall go to hell or heaven." I had no assurance of heaven. I began to think thus: "What is the reason I have not got saved before now?—I want to be in the right way;—Lord, thou knowest that I want to be a Christian,—to go to heaven, and to go thy way;—Christ suffered for me; he died that I, through him, might live for ever,—therefore I love him." These words were applied to my mind, "Believe on the Lord Jesus Christ, and thou shalt be saved." I said: "Lord, I believe; help thou my unbelief." I could believe in him, and my mind was filled with peace. I had no doubt of my acceptance with God. I felt I loved him, and I could feel assured that the Lord was my father, and I his child.

My sins were blotted out; my soul was free; heaven was begun below.

> "My Jesus to know, and feel his blood flow;
> 'Tis life everlasting, 'tis heaven below."

Everything wore a glorious aspect. I expected to live the residue of my days without sorrow, cross, or grief of any kind; had no thoughts about temptations, or an alluring world. I had so little acquaintance with the world that I thought, "Now every one will love me, as I shall endeavor to serve God and do right; my parents will love me, and not disapprove of my actions; and all the world will be like them." Such was my simplicity. I did not know then that Jesus was hated by the world because he testified of it that its deeds were evil, nor that instructive text: "They that will live godly in Christ Jesus, shall suffer persecution." But I soon learned that innocency and simplicity, if associated with faithfulness to truth and God, can never exempt a Christian from the shafts of persecution, but will rather provoke them. For many years now, when I write this at 66, I have been blessed with exemption from this curse, " Woe unto you, when all men shall speak well of you!"

I continued very happy for some time, until one day my dear father threw a stumbling-block in my way,—he was angry with me. I was offended. We met together in class, and I neglected going, thinking I would continue in Christ's service as before,—that I might be as holy out of the class as in it. I neglected it one Lord's day morning; but I never was so miserable in my life. I was like a troubled sea that could not rest. I had taken two steps in the wrong direction. I had taken offence at my father, and thus, by refusing to meet him at the class, my course was downward. If he had wronged me, I should have mentioned it to him; if not, it was wrong to take offence. By punishing him, as I intended, God was offended. For immediately the temptation came, " Why not turn back altogether: I am young yet: by being religious I give up all the pleasures of the world; why may I not have them a little longer, and yet become a Christian before death ?" In going thus far the enemy overshot the mark. I saw the precipice down which I was about to be hurled, awoke from my delusive dream, and cried, "Turn back! What! to sin and hell? Turn back! From whom?—from God, my Father and best friend? Turn back! from heaven and eternal glory? No, never, while I have breath." Here the temptation vanished, and I was comforted, and I seldom stopped away from the means of grace after.

It was about this time I was going alone for a cart load of peat or turf to the mountain Pennel, when the horse took fright, and the cart wheel ran over me. I proceeded however, loaded the cart, and got home dragging at the end of the cart. But I was lame for some time, and ill, more like going into a consumption than otherwise. I could eat little but eggs, and they seemed to save me. I have said but little of my dear mother. She was not saved, although she loved me much; yet at this time, I dare say, my long illness tried her temper. She irritated me by inconsiderate remarks, till one night I almost lost my reason, and if sleep had not come to the rescue, I might have lost it altogether. I could not bear to see her in my room. Let this be a warning to all mothers not to teaze the afflicted. "They have enough to bear" without any additional burden, and it is very dangerous to the afflicted and sensitive.

I had frequently desired a young companion to walk and talk with on my journey through this world to the heavenly Jerusalem. There was no young person in the society at Carlton when I joined it, and they were generally aged Christians. Nevertheless I found the Lord to be my Friend: with him I could walk, and to him I could unbosom myself, and many a blessed quickening, soul-refreshing time I have had with my Lord in secret prayer. But I found a friend of similar views in an aged brother, Ralph Rider. Let his name be mentioned with honor. He only lived across the street from us; so that I often went over to "search the oracles divine" with him, and he seemed to take a pleasure in teaching what he knew to a very young disciple. When I began to strive to enter in at the straight gate, many people said, "Ah, he is but young yet; when he grows older he will lose his religion." These proved good warnings, for I was afraid of losing the great treasure with which the Lord had enriched me, and these predictions were incentives to watchfulness, lest they should be accomplished.

In November, 1818, my father's uncle, Edward Dawson, who resided at West Scrafton, requested me to live with him. My father told me I might either go to live with his uncle, or continue another winter at school. I thought I had as much learning as would be useful, and I accepted the former. Since then I have thought I did wrong, for a little more learning would have been useful in after life. This relative lived upon his own farm; milked four or five cows, and kept several scores of sheep, and one horse. He had only one son then alive, 6 years of age, who lived with his brother, John Dawson. He had buried his wife, and three daughters, before I went to him; and he buried a fourth soon after, and had but two daughters left. One kept his house, and the other was at home at times. Their father had a remarkable love to the English Church, and was a regular attendant. Sometimes, but very seldom, I got him to go with me to hear the Methodist preachers, and I believe he got good while he heard; but it was his decided opinion, that the Methodists, and all dissenters, were the false prophets and false teachers whom Jesus Christ prophesied would deceive, if it were possible, the very elect. When he got a little good, he used to remember these words, and I believe he thought the preacher should not deceive him. Sometimes I used to tell him the Methodists preached according to the Scriptures, and therefore could not be the persons alluded to in that passage; but nothing changed his rooted sentiment. For some time after I went to live with him I grew in grace and in the knowledge of Christ. Religion was at a very low ebb at Scrafton. Very few made any profession, and fewer still enjoyed the gospel. However, two or three were devoted to God, and when we met to honor Christ, his Spirit met with us, and did not leave us comfortless.

A cheerful and jesting spirit was always my besetment, and very frequently it caused me pain of mind when carried too far. I had the following dream: "I thought I was dressed for the cricket ground, and playing with the young men of the village with as much eagerness as any of them." When I awoke, no one can tell what gladness I had in thinking, "It is only a dream." But to me it was a warning. Worldliness and youthful follies were all around me, and I knew that if I could join the society thus employed, I could not retain the truth. There is nothing wrong in such healthy employment with a father or his sons, or a few friends, if they are confined in schools or shops, but as I had enough open-air exercise, I needed it not, and took the dream as a warning. Job xxxiii.14,15. It was made a blessing to my soul, and I was thankful for it; "For God speaketh once, yea, twice, yet man perceiveth not. In a dream, in a vision of the night, when deep sleep falleth upon men, in slumberings upon the bed." But when I applied to my heavenly Father, I found him to be according to his promise, "Ask, and ye shall receive, that your joy may be full." (John xvi.24.)

I used frequently to think, even before I was converted, that I should be at some time or other a preacher of the gospel: I cannot account for it. It was also impressed on my mind after I was brought to know experimentally that Jesus came to save his people from their sins. This impression grew stronger. I began to see undying minds of boundless worth to be in alarming danger, and that it was my imperative duty to warn them to escape from their impending doom, and to exhort them to get saved from self and sin by beholding "the Lamb of God that bears away the sin of the world." But the Lord had much to do with me, and I had a great deal to do with myself, before I would consent. At length I ventured to say a little at Horsehouse, about two miles from Scrafton, from the five wise and the five foolish virgins. I experienced much timidity and backwardness in my own mind at the beginning, but the Lord aided me while I was speaking, which made it happy work. I went soon after to hear a young man preach at Caldbridge, about two miles off. When I got there, contrary to my expectation, I was informed he was sick and would not be there that night. A congregation assembled; and as there was no society at the place, there were few who could carry on a prayer-meeting. Here I saw an opening, as I thought providential, but I did nothing but pray and sing, not having courage to preach. After this I exhorted a few times at Scrafton, and then the enemy got the victory over me in this, and I gave up publicly exhorting sinners to turn to God. I was convinced I was omitting my duty, and became miserable on that account. Sometimes I have been melted down into humility and tenderness at the means of grace; and when returning home have frequently thought that the Lord was good to me and blessed me, and still I was not willing to do his will, but wanted to do my own will; and I saw that it was impossible for me to get on in the service of Christ without doing his will. Convinced that I must either preach as well as I could, or perish, I shuddered at the thought of being miserable in both worlds; first to sin against light here, and then to fall into perdition. My youth and lack of knowledge stood as barriers in the way, so that I had given up all idea of preaching; but I lost my peace with God. How could I pray, "Thy will be done," when I was opposing his will? In this state of mind, expecting God to depart from me, I attended a fellowship meeting at Carlton, and was much blessed. On returning to Scrafton, by the side of the river Cover, concealed behind a hedge, far from human view, I kneeled down, and, with a full heart and weeping eyes, surrendered myself to God, either to preach or not, as it pleased him. My peace of mind returned. This was a solemn, a sublime consecration of my whole being to God—to Christ—to the gospel. While walking in my heavenly Father's favor, his food was sweet to my taste, and I enjoyed that hope that makes not ashamed, because the love of God is shed abroad in the heart. I went on my way, giving glory to God, as I was willing to speak for the Saviour when an opportunity offered itself.

I inherited a quick temper from my excellent father. Lest, as I took part in the religious meetings, Christ's cause in our family should suffer, I resolved not to speak one word while angry. An accident occurred likely to excite wrath. All expected it. My cousin, Mary Dawson, saw the blood in my cheeks, and pointing at me, exclaimed, "See how he boils there!" I was thankful that I did not boil over, for I was silent.

An incident occurred here which may indicate a singular mode of giving reproof. My uncle supplied generally what was needed while shearing the sheep, ploughing, or working on the land; but in haytime, I judged, when we went out with scythes to mow, that a little dry bread and thin or old milk were not sufficient. I contrived the following plan to tell him, what I could not otherwise: He went before, I followed, and only just cut the top off the grass. "John, why thou art not mowing at all." "Who can mow with a little barley bread and thin milk in a morning," was my prompt reply; and it procured all I wished. Of course I returned and did my work well.

During my residence here a young woman attended the meetings, about my own age, a farmer's daughter, Ann Walker. As she had nearly a mile to return home through a lonely road, I used sometimes to accompany her, but nothing beyond Christian kindness passed between us, although it created some talk. I went for a few weeks to Moses Rayner's, a farmer in Nidderdale, but I returned to Scrafton for some months, not liking the situation. In fact, it required a strong man, and I was not more than 17 years of age. However, when the marriage of my cousin, Ann Dawson, to William Utley took place, I was no longer required, as the husband took my situation.

In 1821, I left this home to which I was attached, and engaged myself, at Leyburn market, to the Messrs Wilson, brewers and malt makers, at Coverbridge, a mile and a quarter below Middleham. I continued with them six months. During this time my grace was tried, but my soul prospered in the divine life. Here I met with a few souls living to God, and when we met the Lord was with us, and made us rejoice in his presence. The family with whom I resided were all living in an unconverted state, and they requested me to do different things on the Lord's day which might have been done on Saturday night or Monday morning. Those things I refused to do, being determined through divine assistance to keep a conscience free from guilt. I consequently could not do these things and sin, as I then thought, against my God; but I avowed my religious sentiments when first engaged, and had liberty to attend the means of grace, so that this was a privilege I expected; however I was determined to offend man rather than God, and to leave my situation rather than injure my conscience. This I did in November, 1821. My soul prospered in the divine life, I enjoyed the smile and light of my heavenly

Father's countenance, and felt a growing attachment to the Lord and his cause.

I spent a week or two of this time in working in a slate quarry, owned by a Methodist, but as it seemed likely to be too heavy for me, in a stooping posture to hurl the slate waggon through the confined tunnel, I was obliged to relinquish it, although quite willing, when not needed at home, to do anything which Providence opened up to me.

About six months before this, the Primitive Methodists made their way into Carlton, and I went to hear what their preachers had to say. People called them "Ranters," and I expected them to be a lively, zealous people. I went one night to hear a preacher in the street. On drawing near they were singing one of their lightsome tunes, and my favorable opinion of them was decreased; although, before this, I was very fond of life and zeal in worship, yet 1 loved solemnity in singing. However, I went to hear, the word came with power, my soul got blessed, and good was done. About this time James Farrar came to Middleham.

Some years after this, a division took place at Leeds among the Wesleyans. Two eminent men took different sides on the organ controversy. James Farrar was with James Sigston, against the organ. William Dawson went with the Conference. Meeting on the street one day, Dawson said to Farrar, "How are you getting on?" *F.* "Very well." *D.* "Take care; for we mean to *pray* you down, *sing* you down, *preach* you down, and *live* you down!" They did not effect their object. But this incident shows the spirit of the men. If we would put down division we must do more than pray, and sing, or even preach against it; we must "*live* it down" by living a life of purest love—a love-life.

On Farrar's coming to Middleham, it was announced that he was one of the ablest preachers in the connexion, so I went to hear that holy, happy man. His words were honey to my taste; of a truth God was with him. Sinners were awakened and converted, backsliders reclaimed, believers edified, and God was glorified. Sometimes I thought of joining them; but it was the general cry of all the Wesleyans with whom I had conversed, "They will soon come to nothing: it will soon be over with them." I thought, if I join them and they fall away, it will bring me into disgrace; so I waited for some time. But, contrary to the expectation of their enemies, the work went on prosperously, God was with them, and some notoriously wicked characters, who would not go to any place of worship, went to hear them, and got wounded and healed under the word. I saw the work was of the Lord, and prayed that he would carry it on. Before this time, I had spoken a few times amongst the Old Methodists, but believed it to be my duty to join the Primitive Methodists, which I did in December, 1821. The reason of my leaving the Old Methodists and joining the Primitive Methodists was this: I had been a member of the Society about four years and a half; had attended love-feasts, and fellowship meetings; but during that period I never heard of any souls being converted through the instrumentality of the itinerent preachers. On the other hand, the Primitive Methodist preachers had many seals to their ministry, and much good was effected. Now, I thought, if the Lord was displeased with these people, then he would not sanction their proceedings in such a remarkable manner. I loved them for their zeal in the cause which they had espoused. It was a good cause. Paul says, "It is good to be zealously affected in a good thing." The work of bringing souls to God is a good thing; who, then, can blame their zeal? I could not, while it was according to knowledge. I felt united to them because of their spiritual life. "He that hath the Son hath life."—1 John v. 12. "The Spirit giveth life."—2 Cor. iii. 6. I loved them because of their humility and love. "The Lord giveth grace to the humble." We are commanded to "be clothed with humility." (1 Pet. v. 5.) Their love to God and one another was seen. "By this shall all men know that ye are my disciples, because ye love one another." Now, I thought, whether is it my duty, while I am casting my mite into the treasury, to help and support those men who are winning but few, if any, souls, or those humble men who are preaching Christ faithfully, clearly, affectionately, and constantly, and winning many souls? Here conscience spoke and said, "It is thy duty to help to support and forward, according to thy ability, these men in their work." I saw my way, and said, "Lord, with thy help I will do it." The following also had its weight. My father was intimate with a farmer and miller, who used to lodge the Wesleyan preachers in their fortnightly visits, and he told us the habits of some preachers. Some were like themselves, easily pleased with their food, (and well they might, as the farmer was in very comfortable circumstances, and kept a good table) others, however, and he named one or two of the preachers, prescribed what they would eat: they declined meat pies, which the family sometimes had, and preferred roast beef or mutton, etc. This led me to ask: "While our neighbor is keeping the preachers gratuitously, in love, are they proudly to dictate to him what they are to eat? Why should they not resemble the primitive preachers? It is not my duty to support such pride and lordliness," and thus I left them. Possibly they might have had me longer, but as I determined to preach where the Lord opened a door, and as they did not relish my co-operating with the Primitive Methodists, their narrowness also hastened my decision.

About this time I went to live a few weeks with a family near West Witton, and had a good opportunity of getting to the means of grace. Here I found a young man, some years my senior, who had left the Wesleyans and joined the Primitive Methodists. We had a large room to hold our meetings in, which might hold two or three hundred people. We used to exhort and entreat sinners to turn to God. Large congregations attended, and good effects followed; a society was formed, and God was with us. My soul prospered, and I could rejoice in the God of my salvation. When I began to exhort and preach in public, I felt much oppressed with the fear of man. I got over this one Lord's day evening, when I had done explaining a passage of Scripture, and William Haw was speaking, the young man before mentioned, I got such a view of man in his fallen state, of the exalted privilege and honor of the Christian, that all fear of man was entirely driven away. I saw sinners in the arms of the Wicked One, led captive by him at his will, suspended over the pit of hell by the slender thread of life, that, should this be cut, they would be lost for ever, and O what need of using every possible means in order to snatch them from this perilous condition. I saw it my duty to entreat them to come to Christ, to flee from the wrath to come, and thus to awake from the sleep of sin. From that time I was able to speak with more boldness, and had greater liberty than before. I could never open my eyes while speaking before this evening. For several times I spoke with my eyes closed. It was very painful, as the thought occurred, "The people may be laughing, or making sport of the discourse." Had I opened my eyes I should have ascertained, as it came to my knowledge after, that they were rather serious, and sometimes weeping. I began to speak occasionally for the Lord at different places, afterwards returning home. I had also more time for reading and preaching the gospel. I visited Melmerby about once in a fortnight, on Thursdays, where my dear father opened the meeting by prayer, after which I exhorted. Precious seasons! even to review. I used to go down to Middleham to preach, and many a blessed, soul-refreshing time I have had among the friends at Middleham.

One day I walked about 40 miles, from Coverdale to Burnley, and then went on to see some distant relatives at Bolton-le-moors. At Burnley, I got acquainted with John Moon. He had been a very ungodly man; so very wicked, that as he concluded he must certainly go to hell, he thought he should like rather to be a captain than any subordinate there. With this view he abandoned himself to evil that he might be counted worthy of elevation in the ranks of Satan. But he became so miserable, that he sought refuge from a guilty conscience in the promises of the gospel. He is now a Wesleyan local preacher; a captain in a better regiment than he contemplated.

Having a little money with me I expended some in articles of dress, &c., intending to sell them at home. One day, not being busy, I went to the suburbs of Burnley, to see if my purchases would sell. Going into a public-house, I was told that they would fine me for selling without a license. I had never heard of such a thing before, and was much alarmed. However, I was suffered to go free, and was glad to get back to my friends without being fined.

In March, 1822, I attended the quarter-day at Brompton, along with my esteemed brother William Haw. It was at this meeting I was first proposed to be placed on the Plan as a local preacher. The district meeting at Hull being just at hand, the superintendent preacher was nominated to go, and I was requested to preach for him till his return. To this I stated some objections; but these being over-ruled, I was prevailed upon to stay. The first place I spoke at was North Allerton. The Lord refreshed the people. The circuit was in a very flourishing state, and the Lord was with me, and made me very happy in the work, and as some good was effected, I continued to travel about three weeks, and then returned home, with a longing desire soon to return to spend the rest of my days in this important and blessed work of calling impenitent sinners to believe and repent, and believers to seek and obtain entire holiness of heart. I continued at home a few weeks, speaking for Christ when an opportunity offered, and felt a growing attachment to the Lord Jesus, and to his cause, and servants.

CHAPTER II.

ENTER GUISBOROUGH CIRCUIT—EXTRACTS FROM JOURNAL—OUTLINE OF A SERMON—GREAT SNOW—COMMENCED TO SMOKE—RIPON CIRCUIT—A CAMP MEETING—CONVERSION—OPEN OLDFIELD—REVIVAL—BECKWITHSHAW—HENRY SNOWDEN—MOSES LUPTON'S LETTER—MISS SADLER'S CASE—INSTRUCTIVE DREAM—NEARLY LOST IN THE SNOW—MISS PULLEN—INTERESTING FACTS—JOURNAL, ETC.

AFTER I had been at home a few weeks, I received a letter from Guisborough Circuit, requesting me to travel there. I presented it to the Quarterly Board. A committee was chosen to hear me preach my trial sermon at Middleham. My prayer to God was, "Lord, if thou hast not called me to preach the gospel as a travelling preacher, confound me before them ; but if thou hast, let me have my full liberty, so that I may know Thou hast called and sent me." The Lord blessed me with liberty. I was approved and sent into the Guisborough Circuit to travel along with Samuel Cookman, (Superintendent) and R. Baker. This was at Midsummer. Guisborough had only been a Circuit about a quarter of a year. We had a number of difficulties to encounter but the Lord was with us. I preached about a quarter without any apparent good being done. Sometimes I was cast down, and thought of returning home, thinking that if the Lord had called me to preach, by this time he would have given me some seals to my ministry. This was the end of my preaching. For this I prayed. When I turned out into the vineyard it was the earnest desire of my soul to spend my strength in labor, to promote the honor and glory of God, in the conversion of my fellow mortals, and that the Lord would give me the desire of my heart, but for the honor of his name.

Before bidding adieu to the Christians at West Witton, a dear young sister, who seemed to have some insight into the future of my ministry, said, with deep feeling, "When it is well with thee, remember me." She said it as a Christian sister. No other than Christian unity existed between us. It reminded me of another who said, before he left his sorrowing disciples, "This do in remembrance of me," and while we attend to the Lord's supper to remember him, he will not forget us. Thus I judged I should be remembered while praying for her.

I was now only 18 years of age, but robust, healthy, and joyful in the Lord. If I knew but little, that exceeded the amount of knowledge of the great majority of my congregations, otherwise I was too young and inexperienced for so great a work. My youth was not despised but honored. I preached at the opening of *Ayton* Chapel. So crowded that the candles literally went out, until some one called out, very properly, for fresh air. From here I travelled over the intervening hills towards *Redcar*. From these hills I first gazed on the distant sea, wondering what it was like, whether it would be dangerous or safe to walk near its mighty waves. What a mercy that I saw it now, not in self-will, but with a mind at peace with God and man.

Extracts from my Journal.

Sep. 27, 1822. I came into Friupdale, and had no appointment to-night. But Bro. Venis accompanied me to Castleton, 4 miles from Friup, a place our preachers had tried before, but gave it up last spring. We got a large room for preaching, at the high end of the town, and as no person had previous notice of preaching, we sang through it. Several people followed us up so that we soon had a congregation, serious and attentive. After I had done preaching, I told them we had an opportunity of visiting them again, if they could only provide the preachers with lodging once a fortnight, and that they wanted no superfluities. So we left them with the Lord. The man who lent us the room, sent word he would take in the preachers. Praise the Lord, O my soul. O Lord, " Hold thou me up, and I shall be safe."

Oct. 9. Spoke at *Ayton*, near Roseberry Toppin. A good time. This has been a good day. I feel it is well for me to retire to converse with the Lord and to converse with my own heart. I want to be more crucified to the world—more given up to God.

22. To-day I visited a young man upon his death-bed, who was previous to his affliction an enemy to God and a persecutor of his people. He was a strong, robust, healthy looking young man, but now laid upon a bed of affliction, and his body is wasting away. Now he desires the prayers of those whom he once despised. I asked him some questions about the state of his mind, and received satisfactory answers. He has a pious mother, who has prayed for him many a time. The prayers of the righteous avail much. What a wise God we have to do with! Had the Lord cut him down suddenly, he might have been lost for ever ; but his merciful Creator sent a slow consumption, to convey him into the eternal world, so that he had time and opportunity to believe, repent, and be saved. I see a great need of living every day as though I had to die at night, and give an account to God for my words and actions. My last day in this world is drawing near: how near I cannot tell. Praise the Lord, O my soul, for the prospect thou hast of spending an eternal day, without a night, with Christ and his holy angels.

Nov. 29. Spoke at *Boulby*, from "What hath God wrought?" Of a truth God was with us. Added two to the class in society. The last time I spoke here, a woman was brought to a sense of her danger while I was discoursing from " Choose ye this day whom ye will serve." Joshua xxiv. 15. All my sermons at this time were entirely original. As this was blessed at least to the conversion of one soul, here is the outline.—" Here are two masters, Christ and Satan ; for the world and the flesh are all on Satan's side. In order to choose, you must consider the masters before you, and their respective claims to your service. We judge of a master (1.) By his *disposition*. Is it kind or cruel? Christ displayed his love in visiting our earth and dying for us. Satan is like a roaring lion seeking to devour us. (2.) By the *table* that he keeps Christ provides for body and mind what we need. He is 'the bread of life;' we have only to eat and live for ever. Satan hungers his servants. The prodigal son, a notable example. I would not serve a master that starved his servants. Come to Christ, and you will find rest. (3.) A master may be judged by his service, whether it is *hard* or *easy*. Satan is a hard taskmaster. 'The ways of transgressors are hard.' So Saul of Tarsus found it. 'It is hard for thee to kick against the goads.' Not so the service of Christ. 'Take my yoke upon you and learn of me; for I am meek and lowly in heart; and ye shall find rest to your souls. For my yoke *is* easy, and my burden is light.' All that have tried his service have found it so. He makes all his servants joyful. The more they know of him and the better they serve him, the more joyful they are. (4). Then the *wages*. You know that 'the wages of sin is death.' Hell with all its torments, weeping, wailing, &c. This is the end of the promised pleasures of sin. But what does Christ give?—'eternal life,' 'pleasures at God's right hand for evermore.' The 'Well done,' and crowns, thrones, and kingdoms promised, the everlasting inheritance, &c. Now contrast the two services, and 'choose you this day whom you will serve.' You will not be forced: Satan *cannot* force you, Christ *will* not. His service is a choice. Resemble Mary, of whom it is said, that she 'had chosen that good part, which shall not be taken away from her.' How can any of you deliberately choose Satan—the broad way and its fearful end? Choose Christ, 'the way, the truth, and the life.'" During some part of the discourse I had said: "Some of you have been serving the devil twenty, some thirty, some forty, some fifty, and some sixty years; is it not high time to desert his service and turn to God?" Those words fastened upon the woman's mind, so that she determined to turn from darkness to light—from the power of Satan to God. For about a fortnight she sought the Lord with sorrowful heart, when it pleased him, while she was at a prayer meeting, to set her captive soul at liberty, and now she is going on her way rejoicing, and giving glory to God. "O Jesus ride on till all are subdued."

Dec. 1. Spoke at *Staiths*, at 2 o'clock in the afternoon. Before I went into the chapel I felt my mind disturbed. I felt a longing desire to see souls brought to God, but was tempted to unbelief. With no inclination to give way to the temptation, I retired into secret, and poured out my complaint to Him that said, "Fear not," for "behold I am with you always, even unto the end of the world." I went into the chapel, and, of a truth, God was with us. It was a solemn time. The Lord conveyed the word with power. I was much affected myself while speaking. It was a melting time, and many were convinced of sin, yes, I believe deeply wounded. After preaching, renewed tickets, and admitted 10 on trial; 28 in society.

Robert Southey writes: "Keswick, Jan. 27, 1823. We have not seen the face of the earth here for fifteen days,—a longer time than it has ever been covered with snow since I came into the country."

At this time I was in the Guisborough Circuit, with Messrs Cookman and Baker. The snow was so deep that we could not get to our appointments, but remained in the town, and conversed, and amicably disputed on various topics. One of our themes was: "Is the hope of reward or the fear of punishment the greatest incentive to virtuous actions?" Cookman was an intellectual and devoted man, but delicate. He died early, after leaving this circuit. Baker was of little use in any way. It was at the recommendation of Cookman that I procured the four volumes of Sermons by Samuel Davies, of America, and from that time to this, have always had a taste for superior preachers and authors.

They at once elevate and expand the mind, and when spiritually disposed, lift up the spirit to God and heaven.

While in this circuit, I was indulged with a strong pony when ever I liked. Two of the journeys are memorable. The owner, a kind miller, a few miles west of Guisborough, had friends in Coatham and Redcar, &c., and the Redcar Society wished a chapel. Twelve Trustees were appointed, ground bought or given, and I was sent to beyond Stockton-on-Tees, to order the bricks. Two ship-loads were sent. They were not readily paid for by the Trustees, and for a year or two after I was troubled for this account. This gave me a lesson about chapel building. I have long known that to get into debt for chapels is not the Lord's way to advance his cause: but it is really forwarded by the holy, every-day deportment of his disciples.

The other journey I took was to see my parents. John Harrison was then a preacher at Middleham, and he construed my riding about and appearance into pride, so that when I was appointed the following year for the Ripon Circuit, the older people were afraid of my being lifted up with pride. I labored there, at Ripon and the wide circuit, two years. It would be about 200 miles in circumference, and never had one encouraging word in the circuit town until I came away, and then they wept, as though their hearts would break, as though they would now make up for their unworthy suspicions.

Lofthouse was rather a favorite place with me in the Guisborough Circuit. On arriving, Robert Adamson, grocer, half Quaker, half Methodist, would get his pipe and commence some earnest conversation. On one occasion I asked, "How are you getting on at Lofthouse?" He answered, "One of our number has fallen down into the mire, and the rest are tumbling over him. What dost thou think should be done?" "That is about the worst use you can make of him. Get him up if you can even by soiling your fingers, but by all means avoid tumbling over him." He spoke of him as a man without energy either for God or against him. "If," said he, " a man will serve the devil, I like to see him serve him with some spirit, and then when he gets converted, he will serve God with some spirit." It was this year I began to smoke. I suppose father's example had some weight. I consulted a doctor: he thought a little would not hurt me. This was a wrong step. I smoked ten years, and it nearly killed me.

In 1823, I entered the Ripon Circuit. When in town resided chiefly with Thomas Chapman, grocer. He had not been long married, and his wife was often reminding him that they needed this or that, his constant smiling reply was, "And then we shall be happy." This appeared his mode of teaching her that our happiness does not consist in the abundance of the things that we possess. Another thing was admirable in him. It sometimes happened that we were very strongly opposed to each other's views in the Quarterly and other meetings. He did not conceal his views to please me, nor I to please him. But his nobleness of mind was shown when we came out that we were the same as before. I now see that such meetings are temptations to contention, unscriptural, and should not be held. They set Christians often at variance.

A camp meeting held on Ripon Common soon after my arrival interested me much. In the forenoon, I preached from "Thou God seest me." It was a great weeping time. The superintendent of the meeting about mid-day handed me a note: "Will you preach again?" Not being very well prepared, I thought seriously for a few moments, that a preacher should be always prepared, so I wrote under it: "I will preach." The concourse was now large, amounting to two or three thousand. I preached from, "Then how wilt thou do in the swelling of Jordan?" (Jer. xii. 5.) The people were less attentive. I expected a deep impression, but saw none. I was afraid I had made a mistake in preaching the second time. Some weeks elapsed, when I was accosted by a plain countryman in the street, who seemed to know me. I said, "I do not know you." But he replied, "I know you: did you not preach at Ripon camp meeting?" "Yes." "I was there: I came a careless sinner, was awakened, found peace, and now I am happy in God." "You had been there in the forenoon?" "No, I did not come till afternoon,—the text was, 'Then how wilt thou do in the swelling of Jordan?'" "Where do you live?" "At Oldfield, a village a few miles off." "Have you any preaching?" "Nothing but the Church, and no gospel there." "Have you a house?" "Yes, the largest in the village." "Will you give it for preaching?" "Yes, and welcome." We arranged for preaching, and my brethren went. I was just rising out of a fever, when he told the people the man was coming from whom he had got all his good. The house was crowded. To a deeply attentive assembly I preached the unsearchable riches of Christ. By the Divine blessing on our labors many were saved, and a Society formed. This resulted from my apparently barren sermon.

At BECKWITHSHAW, a farming district near Harrowgate, Henry Snowden, a farmer, came to hear. His wife, as they returned home said: "How did you like Bowes to-night?" He replied, "I like him so well I think he'll make me give over praying." He did give over for a fortnight, and then reasoned thus: "When I prayed, I thought I had some religion: now that I have given over praying, I know I am going to hell." The text and remarks by which the Holy Spirit had awakened him were, "If I regard iniquity in my heart, the Lord will not hear me."—Ps. lxvi. 18. I proved that men had better either give over loving sin or praying, or else by praying they were only adding sin to sin, since "the prayers of the wicked are an abomination to God." At the end of the fortnight he believed the gospel; began to pray in earnest, ere long to preach, and lived and died a few years ago in Wisconsin, where in 1866 I saw his widow, to whom the Lord also made me useful. She is indeed the sister of my dear wife, although the latter was unknown to me for some years after.

The writer of the following letter was President of the Primitive Methodist Conference in 1870:—

LEAVENING, JULY 17, 1824.

BRO. JOHN BOWES,—

May the love of Jesus fill and rule thy heart this day, and thy Brother Moses Lupton's. I now embrace the opportunity of writing, hoping to find thee well, as I am at present. Glory to God! Since I last saw thee, I have had many buffettings from Satan, and many blessed interviews with heaven,—a nearness of access at a throne of grace. I have felt prayer, together with faith in the blood of a crucified Jesus, to be the only support of my soul in the day of keen trial. I see more than ever that it becometh those characters that bear the vessels of the Lord to be holy, as much devolves upon their heads respecting the conversion of souls.

It's quite possible to get a great name as a popular preacher, to increase in knowledge and wisdom, to preach correct and systematical discourses, to be orthodox in our opinions,—and fall wide of the mark. Not having in possession that holiness that is our privilege we may preach, preach, preach, until we die, and never be useful except we live, move, breathe, speak, and walk in God. The Lord help thee and me. O be filled with God. It's prayer that makes the useful preacher. Reading, writing, and thinking, tend greatly to make a man shine; but holiness, much power in prayer with God will make him shine with more lustre and with a greater brilliancy, and he will be more useful in the conversion of sinners. The general enquiry is, "How shall I appear high in the estimation of men?" Let thee and me seek how we may be more useful. Pray more. Not that I would have thee understand that I would cry down or despise ability, no, but rather encourage every God-like method that leads to the attaining it. Let us try to be great preachers, and more so, good, useful preachers. The Lord bless both thee and me. Conference stationed me to labor in the Malton Circuit. They generally are a lively people. The Lord blesses us with souls now and then. Spoke in Newchalton Chapel on Monday, the 5th of July. Quite bound up, but the people felt well seemingly. I believe some were wounded. Held a prayer meeting the night after. Two young men professed to find liberty. We have generally good congregations. Some pretty chapels in the country. I shall, God willing, be at Bold-Kirby on August the 9th and 10th. I will come to Killburn, and if thou write me, thou mayest leave it at the place where you stayed; if thou hast not come, thou mayest send it with the other preachers. Give my love to Samuel Tillotson, and all enquiring friends, not forgetting to accept the same thyself. From thy brother in the gospel,

MOSES LUPTON.

He was born and lived, until he became a preacher, at or near Masham, a few miles from my native place.

While in this Circuit, I got acquainted with Elizabeth Sadler, the daughter of a retired farmer, William Sadler, who was also a local preacher. The preachers were lodged at his house at Monckton. She was one of the most amiable young females I ever saw. She attracted me by her sweet disposition, loved by all that knew her. She said: "I fear I am no Christian; for they that love Christ have all enemies, and people that speak evil of them, while every one speaks well of me," and it gave her undisguised concern. Possibly she did lack courage to speak of Christ openly before his enemies; but others found no ground of complaint. She was the only person that I ever knew alarmed at her own favor in society. Providence hindered our union by the following circumstance: It was her great desire that, should we get married, her father should live with us. This was not a matter for me, to propose. It was therefore agreed between us that she should mention her desire before my return. When I came back in the regular course of my plan to preach, I found her with reason all but gone. She could hardly speak to me, and was under medical treatment for lunacy. She said little, and was very low-spirited. When I got a convenient opportunity, I asked her father if he could assign any cause for this change? He said that she had mentioned her desire that he should live with us, and that he preferred rather a house of his own. This appears to have been too much for her sensitive mind, so that, between her love for me and her very dear father, reason reeled. My presence made her a little more cheerful, but several weeks elapsed before she returned to her wonted composure. I consulted my bosom friend, Thomas Dawson. He said her disease was hereditary in the family, and how distressing it would be if I should have to mourn a family afflicted, or even herself. After calmly reflecting on the matter, it seemed probable that if this trial was too great for her, others more formidable might destroy her reason altogether. I therefore went to the house several times after her recovery, chiefly in my appointments to preach, and refrained from mentioning, or even hinting at, our former intimacy. However, before finally leaving, when we were alone, I ventured to ask, if she was aware of the cause which had led to her state of mind? She was surprised, as I had been often at the house, that I had not mentioned it before. My answer was at hand. I had waited until I felt confident that she was sufficiently recovered to sustain no injury by such a conversation. She confirmed what her father said, and thus left me to wonder, whether one who had been so much attached to me, and was so amiable, should be resigned. Affection yielded to reason, and the subject seemed now quietly settled. After I left Ripon I saw her no more, and never ventured to write her; but was glad to hear that some time after she married a farmer, did well as a mother of several children, and never heard of any second attack. As a preacher of the gospel, often in the company of young women, it appeared to me wicked to trifle with their affections, therefore I spoke to none on the subject lightly, but with the sincere intention, should we be mutually acceptable to each other, as in this case, to be married. Yet Providence hindered. My life has been crowded with deeply exciting events. How Elizabeth Sadler might have gone through them who can say? It was well that she had an easier path.

I always had a great horror of two things: 1st, the company of the harlot, so killing to the bodies, minds, and morals of young men; and, 2nd, the unmanly conduct of any of our sex leading a confiding young woman to become a mother before she was a wife. As a woman's virtue is her brightest jewel, her highest honor, her greatest treasure for this life, to rob her of it is a grievous perpetual wrong, which all honorable-minded young men should shun as they would the dishonor of their own sister. If correct views on this subject were widely diffused, the black catalogue of our illegitimacy would soon be annihilated.

I had another instructive dream in this circuit, which guided me at every step. I had seen it duty to purge the Snaith society from a young woman, who acted as nurse during Mrs. Tillotson's confinement. She hasted to Ripon to report. I dreamed that I was pursued by an active young heifer, black about the eyes, and with considerable horns; but I escaped her. This young woman had very dark eyebrows, and some horn-power with my superintendent. We were five ministers; I was the youngest. The long, healthy country walks of this agricultural circuit, tended to the health of both body and soul. After being unwell, however, I started from Ripon to Carlton, where my parents yet resided. There was no snow at Ripon, but when I came to Coulsterdale to the moors, it was knee deep, and dark; the roads, only sheep tracks at best, had all disappeared. The sweat poured off me. If I stood still I became stiff. I was lost: however, I kept to the right, and the moon arose, so that in the distance I saw the lights of the houses, left the moors, and made for them in the valley; got to James Falshaw's at Caldbridge, where we used to hold the meetings. He brought me out a crust of cheese and bread; my extreme hunger made them the sweetest of any thing I had ever tasted in my life. I had now only two miles to go, over a well-known road. After this narrow escape I trust the Lord will make me of some further use in his blessed service.

Miss Pullen at KNARESBOROUGH, had been led to Christ through my labors, and I called to see her with her parents' consent. Some weeks after our correspondence commenced, she came one Lord's day a long distance to Grewelthorpe to consult me about some steps relating to our union. Her visit annoyed me uncommonly. I was known as only attending to the spiritual interests of the people, and here was a single, unknown female seeking for me. Of course I behaved to her as courteously as I could. Her visit, if intended to hasten our union, retarded it, perhaps hindered it for ever; not that I had ever made up my mind to marriage. We corresponded however until I left the circuit. She ultimately married John Cliff, Junr., tailor and clothier; after which they emigrated to America, where she died. Her husband and children returned to Manchester. (See T. Dawson's letters in future pages.)

At SPOFFORTH, I often preached among a simple, honest people with great delight. One Lord's day morning, while preaching, I remarked that I was thinking about speaking to them about such a thing: "Aye du, lad," cried out Joseph Hebblethwaite, loud enough to be heard by all."

THIRSK was in our circuit. Here a devoted man, in telling his experience, said, when convinced of sin, "I endeavored for some time to give it up, and seemed doing pretty well, but did not know what to do with these others," meaning his past sins. He found Christ's precious blood able to take them away. In a large village, close to Thirsk, on a fine green, and near the parish church, one Lord's day morning while preaching, a pompous little man in black came up, and with a consequential tone, ordered me off. I declined, assuring him that I had authority for preaching in that open place.

At CARTHORPE we had a good work. Many years ago, a man had been converted by the parish minister. Thinking that he might be glad to hear this, after many years, he called to tell him the glad news. The minister laughed at him, and told him he did not believe that anybody could be converted by anything that he said. It was well that he was well grounded in the truth ere he called on his former teacher. Whether he had fallen on the sermon of some evangelical preacher, and had given the people that, or God had owned his own read word, the fact cannot be questioned, both in this and other cases, that some unconverted preachers have been used of God in the salvation of sinners.

At MELMERBY, near Wath, a few miles from Ripon, preached out of doors amid great opposition from the squire and his agents. A forcible attempt to stop the preaching failed. A threatening whip by a man on horseback did not succeed. All this indicates that the aristocracy and clergy think they should be left in undisturbed possession of these rural villages, which, alas, are very ignorant of the gospel. Although there seemed much to alarm one for personal safety, yet, through mercy, divine protection was afforded.

At MARTON-CUM-GRAFTON, near Broughbridge, resided a dear brother and friend, Thomas Dawson; but I was very intimate also with Mark Noble's family. He was a noble man, and used to preach Christ in the market, while attending his butcher's stall. In harvest he attended the chapel when few could be there. "What sort of a meeting had you?" was asked. "Very good." "How many were there?" "Four,—

Father, Son, and Holy Ghost, and I." "How did you conduct the meeting?" "I sung, and prayed, and then exhorted, [I suppose he meant himself, to perform his duties] then sung, and prayed, and concluded." The meeting lasted about the usual time.

Here, also, a young man and woman absented themselves from the meetings under the plea that they were not edifying, and they got more benefit away. It was not long before it was found out that their own fleshly desires kept them from the public services. A child was born. I forget whether they married after. This was one of those numerous cases, where people act from one motive and assign another. It is a bad sign when people absent themselves from assembling together under flimsy pretences.

At GREWELTHORPE, I was hospitably entertained by John and Emma Boddy, his wife, Wesleyans. She was indeed a mother to me, and always as glad, or even more glad, to see me than as though I had been her own son.

When I was twenty years of age, there was a considerable amount of infidelity, although not so bold and eager for publicity as it was twenty years afterwards. The following is Robert Southey's account of it, *Life, Vol. V., p.* 184: "When I call to mind those persons who were unbelievers some thirty years ago, I find that of the survivors the greater and all the better part are settled in conformity with the belief of the national church, and this conformity in those with whom I am in habits of peculiar and unreserved friendship, I know to be sincere." This, of course, he speaks according to his own personal knowledge as a churchman. "A very few remain sceptical, and are unhappy; and these, with the best feelings and kindest intentions, have fallen into degrading and fatal habits, which gather strength as they grow older and older, and find themselves more and more unable to endure the prospect of a blank futurity. Some others who were profligates at the beginning continue to be so." The stream was then setting in towards the masses, and burst out in great fury a few years afterwards. "Accordingly, to my estimate of public opinion, there is much more infidelity in the lower ranks than there ever was before, and less in higher classes than at any time since the restoration." Many, like Gibbon the historian, were styled unbelievers because they did not believe in the priestism of Rome or England.

The following instructive letter is from a brother, Robert Stothart:

Beloved Brother,—

Grace, mercy, and peace be multiplied unto thee, from God our Father and from our Lord Jesus Christ. I remember that a few lines were agreed upon by us when parting among yon trees a little distant from Hardcastle Garth, and most likely you will have looked for them some time since, but believing that you are a person in whose heart are to be found the graces of love, patience, and forbearance, together with so happy an understanding and judgment, as to perceive the fickleness of all sublunary things, and fluctuations, and changes of terrestrial things which will prevent you from hasty decision and uncharitable conclusions, I indulge the idea of pardon and access.

Since I enjoyed the pleasure of your conversation, I have had the honor of visiting Mount Tabor, but did not stay there long, from thence I must spend some time in the vallies of marshes and quagmires, among thorns and briers.

My temporal concerns are as might be expected. I am in a school at Wolsingham, a town about 16 miles north-west of the city of Durham. It is a healthy but not a wealthy little town, close by the side of the river Wear. We have a little church in this town which is not quite so prosperous as it was. I suppose there is a great declension, and from the drift of what I learn whispering and backbiting have done a great deal of mischief, (1) that is to say the want of genuine piety It is highly necessary, my worthy friend, to preach Christ in all his holiness, and to press it with all the warmth of affection. Show the nature of it, and the necessity for it. In doing so you must expect to become an enemy to all lukewarm professors and hypocrites. (2) But God will be your friend. I have been here only a few weeks, and at present think I shall not continue long, I should like to see a few lines from you, and in them be so kind as to give me your address, for I have lost it. I am yours, very dear brother, in the bonds of the gospel of Christ.

ROBERT STOTHART.

WOLSINGHAM, May 12, 1824.

Address to me,—Robert Stothart, Schoolmaster, Wolsingham,.

(1). This always does mischief; but then it indicates the low moral condition of those who will not control their tongues. We should watch against judging any one uncharitably, and should not speak evil of any one in ordinary discourse. When we have to testify against evil, let it be as much as possible to the offenders themselves.

(2). They may be my enemies, but by Divine grace, I will not cease to be their friend, while I abhor their deceit.

This young man married an amiable Quakeress. I have lost sight of them for many years.

Extracts from my Journal.

July 18, 1824. LOFTHOUSE in the morning; PATELEY BRIDGE afternoon. The sun shone so much in our faces that I could hardly endure to speak, or the people to hear. In the evening, preached to a large congregation in the same place. Possibly I might have been more useful had I been more serious.

21st.—Finished reading the Life of Bensom, by John Fletcher, and was much affected when I came to his dying sayings, and could not forbear praying that a double portion of his spirit and faith might rest upon me.

25th.—SPOFFORTH at 9 a.m., and KNARESBOROUGH at 2 and 5, in the market-place, to a large and well-behaved congregation. A gracious, melting influence attended the word. We sang from the market-place to the chapel, where I preached again at 7 p.m.

26th.—Visited, and held a prayer meeting in the forenoon. Some souls in distress. At night, preached at KEARBY-CUM-NETHERBY. Some of the congregation unruly when we began, but the Lord made them feel before we had done. The cause is entirely the Lord's, and I give myself entirely to Him.

30th—TOPCLIFFE, at the Cross. Before I began, I went to some men who sate at a distance from the cross, and invited them to go with me to aid in singing. [I state facts as they occurred, but should not do so now.] They refused. I went up to the cross and prayed. I was much tried, as I did not know one face in the place, and had no congregation. However, I began to sing, till a few children came running up, after them a few old people ventured near, and at length I had a good congregation. After I had preached, I told them, if any of them would accommodate me with lodging, it would save me the trouble of a walk to Thirsk in the dark. A woman gently touched my arm, and made me welcome, as did her husband. He said, we Primitive Methodist preachers were like Wesley and Whitfield of old. Such were our difficulties nearly half a century ago, in our attempts to carry the gospel to the neglected localities of England. What if I had not got one hearer, the gospel might have been carried from house to house.

Aug. 15th.—We held a camp meeting upon RIPON Common. I and William Lupton, (afterwards a Wesleyan minister in Ireland) spoke in the forenoon. I never had such a refreshing time at Ripon. In the afternoon we sang from the town to the Common. A gracious influence rested on the people; but one of the preachers gave us such a long, dry discourse as effectually damped the assembly. Two short and pointed addresses would have been far better. A love-feast held after, in the evening, was much blessed.

30th. KIRBY-MALZEARD. I discoursed on "the love of Christ." J. Horseman on "Quench not the Spirit."

31st.—Attended the Quarter-day here; added 48 members in the circuit, which is prosperous.

Sep. 7th.—BORROWBY, near Thirsk, text, "Then cometh the devil."

14th.—Went to RIPON to see James Farrar. Was much refreshed and profitted by his company and useful conversation. He seems full of love, but what slow progress have I made since I saw him nearly three years ago.

16th.—STAVELEY. Text, Prov. i. 24. One man has obtained a sense of God's forgiving love this week, and went from the prayer meeting through the village, giving glory to God. Our congregations here have increased ever since I preached a funeral sermon, for one of the members.

26th.—Lord's day morning, LOFTHOUSE. Afternoon, J. Myer's Farmhouse, evening, PATELEY BRIDGE. This will show what extensive walks were often associated with three or four sermons on the Lord's day.

Oct. 3rd.—KETTLESING in the morning; text, Zeck. iii. 9,—"Upon one stone SHALL BE seven eyes." Many tears were shed. Yet upon the whole I have seldom been able for many years to adopt a singular text of this kind. Textual preaching should rarely be adopted, and as a rule singular texts should be avoided. Afternoon held a lovefeast at WEST END. Several spoke on what I have repeatedly inculcated, entire holiness. I taught the people to expect now, here, a present salvation from all sin. Evening preached at PATELEY BRIDGE. Retired to rest more fatigued than I ever remember since I began to travel with the gospel. Weary in the great work, but not of it.

10th.—MARTON-CUM-GRAFTON, at 9 o'clock a.m. Held a lovefeast at KNARESBOROUGH in the afternoon. Two souls professed to find the liberty of the gospel.

> Praise is due O God from me,
> When angels give it, Lord, to thee.

Possibly I was too long in my own experience, and should have cut short that of a woman. I want to speak and act just as my Master would in my circumstances.

19th.—KEARBY, near Harewood Bridge. After preaching, we prayed with a man who has lost his peace of mind. He used to pray publicly until tempted about his want of ability. He yielded to the temptation. We prayed for him about an hour, till all seemed swallowed up in God except the man, who felt a little comforted.

21st.—Preached at BOROUGHBRIDGE; not well. One or two prayed after. The presence of the Holiest was so much in our midst, that the class-leader declared he believed had we waited a little longer the Lord would have saved every soul in the place. After preaching got my feet into hot water, drank some hot milk and treacle, could eat nothing, went to bed, but did not sweat.

22nd.—Preached at BURTON Cottages. The Lord has saved a few here. Retired to rest, sweat much. Rose in the morning, nearly well.

23rd.—Walked about 14 miles to BORROWBY, felt a great stiffness in my neck, but as soon as I arrived, I took from my neck the handkerchief in which I had walked, and tied a silk one closely round my neck, and through the Lord's blessing rose well the next morning. Addressed two meetings here, and preached in THIRSK Chapel at night.

Nov. *8th.*—CRAKEHALL, near Bedale. Renewed Tickets.* Added five, two of them saved from the guilt of sin, the rest are seeking this salvation. †

Nov. *9th.*—NEWTON-LE-WILLOWS. We had singing through the long village, and a good congregation, but had not my usual liberty, having had no opportunity for retirement before preaching. It is a good preparation for public duty to read, study, and pray, and thus commune with God, ere we seek communion with men.

15th.—Having preached yesterday afternoon and evening to smaller congregations than usual at KIRBY MALZEARD, I intimated last night, that this evening I would preach on "Love to our neighbor," And to insure a large audience, I commenced this morning to go through the town from house to house, to invite all to the chapel to hear my discourse on love. I was a little timid when I began my visits, but could have invited the king before I had done. Many promised they would come, and honorably redeemed their word. The congregation was large, whom I addressed in these words, 1 John iv. 11,—"Beloved, if God so loved us, we ought also to love one another." I had never studied this text before this morning, but I had the love of which it treats. It was a daring undertaking for a young man of twenty, but in Christ's service we must hazard great things. I never regretted it. The people needed the gospel, and they got it both in my text and sermon. I resolve to give my little all to Him who died for me, and to be near the throne [I should now say upon it], so ably described in Watts' "Death and Heaven," which I have read with great advantage.

21st.—RIPON. Prayer meeting in the morning. Preaching, afternoon and night. Two or three professed to receive entire sanctification. Two or three seeking mercy. One got liberty in the afternoon, when my text was, "The cloud of witnesses." The night was a mighty time, from "Thou God seest me." I had never had so happy a day at Ripon. Jehovah's power brought me over all their prejudices.

---

* Another evil in which Methodism abounds, adding to the Society those who are not yet added to the Lord. It was right to accept the two, whom the Lord had accepted, but the three should have waited.

† This I now see to be unscriptural. The Preacher, or Leaders' Meeting, can withhold as well as give, and thus all hold their membership by a slender thread, whereas nothing but sin can sever us from Christ, the true church, and heaven. Tickets are an unscriptural abomination to raise the Quarterage.

29th.—Our preachers' meeting. At night a fellowship meeting. The best I ever attended. Two experienced the sanctifying power of the Holy Spirit. One, a travelling preacher, John Horseman. [I had more fellowship with his spirit than any of the rest. He travelled some years. His health failed. I saw him a few years after he had located at Sunderland, where he fell asleep in Jesus.]

30th.—The Quarter Day. John Kendall, one of the preachers, suspended.

During this month the following hymn was composed at WELL, Yorks. It will convey some idea of the very happy state of my mind, and what filled it at that time. Healthy in body, full of joyful work in publishing the glad tidings of salvation from a full heart, I thus expressed to Jehovah my overflowing thoughts.

> Giver of grace thyself impart,
>   Manifest THY great power in ME;
> Clear thou my views, and fill my heart,
>   While I now preach and plead for thee.
>
> Come Holy Spirit, assist in PRAYER,
>   Help me to urge the availing plea;
> Thy powerful arm in mercy bare,
>   That blinded souls in sin may see.
>
> Send down thy mighty, softening power,
>   Now break the HARDEST HEART of stone;
> Convince and trouble, Lord, this hour,
>   Then make the troubled heart thy home.
>
> The TEMPTED SAINT in mercy view,
>   Apollyon's fiendish rage control;
> The Christian's foes at once subdue;
>   And ever guard his precious soul.
>
> REVIVE THY WORK, this present time
>   Thy children's every want supply,
> Give them to know thy cleansing power,
>   The blood of sprinkling, Lord, apply.
>
> Let FORMALISTS hear that quick'ning word,
>   Which bids them strive the crown to win,
> And hearing take the two-edg'd sword,
>   And fight till they the conquest gain.
>
> See, Lord, the hearts that ONCE LOV'D THEE!
>   The abject wanderers restore;
> O may they here their danger see,
>   Believe, repent, and sin no more.
>
> The YOUNG in mercy guide and save,
>   Preserve them from the grasp of sin;
> The OLD alarm, should they not have
>   Thy truth, thy life, thy love within.
>
> The NEEDY POOR, true riches give,
>   Treasures that never can decay;
> May RICH MEN to thy glory live,
>   And boldly urge their heav'nward way.
>
> Pour down the Spirit of thy grace,
>   On ALL THE SOULS assembled here;
> That we with joy may run our race,
>   Till crown'd we on thy throne appear.

Dec. 5th. LOFTHOUSE. Preached a funeral sermon for a young man, afflicted 18 months. His illness was self-procured, by being at a dance.* After sweating he came into the cold air, and stood till he was nearly stiff. This brought on his long sickness, during which he began to seek the Lord in earnest. He was made happy, and died saying, "Glory to God and the Lamb for ever and ever!" It was a melting time while I discoursed from Job xiv. 14 : " All the days of my appointed time will I wait, till my change come." Walked to PATELEY BRIDGE, and preached afternoon and evening. A hard place.

6th.—At GREENHOWHILL. Came up amid wind, rain, and snow; got wet, changed my clothes, and preached here for the first time. We have no society yet. To-night I met with an old friend, who told me that I should be obliged to speak lower, or I should soon weaken my constitution. Perhaps there is some truth in the remark. [I am willing to give the Lord all my strength; but have often asked him that I may just speak so long and loudly as will be for the best. He has given me a power over the voice for many years, whether in the open-air or in-doors, which very few possess. To Him be the praise.]

31st.—Thus ends the blessed year of 1824. I have read the Bible through this year, and for six months or more, especially, have been entirely dedicated to God through his truth. At 7 p.m. preached at HUMBURTON. Here a brother is a local preacher, who cannot read! After preaching walked 8 miles into Ripon to the Watch Night.

Jan. 3rd., 1825.—SNAPE in the morning; MASHAM, at 2 and 6 p.m. Some wept, others rejoiced, while I discoursed from Psa. cxlii. 4 : " No man cared for my soul." Some who had heard me on the text before desired to hear me again.

10th.—GRANTLY. Preached a short time, and held a fellowship meeting after. This gives the members an opportunity of unfolding their views of divine truth. I had rather hear this than their own feelings.

20th.—At MARTON-CUM-GRAFTON. Went round from house to house in Grafton to invite people to the chapel. In the evening had good liberty in addressing them. Here a few have been saved, and believers are thirsting after more holiness.

22nd.—ARKENDALE. Spent most of the day in the society of that blessed old preacher, Robert Harrison, who had travelled 31 years among the Wesleyan Methodists, but left them some years ago. My father esteemed him highly. He gave me some advice which will be useful. He recommends to keep a variety of preachers, and to "lay hands suddenly on no man." No doubt this counsel has been departed from. The Primitive Methodists have many efficient preachers, whose usefulness is hindered by being yoked with a very different class.

23rd.—STAVELY at 9; BOROUGH BRIDGE at 2 ; RIPON at 6. This day's labors shows how we scattered the good seed far and near on one day.

24th.—OLDFIELD. A large congregation. Many were much affected.†

29th.—Having preached during the week at Pateley Bridge, Ramsgill, and Lofthouse, I crossed the moors to-day to see my parents at CARLTON. The Lord enabled me to speak lovingly and plainly to my dear mother, yet unsaved. Returned over the mountain, and preached at MIDDLESMOOR at night. Eight in Society.

---

* See my tract on Dancing, No. 161. † See page 17.

30th.—LOFTHOUSE in the morning. One of the most affecting times I have had in this neighborhood. The greater part of the congregation bathed in tears, and I was much moved while I entreated the audience in these words, "Pay thy vows."

31st.—GREENHOWHILL; a very crowded house. I sweat much, although I put off my coat.

Feb. 1st.—Met with an old Methodist Magazine of 1780, in which I read with much edification the lives of Gregory Lopes, a hermit, Thomas Hanby, T. Taylor, Lee, and Mitchell, after which I went to the PLATTS and expounded the Lord's Prayer. I resolve, by the help of God, to be more sparing in words, "slow to speak," to be more watchful, and more earnest in the momentous work in which I am engaged. I preached at LOW LAITHS, and formed a class of seven members.

8th.—At EAVESTONE, where we have a prosperous society of very affectionate people, chiefly farmers.

Before leaving Ripon, the following encouraging letter reached me from my friend Moses Lupton:—

HOVINGHAM. MAY 8th, 1825.

DEAR BROTHER BOWES,—

. . . . I am appointed for Dewsbury Circuit. Let me know particulars, and where you are going to labor for the ensuing year. I hope you are making some advancement in the divine life, growing more like Jesus, living for eternity, breathing in God. Glory, glory be to Jesus! he has my heart, all of it. Praise his name for ever! he has " sanctified my soul." O for more of God—for a filling and letting into God. O, John, live for God and souls! Since I came into this circuit, the Lord has given me many souls; perhaps within the last month I have had 30 souls. In my last round, my first Sunday in Malton, the converts, I think, were past counting; for the cries of penitents for pardon and that of believers for holiness were so numerous that scarcely anything else could be heard. There likewise on Monday night 14 more, all crying for pardon and holiness. They tumble about like ewes on the floor. It continued through the week, and on the Sunday following at Malton, 6 or 10 professed to find the Lord: I think 2 on Monday night, 1 on Friday night, and 2 on Saturday at Coneysthorpe. On Wednesday I got liberty and rejoiced in God her Saviour. Yesterday, at Hovingham, 1 found the Son of David, and many more are wounded. Glory be to God! for he hath done marvellously. "What hath God wrought?" To God be all the glory; for it is he that moveth the waters. Well, my brother, there is yet a fountain open. Thousands more want washing. Take your shepherd's bag and sling; search in the Book of God with prayer for stones; let faith cast them, and Goliath of England shall fall. May heaven help you. O what a blessed work is winning souls. My God help me, John; I want to be useful. Sinners are dying and falling into hell. Cry aloud, and spare not. Pray for me, My soul delights in Jesus. O precious Saviour—what a God! what a King! what a Friend! what a Comforter! Why, He is mine! Glory, glory! I feel him while I am writing, warming my heart. A glimpse of bright glory overpowers my soul. O the Celestial Court, how delightful! May the Lord bring you and me there to dwell for ever. . . . . Give my love to all your preachers and all enquiring friends. Accepting the same from thy brother in the gospel of Christ,

MOSES LUPTON.

Having been two years in the wide Ripon Circuit, I preached farewell sermons in most of the places, many of which are not even mentioned in my Journal, and the following hymn, which I composed for the occasion, was generally sung amid flowing tears, (as it was also in Keighley, with even more feeling, two years later) for very few of us ever met again; nor shall we, till summoned to the marriage supper of the great Bridegroom.

A FAREWELL HYMN COMPOSED BY J. BOWES, ON LEAVING RIPON CIRCUIT, JUNE, 1825.

Farewell to you my brethren dear,
  From you now I must remove;
Oft our Saviour's met us here,
  Oft he's fill'd our hearts with love:
Let's adore him, till we join our friends above.

Farewell sinners, still regardless
  Of your state, and woeful doom;
If you perish, I am guiltless;
  But remember, you're undone.
If rebellious: Hell will prove your lasting home.

Fare-you-well, whose new vocation
  Is the service of the Lord;
Expect foes and tribulation,
  Gird your arms, and wield your sword,
Fight ye warriors! till you win yon high abode.

Aged pilgrims, farewell, farewell,
  Soon you'll quit this vale of tears,
In your blood-bought mansions dwell,
  Dwell with Christ to endless years.
Hallelujah! banish then your doubts and fears.

Fare-you-well, my babes in Jesu,
  Here we never more may meet,
But be faithful, and I'll join you,
  To sing round our Sovereign's seat;
There to cast our glorious crowns at Jesus' feet.

Farewell all my loving friends,
  Soon life's troubles will be o'er;
Soon our glorious Guide will place us
  Where immortals part no more:
Loud we'll praise him! as we land on Canaan's shore.

CHAPTER III.

JOURNAL IN KEIGHLEY CIRCUIT—THOMAS DAWSON'S LETTERS—B. GODWIN'S SERMON—MANY CONVERSIONS—A GREAT REVIVAL—ANSWER TO A CHALLENGE—MISS MARIA BARRETT—LETTER TO MISS S. BELLWOOD—MARRIAGE—JOURNAL CONTINUED—THE APPEARANCE OF WILLIAM CLARKSON TO WILLIAM MANN AFTER DEATH.

KEIGHLEY CIRCUIT.

July 18th.—I visited from house to house at ADDINGHAM, as the Society was disturbed if not rent. I labored to settle all disagreements as well as possible. They have risen principally through the class-leader, who needs more meekness and humility. At 8 o'clock I preached in the open-air to an attentive congregation, after which I met the Society, and put in another leader. I am glad to-night all seemed peace.

19th.—I went to seek up some poor lost sheep, lost, as I have reason to believe principally through the carelessness and rashness of the leader, and left them with 32 in Society. At night I felt it good to wait upon the Lord at WEST MORTON, where I preached and met the Society, 12 in number, but many have lost a great part of the life of God. Some few seem to have an evidence of their acceptance with God.

21st.—At UTLEY very few present. Only eight came I remember once on a very wet night, to this place, and I pondered whether it should be a prayer meeting, but when I considered that those who came expected a sermon, and that they were not to blame for those who did not come, I resolved to give them in full as good a sermon as I could; and this is a good plan. Our Saviour preached to one woman at the well, and, like her, should one get saved out of eight, that one may lead many others to know the glorious gospel. We may look at the mass and despair, but one saved gives joy in heaven.

25th.—Our chapel, KEIGHLEY, preached a sermon to the Provident Society. The chapel was nearly full. I have reason to believe that the Lord touched some of their hearts. At night preached at RYCROFT with more than usual liberty. The people were attentive, and they seem affected, but they have not much life and zeal, apparently. O Lord, "Revive thy work" in my soul and theirs.

31st.—At MORTON BANKS at 10. A mighty moving. Some hard hearts were affected. At KEIGHLEY half-past 1 and 5. A good day this has been to my soul. It was so hot I put off my coat at night.

Aug. 1st.—At 2 o'clock I spoke at FELL LANE in the open-air, (it being their *tide* or *feast*) to a serious and well-behaved congregation. At night at KEIGHLEY, from the Lord's Prayer. Many attended, I believe not in vain, for the Lord was among us in a special manner.

2nd.—At OLDFIELD in the afternoon. We began in the open-air, but the wind was strong and I was weak in body, owing to the heat of the weather and too much labor, so I spoke in the house to an attentive and weeping congregation, but they were much more so at night, about a mile further up. I think I never felt more of the power of God than this night, though I had such pain in my breast that I was obliged to stop and get them to sing a verse till I got a little better.

3rd.—Took a little rest to-day, and attended a prayer-meeting at KEIGHLEY. Got my spiritual strength renewed.

Having discovered that I should be left alone in this circuit, I invited Thomas Dawson to come to my help. This is his reply:—

GRAFTON, AUG. 1st., 1825.

MY DEAR J. BOWES,—

That grace, mercy, and peace may be multiplied upon thy head, and in thy heart, is the sincere prayer of my soul. Amen. I received thy letter on the 14th July, and felt pleasure in perusing its contents. I am happy to hear thou art in health, and affectionately received by the people. My dear John, labor for souls, and in order to have that for which thou laborest, fast so much as the keeping to thy work will admit. Pray much, pray often, pray always; by this means thou wilt always keep in a devotional spirit, always be getting or doing good. Rise early; write much; read more; shake thyself from all filthy conversation, and gossipping fables; act the Christian; play the man; live for God, for souls, and for immortal glory. O, my John, immortal glory shall soon be ours. I am in full stretch for all that can be enjoyed in this life, and am anxiously desiring, yet patiently waiting, the time of my departure. We are all well at Marton, and much as usual. I have attempted getting a few of us to meet together on a Saturday night, to groan before the Almighty for the prosperity of Zion, and adopt measures for the carrying on of the work of God: such as, short and quick singing, short and pointed prayer, fasting at the least one meal per week, reproving sin wherever we see it; and it is my intention, as soon as opportunity serves, to try to get a quarterly fast throughout the circuit, regularly. O, John, we want the work deepening. I think this means will be calculated to answer the end, if attended to. Mark's were not satisfied that thou didst not send thy love to them: they send their love to thee. I believe they would be glad to receive a letter from thee; they respect thee much. I saw J.P. [Jane Pullen] last Sabbath, and got tea at her house. She is well; but I think not quite so lively as usual. I still approve thy choice; but would have thee impress spiritual things much upon her mind in thy correspondence with her. The new preachers in this Circuit are very well received. Thompson is a very good preacher; for anything further, I cannot as yet say. I have not answered A.B.'s letter, but think of answering it next week. There are some things in it I much admire; others there are that say it is only a female. Since I have got the letter, I have sometimes thought there is a Divine Providence in it, and that after all we shall go together. How the matter will end I cannot say. I hope thou wilt write to me again soon, and write me all thy mind. There is a little incorrectness in this letter, but I think thou wilt overlook that, and believe me to be as ever thy faithful friend and brother in Christ Jesus,

THOS. DAWSON.

He afterwards married Miss Slater, a sister in Christ at Newton-le-Willows, who bore him a large family.

7th.—Preached at RYCROFT in the morning, and held a love-feast in the afternoon. It was a solemn, useful love-feast. Some men rather got wrong in setting tunes few of their brethren could sing. This is a sad mistake.

9th.—Having much pain in a tooth, the farthest on the lower jaw, I went to get it pulled out. After the doctor had tried about half an hour and put me to inexpressible pain, I found he could not get it out.

13th.—I have been unable to preach since the *9th*, owing to my mouth swelling to such a degree that I could hardly talk; however, the pain is gone, and I have the tooth yet.

14th.—Preached two sermons in the DUDLEY HILL Chapel, Bradford Circuit, for the benefit of the Sunday School. At night I felt much liberty, and I believe the people felt the power of God. The chapel was nearly filled both times. The sum of £2 10s collected for the school.

15th.—Got to KEIGHLEY, and preached in the chapel, from "To me to live is Christ, and to die is gain." Felt the influence divine. To-day, received this from my faithful friend and brother Dawson:—

OCTOBER 15th, 1825.

MY DEAR BOWES,—

In compliance with thy request, I put my pen to paper once more. I have no fear of our corresponding letters being opened by any but ourselves. On the 17th or 18th of September, P.B. [Philip Bellwood] and myself set off for Leeds. In our way we called at K——, and saw J. P. [Jane Pullen], when we informed her that we were coming to Keighley to see thee, which was then our intention, and I did then think P. B. would not go back to his circuit on account of the unhealthfulness of the country, but come to assist thee, as thou wast in want of help; but when we got to Leeds he was taken ill, and we thought it advisable to move homewards, and did so. When P. B. got home, he received a letter stating that the preacher he left in the Circuit was dead, therefore was determined, live or die, to go back. I expect to hear from him soon. As it regards thy studying the languages mentioned, thou hast my approbation; but I scarce know what to say about thy connection with J.P., only it strikes me, if thou doest right, J.P. is the girl; but I fear thou art a conquered man. Oh, John, do beware; her equal will not be easily found. It is true money is wanting, but I fear that shouldest thou get money in another, yet other things of greater value will not be there. REMEMBER the manner in which you were first brought together; the affection you have felt for each other; and her suitability for a preacher's wife. J.P. still maintains an unspotted character. The work at Knaresbro' is at a stand. We are going to get shot of C——'s, Senr. and Junr, and the place, and I am glad. My advice is, keep up thy acquaintance with J.P. as a faithful lover [See my remarks, p. 20]. Get a young man into the circuit; get it clear of debt; marry J.P. next April or May; then you will stand as usual—one married and one single man for Keighley.

Nothing more has past in my correspondence with A.B. of C——, excepting that I answered her letter. I could like things to be decided, but to have them done honorably. I should like to see thee much. If thou hast not been over to see thy parents, defer thy going till Christmas, and I will endeavor to meet thee there, but will write to thee again first. We are doing well in the circuit: the preachers suit us well, and are useful, faithful, loving men. I was at Ripon on Sunday; they are doing better, and are all well. T. Chapman seems astonished that thou hast not written to him. I have thought of paying my addresses to another person, but shall not as yet.

I have no inclination to go out to travel at present. I think the Lord seems to be opening my way at home a little. We have had some good done at Marton lately. Our congregations increase, and we have favorable prospects at present. I am well and happy, and determined to live to God. Mark's join in love to thee. Do, my dear John, live for God. Labor to enjoy that fulness which is held forth unto thee in the Word of God. Do breathe in a pure air. Keep disentangled. Make a practice of going from thy knees into the pulpit, and do not let thy devotions in private be a mere form. Endeavor every time thou bowest thy knee to catch a few fresh sparks of the living fire. This manner of living will make thee a blessing to the people; for while they stand in awe of thee, they will love thee. I conclude with charging thee to keep up thy correspondence with J. P., assuring thee that I have written according to the dictates of my own conscience, while I still remain thine, as ever, THOMAS DAWSON.

16th.— At WEST MORTON. A full house and a powerful time. Met the class. Renewed tickets. Excluded six and added one. Lord have mercy upon those I have excluded, for they will not obey thy word. I found this one of the means which the Lord blessed in all this circuit, removing unworthy members.

19th.—My colleague went with me to open HARDEN, an old place that had been tried and given up. I spoke in the open-air till it was dark, and then held a class meeting and formed a society of 4 members.

21st.—Sunday. At MORTON BANKS at 10; KEIGHLEY at 1½ and 6. We had a mighty moving in the morning. In the afternoon I felt a heavenly sweetness of soul in preaching the word of life.

22nd.—We had our chapel in KEIGHLEY re-opened by Benjamin Godwin, M.A., Baptist minister. The following is an outline of his sermon:— Nahum i. 7, 'The Lord is good, a stronghold in the day of trouble, and he knoweth them that are his.' The Lord's justice is known by the convulsions of nature. There are only two ways by which we can arrive at a knowledge of God,—by revelation and the works of creation. We could never have arrived at any certain knowledge of God by the latter. I. What the Lord is in HIMSELF. II. What he is TO HIS PEOPLE. To attempt to prove that the Lord is good, is like proving that light comes from the sun, and heat from the fire ; but (1) He is essentially good : all the goodness of men or angels is derived from Him. His goodness is underived. (2) He is infinitely good : we can place no bounds to his goodness. (3) He is universally good. There is no part of his nature defective ; he is good to all. (4) He is unchangeable, and he changes not for the worse ; for the better he cannot. II. What he is TO HIS PEOPLE. (1) A stronghold in the day of trouble. To this point the Christian tends in his distress. Refer to the strongholds of Babylon and Tyre. 'The Lord knoweth them that are his' with a knowledge of, 1st Affection, 2nd Approbation."

24th.—The New Connexion preacher spoke for me at Fell Lane. Not many people.

25th.—Held a prayer meeting in Keighley, after visiting some sick people. I felt in a devotional state of mind.

26th.—I spoke in Eastward Row in the open-air; after which we held a prayer meeting. Some were affected under the Word.

29th.—Monday. Attended the Quarter Day. It was found that the circuit in its present state would not support both a married and a single preacher, so it was agreed that Eli Barroclough should go away.

30th.—Spoke with much liberty at SCARTOP to a large congregation. Here lived John Judson, preacher. Held a prayer meeting for a few minutes after, and I think I felt better than while preaching. I think if we had more praying and less preaching more good would be done. Is not this a mistake? Should we not have more of both?

Sep. 16th.—Spoke in HARDEN. Felt it good within, while Satan raged without. The stones were thrown against the door while we were preaching and praying, and a great noise made without, so when we had concluded, I went up to the disturbers and spoke to them on the shortness of their lives, and was beginning to say a little on the solemnity of judgment, when they all ran off, as though I had come as an officer to take them. The wicked flee when no man pursueth.

18th.—Sunday. Preached at BRADLEY and SILSDEN, in Silsden Circuit. It was a melting time. At the former place, in the morning the congregation was large, and the Lord did not leave many hearts untouched. Held a fellowship meeting at Silsden, after preaching twice, and two backsliders groaned and cried for mercy. When persons have once been in the way to heaven, they can never be happy till they return; if they never return, their misery is everlasting.

19th. At KEIGHLEY. Spoke with good liberty from Psa. ciii. 13, 14, to an attentive congregation.

20th. Spoke at HAINWORTH. A large congregation, and much of the divine presence. The Lord enabled me to be plain, and I trust faithful. This afternoon I attended a funeral, and sung, prayed, and exhorted to the people before the door from which the corpse was taken. Many seemed much affected while I spoke on the solemnity of death, the uncertainty of our continuance here, and the necessity of an immediate preparation for death. O that it may be seen many days hence. Spoke at FELL LANE to a few more people than the last fortnight; but I did not preach with that feeling which I needed. Lord have mercy upon me. To-night I felt a want of more of the spirit and power of godliness. O Lord do thou give me to feel more for lost sinners. Give me the active zeal,—the living, prevailing, conquering faith, the unmoved fortitude, the undaunted courage, the holy resolve of mind which I need for this most important employment of winning souls.

GREAT REVIVAL IN KEIGHLEY CIRCUIT.

[The following mostly appeared in the *Primitive Methodist Magazine July*, 1826. As this is my first appearance in print, I took some interest in it, and believe it was for the Lord's glory, not mine.]

Nov. 5th.—Saturday evening. I attended a fellowship meeting at KEIGHLEY (we hold one every Saturday night). A few persons expressed their determination to seek entire holiness of heart. After the close of the meeting, a man came into the house where I lodge, who was awakened the last Lord's day under the preaching. We prayed with him, but he did not obtain saving faith. We were nearly an hour upon our knees at family prayer, and the head of the family received the witness of the Spirit; which he had not experienced for twelve months.

6th.—Spoke twice at ADDINGHAM; renewed tickets, and was under the painful necessity of either breaking our rules or excluding 7 persons from the society who had not met in society these two or three months, some longer. Churches should be purged from the ungodly only.

11th.—Friday. I formed a preachers' class in KEIGHLEY. Two persons under serious impressions attended. To one I gave a place on trial. [This was wrong if the person was not saved, and if saved, the member should have been received on earth as in heaven.]

13th.—Sunday, MORTON BANKS; where the people were much affected while I cried, "Pay thy vows." Held a lovefeast in the afternoon at KEIGHLEY. Many people attended, and the Master came to the feast. I believe good was done. Many more would have spoken, but as I had to preach at 5 o'clock, I concluded the lovefeast about half-past 4. As many could not speak, I exhorted as many as were determined for heaven to lift up their hands, which numbers did. A large congregation assembled at 5, to whom I spoke, through my Master's help, with much liberty, and I trust the word was rendered useful to many.

14th.—I spoke at KEIGHLEY from the parable of the talents with much liberty. I frequently have good liberty when I retire an hour or two for meditation and prayer. I have heard since that good was done.

18th.—Having formed a preachers' class last Friday, to-night six persons gave in their names, most of them deeply awakened.

19th.—Fellowship meeting. A glorious time : one sanctified wholly.

20th.—Sunday. Spoke at MORTON BANKS at 10 ; at KEIGHLEY at 1½ and 5. The congregation was large in the afternoon, but at night there was more I think by near a hundred than I ever saw. The Lord assisted me in speaking to them. I long to be more useful. I felt happy while speaking, singing, and praying.

21st.—Spoke at KEIGHLEY from 1 Thess. v. 23. I showed, 1st, the nature, 2nd the author, 3rd the effects, 4th the necessity of entire sanctification, and, 5th that believers had many reasons to expect it. The Lord assisted me in the work. This preaching of entire holiness God has always owned.

22nd.—I had much liberty at SCARTOP in recommending entire holiness of heart.

24th.—I spoke to an attentive congregation at INGROW, half a mile from Keighley, from Luke xv.2, " This man receiveth sinners." After the preaching service concluded we held a prayer meeting, and I exhorted none to go away but those who were determined to sacrifice heaven for sin. After the prayer meeting I went into the next house, and found 3 or 4 under conviction. We knelt down again ; hearts were softened, but none got saved. Possibly we depended more on prayer than Christ. Three promised me to come to the class meeting to-morrow night.

25th.—Attended my class. Many present groaned for mercy, but did not obtain a sense of the pardoning love of God. It appears that 40 or 50 are under conviction in the town ; one of our members thinks 100. I feel a little surprised that none of them get converted. Perhaps there is too little faith among believers. To-night I feel a little concern about them, but have felt a degree of confidence while imploring Almighty God to comfort these mourning penitents.

26th—To-night our fellowship meeting was well attended. After a number had spoken in quick succession for about an hour, one man stood up and informed us that he had come expecting to be saved to-night. I asked if there were any more who were seeking the Lord, and if there were, that they would stand up and inform us. A woman got up, with tears starting from her eyes, and said, " I went home from the preaching last Monday night so much affected that I have got little rest since, either by night or day, and I have come expecting the Lord to set my soul at liberty." After this more spoke nearly to the same purport. We kneeled down to implore Almighty God to proclaim liberty to these captive souls. We had not prayed long before a young man believed with his heart unto righteousness. We then sung " Praise God from whom all blessings flow, &c." I then requested this man to go and speak to another man who was in distress. He did so, and very soon that man received the witness of the Spirit. The meeting commenced at eight o'clock, and closed between eleven and twelve ; during which time seven souls obtained the knowledge of salvation by the remission of sins. Many more were in distress. The scene was truly interesting; while sinners wept and cried for mercy, the sounds of praise were heard among believers.

Dec. 3rd.—Saturday evening. At the fellowship meeting, when a few had spoken, I exhorted those who had got liberty the last fellowship meeting, to inform us how they obtained it. Some did so. I then enquired whether any else had got saved this week. "Yes, me, sir," replied a man who had been in the army many years, and in Satan's service much longer. The man's wife got liberty to-night, and her daughter has obtained a sense of pardon during the week. One man who got quit of his burden to-night, lay some time with his face towards the ground, praising the Lord. He wondered that he did not believe sooner, and cried, "It is quite easy to believe; it is quite easy to believe." Three got saved at this meeting, and more were in distress.

8th.—At UTLEY. I spoke without any premeditation on Tit. ii. 14. It struck my mind while we were singing the last verse of the second hymn. I have reason to hope it was rendered a blessing to the small congregation.

9th. Attended my class. It was good to be there.

10th.—Fellowship meeting: more people than usual. A cry for mercy. We concluded, and I exhorted the mourners to stay a little longer. After wrestling and praying some time, two found Him of whom Moses in the law and the prophets did write.

11th.—After preaching twice in the country, I returned to KEIGHLEY; and after Brother Pedley had spoken in the chapel, we called a prayer meeting. At eight o'clock the praying laborers attended at private houses to hold prayer meetings. I was at one of them; the house was crowded; the Lord poured his Spirit; one soul obtained justification by faith. Being asked if the Lord had spoken peace to his soul, he replied, "I know it, as well as I know my right hand from my left."

12th.—Preached at KEIGHLEY; a glorious time. After service we held a leaders' meeting and admitted eighteen persons on trial. During the last 15 days, sixteen souls have been justified, and two or three wholly sanctified, (all in the town).

17th.—Attended a fellowship meeting. Five or six were in distress. There was much divine power in the meeting. Believers seemed overawed with the Lord's presence, and filled with his glory. We continued about three hours.

18th.—Sunday. Had a powerful time at MORTON BANKS in the morning, and a comfortable waiting upon the Lord at KEIGHLEY in the afternoon. At night I spoke to a crowded congregation from Rom. ix. 15, 16. A person sent me a private letter desiring it. I had good liberty. Held a fellowship meeting after; many attended. At 8, I held a prayer meeting: fourteen prayed in the space of an hour and a few minutes; it was a good time. I was almost exhausted.

19th.—Spoke from the fall of Peter. I believe some lasting good was done.

20th.—I was very ill, and confined to bed part of the day. Afflictions are good for me. I examined myself, and thought, now I may die; if so, am I ready to appear before a just and holy God. I have exhibited the enjoyments of a dying believer to others, what do I enjoy? My answer was,—peace of conscience, favor with God, purity of heart; and when I look into eternity, all appears comfortable. Jehovah is my friend, and if I be called to pass through the valley and shadow of death, all will be well. By the grace of God I am what I am.

21st.—I spoke, although weak in body, with good liberty, from the parable of the talents.

22nd. In the Clubhouses to a crowded house, from "I am crucified with Christ." It was a good time.

23rd.—Attended my class, and three more gave in their names to go to heaven with us.

24th.—Attended the fellowship meeting: it was a powerful time. Many attended (as they generally do). It was very solemn while we waited upon the Lord in silent prayer upon our knees.

25th.—Christmas day. Many attended the prayer meeting at 5 a.m.; it was good to be there. I spoke at MORTON BANKS at 10, and KEIGHLEY at half-past 1 and 5. At 5, I spoke from Luke xxii. 19: "This do in remembrance of me." It was a solemn time; particularly at the Lord's Supper: I think about 100 attended. To-night my soul is unspeakably happy in my Redeemer. I give myself into his hands for time and eternity.

26th.—Heard a local preacher out of the Ripon circuit; after which I exhorted and prayed, and experienced the refreshing influence of divine grace.

Thursday night at INGROW. Since I spoke here before the Lord has liberated the man, his wife, and daughter.

31st.—To-day I have been reviewing the gracious dealings of God with my soul during the year, and I find much cause of humility and gratitude. When I came into this circuit the work was at a very low ebb; many improper characters being on the class papers: these I excluded. The congregations continued to increase, and the Keighley Society got quickened, and love was manifested among them. They implored Almighty God to revive his work. We gave special attention to three things, viz.: 1st, Excluding improper persons; 2nd, An union in society; 3rd, Fervent prayer. To these I attribute the late revival. "Praise the Lord, O my soul, and forget not all his benefits." Last Lord's Day three got liberty at a place in the country, and two in the town. To-night a good company attended the watch night, and it was a very solemn time while we renewed our covenant with the Lord.

Jan. 1, 1826, Sunday. Lovefeast in the town. Quick and sound speaking. Many people. Some were crying for mercy in the gallery. I left the pulpit and we prayed with them, and one got liberty; and the last Lord's day three got liberty at a place in the country; and, during the week, two in the town. O Lord, spread the revival through the circuit.

2nd. Preached at KEIGHLEY, from Col. iv. 5, "Redeeming the time;" after which I attended the leaders' meeting, and we received twelve on trial.

13th.—Met my class. A happy time. Four gave in their names. It is nine weeks to-night since this class was formed; and out of the world the Lord hath gathered twenty; most of whom enjoy the favor of God, the rest are seeking it. Lord, grant them the desire of their hearts.

14th.—Fellowship meeting. A man who had been in the Methodist New Connexion eighteen months, having heard that the Lord was saving souls among us, came in to get the blessing of pardon. He got it and went home rejoicing, and other three more. Two more struggled hard for it, but did not get liberty.

15th.—Two got liberty at a prayer meeting.

17th.—Preached at SCARTOP to a large congregation. Met the Society; and, while exhorting them to "Fight the good fight of faith," to pray for, and expect a revival, the Lord quickened us together.

19th.—After speaking to a small congregation at UTLEY, I returned home and poured out my soul to God in secret prayer. I had such a solemn overwhelming sense of the Omniscience and Omnipresence of the Unsearchable Lord God, as I never before witnessed. O, what solemnity pervaded my mind, under a humbling sense of mine own unworthiness. I gave myself unreservedly to the Father, through the Son by the assistance of the Holy Spirit. O that I may enjoy uninterrupted and eternal union with my Maker, Redeemer, Sanctifier, and Judge.

21st,—Fellowship meeting, About one hundred people attended. One woman, a hearer of the Baptists, came three miles in order to get liberty. She received it, and other two persons likewise. More were seeking ; and a class-leader informed us that he obtained entire holiness of heart, (while at private prayer) of which he gave a clear and scriptural account.

22nd.—Sunday, at $10\frac{1}{2}$, at MORTON BANKS, from "Turn ye, turn ye from your evil ways." $1\frac{1}{2}$ and 5, at KEIGHLEY to large congregations. After night service held a fellowship meeting, (we have begun to do this once every month ;) it was a glorious time. At 8 o'clock attended a prayer meeting. A great moving : one backslider made happy ; souls in distress, believers filled with gratitude and praise. Glory, glory: 4 heavy laden souls have found rest in the wounds of Jesus to-day ; sixteen within this last nine days ; thirty-four the last two months, in the town, and six or seven in the country.

Feb. 12th.—During the last fortnight I have been to see my parents, and have spoken to crowded congregations.

During the last week two have got justified, and one or more wholly sanctified. Preached at HAWORTH at $10\frac{1}{2}$ o'clock, renewed tickets and added one. $1\frac{1}{2}$ and 5 at KEIGHLEY. At 5 the chapel was so crowded the people could scarcely get in. I read an awful account of an apparition at Glen Cottage, near KIRBY-MALZEARD, and preached from Matt. xvi. 26, "What shall it profit a man, &c." It was a solemn time ; having preached three times and renewed tickets to upwards of one hundred members, I felt weary in body, but my duty is my delight.

14th.—AT SCARTOP. A good time : two have got sanctified wholly since I preached here before.

17th.—At HARDEN. A large congregation ; I believe the Lord blessed the people. I gave them tickets and received one on trial.

18th.—Fellowship meeting. Nothing extraordinary took place, till it was time to draw towards a conclusion. I then exhorted those who were seeking pardon or holiness, to inform us. After some time a man broke through shame, and informed us that although he had long been a member of our Society, he had been without the evidence of his acceptance two years. And some believers told us that they were seeking to get their hearts made pure. We kneeled down to pray for penitents and believers ; but none got what they sought.

We sung, and I exhorted them to sit down, I got upon a form; and told them, as both justification and sanctification were obtained by faith, if they could believe they might be saved (unworthy as they saw themselves) without any merit of their own,—saved now this moment.

I was interrupted by one who told us that she had got it, and then another and another believed with their hearts unto righteousness, and with the mouth they confessed that the blood of Christ had cleansed them from all sin. I counted to eight or nine who (I believe) got it. But the work was so instantaneous, that I could not exactly ascertain how many got that blessing. In the meantime, two obtained justification by faith. I never was at such a meeting as this before. Glory to the Lord for ever.

15th.—Sunday. At MORTON BANKS at $10\frac{1}{2}$. Preached and admitted three on trial. In the afternoon held a lovefeast at KEIGHLEY. More people at it than on any former occasion. Many spoke clearly and spiritually of justification and sanctification. It was at one of these lovefeasts, perhaps this, at which a farmer's wife, with a sweet heavenly countenance, said, "I dare tell before all our folks that God has cured my tempers." It was little to tell it to us strangers, who did not live with her, but to tell it before her unconverted husband, servants, and children, was a greater thing, and why should not our Saviour save us from all evil temper, and every other sin? He came to "destroy the works of the Devil," and he is able to accomplish it. He that is able to bridle the tongue, "that offends not in word, the same is a perfect man, is able also to bridle the whole body." It is a happy sign of universal victory. At 5 I preached in the chapel to a large congregation, after which I exhorted the Society.

20th.—Preached in KEIGHLEY to as many as the chapel could contain; had good liberty; we held a leaders' meeting, and received seven on trial. At that held three weeks since twenty-three were added.

24th.—Visited some persons who have a desire to obtain salvation, I invited them to my class, which I met to-night; and four gave in their names.

25th.—Fellowship meeting. A glorious time from first to last. Many under conviction; ten or more professed redemption in the blood of Christ, viz., forgiveness of sin. A backslider was weeping and groaning for liberty in a most lamentable manner. When the meeting concluded he refused to rise from his knees. He did not believe while I stayed, the meeting lasted between three or four hours. Being much fatigued I went home; where I had not been long before I heard some people come up singing. I stepped to the door, and was informed that the man had got liberty. Praise the Lord. His promises are sure.

26th.—Sunday. Preached at RYCROFT at $10\frac{1}{2}$ o'clock, in a barn to some hundreds of people. At 2 at SAWOOD, I could scarcely get into the house for the crowd. A solemn influence seemed to attend the word. Some could not get in. Service concluded, I hastened to COLLINGWORTH at 5 o'clock. The house would not contain half of the congregation; but the Old Methodists permitted me to preach in their chapel. This has been a good day to my soul.

27th.—We have had our Quarterly Meeting to-day, and find that we have added seventy souls during the quarter. Lord increase our gratitude.

March 4th.—Fellowship meeting. Two or three saved, and a few more seekers comforted, but not fully saved.

7th.—At WEST MORTON. Crowded house; powerful time.

10th.—At HAINWORTH. Solemnity pervaded the assembly, while I reasoned on the necessity of a speedy preparation for judgment. A full house.

10th.—Preached at Slack Lane Head, three miles from Keighley, in a barn. About three hundred hearers. I believe good was done.

11th.—Fellowship meeting. A gracious influence rested in the meeting. It appeared to me that many were in distress. So I requested as many as were seeking pardon to tell us. One man arose trembling and said, "I came on purpose." Six or seven more spoke nearly to the same effect. We kneeled down to pray for them, and seven obtained peace through believing. More were in distress. My soul has been in its glory to-night.

12th.—Sunday. Attended 6 o'clock prayer meeting. One mourning soul got encouraged, not fully saved. At 9 o'clock preached in the chapel from "Verily there is a reward for the righteous." It was a comfortable time. 1½ o'clock, I attended a lovefeast at MORTON BANKS. The place was crowded, the power of God descended; the hearts of the people melted like wax before the flame. It appeared as though they would have continued speaking for hours longer than they did. It struck my mind to request those who had got liberty during the last four months to confess it in as few words as possible. A goodly company arose, this took up but little time; in the meanwhile one man got up and said, (tears streaming from his eyes,) "The Lord has set my soul at liberty just now." This had a powerful effect on the meeting. I then exhorted those who were seeking pardon to inform us, that we might direct them how to obtain it. More did so than I could count, I then cried, "Are all else pardoned? Is there not another seeking the Lord?" Then some more answered in the affirmative. Three souls got liberty.

I then concluded the meeting, and requested all to go away who had got enough, but those to stay who had not. So many stayed that it was with difficulty I got about the place to seek up the mourners, for they lay about the place in all directions. Two or three more soon got their burden removed; and it seemed that there were more in distress than the praying laborers could attend to. So I cleared three forms, and invited the mourning souls to come forward; and within two minutes they were filled with penitents. It did me good to see them; the praying laborers explained the plan of salvation and prayed with them.

I then retired as secretly as possible, as I had to preach at KEIGHLEY at 5 o'clock. I hastened thither. A local brother gave out a hymn and prayed, while I took a little refreshment; after which I spoke to a crowded congregation. After service called a prayer meeting. Before it began, some friends returned from the lovefeast and informed me that, from the beginning to the final close of the meeting, thirteen souls got liberty; and I have heard of six or seven since, making in all twenty. Praise the Lamb. This has been one of the best days ever my eyes beheld. Although it is nearly four months since the commencement of the revival, I do not know that one of the new converts has fallen back.

The following are a few things which I think have been useful in promoting the revival:—

1. When I came into this circuit last midsummer, it was considerably embarrased, and unable to support two travelling preachers. The circuit wrote to the general committee, requesting them to use their influence in getting another circuit for one of us. A circuit was provided for my colleague, and since then I have had no colleague. There was not work for two preachers in the circuit; consequently when one removed, the burden was lighter, and our temporal concerns grew better.

2. Excluding improper characters (according to rule) from the society.

3. Preachers, leaders, and members got united, and

4. We agreed to give ourselves to God, and pray for a revival, expecting one.

5. Some of our members were successful in inviting their neighbors to the preaching and the class.

19th.—Preached at OLDFIELD at 10 to a large congregation. At 2, to two or three hundred hearers in the open-air. I had good liberty at night at KEIGHLEY, while preaching a sermon to young people.

20th.—To-day a Methodist local preacher came three miles in order to join us. He comes from Harden, and has preached upwards of 33 years among them. He took my place to-night at Keighley: after he had preached, I exhorted a few minutes. One got liberty.

21st.—Spoke at BOTANY, near East Morton, with good liberty to a serious congregation. Three got liberty. Glory to God.

26th.—Preached at RYCROFT at $10\frac{1}{2}$ and $2\frac{1}{2}$; powerful times. At night I preached in the local preacher's house who joined us the last week; crowded to excess; 2 gave in their names. Hastened to KEIGHLEY. Attended a prayer meeting; a happy time; some weeping.

28th.—At SCARTOP. One soul has been made happy since I was here before.

30th.—MILL HEY, near Haworth. I think some scores could not get in.

31st.—At RYCROFT. Called a meeting after to see who would give in their names to join the Harden class; seven volunteers came forward. Rycroft is only half a mile from Harden.

April 1st.—Joined another before I left the place I was at, and left the newly formed class with 11 members in it. Three or four more have joined the other class. Attended the fellowship meeting. One got liberty, and another mourner encouraged.

3rd.—Received a letter from my friend and brother Dawson. A few words are worth preserving:

APRIL 2, "After a delay, as thou wilt see according to the case, I write to thee, hoping thou art well, as I am at present. My Chirstian experience as follows,—I am still a babe in Christ; as a babe I am weak, as a babe I am ignorant, as a babe I am helpless, as a babe I am full of wants, as a babe I am sometimes overcome, as a babe I am looking up to my Father for protection, but as a babe I partake of the same nature as my Father that begat me, as a babe I bear some small share of my Father's likeness, as a babe I love my Father, and as a babe desire to obey him, and to be found loving those that are begotten of him."

6th., LONG LEE in a barn. Many people, and a good prospect, the first time any of our preachers preached here. Our members have held prayer meetings a few weeks. I turned it into a fellowship meeting. It was a good time.

7th.—Attended my class; about 40 people; it was a profitable season. Six persons gave in their names to join.

8th.—To-night the fellowship meeting commenced at seven o'clock, and continued four hours and twenty minutes. One soul saved; more seeking.

13th., At MORTON BANKS. A solemn time at a class leader's house, just joined us from among the Wesleyan Methodists. It was good to be there.

15th.—Fellowship meeting. A glorious time; heaven begun below. One got justified, and two sanctified wholly.

16th.—Sunday. Attended 6 o'clock prayer meeting; one or two seeking the Lord. Hastened to HARDEN to hold a camp meeting. We had as many in the forenoon as could be expected. Some awakened.

In the afternoon about as many attended as could hear, and all behaved well. It was a mighty time. If ever I preached with power divine it was this afternoon. Some trembled; I believe most of the people felt the power of God. Surely he shook the hearts of the people. Tears descended in abundance; and, towards the close, seriousness and solemnity seemed to pervade the camp. I spoke from 2 Cor. v. 20; after exhorting them to be reconciled to God, I urged them no longer to halt between two opinions, but to return home either the decided friends or enemies of God; and as many as were on the Lord's side, and determined for heaven, to manifest it by lifting up their hands. Many resolved, decided, and raised their hands in favor of Christ. At this moment divine glory seemed to rest upon the camp. To me it was a satisfying and an affecting sight; so many acknowledging the Lord among the people.

I then cried out: "As many of you as are determined to serve sin and the devil, and to be the decided enemies of God, lift up your hands." Not a hand was raised. Sinners are cowards; some seemed struck with seriousness; others appeared to be abashed and confounded. Some who were awakened at this camp meeting have since got converted, and have joined the Society. Lord keep them. Doubtless many who were there, do, by their conduct, declare in favor of sin and Satan, and say of Christ, "We will not have this man to reign over us." Then why did they not declare themselves the enemies of God to-day? Were even their infatuated minds struck with horror at the idea of doing that with a hand which they do by the whole of their conduct? O Lord, do thou in thy boundless goodness pour light into these benighted minds.

After the camp meeting we held a lovefeast in the chapel at Rycroft. A mighty moving: some in the gallery were seeking the Lord. After the close of this glorious lovefeast, I returned to Keighley, weary in body but happy in mind.

May 6th.—Fellowship meeting. It was not very powerful till we called a prayer meeting, when three souls obtained salvation through faith in the Divine Redeemer, and one during the week.

9th—Preached at KEIGHLEY in the afternoon, and SCARTOP at night.

One soul received Christ by faith, while I spoke from Rev. iii. 20. It was a powerful time.

12th.—In HARDEN; one of the best seasons I ever witnessed: two have got liberty here this week. I renewed tickets. Thirty-four in society (Rycroft included). About six months ago we had only four.

"The little cloud increases still."

May 14*th.*—Sunday. Preached twice at OLDFIELD to large congregations, and returned to Keighley at 5, to hear John Flesher. I think one of the most popular preachers ever I heard in the Primitive Methodist Connexion.

19th.—Met my class; it was too large, so we joined one out of it of sixteen members. We have upwards of twenty left. It was as profitable a time as ever I enjoyed.

21st.—Sunday. At 10 o'clock at MORTON BANKS. A mighty influence attended the word; one man awakened. A half-past one held a lovefeast at KEIGHLEY. More people than on any former occasion. They spoke so quick, and were so desirous to confess what Christ had done for them, and what the Holy Spirit had wrought in them, that it was difficult to keep them from speaking together; so many beginning at once, that I could not tell either who began first or who ought to speak next. Sinners wept, trembled, and cried for mercy; while, among believers, the falling tear! the sonorous voice! the sweet hallelujah! and the powerful amen! displayed that the Lord was at work among the people. Three souls got plunged by faith in the fountain open for sin and uncleanness. More were struggling to lay hold of the hope set before them, so that, although the preaching service should have commenced at 5 o'clock, it was near six before we could get them from their knees.

29th.—We held our Quarter Day, and have added during the quarter forty-eight, making one hundred and eighteen for the last half-year.

"Who, I ask in amaze, hath begotten me these?
Yea, I ask from what quarter they came?
My full heart, it replies, they're born from the skies,
And give glory to God and the Lamb."

June 4*th.*—We held a lovefeast at MORTON BANKS. I left them praying with the mourners, and preached at KEIGHLEY at 5 o'clock in the chapel; and at 7 by the Low Bridge, in the open-air. A large, attentive congregation; and one got liberty at a prayer meeting held after.

18th.—Attended the camp meeting at KEIGHLEY. About 8 o'clock we held a prayer meeting for half-an-hour in the chapel, then sung through the street as a little army sounding to battle. Our fortitude, courage, and faith, increasing while we sung. The travelling and local preachers led the van; the leaders followed close to them, and the members and hearers brought up the rear. We opened the meeting with prayer, and continued the service with preaching, (about twenty minutes each) and exhorting; and twice we went out for prayer meetings. The manner of conducting the meeting was much the same after dinner; only, about 16 or 18 pages (selected for the purpose), of the "History of the Primitive Methodists," was read, with occasional remarks. This had a good effect; the congregation was very large; souls were awakened on the ground.

But it was at the lovefeast held after the camp meeting, especially, that the power of God was made known. If ever I saw the glory of God rest upon a congregation, or felt it in my own soul, it was at this lovefeast. To all appearance, almost every heart melted before the power of God. We could sing,—

> "Satan feels his power is gone,
> He falls like lightning from his throne,
>   Hosannah to the Lamb of God."

How many were awakened I cannot tell, bu seven souls got delivered from bondage into liberty. The prophet cried, "Unto him shall the gathering of the people be," and they are coming to " the Lamb of God that takes away the sin of the world."

I have preserved the following as worthy of consideration in this age of wars and of duels :—

ANSWER TO A CHALLENGE.

[At a late meeting under a commission of bankruptcy, at Andover, between Mr Fleet and Mr Mann, both respectable solicitors of that town, some disagreement arose, which ended in the former sending the latter a challenge, to which the following answer was returned.]

To KINGSTON FLEET, ESQ.

I AM honor'd this day, Sir, with challenges two,
The first from friend Langdon, the second from you,
As the one is to *fight*, and the other to *dine*,
I accept *his* 'engagement,' and yours must decline.
Now in giving this preference, I trust you'll admit
I've acted with prudence, and done what was fit,
Since, encountering *him*, and my weapon a knife,
There is some little chance of *preserving* my life,
Whilst a bullet from you, Sir, *might* take it away,
And the maxim, you know, is to live while you may.
If, however, you still should suppose I ill-treat you,
By sternly rejecting this challenge to meet you,
Bear with me a moment, and I will adduce
Three powerful reasons by way of excuse:
In the first place, unless I am grossly deceiv'd
I myself am in conscience the party aggriev'd ;
And therefore, good Sir, if a challenge *must* be,
Pray wait till that challenge be *tender'd* by me.
Again, Sir, I think it by far the more sinful,
To stand and be shot, than to sit for a skinful ;
From whence you'll conclude (as I'd have you, indeed)
That fighting composes no part of my creed—
And my courage (which, though it was never disputed,
Is not, I imagine, too, too deeply rooted,)
Would prefer that its fruit, Sir, whate'er it may yield,
Should appear at '*the table*,' and not in *the field*.
And lastly, *my life*, be it never forgot,
Possesses a value which *yours*, Sir, does not ;*
So I mean to preserve it as long as I can,
Being justly entitled 'a Family *Man*,'
With three or four children, (I scarce know how many),
Whilst *you*, Sir, have not, or *ought* not to have any.
Besides, that the contest would be too unequal,
I doubt not will plainly appear by the sequel ;
For e'en *you* must acknowledge it would not be meet
That one small '*Mann* of War' should engage 'a whole *Fleet*.'

Andover, July, 24, 1826.

* Mr Fleet is a Bachelor.

I made one more attempt, while at Keighley, to prepare the way for a permanent union. I was invited occasionally to tea in the family of Mr. Barrett, a manufacturer and hearer, who had several daughters; one only professed to serve my Master—Maria. She was a fine looking young woman; one of the youngest. Whether I acted wisely, or not, facts shall be given. At first, I knew not whether we should be mutually agreeable to each other; in which case, it would be a waste of time to consult her parents, who were indeed reputable, but not avowedly Christian. I spoke to her in private. We met a few times by appointment at one of the member's houses; but before we had sufficient time to conclude, her parents must have ascertained her mind, or mine, or both; for, without any warning, they sent her to a ladies' boarding school, far beyond my reach. I wrote; she wrote; I tried another post office; all our letters were intercepted. She might have been in a convent. Months passed without a line. It thus appeared that I should not be acceptable to her family. I hardly knew whether to herself or not. I was married first, and then she was recalled home, and then they produced all my letters and hers. Then only did she know the truth of the matter. We only saw each other at a distance until 24 years after. She had then been long married, resided in Belgium, came over to see her relations, saw my name placarded on the walls of Bradford, in 1850, to hold a discussion with George Jacob Holyoake, and thought she would like to speak to me after all these years. I was then residing with the late James Grinstead, had passed one night of the most important discussion of my life, my table was covered with books, my head crowded with arguments, and I had but little time to attend to her interesting communications. She blames those who had kept back our correspondence. Her husband was then living; for years he has been deceased. She survives, a widow, left with an interesting family. Providence hindered our union: it was no doubt for the best.

"What He appoints is best."

I had never asked her parents. If I had, it is likely, from the course they adopted, that it would have been in vain. I cannot but thank my heavenly Father for this also.

This seems to be a very proper place, now in old age, before I record the steps which led to my marriage, to impress all my readers with the high, everlasting value of the spring-time of youth. It not only

"Saves us from a thousand snares,
To mind our Saviour young,"

but it leads to ten thousand pleasures,—it leads us to choose such companions as we regret not in after years. It is sad when a companion for life is elected in folly and sin; but most blessed to review, when even the highest wisdom has been sought, and we can say that God "sets the solitary in families," having proved it in our own happy experience.

When any one is converted in early youth, he possesses great advantages over others. In mid-life, when turning to Christ, people have formidable enemies to encounter. Their evil habits have acquired a tremendous power. Intemperance for years may have maintained an ever-growing ascendancy. The passions, and, possibly, illicit associations have predominated. Companions, and partakers in their guilty pleasures have become necessary to them. A sordid love of gain has had time to root itself among other vices in their nature. Habits of novel reading, indolence, and self-indulgence have ripened to maturity. All these, and many more, in the conversions which occur in mid-life, have to be encountered and vanquished; while the youthful convert is wholly free from them, and ere they attack him, whether a few or all, he has grown up to the strength of a young man, has become armed with the great truths of the Divine word, and taught to steer a course which renders such temptations either entirely impotent or less perilous than they would have been had he reached manhood in a state of entire worldliness. Beside; when early years are given to Christ,—to the acquisition of the highest and best knowledge—the mind improves, expands, and often gets filled with varied stores of wisdom; the heart becomes pure, benevolent, god-like, and thus selfishness is slain. The best of man's life is devoted to God, his assembly, and to be useful to society. "Seek ye the Lord while he may be found; call upon him while he is near." If a day lost is an eternal loss, what must years be?

The following is the first letter ever addressed to my present wife:

KEIGHLEY, AUGUST 22ND, 1826.

DEAR SISTER BELLWOOD,

I have of late had some serious thoughts of exchanging celibacy for matrimony, and the chief reason of my not doing it prior to this time is, I have not met with one to my mind. This morning I entered into conversation with my beloved colleague G. J. Sellers, who has given me high eulogiums of praise upon yourself. I immediately felt disposed to write you upon the subject. To yourself I imagine I am utterly unknown, but to some of your near relations I am well known,—as your brother Philip, and sister Snowden, at Beckwithshaw, and sister Mann, at Thorpe. If you are not engaged to any young man in bonds of promise or affection indissoluble, and will accept the proposal, I will (if my Master permit) come to your residence. To say much in my own behalf requires more ignorance and presumption than I am master of; only permit me to inform you that I have travelled upwards of four years,—one in Guisborough, two in Ripon, and this is my second here. I have passed my 22nd year this summer; and you will know more about me hereafter, if Providence permit. I hope you will oblige me with an answer by return of post to the following questions, in short—1st. Are you engaged? 2nd. If not, have you any objection to my coming on the above errand? 3rd. When will you be at home? My prayer to Almighty God is, that he would direct you and me in this momentous affair, which stands so intimately connected with our present and final happiness. Being already prepossessed in your favor, I subscribe myself,

Your very affectionate friend and brother in the best of bonds,

JOHN BOWES.

P.S.—Please to direct for me at John Nuttals, Paper Box Maker, South Street, Keighley, Yorkshire.

Sep. 3rd.—Held a camp meeting betwixt Silsden and Baildon, and a lovefeast at SILSDEN at night. The glory of Jehovah was manifested, and his power to save made known at the lovefeast. Three souls got liberty, and more were in distress. Such a lovefeast has not been held in Silsden for years. It alarmed the neighbors; some of whom came to see what was the matter.

4th.—Preached at STEETON; a good congregation. Called a prayer meeting. Souls in distress. I have heard since that some young men who intended to go to Kildwick Feast got their minds changed.

24th.—Preached three times at MARTON-CUM-GRAFTON, in Ripon Circuit. Spent the day comfortably with my old friends.

25th.—Set off in company with T. Dawson, my most intimate friend, to COTTINGWORTH, where I intend to be married to-morrow. Met my intended wife at York, with her brother Robert and sister Mary.

26th.—To-day I was united in matrimonial bonds at Thoganby or Cottingworth Church, to Susannah Bellwood, youngest daughter of John Bellwood, farmer, with whom I trust I shall be happy. After dinner we all prayed who were in the room. A backslider came in to see my friends, we got him to pray, and the Lord set his soul at liberty. An auspicious beginning. Brother Dawson preached at night, and at the prayer meeting held after it was a powerful time. I wrote to my wife before, but never saw her till the 7th inst. I got acquainted with her by the advice of G. J. Sellers. Knowing that others had suffered much in their preaching excursions through the opposition of their wives, I deemed it requisite, especially as I expected to have much travelling for the Lord, to guard against the trials into which Wesley, Whitfield, and others had fallen, by making an agreement, that whatever service I might have for the Lord that she was not to oppose it. This agreement on her part has now been tolerably kept for 44 years. I have only had occasionally to remind her of it, which has had its influence. The will of God should prevail in the minds of all his servants, and not the will of the flesh. If the merchant who visits foreign shores and ports, or the mariner who sails long voyages over distant seas, for the sake of the reward of wealth which he gets for his self-denial, why should not the proclaimers of the gospel deny themselves for Christ and the everlasting salvation of lost sinners?

27th.—Set off to my circuit, and my wife with me. At night in company with my brethren Dawson and Rumfitt, I attended a class meeting at York.

28th.—Got to SPOFFORTH about 6, and in an hour's notice preached to a large congregation.

29th.—Preached at BECKWITHSHAW, where my children in the Lord, and now brother and sister, Snowden, reside.

Nov. 19th.—At EMBSAY. Preached in the chapel in the morning, and held a lovefeast in the afternoon, but there was nothing remarkable. Good congregations. At night preached in a house crowded with people at EASTBY, a quarter of a mile from Embsay. A powerful time. Called a prayer meeting. One got liberty; nine or ten in deep distress; some cried aloud for mercy. A few weeks have now elapsed since I gave my congregation at Embsay a challenge to produce one passage of scripture saying or proving that Christ did not die for all, and I would bring a hundred to prove that he did. Instead of complying with the proposal, some rigid predestinarians provided one Mr Holgate, from Salterforth (who has a chapel there), to preach and prove that particular redemption was true. I preached in the chapel on a Wednesday evening, to more people than could get in. I spoke, and had good liberty, from Rom. ix. 15, 16. After which he preached in a large house; but instead of bringing reason and scripture to disprove what I advanced, he dealt out abusive language to a very plentiful amount. However, since that time our congregations have been greatly enlarged, and a good prospect opened. [Then our society consisted of 54; no[w] we have between 60 and 70.—*Jan.* 1827.]

Dec. 3rd.—Held a lovefeast at CONNONLEY. While I was praying, [a] man fell from his knees upon the floor apparently senseless. A pray[er] meeting was held in the place a short time after he was taken o[ut.] Solemnity pervaded the assembly. When the service closed, I we[nt] to see the man, whom they had conveyed into an adjoining house. [I] found him laid upon a bed, perfectly sensible, and interrogated hi[m] respecting the cause of what had happened to him, and from his a[n]swers I concluded that it was a sensibility of his dangerous conditio[n] as a sinner which had overwhelmed his frame. I kneeled down [to] pray with him, but had not prayed above two minutes before he rag[ed] and threw himself about as though he would kill himself, and w[as] more than three men could hold. In a very few minutes he came [to] himself, and walked down home. He once had a fit before, when te[r]rified, and only once. He has since joined the society.

10th.—Held a lovefeast at MORTON BANKS. One got liberty. Spo[ke] at KEIGHLEY at 5; after which returned to Morton Banks to hear m[y] wife exhort. The place was crowded. I spoke after she had done.

31st.—Preached two charity sermons for a Sunday school, late[ly] begun in that place. The Wesleyan Methodists have refused to tea[ch] writing, and we teach it, and have a good school. Preached again [at] a quarter past 10, and held a watch night. A wonderfully solem[n] time. I see myself as nothing. I have done nothing for God, f[or] souls, and for eternity to what I might have done; but I am accepte[d] through Christ. One man got liberty at my class on Friday night.

Jan. 3rd., 1827, COLLINGWORTH, a few people, but God was with u[s.] I have not felt more of his love and power for some time. For such [a] visit my humble soul feels grateful. O that I may never forget it.

24th.—During the last fortnight I have visited my parents, wit[h] whom I stayed two or three days. On the *14th*, first Sunday, I spok[e] in the forenoon at SCRAFTON, and in the evening at CARLTON to [a] crowded congregation. It was a solemn time. On Monday I wen[t] with my wife (who accompanied me this journey) to GREWELTHORP[E,] where I preached on Tuesday night, also on Wednesday night at KIRK[B] MALZEARD. At both places my soul was refreshed with the brethre[n.] On Thursday we travelled from Grewelthorpe, where my wife has tw[o] sisters married, to EAVESTONE, where I preached to a large congregatio[n,] after which we held a fellowship meeting. It was good to be ther[e.] The Lord is carrying on a good work in this place. When a reviv[al] broke out while I travelled in the Ripon Circuit, at one time the num[ber in society was 26; before the present revival their number was onl[y] 14, and now it is between 30 and 40. They are a kind people. O[n] Saturday we arrived at home. Attended a fellowship meeting. Tw[o] or three were desiring salvation. One professed that he obtained en[ ]tire sanctification.

Feb. 17th.—Attended fellowship meeting. The people were bac[k]ward at speaking towards the beginning. I proposed to meet as man[y] as would engage at a throne of grace to pray for a revival in our ow[n] souls and others, three times every day, viz., at 8, at 1, and 10 p.m[.] The 6½ o'clock meeting not being well attended. I went round to as[k] them if they personally would attend. All of them agreed to the forme[r] and most of them to the latter. One or two seeking the Lord did not get liberty at the meeting, but while two or three brethren were at prayer after, the Lord set one of them at liberty.

18th, Sunday. Most, if not all of us, who promised, attended at 6½ a.m. A precious season. I talked a little at Morton Banks, at 10 o'clock, and then a prayer meeting. Attended lovefeast at KEIGHLEY, in the afternoon. A good time. At 5 o'clock I was appointed to preach, but took no text. I described

1. The awful condition of the ungodly.
2. The method by which a sinner gets converted.
3. The duty of a person who is brought into the way.
4. The causes which produce backsliders.
5. I contrasted the happy death of a believer with the miserable end of sinners and backsliders.

I was enabled to be serious with the congregation. Attended a prayer meeting. A backslider broke through and prayed and promised me that he would attend the class meeting.

May 6th, Friday evening. Attended a camp-meeting in HARDEN. In the forenoon we broke into praying companies once. The day was unseasonable, it was wet. The people were attentive. I had a precious time in the afternoon at the lovefeast. Three or four got saved. Last Sunday I only preached once in KEIGHLEY. Was unable to attend my own appointment. Both I and the congregation were bathed in tears.

June 17th.—Held a camp-meeting at SKIPTON, near Embsay. Many people. I trust good was done. I held a lovefeast after, and gave the society and others present a farewell. Exhorting, I spoke so long, &c., till I lost my voice.

24th.—Sunday. Preached a farewell sermon at MORTON BANKS, and left a weeping people. When I bade farewell to some of them they were filled too full of sorrow to speak, so was I to see them. At 5 o'clock in the evening I preached my farewell sermon at KEIGHLEY to a crowded congregation. It was a good time; but I think I never left such a sorrowing people. I have had considerable trouble during the last twelve months with two or three of our leaders here. I have been obliged to oppose them in some things, and they have labored to do me much injury. They have been the means of stirring up strife and contention in the church, so that many precious souls have been slain; but one of my most bitter enemies had his heart touched to-night, and, while standing on the gallery stairs, was heard to say, the tears streaming down his cheeks, "God bless him!" I am thankful for two things: first, that they have not been able to drive the congregation from the chapel; and second, that they are now at peace. I have made it a practice to pray for my enemies of late.

25th.—Monday. Set off at 6 in the morning for the Sunderland Circuit, and was accompanied by some kind friends a few miles, and by two as far as Otley, 12 miles. I arrived at my brother-in-law's (Snowden), at Beckwithshaw, in the afternoon. I had not been long there before some of my old friends came from Kettlesing, requesting me to pay them a visit. I preached at Beckwithshaw on Monday and Tuesday nights, and was much refreshed with the spiritual conversation and fervent prayers of this people. On Wednesday night I preached at KETTLESING to a crowded congregation. From thence I went to

RIPON to see a few friends, on my way to GREWELTHORPE. As William Mann resides here, and I and he married two sisters, I introduce the following from the *Primitive Methodist Magazine*, 1826:—

"AN APPEARANCE AFTER DEATH.

"But we preach Christ crucified."—1 Cor. i. 23. "Neither is there salvation in any other."—Acts iv. 12. "For by grace are ye saved, through faith; not of works, lest any man should boast."—Eph. ii. 8, 9. "For if righteousness came by the law, then is Christ dead in vain."—Gal. ii. 21.

"Dear Brother in Christ,—

"On Saturday, Jan. 7, 1826, I set out from Silsden, in company with Joshua Fletcher, one of our local preachers, for Kirby-Malzeard, in the Ripon Circuit, having, according to request, to preach there the next day, being Sabbath. On Monday, the 9th, the following awful account was delivered to me by William Mann, a respectable and religious farmer, of Glen Cottage Farm, near Kirby-Malzeard. He delivered it in the presence of Timothy Bonwell and Richard Morland, both of Kirby-Malzeard, and Joshua Fletcher, of Silsden. I took the account down in writing, from William Mann's lips, in presence of the above named persons; and I with a great number of others, hope it will be thought worthy a place in your widely-extended and useful magazine. Hoping it may prove an effectual warning to all who may read it, I remain yours in the Lord,
"NATHANAEL WEST."

"I, William Mann, do testify, that William Clarkson, lately deceased, did formerly reside and board in my house, and that he was a relation of my wife's; and that he, the said William Clarkson, departed this life about the beginning of last harvest; (that is in 1825) and that on the evening of October 8th, about nine o'clock, the said William Clarkson appeared to me in a narrow lane, between my house and Grewelthorpe. He passed by, looked at me, and smiled, but did not speak. I felt much affected, because I perfectly knew him to be the same William Clarkson who had boarded with me in his lifetime. After this, he came every other night, at about half-past twelve, for near a week. He sometimes smiled, and sometimes looked very expressively. Sometimes he came to the foot, and sometimes to the front of my bed, and put the curtains aside. I felt much agitated, and tried many means to speak, but could not; but as soon as I began to breathe out prayer to God, he vanished.

"After this he came every night for about a month. One time he pulled me half way down the bed; another time he stroked my face with what felt like a cold hand. The rest of the times, this month, he appeared much as before; that is, always accompanied with a gloomy light, much resembling in color the blaze of brimstone. I got out of bed many times in order to try and speak, but could not accomplish it. I felt much disturbed in my mind; I lost my appetite, my flesh failed, and my sleep departed.

"The next time he appeared to me was on Thursday, Nov. 17th, as I was coming from Ripon, in company with my wife and my brother's daughter, about twilight in the evening, between a place called Thieves-Gill and Azerly. As soon as I saw him, I had courage to speak to him in the following words, 'Bless God! what is the reason you torment me so?' He answered, 'Willy, thou hast kept both thyself and me unhappy, by reason of not speaking before now. The reason I have come is, my will was not made as I could have wished; the sale of my goods is going to take place this evening, thou must go and tell Anthony Grange (this was his nephew) to stop the sale if possible. I have no more to say to thee now, but meet me at half-past eleven o'clock, on next Saturday night, in my Far Close, (that is near Grewelthorpe). I must now have something from thee, as thou hast kept me so long without speaking. Thou canst best part with the hearing of thy left ear. On his so saying, I felt a sort of sound in my left ear, and my hearing on that side immediately left me. Before he went away, I asked him leave to bring my brother Anthony with me, to which he said, 'Thou mayest bring him with thee; but he must stand a distance off.' He then disappeared.

"He did not come any more till the time he himself had appointed, namely, the Saturday night following at half past eleven o'clock; at which time my brother Anthony and myself were at the place appointed. Before we set out, we had prayer in my own house, and an excellent time we had; the Lord was present indeed. When we arrived at the place, my brother Anthony stood at a distance, but within sight. The night was frosty and clear; the moon was at or about the full, and it was very light. I walked to and fro for about ten minutes; he then appeared. His appearance at this time was much the same as when he was alive. He spoke as follows: 'Willy, thou'st come.' I answered, 'Yes, I am come.' He said, 'Thou'st brought thy brother with thee.' I said, 'Yes.' He said, 'I wish I could have had my will before I died. I wanted nothing to be disturbed as long as my brother Thomas lived. The legacies were not left in the way I wanted them; some have got nothing; others have got only ten pounds each, and I wanted them to have fifteen pounds each. Also thou'st let them have the bed; and I did not want them to have it: for they could not have gotten it by law if they had tried.' I then asked him what he would have me do. He said, 'It is now too late; thou'st kept me too long without speaking.' I then asked him if his soul was happy. He said, 'I am lost,—lost,—lost, for ever!' I asked the cause of his being lost. He replied, 'I trusted all upon my own good works; but if I had taken thy brother Anthony's advice, I might have been saved.' I then asked him if a certain person,* late of Grewelthorpe, was happy. He said, 'I have him for a companion:' and then added, 'Thou must take care lest thou be a companion of mine also.' He had a most suffocating smell of sulphur, which caused me to step back; at which he remarked, 'Thou must not be frightened; I will not hurt thee.' He then added, 'I will plague thee no more,' and immediately disappeared.

"He told me many other things, but ordered me not to mention them. He detained me in conversation, according to my brother Anthony's account, about a quarter of an hour. My brother Anthony was within sight all the time.

"I protest before Almighty God, by whom I must shortly be judged, that the above account in substance is true.

(Signed) "WILLIAM MANN."

---

* "This same certain person, alluded to above, was once a professor of religion, and joined to a religious society: and, according to report, bid fair for heaven. His chief besetment, by which he fell away, was liquor. A fit of intoxication caused his death. He died the winter before William Clarkson. Drunken backslider! 'Prepare to meet thy God.'"

"We, the undersigned, do declare in the presence of Almighty God, that we heard William Mann, of Glen Cottage, near Kirby-Malzeard, on Jan. 9th, 1826, declare, with tears in his eyes, the substance of the foregoing account.

        (Signed) "NATHANAEL WEST, Prim. Meth. Preacher.
           "TIMOTHY BONWELL, } Of Kirby-Malzeard.
           "RICHARD MORLAND,
           "JOSHUA FLETCHER, Silsden."

"Glen Cottage, near Kirby-Malzeard, Jan. 9, 1826."

"We certify that we have known William Clarkson in his lifetime, and that he did lodge and board with William Mann, farmer, of Glen Cottage, aforesaid; and that he departed this life according to the foregoing account. We also certify that we know personally William, and Anthony Mann, his brother; and that William Mann is a member, and Anthony Mann a leader, in the Primitive Methodist Society, at Grewelthorpe, in the Ripon Circuit. And that these two men bear an unimpeachable character in the world, and are considered truly religious persons. We therefore have no hesitation in believing the truth of the preceding awful account.

    (Signed) "TIMOTHY BONWELL, Kirby-Malzeard.
             "JOHN FRANKLAND,   Ditto.
             "RICHARD MORLAND,   Ditto.
             "ARABELLA TOMLINSON, Ditto.
             "THOMAS THIRKILL, near Ditto.
             "JOHN TEBBS,   " Ditto.

"Kirby-Malzeard, Jan. 9, 1826."

"N.B.—The signatures here annexed are all (save one) from persons who are joined members of religious societies; not of our connexion alone; and from persons too of undoubted credibility. Was it necessary to have any more signatures, I am persuaded scores of others would sign it also."   "N. W."

"FURTHER PARTICULARS.

"This matter being so very extraordinary, we wrote to our respected brethren, William and Anthony Mann, and they sent us the following particulars.

"1. William Clarkson was a farmer in the former part of his life, but losing his sight, he gave up farming, and sold all his goods except a bed and a table, and came and lodged with William Mann. He had been married and had a child, but both died. He had a little landed property, but the income of it was hardly sufficient to keep him; and his custom was to go amongst his friends for two or three months in the year.

"2. He was at Nidderdale when he fell sick; and removed to a place near Pateley Bridge; where, growing worse, he was confined to his bed. And finding his departure to be nigh at hand, he sent to Grewelthorpe for his will, and wanted to alter it; but being blind, and very sick, it was not, it appears, done to his mind.

"3. The sale took place by candle-light on the evening before spoken of; it was by auction; and his landed property was sold for £670.

"4. At the last interview which William Mann had with the deceased William Clarkson, Anthony Mann saw a dark gloomy appearance near his brother William Mann, but the wind blowing sharp, and in a contrary direction, he could not distinguish the words spoken."

"ON THE APPEARANCE OF WILLIAM CLARKSON AFTER DEATH.

"This remarkable account we gave, page 158. Before we inserted it, we wrote to our respected brethren, William and Anthony Mann, and they furnished us with additional remarks. We have since received an account drawn up by the travelling preachers in our Ripon Circuit, from which we shall make a few extracts. On the last appearance but one their account is more at large; it is as follows:—

"'On November 17, (1825) about four o'clock in the afternoon, as I was returning from Ripon Market, in company with my wife and niece, the said William Clarkson appeared to me again in Ripon Lane, between Thieves-Gill and Azerly. I then felt power to speak to him. My wife and niece went on with the horse and cart. I made a stop, and said, "Bless God, &c."'

"The interview at the last appearance has in it something striking and awful. It is as follows:—

"'I walked to and fro for about ten minutes. He then appeared, as though he came from the corner of the field;—very black, but in every other respect his appearance was as when he was alive.'

"There are also a few additional particulars relating to his affairs, and to certain particular persons; but these we shall be excused from inserting, as they hardly would be of general interest.

"At the close of this interview, their account runs thus: '——He then bid me take care lest I should be his companion also. He then advanced nearer to me, and had a most suffocating smell of sulphur, which caused me to step back, &c.'

"At the close are given the signatures of the travelling preachers and other respectable friends.

"This is certainly one of the most alarming and awful accounts it has ever been our duty to record. And the more so as the said William Clarkson was by most looked upon as a good sort of man."

As my dear wife was on a visit at William Mann's at the time, and was present at the prayer meeting held in his house before he and his brother Anthony went out to meet William Clarkson for the last time, I give her statement;—

"Westfield House, Dundee, Jan. 14, 1871.

"This is to certify, that William Clarkson was my mother's uncle. I knew him well, and visited at his house during the time my sister Elizabeth was his housekeeper. She afterwards married William Mann; at whose house I was on a visit, and at the prayer meeting before he and Anthony Mann went out to meet William Clarkson. He and his family left England for America. He said he should never live to see it: which took place as he foretold. He took fever, died, and was buried on the passage. Was this one of the things which he learned, but would not tell to alarm his wife and family? They urged him to go, or he never would have left England. William Clarkson was a great Churchman, but generally regarded as not benevolent.

"SUSANNA BOWES."

I knew William Mann well. He was a solid, sedate man, neither suspected of untruthfulness nor insanity, and, excepting in this singular case, like other Christian farmers. I have said to my own mind, is this narrative true or false? If W. Mann believed it to be true, it must be so, or he was under some delusion, for it is evident that he believed his relation of the conversations to be real.

Apparitions are taught in the Scriptures. Samuel appeared to Saul and talked with him after Samuel's death. Wesley speaks hopefully of the salvation of Saul and his sons, while paraphrasing a part of 1 Sam. xxviii.—

> "What do these solemn words portend?
> A ray of hope when life shall end,
> Thou and thy sons *though* slain shall be,
> To morrow *in repose* with me,
> Not in a state of hellish pain,
> If Saul with Samuel remain.
> Not in a state of doomed *despair*,
> If loving Jonathan be *there*."

Then we have another distinct case in the New Testament, Luke ix., where Moses as well as Elijah appeared and conversed with Christ, This was witnessed by the apostles, one of whom wished to make tents for them and Christ. This idea which permeated the Jewish mind was not rejected by Christ, who in the narrative of the rich man and Lazarus, Luke xvi., tells us that the rich man wished Abraham to send him to the house of his father, "For," said, he, "I have five brothers; that he may earnestly testify to them that they may not also come to this place of torment. But Abraham says to him, They have Moses and the prophets; let them hear them. But he said, Nay, father Abraham; but if one from the dead go to them, they will change their minds. But he said to him, If they hear not Moses and the prophets, neither will they be persuaded, though one should rise from the dead." This kind of warning given by William Clarkson to William Mann occurs in this narrative. The whole teaching of Scripture in reference to a rich man who is not benevolent accords with this case. Mark x. 17—31; Matt. xxv. 31 to 46; 1 Tim. vi. 14 to the end.

I have not cited the case of Lazarus raised from the dead, John xii. 17, nor the widow's son of Nain, &c., &c., as these were so obviously like our Lord's own glorious resurrection, so evidently miraculous. But we may reject the common notions of ghosts, without denying what the Scriptures say of Samuel and Moses, and thus admit the possibility of the dead on particular occasions, and for important reasons being permitted to increase the faith of saints, and attack the unbelief of sceptics, by speaking words of terrible warning to the living; not that they will be always able to prevail against the inveterate unbelief of men, since the Jews generally did not embrace the gospel, after they could not disprove the resurrection of the beloved brother of Martha and Mary. God speaks to men by his ministers, by his word, and even his Son from heaven, nay, he goes further and speaks to them of another solemn state of existence, where such as Samuel, Moses, and Lazarus are happy, and such as the rich man are miserable. Let men hear the voice of mercy that opens up to them the secrets, the rewards and punishments of eternity, and so believe and live as to avoid the one and obtain the other. Without saying that I have the same faith in William Mann's testimony as in that of the Old and New Testaments, I can say I see nothing in his testimony inconsistent with them, and from my knowledge of the person, conclude that he really believed what he said, and, if he was under no mistake, which I cannot prove, I receive his witness.

July 1st., GREWELTHORPE, Sunday. Was joined by T. Dawson, my friend, and P. Bellwood, my brother, from whom before he left I received the following news from YARMOUTH: "Now the work is very powerful. The last week many souls have been saved. Several have been struck down as dead men in battle, and have been carried out by the people. Scores of people will be loath to part with me, but the Yarmouth Committee is so corrupt I cannot bear them." I had reason also to complain of these committees. Why should an evangelist have any Master but Christ. I preached here in the morning, and at MASHAM at night. Had a good day in spirit but not in body, being affected with a disorder in my bowels, something like diarrhœa.

On Monday we came, my wife, Phillip, and I to RIPON, and found them in a divided state. Some had made disturbance about little things, till I am afraid the great duties of the Christian are nearly lost in the contention. We met the coach at DISHFORTH on Tuesday morning, and arrived in SUNDERLAND about 6 o'clock the same evening. Heard S. Tillotson preach a useful sermon. The people here were kind in all respects but one, they gave us a bed so old and infested by bugs that it broke down, they crowded around us in scores; to get any sleep at all we had to leave it and rest on the floor. This was certainly not the way to treat Christ's servants, nor even an enemy. The Lord takes what is done to the least of his servants, as done to himself. No doubt those were to blame who had the rule here, whose conduct we shall soon have to examine, and having concealed the fact forty-four years, it is only published now to prevent others from a similar evil.

5th.—Thursday. Set off for NORTH SHIELDS, where we stayed all night, and took the steam packet for Leith at 9 next morning. Philip Bellwood, my wife's brother, left us here, and went to his circuit at Winlaton. We had a fine sea, but I was sick soon after we crossed the bar, and continued so until we came near Berwick. My wife was sea-sick soon after; and as she is in an advanced state of pregnancy, I was much afraid lest she should be injured; but we arrived safe at New Haven, on the Chain Pier, about 6 o'clock. Thomas Oliver had provided us furnished lodgings.

Before leaving Keighley, I had an offer to go to the West Indies to superintend a plantation there. It was made through Nathanael West, then in Edinburgh; but from his letter, now before me, in answer to mine, I see that I regarded it as a pecuniary temptation to leave the Lord's work for mammon, and gave him a severe rebuke for presenting the temptation before me. He vindicates himself thus: "One of the most eminent ministers in Edinburgh made his fortune there, (in the West Indies) and got his religion in it too. I thought, if you went, you could glorify God there in a very extensive degree, and perhaps be the means of introducing our cause to some of those islands." I have no doubt but my decision was right.

CHAPTER IV.

LABORS IN EDINBURGH, LEITH, ETC.—CONTROVERSY WITH THE SUNDERLAND COMMITTEE AND THE EDINBURGH MISSION—MY LETTER TO THE DISTRICT MEETING PRESENTS THE WHOLE CASE—VISIT TO SUNDERLAND—GREAT MEETING—MANY SAVED AND ADDED TO THE CHURCHES IN BOTH EDINBURGH AND LEITH—T. HARRISON'S CASE—CONLIN'S SINGULAR CASE—SEPARATION OF EDINBURGH AND LEITH THREE PREACHERS AND SOCIETIES FROM THE PRIMITIVE METHODISTS—MY ULTIMATE WITHDRAWAL FROM N. WEST.

EDINBURGH.

EDINBURGH is a Mission from Sunderland Circuit. T. Oliver and the leaders I found divided, also N. West and T. Oliver; so that T. O. was prohibited from preaching. N. West was appointed by the Conference for South Shields Circuit, but the people appeared determined to retain him in Edinburgh, and he to accede to their wish; assuming as a reason, that he had only been six months on the mission, and that he had gained great influence in this city. This he certainly appeared to have. However, on the night I arrived, I made T. O. my companion, as he and he only can now be legally called the Edinburgh Missionary, but when he began to talk of faith going before reason, and told me that he had preached this doctrine, and when I saw his conduct I was led to fear that he was most to blame. However, the principal prayer leaders and class leaders met to consult what was best to be done, and as N. West and Sunderland Circuit were at variance, we judged it best to try to get them to state a sum, what they would take, and either make Edinburgh into a circuit, or give us up to the General Missionary Committee.

8th., Sunday. Mr West lectured in the morning, I preached at 2 o'clock, and N. West in the Grass Market. Large congregation. Attended each time.

On Monday night attended a prayer meeting. A good meeting.

On Tuesday night spoke in the room, Heriot's Bridge.

On Wednesday preached at a place called Sheriff Bray, in LEITH. Large congregations.

On Thursday night I met Bro. Mooney's class. Most of them enjoy liberty.

On Friday night N. West preached at NEWHAVEN. Felt it very good while praying with an old woman after, on the confines of eternity.

On Saturday we met the tract deliverers.

On Sunday morning I lectured in the room, from John iii. In the afternoon met class at LEITH. Two backsliders had got wounded on Wednesday evening and joined this afternoon. At night preached from "Be sure your sin will find you out." When I had done a soldier came and got hold of my hand. He seemed much affected, thanked me for the sermon, and added, "I have never heard a more Christian-like sermon these many years." I exhorted him to profit by it.

On Monday went to visit some who were under deep conviction. N. West and I spoke to them about the plan of salvation, a most gracious influence rested upon us.   We prayed, and one woman got liberty.

N. West preached on Tuesday evening.

On Wednesday I preached at LEITH. A large congregation.

Thursday visited and attended N. West's class. About 43 in it. I spoke over much, or too loud.

On Friday night I spoke at NEWHAVEN to an attentive congregation.

I insert this letter of the Committee, as it gives their view to the Edinburgh Mission :—

DEAR BRETHREN,—

We have duly received yours of the 18th instant, and we are glad that you are for peace, which you may rest assured has (and through grace) ever will be our aim, accompanied with fervent desires for your spiritual prosperity, and far, very far, be it from us as much as to think of lording over God's heritage, or to do aught designedly that may tend to offend the least of Christ's little ones that believe on Him. There is only one thing, we now observe, you err in, (but we excuse you, as events have transpired that have had a tendency to lead you a little aside)—i.e., in causing Brother Oliver to desist his labors as a preacher. There are regular steps to be taken, indeed according to equity, before a minister should be banished from his ministry, and his salary taken from him, or otherwise anarchy and disaster would be the consequence invariably. However, we bear with you. Your letter says that Brother O. has stated to you, that Brother G. Black pre-determined to keep him in the mission for a living. If T. O. said so, he erred very much; because, first, no single individual rules in our church, and, second, we believe Brother Black would say no such thing, and he has more prudence than to vaunt of helping men into such an important office as the ministry for a piece of bread, or to think of voting for a man to remain when it appears he is not in his providential way. Brethren, if you lay aside all grievances from your minds, and calmly reflect, as we are doing at this moment, you will perceive from whence many errors have arisen in the late unpleasant contention. It originated first between Brother W. and Sunderland, and you, as well as Brother O., have been brought to trouble, who otherwise might have been neutral, and at peace, and owing to which much recrimination has been used. When persons are contesting it is not hard to get wrong and speak unadvisedly. You know, if T.O. has incurred your displeasure, it is recently, by abiding by our instructions; and we positively affirm that T.O. never said an ill word in his letters about any one; nor did he encourage any opposition against Brother N. W., which he seems to be blamed for. As a proof, we will give you an extract of his letter, dated May 28th, 1827, sent to this circuit committee : "If you are determined to stand out against Brother W., see that your cause be just, and your proceedings in that cause be according to 1 Cor. xiii., and if your mind does not come to it, before ever you proceed further, let your mind change to this religion, for it will never change to yours, though you should eternally perish." And in the same letter he says his heart is knit to you, and to all the Society. In another letter dated the 9th inst., he says, with reference to Brother Bowes,—"I must acknowledge, with all deference to others, he excels them all, as far as I have seen, in fineness of spirit and holiness of disposition." And again he says, at another time, he prayed for all parties fervently, and this at the very time he was put from his work, and his subsistence withdrawn. But to conclude : Dear brethren, we will not contend with you; only allow him to labor for the present, as Quarter Day is at hand, and then he may be removed, as at this time we have not a station for him; and beside, it will have a tendency to bring about a reconciliation and peace among all parties. Brother West will go, and doubtless will be received in peace, and we have no hardness against him, nor have we against you; and if you are reconciled to your first preacher, we all may again offer our sacrifices, if not together, yet in one spirit at the throne of grace. And may the Lord in his mercy bring us all in the end to our Father's house above.

S. TILLOTSON, President.
H. HESMAN, Secretary.

JULY, 21st, 1827.

It was this forcing of T. Oliver so long on a society that would not have him, that produced immense damage, as the following letter proves :—

BROTHER BOWES,—

I am delegated by our Committee to write, informing you of the decision of our Committee.

Resolved,—"That T. Oliver be withdrawn from the Scotland Mission immediately." You will please to let him have money to defray his expenses down, and account for it to Quarter Day. We have just received a letter from the General Committee. The following is an extract : "The matter is now decided; he is not, and cannot (that is, N.West), according to rule, be recognised as a travelling preacher in our connexion."

Dear brother, from this you will discover your case to be critical, on the face of rule, and you will now have to exercise your fortitude, as well as your prudence, otherwise a conjunction will prove as disastrous as a division. Be cautious; let prudence dictate; and after that enforce with authority. My love to you and wife, Brother Oliver and wife, and all enquiring friends. I remain yours, &c.,

S. TILLOTSON.

Committee Room, July 27, 1827.

P.S.—Send me a few lines, telling me all your mind, by brother Oliver. Keep this letter to yourself, as we expect the General Committee will write soon.

22nd.—Sunday. Lectured in the morning from Rom. viii. In the afternoon the congregation was very large, and I had an extraordinary good time. At 6 o'clock I preached on Leith Links to about a thousand people.

On Monday night I received a letter from Sunderland; more satisfactory than the last. On Tuesday night, charges were preferred against T. Oliver. The leaders' meeting examined him, and found him guilty of many things. He seems to be made up of mysticism, insanity, and perverseness.

29th.—Sunday. N. West lectured in the morning. I preached at 2 o'clock, from Luke xix., 21, 22. After which we observed the Lord's Supper; about 200 communicants; a most precious season. At 6 o'clock I preached to about 1000 people in the Grass Market, about 500 of whom followed us into the chapel to a prayer meeting. We sang, and two prayed; and again sang, and two prayed. I then began to sing again, and T. Oliver began to pray; however the people continued to sing. While they were singing he stepped up to me, and asked me if I did not intend him to pray. As I had before desired him not to minister until Sunderland Circuit Committee had examined the charges alleged against him, I told him that he might pray without praying aloud; but if he was determined to pray he might. However, when we had done singing I exhorted the people to sit down, intending to tell the mourners how they might obtain liberty; but he got upon a form, began to call the leaders wicked men, and told the people I was sent here to assist him, and had joined in with them against him. After he sat down, I said a little to calm the minds of the people; but I am afraid all the good that has been done to-day has now been damped, if not destroyed, by this outrageous conduct. I kneeled down and began to pray; after which, at the same time, he began: after he had done, I concluded the meeting.

30th.—This morning I received a letter (given above) from Sunderland, recalling T. Oliver from this mission immediately. Accordingly, I was exceedingly glad, for he is doing much harm. To-night we held a prayer meeting; as many as usual attended, at which I was much surprised. We had a good time.

On Tuesday morning N. West and I breakfasted with James Haldon, Esq., of Gayfield Square; after which, he took us by the arm and walked up to Edinburgh Bank. We had some conversation about the mission, and he advised us to disentangle ourselves from England, and labor on. I preached to-night, and had an extraordinary good time.

Aug. 1st.—I began to sing at LEITH, intending to preach. We were driven off by the rain, but many followed me to a prayer meeting, held by the sailors in connection with the floating chapel, in the Methodist old chapel. Some were much affected. In addition to the ten families, I visited to-day two sick women; one on the brink of eternity, apparently very happy.

2nd.—In my regular visiting, two or three invited me to pray with them. I visited also a sick man, a butcher, once rich, but now in a wretched condition outwardly, and worse inwardly, having had no passage in his bowels these eight days. He still takes liquor, and when his poor wife cannot get it, he curses most horribly. I talked to him of his sin and danger, and he seemed affected. I prayed with him, and he invited me to call again.

The following shows that South Shields was ready to receive N. West:

TO THE PREACHERS AND LEADERS OF THE P.M. CONNEXION AT EDINBURGH.

DEAR BRETHREN IN THE LORD,—

We have received by the hand of our dear brother West your loving and excellent letter. We cordially thank and salute you in the Lord for the care you manifest for the church of Christ among you in the important city of Edinburgh, aud we hope your society will more and more flourish in number and in grace. By this short epistle we give you to understand that we have unanimously and affectionately received our Brother West. And further inform you, that if you received our last, it was written solely on the supposition that Brother West would not come to us, and we wrote to the same effect to the General Committee. But now he is come, and we hope that sorrow on both sides of the question will end. Wishing you all prosperity in the cause of Christ, I remain, dear brethren, yours on behalf, and by order of, Circuit Committee meeting,

JOHN ROBINSON, Circuit Steward.

South Shields, Aug. 3, 1827.

5th.—Sunday. This has been a good day. Contrary to my expectations, I find T. Oliver's conduct has not done the harm which I feared. Our congregations were as large as usual.

6th.—The families which I visited to-day were principally professed Roman Catholics; but so much ignorance and bigotry I have not witnessed before. Some of them would neither read our tracts, nor permit me to come away without abuse; others did both.

11th.—The first fellowship meeting held among our people was held to-night. It was very rainy. Notwithstanding, we had more than could be expected, and a good meeting. I hope only a prelude to what we may expect.

12th.—Sunday. To-day my wife has been delivered, after much hard labor for sixteen hours, of a fine girl, still-born through the hardness of the labor. It has been a day of great trial to me. However, as all the best assistance which was necessary was got, I will submit.

18th.—Held another fellowship meeting. More people than last week. A mighty time; two found liberty, and more were seeking.

19th.—After lecturing in the morning from John ix., I spoke in the afternoon and at night, and exhorted the Society, with which a great part of the congregation stayed.

22nd.—Preached in the Academy for Seamen's Children, LEITH: not many people.

25th.—Attended the fellowship-meeting. Many present; some seeking the Lord. One man who was seeking last week prayed, and the two who obtained pardon confessed it.

27th.—To-night our Quarterly Lovefeast was held. It commenced at 7, and concluded a little after 10 o'clock; but many being wounded by the Spirit, refused to rise from their knees. When many were gone out, we commenced a prayer meeting, and invited all the mourners to come into one place. About twenty came, and we engaged in prayer for them. I could not ascertain how many were made happy by faith in the Redeemer, but I suppose at least six or eight. Many cried aloud and wept for mercy, and many shouted aloud for joy. Some came tonight to ask for admission who had never been at one of our lovefeasts before, but who were recommended to come by persons who met with them in their different churches.

29th.—Preached in the floating chapel, and had tolerable liberty. May the Lord make it a blessing.

30th.—Began a class. Many attended, and three gave in their names. A good time.

Sep. 2nd.—Preached twice to large congregations, and had particularly liberty in the open-air at 6 o'clock. The greatest part of the congregation followed to the prayer meeting in the chapel.

13th.—Met my class. A most glorious time. One professed to find the Lord.

Received the following letter from Sunderland Committee:—

SUNDERLAND, SEP. 14th, 1827.

BROTHER BOWES,—

These lines come to inform you that we have received the anxiously looked for letter from the Central Committee at last, and sorry we are to say that N. West is not recognised as a preacher among us, on account of his own refusing to go to his circuit; consequently, you must withdraw from acting in cognizance with him, which will peremtorily call upon you to take prudential steps accordingly; there now being no other alternative. But if you should find it unpleasant to make a stand, which we know will be disagreeable for any one, you must return to Sunderland, where you may labor both with peace and pleasure. You must now make up your own mind, and answer accordingly, immediately. An answer from your own mind to the following queries is required,—

1. Will you abide by the Connexion's decision, and preserve the mission as far as possible from monopoly and imposition? &c.; or

2. Will you return to labor in the other parts of Sunderland Circuit, that another may supply your place? or

3. Will you still continue to labor in unison with N. West, as you have been doing since you entered upon the mission?

N.B.—An unambiguous answer is forthwith requested to those queries, which answer we intend to be ground of our future conduct. Do be expeditious in making up your mind, and answer without delay. I remain yours, in behalf of the adjourned Quarter-day,

SAMUEL TILLOTSON.

P.S.—We have written a few lines to the Society Steward along with this, for the leaders' meeting. We hope you will, in this one instance, show your attachment to the cause you have espoused, by acting according to its contents.

23rd.—Opened a church or kirk formerly occupied by Mr. Culbertson, U.P. minister, and recently by Mr. Smart, which, he having opened a new church last May, has since been unoccupied. I preached in the morning, and N. West afternoon and night. At the last service the chapel was crowded.

Oct. 15th.—Wrote the Sunderland Committee. The following only will form my defence against the accusations of the committee :—

"You think that I should have made 'restitution' of the £5 I received from you towards my travelling expenses. Answer: I came from Keighley to Edinburgh to labor as your servant, distance 242 miles, at the rate of 6d. a mile according to rule, so that you have not paid me enough by £1 1s., the cost being £6 1s. In addition to this £1 1s., you owe me also £3 for wages, and £1 10s. which I paid to Bro. Mooney for T. Oliver's removal, making a whole of £5 11s. which is legally due to me up to the time I was your preacher; 2s. you may take from that for magazines which I sold, and I want now £5 9s."

LEITH.

25th.—On the 21st of last month we removed to LEITH, where we have been living since in lodgings. My wife meets a class of 8 members, and I meet one on Thursday nights, consisting of 16 members. There were not more when we came than 10; so that 14 have been added this last month. Our congregations here are good. I visit ten families daily (Saturday and Lord's Day excepted). In consequence of not standing by Sunderland Committee, I received a letter this month, informing me that I was no longer a Primitive Methodist preacher, because I would not make a division and oppose N. West. They have sent over S. Tillotson and T. Oliver, who have attempted to take our chapel in Heriot's Bridge from us, but have been disappointed, and S. Tillotson has returned to England, leaving T. Oliver here. He has not above 6 members, whom we would have desired to keep. On the 15th, we opened a school-room at STOCKBRIDGE for worship, where we preach every Monday night; and we have opened another at the WATER OF LEITH, where we preach every Friday night, and on Sunday mornings at half-past 9.

Last Lord's Day, the 21st, we opened a commodious chapel in Richmond Court, formerly occupied by Christopher Anderson, Baptist minister. It was crowded to excess at night; scores could not get in. We have the three last mentioned places free of charge. Our congregations are large, and our classes weekly increase.

Dec. 21st.—Preached at the Water of Leith. Met the Society, and added 6 young men to the class. Much good has been done here.

24th.—Monday. Attended a lovefeast. Many people; a glorious time. One young man whom I admitted seemed careless when he came in for a note of admission, but he came to me when the lovefeast was closed, and said, with tears in his eyes, "I hope you will not prevent me from attending these meetings in future."

31st.—To-night I assisted in holding a Watch Night in Heriot's Bridge chapel, EDINBURGH. Many people. I spoke first, from Ps. ciii. 2. I noticed God's benefits to the unbeliever and to the believer during the past year, and with what dispositions we ought to review our mercies. Two Leaders spoke, and Mr. West, on the shortness of time and the awful state of the aged. Many appeared much affected, and it was a solemnly profitable time. I renewed my strength and covenant with God.

Jan. 1st, 1828 (Leap year). Attended a lovefeast in Richmond Court chapel. A most gracious season. Many of our members spoke who never did before in a lovefeast. It appears they are growing in grace. Preached at night in Heriot's Bridge chapel. I was plain, and earnest that all might begin the year with God.

Feb. 9th.—We removed yesterday into a house. Some friends in Edinburgh have been very kind, and have assisted us to furnish it. The Lord's work still prospers in the mission, and our prospects are increasingly bright. I begin to feel more attachment to our little flock here. I believe they are growing in grace. One woman, who kept a house of ill-fame, came to the chapel one Lord's Day night in last month, and on the Monday morning following, she dismissed the poor girls from the house, and since then has kept her house free from its former evil practices.

18th.—To-day I have begun to set apart two hours every Monday for conversing in my own house with such as may come enquiring, "What must I do to be saved?" Two persons came, and I had a profitable time while speaking to them. To-night I formed a class after the Monday night prayer meeting. Four new ones. Last night I had a most powerful time at Heriot's Bridge chapel. Many seemed pricked to the heart, and cried for mercy. In the prayer meeting one young woman trembled much, and spoke to me in great distress. Another told me that she was struck by the power of God when I was here about five weeks ago, and that she had experienced the new birth. Glory to the Lamb of God.

March 22nd.—Held the usual fellowship meeting in LEITH. It was a solemn time; some wept, and some rejoiced. Two got into the liberty of God's children. It is now about six months since we opened this chapel here, and we have now 51 members. The increase in the mission for 6 months, 106. Thus the work of God is progressing almost as much as at Keighley.

April 7th.—We held a lovefeast in LEITH. A powerful time. Held a prayer meeting after. Much power. Some think the Scotch will not drink into the spirit of a revival, but I think otherwise; the fault has been in ourselves. The Lord make us more alive. I long to see souls converted.

The following letter to the District Meeting and Conference will explain the whole case of our controversy with Sunderland Committee, and is therefore given at length:—

TO THE P. M. DISTRICT MEETING AT SOUTH SHIELDS, AND FROM THERE TO THE CONFERENCE AT TUNSTAL.

MY DEAR BRETHREN,—

May grace, wisdom, and peace be with you all, from God our Father and Jesus Christ, our common Lord. As a letter can ONLY SPEAK ONCE, and as I am unable to attend your meeting in person, I hope you will take this letter into due consideration. This comes to inform you that I have been excluded from the Connexion by the Sunderland Circuit, and also to lay before you the causes of that expulsion, with my appeal against it, and in order that you may be able to form a correct opinion concerning the subject, I shall give you a statement of facts as full and concise as the nature of the subject will admit.

Early on Saturday morning, July 7th, 1827, I arrived in Edinburgh, went to the lodgings of Thomas Oliver, and obtained what information I could relative to the state of the Mission. He informed me that the leaders had suspended him; but he told me also that one of them was a hypocrite, a second a novice, a third a formalist, &c., &c. I told him to point me out his reasons for giving them such names. The only reason he gave me was this, viz., that they opposed him. The fact is, that they were all against him but one. The same morning I went to the house of N. West, and inquired if he intended to go to his circuit. He answered in the negative. I used reasons. He still refused. I would not hear of his staying in Edinburgh; but urged that he ought to have been at Shields. I only talked with him a few minutes, and returned to T. Oliver, with whom I went to wait upon J. Haldon, Esq., treasurer for the mission. He commenced by charging T. Oliver with many things which he had done wrong, which I forbear to name. For a considerable time the gentleman appeared to take no notice of me. I was afraid that I should not have the privilege of apologising for my appearance in Edinburgh, &c.; but I was agreeably disappointed. He conversed frankly on the state of the mission, and heard me patiently while I showed the evil that might follow the detention of N. West. I went also to the only leader that stood by T. Oliver, and heard what he had to say. At night a meeting of all the official characters on the mission was held. My limits and memory allow me not to mention all that was said; but the meeting resolved to propose to Sunderland, that if they would give up the mission, Edinburgh would repay them the money which they had expended on account of the mission. If this was agreed to, the mission should be offered to the General Missionary Committee. While the leaders sent their proposals, I also transmitted to Sunderland a correct statement of the state of things in the mission, and made opposite proposals to Sunderland, which I thought would be more conducive to the good of all concerned. Their answer to this (my first letter) is dated July 12th, 1827, and I will make a few extracts from it, that you may see the manner in which I was treated, while I was doing what I could for them and the mission. In the first sentence they say, "We are a little surprised at the matter of your letter because of its inconsistency," &c. They proceed, "Again, you are to be kept by them (Edinburgh society), for this reason, because you have chimed in with them, and have actually taken a part in those things which you were to oppose. Was Solomon here with all his wisdom to give us council. we could not understand your zigzag. We hope in future you will write no such empty, high-sounding stuff. We cannot remove T. Oliver yet, *until we see whether we have a preacher in Edinburgh or not!*" I was struck dumb with astonishment when I received this. I came here determined to act, through grace, in accordance with the Bible and rule. So I had acted. I had not taken one step which did not appear to me calculated to conciliate the regard of Edinburgh Society for Sunderland Committee. Indeed I did oppose the ways of T. Oliver, which was crime enough in the eyes of Gordon Black, whose *minion* T.O. was. S. Tillotson wrote this letter, and what harm had I done him? None. But as I have been since informed, Sunderland people talked much in my favor, which (as is now plain) the envy of S. Tillotson could not endure, and so he, having an opportunity of striking a blow at my character, seized the moment, &c.

In my next letter I complained of hard and unjust treatment, which caused another from them, dated July 21st. They acknowledge in this their own fallibility, and that, owing to the dark state of the mission when I entered on it, I was excusable, &c.,&c. During this time I was using my influence to persuade N.West to go to his circuit, in which I ultimately succeeded. The leaders being willing to give him up on the condition that T. Oliver was removed; which also, after much labor, was effected. Accordingly, N. West was thrown off the funds of the mission, and on, or about, the 1st August, he and T. Oliver went to England. Here I may call upon you to remark, (honesty binds me to it or I should not) that while T. Oliver was upon the mission after I came, he did all the injury to the mission that he possibly could, by going from house to house sowing discord, and by his persecuting prayers, &c. In short, he appeared to many to be a compound of mysteriousness, wickedness, and insanity. He threatened to break my head, and tear me in pieces, in my own room!!! Yet Sunderland coincided with him who was a *perfect nuisance* on the mission, and opposed me because I had the misfortune to be acceptable to the society—the principal part being opposed to him.

When N. West was at Sunderland, G. Black told him that I had acted worse than he (N. West). While he was in Sunderland, he requested the Committee to give him either good or bad credentials. But whether he was too bad for a good one, or too good for a bad one, I never yet learned; but they refused. So he came back to Edinburgh, All of the leaders but one had determined to stand by him if he was excluded for standing by the mission.

I heard nothing more from Sunderland till a woman came to our lodgings early one morning, and informed me that two strangers from England waited at their house to see me; concealing their names and business; but withal told me that I was not to see N. West before I saw them. I wondered much who these presumptuous strangers were, that could so calculate upon my weakness as to command me first to go to them, and secondly, not to see N. West before I went. However I was so cautious as not to comply; and so the mystery unravels. S. Tillotson and G. Black were the two "strangers." They had gone twice past our door, slept under the same roof that covered me, and had gone into the suburbs of the city, a mile distant, to see me there! On this clandestine procedure I leave you to comment. But the subject does not end here. They came to my enemies,—to the enemies of the society,—persons who were not in society—with these persons they ate, and slept, and tarried until they departed; while both I and the society were grieved to see ourselves treated with contempt. We proposed that they should examine the charges that stood against T. Oliver. This they declined.

While here they wrote to the General Committee; but neither made me a companion in their work, nor let me see the letter. An answer did not come until they had returned to Sunderland. It was sent after them; I never saw it. All this time I was kept in suspense,. At length I received a letter, stating that they had received the General Committee's letter, and in it they propose the three questions,—"First: Will you abide by the Connexion's decision, and preserve the mission as far as you can from monopoly and imposition? or, Second: Will you return to labor in the other parts of Sunderland Circuit, that another may supply your place? or, Third: Will you still continue to labor in unison with N. West, as you have been doing since you entered upon the mission?" Query: Was I laboring in unison with N. West all the time he was opposed to go to Shields, while there, or while in Sunderland vestry trying to obtain his credentials? I wrote an answer to these questions, which I think it will be necessary for them to produce.

In their next letter came my expulsion. A part of it I shall transcribe for your perusal. They call my letter "virulent and contemptuous," and say, "with all the sophistry and craft you are master of, which is not a little, you cannot prove that you have not purloined from us. They tell me that I am guilty of "treachery, fraud, and sacrilege." They compare me to the traitor "Marshal Ney," to "Achan the Jew, whose conduct," they say, "is similar to yours." They charge me with intrigues and self-seeking;" they compare me to the devil, and say, "you need not now attempt to transform yourself into an angel of light, as you have appeared; the garb is torn off, and you appear in your native deformity," &c. I will pass no comment on this astonishing language; for I think you will all understand it.

Here, then, I must pause. Such is the manner in which I have been treated, and as you have the whole matter before you, judge whether I merited such treatment.

It remains for me to state my reasons for not complying with the two first proposals of Sunderland. The great reason why I could not comply with either proposal was, because compliance must have issued in a division, which I was desirous to prevent. I could not make a stand against N. West without making a division. Hence I could not comply with their first proposal for the following reasons:—

1. Because of my duty to God, by whom I profess to be sent,—not to make divisions, but to "preach the word," &c. My conscience bears me record that, had I been accessory to a division, to Him I should have been an unjust steward.

2. Because of my duty to the Primitive Methodists, who did not call me out to make divisions.

3. Because of my duty to the souls committed to my care. As a shepherd I was sent not to divide and destroy the flock, but to "feed the flock," not with the gall of discord, but with "the sincere milk of the word."

I could not comply with their second proposal, viz., "return to Sunderland," for the following reasons:—

1. Because they proposed sending another in my place to make a division. Hence all the former reasons lay against this proposal.

2. Because of their treatment to me, as stated in this letter, and as they had excluded N. West, and as I "was worse than he," I could expect no less.

3. Because the Edinburgh Society was altogether opposed to my leaving them.

Note, I had only been here a few weeks. Now, mark, the matter stands thus— Our Rules do not authorise any preacher to obey a Committee when they command him to do wrong. It was wrong for Sunderland Circuit Committee to command J, Bowes either to make a division or return to Sunderland, and, therefore J. Bowes acted rightly when he refused to obey Sunderland Circuit Committee. Such is the conclusion to which my logic conducts me. I will only trouble you with a few remarks. 1st. I want of Sunderland Circuit Committee £5 9s. What must I do to get it? £3 19s. and £1 10s. which I lent them to take T. Oliver to England. I sent for it. No answer. But after my letter was read, G. Black rose up and said, that "He (Bowes) is as big a thief as ever was unhanged. I should not regret to see him hanged!!! I have had to do with all kinds of men, but never met with such a villain as Bowes!!!" This is one sample of Gordon Black's fitness for the important office he holds in the church of Christ. I will give you another. The first night after my arrival in Sunderland, I attended a Committee, after which he came to me and said, "No man has a finer opportunity of acquiring honor than you, &c., &c." He referred to the Edinburgh Mission. He spoke of the applause which would be conferred upon me in overthrowing N. West, and much more. I shuddered at the idea of seeking the praises of men. Surely it was the very bait which Satan himself would have used for corrupt nature to catch at. What a mercy that I discovered it, and I hope shunned it, for so I designed to do. But was it not awful for a Circuit Steward to place such a motive before a young minister, merely that I might be instrumental in gaining his point. Dear brethern, you will not think it unscriptural for a minister to vindicate his character when it is maliciously impugned. If you reflect upon the example of Paul, hear me then for a moment while, to use (Paul's words), "I speak as a fool." At the age of 13 I became a member of the Wesleyan Society. From that time I continued with them till about 6 years ago, when I joined the Primitive Methodist Society. I left them "in peace with all men," and no charge was ever brought against me while among them. I joined this body, Primitive Methodists, with the purest of motives. I have been near 6 years a travelling preacher in the following Circuits, viz.—1 year at Guisbro', 2 at Ripon. and 2 at Keighley, and near one I have spent here. During this time I never had a charge brought against me (as far as I remember) of any kind to any Circuit Committee or Quarter Day, where I have labored. No, not at Keighley where my duty called me to oppose some two or three of the most turbulent and revengeful Committee men. Yet I am all at once bad, sentenced, and thrown *overboard*. Be it remembered that when I left Sunderland, neither I nor N. West intended to leave the body of Primitive Methodists. I might have added that the Lord has given me some scores of children in the body, and that I never left any of the Circuits without considerable improvement both in temporals and spirituals.

I have to remark, that if you will not credit the statements made by N. West, the Leaders, and myself, you cannot have a correct knowledge of matters except you were to examine them in Edinburgh, for notwithstanding the strange way in which S. Tillotson has acted, he told me while here that his views of things were so changed after his arrival, *that his views* were exactly like my own. How strange then does this man's conduct appear? He could say when he came to make the division with Oliver that his views of Oliver were such as that he (Oliver) had done wrong, &c., that Sunderland had done wrong. He said this to me, yet he assisted Sunderland, he joins Oliver to effect a division. Does not this betray a base, man-pleasing disposition—where was his principle? where was honesty? Praying that the all-wise God may direct you, I subscribe myself,

Your brother in Christ,

JOHN BOWES.

No. 71 St Giles Street, Leith, Scotland, April, 12, 1828.

April 13*th*.—After preaching a short sermon in Richmond Court chapel, I went to hear Jas. Johnson, from Glasgow, in Heriot's Bridge chapel. He had done his sermon, and was informing them how the Lord had wrought in Glasgow. It was while he spoke blessing rested on us. His conversation while at tea was as profitable as his pulpit talk; it did me good. I see, I feel we are too dead. The Lord make us alive. I did take a text at Richmond Court chapel, but spoke from it without premeditation.

20th.—I had good liberty in preaching a sermon before the Lord's Supper at Heriot's Bridge; also felt much of the presence of God while serving the Tables (as it is called here) with N. West. I preached at night from 1 Samuel, vi, 20th, "Who is able to stand before this Holy Lord God," sinners wept aloud. I held a prayer meeting after the sermon; few went away; conviction had seized many hearts. I recommended the people to clear three forms and exhorted the mourners to come from all parts of the congregation, and we prayed with them, some got liberty. The three forms were filled: I don't know how many got liberty. A man came to me with tears rapidly streaming from his eyes, and said that he was once joined in Mr Clewer's class, but had been twelve months after from the city, had fallen from grace and God, and now promised to live nearer to him, through grace.

24th.—To-day I visited an aged man who had been many years in the army. I inquired what place of worship he attended. He said "Mr Muir's." I asked, "Are you a Member? He answered, "No."

J. B.—"You are now advancing far into years; it is a wonder you have not joined some church before this time."

MAN.—"Many take the Sacrament who are not fit for it."

J. B.—I believe it; but you ought not to avoid the church on that account. There was a Judas and a Peter among the twelve Apostles. Both did wrong; but the rest followed Christ, and religion is a personal thing; if you have it, you will be saved, and if you have it not, you will be condemned. You believe the Bible?

MAN.—"O yes, I acknowledge that it is wrong for me not to join the church."

J. B.—"Certainly, for if you do not join the church on earth, and get made holy by faith in Christ, how can you expect to join the church in heaven after death; for heaven is a Holy place." Here I quoted some passages to convince him of the propriety of joining the church, and of being holy, &c. He listened attentively and appeared convinced of the vast necessity of a change of heart and life.

I visited a widow, and inquired if she had read the tract which I left. "Oh yes, sir, many times over, I have just been reading it, it is in the Bible in Solomon's Song." "Have you got good by reading it? "O yes, much good." (It was the tract entitled, "Address of a Minister to his Parishioners on Prayer), I left her another tract, and said, "Now you must read this carefully over." "O yes, sir, and I will make the little girl read it as soon as she comes in." I spoke to her on the necessity of being born again, &c., she wept, and seemed abundantly thankful for my visit. The greatest number of those with whom I conversed on the nature of faith in Christ, and immediate preparation for another world, &c., answer: "We do what we can," or "We must do what we can."

May 4th.—This morning I should have preached on the Links, LEITH, but as the morning was wet, I preached at eight o'clock, in the Chapel, about 12 people. Lectured at 11, and at 2 and 6 preached in Richmond Court chapel; at night held a Prayer Meeting, many there, but there appeared to be no particular work, till I and another began to speak to one or two who seemed to be affected. One young man cried aloud for mercy, some were made happy.

5th.—Monday night, attended a Lovefeast in the same place, the bar of unbelief was broken; souls in distress; we prayed, two or three got liberty, and when speaking commenced again, they confessed with the mouth; more got liberty, I suppose about ten. Yet one of our Class Leaders got wrong by referring to the experience of another, and this caused us some trouble the night following.

8th.—Thursday, Fast Day in EDINBURGH, went up early in the morning; some cried aloud for mercy; one got liberty at the 8 o'clock prayer meeting. At 11 I lectured on the 51st Psalm; more in deep distress. At 2, I preached in the open-air in Richmond Court; a melting time it was. Many followed into the Chapel to a prayer meeting. Hastened to LEITH to lead my class, some of them saw the necessity of being born again. We had some yet in the class who were anxious, but not saved.

9th.—Friday, Citadel, NORTH LEITH, in the open-air, preached to a large, well-behaved company. I trust good was done.

June 1st.—I preached in the morning at half-past 7 o'clock, on the Links, on the Justice of God, not forgetting his Grace. Lectured in the Chapel at 11, and preached in Heriot's Bridge Chapel at a quarter-past 2 and 6 o'clock, to large congregations. Good was done. Some got made happy in the prayer meeting after, while some cried aloud for mercy.

2nd.—Monday, 7 p.m. held our Lovefeast in Heriot's Bridge. A most glorious time; many more under conviction; some got good; the speaking in general displayed much zeal and knowledge.

3rd.—Tuesday, at Portobello. Open-air, a serious company.

6th.—Friday, at RICHMOND COURT Chapel to-night, from Gal. iv, 18.

7th.—Saturday, this morning when I got up I was ill, such griping pains in my bowels as I seldom felt. Discharged a great quantity of green matter; vomited also most of the day green matter. Took an ounce of salts, vomited them immediately. Took half-an-ounce again, but did not vomit soon after. Doctor Milner sent me a little castor-oil. I took it and vomited some time after. It did no good. I was confined to bed all day, as I got up but could not bear up. I never endured so much pain in one day in my life; I sweat very much; and when I thought of souls being in hell, and if they only suffered as much as I, it would be quite distracting. I thanked God for a better prospect. This illness was brought on by drinking or supping a bason full of milk, after the fatigue of Friday night as I think, and so aggravated by using tobacco.

9th.—Monday, I have recovered a little in body. I received a letter from my brother-in-law saying that this mission was not made a circuit by the conference, and that neither N. West's name nor mine is on the stations of conference. We sent our proposals to the district meeting, but neither has given us an answer.

In June and July we formally constituted the Grass Market Evangelical Mission, published our reasons for separation from the Primitive Methodists in England, and certain doctrines, laws, and Rules in a pamphlet of 42 pages. We had got a little in advance of Primitive Methodism but we were yet bound by laws of our own making. This work was our's not God's; our preaching of the glorious gospel, was His, and in this at that time we had great success, although subsequent events will show that barriers were soon erected in our way.

July 27th.—On Sunday a little after 11 o'clock p.m. my wife was delivered of a fine girl, whom we called Ann.

30*th.*—N. West went by the packet to Sunderland.

August 3rd.—I preached in the KING'S PARK at half-past 7 o'clock to a large congregation. I have reason to think good was done; at half-past 11 I lectured in Richmond Court Chapel, and afternoon and evening I preached two sermons to prove, 1st, the being of a God; and 2nd, the authenticity of the Scriptures. Very large congregations.

11*th*—I set off from Edinburgh for Sunderland by the Chevy Chase coach; a pleasant journey. Entered into conversation with the coachman he was extremely ignorant of divine things, as might be expected, for he had not been in any place of worship he said for 30 years past, except once, and that was when he was married. I exhorted him to repent, I showed him the awful consequences of a life of sin, and I hope that the exhortation was not without effect. He soon after (as usual) took the name of God in vain, I reproved him, he said, "I dont know when I do it," this I believed. It was an inveterate habit. On the coach I had much conversation with an Independent from Hawick; who keeps a shop there, and for many years has preached on Lord's Days. I inquired into the state of religion there. He gave an unfavorable account, and said that the clergyman of the Scotch church there, was an ungodly man. I asked "What marks of ungodliness does he bear?" He did not proceed to state any real marks of ungodliness, as I expected; but to put the matter beyond all dispute he said, "In short, he is an Arminian!" This was the grand climax of his sin. After spending the Monday night comfortably with the brother of my brother-in-law's wife in Newcastle-on-Tyne, I hastened to SUNDERLAND where I met N. West. I preached that night in Number's Garth Chapel; it belongs to the Independent Methodists.

13*th.*—Wednesday, to-night, at half-past 6, we held a meeting in Robertson's Lane Chapel, in order to give an explanation of the reasons why we were not in communion with the people called Primitive Methodists; a crowded place, I suppose about 1000 people. We read the letters of the Sunderland Committee to me, and my answers; showed the anti-christian manner in which we had been treated by the Sunderland Committee, and then stated our reasons for calling the meeting,—that we could not get a hearing in the connexion; our characters were assailed in the most malevolent manner; we were called the worst of names undeservedly. We showed, moreover, how the corrupt discipline of the body produced such evils, &c. The meeting continued till near 11 o'clock. At the commencement of the meeting we had a little opposition from some of the committee; but it was soon overturned, and the meeting gave us repeated and uncommon bursts of approbation for our conduct.

14*th*—Thursday, took Numbers' Garth Chapel. Preached to a large congregation. Formed a church of 12 members.

16*th.*—Saturday, I arrived safe back in Leith. Praise the Lord.

Sep. 1st.—To-day I visited, prayed with, and gave advice to a woman who tied her feet, and got out of a window, and threw herself down the outside of the house. She fell from the third storey, and not a bone was broken. She was very much hurt. It is now eight days ago. She seems sensible of the heinous nature of her offence;

weeps I trust on account of sin; prays for mercy. I hope her repentance and prayers are sincere. It appears from what she says, that her worldly circumstances are not so easy as formerly. Some of her children are unsteady; her husband, however, appears pious, but has been some months without employment.

We held a Lovefeast in Heriot's Bridge. A large company of people. A serious meeting; rather slow speaking; but we had a sweet, glorious outpouring of the Spirit. Many were in great distress of mind, seeking the Lord with strong cries and tears. Many were made happy, and enabled to rejoice with joy unspeakable and full of glory. We concluded three times before the people were all willing to depart. Glory be given to my God. This has been a most glorious night.

26th.—N. West and I made a very Christian agreement to labor together; but as it was not kept on his part, it need not be inserted.

Oct. 8th.—Since I wrote my last in my Journal, N. West has returned from Sunderland, and James Farrar, from London, has joined us, and has taken up his station with us. He arrived in Sunderland, Sep. 12. A letter from there of last week states that they have 40 members and five preaching places.

On Monday night we held our Quarterly Lovefeast. A most solemn and profitable time; there was quick and solemn speaking. I preached a sermon in Heriot's Bridge from Prov. v. 11, 12, which, it appears, has had its desired effect. Many wept to-night. Praise God, for his mercy endureth for ever. We are adding members in Leith, but we have some to put away; they cannot do with the strictness of our discipline. But the increase exceeds the loss.

Nov. 15th.—Last night was in great heaviness of soul, by reason of the conduct of an individual who ought to have known better. I fear his lordly conduct will be pregnant with the worst consequences, both to himself and the infant cause, except the Lord overrule the evil for good in mercy to us. However, I had a most glorious time in preaching and praying in Richmond Court chapel. Afterwards I attended the Elders' Meeting, and desired liberty to meet a class in Richmond Court, as I engaged to spare time for that purpose. I wished the brethren to consider the matter, and was told by N. West that I was "flatly impudent." I did not resent it, but was enabled to look over it; and thus war was prevented.

16th.—I preached in Heriot's Bridge. Afternoon on "Lying," and evening on "Drunkenness." Large congregations.

17th.—I mentioned the state of matters to Mr. Haldon, treasurer to the mission, and asked his advice. I and my brethren waited upon him, and the matters in dispute betwixt Mr. West, on the one hand, and I and T. Harrison, on the other, were adjusted to my satisfaction.

24th.—Last night I had a good congregation while preaching on "Lord's Day Observance," and to-night I have been much edified while reading and meditating on the necessity of the Holy Spirit's work.

I give this letter as a model of singular honesty:—

REVEREND SIR,—

With feelings the most poignant, I now sit down to write to you. I know your heart will be wrung with sorrow when you know the cause of these sensations. You must know, that last Tuesday night I went to our club-house with the intention of doing a good office to an old shop-mate,—viz., to procure him a travelling card from the society. He accused me of villany, and exposed me in some of my old follies and misdoings. Witness the result. Passion rose above reason. I rose from my seat and struck him. A scuffle ensued, and we both came to the floor. This was witnessed by five different individuals, and though, as my friends, they might keep this shameful transaction secret, and you might never come to know it, yet I cannot hide it from God and my own conscience. As my leader, I consider it my duty to make you acquainted with my fall from morality, and to state that I fear that I have never received the real converting grace of God. I fear that my heart is not right, and that I am only in the state of those whom Mr. West describes as the unrighteous, in his sermon upon Isa. lv. 7, where he shows that though the surface of the fountain of the heart may appear smooth, yet, put in something to agitate the bottom, then will the sludge and filth of our evil nature appear and show itself to the world. I had sought for and found something applicable to the state of those who meet in class with me, and was upon the point of stating it, but could not think of coming to lead others in the way which I had forsaken myself. Again, I would have come to Leith, but it is the sacrament, and the members would have expected that I would have partaken. How could I in this state of mind? It would be awful. O pray for me, and recommend me to the mercy of God, through Jesus Christ. You will take my case into consideration, and let me hear from you soon. I am yours sincerely,

RICHARD NOBLE.

This man at that time was noble by his new nature, as well as by name. He was a means of opening our way to Dundee in 1830. This letter is a noble specimen of ingenuous honesty. He had gone into improper company. At such club-houses, especially where strong drink is sold, many fall and are ruined. Let Christians shun them as the high road to ruin,

Dec. 31st.—We ministers met together by Mr. West's desire, and all matters were again made up amongst us, as the evil was as bad or worse after the 17th November. This letter was the result:

We, the undersigned, do declare, as in the presence of Almighty God,—

1. That we have had no intention to make a division, directly or indirectly, upon the Grass Market Evangelical Mission, or any part of it; nor to take any part thereof, or the whole, to ourselves; but that we have labored to promote the general good of the whole mission; all our exertions having been to this END; and that, from this time forward, we will take no measures, directly or indirectly. to secure any part of the mission to ourselves. individually, or so that any one of us shall be injured by the other two acting against him. Note.—This does not refer to any act of immorality; which, if a minister commit, he must submit to the church.

2. That we consult each other in every matter of importance relating to the church, and that no place of worship be taken, or any other important thing entered into that affects the mission, by any one minister.

3. That it is understood the office of Superintendent be respected by the other ministers, and that the office of the other ministers be respected by the Superintendent.

4.—That all unpleasant things now past be from henceforth buried in oblivion, so as not to be referred to in any future argument or dispute by any of us, but that if any one of us transgress inadvertently he shall when reminded of it, make submission.

5.—That we labor to the utmost of our power to support, defend, and guard each others character, according to Scripture, especially in meetings of business before the brethren.

NOTE.—This arrangement does not affect Brother Harrison's marriage, as that matter has yet to be decided upon.

(Signed) NATHANAEL WEST.
JOHN BOWES,
THOMAS HARRISON.

DECEMBER 31st, 1828.

January, 1st 1829.—Held our adjourned quarter-day, and certified the brethren that all uneasiness or differences between N. West and the other two ministers were made up.

23rd.—The tyranny and unpleasantness of Mr West has manifested itself in the same manner as before our last agreement. Mr Farrar also is in great distress in Sunderland for want of money. After thinking how often Mr. West had threatened as though he intended to take Heriot's Bridge (the place that brings in the most money) to himself, and considering how the place was taken in his name alone, contrary to my knowledge, in February 7, 1828, when nothing but peace existed among us, I concluded that only one of the two following things could induce me to continue to labor in unison with him : viz., either because if Mr. Harrison and I separated from him we should not have so much support ; or secondly, the good of the mission. As to the former, I was determined never to preach &c. for gain ; and as to the second, the mission is not in a good state ; 1st, there is a great declension in the spirituality and life of the people. 2nd, the greatest part of our official characters are dissatisfied, many have resigned their offices, and others are about to do it, without a speedy change. So I conclude that as Sunderland people desire to exchange Mr. Farrar for Mr West, as some of our best members have left the Society through him, it would be best for him to remove to Sunderland. If he refuses, then I and T. Harrison can go ; or a division must be made ; for a part of the Mission had better be made peaceable, than the whole be at war. Mr. Harrison and I waited upon Mr. Haldon, who sent for Mr. West. Before night, we determined to hold a general special meeting on this evening. From 9 last night, and from 7 to 8 this morning, was set apart for each minister to pray and examine himself. Mr. Haldon joined us, and as many of the elders as found it convenient. At half-past 7, we met. Mr. West objected to the legality of the meeting. Mr. Haldon presided. The meeting went on. I wished to keep from bringing charges against N. West, and shewed the necessity of a change. He objected to a change, and so I told the meeting the plan I had laid down, as above, and added, that if Mr. West acknowledged his faults before the meeting, and promised amendment, I would not confide in what he said, as he had deceived me twice. However, I agreed to submit to the decision of the meeting, and so did Mr. West. The meeting unanimously gave it as their opinion, that we ought to forgive and continue. After this, Mr. West got up, burst into a flood of tears, and said he believed he had offended us all, came and took hold of my hand (which he felt I gave him coolly), and pressed it sometime, as if to assure me that I might *now* confide in him. He then went to T. Harrison, and gave him his hand. The meeting then moved, that those who had left through the late disturbance, should be invited back.

Feb. 19th.—I have been sick, and never preached since the 8th inst. I have seen the necessity of having Christ in affliction ; for I could sometimes scarcely pray or think for pain. What a wretched situation must those be in who have no Christ, when they can think of little but their sufferings ! The Lord is restoring me a little.

April 8th.—Since I wrote the above, we have had our Quarter Day, which was held on March 16th. Mr. Waugh opposed T. Harrison's continuance in the ministry on the ground of his marriage. Nothing was done all the afternoon. At night, Messrs West and Waugh were out of the meeting about an hour and a half, and we got through the greatest part of the business of the Quarter Day; but the Sunderland Mission not being in a prosperous state, it was agreed that Mr. West and Mr Farrar should exchange in May next. Mr. West objected to this, and stated that he would not go, except the congregation voted him away. There has lately come in amongst us a young man of considerable abilities, named Conlin, who professes to have come from the Roman Catholic Bishop in this city, and that he has been educated for the Roman Catholic priesthood, is of the order of Jesuits, and professes his recantation of that religion. The Quarter Day thought of employing him. T. Harrison agreed to sit down, as a matter of expediency. On Tuesday, 24th, a society meeting was called. Mr. West urged that all minutes of the Quarter Day and financial committee should be read. I was aware that many were grieved that T. Harrison should cease to travel; and some, influenced by N. West, thought that T. Harrison should not be a minister at all. However, I objected to the reading of the minutes, seeing that it was intended to influence the minds of the people against N. West's removal to Sunderland, and against T. Harrison's continuance in the ministry. In the first instance, it seemed to have the desired effect; in the latter, a contrary effect. The meeting continued to a very late hour, and nothing was done. After this a society meeting was held on the 30th, and none of the ministers were to be present. This meeting dissolved the constitution. It was brought forward by *N. West's party*, evidently to secure the property of the mission in the event of a division, which then seemed probable. After this the meeting appointed 12 deacons, all the leaders of classes to stand; proceeded to call their ministers, West, Bowes, Farrer, and Conlin; they called the latter without any evidence of goodness of character; he accepted of their call providing Mr. West and I could agree. I was not present at this meeting, but at the adjourned meeting the night following, when I agreed to their call on the condition that their system of government suited me. Mr. West again engaged to bury past grievances, declared himself satisfied, and Conlin agreed to be the meeting's minister. However, during the week I saw N. West, and he declared he was not satisfied. I asked him why he told the meeting so. T. Harrison had 59 votes for, and 63 against his being a minister. The society meeting adjourned to Tuesday, 7th April, when T. Harrison sent in his resignation as leader and member, or I believe he would have been expelled from both offices, as N. West and Conlin would not labor in a church where he held these offices. I was so struck with this spirit of persecution on the part of N. West, that I was resolved to have no more connection with him, if he succeed in expelling T. Harrison from church fellowship, who twelve months ago was sent for by him, and through him only, to be our minister, and who had no crime alleged against him, but that which Mr. West knew of and advised, viz., marrying his deceased wife's sister. However, the meeting and I were not a little surprised to find that Conlin refused to labor with us, because I had given a certain member a ticket since last meeting. Such inconsistency as that displayed by West and he, I never saw.

The first time I saw Conlin was in Mr West's, No. 6 Heriot's Bridge, Grass Market. At first he spoke of himself as a Roman Catholic, who had doubts of the truth of that religion; he also made strong objections at first to Protestantism. Being at times in Edinburgh, I sometimes conversed with him at Mr West's, when he professed to be at Bishop Patterson's and to have resided there about three months. After a few days' conversation with Mr West, &c., I met with him on March the 4th in Mr West's, when he said he had been in the Chapel as early as 3 o'clock, that he had been at Prayers &c., and that ashes had been sprinkled upon his head; that he had taken breakfast with the Rev. Dr. Patterson, Revs. Messrs Reid and Gillies, that he expressed his doubts in their presence, that the Bishop charged him with heresy, and threatened to send him to Glasgow by the Rev. Mr Gillies, that it was not customary for Catholic Priests to take cream in their coffee on Ash-Wednesday morning, but that it was generally set on the table for any that might be unwell &c., that he took the cream, sugar, &c., and proceeded to take a cup of coffee, at which the Bishop was so much enraged that he took it and cast it out at the window, and he expected that the Bishop would send him into foreign confinement for his opinions. That after breakfast he got out of the house almost by force, and came to Mr West's; after this he never returned to the Bishop's. He professed to be a Jesuit, to have been educated for a Priest, to have refused to take orders in consequence of his scruples about the Roman Catholic Religion; these scruples had been of four years' standing, for two years he had quite disbelieved their chief doctrines, but did not see any way to leave them and keep his life until now, and expressed fears of his life being taken away even now. These doubts about their religion had been produced chiefly by his knowledge of philosophy and reading Protestant works, while engaged in translating them into Latin to send to Rome. His clothes were not good; which he accounted for by saying that he was doing penance; his hat was bad; he had on a dark brown coat, approaching to black; his trousers were nearly the same color, and I never saw his vest, as he kept his coat buttoned up to the neck; I think he had on no leggings, and his stockings were of a bluish color; his shoes appeared good, but not very strong; and round his neck he had a black collar. His clothes, he said, belonged to his order, and he would send them back when he got new ones; but never did, so far as I know. He professed to have on a hair shirt. When he got another shirt, I was desirous to see the hair one, and he told Messrs West and Waugh that he had disposed of it to Mr. Harrison, one of our missionaries; but Mr. Harrison told me he never saw or heard of it. Some days after March 4th he preached his recantation sermon in Heriot's Bridge Chapel, where he preached often afterwards. The Catholic Bill he said had occupied much of his thoughts, and he was most anxious that it should pass into a law, &c. He said the chief articles that had appeared in the "Scotsman" on emancipation, had been written by him, that the Editor was a Catholic. After he had preached his first sermon against the doctrines of the church of Rome, it was remarked to him that the "Scotsman" if a Catholic, might be taking up the subject, and a wonder was expressed that he did not, to which Conlin replied that the Editor was so well acquainted with his (Conlin's) powers as a writer, that he would not dare to meddle with him. At first he was very friendly with me until I requested him to tell me where he came to after he left Dublin? (He stated that he was sent on private business by Dr. Doyle to Scotland.) How long he had been in Glasgow? If he was acquainted with any Catholic or Protestant gentlemen in Edinburgh? He seemed studiously to avoid my company. I wished him to prove that Dr. Doyle, bishop in Dublin, knew him. A letter was written to him by Conlin's consent. I heard it read: it was to know if Conlin had been educated in the College of Carlow, &c. He said that if Dr. Doyle did not write within a fortnight, we might look upon *him* (Conlin) as an impostor. Dr. Doyle never wrote. I became suspicious, and was put off by him and another saying, that he was going to have a meeting with Dr. Patterson. That certain gentlemen were about to prepare for such a meeting, I believe. On April 12th, Conlin had been preaching in Heriot's Bridge chapel that Sunday evening, and four men, from Hume's Close, Cowgate, followed him up to Mr. Wm. M'Lean's 322 Lawn Market, and in the presence of Mrs. M'Lean, accosted him by, "How do you do, Mr. Cane?" and demanded from him pay for a week's board and lodging in Mr. M'Ewan's house, Hume's Close, Cowgate. Conlin pretended to be much afraid of them, and desired Mrs. M'Lean to go for Mr. West, which she did, and Conlin was left alone with the men. Mrs. Monro, a Protestant, who lives next door to Mrs. M'Lean, was entering, and the door was closed by Conlin's order. She listened at the door, and heard Conlin pay down the money demanded; after which he told them that if they did not go away, they should be apprehended. I have seen the men, Mrs. Monro, and Mrs. M'Lean, and taken down their statement in writing. Mr. M'Ewan states that Conlin lodged with him about a week, called himself James Cane, professed the Roman Catholic religion, said that he was a silversmith from Dublin, professed to get work with " Duncan and Kinnear," in the New Town of Edinburgh (we can find no such silversmiths)—he went professedly to work and returned to his victuals for about a week,—that on Saturday, Feb. 28th, he went to his work, as he pretended, but never returned, and they saw him no more until they saw him in Heriot's Bridge, in the pulpit. They describe his clothes minutely, and tell a strange story about his leaving his master's in Dublin. He came finally to Mr. West's four days after the date which Mr. M'Ewan gives of leaving his house. Mr. M'Lean was with me when this statement was taken at Mr. M'Ewan's, from whose house we went to Mr. M'Laren, editor of " The Scotsman." We stated what Conlin had told us; he said that he did not know any person of that name, and that no such person had ever written any article for " The Scotsman." I laid these facts before Mr. West, but as he admitted Conlin to preach in the chapel since, I have withdrawn from him, and have not seen Conlin since, but hear that he is still preaching in Richmond Court chapel, and that he has been preaching strongly against Catholic Emancipation, so that he has soon changed to suit his present admirers. The above are facts that cannot be disproved by any one.—*July 21st*, 1829.

This was written down at this date. N. West said to me, " I do not care for his telling a few lies, providing he is right in the main." As though any man could be " right in the main" who could tell such lies!

How could I remain in union with such a man? Conlin, or Cane, afterwards married the daughter of a baker, and all the sorrow that followed would have been prevented, had N. West only used ordinary caution.

April 22nd.—To-day I waited upon Mr. West in order to make some arrangements for the good of the work, and found him in such a fury that I could get no arrangements made with him; so I came away without making any disturbance, and resolved to have no more communion with him. I see plainly that he is determined by one means or another to have the Heriot's Bridge chapel to himself.

23rd.—To-day I resolved to inform the benevolent friends of the mission that I had separated from N. West.

(CIRCULAR.—CAUTION.)

TO THE FRIENDS OF THE GRASS MARKET EVANGELICAL MISSION.

WHEREAS a printed Report, published by MR WEST, is now in circulation, containing statements *contrary to both truth and righteousness*, the benevolent friends of the Mission are hereby humbly requested to withhold their Donations *from him*, until there shall be submitted to them *a true detail* of the causes why the Missionaries recently in connection with him, have now withdrawn themselves from him, which will be done as soon as convenient.

J. BOWES, *Missionary.*

EDINBURGH,
April 23, 1829.

I also took a place of worship in Edinburgh, viz., the Hammerman's Hall, in connection with T. Harrison.

26th.—I preached at the West Port in the open-air at half-past 7 in the morning, and in the hall the rest of the day. The congregations were not large, it not being fully known that we had taken a place.

The friends sent out the following circular:—

An answer to a printed card purporting to come from a "Congregational Meeting" held April 27, 1829, Heriot's Bridge, Grass Market, and sent out by Mr West. The very title is not true, the meeting was partial not "Congregational," as many of the members did not hear of the meeting till afterwards, and before any explanation was given the members present were requested either to say that they would be Mr West's members or they could not be allowed to sit in the meeting, consequently some withdrew and some would not withdraw, yet those who continued were put down as his members. The meeting is stated to consist of 100 members, and persons who were present state there was not 100 in the meeting; farther, the card is signed by J. Cockburn, Secretary, when it is well known that Mr West was the real Secretary of the meeting. Also we are credibly informed that the "resolutions, &c.," were prepared by Mr West before they came to the meeting. These considerations alone are sufficient to show what credit is due to the statements of the card, the fact is it is a very presumptious hypocrite, as it professes to be what it really is not; it should be considered and treated not as the production of a meeting, but as Mr West's. It is principally about the "Circular.—Caution," sent by Mr Bowes which states that the report was published by Mr West, and there is nothing in the card to contradict it. There are many assertions about Mr Bowes' assisting to prepare the report, not objecting to it when read to him, &c. &c., which are partly true and partly false, for instance there are articles in the report which Mr Bowes never saw or heard of till he saw them in print. It was printed and Mr Bowes' name put down as signing the Report for Leith without his knowledge or consent, which was little better than forgery. Mr Bowes *did object* both to the report and the time of printing it, viz.—when Mr West did not know that Mr Bowes would continue to labor with him another day, in consideration of this we believe that Mr West aimed at deceiving the public by printing the report at that time, we wished to have everything amicably settled before it went out, however Mr West finding himself in such circumstances consented to a settlement when it was printed, *and it was after this settlement* that Mr Bowes consented to circulate some of the reports in Leith, yet about this time Mr West held two private meetings to injure Mr Bowes' character, and when Mr Bowes waited upon him, April 22, to make some arrangements for the good of the work, he found him in a complete fury, he would make no arrangements, but treated Mr Bowes very abusively, so Mr Bowes desiring *no more* disturbance, came quietly away, and seeing that neither peace nor prosperity were likely to attend any further connexion with him, he determined to separate from him. It was after this that he deemed it right to inform the benevolent friends of the Mission that the Missionaries had withdrawn themselves from him. Mr Harrison having sent in his resignation before, *which was cacepted and a vote of thanks given to him for his ministerial labors.* Now the report imports throughout that there *are three Missionaries employed unitedly* in one common work. Was this the fact when two of them had separated from Mr West? No. We say then that after the separation took place the report *did not give a just and true idea of the state of the Mission.* The card refers to Mr Bowes' circulating the report and receiving donations for the Mission in Leith, to which we reply that he was placed in *different circumstances in Leith to what Mr West was in Edinburgh.* He has been the only Missionary that we have had in Leith since September, 1827, whereas we have two in Edinburgh, so that he was only receiving subscriptions for the same object as though he had still been united to Mr West, viz.—for the Leith Mission; whereas Mr West was receiving aid for himself, as he positively refused to give up the subscriptions to pay a legal debt which the Society had directed him to pay to the other Edinburgh Missionary. It was this act, taken in connexion with others, that induced Mr Bowes to send the friends of the Mission the circular, which does not, and never was intended to impugn the "Abstract of the income and expenditure of the Mission." But it is said that "Mr Harrison was put away by a congregational meeting, and afterwards sent in his resignation to another congregational meeting." *This is not true: the meeting was one,* as it adjourned from time to time until it had done its work; and if it must be called "putting away," then all the missionaries were "put away" at the same moment that the Constitution was dissolved; and when Mr. Harrison sent in his resignation, the meeting was sitting, and ACCEPTED IT, as above. But "Mr. Harrison's character was not considered defensible." When not defensible? If before Mr. West sent for him to labor as a missionary, then why did he give him such an excellent character, and become the sole cause of his coming to Edinburgh, when none of us knew him? He has been here more than twelve months, during which time we have not seen anything in his character which requires defence. This article must therefore necessarily recoil upon its author. The lower part of page 2, we deny *in total.*

Now it must be obvious to every decerning mind that the pseudological Card contains primarily and properly Mr. West's "Resolutions," and not the resolutions of the congregation; and he, as their proper father, ought to come forward and own his real progeny. He should have done this at first, and not have covered his proceedings with a cloak. "He that doeth truth cometh to the light." Truth has nothing to fear from "the light," but much to hope. Let us just glance at the 3rd and 4th "Resolutions," when the proper reading is supplied:—"Resolution III. That [Mr. West] on reviewing the conduct from first to last of Mr. West, [he] has every reason to believe him to be a true defender of this mission [!] a laborious, diligent minister of the gospel [!]—an honest and an upright man in all his dealings" [!] &c., &c. He gives himself an excellent character!! "Resolution IV. That [Mr. West] requests Mr. West will do [Mr. West] the favor not to meddle in controversy himself"[!] &c. And he was meddling with it all the time! In future we should expect that he will either do himself "the favor," or candidly declare himself to be the concealed controvertist.

In conclusion, we remark that, in reference to anything which Mr. West may hereafter publish, should we be silent, we hope that our silence will not be construed to proceed from any other cause than a desire to avoid any further disclosures of his character and proceedings. Also the friends of the Mission are informed that both past and future subscriptions will be applied to the purposes for which they are given, and will be duly and properly accounted for.

By order of the Society Meeting for the Missionary Committee.

(Signed) GEORGE DIPPIE, President.
RICHARD NOBLE, Secretary.

EDINBURGH, May 1st, 1829.

May 14th.—I sent a letter to Sunderland Circuit Committee, stating wherein I conceived they had got wrong before, and also myself. It was prepared on the 1st instant.

June 25th.—Towards the latter end of last month T. Harrison returned to England. I also saw Mr. Broadbent, the Primitive Methodist preacher here, who wrote to Sunderland, desiring them to lay aside former prejudices, and again to let the people in Edinburgh unite with us, and so be all united *again*; to which I suppose they object altogether. A few new members have joined us lately; we have three class leaders; very good meetings; some are getting awakened, and one or two have been savingly converted. Having service three times every Lord's day in two places, I am necessitated to have help. I preach every Lord's day morning in the King's Park, open-air, and on Leith Links in the evening. To-night we held our Lovefeast in Edinburgh. It was a most glorious time. Brother Scott remarked a few things that deserve attention. 1. When he began to seek the Lord, his greatest fear was that of falling by his former companions, and for two months Providence so ordered it that he never saw one of them, and by that time they had learned his change, and did not seek his company. 2. He was led to a class meeting by the very stair and door being pointed out to him. 3. He had many doubts about being able to continue, but these all vanished when he said in the class, "I am now determined for heaven." 4. He remarked that we should be kind to strangers, and invite them to meet in the class.

I see I was much supported in this great trial, in being obliged to separate from N. West, writing to P. Bellwood, then settled at Lanchester, 8 miles from Durham, July 4th, 1829: "I am giving myself more than ever to prayer and to God, and the result is, I ask for nothing but I always get it. I value salvation more than worlds. I set myself to do something every day either for the bodies or the souls of God's people, and for ungodly sinners. See that the cares of the world do not choke the good seed, and try to provoke your wife to serve God more and more. J. Broadbent, Primitive Methodist preacher, was for my returning to the Primitive Methodists, and wrote to Sunderland, and Tillotson, who I suppose is secretary of the Committee, gave him a warm reply. God's will be done. I wait to see his will."

A few lines from this letter of T. Dawson's will give an idea of the dimensions of the Primitive Methodist Church :—

. . . The way for those who secede from our body coming back seems nearly made up; nevertheless, though I should like to hear tell of thy coming back, I would say, come back honorably, if at all. Our body at present is tolerably prosperous. I believe the following is the state of the Connexion: 33,720 members, 228 Travelling Preachers, 2491 Local Preachers, and 403 chapels; being an increase of 2110 members, 24 Travelling Preachers, 282 Local Preachers, and 79 chapels. Four missionaries have gone to America. I have some serious thoughts of marrying, but cannot name the time at present. My intended is own cousin to Miss Buckle of Coverdale; her name is Slater. She lives with an uncle and aunt at Newton-le-Willows, near Bedale. Say in thy next thy thoughts on that point freely. Mark's family are all well; they desire to be named to thee. Our family are all well. Give my respects to thy wife, and accept the same thyself, from thine, as ever,

THOMAS DAWSON.

This is perhaps my last notice of N. West. A few years after this he went to America, became a minister in the Presbyterian body, was settled sometime at Pittsburg, and was made a "D.D." He was opposed to instrumental music in churches, had done what he deemed requisite against it, and, after all, the governors in his congregation carried it against him; so on the Lord's Day morning when they introduced a bass viol, he opened the service by saying, "Let us fiddle and sing to the glory of God." When the war broke out, he was made a chaplain in the army. For an account of his death, in 1864, see *The Truth Promoter, Vol. IX. p. 172*. He had respectable talents, but his selfishness spoiled all, and, at least in Edinburgh, seriously retarded the work of God, and no doubt at last occasioned his leaving this country. The Lord made use of him to separate me from the Primitive Methodists, and sectism; so that, after passing through deep trials, at length I had great reason for thankfulness.

July 26th.—Mr. H. Bourne was in Edinburgh. I went to see him, but he sent word that he did not wish to see me, or could not see me; so I sent him a note and requested an answer, but never got one. I also wrote on the 20th to the General Committee, but never received an answer, nor do I expect any. I offered myself again to the body, because, as I never left them by choice, I believed it to be my duty, and shall feel satisfied whatever may be the result. My known opposition to the unwarrantable power of Hugh Bourne and the General Committee, I suspect, as the cause; although perhaps the Lord has something for me to do which will be more to the honor of his name. For His glory I am determined to spend my life.

Aug. 2nd.—Jabez Burns, from London, preached for us.

3rd.—I heard him preach an excellent sermon, and the Committee agreed to invite him, providing that he could give satisfactory testimonials of character, and labor with the same dividend of salary with myself, to which he agreed.

20th.—The Lord seems to prosper whatever we set our hands to. We are adding souls weekly, and sinners are inquiring the way of salvation. The King's Park preaching has been remarkably well attended and blessed. Mr. Burns resides in Leith, and we have removed to Edinburgh.

The following from the Annual Report for 1830 will give an idea of the nature of our visits.

1. THE MEANS EMPLOYED,—VISITING.

"In these visits the Missionaries take a book with them, and in the first entrance upon a district insert the name of the person, the number of children, the number capable of instruction not at school, whether the person has a Bible, employment, &c., and whether they attend divine worship? By this means a knowledge of the wants of the family is speedily acquired. Religious instruction is then imparted, and often from 4 to 10 families are collected together, when the Scriptures are read, an exhortation given, and prayer made with them. Religious tracts are also given; and, in cases of great indigency, relief is either afforded by the Missionaries, or the persons directed to apply to such charitable institutions as may meet their case.

"2. PREACHING THE GOSPEL.—In Edinburgh until last December,

the Hammerman's Hall was used as a place of worship, since then, a Chapel in Carruber's Close which will hold 500 people, has been engaged, where there is service three times every Sabbath, and twice during the week, viz., on Monday and Thursday evenings at seven o'clock. The place is not full, but the Congregations are increasing.

"The place of worship in Leith is situated in the Broad Wynd. (Next to the Dispensary.) Service on Sabbath same as in Edinburgh, and on Monday and Wednesday evenings. The place will hold 200 people, and is well attended.

"Water of Leith, Ladies' School Room, on Wednesday evening; the Congregations are not large, but regular and attentive.

"Stockbridge, Sermon has been commenced on Tuesday evenings in the New Academy, many young people attend, but not many adults.

"In private houses, Friday evening is devoted by each Missionary in preaching from house to house. Congregations at these Sermons are large. Any person who applies, can thus have Sermon in any part of the town; when the Sermon is done the person speaks who would like to have it next, and it is thus published. By this means, many are brought under the Gospel who would otherwise seldom or never hear it. In summer there is preaching at half-past seven o'clock in the morning in the King's Park, and on a week day evening on the Castle Hill, to the soldiers and others. Also on Leith Links on Sabbath evenings."

II. THE NECESSITY OF THESE MEANS.

"Of 80 families recently visited in St. Mary's Wynd and its vicinity, 30 are Roman Catholics, 16 attend no place of worship, 16 have no Bibles, and there are 14 children, capable of instruction, at no school. The necessity of these labors is founded in the ignorance and depravity of the people, which may be seen on the streets and lanes on the Lord's Day; even when the people of God have gone up to worship in his Temple, what numbers are still seen spending their time idly about the streets! The necessity may be seen in their appearance, heard in their language, and read in their conduct. A few brief extracts from the Missionaries' Journals may throw some light on the state of the people.

"Mr. Bowes writes, *Jan.* 5, 1830, 'I visited, in company with Mr. Burns, in St. Mary's Wynd. We met with two poor old women in a lonely garret, one of them apparently unable to work, and has only about eightpence a-week to live upon; the other appears unhealthy and obtains no work; said she had nothing to eat. Such misery is quite affecting. Neither meat nor fire on a cold winter's day.

"*January* 8.—St. Mary's Wynd.—Met with a Roman Catholic family from Ireland. Neither the husband nor wife can read. She lamented this, and added, "It says a great deal for the people in this country, that their children are taught to read. It was not so in my country a few years since, but now it is different; they are beginning to see the value of reading, and there are many schools." I was much pleased with the artless simplicity with which she regretted her incapability of reading, also with the news from such a quarter, that Ireland is awakening to her privilege. Perhaps the Protestant Sunday and Day Schools are producing this. I gathered six families together. Read a portion of Scripture; exhorted from it; and prayed with them. Both Protestants and Catholics listened with great attention. The before-mentioned woman was visibly affected, and united with the rest in returning thanks for my visit. It is a pleasure to be thus employed. On the flat below I had some difficulty to obtain a house to exhort and pray in. At last I prevailed upon a Roman Catholic woman to allow me her house. I asked for a Bible; she had none. I asked for some other good book. She gave me a Catholic Prayer-book. Having prevailed upon other two Roman Catholics to come in, I selected an excellent prayer, treating upon sin and the Redeemer. I expounded it. They paid more attention to what I said than I could have expected if I had appeared to speak to them from the Bible. I prayed, shook hands, and came away. This people are in 'gross darkness.' One man on this flat refused to come in. I asked him if he had a Bible. 'No.' 'The Bible is the best book in the world; it is a pity that you do not possess it.' 'I don't know,—there are many better books in the world than the Bible.' 'Surely there cannot be a better book than that of which God is the author.' 'There are many Prayer-books that I like better than the Bible: it is a dangerous book; many people don't understand it.' 'I agree with you that many people do not understand it, but abuse it; there are many excellent things abused. The fire is a good thing, (it was a very cold day) but it may be abused. Water is a good thing, and if some people abuse it by drowning themselves, it does not therefore prove that it is not the most useful of all liquids.' The man was confounded and speechless, but I fear not convinced. May the Lord take the veil from the eyes of this people."

"It is to be particularly observed, that the Mission is not the organic vehicle or machine of any party. It refuses every appellation but that by which the followers of Christ were first designated, and it attempts not to increase the number of divisions or widen the breaches in the Christian world, but to collect the ignorant and the vile, and make them acquainted with the knowledge and consolations of our common Christianity."

In this year I published my first tract, 8 pages, on "Church Unity." This was widely circulated.

The reason why I gave up spirits was this: One day, while visiting, in Edinburgh, a family without any outward appearance of comfort, hardly any furniture, decent clothing, or fire, I recommended the father of the small family to abstain from whisky. He remarked, "Perhaps you take a little yourself?" "Well, but only a very small quantity, seldom spirits, and if I taste wine, very little." "Oh!" said he, in triumph. "that is just what I do, only perhaps I take a little more than you do." I felt at once the force of his remarks, and that, if I could have said truly, "I never taste spirits,—*do as I do*," I should have had more power with him. Such a man as this cannot be moderate. If he takes any he must take much, and therefore he ought to abstain. Therefore, for the good of our neighbor, as "Love works no ill to its neighbor," I began at once; not that I felt any danger to myself, but there might have been. I never was really intoxicated in my life, but on two occasions I was conscious of being affected by it; once by old ale at Spenithorn, stronger than I expected, and once by spirits. It is now more than forty years since I gave up spirits, and I never regretted it. It was some years later, at Liverpool, that I became an abstainer from all intoxicating liquors.

I prosecuted the study of the Greek language under a tutor, Mr. Turner, himself a student at the college; N. West and I engaged him, as we had not time to attend college ourselves. The reasons why I have prosecuted the study of this language for forty-four years may be thus briefly given. (1.) Those who expound the Scriptures, especially the New Testament, should, if possible, draw their streams from the original fountain, or they must depend upon others for uncertain supplies. (2.) In after years I laid the subject of the languages before the late Dr. Thomas Dick. His opinion was, that there were but few works in Latin worth the time and trouble of getting the language to read them. With this opinion I coincided, and therefore prosecuted the study of the Greek with more care, little thinking, until many years afterwards, that I should ever live to write out a translation of the New Testament with my own hand. Let no one despise the day of small things. I soon became able to give the sense of the original in sermons and lectures, and ultimately commenced, with a few others, a class at Cheltenham, for reading the Scriptures of the New Testament in the original. Our improved renderings on Hebrews appeared in *The Truth Promoter, Vol. V., p.p.* 63, 70. And I published "The New Testament, translated from the purest Greek," in 1870.

CHAPTER V.

RISE OF THE CHRISTIAN MISSION—VISIT TO DUNDEE—OPEN-AIR PREACHING—GREAT CONGREGATIONS—VISIT KIRKCALDY—PREACHING IN FIFE—ACCEPT THE CALL TO DUNDEE—JAMES PATERSON'S LETTER—TOPICS FOR SELF-EXAMINATION—CHRIST'S CHURCH UNDIVIDED—NOTES OF A VISIT TO ENGLAND—CHOLERA IN DUNDEE—GIVE UP SMOKING—SPEECH AT A GREAT VOLUNTARY CHURCH MEETING—ON CHURCHES RECEIVING MEMBERS—WHO OUGHT TO BE MINISTERS—LETTERS FROM AND TO THOMAS ERSKINE, ESQ.—ON PEOPLE BEING IN CONFERENCE—TO LEEDS METHODISTS—PROFESSOR KIDD'S DYING ADDRESS.

RISE OF THE CHRISTIAN MISSION.

(From "The Christian Miscellany and Herald of Union," 1831.)

WHEN any thing extraordinary takes place in the Christian community, those interested in the progress of Christ's kingdom, desire to know both the causes by which it is produced, and the consequences with which it is followed.

That a number of Christians should have resolved to renounce all party appellations, and hold their peculiarities in abeyance—that they should have proceeded so far as to form churches in several places on the same liberal principles, is a circumstance probably unparalleled in the history of Protestants; and, notwithstanding that they embody persons of very dissimilar sentiments in minor points of discipline and doctrine, must be hailed as a happy circumstance by those who are already wearied of the discords occasioned by sectarianism. These will naturally ask, how did the work begin? and how has it proceeded?

To answer these questions, so far as human agency is concerned, is the object of this statement; and it will no doubt be interesting to trace the wonderful developments of the providence of that God who is emphatically "The King of Saints," who has promised great things to his church, and accomplishes them according to the purpose of his own will: this must never be overlooked in the history of Christ's kingdom. When corruption had overspread nearly the whole length and breadth of the Christian profession, and when many were anxiously waiting for a reformation in the Romish hierarchy, and were busily employed in order to bring about a reform in their own way; then did the Majesty of Heaven show that He had a plan of reform in view too, but it was one which, when manifested, was by no means agreeable to the views of those who called loudly for a change in the practices of the dissolute and avaricious clergy. They would have agreed with the principles of reform, if they had only been compatible with their views of continued union in the Church of Rome.

But the way of Divine wisdom contradicted all their settled notions of the fitness of things. A German monk, and not the Pope, was elected to be the principal agent in this great work. An entire separation from the acknowledged abominations, and a complete overthrow of the established order of things, was the way which providence seemed to mark out. And a proceeding similar to this may be traced in the rise of many flourishing denominations of Christians, existing at this moment, as the most prosperous of Christ's church; in this way also have risen up the most of our greatest and most efficient Christian societies. It will not be expected, then, by those who consult the origin and progress of Christ's church, that we shall have much to narrate which will leave behind it something which may lead man to glory in *his* wisdom or in *his* might. It will rather be expected, if the work be of God, that there will be some obvious marks of such a working in this cause, as will leave no flesh to glory in His presence.

[After the events narrated in the foregoing chapter,] a place of worship was still occupied in Edinburgh, and another in Leith; connected with each place there was a church, and the two ministers went on laboring in the word and doctrine, and in teaching and preaching from house to house, when, towards the latter end of May, some domestic circumstance called one minister away to England. This was a great trial to Mr. Bowes, now the only remaining missionary, as betwixt them there always existed the greatest friendship. It was now that Mr Bowes, by a mysterious train of providential circumstances over which he had no control, beheld himself for the first time alone in the ministry. The difficulty now seemed to be, how to obtain another minister for one place of worship, or to obtain a supply until another could be obtained. However, through the kindness of "Him that keepeth Israel," the latter difficulty was soon obviated, for assistance was kindly afforded by preachers of different denominations. During the summer Mr. Bowes preached 4 times every Lord's Day, and four times through the week. Often five of the sermons were delivered in the open-air, to large congregations, in the King's Park, and Castle Hill, Edinburgh, and Leith Links. It was now that a great change was produced in the sentiments, relative to church unity, of Mr. Bowes, of which he gives the following account:

Being quietly employed in actively preaching the gospel, and feeling myself in a kind of happy solitude, even amidst the noise of a city, one day while meditating upon the present divided state of Christians, I said to myself, "What is the reason that Christians in the present day are divided into so MANY different sects?" I resolved, if possible, to find an answer to this interesting inquiry. In order to which, I commenced where Scripture leaves the history of the church, and investigated it down to the present time. I had access to many valuable books, such as Mosheim's History of the Church, Clark's Lives of the Fathers, Cave's Primitive Christianity, Milner's Church History, Jones' History of the Christian Church, Du Pin's History, &c., &c.; but the book which throws the most light upon the ancient discipline of the church, of any that I have seen, is one "drawn by an impartial hand," I believe commonly ascribed to Lord Chancellor King; this book is invaluable, but very scarce. By comparing the present state of the religious world with primitive Christianity, I became convinced that nearly the whole Protestant world had gone wrong so far as they had divided into sects. And I was as firmly persuaded that the first reformers brought with them, from the Romish church, the very essence of those divisions which have so long disfigured the church of God.

I compared this state of things with the Scriptures, and became so fully convinced as to direct my own practice, that points of doctrine and non-essentials in discipline, unauthorised by the word of God, as tests of membership, had been substituted by most of the denominations of Christians extant.

Party names appeared to me objectionable, because as they are not sanctioned by Scripture, so they tend to keep up a spirit of hostility among Christians, who resemble each other almost in every thing but their names.

In September, 1829, I began to lecture on Church History in Edinburgh, and delivered one weekly for twenty-two successive weeks. I endeavored also to show the scripturality of a Church of Christ, united in fundamentals, and exercising forbearance in lesser terms, composed of believers in Christ, giving evidence of their faith by obedience to his holy commandments. The churches in Edinburgh and Leith were small in number, they resolved to adopt this line of proceeding, they were therefore formed on the principle, that believers in Christ ought to compose but one undivided church; they refused every appellation but that of "Christians" and agreed that any person holding the grand essentials of Christianity should be eligible for membership.

The churches being thus constituted, were preparing to employ another minister, when Mr. Jabez Burns,* being at Edinburgh on business, delivered two sermons at Edinburgh and another at Leith. His preaching was approved of, and as Mr. Bowes had been acquainted with him some years, and could recommend him, the churches agreed to invite him to labor in connexion with Mr. Bowes. To this he agreed, and in December, 1829, he and his family arrived in Leith from London. The places being thus regularly supplied with preachers, the congregations began to increase, and members were added to the church, so that in May, 1830, the Mission was able to call a third minister, Mr. Blake, who had labored several years in the same cause with Mr. Burns in London.

For some months previous to this, six or eight of the Leith members had removed to Dundee, and were desirous that a missionary should visit them; accordingly, Mr. Bowes was sent to Dundee. Here we quote extracts from his Journal:—

May 12*th*, 1830.—This morning I came by a steam boat to Largo on my way to Dundee. While in the boat I had some interesting conversation with a Mr. Young of Edinburgh; we dwelt upon the lamentable divisions of the day, and the necessity of union among all the followers of Christ. His sentiments had a strong resemblance to my own; I promised to call on him when I returned from Largo. I walked to Newport, a distance of about 20 miles, from half-past 1 p.m. to half-past 7. Found my friend Mr. Noble and family well.

13*th*.—Thursday. To-day I endeavored to provide a place for Lord's Day preaching, but made no arrangement. In the evening I walked out to the front of the New Coffee Room in company with Mr. Noble, and preached in the open-air to an assembly of about 300, from Luke xiii. 24. "Strive to enter in at the strait gate; for many, I say unto you, will seek to enter in, and shall not be able." The congregation listened with great attention, and I trust the seed sown was accompanied with the softening dews of divine grace. I gave some account of the object of my visit and the plan of our Mission, and published for preaching at the West Port to-morrow night.

14*th*—Friday. I made arrangements for preaching in the Thistle Lodge, Union Street. I also published advertisements for preaching

---

* Now "Dr. Burns," of the Baptist Church, New Church St., Paddington, London.

there next Lord's Day, three times, and in the evening I preached at West Port, to a more numerous assembly than last night, from Acts iii. 19, "Repent ye, therefore, and be converted, that your sins may be blotted out, when the times of refreshing shall come from the presence of the Lord." The people heard with marked attention, and I experienced much enlargement of heart in addressing them from this encouraging passage. The fields appear white unto the harvest.

16th.—Lord's Day. I preached three times to-day in the Thistle Lodge, according to the previous announcement. I suppose there would be about a 1000 people in the hall and adjoining rooms, staircase, &c. I had liberty in preaching the ever-blessed gospel of God. Oh! that his Spirit may attend the word, and deeply infix it upon the minds of the people.

17th.—Monday. Preached at the West Port again; more people than could well hear.

18th.—Tuesday. Walked out to LOCHEE, a village about two miles from Dundee, and preached in the open-air, from "So run that ye may obtain." The people looked about at first with manifest astonishment, but they heard, became serious in their outward deportment, and I hope the labor was not lost.

19th.—Wednesday. Visited from house to house in the Hilltown, distributed tracts, gave exhortations, and prayed with several families; they received me with the greatest cordiality and thankfulness. Domiciliarly visiting is quite a new thing in the Hilltown. In the evening I preached at the bottom of the hill to a large concourse of people.

21st.—Preached before the coffee-room on the Shore, to a large congregation, who heard eagerly, notwithstanding the coldness of the night.

23rd.—Lord's Day. This forenoon I delivered the first lecture on Christian Unity: the people heard it with the greatest attention, although it occupied near two hours in the delivery. Afternoon and evening, as well as morning, quite crowded, and hundreds went away who could not obtain an entrance.

24th.—Preached this evening in the Lodge, it was quite full, notwithstanding that the rain fell in torrents, and I had glorious liberty; truly the Lord opened to me a door of utterance. This people seem athirst for the word of life. Twelve persons were admitted as candidates for membership. May the Lord form a church here, against which the gates of hell shall never prevail.

25th.—Tuesday. To-day Mr. Burns came from Leith to succeed me. I preached with pleasure on the Hilltown; the ground was very wet, but this seemed a matter of no consideration to the large audience. What a responsible situation do I now occupy, so many immortal souls, many of whom are either only formal professors, or entire neglecters of public worship, daily listening to the gospel from my lips! I wish to be in earnest, and to be an instrument in the hands of God in warning them to flee from the wrath to come, and in turning them to God.

26th.—Wednesday. Mr. Burns accompanied me to Lochee, where I delivered the same lecture, by particular request, as on Lord's Day morning in Dundee; the Weaver's Hall was full, the night was rainy and unpleasant. When I returned to Dundee I felt a little fatigued; but it is a good work, and I would not forget that I shall soon have plenty of rest in the grave. I know that this is not the place of m[y] rest, but if I discharge my duty, it must be in the day, but it is happ[y] toil to be instrumental in snatching sinners as brands from th[e] burning.

27th.—Thursday. To-day I left Dundee at 7 a.m., and took coac[h] for Edinburgh. A stranger (to me) who has been a hearer, crossed th[e] river with me, with whom I had some interesting conversation; h[e] professes to have received good under the sermons, may it be lasting i[n] its effects. Arrived in Edinburgh about 3 o'clock, and found my famil[y] well, for which I ascribe praise to the Author of all good. This ha[s] been to me a pleasant journey, of much labor indeed, but if I ma[y] judge from appearances, it has been a time which will not soon be fo[r]gotten by many precious souls. I have been informed that a Deis[t] having heard one sermon, expressed high satisfaction; I hope the wor[d] took hold of his heart. On Tuesday Mr. Burns and I were accosted o[n] the street by a Mr. Lowe, pastor of a Baptist church. He treated [us] kindly, and offered us the use of his church should it be a wet evenin[g] when we propose preaching out of doors, and said that they have n[o] such preaching in Dundee. May the Lord make it a blessing. Amen[.] After this I visited Mr. Lowe again, but notwithstanding that we pr[o]posed to accept of his offer, he told me that he could not grant [it] without consulting the church. I suppose he may be afraid that w[e] shall draw away some of his members.

OPEN-AIR PREACHING.

From the statements in the Magazine of last month, it would b[e] observed that the ministers have hitherto been in the habit of preachin[g] the gospel publicly in the open-air; and it may not be out of place her[e] to remark, that this mode of preaching, although at present uncommo[n] for the clergy of Scotland, is strongly supported by Scripture, preceden[t] and command, especially was the Christian era ushered in by tiding[s] in the open-air. Isaiah foretold of John the Baptist that he should b[e] "the voice of one crying in the wilderness: Prepare ye the way of th[e] Lord and make his paths straight." And did not the event justify th[e] prediction, when "John the Baptist came preaching in the wildernes[s] of Judea?" (See Matt. iii. 1—3.) Nor did the Son of God deviat[e] from the path of his precursor. As the gospel was given that it migh[t] be promulgated—that it might be known and cordially embraced, s[o] Christ's incomparable sermon on the mount was not restricted to [a] limited few in the house. "Seeing the multitudes, he went up into [a] mountain," *and there* "he opened his mouth and taught them." (Mat[t.] v. 1.) More than once the incarnate God both taught and fed th[e] listening thousands, who in the open-air assembled that they might b[e] indulged with so singular a privilege. And if the Saviour set us suc[h] an example as this, who then, among his faithful stewards will blush t[o] tread in his steps?

If farther evidence of Scripture be called for, we refer to the memor[]able day of Pentecost, when Peter preached, and the Holy Spir[it] sanctioned his labors by descending on three thousand persons, an[d] expressed from their pierced hearts the anxious cry of "men an[d] brethren, what shall we do?" And is it too much to say, that if suc[h] preaching were more frequent, aroused auditories would often furnis[h] gospel ministers with an opportunity of solving the same interesting question. Is it objected that such preaching might be useful to a barbarous or illiterate people, but not to those whom civilisation has polished, and learning made wise. Behold Paul, not on the coasts of Galilee, but in the renowned city of Athens, famous for its orators, its statesmen, and its sages. Behold him! standing "in the midst of Mars-hill," and *there* publishing to the Athenians the message of their God. Perhaps it may be said, "But he would do no good to the wise men of Athens by such a method of teaching." Oh, yes; he did good. "Certain men clave unto him and believed: among whom was Dionysius the Areopagite, and a woman named Damaris, and others with them." (Acts xvii.44) The Acts of the Apostles abound with evidence to prove that we have Scripture precedent for this useful practice.

In reference to Scripture commands, we refer only at present to Luke xiv. 21, 23: "Go out quickly, into the streets and lanes of the city, and bring in hither the poor, and the maimed, and the halt, and the blind." "Go out into the highways and hedges, and compel them to come in, that my house may be filled."

Open-air preaching is recommended to us by the example of some of the most efficient ministers of Christ, both ancient and modern. It has been associated with some of the most amazing revivals of religion in America. And in England numbers will have to adore the Saviour for ever, who found them wandering the streets, and never attending a place of worship, till His word was sent to them by man's instrumentality, and by the Holy Spirit, efficiently. Cheering, undeniable instances of its utility are now before us, and before the world. And surely to win souls to Christ—to snatch immortals as brands from the flame, is an achievement worthy of toil and labor, and even reproach, and peril, and death. So thought the Lord Jesus.

We would not be understood, however, to sanction those who preach in the street, but are neither sent nor sanctioned by any church of Christ; and we apprehend that this circumstance alone accounts for the prejudice which exists in the minds of some people against open-air preaching in any form.

In America, ministers of nearly all denominations are zealously employed in this laudable practice. It is recommended also by the example of many fervent and useful preachers in England. If all the people regularly attended public worship, this mode of communicating divine truth might be dispensed with; but while thousands and tens of thousands are to be found who seldom or never attend any church, and are therefore perishing for lack of knowledge, it will remain the duty of those to whom it is committed to "preach the gospel to every creature," to be faithful to the trust reposed in them; otherwise, when the Judge shall arraign them at his bar, it will be found that they are obnoxious to his just indignation. The above considerations will, we hope, be found sufficiently weighty to induce many to lay aside indolence and indifference, and fearlessly, and by all scriptural means, to seek the salvation of perishing men. But to return to the progress of the work of God.

The Thistle Lodge continued crowded every Lord's Day to excess, and hundreds were disappointed and necessitated to retire without admission. This induced the church in Dundee to engage a second place; accordingly, the Episcopal Chapel, High Street, was rented, and on June 27th, 1830, it was opened for religious worship by Messrs Bowes and Burns: both places were crowded to excess, and many could not obtain admission. In the afternoon, the Lord's Supper was administered, and it is believed that the labors of the 27th June will not be soon forgotten. The ministers continued during the summer statedly to preach on Tuesday, Thursday, and Friday, in the Hilltown, Shore, and West Port, always to many hundreds of persons; and it is but due to the inhabitants of Dundee to say, that they always heard with the greatest attention and decorum; and it is consoling to know that many have professed to be quickened and animated in the service of God, who had been lukewarm and indifferent, and some were brought to a concern for their salvation who had been either declared opposers of the gospel, or entirely careless about their eternal interests. Also many godly people have expressed their edification and profit under the different sermons. To God be all the glory; and may his blessing continue to water the labors of his servants. Amen.

The labors of the ministers in the open-air were always on other days than the Lord's Day, in Dundee; and wishing to give proof of the disinterested nature of these labors, a collection was never made at any of the services.

In addition to visiting candidates for membership, the sick, and dying, the ministers visited regularly many scores of poor families in the Hilltown, who received them as messengers of mercy. Almost as soon as a minister was known to be in the neighborhood, the people, knowing or guessing his intention, would assemble to the number of twenty or thirty. He then read a portion of Scripture and expounded it, or addressed them as sinners needing repentance, faith, and holiness; prayer then followed, and a religious tract was left with each family. Visiting in this manner may seem a self-denying work at first, but it is truly a delightful employment. In the beginning of August, a fourth minister was employed, Mr. W. Roseman, from Glasgow; so that another place was visited, and a place of worship opened in it. Here we quote again Mr. Bowes' Journal:—

Aug. 11th, 1830.—Wednesday. I came over to KIRKCALDY, as I had often been requested by a pious man who removed hither from Leith some months ago; my intention was to take a place of worship for Lord's Day, and preach this evening in the open-air. But as the evening was very rainy, I was disappointed. I waited upon the Provost for his sanction, which was soon granted. I also waited upon Mr. Aikenhead, the Independent minister, and in the evening attended a prayer meeting in his chapel. He had been one month in the south of Scotland, employed in missionary work, viz., at Peebles, Melrose, and their vicinity. He read his journal, which was very interesting; it gave an account of the situation of many places, with respect to how they were furnished with ministers; and it appears that in an extensive tract of country in the south, containing many parishes, there is hardly one evangelical minister, but that the people are most ready to hear the gospel when they can.

12th.—I had engaged, if possible, to return to Edinburgh to-day to a church meeting, but the sea was so tempestuous that I was disappointed. I therefore concluded upon preaching in Kirkcaldy this evening.

As it is a long, scattered town, I engaged the town-drummer to cry it through Kirkcaldy, and the bellman of the Links published it there. So that at 7 o'clock I preached at Port Brae to many hundreds of attentive hearers, and gave some intimation of the object of my visit.

13*th.*—This evening I preached on the Volunteer Green to a large audience. May the Lord water the seed! Having engaged the place of worship known by the name of "the Barn Church," formerly in the possession of the Cameronians, I advertised for Mr. Roseman to preach in it three times on the Lord's Day. Then the congregations were exceedingly large.

17*th.*—Tuesday. Lectured in Kirkcaldy on the green before the church, on the necessity of Christian unity. The people heard with amazing attention.

18*th.*—I preached again at the Port Brae, and had a most solemn time, from "The way of transgressors is hard," (Prov.xiii.15) to about a 1000 people. If ever I longed to be instrumental in bringing sinners to God, or had a striking view of their danger while without Christ, it was this night. Many were powerfully affected.

19*th.*—I sent the bellman round Path-head, a populous village contiguous to the east end of Kirkcaldy, and in the evening had many hundred hearers in Mid Street, who heard with as much seriousness as though they had been in a church.

20*th.*—This evening I preached in Dysart, two miles from Kirkcaldy, but as I did not commission the bellman to inform the inhabitants, the congregation did not exceed 200 people, and with the exception of a few from Path-head, they were more unruly and careless than might have been expected from Japanese.

21*st.*—I preached again in Path-head to about 700 people, they showed the greatest kindness and attention. I had a most powerful time, and felt quite at home among the people, and shall gladly embrace an opportunity of visiting Path-head again, if ever one occur.

22*nd.*—Lord's Day. This forenoon I preached on a fine green before the church in Kirkcaldy, to about a 1000 attentive hearers. In the afternoon had about 2000 people, every eye seemed fixed, and not a few looked through the starting tear. "Oh! for a trumpet's voice, on all the world to call;" this was the language of my heart. It came on rain in the evening; I was obliged to take the church. It would not contain more, I should think, than about one-fifth of the people desirous to hear.

23*rd.*—This morning an aged man came into my lodging, and said that he had been looking for this unity among Christians for many years; while conversing with him, a woman in great distress came in. She said that what she heard yesterday had so affected her mind, that she had slept none through the night. I directed her to the Saviour. Praise the Lord! The prospect of doing good in Kirkcaldy is very extensive. May the Lord save by whom he will.

Mr. Kingsford, who had been a preacher amongst the Baptists in the south of England, was invited to visit Edinburgh, and after preaching before the committee, was received to labor in the mission. In order that suitable arrangements might be made, a general meeting of the ministers, and delegates from each station was convened at Dundee, Sept. 14th. The following persons composed the meeting:—

Messrs. Bowes, Burns, Blake, Roseman, and Kingsford, ministers of the mission, and Messrs Dippie, Drummond, Sturrock, Noble, and Brown, as delegates of the churches. Mr. Bowes was chosen President, and Mr. Noble, Secretary. A variety of resolutions were adopted relative to the management of the mission, and the ministers were appointed to labor in the following order: Mr. Roseman, Edinburgh; Mr. Blake, Leith; Mr. Bowes and Mr. Kingsford, Dundee; Mr. Fairweather, Kirkcaldy; and Mr. Burns to open the mission at Perth. On the evening of the 14th, Mr. Roseman and Mr. Kingsford were set apart to the work of the ministry, when Mr. Burns preached the sermon to the people from 2 Cor. iv. 5, and Mr. Bowes gave the charge from Acts vi. 4. The scene was truly solemn and interesting.

As Mr. Paterson, road surveyor, who writes the following letter, was the only Universalist we ever received in Dundee, and as he honestly avowed his sentiments when he sought fellowship, and gave us no disturbance with them afterwards, we had no reason to regret his admission.

MONTROSE, 11th OCTOBER, 1830.

DEAR SIR,

. . . . I formerly stated to Mr. Burns, that on account of my liberality of sentiment, particularly in regard to the extent of the atonement. I was excluded from fellowship with the Baptists, with whom I was formerly connected, and wished fellowship with you as a body of Christians whose views were more similar to my own than any I had met with in this quarter. I gave him a copy of my publication, that he might know my sentiments, (a copy of which I also left with your colleague for you) and for anything further that he wished to know about me, I referred him to the pastors of the Baptist Church in the Seagate, viz. Messrs Gilbert and Pirie, or to Mr. Torbet, upholsterer, their deacon, with whom I formerly had fellowship, and to whom I am well known.

I received Mr. Burns' answer (which I enclose), and called on Wednesday to converse with him, when I learnt he had gone to Perth. I said to your colleague that I expected to be in Dundee on Saturday week, when I promised to drink tea with him, and afterwards we were to call on you. But instead of Saturday I find that I would require to be sooner, and shall try to make it on Thursday, the 21st, and hear your lecture on Ecclesiastical History. . . . . I remain, dear sir, yours in the bonds of truth,

JAMES PATERSON.

Dec. 12*th.*—Lord's Day. Having exchanged with Mr. Burns this day, I preached in PERTH, in the Taylor's Hall. The morning congregation was only small; in the afternoon it was full, and in the evening it was crowded to excess, and numbers went away who could not get in. I had a gracious day, especially at night, while speaking from Rom. viii. 28. Many were in tears of joy, or sorrow. It was a moving season.

13*th.*—I lectured on the necessity of one undivided church. Endeavored to show the anti-scriptural nature of so many hostile sects, and to prove by argument the possibility of free and undisturbed communion.

Soon after this the churches were to elect their own pastors. Mr. Burns had about a dozen votes, chiefly those immersed; I did not see immersion at that time; all the rest called me. I did not wish to settle down as a pastor, but I saw no better way then of sustaining the great work in progress, and for which the last three years of trial and research had been preparing me, than accepting the invitation, which, however, detained me in Dundee for nearly seven years. I here express my conviction, that the Annual Meeting made a great mistake. It was in the midst of a glorious work of God, when this change was made. Many places were opened; crowds heard the gospel, and it was soon discovered that a preacher, able to supply a place with others, had not gift to keep either a church or congregation together long when left to his own resources. Beside, there is not a word in Scripture to warrant churches to elect their own pastors. Mr. Roseman, now and for many years Congregational Minister at Bury, went to Kirkcaldy, and remained there until he was invited to Dalbeatie. The second congregation in Dundee, under the care of Mr. Kingsford, did not last long, and several others failed, my conviction is, in consequence of this one wrong step. In some respects it was good for me to have seven years of study, for in addition to my contributions to our Magazine, and other publications, I was preparing for my work on "Christian Union," published in 1835. Let brethren to whom the Lord has imparted the evangelical gift, beware how they settle down in a place. Few have the rare gifts of both pastors and evangelists, and every one should know his own proper gift. My connection with the church in the Nethergate Chapel (now Union Hall), was very happy, only I longed to carry the gospel to other places, when the church had no such idea of their pastor.

I wrote out and published these

TOPICS FOR SELF-EXAMINATION.

1. Where have MY THOUGHTS dwelt most this day; upon earth or heaven, upon Christ or sin?

2. What HAVE I CONVERSED UPON; this world only or the heavenly world, things temporal or things spiritual; have my words been few and useful, or many and sinful?

3. What HAVE I DONE to-day for the BODIES and SOULS of men. As I should never pass over a day without attempting at least to do some good, have I been careful to improve every opportunity of being useful?

4. What were MY VIEWS AND FEELINGS while at SECRET PRAYER? Did I feel myself needy and helpless? Did I view Christ as willing and able to bless me with holiness and strength, or was I content with the form of devotion, while I experienced not the power? Did I offer my petitions with FAITH and EXPECTATION, or were they void of both?

5. How did I perform FAMILY WORSHIP, with zeal or with indifference; could my domestics perceive that I was in earnest, or did they see evident marks of lukewarmness?

6. Have I lived BY FAITH in the Saviour this day, and has it been evinced by MY EXAMPLE?

7. Have I lived this day as though it were my LAST; have I kept death and judgment in view?

8. Can I close my eyes to sleep this evening with the well founded hope that if I open them no more in this world, that I shall not lift them up IN HELL BUT IN HEAVEN?

FOR THE LORD'S DAY.

1. How did I begin this precious DAY OF REST; by reading the Scriptures, examination, and prayer?

2. Was I present at THE MORNING SERVICE? What did I hear: was I convicted of any sin; am I willing to give it up; was I aware of having omitted any duty? If so, can I say "thy will be done?"

3. Did I SING with the spirit? Did I PRAY as well as the minister? Did I hear with HUMILITY, CANDOR, PERSONAL APPLICATION, FAITH, AND LOVE? Are my affections more fixed on heaven than they were? Have I prayed that God would bless the word to my own soul and also to others?

4. Does THIS DAY REMIND me of an ETERNAL REST? I have closed my shop for a day's rest. I shall soon close it for an eternal Sabbath. I gave up worldly business for this divine employ. Am I reminded that I shall soon give it up to return to it no more for ever?

These few topics can be easily written out by the reader, and referred to at any time.

MY INDUCTION IN DUNDEE.

On the evening of the 20th April, 1831, I was inducted to the pastoral charge of the first church of the Christian Mission in Dundee. Mr. Fairweather, of Newburgh, opened the service with prayer, after which the passages which refer to the duties of the ministerial office were read by Mr. Hart, of Aberdeen, who also asked the usual questions, and afterwards delivered the charge from 1 Tim. iv. 16. The service was concluded with prayer by Mr. Roseman, of Kirkcaldy.

On Friday evening, the 29th, a Missionary Meeting also was held, when Mr. Kingsford was called to the chair. The following resolutions were proposed and carried:—

"1. That this meeting views with regret the numerous sects into which Christians are unhappily divided, and deems it a most desirable object that they should again be as much united as the churches of Christ in the first centuries.

"2. That Christians, in order to bring about the desirable object of Christian unanimity and concord, must communicate information, and that delivering lectures and establishing churches on this principle, are the most likely means to carry conviction to the minds of the people.

"3. That in reviewing the endeavors of the Christian Mission to promote unity, we would be thankful to Almighty God for so remarkably blessing the means used, and would distinctly recognise the necessity of divine influence to make the future labors of his servants successful."

The speakers were, Messrs Hart, of Aberdeen; Burns, Perth; Roseman, Kirkcaldy; Fairweather, Newburgh, and Bowes, Dundee.

A similar meeting was held in Perth, on the 4th May, in the Baptist Meeting House, which was kindly given for the occasion. Mr. Wm. Taylor in the chair. The congregation was large and attentive, and seemed highly interested in the speeches which were delivered.

I published this article in "The Christian Miscellany,"

CHRIST'S CHURCH UNDIVIDED.

DURING many dark and long ages, it was the bane of the church, that men implicitly credited, and credulously followed, the instructions of a bigoted and blind priesthood, who found their own worldly interests largely promoted by keeping the people ignorant of the mind of God. And, although on this ground now men loudly condemn popery, yet it is not a little surprising to find such numbers connected with churches professedly reformed, who evidently give themselves no concern as to what is the state of Christ's militant church, nor do they trouble themselves to ascertain what that state ought to be. The slightest reflection might serve to convince them, that it is of the greatest importance that Christians should follow the counsel of Christ, and imitate those first Christians, who through faith and patience now inherit the promises. Amongst them we search in vain for numerous sects, having separate places of worship, different names, and clashing interests. It is true, in the church of Corinth a spirit of division early displayed itself, but it was severely reprehended by the Apostle Paul, who considered their schismatical spirit as a plain evidence of the carnality of their minds. "For," says he, "ye are yet carnal; for, whereas there is among you envying and strife, and divisions; are ye not carnal, and walk as men?" 1 Cor. iii. 3. This epistle, far from giving countenance to the existing evil, tended greatly to suppress it: he felt keenly for the welfare of the Church. He therefore, in the most solemn and affectionate manner thus addressed them:—" Now I beseech you, brethren, by the name of our Lord Jesus Christ, that ye all speak the same thing, and that there be no divisions among you : but that ye be perfectly joined together in the same mind, and in the same judgment." 1 Cor. i. 10. Here then is our first argument. It is reasonable to suppose, that when the Lord Jesus Christ by his Apostles founded the Christian Church, that it was founded on the best of all plans; but it is quite plain that the Church of Christ was one Church for about two hundred and fifty years, and it ought therefore still to be one. Modern Christians then have erred grievously in forming discordant churches, with opposing claims, opposing interests, and different names. This conclusion, I think is fairly drawn from the above argument.

2ndly, Christians are taught in numerous passages of Holy Scripture that they ought to "love one another ;" to instance a few, "Let brotherly love continue." " He that loveth his brother, abideth in the light, and there is none occasion of stumbling in him." " We know that we are passed from death to life because we love the brethren ; he that loveth not his brother abideth in death." From these words I ask the sectarian professor of religion, whom do you regard as a "brother ?" "All that believe in Christ and obey him, of every sect and name." If this is your answer, I say very well. But if you admit there are brethren beyond the pale of your church, then are you bound by Christ's law to love them, and show one of the most evident marks of love, undisturbed communion. If they apply to you for a seat at the Lord's Table, you must not refuse to celebrate the love of Christ in their company ; if you do refuse, you obviously throw contempt on the religion of love, and your profession will be regarded as a mere name. But you will tell me that these people do not think with you upon some point of doctrine, upon some ordinance, or upon some point of church government or discipline ; all these you say, or some of them are of great importance—OF GREAT IMPORTANCE! but are they of MORE importance than brotherly LOVE ? Must almost everything in religion take the precedence of LOVE ? Is everything in religion to be regarded but LOVE ? Faith and hope must be allowed higher ground in the Christian system than many other things; without these a man cannot be saved—without these I cannot regard him as a brother. But invaluable as they are, Paul exalts LOVE above them. "Faith, hope, love, these three, but the greatest of these is love," so says the Apostle to the church inclined to schism. Let modern schismatics remember his words, and give love its proper place in the church of Christ.

How superlatively PURE, SCRIPTURAL, and EXCELLENT, do many conceive their church to be, and what dishonor their church throws upon Christian LOVE. Can those ministers be said to love one another as fellow-laborers in the gospel ought, who will not preach for each other? Or can those human systems be accordant with holy love, which forbid their ministers, upon pain of expulsion, to receive their brethren of other names into their pulpits.

3rdly. As the original formation of the church, and the love which Christ requires his people to evince to each other, prove that the church of Christ should be really united, we conclude that it is both irrational and disgraceful for Christians to divide.

IT IS IRRATIONAL. The very nature of the human mind shows that in this world there will be higher and lower attainments in knowledge; yet even those who are exalted the highest in the scale of knowledge, only know in part, and see through a glass darkly; and they are now more intelligent than they were once. Some are mentioned in Scripture who were "unskilful in the word of righteousness;" but they are called "Babes in Christ?" and is it reasonable to measure the babe by the same standard as the man? Is it reasonable to demand from him the same views, the same justness of thinking which characterise the "Father in Christ?" Is it reasonable for a man, who "knows only in part," to treat others as though he knew every thing? If these interrogatories are fairly weighed, I think they will produce the conviction, that a Christian should have such humbling views of his own attainments, as to induce him to exercise charity towards those who differ from him, especially if they are only "babes;" and that it is irrational to expel a man from the church, or forbid his entrance into it, whom I regard as a Christian, merely because he does not yet see spiritual things as I do. Would not a father act as rationally to require his son of two years old to be as tall as another son aged twenty years; and if he was not, proceed to exclude him from his family for his diminutiveness of stature.

Farther, it is as disgraceful for Christians to divide as it is irrational. What should we think of a schoolmaster incapable of reading a chapter of the New Testament? We should think it a disgrace to his profession. What should we think of a medical doctor, ignorant both of the nature of diseases and the proper method of cure? We should think his ignorance a disgrace. And what do we think of a man, pretending to be like Christ, professing the doctrine which requires him to love "all the saints," the doctrine which knows nothing of modern distinction, but which demands him to love all that are "born of God?"—What do we think of a man professing this doctrine, neglecting the practice of brotherly love, and giving manifest proof of his disrespect to all Christ's flock who think differently from himself?

What do we think? We think it is disgraceful. It is so in our estimation. It is so in the view of infidels. It is so in the sight of the immoral; and, above all, it is so in the sight of God. Such conduct is bigotry. And what is a bigot? Often very ignorant. Like the owl, he runs his head into darkness, to avoid the light. Like those creatures which burrow under the ground, he seldom moves execept it be to do mischief. I compare him to those mischievous animals which subsist best in the night. He walks forth in the most security in the greatest darkness, and would perhaps have attained considerable honor in the fourteenth century; or he might still be styled an intelligent Christian by the inhabitants of Spain. But here, in this century, his hypocritical cloak shall be torn from his shoulders. The appalling sentence which Christ pronounced upon his ancient brethren, shall now pursue him and his companions—"Ye serpents, ye generation of vipers, how can ye escape the damnation of hell?" Hundreds and thousands lament that divisions and sects are so numerous; but they do not see any remedy. They ask, "what can we do—can we produce a change?" No; if you remain inactive, if you do nothing, you cannot produce a change; nor can you do it by good wishes and good desires. Was the Reformation effected by doing nothing; or, what is the same thing, by good wishes? Was it not a work which laid under contribution the bodies and souls, the time and talents, the tongues and pens, the prayers and actions, of the reformers? Yet the Reformation, though in its commencement more inauspicious than the unity of Christians, ultimately succeeded. If we would contribute to the unity of the church, we must pray for it in the closet, in the family, and in the church.

We must disseminate knowledge by preaching, writing, and conversing.

We must add EXAMPLE to argument, and show how highly we value it. Churches formed upon the principle of admitting all real Christians to membership, and having no party appellation, would go far to do away with sectarianism; nor could churches formed upon this principle be charged with being sectarian, because they keep no real Christians out of the church, which is the case with all sectarian churches. Let this simple principle be adopted by all Protestant Churches, to exclude none from the church on account of their peculiar sentiments, but receive all that Christ has received, and give up for ever their different *names* of Episcopalian, Presbyterian, Independent, &c., &c.; and, after this relinquishment, what room would there be for disunion?

But it is objected, "such a union as would merge all party distinctions, and bring even all orthodox Christians into one church, would be a heterogeneous mass." This is a term which has often been employed to designate churches free from party principles. But I would ask such objectors, who compose the church of Christ upon earth? Are they not all believers in every part of the world, and in all churches? "What a heterogeneous mass!" you exclaim, "is the church of Christ, the bride of Christ, the kingdom of Christ." And how dare you apply this term to Christ's church, in contradiction to the bridegroom, who regards his church as glorious, and like the "king's daughter, all glorious within." But if the term "heterogeneous mass" will not apply to the church of Christ in general, neither will it apply to any particular church which admits all those to membership who apply, of every name and grade, when convinced of their Christianity.

But it is farther objected, that "in a church so constituted, the members could not live together in peace." Hear this objection, all ye disciples of the affectionate Lord Jesus, "ye cannot live together in peace." Ye who profess to love each other with a peculiar affection—ye who are disciples of the same Lord, as the first Christians so celebrated for their love and peace—ye who profess to be servants of the same Master, believers in the same doctrines, recipients of the same grace, expectants of the same heaven, "ye cannot live together in peace." If the objection were true, I would say that you are not Christians. But it is false. Churches are formed in various places on this principle, and they find no difficulty in "living together in peace."

It is further objected, "that churches so constituted could not stand long, and would soon fail." So it has been said of most of the Bible and Missionary Societies that have originated within the last seventy years. Open enemies and timid friends have said, "these Bible and Missionary projects are chimerical, and therefore will soon fail." And have they "failed?" No. They have been progressing up to this hour, and with accelerated motion they march on.

And shall churches "fail," which are founded on the plan of Scripture, and distinguished by LOVE? "Love never faileth: but whether there be prophecies, they shall fail; whether there be tongues, they shall cease; whether there be knowledge, it shall vanish away."

But it is again objected, "Have any of the ministers of the gospel, high in rank—in talent—in title—in riches, embraced these sentiments; for, if they are scriptural, surely they ought to be the first to exemplify them." In answer to this, I remark, that it requires more Christian disinterestedness than men in general apprehend, to resign a great salary purely for the love of Christ and the glory of God. Most of the ministers of the gospel referred to, would doubtless inquire into the provision and support to be expected from an "United Christian Church," and we may not be able to give such satisfaction to their inquiries as they demand. However excellent such ministers are in their private and public character, they are interested parties, and these are not the most likely to judge candidly on any subject who are interested. Highly endowed clergymen, in general, have not been the first to propose or adopt measures of reform in the church. The pope and his cardinals, the bishops and archbishops of the Church of Rome at the time of the Reformation, are plain proofs of the correctness of these remarks. And at this moment, are the Right Reverend prelates of the English and Irish Episcopal churches the first to propose a Reform, which other people see to be both desirable and inevitable? If not, then as soon might we expect a number of interested borough-mongers and sinecurists to be the first proposers and firm supporters of Reform in Parliament, as to expect many ministers of the gospel to be the first and firm supporters of Christian unity. Many ministers who are disinterested, may be expected to embrace it among all denominations. But as for the rest, we may expect them to oppose such Christian concord, and to support the *stately* walls of their several portly temples, until they are either deserted or crumble upon their heads. I say to all Christians, Flee! Flee speedily! the mystical Babylon hath surrounded you with party walls, but they are destined to perish. Behold! the accomplishment of prophecy hovering in the prospect. Hear! the sound of our Lord's triumph approaching on the wings of surrounding events, "Babylon the great is fallen! is fallen!"

I pray that the Lord may bless to the reader what has been already said.

J. BOWES.

Dundee, July 7, 1831.

In October, 1831, we published "An Appeal to Ministers and Churches on Unity." This was chiefly my production. We then hoped that ministers would consider this great subject and find our spiritual arguments all-powerful. It was not until years afterwards that the painful conviction forced itself on us that many ministers would do nothing that would endanger or diminish their salaries. We have found only a few happy exceptions to this rule.

AN APPEAL TO MINISTERS AND CHURCHES ON UNITY.

DEAR BRETHREN,

Every thing which relates to the prosperity and happiness of the Church of Christ, is, in your estimation, of great importance; we may therefore anticipate a candid and dispassionate hearing, while we attempt to offer to your consideration a view of the present state of the Christian church.

We rejoice to behold among the various denominations of Christians, a greater degree of zeal than hath been manifested for many centuries; we trust also, that this zeal springs from the stock of living faith, and the flame of holy love. We farther joy to hear of the success which our divine Lord is graciously imparting to the use of Scriptural means, both among ourselves and abroad, so that we hear tell of the faith and conversion of those who were living without hope and without God in the world. We see also great cause of thankfulness and satisfaction in that growing affection and harmony which appears to have been produced by Christians meeting each other in those Bible and Missionary Societies, where party names and creeds are forgot, and where it is only remembered that they are serving the same Master, and aiming to promote the same grand object—the conversion of the wicked.

But while we behold so much to produce feelings of satisfaction and gratitude, we must not conceal that there exists in the present state of the church sufficient reasons for humiliation and sorrow.

If we look at the real state of the churches at home, do we not behold an immense leaven of worldliness mingled up with the profession of the religion of Christ? Is there not even a world within the church, as well as a world without the church? Where do we behold the conversation that is always with grace, seasoned with salt? What a dearth of spirituality do we find in religious society! And in looking at the results of missionary effort abroad, do we find our success corresponding with the labor bestowed, and the money expended? Those who have studied the subject, must acknowledge that there is a great disparity betwixt the means and the end. And whence does this arise? Can we be laboring agreeably to the mind of Christ, and yet have little love, *so essential* to success? Does not the cause of our limited success lie in our divisions and sectarianism? We think it does. And that until Christians are gathered together into *one Church*, "disappointment will laugh at hope's career." This sentiment we bring to the test of

Scripture, from whence alone we would draw the wisdom which is profitable to direct. The unity of the church was a subject of such importance in the estimation of Him who purchased it with his own blood, that a little before he suffered, he prayed for it in the most distinct and importunate manner. "Neither," (said he to his Father) "pray I for these alone, but for them also who shall believe on me through their word. *That they all may be one*, AS THOU FATHER ART IN ME, AND I IN THEE, that they also may be ONE IN US: *that* THE WORLD MAY BELIEVE THAT THOU HAST SENT ME. And the glory which thou gavest me I have given them; THAT THEY MAY BE ONE, EVEN AS WE ARE ONE. I in them, and thou in me, that they may be made PERFECT IN ONE, and that the world may know that thou hast sent me, and hast loved them as thou hast loved me." John xvii. 20—23.

If Christ did not pray in vain to his Father, then we learn from these remarkable words, *First*, That all real Christians are to be ONE. *Secondly*, Their union is to resemble that of Christ and the Father. *Thirdly*, In order that they might become ONE, the glory which the Father gave to Christ he gave his church. *Fourthly*, That the world, beholding this unity among Christians, will believe that Christ is sent of the Father. This doctrine of the unity of the church is taught also in Romans xii. 4, 5; also xv. 5, 6; 1 Cor. i. 10; also iii. See also the whole of the 4th chapter of Paul's Epistle to the Ephesians; nor does it appear possible to explain the above and similar passages in any other way than that which establishes this truth, *That all real Christians should form one Church*.

It is essential to the unity of the church that this general principle should be recognised. That each church admit to membership such as Christ hath received—" receiving one another as Christ has received us," so that no real Christian should be excluded in consequence of his peculiar notions; and, secondly, that all sectarian appellations should be renounced, for the family name of CHRISTIAN. These simple principles, if acted upon, would go far to unite the *whole of Christ's people*.

[I should have been glad to give the whole of this pamphlet which contains many extracts from excellent authors, but conclude with this urgent appeal.]

And Christians, if you will not labor for the *union* of the church, and pray for it, and set an example of it, "you throw to an immeasureable distance the period of Zion's joy;" you put in peril an enterprise which would fill the minds of millions with unutterable joy. We beseech you, for the sake of immortal souls, to lay aside animosity, and love as brethren. We beseech you, by the sufferings and death of your Lord, who once agonized, and bled, and died, that the world might be saved. We beseech you, *by the fearful consequence of others dying in unbelief and sin*—by the miseries of hell, endeavor to use the plan recommended in Scripture for snatching sinners as brands from the burning. We beseech you by all that is lovely and glorious and attracting in the religion of love. We beseech you by the glories of heaven. In fine, we entreat you by the love you bear to Christ, to evince that you love his spouse, and act towards her as he has enjoined. Are you decided what to do? the way of duty is plain before you. Set an example of what you wish to recommend to others. Let your conversation tend to promote unity;

furnish yourselves with arguments. You never heard of the accomplishment of a difficult enterprise, by wishing, and hoping, and doing nothing; nor need you expect discord to flee away without activity; some of you can deliver lectures on this subject, others of you can write upon it. "If I had to live my life again (we believe, it is said by Cecil) I would write more books; they should not however be folios, but penny tracts. The folios are read by your tens, your penny tracts by thousands."

On June 26th, 1831, died George IV., who was no honor to monarchy.

We had an occasion in 1831 to show our regard to Christ's law of love by assisting the poor during the Irish famine. The following letter shows also that much was done in several parts of Great Britain to aid the suffering poor in the sister isle.

EXETER HALL, 9th July, 1831.

SIR,

I am directed by the Western Committee for the Relief of the Irish Poor, to acknowledge the receipt of £7, which has been paid into the hands of Messrs Drummond & Co., and to thank you sincerely for it. At the same time, I have the satisfaction to state that from information which they have received, they feel satisfied that the supplies already forwarded, and those in progress, will be sufficient to meet the pressing wants of their distressed fellow subjects until the potato harvest, and they have therefore given public notice to this effect.

I am, dear Sir, your obedient servant,
J. BARTLETT, Secy.

REV. JOHN BOWES, Dundee.

In January we commenced the "Christian Miscellany and Herald of Union." Between three and four hundred copies were circulated in Dundee. The largest number were taken where the churches were the largest.

This year died Andrew Thompson, of St. George's, Edinburgh. He was very zealous for a pure Bible Society. I have heard him deliver powerful speeches against the London Bible Society's allowing corrupt versions to be circulated on the Continent.

It was in 1831, I published "A Sermon on the Causes and Cure of Drunkenness, illustrated with facts, preached in the Episcopal Chapel, Dundee, by John Bowes, minister of the gospel. Sold by Donaldson, Sime, and Livingston, booksellers, Dundee, for the Temperance Society. Price Three-halfpence. The above sermon contains a variety of important observations on the sin of drunkenness. It is illustrated by many interesting facts, and supported by powerful and convincing arguments. We hail it as another useful tract, which is likely to advance the interests of the society for whose benefit it is published. We would advise all our readers to lay out three-halfpence in purchasing it, and can assure them they will have enough both of quality and quantity for their money. Its cheapness is the only reason why we have not furnished extracts from some of its striking statements."—*The Christian Miscellany*.

On September 14th, I addressed a Missionary Meeting in Ship Row Chapel, Aberdeen. Its object was to promote union, and the knowledge of the gospel in these kingdoms.

In November I published "An Address" of twelve closely printed pages "to the spirit-dealers of Scotland." I had previously delivered a course of sermons against drunkenness. Many were afraid that they would drive away some of our seat-holders and hearers. Some they did, but I kept to duty, and some spirit-dealers left us. For more than 40 years we should not have taken into any of the churches where I go a spirit-dealer.

This article appeared in the Christian Miscellany, vol. II. page 6.

ON CHURCHES RECEIVING MEMBERS.

When the disciple of the Lord Jesus Christ looks abroad into this professedly Christian land, he sees much reason to commiserate the dishonored church of God. Hundreds and thousands of professors present themselves before Him along with palpable evidences that they possess nothing of the religion of the Saviour beyond the mere form. This judgment, charity itself, however extended, is compelled to form. Numerous reasons may be assigned for this awful state of things. In Scotland, nearly the whole population professes Christianity. And there is a considerable degree of disgrace connected with not professing religion—and not being a member of some church. Hence many become members of the church, through the influence of custom, through fear of reproach, or through motives of worldly profit. These reasons are the foundation of an extensive difference between primitive and modern Christians. By the former, Paganism or Judaism, had been professed, and to embrace Christianity, was to undergo a wonderful change in the great objects of real or pretended faith. The latter are trained up in the belief of the doctrines of Christianity. The former had to fear reproach in the Christian religion, while honor awaited them in Paganism or Judaism; the latter discover that worldly honor is now closely connected with church membership. The former had to hazard their property, and even their lives, in professing the religion of Christ; the latter have more ample opportunities of becoming wealthy in the church, than out of it. These are the reasons assignable for such extensive corruptions in the church, as that which we deplore. Because the "United Christian Churches," receive as members, persons from all orthodox denominations, it is therefore said by some sectarians, "that this church receives all kinds of applicants." If, by this objection, it is insinuated that we make no difference betwixt a believer and an unbeliever, a moral and an immoral man, we wholly deny the charge; but if the objection means that we receive all whom Christ has received, as far as we can ascertain, we acknowledge it, and glory in it. But we would do all that we can in order to ascertain this. I am convinced that our churches must be considerably influenced by our manner of acting in reference to candidates for membership. If in this age of profession we are satisfied with the candidate's saying—"I believe in Christ." We shall easily obtain members who never believed "with the heart unto righteousness." The question is, does their "faith work by love?" Is it accompanied by the indwelling of the Holy Spirit? Has "God sent forth the Spirit of his Son into their hearts, crying, Abba, Father?" And do they show their faith by their works, by all "holy conversation and godliness?" It appears to me necessary, that candidates for membership should understand the duties which will arise out of their proposed connection with the churches. Not only should they be taught their duty to God in the Church, but also their duty to their brethren in the church. Of this I am certain, that many are members of different churches, who cannot give a satisfactory reply to the question, "What is the duty of one member of Christ's church to another?" And if they do not know their duty, they cannot do it. A brother may be sick, but they will not visit him—in need, they will not minister unto him,—he may sin from day to day, and from week to week, under their immediate notice, but they never think of going and telling him his fault, according to Matt. xviii. 15-17, but leave him to disgrace the church, to be a stumbling block to the weak, and a prey to the destroyer.

If all our members were well instructed in their duty to one another, and disposed to attend to it, who can calculate on the blessed results? The church would discipline itself, and by the blessing of God purge itself, and shine brilliantly before an ungodly world, to the glory of divine grace. It appears to me that for a minister, elder, or deacon, to listen to an evil report in the church, against any brother who has not been treated according to Matt. xviii. 15, &c., is to encourage the breach of Christ's published law, throw the church into confusion, and endanger its purity.

Unity and purity must proceed together, the one is as essential as the other, and both are indispensable. I would not forget, however, to notice that in the present state of things we may expect imposition. If the Apostles were imposed upon by Simon Magus, and Ananias and his wife, when there were no real inducements of a secular kind to attract men to the form of godliness, how much more likely are ministers now to be imposed upon, after all their prayer and investigation, when there are reasons innumerable, of a secular kind, for men becoming professors of religion.

The church has to guard, on the other hand, against a forbidding attitude—against making sad those whom the Lord hath not made sad—against driving from the church a sincere but feeble Christian. Should our churches acquire the character of impurity, which God forbid, such a character would be a warrant for the unholy to apply for membership. Should they, on the contrary, assume the appearance of forbidding and narrow stubbornness, many real disciples would turn away from them, being afraid to undergo the dreaded ordeal.

May the Lord make our churches powerful by his life-giving presence in all our sermons and assemblies—honorable, by their scriptural order and purity—and attractive, by their compassion and hallowed love. Amen.
JOHN BOWES.

Dundee, Dec. 13, 1831.

Jan. 22nd, 1832.—Lord's Day. After a pleasant day in His service, my wife and I were taking supper, and talking of the services of the day, when our youngest child, Elizabeth, got a little cheese crust into her throat. We were all alarmed, my dear wife especially; she endeavored to get it out in vain. The face of the dear little infant was becoming black. I tried to make her throw it. All hope was nearly gone; my efforts failed. I tried once more; put my finger down her throat, and thrust down the cheese; but still she drew no breath. I then laid her breast on one hand, and clapped her back with the other, when she threw it up. For this mercy we kneeled down and thanked the Lord. May we never forget his goodness.

I would notice also here, that during the last year one of the brethren, Mr. James Paterson, residing at Montrose, died of apoplexy while at Brechin, and has left behind him a wife and six children. His widow is a most intelligent and amiable Christian, as are also some of her children. Being at Montrose a few weeks ago, lecturing for the Temperance Society, after the lecture I called the family together, read a portion of Scripture, and endeavored to inculcate upon the fatherless children their duty to God, their mother, to each other, and to all men. While showing them that God would be their Father and guide, and that by believing in him and obeying him they might expect his blessing, we were all much affected. I then experienced much liberty in spreading their case before the Lord. May He bless them, and make them a blessing.

On the 1st of this month, I was invited to take tea with Mr. Saunders, hatter, who has had much affliction in his family by the fever during the last few months. One of his daughters has been removed into eternity, and another and himself have been mercifully snatched from the gates of death. I have visited him during his affliction, and trust that the Lord has sanctified his rod. After tea, I told them that if they had no objections, and would call the family together, we would try to improve their late affliction. To this request they frankly acceded, and I read and expounded the case of the ten lepers, and dwelt particularly upon the leper that returned to praise the author of his cure. I endeavored to impress upon the minds of my affected and serious auditors that they had special reasons to be thankful to the Lord for sparing the father of the family. I hope the Lord will bless this endeavor.

March 5th.—Yesterday, having been unwell with a cold during the preceding week, I felt unwell in the morning, and with difficulty expounded the first chapter of Matthew; but through the kindness and care of one of the members and my dear wife and servant, and the blessing of the Lord, I was able to preach three times, growing stronger each time. I took dinner and tea in the vestry, and never went home till after the evening service. It was a pleasant and precious day, although the congregations were smaller than usual. For some time past the Father of mercies and God of all consolation has been quickening my soul, and leading me by his Spirit, to see the vanity of the world, and the excellency of the grace of our Lord Jesus Christ, in whom I desire to trust for time and eternity. I have been melted into sorrow by reviewing the present state of professors of religion in this town,—drunkards, swearers, liars, &c., are members of the most numerous churches. There are a few among all denominations that "sigh and cry for the abominations done in the land," but among them there appears generally too much apathy and deadness. Importance is attached to the little peculiarities of a party, and time and talent wasted in maintaining them, while souls are allowed to perish, without any general attempt to rouse them from their fatal security. I have sought to convince the church of the necessity of purity of discipline, persevering prayer, and zealous efforts. May the Head of the Church prosper the attempt.

7th.—(I find this entry.) I resolve to pray in secret to the Lord for myself, the church over which I am placed, and the world, daily at 10 o'clock, a.m. This appears to me the best time for the present.

May 2nd.—The Annual Meeting was held in the Maygate Chapel, Dunfermline, in which I preached several times, as well as in the open-air. While here I was consulted by brother M—— concerning a Christian wife. I recommended a Dundee sister, who had been compelled to divorce her husband. They both lived in Dundee several years after this, met, but never spoke: they were dead to each other. Brother M—— was permitted to come to Dundee; they were pleased with each other, and soon after married. To her daughter he became a kind father. The marriage was a very happy one.

EXTRACTS FROM NOTES OF A VISIT TO ENGLAND.

I left Dundee with my family in the brig *Thistle*, on the 19th of June, and arrived in the mouth of the Tyne, about 4 o'clock a.m, on the 21st. The first Sunday I spent in Durham. Not being able to procure the promise of chapels in time on Saturday, I sent the bellman to announce that I should preach in the market-place at 9 a.m., half-past 12, and 4 p.m.

24th.—Sunday. Commenced divine worship at 9 o'clock. Had not proceeded far, before a person commanded me to desist; saying, "You cannot be allowed to preach here." I shall here give the substance of the conversation, according to the best of my recollection:—

MINISTER.—The law of the land allows me to preach here, and I shall proceed.

OFFICER.—You cannot preach here. You must go before a magistrate.

M.—I have no need to go before a magistrate. This is public property, and I can preach anywhere on public property, if there be no disturbance, and the highway be not obstructed.

O.—The authorities will not allow it: you must go with me.

M.—Who are you? Who sent you to interrupt me in this manner, or by what authority do you act?

O.—There is my authority, (pulling a constable's staff from his pocket.)

M.—Well, that is no authority at all for this interruption. I must proceed with the discourse.

O.—(Taking the minister by the collar very unceremoniously). Then I must take you into custody.

(Here some of the audience remonstrated, but Joseph Liddle was inflexible.)

M.—(To the people). Well, I cannot preach to you if the officer uses force. I must go with him to a magistrate, but I expect to be with you in ten minutes;—if I am longer, I shall preach here when I return.

I accompanied the officer to —— Fenwick, Esq., followed by a great part of the assembly. As we were on the way, I said to him, "Are you not afraid *thus* to interfere with a servant of the Lord Jesus Christ?" He replied, "It is not my will to do it; but when any preachers have been allowed to preach in the open-air, we are found fault with." When we arrived at Mr. Fenwick's house, the officer said, "Here is a gentleman, sir, who has been haranguing the people in the market-place."

MAGISTRATE.—Was there any disturbance?

OFFICER.—None.

MAG.—Where was it?

O.—At the low end of the market-place.

MAG.—(To the minister.) You should keep off church hours, sir, if possible.

MIN.—That I have done; but there is no law to that effect. The law allows preaching on public property.

MAG.—The fact is, there is no law against it. (Here Liddle got a slight reproof.)

MIN.—The time is passing, sir, and I must hasten to finish my discourse before church time.

The magistrate accompanied me to the door; the people bowed and thanked him; and, after this, we finished the morning service in peace. At half-past 12 o'clock, we had not been long engaged before I was again tapped on the arm, and ordered to come down by a clerical magistrate.

CLER. MAG.—You must come down, sir; you cannot preach here.

MIN.—I intend to go on, sir. I can preach here lawfully, and will not be interrupted.

C. M.—What are you, and where do you come from?

M.—*Who are you*, sir; and who gave you authority to ask me that question?

C. M.—My name is Davison. I am a minister of this church, (pointing eastward) and a magistrate of this county.

M.—I have been before a magistrate this morning, who agrees with me, that there is no law against preaching on public property.

C. M.—This is my property. It belongs to my church.

M.—If it belongs to your church, why do you not fence it in? Here is no enclosure—it is the market-place; but I must go on with my discourse, sir.

Which I did, and finished in peace. The Rev. Mr. Davison went away not a little mortified. At 4 o'clock, we had persons of nearly all ranks in the city, to whom I endeavored to show the evils of divisions among Christians, and the scriptural nature and advantages of unity. In conclusion, I referred to the tyrannical opposition which I had met with that day; and told them it was a disgrace to their city. I had preached the Gospel in the open-air in Edinburgh, Dundee, and other large places, both in England and Scotland, and had never met with such intolerance; but that I did not expect much better while ministers of the Gospel were *civil* magistrates; but there was a time coming when this combination of offices would cease, and then the proud, drunken, and indolent among the clergy would be discarded, and those only employed who would visit their flock, as well as preach to them.

On the 25th, I preached in LANCHESTER, with great liberty, from Rom. viii. 16. The people are very lively and zealous.

On the 26th we took coach for York, and arrived in the evening at the house of my father-in-law, Mr. J. Bellwood, WEST COTTINGWORTH, ten miles beyond York.

On the 28th, I preached in the Wesleyan chapel on the parable of the barren fig-tree. The people were serious. There is great excitement and alarm felt here from the appearance of the cholera in Selby and York; some scores have died. In most places, drunkards and common prostitutes, or infirm people, are its common victims, but I have heard of sober, healthy, and respectable people dying of it in Selby and York, some of whom were decidedly religious. May we all be ready for heaven—then death will not injure us.

On the 29th, we took coach at York for Harrowgate. While on it, a circumstance occured worthy of remembrance. I sat on the front of the coach; on my left was a young gentleman, apparently a great traveller either for pleasure or improvement; before us, next to the driver, was a shrewd, but kind, gentleman of about forty years of age. They conversed on a variety of topics, in which I occasionally joined. Both appeared to be acquainted with politics. The gentleman of forty thought the practice of flogging inhuman, and expressed his anxious desire for its abolition. The young traveller thought it a good mode of correction, and, in short, the best that could be devised. That subject ended, the cholera was treated upon, and other diseases adverted to, and the use of medicine in cases of cholera questioned. The young traveller said "I never take physic; indeed, I have never taken any since I was at school." The gentlemen of forty replied, "A birch dose, Sir, I suppose, as you are so very fond of flogging." This rejoinder, coming an hour after the young traveller's observations were made in favor of flogging, was like a thunder-bolt to us all. It produced no reply. The young man was struck dumb, and remained so nearly the whole of the remainder of the way. I think from the effect produced at the moment, that he will never advocate flogging any more in any company.

The second Lord's Day I spent at MIDDLEHAM.

On Saturbay, the 30th, we arrived at Middleham, a little past nine o'clock in the evening, the residence of my father and mother. In half an hour I visited Mr. Rogers, superintendent of the Middleham circuit, and Mr. Digby, circuit steward—an excellent Christian, whom I have known many years. I solicited the chapel for one sermon on the Lord's Day, and for the Monday evening, which was soon granted; as was also the Primitive Methodist chapel for the evening sermon.

July 1st, Lord's Day. I preached in the only two dissenting chapels in Middleham, and my heart was gladdened by the presence of many Christian friends, with whom I used formerly to take sweet council. After the two o'clock service, the superintendent, Mr. Rogers, and Mr. Digby, came over to the house of my father, and kindly invited me to preach again in the evening, in the Wesleyan chapel; but having engaged to preach in the other chapel, I declined. O what a blessed principle is Christian love! It leads all who love Jesus Christ to love one another. May the Lord prepare me to follow him.

6*th*.—We bade farewell to our relations in Yorkshire, after commending them to the grace of God.

The third Lord's Day I passed at NEWCASTLE.

8*th*.—Preached in the morning and afternoon in Mr. Graham's chapel, Wall Knoll; and in the evening, lectured on the unity of the church, in Mr. Pullar's congregation, Felling Shore. The chapels were crowded with attentive hearers.

The labors of Messrs Graham, Pullar, and Adam are abundant. They preach four times on the Lord's Day, and almost every night in the week: but the results are answerable to the labor bestowed.

9*th*. Lectured in Wall Knoll chapel at seven o'clock P.M., on the necessity of Christ's disciples being one. A large, attentive congregation.

10*th*. Attended a Missionary meeting in the before-named chapel. It was quite crowded. The people were attentive to the last. I was particularly satisfied with a remark made by Mr. Pullar. He had long thought that Christ's church should be one: but there was one difficulty he could not get over—there was one thing which, up to that hour, he thought he could not part with. It was the name which was associated with the views he entertained of a church of Christ, scripturally organised. He had thought that certain distinctive principles should be known by certain names; but since he had entered this meeting, his love to the last vestige of sectarianism was gone, and he now declared, that if ever he was destined to be a minister over a church, it should be denominated only from Christ. This assertion produced a general burst of approbation; from which I conclude that the people entered warmly into, and approved of, the sentiments [how soon Mr. Pullar's mind changed; he joined the Congregationalists, and I believe is with them still at Hamilton in Canada]. It was altogether the most Christian and powerful Missionary meeting that I ever attended. May the effects be seen many days hence.

The meeting opened with singing and prayer; after which, Mr. Adam was called to the chair: when it was proposed by Mr. J. Graham, seconded by Mr. G. Pearson, and resolved,

1. That this meeting, contemplating the numerous population on the banks of the Tyne, and the villages around Newcastle, destitute of, and partially supplied with, the means of grace; and the consequent depravity and wickedness that so lamentably prevails, recognise the importance and necessity of adopting means to supply the deficiency.

Proposed by Mr. J. Bowes, and seconded by M. Graham, Jun.

2. That this meeting expresses deep regret and sorrow at the many divisions existing in the professing Christian world; ardently desires a speedy union in affection, communion, and enterprise, among all real Christians; and earnestly hopes that the means will not be wanting for assisting in the preaching of the Gospel, and the formation of churches on the broad basis of Christian, in opposition to party communion.

13*th*, Friday. Came by the Ardincaple steam-packet to Leith; and on Saturday morning, the 14th, came by the Lady of the Lake steamboat to Dundee, after a pleasant and profitable journey; and found an affectionate flock grateful for our safe return.

As the important subject of Church Purity is set forth in this article, it will be a key to keeping apart from all churches who have discarded this vital principle, whether north or south of the Tweed.

WHO OUGHT TO BE MEMBERS OF THE CHURCH OF CHIRST?

This inquiry is of the first importance to the interests and well-being of Christ's Church. And if we can arrive at a scriptural solution of the question, it may serve to direct our practice, and confer real benefit on the church.

Were we to take the Word of God for our only guide in questions of this nature, we should not be much embarrassed in our attempts to arrive at satisfactory conclusions; but, unhappily, for the interests of the Saviour's kingdom, we are too much under the influence of educational prejudices, and the practices of such churches as we have been accustomed to regard as Christian, so that we do not discover the order, beauty, or utility of New Testament principles. But it is to the word of God alone, that I desire to appeal in this investigation, believing that it has decided the matter for the direction of all the followers of Christ. I think, then, that it may be laid down as an established truth, that those only ought to be members of the church of Christ, who believe in the record which God has given of his Son. It is not necessary here that I should fix the meaning of the term " believe ;" some think that Faith is nothing beyond crediting a testimony ; others, that it is something more, when a man is justified by it; but both agree that there is a faith in the Gospel by which a man is justified and introduced into the favor of God,—this is enough for my present purpose. I assert, then, on what authority it shall be seen, that those only who believe to the saving of the soul should be admitted into the church. In Acts ii. 41, &c., we have an account of thousands being added to the church, and their qualifications for membership are mentioned : " Then they that gladly received the word were baptized, and the same day there were added unto them about three thousand souls. And all that believed were together, and had all things common." That those that believed were saved, is manifest from the last part of the 47th verse, which, when correctly rendered, reads thus : "And the Lord added to the church those who were saved."

A remarkable effect followed the awful death of Ananias and Sapphira; Acts v. 13, 14, "And, of the rest, durst no man join himself to them ; but the people magnified them. And believers were the more added to the Lord, multitudes both of men and women." This passage is remarkably instructive ; it shows us that while the startling death of the liars before mentioned, deterred the unconverted from joining the infant church, it was a powerful inducement for believers to unite themselves to the Lord.

These passages are sufficient, were there no other, to prove that none but converted or believing souls should be received into the church.

Again, the Apostle addresses the churches in such language as plainly indicates that they were composed of converted men. When writing to the Romans he only directs his epistle "To all that be in Rome, beloved in God, called to be saints," Rom. i. 7. When writing to the church at Corinth, he uses language of equal strength and perspicuity : " Unto the church of God, which is at Corinth, to them that are sanctified in Christ Jesus, called to be saints," &c., 1 Cor. i. 2.

He addresses his epistle to the Ephesians thus : " Paul, an apostle of Jesus Christ by the will of God, to the saints which are at Ephesus, and to the faithful in Christ Jesus," Eph. i. 1. He uses similar appellations in reference to the Colossians : " To the saints and faithful brethren in Christ," Col. i. 1. To the same church he writes thus : " Forbearing one another, and forgiving one another, if any man have a quarrel against any: even as Christ forgave you, so also do ye," Col. iii. 13.

Now, except it can be proved that unconverted men are beloved of God, called saints, sanctified in Christ Jesus, faithful brethren in Christ, and forgiven of Christ, they are unfit for the church.

Again, the duties required of Christ's church, are such as believers only can perform. Christ's disciples are commanded to "Let their light shine before men." To them Christ says, "Love your enemies." "Do good to them that hate you," "Pray without ceasing," "Rejoice evermore," "In everything give thanks," "Glorify God in your body and in your spirit, which are God's." Now, I ask any candid and reasonable Christian, if any unconverted man can attend to and obey these injunctions, and a host more of the same kind? If not, then such a man is plainly unfit for a community where such obedience is indispensable.

Again, the very nature of the Lord's Supper implies the necessity of conversion, in order that it may not be received unworthily. In that precious ordinance we celebrate the love of our Master, and by it our conceptions of his love are enhanced, and our meditations carried forward to his second advent. How then can a man be supposed to communicate worthily, whose heart is the seat of enmity to the being whose love he professes to celebrate? How can he be supposed to have any delight in thinking of Christ's second coming, who has never appreciated his first?

To speak out, such conduct is odious hypocrisy. What should we think of a man opposed in heart to Nelson and Wellington, attending with the respective admirers of these celebrated men, and professing to mingle in the enthusiastic applause given to the heroes of Trafalgar, and of Waterloo,—should we not regard such a man as a detestable deceiver? And in what other light can we regard a man, whose heart and practices are opposed to Jesus Christ, when he has the audacity and hardihood, in spite of the curse pronounced upon such men, to sit down among the friends of Christ, and join in the celebration of an event, the most impressive, important, and beneficial, that ever occupied the attention, or engaged the praises, of man? Oh! that men would be wise for themselves, and study the import of God's word, that they might be led to hate and abandon practices as much opposed to their own interests, as they are to the spirit and tenor of the word of God. See 1 Cor. 11th chap., from 27th verse to the end.

I cannot close this article without referring to the practices of many Christian churches in receiving members. They do not even profess to receive only those that they have reason to think Christ has received: on the contrary, they admit those who may have a tolerable moral character, if they do not deny the doctrines of the Bible. Some churches require that candidates for membership should manifest a desire to flee from the wrath to come; but, I ask, may not a man be tolerably moral—an assenter to the truths of inspiration—a professor of a desire to flee from the wrath to come, and yet be unjustified, unsaved, and unchristian? That there are thousands of this sort of people in the church, every Christian who observes its state must know. They enter the church unconverted—they live to disgrace it, some by pride, others by covetousness, others by drunkenness, lasciviousness, and so on.

And this is not all, they die unconverted, and consequently go to hell, but not until they disgraced the church, and made many, many infidels who have been shocked by their daring hypocrisy.

How is the church of Christ burdened with such men? and by what means are they brought into it? The reply is easy. They are received unconverted, and are allowed to remain in the church, even after they have given evidence of their unrenewed state. I know it is common for the advocates of a lax discipline to allege in its favor the parable of the tares and the wheat. "Did not our Lord," say they, "tell his disciples not to root up the tares? did he not say, 'Let both grow together until the harvest?'" To which I reply, certainly our Lord did so speak; but does the parable apply to the church or the world? I think to the latter: "Let both grow together;" viz. the righteous and the wicked. Let there be no separation of them, "the field is the world," let them live together, and have trade and commerce together, until the harvest. Concerning what is meant by the harvest, there can be but one opinion. It appears, then, that Christ neither said nor meant, let both the wicked and the righteous grow together in the church. His word says quite the reverse. See 1 Cor. v. 11, 12; Rom. xvi. 17; 2 Thess. iii. 6, 14; 2 Tim. iii. 1—5; Gall. v. 10—12; Rev. ii. 1, 2, 14, 15, 20. But supposing that it were admitted that the parable in question refers to the church, then it condemns the practices of nearly all churches, for I am not acquainted with any which retain murderers in their communion. But if both are to grow together, then are we prohibited from excluding even the most worthless. But before I dismiss this subject, I would just remind the advocates of laxity in the church, that when "the servants of the householder came and said unto him, 'Sir, didst thou not sow good seed in thy field? from whence then hath it tares?'" that, "he said unto them, 'an enemy hath done this.'" So that if the parable refers to the church, then those (be they ministers, elders, deacons, or churches,) who bring into the church the tares, are plainly enemies to Christ and his church. And as they gaze at their unconverted members, and endeavor to satisfy their consciences by one part of the parable, viz. "Let both grow together until the harvest," I would disturb their tranquility by another part of the parable, and place before them those fearful words, "an enemy hath done this." Perhaps in no part of the world where the reformation from Popery has prevailed, are there more evidences of hypocrisy than in Scotland.

The greatest part of the population profess the Christian religion, and is united with some denomination of Christians. In England and America great numbers profess no religion at all; the result is, that when men join the church, they generally do so out of love to its Head. But will the most extended charity allow us to say that this is the case in this country? On the contrary, thousands join for no other reason than that they may obtain what is termed "Church Benefit,"—that is, that they may have children baptized, and, if they please, partake of the Lord's Supper; consequently, churches are crowded with unconverted men, to the great dishonor of religion, and to the grief of those holy men who are to be found, I hope, in all churches. I would seriously advise all those who propose to unite with the church, to consider dispassionately their motives, and if they do believe in, and supremely love, the Lord Jesus Christ, it is their duty to become members of his church, without which they cannot observe the ordinance of the Lord's Supper, and consequently must be found guilty of transgressing that plain command, "This do in remembrance of me." But if their sole reasons are, obtaining baptism for their offspring, and being like their neighbors, I advise them to consider, in addition to what has been said before, that baptism cannot save their children, and that their children can have no right to it, when they themselves are unbelievers; and, consequently, it will be better for their children, for themselves, the world, and the church, that they should not take upon themselves the Christian name, until they are true Christians.

J. BOWES.

Dundee, July 31, 1832.

This article shows the value which I always attached to a pious and competent ministry, long before I gave up hire in either theory or practice.

WHO OUGHT TO BE MINISTERS OF THE GOSPEL?

In order that sinners might be brought under the blessed influence of the Gospel of Christ, he has wisely made arrangements to secure to his Church a succession of faithful men, able to teach others his grand doctrines; and that there might be no misconception as to the persons who ought to be employed in this important work, we are furnished in the Scriptures with sufficient marks by which to know what qualifications are necessary for ministers of the gospel.

It perhaps may be allowed, that some have not the qualifications necessary for bishops, elders, or pastors, who ought, nevertheless, to show unto others the way of salvation; but without determining this, it will be sufficient to remark, that this present investigation is to be confined to those whom the Scriptures style "bishops or elders," and who are in modern phraseology designated, "Ministers of the Gospel."

I. Those only ought to be ministers of the gospel who have been *regenerated* themselves, and who give unequivocal evidence of their *decided piety*.

The apostle Paul mentions his conversion as a preparatory requisite for preaching Christ "among the heathen." "But when it pleased God," says he, "who separated me from my mother's womb, and called me by his grace, to reveal his Son in me, that I might preach him among the heathen, immediately I conferred not with flesh and blood.—Gal. i. 15, 16. The appeal made by this apostle in behalf of himself and his brethren in the ministry, to the Thessalonians, in the following passage, evinces the piety of the first preachers of the gospel:—"Ye are witnesses, and God also, how holily, and justly, and unblameably we behaved ourselves among you that believe. As you know that we exhorted and comforted, and charged every one of you, (as a father doth his children) that ye would walk worthy of God, who hath called you into his kingdom and glory."—1 Thess. ii. 10—12.

When we consider that the tree is known by its fruit,—the heart by the life,—we cannot conceive how ministers can behave "holily, justly, and unblameably," without decided piety. Nor can we understand how they can *exhort, comfort, and charge* the church, (as a father doth his children), unless their own hearts enjoy divine love. It is necessary that ministers should pity and love the immortals whom they address, otherwise they are not likely to be successful; but "All men are orators when they feel," and this accounts for the uselessness of some ministers, and the success of others. It was a beautiful picture which a deistical physician drew of the late Dr. Gillies of Glasgow, when he said, "I believe that John Gillies would be glad to carry all mankind to heaven in his bosom."

The following instructions, given to Titus, indicate the imperative necessity of piety in ministers:—"In all things showing thyself a pattern of good works; in doctrine, showing uncorruptness, gravity, sincerity,—sound speech that cannot be condemned; that he that is of the contrary part may be ashamed, *having no evil thing to say of you.*"—Tit. ii. 7, 8. The same important truth is taught in the qualifications which the Apostle Paul describes as necessary for a bishop, and which he concludes by saying, "Moreover he must have a good report of them that are without; lest he fall into reproach, and the snare of the slanderer." (See Tim. iii. 2—7.

Again, the Lord's people are pointedly guarded against ungodly ministers,—a circumstance which leads us to infer that the Almighty does not approve of them,—"Beware of false prophets, who come unto you in sheep's clothing, but inwardly they are ravening wolves,—ye shall know them by their fruits."—Matt. vii. 15, 16. "Cease, my son, to hear the instruction that causeth to err from the words of knowledge."—Prov. xix. 27.

Unconverted ministers resemble the Pharisees of old; and the awful effects mentioned by Jesus Christ, of their guidance, are still produced by those who resemble them. He said to his disciples, "Let them alone: they be blind leaders of the blind. And if the blind lead the blind, both shall fall into the ditch."—Matt. xv. 14. From these words it is plain that a blind minister is most detrimental to the interests of the church; and that instead of leading men to Christ and heaven, he leads them into error and perdition.

And what else but misery and ruin can be expected from unconverted guides? How can they teach, with success, a gospel which they neither understand nor believe? or be expected cordially to invite men to partake of the blessings of a Saviour whose excellencies they neither see nor admire? To be a useful guide in the narrow way, acquaintance with it is essential. When will the Church learn to cast off that enormous load which now presses down its energies—*an unconverted ministry?* The *boldness* required of ministers, implies that they should be holy. They are sometimes called upon to reprove sinners, as John the Baptist reproved Herod;—and if, at present, the law preserves their heads, it does not shield them from the attacks of malevolence;—and if they wish to have the favor of the rich and honorable, they must be tender of their vices, or they will soon provoke hostilities. A Christian will be faithful in the midst of hostile men, but a hireling will flee before opposition. The Apostle of the Gentiles felt the necessity of boldness, and requested the Ephesians to pray that he "might open his mouth boldly to make known the mystery of the Gospel." Eph. vi. 19. It is the duty of Zion's watchmen to warn men faithfully, whether they will hear or not. Will unholy ministers do this? No! They swim with the stream, afraid of offending the rich and the honorable sinner,—ashamed to beg and unwilling to work,—"they crouch for a piece of silver, and say, put me into the priest's office, that I may eat a morsel of bread ;—they teach for hire, and divine for money :" and on this account they are branded as "greedy dogs that can never have enough, as shepherds that do not understand, looking every man for his gain from his quarter."

The evil practices of unholy ministers have done incalculable mischief to the church in all ages. *They* have stumbled and turned out of the way the weak members of the church,—have prevented those from entering the church who were about to become members,—have caused the enemies of Christ to blaspheme,—kept the Church in fearful darkness, and subserved the interests of Satan's kingdom much more effectually in the Church, than they could have done if they had remained the professed abettors of that kingdom. It is therefore high time for every lover of Zion to speak out on this subject, and attempt to rid the Church of one of its greatest evils,—and thus divest Satan of one of his most efficient agencies.

II. Those only ought to be ministers of the Gospel, who, in addition to piety, have talents suited to the office. Many a man is unquestionably pious, who is, nevertheless, incapacitated for the ministry; and many a man is possessed of suitable talents who is unfit for the ministry in consequence of his want of piety.

Paul said to Timothy, "The things that thou hast heard of me among many witnesses, the same commit thou to faithful men, who shall be able to teach others." 2 Tim. ii. 2. And the same Apostle, in enumerating the qualifications necessary for a Bishop, says, that he must be "apt to teach,"—1 Tim. iii. 2,—by which we may understand, that a Bishop should have a capacity to teach, and apply himself attentively to that work. As it would lengthen this article beyond due bounds, to enlarge upon other endowments which the Apostle enumerates, as necessary for a Bishop, it may suffice to refer the reader to the 1st Epistle to Tim. 3rd Chap. from the 1st verse to the 7th, where he will see that a Bishop must be blameless, vigilant, sober, of good behavior; given to hospitality; not given to wine; no striker; not greedy of filthy lucre, but patient; not a brawler; not covetous; one that ruleth well his own house, having his children in subjection; not a novice, &c.

When ministers of the gospel lack either piety or other suitable endowments, they necessarily degrade the office which they sustain, and inflict deep and lasting wounds upon the Church. From this fruitful source of evil arises indolence, bigotry, pride, avarice and a host of other ills.

It may be useful to reflect upon the causes which produce an inefficient ministry, and show how this enormous evil may be remedied.

Many churches and families send their sons to the college, with a design to have them made ministers, without any regard whatever to their piety or talents; so that they may have the one and not the other, or they may be destitute of both. In order to prevent those who are not pious from directing their attention to the ministry, parents and churches should never even think of young men filling such an awful situation until they first give evidence of the new birth. Parents would have more real satisfaction, and would be more in the way of duty, in bringing up their children in the humblest occupations than in pushing them forward into a situation in the church, which they can only occupy to their own hurt, and the injury of others. It is the duty of the church to pray for a pious and laborious ministry; and if prayer is offered up constantly and fervently, the Lord will give his people the desire of their hearts, and consistency will urge them to use all prudential measures in order to realise their requests.

How much is that *poor young man* to be pitied who has been set apart to the pastoral office by his parents, and who is seeking preparation for it within the walls of a college, and all the time destitute of the love of God! Who will show him his danger? Who will endeavor to rescue him from acting the "direst, deepest tragedy that ever was performed by man, since it ends in the eternal death of the performer?" Let parents and churches set their faces against this prevailing evil, and they will, in the end, banish it from the church. And in order to prevent untalented men from spending eight or nine years in preparing to fill an office for which they are utterly disqualified, let candidates for the ministry exhort or preach to the poor ignorant people who crowd the closes and lanes of our densely populated towns, and destitute villages, and let their own ministers or brethren in the chnrch hear them, that an opinion may be formed of their fitness to engage wholly in preaching the gospel.

Perhaps it will be objected to this plan, that it is defective, inasmuch as it supposes a young man to be able to teach before he has obtained the requisite education. To this objection it may be replied, that if a Christian is incapable of instructing the most ignorant part of our population in the elementary principles of Christianity, it may be doubtful whether he will ever be "apt to teach."

Should a Christian consider it to be his duty to preach the gospel, he might easily communicate his thoughts to the pastors, who, by directing his studies, and other friendly attentions, might bring forward his talents; and if he was found "able to teach others," the necessary steps might be taken in order to introduce him into the ministry.

Perhaps the greatest number of our modern systems of ministerial education ought to be objected to, because they do not always give sufficient encouragement to men of talent. Merit, rather than either friendship or wealth, should be the chief recommendation to this holy office.

In some denominations in North Britain, it is essential that a candidate for the ministry should receive his education in one of the Scottish colleges; so that, if he had been a number of years at Cambridge, Homerton, Oxford, or Hoxton, he would have to remain the usual time at Glasgow, Edinburgh, St. Andrews, or Aberdeen, before he could obtain a license to preach! This arbitrary and unreasonable law needs only to be understood in order to be reprobated. Candid men of all parties must allow that it is immaterial where a student has got his learning, whether at a university, academy, or school, provided that he has what is necessary, The question to be proposed rather should be, "What learning have you?" not "Where did you get it?" Moreover, it should be carefully remarked, that a person may have both piety and learning, and yet be deficient in some other qualifications essential to a minister. For instance, learned and pious men are not always "apt to teach."

Those who are truly pious ministers when they enter upon their work, are much more likely to improve their talents than those who are destitute of piety. They will feel that they are bound to consecrate all their time to the service of the Head of the Church, and that they are not at liberty to spend one hour uselessly. They will therefore increase in knowledge as well as in grace, and be increasingly useful both to the church and to the world; whereas those ministers who are not careful to please God, will spend their time in any amusement, worldly society, or engagement, likely to consume time and draw off their attention from the drudgery of their proper work. Bishop Jewel, after speaking in reference to such anomalous characters, offers up the following appropriate petition:—"God grant such idle and slothful ministers grace to know their office and do it; if not, God give the people grace to know them, and shun them, and fly from them."

J. BOWES.

Dundee, Sept. 10, 1832.

THE CHOLERA.

During this summer about 750 were afflicted of Cholera in Dundee, of whom about 500 died.

I published a Tract of 12 pages on, "Sin, the cause of the pestilence; or CHOLERA MORBUS; reformation, the cure," from which I extract the following:—

"In the midst of numbers of the dying and the dead, I take up my pen to address the living. O, that I could say something as important— as solemn—as powerful as the occasion demands! Wherever we turn, death or his attendants meet our eye; while we sleep, others are sickening and closing their eyes in death. They bid farewell—often an involuntary farewell, to life, and if unprepared for their journey, how alarming their circumstances—how fearful their end!

"I visited a pious woman, afflicted with this disease about nine o'clock p.m. on Lord's Day, I asked 'If the Lord should restore you to health, do you think you would be more zealous in his cause?' With pleasure beaming in her eye, she elevated her feeble arm and replied, 'I would run to do his will.' David expresses himself in similar language, 'I will run the way of thy commandments, when thou shalt enlarge my heart.'

"We should all be humane and attentive to the bodily and spiritual necessities of the sick and dying. The following facts may evince the importance of this advice.

"*Sept.* 11, 1832.—I was called up this morning, betwixt five and six o'clock, to visit a *Cholera* patient in the neighborhood of the Magdalene yard. I passed through a room where a child of four years of age was laid dead of the disease, in the next room the only remaining one in the house, was lying the mother, a strong woman, apparently about 35, but alas! she was fast sinking into the arms of death; she was seized yesterday, her mouth and eyes were black, her right arm bended with the cramp, her finger ends were cold and withered, and she was unable to speak, but gave signs, to indicate to us that she was capable of understanding what we said. I exhorted her to flee from the wrath to come, as she would in a few moments be in another world; I prayed. Two of her sisters were in the room, they wept much. I exhorted them to confess and forsake sin, and seek the favor of God. The neighbors seemed all very much alarmed; as I came away, a woman with consternation in her countenance, informed me that a man in the same land had been crying out with pain all night. I went into the room alone. The woman at my request opened the window, and sprinkled vinegar on the floor. O, in what a pitiable state was this man; his wife away at the harvest, none of the neighbors have ventured to do anything for him, with the exception of this woman, who has only given him twice a drink of water. I spoke to him about the state of his soul; before I commenced, he said, in the most affecting tone, 'Please, Sir, give me a drink of water?' The pitcher was empty; got it filled, and complied with his request. I exhorted him to pray, and look to Christ for mercy, in this the time of his extremity. Oh, how hardened was this immortal soul! I warned him of his danger, invited him to come to the only Saviour of sinners, and prayed with him. I was the only person in the room with him, the neighbors stood and heard me in a distant part of the passage; he expressed a wish to have some hot irons applied to his cold feet, I endeavored to persuade the neighbors to obtain them; none but the woman before mentioned, seemed inclined to do anything for him, and she was unwilling, without their co-operation. I endeavored to show them their duty, and urged upon them the necessity of waiting upon him, one hour alternately; one woman seemed hardened. I called upon her to do her duty; she melted into tears, and said, 'I have four children, my husband is from home, I would do something for him, but I am afraid for my children.' I told her to do her duty, and God *could* preserve both her and them, and if she would not, He *could* easily send it to the family. The man had received no medical assistance, so I went and ordered a strong dose of castor oil. I have learned since, that both the man and the woman died in a few hours. Every reader will see the inhumanity of allowing a dying man to remain a whole night in a solitary room, without medicine or attendance."

During this year I abandoned smoking. Some say, " But my doctor recommended me to smoke;" so did mine, more than forty-eight years ago, on account of flatulency on the stomach. I smoked ten years on the doctor's recommendation; and because I began to *like* it. I left it off more than thirty-eight years ago, and found my health much improved by discontinuing it. Indeed, I had often dreadful pains in the bowels, some of them not recorded, but after I gave up smoking, they never returned. It, no doubt, would have slain me many years ago, had I not renounced it. Some fear, that if they should give it over suddenly their health might suffer. I gave it over at once without sustaining the least injury. A few months after, during the raging of the cholera, as I had visited the sick and dying, and entertained the old notion that it would ward off infection, I smoked again for a few months, intending to become a gradual abolitionist. I commenced by taking one week, four pipes per day; next week three; and the next one. I had got to one, when I was called to preach in Aberdeen, where resided a minister, an inveterate smoker. I had to spend a few days chiefly in his society. The pipe was seldom out of his mouth. I smoked again in self-defence. Thus my plan of gradual abolition failed; when I returned home, I became an immediate abolitionist, and have never smoked a pipe since. I have been often invited to take snuff, but feel it better to decline, than give it the least countenance. I remember a fact recorded of a negro, who had the snuff-box presented to him, with the usual invitation; he gave a very sensible answer to the gentleman who solicited him: "No, tank you, massa; me nose no hungry!" was his forcible reply. Persons tell us they can do longer without food by using narcotics: this may be, but as they contain no nutriment, they cannot support the body.

On Sept. 24th and 25th, I addressed Missionary Meetings in Dundee and Perth, intended to promote the union of Christians, and the spread of the gospel.

On Oct. 24th, having received an invitation from Mr. Robertson secretary of the Forfar Temperance Society, to attend their annual meeting, Nov. 12th, I attended. It was held in the United Presbyterian Church, and led to my going there some years after to preach in Forfar.

In 1832, I had two excellent Bible Classes, one of males, the other of females, so that they were early interested in bible truth. They formed nurseries for the church, as well as educated farther in Christian truth those already saved and in fellowship. I generally gave them one text as the theme of a subject, and they were to find out other texts by the next meeting.

This year died Dr. Adam Clarke.

Jan. 23rd, 1833.—This morning our dear Elizabeth died, after an illness of sixteen days, caused by water in the head. She was the most intelligent and most amiable child I ever saw. Sometimes I have heard her crying in another room, and have sat still in my study calling her to come. She always came, confessed her fault, and promised amendment, although only about two years old. I never recollect correcting her in any other way than by verbal reproof. May the Lord sanctify this loss to our good.

Feb. 10th.—While preaching at Kirriemuir, my wife was delivered of our first-born son, whom, in memory of God's goodness, I have called Ebenezer.

11th.—KIRRIEMUIR. To-day Dr. Easton, parish minister sent for me, and gave me some account of a meeting of the inhabitants of the town, to be held this day in the parish church. He likewise intimated that I might usefully address the meeting. I did so; showing that the following things tended to lead men wrong on the Lord's Day,—the immorality, covetousness, and divisions of professors of religion. The meeting was called to petition Parliament to adopt such measures as might appear necessary in order to a better observance of the Lord' Day. In the evening I lectured to an overflowing house on the unity of the church.

17th.—DUNDEE. I preached this afternoon on Mark x. 21, evincing that Christians ought not to lay up treasure on earth. This sermon is printed. In the evening, I commenced a course of lectures against Popery, contrasting Protestant Churches with the Church of Rome.

19th.—Tuesday evening. Conversed with applicants for membership. One young married man I asked to tell me what Jesus Christ died for? "To repent," said he. "Where did he die?" "*In heaven*," was the answer. "Where did he die?" said I, thinking he misunderstood the question; "In heaven," he replied again! On a former occasion, a man applied for membership, and I asked him if he knew the meaning of the bread and wine in the Lord's Supper? "No, sir." "Have you never been present to see that bread and wine are used in that ordinance?" "No, sir." "Have you lived in Scotland all your life?" "Yes: at Ayr, Glasgow, and Dundee." "Do you ever pray?" said I to him on another occasion. "Yes; I say grace before meat," said he seriously. Scotland, with all her boasted knowledge, contains as ignorant persons as any part of England that I have ever seen. On another occasion, a fine looking young woman came to converse with me, desiring to become a member. In order to convict her of sin, I asked her if she had kept the commandments? "No, sir," she replied, "I have not time!" "You have not time to keep the commandments," said I, "what do you mean?" "I have not time," she answered, "because we work such long hours just now." She was working at a mill where they work about $13\frac{1}{2}$ hours a day. She was an orphan.

March 10*th.*—My only brother, Edward, was married to Hannah Beanland, Bradford, Yorkshire.

In the January number of the "Christian Miscellany," a correspondent, signing himself "Aliquis," attacked our system of all Christians being united, and as no one replied to him, I deemed a reply necessary, and sent the two following letters to the editor.

LETTERS TO THE EDITOR OF THE "CHRISTIAN MISCELLANY" IN REPLY TO "ALIQUIS."

Mr. Editor,—

Having waited two months, hoping that some of your correspondents would make observations upon the communications of "Aliquis," inserted in your first number for the present year, and finding nothing in your pages of this kind, I feel disposed, for the sake of promoting the great cause of Unity, to offer a few remarks upon that communication.

"Aliquis" asserts that "Your system is either too contracted, or too extensive." "It is too contracted," he says, "if you wish all who assume the Christian name to be united in one body." This assertion would be true if the supposition contained in it were not untrue; but that it is untrue, might have been apparent to "Aliquis" himself, as it appears that he "has seen the few doctrines which you deem essential." These doctrines evince that the United Christian Church *does not* "wish all who assume the Christian name to be united in one body." For example, Unitarians or Socinians call themselves Christians, but they do not believe in the "divinity and personality of the Lord Jesus Christ, and the Holy Spirit, and the Redemption of man by the obedience and death of Jesus Christ," &c., &c. But doctrines apart, "Aliquis" should know, that our churches believe that many "assume the Christian name," whose practice is so anti-christian, that our churches are as unwilling to admit them into their fellowship, as they are hostile to the admission of Socinians. Hence, from both these facts, he might have known better than even to suppose that we "wish all who assume the Christian name to be united in one body."

But your correspondent himself does not think that our "system is too controlled." He shall speak for himself. "But, sir," says he, "I rather think, though I thus write, that your system is too extensive;" consequently, as he is willing that all he had said should go for nothing, I have no objection, but must candidly consider what he says in reference to the system which "is decidedly too extensive." "It is impossible," says he, "that people can walk together who are not agreed, and in the Christian Mission there appears two attempted agreements which, in my opinion, are incompatible with each other. The one is a matter of faith, the other is a matter of practice. The matter of faith relates to the extent of the atonement, or the salvability of all men. Those believing this are denominated Arminians, and those denying this are denominated Calvinists," &c. In reply his "Remarks on the unity of the Christian Mission" appear to have been made to this, I observe, that I do not object to the sentiment, "it is impossible that people can walk together who are not agreed;" but I do object to the use he makes of it,—viz., that Calvinists and Arminians cannot walk together in church fellowship, because they do not hold the same sentiments. This, I think, is his meaning; or perhaps he goes farther, and concludes that there can be no church fellowship unless all the members think alike in doctrinal, experimental, and practical subjects; and if he does not go this length, the sentence in question loses its force. For if persons may enjoy church fellowship who are not agreed on all theological subjects, then it follows that it is not necessary for them to be agreed in all matters in order to dwell together in brotherly communion; and that this is the fact of the case will appear, if we refer—

1st, To the Scriptures. That different opinions existed in the first churches is plain, for Paul says, " For one believeth that he may eat all things; another, who is weak, eateth herbs." And again, "One man esteemeth one day above another; another esteemeth every day alike," see Rom. xiv. 2—5. Now what did Paul do in these instances? Did he tell the members at Rome that they could not walk together in church fellowship, unless they were all agreed in reference to the things about which they differed? No such thing. He said what we say, "Him that is weak in the faith receive ye, but not to doubtful disputations." "Let not him that eateth, despise him that eateth not; and let not him who eateth not, judge him that eateth; for God hath received him," Rom. xiv. 1—4. We wish to do what Paul enjoins, viz., receive into our communion all that "God hath received." But God has received Arminians and Calvinists, and who are we? that we should say to any man, "We believe that God has received you into his favor, but that is not enough for us. He may indeed admit you to his communion with all your errors in doctrine, but that is no reason why we should admit you to ours." Does "Aliquis" wish us to pretend that we are holier or wiser than God; so that persons graciously admitted into his fellowship ought to be kept out of ours? If not, then let him allow that our practice is Scriptural, or else deny what I am sure he cannot prove—that no Calvinists enjoy communion with God.

I shall only adduce another passage at present to prove that the first Christians were not all of one opinion in reference to religious subjects, and that this did not prevent them from walking together in church fellowship, it is Phil. iii. 15, "Let us, therefore, as many as be perfect, be thus minded; and if in any thing ye be otherwise minded, God shall reveal even this unto you." From this it is plain, that there might have been some members in the Philippian church who were not agreed with Paul himself and his "perfect" brethren; but the apostle was far from saying, "As you and I are no longer agreed, we cannot walk together in the church."

2nd. The general practice of churches evinces, that they do not require agreement among themselves in every thing connected with Christian doctrine, for I suppose it will be granted that it is difficult to find a church consisting of twenty thinking and studious members, in which there exists a perfect unanimity of sentiment. But if differences of sentiment already exist among Christians of the strictest sects, and yet if they walk together, why may not similar differences exist among us, without destroying our harmony and brotherly love? Your correspondent seems to have a particular hostility against our churches receiving Calvinistic members, because he does "not know of a more God-dishonoring and sin-serving creed" than that held by Calvinists. Perhaps he may not, but if it would not swell your pages unduly, I could inform him of creeds which dishonor God in the person of his Son, and serve sin, much more than that which he impugns. There are certain doctrines which all orthodox churches make tests of membership, while they allow their members to receive or reject other doctrines, but this is an improper mode of procedure, if it is essential to church communion that all its members think alike; and if this is not essential, it is important to draw accurately the line of distinction between the doctrines which are fundamental, and are *therefore* made tests of membership, and those which are not fundamental, and are therefore made matters of forbearance. If we make those doctrines tests of membership which a man may either believe or not, and yet be a justified and regenerated man, calling God Father by the Holy Spirit, then we exclude from God's church his own children, and place ourselves in awful circumstances, and incur a fearful responsibility which few Christians, I apprehend, would wish to sustain. On the contrary, if we make only those doctrines essential which Christ has made essential—those doctrines which, if a man believes not, he cannot enjoy salvation and eternal life, even if he should err in some other important, but not essential matters of faith. If these observations are just, then we have only to ascertain whether a Calvinist believes all the doctrines which are essential to salvation, or he does not. It is commonly admitted by all orthodox Protestants that Calvinists in general do believe in all those doctrines which are fundamental to salvation. So the United Christian Church thinks, and therefore receives them, other things being equal, as brethren and "fellow citizens." I ask "Aliquis" if he really believes that there are no pious men among the Calvinists, as he calls them? For my part, I believe that there are hundreds and thousands, and I wish to be one with all who are one with Christ.

"Aliquis" has fallen into a very palpable mistake in asserting, that "in the system of the Christian Mission there appears two attempted agreements, the one a matter of faith, the other a matter of practice." By the "matter of faith," he means that which is in dispute between the "Calvinists and Arminians." But when or where did he ever find the "Christian Mission" attempting to make "Calvinists and Arminians" agree in matters of faith? For my part, I never heard or read of any such attempt. We rather endeavor to bring persons of such sentiments to make them matters of forbearance, than to set them to determine existing controversies by argumentative discussion. This has been tried for several centuries, and it has failed. We therefore say, let the Calvinist and Arminian, the Baptist and Pædo-baptist, maintain their peculiar sentiments, but let them live together in peace. "Aliquis" speaks as though he thought that the God and Father of our Lord Jesus Christ had given us the Bible with the same intention that persons sometimes have when they throw a bone to the dogs,—that they may fight about it. But rather think, that when we fight about the doctrines of the Bible, we contravene the design of God in giving us that invaluable boon. He gave it that men might believe it, understand it, obey it, avoid its curses, and secure its blessings. Oh! that men were wise. Oh! that they understood God's will concerning them.

I wish "Aliquis" would give his real name. I suspect that I know him, but I may be mistaken. If he is a Christian brother, I should rejoice to call him by that endearing appellation, and I would say to him, "Brother, let us not sit at the feet of Calvin and Arminus to learn their doctrines; they were but frail and fallible men like ourselves. Let us go to the feet of Immanuel. He was God—is God—and he ever shall be God. Let us hear him; let the church hear him; let the authority of Calvin and Arminus fall lower, and yet lower still, but let the authority of Jesus Christ be exalted and extolled, for he only is worthy of all power and dominion! Let the churches hear him and obey him. Then shall they prosper under his smile, conquer under his banner, and ultimately enter into his joy!"

Being afraid, Mr. Editor, lest I should trespass upon your patience, I will add no more at present; but I propose in your next to animadvert upon what "Aliquis" calls "your matter of practice in reference to baptism." In the meantime, I am, &c.,

J. BOWES.

Dundee, March 19, 1833.

LETTER II.

MR. EDITOR,—

In my last letter I promised "to animadvert upon what 'Aliquis' calls your matter of practice in reference to baptism." It was the object of my last letter to evince that Arminians and Calvinists might be admitted, on scriptural grounds, into any Christian church; that its unity need not be impaired by their admission; and that, therefore, "Aliquis" unjustly charges the "system of the United Christian Mission with being too extensive."

It shall be my aim, in this letter, to manifest that our "system" is not "too extensive," as regards the "matter of practice." In order to prove that it is "too extensive," your correspondent tells us *what* the "Baptist" believes, and he also tells us what *he* believes not, viz. "that faith and baptism are connected—that there is only one baptism, as there is but one Lord and one church." All this I believe, and have therefore, no controversy with him on these particulars. But he says, "that sprinkling the faces of infants is not baptism, but a mere invention of man." &c.

In looking at this assertion, and some others, I am constrained to observe, that rather to subserve the cause of the Arminians and the Baptists, than to prove that Christian union is untenable. And I must inform him, that he will not lead me into this sought sectarian controversy. I know that it is common for sectarians to employ too much of their time and talents, in order to bring over Christians to Sectarianism, while they evince little anxiety for the conversion of the wicked. For instance, it is very common with some "Baptists" to spend hours in reasoning with a Christian of other sentiments, in order to bring him over to their own; and this, too, while they have no doubt of his Christianity, while they do not spend one fourth part of their time, nor take one fourth part of the labor, to bring real and acknowledged sinners to Christ. Yet all this time they cry, " the truth! the truth! we must be zealous for the truth!" These people may be instructed by the following illustration: One of their neighbors is dying of a raging fever. Another is very well, with the exception of a small pustule on the skin of his face, which his sagacious and philanthropic neighbors think is much disfigured by this unsightly blotch. They have a remedy in their possession for both cases, but they pass by the man in the fever, and as they are commanded to love their neighbors as themselves, they interpret this injunction to mean, that they ought to convince the man with the pustule, that it makes him look very ill—that although he can eat, work, and sleep well, it is alarmingly dangerous, and that he ought to apply the remedy which they propose to him. "Why," says he, "gentlemen, if, as you say, I am dangerously ill, how do you account for my symptoms of health. I see no reason to converse any longer with you on this subject, as I do not believe, although you have spent four hours to convince me on this occasion, and as many hours together on former visits, that this pustule mars my beauty, or injures my health." Now, mark these philanthropic men, they are most anxious to cure *him*, but they never go near the dwelling of the man who is dying of fever, and, therefore, he dies because they do not tell him of the remedy with which they are acquainted. Now, although I firmly believe that there is more authority in Scripture for the baptism of the infant offspring of believers, than for leaving them unbaptized until they shall have grown up, yet for the sake of making a concession to "Aliquis," let it be granted, that in his estimation infant baptism is a pustule upon the visage. Let us also admit that he could set right a brother on that subject, by arguing the point with him again and again, and that he could ultimately make him a Baptist, what has he gained? The man most likely was a Christian before; he was a believer—a justified and regenerate man, walking in the narrow way to heaven, and therefore safe enough; but if he was no Christian before, mere immersion, I apprehend, would not make him one. Then, I ask "Aliquis," in either of these cases, how Christian benevolence appears, especially when we take into the account, that the time and talents devoted to the proselytising system, might have been employed in making known to sinners, who are dying of a worse disease than a raging fever, the true and only remedy which God has appointed for their recovery and salvation? And what can we think of the benevolence of those who are more zealous to make men Sectarians than Christians— to bring men into *their* church, than into the church and kingdom of Jesus Christ? For my part I will not throw away my time and talents in making men Sectarians. If I can be useful in turning sinners from darkness to light, and from the power of Satan to God, and of building up and uniting the church, I shall rejoice. But with the views I have of my duty, I cannot enter upon a controversy relative to immersion; and if I was disposed to do it at all, I would not bring down the pages of the "Herald of Union," and make *them* the vehicle of Sectarian sentiments. I hope this apology will be deemed sufficient for not here entering upon the Baptist controversy.

What I must now evince is, that Baptists and Pædo-baptists ought to be united in the same church, which "Aliquis" denies. I prove it thus. Take it for granted, 1. That a Baptist may be a real Christian; this, I suppose, your correspondent will not question. 2. That a Pædo-baptist may be a Christian; and this "Aliquis" cannot deny, even upon his own letter, for he says, that "a consciencious Baptist believes that believers only should, or ever can really be baptized;" consequently a man must be a believer before he is immersed. Hence he may believe, nay, must believe, before he attends to baptism; consequently he may be a Christian, and not be baptized at all, according to "Aliquis." Well, then, if both may be Christians, what are they to do? What advice will "Aliquis" give to Christ's family? Would he say to the unbaptized believer, go to your own company, but you cannot come with us unless we immerse you. "My own company," might the converted soul exclaim, "I hope the company of my Master's family are, and ever shall be mine. And are not you and your brethren, "Mr. Aliquis," children of my Father, and do you not belong to my company; and may we not love, and hold communion together as brethren?" Perhaps "Aliquis" will inform us what reply he would give in such a case? It appears, then, a man may be a Christian, or what is the same thing, according to "Aliquis," a believer, who is not baptized, i. e. is not immersed, and also he will grant that an immersed man may be a Christian, a true disciple of Christ, what are these two brethren to do? Christ tells them to "love one another." He says, "A new commandment I give unto you, that ye love one another; as I have loved you, that ye also love one another," John xiii. 34. How then did Christ love his disciples? It is only necessary for our argument to assert, that he held communion with them, observed the Lord's Supper with them, and acted towards them in all things as brethren belonging to the same church; but, says Christ,—"As I have loved you, that ye also love one another." Can any thing be more plain than this, that all Christ's disciples should hold communion together, as they have opportunity.

Nothing is more frequently, largely, and urgently insisted upon, in the New Testament, than brotherly love; but it is a doubtful matter, at least to the world, whether those can be said to love one another, as Christ loved his disciples, who cannot and will not, hold fellowship with each other. Nothing should be more visible and well known than our love. It should be seen, and distinctly recognised, wherever Christians dwell. Christ inculcated this immediately after the words already quoted, "By this shall ALL MEN (mark these words) know that ye are my disciples, if ye have love one to another," John xiii. 35. All men were to know the disciples of Christ, by what mark? by their Arminianism, or Baptism? No, but by this, says Christ, "if ye love one another." And if all men are to know who are Christ's disciples, by their love one to another, does it not follow that all men are to know that, when love is wanting, whatever other qualifications may be possessed, or whatever pretensions to discipleship may be made, by this shall all men know that they are not my disciples, because they do not love one another. "But it may be" says your correspondent, "You will ask, will none but immersed believers enter the kingdom of God? Search the Scriptures for an answer; and if God's book be silent, it becomes me to be so too." If this paragraph gives the real honest views of its writer, he is uncertain whether any but "immersed believers can enter the kingdom of God;" and he is so ill-acquainted with his bible, that it is a moot-case with him whether it has decided the matter. And does he really doubt whether the following Christians are in heaven, viz.:—Luther, Melancthon, Beza, Calvin, Junius, Zuinglius, Wishart, Knox, Latimer, Bradford, Philpot, Halliburton, M'Culloch, Owen, Baxter, Bates, Howe, Fletcher, Wesley, Whitfield, and a host of other worthies who were never immersed?— And is it doubtful, to the narrow soul of your correspondent, whether all the ministers and Christians now living unimmersed are not on the road to perdition? And does he doubt whether immersed Calvinists can go to heaven? If so, as the number of immersed Arminians is very inconsiderable, I doubt that millennial glory is far, far in the distance.

But I will bring one or two passages of Scripture to his recollection, which perhaps may help to settle his doubting mind, or enlarge and warm the views and feelings of his soul. Will he favor us with an account of the immersion of the penitent thief, to whom Christ said, "To-day shalt thou be with me in paradise?" Did not this thief unite with the other, in deriding Christ up to the time of the crucifixion? How then could he be immersed? And if immersion is essential to salvation, what hope can there be of the salvation of Abel, of Enoch, and indeed of the most, if not all, of the Old Testament saints? But we need not go to the Old Testament for proofs; Christ said, "He that believeth on the Son hath everlasting life: and he that believeth not the Son shall not see life; but the wrath of God abideth on him," John iii. 36. If then, salvation, yea, everlasting life, is frequently promised to faith, and if eternal punishment is threatened as the consequence of unbelief, is it not incredible that all those will go to perdition who have not been immersed, and although they may have faith, justification, and sanctification? The idea is too absurd for reception. But we need go to no other authority than "Aliquis" himself, in order to prove that a man may be saved without immersion; and if he would only study a part of his own creed, it would effectually overturn the part in question. He says, "A conscientious Baptist believes that believers only should, or ever can really be baptised." I suppose he will grant that believers are justified, enjoy the favor of God, and are made his children. Well, then, supposing a believer dies after believing, but before immersion, a circumstance by no means of rare occurrence, either a man may go to heaven without immersion, or we must entertain the horrid idea that the God of love will send one of his own children to hell, and that, too, notwithstanding his own promise of everlasting life.

Your correspondent wonders "how" the Baptist "can tolerate what he believes to be anti-scriptural." What a mercy that "Aliquis," and persons of his views, are destitute of legal power, as it seems that if he was on the throne, surrounded by a number of persons like himself, that the fires of Smithfield would be again kindled, our prisons filled with victims of intolerance, and foreign shores crowded with our Pædobaptist exiles! The word "tolerate" signifies " to allow so as not to hinder—to suffer;" but "Aliquis" would not have the Baptist to "tolerate" what he believes to be anti-scriptural: consequently had a Baptist of these sentiments power, he would not suffer Calvinism, Episcopacy, Presbytery, Methodism, or any other thing judged by him anti-scriptural. AWAKE, YE CHRISTIANS, who have so frequently offered your eulogiums upon our mild and tolerating laws, and, under the new light of the throne of "Aliquis," repent of your folly, and execrate your former foolish encomiums! SAGE PHILOSOPHERS, cease your vain musings, and learn, in the plentitude of new wisdom, no longer tell us that every man should have liberty to worship God according to the dictates of his own conscience, and inform posterity that the Baptists only should be tolerated. POETS OF GENIUS, polished by the adornings of art, bring down your imaginations, and let your souls no longer chant the acclaim of toleration. It is unworthy of your attention. Sing now of Baptist intolerance: here is a theme worthy of your highest powers, worthy of your noblest song. Believe "Aliquis," (all depends upon your faith in him,) and you will cease to praise God for your privileges, and no longer pray for their continuance.

I am willing to allow that some difficulties stand in the way of all CHRISTIANS being united; but they arise more from the ignorance and prejudices of men, than from the nature of the subject. "Aliquis" mistakes when he supposes it is essential to Christian Union that the Baptist should be silent on his peculiar sentiments. He may preach upon them, and write upon them, if he can find no better work, and that as often as he pleases. If he is a Minister, other Ministers will not hinder him from preaching these sentiments to his own people. It would seem to be necessary, however, in the present state of the Church, that if an Arminian or Baptist preacher should be called upon to preach occasionally for a congregation of other sentiments, that it should be understood that he would not preach his peculiarities at that time. And why should he? He may preach those truths by which a sinner may be saved, without adverting to the one or the other.

But I apprehend, from my own knowledge of Calvinistic, Arminian, Baptist and Pædobaptist preachers, that their sermons resemble each other much more than what is commonly supposed; and if printed without the names of the authors, Christians would be unable to assign the real origin of any given sermons.

The Christian Mission does not prohibit Ministers from teaching whatever they regard as divine truth, providing that they do not teach heterodox doctrines. But they are of opinion that the true way of being useful is to hold up frequently and faithfully to public view, those grand truths about which all orthodox Christians are agreed, while other less important matters should be treated according to their true importance in the Christian system. Your correspondent states, that "there are many other inconsistencies in the plan of Unity, as advocated by the Christian Mission." If he would have the goodness first to make himself *sure*, that what he regards as inconsistencies are really so, and not delightful, useful, and scriptural verities, I shall be happy to hear from him soon, hoping that he will point them out. In the meantime, I must inform him, that the divisions and contentions of Christians are *unnatural, unscriptural, irrational*, and without a parallel in heaven, or earth, or hell.

> "O shame to men! *devil* with *devil* damn'd
> *irm concord holds, men* only disagree
> Of creatures rational, though under hope
> Of heavenly grace; and, God proclaiming peace,
> Yet live in hatred, enmity, and strife,
> Among themselves!"
>
> *Par. Lost*, B. ii. 1. 496.

Praying that the time may soon come when Christians shall learn to "love the brotherhood," the whole "brotherhood," I remain, &c.

J. BOWES.

Dundee, April 30, 1833.

We not only opened the Table of the Lord to all Christians, but also our pulpits to all godly ministers. The following letter from Thomas Erskine, Esq., of Linlathen, demonstrates this:—

DEAR SIR,

I trust the Lord will bless you and your deacons for opening your pulpit to His servant, and that he may pour out a blessing on your people also, through the word that may be given him to speak to them. There is one change which I should like to have made, and that is, that he might have the morning and afternoon, instead of morning and evening, as he is desirous also to preach in the Ferry, which he could not well make out according to the present arrangement. If you are not at home when this note arrives, pray just have the goodness to put your answer into the post office. I however have such confidence that you will grant this, that I shall take steps for warning the Ferry. I remain, with many thanks, yours very truly,

T. ERSKINE.

LINLATHEN, JUNE 21st, 1833.

I most readily accept your kind offer to have bills printed and put up. The form of the bill might be thus, but you will judge:—"Sermon. The Rev. David Dow, late of Irongray, will preach in the Rev. Mr. Bowes' chapel, High Street of Dundee, on the morning and afternoon of Sabbath, the 23rd June, at the usual hours; and at half-past six o'clock in the evening of the same day, in the small chapel at Broughty Ferry."

I had some very profitable correspondence and conversations with this estimable gentleman. The following letter of mine, is in reference to one of our interviews.

MY DEAR SIR,

Having an opportunity of sending you a few lines, I think I ought to inform you, that I have found your visit yesterday exceedingly profitable, especially that part of your conversation which related to the dishonor done to our Lord Jesus Christ by the "idolatry of talent." I thought of this, and in the evening preached from Col. iii. 11, "Christ is all and in all." The congregation was large and deeply serious. I endeavored to show the dishonor put upon Christ, by the people, in all the institutions of his church,—making the ordinances of the Lord's Supper and Baptism more than Christ, and placing them above him; also putting the minister in Christ's place, and even above him,—going to hear the minister, rather than Christ; and as a proof that Christ was not "all," thinking and speaking more upon the good sermon, the fine sentences, the beautiful ideas, and the chaste action of the preacher, rather than of Christ. Whereas ministers are nothing, and "Christ is all." Ministers are only men by whom "ye have believed,"—poor servants of Jesus Christ. I was also led to show, that as the churches had put dishonor upon Jesus Christ by exalting other things above him, it was not to be wondered at, since He has declared, "They that honor me, I will honor; and they that despise me shall be lightly esteemed;"—that He should have left us to struggle in the forms of religion without its power,—to combat the world, and the flesh, and the devil ALL ALONE; whereas Paul could say, "I can DO ALL THINGS through Christ strengthening me." May the Lord pour out his Spirit (my dear sir, let us pray for this) upon the churches; then Christ will be exalted; there will be life in every member, and we shall think less of self, and more of God. That expression, being "FILLED with all the FULNESS OF GOD" is a form of prayer which we ought to use. Feeling, as I have often done, that there is a savor of godliness in the conversation of you and your brethren, (perhaps I may call them my brethren, for I wish to be one with all who are one with Christ) I shall be always happy to be favored with any of your visits, as well for my own profit as God's glory. As you propose going from home, I hope you will be made a blessing in godly conversation, to every one you shall converse with. But lest there should be deception in those who speak with voices, ought we not to take heed to the caution, "Believe not every spirit," &c. Praying that what is of the Lord may be established, and all else overthrown, I remain, dear sir, yours in the communion of the Gospel,

JOHN BOWES.

Dundee, Aug. 15th, 1833.

This letter appeared in the "Christian Advocate," Dec. 9th. It uses terms, such as "laymen," &c., which I have long abandoned as unscriptural. It and other letters and aid, prepared the way for the Association in 1835.

WHY AND HOW LAY DELEGATES SHOULD FORM A PART OF THE CONFERENCE.

Mr. Editor,—

I am happy to see that the members and lay office-bearers in the Methodist Society are beginning to be awake to the importance of introducing Lay Delegates into the Conference; but I have not yet seen any plan which promises to be efficient for bringing about this desirable event. I therefore propose—

I. To evince the importance of the measure.
II. To unfold a plan whereby it may be accomplished.

First, as to the importance of the measure. Had not one of your excellent correspondents for November 18th, referred to the scriptural nature of the proposal, I might have adduced scriptural precedents in its favor; but, as I do not wish to go over the same ground, I appeal,

1st. To the example of the primitive church. Cyprian, Bishop, or Pastor of Carthage, who flourished A.D. 250, tells us that "He did nothing without the knowledge and consent of his people. When any letters came from foreign churches, they were received and read before the whole church; and the whole church agreed upon common letters to be sent to other churches." And as to all matters relating to the policy of the church, they were managed "by the common advice and council of the clergy and laity."

These quotations show that, in managing ecclesiastical affairs, in a single church, the laity and clergy were united. But what we wish particularly to know, is this: Whether laymen were present at any of the ancient Synods and Councils? "At the great Synod of Antioch, that condemned Paulus Samosatenus, there were present Bishops, Presbyters, Deacons, and the churches of God;" that is, laymen that represented the people of their several churches. When there were some disputes in the Church of Carthage about the restitution of those lapsed members who had appostatized during the persecution, Cyprian writes from his exile that the "Lapsed should be patient until God had restored peace to the church, and then there should be convened a Synod of the Bishops, and of the laity who had stood firm during the persecution, to consult about and determine their affairs." To this opinion not only the church of Carthage, but also the whole church of Rome agreed; and, accordingly, at that great Council held at Carthage, A.D. 258, there were present, "87 Bishops, together with Presbyters, Deacons, and a great portion of the laity."

These quotations prove that the practice of the Primitive Church was very different from that of the Wesleyan Conference. Other quotations from the Fathers might be adduced, but they would crowd your pages too much. As the Primitive Church stands opposed to the present constitution of Conference, so,

2ndly, Nearly the whole of modern churches are decidedly opposed to its high claims. I need not refer to the Independents and Baptists; it is well known that, among them, the minister and the whole church manage all their affairs. But look at the Presbyterians; their Kirk Session is constituted almost like a Methodist Leader's Meeting, and consists chiefly of laymen; and their Synods, or General Assemblies, as well as their Presbyteries, are composed of about an equal number of ministers and Lay Delegates. I need not refer to the Methodist New Connexion, to the Primitive, or Wesleyan Protestant Methodists, as they have all separated from the Old Connexion in consequence of the power and tyranny of the Conference Preachers. Among the Episcopalians, laymen have frequently the power of putting ministers into parishes; and, as the English Parliament is composed of laymen, and as it can control the revenues and government of the Church, even the Episcopalian clergy must yield the palm of power to the Wesleyan Conference. In short, there neither is now, nor ever was, anything so monstrous in the religious world, if we except the Church of Rome, and the mighty power of his Holinesss at Rome, as the domination assumed by the Wesleyan Preachers. What, then, must be done, in order to reduce this overgrown power, which, like that of the Inquisition, has made thousands tremble? Some say, Stop the supplies. I say, not yet; it is too soon. That should be the last measure—the dernier resort; to be tried when all other means have failed. I have promised,

II. To UNFOLD A PLAN WHEREBY IT MAY BE ACCOMPLISHED.

1. Let a lecturer be employed to go through the length and breadth of the land, making known the power of the conference, the power of Superintendents, evincing the evil conseqences of this power. The Minutes of the Conference will prove the former; facts will testify to the latter.

2. Let Societies be formed, denominated as may be deemed proper. Their real object will be to promote Religious Liberty among the Wesleyan Methodists. Two plans have presented themselves before me for constituting these Societies. The first is this:—Let them be composed of Wesleyan Methodists only. This plan has some recommendations and some defects. As to the former, Wesleyan Methodists are those most interested in its accomplishment; and the Preachers would hardly refuse, at least, to hear them. But then, on the other hand, would not the Preachers exclude from their Connexion the first men who shall give their names to such a Society, no matter how numerous or respectable, and by this means crush it in its bud? Would they not raise the old cry, "These meetings are immethodistical?" The second plan has its advantages and defects. It is this. Let the Societies be formed of all those ministers of churches who are favorable to their design. In which case, many ministers of the Gospel, and members from the other ranks of Methodism, as well as from the Independents and Baptists, would join them. In either case, let measures be adopted for giving in your journal, to every member of the Wesleyan Society, an accurate view of the design of the associations, to report progress, adduce arguments, and forward the great cause. If this plan should be adopted, the Wesleyan ministers will hardly venture to cut off those members who may join the Associations; and, if they do, the Lecturer will report it "the kingdom through." By this means, the power of the Wesleyan laymen would be concentrated. Hitherto, they have murmured and complained, and seen the Connexion split up into discordant sects, and they have done nothing, chiefly because they were afraid to encounter, alone, the monster, priestly domination; but they would then be in a condition to speak fearlessly out. And, at the next Conference, Delegates might be sent from all parts of the Kingdom to the place of its meeting, in order to demand redress, after the same manner as the Anti-slavery Delegates assembled in London to express a nation's wish. If the Association shall include ministers of other names, the Preachers must either treat them respectfully, or forfeit their own character; and they would become witnesses for the people. They might also preach, as they would obtain chapels; and, if it should be thought prudent, call meetings to report progress. If this plan be adopted, it can do no harm, and it may introduce Lay Delegates into the conference, at farthest in two years. If it may be approved, let those most interested in its execution set about it immediately.

The Preachers are united, and therefore powerful. Let the people unite, and they will be still more powerful. I am aware that many other evils exist in the Wesleyan Methodist Connexion, besides the tyranny of the Conference; but it is well to aim at the root. Let Conference be set right, and then we shall hear less of the misrule of Superintendents; the Toryism of leading ministers; the exclusion of laymen from commanding committees; the unchristian and persecuting proceedings of the ministers of Christ, "THE PRINCE OF PEACE;" and "the pious frauds" of "Model Deeds."

While I am writing, I cannot pass over the persecution, begun by the Conference, and carried on by the Book-Committee, against you, and your journal. It does appear to me that, if the men who originated and sustain it had power, to say the least, they would suppress your paper, and seal up your press. They feel that they must either put you down, or you will lift up the Methodist laymen to an equality with them. If these allow you to fall, spectators may lament their infatuation and cowardice, but cannot pity that future vassalage which must attend the continued reign of men who triumph over their fallen liberties, and cease to love any of those who have Christianity and religious patriotism enough boldly to assert them.

I am a constant reader of your paper, along with a few more subscribers; but hereby order a copy for myself. I do this not only because of the persecution under which you are suffering, but because I regard it as the most spirited, the most independent, the most talented, the most interesting, and the most useful, of any paper that I know.

A MINISTER IN NORTH BRITAIN.

Dec. 3d, 1833.

P.S. I must express the satisfaction I feel in the interest you manifest in the

Temperance cause. Your column, which I may call your Temperance column, is a very important and useful one, and may furnish the advocates of Temperance with striking facts for public meetings.

During this year, J. R. Anderson, from North Shields, came to labor at Forfar and Kirriemuir, under our auspices, but he did not succeed.

Jan. 29th, 1834.—In writing to my brother, Philip Bellwood, I say: "I go frequently one or two nights a week to the country about seven or twelve miles. The people are thirsting for the gospel in many parishes. They seldom hear it in the Established Church. Dundee contains about 50,000 inhabitants, and Lochee about 9,000."

Feb. 13th.—A letter from my very dear Father contains the following: "The Lord hath been my helper. I have often felt myself overwhelmed with trials; but when I look back at my Lord and Master, when he was falsely persecuted, spit on, buffetted, crowned with thorns, crucified, his hands pierced with nails, blood and water streaming from his side, the effect of a poor mortal's spear, how shall I mention my trials or give them a name, when the Lord expressly tells me 'all things work together for good?' What I know not now, I shall know hereafter." He then mentions the birth of my only brother's first child, and goes on to say: "I consider the gratitude which is due from me to Jesus for his goodness and mercy towards you all. I always feel my mind to be at rest on your account, because the Lord has promised never to leave them that put their trust in him. I always bear you on my mind in prayer. I trust you do the same as to me. One thought can reach the knowledge of the Lord as well as many words, for he knows the secrets of all hearts." This explains what blessing we had in a a father's prayers, and what comfort he had in our being the children of God, and therefore the objects of our heavenly Father's tenderest care. Whatever trouble we had given him in our sins, it all ended, and we gave him no more when we were born from above. Not another hour of sorrow had our earthly parent with us after that. He knew his children were cared for by God, and in his hands he quietly left us.

Mar. 24th.—I addressed the Annual Meeting of the Wesleyan Sabbath School, and gave reasons why the teachers should

"Try every art, reprove each dull delay,
Allure to brighter worlds, and lead the way,"

because "That charity is the best whose consequences are most extensive. Out of one such school had arisen ten ministers of the gospel. Converted teachers only should be employed, then we may expect them to be deeply concerned for the conversion of their pupils.

David Boon had drawn together a number of hearers at Methill, in Fife, and I went over and preached there, but the results I never learned.

This letter will show how far we had got towards New Testament unity and forbearance. It is from our Annual Assembly, but drawn up by me.

TO THE WESLEYAN PROTESTANT METHODISTS, LEEDS.

EDINBURGH, June 26th, 1834.

DEAR BRETHREN,—

A letter from you, dated Jan. 12th, 1833, was laid before the Annual Meeting of that year, and it directed the President and Secretary to reply to you.

The Annual Meeting, held in Edinburgh, June 25th, of this year, enquired whether this had been done; when its members found to their sorrow, that in consequence of the President having been in England a great part of the year, the letter had not *yet* been answered. Having stated the facts of this case, which we exceedingly regret, we hope that you will accept of this apology, and we shall endeavor to provide against the recurrence of such an omission in future.

The letter to which we refer is signed "M. Johnson, President; Joseph Blythman, Secretary," and is addressed to Mr. Bowes, who had given you a brief outline of our religious principles. We are glad that you "maturely considered" them "with much prayer," but regret that you cannot yet see the possibility of Calvinists and Arminians keeping "the unity of the Spirit in the bond of peace." You ask, "Would not the preaching of the doctrines of Arminus and Calvin in the same chapel be productive of many evils?" To this we offer the following solution, as it is a difficulty which will naturally occur to any one not perfectly informed in reference to the practice of our churches. The union which we have adopted does not necessarily imply that both the sentiments of the Calvinist and Arminian will be promulgated from the same pulpit. For example: that church which is imbued with Arminian sentiments is not compelled to accept of a Calvinistic pastor: it has its choice; and if it elect an Arminian pastor, he is not compelled to admit a Calvinist to his pulpit, although of the union. Were he to do so without the Calvinists being understood to preach doctrines upon which they were mutually agreed, evil consequences might follow. In farther illustration of this difficulty, be it observed, that if your societies, or your whole connexion, should resolve to act upon our principles of receiving all acknowledged Christians—all that God has received—into their fellowship, and to be called by no name for which they could not point to chapter and verse, they would be expected to send representatives, if possible, to such meetings as might be fixed upon for propagating the gospel and extending the cause;—and should a Calvinist apply to them for membership, of whose piety they were satisfied, with the understanding that he should "*hold the truth* IN LOVE," they would be expected to recognise him as an "heir of the same inheritance," but they could use their own discretion as to the admission of Calvinistic ministers into their pulpits. Class-meetings, fellowship meetings, lovefeasts, &c., &c., could be continued; only if any man desirous of joining the church should feel conscientious scruples against class-meetings, so that he could not attend them, which is the case with many godly people in Scotland, he would not be compelled to attend the class in order to his being a member.

We may briefly narrate our principles. We have no *Creed* but the Scriptures; no *Name* but Christian, and some of us would almost suffer martyrdom rather than perpetuate sectarianism by being called by any party name whatever. We maintain that no doctrines should be made tests of membership, but such *as must be believed* in order to justification, sanctification, and glorification,—that we have no scriptural warrant to exclude from his Father's table an acknowledged child of God, because he is a Methodist, or Calvinist, a Baptist, or Pædo-baptist. We maintain that all real Christians are already united in faith and practice, especially in all matters essential to life and godliness, and that it is a sin therefore to exhibit Christianity to the view of the world as a forbidding thing, merely for the sake of what is confessed on all hands to be of minor importance. We only expect the conversion of the world to be realised through the intervention of the efforts of an united church. How the Lord will bring his people into one *visible* family and fold, it would be presumption to assert. Perhaps all great bodies, such as synods and conferences, will be broken up into parts, and afterwards these parts will become one (the present aspect of Wesleyan Methodism seems to favor this idea); or perhaps they will continue to become more and more under the influence of New Testament principles and brotherly love, until, as bodies, they renounce every remaining vestige of intolerance, bigotry, contention, and sectarianism. In the meantime, *let us pray* after Christ, (see John xvii. 21—24) that his followers may be one. Let us be deeply serious in our prayers, as well as believingly fervent. Let us pray for it, in the closet, the family, the prayer meeting, and the pulpit. Let us promote *brotherly love* to the utmost extent of our ability, and *hold communion* with all the children of God to the utmost extent of our opportunities.

As you express a willingness to maintain a "friendly and Christian correspondence," and "an interchange of preachers on special occasions," to this we agree cordially, and if we can assist you at any point, shall be glad to do it. We hope our beloved brother Cruikshank will be made a great blessing to your societies and to the world. We received your magazine safe, although we shall not be able to promote its sale among our congregations, in consequence of its having a sectarian title, but if any plan could be adopted to suit it to our members and hearers, we would gladly promote its sale.

We have the prospect of adding some ministers and churches to the union this year. A second church has been formed in Dundee, under the pastoral care of the Rev. Wm. Menmuir, which meets in the Trades' Hall. Could you conveniently send a deputation to our next meeting, to be held in Dundee in the month of April next, we should be happy to receive that deputation, whether consisting of one or more. We sympathise with you in your sufferings from the tyranny of Conference, but we hope that God has overruled them for your good and his glory. He does wonderfully, and we do not yet understand all his ways.

If anything could be done to arouse Christians generally to promote union; if societies could be formed, or a lecturer or two sent out from city to city, and from town to town, we would gladly bear a part of the burden. We are, dearly beloved Christian brethren, in the name of the Annual Meeting of the United Christian Church, yours with Christian love,

JOHN BOWES, President.
————— —————, Secretary.

SPEECH AT THE VOLUNTARY CHURCH MEETING.

This speech was delivered, as the first, at a very large meeting of the Dundee Voluntary Church Association, held in the United Secession Church, School Wynd, July 30th, 1834, Mr. James Wilson, manufacturer, in the chair. The other ministers who spoke were, Messrs Young, Perth; Stirling, Kirriemuir; Peter Davidson, Arbroath; Adam Blair, Tayport; Marshall, Cupar Angus; Lamb, Errol; Cross, Dundee; also William Menmuir, James Small, and Andrew Adam.

"The Rev. John Bowes, of Dundee, proposed the first resolution.—'That Civil Establishments of religion derive no support, either from the Scriptures of the Old or New Testament.' The motion which I have just read comprehends a great deal. It asserts 'that civil establishments derive no support from the Scriptures;' and if I and the seconder of this motion can prove what is here asserted, we shall leave very little for succeeding speakers to do; for if we can prove that establishments are nowhere sanctioned in the Old or New Testament, I know not where else their advocates can look for proof of their divine origin.

"Before I enter upon the proof of what is contained in this motion, I would offer a few preliminary observations, as to the spirit and temper in which this controversy should be carried on. As it is a controversy between professedly religious men, it should be carried on in the *first place* in a spirit of piety; and if this is attended to, the religious interests of both parties may be promoted,—if it is neglected, they will be deteriorated. And it should be conducted in the *second place* in a spirit of charity, and mutual good will; common humanity teaches this, and if we neglect it, the beasts of the field will reprove us. For—

"Beasts of each kind their fellows spare,
"Bear lives in amity with bear."

Then as we are all the subjects of affliction, and destined to yield to a common mortality, does it become us, who shall so soon be in the tomb, to manifest bitterness and hatred towards each other? But we might urge the necessity of charity and mutual forbearance on still higher grounds. We all profess to be followers of Jesus Christ, the Prince of Peace, the God of love, and we ought therefore to love one another, even as he has loved us, and for his sake. Yes, if we differ in our opinions, let us agree in our affections. If we cannot think alike, let us love alike. Nay, if possible, let us be even more kind and attentive now to the advocates of establishments than we ever were before, that, if there shall be divisions, all men may see that they do not originate with us.

"But to come at once to the motion, I know that it is common for the friends of civil establishments to aver, that they are founded in the Old Testament, and that the Jewish Church was an example. This I deny, and shall endeavor to prove that there never was, in any age or country, from the beginning of the world until this hour, a civil establishment of religion instituted by God. Those that would make this subject intelligible must define it.—What is a civil establishment of religion? I have never met with an answer to this question that gave me entire satisfaction, and, perhaps, the definition which I am about to offer, may not satisfy every one: I have endeavored to make it as laconic as possible, that it may be remembered: 'A civil establishment of religion is the legal provision made by the state or government of a country for the support of religion.' Now, if we glance at a few of those passages which are commonly adduced in favor of civil establishments, we shall be able to determine whether they were contrived by God or man. We begin with the Old Testament. In order to show their scriptural nature, the advocates of tithes and establishments go back to the time of Melchisedec, and refer to Gen. xiv. 20, in which it is stated that Abram 'gave him (Melchisedec) tithes of all,' evidently referring to 'all' the spoils which he had recently taken in war. Of these it is granted that Abram gave tithes to the king of Salem, but then it was a voluntary offering on Abram's part to him, because he was a benevolent king, who 'brought forth bread and wine,' 'blessed Abram,' and was 'the priest of the most high God.' The offering of Abram was an offering of gratitude to God and to his priest. We read of no law to enforce it. We read of no establishment at all. It does not even appear that Abram lived in the king of Salem's dominions. Yet, the friends of civil establishments think because Abram paid tithes voluntarily, we ought to be forced to pay them whether we will or not. We have no objection that they should give a tithe of their property to their ministers; nay, we shall not find fault with them if they give one half, and pay their minister as large a stipend as is received by his Lordship of Durham, if they pay him themselves without compelling us; and I ask any man of candor or justice if it is not right and just that every church should pay its own minister?

"After the case of Abram, they allege the Mosaic economy; and assert that the Jewish Church was Established, and that tithes were paid to its Priests, in consequence of which they claim tithes or tiends. Observe, sir, the Jewish Church *was not* a civil establishment at all. It was founded and regulated by no earthly power. Its institutions and laws, were all given by God himself to the children of Israel: and the Jews, strictly speaking, lived under a theocracy,—God was their king. In fact, the whole Mosaic institute was typical; the offices of the prophet, the priest, and the king, were all sacred, and typical of the prophetical, sacerdotal, and regal offices of Jesus Christ.

"The institution of the tithes did not take place until the children of Israel took possession of the fruitful land of Canaan. Then God committed the priesthood to Aaron and to his sons for ever, and appointed the Levites to assist them in the service of the tabernacle, and that was to be their entire employment, hence they had no portion in the land of Canaan. 'And the Levite that is within thy gates, thou shalt not forsake him; for he hath no part nor inheritance with thee. At the end of three years thou shalt bring forth all the tithe of thine increase the same year, and shalt lay it up within thy gates. And the Levite, (because he hath no part nor inheritance with thee,) and the stranger, and the fatherless, and the widow, which are within thy gates, shall come, and shall eat, and be satisfied; that the Lord thy God may bless thee in all the work of thine hand which thou doest.' Deut. xiv. 27, 28, 29.

"Now let it be carefully observed, that when the land of Canaan was divided, the eleven tribes were all provided for, but the Levitical tribe had no portion in the land—their portion was given away to their brethren; then, as they were appointed to serve at the altar, *for the other tribes*, it cannot be thought that they got too much when they got a tenth, as they had already given up a twelfth of the land, which their brethren had divided among them, and, consequently, when they received the tithe, it was their own, which they received in kind, because they had not time to cultivate the land. Let us apply this. Have our established ministers given up all their personal property to the nation? If so, we acknowledge that their case is so far similar to that of the Levites, but if they have absolutely given up nothing, how come they to put their claim to the tithe upon an equality with that of the Levites, who gave up all?

"Now we assert, that the institution of the Aaronic priesthood, and the service of the altar, which was confined to the Levites, and in short the whole ceremonial institutions of Moses, are abolished. The ministers of the establishment say, Yes; with the exception of tithes. But why except tithes? Can they shew that any other land besides Canaan was ever tithed by God, or that any other persons were to receive it besides the sons of Aaron and the Levites? If I meet a minister of the establishment, I say to him, Sir, are you a son of Aaron? He replies, No. Are you a Levite? No. Do you reside in Judea, and do you serve the tabernacle? No. Then you have no more right to tithes of any kind than you have to another man's property. But granting, what we deny, that tithes ought still to be collected, how comes it to pass, that the stranger, the fatherless, and the widow, do not get their share?

"From the law of Moses our opponents come to prophetic vision, to Jewish prophets looking forward, and telling of gospel times and gospel benedictions; and they adduce Isaiah xlix. 22, 23, in favor of their cause. 'Thus saith the Lord God, Behold I will lift up mine hand to the Gentiles, and set up my standard to the people: and they shall bring thy sons in their arms, and thy daughters shall be carried on their shoulders. And kings shall be thy nursing-fathers, and their queens thy nursing-mothers.' On this passage they rear a mighty fabric. They say, It is the duty of a man to be religious, and to promote religion: when he becomes a father, he should promote it in his family; when a magistrate, among the community over whom he presides; and when a king, in his kingdom. Now this is good, and to the whole of it we agree: but they go farther, and say, that kings and queens are to nurse the church by endowing it. Ah! these endowments, they can find them, so clear-sighted are they,—such lynx eyes have they, that they can find them, where a simple hearted reader can see no such things.

"Let us read this again, and see if we can find any thing about tithes, tiends, stipends, or endowments in it. [Here Mr. Bowes read the passage a second time.] The idea is a domestic one, the father and mother endeavor, by nursing their infant offspring, to promote their growth, health, and comfort. Nursing signifies to encourage, to deal tenderly with. Now kings and queens may do this without civil establishments. Let us suppose our King and Queen to be members of some Independent or Secession Church, could they not nurse it by being kind to its young members, by contributing to its funds, and to the funds of other churches and missions, out of their own private resources? And is not that far more like nursing, than making one part of their subjects support both their own ministers and churches and those of the state? What kind of nursing is that which makes the poor pay for the ministers of the rich? which lays up kind obedient children in city jails, and drives away the last of their property and cattle with an armed force, to be sold for the minister? Had my father and mother nursed me as some of the kings and queens of England have nursed Cameronians, Nonconformists, and other dissenters, I had never troubled civil establishments, either by my presence or arguments.

"Other passages of the Old Testament are sometimes mentioned as favorable to establishments, but we must pass on to the New Testament. I once heard a minister assert that establishments received countenance from the New Testament! A voice cried, Proof! proof! 'I will give proof,' said he, 'Jesus Christ paid tribute to Cæsar.' I need not say how this was received by the meeting. But if Jesus Christ's paying tribute to Cæsar proves that he favors establishments, then by the same process of argumentation I can prove that all the ministers now around me, and all this meeting, are favorable to establishments. The word tribute signifies a tax. You all pay taxes, either directly or indirectly: *Ergo*, you are all favorable to establishments.

"When we wish to prove the scriptural nature of any institution, we have recourse either to scriptural commands or precedents.

"1st, As to commands; Is the established system commanded, or the voluntary one? I have read the Scriptures and no where can I find any thing like a command for the established system. I have read that the kingdom of Jesus Christ is not of this world, by which I understand that as to its origin, constitution, and office-bearers; it is not a worldly kingdom. When Christ first sent out his twelve disciples, he gave them this commission, 'As ye go, preach, saying, The kingdom of heaven is at hand. Heal the sick, cleanse the lepers, raise the dead cast out devils: freely ye have received, freely give.' Matt. x. 7, 8. By which cannot be meant that they were not to give at all until their hearers, and those who never would hear them, were compelled by law to give them an ample maintenance In Luke x. 7, 8, Christ said to his disciples. 'And in the same house remain, (the house which had first received them), eating and drinking such things as they give: for the laborer is worthy of his hire. Go not from house to house. And into whatsoever city ye enter, and they receive you, eat such things as are set before you.'

"You will observe, that it is not said that the loiterer, but the laborer, is worthy of his hire, and that it is said eating and drinking such things *as they give*, meaning such things as they voluntarily offer, not such things as ye take by force.

"Let us look at 1. Cor. ix. 7, 'Who goeth a warfare any time at his own charges? who planteth a vineyard, and eateth not of the fruit thereof? or who feedeth a flock, and eateth not of the milk of the flock?' If the ministers of the establishment would only eat the fruit of their own vineyard, and drink of their own flock, we should find no fault with them; but when they come to compel fruit from our vineyard, which they never planted, but which we plant; and when they come to eat milk of our flocks, which they never feed, but which we feed; we complain of the unscriptural and oppressive nature of their exactions.— There are several other verses in this chapter, which illustrate and establish the principle of voluntary support, but I have not time to mention more than verse 11th, 'If we have sown unto you spiritual things, is it a great thing if we shall reap your carnal things.' Here the apostle supposes two things, First, That he and his brethren had sown unto the Corinthians 'spiritual things.' Secondly, that it was not 'a great thing' if he and his brethren should reap their 'carnal things.'

"Now this is the arrangement for which we contend, and which we wish to see everywhere established, but to this the ministers of the law-church are opposed. They do not minister to us in 'spiritual things,' yet so attached are these spiritual men to our 'carnal things,' that although we never hear their sermons, they will have our 'carnal things,' however unworthy we may be. Our 'carnal things' (to which according to this book they have no right) are too valuable to be lost.

"In the New Testament you will find no commands for the propagation of religion in any other way, than that adopted by Voluntary Churches.

"Come, 2ndly, to scriptural precedents, the advocates of civil establishments will not say that the first churches were established. They will not say that kings and senators, in the days of Christ and his apostles, endowed the churches of Jerusalem, Antioch, Corinth, Ephesus, Philippi, and Rome. We on the contrary appeal triumphantly, and beyond the remotest fear of contradiction to scriptural precedents. All the churches established by Christ and his Apostles were voluntary. The first at Jerusalem was of this kind, and every other that succeeded it, during the first three centuries, whether in Asia, Africa or Europe.— On this rock then I take my stand, the churches founded by inspired men were voluntary: on this summit I look around me, asking any one that would lift the voice of opposition against the voluntary system, 'Where else away from our churches will you find a scripturally constituted church? Were the first churches connected with the State?' He is dumb; an answer he cannot give. Now, I do feel that we have the vantage ground here, the advocates of established churches also feel this; among all their speeches when was it heard, among all their pages when was it read, when was it seen that they denied the scriptural nature of our churches, or asserted that the first Christian churches were established? No, among all their strong and sweeping assertions, not one of them has gone to assert, that the Church of Christ at first was established by the state.

"My motion denies that established churches are founded on scripture. But you never heard a motion, in a Church of Scotland meeting, (and I dare venture to say you never will), asserting that voluntary churches are unscriptural, having no foundation in the word of God.

"I have dwelt the longer on this point, for I think it has never yet been set in a point of view sufficiently plain. Here then the whole matter might end; for, it is reasonable to suppose that when Jesus Christ and his Apostles founded the first churches, they founded them on the very best plan, but, as we have seen, and as our opponents allow, that they were all voluntary churches, therefore the churches of Christ should be voluntary still.

"Now, if they say that civil establishments are upon a better plan, do they not say that the advocates of these modern institutions display more wisdom than Christ and his Apostles? If they say civil establishments are inferior, because they depart from the original model, they yield the palm to voluntary churches, and proclaim that their churches are less scriptural than ours, or in other words, that ours are scriptural, but theirs unscriptural.

"In making a few concluding remarks, I would observe that if civil establishments have no place in Scripture, in all cases when men are compelled by law to pay for civil establishments, an act of flagrant robbery is committed upon their property. No human laws can make that morally right which in its own nature is morally wrong. Take an illustration from the slave trade. The word of God had said, ' He that stealeth a man, and selleth him, if he be found in his hand, shall surely be put to death.' Ex. xxi. 16. Our government at one time legalised the traffic in human bodies and souls. It was sanctioned by human laws: was it, therefore, morally right? and was it no longer stealing? The nation has answered these interrogations. If it was wrong for one man to steal another, it was wrong for a thousand; if for a thousand, it was wrong for a nation. The same remark applies to the taking of another man's property without his consent for the support of the church, it is robbery in the eye of the divine law. And if churches can enjoy the smile of God, and flourish by robbery, then may our established churches enjoy prosperity.*

"Again, I infer that it is right to take that part of the property which the church holds from the nation, and to apply it to national purposes. Should the present connexion between the church and the state cease, justice should be done to individuals, to churches, and to the nation.

"Church property may be divided into the following parts:

"1st, That which was given or bequeathed by individuals or families of the Roman Catholic Church before the reformation.—This belongs to them, and they ought to have it returned by its present occupants.

2nd, That which has been given or bequeathed to Protestant establishments by individuals or families since the reformation, this belongs

---

*"The Moderator and Clerk of the General Assembly of the United States, say, in behalf of the Assembly, 'The question is settled, thoroughly settled, by the experience of this country, that the Presbyterian Church flourishes more without any connexion with the state than when made a part and parcel of civil polity.'

to them ; and they have as much right to it as voluntary churches have to the chapels they have built and endowed.

3rd, There is a third kind of property intrusted to the keeping of the church by the country, and voted by acts of Parliament, this is national property, and should be returned into his majesty's exchequer. Now this is the kind of property which established ministers are so much afraid of losing, this is what is meant, when the cry is raised, 'the church is in danger.'

"A friend of mine got a ticket to attend the hole-and-corner meeting in the Thistle Hall; as he came down the stair, he was accosted by an old man who expressed great surprise at what he had heard. 'I did not know till now' said he, 'that the church was in danger,' and he seemed quite amazed at the discovery made at the meeting, 'Don't be alarmed, guid man,' said my friend, 'Don't be alarmed; the church is safe enough. She is in no danger. These young men's stipends are in danger, that is what they mean.'

"In fine, if civil establishments are contrary to the word of God, we need not wonder at their corruption, persecution, and illiberality. In proof of their corrupt character, I will only refer to one thing, viz: the temptations to indolence which they hold out to their ministers. Churches ought not to be sources of temptation to abandon duty, but of excitement to perform it. But when the minister knows that his pecuniary reward is sure, whether he is a laboring bee or an indolent drone,—when he knows that he is independent of the people of his charge, it frequently impairs his usefulness. One of my deacons is a weaver. We happened to be speaking about this all-absorbing controversy. I said to him, 'Do you think if the weaving trade was established by government so that you should receive the same amount of wages whether you wrought little or much, that you would work as hard and weave as much as you do now?' 'I do not know,' said he, but of one thing I am sure that we should not get up quite so soon in 'the morning.' Then, as to their illiberality I have not time to speak of it. I will say nothing of their Sectarian City Missions, Sabbath Schools, Tory predilections, and their known hostility to the civil liberties of the people,—of those things I will not say one word, but glance at their persecuting spirit. Establishments have done such deeds of blood, as are calculated to overwhelm the heart with pain and sorrow. What murdered the Son of God, and stained the Roman Empire with the blood of the most valiant and noble sons of the church? Establishments. What imprisoned and destroyed the unflinching adherents of orthodoxy during the Arian persecutions? Establishments. What confined the light of divine truth in mountains and glens during the dark ages? Establishments. What now excludes Christianity from Turkey, China, and other heathen and Mahomedan countries? Establishments. What excludes the light of the reformation from Spain, Portugal, and Italy? Establishments. What are contributing in our country to bring the Christian religion to reproach, and contempt as though it favored injustice, tyranny, and robbery? Establishments. Voluntary Churches could not persecute if they would; they could not imprison men's bodies, and confiscate their property.

"Having these views, I can as a Christian and as a minister state, that if this were the last hour of my life, and this the last speech that

I should be permitted to address to mortals, so conscious am I of the goodness of our cause, that I should retire from the world with a consciousness of having done my duty, and with this consciousness I now sit down."

I was never prosecuted before a court of law but once—this year—at the instance of Mr. Jabez Burns, then editor of the "Christian Miscellany," &c. He was liable to the printers for goods for which the churches should have paid him. They were to take old stock, &c., at a small price. He sent me some at full price. I, never expecting a prosecution, had not the good sense to send all back; so that the court decreed that I should pay the amount, and fall back on those upon whom I had a claim. However, I got the matter submitted to arbitration after the award of the court, and was quite satisfied with the result.

Mr. James Silk Buckingham's Committee, appointed by the House of Commons, sat on "Drunkenness," from the 9th of June to the 28th of July, 1834. It did good service to the cause of Temperance, and spread widely important views on this great question.

On 1st August, 1834, slavery was abolished in the West Indies, by the authority of the home government and parliament.

As I preached often to vast congregations in Hugh Hart's Church, Ship Row, Aberdeen, with much blessing, I ought to say why I was obliged to abstain from going. It will be seen that I held views on church purity widely different from many. He did not act on the principle of purity of communion, and therefore, although he professed the principle, I was obliged to withdraw. It was while going to one of these communions that the following incident transpired:—Dr. Ritchie, of Edinburgh, had lectured in Dundee, and Mr. ———, of Montrose, had been one of his hearers (he was an Established minister). He was so fiery and zealous against the lecturer on voluntary churchism, that I remarked, "If it were lawful to send off voluntaries out of the country, I was afraid he would send them off to foreign countries, as had been done when Nonconformists were transported to foreign parts, such as America." He remarked, "Yes, I would, and Dr. Ritchie should go with the first ship-load!" I was much astonished at the intolerance of this minister, and afterward did not marvel much to find him leading the "hissers" after one of Dr. Ritchie's lectures in Aberdeen.

Two preachers in Aberdeen attribute their conversion to my visits to Ship Row Chapel,—Gordon Lyall, and Mr. Stewart, who afterwards became a minister in the Free Church. It gives one great joy to be used in imparting the gospel to others who become preachers, and scatter the good seed afterwards in various parts of the world.

I have been reading in the "Revivalist" of a good work at Eccleshill, in Yorkshire. God was with me in the lecture. I have been too formal, unbelieving, and proud, both in private and public. May the Lord forgive me. Four of the members prayed with more energy than usual. I was blessed in catechising the young, from 7 to 8, before the public service. I think prayer meetings might be held more frequently. The Lord fill me with wisdom, that I may know how to promote a revival of his work.

In the month of August I visited ELIE, and preached on Unity, in the open-air, to a large company; also the night following at METHILL, and the night afterwards at LEVEN, to about a thousand people, near the New Relief Chapel. The congregation seemed much affected. Several desired me soon to come back again. I will the first opportunity. In returning by the *Rothsay* steamer, a man fell overboard into the open sea. The vessel was stopped as soon as possible, but not until she had got to a considerable distance from him. The small boat was lowered, and the vessel put back. Happily the man could swim; but we observed that he began to appear much exhausted. A rope was thrown, and he endeavored to catch it. We ordered them to stop the steamer, as the motion caused by the wheels was too strong for him. At last the small boat picked him up. When he got on board, after a convenient time had elapsed, I asked him if he was not almost spent?" He said he could not have kept up three minutes longer. I said, "Are you not thankful that after being so near eternity, the Lord has spared you?" He expressed great gratitude.

I had a kind invitation, September 1st, from Alex. Workman, Pitmidle to preach in that part of the country. I went several times, and preached to very attentive congregations, as did several other brethren.

Sep. 20th.—Two weeks ago, we commenced a Lord's Day school, which is doing well. The prayer meetings of the church are better attended than ever I saw them, and the brethren pray with great energy and life. May the Lord revive his work.

Oct. 9th.—To-day I waited upon the unfortunate man, A. Marshall, at present under sentence of death. He received me kindly. He again and again asserted his innocence of the crime laid to his charge. I said that the judge had pronounced such a sentence as seemed to him just from the evidence—that he was accordingly condemned, and that all that I had to concern myself with as a minister of Christ was the salvation of his soul. He acknowledged that he had been a great sinner, independently of the crime falsely laid to his charge. As to the divine commandments, he pleaded guilty of trespassing all. I then spoke of the goodness of God to him, and asked him if he did not feel sorry, and told him the plan of salvation. I then asked him if he believed in a heaven and hell, and that the only way of escape from hell was by the merits of Jesus. He assented with apparent hesitancy; on which Mr. Dow remarked that he did not seem to be free in his remarks. I explained to him the way of salvation through Christ; and he said that he had no hope of salvation but through faith in the sufferings of Jesus Christ. Mr. Dow stated that he had never heard him express so much before. He said that his life had been sworn away by false witnesses. I said, "I cannot enter into that; but I may just remark to you, that if you are really guilty, and deny it, you can never have pardon from God." This he acknowledged. I advised him solemnly never to deny his guilt if he was guilty, and if he did not choose to confess it, the best way would be to say nothing about it. He said, "I was in my younger days rather revengeful and unforgiving. I regret that I did not observe the sabbath day; and even after I was condemned, I felt as I should not have done against the witnesses; but now I forgive them all." I asked him before prayer, what I should pray for. He said, "For the Lord to give me patience and grace." He was condemned for murdering his wife, but not executed.

In December was cut down suddenly by fever, Stewart Peterkin, the son of an avowed infidel. What the father thought when he saw the conversion of his son, and that he became a preacher, I cannot tell; but ever after he spoke to me very kindly. The son preached well, but was soon taken away from the evil to come.

The following was received, in answer to ours, from the Wesleyan Protestant Methodists, Leeds. I give a part of this. The writer was the celebrated " Dundee Carter." He became a successful Temperance lecturer, and preacher, and was sent from the Dundee Church to Leeds.

LEEDS, Dec. 9th, 1834.

DEAR BROTHER,—

I have been requested to answer the letter of your Yearly Meeting, which was addressed to our Yearly Meeting, dated June 26th, 1834. I am sorry to say that it was mislaid, and has been just now forwarded to our Contingent Fund Committee, by our President. I assure you that we feel very sorry that anything like neglect towards your body should have taken place, as nothing but the distance between us could prevent a more friendly intercourse. Dear brother, there is much of your letter with which, as a body, we heartily agree and practice. We admit all evangelical preachers to occupy our pulpits. Since I have been in Leeds, our pulpits have been occupied by Independent, and Baptist, as well as preachers from other denominations. And I can assure you that our pulpits will be open to you, or any who are known to belong to your body. Our communion is open to all who profess to be Christians. Our lovefeasts, fellowship and public band meetings are open to all Christians; their testimonials of membership in their own society admit them to our ordinances. But I must inform you that our people could not be brought to abandon the name of Methodists on any account whatever; at least with their present views, and under their present circumstances. Nor is it possible for our preachers to leave the scene of their labors hardly for a day. However, while on this subject I may just say, that if circumstances be favorable, I do wish very much to visit Dundee in the course of next summer; for I assure you my heart yearns towards you, and I believe that I might be indulged in my wish sooner than any other of our preachers, and that for two reasons: first, because my place could be more easily supplied in Leeds than elsewhere, and second, because the people are more accustomed to be without me, as I am already so much called from home. . . . I have very little time, as I preach very often eight times a week, seldom less than six. I have the pastoral care of 1400 souls; I deliver lectures monthly on the art of study and the composition of sermons, and I have to assist at the leaders' meeting weekly, and the meeting of the circuit committee. . . . I beg an interest in your prayers, and the prayers of the church. Yours in the Lord,

WM. CRUIKSHANK.

" FAREWELL ADDRESS

found in the repositories of the late Professor James Kidd, D.D., minister of Gilcomston Church, who died 24th December, 1834.

"Aberdeen, 3rd Oct., 1833.—I feel myself fast advancing to the grave, and upon a back look of past life, I can say in truth, that God hath been very merciful to me, and I now leave my testimony to his providential care of me, from my infancy hitherto—he has given my heart's desire to me in my standing in society, and I bless and praise him for all, and am willing to lay down my Professorship and my ministry when he may please to call me to do so.

"I now bid adieu to the Universe, and to all things beneath the Sun. Farewell, ye Sun, Moon, and Stars, which have guided my wanderings in this valley of tears—to you I acknowledge much assistance in all my attainments!

"Farewell thou Atmosphere, with thy clouds, and thy rains, and thy dews—thy hail, and snow, and different breezes, which contribute so much to my life and comfort!

"Farewell, ye Earth and Sea, which have borne me from place to place, where Providence has ordered my lot; and with your productions have supported my bodily wants so often and so long!

"Ye Summers and Winters, adieu!

"Farewell my native Country, and every place where I have had my abode! Adieu, Aberdeen! May peace and prosperity for ever be in you—to all your inhabitants I bid farewell!

"Farewell Marischal College and University, in which I have had the honor of a Chair so long. May Learning and true Religion flourish in you till the latest posterity. Adieu, ye Members of the Senatus Academicus! May you enjoy many years of health, peace and prosperity!

"Farewell, all ye who ever Studied under my care! May you be useful, faithful, and successful Ministers of the Gospel.

"Farewell, Chapel of Ease! May peace be within thy walls. For my friends and brethren's sake, peace be in thee, I say.

"Adieu, ye Eldership—ye Heads of Families—ye Young! May the Lord in tender mercy bless all I have baptized, and all I have admitted to the Lord's table for the first time. I follow all with my most earnest prayers as long as I live.

Farewell, ye Little Children, in general all around whom I have so often met in kindness and saluted with my best wish for your good! May all good be your portion in this world and the next.

"My own Children—I commit you to God in life, and in death. May he fulfil to you the promise, Psalm xxvii. 10. With mixed distress I leave you under the care of Him that is able to keep you from falling, and present you faultless before the presence of his glory with exceeding joy. Farewell!

"I bid adieu to my Library, and to my Bible, which has been my companion from my earliest days. I leave the Volume, but I carry with me, as the ground work of my sure hope, the contents found in Psalm lxxiii. 23—28; John xiv. 3; Psalm cxxxviii. 7, 8; and Psalm xxii. These I take, before God, as my dying support and comfort.

"Farewell Time! Welcome Eternity!—Farewell Earth! Welcome Heaven!—Amen and Amen."

(Signed)   "JAMES KIDD."

CHAPTER VI.

MARK DEVLIN'S CASE—SENTENCED TO DEATH.—ROBERT NEWTON'S SERMON.—TESTIMONIALS.—REVIEW OF "CHRISTIAN UNION."—DR. DICK'S LETTER.—DEPUTATION TO ENGLAND—JOURNAL—UPROARIOUS MEETINGS—TENT PREACHING—PETITION TO PARLIAMENT.—LETTER.—EDINBURGH CONFERENCE.—MY LETTER ON THE MINUTES OF THE WESLEYAN METHODIST ASSOCIATION.

Feb. 22nd, 1835.—After preaching at PITMIDDLE, Mr. Gordon C. Lyall went to the parish church of Kinnaird to hear Mr. Spence, who ascended the pulpit with an air of uncommon lightness; after which he announced the psalm with the utmost apparent carelessness. This being over, he folded his arms and laid himself down upon the front of the pulpit, and there he lay for three quarters of an hour, pretending to pray, during this long period he used many vain repetitions, and several expressions as much at variance with sound sense as with sound theology. When the prayer was ended, he read the 40th chapter of Isaiah, and exhorted his audience to repent, remarking, "You cannot do much, in consequence of the depravity of your nature, but you must do as well as you can." When he came to the 12th verse he said, "*If there be such a great being* as 'hath measured the waters in the hollow of his hand,' it would be an easy matter for him to raise the dead at the last day." His reading of the chapter and the whole discourse was concluded in the course of twenty minutes. His whole proceedings were calculated to make the audience view him as an infidel, and religion as an imposition. I have heard similar reports of this minister before.

In a letter from my father, March 5th, addressed to his "son and daughter," he says: "Still, being persuaded that you are living to the Lord; and I hope you are doing all the good you can to your fellow creatures." After stating the comfort afforded him by the promises of God under deep trials, he adds, "But you may say, 'Is the promise for thee?' I answer, 'Yes; for I love the Lord Jesus Christ, and though worms destroy this body, yet in this flesh I shall see God for myself and not for another. I know

'My trials here,
Will only make me richer there,
When I arrive at home,'"

MARK DEVLIN'S CASE AND EXECUTION.

May, 22*nd*, Friday. I resolved if possible to obtain an interview with Mark Devlin, the Irishman now under sentence of death for rape committed upon a young girl in this town, about fourteen years of age.

I went to the iron gate and found Mr. Dow the jailor there, who after hearing my errand, stated that I could not obtain admission without the consent of the Chaplain. Mr. Macalister; I waited upon him at his own house, requested his consent, and stated that my object was to communicate religious instruction with the hope that the unfortunate young man might derive some spiritual advantage. But Mr. Macalister would not give his consent; he stated that he had only introduced Dr. Addie, &c., Mr. Jaffray, and that Mr. Roxburgh had seen him of his own accord. I stated that if the unfortunate man was willing to receive instruction, it was well that different ministers should be admitted, as he might derive advantage from some out of the many. He stated that he could not give his consent, as some fault had been found when Balfour was under sentence of death, because too many persons had been admitted; but said he, "I'll tell you to whom you may apply, the Priest can give you liberty, or the Provost." Having little hope of the Priest's admitting me, and regretting that one Protestant minister should refuse to admit another, I determined to consult one of the Bailies; I stated the case to him, and as the Provost was from home, he most frankly gave me a line to the jailor, who after looking at it, stated that it was quite satisfactory, and that I could see him to-morrow morning at eleven o'clock.

23rd, Saturday, eleven o'clock. On going to the Town Hall, I met Mr Dow, the jail keeper, who, with the turnkey, informed me that the Priest had been there yesterday, after I came out, and the prisoner had stated to him (the turnkey), in the presence of the Priest, not to allow any one to see him but the Priest and Mr. Jaffray, who was understood to be acting for the Chaplain. I had now given up all hope of seeing the prisoner.

25th, Monday. Walking by the Town Hall to-day I met with another of the Bailies; I stated the case to him; he said he understood that the prisoner had given orders to the jailor not to prevent any person from visiting him; "but," said the Bailie, "call here to-morrow forenoon, and we will endeavor to obtain admission.

26th. This morning saw the Bailie; visited the jail which was now readily opened. Before I went in I saw the turnkey, who stated "that Mark was now willing to see any one." Just as I was entering Mr. Jaffray came in; Mark was reclining on a bed on the floor; he sat up when we entered. Mr. Jaffray spoke to him a little and then gave place to me; I stated that I had come as a minister of the Gospel who wished well to his soul, "I am aware that you are a Catholic and that we are Protestants, but the question is not whether is the religion of the Catholics or that of the Protestants right, but what must I do to be saved?" He said, "I do not mean to change my religion, but to die in the Catholic faith, but I am very happy to see and hear any friend." "We look upon you as a fellow mortal—as a partaker of the same flesh and blood with ourselves—as destined to meet death as certainly as we are ourselves—as a sinner like us, and capable of being saved, and on these accounts we take a deep interest in your salvation." I then proved to him the fallen state of man, and remarked, "that when I say that you are a sinner, I do not refer to the crime on account of which you are here, but I mean apart from that, that you are a sinner, just as I have been a sinner, and as we have all sinned." He shook his head and appeared serious and devout, I then pointed him to Christ, and showed that he was able and willing to save to the very uttermost, that the greatest sinner on repenting and trusting in him would have all his sins blotted out, and that as he had but a short time to live, and as there was no hope for either a reprieve or a commutation of his sentence, he ought to be ready for his approaching doom, that he should greatly desire his salvation. "I should think," continued I, "that if you could obtain a reprieve, and especially could you obtain a pardon, that you would be greatly delighted," he said " No, I do not even desire to live;" he had no hope, and he rather desired to die for his sins. " Well " said I, "then you may suppose that many a man in your circumstances would greatly desire pardon, and an exemption from suffering, and if he would desire to be exempt from temporal death ; how much more should you desire exemption from eternal death, and the possession of eternal life." I then urged him to love Christ, in words to the following effect —"We love those that are kind to us ; and if you had been drowning in the Tay, and any one had thrown himself into the river after you, and risked his life to save yours, would you not love him? would you not cherish the most grateful recollection of his kindness? Oh! then, what love should you have to Jesus Christ who died to save you from sin and hell, and expired on the cross to save you? Only love him, and you may rest assured that he loves you, and that you are saved. Heaven, however, is a very holy place, and God is holy. Do you ever think what a solemn thing it will be to enter into his presence? And the exercises of heaven are holy, and if you are prepared to enjoy them it must be here. We cannot enjoy that for which we have no relish, no taste." About this part of the address he lifted up his voice to God in solemn prayer, and said, "O Lord change my heart and prepare me for death!" He put up a similar prayer to this while Mr. Jaffray was addressing him. I then remarked that none of us need fear death if we were ready for heaven ; for my own part, I should rejoice to go to heaven before Sabbath, if I knew that I was prepared for heaven ; no poor cottager fears going to a great estate, and if you get ready for heaven—if your sins be blotted out—if the love of God fill your heart —if you obtain peace through believing in Christ, and none of us have any merit of our own, and if you have good hope through grace, you need not fear death, 'For so an entrance shall be ministered unto you abundantly into the everlasting kingdom of our Lord and Saviour Jesus Christ.' When you die you will not find heaven closed against you, but an entrance will be ministered, served out to you by ministering angels 'abundantly,' the gates of heaven will be thrown wide, abundance of angels, and honors, and joys will await you ; but without holiness this felicity cannot be entered, without holiness fearful torments which never end await you ; and O! it is a solemn thought that God is here, and he will call us to an account in the last judgement, when we shall stand side by side with you, not only for this interview but for all the deeds done in the body."

Mr Jaffray gave him a useful address, and expressed a willingness to be locked up with him for a short time that he might not detain the jail-keeper, after my withdrawal. This he peremptorily refused, saying, "No one shall be locked up with me but my own priest: I do not wish to change my faith." Before we left him, Mr. Jaffray prayed. I obtained his Testament, the Douay Testament, and desired him to read the Scriptures, remarking, that many of his visitors might recommend religious books, but as his time was short, I would recommend him to read the Bible. A friend had put into my hands a sermon by Mr. Jonathan Watson, pastor of a Baptist Church in Cupar, preached on the execution of Henderson. This he said he had read; but I might leave it. I did so. May the Lord so bless his own Word, that the soul of this son of Adam may be free from the penalty of a broken law.

27th.—Yesterday I saw the jailor, who informed me that as this was the day on which the chaplain would visit the prisoners, he was afraid I should not be able to see Mark Devlin; but I might call about 12 o'clock. I did so, and was admitted. He said he slept soundly five or six hours every night, and was very well. I asked him if he had read the chapters I had pointed out to him. He said he had. I remarked, that I was anxious to fix his attention upon John iii. 14—16; for here he read that by faith in Christ any perishing sinner might be saved, and should not perish. He said Christ was his only hope, and he trusted in him alone. Then he gave me a book containing several passages of Scripture, and desired me to read a page. I did so, and remarked especially upon one text, Heb. xii. 9: "Furthermore, we had fathers according to our flesh who corrected us, and we gave them reverence, shall we not much rather be in subjection unto the Father of spirits, and live." I observed: "You see from this beautiful passage that we have two fathers, our father according to the flesh, and our Father according to the spirit. Two interests—the one relating to the body, the other to the spirit: the one relating to time, the other to eternity. Our fathers are chiefly concerned about the welfare of our bodies; our heavenly Father is chiefly concerned about our spirits. He may allow our worldly interests to languish, in order to promote those of our spirits. His aim is to purify and save them; and hence the soul is sometimes in the most prosperous circumstances, when the body is sick, or when it dies, and if you look up to him, and know that he is your Father, and that you are his child; then you will be able to rejoice with joy unspeakable. I hope, Mark, that you have been deeply sorry for your sin." "Yes I have, sir, and I bless God for putting it into my heart to be sorry for my sins. I see that I deserve to suffer for my sins, and I am quite resigned to die for them." "I am delighted to hear you say that you thank God for putting sorrow for sin into your heart; it shows that you regard any good in you as from the Lord, and you may depend upon it that you will never repent having indulged this sorrow, 'for godly sorrow worketh repentance to salvation, not to be repented of.' You will not repent of this sorrow, either in death or judgment. I hope, Mark, that you really forgive all your enemies, or any that may be supposed to have been connected with your present condition." "I forgive them from my heart," said he. "But I trust you feel that you have been guilty, that you have done many things wrong, and that you need forgiveness from God." He confessed that he had done many things wrong. "I hope that you are resigned to die, and that your confidence and hope grow stronger as you approach the eternal world." He said, "I do feel strong faith, and I hope that I love my Redeemer, and that he loves me; I feel stronger and stronger every day, and I bless God for bringing me into this place, and that I am going to suffer for my sins." I asked him if he desired me to pray with him; to which he assented. After prayer, he said feelingly: "An excellent prayer: I hope that God will bless to me all the prayers offered up for me, and all the endeavors made by every person for the salvation of my soul." I said, "I do not know whether

I can find time to visit you to-morrow or not, but if I can, do you desire to see me? He expressed his thankfulness for my visit, and desired me to call to-morrow. Before prayer, I exhorted him to lift up his heart to God for his blessing, while I was employed in prayer; after recommending him to pray for himself, and to believe in Christ, I came away. Mr. Matthew Fraser, U.P. Church, was going in as I came out. He read to him some of the first verses of the fifty-first Psalm, to show him the evil nature of sin. He listened with great attention, gave appropriate answers to the questions proposed, and when asked, whether he was satisfied of the justice of his sentence, he replied in the affirmative, observing, "Jesus Christ suffered for our sins; why should we not suffer for our own?"

He is about 26 years of age, a little man, quick, and more intelligent than might have been expected. He was a weaver to trade; his father and mother living, and he had one child. One man, who was taken up and sentenced to 7 year's transportation, was admitted to see him before he went off, and they said that they forgave every person that had injured them: they did not speak as though they had injured any. He was executed in the High Street, Dundee.

The remarks that follow were delivered to our congregation as

AN ADDRESS,

after the execution. Happily, our laws now are less sanguinary, and murder is the only crime for which capital punishment can be suffered.

"1. Such a death as this is very *unnatural* and *shocking*. When we die in the ordinary course of nature, we know not the hour; our sensibilities may be wasted by disease, even if our minds retain their wonted vigor; or our minds themselves may be rendered incapable of rational thought, and we may pass into eternity gradually without knowing it; but in this case, a man, in the bloom of life, has the day and hour of his death before him for several days, and although he expects to meet it, he has no hope of a reprieve—no hope of escape.

"2. It is *peculiarly affecting*. There is something affecting in death under any form, and in all the circumstances of its approach. But when we see the young depart by the power of disease, or accident, we are more impressed than by the death of those whose race has been long, and stained by many blots of sin. But to see a man in health, at 26, meet death in consequence of a crime for which he solemnly professes his sorrow,—to see him meet it, not with careless indifference, but with an anxious solicitude about his welfare in that eternity into which he is about to be plunged,—to see him clothed in black, with 'weepers' upon his dress, and a white cap upon his head, leading the solemn procession to the fatal drop,—to behold him look firmly and seriously at the congregated thousands who have been assembled to witness his last moments, and then fall upon his knees, with his spiritual guide, and with his hands spread out, or clasped to his heart, appear devotedly breathing out his soul to God,—to behold him ascend the fatal drop, while the hangman, veiled in black, fastens the killing rope leisurely round his neck, and draws the cap over his face,—to see him lift it up with his own hands, and look upon the surrounding spectators, and give them solemn warning, and then to behold the tears of sympathy glistening in thousands of eyes, while he takes his last look on the world he's leaving, draws over his eyes the cap, bids farewell to the world, gives the last signal by the falling napkin, falls into death's agonies, and plunges into eternity!—this is surely a very affecting death.

"3. It is *humiliating* and *instructive* as to the ruinous effects of sin. To gaze upon man, created in the image of, and designed to hold communion with, his God—upon a man with a capacity for knowing, loving, and enjoying God, and the society of the Redeemer and the redeemed,—to behold him departing out of life because the laws of his fellow-men have pronounced him unfit to live, unfit for the society of men, and only fit for a death, the terror of which may inspire others to dread his fate and avoid his example. Oh! sin, what hast thou done? but for thy blasting, deceiving, destroying influence, here is a man who might have lived long to guide his children into the paths of holiness—to bless society by his instructions and example, and to make honor and glory redound to his God. Look to this, and think where your sabbath dram-drinking may end. Look to this, ye 'gay dreamers of gay dreams,'—ye dupes of sensuality, and see where your sin may end!

"4. And how miserable are many of those that die a natural death! Their eyes are opened to behold the fearful gulph into which they are about to plunge. They see that their own sin and folly has closed against them the gates of paradise, and their misery is inexpressible. We have heard of many such cases."

June 26th.—In the Wesleyan Chapel, heard the justly celebrated Robert Newton. He is very popular in England, and draws vast congregations. Here, he had very few to hear him, and he seemed to feel it; for, even during his prayer, he opened his eyes several times and looked at the door; yet he gave (as he generally does) an excellent evangelical sermon, of which the subjoined outline can only give an imperfect idea. "Rom. xiv. 17: 'For the kingdom of God is not meat and drink; but righteousness, and peace, and joy in the Holy Spirit.' I. Point out some erroneous notions concerning the kingdom, or spiritual Christianity. (1.) It does not consist in external ordinances, however excellent, such as baptism and the Lord's supper. (2.) Not in opinions, however correct. (3.) Not in external observances, or morality in the popular sense. II. What it is in reality. (1.) Righteousness; of faith in justification; internal righteousness, or true holiness. Righteousness of actions; trees of righteousness, and fruits of righteousness. (2.) Peace: if at peace with God, the man is at peace with himself, and with mankind. (3.) Joy, produced by the Spirit—pure joy; it differs from worldly joy and carnal joy in its relations, in its honors, its wealth, and its health—it is everlasting. Remarks.—The text furnishes, 1st. The standard of true Christianity. 2. The acquisitions of a Christian. 3. The conviction of the text. Have you this kingdom? Have I? Have we those excellencies—marks of our having the kingdom of God?"

As I intended to travel and lecture on Union, the following testimonials were given.

DUNDEE, APRIL, 1835.

Having been on a visit to Scotland on behalf of our Irish Mission, I had the pleasure of hearing the Rev. J. Bowes lecture on Christian Union, and of seeing its good effects. I was privileged to preach in his Chapel and received support and kindness. I can corroborate Dr. Dick's statements, and I pray that Christian love and union may universally prevail.

JAMES ARGUE, Irish Missionary.

GLASGOW, 25th JULY, 1835.

These certify that the Reverend John Bowes of Dundee has been known to me for several years as a devoted, faithful, and efficient minister of the Gospel. As the result of his zealous and indefatigable labours in preaching and visiting the poor and neglected in the populous town of Dundee, a church has been collected, which under his pastoral superintendence, continues abundantly to prosper and increase. Many of the members of that church, and others now connected with kindred communities have reason to regard him as their spiritual father. His efforts for the honor of his Lord and the salvation of human kind are not limited to one place; in various parts of the country, as Providence opens a door, he proclaims the unsearchable riches of Divine Grace. His exertions in the open-air have been attended with happy results, especially in the place where he statedly labors. In consequence of his zealous ministrations in this department and his growing acceptability as a servant of Christ, the place has become too strait for his congregation; for years the necessity of larger accommodation has been felt. I doubt not the friends of the Redeemer in various parts of the country will aid the efforts he may make to procure for his people a more ample place of worship.

THOMAS PULLAR,
Pastor of the Congregational Church, Albion Street.

REVIEW OF MY "CHRISTIAN UNION."

"'*Christian Union:* Showing the importance of Unity among real Christians of all denominations; and the means by which it may be effected. By JOHN BOWES, Pastor of a Christian Church, Dundee. Pages, 310. London: Simpkin and Marshall.'

"This is really a good book, and ought to be in everybody's hand. The writer evidently possesses two of the rarest qualities imaginable in writers upon ecclesiastical polity,—viz. good sense and benevolent feeling. In prosecuting his task, the author traces the rise of the different sects into which the religious part of mankind is divided. In doing this, he shows that what is called *the church* has generally been at fault; and that priestly intolerance, and the union of the Church with the State, have produced nearly all the divisions which have taken place. He then shows the evil consequences of these divisions, and points out the nature of the union which ought to exist,—advances a number of arguments for the union of the Church, and shows by what means this unity may be obtained. These subjects have been treated with a degree of minuteness and to an extent which have rather surprised us. The writer is quite at home in his work, and appears perfectly master of his subject. [Here follow some extracts from the book.] Thus we are taught that nearly all the divisions in the Church of Christ have arisen from priestly intolerance. By the facts here laid before us, we see at once the truth and fulfilment of Holy Writ. '*My people* have been lost sheep; their SHEPHERDS have caused them to go astray; THEY have turned them away on the mountains: Many PASTORS have destroyed my vineyard; THEY have trodden my portion under foot; THEY have made my pleasant portion a desolate wilderness.' These are monitory lessons; but the evil still continues. Wherever power has been placed in the hands of the clergy, it has, with little exception been abused.

For one clerical body, *unlimited, unamenable power, has recently been claimed, and conceded* in our highest courts of law; and the body thus honored is using this power in desolating the heritage of God, with fearful rapidity, by means the most despotic and arbitrary. As a powerful means of checking such evils—of inducing professors of religion to attend more to the Holy Scriptures, and of teaching them to trust more in God and less in men—we hail the appearance of this valuable work. To all religious characters it will prove an acquisition: it will show them the importance, possibility, nature, and way to secure and maintain Christian unity in the Church of God; while the good sense and tone of deep piety which pervade the work will benefit the minds of those who read, and lead them to pray and to labor for the time when the envy of Ephraim also shall depart, and the adversaries of Judah shall be cut off; Ephraim shall not envy Judah, and Judah shall not vex Ephraim."—CHRISTIAN ADVOCATE.

Having been very intimate with the late Thomas Dick, L.L.D., I have often regretted that no Memoir has been written of him. I have pleasure in giving this letter.

BROUGHTY FERRY, 18th July, 1835.

DEAR SIR,—

I have perused, with much pleasure, your excellent work, lately published, on the subject of Christian Union;—and, without pledging myself for the accuracy of every sentence it contains, I have no hesitation in declaring, that it is excellently calculated to arouse the attention of Christians to a subject of immense importance, which has, hitherto, been almost overlooked, and to promote the peace and harmony of the visible church, and the efficiency of its efforts for promoting the best interests of mankind. The history you have given of the rise of the various sectaries into which the Church has unhappily been divided, will afford some new information, as well as instruction, to many of your readers; and the many excellent extracts you have given from the writings of the most eminent characters that have adorned the church both in ancient and modern times, will tend to show that all enlightened and right-hearted men have but one opinion on this subject, —whether they have been classed as Methodists, Independents, Baptists, Presbyterians, or Episcopalians,—and that they all lamented the divisions of the Christian Church, and ardently desired to behold an approach to that "unity which is the bond of perfection." The evils which have flowed from disunion are numerous and almost incalculable, and it is amazing with what apathy and indifference Christians have rested contented in their sectarian compartments, without arousing themselves to put an end to such evils, which strike almost at the foundation of religion, and to hold out to each other "the right hand of fellowship." The arguments for Unity which you have brought forward, supported as they are by Scripture and by the reasonings of the most respectable writers, are more than sufficient, if impartially weighed, to determine all liberal and enlightened Christians to concert measures for bringing about a "consummation so devoutly to be wished."

I have long entertained sentiments similar to those which you support, and have occasionally presented them to the public, some of which you have done me the honor to extract. I have long deeply regretted the sectarian spirit, and the consequent divisions of the Christian Church, and I would fain hope that the time is fast approaching when the "breaches of Zion shall be healed," when the Church shall be visibly united in one grand and harmonious body, and when "the name of the Lord shall be ONE throughout all the earth." But, in order to this happy consummation, it is requisite that the attention of the Christian world be aroused to this subject, and proper measures concerted in order to bring about union in the church on liberal and scriptural principles. I entertain little hope of such an union, till the "doctrines and commandments of men" be entirely set aside, and appeals be made, on every question, *directly to the Sacred Oracles*. It is truly lamentable to reflect, that, among certain denominations of Christians, when attempting to settle points of divinity, appeals are made to the writings of the Fathers, of Luther, of Calvin, of Arminius, or of Wesley; and to confessions, liturgies, books of discipline, acts of assembly, and acts of parliament, while no direct appeals are made to the "Acts of the Apostles," and the original record of Christianity; and while "the commandments of our Lord and Saviour," and of his holy Apostles and Prophets are entirely overlooked. In regard to every thing which relates to the present comfort and eternal happiness of man, the Bible is the most plain and perspicuous book I have ever read; and, therefore, it is not a little surprising, that so many different and opposite opinions should have been adduced from it. This is owing in a great measure to the ignorance, self-conceit, and perversity of man, and to the *selfishness* of many religionists in making Christianity subservient to their vanity and the promotion of their worldly interests. The Bible, indeed, contains "some things which are hard to be understood," from the very nature of the subjects treated of,—just as the system of nature contains facts and mysteries which are inexplicable—but, instead of waiting till our faculties be expanded, and the light of heaven burst upon our understanding, we have fixed our attention upon such inexplicable subjects, and raised disputes and contentions respecting them, while we have, in a great measure, overlooked all that is grand, interesting, and ennobling, and which is expressed in language that is plain to the meanest capacity.

I expect no cordial union till more importance be attached to the **exercise of Christian LOVE**, and the manifestations of Christian dispositions and conduct, than to mere opinions on doctrinal subjects. And, while I would allow a considerable latitude of sentiment on such subjects, I would be more strict in inquiring into the Christian principles and dispositions of candidates for church membership, than what accords with the practice of almost any existing denomination. Instead of inquiring whether they agree in sentiment with Luther, or Calvin, or Wesley, I would endeavor to ascertain whether they indulged hatred, malice, or revenge—whether they were given to "evil-speakings and hypocrisies," or cultivated a kind and forgiving disposition,—whether they harbored in their minds the principle of "covetousness, which is idolatry," and whether the general train of their actions is such as "becometh the gospel of Christ," and the conduct of those who profess to be "strangers on earth" and travellers to a blessed immortality. Where the fruits of Christianity are uniformly manifested in the temper and conduct, there is little danger of the doctrinal principles from which they flow being erroneous, or very different from those of the gospel; and it is a maxim laid down by the highest authority,—"By their FRUITS [not by their *opinions*] ye shall know them."

If the members of the visible church had comprehensive and impressive views of the perfections of God, and of the love of Christ, of their ignorance and depravity as sinners, of the beauty of holiness, of the evil of pride and self-conceit, and particularly of the great realities of the eternal world to which they are advancing,—we should find fewer contentions and animosities about comparatively unimportant matters, than we now do among the great body of those who profess the religion of Jesus. It is recorded by a worthy person who kept a journal of the Plague of London in 1665, that, during that calamity, "Many consciences were awakened, many hard hearts melted into tears, and many a penitent confession of crimes long concealed. The people showed an extraordinary zeal in their religious exercises. Many of the clergy were dead, and others had left the city, but such of the churches and meeting houses as were still open were crowded with the people. And it is worthy of notice, that differences on religion were now little regarded. A near view of death reconciled men to each other, and made them forget those small matters about which they contend so eagerly when their situation in life is easy." "In heaven," adds the author, "whither I hope we shall come from all persuasions and parties, we shall find neither prejudice nor scruple, but shall be of one principle and one opinion; and that we cannot go hand in hand to the place where we shall unite in complete harmony, remains to be lamented."

When men approach to the confines of the eternal world, their creed is generally much simplified and contracted They do not so much inquire whether Luther's or Calvin's system be the true one, as whether they have exercised "repentance towards God, and faith in our Lord Jesus Christ," whether they have spent their lives in folly and dissipation, or consecrated their powers to the service of God; whether they are still in the "gall of bitterness," or have been renewed in the spirit of their minds; whether they are "meet for the inheritance of the saints in light," or for the regions of darkness,—and such important considerations should at all times occupy our attention more than "questions which gender strife rather than godly edifying." When Episcopal, Methodist, and Independent missionaries meet at parts of danger in heathen lands, they make no scruple in joining with each other in all the solemnities of divine worship. And how glaringly absurd and inconsistent is it, that they refuse to do so in their native land? as if the mere circumstance of a difference in locality ought to set aside the fundamental laws of Christianity. Man is an inconsistent creature;—and something must be wrong where such incongruities exist.

Wishing an extensive circulation to your volume, and much success in your endeavors to promote the cause of Christian unity, I am, dear sir, yours very truly,

THOMAS DICK.

DEPUTATION TO ENGLAND.

The most of this appeared in the CHRISTIAN ADVOCATE, October 5, 1835.

The Annual Assembly of the United Christian Churches, which met in Dundee, April 25 and 26, 1835, having appointed the Rev. William Menmuir and me to visit England, for the purpose of endeavoring to promote UNITY among real Christians of all denominations; and being anxious to promote the object of our visit, we conceive that a brief narrative of our tour may be both interesting and useful to many Christians in different parts of the kingdom.

July 20th.—DUNDEE. Both our churches met this morning at 6 o'clock in the Nethergate Chapel, to implore the blessing of the Lord to attend the deputation. It was a refreshing season.

22nd.—Went on board the Ardincaple steam packet at Newhaven, for Newcastle. We had the company of a Deist, from the neighborhood of Doncaster; he soon informed us that he had no faith in the Bible—and that it was evident to the eye of every one that Christians were the worst sort of people. We admitted the selfishness and hypocrisy of many professors of Christianity, but denied that they ought to be called Christians. We adduced several arguments to prove the truth of the Holy Scriptures, and answered his objections. He said "The Bible is not fit for every one to read, there are many bad things in the Bible." We requested him to point out just one bad thing. He was in apparent confusion for some time, and endeavored to waive the subject; we solicited him kindly but earnestly to inform us what he had discovered in the Bible calculated to do harm, at length he said " I cannot recollect exactly now where they are"!! We wished to know how he could assert what he had done, without being able to fix upon one single bad thing in the Bible. He said "I have not read it for eight years." We never saw so much apparent honesty in any Infidel. He was once numbered among the professed followers of Jesus : became disgusted with the hatred, selfishness, and strife of some corrupt professors, and unhappily for himself, joined the ranks of the enemies of the Lord Christ. Several of our observations seemed to make a deep impression upon his mind : we treated him kindly—as all men even infidels ought to be treated—and parted with mutual expressions of good will. He promised to give several of our observations a serious consideration, and we cannot but indulge the hope that he will one day be disentangled from his present errors.

23rd.—We landed in Newcastle this morning about one o'clock; found Mr. David Adam, who had formerly been the pastor of one of our churches, and family well; he is now a town Missionary : he preaches in the open-air, in school-rooms, and wherever he can obtain a congregation, also for several of the dissenting bodies ; he endeavored most affectionately and zealously to promote our object. This evening Mr.

Menmuir preached in Mr. Jack's congregation, North Shields.

26th—Lord's Day. NEWCASTLE. Mr. Bowes preached in Mr. Pengilly's Chapel in the forenoon, (after preaching at nine o'clock, in the open-air, for Mr. Adam, on the Quay), and Mr Menmuir in Mr. Orange's. SOUTH SHIELDS.—In the afternoon Mr. Bowes preached in Mr. Lawson's, and Mr. Menmuir in Mr. Tapscott's, and in the evening again in Mr. Jack's, NORTH SHIELDS, while Mr. Bowes went on to Sunderland and preached in Mr. Richardson's; the congregations were generally large. Several of the ministers at Shields had preached on the Unity of the Church in the morning, and had thus prepared the way for our discourses.

27th—SUNDERLAND. Held a public meeting this evening in Mr. Muir's Chapel, Mr. Watkinson, a pastor, took the Chair. After we had delivered addresses, he announced to the meeting that the ministers of different denominations then present, amounting to eight, by whom he was surrounded, had requested him to say that they approved of the principles advocated, and would bring the subject before their next Monthly Missionary Prayer Meeting, in order either to form an association, or to adopt some other plan for promoting Unity among Christians.

28th.—NORTH SHIELDS. Held a Public Meeting in Mr. Gilmore's Chapel, he took the Chair. Mr. Lawson addressed the meeting in a very clear and convincing speech, and stated that he had been of our sentiments ever since he was at college. On a former day, Mr. Lawson accompanied us to Mr. Tapscott's, when we solicited his Chapel; Mr. Tapscott made some becoming enquiries in reference to our object, and said he could not exactly understand it. Mr. Lawson with a noble freedom of manner, said, "Well, I understand, Sir, that their object is to convert the world by uniting the church, something like the Americans." This remark conveyed to Mr. Tapscott all the information he seemed to require.

29th.—NEWCASTLE. Held a Public Meeting in Mr. Pengilly's Chapel. Mr. Pengilly took the Chair; the meeting was addressed by Mr. Adam in a lucid speech, in the course of which he observed, "that as to Christians sitting down together at the Lord's Table, I as a Baptist, may, and do believe that all believers should observe believer's baptism; but if we cannot bring our Pædo-baptist brethren to do the whole will of Christ, are we to prevent them from doing that which they are disposed to do? Surely we ought to rejoice that they are willing to obey the Saviour in this command, "This do in remembrance of me." Mr. Chester, Wesleyan Protestant Methodist, addressed the meeting, approving of the object. After this interesting meeting, several Christians accompanied us to our lodgings, and desired us if possible to form a committee and get up an association before we left them; this we could not do as we were necessitated to take coach for Leeds next morning.

We cannot pass over these northern towns without remarking, that in general we were received by the Secession, Independent, and Baptist ministers and churches with warm Christian kindness; their pulpits were readily granted us, and in several instances they took part in the public meetings. We also learned that in some places the Cholera had led Christians of different names to form Union Prayer Meetings, and we could not forbear remarking, that if Christians will not be drawn together by scriptural motives and persuasion, *the judgments of God may drive them together.* May the Lord increase the love and concord of his people, in these places, a hundredfold.

Aug. 2nd.—LEEDS. Mr. Bowes preached in the morning in the Wesleyan Protestant Methodist Stone Chapel. We proposed preaching in the Market place at half-past one o'clock; as Mr. Menmuir was about to open the service a man came up to him and told him that *the Market place was private property*, and that he was instructed by the proprietors and the Mayor not to permit preaching there. The Market place was spacious; no passengers would have been interrupted—hence the prohibition seems to be levelled against the preaching of the Gospel. What are English Christians about, to allow such restrictions on open-air preaching? We should not have met with such interruption in any part of Scotland. We were conducted by the people to the Fish Market, in which Mr. Bowes preached to a numerous and deeply affected assembly. In the evening Mr. Bowes preached in the (parade) Baptist Chapel, and Mr. Menmuir in the Wesleyan Protestant Methodist Chapel.

3rd.—Mr. Bowes lectured on unity in KEIGHLEY; in a few hours notice had a considerable number of attentive hearers, several of whom solicited him to spend a Sunday among them, to which he consented, on their procuring him three Chapels, belonging to three different denominations.

4th.—We held a Public Meeting in Leeds, as we could not obtain a Chapel we rented a splendid Hall, used for public meetings, called "The Commercial Room." Mr. Walker, a deacon of Mr. Ely's church, took the Chair; the following resolution was unanimously adopted:—
"That considering the evils which have resulted from divisions among Christians—that the first Christian churches were united—and that sinners generally are only to be converted by the labors of the Church when united: it is desirable that an association be formed for the purpose of promoting union among real Christians of all denominations." A committee of seven, connected with the Independent, Baptist, and Methodist communities, was elected to form an asssociation. In Leeds we could not obtain one Independent Chapel, for either Sermon or Public Meeting. The Wesleyan Methodists have great influence here. There is a Union Prayer Meeting here, composed of some denominations of orthodox Christians, from which it would seem others are shut out; let the Christians of Leeds see to this.

5th.—BRADFORD. Held a public meeting in Mr. B. Godwin's Chapel, who took the chair; he had been for many years classical tutor of the Baptist Academy here, but has resigned the office. He treated us very affectionately. as did Dr. Steadman, the Theological tutor, an aged and venerable man, who was present at the meeting. As the public notice was short, the congregation was not large.

6th.—MANCHESTER. Several of the ministers were not in town. We did not find that union among the different denominations which we anticipated. Mr. Menmuir preached in Grosvenor Street Chapel, Mr. Fletcher's, who treated us very affectionately, as did Mr. M'Kerrow. Mr. Bowes visited Liverpool, but found that most of the Chapels were to be occupied for the London Missionary Society.

9th.—Ashton-under-Lyne, Dukinfield, and Staley Bridge. Mr. Bowes preached in the morning in Mr. Ivy's Chapel, Dukinfield, in the afternoon in a Chapel recently built by a society under the pastoral care of Mr. J. R. Stephens, and in the evening in his place of worship, Ashton.

10th.—Mr. Bowes lectured on the Unity of the Church, in Ashton, in the same place, to a large congregation.

11th.—Held a public meeting in Dukinfield, at which Mr. Ivy presided; a crowded place. Mr. J. R. Stephens delivered an effective speech, in the course of which he made the following observations, " I have long regretted the existence of divisions in the Church. We have all been guilty; I will not exonerate myself, but I never felt so sorry on account of the state of the Church as since the brethren have come from Scotland. The brethren have not been well used in all cases; they have not had free liberty to deliver their sentiments; they have not obtained Chapels in certain cases, when they ought to have obtained them. The chapel deeds might be in the way. If you would be a minister among the Wesleyan Methodists, you are asked, ' Will you preach according to the first four volumes of John Wesley's Sermons, and his Notes on the New Testament;' or if you desire to preach in some Independent chapels, you are required to subscribe the Westminster Confession of Faith. When Jesus Christ came in the flesh, he was seldom prevented from delivering his sentiments, and his ministers ought not now to be prevented; but were he to come again in the flesh, I speak it by way of supposition, and with all reverence, should he wish to preach the gospel among the Wesleyan Methodists, he would be asked, ' But will you preach according to the first four volumes of John Wesley's Sermons, and his Notes on the New Testament ?' or should he wish to exercise his ministry in some Independent chapel, ' Do you believe in the Westminster Confession of Faith ?' " Mr. Stephens subsequently proposed, and Mr. Rose, a Moravian preacher, seconded, the following resolution:—" That the thanks of this meeting be given to Messrs Bowes and Menmuir for the intelligent, powerful, and affectionate appeals they have just made on the necessity of union amongst Christians of all denominations, and that this meeting pledges itself, by God's blessing, to carry into effect the great truths on this subject, which have been advocated before it.—(Signed) R. Ivy, chairman of a public meeting held in the Sunday-school Room connected with Providence Chapel, Dukinfield (the chapel itself being under repair), to promote the object which the above brethren were deputed to advance.—Aug. 11, 1835."

Aug. 12th.—Mr. Menmuir separated from Mr. Bowes at Manchester, intending to return home by the West of Scotland. Called at Warrington, with the view of preaching and holding a public meeting. Found the chapels engaged for Mr. Wilson, of Malta, who was to preach for the London Missionary Society. He preached, however, on the 16th, in Mr. Seveir's (Independent) chapel in the morning, and in Mr. Philip's (Independent Methodist) chapel in the evening. Assisted at a public meeting, held on Monday, in aid of the London Missionary Society. The two Independent ministers and the minister of Lady Huntingdon's connexion here, act in perfect harmony, which was unknown among the ministers, before their recent settlement. Their union is visible; for they are seen preaching for each other, holding monthly lectures and prayer-meetings in each other's chapels, and on Lord's Day mornings they preach in the market-place, all three taking part in the service. They also correspond with Mr. Philips. United efforts to do good are necessary here, and they have already been followed by good effects.

16*th*.—KEIGHLEY. Mr. Bowes preached in the morning in the Baptist chapel, in the afternoon in the Wesleyan Protestant Methodist chapel, and in the evening in the Primitive Methodist chapel, EAST MORTON. The Baptists and Independents, as well as the Primitive Methodists, preach in this chapel. When a chapel stands in a thinly populated village, in which may be found persons of various denominations, the cause of Christ sustains great injury when that chapel is closed to all but one sect, and when it is standing unoccupied, while the minister of another sect is preaching in a house or barn.

18*th*.—Lectured in Mr. Clarkson's chapel, BINGLEY. The congregation was small, as the people were preparing for the Feast. Mr. Taylor, Baptist minister, prayed after the lecture. Mr. Clarkson and family treated Mr. Bowes with great Christian kindness.

23*rd*.—HULL. Mr. John Spencer, sailor's missionary, an old acquaintance, received Mr. Bowes with great kindness, and aided him in procuring chapels. Mr. Bowes preached in Mr. Sibree's in the forenoon, Mr. M'Conkey's in the afternoon, and in the floating chapel in the evening. He could not obtain the co-operation of many of the Hull ministers. One of them acknowledged that our object was good, and that Christians ought to be united, but remarked, "This is not the time." Which was like saying, this is not the time to do right!

25*th*.—Held a public meeting in Mr. M'Conkey's chapel, and he took the chair. In the course of his speech, Mr. Bowes endeavored to answer the objection of the Hull minister: he observed, "It is granted that we are laboring to accomplish a *right thing*, but it is said, 'This is not the time.'"

About the New Year of 1836, I attended two soirees. One by the church. The members of the congregation and other Christian friends took tea, and spent a few happy hours together. I have not heard of any similar congregational meetings. It was a blessed time.

April 10*th*.—To-day I have been exceedingly affected with the barrenness of the church; few sinners get saved; the people of God generally, and I in particular, have been too formal. I mourned and wept in secret before the afternoon service, and went to the pulpit with a heart of tears. Preached from "Ye did run well, who hath hindered you?" It was a moving season. Evening service.—As I have been in the habit of preaching too long, especially in the evenings, I resolved this evening to preach a shorter sermon, and stay the usual prayer meeting myself. I did so; and two or three times as many as usual stayed. I hope that the Lord will revive his work. I recommended all the brethren to pray for it.

11*th*.—I feel travailing in birth for souls, until Christ be formed in them. A Christian brother accompanied me, and prayed after I had spoken. I had joy and liberty in recommending repentance and faith. Have got great good in reading "Abbot's Young Christian," and the second volume of "Reid and Mathewson's Visit to the American

Churches." It appears to me that the American revivals, like all others, are effected by the use of means: 1st. The people of God, secretly, in the family, the social prayer meeting, and in public worship, earnestly praying for an outpouring of the Spirit, and a consequent revival of religion. 2nd. Working. Their prayers are followed by corresponding exertions to promulgate divine truth,—they are laboring privately and publicly to do good.

17*th.*—Had a gracious day. Preached with great liberty from Heb. ii. 2—4, and in the evening lectured on Rev. xx. 11—15. Nearly one half of the people continued at the prayer meeting.

18*th.*—Held a fellowship meeting. On the Lord's Day, I recommended the church to pray that the Lord might do us good. We had more than I expected. About two years ago we had not a fifth part as many.

25*th.*—This evening attended George's Chapel, in which Dr. John Ritchie delivered an address on Voluntary Church principles. There was great disturbance at one of the gallery doors. Three advocates for Establishments opposed him. The meeting was most uproarious. I have attended four meetings now of this kind. The first was in the Steeple Church on " The Sabbath Question," to petition parliament for a bill for exempting London bakers, etc., from Sabbath-day work. Few of the speakers could be heard; the " roarers " prevailed. The second was held in St. Andrew's Church, to support the Establishment, and only one was allowed to speak; the meeting was in a state of hubbub for three hours, and was only restored to order by the election of a new chairman. The third was held in the High Street, on the water question; the Town Council and Joint Stock Water Company being hostile to each other in reference to supplying the town with water. And the last was the meeting on the 25th, in which neither Dr. Ritchie nor the church party could be heard, at times, though the former was better heard than the latter. Such shouting and roaring tends to suppress the truth, confuse the minds of an audience, and disgusts all sensible people. If men would judge of a question, they must hear both sides.

June 8*th.*—EDINBURGH. Walked with a friend to a place in the High Street, opposite Bank Street, where I intended to preach in the open-air. Mr. Flockart, an old friend, was praying, and about to preach. I stepped up to him, and informed him that I was passing through Edinburgh, had only one night to spend, and that, not knowing that he was to preach there, I had intimated to a few friends that I should occupy the place, I requested his " pulpit " or stand. He said he could not give it up till nine o'clock; so we repaired to Princes St., asked a chair from Mr. M'Lean, which he kindly carried over himself, and heard the sermon. I preached from, "Go ye out into all the world," &c. I told them who I was, and secured the attention of rich and poor. Many seemed deeply impressed. After preaching, Mr. M'Lean read me and several friends a curious worldly letter from N. West, of America. He has joined the Presbyterian Church. I fear he *still* makes gain of his religion.

9*th.*—Took coach for Dumfries; it was crowded with people and luggage. The rain came on when we had only got a few miles from Edinburgh. A middle-aged gentleman sat near me, I think a minister (certainly an advocate) of the Established Church; when the rain descended he gave several anxious looks round and upwards, and then said, "I fear we are going to have a very unpleasant day, Sir."—"Many an inhabitant of a city would greatly enjoy our situation to-day, and feel pleasure in witnessing the mist encircling the mountains, and the tempest sweeping over the land." "I confess," said he, "I am not sufficiently stoical for that." The heavens became blacker and the rain fell thicker than before. The gentleman, looking concerned and dissatisfied, and getting his cloak closely round, said to me, "Not much pleasure to-day, Sir." "Not much, Sir," said I, "only some persons enjoy pleasure in seeing how patiently others endure pain." I think we had not one unpleasant or discontented word from the general passengers, till we entered Dumfries. We talked about parishes, ministers, preaching the gospel every where, and *by every person* that *knows* the gospel; about piety, temperance, &c. A carter under the influence of drink was taken up; he laid down on the luggage and fell asleep, lost off his hat on the common or muir, just before we entered the Delveen pass. The storm raged furiously upon the head of the carter but did not waken him out of his sleep; the driver was informed, but he slackened not his pace, until I offered to get off the coach in pursuit of the hat flying before the wind; I secured it and placed it upon his head, but he awoke not until some time afterwards, when the passengers informed him what I had done for him. I was in hopes that he was some generally steady carter who had been induced to take large quantities of spirits in consequence of the inclemency of the weather, and that we should find some good thing in him; however, I was grievously disappointed; when he awoke he began to swear and rage fearfully. He left us at Thornhill. We arrived in Dumfries about seven o'clock, having been about twelve hours on the road. A more stormy day I never had, and never spent a day more pleasantly, in consequence of the general intelligence, and I trust, piety of the passengers. I was taken, the same evening, amid torrents of rain, in a gig, to Dalbeatie, which I reached soon after nine o'clock, wet, and happy in the Lord.

10*th.*—Fast day. Preached twice.

11*th.*—Preached twice again.

12*th.*—Lord's Day. About 2000 people, or upwards: Mr. Roseman delivered the first sermon in the tent, I made a few observations on the characters of whom a Christian church ought to be composed. While we were seated at the first table a shower of rain descended, it continued during my serving the second; the people put up their umbrellas, but I do not know that one person left the ground. In the evening I preached; the services were finished about eight o'clock, the people having been together ten hours, except one, from four to five o'clock we took a little refreshment.

13*th.*—I preached in the morning, and proved that "We gain more by Christ than Adam ever lost." After sermon I gave such counsel as I judged necessary and useful: I brought prominently forward the following truths :—

1st. That all believers are safest by "believing the truth," which is the great medium of purity, and consequently our faith and love are augmented by an increasing acquaintance with the character of God.

2nd. That he that "Believeth hath the witness in himself," and consequently hath joy, great joy in his religion, and that this is the privilege

T

of every Christian who may be expected to have the witness of the Spirit, unless he has been erroneously taught or is affected with some mental malady.

3rd. That none but such as we have reason to regard as believers, regenerated, or justified persons ought to be admitted into the church. We are warranted to admit hypocrites when their hypocrisy cannot be detected.

4th. That all Christians should be united together in one harmonious community, and not divided into sects as at present.

5th. That we should exert ourselves in every possible way to make the gospel known to others, not depending solely upon the exertions of the ministers, but that every parent should teach Christ to his children, every master to his servant, and every Christian to all with whom he converses, as he has opportunity.

6th. To render sinners without excuse, I proved that every man can come to Christ if he will.

In the evening we had a voluntary church meeting, and had present Christians of various denominations.

15th.—I set off at three o'clock in the morning from Dalbeatie, part of the way I walked, and rode the rest of the way to Dumfries in a carrier's cart, where I took the coach; had a pleasant ride by Thornhill, through the beautiful Delveen pass, by Biggar, &c., to Edinburgh. Miss Duncan, an interesting young lady, the daughter of Dr. Duncan, minister of Rothwell, who has two sons ministers in the Established Church, gave me some pleasing details of the Lord's Day schools in that parish. The minister meets the teachers and holds a catechetical exercise once a month; this must increase the knowledge of the teachers, and fit them for their high duties. I told her my residence and name, and that I should preach on the Mound, about the middle of Princes Street, the two succeeding evenings.

16th.—I preached to a large congregation, I think Miss Duncan was in the crowd.

17th.—Preached again in the same place to about as many people, after having taken tea with Mr. M'Lean's family, Mr. Milne, teacher of the Infant School, and several other Christian friends; after tea Mr. M'Lean introduced the Bible and Psalter and we had family worship. A young woman followed me this evening, as some persons had done on former evenings, she wanted to know where my place of worship was; I told her where I should be preaching on Lord's Day, she artlessly asked if every body was admitted.

19th.—Lord's Day. This day I spent in Heriot's Bridge Chapel, Grass Market, the first place that I preached in when I came to Scotland, about nine years ago. A little more than twelve months ago N. West left for America. Before he removed, the congregations had fallen off considerably; they almost fell to nothing under Mr. James Young, but under Mr. John Reid they are good. Held a prayer meeting in the evening; a blessed season.

This Petition will explain itself.

"TO THE HONORABLE THE COMMONS OF GREAT BRITAIN AND IRELAND, IN PARLIAMENT ASSEMBLED.

" The petition of the Christian Church and congregation under the pastoral care of the Rev. John Bowes, Dundee,

"Humbly sheweth,—

"That your petitioners have learned with considerable astonishment and regret, that petitions have been presented to your honorable house, requesting increased church accommodation in the Established Church of Scotland at the Nation's expense: That your petitioners are grieved at the misrepresentations contained in some official documents, which have been, no doubt, submitted to your honorable house, in which the Established Church is set forth as containing accommodation for a very limited number of the inhabitants, while the greater part are represented as 'living in a state of entire exclusion from all the outward and ordinary means whereby are communicated the benefits of redemption;' whereas, it ought to be well known, that in some of our largest parishes, the Dissenters are more numerous than the Established Church, and consequently may be expected to give more Christian instruction, although the official documents in question take no notice of their existence: That your petitioners are convinced, that in many places there is already a surplus accommodation, and in such as exhibit a deficiency, its supply may safely be left to the voluntary exertions of the friends of Christianity. We hold that it is both *manifestly unreasonable* and *palpably unjust*, that Dissenters, after supporting their own ministers, and building their own chapels, should be compelled to pay taxes to support the ministers and build the chapels of another community, of which they conscientiously disapprove. We have been lately very much confirmed, by the course of events, in our opinion that the Church and the State would be both benefited were they separate; so that your honorable house might be at liberty to confine your attention chiefly to the secular affairs of the kingdom. We have been grieved to observe, that you have had to spend that time and those talents which, in other circumstances, might have been dedicated to the civil interests of the empire, in legislating, day after day, month after month, and year after year, about the Irish, or some other Established Church.

"May it therefore please your Honorable House, to take the premises into your consideration, and to resist firmly all petitions for national grants of money for ecclesiastical purposes, and to adopt such measures as will leave you more leisure to lighten the burdens, promote the commerce, and extend the influence of this great nation."—*May 20th*.

LETTER TO MY BROTHER-IN-LAW.

DUNDEE, 27th June, 1836.

MY DEAR PHILIP,—

. . . . We too are endeavoring to apply our minds to divine truth as the only medium of purity and peace. Babes in Christ are to desire "the sincere milk of the word" that they "may grow thereby," and as it was by becoming intimately acquainted with the doctrines, precepts, and promises of the gospel, that our souls prospered immediately after our new birth; so we have now no other means of growing, sufficiently effective to exclude this. When the Lord Jesus prayed for those who had been some years disciples, he said, "Sanctify them through thy truth; thy word is truth." Let us, therefore, my dear brother, apply ourselves to READ a portion of this truth DAILY. Let us study prayerfully what we read, and add to our reading—hearing, for faith not only comes, but is greatly strengthened, by devout hearing of this truth. And let us farther add to this— conversing with the people of God in reference to this truth; for when we converse about anything, our thoughts are called into exercise, we become better acquainted with the subject, by viewing it in a variety of lights, and thus divine truth will live in our hearts. "Thy word have I hid in my heart, that I offend not thee," says the Psalmist; and we shall be kept from sin by principle. What is the reason that many people resolve to break off sin, but they do not accomplish it?—their resolutions are scarcely made ere they are violated. The reason is this, —they have not the truth of God in them. "Wherewithal shall a young man cleanse his way, by taking heed thereto according to thy word." I am far from asserting that the word will sanctify us by itself, without the Spirit, but it is the instrument by which the Spirit works, and when He operates on our minds, it is not to enable, or to induce us to believe *without* reason and understanding; but it is to enable us to feel the force, reason, and propriety of divine truth, so that it takes hold of our mind and our heart. Good books, sermons, class-meetings, love-feasts, and conversations are just so far valuable as they are aids or helps to a better understanding of the Scriptures. All true religion is founded in knowledge, and all saving knowledge relates to God, as the object known. If we wish an increase of FAITH, we must study "the truth," which testifies of God, and then we shall see that God is worthy of being believed. If we wish an increase of love, we must become better acquainted with God, and then we shall see that, being infinitely lovely, he is worthy of our supreme regard and highest ascriptions of praise. A proper view of God will also stimulate us to exertions for his sake, especially when we view him in Christ, reconciling the world to himself, and giving all the honors, riches, and pleasures which are comprehended in that at present incomprehensible term—"eternal life." You mention the divisions among the Methodists; rest assured that, sooner or later, the Conference tyrants must bow, or the connexion will be rent into fragments. I am glad to hear of the success of the Reformers. . . . Yours in the kindest bonds of affection,

JOHN BOWES.

EDINBURGH CONFERENCE.
(From the "Christian Advocate," Sept. 26, 1836.)

We have received the following account of a Conference between the delegates of the "United Methodist Churches" of Scotland, and the delegates of the "United Christian Churches" of Scotland, from the Secretary of the latter :—On Thursday, the 15th instant, a meeting of the delegates of the "United Christian Churches" of Dundee, Edinburgh, and Newburgh, was held in the Rev. John Reid's Chapel, Heriot's Bridge, Edinburgh, consisting of Messrs. Bowes, Mitchelson, Wood, Ogilvie, Stratton, and Bathie, from Dundee; Messrs. Duncan, Reikie, and Grant, from Edinburgh; and Messrs. Anderson and Todd, from Newburgh. Dalbeatie and Castle Douglas church sent a letter to the meeting. The Rev. John Bowes was chosen President; and Mr. Peter Stratton, Secretary. The number of members in each Church was as follows:—Dundee, 340; Edinburgh, 175; Dalbeatie and Castle Douglas, 128; Newburgh, 20; Total, 655. The Dundee church has three preachers in addition to the pastor. A copy of the regulations of a missionary society connected with the Nethergate church and congregation, Dundee, having been read, it was unanimously agreed that a copy be transmitted to the Edinburgh, Dalbeatie, and Newburgh churches, by the Secretary, and that it be strongly recommended to each church to organise a similar society, leaving the construction of the rules to its own discretion. It was unanimously agreed that the Rev. John Osborne is not a minister of the United Christian Churches, and that the above resolution be transmitted to the Dalbeatie church, with official permission to tender it to Mr. Osborne, should they deem it advisable. It was resolved,—That a communication be sent to the delegates of the "United Methodist Churches," requesting them to appoint a committee to meet one of ours to consider the method of negotiating a union of the two bodies. The following communication was sent:—

"Sept. 15th, 1836.

"DEAR BRETHREN,—

"The Delegates of the 'United Christian Churches,' having met in Heriot's Bridge Chapel this morning, and considered the correspondence which has taken place between Mr. C. J. Kennedy, secretary of your May meeting, and Mr. J. Bowes, secretary of our Connexional Committee, also the information supplied by Mr. D. K. Shoebotham, of Dundee, in reference to a union between your churches and ours, have agreed, upon that correspondence and information, to appoint a committee, of either three or five of our number, to meet one of yours, for the purpose of arranging the method in which the negotiation should be conducted.

(Signed)   "JOHN BOWES, President,
"PETER STRATTON, Secretary.

"Heriot's Bridge Chapel."
"To the delegates of the United Methodist Churches, met in Chalmer's Close Chapel, Edinburgh."

Messrs. Kennedy, Horsburgh, and Cochrane, from their delegates, met Messrs. Bowes, Anderson and Stratton, as a committee from ours, in Heriot's Bridge Chapel, at eight o'clock p.m. Mr. Horsburgh said they would like to understand the basis of our union; on which our committee tendered them the printed "Epitome of faith and essential principles," published by us; also, the questions proposed by our Connexional Committee to the Rev. D. K. Shoebotham and Mr. Kennedy. The following is a copy of the latter document:

"The Committee met, and a letter was read from Mr. Kennedy, of Paisley, in reference to a union with the 'United Methodist Churches.' Mr. Bowes also stated the substance of a conversation he had had yesterday with the Rev. D. K. Shoebotham, in explanation of the views of that body, from which it appears to us that it will be proper, before we call a meeting of Delegates, to meet theirs in September in Edinburgh, that information should be solicited on the following subjects:—

"1st. Whether the Association and United Methodist Churches act upon the principle of receiving none to membership but such as can be regarded as believers, disciples, children of God, and Christians? The rule referring to this topic, read by Mr. Shoebotham was not well understood by Mr. Bowes.

"2nd. Whether the United Methodist Churches, &c., will apply the same principle of FREE communion to the ministers which they do to the members of the church? or, as this is a principle, which we CANNOT give up, having felt no difficulty in the practice, will they allow us to hold communion with all Christian pastors?

"3rd. As to a NAME. Less difficulty is felt here, in consequence of the Association and United Methodist Churches having different names; but will the latter engage, that, if we do not obtain a satisfactory name at Liverpool, they will unite with us in demanding that no sectarian name be urged upon us?

"4th. If satisfaction be obtained on these points, that a meeting of Delegates be called to meet the Delegates of the United Methodist Churches.

(Signed)   "W. MENMUIR, Moderator.
"JOHN BOWES, Secretary."

"Dundee, August 27th, 1836."

Our committee stated that satisfactory answers had been obtained to all the queries but the second, and that, while the first part was answered in the negative, and was consequently not satisfactory, the second part was answered in the affirmative, and was quite satisfactory. Their committee stated that they had no power to accept or reject our proposals, but would submit our documents to the delegates on the following morning, and remit us official information as to what time the confer-

ence should take place. Our committee earnestly recommended that the conference should be conducted in the presence of all the delegates of both bodies: or, if that proposal did not meet their approbation, our committee was prepared to consider any which they had to offer. They could not think of any better plan, and promised to lay it before the whole of their meeting. After their departure, the greater part of the minutes of the Delegates' Meeting at Manchester, held in August, was read; also the whole minutes of the " United Methodist Churches" resolved and unanimously adopted by them in this city, in the month of May. They were considered *seriatim*. Out of fifteen, ten were found unobjectionable; and the following improvements to the rest were suggested to form a basis of union. The first preliminary reads thus :—

" 1. That it is highly desirable to form a union among those Methodists in Scotland who have seceded from the Wesleyan conference, that they may thereby more efficiently promote the genuine object of Methodism—the spread of Christian holiness throughout the land."

Amended thus—

" 1. That it is desirable to form a union among *all Christians* in Scotland, that they may thereby more efficiently promote the genuine object of *Christianity*—the spread of holiness throughout the land."

Principles agreed upon :—" 1. That we retain those doctrines believed and taught by the body of Methodists."

Amended thus—

" 1. That we retain those doctrines believed and taught *formerly* by the United Methodist and the United Christian Churches."

" 2. That, in general, the same hymns be sung, the same social means of grace attended to, and the same form of worship observed, to which as a part of the Methodist body, we have heretofore been accustomed."

Amended thus—

" *Psalms* to be put in before hymns, and *the two bodies* substituted for ' as a part of the Methodist body.' "

" 8. That the church shall admit to fellowship only such as afford to it adequate evidence that they earnestly desire to flee from the wrath to come, and rely, through divine grace, on the Lord Jesus Christ, and Him alone, for salvation."

Amended thus—

" 8. That the church shall admit to fellowship only such as afford to it adequate evidence that they *are believers, disciples of Christ, children of God, or Christians.*

" 11. That a token of church-membership (a ticket) be given to every member of the united churches, to be renewed each quarter."

The following amendment to be suggested—

" *That this rule be submitted to each church for its approval.*"

" 12. That the name by which the union be designated be ' The United Methodist Churches.' "

Amended thus—

" The name to be ' The Associated or United Churches of Christ.' "

On the second day, September 16, a letter was received from Mr. J. Lees, Secretary of the United Methodist Churches, acceding to our request of a full conference, and appointing it to be held in the Chalmer's Close Chapel, at eleven o'clock a.m. The Conference of the whole delegates being assembled, the Rev. D. K. Shoebotham was appointed President, and Mr. Peter Stratton and Mr. Horsburgh, Secretaries. The President gave out a hymn, and called upon Messrs. Rutherford and Bowes to engage in prayer. A private letter from the Dalbeatie church was read, from which the following is extracted:—

"We are delighted to hear that all the churches are to be independent. Consequently, that public meetings will be consultative. We have suffered much from Presbyterian domination, and have been led to discover that the authority that they exercise is usurped and unscriptural. We would not submit to it, or any other power that would again deprive us of our privileges, even for the sake of connexion. We are also glad of the information imparted with respect to 'who should be members; but we felt satisfied on this subject from Mr. Kennedy's published sentiments, and his strenuous advocacy of purity of communion, and his connexion with the Association was a sufficient guarantee that this would be attempted as far as possible. The principle of free communion, with respect to both ministers and members, is important; and, if our friends could not pledge themselves to it, it would be necessary that it should be so secured to us, that we could FREELY communicate with all we believed to be God's adopted children. With respect to a NAME, less difficulty appears to be felt in the north; but it is very different in the south. For our own part, we have given up, and we wish entirely to have done with, sectarian names. The feelings of this county are not averse to sectarian appellations, but to that of Methodists they are decidedly averse; and, as we have raised much opposition against ourselves, and have encountered long-established and deep-rooted prejudices already, by openly avowing as our belief, and defending the gloriously extensive range of Christ's death, together with the principles of free communion; and as, through mercy, we have been enabled to go forward, notwithstanding this opposition, and we trust are still going forward in removing these prejudices, we do not think it would be right to place ourselves in a more disadvantageous position by adopting a name that the people are so much prejudiced against. We do not say, neither do we believe, that these prejudices are well-founded; for it consists with the knowledge of many of us, that a more zealous, useful, or devoted body, as a whole, it would be difficult to find. Still the name we cannot receive. We wish our own to be adopted in preference to any other. We desire a union of both, because we believe it would be of mutual advantage, and by strengthening the body, it would afford greater encouragement to ministers and churches who are tired of the yoke under which they groan, to unite with us. We also desire the union, because it would show to those men who have nobly struggled, and sacrificed Connexion in order to break the bonds of tyranny, that their noble conduct is highly appreciated by others, and that there are others who, not suffering under such yokes, are still willing to unite with them, that they may thereby strengthen their hands."

Our delegates were now asked if they had any plan of union. They stated that they would either take the resolutions of the May Meeting of the Methodist churches, or their own published epitome of faith and essential principles, as a basis of union. The latter was unanimously preferred. The doctrines were then considered *seriatim*. The first six were unanimously adopted, with some inconsiderable alterations. The seventh was read, which stands thus:—

" We believe in the redemption of mankind by the incarnation, obedience, sufferings, death, resurrection, ascension, and intercession of Jesus Christ, whom we regard as both God and man."

The doctrine excited some discussion. Mr. Kennedy desired to know if the article was for the admission of members or ministers? Mr. M'Kenzie, of Edinburgh, requested to be informed whether the " United

Christian Churches" with those who hold Calvinistic doctrines; for his part, and for the part of the Edinburgh church, he would say that no Calvinistic minister should enter that pulpit (pointing to the pulpit). Mr. Bowes replied to Mr. Kennedy's question by referring him to a paragraph in the Epitome which asserted that the doctrines "are not considered to be as a creed" for either minister or members; but that they are merely to express to the world the faith of those at present in the union. As to Mr. M'Kenzie's question, Mr. Bowes replied that the doctrine was so framed as to admit both Calvinistic and Methodist ministers; and that both are, or may be, *part* and *parcel* of the union. Mr. Wood, of Dundee, corroborated Mr. Bowes' statement, and added that this was a principle which we could not give up. Mr. Anderson, of Newburgh, stated that it was not merely *occasional communion* to which his brethren had been referring, but that such ministers preaching for us, sat down at the Lord's table with us, were eligible for members of our Connexional Committee, and would sit in the annual assembly, with the same privileges as other members. Mr. Bowes stated that it appeared to him quite consistent to apply the same principle of free communion to the ministers as to the members; and that it was decidedly inconsistent in the Methodist churches to admit a Calvinist to fellowship as a member, and, should he evince preaching talents, such as a Hall or a Wardlaw, then proceed to expel him, after meeting with him in the various means of grace. Thus violence would be done to Christian feeling, and great injustice to the preacher. They would not be consistent without either keeping out altogether a Calvinist from the membership of the church, or, after his admission, allowing him all the rights and privileges of other members. That, although those were his sentiments, in which his brethren concurred, yet, since the Methodist Churches could not allow Calvinistic ministers to enter their communion, he did not wish to base the union on such a proposal. He and his brethren were willing to unite with the "United Methodist Churches," if the latter would allow them to exercise, so far as the pulpits and ministers of the United Christian Churches were concerned, the *same liberty* to which they had been accustomed. But he could not submit to have that Christian liberty fettered, and no man should prevent him from holding full and free communion with all Christians; no man should prevent him from thus boasting in all the regions of Scotland. Mr. M'Kenzie thought that if Calvinistic ministers were received into union with the United Churches, and if the Methodist Churches were united to them, it would be almost like admitting them into their own pulpits; and, as it regarded what had been said about Calvinistic ministers making their own peculiar sentiments a matter of forbearance, he never heard a Calvinist preach, but he saw Calvinism like a line run through the whole discourse. Mr. Cochrane, of Glasgow, did not participate in the sentiments of Mr. M'Kenzie; and he would remind him that Dr. Warren had occupied the pulpit of a Secession minister in this city, and Dr. Wardlaw's pulpit in Glasgow. Mr. Kennedy had no objection to occasional communion with Calvinistic ministers. Mr. Bowes desired Mr. Kennedy and Mr. Shoebotham to explain what they meant in their answers to the questions of the Connexional Committee when they said, that they would "allow the United Christian Churches to hold communion with all Christian pastors." Mr. Shoebotham replied that he meant only occasional communion; to the same effect spoke Mr. Kennedy. Mr. Bowes thought that Mr. Kennedy's letters went much further. Mr. K. allowed that such a construction might be plainly put upon them; but they were written in haste, and when he saw the extensive communion proposed to be held by the United Christian Churches with Calvinistic ministers he now concurred in opinion with Mr. Shoebotham. Mr. Hillier, of Edinburgh, thought (to use a phrase of Mr. Shoebotham's) that the United Christian Churches were like a man who wished to have *two wives*. "They wish," said he, "to give us the one hand, and Calvinists the other, and to be united to us both. This we do not wish: if they come to us, we wish them to come altogether, to give us all their *influence*, and all their *affections*, and all their *energies*, and not divide them with others." Mr. Bowes was glad that Mr. H. understood the position which he and his brethren desired to occupy. He felt pleasure in reasoning with such a gentleman. "We," said he, "do wish to give *you* the one hand, and Calvinists the other; and when Mr. H. claims for you *all* our *affections* and *energies*, he claims what we cannot give." "Brethren," (said he, looking over, evidently under strong emotions, to the Methodist Delegates,) "Brethren, for we regard you as brethren, but know that we have other brethren besides you: them we are commanded to love as well as you. If they are sick, we must, and will visit them; if they are naked, we will clothe them; if they are hungry, we will feed them; as our Divine Master has given us commandment; and, were we to give you all our *affections*, we should act most unscripturally. The demand itself is most *Sectarian*, with which we can never comply." It was now proposed that each body should consult its own Delegates for the purpose of coming to an unanimous conclusion. The Delegates of the United Christian Churches retired for a few minutes, and unanimously agreed to adopt the following resolutions:—

"The delegates of the United Christian Churches have unanimously agreed to hold it as an indisputable principle, that they will not give up the principle of holding FULL communion and fellowship with Calvinistic ministers and churches; but that they leave the United Methodist Churches to act according to their own discretion in this matter."

The Methodist delegates read the following resolution:—

"That we cannot admit Calvinistic ministers to our union."

Some other resolutions were passed by the Methodist delegates, which we have not been able to obtain from their secretary. The President considered the resolutions of the two bodies would prevent their union, and that the Conference was broken up. Mr. Kennedy did not think that it was yet necessarily broken up. Mr. Bowes moved, and Mr. Cochrane seconded, the following resolution:—

"That we are mutually satisfied with the present conference, and hope that it will tend to remove misrepresentations; and, although the union cannot be effected now, that, at no very distant period, it may be both prudent and profitable."

Mr. Shoebotham, in summing up the proceedings, protested against Mr. M'Kenzie's sentiments being understood to represent more than those of the Edinburgh church, and expressed his own willingness to hold occasional communion with Calvinistic ministers. Mr. Shoebotham highly eulogised Mr. Bowes' work on Christian Union, and recommended it to the consideration of his brethren. The following extract (see book, p. 172) was then read, being part of the speech of Dr. John Brown, of Edinburgh, made at the centenary of the Secession Church:—

"The faithful part of the church would naturally connect themselves with those, who, in their view of Christian truth, are of one mind and heart with them; and may we not hope, that, ere another century revolves, even this name shall be felt as unduly sectarian; that under the clear and genial influence of a millennial sun, the true followers of Jesus Christ of every denomination shall be made to see eye to eye, that there shall be a general return to the purity of primitive doctrine, the holiness of primitive discipline, and the simplicity of primitive usage; that Christians shall only be known by names expressive of their subjection to the Lord, and their love to one another, that sects and party names shall fall, and Jesus Christ be all in all; that it shall no longer be the Established church and the Secession church, and the Relief church, and the Congregational churches, and the Baptist churches, but the church of Christ in Scotland; that, in our land, as in all lands, there shall be but one fold, as there is but one Shepherd."

He then gave out another hymn, and Messrs. Kennedy of Paisley, and Anderson of Newburgh, concluded by prayer. A vote of thanks was unanimously passed to the Rev. D. K. Shoebotham, for his impartial conduct in the chair. It was unanimously appointed by our delegates, that Mr. Anderson of Newburgh, should be ordained on the Tuesday after the Dundee communion: and that, previous to his ordination, he should be examined according to rule fifth of our organisation. It was agreed that our Secretary furnish the editors of the *Christian Advocate* with a copy of the whole proceedings. The Rev. John Reid, of Edinburgh, and the three delegates, took part in our proceedings, only so far as they were connected with our own churches; not being empowered to do more, in reference to the union, than hear and report to the Edinburgh church. The next two letters are mine.

THE MINUTES OF THE WESLEYAN-METHODIST ASSOCIATION.
[To the Editors of the CHRISTIAN ADVOCATE.]

Gentlemen,—When a religious denomination publishes its sentiments to the public, and appeals as the "Wesleyan Association" has properly done, to "the Holy Scriptures, as the only and sufficient rule of faith and practice, and also of church government," its rules and opinions become public property; and if any excellencies, or defects, can be pointed out to other bodies, or to itself, confidence may be inspired in what is scriptural, and new energies may be awakened to remove what is unscriptural. In my present review, of the "Minutes of the Annual Assembly of the Delegates of the Wesleyan Association, begun in Manchester, on Wednesday, August 3, 1836," I must disclaim any intention of lowering the Association in the estimation of your readers. It stands far higher in my own, than any other body of Methodists, if I except the "United Methodist Churches" of Scotland.

I. I shall begin by directing attention to some of its excellencies.

1. And, as is apparent from its address to the "Methodist Conference," it has made a noble stand against the usurping domination of that body. The Reformers have determined not to remain in a confederacy, whose members are no longer at

liberty to act according to the dictates of a pure, peaceable, and an enlightened conscience, but must either openly support, or at least not oppose the English State Church, one of the harlots mentioned in Revelations (see xvii. 5), whose mother was the Roman hierarchy while under state patronage and state pay, called "the mother of harlots," and whose sin of fornication is expressly said to be "committing fornication with the kings of the earth." Rev. xviii. 3, 9. By receiving her laws, and office-bearers, and pecuniary support, from secular authority, the English Church hath demonstrated her harlotry. And at the wickedness every Wesleyan or Conference Methodist must wink; he dares not speak against it; but has strong, alas! too strong for many giddy heads, temptations to speak for it. But from this abomination the Association has purged itself, and proved, that the Wesleyan preachers have no right to make its members bow down either before the image of its favorite "beast," (I speak scripturally), or before the ghostly authority of the "collective pastorate," which, if it were not out of my course, I could easily prove to be no scriptural pastorate at all. In resisting the unscriptural power of the preachers, the Reformers must have no small degree of pleasure from the smiles of an approving conscience and an approving God.

2. It has affirmed, more clearly than any other body of Methodists, the great Protestant principle of the sufficiency of the Holy Scriptures, as "a rule of faith and practice and also of church-government." See General Principles, page 15. And as a legitimate consequence of this affirmation, it has refused to give to the Annual Assembly that power which Christ has delegated to no body of men or angels on earth, or in heaven—power to legislate for the church. The Conference, the New Connexion, and the Primitive Methodists, are all wrong—far, awfully wrong in allowing their Conferences to give law to the Church of Christ, deposing thereby, or attempting to depose, Christ from being law-giver in his own church. I am sorry that the New Connexion did not abandon this ground, in their recent attempt to unite with the Association; but, if they cannot be reduced, at once, to abandon it, might they not be received by the Association, on its own grand principle of liberality, to a general meeting of delegates of both bodies, to be held annually for consultation mutual assistance, exchanging of preachers, or calling them from one branch of the body to another. From the high vantage ground taken by the Association, it can never recede without disgrace.

3. It has recognised the independency of particular churches, societies, or circuits. Mr. Leach, without a shadow of evidence from Scripture, writes against this principle; and, in doing so, he opposes the Scripture. See Acts vi. 1-7. 1 Cor. v. throughout. If Christian churches give away to other hands than their own, the management of their affairs, it matters little whether they commit them to an assembly composed entirely of preachers, half of preachers and half of laymen (as in clerical phrase, the brethren are called who preach not on the itinerant plan), or of two laymen and one preacher. They will necessarily be mismanaged; but, as the liberty in question, although a great blessing, may not be appreciated, many of the seceding circuits not being prepared to enjoy it, the plan of itinerancy generally adopted by the Association may give satisfaction, and be useful. But I should certainly say, that the most scriptural plan is that of evangelists going from church to church, and building up the churches, or planting new ones, in connexion with a settled ministry, combining the excellencies of that of the Independents with that of local preachers. I have been much interested in the Sunderland Reformers. They seem, like their northern brethren, the "United Methodist Churches," to entertain tolerably correct notions about the congregational form of church government. I wish they were more closely united with these northern churches. "A Lover of Free Discussion," in a recent number of your paper, mentioned, however, in an admirable letter, that, although the Association was more approved, they had some thoughts of joining the New Connexion. At this I greatly marvel. What! will they sacrifice principle to expediency, and what they do not approve, because the New Connexion have preachers in their neighborhood whom they approve. Disapproving, as they do, of legislating for the church, will they join a body whose Conference, as a court, sits like the Wesleyan Conference, to give law to the whole inferior courts—yea, to the whole Connexion? And will they make a part of that court, and submit to its mandates!!! This would be certainly doing evil that good might come. I have been led into these observations, because of the intimate connection subsisting between the Sunderland case and my subject.

4. The Catholic spirit of the Association must be a powerful recommendation, in the estimation of every enlightened Christian. I have great pleasure in quoting the whole of its second great principle. "Second. That the members of this As-

sociation are desirous of cultivating, to the utmost of their ability, a catholic spirit, and to live on terms of the most affectionate Christian communion with all who love our Lord Jesus Christ; but they especially desire union with all the branches of the Methodist family." The first part of this expansive resolution, which cannot be too highly praised, gives honor to the understanding minds and feeling hearts of the members of the delegate meeting. It is the first resolution in the history of Methodism, which holds out the olive branch of peace to the whole church; and, when the evanescent sects of the present day have disappeared, and shall no longer disfigure the church of the living God, and when the future historian of the church shall sit down to write a history of its return to union, he may point to the Delegate Meeting at Manchester as the first dawn of the morning of union in the Methodist community. I hope, Messrs. Editors, we shall see this catholic, this emphatically Christian spirit, which breathes in this resolution, everywhere evidenced by the members of the Association. The Association deserves the unfeigned regard of every bosom that longs for the union of the church. It is the first Methodist body that has ever said, "We desire union with all the branches of the Methodist family." This, I think, should be its first work, to lay down a New Testament form of union, capable, in the first place, of receiving all the Methodists; and, secondly, capable of receiving all Christians in the expansive spirit of this resolution, this blessed resolution—for it aims at peace, "and the God of love and peace" will be with its authors. Let the Association go forward, not looking back to the "beggarly elements" of human legislation; not turning aside—no, not for the sake of an unscriptural union with the New Connexion, and they will deserve the respect of every Methodist community, and of all the churches of Christ. But I must say of the "United Methodist Churches," whose general liberality exceeds that of the Association itself, and that is saying a great deal, that I think they violated both the spirit and the letter of this resolution, in refusing to unite with "the United Christian Churches." From the resolutions passed by both bodies, it appears that the latter only wished to continue the exercise of free communion towards all real Christian ministers and churches; but that the former not only resolved that they could not "admit Calvinistic ministers to their union," but that they would not admit to "their union" those who hold communion with such ministers. Now, I ask the "United Methodist Churches" if this shows that they "are desirous of cultivating to the utmost of their ability a catholic spirit, and to live on terms of the most Christian communion with all who love our Lord and Saviour Jesus Christ?" Here was an opportunity afforded of living "on terms of the most affectionate Christian communion" with the United Christian Churches, and yet it was declined, because those churches spurned the idea of having their Christian liberty restricted—a privilege which, if they had given up, considering the broad basis of their churches, and their abandonment of every vestige of sectarianism, they would have plunged themselves into a position, to them ineffably dishonorable. But perhaps the United Methodist Churches are less catholic than their brethren in the south, and do not approve of their golden resolution; or perhaps they may soon retrace their steps, as I have some reason to think they do not entirely disapprove it. I recommend to their serious and prayerful consideration and practise, the following part of an address to themselves, by the Association, in reference to a GENERAL UNION:—"Such a confederation as is contemplated," says the latter, "whilst it proposes a combination of council, of strength, and of co-operation, in plans of general usefulness, disavows in the most explicit manner, all attempts to give ascendency to any individual section of the church over the rest, OR POWER INDEPENDENT OF THE PEOPLE, *even in the Annual Assembly, to enact rules for the Association at large, which shall interfere with the right of any society or church to govern itself by its own local regulations,* so far as they are compatible with the general principles of the Association."—*Minutes of the Annual Assembly,* p. 33.

Thus I have enumerated four excellencies; three of which do not belong to any other extensive community of Methodists; and these are not petty principles, having no bearing on the exertions and internal arrangements of the church: they are vitally important principles. The *second* that I have named points to the word of God as supreme authority in the church. The *third*, in conformity with the second, places the power of regulating the church in itself under its head, in accordance with his revealed will. In the *fourth*, the Association recognises every Christian church as a sister, and every man that bears the image of Christ as a brother—a glorious principle, the practical and effective working out of which would go far to unite together the scattered fragments of Messiah's temple. It is exceedingly honorable to the hearts and heads of the Christian men of the Association, that, at the very time when they were expelled, or under the necessity of withdrawing from the Conference, they have evinced, that they were so far from being men of a divisive spirit, that they both understood, and were willing to practise the communion of the saints, and promote their extensive union.

II. WE MUST CONTEMPLATE THE DEFECTS OF THE ASSOCIATION. Having dwelt so long on the pleasing part of my subject, I shall, happily, not have much room in this letter for the painful part; but I can assure the judicious members of the Association—and I regard them as the most judicious part of the Wesleyan community—that I shall touch those *defects* with the hand of a friend; and, while I may wish their extinction, and labor to effect their removal, it is out of love to my brethren in the Association—for every Christian is my brother—and, if he err, love should induce me to tell him the truth in love.

1. The name is *defective*, or blameable. I find no fault with the term Association, considering the circumstances of those whom it designates; but with the term "Wesleyan" I find nothing else. Who was John Wesley, that he should obscure the name of Christ? He was a good, laborious, talented, useful minister of Christ indeed; but to exalt his name, as both the Conference, and after them the Association, do, into its present situation, is an appropriation which belongs to no name but that of Jesus; and, could John Wesley come down into the midst of his admirers, I have no doubt but, with a frown of holy indignation, he would say, "Who is Wesley? Was Wesley crucified for you? Were you baptized in his name? Christ is all in all." Two reasons, at least, may be assigned for laying aside this offensive term—first, it unduly exalts a creature; secondly, it dishonors Christ. It is dishonorable that His followers should make the name of a fellow-servant their designation and their watchword, rather than the name of their Master.

2. The term "societies" should give place to the term "churches," at least if the Association intend to pay any attention to my last letter, or to the character of their members. I took the liberty of showing, that the standard of most of the Methodist communities is too low. I did not quote the Scriptures to prove it, as I had done it in a former letter: but I am prepared to demonstrate, and I state it in the face of every Methodist preacher and member that read your paper, that none ought to be a member of a Christian church who does not afford it sufficient evidence that he is a child of God, or a Christian. This position none of your correspondents have ventured to assault. Now, I hereby call upon all Methodists either to disprove it, or abandon the practice of receiving unconverted, unpardoned men to membership. If the "societies" are not "churches of Christ," then the Methodists have no Christian churches among them; and, if they have not, why do they administer Christian ordinances; and, if they have, why not call them by their proper name? "Society" is not a scriptural name; and the Association "holds, as the only sufficient rule of faith and practice, and also of church-government the Holy Scriptures." By this rule, let all their Minutes be tried. Can they show from the Scriptures, that "Wesleyan" and "societies" are proper designations for Christians? They cannot. I know they cannot, and therefore I boldly affirm it.

3. Their third general principle is faulty. Here it is :—"That, on subjects of doctrine, they entertain views according with those which were generally taught by Mr. Wesley, and are admitted by the various branches of the Methodist community as consistent with the Holy Scriptures." Here Mr. Wesley is again dragged into undue notice. What a pity that Methodists will not let the good old man rest! They had just affirmed on the same page (15th) that they held "the Scriptures as the *only* and *sufficient* rule of faith;" and yet in this resolution "Mr. Wesley's views," and also those "of the various branches of the Methodist community," are brought in as a rule or rules of faith. Now, dear sirs, could any thing be more palpably evident than this—that, if the Scriptures were the *only* rule, "Mr. Wesley's views" are *no* "rule of faith;" and, if "the Scriptures are a *sufficient* rule," then it is superfluous and palpably inconsistent to drag in either "Mr. Wesley's views," or those "of the various branches of the Methodist community." "Out of thine own mouth will I condemn thee." Referring to Mr. Wesley at all, as a model or authority in doctrine, was a very unhappy circumstance, after so nobly recognising the Holy Scriptures.

These are a few of the faults that I marked when reading over the "Minutes" (some few others, of a minor kind, I may never mention); and I freely grant they are small and inconsiderable, when contrasted with the very great excellencies to which I have called attention.

As the Minutes are open for improvement, let me suggest the propriety of the "Home Mission Fund" being employed in supporting a settled ministry, when desired by a church, as well as the itinerancy also; that the tickets, like the Old Methodist tickets, have on them the pure word of God, and no sectarian name whatever.

Gentlemen, when you look at the noble stand made by the Association for NEW TESTAMENT PRINCIPLES, you must feel no ordinary delight in reviewing the labors of your pen. The Association is, indeed, the child of Providence; but it has been brought into being, as to instrumentality, chiefly by your valuable labors: and the Conference preachers know it; and, therefore they hate you. I hope you will continue fearlessly to give your counsel when it is needed; and, in a few years, you may have the very great happiness of seeing the immense mass of rubbish which has long blinded the eyes and crippled the energies of the church, removed, and succeeded by light and love, while thousands of renewed souls will walk therein in one church. Yours with growing regard,

Nov. 7, 1836. A MINISTER IN NORTH BRITAIN.

P.S.—Mr. Kennedy thinks that "some sort of union" should be formed between the "United Methodist" and the "United Christian" churches; but he does not define what "sort" he means. He should inform them.

WHO SHOULD BE MEMBERS OF THE CHURCH OF CHRIST?

Gentlemen,—As it is my object in addressing you to promote scriptural views of church polity, it affords me great pleasure when I find your correspondents appealing to the Holy Scriptures in proof of their doctrinal or practical sentiments. It is an utter waste of time to write and read communications, in which one human system is arraigned against another system; instead of all systems being brought to the test of the inspired record. Your Paisley correspondent, Mr. John Rea, endeavors to support his views of the admission of members, by an appeal to this record, and, whatever opinion I may form of his success, I cannot fail to commend the propriety of the measure. The question between us is this:—"Is it scriptural to receive to the fellowship of the church, any who are not believers or children of God?" I maintain that it is not. Mr. Rea maintains that it is. He makes use of the term "justified believer." I do not remember having ever read in the book of God, of a believer in the Lord Jesus Christ who was not justified. Has Mr. Rea? This is the great mistake throughout—going upon the supposition that a man can believe in Christ without being justified; whereas, the word of the Lord says, "All that believe are justified from all things, from which ye could not be justified by the law of Moses."—Acts xiii. 39. The "just" God is said to be "the justifier of him that believeth in Jesus," (Rom. iii. 26) and "He that believeth on the Son of God, hath the witness in himself." (1 John v. 10.) I freely grant, that many profess faith in the Gospel who are not justified, but their profession is false; and I no more believe that a man has faith because he says so, than I do that he has love, because he loves in "word and in tongue." I know that it is common for certain divines to puzzle their hearers by the notion of many kinds of faith and unbelief; but, like the legislation of Conferences, they are the figments of human error. How read we? "He that believeth on the Son HATH everlasting life, and he that believeth not the Son shall not see life, but the wrath of God abideth on him."—John iii. 36. As a believer is justified and has everlasting life, and is a Son of God, (see John i. 12), it follows, that to talk of a "justified believer" is tautology, and erroneous phraseology, calculated to foster the untenable notion, that a believer in Christ may be unjustified.

Your correspondent thinks, that "according" to my "demonstration" "all the children of God are to be born on the outside of the church." What does Mr. Rea mean by the church? Had he in his eye four stone walls and a steeple, in the nomenclature of many denominated a "church?" If so; I deny the propriety of the name, because the word is never so appropriated in my rule of practice. However, I freely grant, that in buildings *improperly* called churches, many have been born again, though, I fear, fewer than most people imagine. But if by the church he understands "a community of believers," the New Testament meaning of the term, common sense and Scripture dictate, as we shall soon see, that a man must either be a believer, that is "born," before he enters that community, or he will deteriorate the community; and a number of such admissions would destroy the church, unless it be thought as good a definition of a church to say, that it is "a community of *un*believers!" Mr. Rea refers to the "word" to evince that the church is the mother of believers. With this view I have no controversy. *But a child must surely be born before he is entitled to call any one mother!* This is what I contend for, but Mr. Rea would introduce men into the church who are not "born," and can neither say "Abba," Father, to the God of heaven, nor "Imma," Mother, to the church. Are not all believers, or the members of the same church, designated "brethren," because they have a common parentage? but how can an unconverted man call the "sons of God brethren?" Or how can they treat him as a brother, who, alas! is yet unborn!! I conclude then, because every child is born before he can use the endeared name of "mother," so must every one be born again before the church is his mother; and, as every brother, in a natural father's house, must be born before he can be entitled to the designation of brother, so no man can be recognised as a "brother in Christ," before he undergo the new birth. Were the three thousand on the day of Pentecost made members of the church before they had faith and salvation? We are told in the chapter which records their conversion, "And the Lord added daily to the church those who were saved." (Acts ii. 47; see Doddridge's Translation.) The case of the eunuch is a beautiful illustration of my position. When he said to Philip, "See, here is water; what doth hinder me to be baptized?" what was the evangelist's answer? "If thou believest with all thine heart, thou mayest?" And he answered and said, "I believe that Jesus Christ is the Son of God." (Acts viii. 36, 37.) Now, whether baptism is to be regarded as an initiatory ordinance or not, it must be allowed that the qualifications for it are not greater than for the Lord's Supper; but as Philip was not satisfied with his having merely "a desire to flee from the wrath to come," but called for an explicit avowal of his faith, so should we, ere we admit a man to the privileges of church-membership. Did not the jailor and his house believe in God, and rejoice and participate in the blessings of salvation, before they were added to the church? (Acts xvi. 30—34.) But it is needless to offer more examples at present. I call upon Mr. Rea to show me *one single scriptural example*, of a man's becoming a member of a Christian church before he was born again?

It was to be regretted, that he gave himself the name of "Simpleton," as the word signifies "a silly mortal," "a trifler," "a foolish fellow." Now, I trust, he did not "trifle" with the Scriptures he quotes; although they are certainly misapplied, when dragged in to prove the eligibility of unsaved men for church-membership. Psa. li. 17, is referred to, which says, "The sacrifices of God are a broken spirit; a broken and a contrite heart, O God, thou wilt not despise." The advocates of purity of communion do not despise "a broken heart;" far from it. We rejoice to see it. We would not "despise" a Mahomedan, who begins to listen to Divine truth with deep seriousness, although many doubts may linger on his mind about the truth of the Koran; but we would not receive him into the church until he had renounced all dependence upon its errors, and professed complete dependence upon our Divine Redeemer. But, to be concise, to prove that this passage is favorable to his views, he must show: First, That a "broken spirit and a contrite heart" may be possessed by an unregenerate man. Second, That not to despise him, is equal to a warrant for his admission to the membership of the church. Nearly the same remarks apply to Isaiah lvii. 15; lxii. 2. Isaiah l. 10, applies to *providential* darkness, not *moral* or *spiritual*, and is quite compatible with the highest degrees of grace. Isaiah lv. 1—3, refers to such as "spend money for that which is not bread, and labor for that which satisfieth not." Would Mr. Rea admit these into the church? He would not lack members!! For alas! the multitude may be thus characterised. Matt. xi. 23, (I suspect he means the 28th) proves nothing to the point; neither does John vii. 37, nor Rev. xxii. 17. But let us listen to Mr. Rea's commentary on these delightful invitations and addresses to sinners, that they may participate in the blessings of gospel grace. "These show us," he observes, "that all they who are desirous of spiritual blessings, are invited to come and be made partakers of them; for Christ had shed his blood for them, and the privileges of the gospel were granted them." This is strange divinity, if adduced to prove the position with which our author set out; and, if not so adduced, why did he write such nonsense. If all "who desire spiritual blessings are invited to come" to church-fellowship, as one "spiritual blessing;" and if all "for whom Christ shed his blood" are to be received into the church, then will drunkards, swearers, and adulterers, desire church-fellowship, and must be admitted. And as Christ "died for all," "gave his life a ransom for all," "tasted death for every man," and was a "propitiation for the whole world," all kinds of characters may enter the church!! As to what he says about "weak faith," the first part of this letter proves, if I mistake not, that, where real faith exists, however weak *it saves*, consequently, such a man as possesses it is a "babe in Christ," and is admissible.

I do not know what to make of Mr. Rea's letter; it appears to me to answer or contradict itself. "Faith," says he, truly, "in Christ is the condition of salvation, and of course becomes the proper condition of church-membership." This is correct and scriptural, and answers the whole; for "by grace ye are saved, through faith." So then Mr. Rea gives up the whole point at issue, and believes with me, that FAITH which HAS SAVED is "the only condition of church-membership:" for I have shown, a man cannot possess faith without being saved.

Perhaps I ought to apologise for replying to this letter. I assign three reasons—

1. It respects and appeals to Scripture; and with me, in these times, this is an important matter.

2. It refers to a point of immense magnitude to the church, and especially to Methodists of all kinds, who are generally alleged to be too careless or indifferent, as to the kind of members they receive, although I believe they exercise a vigilant eye on them afterwards; but it is better to KEEP out, than PUT out, the wolf.

3. I had considered the point as settled; and, by way of proclaiming it settled, after being maintained and standing invulnerable in your pages, I had given a challenge to any minister or member of the Methodist community; and, had I been silent, some would have considered the letter of Mr. Rea unanswerable.

I beg to recommend to the notice of your readers interested in this controversy, a few observations, which occur in one of my letters of Feb. 15:—"The churches of Rome and Corinth were addressed as SAINTS and SANCTIFIED in Christ Jesus. (Rom. i. 7; 1 Cor. i. 2.) Similar and equally characteristic appellations are applied to the Colossians. 'To the SAINTS and FAITHFUL BRETHREN in Christ.' (Col. i. 2.) 'Forbearing one another, and forgiving one another, if any man have a quarrel against any; even as CHRIST FORGAVE YOU, so also do ye.'

"What, then, may we learn from these sacred words? That all Methodist Reformers should be united together? No; but that all the 'saints,' or 'saved,' or 'forgiven' among them, should be united. Or do we learn that none but Methodist Reformers should be received into the union? No; but that all the 'saved,' &c., should be received. If an Episcopalian, Presbyterian, Baptist, or Independent be 'saved,' we transgress the law of God if we reject him, or refuse to admit him into the church. Our brother may be in error, he may be weak, but so long as he is a 'child of God,' however erroneous his views in other respects, we are obligated to receive him. 'Him that is weak in the faith receive ye;' and the reason is given, 'For God hath received him.' Rom. xiv. 1—3. Sooner let my right hand forget its cunning, than that I should be accessory to the keeping out of Christ's family, one of *his own children*."

To conclude my reply; as the first churches were composed of the "saved," the "saints," "faithful brethren," persons whom "Christ" had "forgiven;" these persons were surely converted; and, if so, then men composing Christian churches should be now of the *same* kind, or they are not following New Testament models. It is of the utmost importance to the well-being of the Christian interest, which ought to be dear to all our hearts, that the character of the membership should not be vitiated. Let that be kept pure, and we may expect a pure deaconship, or leadership, a pure ministry; and, as the church is the light of the world, she will emit a pure, heavenly light. Then, I apprehend, we shall have fewer lords over God's heritage—fewer letters in religious periodicals, vindicating an unchristian spirit—fewer organs in chapels, and more divinely attuned hearts and voices—less wantonness among ministers and people, and more spirituality of conversation and affection—less spiritual sloth among the members of the church, and more tender, soul-moving pity, for perishing sinners, and greater exertions at home and abroad that the gospel may be verbally and *practically* "preached to every creature."

On the other hand, if worldly members continue to enter our churches in *shoals*, what can we expect but a money-loving, indolent, time-serving church? The absence of manly decision, of Christian dignity, of elevated piety, of warm benevolence, and martyr-heroism! The world, as it has been, and I fear still is, in thousands of churches, will be the Alpha and Omega of our religion. From such a state of things, ye ministers of Christ, ye guardians of souls, save us! And save us, O Thou that keepest Israel, from sacrificing the power of thy church at the shrine of human policy, and from debasing its purity for the sake of *numbers* and *pomp!* Amen.—Dec. 26, 1836.   A MINISTER IN NORTH BRITAIN.

CHAPTER VII.

MY LETTERS TO THE DUNDEE ADVERTISER ON NATIONAL EDUCATION AND CHURCHES—REMOVAL TO LIVERPOOL—R. AITKEN'S LETTERS, AND HIS CONDUCT—PUBLIC MEETINGS—HOW I BECAME A TOTAL ABSTAINER—VISIT TO BIRMINGHAM—SOULS GET SAVED—DISCUSSIONS WITH INFIDELS.

THESE letters, which appeared in the DUNDEE ADVERTISER, will prove that I advocated, in our most popular assemblies and newspapers, a National System of Education, and political freedom and courteous treatment to Roman Catholics, thirty-four years ago.

THE REVEREND DOCTORS COOKE AND STEWART.

Mr. EDITOR,—

The two meetings which have been recently held in the Old Church and Thistle Hall, on Irish Education and Popery, I have attended. The Reverend Dr. Stewart, although obviously against the civil liberties of the Roman Catholics—for he exclaimed with apparent horror, "We have one Roman Catholic Judge!"—(he did not say how many Protestant Judges)—seems the most moderate man of the two deputies. The Reverend Dr. Cooke seems inferior to Dr. Stewart as a theologian, though superior as a speaker. His speech in the Old Church, which he recapitulated in the Hall, was a tissue of calumny against the Government scheme of Education. This was not candid and honest. Why did the bills not declare that the Doctors would deliver addresses against this scheme, as this was palpably their object? Let us examine all the charges brought against the object of their abuse.

1. "During four hours of the day the Bible is excluded from the school.' Well, admitting the truth of the objection,—which, like all the rest, was not proved by a reference to the proper documents,—does the schoolmaster of Scotland keep the scholar at the Bible during every hour of the day? Is no time allowed for other reading, for writing, arithmetic, geography, &c.? The Doctor endeavored to play upon our feelings by saying, "that during the four hours the child might die." And what if it did? Although the Bible might not be in the school, might surely be obtained. But if it be the object of the Government which the reverend Doctor assails to diminish Bible reading, they have defeated their own purpose; for, according to Dr. Cooke's own confession in the Church, "the Bible is more read now in Ireland than ever it was!" Mark this, intelligent reader. If the Government aimed at this, they have effected their object, Dr. Cooke being witness! Yet the Doctor is ill pleased. Wonderful logician! Curious Protestant!

2. "Protestant ministers cannot preach in the school-houses built." I answer: neither can the Catholics. Had both been allowed, we should have heard of the school-houses being turned into mass-houses. They are not built for preaching in, but for purposes of education. Dissenters in Scotland have as good reason to complain, that they are excluded from preaching in schools built by the nation's money in Scotland. Will the Established clergy of Dundee open such schools to me for week-night preaching? If not, it is a great hardship, on Dr. Cooke's showing, and especially as the Established clergy are at liberty to do what the Irish Roman Catholic priests cannot do,—viz., to occupy them themselves; which, however, I believe is seldom done.

4. The Doctor complained that the Board consisted of different parties. And is the education not for all parties? The Board is not to be formed like the Synod of Ulster—altogether of religious men; but here comes out that intolerant and exclusive spirit in which the Doctor and his party act. They wish other people to *contribute the money* for education, *regium donum*, and tithes, and *they*, the friends of Establishments, will *dispose of it.* These are all the formidable objections

brought against the scheme under review, except the one about "extracts from the Bible" being used; which, being of less moment, I pass it over. These objections are easily answered, and some of them, as I have shown, were answered by Dr. Cooke himself,—the greatest Protestant Reformer in the world, if we may believe himself; for he assumed publicly nothing less. What egotism!

Let me seriously ask, Why these reverend gentlemen did not give the Government credit for good intentions? When its members approached the subject of Irish education, was it not thick-set with difficulties? The Irish Catholics and Protestants had stronger prejudices and feelings against each other, than the English, which formed the main obstacle to any system that could be devised. And, is it nothing that the Government have effected much in removing prejudice and in educating Ireland? Are there not more people by far under education at this moment in that suffering isle than any former period could ever boast? Is this *nothing* to our Irish Doctors? Had they rather see Ireland uneducated than not have the glory of doing it by the Ulster Synod's schools? Dr. Cooke acknowledged that he had some weight with the Government. Why did he not employ it in endeavoring to remedy the defects of the system which he maligns, instead of setting himself against both? The Doctor seems to have a great dread of "walking arm-in-arm with a priest," even when going to ask for money in aid of education. Why should he fear the company of a priest? Jesus Christ feasted with a Pharisee; and of him also it was said, "He receiveth sinners and eateth with them." Why may we not receive from a Roman Catholic, and reciprocate, civil and benevolent offices? Suppose that Dr. Cooke falls overboard and is drowning in the Tay, while a priest, an expert swimmer, and a kind-hearted man (for even priests may have kind hearts), dashes in after him, and brings his Reverence in triumph to the shore, almost drowned, indeed, but alive; and, conscious of his deliverer's philanthropy, would the Doctor refuse to be saved by a priest, and perish? Would he not rather thank him; and, taking hold of his arm, walk home with him? or would the feelings of the bigot obliterate those of the man?

Some may say, "Why did you not state all this in the Doctor's presence; you can talk when he is gone?" I did stand up in his presence to ask a question when a motion was about to be put. The question was this,—"Will you not hear both sides?" It was answered in the negative, and I sat down, or I was prepared to say more. This gave rise to the following attack upon me, which appeared in the pages of the *Chronicle*:—

"The confusion at this moment became a little alarming in appearance, and was increased by the clamor of a new actor on the stage of disturbance, viz., an individual who calls himself the *Reverend* John Bowes. If notoriety be the object of this man, and it seems evident, we can assure him that he has had enough of it; for not a few inquiries have been made concerning his history since the celebrated Cowgate meeting, where he earned such black and dismal laurels. The interruption of this man and his Popish coadjutors was firmly met, in support of the Chairman, by the Reverend Mr. Duncan; to whose conduct throughout, and particularly for his judicious arrangements for holding the meeting, the friends of Protestantism here are much indebted."

I have thus stated this attack without note or comment; and I shall leave your *judicious* and *Christian* readers to make their own remarks, after informing them, *on the best authority*, that the author of the whole report, and of the above paragraph, is the Reverend Alexander Duncan himself, of Dundee. The next week I shall prove, with your indulgence, that the late Protestant meetings, instead of promoting, *were adapted to injure the cause of Protestantism.*

JOHN BOWES.

Nethergate, January 16th, 1837.

THE REVEREND DOCTORS STEWART AND COOKE AGAIN.

Mr. Editor.—

It shall be my object in this communication, as I intimated last week, to prove, " that the late *Protestant meetings*, instead of promoting, *were adapted to injure the cause of Protestantism.*" It may be promoted either by conciliating the Romanists to hear dispassionately our arguments, or by their being induced to abandon the errors of their church, by the light of truth finding its course to their understandings and their hearts. Or it may be promoted by Protestants being warned in the spirit of Christian affection against the errors of the Romish Church; thus the evil of their going over to that Church may be prevented; or, farther, it may be promoted by their being aroused by powerful motives, such as the sacred Scriptures amply supply, to exert themselves to disseminate Divine truth, and chase away soul-defiling error both from the minds of stupidly ignorant men in their own Churches and that of Rome. But each of these ends has been defeated by the late meetings. This opinion derives its importance from the evidence which follows.

1. The conductors of these meetings have injured the cause which they professedly wish to advance, and have drawn forth against their measures a considerable number of Protestants as well as Catholics, in consequence of having *linked* their hostility to Popery with their reiterated opposition to the Government scheme of national education for Ireland. If they sincerely desired to advance the cause which all true Protestants must have at heart, why did they adopt a plan of procedure which prevented all Dissenters from acting along with them? If they wish to assail Rome with success, they cannot afford to leave behind them, much less to have opposed to them, more than one half of the Protestants of the empire.

The Government scheme of education approves itself both to Whigs and Tories. Sir Robert Peel himself, the oracle of the latter, gave it his sanction. Then, as to the Romanists, they know well that it was designed to exalt them and their children, by putting the blessings of literature, of which they had so long been deprived, into their speedy possession. And is it likely, I would ask, that Doctors Stewart and Cooke could expect a candid and unruffled hearing from men at whose civil privileges they aimed a deathblow? which, however, I hope has been parried, and wasted "on the desert air."

That Government, whose measures were so unmercifully oppugned, is dear to the Catholics, who have discernment sufficient to understand that the men who could brave the greatest storm of opposition which the Tories could get up against "the appropriation" for purposes of education, of the surplus revenues of the Irish Church, and are willing to endure more that Ireland may be educated, deserve the appellation of the *Friends of Ireland*. And is it the way to convert the Catholics to sink the reputation of their friends? Perhaps our Irish visitors and their Dundee "coadjutors" regard themselves as the *best friends* of the Catholics; this they claimed, but concealed not their hostility to the priest,—another fatal blunder which they committed. Will the Catholic be gulled by hearing a man exclaim "We *love* you, but *hate* your priests!" If the priests are wrong, are not the people to blame to follow them? Protestants should love both priests and people, and hate whatever is unscriptural in either. But the Catholics must be allowed to judge for themselves who are their best friends.

2. The conductors of the Thistle Hall meeting have laid themselves open to a serious charge, which may well arouse the indignation of the Catholics, when in the resolutions of the meeting it is affirmed that the "system (of Popery) threatens destruction to the Protestant character and *liberties* of these realms." This resolution was moved and seconded by the Reverend Mr. Arnot and the Reverend Robert Thompson, Wesleyan minister; and, as they did not offer any evidence to the meeting in proof of this proposition, I should think consistency requires them now to bring it forward. Is it not ascribing too great consequence and importance to Popery, and attributing too little to the intelligence, stability, and piety of Protestantism, to maintain that it threatens destruction to the *Protestant character*? That character must be a very weak, evanescent thing, if it be so easily destroyed. What harm can Popery do to a real Protestant's Christian character? None in the world; and, if a man be not a Christian, it matters little whether you call him Protestant or Catholic, he will subserve the interests of neither. Nor does Popery "threaten destruction to the liberties of Protestants." I am quite astonished at the temerity of the men who could come forward and maintain this proposition before a British audience. I am desirous of using measured terms; yet I must at once say that it is not borne out by the fact. Have not the Catholics in our day, as a body, *always supported the rights and liberties of these realms*? Was it not chiefly by their influence that the reform, anti-slavery, and municipal bills passed into law? Are they not now the advocates for granting an exemption to the Dissenters from Church rates and other grievances? In truth, they are the champions of our liberties, as well as of their own; therefore, the two gentlemen who moved and second-

ed this resolution, must either prove it, which I believe they cannot, or stand confessed as not only affirming a proposition they cannot prove, but as calumniating the Catholics. Now, Sir, such conduct as this I hold is calculated to give the Catholics a low opinion of our religion, as though it could only be supported by misrepresentation and calumny. Is not such conduct injurious to Protestantism? Mr. Arnot regretted the manner in which some persons had been treated who have withdrawn from the Church of Rome. So do I, believing, as I do, that the Romanists hold several dangerous errors. I rejoice when I hear or see of priests or people turning away from them, on enlightened and Christian considerations; but then it is wrong to make these proselytes the agents of a party, and to play them off against the Government.

3. The Catholics appear to have a great hatred of Toryism; and, according to the Reverend Alexander Duncan's report, they charged the chief conductors of the meeting with nothing less, and affirmed that "they were Tories, hired pleaders against the Catholics, and receivers of the *Regium donum.*" Now, without examining any other charge than the first, can that be established? Dr. Cooke's Toryism will not be denied, after his recent speech at the Irish meeting of Orangemen. The disposition of the Established clergy to the same party was plainly manifested by their vexatious prosecution and persecution of Dr. Brewster for attending a Whig festival, and by *forty-seven* attending that of the Tories just held in Glasgow. It certainly does appear, from all the evidence of facts, that the political bias of Established clergymen is in favor of Toryism. And these are the men who tell us that Popery threatens our liberties! while in reality they are stirring earth and heaven against them. Do your readers think that, had Sir Robert Peel, instead of Lord Melbourne, been Prime Minister, that the Reverend Doctors would have raised the "No Popery" cry in Dundee, or lifted up their voice against the Government scheme of education? If they do, I differ from them, and believe that their visit is intended to give a deadly thrust at the present Government, by directing the prejudices and fears of Protestants against it under the idea that it favors Popery. They would do nothing to embarrass a Tory Government. The present is perhaps too Liberal! What did Mr. Arnot mean by the "spirit of the age," which he denounced, but the spirit of civil and ecclesiastical reform? But were we to allow, for argument's sake, that this charge made by the Catholics is ill-founded, we should be obliged to concede, that, however mistaken they may be, while they hold the opinion that the advocates of Protestantism are Tories, it must prejudice them against the truth.

4. The meeting in the Thistle Hall was not only convened and addressed by the advocates of civil Establishments of religion, against which the generality of Catholics have set themselves in common with many Protestants, but the Chairman of the meeting palpably *endeavored to support such institutions*, if we may believe the report of his speech, which bears marks of being furnished by himself. He gave utterance to the following remarks. "The whole matter, my friends, is a question of national responsibility; for, if it be the truth of God that nations are dependent upon him for being and happiness, and bound therefore to govern themselves by his revealed will—if it be true that the nation that shall not serve him shall perish and be utterly wasted, &c. . . . We must continue to insist, by every means in our power, for the purity of national religion, if we would not be landed in the intolerable mischiefs, moral and political, of national irreligion, or a national neglect of our duty to God." If I correctly understand this language,—and, considering from whom it comes, I cannot be mistaken,—the author regards the questions before the meeting as amounting to this,—Established Church or no Established Church, endowment or no endowment; or, to use his own words, "national religion or national irreligion,"—supposing, no doubt, that the Government which supported "the appropriation clause," and the national system of Irish education, is not sufficiently friendly to "national religion," or an Established Church. And what has this to do with Popery? I must tell Mr. Roxburgh, that it is possible to suppose a case in which there should be no national church in the realm, and, at the same time, no Popery. It is "true that the nation that shall not serve God shall perish and be utterly destroyed." But does he mean to say that a nation cannot serve God without an endowed or an Established Church? I ask him if there is no service presented to God unconnected with the Established Church? And I further ask, and wish him to mark the question,—Admitting that "the spirit of the age" shall destroy the connexion between the church and the state, and the truth of God find its way to the mind and heart of every human being in the kingdom, so that all shall repent, believe in Christ and love God and

man, would Mr. Roxburgh say that the nation could not be said to serve God, because destitute of an Established Church? Let him understand that as men sin as individuals, so as individuals they believe, and shall be judged. And, if the time shall ever come when the whole nation shall be on the Lord's side, it may be called a righteous nation, serving and glorifying him, although there shall be no State-endowed churches or State-paid ministers. The Government of Britain regards our civil interests, the Government of the Church our spiritual interests, and the former may not interfere with the latter with impunity.

The Catholics think that it is unjust that they should pay their own priests and then be forced to pay men who hold them up to public ridicule. They pay their share of the *Regium donum*, and so do I and all Dissenters, in paying taxes, 100*l*. of which Dr. Cooke receives annually. They are compelled to pay tithes, and English Dissenters are urged to pay church rates. I really wonder that Christian ministers should be so much alarmed at Popery and not be alarmed at the flagrant injustice of taking money from persons that never hear them and do not approve of their church! Perhaps I shall be told, "It is their own fault; the churches are built (partly with our money) and open for all." I will tell you a fact, Sir,—a fact which shall be my ratiocination,—I state it on the authority of J. B. Smith, Esq., of Manchester. In a certain parish, a Quaker by profession a barber, received one day a note for Church rates for the year 1835, 5s. 6d. He shortly after called upon the clergyman of the parish with the note, and said, "Friend, what do'st thou mean by this note?" "Why, it is for Church rates, don't you see?" "Yes, friend, but what is that for?" "Why, for the repairs of the church and the decent maintenance of public worship, to be sure." "Well, friend, but what have I to do with that; I do not attend thy church?" "That don't signify; the church is always open; it is your own fault if you dont come; besides, it is the law, and you must pay." "Well, friend, I take leave to tell thee that it is a very unjust law which obliges me to pay for a church and a religion which I do not attend. Fare thee well!" A few days after, the barber, by way of straightening accounts with the priest, sent his Reverence a note. "Dr. —— to Timothy Broadbrim, to shaving and hair-cutting, 1835, 5s. 6d." The receipt of this note by the clergyman, very quickly brought him to the barber's shop, and not in a very good humor. "You scoundrel, what do you mean by sending this note? I owe you nothing; you never cut my hair and you never shaved me in your life." "Nay, friend, but thou knowest my shop was always open; it is thy own fault if thou hast not been to be shaved." This fact will evince, that, as it was unjust for the barber to make a charge when he had done no work, so it was equally unjust for the minister, and for the same reason. Now, as Catholics and many Protestants have a high sense of the injustice—the *positive moral wrong*—of being taxed for the support of Established Churches and ministers, and as the recent opposition to Popery of the latter has been associated with the defence of Establishments, *i. e.* with the defence of injustice, and as this injustice is defended by Protestant ministers, who profess to be servants of the ineffably benevolent Son of God, if the defence of injustice will injure a cause, the cause of Protestantism has been injured in Dundee.

But this letter is long enough: The next week I shall probably finish, by pointing out such measures as may benefit Ireland and convert Catholics, by reviewing the spirit of the Thistle Hall meeting, and by making a few observations on *meetings of uproar* in general. In the meantime, I can assure you, whatever I say against false systems, *I am the friend of all men, and the enemy of none.*

JOHN BOWES.

NETHERGATE, January 23, 1837.

HOW IRELAND MAY BE BENEFITED AND CATHOLICS CONVERTED, ETC.

Mr. EDITOR,—

Hoping that both Doctors Stewart and Cooke, and the ministers who countenanced their proceedings, sincerely desire the conversion of Catholics, it may be useful briefly to specify such a line of conduct as will be successful; and, as there is a system in active operation in Ireland *far more injurious* to the best interests of its teeming population than the government system of education can be,—viz., the system of the *overgrown Irish Church*,—the first step for pacifying Ireland and converting Catholics should be to abolish its tithes, its imprisonments, and its oppressions, and to put an end to its murders. In close connection with this, there should be the constant preaching of the gospel, and an unequivocal expression of affection towards the Catholics, accompanied by consistent Christian conduct. Protestants are living books, and Catholics will judge of their religion by them.

Now, suppose that I go to Ireland and preach salvation through Christ, in the pungent and forcible manner of Felix Neff, who gained more converts from Rome than any of his contemporaries,—that I visit the sick in their poorest cabins, and, according to my means, relieve the wants of the afflicted and necessitous,—shall I not be more likely to succeed, than by all the means of coercion that ever mortal commanded? But if I should not succeed, suppose that I relinquish my first plan —apply for Episcopal ordination, and obtain a salary of £1500 per annum, chiefly from tithes—my Catholic parishioners refuse to pay me—I point to Acts of Parliament as my authority—still they refuse to pay—I call in the aid of the tithe-proctor and the military—still the people will neither believe my doctrines nor "pay me my tithes!" but they assemble in crowds—the soldiers fire—some of the people fall!—some are wounded!—some are killed!—so that in my parish are enacted over again the blood-red scenes of Newtonbarry and Rathcormack. Some of the people I send to *prison*, some to *heaven*, and *some to hell!* and *then* I preach Protestantism to the Catholics! Would they then be in a temper to hear me and receive my opinions? No; they would execrate me as the murderer of their husbands and the sons of their widowed mothers, and cleave with new affection and tenacity to their own Church.

I know it is common for our Northern advocates of Establishments to allege that they do not defend the evils of the English and Irish Churches; but, if they do not defend, neither do they *assail* them. Why do they acknowledge, with us, that great evils exist, without writing one petition, or delivering a single speech, or taking a solitary step for their abolition? Did Doctors Stewart and Cooke say a word or utter a syllable condemnatory of the Irish Church? Not one. If they would be Reformers, let them call meetings, deliver speeches, and get up petitions against the enormities of the Irish Church; and let our Established Clergy join them. The Dissenters have already done their duty, and have spoken plainly out against the proceedings of that blood-stained hierarchy.

Again, if they would convert the Catholics, they must not evince towards them a spirit *deeply impregnated with asperity;* but on the contrary, a spirit of real affection,—visiting them when sick—not with law-officers and tithe-proctors, but with sympathetic feelings,—feeding them when hungry,—not with powder and shot, but with the bread that perishes, and also with the bread of life,—and clothing them when naked,—not with the walls and bars of a prison, but with comfortable apparel. I have been long convinced, that before Roman Catholics and Infidels will be induced to adopt our faith and practice, we must be more affectionate towards them. It was a wise observation of the late pious and amiable Dr. Bogue, that "when anything arduous is to be done, if love cannot do it, nothing else can." I have already admitted that the Roman Catholics are in error—great, *dangerous error;* but what error or heresy can be *greater than the want of love?* If Paul affirmed, "Faith, hope, charity—these three—but the greatest of these is *charity*," or *love*, then may we safely infer, that, of all errors, the want of love is the greatest and most dangerous! The most effectual measure for the conversion of Romanists would be the cessation of all hostilities among Protestants; and, were this desirable event to transpire, and to be followed by the cordial union of the wise and good into one vast and harmonious community, it would do more for the conversion of the Romish Church than has been effected since the time of Luther. Who does not know that our divisions render our religion hateful in their sight? To use the words of a writer in the *Edinburgh Review* for April, 1836, "Catholics contemplate our multitude of obscure and vulgar sects with pre-eminent disgust." Let us preach against them, and pray for their removal if we wish to remove error from Romanists.

Spirit of the Thistle Hall Meeting, held January 13th.

This is the next subject of review. It is well known that the "resolutions" were hurried through the meeting without discussion or deliberation. Their wisdom could not be questioned! and reasons against them could not be heard! their authors sagely judging, no doubt, that to reason against them would be their ruin! Accordingly, at a subsequent meeting, in which both sides were heard, counter resolutions were carried by "nineteen-twentieths of the meeting." Now I hold Sir, that all meetings of a public nature, in which motions are submitted, should be open for deliberation and observation; otherwise, if reasons are not heard, motions are of no use; and, consequently, I regard the resolutions of the Thistle Hall meeting, held January 18th, as utterly worthless.

The meeting was led to expect, from Dr. Stewart's saying, "First lend me your ears and then your voices," that he meant to hear Catholics in reply; but they were not allowed a hearing. Hence, exclaimed one of them, "If you will not hear us, where is the light?"

Protestants have no just right to refuse a hearing to Catholics, especially when the latter are the assailed party. But violence, absolute violence—was used by the Church party, not only against Catholics, but against others. When I stood up to ask a question, one young man on one side, and another at another, pulled violently at my cloak; but the cloak being good, it did not tear! and, as I was not weak, I did not fall! I do not know the names of these *champions of the Church!* or I would certainly have given them. Oh ye wise men of Dundee! *are these* your arguments for Established Churches and Protestantism? But we must speak next of

Meetings of Uproar.

I refer not to political meetings, with which I never interfere, but to professedly religious meetings; and, as several in Dundee have been very tumultuous, let us first try to ascertain the cause. If I am not mistaken, the great—the only cause —is the *suppression of free* discussion. The Cowgate meeting is perhaps the most striking illustration of our subject that we could select. It was called by the friends of the Church,—all friendly "to the establishment of the true religion, according to the Word of God," were invited. Dissenters thought themselves as favorable "to the establishment of the true religion according to the Word of God" as their brethren of the Establishment, and attended in great numbers. Attempts were made to pack the meeting with the friends of the State Church. The Chairman announced that none else would be heard; and what resulted? Two speakers were heard in favor of the Church. A Dissenter arose not far from where I stood; he was refused a hearing; and, as the ministers would not hear *him*, the assembly would not hear *them*. The meeting got into the utmost uproar, and had been in such a state as this for about half an hour. When I judged that if I, a Dissenter, presented myself, I should be able to restore order, by saying, "that the assembled ministers ought to be heard,—that, if they are about to speak the truth, they will deserve a hearing; and, if *error*, we shall have an opportunity at *this*, or another meeting of exposing it." The ministers about the chair hissed and clamored so that I could not be heard. I do not think that hissing at public meetings is a practice very becoming in Christian ministers: It is one which I never adopt, and which I repudiate. The meeting remained in a state of confusion for two or three hours. Another Chairman was chosen, and from that moment we *had free discussion*; and a more orderly and peaceable meeting I never attended,—both parties were heard, and the advocates of New Testament Churches carried their resolutions in the most triumphant manner. From what I saw in the meeting, I incline to think that hearing both sides fully and candidly would put down tumult. If this will not do it, I know of no other remedy. If the friends of good order and liberty will not use their efforts to apply a remedy to these meetings, the town will be absolutely disgraced. For my part, I hate such meetings, with a perfect hatred. They are a reproach to rational beings not to say Christians. They originate in folly, and injure the cause whose interests they are intended to subserve. Why are men afraid of hearing both sides? Are they afraid of the truth? If not, they need not be afraid to hear Catholics oppose Protestantism, or Dissenters publish their views of State Churches, or the latter express theirs against Dissent.

If the views expressed in these letters are correct, the national system of Irish education is good,—it may have errors, but perhaps not so great as the Scottish parochial system. There are two classes of persons in this empire: The first would have the education of the country to continue under the entire management of Established clergymen and churches, while the *nation contributes the funds*. The second—and to this class I blush not to avow my adhesion—would have a NATIONAL SYSTEM OF EDUCATION FOR SCOTLAND AND ENGLAND, as well as for Ireland: so that Dissenters of every grade and churchmen of every hue might have access to the national fount of learning, and their intelligent youth be eligible for teachers in its schools, and their fathers for being directors. It is time that an effectual end be put to the system which taxes us with the funds which supply education, and banishes our children and ourselves from most of its privileges. Were this done, the parish minister would have less power over the parish teacher; and his place would be supplied by a number of judicious lay-directors from all parties. Hoping soon to see the accomplishment of this desirable object, and the cause of Protestantism advocated with Christian temper and spirit,

I remain, yours respectfully,
JOHN BOWES.

NETHERGATE, DUNDEE, January 30, 1837.

It will be seen that I had taken the oversight of the Dundee Church, with the intention of again itinerating as soon as Providence opened the way. My book on Union as well as other labors prove that I had at heart the union of Christians. The following correspondence opened my way to Liverpool, and to many trials and blessings there, as the reader will find as he proceeds, as it led to my removal with fair prospects of great usefulness, it may be given at some length.

LIVERPOOL, 14th February, 1837.
14 Bedford Street, Abercromby Square.

Dear Sir,

Your communication afforded me unfeigned satisfaction, not simply because your views on the subject of Christian Unity of Communion so fully accorded with my own, but because of the joyful intelligence that a truly Christian Church was beginning to rear its head in my native land. During the space of four years subsequent to my conversion to God, it was my daily prayer, "Lord undertake for poor Scotland;" and it was my daily request, "Lord send me." It pleased God to send me into a different field of labor; but blessed be his name, the perusal of your letter satisfied me that he had not only heard, but answered my cry, and the conviction has been revived that in his own good time, he will open an effectual door for me to preach the unsearchable riches of Christ amongst my poor benighted pharisaical countrymen.

I have a hundred questions to put, and I dare say you have as many that you would like me to answer, and we can say more in one hour than we can write in a week; but it is impossible for me to leave home at this time, owing to the multiplicity of my engagements. Dare you undertake a journey to Liverpool? we will most cheerfully pay your expenses, on Sunday the 26th. I have an occasional sermon to preach in Staffordshire; will you on that day take my pulpit? I leave the matter with you and with God, but I trust you will do your utmost to meet our wishes. I took the liberty of reading your letter at our Leaders' meeting last night, and the result was a cordial and unanimous invitation from the meeting for you to preach on that day, and to spend a week with us if possible. We have about one thousand members in society in Liverpool, the greater part of whom have been gathered out of the world during the past year, and all of them profess to be justified by faith, and to have peace with God. Our Chapel will seat about fourteen hundred, but our congregations inside and outside of the house generally exceed two thousand. My brother, do you carry out what is commonly called the revival work? Do you hold penitent meetings after your sermons? And do you make a point of calling upon the church to humble themselves before God if souls be not saved at every service? Are you doing your utmost to raise the standard of personal holiness, which is lamentably low in most Christian churches? If you indeed love the Lord supremely, and if this be your mode of procedure, your reception here will be even more cordial than the invitation that has been given you. But should the case be otherwise—it is not according to my expectation—and any attempt at union, further than the meeting together at the Communion Table, on the common ground of being the children of God, is entirely out of the question. I would not admit a minister to my pulpit simply because he may have correct views of scriptural truth; he must work the work of God; he must preach with the unction of the Holy One and with power; he must in the strength of the Spirit awaken sinners and edify the church, else he cannot minister amongst us. I have thought it right to be thus explicit that there may be no mistake.

Believe me to be your brother in the Lord,
R. AITKEN.

An immediate reply will greatly oblige me.

41 BEDFORD STREET, 4th March, 1837.

MY DEAR BROTHER,

I submitted your communication to the consideration of our Leaders, yesterday, at our Quarterly Meeting, but my engagements are so numerous, and my arrangements connected with my own removal so important and pressing, that I have but a very limited period either for consideration or writing on church affairs. In the first place, I beg to refer you to the declaration contained in my former letter, that I have no power to legislate for the society, I can neither make new laws nor cancel old ones, because the churches are strictly connexional and not independent; and should you desire that our laws and regulations be absolutely and *bona fide* a dead letter, you make a demand upon me and the church that it is entirely out of our power to comply with, we have no such power vested in us, but if you merely wish us to understand that you entertain conscientious scruples touching the observance of certain regulations, which you deem unscriptural; there is a hearty disposition both on the church's part and on mine to meet your views to the extent of our ability; and I have no hesitation in reiterating my former declaration—that the work of God is everything, and that laws are comparatively nothing, either to the society or to myself. And with that openness which ought to characterise every action and procedure of a man of God, I declare to you, that had I not been convinced that there was nothing in us as a body that could retard your usefulness amongst us, and that your Catholicism of spirit was kindred to my own, I never would have consented to have given you an invitation to the highly responsible situation that you have been called upon to occupy. I cannot help feeling and saying, my beloved brother, that while I have many things to cry to God for, you appear to me to have but one thing, and that is that you may be enabled by the grace of God to come up amongst a people full of the Holy Ghost and power, and prepared every way to help you in the fulness of that spirit of power which alone can qualify you for the extension of the kingdom of our blessed Redeemer. I am sorry that the society cannot send you a larger remittance, but they have my family to remove to London, and brother Newcombe's from Nottingham, and consequently their funds for the moment are comparatively low; we are but an infant society, and I thank God that we are able to do so much,—as I never have saved, and never will save one penny either of my private income or of what I may receive from any church. I cannot leave my furniture else I would have gladly done so. If you can convey your furniture to Liverpool at a moderate charge, you had better do so, than dispose of it at a disadvantage. I am very anxious that you should be in Liverpool by the 15th. even should Mr. Parker follow with your family a week after, as I must of necessity open my chapel in London on the 23rd. Mr. Collinson and myself have been traversing the town this morning in search of a suitable house, and we have two or three in our eye, and one of them shall be taken for you. For your strengthening and comfort I beg to state that prayer is being made for us both, of no ordinary character, and I feel the utmost confidence, I believe induced by the Spirit of God, that our union will be for the glory of God, and for the good of thousands of souls.

I am my dear brother, yours very affectionately,

R. AITKEN.

7th March, 1837.

MY DEAR BROTHER,

I have not time to enter into any detail as I am just about to set out for Preston, but I cannot deny myself the pleasure of communicating the fact to you that last night, at our Leaders' meeting, it was unanimously resolved that full power be given to me to enter into negotiations with you on the subject of your becoming the pastor of the Hope Street Chapel Congregation. Much prayer has been offered up that a suitable pastor might be found, and I trust you will see it your duty to give the matter your most prayerful consideration. I believe your sphere of usefulness would be greatly enlarged, and that you will prove the coadjutor that I so much need in reviving vital godliness throughout these lands. I should think that Mr. Reid would be a very suitable person to succeed you in Dundee, but of course all these matters must be subjects of future deliberation.

Give my best respects to Mr. Parker. You may expect to hear from me in the course of ten days, when I shall be able to lay the matter fully before you.

I am your brother in the Lord,

R. AITKEN.

20th March, 1837.

My Dear Brother,

I have received your letter of difficulties and truly it could not have fallen into better hands, I have been so much accustomed to deal with such commodities of late that they must be monster like indeed if they prevent me from grappling with them—Talk of difficulties to a minister of Christ! My brother, if we are to walk in the footsteps of Paul and Apollos and Cephas, of Luther, Wesley, and Whitfield, like them, looking to God we must laugh, not at difficulties, but at impossibilities, and cry it shall be done. Difficulties! I could scarcely keep my soul alive without them; they are my continual schoolmasters, driving me to Christ. Let those choose the shallow waters, whom shallow waters suit; blessed be God, he has taught me to like the rocking of the battlements, and the higher the wind, and the rougher the billow, so much the more do I admire the skillfulness of the Pilot, so much the stronger do I feel my security in the faithfulness of my God. You need not tell me that you will find it a difficult and a painful matter to tear yourself away from your beloved flock at Dundee; It was a painful thing for me to withdraw from the Church of England,—It was painful to leave my sweet and comfortable retirement in the Isle of Man,—It was painful for me to stand out against the Christian world, on the broad principle of salvation or no salvation,—and the most painful circumstance of my life now lies before me, that of being separated from the men who have stood by me in many a hard fought engagement, and from about a thousand children, whom in Christ Jesus I have begotten through the Gospel. I ask of your children, if they be not ricketty ones, more given to talking than to walking, if they ought not by this time to be able to go alone? but as for mine, poor lambs, they are most of them under twelve months old, and my heart is full and my eyes are now flowing at the very thoughts of weaning them. My brother, our beloved Master left the bosom of his Father, and I leave my Liverpool children that God may be glorified in the salvation of sinners and in the conversion of the world. And if you cannot leave Dundee from the same motive and on the same errand, stay where you are, we covet not such assistance. It does not require two minutes to satisfy the man who has lost his will in God's, that your sphere of usefulness would be greatly enlarged by coming to Liverpool, and that is the chief thing which the man of God must look to. We have but once to live, though we must live forever, and amidst the general carnage that Satan is making of immortal souls, that faith is the safest and the best in which we can lead most sons to glory. I defy you or any other man to go beyond me in love to Scotland, but with your limited resources both of men and means what can you do for her; let us but get a good cause in England and this will enable us to support an effective mission in Scotland; you shall then see who shall be first in the field and who shall be the last to quit it, in the struggle for the conversion of my beloved countrymen; a struggle it will be, and a most fearful one, you may depend upon it, before anything like an impression can be made upon Scotland, and it is vain to try the attempt without adequate means; here, and throughout England generally, the fields are truly white unto the harvest, and it is only thrust in thy sickle and reap; but in Scotlond the fallow ground is yet to be broken up, and it is a fallow of so peculiar a quality that every ploughshare will not touch it. If your church be disposed to unite with us it must be heartily and truly; in that case they may have a trial of Mr. Reid for one month, and if the work of God extends under his ministry he may remain, if not, he shall resume his labors at Preston, but I anticipate just as much trouble in removing him from Preston as you from Dundee; the church at Preston are devotedly attached to Mr. Reid and not without reason, he has, in the space of nine months, raised a society out of the world of one hundred and fifty members, and erected a comfortable chapel, and of course, like you and myself, he dearly loves his children; should his arrangements meet the views of your church, I shall do my endeavor to visit them every six weeks in common with our other churches, and do my utmost to help forward the word of God amongst them. In that case we shall commence a society both in Edinburgh and Glasgow as soon as possible, that our journey to the north may serve for all, and that the expense may not be felt by the church at Dundee, but should they prefer their present independent position, and if they can provide themselves with a suitable pastor, I have nothing to urge in the way of objection. It is preachers of the right kind and not congregations that we want, and we can ill spare Mr. Reid in the present increasing state of our society. I have no ambition to increase our number by the addition of one or two churches of saved souls. My object is, and ever will be to do my utmost for the conversion of a sinful world. To draw this part of our subject to a conclusion, I beg to say, that if your present church cannot enter fully into our views, and spiritedly and determinedly take up the conversion work, they will be better without us, and we will be better without them; if, on the contrary, they be men of zeal and devotedness to God, and willing to go all lengths, and to make sacrifice of minor matters for the sake of the cause of God, we shall hail their union with thankfulness, and look upon them as a breach already made in the high wall of prejudice and pharisaism, inviting and demanding a spirited and determined attack upon Scotland. You will easily perceive from the connexional construction of our society, that it is impossible for me to make an advance to meet your own wishes touching matters of polity. But I shall most thankfully lend you my best assistance at our next convocation to improve and amend our laws and regulations, wherever they are found to be unscriptural or ineffective. I thank God, laws are nothing to me, and they are nothing to our societies; and those that have been drawn up will be only a dead letter so long as the word of God continues to progress amongst us, and our hearts continue to be filled with the love of God. Laws are made for evil-doers and men that are filled with the Spirit will neither need them nor be trammelled by them, and if you keep the church alive and direct their energies in attacking the world, and lead them out to strong travailings in birth for the conversion of sinners, you will not need to consult our laws should you be spared to minister amongst us for fifty years, only keep the chapel hot enough and all unruly walkers will quickly expel themselves, they cannot live, my brother, in the holy atmosphere.

The salary that has been fixed upon for the Liverpool preacher is £200 per. annum; we have however taken a Baptist Chapel on loan, in the north end of the town, and Mr. Newcombe, intended for it, must be supported out of the Hope Street funds until by your assistance a society sufficient to support him be raised in that quarter; and I have been requested by the deacons to ask whether you would be satisfied for the first year with £160, on the understanding that the following year it will be raised to £200, of course Mr. Newcombe will be under your direction. You perceive it is the day of sacrifice. I have given up my salary of £200 from Hope Street, and I do not yet know of two members in London to commence with, nevertheless I have no misgivings, God has hitherto supplied my every want and I am satisfied he will go with me to the Metropolis, indeed already I have had ample proof that he has opened a wide and effectual door for me which no man shall shut. Last week I received a letter from a friend in London stating that he had taken a large chapel for me, capable of accomodating two thousand persons, on a lease for twenty-one years, at a very moderate rent. I write from Doncaster, where yesterday we commenced a society with every prospect of success. My interruptions have been very many, and I have written in a haste little suited to the importance of my subject, I must now however leave the matter with you and with God. If I had not the strongest conviction that it is your duty to accept of the call that has been given you, I would not thus have pressed the matter upon you; you must be answerable for your decision at the judgment seat, and no man nor church can share the responsibility with you. I expect to hear from you as soon as possible, and I trust you will be able to take my place, not on Sunday first, but on the following Sabbath. Mr. Reid will supply your place should your people desire it. May God grant that our union may be for the glory of God and our mutual com fort. Amen.

I am, my dear brother, yours in the Lord,

R. AITKEN.

Who, after getting this excellent letter of promise, could have doubted? Nearly all the promises were broken, instead of coming to Dundee once in six weeks, he never came at all.

Extract from my letter of March 27th, 1837, to which the Leaders' Meeting agreed, as well as Mr. Aitken:—

"That we mutually and prayerfully consult about any minor regulations which may bring the United Christian Churches of Scotland, and the Christian Churches of the South of England to be one community, and also to bring all other Christians to union as we have opportunity."

1st April, 1837.

MY DEAR BROTHER,

I have been from home and consequently could not notice your letter sooner. To prevent you from feeling any uneasiness at my silence I have thought it right to drop you this hurried note. Our quarterly meeting will be held on Monday, and *Deo volente* I shall write by Tuesday's post, as it is already advertised that my chapel in London will be opened on the 23rd, if possible you ought to be here on the 10th. I cannot consent to invite Mr. Kennedy to take a part at your ordination. Mr. Kennedy is not only without ordination of any kind, but the body to which he is attached are opposed to ordination in any form, and if we have any regard to consistency either on his part or our own, we can neither give nor can he accept of the invitation. I cannot close my note without saying that I value the compliment as to the youngster's name, we shall have a relationship now both in reality and in name. And Satan, I trust, will have something to do before he can find a spot where the seeds of dissension will grow betwixt parties so united.

I am yours very affectionately,

R. AITKEN.

A few lines from this will show how Mr. Roseman received this step.

DALBEATTIE, 7th April, 1837.

MY DEAR SIR,

Allow me to congratulate you upon your call and the sphere of usefulness and increased comfort on which you are about to enter, most sincerely do I wish and earnestly pray that you may be used as an instrument of good to many souls, and a blessing to the Christian generally. I should have liked more particulars with respect to what they were? with whom connected? and whether or not we were to lose a friend whilst you gained a larger church? or whether we were certain this would lead to a more close and endearing connexion? I flatter you not when I say I have confidence in you, of Mr. Aitken I have never heard much, but what I have heard is favorable; I hope that in the movements that are found in that chapel, call them "Revivals," that there will be found a large proportion of real conversions, though over many of those Christians that are made so easily and so fast, I often rejoice with trembling. . . . .

I remain, my dear Sir, yours as ever,

WM. ROSEMAN.

Mr Kennedy was the Association's minister at Hull.

HULL, 10th April, 1837.

MY VERY DEAR BROTHER,

Since writing you, a thought has entered my mind and has become the subject of my prayerful consideration, I deem it so important as to warrant my troubling you with a letter to state it, that you may reflect upon it, and give me your views as soon as you can form a conclusion on the subject.

It is this:—Could we not form, and through the Divine blessing and our mutual counsels and joint efforts, execute a plan for uniting—first, the Methodist churches, and finally, all the other churches in Britain on the principle of *pure* and *catholic* Christian communion? Your new position will give increased facilities and power to promote that consummation so devoutly to be wished; could we receive the full concurrence of the Rev. Mr. Aitken I would feel sanguine hopes regarding the success of such a project.

Purity of communion I now see must be the first point carried. No proper amalgamation can be effected between the pure metal of converted souls and the dust of the unconverted in the impure and to a great extent nominal churches.

The terms of communion in the Association, I now find by observation and experience, to be far too low. I thought sometime ago the practice would be better than the rule, I now see cause to expect it to be much worse.

It is well that Mr. Aitken has come up to the scriptural standard, perhaps he has expressed that standard in terms admitting of some safe abatement, but he has erred, if at all, on the safer side, so I now think, after seeing the working of the Association system, (you see I am willing to learn) as you are leaving Scotland, if no other worthier and stronger hand take it up, I should like to unfurl there the standard which you have had the honor to bear aloft, its motto Purity and Unity in the Churches of Christ. My views are not perhaps entirely yours, conviction alone can alter my procedure, but I am open to conviction, and long, my dear brother, for a letter from you on the subject of this.

I am yours in the bonds of Christian love,
C. JOHN KENNEDY.

At an Elder's and Deacon's meeting held in Mr. Collinson's, 15 Mount Pleasant, on Thursday, 18th April : present, Brothers M'Conachie, Beatty, Pinnington, Storey, Parnel, Onions, Collinson, Hall, and Newcombe,—the whole of the correspondence between the Rev. R. Aitken and myself, in reference to my becoming the pastor of the Hope Street Congregation, being then read, it was unanimously resolved—"That this meeting will not urge upon Mr. Bowes any single practice in our rules, which he may deem inconsistent with the word of God, and that Mr. Bowes is not to alter any of our accustomed practices, until effected in a constitutional way."

The above resolution was unanimously passed at a Leader's meeting, held April 24th, 1837. I asked, "Do this meeting receive me as the pastor of Hope Street congregation on the conditions stated in my correspondence with the Rev. Robert Aitken ?"

It was unanimously agreed that the whole correspondence be now read, after the reading of which the following answer was unanimously returned.—

"This meeting does receive Mr. Bowes on the conditions expressed in the whole correspondence, with the following exception."

Moved by brother Collinson, seconded by brother Stubbs.

Resolved, "That Mr. Bowes consult the Leader's meeting, when he has an opportunity, before he go from home on the Sabbath, or invite any other minister to preach in Hope Street Chapel, but in case of emergency he supply the pulpit according to his own discretion."

LIVERPOOL, May 8th, 1837.

MY DEAR PHILIP,

You may be surprised if you have not learned that I and my family have removed to Liverpool. I am now the pastor of a Christian church, assembling in Hope Street Chapel, capable of seating near 2000 persons, often containing 2500; built last year. The members, who were chiefly gathered by the blessing of the Lord on the Rev. Robert Aitken's labors, number about 1100. We opened a second chapel in another part of the town on the 23rd of April, the first day of the Lord after my arrival, which was on the 20th of April, with wife and four children, three sons and one daughter; the youngest son, a month old when we came, we name Robert Aitken Bowes. I received an invitation to supply the Hope Street pulpit one Sabbath, which I did on the last Sabbath of February, the result was an unanimous invitation to become their pastor.

Mr. Aitken has opened London, with a Chapel capable of containing 2000 persons; it has only been opened three Sabbaths, and the members exceed 100. About sixty have found peace through believing since I came to Liverpool. We have societies, and generally chapels in Preston, Manchester, Hanley Burslem, Congleton, Leigh, &c.

I left Dundee with regret. When I preached my farewell sermon to the church, half of the people could not get into the chapel. And when I preached my farewell sermon to the town, which I did on Monday morning, 17th April, at 8 o'clock, in the open-air, I suppose we had 2000 people present. The church will go on, and build a new chapel this summer. We added 19 members after it was known that I should leave. May great grace rest upon them all, and may the Lord send them a suitable pastor.

Labor to convert every sinner you meet. There is some talk of an union with the New Connexion Association and the Christian Society. I know not the result.

The Methodists do wrong in receiving unjustified, unsaved persons to membership; this we do not, and will not do when we know it.

To P. Bellwood.   JOHN BOWES.

It began to appear thus early, as this letter testifies, that our objects were different. I wished union with all Christians; he, to establish a Connexion, of which he was to be the head, as much as John Wesley was over his societies.

                      9 BARRATT GROVE, KINGSLAND ROAD,
                                16th May, 1837.

DEAR BROTHER,—

I am thankful that, as I have had no official communication from the elders of the church in Hope Street respecting your overtures to the Wesleyan Association, I feel myself at liberty to write to you in confidence, as a friend and brother, and not as minister of the district. The private intelligence that I have received has exceedingly surprised and pained me. From Mr. Collinson's letter, I concluded that you had pledged yourself not to disturb our order, nor interfere with our polity, until Convocation, when you would have the opportunity of submitting your views to the consideration of your brethren. This arrangement was so perfectly satisfactory to me, and knowing, as I did, that the church was in so healthful a state, I had everything to hope, and nothing to fear, for your success, and for the prosperity of the cause of God in Liverpool. In the midst of labors, anxieties, difficulties, and persecutions of no ordinary kind, but which I had fully made up my mind to meet and to grapple with in London, it was the continued solace of my mind—the battle is fought and the battle is won at Liverpool—judge ye what my feelings must have been, when I received the information that the church which was my comfort and my joy, was attempted to be agitated by a question of union, and with whom?—Why, with a body of men of whom it is not too much for me to say—that it is my conviction that neither the church in Hope Street nor myself have one feeling in common.

Had I and the men who united with me to form the Christian Society, been capable of drinking of the spirit of the Association, and of acting in concert with them, the Christian Society would never have had an existence through our agency. But enough,—I have not time either to write or to read long letters, and I will not have my mind diverted from the great work to which my Master has called me by discussing the expediency of an union as unpracticable and ridiculous as would be the attempted incorporation of fire and water—life and death. I beg of you as a friend, a Christian, and a minister, to direct your own energies, and that of the church, to the salvation of the thousands of perishing souls round you. If at our Convocation you are satisfied that you would be more useful in a different sphere, there is nothing to prevent you from pursuing your own course; but I am convinced that you are where God would have you to be, and that there are few ministers in England who have such an opportunity of exercising their ministry so profitably, and with so much comfort.

If you are determined to persist in your present course, tell me with that openness and candor which ought ever to characterise the proceedings of a minister of Christ and a man of God, and I will immediately resume my station in Liverpool until I can procure a suitable minister for that important charge. I thank God that he has already raised up several preachers here, and although the cause will unquestionably suffer a temporary injury by my leaving it, still the work will not be undone that has been done. My mind is fixed, and upon your answer will the course of my procedure entirely depend. In the hope that God will direct you in this and in every matter, I am, your brother in Christ,

                                               R. AITKEN.

---

                                11 VINE STREET, LIVERPOOL.
                                       14th June, 1837.

DEAR BROTHER,

I did not answer your letter of the 16th of May, as I conjectured that it arose from mis-information, and by allowing a little time to pass I concluded the mistake would be corrected, especially as at the time of your writing you had not received my letter giving some account of the state of Liverpool, Leigh, Manchester, &c. And as I submitted the letter to three of the Leaders, who assured me that they would write and give you correct information, &c., that it had been supplied by others, they also desired me to delay writing. However as you take no notice of having ever received a letter from me, and as you do not write to tell me that you have got other information, I shall proceed in the fear of my Master to answer yours of the 16th of May. You say, "The private intelligence I have received has exceedingly surprised and pained me." To this I can only say, that when I know who communicated that intelligence? and what it was? I can tell better how to treat it. As it regards the prosperity of Hope Street, and there being nothing to fear from the church. I readily acknowledge with gratitude to God that there was prosperity, and had the Leaders and other office-bearers had the correspondence on which I came, read and explained to them before I came, &c., had they agreed to that correspondence, several painful things through which I have passed perhaps would never have occurred. Sometimes I am told that every mind is satisfied in the society, and that all is well; and anon, by a few I am viewed with suspicion, but I mind it not; I am the Lord's servant, and as various opinions and unworthy suspicions were entertained about my Master, why should I, his servant, complain; I am prepared to suffer his will, and if I mistake not, to die if necessary in his cause.

I know you must have had a great deal to endure in opening London, and I have spared your feelings as much as I could, for we should rather "bear each other's burdens" than make them heavier.

As to the proposal of union with the Association of which you speak, take the following brief narrative of facts. I wished to establish an *open-air preaching union* among all orthodox Christians, the minister of each chapel taking his turn at a given place. Mr. Jackson of Manchester and I waited on Messrs Peters and Jones the only ministers known to me excepting Dr. Raffles, who was, and is out of the town. In addition to the open-air preaching, I proposed that they should assist me in getting up a Union Love-feast, to be held quarterly in any large chapel belonging to any Christian denomination willing to accept it. This was all the union that I ever proposed to the Leaders in Hope Street, or to Messrs Jones and Peters. They, however, suggested the propriety of an occasional exchange of pulpits as a preparatory step, and declined the other till it should be taken. I saw no objection to their proposal, and as they promised to submit the whole case to their Leaders' meetings, I promised to bring before ours, open-air preaching, a union Love-feast, and to state their proposal of an exchange of pulpits. The result was that our Leader's meeting agreed to the open-air plan without a dissenting vote, *twelve* voted for the union Love-feast, and *sixteen* against it, and as nearly the whole seemed against an exchange of pulpits the subject went to quiet sleep, and thus it might remain, but as some of your expressions are strong, and to me unaccountable, perhaps I may be allowed to solicit explanation. You say, concerning the Association, "It is not too much for me to say, that it is my conviction that neither the church in Hope Street nor myself have one feeling in common." I would say, if I understand this sentence, then either the one party or the other cannot be designated "children of God." If you and the Hope Street people and the Association generally, are not children of God, my views are too charitable, and if you are, have you no feeling in common? Paul will tell, "Endeavoring to keep the unity of the Spirit in the bond of peace. *There* is one body, and one Spirit, even as ye are called in one hope of your calling, one Lord, one faith, one baptism, one God and Father of all, who is above all, and through all, and *in* you all." Eph. iv. 3 6. If you are *one body*, influenced by *one spirit*, if you have *one hope, one Lord, one faith, one baptism, one God and Father*, then I think you must have many feelings "in common."

You ask, "If you are determined to persist in your present course, tell me with that openness and candor which ought ever to characterise the proceeding of a minister of Christ and of a man of God, and I will immediately resume my station in Liverpool until I can procure a minister for that important charge?" To which I reply, "I am determined to persist in my present course," and that, by God's grace, to my life's end. If that course has been misrepresented to you, it is no concern of mine; and it is because I am convinced that I have acted honorably and faithfully to Christ, that I say I shall go on. Nevertheless, if I have erred in any matter, I say to God and men, "What I know not, teach me." I might say more, but as I expect to see you soon, let this suffice; and let me hope that you will be prepared, when we meet, to consider, or offer for consideration, some plan by which we may mutually understand each other, that the cause of Christ may advance.

June 4th, I preached at HANLEY in the morning; BURSLEM, in the purchased chapel, at 2 and 6. Three gave themselves to God. At half-past nine in the evening, I preached, the fourth time, in the market-place. Also on Monday evening at 7½. One young gentleman, who for years had listened to the Independents, while I proved in the evening sermon that every man can obey God if he will, felt he had been wrongly taught. June 5th, in Hanley market-place; about 2000 people; seven found Christ in the penitent meeting. June 6th. At STOKE; preached in the room, made the collection, and then preached to several hundreds in the street; several penitents. June 7th. Lectured on the necessity of the Lord's people uniting in order to convert a guilty world, in BURSLEM new Sunday-school. June 8th. Preached at TUNSTALL at mid-day, to several hundreds, in the market-place. Also at Congleton market-place at 7 p.m., to about 1000 people. A constable ordered me down, asserting that the road was stopped, and it was nearly stopped from side to side, but the people made way; the constable threatened to take me into custody. I took the vote of the congregation, whether the road was stopped, and nearly all held up their hands to the negative of this proposition. This silenced him, and I finished in peace; and at 8½ preached in the house, which was crowded. June 11th. Three times in the chapel, PRESTON; at 4 p.m. in the market-place. A full chapel at six. June 12th. Market-place at half-past 5 in the morning. Orchard, at mid-day; scores of Catholics, and some opposition. *A shower of love* in the chapel at night. Glory be to God. Yesterday I returned home, having preached 12 times in five days in the Potteries, and 7 times in two days at Preston. You see, therefore, that I have now visited, at your request, every church, except Altringham, and they are hopefully prosperous. Let ministers of the *right sort* be obtained for the places that shall in future be opened, and a few changes be made in the regulations of the society; as for instance, leaving out—"The Christian Society in connection with the Rev. R. Aitken," * and also taking Mr. Wesley as an authority in doctrine, and I hope great things. Your *misrepresented* or *misunderstood* fellow-laborer in Christ,

To R. Aitken. JOHN BOWES.

P.S.—Your letter to the Leaders, &c., was duly read to them, and I understand they have agreed to consider it at the Quarter Day. I have been from home at the last two meetings. Mr. Reid has spent two Sabbaths with my late beloved flock.—J.B.

HOW I BECAME A TOTAL ABSTAINER.

The Temperance Society was about to hold its Annual Festival. A deputation waited on me to ask me to preside. My objection was that there might be some little nutriment in ale, porter, and wine, and as the society's pledge condemned all these, our principles were at variance, and if the speakers should say any thing contrary to my views, I might express my sentiments. They said I was already very near them, that I took so little, and that they would be glad that I should preside, giving me all possible latitude, even to oppose them, if I saw any reason. I consented. The meeting was large. Edward Holmes was an early speaker, a young married man, with two children; he addressed the meeting with a cheerful countenance, but sometimes with weeping eyes, in, as nearly as I can recollect, the following terms:—"When I and my wife got married, we had a little money, but it was going fast, as I drank, not so much as some, but too much. One night I was passing ——— Chapel. There was a Total Abstinence meeting. The speeches convinced me that I was wrong. I signed the pledge. When I got home, I said to my wife, 'What do'st think?' 'I don't know.' 'I've signed teetotal.' 'Thou'lt keep it till morning.' It was then too late to go out and get any more drink. I went up stairs, half drunk as I was, kneeled down, and if ever I prayed earnestly to God for

---

* To show him personal regard, although I was unwilling to put his name on God's church, I had called my son after him.

anything in my life, I prayed that God would help me to keep it, I knew I could not keep it myself. About a fortnight after I was passing the same chapel again. It was a sermon; I thought as I got good before, I might again; the preacher was showing that sinners, great sinners might be saved since Jesus died for the chief of sinners. I got hope, believed in Christ, and found peace. When I was converted there was not one of our large family in the way to heaven, and now we are 16 of us, and nearly all here to-day." I know several of this large family; several have gone to heaven, some are in America, some yet in England; some of them for 34 years I count among my dearest friends.

I saw this society was accomplishing objects on which I had set my heart; making men sober, and after that becoming rational, they were led to the Gospel and to Christ. I said, "If you go on this way I will join you till Christmas." So I did, here is the pledge :—" Temperance Society, Hope Street Chapel. Total Abstinence Pledge. We agree to abstain from all Intoxicating Drinks; such as Rum, Brandy, Gin, Whisky, Ale, Porter, Cider, Spirit Cordials, and Wine; except used Medicinally, or in Religious Ordinances; and to discountenance the Cause and Practice of Intemperance.—JOHN BOWES.—Liverpool, July 19, 1837."

I joined the general society July, 21st 1837, without any limitation as to time, and never regretted it.

Sentiments uttered by the Rev. Robert Aitken, A.M., at the Convocation, September, 1837.

"Mr. Bowes never had the spirituality to be a minister of this church. I believe him too full of pride. [To Mr. Bowes,] You have spoken like a natural man; if you had got more of the Spirit of God you would unite with us. An union in the way Mr. Bowes views it would be death. Mr. Bowes is only probationary with us and should sit and hear. If I am to be minister of the District I must have power; the controversy is about power; Mr. Bowes and I differ on this subject. You must come to us, we will not come to you. [In reference to the people expressing an opinion about a minister's removal,] I do intend to set my face against any such radical proceeding. My determination is to look for a supply of our pulpits from those men of the Episcopal Church who have been accustomed to subordination. I will not have the societies made nests of political demagogues. Before I would suffer that spirit to come into the society I would separate from it. Many of the people coming over from Methodism are Devils. I am as perfectly satisfied that Teetotalism is from hell, as Brother Bridges."

TERMS OFFERED AT CONVOCATION.

1. The conditions upon which the Christian Society and Mr. Bowes can be united, as required upon the part of the Christian Society, are as follows, viz:—That the Rev. Mr. Bowes shall, for *one whole year*, refrain from agitating the Union either in public or private, with members of the Christian Society, and shall confine himself to preaching the truth of the Gospel of Christ.

2. That the Rev. Mr. Bowes shall be under the minister of the District, whoever that minister may be, and shall submit to whatever regulations and plans the minister of the District may lay down.

3. The Convocation is united in its decision that no alteration shall be made as it regards the title affixed to the rules, to which decision the Rev. Mr. Bowes is also expected to comply.

Mr. Bowes cannot accede to any of the above named propositions,

11 VINE STREET, LIVERPOOL,
November 10, 1837.

MY DEAR BROTHER,

I herewith send you £5. Come as soon as ever you can. Mr. Matthews has not come nor is he likely to come. Perhaps you may spend a few weeks with us in Liverpool before you open any other place. We have preaching every night in Cockspur Street, souls are being daily saved. Give our kindest regards to all friends; can you not bring letters from Messrs. Menmuir, Allan, Stratton, &c., also to Mrs. Bowes from Mrs. Barrie, Saunders, Mitchelson, &c., also from the Rev. George Reid.

I should think you may be here by the next Friday or Saturday. I was laying the foundation of a new chapel at Altringham last Monday. We are now all exceedingly agreeable and happy in Liverpool.

The Lord come with you. Amen. I bless God for sending me the £5 from a very unexpected quarter.

Yours in Christ forever. Amen.

JOHN BOWES.

To P. G. Anderson.

[OFFICIAL.]

November, 20, 1837.

DEAR BROTHER,

We have found it a more difficult matter to supply Mr. Matthew's place at Bedford, than we had expected. I go to Bedford to expedite the arrangement, and if Mr. Matthews cannot be with you before this day fortnight, Mr. Bridges, whom God has evidently called to the ministry, will supply his place at Liverpool, until he can take his own appointment. I write merely to allay your anxiety. I am greatly better as respects my health, blessed be God.

Yours very affectionately,

To J. Bowes.
R. AITKEN.

LIVERPOOL, Nov. 28, 1837.

DEAR BROTHER,

Your communication of the 20th, in reference to the Rev. Mr. Matthews' or Bridges' coming to Liverpool was submitted to our Leaders' Meeting last night, when it was unanimously resolved "That as Brother Storey has agreed to assist Mr. Bowes in the delivery of the tickets, and as we expect Mr. Aitken to visit us in the course of the next month, according to promise, that we remain without any farther ministerial assistance until the next quarter-day, when we shall take into consideration the propriety of employing another minister if our funds will allow it. And that Mr. Aitken be requested to reply to the letter of our Secretary, Mr. Fletcher, as soon as possible, fixing the time when we may expect him."

The feeling of the meeting was that should another minister, whether Mr. Bridges or any other, be deemed necessary, in the event of Mr. Matthews not coming, that he should be elected by the Leaders' meetings.

Yours in the bonds of brotherly love.

To R. Aitken.
JOHN BOWES.

3rd December, 1837.

DEAR BROTHER,—

I have been much distressed by the obstacles that have arisen to Mr. Matthews' removal from Bedford. The lady who has the mortgage upon his church, persists in her determination to call in her money if Mr. Matthews be removed, and as the premises are not worth the amount of mortgage, at least would not sell for the amount, the trustees would be most seriously injured by such a mode of proceeding. Until a final settlement can be come to, it will be well to secure the assistance of Dr. Burrows; he can still attend to the duties of his profession and assist you on Sundays, and occasionally on week nights. On the subject of remuneration for his services, I would say that until he is regularly received amongst us as a preacher, he had better leave the matter entirely to the church, and if the church give him ten pounds per quarter, I would consider it a fair remuneration; because the Doctor would have his own business to depend upon, and the prospect of enlarged usefulness. This arrangment would give you a fair opportunity for recruiting your funds. I will furnish the Deacons with a list of the places to which the Rules were sent, at my earliest convenience. The work of God is steadily progressing here. We have built three new vestries, and we are now in better working trim as to room than you are in Liverpool. We have not less than fifty conversions weekly; but we cannot now accommodate them at White's Row; there we are full. We have three smaller chapels, and are commencing in earnest to raise funds for our new chapel. But what we have most to be grateful for, is the state of the society. A number of our members have evidently received the teachings of the Spirit, and the church *en masse* is earnestly panting after it. Glory be to God. I will give you a week's notice before I visit you, and shall do my utmost to name an early day. I think it will be on the second Sabbath in the year. Yours in haste, but very affectionately,

To J. Bowes.   R. AITKEN.

DEAR BROTHER,—   26th Decr., 1837.

As I must spend some time in the Potteries, I shall not be able to reach Liverpool before Sunday the 21st; you may advertise me for that day. I thank God that the Lord's arm is indeed made bare in London. The spirituality of our older members is beyond anything I have ever heard or read of, save in the Bible. Truly the Apostolic day is returning, and God is being glorified in a holy people. Yesterday morning at 5 o'clock, a lovefeast was held, and the body of the large chapel was well filled, and the experience of the speakers was such as I am persuaded has not been known in the church for centuries. To God be all the glory. Our services yesterday were attended with extraordinary unction and power, and the attendance was as crowded throughout the day as on Sunday. I should think that we have from 800 to 1000 communicants. The number of penitents every meeting seldom under twenty, and oftentimes double that number. We only want ministerial aid to plant churches in every part of the metropolis, and numbers who have been converted at White's Row, but who cannot meet with us on account of the distance, are waiting with anxiety to rally around the standard whenever an opening shall be made. I have at present a young clergyman with me who has lately been converted to God. He has preached for me, and will continue to do so occasionally; but he has everything to learn. He finds it hard work to throw away his notes, but I have good hopes that he will be an useful man. To raise the gospel standard, the ministerial standard must first be raised, and from henceforth no man shall be admitted a minister amongst us unless he be eminent for holiness Mr. Courteney, the clergyman alluded to, is decidedly pious in the true sense of the word; he is a single man, and of liberal fortune.

On the subject of Mr. Anderson, you are already in possession of my opinion. I am quite sure that, in his present state, he is not qualified to raise a cause in Chester or anywhere else. As to his assisting you in Liverpool, the thing is entirely out of the question, and it has my most decided negative. We hold this day (Tuesday) as a fast day for the whole church, and there will be services from 9 in the morning to 10 at night. This will be the third successive day spent by our dear people in the house of the Lord. Read this hurried epistle at your Leaders' meeting, it may stir them up to increase their efforts to promote the cause of their Redeemer. Your brother in Christ,

To J. Bowes.   R. AITKEN.

This letter will explain both Mr. Aitken's claims of authority, and how we met them.

LIVERPOOL, Dec. 29th, 1837.

DEAR BROTHER,—

As everything has gone on comfortably and prosperously since the Convocation, and being loath to hazard anything before the Leaders' meeting which might cause needless agitation, I deemed it prudent to submit your letter of the 26th to the consideration of an Elders' meeting, which was held last night in Hope Street. The result is, that I was unanimously requested to state to you, that they think it almost certain that you must have been the subject of mistake or misapprehension when you penned the following part of your otherwise acceptable letter. —"And from *henceforth* no man shall be admitted a minister amongst us unless he be eminent for holiness. . . . On the subject of Mr. Anderson, you are already in possession of my opinion. I am quite sure that in his present state he is not qualified to raise a cause in Chester or anywhere else. As to his assisting you in Liverpool, the thing is entirely out of the question, and it has my most decided negative. . . . Read this hurried epistle at your Leaders' meeting." The Elders suppose that you have not been informed that the Connexional Committee, appointed by the Convocation to manage matters in the North District, have unanimously requested Mr. Anderson to become a preacher or minister among us, in consideration of his having lost his late charge through supplying one of our pulpits; and some of the elders thought it possible that, if you had been informed of what the Connexional Committee had done, you might be ignorant of what the Liverpool Leaders' Meeting had requested, viz.—that Mr. Anderson labor among them till Quarter Day, on the understanding that he might then be either continued or not. You remember, Convocation appointed this Committee to consist of Mr. Matthews, myself, and Mr. Newcombe. In the absence of Mr. Matthews, we appointed Mr. Bertram to act in his place. You remember that one particular part of the business of this Committee was to examine and call out ministers, (to be subject to the refusal or acceptance of Convocation) as well as to appoint missionaries for new fields of labor.

Now you will easily see that, according to the appointment of Convocation, if the Committee meet and do business, and expend money for the conversion of souls, and the glory of God, it will not be consistent with our "striving together for the faith of the gospel," for you to attempt to undo what has been constitutionally done, or prevent the free choice of the Leaders' Meeting. We are as anxious as you can be on the point of piety, and shall do all we can to prevent any man whose piety—not to say moral character—is dubious, from having any place among us. As to Mr. Anderson's piety, my acquaintance with him is not that of a day. I have been acquainted with him for several years, and a more devout, consistent minister, and one that spends so much time in communion with God, I have not known. I have confidence in God, that he will overrule this, and all other matters, for his own unperishable glory and the furtherance of his blessed gospel. In the bonds and love of which I am yours,

To R. Aitken. JOHN BOWES.

P.S.—We shall advertise for your being here at the time specified in your letter, and may the Lord bring you " in the fulness of the blessing of the Gospel of Christ." J.B.

This year I published—" Christian Union: Two Lectures on the Unity of the Church; delivered in the Nethergate Chapel, Dundee, Nov. 28th, and Dec. 12th, 1836. Reprinted from the *Christian Advocate* Newspaper."

January 3, 1838.

My Brother,

In reply to your letter I beg to say that I cannot recognise your appointment as minister of the Northern District, by whomsoever it may have been made, and without a minister of the District there can be no connexional committee. I have again written to Mr. Matthews to insist that he shall either without delay take his station at Liverpool, or officially resign his appointment as minister of the District, that another may be appointed in his place, but until this be done by the preachers of the District, whose province it is to elect the minister of the District, I feel it my duty to protest against the proceedings of the self-constituted connexional committee; and, as president of the Convocation, I also protest against the attempt that is being made to appoint Mr. Anderson, a preacher in the Liverpool circuit; as I am responsible to Convocation for this exercise of authority, you will see a good reason why I thus write to you officially, instead of condescending to terms of entreaty, which, under different circumstances, would have better suited my spirit and inclination.

I am your brother in Christ,

To J. Bowes. R. AITKEN.

As my communications with Mr. Matthews and the preachers of the Northern District may retard my anticipations for leaving London, you must not advertise me for Liverpool until you again hear from me.

This letter proves, as well as others, that my dear, and only brother was trusting in the Rock.

BRADFORD, January, 26th, 1838.

DEAR JOHN,—

It is now a long time since I had the pleasure of hearing from you. I had intended to have come over to Liverpool this Christmas, but the weather came on very severe which put a stop to my intended journey. I still feel determined to live more to God, and to give him all my heart; there are but two places for us after death, we must either go to heaven or hell, and I feel determined to live for heaven; I have felt the Lord blessing my soul while I have waited on him; it is a great mercy that the Lord has spared me, and has not cut me off in my sins, while I was trampling on his precious blood. O how many years have gone into eternity, and gone forever, which I have lost; may the Lord help me to live to him for the future.

. . . . We are doing pretty well both for this world and the next, may the Lord keep both you and me and all our families from evil.

From your loving brother,
EDWARD BOWES.

LIVERPOOL, January 31, 1838.

MY DEAR BROTHER,—

As you desired me to write if anything extraordinary occurred on Mr. Aitken's coming down, I cheerfully do so, though with a heavy heart.

Mr. Newcombe was with him nearly all the day on Saturday; on Sabbath morning in the course of his sermon he referred to a minister having less holiness than he (Mr. A.) thought requisite, and Mr. Aitken said, he would not only destroy the life of religion in the church where he resided, but also in other towns, "therefore" said he, "cast him off," and he called upon the church to cast him out, and as many of our brethren here say, he meant what he said, and wished the church here to cast me out; whether two or three of the brethren thought they should please him by attempting "to cast me out" or not, I cannot say, but on Monday they requested about twenty brethren to meet him at Mr. Goff's to take tea, and there a plan was laid for effecting his purpose. I knew nothing of all this; evening arrived, I was opening the Leaders' meeting when the doorkeeper informed me that Mr. Aitken wanted to speak to me, he stated, on my going, that twenty men had waited upon him, and stated, that either I must be removed, or they would leave, and put it to me whether I would not leave, as they would give me £40 or £50 if I would. I referred the matter to the will of God, and returned; the business went on agreeably, as all our business now does, except when disturbed by his letters, until past nine o'clock, when the matter began to be opened; but instead of twenty men stating that they would leave the society, if I did not leave, only two or three had stated it, so that there was an attempt made to impose upon me; Mr. Aitken himself got so ashamed of it that he said he would not have entered into the business had he considered me a pastor, but he did not, although, as you know, that office I brought with me, and have exercised ever since, as well as for many years before; he charged me with some false things about dividing the classes and increasing the trustees, and bringing Mr. Anderson, and denied that there had been much writing between him and the brethren of the twenty, and said some awful words, such as, "From this night either you must leave, or my connexion with this church ceases." "I must now state that I can no longer regard Mr. Bowes as a brother." The result is that everything is thrown into excitement. Those that speak to me say that the proceedings of the twenty were so wrong that I have nothing to fear, and that I ought to stand my ground and not resign; this I feel determined to do by God's grace, I am a shepherd and shall not flee as an hireling when there is danger. I am wonderfully supported although I feel much for the church, may God send deliverance, he is with me and my righteous cause, and takes what is done to me as done to himself. "Gird up your loins my brother," and if Mr. Aitken call the ministers of the District to a meeting, which he talks of doing, he will not perhaps call me, in that case perhaps you will let me know. I consider myself a minister of the connexion and shall act as such. I told Mr. Aitken and the Leaders' meeting that if I thought that it was the will of the members and ministers of the society to submit to his will as the only law, and that we should have no government but his will, I would not submit to be in the body, but I did not believe that the ministers and members were so minded. He goes to Leigh to open the chapel on Friday, Manchester on Sunday, Altringham on Monday, Newcombe on Friday; I go on Sabbath, and you on Monday. It may be necessary for the committee to meet at Altringham on Friday or Saturday, but I will write you if necessary; I hope you will come to Altringham as early on Monday as you can. Let us pray much, commit our cause to God and all will be well. I shall not allow myself to speak all I think about the shameful proceedings of Mr. Aitken and his friends, but I shall keep a record of them, and publish them, if for God's glory.

Your very affectionate unslain brother,

To the Rev. J. Bertram.   JOHN BOWES.

"On Feb. 2nd, 1838, at a special Leaders' meeting, held in Hope Street Chapel, Rev. R. Aitken in the chair, it was unanimously resolved that the Rev. J. Bowes be sent to mission Birmingham, and that his salary be paid until he can raise a Society to support his family; it being understood that his appointment by the Convocation be not meddled with.   (Signed) R. AITKEN."

"Copy of the Resolution given him (Mr. Bowes) by order of the Leaders' Meeting, Feb. 13th, 1838.   CHAS. PURNELL, Sec.'

MY BROTHER,—

I beg that you will forthwith proceed to Birmingham; else you will entirely put it out of my power to assist you in any way. I know not what construction to put upon your conduct. I can account for it in no other way than that your mind is distracted by the occurrences of last week, and you know not what you are doing. For your own sake, and for the church's sake, I entreat you to leave Liverpool with all expedition, and let us have no more of these heart-rending proceedings. Your friend and brother for Christ's sake,

Sheffield, 6th Feb., 1838.   R. AITKEN.

To J. Bowes.

LIVERPOOL, Feb. 9, 1838.

REVEREND SIR,—

We have received a communication from Mr. Aitken, requesting us to act upon the Resolution passed at the Trustee Meeting on the 31st January last, which was as follows:—Resolution, "That Messrs Boumphrey and Beatty be appointed to prohibit the Rev. J. Bowes from occupying the pulpit of Hope Street Chapel, should Mr. Aitken find it necessary to advise such a proceeding." Therefore, in accordance with the above resolution, we hereby respectfully request that you will forthwith vacate the pulpit. Yours respectfully,

JOSEPH BOUMPHREY.
ROBERT BEATTY.

To J. Bowes.

[REPLY TO TRUSTEES.]

DEAR SIRS,—   Feb. 13th.

Yours of the 9th curt., prohibiting me "from occupying the pulpit of Hope Street Chapel," would have met with earlier attention, had I not been from home the last three days. I write to say, that it is an unwarrantable interference, with which I cannot comply, for the following reasons:—

1st. At a special Leaders' Meeting, at which the Rev. R. Aitken was present, held Feb. 2nd, 1838, it was unanimously resolved—"That the Rev. J. Bowes be sent to mission Birmingham, and that his salary be paid until he can raise a society to support his family: it being understood that his appointment by the Convocation be not meddled with."

2nd. I refer you to the Minutes in the large Rules, page 48, anent Trustees, &c.

Yours very truly,

11 Vine Street.   JOHN BOWES.
To Messrs Boumphrey and Beatty.

"Hope Street Chapel. Special Leaders' Meeting, Feb. 13th.

"Resolved—that the Rev. J. Bowes take the Chair. A letter read from Rev. R. Aitken concerning Mr. Bromley.

"Resolved—that brethren Landers, Goff, and Varty, be a deputation to wait on the Rev. Mr. Bromley, requesting him to preach in Hope Street Chapel next Sunday, 18th curt. Brother Purnell to go if Brother Goff cannot get away.

"Resolved—that rule on 48th page, beginning 'Trustees shall not attempt, &c.,' be abided by.

"Resolved—that a society meeting be held in Hope Street Chapel, on Tuesday next, at 7 o'clock. Notices read at Hope Street by Brother Pearson; Heath Street, by Holmes; Cockspur Street, by Purnell. Form of minute—'That a meeting of Society be called on Tuesday evening, at 7 o'clock, according to Rule on page 48, anent Trustees, &c., to consider whether the Rev. John Bowes be retained Pastor of Society in Liverpool or not.'

"Resolved—Brethren Landers and Crannel be door-keepers, and Brother Bowes be present at Society Meeting.

"JOHN BOWES, President.
"CHAS. PURNELL, Secretary."

Monday, 13th February, 1838.

DEAR BROTHER,—

Your letter has greatly relieved my mind, although I cannot help thinking that you acted inconsiderately in bringing subjects before the people which were sure to cause agitation and strife. If you will shew this note to Mr. Goff he will immediately, on my responsibility, advance you the money subscribed for the Birmingham Mission. As I have much work on hand you will oblige me if you do not call for my assistance at Birmingham until ten days or a fortnight after your opening.

Your brother in Christ,
To J. Bowes.   R. AITKEN.

OPENING OF BATTY'S CIRCUS, BIRMINGHAM, FOR PREACHING THE GOSPEL.

Feb. 18*th.*—Preaching in such a building as this, is an occurrence so rare, if not unprecedented, as to call for some explanation or reason.

1. My brother and I have been sent hither to preach, under the conviction that ministers of the gospel have a travelling commission: "Go ye out into all the world," &c. But if this be a reason for our coming to BIRMINGHAM, from Liverpool, it is perhaps not evident that it justifies our appearance in this place—a circus.

2. We traversed this populous town for a considerable part of two days, and could not procure any chapel, hall, or large room, in which to proclaim the unsearchable riches of Christ, and therefore it was necessity that compelled us to take this place.

3. The *novelty* of the proceeding is an argument in its favor; for the very novelty may arouse the torpor of sluggish minds—sluggish I mean as to the claims of our holy religion, and lead them to hear that gospel in this place, which they refuse to attend in regular places of public devotion, and if souls get renovated by the word and Spirit of the living God this day, or on any other future occasion, facts will vindicate and justify our proceedings.

4. If I shall be told, that this place is not holy, and that religious services should be conducted in holy places, I reply, that, as to absolute

holiness, I have yet to learn that one plank, or window, or roof, or building, of brick, stone, or wood, is holier than another. God says, "Wherever my name is recorded," and it will be recorded here to-day, "I will come unto thee, and bless thee." Dismiss from your minds the idea that holiness, which in God is moral excellency, and in his creatures, obedience to his law, can exist in unconscious matter, such as wood, and lime, and stone. Dismiss from your minds the opinion, if such you ever entertained, that God cannot enlighten you here. He is not confined to temples made with hands. In the days of Wesley and Whitfield, not a few were reclaimed by hearing of Christ in the fields, lanes, and market-places, and we cannot regard this place as more unfriendly to our object. Only let the Lord's people keep serious, stay their minds on God, pray to him as fervently, and sing as gratefully as they would do in a regular church or chapel, and I promise them as great a blessing from my Master as though they were convened in the most superb cathedral, or splendidly adorned chapel.

And as to those of you who do not yet rank in the honored class of children of God, I address you as men, as reasonable beings. As you have not yet obtained holiness of heart, notwithstanding your attendance on public worship, for you to pretend that such is your love of holiness that you can derive no spiritual advantage from the services of this place, would be no better than downright hypocrisy. If you have such a great regard for holiness, why do you not get it into your hearts? If you pay such deference to holy places, why do you not get your heart made clean, that it may be a place for God to dwell in?

Let all keep their minds stayed on what may be read, preached, or prayed, and no doubt God will respect us here, and bless our preaching, as he did Paul's at Athens on Mars Hill.—*My Apology before sermon.*

LONDON, 19th February, 1838.

To the Rev. John Bowes,
SIR,

It is my most painful duty to suspend you from the office of stipendiary minister to the church and congregation, assembling in Hope Street Chapel, Liverpool, to which you were appointed by Convocation, and you are hereby suspended until the District meeting shall investigate your conduct in reference to your late proceedings in the church, assembling in Hope Street Chapel. Witness my hand this 19th day of February 1868.

R. AITKEN.
President of the Convocation and acting as minister *pro tem.* of the Northern District.

(Witness.) W. Collinson.

BIRMINGHAM, March 1, 1838.

To the Rev. Robert Aitken. A.M.
DEAR SIR,

Yesterday, by the hands of Messrs Goff and Varty of Liverpool, I received a letter from you, dated the 20th of February, with that date scratched out in two places, and the 19th put in. Without staying to inquire why a letter containing my expulsion, or suspension, should have been known by the Liverpool Leaders' meeting, and caused the expulsion of from twelve to twenty Leaders *at your request*, several days or near a fortnight before I received it, I proceed in the fear of God, and in the eye of my Master, Christ, to bring to your remembrance *a collection of facts.* It was twelve months ago the last Lord's day, since, at your request, I came overfrom Scotland; in the course of a few hours' interview you informed me that it was probable the Hope Street Church would give me a call, this led me to state that I had read over your rules, and that of several things I disapproved, such as your name being attached to the society—the power of the minister of the District to suspend a minister, &c. &c. &c.

This last, you endeavored to persuade me, only applied to cases of immorality, and would never affect me, however we might differ in our views.

Now you suspend me on this identical rule! of course, this is one reason why I shall not consider myself suspended.

2ndly. *You are not the minister of this District*, and cannot suspend me, for according to a letter of your own, in my possession, a minister of this District must be chosen by the ministers of the District, which has not been done, and according to Rule, cannot be done.

3rdly. When I asked, at a Leaders' meeting hereafter named, if you or the Leaders had any charges against me as reasons why you wished me removed, both you and they, again and again, said *none*, now it seems a strange proceeding to suspend a minister of Christ without a charge!

4thly. I dare not resign my charge, for at a church meeting last week, I am told by letter that a motion was carried by "the great majority" of the church for my continuance as their pastor.

But to return to my facts; I had not been long at home in Dundee before you informed me that the Hope Street Leaders' meeting unanimously requested me to become their pastor, I wrote back, giving a full explanation of my principles, and *objecting to the call*; you endeavored to remove my objections by the longest letter I ever saw from your hand, stating that your "laws would be to me a dead letter," and promising your best assistance at Convocation to make them agreeable to me. On your promise, and my own conditions, I came, not to be merely a "stipendiary minister" removable at *your pleasure!* but the pastor of the church assembling in Hope Street. When I arrived in Liverpool I found that you had endeavored to shake the confidence of the Leaders in me, because you knew from my principles, and our conversations, that I was friendly to the Wesleyan Association, which, in your own room, you stated (before I came,) you would not object to join on certain terms which I laid down, though now you speak of that body in a spirit which leads me to conclude that you do not love them as brethren in Christ. Soon after my arrival you threatened to resume your station if I did not conform to your wishes, I told you I could not, and you remained in London.

A few months after you came down and told me many things you had against me. This was done in the presence of a full Leaders' meeting, I standing to defend myself, as at your bar, before the meeting.

A second time you came to Liverpool, and for several days never looked near my house, although you passed through the same street. The Convocation was now held, you did not redeem your pledges as contained in letters to me, but labored to make me submit to *your authority* and to that of the *Rules*, which I had expressly stipulated should be a dead letter.

Deceived, and used from month to month in the most unbrotherly manner, I would have left you then, but I looked forward to God's Providence either to open my way *among* you or *from* you. At the eleventh hour you made some concessions, and I remained, being at peace with the Leaders' meeting in Liverpool, for three months, undisturbed by you, souls got saved in scores, the circuit enlarging, and all was well, until you disturbed our tranquility by opposing the measures of the Connexional Committee and the Liverpool Leaders' meeting, stating that the Rev. P. Anderson, whom they had called, you could not approve of; this aroused your friends, but the Leaders' meeting would not dismiss him, either for your opposition or theirs, for it appeared tyrannical and unreasonable *for your will to be the only law in the society*.

Towards the end of January last you visited Liverpool a third time, you and a few of your friends formed *a secret plot*, held a secret meeting of which I and two thirds of the Leaders knew nothing. The *same evening* you told me, calling me out of the Leaders' meeting, that twenty men had resolved to leave the society if I remained; this was proved to be untrue in your presence, when first one and then another of the twenty contradicted you, and it came out that only *a very few, five or six at the most*, had said so.

How will you answer to God and men for this? At our private interview you stated that if I would go away £40 or £50 would be given me, I scorned the bribe.

In the Leaders' meeting you and your friends opened the plan for my removal, you said, "From this night either you (Mr. Bowes) must leave or my connexion with this church ceases." "I can no longer regard Mr. Bowes as a brother." Thus attempting for several hours together to divide God's church; you failed, blessed be God. May he again frustrate your divisive purpose. Three days after, I felt offended at your conduct, and called on you according to the xviii. chap. of Matt. you satisfied me, and prevented me from proceeding further. The same day you proposed I should mission Birmingham, without resigning my present charge; for the sake of peace, I agreed; the Leaders agreed. But before I came you had met the Trustees of Hope Street, *to get them to expel me from the chapel.* You succeeded with a majority, and the same night used words *to my much lamented brother Stubbs an Elder, Leader, and Trustee, which robbed him of his reason, and in fourteen days sent him to an early grave. May the Lord be a husband to the distressed widow.* Before I left for Birmingham you sent a preacher without consulting me to take my pulpit, and ordered the trustees to exclude me from Hope Street Chapel. You again and again promised to preach the first or second Sabbath in Birmingham, if I would only go thither. I invited you to fulfil your promise, you never answered me, and never came. And now you have suspended me!! For my own comfort I might wish our connexion to cease, for I have been treated by you in a most *unbrotherly*, not to say *cruel manner*. I have kept my reason, thank God, but have suffered a mental martyrdom from you. May God open your eyes to see what you have done, not to me only, but to others; a member of brother Varty's class has also lost her reason through this matter; I had this fact from brother Varty's own lips yesterday. I beseech you pause, remember that "Love worketh no ill to his neighbor," and "Follow the things which make for peace." If you have no mercy upon my dear wife and four innocent little children, have mercy upon God's children, and his church. With all speed I shall go to resume my charge at Liverpool, to which a great majority, said to be three-fourths of the people, have just called me, and will you endeavor to expel me from my charge by force? shall God's house, instead of being a house of prayer, be a scene, not of martyrdom, but of an attempt to expel a shepherd of Christ from feeding his flock? To prevent this, let a church meeting be called, let the whole facts of the case be stated, and let both sides be fairly heard, and let God by his people decide.

And if we part, let us part like Christians, and like ministers of Christ. I implore this for Christ's sake, for the sake of his church, for the credit of our common religion, and to prevent any more from losing their reason and their life. An early answer to this letter, which I request you to read to your Leaders' meeting in London, that you may have their advice, may prevent future evil. If I get no satisfactory reply and reparation in a few days, I shall hold myself at liberty to publish the facts of this, and other letters to "The Christian Society," and the whole Christian church, that your conduct and principles may be understood.

Yours for Christ's sake,

JOHN BOWES.

LIVERPOOL, March 2, 1838.

I have just met the Leaders, and a church meeting for stating the whole facts is fixed for evening. I give you this official notice that if you chose you may attend.

J. BOWES.

LIVERPOOL, March 6th, 1838.

DEAR SIR,—
The expelled Leaders and I have called a Society Meeting, to be held in Music Hall to-morrow evening, at 7 o'clock, when the facts, on both sides, connected with my suspension will be stated. I and the brethren cordially invite you to attend, and state your own case. Yours respectfully,

To the Rev. R. Aitken. JOHN BOWES.

P.S.—If I receive no answer to my last in the course of to-morrow, I shall send a copy, with my expulsion or suspension to every Society or Circuit in the Connexion. I give you notice, that you may not complain afterwards. J.B.

At a public Church Meeting of the Christian Society, members of Hope Street Chapel, Liverpool, held in the Music Hall, on Wednesday evening, 7th March, 1838, Mr. Landers, an elder and leader being called to the chair, the following resolutions were unanimously passed:

"That it is the opinion of this meeting, that the Rev. J. Bowes has done nothing worthy of suspension."

"That this meeting cannot consider that any meeting of Convocation can expel Mr. Bowes without breaking faith with him, as he objected to any such mode of expulsion before he came, in his correspondence; to which both Mr. Aitken and the Leaders' Meeting agreed."

"That this meeting recommend the expelled leaders, so called, to continue to meet their classes, and promises to give them their support."

"That Mr. Bowes be requested to take his appointments according to the Plan."

"That twelve or twenty be chosen out of the body of the members to form a Provisional Committee, with the Leaders, to advise with and assist Mr. Bowes in the present state of the society."

"That the minutes or resolutions of this meeting should be printed or written without loss of time, and transmitted to every society in connexion with the Christian Society."

"That all the class-leaders in the society pay over the amount of their collected subscriptions, as received, to Mr. Purnell, treasurer, for the use of their pastor, Mr. Bowes.

"That tickets be issued by the Rev. Mr. Bowes to the members of this society, in the form of those being now issued, with the exception of the initials being omitted, and that the heading be similar to the December 1834 tickets."

WM. J. BROADLEY, Secretary to the Meeting.

At a meeting of the Society, March 14th & 15th, when the proceedings of the meeting were nearly over, Messrs Mitchell and Campbell appeared for Mr. Aitken, and being asked, if Mr. Aitken or Mr. Clarke had the power to suspend or expel a minister, did not answer. It was moved, "That all who thought the possession of such power by Messrs Aitken and Clarke unscriptural, should stand up." Nearly all the meeting stood up. It was then put the contrary way, and Mr. Mitchell only stood up.

STATEMENT AND EXPULSION.

The first time Mr. Aitken came down from London, he and one of the elders were talking about me, and Mr. Aitken expressed himself satisfied with my honesty of principle, but added, " He is in a low state of grace." Think of the effect of this: he had never said one word of the sort to me.

At a Leaders' Meeting on Monday, March 4th, instead of a District Meeting to try me, Mr. Aitken stated that he would call a Convocation, to be held on Friday, the 16th, but instead of calling either the one or the other, on Sabbath, the 11th, in the forenoon, it was intimated in Hope Street that the Quarter Day would be held on Thursday, the 15th; but in the evening he had changed his mind again, and instead of having it on the 2nd of April, according to the printed plan, or the 15th, it was published in the evening for the 16th—the day previously fixed for the Convocation.

Well, then, we had a Quarter Day. I attended. The meeting being opened, Mr. Aitken stated that an individual was present that he was surprised to see in that meeting—that he could do nothing with him, and had put him into other hands. He then adjourned the meeting for an hour. I and my friends sat still. A deputation waited on me, and said, "What do you and your party mean to do?" I said, "What do you and your party mean to do? We intend to remain." They then came back again, and it was proposed—"That the Rev, John Bowes be forthwith expelled from the Christian Society in connexion with the Rev. R. Aitken, and from this meeting." I observed, that if they were going to put me on my trial, I should like to say a few words in my own defence. "I will not allow you to speak one word;" said Mr. Aitken, "I will not suffer you to arraign my conduct." Neither I nor my friends were permitted to speak, and in five minutes I was expelled without a hearing. Mr. Pearson said to Mr. Aitken, "You can come here, and call a quarterly meeting or convocation just when you please!" Mr. Aitken replied, "If I could not, there would be no discipline in the society." In answer to the question, whether he intended to retain the same power of suspending a minister in future, he replied, "Whilst I am in the office I now hold, I will suspend a minister until the District Meeting." Mr. Aitken expressed himself in a similar manner at a Trustee Meeting.

Sometime after I was expelled, they began to try the Leaders, much in the same way as the Inquisition of Spain! In the course of this trial, I was requested to read a part of the correspondence, which I did, but when I was about to come to the most important part, I was stopped. I said little more to the meeting.

By and bye, a spirit of apparent kindness seemed to come over several in the meeting, and there was a motion made, that I and my friends should retire, with the view of agreeing to such propositions as might heal the breach. My friends sat still. Mr. Aitken favored the measure, and said, in reference to my restoration, "We shall restore an useful brother." As one leader threatened to abandon the society should this motion be carried, it was given up, and another adopted.—"That the Rev. J. Bowes should testify his repentance by withdrawing from the meeting, as a first step towards anything being effected." I then stood up and said, "If my going out shall be understood to express my repentance, I shall not go; for I am not convinced that I have done wrong. And before I can listen to any proposals of peace, Mr. Aitken must withdraw his letter of suspension; and I may also intimate that I shall demand my salary till the convocation." This ended the matter.

The following was sent to me from the Arbitrators of different denominations. Thomas Freme, Esq., a Baptist, and Dr. Burrows, a Wesleyan.

"At a meeting held at Thomas Freme's Esq., 26th March, 1838, it was moved and seconded, that it be recommended to the church at Hope Street to allow the Rev. J. Bowes and his party the sum of £500 (five hundred pounds), on condition that he and his party cease to agitate the above church, and fish or use dishonorable means to draw away members from it, on pain of forfeiting the stipulated allowance.

Should the fact of any member having been drawn away from Hope Street church from this date, be proved to the satisfaction of this meeting, the sum of money granted shall be withheld, and if it has been received it shall be refunded to the above church.

JOHN BURROWS, Chairman.
THOMAS FREME.
J. BENSLEY.
SAMUEL KENT.
JAMES PEARSON.

---

20 BOLD STREET, March 16th, 1838.

REV. SIR,—

I have just received your note, inviting me to a meeting at Mr. Freme's this evening. It is now half-past 6, and having been engaged in a dirty job all day in pulling down old buildings, I am quite unfit to appear in your company. Should you have another meeting during the week, and request my presence, by giving me further notice, I shall feel great pleasure in rendering you any assistance in my power to restore peace and harmony in the Society.

Yours respectfully,

To Rev. J. Bensley, 16 Clarence Street.   W. COLLINSON.

REV. SIR,—

The annexed copy of an original resolution, drawn out by Dr. Burrows, and signed as purported, now in the hands of Thomas Freme, Esq., was directed to be transmitted to you as pastor of Hope Street Chapel. The copy of note above, from Mr. W. Collinson, though not the exact words, are in substance his reply to our invitation to be present at the meeting.

I am, Reverend Sir, yours respectfully,

For J. BENSLEY, Secretary,

16 Clarence Street, 27th March, 1838.   WM. BROADLEY.

To the Rev. J. Bowes.

All the chapels of the Methodist New Connexion were open to me. The ministers and people were all very kind. No Christians in Liverpool showed the same disposition to open their chapels, in the cold month of March, when many of our services were held out of doors. Bethesda Chapel we occupied weekly; the Park and Scotland Road a few times. A meeting of sympathy for me, and censure of Mr. Aitken's conduct, was held by members of our society and members of other churches.—

"At a Church Meeting of the Christian Society, and Members of other Churches, held in the Music Hall, Liverpool, on Wednesday evening, 21st March, 1838, for the purpose of hearing the documents read, and the facts explained, connected with the Rev. R. Aitken's suspending the Rev. John Bowes, Pastor of Hope Street Chapel, Liverpool. The Rev. J. Bensley, chairman. The following resolutions were passed:—

"1. 'That it is the opinion of this meeting, that the powers claimed and acted upon by the Rev. Robert Aitken, A.M., of suspending a minister at his own pleasure, causing his expulsion without charge or trial, as in the case of the Rev. John Bowes, is highly dangerous to the religious liberties of the people of God.''

"2. 'That it is the decided conviction of this meeting, that for any Leaders' Meeting to expel a number of Leaders, without charge of sin or trial, at the request of Mr. Aitken, (as the Hope Street Chapel Leaders' Meeting has done), for the expression of an opinion against

Mr. Bowes' suspension, is a most unwarrantable stretch of power, subversive of the rights of private judgment, the glory of Protestantism, and that this assumed power should be checked by all the friends of religious liberty.'

"3. 'That seven Christian brethren, ministers and laymen, connected with different denominations, be chosen to act as mediators, to heal the breach at present existing in the Christian Society between the Rev. Robert Aitken and the Rev. John Bowes.'

"4. 'That the correspondence and documents connected with the business of this meeting be published.'

"5. 'That the above Resolutions be printed, and circulated at the discretion of the Committee appointed on the 7th March, and that Collectors be now appointed to aid the Society's funds for carrying on the work of God.'

"J. BENSLEY, President."

The following Leading Article and Letter appeared in the *Christian Advocate*, March 26th, 1838 :—

"THE REV. ROBERT AITKEN has never been a favorite with us. All our knowledge of him is in his public capacity, in respect of which alone it is that we speak of him. He may be, and we doubt not is, a very amiable man in private life; but, when men obtrude themselves upon the world as public characters, they must not expect that their private virtues will shield them from merited animadversion.

"Our first acquaintance with Mr. Aitken was as the self-appointed mediator between the Wesleyan-Methodist Conference and the Wesleyan Methodist Association; and the manner in which he went about this self-imposed undertaking, did not tend to give us any favorable impression as to his temper and judgment. His suggestions were the crudest and most impracticable imaginable; and he contrived to disgust, by the grossest insults, both the parties whom it was his professed aim to conciliate and bring together. Failing in this ridiculous attempt, our mediator turned apostle, actually dubbing himself, modest man! with this title. We dare say he has not forgotten, whoever may, the account we rendered of his absurd, arrogant, and abortive efforts at constitution-making. Suffice it, for the refreshment of treacherous memories, to observe, that he proposed, amongst other things equally characteristic of his sober-mindedness, the revival of the apostleship, and of the gifts of prophecy! After having seen Mr. Aitken's performances in this line, it only remained that we should hear him preach, and 'behold the order' in which he conducted the services of the church. We therefore embraced an opportunity of doing so; and—But, as there are some for whom we have great respect, who differ from us on this subject, we will only say, that his conduct in the pulpit did not increase our confidence in the soundness or sobriety of his understanding.

"What has happened at Liverpool, consequently, has not taken us by surprise. We have long had the pleasure of knowing the amiable and single-minded Mr. Bowes, and may now confess that it was with equal surprise and regret that we heard of his connecting himself, however guardedly, with so eccentric a person as Mr. Aitken. It will be well if his conduct towards that gentleman, and the conduct of his immediate partizans towards that gentleman's friends, as recorded in another column, lead other respectable individuals who, in unsuspecting confidence, have linked themselves with this soi-disant 'apostle,' to 'look before they leap,' into the bottomless pit of chapel-trust engagements for the behoof of a man who, publicly considered, has hitherto failed to win, or at least to keep, the good opinion of any respectable section of the Christian church."

THE REV. R. AITKEN IN LIVERPOOL.

[TO THE EDITOR OF THE CHRISTIAN ADVOCATE.]

DEAR SIR,—Nothing having appeared in the *Advocate* under the head of the "Aitkenites" for a long time, I send you the following, of which you may make any use you think proper, if a better account does not reach you from another hand.

I am, dear Sir, yours truly,

J. BEYNON.

The Christian Society, established by the Rev. R. Aitken in this town, is now undergoing a state of extraordinary excitement. It will be recollected, that, after the attempt had failed to bring Mr. Aitken out as a travelling preacher in the Wesleyan Connexion, he hastily hazarded the project of forming a new society under the immediate auspices of himself and at a point of time when considerable agitation prevailed in the Wesleyan Body. Not long after he had gathered a society in Liverpool, and drawn up a code of rules, he settled in London, with a view of extending his connexion there. The congregation here consented to his removal, upon the condition that the Rev. J. Bowes, of Dundee, should assume the pastorship of Hope Street Chapel as the successor of Mr. Aitken; and, after the necessary arrangements had been made, he became the pastor of the congregation. Mr. Bowes had the penetration to perceive that the rules drawn up by Mr. Aitken were of so fungus a description, that he expressly stipulated that he would not be bound by them, and that, as far as he was personally concerned, they should be a dead letter, to which Mr. Aitken and the society at Liverpool agreed. Mr. Bowes also declared that he could not give up one principle in the government of a Christian church which the Scriptures warranted, nor could he relinquish his peculiar views in favor of promoting a general union among all orthodox Christians. It appears, however, that the sentiments of the society in Liverpool could not be brought to harmonise generally with those of Mr. Bowes on these subjects; and, in consequence thereof, a party spirit was generated among the members. This state of things might have been innocently tolerated by mutual consent, but the party opposed to Mr. Bowes, being in the confidence of Mr. Aitken, determined at once to remove the former from the pastoral office at Hope Street Chapel. "Private intelligence," and exparte statements, at length induced the Rev. R. Aitken to issue a mandate addressed to Mr. Bowes, to the following effect:—"I am under the necessity of suspending you from being the pastor of the Christian Society at Liverpool, and you are hereby suspended accordingly, till the next District meeting." This extraordinary proceeding induced the friends of Mr. Bowes to recall him from Birmingham, whither he had gone to open a mission in that town; and it appears that a majority of the congregation were in favor of his continuing among them as their minister, at this juncture Mr. Aitken arrived from London, and steps were immediately taken to procure the expulsion of Mr. Bowes from the Christian Society. It was resolved at first, that a special Convocation should be called, without waiting till the District meeting; but it was finally arranged that the most expeditious mode would be to effect this object at an irregular Quarterly Meeting, which was held on Friday evening last. Mr. Bowes appeared at this meeting, and Mr. Aitken expressed surprise at seeing him there. A resolution, however, was carried, that Mr. Bowes be expelled forthwith; and when he attempted to offer some remarks on such a proceeding, Mr. Aitken said, "I will not allow you to say one word; my conduct shall not be arraigned at this meeting." Thus, without a charge or trial, was Mr. Bowes expelled from the Christian Society, the natural result of which was, that his friends rallied round him, declaring that they never would submit to such arbitrary conduct.

A church meeting was held in the Music Hall, on Wednesday last, at which about 1,000 persons were present, comprising members of the Christian Society, and other Christian denominations. Mr. Bowes entered into a full and most satisfactory defence of his conduct, which was denied him elsewhere; and he proved, by going through the whole of his correspondence with Mr. Aitken, that the pledges which had been given him when he undertook the charge at Hope Street Chapel, had not been redeemed. He showed also, from other documentary evidence, that some of the ministers in connection with the Rev. R. Aitken are justly alarmed at the extraordinary powers which he claims to exercise over them. During the reading of the letters it was necessary to authenticate them by persons on the platform, who could, from personal knowledge, identify the handwriting; because it had been said, out of the meeting, that the letters to be produced by Mr. Bowes were forgeries. Several disclosures very characteristic of Mr. Aitken's rashness of assertion were elicited. The following may be taken as specimens of this modern apostle:—Speaking of an union with the Wesleyan Association, he said, "it would be like mixing fire and water together; for I hold *not one principle in common with them.*" He said also, " that tee-totalism came from *hell*;" and " that many who had come over to him from the Wesleyans were devils."

Mr. Kent also addressed the meeting, and stated the manner in which himself and thirteen other Leaders had been expelled from the Christian Society. The practice adopted was similar to that of the memorable transaction at Leeds. A test was applied to the Leaders' meeting, and fourteen were found on the side of Mr. Bowes, who, for no other crime, were summarily ejected by the majority. It was proved that Mr. Aitken had broken his own rules in regard to pastors, deacons, and Leaders; and it was demonstrated, that for priestly despotism, nothing has surpassed him, in the conduct of the preachers in the Wesleyan Connexion during the late agitations.

Before the meeting concluded, resolutions were passed condemnatory of Mr. Aitken's assumed power of expelling a pastor, as a thing unheard of in a Christian church, and it was also resolved that Mr. Bowes was worthy of the confidence which had been reposed in him. A very large number of the Christian Society have joined Mr. Bowes, to whom, as the minister of their choice, he is fulfilling the duties of a Christian pastor.

Liverpool, March 28, 1838.

We understand that the Rev. J. Bowes will preach, the next Sabbath forenoon at Bethesda Chapel, Duncan Street, East, and at the same place every Thursday evening, at seven o'clock. We hear that three-fourths of the society, as well as those of other churches who attended at the Music Hall, are on the side of the suspended and expelled minister.—*Liverpool Mercury.*

TRUSTEE MEETINGS.

"At a Trustees' Quarterly Meeting, held in Hope Street Chapel, on 5th April, 1838, at five in the evening,—present, C. E. Rawlins, in the chair, Messrs Collinson, Pearson, Lewis, Purnell, Boumphrey, and Johnson,—resolved: 'That Messrs Rawlins, Lewis, and Purnell, be appointed a sub-committee to examine the drafts of the Deeds of this chapel, to ascertain if there is inserted therein, that it is "for the Rev. Robert Aitken, and the Christian Society in connexion with him," or words to that effect,—and that they do report thereon at an adjourned meeting, to be held here on Saturday next, at 6 p.m.'

"Charles Edward Rawlins, Chairman."

"Adjourned Quarterly Meeting, held as above, on Saturday, 7th April, at six in the evening. Present, C. E. Rawlins, in the chair, Messrs Cole, Pearson, Collinson, Johnson, Purnell, and Lewis. The sub-committee reported that they had been to the Town Hall, and had there seen in Mr. O'Kill's office, the counterpart of the Conveyance of the Land on which this chapel is erected,—that, at their request, the clerk read the conditions, &c., therein, which bind the purchasers of the land—Messrs Collinson, Boumphrey, and Purnell—to erect thereon, before the expiration of seventy-five years, a building, or buildings, of greater value than the cost of the land ; but no mention is made therein of any chapel. The sub-committee then proceeded to the office of Mr. John Caton Thompson, who has the draft of the mortgage deed. Mr. Thompson was so closely engaged that he declined looking out the draft of the deed; but being informed of the object for which the sub-committee wished to see it, stated that there was no such claim in the deed, nor words to that effect,—Mr. Aitken's name (but as a trustee) was not mentioned in it, nor that of the Christian Society ; that apprehending differences might arise among the Trustees, a proper regard to his clients' interest induced him not to insert any such limitation.

"The chairman reminded the Trustees present that, by that information, it appeared that they were Trustees of the Chapel for the use of the Christian Society simply, and consequently for the whole of that body : the Trustees could not therefore identify themselves with any divisions which had unhappily taken place among them; neither could they permit their authority over the chapel to be interfered with by one party attempting to exclude another from the use of it, or to secure it for their use only.

"Resolution proposed by Mr. Pearson, seconded by Mr. Purnell,—'That the use of this chapel be granted to the Rev. John Bowes once on the sabbath, and twice during the week; and that the same use thereof be granted to Mr. Bromley,—both under the arrangement of the Trustees.'

"Amendment proposed by Mr. Johnson, seconded by Mr. Collinson,—'That the Chairman write to the Rev. R. Aitken, with a copy of the above proceedings, requesting him as early as possible, to resume his *permanent* ministry at this chapel, and that in the event of his not doing so, the chapel be sold forthwith, and that Mr. Aitken be requested to favor the Trustees with an early reply.'

"After some time spent in discussion, Mr. Cole stated that he was obliged to leave the meeting, but expressed his opinion that it would be impossible to carry the resolution into operation if passed. After some time the Resolution was consented to be withdrawn, and the Amendment unanimously adopted instead, hoping that Mr. Aitken's compliance will prevent the Resolution being passed eventually.

"Resolved—'That a copy of these proceedings be sent by the Chairman to each of the Leaders' meetings, and that this meeting be adjourned to Thursday next, 12th instant, at 5 o'clock in the evening, hoping then to have Mr. Aitken's reply.'

"CHARLES EDWARD RAWLINS, Chairman."

SIR,—
In obedience to the directions of the Trustees of Hope Street Chapel, I herewith transmit to you, for the information of the Leaders who are Friends to the Rev. J. Bowes, a copy of certain resolutions passed by them, which you will please to lay before the Leaders at their next meeting. I am, Sir, yours respectfully, C. E. RAWLINS, Chairman.
4 Blackburn Terrace, 9th April, 1838.
To the Chairman of the Leaders' Meeting, Friends of the Rev. John Bowes.

11 VINE STREET, April 14th, 1838.

DEAR SIR,—
Your Christian and business-like communication of the 9th curt., was submitted to a meeting of Leaders and Committee, of the same date, and they

directed me to address a letter to you, expressive of their approbation of the course you, as Trustee, intend to pursue, believing as they do, with you, that justice requires that "one party" should not attempt "to exclude another from the use of the chapel, or to secure it for their own use only." The Committee trust that the generous and equitable principles of our mutual Christianity will teach us to forbear with and love one another, at least to such an extent as to settle the differences that exist among ourselves, without having recourse to *civil law*. And we doubt not, if the Trustees will only act upon the just principles recognised in your communication, that this result will be realized. If we were acquainted with any method by which to hasten such a consummation of this case, as would place both sides in more comfortable and agreeable circumstances, we should be happy to adopt it. As for ourselves, we have been repeatedly compelled to assemble in this cold season in the open air, when we have not been invited, through Christian compassion, to the chapels of our brethren of other denominations. But we trust that the motion—"That the use of this chapel be granted to the Rev. J. Bowes once on the Sabbath, and twice during the week; and that the same use thereof be granted to Mr. Bromley; both under the arrangement of the Trustees," should Mr. Aitken not accept of the permanent charge of the Hope Street Society, will be "eventually passed." This would be equity; but should we obtain the exclusive use of the chapel, without any recompense to the other side, *we* should be guilty of palpable injustice. Praying that the Head of the Church may direct and overrule all these matters for our common benefit, and His own glory,

I am, on behalf of the above meeting, yours very truly,

JOHN BOWES.

To C. E. Rawlins, Esq., Chairman of Trustees' Meeting, Hope Street Chapel. Held April 5th & 7th.

This was printed and sent out as a Circular:—

TO THE MEMBERS OF THE CHRISTIAN SOCIETY, HOPE STREET CHAPEL.

CHRISTIAN BRETHREN,—

It is with no ordinary feeling of concern and regret that I have witnessed the unhappy separation which has recently occurred among you. To express this sentiment, however, without offering some counsel, would ill comport with your circumstances, and with the object of this communication. Perhaps the ordinary principles of Christian brotherhood might justify this liberty; but feeling that no apology can be requisite either to the Friends of Mr. Aitken or to those of Mr. Bowes for this step; and that both alike require and expect from the Trustees the faithful discharge of their duties, I do not hesitate to address the friends on both sides, entreating you not to cherish a spirit of animosity towards each other, but to suppress all evil speaking; not to allow the enemy to divide and conquer, retrace your steps and strive to come together again in the spirit of your common Master; union is essential to success, "but if ye bite and devour one another, take heed that ye be not consumed one of another." Strive to exemplify that Charity "which thinketh no evil, beareth all things, believeth all things, hopeth all things," as you all profess the same Faith in Christ, to be the subjects of the same Grace, and to be journeying to the same country, ought you not carefully to cherish the Spirit of Love towards one another? Recollect the eyes of other Christian communities are upon you; you have been as a city set upon a hill; you have been taught, and have professed to attain, no ordinary degree of Holiness; think then, brethren, how other Christians must lament, and how the foes of our common Christianity will triumph when they hear of your contentions and separations.

If I might descend from Scriptural considerations to those which are far lower, I would entreat you to consider, that should dissentions among you continue, the chapel must get into disrepute, the seat rents will diminish, and thus bring the Trustees into embarrassment, which may probably render the retention of the chapel by either party extremely hazardous. To avert consequences therefore so painful, I would enjoin a speedy and amicable adjustment of all differences; let us hope that "your union has only been broken off for a moment, that it may be cemented for ever."

If, however, you find that all hope of reconciliation has fled, endeavor promptly to make such arrangements, as, while they shall be equitable, will suit mutual convenience, and thus relieve the Trustees from proceedings, which might, if adopted, be to all a source of mutual dissatisfaction, and lasting, but remediless, regret.

Hoping that you will seriously consider, and promptly act upon these suggestions. I remain, Christian Brethren, yours faithfully,

C. E. RAWLINS, Chairman of the Trustees.

Liverpool, May 17th, 1838.

Aug. 22, 1838.—The last week I have been in BIRMINGHAM and OLDBURY. I preached in Allison Street Room, in the former place, on the 23rd; four or five professed to give their hearts to God

24*th*.—I preached again in Birmingham, in the open-air, Bull Ring. I reasoned against Socialism before several hundreds. The last time I was here I was driven off the ground by a number of Socialists and Catholics, and P. G. Anderson and I had to flee for our lives. To-day they were tolerably quiet; after preaching held a penitent meeting in the Room, one or two professed to believe in Christ.

26*th*.—This morning heard Robert Eckett Esq., of London preach an Evangelical sermon, at the opening of a new chapel in Oldbury, called "Methodist Tabernacle;" collection, £60. At 2 o'clock I preached to an overflowing congregation, many not being able to obtain admission, on Luke xxiv. 46-47. "Thus it behoved Christ," &c. A powerful impression was made on the people, may the seeds be seen many days hence. Collection, £54. In the evening I rode to Birmingham, and preached to an attentive audience, my beloved brother Anderson having preached out of doors before I began in the house; several were saved.

27*th*.—Held a public meeting, to explain the reasons why I, Mr. Anderson, and the churches under our care were not connected with Mr. Robert Aitken. A vote of thanks was passed to us for our conduct in opposing Mr. Aitken's tyrannical conduct.

28*th*.—Returned to preach at Oldbury; Mr. Cocker, New Methodist preacher, Madely, had preached in the new chapel in the evening, Lord's Day. Collection, £37. Mr. Eckett again on the 27th. Collection, £10. This evening I preached. Collection, £13. Total, £175. By far the largest sum ever collected for one religious object in three days, probably since Oldbury stood.

The Lord consecrated the place by saving about 5 souls; more might have been saved but the impression made by the sermon was weakened by the singing of one female at once, and then again a choir, while the violins were heard, and all the congregation stood mute!

Thank God, new chapels are being erected in various parts of this, and in other lands. (So I felt at this date.)

29*th*.—Arrived in LIVERPOOL safe by the railway, and heard Mr. Dickson preach in my appointment at Edmund Street, he is a young man of promising talent.

30*th*.—Spoke in Wavertree, Zoar Chapel in a crowded Temperance meeting.

31*st*.—Preached at the Pier-head, in the open-air, and held a fellowship meeting after in Edmund Street Chapel.

Sept. 2*nd*.—Preached at Edmund Street in the morning, renewed tickets in the afternoon; got the members to form two prayer meetings, one for the men, and another for the females. Was greatly encouraged by the good effected under the open-air services.

At six o'clock preached to a large congregation in the Hay Market; many followed to the penitent meeting in Edmund Street, some got saved.

Between the morning service and that of the afternoon, as I did not go home to dinner, I took a walk towards the shore and passed from twelve to twenty persons, male and female, selling fruit, I only passed one without speaking to them ; they all behaved courteously, and acknowledged that it was wrong to sell on the Lord's Day ; one pleaded poverty, I answered "so might the robber, but that did not acquit him of crime." One man said he had been at service in the morning, I told him it was of no use to attend God's house one part of the day, and work all the rest.

(I give facts, but should not act so now).

During the last week I have resolved to visit at least one family every week, that I never visited before that I might teach that family the way of life.

9th.—Preached a short sermon in the open-air, close to the Queen's Dock, from Psalm l. 14. "Pay thy vows." The morning was calm, the people attentive, the season deeply affecting. Adjourned to Bethel Room, and preached again to a full place, from John ix. 4. One young man gave his heart to God; a young woman was broken down, and got saved in the afternoon. At 2 o'clock delivered tickets ; only two saved since the last quarter, both from open-air preaching. At six preached at Edmund Street, to a crowded congregation, against Socialism : two or three saved.

10th.—Heard one of our brethren preach, the sermon was so dry common-place, and ineffective, that it was calculated to do harm rather than good. Preachers, like Total Abstinence advocates, should be instructive, and throw their whole soul into the subject, and then their congregations would be interested, and great good would result.

11th.—At half-past 6 or near 7 o'clock, preached for near an hour in the open area near St. James' Market, and again at 8 o'clock at the Bethel Room, Watkinson Street; both congregations were large, and at the later five or six professed to give themselves to God.

12th.—Commenced a course of sermons on the Lord's Prayer, in Edmund Street, and after preaching, visited a sick woman deeply concerned.

13th.—Visited a family in which I never was before, a newly married female promised to turn to God. At half-past six preached to a very large audience in the Hay Market, from Matt. xxiii. 33. "Ye serpents, ye generation of vipers, how can ye escape the damnation of hell." In the course of the sermon a Socialist asked me if I believed "that man's belief did not arise from his organisation at the birth, and the circumstances attending it afterwards, rather than from his own will, and if he was responsible for his belief?" I refused to answer him till the sermon was done, then I answered him, although he had left the place without leaving his name. Those who thought the answer satisfactory and complete, I requested to show their hands, nearly all did. Those who thought the reverse were then asked to show theirs, not one was lifted up. This tends to silence the unreasonable.

14th.—Visited three sick families ; one woman whom I prayed with on the 12th got saved that evening, and has rejoiced in God ever since, her body is recovering. Visited another, who, with her husband had wandered from God some months, he has afflicted her for fourteen days, on the 8th she got restored to peace and has been growing better in body ever since.

15th.—Commenced a fellowship meeting in Tyzack's Academy, Park Road.

16th.—Lectured at half-past 10 in Edmund Street, from Rev. iv. ch. and preached from Is. xxxii. 8. "The liberal devises liberal things, and by liberal things shall he stand." The congregation was large, and the season unusually elevating. At 2 o'clock renewed tickets to three classes, in one a young man was saved at the Amphitheatre.

We took the great Amphitheatre for several Lord's Days, and often had large congregations in it; the weather being cold however, the people came better in the afternoon and evening than on other parts of the day. At the time I thought it a great hardship to go into it and small chapels and rooms, instead of the great chapel, but I think otherwise now, and that often more good is done in the former than the latter. Thus we were forced into the best means of usefulness. At 15 minutes past five preached in the open-air, and at 6 to a crowded congregation in the Academy; four or five souls professed to believe in Christ, one was saved at a class in the afternoon.

17th.—Attended a committee meeting at 6, heard a good sermon at 7, and met the elders at 9; they requested me to preach from the xviii. chap. of Matthew, 15 and following verses, I agreed, and mentioned the slander of the Methodist Societies, and the impropriety of leaving out members because of poverty. Let those really negligent be treated according to this passage.

18th.—Preached at St. James' Market, from "No man can serve two masters;" and an hour after to a full house in the Bethel Room, Watkinson Street, only one professed to obtain peace, but nearly half a dozen promised to turn to God.

19th.—Was desired to visit WEST DERBY, about four miles off, to see a sick woman; I preached once, some months ago, in the open-air, near her door, she did not know my name but described me as standing and preaching before the window; from that sermon she had been changed though she did not profess a sense of God's forgiving love, her nurse I found also in a backsliding state, they both wept and prayed, and I trust, believed.

Second sermon on the Lord's Prayer, "Thy kingdom come." It was a powerful season. I proved that civil establishments of religion were real obstructions to the coming of that kingdom.

20th.—Visited a number of families, several promised to come to the class and unite with the church. Preached in the evening in the Academy, after a short sermon in the open-air; two professed to find peace.

21st.—Preached in the open-air, Dryden Street, Scotland Road; a serious congregation. At 8 o'clock attended a fellow-ship meeting, and read my journal from the Primitive Methodist Magazine, of July 1826.

22nd.—Attended a fellowship meeting in Tyzack's Academy, Hill Street, one soul saved; more people than last week.

23rd.—Academy full in the morning. Found at the renewing or tickets in the afternoon, that about ten souls had got saved in three classes during the quarter. In the evening three professed to obtain peace.

24th.—Monday, very few at class; expected several new members, none came; some of my own members, in waiting upon them, waited too long and missed the class.

To-day, wrote a letter to the Socialists, accepting a challenge to a public discussion, which they had repeatedly given.

25th.—Very much perplexed in preparing for preaching, none of my old sermons pleased me, they are defiicient in point and warning to sinners. At length after prayer and much thought, I fixed upon 1 Pet. iv. 17, and preached from it at the Bethel Room; crowded place; solemn time; little noise, but a deep work. Eleven souls professed faith, and that they obtained the remission of their sins: several more determined to seek the Lord, indeed almost all the sinners in the place seemed deeply affected.

26th.—Delivered the third Lecture on the Lord's prayer, one backslider reclaimed.

27th.—Tyzack's Academy, more people than last week; three or four saved.

28th.—TRANMERE, CHESHIRE; several strangers; renewed tickets; added one.

29th.—Have been reading over my journal, and am impressed with the fact of not spending more time at any place than while sinners get converted to God. A great work was accomplished in forming a church on New Testament principles, at Dundee, but I am not sure if I did not stay there too long, for my own general usefulness.

1. I think I may be useful in meeting the school teachers one Lord's Day a-month.

2. In meeting frequently, an hour before preaching, the children of all the members of the church.

3. In being more pointed than ever in my remarks from the pulpit. The Lord help me.

4. May I not set apart some time for conversing with the awakened in my own house, as I did in Scotland?

I am distressed, on reviewing the last nine years that I spent in Scotland, that no more good was done. In forming a few churches on New Testament principles, I believe I acted scripturally; but I am not sure, after reading "Finney's Lectures on Revivals," but my original plan of calling sinners to the penitent form, might have been attended with success even in Scotland, but of this I am not certain. I will now endeavor to give all my future time to God's glory.

This evening three souls got saved; about twenty five through the week.

30th.—In the evening Tyzack's Academy could not hold the people, about six souls saved.

Oct. 1st.—Brother Taylor preached a good sermon.

2nd.—Bethel Room, 8 or 10 souls saved. I got more light than ever I had on the importance of telling a sinner the whole truth and setting to work to convert him by it.

3rd.—Edmund Street. "Forgive us our debts as we forgive our debtors." Five saved.

4th.—To-day I attended a meeting of the so-called Protestant Association, it is mis-named, it should be called "An Association for the support of civil establishments of religion." The meeting breathed a bitter spirit against civil liberty. Mr. M'Ghee endeavored to prove that the Catholic members of the House of Commons are perjured men, and had broken the oath taken by them on entering the House. His arguments convinced me that no oaths ought to be tendered at all. I did not stay to hear Hugh M'Neale, I heard him on the 2nd curt. endeavoring to prove that the Pope is the author of the present cry of liberty in Britain. A speaker followed him and highly eulogised Great Britain for granting liberty to the slaves of our colonies, and thus left the meeting to judge whether the Pope or a Protestant Nation is to have the honor of that cry.

This evening preached at Tyzack's Academy; admitted eleven members to the church; it was our quarterly meeting. 304 members, 16 increase. £13 debt.

5th.—Heard the celebrated Joseph Wolfe, LLD., in Trinity Church; at eleven o'clock; a very limited attendance; proved from Acts vii. that as the Jews at first rejected Joseph and Moses, so they had rejected Christ, although plainly foretold. He is a corpulent man, apparently near sighted, and may be known, by his imperfect pronunciation, to be a foreigner.

6th.—Had a gracious and sweet season at the fellowship meeting; while I was there Messrs. Finch and Green called upon me to arrange about a discussion on Socialism, and left the terms.

7th.—This morning lectured on the history of Joseph, and preached from Eph. ii. 18; at 2, held a lovefeast; a powerful time. One of our members spoke last night, and said that he had only been doing boy's work instead of man's work. I fear many are to be found among professors just like him, the age is not manly and brave for Christ, but formal and weak. Six souls seeking mercy.

DISCUSSION WITH A SOCIALIST.

Oct. 30th.—To-day the Discussion with Mr. Green, socialist, commenced, in the Queen's Theatre, Liverpool. Admittance by tickets. Robert Guest White, Esq., late High Sheriff of the City of Durham, in the chair. Probably about 2500 present. The correspondence between Mr. Finch and myself was first read. I then spoke for half-an-hour, shewing that Robert Owen was an inveterate Atheist, and that, in opposition to him, there is a God. This I illustrated and demonstrated from the formation of Man, and marks of unexampled Design in all God's works. I introduced a wheat sheaf, a rose, a pair of spectacles, as evidences of Divine skill.

Mr. Green next introduced himself, by admitting the being of a God. I then congratulated the meeting on our success, in being able to set against Owen, Mr. Green, now on our side. Mr. Green then said, " I neither admit nor deny the being of a God. His vacillation produced great dissatisfaction among the audience. As Mr. G. knew nothing about God, I proceeded to instruct him. He then attacked revelation—the sun standing still, the arguments from geology of the death of animals before the entrance of sin, which, he said, was opposed to the Scriptures: also to hell being below us—"for if it is below to us, it must be above to the antipodes." To the first I answered in my next speech by saying, that Joshua spoke in the universal language of the world; that I had conversed with the learned and illiterate, and was not aware that the greatest astronomer ever said, on the appearance of light in the morning, "The earth is rising," or on its disappearance in the evening, "The earth is setting." The argument from geology I answered by a reference to Genesis ii. 14, "But of the tree of the knowledge of good and evil, thou shalt not eat of it; for in the day thou eatest thereof thou shalt surely die." No where do we read in scripture that the death of animals is attributed to sin. The last argument, about hell being low, I answered by a reference to our mode of speaking: "Did Mr. Green never hear of a *low* man, except he was low of stature? Did he never hear of a *low* house, except one whose roof was only elevated a little above its foundation? Did he never hear of a degraded or naturally low house? Had he never heard of a low Street? or if he had, did he always suppose that it must be near Whitechapel, and could not be near the top of Mount Pleasant? I then proved the system to be grossly immoral; I referred to what both Owen and Finch had written, and showed they were aiming at a community of wives, as well as property. When I had done, and Mr. Green had done, the popular indignation at the immorality of the system was great, it was evidential of a healthy tone of moral feeling; Mr. Green could not be heard in defence; I had to request the meeting to hear him; he was heard for about five minutes, when he made an indelicate statement which exhausted the patience of the audience, and as it was now five minutes past ten o'clock, Mr. Green requested an adjournment and promised to show the next night that I had misrepresented the system.

31*st.*—The meeting was not so crowded this evening, as no notice had been given of the discussion by public advertisement; I was glad that we had more comfort. Through the denseness of the crowd the preceding evening, it was oppressive speaking. Mr. Green delivered the first speech, which consisted of little more than reading the books of socialism. I replied to his speeches the preceding evening. His next speech consisted chiefly of reading accounts of the excellency of of Mr. Owen's plans in New Lanark. I answered his speech by denying that the social system had ever been established at New Lanark, and by admitting, that wherever schools were establish good would result, and that such had been the beneficial effects of education at New Lanark, that the people had the good sense to reject Owenism, and I did not believe that there was existing a single Socialist at New Lanark. While Mr. G. was speaking, Mr. Carlyle, bookseller, Bold Street, stated to me that he had been to New Lanark, and that he could prove Mr. G. was wrong. Him I called to the platform to prove my assertions. He did so, to the great annoyance of the socialists. I then asked Mr. G. if he meant to reply to my arguments on the being of a God. He answered, No. I warned Mr. G. that if he did not redeem his system from the charges which I had brought against its immorality on the preceding evening, in his next speech—for he never once hinted at the subject in his last two speeches—that I should, on rising again, propose a resolution to the meeting, that it might express its opinion on the immorality of the system. I then proceeded to attack the doctrine of *necessity*, which they hold, and to prove, in opposition, the doctrine of Man's Free Agency. Three out of their five fundamental facts I characterised as *fundamental falsehoods*, and the other two truisms which a schoolboy might write. When I first approached the subject of men's free agency, the Socialists cried "That's the question," which was reiterated by the audience. Mr. Green had wearied out the patience of the people by reading an extract from Blackwood's Magazine, in reference to Hope Street Chapel and its penitent meetings, as I had left the Chapel several weeks before, I showed it could not apply to me.; Mr. Green endeavored to prove that men are mere machines, and asserted that no man could multiply motives to himself. I asked him if he would risk the whole controversy on that assertion, and if I could prove that man could multiply motives to himself, that he was therefore a responsible and free agent; He replied "Yes," but by and bye retracted it, I think at the suggestion of certain friends sitting near him. I proved that man could multiply motives to himself by a reference to his industry: referred to the industry of Sir Isaac Newton as an evidence of the truth of the position.

At the close of the second night's discussion, the following resolution was triumphantly passed, with only about 20 dissentients. Moved by Mr. R. Gorst, seconded by Captain Purnell: "That the Rev. John Bowes has most satisfactorily proved that the Social System advocated by Robert Owen, and his followers, is the most *unreasonable, injurious*, and *contemptible* ever proposed to the reason of man." Moved by the Rev. J. Bowes, seconded by Mr. J. Pearson: "That there is an intelligent being, the first cause of all being, himself uncaused, which we call God." Moved by Mr. R. Gorst, Wesleyan Association preacher, seconded by Captain Purnell: "That it is the opinion of this meeting that the principles of the Social System are calculated to promote the grossest licentiousness, and ought to be discountenanced by every friend of good morals and social order."—ROBERT G. WHITE, late High Sheriff, City of Dublin, Chairman.

The first Lord's Day in November, Mr. R. Gorst preached in the Theatre in the morning, and I preached afternoon and evening to overflowing congregations, on the "Truth of Revelation." Some souls were brought to God during the evening sermon.

During the month I visited Dundee, and delivered Temperance addresses in Glasgow and Edinburgh. (*)

---

* See APPENDIX, Note A.

CHAPTER VIII.

LETTERS.—MY IMMERSION.—THE MALTSTER.—JOURNAL.—VISITS TO BRISTOL.—LETTER TO ITS MINISTERS.—EXETER—PLYMOUTH—BARNSTAPLE—LONDON.—LIVERPOOL SECOND DISCUSSION.—TESTIMONIALS OF MINISTERS.—DISCUSSIONS IN DUNDEE AND GLASGOW.—DUNDEE TRIALS FOR OPEN-AIR PREACHING.—LETTER TO THE MAGISTRATES.—FAILURE OF R. AITKEN'S PROJECT.—REMOVAL TO ABERDEEN.—1839, 1840, 1841.

I had some interesting correspondence with the writer of this letter, Sir Culling Eardley Smith.

BEDWELL PARK, HATFIELD,
March 7th, 1839.

DEAR SIR,—

Your letter was forwarded to me, after the lapse of a short time by Captain Pievor. I have delayed answering it until I could have an opportunity of shewing it to one or two friends, who, I knew, sympathise ardently in our object of Christian Union. The result is, my conviction that the time is not yet come for organising an *extensive* society for the promotion of that object. The subject is not yet sufficiently appreciated even by those unconnected with the National Establishment. A premature central movement would defeat its own object. I would rather wait to see local unions established in several of the great towns, which should lead Christians of every name in those places to occasional acts of united worship and communion. I should like to see the subject amply discussed in religious periodicals, and above all I should wish to see and know that united prayer had been offered in the matter, before I should like to stir in the promotion of it.

As a first step, I think prayer most important. When the glory of God and the accomplishment of his kingdom is concerned, what might not be expected from a believing concert in prayer! With this view I had, previous to the receipt of your letter, contemplated inserting an anonymous advertisement in the papers, urging Christians to devote an hour in the morning of the 1st of May, to praying *unreservedly* that God would, in his own way, promote the union of his true disciples. I shall probably also circulate copies of the suggestion, with my name to it, among those who are likely to sympathise in the object.

For the present, therefore, I think your kind offer of itinerating, yourself, and lecturing on the subject, cannot be carried into operation. We shall see what my proposal leads to. I "cast my bread upon the waters" in the confidence that, if it be the will of our Heavenly Father, something will result from it. "Not by might, not by power, but by my Spirit, saith the Lord." I will take care that you receive a copy of the circular.

Believe me, dear Sir, yours with sincere Christian esteem,

CULLING EARDLEY SMITH.

My only brother loved me much. My way might have been easier, had I been able to join a sect.

BRADFORD, March 13th, 1839.

DEAR BROTHER,—

I received your letter last night, and, according to your request, I have sent you £10. I feel very much for you. I have no doubt you have many trials to go through, and if you are where the Lord wishes you to be, He will make a way for you, for he is mindful of his own children. It is not for me to judge whether you are in your right place or not, but why can you not be so useful among any sectarian denomination? Do you think that the Lord would not own your labors and save souls under a sectarian name? May the Lord keep you, and stand by you, and uphold you under every trial. I often think of you, and do not forget you at a throne of grace. I have not been so scarce of money for a long time as I am at present. I have had a great many losses this last year; it has been the worst I ever had, and I have lost more this year than ever I did since I commenced business; yet, notwithstanding this, I feel very thankful that I have it in my power to send it. Money is very bad to come at here at the present time. If you could send it in the course of a few months, I shall be much obliged to you. . . . .

Your affectionate brother,

EDWARD BOWES.

MY IMMERSION.

In the Spring of this year, 10th April, 1839, I was baptized, the circumstances may be seen in a tract on the subject—"Scriptural reasons for the giving up the sprinkling of infants, and adopting the immersion of believers as the only Christian baptism."

It was on the 3rd. month, 10th, when sister Jones, Dale Street, walked a short distance with my wife and me, after the Lord's Day services, saying, "I wish to be baptized." "I have no objection." "But I wish you to baptize me." "I do not object to that, if you can permit one to baptize you whom you think not baptized himself." "Nay, I wish you to be baptized first." I said "My mind is settled on the question. I have read all that is necessary on the subject." After talking a short time, and shaking hands, among her last words she said, "Study the Bible alone this time on the subject." These words fastened on my mind; had I, amid all my reading of Wardlaw, Carson, and others, ever studied the *Bible alone*? I had not. After the family had retired, I took down the Bible, Greek, &c., and read till I was convinced that believers only were baptized, and that immersion only was baptism. What a discovery! before I slept I was decided; but a new difficulty arose, would not this close up my way of usefulness? I could not join the Baptists, for I had long ago done with sects forever; I said, "Well, I never did serve God for bread and cheese, and I never will." I never had a larger family, or more expenditure, or so heavy a house rent; the house was taken for me by the church. The next time I entered the pulpit I preached on Acts ii. 37—41, and thus expressed my change of mind on baptism, but said, if they could convince me from Scripture, I would not be immersed, but if not, I should, and I appointed a time; none tried to convince me but the Treasurer and the Secretary of the church, who expected that the funds of the church would suffer. "Have you no Scripture against it?" "No." "Then I have settled that matter already." Accordingly, on the 10th April, 1839, in Soho Street Chapel, I and several more were buried with Christ, by immersion, by C. M. Birrel, I preferred him as he agreed with me that the Table should not be made a Baptist Table, but the Lord's. Soon after this, I saw a salary to be unscriptural and gave it up. I had about £100 worth of books, and intended to open a shop to sell them, by which I expected to keep my family a time; on going to ask for one in a very public street, I was asked if I would vote for a Conservative or Tory member of Parliament; I had never meddled much with politics, and was never a Tory, at any rate I could not give such a serf-like pledge. I continued to preach, and the Lord to support me, and most of the books were sold by private contract.

This letter is valuable because it contains information, from one of the most influential preachers, in answer to a letter of mine, of which I have no copy, as to the General Baptist Denomination.

DERBY, May 6th, 1839.

DEAR SIR,—

On my returning from a three weeks' missionary journey on Saturday evening I found yours lying at my house, I am now so engaged with a multiplicity of business, that I must beg you to excuse me if I answer your questions more briefly than I otherwise might do.

1. As far as I know, our churches universally require saving faith and conversion as the ground of membership. They may be often deceived, but this is their principle, and I conceive the only scriptural one. I look on Christian Churches and little assemblies of religious inquirers as completely distinct things.

2. Our churches generally maintain strict communion. Of the 126 churches in our union, there may be one or two that admit unbaptized persons to the Lord's table, but I cannot for certain mention one. From what I have known, I think our Annual Association would not receive a church that allowed mixed communion. I am merely giving you here a statement of facts. As an individual, I should feel no serious objection to occasional communion with Pædobaptists, yet am not a friend to the system of mixed communion churches.

3. There is no rule compelling friends united with us to adopt the name of General Baptist. Some of our friends are sticklers for the name; others do not like it; I am one of them. "Baptist" suffices for me, and I scarcely ever use the expression "General Baptist" when I can avoid it. In some cases we cannot avoid it, as in the name of our Foreign Missionary Society, "Baptist." alone would not do there, as there is another Baptist missionary society.

4. The subject of your fourth query excited considerable altercation some years ago, and many leading friends were favorable to such plans as you refer to. Our body are anxious to plant new churches by sending out Home Missionaries.

5. I should like to know who you refer to in your fifth query. We knowingly admit no unholy man to the ministry. No student is admitted for theological studies if not believed to be truly pious. Our ministers would not unite in the ordination of one they believed an unholy man; though on the Congregational system it is possible for a church to choose such a man, and keep him, in defiance of neighboring churches and ministers; yet our Association has a rule for proceeding against, and if needful, excluding from our union such a church. If you write again, tell me the person's name you refer to.

6. Any application for union should be made to the Secretary of our Association, which meets this year at Nottingham, on the last Tuesday in June. The present secretary, is Rev. H. Hunter, Nottingham.

Excuse the brevity of this, and if you want further information, write to me at pleasure. I am the Secretary of our Foreign Missionary Society. Our brethren labor in a wide and promising field in India. Would your friends, as you have no such society, be willing to assist us? We greatly want help. Could anything be done in Liverpool by your friends on the Society's behalf?

Mr. Hunter formerly belonged to the New Methodist Connexion. He is a friendly and valuable man, and has been with us about ten years.

Believe me, dear Sir, yours truly in the gospel,

To J. Bowes. J. G. PIKE.

The Secretary of the General Baptist Association sent me a kind invitation to join them, but as I explained my unsectarian principles, although I expressed my willingness to preach among them, I had no more letters.

11 VINE STREET, LIVERPOOL,
July 1st., 1839.

DEAR SIR,—

I am sorry to learn that you have thrown yourself into the army of the *blood-thirsty* Chartists. In most of their views, as to the objects they seek, I agree with them; but as to the recommendations that have emanated, even from ministers of peace!—to arms!—use physical force, and take peoples' property by violence!—I heartily disapprove these objects, as every man of God should do.

I write at present to give you an opportunity of purging yourself from a charge of deception which appears to stand against you. When Mr. Kent and I came over to Stockport, the Christian Society charged you with "preaching political sermons." You denied it, and endeavored to convince us that it was not true, on account of which we took you by the hand. *Now* you have proved that the Christian Society did not say too strong things about you. You have deceived Mr. Kent and me, and led us to deceive other. Now I ask you why you did not, like an honest man, tell us *your intentions* and your actions? then we should have left you to your own downward career, following you only by our remonstrances, our prayers, and our tears. I once loved Mr. Stephens much, as a bold asserter of religious liberty. He has *derided conversion*. Witness his own political sermons. It will not do for you to say the reporters have misrepresented him, when he issues a publication himself. I once more *warn* and beseech you, for Christ's sake, to mind your Bible, the work of proclaiming the gospel of pardon and holiness to a guilty world, that all may hear, repent, believe, and live. I pray God to bring you to repentance, that your best friends may rejoice, that Satan may be disappointed of his prey, and that many souls may be led to God through your agency. Believe me, that it is with sincere sorrow that I tell you, that if you will send me all the books you have of mine, as soon as convenient, perhaps with Mr. Grinstead, it is probable that this is the last letter which you will receive from one that loved you as a brother in Christ, but must now regard you as an enemy to God, his Son, his church, and your race. Yours, &c.,

To Mr. Wm. Essler.   JOHN BOWES.

I also held a discussion on Socialism at STOCKPORT, Lloyd Jones and another defended it, one each evening. I also baptized six persons in the river, and preached; there might be from 5000 to 8000 persons present. I preached in the evening, and several souls were brought to God.

A statement was issued July 22, from which this is taken.

"A STATEMENT"

"Of the means employed by the Christian Church under the pastoral care of the Rev. John Bowes, for promoting the glorious Gospel of the blessed God, and for the conversion of sinners from the error of their way."

"Since we became separated from Hope Street Chapel, we have found great difficulty in obtaining suitable places of worship. We at present occupy Edmund Street Chapel; in which we have preaching every Lord's Day; and Hill Street Room, Toxteth Park; in which we have two sermons preached every Sabbath, when the weather does not permit Mr. Bowes to stand in the open-air, he delivers two sermons on Wednesday and Friday evenings. He preaches in the following places in the open-air; on Sabbath days, at three o'clock, at the Prince's Pier Head, near the old church, to a congregation sometimes amounting to a thousand, or fifteen hundred hearers; on Monday evening, in the open area near St. James's Market; also at the same place, on Friday evening; on Tuesday evening, near the New Custom House; on Thursday evening, in the Hay Market; and on Saturday evening, sometimes in Queen's Square, or Scotland Place, or at some of the preceding places. Several young men connected with the church, proclaim the 'glad tidings' of salvation, in various parts of the town. Several souls have been led to *know, love,* and *obey* the truth, by the open-air sermons. The success which has attended them fills our hearts with unutterable gratitude to God."

Aug. 2nd.—To-day I visited BIRMINGHAM, spent an hour with my beloved brother Anderson, and saw the building in the Bull Ring burned down by the Chartists. How soon is property destroyed by an infuriated people, when the Lord does not restrain them.

Called at Oak Farm Foundry to see brother Burrows, formerly a member with us at Liverpool, now a local preacher with the New Connexion. As I had received more light from the Lord on the subject of baptism since I saw him, he and his neighbors came in, I read and expounded the Scriptures referring to that subject, as well as to faith and regeneration. He lives at Wallheath, four miles from Dudley.

THE MALTSTER.

3rd.—Brother Burrows observed to me, that as drunkards could spend several days when they thought proper in drinking, he would give up the Saturday to the Lord, and labor to get up a Temperance Meeting ere I should return ; he proposed to ask their chapel, the most influential trustee was Titus Fellowes, a maltster ; he wished us to consult him first, but as it was like asking him for a chapel to demolish his own trade, I was reluctant to go, but was told he was the only man to whom we could properly apply, among the trustees of the Pensnett Chapel. I had little hope of success, especially when he thought that my friend Burrows had done wrong in bringing the subject before some fellowship meetings. He rather proposed that application should be made for the Established Church School, to which we agreed. He received us very graciously, and asked me to preach in the chapel on Lord's Day morning ; I offered to give them two sermons instead of one, if they would get me an open-air congregation at 9 a.m., then I would preach in the chapel at 10½ ; they agreed.

4th.—Mr. Round, my host, of Tipton, took me in his conveyance to Pensnett, the morning was delightful ; the teachers and scholars of the Lord's Day School and many hearers convened on a hill, in a green field from which the hay had been carried a few weeks before. The high praises of God were sung melodiously ; I preached to a deeply attentive and devout congregation, who during prayer kneeled down on the grass, after the service they sang a hymn as they walked to chapel. The maltster, warmed by the service, eagerly grasped my arm as we walked with the assembly, when dear brother Burrows came up to inform us that the clergyman said we could not have the school, as I did not belong to the Established Church. The maltster said, might I not have the chapel ? If I would only mention it to the congregation it would be granted. I said, " No, I am willing to preach or lecture on Temperance to you, but I am unwilling to interfere with the internal management of your affairs." Some one said, " Mr. Fellowes, you can do it ;" he agreed. The congregation was large ; the interest deep ; after the sermon, before either singing or prayer, he ascended the high pulpit steps, and asked if they would give this " babbler " the chapel for a lecture on Temperance to-morrow evening, if so, to lift up their hands. All hands up. Those against it. No hand up. " There Sir," said he, " you may have it." The scene was heightening in interest ; a maltster asks, and gets a chapel for destroying his trade ! " I have seventy or eighty miles to travel in my gig to-morrow, Sir," said he, " but I should like to hear your lecture, and if I can I will get back to it." A good apology, thought I, for coming in late, or possibly not hearing it at all

5th.—My fears were groundless; the maltster was in his pew when my lecture began. I labored to show the inutility and pernicious consequences of intoxicating beer, and every argument struck at his trade. The miners here take their kegs of beer into the pit with them, and are thus demoralised; so that I expected the arguments would be too hard for him, and possibly might drive him away; at last I saw him rise and leave his pew, and to me he was unseen till the lecture was finished. A gentleman then came forward and proposed a vote of thanks for the lecture. A voice from the congregation said "I second it." I looked eagerly, the speaker advanced to the pulpit stairs, it was the maltster, with a deeply solemn aspect, with a confessor's firmness, andwith a martyr's step; he ascended the pulpit stairs, stated his former views, that he had long had doubts of the lawfulness of his trade, that my arguments were unanswerable, and had so deepened his convictions, "that," said he, " you all, or many of you know that I sell, as agent for Messrs. ———, about 4000 bushels of malt, per annum, to-morrow I shall write a letter requesting them to appoint another agent," and in three months he promised, and kept his promise, to relinquish the trade. The moment was sublime. Here was interest sacrificing to the power of principle; conscience yielding to truth and a strong sense of duty. What were the lecturer or the hearers compared to this noble man. I had spoken, they had heard, but he was *doing* truth. At that moment I could almost have wished myself a maltster, that I too might have made a similar sacrifice. Two class-leaders, and twelve more hearers, 14 in all, formed a society. Got to Tipton about 11 o'clock.

Often since then I have inquired about, and a few times seen, Titus Fellowes. I have understood that he lost nothing, but rather gained, by his conscientious change, and has not been unmindful of that most blessed of all causes, the cause of Christ.

In the afternoon of the 4th, Mr. Bennet, a local preacher, who prayed in the morning heartily for the unity of the church, gave out the hymns for me at Tipton. God was with us. In the evening we had much of the power and presence of God. It was a solemn time, and several souls gave themselves to God.

5th.—This morning the servant of the house where I lodged, wished me, without invitation, to take her name as a member of the Total Abstinence Society. I wrote out a pledge, saw a few friends, and then went in search of Richard Noble. I found him at Lower Gornal. He has fallen from grace. He told me he did not believe in the everlasting torments of hell. I soon learned that he had been several years in Dublin, and had scarcely ever gone to a place of worship. His wife took too much strong drink; this led him to drink, and for four months they were parted. What a curse to Britain is intoxicating drink! I got him to promise to return to God, and I hope his wife will grow better. I recommended him to the notice of the brethren. It was through this now fallen brother that my way was first opened to Dundee, to form the Christian Church there. During the day, a draft of the chapel deed (Tipton) was shown me. It is not intended to base it on any sectarian principle.

6th.—I rose this morning at 3 o'clock, in order to reach Birmingham in time for the 6 o'clock train. A little beyond West Bromwich we overtook a lady, who desired to ride with us. She was going to the funeral of her brother, who had died near Chesterfield very suddenly, about 40 years of age, and had left 13 children. His wife died a few months before, so that they will be orphans. Yesterday, she informs us, a gentleman was taken ill and died in a few seconds, while at one of the chapels in West Bromwich. In the midst of life, and the means of grace, we are in death. A few weeks ago I had a very solemn dream, which I felt it my duty to relate to several of my recent congregations. I was in company with some other friends, when a doctor came in and looking at me, said that I looked well, but was the subject of two incipient diseases, which would soon carry me to the tomb. I said, "Doctor, you must be mistaken, I enjoy excellent health, look at my tongue;" he examined it, and saw no danger from it, yet still adhered to his previously expressed opinion. Well, the Lord's will be done, through Christ I do not fear the king of terrors, but believe that my death will be eternal gain. Or perhaps it may be intended to keep me in constant readiness and watchfulness, that I may be always ready, and preach such solemn and awakening truths as may lead to make others ready.

11th.—Received a letter from one of our preachers, to whom I wrote last month warning him against the Chartists.

Chester Castle, August 10, 1839.

My Dear Brother,—

You will no doubt have heard of my arrest and removal to Chester until the trial, which will be next week, for anything I know. The reason why I am not out on bail, is because I thought it not worth while, considering the time is so short. You will be surprised to hear that the charge against me is "conspiracy and sedition," especially when you reflect that I am no party man, and that I never was a Chartist; that I only attended some few of their meetings in an obliging way, before they became so violent, as of late, and that I am a Tory in politics, and therefore quite the reverse of Radicalism. But the secret is,—our manufacturers hate me because I have opposed the Factory system, and their cruel treatment of the factory children, and all their other oppressions of the poor, which, as a minister, I thought it my duty to do. This is the cause. But I have no doubt God will deliver me out of their hands, and that I shall be able at the trial to prove their allegations false. The attorney has given me much encouragement. He says it will be impossible for them to prove that I have any connection with the Chartists.

I well recollect your kind advice the last time you was at Stockport, and am very sorry that I have not acted upon it fully. O do forgive me this wrong, and let me have your prayers and advice at this very critical time. If it is in your power to come to Chester and speak in my favor, you would do me a lasting kindness. The accommodation is quite as good as I could expect in prison, indeed the Governor, &c. are all as kind as possible. My mind is very low at present, but God is my helper, in him I have put my trust, and believe he shall deliver me out of all my troubles in his own good time. Give my love to Mrs. Bowes and to Mr. Hacking, you may let him see this if you please. Remember me to Mr. Kent, and tell him I have that book on the Earth in good keeping, and shall return it to him safe, with many thanks. I want very much to see you on important business, and if you come here in the beginning of the week, I have no doubt you will be permitted to see me.

Yours as ever,

To J. Bowes. W. ESSLER.

Sept. 9th.—We held this day as a fast day, that God might be pleased to hear us, and unite the church, and convert sinners, send us good harvest weather, as the weather has been wet recently, and direct us in deciding upon the following propositions which I submitted to the church:—That I should be permitted to go from home, either to lecture on unity and form Christian union societies, or plant Christian churches on New Testament principles. That I should take only half salary from the church and trust God for the rest, and with the other half they should employ an assistant, either a young man, or a married man without family.

At five o'clock this morning in the prayer meeting, God was graciously present, and also at my house at 2½ p.m. We had a full church meeting at eight.

After returning home from preaching last evening, I received a letter and a parcel of books from Henry Craik, one of the teachers of the assembly at Bristol. He also sent me George Muller's life or "The dealings of God with G.M." I had heard of the labors of these brethren, and that they had formed a church or churches on similar principles to those which we held.

This letter was in reply to one of mine.

18 Paul Street, King's-down,
Bristol, September 5, 1839.

My Dear Brother in Christ,

Your letter reached Bristol while I was absent from home, I had gone for a few weeks to visit my friends in Scotland, and since my return I have been hindered from replying to your communication, partly by indisposition of body, and partly by pressure of engagements. You have been rightly informed respecting the principles upon which we meet. We welcome amongst us all believers walking orderly, according to their light, and there are between 400 and 500 in fellowship with us.

I need not enter at large into a particular exposition of our principles of fellowship and church polity, as I intend to transmit to you copies of certain little works, by the perusal of which you may be able more fully to understand the way in which our gracious Lord has led us and our brethren. There is a brother in Liverpool, Mr. Price of the Mechanics' Institution, who has been for years past on intimate terms with us. He is a very excellent person, and would most fully sympathise with you in your efforts "to gather into one the children of God which are scattered abroad." Should you feel disposed to call upon him, he would be able to furnish you with further information respecting the body of believers with which we are connected in Bristol.

The Lord is indeed blessing us. There is a considerable spirit of prayer amongst us. We have also constant accessions to our number. There are also several amongst us qualified for edifying the saints publicly and privately; still, we have abundant reason for self-abasement before God, in that the truth which he has taught us, has yielded so small a return of fruit to his glory. We go on in the way of confession and prayer, waiting upon him for more of the energy of His Spirit. Brother Muller and myself are both of us much hindered by bodily infirmity from more active engagement in the work of God, both among believers and unbelievers; but there are several coming up to supply our places.

With regard to your "essential principles," I would, with brotherly freedom, give you my mind. I object not at all to the first, or second, or fifth. In regard to the fourth, I should like an express reference to the teaching of the Spirit. I do not see any thing in the New Testament sanctioning the election of pastors by the church. The call of God can alone qualify for the pastoral office, and all that the saints have to do, is just thankfully to acknowledge, and gladly submit to, the gifts which the Lord may have bestowed. I would request you prayerfully to read and consider the principles set forth in the tract on Church Government, the Account of the Orphans, the tract on the Young Men's Society, and particularly the Dealings of God with G. Muller, (all of which I propose sending you immediately) and then to give me your thoughts upon them. Praying that the God and Father of our Lord Jesus Christ may continue to water your soul with His heavenly grace, and hoping soon to hear from you,

I remain affectionately yours in Christ,

To J. Bowes.

HENRY CRAIK,

When the church met, I gave an account of the way in which the Lord led these brethren, and requested the church to wait on God, that he might direct us how to proceed; nearly all the brethren that spoke had faith in God, that he would direct and help the church; should he take me away for a time, only two doubted that my going would break up the church. After much Christian and believing conversation it was proposed, that all the brethren that were determined to stand by the church, however the Lord might order matters, should stand up, all the church stood up, but two or three. It was a solemn meeting; several of the brethren then expounded their conviction of the importance of doing something more under God for the union of the church and the conversion of souls, and, as I was the Lord's servant, that they should leave me to the Lord, and also leave the matter of supplying with the Lord; this was also nearly unanimous. I then desired the brethren to pray that the Lord might put it into the hearts of some of the brethren to commence a day school in Edmund Street, to instruct such poor children as cannot afford to pay anything, taking one penny per week, twopence, or as far as ninepence from those who can afford it. At this meeting it was unanimously resolved that we should have no collections from the wicked, but depend upon God and his church for support, boxes were therefore ordered to be got for the offerings of the church.

10*th*.—A sister has been praying much about the school, and the Lord has put it into her heart to offer herself as a governess. Preached this evening on the shore, Bridgewater Street, and related what God was doing in Bristol, after which I went to Edmund Street Temperance meeting, Lawrence Heyworth Esq. in the chair; I mentioned the school, he said he would give his mite. A crowded chapel; three scholars promised.

It will be seen from this that I had proposed that P. G. Anderson should return to Liverpool.

BIRMINGHAM, 9th Sept., 1839.

DEAR BROTHER,—
Never did any of your correspondence give me so much concern and anxiety as your last. When you wanted me to preach the gospel at first, although with reluctance, from a sense of my own inability, I did consent. When you sought me to go to Newburgh, and after a revolt, turned me back to that charge, I did so. When you sent for me to come to England, I felt delighted to comply with the openings of Providence. But now, what to say, or how to act, I know not. In the aspirations of your magnanimous and Christian-uniting spirit I do participate. When I see how one church shuts out another from places of worship, school-rooms, and other places and privileges, because not of "our sect;"—when I see the weak and puny efforts, though sincere and pious desires, churches can make when alone, and the overwhelming amount of influence of property, power, and wisdom when united;—when I find the difficulty of subscribing to this creed, and that dogma, and human explication and statement not found in the Word of God, and without which subscription there can be no communion,—and when I daily meet with the impenitent, stoutly resisting the gospel, because they know not where to go, and many other evils arising from divisions,—I cry, "O that Christians were one." But this is the difficulty,—*How is this to be effected?* Your plans are good to read,—*Are they practical?*

In the plan of my coming to Liverpool, I can have no possible objection to the thing itself; nay, I should like to be wholly engaged in preaching and the duties of a Christian minister, and, above all, to enter on a church of your training; but, O, the *circumstances* are awfully forbidding. 1st. Many who are now united with you, may be so just from your personal usefulness; and are likely to withdraw on your personal departure. 2nd. How could I walk in your steps, or at all follow you as a preacher! Your intrepidity of spirit, your influence of learning, your zeal as a Christian, and talents as a preacher, leave *me* far in the distance, and forbid any hopes of imitation. 3rd. It is wrong, I grant, to harrass our minds about the future, yet still a prudent foresight is a grace. It is likely a few months will roll you round again on the Liverpool society, and with all the fair prospects of success and aid from these ministers mentioned, you may not be continually employed as a lecturer, and what is then to be the result,—with the decrease of the society already alluded to, and two families to support, where can that support come from? Not that I would be unwilling to commence school keeping again, if necessary; but I can tell you, Brother Bowes, it is hard to be beginning the world all your life.

I have shewn your letter to several, who all appear concerned for the divisions of the church, and long for the union; but your plans, partaking so much of the sanguinity of your mind, they cannot entirely follow up; yet it is blessed to see the principle spreading. My friends in Brierly Hill are very liberal. The Birmingham Missionary Auxilliary has just commenced its meetings yesterday. Instead of the heading of the bills being "London Mis. Soc. Auxil.," it is "Christian Missions." Thus the spirit and signs of the times are going "a-head." I have shewn to Mr. Waller your plans. He drinks into the same spirit. Indeed it is difficult to say, but he will separate from the New Methodist Connexion on this very point; but still, even for him you are fast. Of course you ask for improvements upon your plans, or a better set as a substitute. Dear brother, my mind was never made for device, and *now* I shall submit none to you. But if all is well, and the Lord will,- I intend taking a trip to Scotland next week. In the passing I may be able to spend an hour or two with you. I intend leaving this on Thursday, and passing on to Scotland, so as to return hither by next Sunday or Monday week after. I don't expect to spend a sabbath with you, except perhaps on my return. Farewell. I am far from giving a "decided negative" to your proposals, and perhaps when I see you, you may be able to obviate some or all of my difficulties. I feel willing still to make sacrifices for God. When His ways can be traced; there His goodness can be trusted. My love to Mrs. Bowes, the family, and all friends. Mrs. A. is pretty well, and still more and more willing to embark, even to hazard, in any good cause. Yours in the Lord,

To J. Bowes. P. ANDERSON.

11*th*.—Wednesday. Mr. Dixon called on me to-day, to express his satisfaction with the change in my views; he was passing last night when I gave the statement in the open-air; he meets with three or four brethren to break bread, every first day of the week.

After preaching at Edmund Street, brother Taylor said he believed the Lord had sent him, that I might visit a dying woman, I went to a dark cellar, it was so even morally. May the Lord give light; as we were going we met Mr. Dixon; attended a Temperance Committee, afterwards.

12*th*.—Have determined to trust God for the support of my family, and not depend in any way upon the ungodly. Preached for a short time in the rain in the Haymarket; a gentleman going off by the train wished my name and address, the former was given by a hearer.

13*th*.—Met my class, two new members, both had been led to the consideration of the truth by open-air preaching. Seven shillings given this evening at the meeting, thus is God opening the hearts of the church. The following note was sent by a Christian brother in Bold St., who was aware that I had given up all claim for salary, being willing to receive whatever the Lord, by his people, might supply, and that the Lord's cause among us received pecuniary support from the free-will offerings of the people.

"Dear Brother in Christ,

"Having had my mind much impressed with that portion of God's Word in Luke xi. 41, (Give alms of such things as ye have; and, behold, all things are clean unto you,) and feeling something of the force contained in it, as coming from the lips of Him whom I trust I love, but whom I desire to love more ardently, accept of these two articles, for the cause of God, in any way you think most glorifying to his name.

"Yours in the bonds of Christian love."

(We omit the initials.)

"*Mr. Bowes*, 131 *Vine Street*."

The two articles were an *Accordion*, i. e. a musical instrument, and a *Watch Seal*. The former sold for £1. Since we got the above, several members or friends have aided us by sending in several small articles, which have been sold for a few shillings.

I received these in answer to the prayers that have been made. This evening I expounded the Word of God and held a fellowship meeting after.

For some days past Mr. Bertram and I have conversed about going to Bristol, where he has been laboring; after praying about it, we walked to the shore to inquire for a conveyance, we were directed to Captain Hill, as soon as he saw us he said, "Mr. Bertram, Mr. Bowes;" he had heard Mr. Bertram in Bristol, and me in Liverpool; we made our inquiries, he said, "If you go with me, I will take you for nothing." Thus has God inclined the hearts of his servants.

15*th*.—To-day we commenced depending on God and his people for support, and abolished collecting. One soul brought to God in the evening.

16*th*.—A blessed church meeting; I taught them to observe the Lord's Supper on the first day of the week, and that class meetings ought to be called fellowship meetings; one brother, viz. Mr. J Currie, proposed that a depositary should be provided, to which the church might send articles, to give alms of such things as they had. It was agreed that we should have a fast day to-morrow in reference to the harvest, and sending out and supporting ministers to preach the word in Bristol and other places.

19*th*.—Liverpool, a little past six o'clock this morning I and brother Bertram, and sister Richardson, whose husband was preaching in Bristol, sailed in the "Swift," Captain Hill, from Liverpool. We had a fine day, and at 7 all hands met, for singing, and reading and expounding the Scriptures in the cabin; brother Bertram and sister Richardson were sick, I conducted the worship, Captain Hill prayed.

20*th*.—To-day I was well, and conducted worship in the evening.

21*st*.—This evening I was sick, Captain Hill conducted the worship.

22*nd*.—This is the first Sunday I ever spent at sea; endeavored to make it as useful as possible to the sailors. We have prayed for favorable winds, and the Lord has sent them.

23*rd*.—This evening we had a new gracious influence in the cabin, I trust some of the sailors will never forget this voyage. Lord make me useful to sailors. We are now in the Bristol Channel.

24*th*.—This morning, arrived about nine o'clock within 12 miles of Bristol, as the vessel would not reach Bristol till seven in the evening, brother Bertram and I walked, arrived at 20 minutes past two o'clock; I preached in the evening in Guinea Street, from Is. xliii. 4, and had a gracious season. Found a letter to brother Bertram from Delany of London; he does not see his way clear to go to Sheffield where he is stationed.

25th.—This evening I preached out of doors, near the draw-bridge, from these words,—Luke xiii. "Cut it down, why cumbereth it the ground?"

26th.—To-day I received a letter from Bradford, informing me that my only brother died on Monday evening about 10 o'clock in the full assurance of faith. He is to be buried on Friday.

BRADFORD, Sept. 24th, 1839.

MY DEAR BROTHER,—

I have to inform you that my husband departed this life last night at ten o'clock, after a severe trial; but died in peace, and in the full assurance of entering into the rest that remains for the people of God. Your father feels very sorry that he is not able to write himself; and father and sister hope you will be able to attend his funeral on Friday, the 27th inst. Your dear father thinks of stopping here until the funeral is over. Your dear brother in the Lord, for

To. Mr. John Bowes,   H. BOWES.
    Guinea Street Chapel, Bristol.

It was one of my greatest trials, that I did not see my dearest and only brother alive, and that my positive engagements at the distant city of Bristol, hindered me from following his remains to the grave; but we shall meet again, when my work is done. The next month, my father, who had been with him four days before his departure, wrote, "I think a happier Christian I never saw go out of the world, he was a pattern to all who saw him; he broke out, the afternoon before he died, with singing, which brought people out of their houses to hear where it came from; he said, "do not fret for me father, prepare to follow me, I am only going a step before you, I will meet you when you come; tell my mother to live to the Lord. He was desirous to see thee before he died."

He was in his 28th year, and left a widow and three children; only one now survives, the mother of several children, she has been married twice.

This day brother Bertram and I had an interview with Messrs. Craik, Hull, and Stancombe, chief men among the saints assembling in Gideon and Bethesda Chapels; I learned with pleasure that they and several other churches are not Sectarian, and wish to promote the unity of the church. This evening I preached again in the chapel; brother Stancombe affectionately invited me to make my home at his house. I preached from "The king's daughter, all glorious within." A larger congregation than on Tuesday evening.

27th.—Friday, should have had a large congregation out of doors, the rain drove us off after I commenced my sermon; attended a church meeting after, the church approved of Messrs. Bertram and Richardson withdrawing from Mr. Aitken's society. I taught them several truths which the Lord has lately taught me; it was a gracious meeting.

28th.—Saturday, spent this day in reading and prayer, and in preparing for the Lord's Day.

29th.—The chapel was about three parts full; I expounded Esther iv., taught the church that we should come to the Scriptures, not as judges, but as learners, we may judge other writings, obey the Lord; may the Lord bless us with a teachable spirit; likewise pointed out the influence which Christ's life has over our life.

2½, Brother Bertram preached a short sermon in his gown, I preached on baptism after; about as many people as in the morning. Had a short interview with brother Craik on Saturday; I am much profited by the spirituality of these brethren: this evening he preached on the unity of the church, I preached on 2 Cor. vi. 2, and was mightily assisted by God; the chapel was crowded, about 17 souls were seeking mercy, ten or twelve professed love to Christ, and faith to the saving of the soul. Thanks be to God.

30th.—Delivered a Temperance speech in the Taylors' Hall, the place was crowded, I replied to a tract against the Temperance society, by Mr. Withy, who has withdrawn because he has conscientious objections against it.

Oct. 1st.—To-day met Messrs Craik, Hull, &c., to converse about the unity of the church. We seem to be of one mind. Preached out at six o'clock, and then heard a sermon in Guinea Street by a Mr. Burton. The matter was good. I spoke a few words afterwards.

2nd.—Visited Mr. Probert, and Mr. Birt. The former has been for years of free communion sentiments; not so the people of his charge. He seems unwilling to do anything till he has studied the subject six months. We learned from him, that in a certain large church, a meeting is held for praying for the unity of the church. Mr. Birt thought the churches were in a very comfortable and happy state. In the evening heard Mr. Richardson out of doors.

3rd.—Brother Craik and I called again on Mr. Birt, as he had requested me to call any day upon him. He seemed only anxious to ascertain my personal biography. I satisfied him, and we all prayed together. If these ministers (Baptist and Congregational) will not lead God's people together, may the Lord bring them together without them. To-day I groaned in spirit and wept before God for the state of the church, and have a strong hope that in Bristol there will soon be a movement to bring the saints together. At 6 o'clock preached out of doors to a large assembly, and at 7 delivered an address to an extensive congregation in Gideon Chapel. Afterwards attended a church meeting in Guinea Street.

4th.—This day had an interesting interview with Mr. Roper, Independent minister, and laid fully before him my plan for the unity of the church. He heard me patiently, and seemed to desire union, but not the entire union of all the saints at once. He mentioned to me a meeting of ministers, to be held in Mr. Birt's on Monday, of Baptists and Independents, and thought I might be permitted to address them on the subject of union. At 7 o'clock preached a sermon on Baptism, to a crowded congregation in Guinea Street Chapel, and baptized Messrs Bertram and Richardson, ministers; Messrs Daniels and Jones, open-air preachers (all these became pastors of churches); one Leader, and three more brethren,—eight in all. The two first brethren gave their reasons for baptism.

5th.—This morning I waited on Mr. Birt again. He is still not inclined to do anything for the unity of the church, but would do anything to oblige in the way of personal kindness. He did not think an address to the ministers would be productive of good; but, should I write, would present my letter. During this week have read several pages of Payson's life. During the early part of his life and ministry he seems to have had very defective views of the salvation of the gospel.

6th.—Lord's Day. This morning attended Gideon Chapel; read a part of Eph. iv., and expounded it, also 1 John iii. 1—3. It was a gracious season; the chapel was three-fourths full. The singing was dull and heavy. At half-past 2 preached at Guinea Street, from Luke xxiv. 46—47; it was a precious season; chapel quite crowded. Felt solemnly, and could weep for sinners during the first prayer. About 13 souls professed to get blessed with a sense of God's forgiving love afterwards. I preached either too loud or too long, for my breast felt a little pained.

7th.—Presented my letter to the Independent and Baptist ministers of Bristol, which is as follows:—

TO THE CONGREGATIONAL AND BAPTIST MINISTERS OF BRISTOL.

Dear Christian Brethren,

Looking upon you as the shepherd's of Christ's flock, whose duty and privilege it is "to take heed to all the flock;" and believing that God, our Saviour and common Master, wills that all the saints in Bristol and in the world should be united, I address you on this great subject, praying that the only wise God may favor me with his guidance. For some years I have endeavored to stir up the minds of Christians to pray and labor for the unity of the church; hence in 1835 when I was the pastor of a Christian community in the Nethergate Chapel, Dundee, I and another minister spent six weeks in England to promote the unity of the spirit, by sermons, lectures, and public meetings; Our Journal was published in a periodical of that date.

The Lord previous to that time had used me in forming a few Christian societies, without anything Sectarian in their constitution or name; you may have seen an account of them in Dr. Harris's work on Union, page 204, or the Congregational Magazine for October and December, 1836, the latter number of which contains a letter of mine, relative to their sentiments and order. Having been pressed in spirit to visit other places than Liverpool, where I have labored in the Gospel for more than two years, the Lord has directed my way to Bristol, and here, as every where else, I wish to do something by the Spirit's aid, towards "gathering together in one, the children of God that are scattered abroad." I have conversed privately with eight or nine ministers of the Gospel in this city, and with three or four of your number, the kindness which I have experienced from them, the importance of the subject, and a sense of my duty to my only master, induce me to request that you will prayerfully consider the following passages of Scripture, and either individually or collectively inform me if you feel that it is your duty to do anything to unite the church.

1. Is it not the will of God that all his people in this city should be united together, and form but one visible church, that it might appear one to the world, as did the church at Jerusalem, or Rome, or Corinth, or Ephesus, and not be divided into party conventions, having such names as are unauthorized by the Scriptures. The mind of Christ may

be ascertained from John x. 16, "Other sheep I have which are not of this fold; them also I must bring, and they shall be one fold and one shepherd." Dear Brethren, if you will hear the Saviour's voice, you will speedily come into one fold. In John xvii. 21—23. Christ says to his Father in prayer for his people, "That they all may be one, as thou Father art in me and I in thee, that they also may be one in us, that the world may believe that thou hast sent me," &c. May I request you, beloved brethren, not only to join the Saviour in this prayer yourselves, but also to bring it before the saints, that they too may pray after Christ's example.

2. Were all the people of God gathered into *a oneness which the world could see, would not the world believe* that Christ was sent of the Father? The invisible oneness of the saints arises from faith, which the world cannot see. The Saviour did not pray for *invisible* oneness; for all believers are invisibly one with Christ and each other, as members of his body, *by necessity of their spiritual nature*, being members of the one body, by faith. If Christ prayed for a visible unity to be manifested before conversion, the manifestation of which was to produce faith in the world. Do not those keep back or hinder the world from faith, who keep the church divided? See John xiii. 34, 35.

3. Should you ask who would teach and rule the church when visibly united? I would refer you to Christ's authority and word; "He gave some apostles, and some prophets, and some evangelists, and some pastors and teachers." Eph. iv. 11, &c. "And God hath set some in the church; first, apostles, secondarily, prophets, thirdly, teachers, after that miracles, then gifts of healing, helps, governments, diversities of tongues." 1 Cor. xii. 29, &c. Some of these orders have ceased, others remain. I refer to these passages to prove that God, not man, has set teachers or rulers in the church, in this case they are teachers or rulers to all the church, and that this under Christ the head, would preserve the unity of the church, "All the members of the one body, being many, are one body, so also is Christ." So that there would be union in receiving members, union in teaching and ruling, and union in discipline; a member once received would be recognised as a brother by all the saints in Bristol; a member once expelled would be regarded by all as "a heathen man and a publican," so that the church and the world would be exhibited as two great antagonist associations, the union of the church being not oneness of opinion but *Love*.

If it be your Master's will that his children should unite, that the world may believe, and that they should be kept together by scriptural teaching and rule, ought not you, the shepherds or overseers to be the first to lead the sheep into one fold. I grant that it is the duty of all Christians to unite, whether their pastors unite or not, for no law emanating from pastors can set aside the prior law of the King of kings, and Lord of lords. Therefore in all humility, Christian brethren, let us obey the will of Christ, as expressed by his servant Paul, 1 Cor. i. 10. "Now I entreat you, brethren, through the name of our Lord Jesus Christ, that you all speak the same thing, and *that* there may be no schisms among you, but that you may be put in perfect order in the same mind, and in the same purpose."

What a lovely sight would it be for the under-shepherds of Christ's flock, to lead the people committed to their care into one fold.

Dear brethren, if you, or any of you, desire the unity of the Church, and could bring the subject before the people of your charge, or furnish me with an opportunity of bringing it before them: or if you are willing to attend a public meeting to promote it, or can propose any speedier mode, than that of all the saints being invited by written or oral addresses to come at once together, I shall be glad to hear from you at your earliest possible convenience. Praying that you may see it to be your immediate duty to come together, in the spirit of tenderness and love, and say to the sheep, follow us as we follow Christ, I am, dear brethren, your unworthy brother in sorrowing over the division of his church,

JOHN BOWES.

"We follow therefore after the things which make for peace, and the things for mutual edification."—Rom. xiv. 19.

3 Upper Camden Place,
BATH, Oct. 15th, 1839.

DEAR BROTHER,—

I desire to commend to your Christian notice a brother, (the bearer possibly of this) who has been long, it seems, laboring for the Lord to awaken the Church at large to a sense of its want of union, and who expects to visit Dublin on his way to Plymouth. I felt some little reserve in my mind towards him at the first, knowing how many unscriptural theories are abroad on the subject; but was both surprised and delighted this evening to hear him lecture to a large body of persons, I hope Christians, at the Guildhall. His principles on this point seem quite identical with those we see, and both Moreshead and I felt to-night there was no position he stated in which we could not heartily agree. Indeed, I look confidently to much blessing through it. I believe him to be low in doctrine, but to have a true love to the Lord, and he has been owned, it appears, in gathering out many in Scotland and North of England. That he may receive much profitable instruction (which he needs, chiefly on the heavenly calling and the Lord's coming) from the dear brethren, and their hands be strengthened through his means, I heartily pray. The Lord bless your intercourse with him.

Affectionately yours in the Lord,

To Mr. Bellett. HENRY YOUNG.

20*th.*—LIVERPOOL, this forenoon had a full room at Hill Street, and a gracious season; also a good Love-feast, it was indeed a feast of love; I read Romans, xii. chapter. At 6 o'clock preached at Edmund Street; no souls visibly saved.

21*st.*—This evening I lectured on the duties of those who have left the sects, also on the duties of those that remain in them; while pointing out the common blessing of believers in which they have union, felt that it was good to be there; congregation was large; a church meeting after, where it was resolved to have the Lord's Supper every Lord's Day morning, for the present, at each place. I had tried to secure this in Dundee; the majority would neither do it themselves, nor allow us, a considerable minority, to observe it.

22*nd.*—As William Essler and Mr. Knight from Stockport were at my house while I was at Bristol, desiring to see me, and as the doctor recommends Mrs. Bowes to travel, as Mr. Knight invited her to Stockport, we set off and called at Manchester. I explained our principles to a Mr. Seargeant, Moss-lane, Deansgate, who wishes to be employed among us; he is the son of a Methodist preacher, who was killed some years ago while going to, or returning from Conference. I had some doubts of Mr. Seargeant's sobriety.

As I was going among strangers, I judged it best to take letters of recommendation with me.

LIVERPOOL, 22nd, Nov., 1839.

We cheerfully comply with the request of our brother, the Rev. John Bowes to state that he is a faithful and laborious preacher of the gospel in this town, and that we cordially recommend him, and the object of his journey to Christian friends in all parts of the country.

CHARLES M. BIRRELL,
(Minister of Pembroke Chapel.)
MOSES FISHER, Liverpool.
DANIEL JONES, Do.

These were all immersed ministers, as well as Mr. Lister.

Soho Street, 23rd Nov., 1839.

MY DEAR SIR,—

I find that you are going hence for some time on a preaching tour on the subject of union among Christians. I wish you all success in inducing Christians of all denominations to love each other, and shall be happy to learn that you have not labored in vain. I am, dear sir, yours truly,

JAMES LISTER.

LIVERPOOL. Mechanics' Institute,
December 18th, 1839.

To any Brethren in the Lord Jesus.

Dearly Beloved,—

I send these few lines by our brother, John Bowes, whom I commend to your affectionate regards in the Lord, as one whom I judge to be sincerely in earnest in desiring to serve the Lord in His church, although I differ from him in judgment as to the mind of the Lord in some particulars of service. It is a most interesting feature in his case and character, that he is *quite aware* of *having suffered much from previous ill-teaching and wrong systems*, and that a main purpose in his present journey is to *confer with experienced and gifted brethren with a view to obtain further instruction*. May the Lord be with you and him in any converse you may hold on these momentous subjects, and direct you according to his written word. I am here for two years past, struggling through difficulties, with a very small gathering of disciples, meeting simply as such, (as at Exeter, Bristol, Plymouth, &c.,) and earnestly desire the prayers of all who love our Lord Jesus in sincerity, that I may walk and act in the Spirit, who has graciously delivered us from much evil, and there appears just now to be an especial opening for good. Praise the Lord also with us. Yours affectionately in Christ Jesus,

JOHN PRICE.

My visit to Bristol was much blessed. After this, F. Daniel, the writer of the following letter, labored at Carlisle, in Scotland, &c., and attended college at Glasgow; he became a medical doctor, and removed to Melbourne.

BRISTOL, Nov. 18th, 1839.

DEAR BROTHER BOWES,—

I had given up my business some days previous to my receiving your kind letter from Brother Bertram. I should have answered immediately had I not expected to have been with you in a few days. I fully intended being in Liverpool this week, but circumstances over which I had no control prevented me. I shall be with you, the Lord willing, some day next week. I consider your letter as an especial answer to prayer, as I had been crying to the Lord to open my way, and had just risen from my knees when Brother Richardson came in with the news of the letter for me from you. I have been giving myself, I trust, more than ever to the Lord. I feel myself very weak and unworthy, but I know that our sufficiency is of the Lord. I do earnestly pray that if I come I shall come qualified by the Holy Spirit, that I may preach the gospel with the Holy Spirit sent down from heaven. I do beg of my dear Brother Bowes, and of all the brethren that I have not seen in the flesh—as Paul, the Apostle of the Gentiles did—that they will pray for me, yea, with all prayer. The Lord is with us : glory be to his holy name. Many of the brethren and sisters have been baptized; I believe nearly seventy. We had a glorious time on Sabbath evening last; the fire began to burn in the afternoon at the lovefeast, then were many pricked to the heart in the evening, and cried, "What must I do to be saved?" Truly the Lord made bare his arm. I am sorry I cannot come this week, but the Lord's will be done. It is published for Brother Hinton to preach two sermons on Sabbath next, when collections will be made to assist the friends in the rent of the chapel. I wish they had nothing to do with them. There will be a serious disappointment if Brother Hinton does not arrive. I have seen the Stancomb's, and they are all well. I am happy to inform you they have been holding meetings for enquirers after the sermon on Sabbath evenings; they dismiss all the believers. How far that is right I leave you to judge. There has been some conference between us respecting the union, but not much done. My kind love to you and Mrs. Bowes, and all the brethren and sisters. Brothers Bertram, Stancomb, and Richardson, send their kind love. I remain, dear brother, yours affectionately,

To John Bowes.   FREDERICK DANIEL.

Towards the latter part of November the following circumstance occurred in Liverpool:—Brother Grinstead, a beloved brother in the Lord, had a young brother who fell from a window three stories high, and broke his thigh ; his mother, unconverted, came over from Stockport to see him; she was affected on visiting him, but on the Lord's Day evening she came to Edmund Street, sought the Lord, and found him. It was delightful to see her converted son and she embrace each other when they became related in the Lord. "Now," said she, "I know why my dear boy was permitted to break his leg," &c. She said it was that the Lord might bring her to himself.

Dec. 1st.—To-day I preached at 6 p.m. at Hill Street, from Matt. xvi. 26 ; about seven souls got blessed; this is the more refreshing, as of late we have not had so many saved at once. I have lately felt convinced that the Americans excel us in believing for revivals and expecting them assuredly. May the Lord enable me always to preach in faith and pray in faith.

15th.—To-day, preached in the morning in Edmund Street, and in Hope Chapel, Seacombe, at 2¼. The Lord has brought a few souls to himself at this place, which we entered on November 15th. One night, after preaching, a man could not rest in his bed. In the evening I improved the sudden death of a dear brother, who was killed at the railway, down Park Lane, on the 5th curt. He seems to have had a premonition of his approaching end. On the previous evening at family prayer, he said to the Lord, "If thou shouldest call me away suddenly, sudden death would be sudden glory." He had given directions what hymn we should sing over him. He was highly respected by the workmen, nearly 100, some of whom requested to carry him to his grave. I preached from 2 Cor. vi. 2 ; about eight souls professed to embrace Christ; several backsliders were restored.

16th.—This evening had an invitation to attend a Temperance Festival at the Isle of Man ; I wish to go south this month, and have many cares at home.

17th.—Felt nearly overwhelmed this morning with the state of matters, but kept hold of the Lord ; was encouraged by a refreshing letter from Sir Culling E. Smith, Bart.; also by conversing with a dear brother. Asked the Lord for temporal supplies and wrote about this time to Birmingham and Bristol, that I should be in the former place on the 20th, and the latter on the 21st; this was done in faith, for I had not the means of going.

PORTSMOUTH, December 14, 1839.

DEAR SIR,—

I would readily promote your objects, if I had not at this moment several efforts, of the deepest interest, which require every assistance which I can bestow, and prevent me from doing as much as I could desire for other things.

I am glad to hear every account of an increased desire for union among the people of God. I believe, with yourself, that, in order to attain to it, we must commence anew, with the new Testament in our hands, and organise Christian societies with an entire forgetfulness of what this or that sect are doing. I believe the practice of nearly every sect is more or less tainted with sacerdotal heresy; for, though I conceive the office of overseer was intended to be perpetual, there appears to be no warrant in the word of God for a clerical caste! I should, perhaps, differ from you with regard to the pastoral office: I think there ought to be stated pastors, whose main function should be, to watch the conduct of associated believers, and to keep them up to their duties in the Redeemer's cause.*

However, dear sir, let us not dogmatise; we are all very much in the dark, this only being clear, that Christianity is a far more simple, and a far more absorbing principle than priests and divines have made it. The direction in which humble believers ought to move is, apparently, towards greater simplicity in externals and in organisation, and greater activity in doing all sorts of good, on the part of individuals and of societies. The dust of centuries is still in our eyes, but we begin to see men as trees walking. Let us move on steadily, waiting on God, borrowing each other's light, but avoiding, as far as possible, settling down into any crude or half-matured theories. Let us not discard antiquity merely as such, nor seek novelty merely as such. That passage appears to be our sheet-anchor, while making our way out of human investigations, into the old paths of the primitive Christians—"To him that ordereth his conversation aright, will I show the salvation of God." Let us understand the injunctions of holiness and usefulness in their literal and full sense; let us stir up those connected with us to these things; let no indolent, inactive person continue our recognised associate; let us look upon questions of church order as thoroughly secondary; they are but means to an end, that end being the sanctification of ourselves, and the conversion and happiness of the world.

In striving at these ends, I feel convinced other things will find their level; and, provided we judge calmly for ourselves, and refuse to travel in the mere beaten path of prescription, we shall, in a few years, find out what the Lord would have us to do in respect of pastors, the mode of edifying the church, and reclaiming the ungodly, and the extent to which we are to stand aloof from the world. It is possible to go to extremes in every thing. I do desire earnestly, for myself and those I respect, that they may be kept equally from the Scylla of antiquity, and the Charybdis of novelty, holding our opinions, to use a chemical term, in a state of suspension, and seeking that they may not be prematurely precipitated.

I sincerely hope that God will bless you in your labors of love, for the sake of that glorious Redeemer whom you desire to serve. I shall be glad to hear, from time to time, how you find any plan succeed—by those only true tests of success, conversion from the world (not from other systems), and the increased holiness of the brethren. Believe me, dear sir, sincerely yours,

CULLING EARDLEY SMITH.

My visit to Bristol was a means of leading my beloved brother Anderson to find out a few Christians at Birmingham, who met simply in the name of the Lord.

BIRMINGHAM, December 14, 1839.

DEAR BROTHER,—

I have deferred writing you these weeks since you were here, because, having made engagements with other Christians, I could not find opportunity to

---

* New Testament bishops, or elders, were generally both teachers and rulers—"Let the elders that rule well be counted worthy of double honor, especially they who labor in word and doctrine," 1 Tim. v. 17. I do not differ from the sentiments of the Letter, if "teaching is implied in the view given of the "pastoral office."

meet with the brethren. On the 24th ult., I and my wife broke bread with them in the name of the Lord, and have continued to do so "on the first day of the week" ever since. We have taken a few others with us, and I believe more will follow. Our brethren meet in a room in Union Passage, near Jones' Commercial Traveller's House. They are rather *still* for me; but seem willing to be led forth into action. I have never had an opportunity of speaking among them yet, having judged it better to allow them to go on than to put myself forward. Our dear brother Hargrove, administered the word and ordinance to us last Lord's day. It was a day of refreshing from the presence of the Lord. About thirty heard him at night. He called along with S. Lloyd, Esq., and Mr. Howard, of Tottenham, son-in-law to friend Lloyd, on me on Monday last. He talked very spiritually, and much, much on the Scriptures. He mourns over the divisions in the house of the Lord. I believe I have not been so much in the Scriptures of late as I should have been. But O, he reminds me much of our first months in Birmingham. May the Lord lead us more into Scriptural simplicity! He does revive his work in our souls, and I am believing for great things.

Have you read the "Inquirer" for this month? Are you still continuing the "Patriot." Have you thought of the first Monday of the year for fasting and prayer? Are not the revivals and union of churches a gracious sign of the times? I rejoice in your fellowship and order. The Lord bless you, is my frequent prayer.

In reference to my coming to Liverpool: I could only spend two sabbaths with you at the very most, and would have to be back here on the Monday morning after Christmas, as we only give a week for holiday. And even that would not suit me well, as many things have been let stand till Christmas, which will now require to be done. Nevertheless, on the conditions you mention, I might come and stay over the two Sundays with you. . . . . Yours in love,

P. G. ANDERSON.

18*th.*—To-day a gentleman, unknown to me, gave me £5, £1 for the cause, and £4 to be used in the Lord's work, in any way I deemed proper; my soul was astonished at the goodness of my Master. This enabled me to pay off some little bills which weighed heavily on my mind.

19*th.*—This morning I asked the Lord to give me as much as he did yesterday, as I saw it was needed. I went to the Dingle to call upon a brother Preacher, also to see a few Christian friends, to whom we had sent a "Statement" of our labors. One gentleman had not risen; I waited on him about half an hour without seeing him, and then rose and went out; found John Cropper, Esq. on the road, who inquired concerning our welfare, and gave £5 for the cause, this enabled me to pay the rent of Edmund Street Chapel for three months. The receiver gave 5s. and a friend 10s., making £5 15s. sent in this day. Thus the Lord has opened up my way for this journey, thanks to his holy name; also answered prayer.

20*th.*—Reached BIRMINGHAM to-day; was impressed while conversing with S. Lloyd Esq., he gave £1 towards my travelling expenses while laboring in unity, of course without being asked.

21*st.*—Arrived in BRISTOL wearied and wet; read 1 Cor. ii chap. however the weather these two days has been better than on any former two days lately.

When I got to Bristol I found that no arrangements had been made towards a public meeting.

22*nd.*—Broke bread this morning at Bethesda; G. Muller and I addressed the saints; at $2\frac{1}{2}$ read Romans xvi. nearly through, and expounded it; took the Lord's Supper at Guinea Street, this ordinance is now observed here every Lord's Day. I had a gracious season in the afternoon; preached in the evening at Guinea Street from the Jailor's question, "Sirs," &c.

23rd.—Monday, met a few of the brethren or elders at Gideon Street and Bethesda, who gave me their reasons for not granting Bethesda for a lecture on Union, and not publishing last night that I should lecture in Guinea Street on the 24th. The reasons related to something of which they could not approve in Guinea Street; I was not satisfied. Attended a meeting, held weekly by a few friends, in one of the Orphan Houses, Wilson Street, to pray for the unity of the church; held at five o'lock. Evening, attended a Scripture reading meeting at Gideon; Matt. xiii. parables of the Mustard Seed and Leaven were read, the Leaven was regarded as evil. The following scriptures were read, Ez. xvii. 5—9, Ez. xix., Ez. xvii. 22, 24. I endeavored with great tenderness, I trust, to express my dissent from the view, by showing that as Kingdom of God is used in Mark iv., and as in all other parts of the chapter it is used in a good sense, that something else than bad must be intended. I liked this meeting well.

24*th.*—Set before the people John xi. 51, 52.

25th.—At 10½, glorious season of liberty at Guinea Street.

This morning, brother Bertram, 5s.; this day called on several brethren, brother Willey gave me £1, brother R—, £1.

26*th.*—Had a long interview with G. Muller; although he seems to have stood in the way of a public lecture in Bethesda, he seems to have a fine spirit; he said, "You have before you a long journey, how does your purse stand." I stated I had between three and four pounds, "That," he said, "is little." He gave me 15s, saying, "There, dear brother, I will divide with you," showing he had just the same left. All this without asking any one. It rained much on the way to Bath.

At 7 Attended at the Free Masons' Hall, where the brethren are in the habit of meeting; Moreshead prayed as though some were in great trial. I was led to Romans viii, 28, felt great liberty in expounding it.

27*th.*—To-day called on Mr. Cater, Baptist Minister; had a pleasant interview with him, he seems to have no Sectarianism about him that he is not willing to give up.

28*th.*—On the 26th I called on Mr. Jay, a fine old man of 70, a total abstainer of six years, and nearly so for 25. I have seldom seen so strong a minister at his age. He is not prepared to act for union. This morning I knocked at his door at 7 o'lock, as I had left my pocket book; he was preparing to write, and had been in Bath between five and six; he rises early. He said, "All your papers are just as you left them, for I remember a saying of Lavater, 'Never trust that man that would look into your papers in your absence.'" He did not know that the Wesleyans recognise persons as members who are not children of God. Took the Mail coach for EXETER, the Guard put me inside all the way; a lady rode a few miles, with whom, after a difficult introduction, I had some profitable conversation. A gentleman from Prussia rode from Bath to Glastonbury, and stated that in Prussia, in one place Roman Catholics and Protestants meet in the same Chapel, and were more kind to each other than in this country, the Government being Protestant, about one half of the population Catholic.

Exeter, Lord's Day, broke bread with brethren. Mr. M'Adam read and expounded unprofitably. The bread seemed to be a loaf cut in two, each took a piece; when the brethren were all seated I rose to speak, and just uttered, "Beloved brethren," when Curzon, my host, pulled my cloak, and stated the wine was not quite round, after that they would make a collection; I sat down, and a hymn was sung, the collection was made just before the end. I rose no more, as the whole service showed that there was not liberty of ministry, each service following the other with a rapidity which precluded it. There was Mr. Morris from Plymouth present, who had been an Independent minister but went over to brethren, with about 50 members, and never spoke in their meetings for about six months. In the afternoon expounded Eph. iv. I preached from Romans viii. 28, in Bartholomew's Chapel, minister, G. Offord; felt at home; a large number present. In the evening at six, heard Mr. Morris in the Room in Paul Street; he stated the ground of a sinner's acceptance by faith clearly, but denied the propriety of repentance in the commonly received sense, and said concerning a sinner's reading, hearing, and doing in order to be saved, "These are your blackest sins." Remark this: he showed how all sinners are alike in debt and equally unable to pay, so that both must be equally indebted for forgiveness.

30*th*.—Attended prayer meeting and exhorted at six o'clock a.m., it was a melting time. In the evening attended again; about 200 present; expounded the scriptures.

31*st*.—Six o'clock a.m., prayer meeting at Mr. Offord's Chapel; met with a Mr. Cann who has been with brethren; about a dozen break bread at his house; he was silenced by other brethren, one here, others at Plymouth. This case seems to show that there is not liberty of ministry among them. Mr. Cann objected to brethren being brought in from other places to decide on his case. At six, spoke at a prayer meeting in Mr. Anstie's Chapel, South Street; a gracious season. At 10½ met at Bartholomew Street Chapel. Mr. Offord preached from "Prepare to meet thy God," I, from "Knowing the time." It was a solemn season.

LIVERPOOL.—In this town we are not now hindered by the "powers that be," though I was forcibly taken down, and haled away to the police-station, near Scotland Place, when I commenced my labors in Liverpool. I laid the case before the Watch Committee; solicited and obtained similar protection to that which I had experienced for seven years in Dundee; so that for more than two years drunken men have not been permitted to disturb either the preacher or his hearers.

The Sunday School, containing about 200 children, has gone on as before.

We have commenced a Day School, in which about 100 are taught to read, and are instructed in the principles of our holy religion, *whether their parents can pay for them or not*.

At the Temperance Meetings connected with the Church, about 1300 persons have signed the Total Abstinence Pledge. Some are now members of the church, who first became Total Abstainers, then hearers of the Gospel, after that believers.

We are not aware of any particular changes in our Church Order since the last "Statement" was issued, except that we have now "The

Lord's Supper" every first day of the week, after which a collection is made for the poor saints.

During the last ten years, I lectured on the unity of the church in Edinburgh, Glasgow, Aberdeen, Perth, Montrose, Leith, Paisley, Greenock, and several other large and small towns. In England, I have declared its importance at Stockport, Congleton, Burslem, Hanley, Stoke, Preston, and other places.*

Jan. 1st., 1840.—EXETER. Preached from 1 John iii. 2, in South Street. Heard that Dr. Payne was interested in my visit. Called on him, supped, and prayed with the servants and family. He fears that efforts to unite Christians will do harm, and thinks Baptists and Independents should form one body. When I got to my lodgings, conversed with two friends on the extent of God's love to the world. Wrote home to my dear wife as follows:—

EXETER, Jan. 1st, 1840.

MY DEAR WIFE,—

A holy and happy New Year to you, and all our little ones, and the brethren. I wrote you from Bath on the 27th. I came hither by the mail, and was very comfortable, for the Lord disposed the guard to put me *inside*, though I only paid outside fare. On Lord's Day morning, I sat down with the brethren; about 180 present. Heard their exposition, &c., but felt little profit. In the afternoon I preached to a large congregation in a Baptist chapel; had a gracious season. Evening, heard Mr. Morris, recently an Independent minister, who has joined those call "brethren." I wished to see all their movements here, without doing or saying much among them, and I like their proceedings less than at any other place I have visited. Here they are in two bodies, and have two tables; in short —are divided. . . . Yesterday I received Mr. Anderson's letter, and was glad to hear of your prosperity. The question of Unity is exciting considerable attention in Exeter, and I hope good will be done. The Lord has blessed me, and made me a blessing. The congregations in which I have been most especially at home, have both early meetings, and have thought whether the Lord has not sent me in answer to prayer. I preach this evening, and on Friday or Saturday morning shall proceed either to Barnstaple or Plymouth. I shall be glad to hear from you, or from dear brethren Curry or Williams, directed to me, Post Office, Plymouth. Let me know how you are. I hope the brethren pray for me. I find God wonderfully opening up my way. Praise his holy name! Give my love to all the holy brethren, and to dear brother Price, Dr. Burrows, and all friends. My hopes were never higher as to the subject of union. I have some fears that the brethren are sectarian, in Exeter at least. I hope I shall get a better impression of them at Plymouth. I trust the brethren will take care that no appointments are missed. Either Brother Gorst, or Dr. Burrows will help them. My health is exceedingly good, and brethren are very kind. I am now a little in the country, and could not get a better sheet of paper to write upon. I mean to serve the Lord this year, if possible, better than the last. Much love to the dear brethren. Yours always,

JOHN BOWES.

2nd.—Lectured on Unity in South Street chapel; a good audience. "The brethren," many of them would not come because I lectured in a Baptist Chapel! To conciliate the prejudices of those that did come, and engage them to sing and pray with their brethren, I mentioned that the chapel was our own for the night, having been kindly granted for the use of Christians of all denominations. The sum subscribed for expenses was £1 1s.

3rd.—Went to PLYMOUTH. Mr. Harris, whom I saw, was kind.

4th.—Met with Newton and Harris: they had received a letter of my

---

* See APPENDIX, Note B.

proceedings in Exeter, evidently showing that their brethren were not pleased that I had acted with other brethren and not with them.

As at Exeter I stated that I could not be idle on the Lord's Day, and that if they had any place to preach to sinners in I should gladly meet with them. But while I was quite welcome to the Table of the Lord, they could not recognise my teaching; Mr. Young of Bath had given a favorable testimony as to my gift of teaching, which satisfied Harris, but hardly Newton.

Mr. Nickelson, late a Baptist minister, but who, with the flock committed to his care, has abandoned Sectarianism; both asked me to preach, and offered me the use of his chapel for a lecture. Mr. Hine, Independent, also invited me to preach.

Mr. Craik writes of the Lord's work in Bristol:—" January 1, 1840.—During these seven years and eight months that we have been in Bristol 573 have been received into the fellowship: 68 in communion when we came; 641 would have been the number had there been no changes; but 40 have fallen asleep; 33 have been separated; 38 have left us and are still in Bristol; 55 gone from Bristol:—475 now in fellowship."—" Craik's Diary and Letters," p. 203.

5th.—Lord's Day. This morning I preached to an excellent morning congregation in Howe Street Chapel, from 2 Cor. vi. 2. Afterwards declined preaching for Mr. Hine, to hear the Plymouth Brethren at Raleigh Street. There was a large congregation, but no singing, Mr. Saltau prayed after reading, and then expounded Acts xxvii., and applied Paul's voyage to Rome to the state of the church now!

I met Mr. Bertram on the streets, he went with me, but went out before this strange exposition was through.

In the evening heard Mr. Smith deliver a heart-searching or powerfully awakening sermon from " This year thou shalt die."

6th.—This is the day set apart by American and many British Christians for fasting and prayer, for the Spirit to be poured out and the world to be converted. The Wesleyan, Independent, and Baptist denominations unite; I prayed with them at Howe Street, after which I visited Davenport, and at 6½ had a great meeting in the Independent Chapel, might be 1000 persons present; several ministers prayed. I was requested to take the concluding prayer: I felt great enjoyment. Mr. Orange, whom I saw in Newcastle in 1835, was supplying here, and was remarkably kind. I obtained Mount Street Independent Chapel, for a sermon on Wednesday night, and gave it out this evening. Felt much enjoyment of heart, and my soul stirred up to act for the conversion of sinners.

7th.—Tuesday. Lectured in Plymouth, at the Mechanics' Institute; a very respectable audience. A few of the brethren expressed their concurrence with my views; Mr. Nickelson prayed. In this lecture, for the first time, I pointed out the wrong of those who have abandoned a Sectarian name, but retain a Sectarian spirit. Subscriptions, £1 1s.

8th.—Wednesday. Crossed into Cornwall, the last county in England. Preached on unity in Davenport; the Lord was with us.

9th.—Thursday, set off from Barnstaple, across Devonshire, from sea to sea, reached it about seven o'clock: on the coach 11 hours, felt fatigued. Dear Chapman had collected a good congregation and I delivered a short address. Felt blessed in his company afterwards. He conveys the impression to me of being the holiest, most loving minister I have ever met with. There is nothing Sectarian in his spirit that I could detect. The church in Barnstaple and several other churches, all around, one of 150 members, are nothing more than Christian churches. This indefatigable man often walks 10 or 11 miles to preach at Ilfracombe, and then back again when he has done; these are the times he says, "while walking home after preaching that I take to pray for the unity of the church." Brethren gave £1 10. I regret exceedingly that I cannot stay a week, and sit at Chapman's feet to learn what the Lord has taught him. He holds a meeting every morning in the vestry for an hour, to pray and expound the Scriptures. May the Lord bless his labors. He gave me a letter of introduction to his brother in London.

10th.—Friday, about 9 o'clock left dear Chapman and Barnstaple to go 200 miles by coach to London. While the coach stopped for dinner at Taunton, I walked on, dining on apples and biscuits; when I got some distance I felt in my pocket for my purse and found a hole in the pocket and all my money gone; I was concerned, as I had guards and coachmen, who changed frequently, to pay all night, and to go into London the first time without a penny seemed a great trial; I turned back, snow being on the ground, met some people, but no one saw anything of my money; the coach would now soon appear, and I without supplies, my fare paid to London, I must go. I pulled off my boot, and all my cash in half sovereigns and silver, £1 3s. 6d. turned out; I never was more thankful. I had time to put on my boot when the coach came up, and with joy I took my seat.

We took supper between 12 and 1 o'clock at Salisbury, and crossed Salisbury Plain at midnight; although it was very frosty and cold the Lord preserved me from harm: it is about 13 miles across, where we crossed it, although in other places it is said to be 24. Reached London about 12 o'clock.

I had a letter of introduction to John Chapman, Esq. of Blackheath Park, and as he had left his office in Leadenhall Street, I went out 7 miles to see him. He pressed me to preach twice for him, in a chapel he has erected at his own expense at Leigh: I had a very gracious day, and have no doubt but the Lord sent me hither. They take the Lord's Supper every Lord's Day evening.

Blackheath Park, LONDON,
January 12th, 1840.

BELOVED WIFE,—

I arrived in London yesterday. Left Barnstaple, 200 miles off, last Friday, at 9 in the morning, and got to London by 12 o'clock, noon, the next day. I was out all night on the top of the coach. I am just now at a gentleman's house, seven miles from the heart of the city. I preached in a chapel here which he built, and in which he preaches himself. I never ventured to come to London till I was sure of the Lord's mind. I have no doubt God sent me to this brother's house. He does not see entirely with the Plymouth brethren, but he holds our views of Church Unity. I was introduced to him by his brother, Robert Chapman, a minister at Barnstaple. After this journey we shall have hundreds praying for us that did not before. I saw Miss Clemesha yesterday, and Messrs Delany and Gibson; they have two chapels in London, both separated from Mr. Aitken. Mr. Chapman will introduce me to one or two ministers to-morrow. I have already much work opening up here; but I must come home this week some day, if the

Lord will. I am well in health, and happy in God. I should think I may be at home on Friday or Saturday. I have not time to write much more at present. If you have anything to write, direct for me at John Chapman's, Esq., 2 Leadenhall Street, London. . . . . Give my kind regards to all the holy brethren and to our dear little family. Yours, very dear wife, with a husband's love,

JOHN BOWES.

P.S.—I often pray for you, and I trust you remember me.

13th.—In the morning I called on Mr. Sherman of Surrey Chapel; he gave me a note of introduction to a meeting of the Directors of the London Missionary Society, that I might see several ministers, but I got so engaged that I could not attend. I called on Mr. Herschell, a converted Jew, and apparently a fine spirited man.

14th.—Attended a meeting at 12 o'clock, held the second Tuesday in every month, of ministers of various denominations, in the Religious Tract Society Depot, Paternoster Row, to promote union among Christians. Dr. Reed introduced me to the meeting. G. Clayton read 1 Cor. xii., and prayed. A French minister prayed earnestly for the unity of the church. Those who expressed themselves most friendly to union, were—Drs. Harris and Steinkopff, and Mr. Young, of Albion Chapel, who seemed to entertain similar views to mine. I felt thankful to God for directing me to London, when this meeting was held, though I did not know of it before I reached London.

I set before the brethren the way in which Christians might be united. G. Clayton, as President, wished to know what was meant by union in teaching and ruling; I explained. Mr. Burgess, a Methodist minister who almost broke up the union prayer meeting, which is held by Independents, Baptists, and Wesleyans at Plymouth, thought my views would interfere with denominational discipline. Others thought that the object of the meeting was to promote union among Christians without interfering with denominational peculiarities. Dr. Steinkopff delivered a very affecting speech, showing the importance of more unity. Dr. Harris thought they should continue to meet and not give up because of discouragement. Mr. Hopton, a Baptist minister, read an extract from a church tract to show that the pious part of the Episcopalian church are meeting together to seek for union by prayer: he defended the feelings and coming towards union of the strict communion Baptists. Mr. Young of Albion Chapel had always been profited by these meetings, he sympathised with most of what Mr. Bowes said, and thought the time was coming when such changes as he proposed must be adopted. He would continue this meeting if only two continued beside himself.

In the evening I supped with Mr Dorman, he entered into conversation on the second advent; I told him my plan was to converse about these prophetical and disputed subjects seldom, and that it would probably please Satan well to see us spending our time thus, instead of conversing about the unity of the church and the conversion of guilty sinners.

15th.—Wednesday, set of from London at 1 o'clock, reached Birmingham by 6; spent a comfortable evening with my dear brother Anderson.

16th.—Thursday, rose at half-past four; set off at 6, got home about half-past 11, well in body, and thankful to find my family well.

1st. This journey has convinced me that the brethren in Exeter and

Plymouth are Sectarian in withdrawing from all intercourse with the saints in the Sects. I requested some of them to attend a meeting for prayer at 6 o'clock a.m. in Bartholomew Street: they refused. Instead of separating from evil, by keeping away from God's dear children I fear they go into the evil. Besides, if we must really separate from all evil in every church, we must separate from our own, for in what church is not evil? If their principle be right, the monks and hermits were right.

2ndly. In refusing to allow those to minister among them who do not believe in the pre-millennial advent of Christ. I had heard repeatedly that Mr. Newton affirmed that no man was called of God to teach that denied the pre-millennial advent; I put it to him and he admitted it. Now, as this admission was made in the presence of Harris and Saltau I have no reason to doubt its truth. Neither would he allow a minister of Wesleyan sentiments to minister among them.

3rdly. They have a dogmatism or confidence in their own views, approaching to infallibility; those who are initiated into their mysteries are called "instructed brethren," and these are supposed to have the spirit of judgment. Robert Chapman, who in the deep things of God seems to know more than many, they deem uninstructed.

4thly. I have been gladdened to hear of their care of the poor. A Baptist minister named Mozely had got into debt in planting churches, opening preaching places, &c.: Sir. A. C. inquired how much would clear his debts, and was informed £4,000; £1,500 of which he could raise by personal property. £2,500 Sir. A. C. put into the hands of Mr. Offord to pay the rest, saying that if Mozely should ever be able he might return it, and if not, he lent it to the Lord.

5thly. Mr. Groves gave up £1,200 per annum, as a Dentist at Exeter, to devote himself to missionary work. Yet many of them will not support this good man because his spirit is too catholic.

Feb. 4th.—MANCHESTER. Lectured in the Corn Exchange to a large congregation. This meeting was got up at great expense—I should think seven or eight pounds, the whole of which, and my travelling expenses, were paid by a few Christian friends. I could not have got up such a meeting without them, or similar friends. The following is a copy of the intimation:—Unity of the Church. A lecture on the union of Christians will be delivered (if the Lord will) in the Corn Exchange, Manchester, on Tuesday evening, February the 4th, 1840, at seven o'clock, by John Bowes, minister of the Gospel, Liverpool, who has delivered lectures on the subject in many of the large towns of England and Scotland. All Christians are affectionately invited to attend.— P.S.—The union to be recommended is the same as is detailed in the "Christian Union," p. 311, by J. B., and in the *Congregational Magazine* for October and December, 1836, and which is noticed by Dr. Harris on "Union," p. 304.

5th.—BURY. The Commercial Room was crowded. Ministers of various denominations stayed after; and as no united prayer meeting existed, it was agreed that a Monthly Prayer Meeting should be held in each chapel alternately, to pray for the unity of the church; to commence next Monday, in the New Connexion Chapel: the Wesleyan superintendent concurred in this arrangement. I am thankful to God for this practical benefit resulting from the lecture. A few friends here paid the expenses. It would give me great pleasure if I could go on lecturing without ever mentioning pecuniary matters, that all might see the object to be the spiritual welfare of a divided church.

At this time I expected the conversion of the world by the unity of Christians.

BRISTOL, 7th Feb., 1840.

MY DEAR BROTHER,—

After prayer and consideration, we have thought it well to transmit your letter to the brethren at Plymouth for their perusal. . . . . We are not sectarian, because we hold out the right hand of fellowship to all the people of God, and oppose no human restraint upon the exercise of the gifts of the Spirit; yet we may *appear* to be sectarian, because we repress that which we deem to be of the flesh, while the brother, upon whom the restraint has been laid, may fancy himself led of the Spirit. If the brother be right, then the sin of sectarianism lies with us; but if the brother be under a delusion, then his own error is the real cause of the disunion. Dear brother, the church at large has every where departed from the Scriptures. Purity in doctrine and practice can alone gender a permanent union. The lack of Scripture; lack of prayerfulness; worldly conformity, &c., &c., must be, in a good measure, exchanged for the opposite features of character, before much can be expected in the way of union, The way in which we may promote union most effectually, seems to me, by cultivating much intercourse with God in secret, diligent enquiry into truth, and subjection to the Scriptures: seeking deliverance from educational and other prejudices, remembering that every error in doctrine or in practice which, through carelessness and indolence, insincerity, or from any other unworthy cause, we maintain, constitutes *in us* a barrier to our full fellowship with God, and consequently to our union with those who possess most of His mind. I do not know whether I have expressed myself with sufficient clearness. I shall be glad to hear from you again, and not sorry to learn that as, for years of your ministerial life, you had maintained Infant Baptism, and afterwards had grace to renounce it, so you were resolved to give yourself to a fresh examination of all that you now profess as truth; that in your zeal you may spread not that which lendeth to disunion (which all false doctrine doeth); but that which contributeth to godly edification, because it is agreeable to the oracles of God.

Yours affectionately, very dear brother,

To John Bowes.   HENRY CRAIK.

BARNSTAPLE, Feb. 14th, 1840.

MY DEAR BROTHER,—

I thank you for your kind letter, and rejoice with you in all the goodness and truth that God has shewed you. We of Barnstaple are but feeling after the Lord's uncorrupted ways, and I should not like any narration to be made of us beyond this,—that we see the church's unity, and aim to walk in that path. We have been afflicted lately with much sickness of body, and have had humiliation by the evils of certain of our number; but God will exalt us if we bow before Him, under his mighty hand. Would we could help you in the collection: the saints I think are willing beyond their ability, but have not the power, present burdens considered. I hope to re-visit Spain; help me by your prayers for guidance. My love in Christ to all the saints with whom you assemble. I wish them the flesh and blood of Christ as their meat and drink,

Your affectionate brother,

To John Bowes.   ROBERT CHAPMAN.

25th.—Sir Culling Eardley Smith sent £2 in a letter, in which he says "you are of course aware of many Christians having agreed to make 'Union' the special subject of their intercessions every Saturday."

March 5th.—I concluded a course of five lectures on Socialism and Christianity, which were delivered in the Music Hall. They were well attended: one man professed to be convinced, and he renounced Socialism.

I published this month a pamphlet, entitled "The 'Social Beasts;' or an Exposure of the principles of Robert Owen, Esq., and the Socialists," from which the following is extracted:—

"A letter to the *Leeds Mercury* begins thus:—'Important and interesting proposal, addressed to Robert Owen, Esq.

"Most Philosophical and Greatest of Beasts,

"Your lofty and philosophical intellect, exalted so far above the prejudices of *men*, will prevent you from being shocked by this new style of address, from one of your admiring disciples.

" . . . As we have already discarded every thing which men hold as their distinguished attributes, and of which they are stupidly proud, why should we continue to own relationship to a race of which we have nothing in common but outward shape, and the animal propensities, (which propensities they irrationally control and repress)? Why not take a name that would better indicate our nature? We are the citizens of a 'New Moral World,' why retain the empty '*titles* of the *Old?*' I shall submit a formal proposal,—that in our various communities,— or I should prefer calling them *herds*,—we henceforth designate ourselves as 'THE SOCIETY OF BEASTS.' Your unrivalled compositions I shall propose to denominate 'THE SCRIPTURES OF THE BEASTS,' or the 'BEASTLY SCRIPTURES.'

"That we ought to vindicate to ourselves the nobler title of BEASTS may be best proved by those moral and physical considerations so amply suggested in your own immoral writings. Let us, aided by those lights, examine the distinguishing characteristics of *Men* and of *Beasts*, and the result will establish, beyond dispute, that we belong to the latter race, not to the former. I will put the arguments in a logical form, as follows:—

'1st. *Men* believe in and worship a God; *Beasts* do not. Neither do *we*. Therefore we are not men but BEASTS.

'2nd. *Men* think they have immortal souls, distinct from their animal organization, and living after the body; *Beasts* have no souls; our system recognises no such thing. Therefore we are not men, but BEASTS.

'3rd. *Men* believe in a future state of reward or punishment, and have a notion of responsibility; *Beasts* care only for the present state, and die like dogs; so do *we*. Therefore we are not men, but BEASTS.

'4th. *Men* obey Reason, even when it opposes instinct; *Beasts* follow instinct only; so do *we*. Therefore we are not men, but BEASTS.

'5th. *Men* prate about *free*-will; *Beasts* follow mere impulse, and obey their organization; so do *we*. Therefore we are not men, but BEASTS.

'6th. *Men* practise marriage; *Beasts* live promiscuously with their females, and leave them when they cease to like them; so do *we*. Therefore we are not men, but BEASTS.

'7th. Men train up their children in families; *Beasts* do not, though they train their offspring for a while; *we* do not let parents train theirs at all. Therefore we are not men, and may rank as a *superior* class of BEASTS.

'8th. *Men* live in those "dens of selfishness and hypocrisy"—single families: *Beasts* do not; no more do *we*. Therefore we are not men, but BEASTS.

'9th. *Men* have what they call "Ministers of Religion;" *Beasts* have none; neither have *we*. Therefore we are not men, but BEASTS.

'10th. *Men* every where appoint chiefs, or magistrates; *Beasts* do not, with the exception of bees, and other anomalous tribes; no more do *we*. Therefore we are not men, but BEASTS.

'11th. *Men* live under laws; *Beasts* have no laws; *we* deny all moral responsibility, and therefore banish law. Therefore we are not men, but BEASTS.

'12th. *Men* trade among each other, use money as a representative of value, and allow competition, so that an industrious and skilful man gets more than an idle or stupid man. *Beasts* do not trade: they have no money, and some tribes seem to work not for the individuals, but for the community, (though others, it must be admitted, act on the competitive system). We proscribe traffic, money, and competition. Therefore we are not men, but BEASTS.

'13th. *Men* accumulate property; *Beasts* do not; no more do *we*. Therefore we are not men, but BEASTS.

'14th. *Men* have classes and gradations of society; *Beasts* have none. We repudiate all distinctions. Therefore we are not men, but BEASTS.

'15th, and lastly. *Men* collect together in towns and cities; *Beasts* prefer the woods and fields; so do *we*. Therefore we are not men, but BEASTS.'

"Here, then, are irrefragable proofs, which I may call, in humble imitation of you, 'Fifteen Fundamental Facts and Laws, distinguishing Beasts from Men.

"BEASTS we are, and BEASTS we will be called. Our society shall be known as—'The Society of Beasts,' and we will glory in being known as beings who have no *Wives*, no *Families*, no *Laws*, no *Priests*, no *Souls*, no *Consciences*, and NO GOD!

"I am, O Beast of BEASTS, your admirer and Disciple,

"Leeds, Feb. 27, 1840.   "A SOCIAL BEAST."

22*nd*.—Preached three times in DUNDEE, in the New Chapel, Lindsay Street, to large congregations. My successor, G. C. Reid, divided the church and would not come into this chapel. Then he embraced A. Campbell's views of baptism, and again divided the church. Now he has lost the chapel which we have occupied for about ten years; this reminds one of Diotrephes in 3rd John.

23*rd*.—Monday, commenced a course of four lectures on Socialism in the Thistle Hall, and our chapel, Lindsay Street.

25*th*.—Heard Mr. King of Glasgow deliver a clear, but uncharitable sermon against the movements of the Established church. The voluntary church controversy, (and all other religious controversies) must either go on in peace and love, or it had better subside.

27*th*.—The interest taken in these lectures has been deep. The Socialists published a bill, in which they challenged me to debate. I believe truth has nothing to fear from examination, therefore I have accepted the challenge.

29*th*.—Lord's Day. Commenced having the Lord's Supper every first day of the week. Afternoon: adduced twelve arguments for the truth of the Bible. Evening: answered twelve objections, and preached Christ, freely.

30th.—Commenced a course of five lectures against Socialism in GLASGOW. This evening the congregation was not large; the public expected no discussion, as the Socialists published a bill, saying. "The Socialists again intimate to Mr. Bowes that they will not meet him at the conclusion of his lectures."

31st.—This evening a Socialist opposed, viz., Thomas Taylor. I read the bill, and he declared he would not come to-morrow night.

April 1st.—Thomas Taylor came again and opposed, notwithstanding his declaration last night, that he would not come!

2nd.—Three Socialists occupied fifteen minutes each, notwithstanding their published placard!!

3rd.—One Socialist opposed. From this proceeding one may judge what confidence is to be put in what they say. The meetings have been held as follows,—two in the Relief Church, Regent Place, and three in Albion Street Chapel. They increased much in interest.

5th.—Had a gracious day among my old affectionate Christian friends and children in DUNDEE. Let any now sow the seed of the gospel faithfully and in faith, and reap such a harvest as I have, and he will be stimulated to go forward in the Lord's work. This evening lectured on the unity of the church. The subject, as intimated by bills, was "The Scriptural ground of union; the progress of the cause in various parts of the world, and the hindrances in established and dissenting churches."

6th.—Public Discussion with John Farn, Socialist missionary. Upwards of 800 tickets sold, and many more could have been sold. Alex. Easson, town councillor, was my chairman; Alex. Peterkin, shoemaker, was his. The subjects were—first night: "Is man's character formed for him or by him?"—second night: "Is Socialism adapted to the wants of mankind?"—third night: "Is Socialism of a moralizing tendency." At the close, I moved that it had been proved, 1st: "That man's character is partly formed for, and partly by, him;" 2nd: "That Socialism is not adapted to the wants of mankind;" 3rd; "That Socialism is *de*moralizing in its tendency;" which was carried, in opposition to an amendment moved by Mr. Farn, by a very large majority, perhaps four or five to one.

OAK FARM WORKS,
April 8, 1840.

DEAR BROTHER IN CHRIST,—

. . . . The object you have in view is my glory. I long for the time when names and sects and parties shall fall, and Jesus Christ be all in all. But I despair of the day arriving during the present dispensation. However that should not set aside the use of means. There is a glorious period coming, (I mean that of the Millennium) when all flesh shall see his salvation together, when the earthly Jerusalem shall be rebuilt and made a blessing among the nations, when the law shall go forth out of Zion and the word of the Lord from Jerusalem. For this period the earth itself is waiting. The whole creation is groaning and travailing in pain until now, waiting, to wit, the redemption of the body. You may not agree with me in my views, at the same time I should wish to be put right by any person who can from Scripture convince me I am wrong. I am a baptized Millenarian, but a member of New Connexion.

I must beg pardon for not fulfilling a promise I made to you when you were over last summer, but I think I have a sufficient excuse. I did not know your address. You recollect I promised to send you a Skeleton of Sermons. I have often thought about it, and spoken of it. You shall have it shortly. I am in haste and must close, earnestly desiring for you, myself, and all the church of Christ peace in this life, eternal blessedness in the life to come. There, in heaven I mean, will be seen the advantage of union. With my kind respects to you and all friends, I remain yours affectionately through life,

To J. Bowes.   H. BENNETT.

12th.—Preached again on the evidences of the Gospel, afternoon and evening.

13th.—A final night's discussion on Socialism, perhaps the most triumphant of the whole. I laid down the Bible, recapitulated my arguments in its favor—which Mr. Farn had not even attempted to answer, and challenged him to answer them.

14th.—At 7 o'clock p.m. preached salvation through faith in Christ, in NEWBURGH: at 8 lectured on the unity of the church in the Town Hall to a considerable number.

                                                           April 14th, 1840.

BELOVED FRIEND,—

Forgive me for only dropping these few lines. I am just about to sail up the Tay to Newburgh, where Mr Anderson used to preach. I assure you I am quite at home among my children in the Lord, and brethren and sisters greatly beloved. The congregations have been large. The Discussion against Socialism triumphant. We had a fourth night last night. My arguments for the truth of the Scriptures were not touched. I return by Glasgow either next week or the week following. With kindest regards to Mrs. Broadley, I am with more regard than I can express, yours in the Lord,

To Wm. Broadley.   JOHN BOWES.

16th.—Fast-day. aThe annual meeting of the congregtional union being held to-day, I attended in the morning a prayer meeting. One young man named M'Roberts, from Cambuslang, prayed earnestly, the rest, all young ministers, were called up by Dr. Russell, and prayed on a platform and then retired like an actor on the stage. The Spirit of God might have called others to pray but there was no room. For ministers to limit God either to work and speak by them, or not at all, makes me heartily sick of the one-man-system. Why should a paid minister be more honored than one *un-paid*, provided that other things are equal? Preached twice in the open-air, and three times in the Chapel.

17th.—Friday, to-day I visited, at Arbroath, George Menmuir, who has always approved our principles: I hope the Lord will make him useful. On returning by Glasgow, I had two nights' discussion with Lloyd Jones, Social Missionary, on Christianity as it is, and, Socialism as it is. The main strength of my opponent was the inconsistencies of professors. These, I showed, were not Christianity, but the reverse, and proved from the Scriptures, that Christianity condemned such practices.

Before leaving Dundee and going south, I wrote the following letter to G. C. Reid:—

                                                        VAULT, DUNDEE,
                                                              April 17th, 1840.

DEAR SIR,—

Your letter of April 7th I almost answered when I saw you, for you would perceive that my chief difficulty consisted in recognising you as a Christian. It is true you profess to be a child of God, but then I do not know that you give evidence to satisfy a candid mind that you are a Christian man. This is the first point to be settled. Convince me that you are a Christian by your spirit, your words and your actions, and I will speak to you about the things of the kingdom. In conversation I mentioned the following reasons for doubting your piety.

1. That you had divided the church twice, with the oversight of which either God or his people, or both, had put you in trust. On this subject the Lord's word is plain, "Mark them who cause divisions and offences contrary to the doctrine which ye have learned, and avoid them."—Rom. xvi. 17.

2. I mentioned your sin in keeping out of the church or putting out the Lord's people, and read you as follows—"I wrote unto the church, but Diotrephes who loveth to have the pre-eminence among them receiveth us not. Therefore if I come I will remember his deeds which he doeth, prating against us with malicious words, [the very thing you have done] and not content therewith, neither doth he himself receive the brethren, and forbiddeth them that would, and casteth them out of the church."—3 Ep. John 9, 10.

3. I objected to your doctrine that a man can only get to heaven through baptism. I mentioned that "Abraham believed God, and it was counted to him for righteousness. Now to him that worketh is the reward not reckoned of grace but of debt; but to him that worketh not, but believeth on him that justifieth the ungodly, his faith is counted to him for righteousness."—Rom. iv. 1—5.

(2.) Your doctrine opposes justification by faith. But Christians as well as Abraham are justified by faith, and have "peace with God through our Lord Jesus Christ."—Rom. v. 1.

(3.) The doctrine is foolish as well as dangerous, for if a man sin after baptism, must he be baptized every time he sins? If there be no remission without baptism he must. This heresy is dangerous, because calculated to destroy Paul's great and glorious doctrine of justification by faith.

(4.) It brings the ordinance of Baptism into contempt, when believers are immersed twice over.

4. You have spoken "perverse things, to draw away disciples" after you, (Acts xx. 30) instead of allowing an united people to worship the Lord together.

5. You have acted unjustly and dishonorably to the Trustees, and led others into error, for, whereas a part of the people could not get on with the chapel, the whole united people would by this time have finished it. When you would not go into the new chapel, honorable Christian principles would have led you to say, "Dear brethren, I became the pastor of this church knowing that you had engaged to build a new chapel; as I am determined not to enter it, and as men of honor, and in common justice, you are bound to support the trustees who began to build for you, I resign my charge;" or rather, as the chapel was settled for before you came, you ought not to have come at all, if you intended to act in the strange manner you have done.

These lines convey my sentiments, and also much of the Lord's truth. If you allow the Lord to bring you to repentance, and act differently, I shall regard you as before; until then, discussion with you about the Lord's church is out of the question: the Lord's word to you is,—Repent, and restore what has been taken away. Hoping you will read this to the disciples you have drawn after you,

I remain, your soul's well-wisher,

To G. C. Reid. JOHN BOWES.

May 5th, 6th, 7th, and 27th.—LIVERPOOL. By way of redeeming their cause from a defeat which they at length acknowledged, John Green, their Missionary sustained, in the Queen's Theatre, about eighteen months ago, when he attempted to meet my arguments; and also, to redeem their system from the charges which my lectures contained against it, the Socialists brought forward Lloyd Jones to Liverpool, we need say nothing as to the result, as the discussion is published by Ward & Co., London, price one shilling. One circumstance deserves notice, Lloyd Jones affirmed that Christianity was of a persecuting character, and quoted the second Epistle of John, verse 10, to prove it. I showed that it referred to a teacher, who ought not to be received in that character, and offered to try Lloyd Jones and the Socialists, and see whether they would persecute or not. I said, "They have got a hired house, in the midst of hired houses, in Lord Nelson Street. They call it a Hall; I call it a house; if I should come to it, and bring the doctrine of Jesus Christ, and not the doctrine of Robert Owen, will they receive me? if so, I will preach there, if the Lord will, the next Lord's Day. They must either admit me, or, according to Mr. Jones, they have a persecuting spirit." After some consultation the request was granted. On the Lord's Day following, I preached in the Hall of Science to a large assembly of Socialists and Christians. The Lord assisted me to expound Rom. xii. chap., and to preach justification through faith in the blood of Christ, from Rom. vi. 6, 10. One man was soon after seized with affliction, who resides in Heath Street, Toxteth Park, he renounced Socialism and turned to Christ.

During the whole of the first nights of the debate three of my children were sick with the scarlet fever; Ebenezer died. On returning from Scotland, John, the second son was all but gone, his mother met me in the passage weeping, and said, "I thought your dear little John would have been gone before you came home, and that you would not have seen him alive." The fever was very malignant; for about one month, some part of the family, or our sisters in the church, were up night and day.

June 16th.—I sailed by the Royal George steam-packet a second time this year, to Scotland. The night was very tempestuous, I was very much affected with sea-sickness, but the Lord strengthened me to preach on the evening of my arrival, the 17th, to a large congregation, near the green, GLASGOW; probably from three to five thousand heard the plan of salvation through Jesus Christ. The next day, 18th, I preached three times; morning, afternoon, and evening, at the same place. As the people were working, the morning and afternoon audiences were small, but the evening as large or larger than before. About ten followed me to my lodgings, and wished that a church might be founded in Glasgow on the New Testament principles of church order and unity which had been advanced. They stated, that scores of their acquaintances would be disposed to act upon those principles. The harvest is white, may the Lord send forth laborers.

When I arrived in Glasgow I had not a farthing in my pocket, I therefore judged it to be the Lord's will that I should stay in Glasgow till the Lord opened my way. During these two days, as many of my publications were called for as came to about 6s. The next day I hastened off to Edinburgh, when I arrived I found I had only a few pence left. Two friends bought some of my books, and gave for them 2s. I did not yet know how to get to Dundee, but just as I left, an old friend and brother in Leith, put 2s. 6d. into my hand, (I do not remember that he ever did this before, or since).

AN ACCOUNT OF MY TRIAL FOR OPEN-AIR PREACHING

BEFORE THE MAGISTRATES OF DUNDEE, JUNE 22nd, 23rd, 24th.

June 20th.—Saturday. Arrived in DUNDEE, and preached in the Greenmarket. A police officer informed me, in the course of the sermon, that he had orders to take me to the office. He permitted me to finish my discourse, when I was taken to the office by two policemen, who behaved very respectfully. About 1000 people followed us, obviously displeased with the police; some of them said, "Do you not want to go? do not go; they cannot take you." I said, "I have promised to go; I wish to go, and you must not interfere." The police seemed much afraid; I felt calm; waited on God: rejoiced that I was taken up for preaching Christ, and believed it would end well. When I got to the office, I was asked my name and address. An Officer: "Are you likely to remain any time in Dundee?" J. B.: "I do not know; I am the Lord's servant, and I shall remain so long as my Master has any work for me to do here. By whose authority am I brought here? Is it by the authority of the Magistrates?" Officer: "By the authority of the Superintendent of Police." Lieutenant of Police: "I have heard you, *not* in the open-air, but in other places." (Here some conversation took place between us.) I waited till they gave me a summons, to appear in court on Monday.

21st.—I preached in the open-air, and in the chapel, and had a precious Lord's Day in the open-air; several of the police looked on; but did not interfere.

22nd.—Monday. When I got into court, several persons were tried before I was called. The crimes charged against them were *drunkenness, quarrelling, fighting*, &c. When I was called, heard the charge for the first time which was brought against me, namely, *collecting a crowd, and obstructing the thoroughfare*, or street. This I denied, so far as the obstructing of the thoroughfare was concerned, but admitted that there might be two or three hundred people present.

POLICE OFFICER BROWN stated that the reason why they did not offer to take me away by force was, that they were afraid of the people, therefore they allowed me to conclude.

Superintendent Corsterphan asked WILLIAM HIRD: "Did Mr. Bowes use any expressions which might cause the crowd to hiss the police, and prevent them from taking him away?" HIRD: "Yes, he did." *Cross-examined by me:* "What were the precise expressions that I used to excite the people? Do you remember any?" HIRD: "Yes; you said, 'If a man smote you on the one cheek, you would turn to him the other also.'" (Laughter in the court.) CORSTERPHAN said: "These observations were not likely to keep the people quiet." On being interrogated, he said, "It is the effect of the expressions we have to do with, and not with the expressions themselves." Brown said about 1000 persons followed them to the police office.

The Magistrate said, that if I would promise not to repeat it, he would dismiss the case. I said that I was a peaceable subject, and would most willingly yield obedience to the magistrates in all civil matters; but that in religious matters I acknowledged no law but the Bible, and no king but the Lord Jesus Christ.

I protested against going on with the case until I had time to consider the charge, which I heard for the first time read in court this morning. I requested a week to call witnesses, and, if necessary, consult with friends. This could not be granted. I mentioned that I did not know how the law stood here, but if the officer had interrupted me in England, he would have exposed himself to the penalty of £10.

Corsterphan said I wanted a week that I might have all the services over that I had intimated. This I denied.

I observed Edward Baxter, Esq., Justice of Peace for the County, come into the court, pass before the magistrates, as though he were coming to give me his hand, but he suddenly retired, went round the court, and sat down with me in the culprits' box; was concerned for me, and offered to employ an agent. I had some hesitancy, arising from our Lord's words, "But when they deliver you up, take no thought how or what ye shall speak; for it shall be given you in that same hour what ye shall speak. For it is not ye that speak, but the Spirit of your Father which speaketh in you."—Matt. x. 19, 20. But as my friend urged "that I did not know the provisions of the police act," he engaged J. Shiell, Esq., solicitor.

23rd.—My trial came on this morning, before the magistrates Adamson, Martin, &c. Adamson presided. The court was crowded, and many persons were unable to get in. Some of my witnesses were kept out of the yard a considerable time; and a friend, whom I had engaged to report the proceedings, intimated to the door-keeper that he was engaged to take notes for me, but this made no impression on the keeper of the yard, and my friend had the mortification to see several others admitted, while he was kept out. J. Shiell, my agent, requested a chair for me, as a person in my circumstances, he said, ought not to be treated like most persons brought to that court. This request was denied by Corsterphan; also by the Magistrates. J. Shiell, said, "Will you give me a chair, then?" One was handed to him. I continued standing a short time, when the Magistrates said, "Mr. Bowes may sit down in the front sitting," (the box in which culprits generally stand). I sat down.

J. Shiell asked if they meant to take into consideration the evidence adduced by the witnesses on the previous day, or to recall the witnesses, and was answered in the negative. The only witness called on the side of the prosecution, was John Matthew, policeman. Examined by the Superintendent:—"Was you near the Public Weigh-house on Saturday? Did you see Mr. Bowes?" "Yes." "How large a space might the congregation occupy?" "I measured it, and the ground on which the congregation stood was an area of 130 yards."

Superintendent.—Have you any questions to ask this witness?

J. Shiell.—*None.*

The following is extracted from the *Dundee Chronicle*, of June 25th, 1840, which gave an impartial account of the trial.

For the defence—Mr. Edward Baxter, Merchant.—Knew Mr. Bowes for seven years, and for a considerable portion of that time, he knew he was in the habit of preaching in the open-air. Knew him to be a useful, pious, and efficient minister of the Gospel; and believed, that by preaching the Gospel in the open-air, he had been the means of leading many immortal souls to Christ; Mr. Patrick Watson, Draper, High Street, was next called. The Dean of Guild said, "by these witnesses you wish to prove the excellency and respectability of Mr. Bowes' character?" Mr. Shiell—"I do, and that his case ought not to have been brought to this court." Dean of Guild—"We are quite satisfied of Mr. Bowes' respectability, and believe him to be a very worthy man."

John Kelly, minister of the Gospel,—stated that Mr. Bowes had come to officiate in Lindsay Street Chapel. That the Green Market was broad where he preached—he saw persons passing and re-passing, when Mr. Bowes told the people there was an order from the Police Office to take him thither—the people cried *shame*.

WILLIAM G. BAXTER, (brother to E. Baxter, Esq.,) saw Mr. Bowes standing on Saturday, the shops in the neighborhood where he preached were all shut up. Should say decidedly, there were two hundred people at least. One cart could easily pass another on the street.

GEORGE WHITTON, Collector of Customs.—Has often heard Mr. Bowes in the open-air. He selects his places of preaching judiciously. *Friday was a week he (Whitton) saw in the same Market, two or three times as many people round Mr. Methven, the Auctioneer.* When Mr. Bowes preached, two or three carts might have gone by.

MR. SCRYMGEOUR, Slop Seller—keeps a shop opposite, in the Green Market,—saw no obstruction—there was no pavement where the congregation stood—people and carts could pass. The doors were all closed. The Superintendent asked the witness, if persons passing down to the Shore from Crichton Street, could go in a straight line? Witness— *No, if you meet only one person, you are obliged to turn aside from a straight line?*

MR. MEITCH, Tailor and Clothier, also keeps a shop in the Green Market. The crowd left twenty-four feet of free passage between them and the Fish Market—and fifty feet to the opposite side of the Green Market.

SUPERINTENDENT cross-examined this witness.—"Could any person wanting to go into the Warehouse have got in? Witness—"*I suppose Mr. Bowes would have been civil enough to let him in.*"

JAMES LAW, Chapleshade.—Has heard Mr. Bowes at different times—knows that he takes no money when he preaches in the open-air. Three carts might pass the crowd—there was no obstruction.

J. SHIELL said he had many more witnesses to examine, if the Magistrates were not satisfied with the evidence he had adduced. They expressed their satisfaction, and he, therefore, declined to call any more witnesses.—*Dundee Chronicle*.

The SUPERINTENDENT, as Prosecutor, then addressed the court, saying, "The charge I make against Mr. Bowes is wilful obstruction to the public thoroughfare. A report has gone abroad that I am taking up this case to put down street preaching. This I deny, I never called in question Mr. Bowes' respectability. Is it then to be tolerated, that because Mr. Bowes is a respectable man, and supported by respectable men, that I am to allow obstruction."

J. SHIELL rose to address the court in reply.—I have got a very plain and simple case. It is the duty of the Superintendent of Police to bring up cases of drunkennesss, &c.,—in ninety-nine cases out of a hundred, the Bench feel it to be their duty to support the Superintendent. I am entitled to ask this Bench, if respectable characters, who devote their time to the benefit of the community, and to prevent such cases from coming into this court, are to be treated in the same way? This Bench should be a terror to such characters as are commonly brought hither, and a praise and protection to such as Mr. Bowes. I hold Mr. Bowes is entitled to preach the gospel in the open air, if he do not obstruct the people while going about their lawful calling. Mr. Bowes exercised sound discretion in the selection of the place of preaching. He does not wish to interrupt business—or obstruct the thoroughfares—or break the laws *—but to make his hearers useful members of society. Had he chosen any of those positions in the Seagate or Murraygate, mentioned by the Superintendent, it would have been very indiscreet. But I do declare that, had I wished to instruct the people of Dundee on any lawful subject, I could not have chosen a better place than that selected by Mr. Bowes. The Captain has said, that people might have wished to go into their warehouses, but this, it is proved by a witness, does not take place one night in three hundred and sixty five. A person could not have gone down in a straight line from Crichton Street for the auctioneer, but is such a slight inconvenience as this, to hinder ten thousand times ten thousand more good, than could arise from a person moving in a straight line? As there was a clear passage for individuals, carts, and carriages, I am entitled to an acquittance. Mr. Kelly gave his evidence with hesitancy, but the hesitancy of a witness, it is always held, does not make his evidence the less to be relied on.—I had forgot that Meitch mentioned *fifty feet* clear beyond the congregation. If not only these witnesses, but William Gornal Baxter, states that there was no obstruction, I need not trouble myself about the result. Had Mr. Bowes not been a man of undoubted and spotless character, he might have been classed with those who preach merely to collect a few pence. But his sole object was philanthropy, to reclaim souls, and bring them to Christ, who seldom attend any place of worship, and he is, therefore, fairly entitled to the favor of the court.

The presiding magistrates were ADAMSON, MARTIN, &c. After some consultation, they fined me one shilling. I said I should not pay it, as I considered it wrong to admit that I ought to pay a fine for preaching the gospel of Christ.

J. SHIELL.—I will pay it.

J. Shiell delivered a very reasonable and appropriate speech, of which the above is an outline.

An Auctioneer was subsequently called up for selling goods at the West Port, on whose case the Superintendent stated, that the Magistrates had granted the Green Market for selling goods. And if a passenger is often prevented from going in a straight line through the Green Market, the Magistrates are to blame for granting it to Auctioneers. But almost every body knows, and the next day's trial will show, that the alleged charge against me was not the real cause of my trial.

THIRD DAY'S TRIAL.

Copy of the Charge is still in my possession.

"David Corsterphan, Superintendent of Police and Prosecutor—Fiscal of Court for the Public interest—*Against* John Bowes, Preacher, from Liverpool, Defender; for having on the evening of Tuesday, twentieth day of June current, been found haranguing a crowd of people then assembled round him at the Green Market, Dundee, in consequence of which harangue and said crowd, the free passage of the public Street in said Market was obstructed and incommoded, the same being in contravention of the Police Act, section seventy-second; and the said Defender was on the said day convicted before the Police Court for a similar offence, *There-*

---

* Here J. SHIELL read the law, and stated that the Act said, that there was to be no wilful obstruction, and no such obstruction had taken place.

forte, the said Defender ought to be punished, or such other judgment given as the case requires. In the meantime, warrant is ordered to apprehend and take into custody the said Defender, and bring him into court for examination, ACCORDING TO JUSTICE, &c.

     (Signed)   DAVID CORSTERPHAN.
            By GABRIEL MILLER, Clerk.

Dundee, 23rd *June,* 1840.
  Certified as a true Copy.

"The same evening, 23d," says the Chronicle, "Mr. Bowes, preached to a considerable audience in the Green Market, and at the close of his sermon he received a summons from the Police to appear in court next morning. Accordingly he appeared yesterday forenoon (24th). The court was equally crowded as on the previous days, and the audience seemed to regard the proceedings with very great interest. Several witnesses were examined in support of the charge, who spoke to the fact of the preaching, and of the crowd being collected. Mr. Bowes called a variety of witnesses, who spoke as to the orderly proceedings and that no obstruction was caused. It appeared, from the testimony of some of the defender's witnesses, that leave had been asked of some of the inhabitants of the neighborhood, and that Mr. Bowes had taken a show of hands whether there was any obstruction or not, and the audience were unanimously of opinion that there was none."

The Magistrates, Johnson, Adamson, and Boyack, would not examine one-third of my witnesses, although I requested them to hear more evidence.

The witnesses called by the Superintendent were policemen James Brown, William Hird, John Matthew, and Adam Dow, a spirit-seller, all proved that there was no obstruction; that both "people" and "carts" could pass the crowd.

The witnesses called by me were—Dr. John Mudie; William Cruickshank, of the Crown Hotel; William Hutton, Junr., tar and paint warehouse; James Allan, hair-dresser; Oliver Jones Rowland, merchant, and two of the witnesses who bore evidence yesterday. I had many more ready. WILLIAM HUTTON said: "I will not only give Mr. Bowes liberty to preach outside his warehouse, but open the door, and let him and the people come in, if he pleased." (Cheers in court.)

I conducted the defence this day myself, as the Lord enabled me, and from the notes of a friend, and my own recollection, furnish the following outline of my address to the court. I observed:—

"The case which you have now under consideration is one of the greatest importance to the interests of Christianity in this town, and therefore deserves your serious attention.

"The law, which it is pretended, I have broken, was in existence ten years ago, when I commenced preaching in the open-air in this town; for seven years I preached unmolested, nay more, I was even protected by your predecessors in office; so that, when I removed to take the oversight of a Christian Church in Liverpool, and met with interruption in my open-air labors there, I referred to the conduct of the Magistrates of Dundee, as to an example worthy of being followed in Liverpool. It has been followed; for since then I have not only been protected, but if a drunken or disorderly person disturb the congregation, he is taken away by the police. How does it happen that you are so changed? For seven years together I preached in the very places where you will not now allow of preaching, and no complaint was made of any obstruction. And now that I am brought before you, Who were the witnesses to prove obstruction? Were they the inhabitants who could not get through the market to their business? No; but policemen, who, as was shown yesterday, when they once engage in a cause, are interested in giving such evidence as may acquit themselves and convict the person whom they oppose. Yet even the evidence of the police shews that there was no obstruction. If the inhabitants have been injured by my preaching, how comes it to pass that they, as witnesses, are not all against me, instead of being on my side? Surely this will weigh with the court.

"I can assure you, my continuing to preach is not understood, if it is construed into contempt of court. I am a peaceable subject in all civil matters, as is known to you all, and to all the inhabitants of this town; but in spiritual concerns I do not acknowledge the authority of this court; I acknowledge no king but Jesus Christ, and no law but the Bible. You forbid me to preach in the open-air, but my King says, 'Go ye into all the world, and preach the Gospel to every creature.' He sends me into the streets and market-places, enjoining me to 'compel men to come in, that his house may be filled.' And you may remember, that when the magistrates of old prohibited the preaching of Peter and John, they answered 'Whether it be right in the sight of God to hearken unto you more than unto God, judge ye.' These apostles did not obey the magistrates, but God. When Peter was imprisoned by the former, 'the angel of the Lord opened the prison doors, and brought him forth, and said, Go, stand and speak in the temple to the people all the words of this life.' Here we have the Lord working a miracle, and commanding his servant to preach in the face of the civil power. In like manner, I would gladly obey you, when I can without disobeying God; but when I must either disobey you or God, I do not hesitate a moment. Were I addressing Heathen, and not professedly Christian magistrates, my line of defence would be different; but you profess to serve the same Master with myself, and to be concerned for the spread of his religion; and what will the Socialists and Infidels say after this? Will they not say, 'Here are the magistrates of Dundee fining and persecuting their brother, whom they profess to love, and persecuting him for preaching that very religion which they all profess to enjoy.' What a wound to the cause of Christianity! The magistrates should be a terror to evil-doers, and anxious that those who by vice and crime cause much trouble and expense to this court, should be reclaimed. Open-air preaching has saved this court much trouble in this town, and you therefore should give all possible protection to open-air preaching." I said many other things which are not preserved.

BAILLIE JOHNSTON said, that my case was quite different from the apostles'; that if the magistrates had done wrong in allowing auctioneers to sell their goods in the market, that would not clear me—two blacks would never make a white; and if they allowed me to preach, Socialists, Chartists, &c. would claim the same privilege.

The magistrates did not deliberate long before they passed the following sentence, a copy of which is in my possession:—"No. 1427,

In the Complaint, Superintendent of Police, against John Bowes, dated 23rd June, 1840.

"Dundee, 24th June, 1840.

"Having considered the said complaint, examined the Defender, and heard the evidence adduced for both parties (this is not true: the magistrates did not hear *all* the evidence adduced by my party) finds the Complaint proven.

"Therefore decerns against the Defender for the sum of forty shillings, in name of fine and forfeiture, payable to the Superintendent of Police, Pursuer, and to be applied as the statue directs; and, in default of immediate payment or consignation thereof, grants warrant for committing the said Defender prisoner to the jail or Tolbooth of Dundee, therein to be detained till payment or consignation of said sum; or, failing such payment or consignation, till the lapse of forty days from this date, if such payment or consignation be not sooner made.

———, and decerns.

(Signed) "ROBT ADAMSON, D. G.

"Certified as a true copy, by Gabriel Miller, Clerk."

I refused to pay the fine, for the same reason as yesterday. Andrew Low, Esq. said, "I pay the fine, under protest."

When the trial was over, the Superintendent came over to me and assured me it was not his fault. The men at the office said at first, it was by his order. Be that as it may, he had only been in office a few months, and, like the new king who "knew not Joseph," he knew not my seven years' labor in Dundee; but God and the Christians knew, and protected me from prison. How will these magistrates meet God at last?

The same evening, the 24th, I preached in the Meadows, out of doors, to a very large and respectable congregation. Edward Baxter, Esq stood with me in the cart, and when the rain fell for a few minutes, covered my head with an umbrella. May the Lord reward him, and all other Christian friends, for all the kindness they have manifested to his unprofitable servant.

I continued to preach in private houses at three o'clock, and in the open-air in the evening, as before, and met with no further interruption from the police. May the Lord bring them and the magistrates to true repentance, before they stand before God, in the last judgment!

REMARKS ON THE WHOLE TRIAL.

The alleged charge against me was, "obstructing the free passage of the public street;" that this was not the real reason of the persecution, will appear by considering—

1st. It was proved that the Magistrates had granted the Green Market to Auctioneers, and that one was standing up with a crowd round him the first evening that I preached, therefore, the magistrates cannot seriously consider such a crowd an obstruction in the Green Market, or they would not permit it, which they have done for many years, and which Baillie Johnston acknowledged. And if "two blacks will not make a white," "two" whites will not make a black. If the magistrates be "white" in granting the Green Market for crowds, I am ",white" for having addressed one "on the glad tidings of great joy," which are the best and the most glorious that dying sinners can hear,

2nd. It could not be for " obstructing the streets," &c., because of the vindication set up by the magistrates, that "Socialists, Chartists, &c. would claim the same privilege" of preaching. Then if they fine me lest the Socialists or Chartists should preach or teach, it was not for obstructing the streets. This is like saying, " we must prevent honest men from walking on the Queen's highway, lest thieves should walk on it." If the Socialists and Chartists do wrong, let them suffer for it; but let not the innocent suffer for the guilty, lest somebody, sometime should be guilty. It is a curious circumstance, that the Chartists did hold public meetings in Dundee, in the open-air, and the Magistrates did not interfere, but with the Gospel they did.

3rd. All the witnesses, on both sides, proved that both carts and persons could pass; therefore, there could be no obstruction.

4th. Usage was entirely against it, the Act had been in existence many years. I had commenced preaching ten years ago, and for ten years no one complained of obstruction; therefore it is not credible that it was for obstruction that I was fined.

The new Superintendent was not acquainted with my seven years' labors previously in Dundee. He and the authorities had fined a preacher 5s., only a few days before my arrival, and as he refused to pay, and would not promise not to preach again, he was taken to *prison for ten days*, and there *his head was cropped!* and this in the nineteenth century!

It appears, from the two letters of the late zealous Henry Wight, himself an useful open-air preacher, that what was considered an offence against law in Dundee was tolerated and even applauded in Edinburgh. They are both addressed to my friend Patrick Watson, Esq., with the opinion of the Sheriff substitute, which I have no liberty to print.

EDINBURGH, 27th June, 1840.

MY DEAR BROTHER,—

I received your letter this morning, and was sorry to find that the inclination to oppose street preaching, of the existence of which in Dundee I heard last summer, at the time young Burns was there. An attempt was made to stop me in Edinburgh; the complaint having been made by spirit-dealers. At first the Sheriff sent me a message, requesting me to take some other spot; but as my principle is only to preach in thoroughfares and crowded places, I declined to comply, and said that, as I considered it a point of great consequence, I would try the question, and they might summon me for the purpose. I had to appear two days at the police office; the Sheriff having gone himself to inspect the scene of operations. After evidence being led which shewed that there was room left for a cart on each side of the crowd, decision was given in my favor; the Sheriff observing, that what I was doing, instead of being an obstruction, was a great public benefit. There seems, however, to be a material difference between my case and yours, in this—that the Sheriff and police officers were all in my favor, and anxious to encourage me, whereas it seems to be the reverse with you. I have no doubt that the magistrates are exceeding their powers, and when I heard of their conduct to young Burns, I had intended to have written to him to preach in spite of them, which I certainly would do, as long as I was persuaded I was not transgressing the law. You will perhaps find it difficult in your case to make good your point, but if you persevere, you will have the public voice with you, and they will be obliged to give way. It has occurred to me, on looking at the plan you sent, that if the preacher were to take his stand in or near the centre of the piece of ground (the Greenmarket), they could make less objection. I always endeavor to select such spots, and to preach at such times, as to prevent any charge of obstruction, and I consider that I have as good a RIGHT to preach in any street or area, as any auctioneer or mountebank to display his goods or agility. As to the law, I do not know of any way of appealing from the magistrates, as I suppose the Act makes them the judges of what is and what is not obstruction; but I shall endeavor to find out about this. The only way that occurs to me, is for a preacher, when he is fined, to let himself be imprisoned for the non-payment of the fine, and then sue them for wrongous imprisonment. You had better look at the Act and see this. However, if the thing can be managed without coming into collision, so much the better. Were I on the spot I could judge better how that could be done. Another thing you must resort to in this case is PRAYER, for it is a point that must not be conceded. Believe me, yours very truly,

HENRY WIGHT.

P.S.—I shall probably write to you on Saturday again about the law.

To Patrick Watson, Esq., Dundee.

EDINBURGH, 27th June, 1840.

MY DEAR BROTHER,—

I received your letter this morning, along with the newspaper. I enclose you a note I had from a friend of my own, the best qualified to tell whether there be any legal redress in such a case, as he is sheriff-substitute in Edinburgh. Make what use you like of what he says in his note, but I would rather you should not make it public. I am really at a loss what to say. You may perhaps yet reason the Superintendent of Police into giving up his opposition. I have read the evidence brought against Mr. Bowes, and I can ditsinctly say, that it is less obstruction than that which the Sheriff here declared no obstruction, and for which, he said, I deserved thanks. You proved there was room for two carts, whereas I could only prove there was room for one. Besides, what right have magistrates to give leave to auctioneers to obstruct the streets, and deny it to preachers? I think you should by all means shew determination to maintain the right; but I really feel at a loss to say any more as to how this is to be doue. All this makes me thankful I am so well off here, in the protection I enjoy at the hands of the authorities, and perhaps when the Dundee ones are told how the Edinburgh ones do, they will be ashamed of themselves. Believe me, yours in haste,

To Patrick Watson, Esq., Dundee.   HENRY WIGHT.

During the five Lord's Days which I spent in the chapel in Lindsay Street, the blessing of the Head of the Church rested upon us, and some souls were saved. I also visited ARBROATH twice, and lectured and addressed public meetings, both in the open-air, and in the chapel and hall, on the Gospel, Total Abstinence, and the Unity of the Church.

July 11*th.*—To-day my DUNDEE friends presented me with a new suit of clothes, hat, and travelling cloak. I had resolved to wear out my old suit as long as they would wear, rather than get into debt, and I had worn them longer by two months than the year, for I commonly get one new suit in twelve months. [Since then a new suit lasts me two or three years.] I received them as from the Lord, intending, should He give me health, to wear them out in His service. I was not uncomfortable in my old ones, believing, as I do, that ministers should be willing to wear poor clothing, if necessary, and glory in suffering exposure to "nakedness and hunger," as Paul did, rather than go to the world for support. Thus does the kindness of beloved brethren in the Lord gladden the heart amid the bitterness of persecution.

20*th.*—A letter was received by brother Allan, one of the elders here, from the elders in Liverpool, requesting that I might remain in Dundee, and J. Peart, who has supplied for me these five weeks, and a former five weeks, remain in Liverpool. This gave me much concern, for as his way is not open here, and as I had opened his way among us, hoping that he might be useful to the churches, and be a blessing to him, and as he knew I did not intend to leave Liverpool, I regarded it as unkind and selfish.

21*st*.—Having previously arranged to be in EDINBURGH to-day, I attended a great Temperance Tea Meeting, held in a kind of circus; there were about 1600 persons present. George Troup, Esq., of Aberdeen in the Chair. The meeting was addressed by Mr. Ballantyne, of Galashiels, and others. The chief speakers were Wm. Lloyd Garrison, Mr. Rogers, of New Hampshire, and a gentleman of color, forming a deputation to Britain from the American Anti-Slavery Society. The latter gentleman objected to a part of my speech in which I asserted that, "the slavery of the drunkard was worse than negro slavery." It appeared that we were both right in different senses. The interest was kept up till half-past one in the morning, from seven the previous evening, and probably not more than a hundred left before the close. It was too long, even granting that persons were present from different parts of the world.

26*th*.—Had a gracious day with my brethren in LIVERPOOL.

Aug. 9*th*.—Preached with considerable liberty in the floating chapel, from Rom. viii. 1—18. I have lately changed my mode of preaching. I now generally take a whole chapter, or a considerable part, and expound it. This evening, instead of calling penitents up to the form, I desired them after sermon to go into the next room.

12*th*.—This morning, about 3 o'clock, my wife was delivered of her eighth child, a son. We call his name Edward, after my dear departed and only brother. In the afternoon, as a Christian sister lifted him from the bed, his breath stopped, his face turned black, and three of us concluded him to be dead. I commenced gently rubbing his breast, and immediately wind came up at his mouth, and in a few seconds he came to himself again. Praise the Lord.

16*th*.—This evening I adopted the same course as last Lord's Day evening. Six persons gave in their names for membership.

Sept. 7*th*, 8*th*, 9*th*.—Visited HYDE, in Cheshire. Addressed Total Abstinence meetings, the Annual Meeting of the London Missionary Society, preached the gospel in the open-air, and lectured on the Unity of the Church, in the New Connexion Methodist Chapel; after the lecture, several brethren agreed to meet in the name of Jesus, on the principles of the New Testament.

10*th*.—BRADFORD. I visited the widow of my only brother. He was a Wesleyan; I sent for his leader, and learned, with thankfulness to God, that he never witnessed so happy and triumphant a death. Though older than he, I am the only one of the family left. May my life be devoted to Christ, my blessed Saviour and Master, and to the service of my generation, according to His will. If my life be holy and useful, my last end will be blessed, like his.

12*th*.—Yesterday met my father at Leeds. To-day, as we journeyed north, we passed the *new palace* which is being erected for the new Bishop of Ripon; it is to cost £12,000! Could not help asking, "Would Paul have collected money from the first churches to build such a palace for himself?" The interest of the sum would support three or four missionaries to the end of time! Towards evening, after seven years' absence, saw the peaks of my native mountains. The last time I was at Middleham I preached in the Wesleyan Chapel. As I had little time to procure it, and as I intended to preach the whole counsel of God, I sent the bellman round.

13th.—MIDDLEHAM. Lord's Day. Attended a Wesleyan prayer meeting at nine o'clock, and was melted down in tenderness at prayer; at half-past ten preached to a large assembly at the Market Cross; at one o'clock at the rural village of East Witton, on the Green; at five o'clock, at Middleham Cross; and at 6 in the Primitive Methodist Chapel.

15th.—Preached at CARLTON, where the Lord converted my soul about 23 years ago. I passed by the place in which I first bended my knees in penitential prayer, and cried, "God be merciful to me a sinner," "Lord save, or I perish."

16th.—I preached again in the Primitive Methodist Chapel, Middleham; a number of believers engaged to meet on the principles of the New Testament, the next Lord's Day.

Oct. 5th.—John B. Burrows, Esq., surgeon, and I attended NORTHWICH Total Abstinence Festival. The society seemed to be in higher spirits, and a better state than last year. The Wesleyan Association Tabernacle was crowded. The two ministers are total abstainers.

6th, 7th.—HYDE. I preached, in Flowery Field school-room, two sermons on the Unity of Christ's Church. The brethren here are going on with great spirit and activity, and are likely to do much good. They seem to have much of the love of God.

8th.—MANCHESTER. Delivered a discourse to a very crowded congregation in Hardman Street room, where a number of brethren are meeting on New Testament principles. There is a Sabbath School connected with it of about 120 scholars. Also a very flourishing Society of Total Abstainers. About 1,600 have signed the pledge since June last. Brother Platt has been exceedingly active and successful in this society,—he has got 610 signatures.

9th.—Had a meeting of several friends in Hardman Street, to consult about the unity of the church, which was very pleasing.

BIRMINGHAM, Oct. 29th, 1840.

MY DEAR BROTHER BOWES,—

I should be very happy that you saw the truth on the Lord's Second Coming; for it would unlock many passages of Scripture that to you must seem very obscure. It would place you in a more separated place from the world, and qualify you far more for a teacher in the body of the Lord. Much as you have been honored here, in "adding to the church," and "edifying the body," I believe that far more glory (though the Lord's glory) is awaiting you, when you perceive this blessed teaching of the Scriptures of truth. And the way the Lord has already led you to privation and renunciation of self, in following him, leads me to think, that when this sweet truth comes before your mind you will also be led sincerely and simply to embrace it. O it is a blessed thing to have power of grace over ourselves; to have the old man crucified in every thing, "that no flesh," nor anything of the flesh—its wisdom, or power—"may glory in His presence." May the Lord give us more and more to know that we have been crucified with Christ to all that this world acknowledges or knows,—that "as He is, so are we in this world." He is now the rejected stone; the owner and heir of all things, yet the possessor of nothing, till the times appointed of the Father, save a fulness (Eph. i. 21) of a body which is being formed of poor destitute ones, who, not having seen, yet have believed the testimony given by God of his Son, and wait the time of the redemption of the purchased possession (Eph. i. 9—14; Rom. viii. 18—24; 1 Thess i. 10.) And thus, while walking through this world it is at once our prison and our property, bought and paid for by Him whose right it is, though now He allows the prince of this world to usurp His place, we look for the time when he will take to Him his great power and reign. This world began its mad career in Adam, and Adam under sin is traced down through Cain, Babel, Nineveh, Babylon, and perfected in the Man of Sin; while Adam under grace is traced through Seth, Enoch, Noah, Abraham, Israel, the Church, Jesus being the securing party of all blessing, and centre of all hope. This distinction between man in sin and man in grace seems ever to be before the mind of God, though sad perversion and deep depravity have led even the gracious into the path of the graceless (Gen. vi. 1. 2). Hence Israel has become the degenerate plant of a strange vine, and even the Church has fallen from the grace wherein she was established. Yet the Lord has always overruled evil for the good of His own children, and manifested forth more and more of His glory by man's failure. Still the world remains the same: its Cain-like character is unchanged; it still prefers a robber or a murderer to the Son of God (John viii. 44, with x. 40). GOD HAS JUDGED IT (Rom. iii. 19); judged it in its prince (John xvi. 11), in itself (xii. 31), in its state (1 John v. 19), and in its character (John vii. 7). All are involved in this judgment which is committed into the hands of the Son; but, blessed be God, the sentence is yet suspended! a reprieve, a pardon, a glorious deliverance is offered to every sinner, and whosoever believes God's testimony concerning Jesus is transplanted out of the death and judgment of the world, into the heavenlies and the glory (Heb. ix. 27, 28; Eph. ii. 4—7), by whom the Lord will shew to the ages to come the exceeding riches of his grace, and thus prove to Jew and Gentile that Christ crucified is the power of God and the wisdom of God. Then I expect the blessing to this world, when Satan shall be bound, the Jew restored to blessing, the law proceeding from Jerusalem, the nations receiving blessing through the Jews (Is. xl. 1, 6), and among whom Jesus shall reign as a Priest on His throne; while the Church in the glory, the first-fruits of His creatures, the bride of His love and espousals, shares with Him the glory of reigning over the earth (James i. 18; Rev. xxi.; Song of Solomon; Isa. iv. 5; Rev. v.; 2 Tim. ii. 12; Rom. viii. 15—18). Hence we are strangers and pilgrims here, and can look on this world as Sodom and Egypt, where wickedness and oppression are united, and coming to their climax,—see it at the grave of Jesus, and long for the restitution of all things, and that same Jesus back to us again, or rather, we taken up to meet Him in the air (Acts iii. 20; 1 Thess. iv.), that where He is, there we may be also.

Dear Brother, I often feel great power in thus presenting Jesus to the poor, ruined sinner, as a blessed contrast to all the world can offer or he himself effect,—in shewing him that the risen Jesus is his title to glory, and because Jesus is risen there is evidence of the poor sinner's acceptance with God; and all who believe are justified from all things, from which they could not be justified in any other way. Thus the door closed on man's sin is opened by Jesus' righteousness. O that we had more of the power of the testimony of Jesus in our own souls, that we might present him with more effect to a ruined world. Amen. .... I hope the Lord is opening your way more clearly. Love to all the saints.

To J. Bowes.   P. G. ANDERSON.

Nov. 15th.—To-day, as for several previous Lord's Days, we have either proposed or received new members; received one, proposed four. At three o'clock, I, after another brother had preached, was led to shew that while the Roman Catholics were unscriptural in "forbidding to marry, and commanding to abstain from meats," (1 Tim. iv. 3.) that at some of the recent meetings, the Protestant Reformation Society has carried matters so far as to impress the mind of the Roman Catholic with the thought that he was hated by them. That religion which teaches one man to hate another can never be of God, but must be from Satan, and in as much as all the Scriptures insist upon love being the greatest grace, and hatred the greatest sin, it follows, that those Protestants who are destitute of love to Roman Catholics, or really hate them, are doing great injury to the cause of the Reformation. I adopted this line of argument with great advantage.

16th.—Spoke at MANCHESTER; two or three additional names were given in, to meet on New Testament principles. The last Monday evening a large congregation assembled to hear me, but I was confined at home several days by a severe cold, which I think I caught by putting on wet clothes only a few hours after I had put them off. James Grinstead also said some interesting things as to the principles upon which we act.

17th.—Visited STOCKPORT, and delivered several of the tract called "New Testament principles of church order and unity," which were printed by the Hyde brethren; 1000 being taken by them, 1000 by the brethren in Manchester, and 1000 in Liverpool. The tract I wrote at the request of the beloved brethren in Hyde. Walked through the wind and rain to Hyde, in which I expounded New Testament principles to saints, and preached to sinners. It was a refreshing season.

18th.—Met the brethren in fellowship in Manchester, and exhorted them to be more zealous for Christ than for total abstinence.

19th—Attended a large total abstinence meeting.

20th.—Having sent out copies of my Journal, &c. to several Christian friends, called on Patrick O'Leary, formerly a priest in the church of Rome, educated for some years in Italy, and for several years a priest in the church of Rome in Dublin, now minister at St. Jude's church, Manchester. He has not published his reasons for coming out of the Romish Church, and refuses to lend himself to that political party, who are carrying the "No Popery" cry through the land, it is to be feared only or chiefly to subserve the purposes of Toryism. I understand his ministry has been useful to many, and that poor Roman Catholics often listen to his discourses on Lord's Day evenings. May the Lord hasten the day when such men as he, and all other saints, shall form but one church. He had heard me preach the gospel in Liverpool in the open-air, during this summer. Dined with three dissenting ministers; one, a Baptist minister of open communion sentiments, stated that he had stipulated to be at liberty to express his views on that question when he became the pastor, and that he had never since disturbed his strict communion church. I said, "I should either teach my sentiments, or resign my charge." Every minister of Christ should boldly advocate what he believes to be essential to the prosperity of the church, without fear of man, and without calculating consequences.

21st.—Had some interesting conversation with Mr. Smith, who, I believe, was the means of erecting Tipping Street Chapel, and preaches in it himself. May the Lord raise up men to plead His own cause.

22nd.—Hardman Street Room at half-past ten. Read Rom. xii. and preached from 2 Cor. vii. 1; and at half-past 2, in the open-air, at the bottom of Market Street, near the Exchange. The congregation was large, but not so orderly at first as our Liverpool congregations. Two drunken men interrupted by making a noise; the police removed one at my request. A gentleman, in appearance, who talked like a Socialist, said, "Is that your Christianity?" I replied, that it was the duty of the public to take care of *madmen*, and men who had lost their *reason* by drink. He seemed offended with the tide of evidence which God enabled me to furnish of the truth of Christianity, and continued to talk. I left my stand, went into the crowd, and spoke to him; he was furious, but by kind words he was melted down. I showed the loving, uniting tendency of the gospel, and finished in peace. At six o'clock, preached in Hardman Street Room, to a crowded congregation, from the parable of the Barren Fig Tree. It was a time of weeping and solemnity.

23rd.—Had some interesting conversation with John Smith, a Manchester merchant. He exercises the office of an unordained pastor in the Congregational denomination. He seems to have suffered much in his endeavors to do good. Of course it is not common for a merchant to be the pastor of a church. Why not?

24th.—This day has been one of blessing. One dear soul, Mrs. B—, gave a sovereign to the cause, and, with tears in her eyes, especially desired us to pray for her. Heard ROBERT NEWTON, in Oldham Street chapel, from Phil. iv. 11: "For I have learned in whatsoever state I am, therewith to be content." He said: "(1) This contentment did not arise from the schools of philosophy. At the very time Paul lived, men were teaching, that men, by philosophy, might be superior to pain; yet still there was a difference between pleasure and pain, health and sickness, which philosophy did not provide for,—stoical apathy was not equal to it. This contentment (2) is different from what is merely constitutional. Some men have a deal of caloric in their constitution; they are all fire—all activity; others are phlegmatic, and are always dull and slow. But this contentment is happiness, satisfaction, &c. (3) It was not natural, it was acquired. It was an exotic, a foreign plant,—not learned in the schools of the philosophers—in no school but Christ's. (4.) It excludes *envy*. No man is content who envies another. He who has this contentment is satisfied with Christ and his portion. Then doubtless he was not *doubtful*, but *doubtless*. There did not exist a doubt—they were all gone. But let us put Paul to the test,—1st, He had a *thorn* in the flesh. He besought the Lord. What this thorn was, has been a *thorny* question to commentators. It was something which gave him pain, no matter what. He learned to bear it, to endure it, yea, even to *glory in it*, that the power of Christ might rest upon him. 2nd. See him in the jail at Philippi, &c. 3rd. Going bound between two soldiers, as he expected, to spill his blood. Are you *then happy*, Paul? Yes: 'None of these things move me.' If you had a thousand changes of raiment, you could only wear one at a time. If you had even so many rooms in a house, you could only be in one at the same time. II. THE MEANS. (1.) Get regenerated. (2.) Get your faith fixed in a *special providence*. Some of the ancient heathens, as well as the moderns, believed that one god reigned over one territory, and another over another, and that all they had to do, was to remove from that territory into another god's, if he had offended one. How would the heathens rejoice when they got free? (3.) Matters might have been worse. Some have said,—My case is worse than that of any one; I have nought but sorrow and troubles. Put your troubles on one side, and your *blessings* on the other, and see whether predominates. These are two mistakes. The same sorrows have been accomplished in your brethren on earth, as well as those in heaven. (4.) Others are in *worse circumstances*. (5.) Your *needs* are few. (6.) Your *time* is *short*. 'The fashion of the world passeth away.' (7.) You *deserve* more suffering. (8.) Christ suffered more for you. His life threw all the riches and honors of the world into the shade. Contentment will make you more happy, and more *useful*. We should be living epistles read and seen, &c.,—not *badly* written, not *hard* to be read, not *blotted*,—but so clearly written that he that runs may read. Discontent is *infectious*, and may spread from one to another till all are affected. A *father*, or a *family*, may get into the habit."—*Outline of Sermon.*

Dec. 9th.—To-day I was invited to meet, Mr. Harvey, Baptist minister, from Bradford, with a number of his friends and relations. The conversation turned upon open and strict communion. I trust it was profitable. Mr. Harvey slipped half a sovereign into my hand, while shaking hands with me on leaving the house.

11th.—Heard Hugh Stowell, on Luke vii. 22. *Outline of Sermon*—" This was a striking evidence of our Lord's Messiahship, by which he wished to answer the question of John's disciples, 'Art thou he that should come?' We make two plain assertions. I. The gospel is adapted to the poor. II. It is glad tidings to the poor. When we say it is adapted to the poor, we do not mean to say that it excludes the rich. It saves all that trust in it, and possesses depths and mysteries to occupy the learned. (1.) But it is adapted especially to the capacities of the poor. Is the poor man a *shepherd*; his heart is gladdened by the reflection, 'The Lord is my Shepherd, I shall not want; he maketh me to lie down in green pastures; he leadeth me beside still waters.' Also how is he gladdened by the promise, 'I am the good Shepherd, and know my sheep, and am known of mine.' Is he a *gardener;* as he plants the beautiful lily, he is reminded of the Lily of the Valley; or as he smells the fragrant rose, he is instructed to remember the rose of Sharon. Is he a *husbandman*, following the plough? he knows that he that sows to the flesh shall reap corruption, and he that sows to the Spirit, life everlasting. The harvest is the end of the world, when the wheat shall be gathered into his garner, and the tares shall be burned with fire. And so of almost any other trade or situation among the poor. The cottager's child, under the thatched roof of his father, while he beholds the sparrow building her nest in the thatch, may be taught the care of his heavenly Father,—'Are not two sparrows sold for one farthing, and not one of them is forgotten,' and from the beautiful lily in the father's garden. (2.) The gospel is adapted to the *means* of the poor. The gospel requires no money. It furnishes a price so great in the blood of God, manifested in the flesh, that all attempts to add to its value insult God. We are not *redeemed* with corruptible things. They have only to repent and believe, and they are saved as surely as the rich. (3.) It is suited to the *opportunities* of the poor. They cannot spend much time or money on books, the arts and sciences; but they can serve God in their calling, whether they plough the field, sit on the loom, or ride on the waves of the stormy ocean. They can read at home, and pray, and He will hear. II. The gospel is glad tidings to the poor. (1.) Because it enlarges their capacity of mind. Many a poor man, before he believes, has scarcely a second idea; but the gospel makes him conversant with great thoughts of death, judgment, heaven, hell, Christ, salvation, and thus his capacity is enlarged. The gospel may be understood by the poor, as well as the rich. It has both its deeps and its shallows, as a prelate of our own church remarked, 'It is so deep in some places that an elephant can swim, and so shallow in others that a lamb can walk.' (2.) It ennobles the heart. There is something in the very pride of human learning, and in the riches of the world, which demoralize the heart, and it is more owing to the state of the heart, than the mind, that men reject the gospel. From many of the errors of the rich, the poor are free. It refines the heart, so that some of the finest feelings of the heart may be found among the believing poor. They are often more charitable, and give more, and make greater sacrifices than the rich. (3.) It *comforts* them in their trials and poverty. Much no doubt of the miserable poverty of the land is not to be traced to the Divine decrees, but to men's profligacy, drunkenness, &c. But we know that, were mankind ever so virtuous, the poor we should have always with us. There would be poverty existing from divine visitations. The Christian man knows, that if his place is in the thatched cottage, 'the Son of man had not where to lay his head,' and that his poverty does not equal his Saviour's. The rich must become poor, and rich in their poverty,—*poor in spirit* and *rich in good works*. The poor must become rich. You have heard of the sacrifice of Christ being completed; and so it is; but it will do you no good unless you bring a second sacrifice—the sacrifice of a broken spirit; 'A broken and a contrite heart, O God, thou wilt not despise.' The poor see the providence of God more plainly than the rich, as a poor cripple girl said, when the Lord had supplied her wants. How plainly do the poor see the hand of God; from the rich it is obscured by second causes."

14*th*.—Rose at four o'clock, and attended the prayer-meeting at five. I felt it profitable to deny the flesh, rise early, and hold communion with God.

WARRINGTON. In the evening, I discoursed on the Unity of the church in the Independent Methodist Chapel. These people left the Wesleyans about forty years ago, have increased considerably since, and have had their chapel several times enlarged. My congregation chiefly consisted of Christians; was refreshed by the truth and Spirit of God. Lorenzo Dow resided here when he visited England, from America, and labored in the surrounding district with considerable success, more than thirty years ago. His labors are finished. My visit to this place arose thus:—I was invited to visit this chapel and preach their Sunday School Sermon; I agreed to come if they would have no collection; they could not agree to this, but invited me to give them a sermon, by their chief minister, Peter Phillips, brother to John Phillips, about forty years a pious Wesleyan minister. Peter Phillips pleaded hard with me to come on a Sunday, and make a collection, as it was not for the support of ministers, but for such a philanthropic object as a "Sabbath School," but I could not think of saddling the Gospel with a collection.

15*th*.—Rose between five and six o'clock; was kindly lodged by Mrs. Richardson, who sometimes preaches Christ. She is an intelligent woman, advanced in years. At seven a.m. took coach for Manchester, had an interesting conversation with a Mr. Hague, a Baptist, from Huddersfield. I gave him one of the tracts on New Testament principles of church order and unity; having read it, I gave him a few more to distribute in Yorkshire. A gentleman named Watts requested one, the conversation was not unprofitable.

In the evening I delivered an address on total abstinence to a crowded meeting, in Hardman Street Room, MANCHESTER. When I arrived in Manchester, dear brother Grinstead, from Hyde, was there to request me to visit Hyde.

16*th.*—This evening I met the brethren, who are now meeting in Christ's name alone. Some of them seem to be gathering more of the will of God, and to be getting more divine life.

17*th.*—HYDE. I read and expounded Phil. iv. Met the church after, now about thirty members. They asked me several questions on church order; one brother asked if they ought not to have tickets the same as the Methodists; another thought that the brethren should be received into the church by making a confession of their faith. I handed each of them a Bible to prove the points to which they referred, but neither of them opened them. Then a brother asked how were the first Christians received? I answered at once, "by baptism," and the confession which the believer made was before baptism, as in the case of the Ethiopian Eunuch. It was a most refreshing meeting, and we agreed to meet in the morning, for prayer at five o'clock.

18*th.*—Rose between four and five. We were not very numerous at the meeting. The people in this part of the county, who work in the factories, go between five and six in the morning, and stay till between seven and eight in the evening. Such long hours are neither favorable to the bodies, minds, nor morals, of the people. After mill-hours, their spirits flag, and they have no heart for either religion or any thing else.

19*th.*—Dined at a Wesleyan Leader's house; he gave me an account of his conversion, worth preserving. About 16 years ago he was in Hull working, and lodged a day or two in a public house. He went out to seek private lodgings, he went into an eating house; they told him they were very particular whom they took in, but agreed to try him a week. The first Lord's Day he did not go with them, owing to a prior engagement, but the next Lord's Day attended with these Christians at a Wesleyan chapel, the late David M'Nicol preached the word, it was sent home to his heart by the Spirit of God. When he got home the family saw that he was affected; he was dressed like a gay worldling, he took off a front or neck and put it in the fire; in the afternoon he accompanied them to a class meeting, believed that Jesus Christ died for him and rose again, and was able to rejoice in the liberty of the children of God. He has been some years a Leader. Thus may pious people first lead a lodger to hear the gospel, and this may lead him to Christ, usefulness, and heaven.

In the evening I expounded Eph. iii. We had much of the Lord's presence.

25*th.*—LIVERPOOL. Have attended the five o'clock meeting each morning lately, and have found it profitable. At two o'clock we had a meeting of the brethren, for mutual edification. Brother Hawthorne, after giving us a scriptural account of his conversion, and of his present faith in the Gospel, spoke nearly as follows, and apparently with deep feeling:—"For the last few weeks I have been out of work and unwell, and have been cast as a burden upon you, and you have liberally supplied my wants. 'I was an hungered, and ye gave me meat; I was thirsty, and ye gave me drink; I was a stranger among you, and ye took me in; naked, and ye clothed me; I was sick, and ye visited me.'

I have not been able to work these few days back, but I have remembered that my brethren were working for me, and at mid-day I have gathered my family together, and we have prayed for you." How delightful it is to see a number of working men put by their sixpence or shilling per week, that they may have to give to him that needeth!

Jan. 1st. 1841.—Had a large, serious congregation at the Watch-night. On reviewing the past year, find much cause for applying penitentially to that blood which cleanses from all sins—of sloth and inactivity, &c. I desire to begin and end the year with God; not to loose an hour in sleep, useless conversation, or unprofitable reading. The church is divided, and needs instruction in the duties of love and union. Sinners are perishing by tens of thousands yearly. Christ has saved me from the hell to which I was exposed, and planted in my heart the hope of glory. Every consideration of God's goodness, in creating, supporting, and redeeming me, by the precious blood of Christ, should stir me up to work while it is day, for the night cometh, when no man can work.

Death is near. My sisters are gone hence—my only brother has passed into the skies. What I do must be done quickly, or left undone forever. The rewards of obedience are transcendantly great—the approbation the of Judge—the crown—the throne—the kingdom—the companionship of the spirits of just men made perfect, and of angels, are all before me! If God spare me, I intend this to be a year of self-denial, prayer, travels, and toils, in the name of Jesus, for the glory of God, and the benefit of mankind. Lord help—for without thee I can do nothing! Thou wilt help, according to thy own unchangeable promise, "Ask, and ye shall receive; seek, and ye shall find."

131 Vine Street, Liverpool,
January 2nd, 1841.

Dear Sir,—

In your letter dated Nov. 29th, 1840, you say: "I did cherish a faint hope that your *self-confidence* might have induced you to fulfil your engagement, made in November, 1839, through our mutual friend Dr. Burrows, that upon receiving such explanations as that letter contained, you would hazard a discussion of the points at issue between us, with me." You further say, "You wisely, though not very *honorably*, shrunk from a debate," &c. If by a *discussion* with you, you mean a *public one*, before an assembly of any kind, *I never engaged to hold such a discussion with you*, and it was only on the condition of your regarding the Holy Scriptures of the Old and New Testaments as a revelation of the mind of Jehovah, and consequently *true*, that I ever engaged to write a few friendly letters to you. Now, when I have found that you only believe those passages of Scripture which *appear to you* favorable to your own views, and that you positively reject and discard such passages as I have adduced against your doctrine, I see no need of controversy, but direct your attention to such unanswerable works, with which our language abounds, as demonstrate the truth of the Scriptures. When I adduced John Finch as an example of unbelief, I only stated a fact, but never dreamed that it could give you offence.

With this, then, let the subject close. I cannot spend time to prove to you the truth of a doctrine from the Scriptures when you REJECT the Scriptures which prove the doctrine. I have no unkind feeling towards you, but have now an additional reason for declining any further controversy on your views, in the *spirit* and *language* which you have indulged, and which I should not have expected from you. Nothing but error could have led you to boast of a victory where there was no contest. Dr. Burrows has seen your letter to me, and distinctly disclaims any recollection of ever having said to you, that I would hazard a discussion with you

This he wishes me to state. I pray that Jesus Christ may assist me by his Spirit to write you a few lines which may be useful to your soul.

1. Remember, dear sir, that time is short, and that ere long we must give an account of our stewardship; let it therefore be our business to understand the Scriptures by searching them daily, depending upon the Spirit of truth, who has promised to guide us into all truth.

2. Instead of disbelieving or opposing any truth contained in the inspired volume, we ought to " receive with meekness the ingrafted word, which is able to save our souls."

3. Let us listen with believing attention to the message of the angel to the shepherds: "Behold I bring you good tidings of great joy, which shall be to all people; for unto you is born this day in the city of David a Saviour, who is Christ the Lord," then shall we be able to say, "In whom we have redemption through his blood, the forgiveness of sins, according to the riches of his grace."

4. When we know that our sins are forgiven, through Christ, we shall "love much because we have had much forgiven," and the "love of God shed abroad in our hearts by the Holy Spirit which is given unto us," will lead us to "glorify God in our bodies and spirits which are His,"—" whether we live, we live unto the Lord, and whether we die, we die unto the Lord."

5. We shall "love the brotherhood," *i. e.*, all the children of God, and manifest our love by "feeding the hungry, clothing the naked, and visiting the sick." Thus shall we show that we dwell in God, by dwelling in love with our brethren.

6. To our enemies we shall be kind, and instead of using bitter words against them, railing against them, or killing them, even in self-defence; when smitten on the one cheek we shall turn the other also, and if our "enemy hunger, we shall feed him, if he thirst, give him drink."

7. In ourselves we shall be sober, temperate, patient, gentle, easily to be entreated, full of mercy and good fruits.

8. Our lives will be cheered by the hope of Christ's second coming, when we shall be like him, shall see him as he is, and be forever with the Lord; and when the judgment shall come, instead of being at the left hand of the Judge, among the goats, we shall be placed at his right hand, among his sheep; instead of going into outer darkness, where their worm dieth not, and their fire is not quenched, we shall "enter into the joy of our Lord,"

My prayer is that your faith in Christ may be such as to purify you, even as He is pure, and that I may meet you in that world to which all the humble, holy, and spiritually minded will be exalted. Amen.

Your soul's friend,

To S. Tucker. JOHN BOWES.

11*th*.—HYDE. Set off from Liverpool at seven o'clock—a considerable quantity of snow on the ground—more falling. I was afraid the railway train would be hindered from proceeding, but men were employed with besoms to keep the rails clear. While waiting in MANCHESTER for the Hyde coach, Henry Bannerman, author of the book called "The Temple of the living God," presented me with a copy. Lectured at Hyde against Socialism, some Christian friends had requested me to deliver these lectures. The attendance was not large.

12*th*—Second lecture in the same place, the Working Man's Institute, built by the working men. A Socialist opposed, but with feebleness; he said, "What the Socialists want, is to see Primitive Christianity carried out." I showed that they wanted to overthrow Christianity, and had endeavored to accomplish their wishes; but having failed, they were now glad to retreat beneath the protecting wings of that Christianity which they had in vain attempted to destroy. He denied that Robert Owen's lectures on the marriage system were acknowledged publications.

13*th*.—Was advertised to lecture on Socialism and Christianity in the Temperance Hall, STALEY-BRIDGE. The Socialists seem few and declining here, therefore I dwelt chiefly on Christianity. A friend of

George Mather, who, with James Grinstead, accompanied me, invited us to supper, after which we walked home through the snow to Hyde.

14*th.*—This evening was invited to take tea with James Walker, City Missionary for the New Connexion Methodists, at James Taylor's. He heard me preach at the opening of Oldbury Chapel. Six of us sat down together, not at tea, for we all took *milk, water, and sugar*. This family never use tea. I have now done without for three months, and feel my health improved. I used to be subject to bilious attacks, which have left me since I ceased to use these nervous beverages. When I first read Finney's remarks against tea and coffee, I thought them uncalled for and enthusiastic; now I believe them to be just. Sister Taylor is the first female I have known to abandon tea, though I understand several Christian females in this neighborhood have given it up. I have seldom spent a more profitable afternoon. Mr. Walker, like myself, is opposed to law-swearing or taking oaths, to war, going to law, and clubs or benefit societies. I have spoken against them in Liverpool sometimes. They are unscriptural: 1st. Because believers are "unequally yoked together with unbelievers." 2nd. Because it is laying up treasure on earth. 3rd. It argues a want of confidence in God, who says, "Take no thought for to-morrow," "Be careful for nothing." 4th. It hinders benevolence; for you cannot give the money which you give to the club. 5th. It hinders the formation of a church fund for the poor. 6th. You must conform to their method of dressing. I am glad to record the following fact of Joseph Barker, told by Mr. Walker, his friend: "J. Barker's wife had saved about three pounds to buy a carpet with. She told him, and invited him to go with her and buy it. As they were going, he desired her to walk on. She had given him the money. He called upon several poor families that wanted bread. To the first, he gave half a sovereign; to the second, a sovereign, and thus he went on till all the money was gone. He met with his wife near the shop door. She wished to go in and buy a carpet. He then told her what he had done with the money,—that he could not think of walking on a carpet, while many of the poor wanted bread. She went home quite satisfied with her husband's reasons. This evening I contrasted Christianity with Socialism. After I had disposed of Socialism, I dwelt on the system of union and church order set up in the New Testament. When I had done a socialist opposed. He said that he agreed with all I said, but I was short as to communities. He threw out a sneer about hell, which I met by argument. I took up the book of the "New Moral World," but they declared it was not an authorised publication. This I never heard before. The socialists are now ashamed of Owen's writings. Both here and at Hyde they offered to bring a lecturer forward, if I would come again and meet him in discussion. This evening I walked to Hyde, which we reached soon after midnight. I was tired, and thanked God for supper. This has been a day of blessing. I trust the seed sown will be seen after many days.

15*th.*—OLDHAM. The brethren, Grinstead, Mather, and I, walked through the snow to Oldham—obtained the Independent Methodist Chapel—sent the bellman round. He is a blind man, named Howarth, who has been many years a Wesleyan Local Preacher. Called on three Dissenting Ministers, learned with joy, that they, and William Fullerton Walker, incumbent of one of the town's parishes, meet together at each others houses every fortnight, to pray and converse together on the affairs of Christ's kingdom. It would be cheering to find Christ's ministers of all parts of the church, often meeting together in the Lord's name. Had a gracious season in the evening. Was dissolved in tears, while I spoke of the condition of Christ's poor among the different denominations. I wonder how any Christian can take his food comfortably, when he knows any real Christian brother has nothing to eat. Brother Grinstead spoke profitably when I had done. One brother said he had been expecting such a movement as this for some time, it had not taken him by surprise. Several met to converse with us after the lecture. As none of the Lord's people invited us to lodge with them, and one of the brethren felt too unwell to walk back to Hyde through the snow, we went to two Temperance Hotels, they were closed. We slept comfortably at the Albion.

16th.—Rose this morning at six o'clock. After a four or five miles fatiguing walk through the snow reached Dukinfield. Called on the minister at Providence Chapel, who gave the chapel in 1835. He seemed unwilling to give the chapel without consulting others. After going supperless to bed, and having an eight miles' walk before breakfast, brother Grinstead and I bought two biscuits each. We got to Hyde about nine o'clock.

17th.—HYDE. Lord's Day. Attended the morning prayer meeting at 7 a.m. At ten o'clock the brethren met to break bread; it was truly refreshing to meet these saints. One of the brethren wished to have my discourse written down. I have not time to write copies, and I have not money to print all that I could wish to print, and, perhaps, we have too many books already. I read the Bible more, and other books less than formerly; it is more to be desired than gold, and sweeter than honey. NEWTON-MOOR at two o'clock. I trust the seed sown in this place will be seen after many days. How often we wish to sow and reap together! whereas it is in the church as in the worldly farm, —a considerable time elapses between the seed-time and the harvest. Let us sow in hope. STALEY-BRIDGE at 6 o'clock, in the Temperance Hall. After the discourse, a few agreed to meet the next Lord's Day in the Lord's name, and still to retain their connection for the present with their respective denominations. If Christians would only meet together weekly in Christ's name, they would soon be increasingly dissatisfied with the present divided state of the church.

18th.—HYDE. Read Eph. iii., and expounded it and Luke xv. One or two were led to Christ here last night, under a sermon by brother Grinstead. One had attempted to hang himself, and afterwards cut his throat. He had been *drunk* the day before, and has a wife and eight children. Brother Grinstead was sent to pray for him afterwards: he was speechless. The neighbors assembled in a very large congregation, and our dear brother, after speaking to the man, preached Christ to them. In a few days he recovered, and signed the total abstinence pledge, with two or three of his children. He has attended the preaching here, and last night professed to trust in Christ, and this evening seems happy in God.

19th.—ASHTON-UNDER-LYNE. In the Independent Methodist Chapel. Read and expounded 1 Cor. xii. We had much of the presence of the

Lord. Several conversed with us afterwards, and appeared to approve our sentiments. One man said, "I once had £10, which I offered to give to any church that would provide for the poor, but no one would accept it." Christians should always take care of the poor. The brethren Grinstead and Plews, spoke usefully on Christian Union, and on brotherly love leading us to feed the hungry, and to clothe the naked.

Feb. 2nd.—This morning I received a letter from my beloved brother Anderson, part of which follows :—

BIRMINGHAM, Feb. 1st., 1841.

DEAR BROTHER,—

. . . . In your first Journal of your tour through England, viz—to Bristol, Bath, Exeter, &c., you say of Plymouth, "The Brethren originated here." Now this is wrong, for Jesus originated the term "all ye are brethren,' and therefore Paul wrote to the "holy brethren," &c.; but besides being wrong in itself, it is unfair in its application, because you give them an epithet which they disclaim, they wishing only to be considered brethren, without any distinctive particle to separate them from the whole body of believers. Now I think it fair to call a man Methodist, Baptist, or Congregationalist, if he takes the name himself; but when he disclaims such titles, and wishes only to be one with the Lord's people, in *Jesus' name*, it is unfair, it is unkind therefore, to call persons by sectarian appellations which they renounce. I could not feel warranted to call you Baptist, Anti-Millenarian, Anti-swearer, &c., though you give the respective doctrines a prominent place in your teaching. Let us then "love as brethren, be pitiful, be courteous."

Closely allied with this subject, is that of membership in the church. Please to excuse the familiarity I use, but I think it proper to have right and definite notions of the things of which we speak. The members of the church are never spoken of in the New Testament but in connection with the whole body, or of Christ, the Head. It is never said,—so many members of the church at Corinth, Ephesus, &c.; yet often the membership in Christ Jesus is spoken of. The fact is, the Holy Ghost looks at the church of Christ as including all believers as one body, having many members, yet all so placed as to fill up what every joint supplieth, and if one member suffer, all the members suffer with it. Consequently the true idea arising from all this is, not how many members are in this or that church? but, how many members has the body of Christ? And thus we are associated with every member of that body, in Birmingham, Liverpool, the world. So, our church not only numbers the few brethren that meet together in the Athenæum, Temple-row, but all in Cannon-street, Carr's-lane, Ebenezer, or elsewhere; where there is a soul renewed by Divine grace, there is a member of the same body to which the Lord in his grace hath joined me. Now, a few or many of the members or brethren, may meet, to suit their locality, but the idea of being members of this church, or of that church, of this or that place, has not entered our mind. I met a member of Cannon-street (as he called himself) some days ago. "Well, are you increasing?" said he; "O yes," said I, " wherever there is a soul converted to God, it is an addition to our number, whether in Asia, Africa, or America." "What," said he "are you spreading through Africa?" "I mean to say, when a soul is added to the Lord in Cannon-street," said I, "it is added to us." "O now I understand you," said he; "Well, well, that is a very general way of talking, and certainly a way of thinking that destroys the very essence of party spirit." By this, dear brother Bowes, you will perceive my drift. Special membership we have none; yet, let the Lord be praised, the sweet fruits of brotherly love are daily being manifested. . . . . Yours in love,

To J. Bowes. P. G. ANDERSON.

In my *Second Report*, I wrote the following remarks on the above letter :—

1. I used the words, "The brethren originated here," without intending the least offence. I did not say "*Plymouth* brethren," lest I should give pain.

2. I would not call real Christians, who had really abandoned the *name* and *spirit of sectarianism*, by any other than New Testament appellations; but when I find any mistaken professors, who have abandoned the *name*, and retain the greater *evil*,—*the vile thing*, I feel grieved, and wish to warn them, and guard others against falling into the same thing. The followers of the late Edward Irving profess to put away the name, but they have obviously the *thing*. The same may be said of those who agree in sentiment with A. Campbell, of America; they decry *the sects*, but refuse to admit to their communion unimmersed believers.

"The brethren" (I use not the word offensively) to whom my Journal refers, in Exeter and Plymouth, could receive me as a "dear brother," but *I had not liberty of ministry among them*. I had it among Christians called Baptists and Independents, in the south of England. Why this difference? Why did I not point out the same evils among "the saints," "the holy brethren," at Bristol, Bath, and London? Because, they neither professed the restrictive sentiments, nor acted on them, which a *few leading men*, though not all, at Exeter and Plymouth avowed. However, if there has been any misunderstanding, I shall do my best to have it removed.

1stly. At Exeter I could not obtain a place to lecture on the Unity of the Church, or preach in, though I applied for it to those who profess to have renounced sectarianism; but I obtained *Baptist chapels*.

2ndly. I had not liberty to teach at the breaking of bread.

3rdly. At Plymouth, *a chief brother* could not give his consent to my preaching, and when I pointedly asked him the question, "Have you not said, that if any man denies the doctrine of Christ's advent being pre-millennial, that he is not called of God to teach?" To this, after some delay, I received an affirmative answer. Again, I asked, "If a Wesleyan minister in doctrine, renounce sectarianism, so as to hold your views of church order, &c., but retains still his doctrinal sentiments, would you consider him called of God to teach or preach?" This brother answered, "No." Now, while he holds these sentiments, and acts upon them, and is permitted *to govern* the church, as he did while I was there, so as to prevent me from teaching or preaching in Raleigh-street; and while the church permits this mode of proceeding, am I not warranted to conclude, that while the name of sectarianism is abandoned, the *spirit* is retained.

Whither could I, with my post-millennial views, or any Wesleyan minister in doctrine, go, if God should cast our lot at Plymouth? If we should worship where this brother teaches and preaches, we must be silent! But God has given me his gospel to preach, and I cannot be silent at any man's bidding; therefore must meet with *any* brethren who would not hinder the liberty of the Spirit. Thus, two bodies or sections would be formed. Whether would be schismatical?

However, I say again, if there be any misunderstanding, let it be pointed out. I used means to ascertain if any change had taken place in the views of the brethren at Plymouth last year. If the Lord will, I shall send them a few copies of this (Report) both to Plymouth and Exeter, and hereby desire them to point out any error if any exist. If they remain silent, I shall consider that I did not misunderstand them;

and if there has been any mistake on my part, I shall gladly acknowledge it.

May I further ask, Is it not sectarian for a church to call in neighboring brethren, teachers, or rulers, from other places and churches, to sit as a kind of presbytery over a brother, and silence him, when many of the faithful among whom he teaches, wish him to continue?

TO THE MAGISTRATES OF DUNDEE.

VINE STREET, LIVERPOOL,
Feb. 4th, 1841.

FRIENDS,—May you seek the peace of God. Several months have now elapsed since you permitted, or ordered, the police officers to summon me before you. Four times I was at their office. Three days together I was harrassed, by standing a trial before you, for preaching Christ's holy gospel in your streets.

The last few months have been memorable to Dundee. Twice you fined me, and threatened to imprison me forty days, if the fine should not be paid. One preacher you imprisoned ten days and had his head cropped!

Instead of being "a terror to evil doers, and a praise to them that do well," have ye not made yourselves "a terror" to holy men, and "a praise" to persecutors? What had I done, that ye persecuted me? Was it because for seven years I preached out of doors to the poor perishing outcasts, that seldom or never go to any place of worship? Was it because, when that awful disease, the *Colera Morbus*, raged in your town, and laid prostrate in the grave five hundred of your people, I visited the cellars and the garrets wherever my services were required; and even sometimes supplied the wants of dying bodies whom others deserted, and poured the light of truth into their immortal but departing spirits? Was it because I visited the sick for seven years together, undeterred by fevers and contagious disorders whenever I was called upon, trusting that God would either protect me or take me to heaven? Was it because I left behind me many souls, once benighted, unholy, and miserable, who, by listening to the good news of pardon and sanctification through the death of Jesus Christ, and by the Spirit of our God, could call me father in the gospel, some of whom continue to this day, and some are fallen asleep? Was it on these accounts that on the very first evening that the Lord enabled me to return to Dundee and preach, I was haled away to the place appointed for evil doers?

I shall take no means but such as Christianity sanctions to bring you to a sense of your sin. Punishment is God's, who has said, "Vengeance is mine, and I will repay, saith the Lord." I wish you well, and pray for you. But you shall find it a "fearful thing to fall into the hands of the living God." "FOR OUR GOD IS A CONSUMING FIRE," as well as "a God of love." Have you not seen this? Has God not spoken to you awfully in flaming fire, by the burning down of the "Three Churches," as they are called. You were seated comfortably in one of them, and you persecuted those who carried the glad tidings of salvation to the *outcasts ready to perish*, and God has *burned you out*, for without His permission, the fire cannot burn; so that ye must either hear the gospel in the open-air, or seek refuge in other places of worship. Eight months had not elapsed after your *fines* and *imprisonment* of

God's servants, before a judgment, perhaps unequalled in Dundee, overtook you. Unbelief may laugh at considerations like these; but be warned in time. The fire of the three earthly buildings has gone out, but there is another fire which never goes out, in which you shall be tormented forever, if ye cease not to oppose the servants of God. *Repent*, therefore, of your evil ways. Come to the Saviour believing his doctrine, and evince your faith by yielding obedince to his commands. You that are rich in worldly wealth, be rich in good works. Feed the hungry, clothe the naked, and do good to them that hate you. Then, when you get "a new heart" and a loving spirit, you will confess with tears of sorrow your great sin, and God and good men will forgive you.

I shall visit you again very soon, if the Lord will, and shall continue to preach Christ crucified in the open-air.

You cannot send me to prison without my Master's permission, and if he allows you to proceed to extremities, he can get honor to his name by it; and if God be glorified and society benefited, I shall be satisfied, even if I should leave my bones in your prison.

Hoping that you will prepare to meet me before that AUGUST TRIBUNAL OF ETERNAL JUSTICE, to which, *from your decision*, I appeal, and praying that God may give you repentance unto life,

I remain, your sincere friend,
JOHN BOWES.

To the Magistrates of Dundee who were active in the late persecution, especially Dean of Guild Adamson, and Baillie Johnson, &c., &c.

THE TRANSFERRING OF HOPE STREET CHAPEL.

At a church meeting held in Hill Street Room, Toxteth Park, to take into consideration an advertisement which appeared in the "Liverpool Mercury," on January 18th, in reference to Hope Street Chapel, the following address was agreed to in reference to the before named advertisement.

1st. It sets forth that the "Trustees have consented to resign their trust, on certain conditions, with a view of Hope Street Chapel being connected with the Established Church of England." Was it for this that subscriptions were originally obtained from us and others? No; it appears, from a prospectus, dated Liverpool, January 28, 1836, that these subscriptions were originally solicited for the Christian Society, of which for some time we made a part. That society, in its prospectus, avowed principles the very opposite of the Establishment. (1st.) It invited the "co-operation of every follower of Christ." The Establishment refuses all such co-operation. (2nd.) It disclaimed "exclusive communion on the ground of peculiarity of doctrinal views," and affirmed that "by a fundamental law of the society, every child of God possesses a right of communion with the society, and the liberty of co-operation in the great work of saving souls." The Establishment makes no provision to exclude the ungodly from her communion, since it is notorious that many of her ministers themselves are fox-hunting, gaming, pleasure-taking men, and even godly ministers are obliged, when they commit a drunkard to the grave, to state that they do it "in a sure and certain hope of his glorious resurrection to eternal life.'

(3rd.) The society engaged to set itself to unite Christians, "and to counteract formality in worship," and you propose to make over the Chapel to an association called a church which pays one clerk in every church to call out "Amen," at set times and parts of the service. In fact, the whole groundwork of the prospectus put forth by "The Society in connexion with the Rev. Robert Aitken," shows that funds were collected from us and others with specific views, altogether at issue with a Civil Establishment of religion. You may indeed say "but where is the Christian Society in connexion with the Rev. Robert Aitken" now? This we cannot answer, but we know where it was, till we were compelled to leave the chapel which our own money had assisted to erect.

2nd. One of the conditions on which you resign your chapel is "your being liberated from all liabilities." Now we submit that in 1838 a great portion of the society were forced away from Hope Street Chapel, or withdrew, and that we were among the number. J. Bowes was our pastor before we left and after we left, we then considered that we had claims upon the chapel, and still say that you are liable to us thus far. 1st. For all the subscriptions which we paid, whether in large or small sums. 2nd. Inasmuch as those who came away with us collected or obtained the greater part of the subscriptions. 3rd. For the monies which we gave in collections, &c., which were never intended to support an overgrown hierarchy. If you ask us how much we claim, we answer, the arbitrators appointed at the suggestion of friends on both sides shall tell. We give a copy of their letter to us with this. That this was reasonable we infer, inasmuch as you met soon after and resolved that we "should have Hope Street Chapel every other Sabbath, and two nights a-week, unless at least £400 should be paid." Now as neither of these sums has been paid, nor any part, and as we have not had the use of the chapel as you agreed we should, the other party having hindered us by force, we have an additional right of compensation. If the chapel is worth £100 per annum we have sacrificed £50 per annum in being kept out of it, which, in three years, the time we have been kept out of it, amounts to £150 more. Nay, more, this grant of the chapel which was given by you in the handwriting of C. E. Rawlins, proves that in your view at that time with the party which has held it per force, consequently that equal claim should not be forgot now, unless you mean to give them the chapel entirely, as a reward for having broken through your resolutions, by unjustly witholding the chapel from us. Perhaps you may allege that the arbitrators took into account Mr. Bowes' salary, and since he was promised by Mr. Aitken, as agent for the society, £200 per annum after the first year, the first year being £160, and £29 of that year not being paid. Well, suppose we take Mr. Bowes' loss at £200, and we are persuaded £200 would not cover it, that will leave due to us £450. The account would stand thus: Arbitrators decision, £500
Half rent of the chapel for three years, 150

£650
Deduct off J. Bowes' loss of salary, 200

Due to us, £450

You will perceive how we have gathered the *data* upon which we conclude, not from ourselves, we might be interested, but from the arbitrators and from yourselves. We shall therefore decline mentioning any sums that we have paid in by either collections or subscriptions, but request that the above sum of £450 be handed over. We cannot say that we hope, that R. Aitken and the Leaders will give J. Bowes the sum he has lost, by his dependence on R. Aitken's letters, but that they ought to give it.

As most of you, we believe all, profess to be religious men, we would conclude by observing, that as the granting of the chapel to the Establishment is unjust to the subscribers, we say so still, many of them may never see your advertisement till after the second of March, since we know some of them are from home, but in this grant you act unscripturally. In Rev. xvii 5, we read of "BABYLON THE GREAT THE MOTHER OF HARLOTS, AND ABOMINATIONS OF THE EARTH." Nearly all the Established clergy say that Babylon signifies Rome. She is the "mother of harlots," but who are the daughters? That the English Establishment is one of the daughters, will appear by considering that the harlotry is "committing fornication with the kings of the earth." Rev. xviii. 2. And instead of going into such an unholy connexion, the word of God says "come out of her my people, that ye be not partakers of her sins, and that ye receive not of her plagues." Rev. xviii. 4.

Should any of you believe that hundreds of members contributing to the erection of a chapel, and forced to retire from it, have no claim to compensation, but that you are at liberty to make over their contributions to other purposes, than those for which you were entrusted with them, we are quite sure that our labor must be in vain. We are equally sure that "all liabilities" arising from your trusteeship will not be discharged until we shall have been paid.

You will accordingly return us the before mentioned sum of four hundred and fifty pounds.

    Signed by ordered and on behalf of the before mentioned
    Church Meeting.

Hill Street Room, Toxteth Park,
  Feb. 23, 1841.

 DEAR FRIENDS,—

Having observed in the Liverpool *Mercury* of last week an advertisement headed, "HOPE STREET CHAPEL," which states that "The Rev. R. Aitken, together with the leaders and congregation of Hope Street Chapel, having applied to the Trustees, with a view to its connexion with the Established Church of England, and the Trustees having consented so to resign their trust, upon being liberated from all liabilities."

You are aware that at the request of the Leaders meeting, and Quarter day, in April, 1837, I became pastor of Hope Street Congregation, at the *Quarter Day*, or Quarterly Meeting. You took your seats as members of the meeting, by virtue of your being Trustees, and it is presumed concurred in that invitation. Accordingly I received from you, when you wished me not to occupy the chapel, the following year, a letter, of which this is a true copy—

              "LIVERPOOL, Feb. 9th, 1838.

 "REV. SIR,—

"We have received a communication from Mr. Aitken, requesting us to act on the resolution passed at the Trustee meeting on the 31st of January last which was as follows:—'That Messrs. Bomphrey and Beatty be appointed to prohibit the Rev. J. Bowes from occupying the pulpit of Hope Street Chapel, should

Mr Aitken find it necessary to advise such a proceeding.' Therefore in accordance with the above resolution we hereby respectfully request that you will forthwith vacate the pulpit.

Yours respectfully,

JOSEPH BOUMPHREY,
ROBERT BEATTY.

It is true that at a subsequent meeting, you agreed that I and my friends should have the use of the "chapel every other Sabbath, and two nights in the week until at least £400 should be paid."

The salary that was agreed upon while I was in Scotland, and after my arrival may be gathered from R. Aitken's letter of "March 20th, 1837," in which he says, "The salary that has been fixed upon for the Liverpool preacher is £200 per annum. I have been requested by the deacons to ask whether you would be satisfied for the first year with £160, on the understanding that on the following year it will be raised to £200."

You are aware that my salary of £160 for the first year has not all been paid, but that I still want of that year, £29; and were you to reckon the stipulated sum for the last three years it would give £600 as still due to me, but as I am only willing to charge you what I have *really lost* by depending on Mr Aitken's letters, and being pastor of your chapel, I shall be satisfied if you give me £200, and I hereby put in my claim for the above sum of £200, for the above named reasons, and because I was called from a permanent situation, which I had filled with comfort seven years, and which if I had either continued to occupy, or if the promises made me in R. Aitken's letters had been made good, or realized, I should have received £200 more this day, than I have yet received.

Had I not had a wife and four children depending on the before named engagement, as well as myself, its breach would have been *less* felt.

Hoping that you will not sign away your right to the chapel, till you have done *justice* to all concerned, and seen all "liabilities" *honestly* discharged,

I am yours respectfully,

JOHN BOWES.

To the Trustees of Hope Street Chapel.

131 Vine Street, LIVERPOOL,
Feb. 24th, 1841.

I did not even suspect Mr. Aitken's plan of placing himself at the head of the Societies formed, but it will be evident to every considerate reader of the correspondence. Mr. Matthews, of Bedford, a devout, laborious, and unassuming proclaimer of the gospel, was selected by Mr. Aitken to be a helper, because an ordained Episcopalian clergyman. But while Mr. M. was zealous for the conversion of sinners, he evinced no desire to lord it over other ministers, and as he could not be used as a tool for Mr. Aitken's lofty purposes, he was soon laid aside. The Lord used my firmness to principle to scatter to the winds the scheme of the Christian Society in connexion with the Rev. Robert Aitken, M.A. He indeed carried over Hope Street Chapel and a few people to the Established Church. Discomfitted outside, he retired into his shell; but Hope Street Chapel never acquired stability as an Episcopalian establishment, but had to be sold; while the remnant of the congregation was dispersed. London, Sheffield, Manchester, Preston, and every other society, unaided by his uncertain care, dwindled away. Had he been content to preach Christ as he did at the time I removed to Liverpool in 1837, and left the churches as free as the Scripture leave them, promoting kindly feeling among all other Christians, few men in England would have been more useful. He was exceedingly popular, as well as useful, in preaching. Methodists of all classes flocked to hear him. But he had no judgment to rule. Hence all his chapels have been sold, or slipped away from him, and all the preachers, after his doings in Liverpool, lost confidence in him. Since then he has been known as a clergyman of the Church of England; at once of High Church, Puseyite views, and of Evangelical sentiments! People have been at a loss all along how to regard him. Perhaps the most correct account of his standing would be, at once High Church and Low Church,—his clerical notions as high as the highest, and his sermons often of the old stamp, powerful and awakening.

His aims to set up a second society, like John Wesley, of which he was to be the head, speedily failed, through his own want of judgment. He had feeling, but lacked the well-balanced mind needed to govern in any church. How he will account to the Great Judge for his treatment of preachers and their families, of promises freely made (as this correspondence discloses), but never kept, I know not.

On the review of the whole, I am thankful that the Lord used me in hindering the formation of another clerical and rigid sect, and led me to see more of his truth. This narrative will not be read in vain, if young preachers are led to trust God and follow truth at all hazards, even although opposed by men of renowned ability. Numbers and power may be against us, and against truth, but it and Christ's Spirit are greater than all opponents.

LONDON, Feb. 27th, 1841.

MY DEAR SIR,—

I have only just received this evening your letter of the 20th. At foot I have made a formal claim for the return of my subscription to Hope Street Chapel, which I will thank you to obtain for me, and *keep* till I determine what I may do with it hereafter.

I send you herewith my very much esteemed friend Mr Spencer's tract, (a clergyman of the Establishment), on the Corn Laws and the Prayer Book, which I hope you will receive in good time to be useful to you in the good and godlike work you have undertaken; for surely it is godlike to teach our fellow creatures that if selfish laws were abolished, which are enacted purposely to make bread dear and scarce, they would have what we are taught to pray for. God in his great goodness to his creatures has always provided an overflowing abundance in one country or another, for which the produce of the English laborer might always be exchanged advantageously for food for him and for clothing for them, and thus men would be doing each other good, as brethren of one family having God for their reconciled Father in Christ, and abundance would crown such righteous intercourse between man and man, and between nation and nation, and they would learn war no more, for the love and mutual dependence they would have towards each other.

I am my dear Sir,
Yours sincerely,
LAWRENCE HEYWORTH.

Feb. 27th.—Saturday. Came to HYDE. Called at Manchester, and saw a city missionary, who gave me in substance, the following account: "In his district lived a married woman whose husband was ill and out of employment. She prostituted herself, with her husband's consent, to obtain bread. She continued in this way, till, by the missionary's labors, she saw the evil of her conduct, and embraced the purifying gospel of the Son of God. One of her former visitors called on her, not knowing the change. She was proof against the temptation. He was a professing Methodist, and when he saw the change left her £5." One of the City missionaries has given up, because he cannot be the servant of man; his name is Goold. Had a very interesting conversation on the coach with several persons, strangers. I am seldom able to enter into conversation with strangers and conduct it to my own satisfaction, but the Lord enabled me to-day. I commenced thus (I and another gentleman sat higher on the coach than the rest of the outside passengers), I remarked, that though we were elevated above the rest, it was not of our own seeking, so that we should have nothing to fear from being required to take a lower place. He understood the allusion, and the conversation on religion commenced. Before us sat a Mr. Hardie, a Quaker, and an old soldier who had been in the navy many years. He and I conversed, till I had set before him the plan of salvation, of which he was quite ignorant, and at first, proud, haughty, and angry. When Mr. Hardie left us at Denton, he said, shaking hands with us all most feelingly, "May we all meet in heaven." The quaker, who had scarcely spoken before, now turned to the old veteran, and said, "I should think thy feelings are much better now than when thou didst get upon the coach." The man was a little offended with the style of his address, but that soon evaporated. May we all profit by this conversation. The difficulty was, to keep the soldier from deriding all religion through the conduct of its professors. I endeavored to lead him to the Scriptures and to Christ.

28th.—HYDE. Sat down to break bread, and discoursed at STALEY BRIDGE afternoon and evening. After which, a number of believers agreed to meet in the Lord's name.

29th.—Monday. Preached by request from "Give us this day our daily bread." The discourse was against taxing the bread.

March 1st.—Lectured on Total Abstinence in the Wesleyan Methodist Chapel, GEE-CROSS.

22nd.—Came by the *Commodore* to Scotland. There was much drinking and awful cursing on board among some of the sailors. Oh that Christians would turn their attention still more to this neglected class of men.

23rd.—Arrived in GLASGOW between 9 and 10 o'clock. Had an interesting conversation with Mr. Mitchell, of Liverpool, a member of the Secession Church, and a total abstainer.

24th.—Saw several friends, and was invited to stay over the Lord's Day, and preach to the United Methodists.

25th.—Heard Dr. Wardlaw at 7 o'clock. Few attended to what one might have expected. He prayed and spoke feebly. He called upon three young men to pray who were not there, and then upon an old man, who prayed in such a rapid and low tone of voice that I did not hear three complete sentences. I am more than ever convinced that a one-man ministry tends to formality. Spoke at the University Chapel for a few minutes. I had several requests after. I declined attending a tea meeting, because they will have singing of songs. To-day I sent James Morrison, of Kilmarnock, a copy of our principles.

26th.—Attended a Total Abstinence meeting in Spreull's Court chapel, which was a good useful meeting. The Scotch total abstinence meetings are more orderly than the English.

27th.—Preached at six o'clock before the Glasgow Green, and near the High Bridge; a very attentive congregation. Spoke from the Prodigal Son. At 8, attended a Total Abstinence meeting in the New Vennel. Mr. M'Lean spoke well when I had done.

28th.—Lord's Day. As the congregation to which the late talented J. H. Roebuck preached are destitute of a pastor, and having some reason to hope that I should have an opportunity of inculcating many precious truths which they are not in the habit of hearing, I agreed to stay over this day and preach to them. At 8 a.m., I preached on the Green to a very attentive congregation. At 11, 2, and 6 o'clock, preached in Spreull's Court Chapel to attentive congregations. J. H. Roebuck was cut off suddenly, aged 25 years. The Lord's ministers should work while it is day.

29th.—Preached at six o'clock in the open-air. At half-past eight, addressed a crowded Total Abstinence meeting at Cowcaddens, and at half-past nine, a Soiree in Spreull's Court.

30th.—PAISLEY. J. C. Kennedy delivered a discourse on Unity, as I was so hoarse that I could scarcely be heard. He remarked that "many persons viewed church laws in the same light as the laws of friendly societies, which may be changed or altered at pleasure." He proved that Christ's laws are unalterable, and that He is the only authorised Legislator of the Church. I spoke with much spiritual comfort when he had done.

31st.—Learned to-day that several believers are consulting about forming a church to which neither members nor ministers can be admitted without they totally abstain from intoxicating drinks!

April 1st.—Came by railway nearly to Linlithgow. The steam engine went off the rails, east of Airdrie, and the train stopped at once. The passengers felt a slight shock, but no harm was done. Saw a few friends in Edinburgh, especially a beloved brother, G. Bissett, and his wife, who were very kind and exceedingly glad to meet with me.

2nd.—Had a delightful passage by sea to DUNDEE. Met with Robert White, a young man who seems anxious to be employed for God.

SECOND TRIAL BEFORE THE MAGISTRATES OF DUNDEE FOR PREACHING IN THE HILLTOWN.

4th month, 3rd, 1841.—DUNDEE.—Preached out this evening before the Seminaries. A rumor was abroad that the Magistrates intended to imprison me, but this evening the Police did not interfere.

4th.—Preached at ten o'clock, A.M., in the same place, to a large congregation; also at four P.M.

5th.—Preached again in the same place.

6th.—In the Hilltown, two Police officers heard about half an hour and took down my address.

7th.—Preached on the Shore without molestation, but got a summons to-day to answer for preaching the last night.

Superintendent Corsterphan called the following Police officers to prove that there was an obstruction of the parapet, viz.:—William Hird, Shaw Cattanach, and James Smith. I was then asked if I had any witnesses to call. I stated that I had, but that one, with myself, questioned the propriety of Christians taking an oath. This arose from what is said in Matt. v. 33—37, and James v. 12, that I did not feel free to call any witnesses to swear, but they might be called in, and please themselves whether they took the oath or not. The Magistrates said this would be a very proper course.

Andrew Smith called—Refused to take the oath. The Magistrates

—"Are you a Quaker?" "No." "Is it only in this case that you refuse to take the oath?" "I refuse it in every case." Dean of Guild Adamson—"Are you aware that if the Superintendent had summoned you that he would have forced you to swear?" "No; no man could force me to swear, because I believe it is unscriptural." "Will you swear him, Mr. Bowes?" "No; I think with him that swearing is unscriptural, but I request that his evidence may be taken without an oath." A. Smith—"I will tell the truth just as much as though I were upon oath." "Saw no obstruction; the people were all quiet and orderly, with the exception of a drunken man who should have been taken up by the Police." "Could you have got along the crowd?" (Here the Superintendent tried to make the witness answer to suit his purpose.) "I did not try it to know." Adamson.—"*If you do not answer the question, I will lock you up.*" "There were some on the pavement, but if the people had given way, as I have seen them, a person might have got down the pavement. There was room enough for the congregation between Mr. Soutar's house and the street. I was at the measuring of it, and found that there were sixty feet of space, and about fifteen and a half from the house to the parapet of private property, and about thirty-six feet of private property lengthways."

Andrew Lindsay, Commissioner of Police—'Thought there might be a hundred people; could have got through the crowd; had gone through a stronger crowd without obstruction." "Can you, on your oath, say that you could have got freely and easily through the crowd?" "I could have got through without much difficulty, but there would have been no difficulty at all had there been no crowd." The case of the two drunken men was referred to. "The conduct of the Police was disgraceful in reference to them."

William Cruickshank, a Minister from England, who has returned to Dundee—"Knows the place where Mr. B. stood; should say that five or six hundred people might hear without interfering with the pavement if they stood lengthways; has preached the Gospel out of doors at York, Barnsley, Leeds, Stockport, London, Liverpool, and Sheffield, and was never but once interrupted. Also, has lectured lately on Temperance out of doors at Beith and Stewarton without interruption, and is of opinion that in no other town in Scotland or England would Mr. Bowes have been interrupted on a similar plat of ground."

The Superintendent said the foot-pavement was obstructed; Mr. Bowes had offended in a similar way before; he, therefore, claimed a conviction.

OUTLINE OF JOHN BOWES' DEFENCE.

"I was pursuing no new course. I have not changed. The Magistrates and Police have changed. Former Magistrates and Police never interfered with me, but rather protected me. Why are you so changed? For seven years together I preached on the Hilltown, at stated times, without molestation. My reason for taking the place on which I stood was a desire to give no just cause of offence to the Magistrates, as it was an open space, and private property. (I then read some of the Regulations of the Dundee Police, showing that they had not done their duty.) I have reason to know that, if I had been preaching in any place not acceptable to the Magistrates, in the time of former Superintendents, they would have acted very differently from the present Superintendent—they would have given me private notice. It has been proved that both carts and persons could easily pass up and down the street, and there was no obstruction; but if my hearers had caused an obstruction, this is no uncommon occurrence in this town. When Earl Durham visited this place some years ago, he addressed a congregation before the Town Hall, and, then, both the parapet and High Street were obstructed. *This was done by the sanction of the Magistrates.*

"I remember, on another occasion, a great meeting was held on the Water Question, when the crowd was so great that persons could not pass along the High Street nor on the parapet. The Magistrates sanctioned this. Again, the last year an Anti-Corn Law Meeting was held in the same place under the auspices of the Magistrates. Now, suppose that any one had been disposed to bring the Magistrates before this court for breaking the law, would they have been fined? Who would have convicted them in this court where they would have been their own judges? If I have broken the law, the Magistrates have set me the example. Yesterday it was broken (according to your views of the law) by an Auctioneer who was selling goods in the Green Market. The last night, after I had done preaching on the Shore, as I came up Crichton Street, some persons were playing on musical instruments, and that narrow street was blocked up from channel to channel; and several persons were standing on the parapets, but no complaint was made.

"I would willingly have concluded, after the last trial, that, after all, you were not against open-air preaching— against the Gospel, and against Jesus Christ—but I confess these appearances are against you. Yes, auctioneers may collect crowds, the Magistrates and others may obstruct the streets by public meetings, ballad-singers and musicians may crowd your narrow streets, and all without offence. Preaching the Gospel in the open-air is the only unpardonable sin. (*Applause, and great sensation in the court*) Have I not as good a right to collect a congregation that I may introduce among them the water of life, as the Magistrates have for calling meetings to introduce the water that perisheth? Have I not as good a right to stand and cry—'Ho every one that thirsteth, come ye to the waters,' to set forth Jesus Christ as a Saviour before the perishing people, as auctioneers have to sell their goods?

"You may have a strong police force in this town added to your magistracy, you may also have soldiers stationed in your neighborhood, and be farther supported by the *shore carters* being sworn in constables, but what does this prove—that you are a civilised, religious people? Far from it. All these may exist, and have existed, where there is the greatest ignorance and barbarism. If you would civilise the people, you must educate them, and teach them the truths of Christianity. Not first license public houses to make the people drunk, and then employ a great police force to deter them from the drunkenness which you have previously occasioned. Physical force will never reform the people— moral means must be used. If the Magistrates, instead of threatening with fines and imprisonment open-air preachers, would give them protection, and if all the ministers of the gospel would turn out and preach to the people, they would do more to reform the population than the whole of your physical forces put together. Can the magistrates be cleared before the Judge of the world for preventing open-air preaching? Did you not hinder from preaching that man of God, Henry Wight, of Edinburgh, a man whose labors God hath blessed? Now, I do say, if persons would have heard him and been saved (whatever you may think of my labors), but have been prevented by this court—if those persons perish, their blood will be found in your skirts.

"To conclude, if the Magistrates differ from me in opinion as to the place of preaching in the Hilltown, as I have not returned to the Green Market since they fined me, so I can get other places to preach in the neighborhood, and if they think it is an improper place, I shall not return thither."

The DEAN of GUILD said that the case had been clearly made out and he was sorry that Mr Bowes had not profited by what had occurred on the two former occasions. *He would subject Mr Bowes to the same fine as before (40s., or forty days' imprisonment), and said—" I regret that this is all the Act allows, or it should have been more."*

I was only kept in the Court a few minutes when some Christian friends paid the fine.

12th.—Monday. This evening read over the evidence of the Trial, &c., in the chapel, and had a profitable season. The last Monday, several of the followers of A. Campbell desired a conversation with me. We met in my lodgings, and conversed for some hours on "Baptism." They maintained that it is the only way by which sin can be forgiven, and by which we enter the church. In opposition to both these views, I declared—1st. "That, through his (Christ's) name, whosoever believeth in him shall receive remission of sins." (Acts x. 43)—2nd. That as they professedly baptize *only* believers, they baptize persons who are already justified and pardoned. (Rom. iii. 24, also iv., and v. 1.)—3rd. I asked, "Suppose a man sin the day, or a few days, after baptism, is he to be rebaptized to get pardon?" We adjourned to the Hammerman's Hall on the Wednesday night, and then again to the Friday night. It was a friendly conversation, but some of them manifested a bad spirit, not to me, but to each other, and the impression which I have is, that there is very little religion among them!

13th.—At 11 o'clock set off for BLAIRGOWRIE. Had an interesting conversation with two or three passengers on believers knowing that their sins are pardoned. One of them was William Dalgleish, cork manufacturer, from Dalkeith, to whom I gave some tracts, and who invited me to call on him, should I ever go that way. At the request of the Total Abstinence Society I lectured this evening in the Independent Chapel.

14th.—Rose early this morning, and was accompanied by Thomas Mitchell and Mr. Saunders, to see the beautiful scenery around Craighall, the seat of Robert Clerk Rattray. Understanding that his wife is a pious woman, I left several tracts at the hall. It stands upon a high rock, about 280 feet above the level of the river *Ericht.* It is awful to look down from this amazing height, for the rock is nearly perpendicular. The river, which is considerable, a little above the hall rushes down the rocks, and in one place almost looses itself by rocks, which overhang its bed. This is some of the most sublime scenery I have ever witnessed. Lectured in the Secession Church (or Chapel) on New Testament principles of Church Order and Unity. I was refreshed by enlarged and liberal views of several brethren here.

15th.—Fast Day in DUNDEE, more properly a "preaching day." People leave their work, the places of worship are opened, and ministers from a distance preach, preparatory to the Lord's Supper, which is delivered every six months. Preached along with James Johnson in the open-air at 10, and afterwards adjourned to his chapel, Baltic Street, after 11 o'clock. Addressed a meeting in the same place at 2. At 4, he and I spoke out of doors, and at 6, addressed a meeting in Lindsay Street Chapel.

16th, 17th, and 18th.—ARBROATH.—Found a number of believers much disposed to come out of the sects for the following reasons:—1st. The ministers and many of the members encourage the drinking of intoxicating liquors, and give them at the Lord's Table, and refuse to countenance the Total Abstinence principle. 2nd. Because the gifts of the Spirit in the Church are shut up and confined to a one-man ministry. 3rd. Because they regard schisms and divisions among Christians as unscriptural, and desire that all believers may become "one flock," under "one shepherd." Some of the brethren wished only to admit Total Abstainers: but on finding that this would not diminish the sects, but add a teetotal sect to the number, and that should a believer mistake his duty after the church had admitted him, and return to the injurious practice of taking a little wine or strong drink, in the mistaken notion that it would strengthen him, yet, if he remained a believer, they had no right to excommunicate him. They cordially adopted the principle of receiving to fellowship all believers; and after two or three meetings, during which the brethren professed before each other their faith in Christ, and, being satisfied with each other as brethren, on the 18th, thirteen of us sat down together to break bread. Thus a number of believers, with two or three teachers or preachers among them, have met in the Lord's name to observe his ordinances and commandments, and to pray and labor for the union of all his saints in Arbroath, and to continue in these exercises until the church shall become one, or they die, having scripturally made the attempt. May the Prince of Peace smile upon this plan of peace, that brethren may soon reap the reward of unity, according to Psalm cxxxiii. 1, "Behold how good and how pleasant it is for brethren to dwell together in unity." Preached at 4 o'clock on the Battery. Hundreds came round us, but as the rain came on they hurried away home, with the exception of a few scores, who remained till I finished. At 6, had a solemn and impressive season. Spoke from the barren fig tree. Two interesting young men, members of the Secession, were deeply affected; I trust it will be lasting. They approve the plan of uniting Christians. I urged upon them decision in the great question of personal salvation.

21st.—DUNDEE. Was much refreshed by the coming of brother James Grinstead, who brings good news as to the state of matters in England. Thomas Smith, a Wesleyan local preacher, has begun to publish John Wesley's sentiments on the right use of money. Thomas Sturges, itinerant minister in the New Connexion, dreamed one night, that John Bowes was outside of his chamber-door, kneeling down and praying, "O Lord remove that greatest of all curses to the spread of thy gospel,—sectarianism." He said in a loud tone of voice, "Amen."

This young man has sent word, that if I will go over to Gateshead, he will keep me a week. Preached this evening, without a text, to a considerable congregation below the Greenmarket; after which held a friendly conversation with a number of Baptists, who baptize for the remission of sins.

22nd.—Preached from and expounded John xxi. Out of doors at 7. Lectured in the chapel from 2 Pet. i. 6, at 8 o'clock. After which met a number of baptists to converse on open and strict communion. We also considered whether God the Spirit ever works on man without the Word. I referred to the works of creation, to the effect of Christ's miracles, and the operation of God on the mind of heathen kings, such as Pharoah, Artaxerxes, &c., and asked whether the dreams of Pharoah's chief butler and baker were from God?

25th.—Preached out near the Seminaries at half-past nine; in the Operatives' Hall, at 11 and 2, and in the chapel at 6. A second lecture on the Popery of Protestantism. Had much blessing through the day.

26th.—Several of the dear brethren and sisters came to bring presents and bid farewell to me. Some wept at parting.

26th.—Sailed by the *Benledi*, to Granton. James Johnson was on board. Preached to a large congregation on the Mound, EDINBURGH. I think a Christian church might soon be gathered here.

28th.—Took an early walk, having slept at the Temperance Coffee House all night. I find it very trying to be so long away from my family. I trust I forego the comforts of home for the kingdom of heaven's sake. In the evening preached on the Green, GLASGOW. Had a large congregation.

May 1st.—Saturday; in the same place.

2nd.—Lord's Day; 7½. Had a very attentive congregation; several other congregations were out. The Christian Instruction Society commenced its summer labors in a tent, where ministers of various denominations preach. At 11, attended at a Scotch Baptist Meeting, for exhortation; several prayed; one exhorted, he was rather tedious. The Scriptures were read, one chapter in the New Testament and one in the Old. 2 o'clock, same place; many more people. I preached from Rom. viii. 28. It was a refreshing time. At 4, on the green. I felt the mighty power of God, as I have never done in GLASGOW. I exerted myself too much. Text, 2 Cor. v. 20. Surely the fruits of this sermon will be seen in eternity. At 6, Lectured in the Mechanics' Institution, North Hanover Street, to an attentive congregation, on the Unity of the Church.

3rd.—In a letter, dated 23, St. Alban's Street, Leeds, May 2, 1841, Thomas Smith, author of several valuable treatises on the right use of property, and the benevolence required by Jesus Christ, writes:—

"I have read several times your 'New Testament Principles,' &c., and, so far as I see at present, I agree in most of the points therein stated. I do think, my dear brother, there is a *preparatory process* going on in many parts of the country (in which the hand of the Almighty may be discerned), which must ere long result in important and glorious reforms. It appears to me pretty evident that we are taking another retrograde movement towards the simplicity and purity of our holy religion. May the unerring Spirit direct us in all our inquiries and decisions."

Preached before the Green to a very attentive congregation, after which read the Constitution and Rules of the Ancient and Universal

Benefit Society, established by Jesus Christ. Read and expounded Rom. iv. and v. 1 and 10.

4th.—Preached on the Green at 7, and I and Thomas Brown lectured on New Testament principles at 8, 280 George Street; several seemed willing to act upon these principles.

5th.—Preached again on the Green, several attended me to my lodgings to converse.

6th.—On the Green at 7, and held a conversational meeting afterwards in a Room in Spreull's Court. It was a refreshing season. A few in Glasgow seem willing to act on the principles of the New Testament.

7th.—Came by Paisley; saw John C. Kennedy. Got the second edition of the Principles from Alexander Gardner. By railway to Greenock, and forward by the Royal Sovereign; had a good passage.

8th.—At sea.—Since yesterday, on the way to Liverpool from Greenock, I preached on board the Steam Packet. As I had a few brethren with me, especially Hopewell from Wales, and Lundie from Stockport, we opened with singing. The Captain gave his consent to the sermon. I preached on the steerage part of the deck. Several of the cabin passengers made a part of the congregation. They were serious and attentive. Perhaps eternity may show that Jesus Christ was not set before the people as crucified for their sins without good results. "Cast thy bread (corn) upon the waters, for thou shalt find it after many days." "In the morning sow thy seed, and in the evening withold not thine hand, for thou knowest not whether shall prosper, either this or that, or whether they both shall be alike good." Eccles. xi. 1 and 6. When the Captain came round to take the fares I desisted, and finished when he had done. Arrived at home safely about 15 minutes past twelve; found my family well.

11th.—Wrote the following letter to Mr. Sage who had been a minister in the "Christian Society."

12 NORTHUMBERLAND STREET,
LIVERPOOL, May 11th, 1841.

DEAR FRIEND,—

I have been nearly seven weeks in Scotland. My family reside here. "The Christian Society" is dissolved; R. A—— has returned, like "the dog to his vomit" again. He preaches in Hope Street Chapel. There has been a considerable secession of members since he came. Mitchell, Campbell, Cubbin, &c., meet in another place. I am glad to hear that souls have been saved in Ireland; but you have gone to a sect, and put them in a sect, for which the word of God gives you no authority. I never thought that, in joining the New Connexion, you were guided by love to Christ's truth, or respect for your views of God's truth: it seemed as though you regarded it as offering you an opportunity to be a hired priest or minister, and you eagerly embraced it: therefore your disappointment is only what one might have expected. Let any man obey God, and do right, according to the light he has, and God will make him happy and useful. When you have read these "Principles," you can tell me what you think of them; also whether you are determined to be a New Testament preacher, and a pure, decided follower of Jesus Christ. If you approve these principles, you can ACT on them in Ireland. Rumor says that three New Connexion ministers in England will be either turned out, or come out, this Conference. They hold similar views to myself. Truth is going on rapidly in England. Yours in Christ Jesus,

JOHN BOWES.

To Mr. John Sage,
   Ballyclare, Ireland.

17th.—I preached at Scotland Place at seven. In Crosshall Street at eight.

18th.—Near James's Market at seven, and in the Hill Street Room at 8, on spirits, evil and good, on witches, visions &c., in consequence of a woman, named Sarah Orme, about 21, professing every night to converse with departed spirits. Her brother and father-in-law were present. I conversed with her for about an hour through the day, but was far from being satisfied with her views.

19th.—At Jubilee Street, a houseful. Several gave in their names to meet in fellowship, and one soul professed to give herself to the Lord.

20th.—Hay Market, at 7; Great Crosshall Street, two or three souls seemed impressed, one was made to rejoice in a sin-forgiving God.

21st.—St. James' at 7, Room at 8; another soul or two were blessed, one woman who attended a sick brother whom I visited.

22nd.—As I could not preach out for the rain, I called on Sarah Orme, although she had invited me to call and see her, she would not see me. The reasons assigned were the searching questions I had proposed to her, and my sermon, which she construed to be against her, though I never mentioned her case. This is a sufficient proof to me that she is afraid; she turned out as I supposed.

23rd.—Lord's Day. Had a gracious season at the breaking of bread. At a quarter past 2 addressed the school; it is increasing. At 3 preached at the Prince's Pierhead, to a large and attentive congregation. At 6 in Hill Street, six persons came forward to be instructed, one was a Roman Catholic who heard me in the afternoon, (another Roman Catholic came also on the 21st.) Four professed to love Christ, and to submit to God. It was a glorious night, praise the Lord, for saving souls. May I ever preach for saving souls.

24th.—Preached in the Hay Market at 7. A large congregation at Crosshall Street after, two professed to receive the Lord, one, an old grey-headed sinner.

25th.—Hill Street Room. The Lord was present, blessing his truth. While I was speaking, Jane Marsh, our servant, cried aloud for mercy; indeed, the whole place seemed moved by the power of God. It was a pentecostal time. Five souls professed to believe in Christ, and to find redemption in his blood—the forgiveness of their sins. The Lord has been carrying forward his own work gloriously since the 19th. It began thus—After I had finished preaching in Jubilee Street, in a private house, one woman, under soul concern, returned to speak with me about salvation. She had not been in any place of worship except twice, and at marriages or funerals, for eighteen years. She stated the same of her husband. How important, then, is preaching in the open-air, "publicly, and from house!"

June, 9th.—Was cheered to-day by the arrival of a letter from John Wood, Middleham, part of which I give:—

"I see too that the only way for those who have left the sects, to maintain the purity of Christian principle, is to make the Word of God, and especially the New Testament, our only reference book, and our only authority in all matters relating to faith and practice. It is a most important and a most valuable fact, in my mind; a fact which makes the Holy Scriptures appear to me to wear the indisputable mark of Divine authenticity, that the Holy Spirit in dictating his word has admirably adapted its spirit and precepts to the state and conditions of all men, in all ages and climes, so that we need not legislate afresh, and set up a conference authority to lord over God's heritage under the pretence that things have undergone a change."

A number of believers intend to meet together to break bread every Lord's Day.

16*th*.—Scotland Place,—out of doors. When I had nearly finished, a little pert looking man said aloud—"Who gave you authority to preach?" *Ans.* 'About twenty-four years ago, I saw myself to be a lost sinner. I repented of sin, and believed in Jesus Christ. When I got saved, I felt great pity for other sinners, and believed it to be my duty to direct them to Christ. Since I commenced, scores of sinners profess to have been led to Christ by my labors. By this I know that God has called me to preach. I have got ability to speak to sinners, and God requires me to use that ability. Now, you have asked me a few questions (he had asked others besides this), permit me to ask you a few. Do you love Jesus Christ?" "No" "Do you love God?" "No." "Do you believe that God made you?" "Yes." "And yet you do not love your Maker? Then, as it is natural for a child to love his father, if you do not love God you are an unnatural child. Are you a father of children?" "I am." "Suppose that one of your children should be asked—'Do you love your father?' and he should answer—'No;' what would you say?" "I should be satisfied." "Then, you are a most unnatural father; for all good fathers wish to be loved by their children." After this, he endeavored to disturb the congregation by his remarks which were inaudible to me. I desired my friends not to speak to him, assuring them that he would soon be tired of talking to himself if they took no notice of him. He was silenced.

13*th*.—This morning, baptized nine believers in the river. Had several souls blessed after preaching in the evening.

14*th*.—Monday, assisted at an open-air congregation, Hay Market. Spoke in Great Crosshall Street Room, also, on Tuesday assisted at two open-air congregations; some souls professed to give themselves to God. I should think about forty souls have professed to give themselves to God, during the last month.

15*th*.—Sailed by the Commodore, for Scotland, at 8 p.m., having had several letters of invitation from Aberdeen, and money sent to bear my expenses. Thanks be to the Lord for the good work we have had in Liverpool during the last month. The brethren have been greatly revived and comforted. One plan of usefulness may be mentioned. First of all, during week nights after a short sermon in the open-air, we have adjourned to the preaching room. Many have followed us, and some of these have received the truth. Another plan which the Lord hath blessed has been speaking to such as appeared serious, and addressing them on the plan of salvation by Christ.

17*th*.—Arrived in Greenock at two o'clock, and got to Paisley soon after four, by railway. Ordered a tract on baptism to be reprinted. Addressed a Total Abstinence meeting of about 3000 hearers, in the Bazaar.

18*th*.—Went up to Port Dundas to go by canal to Edinburgh; forgot my cloak; was obliged to stay from 9 to 12 oclock; hoped that this might be for the glory of God. Several elders returned in the boat from the Secession Synod, from whom I learned some important information, laid New Testament principles before them, and gave them each the tract. Perhaps it was on this account that I forgot my cloak.

19th.—Rose at half-past four. Took coach at half-past five, and boat at 6, for Aberdeen. The sea was rough, many were sick; I was very comfortable. Arrived in Aberdeen about 15 minutes past 5.

20th.—Preached in George Street Hall to about 400 hearers, from Ps. xlv. 13. At 2½, in Frederick Street Hall, to about 500 hearers, on 1 Tim. iii. 15, New Testament principles. Evening, in George Street Hall, from 2 Cor. vi. 2, to a crowded congregation.

21st.—On the Inches to about 500 people. The word seemed to take great hold of the hearts of the people.

22nd.—Was desired last night to go and see a sick woman, found her looking to the Lord. She said she had a neighbor, a non-intrusionist, who would be glad to come in, "but," said she, "if they would take your plan, they would have no intrusionists, I'll promise them, for there would be nothing to intrude for."

23rd.—Both these evenings, preached in the open-air, Castle Street, to large and attentive congregations. Attended a Total Abstinence Soiree, and spoke with considerable liberty, in the course of my speech, I said, "I say nothing against the ten ministers in Aberdeen who have joined the Society, they have done their duty, I speak against those who have not joined, and upon them, and other influential members of society, I charge home the murder and ruin of sixty thousand drunkards annually." Because &c. This statement was called in question by Mr. Sime, a Total Abstainer Agent, but I did not retract it, but proved it, by showing that if all respectable parties would abandon it, drunkards would be prevented and reformed, and that these ministers &c. did not design to do the injury with which I charged them. A gentleman said that Finney had made a still stronger statement, declaring those ministers hands to be red with blood, who did not come forward and do their duty.

24th.—Inches; preached, and then addressed a Total Abstinence meeting out of doors.

25th.—Hall, 38 George Street, from Eph. iii. 11, and conversed with several about membership.

26th.—Preached on the Inches. A great political meeting was held not far from me, but it did not much disturb me.

27th.—During the night I dreamed, for the first time that I was dying; the spirit seemed struggling to quit the body, with a little of "the pains, the groans, the dying strife," and all became tranquil when I seemed to be receding from the world, and eternity, with its swift winged messengers, were approaching. I thought, I have heard of others dying, now I am dying myself, I have desired others to be ready, am I ready? I thought, well, I can trust in Christ, he is my only stay and confidence, and a few moments now will show whether I am accepted of him. I was very calmly and composedly waiting for the opening of a veil, which seemed to be between me and some invisible angels, who were drawing nigh, when I awoke, and found myself still in the world. This seems to preach to me, "Be ye also ready, for in such an hour as you think not," &c.

Preached three times in Frederick Street Hall, and at half-past seven,

In the Baptist Chapel, John Street. The Chapel was crowded—the aisles, vestry, windows outside, and the street. Many had to go away who could not get in. The minister, and one or two females, were with me in the pulpit. Text, Luke xxiv. 47-48. In the morning I had Ps. i. 18, "O Lord I beseech thee, send now prosperity." Also afternoon, Ez. xviii. 31. "Make you a new heart."

July 3rd.—Large congregation and considerable liberty in Castle Street. This afternoon I took "purity," (so we call hot water, milk, and sugar) with widow Murray, who gave me the following remarkable account: "More than eight years ago, a few months after their marriage, her husband was wasting with consumption. She was disconsolate, and not able to give him up. She used to go to her wonted place of secret prayer, but could not say one word. She could eat very little in consequence of sorrow. One day I was preaching in the Ship Row Chapel. Her husband said, 'Go with me to hear Mr. Bowes, I am sure you will get good.' She was afraid to venture with him on the street, he was so weak; but he would take no denial. When most of the people had gone to their places of worship, she came with him. I was praying, after which I read out this text, 'It is the Lord, let him do what seemeth him good.' Her husband gave her a gentle push, as though he would say, 'That is for you.' The text and sermon made such a powerful impression on her mind, that she retired resigned and happy; and although she had not tasted food that day, she returned and took her dinner cheerfully. Her husband was a blessed man, and used often to exclaim aloud, 'Sudden death—sudden glory!' and even pray that he might depart suddenly. One day he walked out a short distance from the door; said to a few persons standing by, 'Take hold of me,' as he was falling; they endeavored to get him home, but he died in their arms. He had broken a blood vessel. When his wife saw him a corpse, she was comforted by the text, 'It is the Lord, let him do what seemeth him good.'" She wondered whether she should ever see me again, as she had frequently gone to the chapel, but never met with me.

8th.—Lock Street. Met a number of brethren, who profess to meet nearly on our principles, but we differed in judgment about the admission of members. They receive all who profess to believe in the fall of man, and his recovery by Christ Jesus. I would not receive those who are not born of the Spirit, or who do not believe with their hearts unto righteousness.

9th.—Preached to a large congregation in front of the Infirmary, and afterwards about nine persons met with the view of coming together in the Lord's name, to promote unity among Christians, and to observe the Lord's ordinances as a church. Five were satisfied to meet each other as brethren. I was much refreshed by Alex. Stewart's narrative of his conversion. He was led to the Lord about eleven years ago, while I delivered a sermon in Aberdeen; he has passed two sessions at College. Three, out of the five believers who are to meet together as brethren see it to be their duty at present to remain in the denominations in which they have usually been. Three or four are seeking the Lord.

10th.—Lectured in the New Temperance Hall on Total Abstinence. I had some hesitation about agreeing to the request of the committee, lest I should be hindered from delivering an open-air sermon; but I found I had been directed of the Lord, as it rained much.

11th.—Prayer meeting at 7; one seeking the Lord. At 11 o'clock, explained the principles of the church, and preached from 2 Pet. i. 1. At 2, from Num. xxxii. 33, "Be sure your sin will find you out." A most powerful time. At 6, on 2 Pet. i. 4, "Exceeding great and precious promises." One young woman came in after the prayer meeting in great anguish of soul. We prayed with her, and spoke to her, but she did not seem comforted.

12th.—Visited her. She states that she has not been in the habit of attending any place of worship for three years, till she heard me in Castle Street. Preached out of doors, near the North Church at half-past 7; a large congregation. At half-past eight in the hall; a prayer meeting after. Invited all those who wished to learn the plan of salvation, and were seeking the Lord, to come together to the first form or pew. We had between twenty and thirty seeking mercy. A few professed to believe in the Lord Jesus Christ. This was a glorious night! The work is now as powerful as it was the last month in Liverpool.

14th.—Set off by steam to PETERHEAD. Was advertised to lecture on Total Abstinence in a hall. Though not sick, the sea voyage made me unwell, but I got better before I finished a two hours' lecture. Large congregation.

15th.—At half-past 2, preached to the fishermen on the shore, from Mark i. 17, 18, "And Jesus said, Come ye after me, and I will make you fishers of men. And straightway they forsook their nets, and followed him." The men listened attentively. I remembered that the apostle Peter was a fisherman. Many of them are sunk very low by drink. There are now probably six or eight thousand persons here from different parts of the county engaged in the fishing trade. In the evening at 8, in the Keith Masons' Lodge; a gracious time.

16th.—Preached once more to the fishermen. In this I have much pleasure. If these men were only delivered from strong drink, snuff, and tobacco, and if they were led to know Christ as a Saviour from sin, they might resemble that warm-hearted fisherman preacher, Simon Peter, his brother Andrew, and the two sons of Zebedee, James and John. But they do not seem to know that they have any talents which the Spirit of God could use for the honor of Jesus and the benefit of mankind. At 8 o'clock, preached at the Market-cross to about 1500 or 2000 people. I addressed them for nearly two hours with the greatest liberty. The truth seemed to bear down upon them with great effect, and to carry all before it. I expect a rich harvest in eternity from this night's discourse. After sermon, I met those who are favorable to the union of Christians.

17th.—Attended a Total Abstinence meeting at Woodside. I have been able to preach and address public meetings thirteen times these seven days; this I could not have done without temperance and good health. Praise the Lord! The parish minister and the Independent minister were present, both total abstainers, and both leading on the people by their instructions and example. A large meeting. This visit to Peterhead was partly undertaken by the desire of G. Pegler, and the President of the Total Abstinence Society.

18*th*.—ABERDEEN. Lord's Day. A gracious time at the prayer meetings at seven o'clock. To-day, after previous meetings, eleven of us sat down to break bread, and thus observe the Lord's Supper. Eight see their way clear to profess to be *Christians only*, the rest will meet with them *without* resigning their denominational designations. After the evening sermon, in the prayer meeting, fifteen came forward to seek mercy and receive instruction. Two or three professed to be saved.

20*th*.—Preached in Castle Street to the largest congregation I have seen here out of doors. I spoke too long and loud. I have since learned that one was made happy in God under the sermon. While I was speaking about an elector changing sides, and not voting for Bannerman or Innes, and applied it to a sinner leaving the world and choosing Christ, she came over to Christ.

21*st*.—A meeting for enquirers. Three applied for membership; two of whom have got saved since I came.

22*nd*.—Fast Day. Heard the minister of the North Church, Mr. Murray. He praised the dissenters of the last century as preserving religion alive in the nation, when the church was asleep. He complained much of the manner in which the General Assembly's Fast is this day disregarded. I suppose the people know, that if the ministers would decline to receive their stipends from the State, that there would be no more intrusion, and consequently no more word about non-intrusion. At half-past two, went with a dear sister to the college church to hear A. Gordon. Much gospel, but little of the sinner's duty expressed; in a good spirit, but with his eyes shut, which spoiled the discourse. Many of both congregations were asleep. The congregations in Scotland are the most sleepy I ever saw! At 8, I preached near Union Street Bridge, to an attentive congregation.

24*th*.—A large attentive congregation at Castle Street. My disappointment to-day has been considerable, in consequence of my wife not arriving from England.

25*th*.—Lord's Day. About 50 present at the 7 o'clock prayer meeting. In the evening preached from Rom. xiii. 11. I fear I spoke too long and too loud. About twelve seeking the Lord. Some got blessed.

26*th*.—Conversed with candidates for membership. One man applied who says he was excluded from an Independent church without a hearing; I have not great confidence in his piety. A woman, a member of the Established Church, attended, who states that she has been a member of the Established Church about 17 years. She attended at the Lord's Supper, when she knew nothing of the meaning of it. She professes to have got more good the last few weeks than in all her life before. This evening preached with great liberty from 1 John iii. 1, 2. The glory of the Lord seemed to fill the place. I was abundantly happy, chiefly by looking at the death of Christ as taking away my sins, and looking forward to the coming glory of Jesus Christ.

27*th*.—This evening preached above the Chain Bridge, close to the river Dee. Many thousands came to witness the baptism. I preached from Rom. vi. 1—3. The young people and boys were so disorderly that after I had preached the sermon, I dismissed the congregation, and informed them that, as we could not observe the ordinance with comfort, we should postpone it.

30*th*.—Near the Infirmary. The evening was wet. I had no intention of preaching; but as I walked out to the place about half-past 8, the people were standing in groups, and some had gone away. I was encouraged, and preached. Received the following interesting letter from Mr. Thomas Sturges:—

BROADBOTTOM, July 29th, 1841.

MY DEAR BROTHER BOWES,—
Yesterday I received yours of the 26th, and was happy to hear from you. I always experience great pleasure in reading over your letters, and generally learn from them some useful lesson. Having always been accustomed to the sects it is with difficulty I can prevent myself from speaking their language, and moving in their beaten path; so that, where you find any expression in my letters that is not in accordance with gospel truth, you will know how to account for it. When you discover any obliquity in my conduct from the requirements of truth and duty, do not attribute it to a want of disposition to walk uprightly, but rather to a want of light. There is a good deal of difference between you and me in this respect. You have long thrown off all human shackles, and have as long enjoyed, and walked in, the full light and liberty of the gospel; whereas, I have but just begun to see,—but just begun to enjoy the blessings attaching to the Lord's freemen. This therefore will account, in some measure, for my saying in my last what I did, in reference to "the people here having appointed me as minister over two societies." I fully concur with you when you say that if "the Lord had not sent me, I should do them no good," and if I was not convinced that the Lord had sent me among them, I would not stay. In reference to Hyde, I have no idea that there will be much good done there by way of Union. . . . .

I see more clearly now, the ground you take, and the ground we ought always to take, viz., "Is it the Lord's will that I should go to so and so?" and if it once becomes the Lord's will, then nothing ought to form a sufficient reason for not going and doing his will, but a direct prohibition from the Lord. I am quite of opinion with you, that there has been too much of "man's interference with the Lord's work!" I believe it is for God to send, but for man to recognise those who are sent. "I have not sent them, therefore they shall not profit them." Would you be so kind as send me word, what you consider a sufficient criterion, when you are to go, and when to stay. The "Christian Investigator" is out, it has been out nearly a fortnight; there is a good deal of work laid out in the first article. "Mossley Circuit" has done nothing particular, they have resolved to maintain but one preacher. "Staleybridge Circuit" is still considered perhaps as a New Connexion Circuit, though Newton, Mottram, Dukinfield, and part of Staleybridge have left. They have taken the Temperance Hall, at Staleybridge, and Joseph Barker opens it next Lord's Day; nearly 200 have left there; they style themselves an "Independent Christian Church." A man named Newcombe, who used to preach for R. Aitken, is to preach on the Sunday evening, and if they approve of him, it is likely that he will be employed by them for a time. This I had, as I have given it you, from one of the principal men. It is expected there will be a breach in the Ashton Circuit. Barker is appointed to preach next Lord's Day afternoon and evening at Dukinfield, and the second preacher is appointed there that day, and he intends trying to prevent him takng the pulpit! How vain! His name is Merchant. He came from the same circuit as Walker and I, (Dudley). Gateshead has almost all left, with the exception of eight or ten; I heard they had all left. The country places have nearly all left, and those that remain are divided. Newcastle has all left, I believe, and all the country places, except two, I think. It is the same at Bradford, I believe. They are very much dissatisfied at Chester, Manchester, Fenton, and Dudley, and other places. "The Dream" you mention was correct, only I think you prayed that God would "remove that greatest of all curses from the churches—*a paid ministry.*" J. Walker has the letter I sent him containing the account. I have not yet "set our people to pray for the union of all the Lord's people" on any given day. Though I have of late been praying for it myself, both in public and in private, I intend to set them to do so the first opportunity. . . . When shall you come up to Liverpool again? and when you come, do you think it is probable that you will visit this neighborhood? If you do, I beg you will give us a call, and deliver a lecture or two on the "Constitution of the Primitive Christian Church," and on the necessity of union among God's people in order to the regeneration of the world. I am anxious to join heart and hand with you in carrying out the glorious designs of Christ. I cannot say that our people here are fully prepared for union as I have not tested them. I have circulated pretty freely those "Principles of Church Order and Unity," and have requested them to read them, and several have expressed their entire approbation of them. . . . I am studying the New Testament now. My plan is, to read *through* a narrative, or epistle, and make an observation or two, in writing, on what the *object* of the writer is, in writing the epistle, and then I turn back and carefully read it over, verse by verse, and sentence by sentence, and word by word, and as I get what I think is the meaning of the Holy Ghost, I set it down. In this way I trust I shall get to know what the great truths are which are contained in the Scriptures. . . . . Yours, &c.

To J. Bowes. THOMAS STURGES.

31st.—Castle Street; evening, a large congregation. This morning, met at 4 o'clock at the Dee side, and baptised several, (9), at this early hour, a considerable number of serious people attended.

Aug. 1st.—At 7 a.m., about 50 at the prayer meeting. At 11, read Acts iv., and preached on backsliding, from Ez. xxxiii. or xviii. At half-past 2 had a most solemn and refreshing season, from Ps. ix., "The wicked shall be turned into hell, with all," &c. At 6 the Hall was full, from Acts viii. &c., the Baptism of the Eunuch; 12 seeking mercy. One young woman seemed in deep anguish, and could not forbear sobbing aloud; she got made happy; when I went to speak to her, she expressed her confidence in Christ, and, with a smile of great sweetness, said "Dear brother, pray for me." Some more believed in Christ.

2nd.—Preached twice. Eight seeking mercy; a few blessed.

3rd.—Castle Street. Had great enlargement in preaching, but feel a strong sense of God's great goodness, considering my own unworthiness.

4th.—Lock Street, enquiry meeting after; it was crowded. One seeking the Lord, who was awakened under the open-air sermon, last night; this is very encouraging. Several more were seeking the Lord.

5th.—This day I thank God for his great goodness to me, and intend to devote myself to his glory. I could vow by his grace to do all I can to honor him, who has loved me so much, may he keep me faithful in his service to the end. Amen.

LIVERPOOL, August 5th, 1841.

RICHARD DAVIES, a disciple of the Lord Jesus Christ, and JOHN JONES, our brother, unto JOHN BOWES, our dearly beloved brother and fellow-laborer in the cause of Christ. Grace to you and peace, from God our Father and from the Lord Jesus Christ.

We received your very welcome letter last Lord's Day morning, and were very much refreshed in hearing from you, that your body is in good health; but it affords still greater satisfaction when we hear of the health your soul enjoys, the zeal you manifest for your Master's honor, your great love for poor sinners, and your unceasing endeavor to bring them to Christ. Oh, dear brother, never get weary in this good work, for "this man receiveth sinners" still. Last night, at Hill Street Room, brother George Mather was disposing of some of Joseph Barker's works. I was rather sorry when I heard that his friends had formed themselves into an "Independent Christian Church." This is not the exclusive authority of Christ: we are dependent on him for everything, "for without Him we can do nothing." It is a pity that they lose sight of believers' Immersion, a doctrine so prominent in the Holy Scriptures, that a wayfaring man need not err therein. Our brother Barker, and his friends, have made great sacrifices, comparatively speaking, and have been rescued from many prejudices. I pray God that they may be led before long to see the Christ-like beauty that this doctrine holds forth. For my own part, it is with great pleasure I look back upon the time when I began to examine these most important matters. Then they appeared strange,—

now familiar; then hard,—but now congenial. Oh how I love the principle of Unity among Christians." How good the Lord has been in bringing me under your ministry.

"May you still freely give what you receive,
And preach the death by which you live."

Last Lord's Day, we met for tickets. Our brother Curry stated that we would first be at liberty to tell of the goodness of God to our souls, and afterwards receive our tickets, then whatever we had to give to the Lord, we put it in the box going out. This seems more comfortable to those who wish to give and yet cannot. We should always remember the poor. The season was a happy one indeed. Never before did I enjoy so much of the pleasantness of thus dwelling together in unity. I was reminded of the time when the disciples were all with one accord in one place. Oh that we may keep the unity of the Spirit in the bond of peace. I feel I love the brethren. I love the Saviour because he first loved me, and I am determined to act as Paul did, when he said, "Lord, what wilt thou have me to do?" with reference to going to Scotland. I cannot see my way clear to determine, for these two reasons: first, I want to be taught the way of the Lord more clearly myself; second, I want to be perfectly disembarrassed from the world. Of this one thing I am confident, that if I "acknowledge God in all my ways, he will direct my paths." Thy will, O Lord, be done.

Dear brother, we are co-operating together in our usual loving manner. Our Elders' meetings are remarkably loving and delightful. In arranging church matters none "strive for the mastery," for we have no master, but Christ. Dear brother, this is the first time I have written to you, therefore you will bear with me for being so tedious, and, in concluding, I beg you will favor brother Jones and I with an answer, and send us some more instructions, for we require it all. Oh, that we all may be very familiar with the Holy Scriptures, "which are able to make us wise unto salvation," is the prayer of your unworthy brother,

To J. Bowes. RICHARD DAVIES.

6th.—ABERDEEN. Preached near the infirmary to an attentive congregation. I trust good was done.

7th.—A very large congregation in Castle Street.

8th.—Lord's Day. About 6 at the 7 o'clock prayer meeting; 25 sat down to break bread; 12 were seeking salvation, after the evening sermon, some found blessing. Texts, morning, Gen. v. 24, Enoch; afternoon, 1 Tim. iv. 8, Godliness &c.; evening, 2 Cor. v. 20.

9th.—Preached near the North Church at half-past 7, and at half-past 8 in the Hall; only two seeking mercy, but it was a very refreshing season.

10th.—Castle Street. Took no text. A very large attentive congregation.

11th.—At the Port, Park Street, a very wicked part of the town; sin has committed dreadful ravages in this neighborhood. Had a large meeting afterwards at 73 Upper Kirkgate.

BROADBOTTOM, Aug. 11th, 1841.

MY DEAR BROTHER,—

I received yours on the 7th, and was glad to hear from you. On the same day that I received yours, in the morning, one of the local preachers of the Association came to borrow my "Finney's Lectures to Professing Christians," and we had a good long conversation together about the Church and its present divided state. A few days before, I had left him one of the tracts "New Testament Principles, &c., and he had read it, and he told me what he thought about it. He did not know that I had a friend Walker and a friend Bowes engaged in that Church, so that what he said I thought the more of, on that account. He said he had not seen anything, that he knew of, that had come so near his views as the principles contained in that tract. He had long been thinking of salaried priests and provision for the poor members, and that seemed the nearest to his views of any that he had ever seen. I then began to tell him how the principles were taking root in England and Scotland, and the fruits that already appeared as consequents of their adoption. Yesterday, James Walker and I went to see him at his own house, as I wanted to engage him to preach for me, and we had a long conversation again. He told us how he had been talking the subject over with the leading men in their circuit, and that, while some approved, others said no; also that he intended writing a piece to their magazine on some of these subjects. He is a blessed man. He has a brother living with him who is a local preacher in the Wesleyan body. He is full of desire for union. It is a heart-cheering consideration, and my brother Walker and I could not help remarking to each other, that these principles seem to be taking hold of the minds of the people almost the whole country over; go where you will, we can hear of some one or other approving them. James had a blessed day on Sunday; there were several that found peace, and others were seeking. One local preacher had left the Association, and has joined the brethren at Hyde. The room was crowded, nearly to suffocation, on the Sabbath evening. He intends going to Gee-cross and other places to get those of the brethren who feel disposed to meet, to work. I went down to Hyde again last Saturday evening, with James, and we held a Temperance meeting in the open-air. Such attention I hardly ever saw. The people seemed as though they were almost cemented together, and after we concluded, they still stood, as though they were afraid to go till we had gone lest they should miss hearing something. I have the fullest confidence, that God will raise up a flourishing church at Hyde. I was down there myself the Sunday night before. I preached at 6 in their room, and at half-past 7 in the open-air, at the Market place.

In reference to Staleybridge and its retension of a little of the sectarianism of the day. It is a strange thing how men cling to it; and most of all I am surprised at J. Barker. I was at tea with him at Hyde last Tuesday afternoon, and in the course of a conversation which passed, the subject of *leaving the Connexion* came up. Some of the preachers had been charging some of the members about *leaving* them. Barker said they had *not* left them, they were *still* the NEW CONNEXION! They, like others, had departed from the original principles of the Connexion, and they (Barker's friends) had adhered to them; so that they were "still the New Connexion." I was surprised to hear it, especially when I considered what he had said at Staleybride *two days* before, and, by the way, what he said the *very same evening* in the Working Man's Institution *after* he had made this statement, viz., that *all* the difference that there was between them *now*, and what they lately had been was, that they had substituted Jesus Christ for the Conference! Now this was either true or otherwise: if true, then they could not be the New Connexion, because they cannot be the New Connexion without a Conference; if otherwise, then why say that they had substituted Jesus Christ for the Conference when they still adhered to the Connexion!

My dear brother, you ask me whether I am "come fairly out of the sects" or not, and whether I can say of myself and those with whom I meet, 'We belong to the Church of Christ, and all His people are members of our Church. I answer: as far as I myself am concerned, I can say so; I am not aware of any sectarianism attaching to myself as an individual: I feel that I am the Lord's free-man, and am willing to do his will,—

"Where He appoints I go."

I do not remember having had a more blessed sense of the approval of my God for months than I feel at this moment while writing this epistle. I never felt more anxious in my life for the spread of truth. Once I was afraid to be singular for God; now it is my glory and joy. Once I was afraid to stand up and preach Christ out of doors, at least was rather backward to do so; now I glory in doing it. I wish to be a star, if not a sun, *i.e.*, I wish to give light to my fellow-men respecting the great truths of the gospel, and, I trust, am not spending my strength in vain. I am resolved to do all I can to kill and bury sectarianism, and remove every barrier (existing in the church) to the spread of God's truth. I am anxious to see a growing church, and that in more senses than one;—I wish them, first, to grow in grace, and in the knowledge of the truth; there are too many infants, weak, staggering children in the church, liable to fall over every straw,—I wish them to grow up into Christ "till they all come in the UNITY of the faith, and of the knowledge of the Son of God, unto a perfect man, unto the measure of the stature of the fulness of Christ; that they henceforth be no more children, tossed to and fro, and carried about by every wind of doctrine, by the sleight of men and cunning craftiness, whereby they lie in wait to deceive; but that they may grow up into him in *all things*, which is the head *even Christ;*" and when this is the case, we may expect to see,—secondly, the church growing in numbers,—hundreds and thousands falling prostrate at the foot of the cross, acknowledging Christ to be Lord, to the glory of God the Father. As I said before in a former communication to you, I dare not say that all the people here are as free from it as is desirable, yet I do not see *much* sign of its existence amongst us. I believe that they are quite willing to learn their duty, and have no doubt they will be willing as fast as they learn it, to reduce it to practice. . . . . I hope you will write soon, and tell me how you are getting on; your letters do me much good. Yours in the Lord,

To J. Bowes. THOMAS STURGES.

12*th*.—This morning rose at 2 o'clock, and baptized about half-past 3 o'clock; 13 were buried with Christ in baptism. Evening; preached again without a text, on the excellencies of Jesus Christ, near Union Bridge. During the last few days my own mind has been much refreshed, by considering the great love of God, and the great dignity and elevating tendency of the inspired writings. I wish to have Christianity entire and unimpaired, even as I see it in the Scriptures, and not as I see it in the sects.

13*th*.—To-day, Peter Anderson, a beloved brother from Birmingham, who has spent a few weeks at Dundee, &c., arrived in Aberdeen. While in Dundee he had got one page of a letter written, to tell me that he was about to return to Birmingham, and *not* come to Aberdeen, when he became so unhappy that he could not proceed with his letter. He retired to pray, and was convinced that he ought to come; he came at a time when he was much needed. He preached out this evening to a large congregation near the Infirmary; they continued amid the rain.

14*th*.—To-day visited PETERHEAD, and preached to the fishermen; a large congregation.

15*th*.—Heard a tolerable good sermon at the Independent Chapel, in the forenoon, having delivered a discourse in the Hall at 9 o'clock, to a large congregation. At 1 o'clock, preached at the cross to a tolerably large assembly. At half-past 2, heard a sermon in the secession church, the whole service was dry and formal. At 4 preached in the Hall. It was nearly full. At 6, at the cross, to near 2000 people. The Lord gave me great liberty, at 8, in the Hall, to a great crowd. During the day I have endeavored to bring before these willing hearers, all the truths of God, likely to benefit their souls.

16*th*.—This morning preached at the Cross, or Market-place, at 7 o'clock, to some hundreds. How pleasing to see so many in the open-air at this early hour. Took the mail for ABERDEEN as soon as the sermon was over; preached at the North Kirk, also in the Hall, afterwards, brother Anderson and I spoke. Seven or eight souls were seeking mercy, and some found peace through believing.

I have now been eight or nine weeks here, and the Lord has commenced a great work. I trust it shall go on till thousands shall be brought to the Lord.

17*th*.—Sailed for EDINBURGH at 8 o'clock, arrived about 5; took coach for Glasgow, arrived soon after 10.

18*th*.—Saw a few Christian brethren, especially Thomas Brown, and advised him to come out of the sects. Sailed for Liverpool from Greenock, having gone thither by railway.

The remaining part of this month I spent in LIVERPOOL, preaching to large congregations.

Aug. 5th.—Lord's Day.—Visited Hawarden, in Wales, with George Mitchelson, at the request of several brethren, who have withdrawn from the Methodist New Connexion, in consequence of the last Conference having expelled or suspended Joseph Barker, William Trotter, and Thomas Sturges. On the Lord's day I had attentive congregations, in considerable numbers. The chief part of the people whom we addressed are great admirers of Joseph Barker, and I fear some of them extol him, and speak of him, more than they praise and speak of Jesus Christ. When souls have received much spiritual benefit from any minister, how prone they are to put him too high! Oh that we could see more of God in our salvation, and less of men! These men, however, have left the sect, and seem anxious to answer the question, "What is truth?" If they will follow the true light, they will be guided into all truth.

In the forenoon of the 5th, at EULOE; G. Mitchelson spoke, with me. At two o'clock he preached at MOORE; I, at Lane end, BUCKLEY MOUNTAIN. Evening, we both preached in a green lane, HAWARDEN. About 100 people have come out of the New Connexion in this neighborhood.

7th.—To-day sold several remaining articles of furniture, and books in Walker's Sale-rooms.

8th.—Attended meeting in Jubilee Street, where the Lord has been lately blessing immortal souls.

9th.—This morning my family set off for Yorkshire.

12th.—Preached farewell discourses in Liverpool. One or two souls professed to be blessed with peace through believing, after the evening discourse.

13th.—Came by railway to MANCHESTER; several brethren and sisters agreed to have a prayer meeting at five o'clock, to implore the divine blessing upon my journey. Several accompanied me to the railway, and obeyed the Apostolic command, "salute each other with an holy kiss." On arriving in Manchester found that the prospects of the church were brightening, some souls had been added, and Thomas Storey had been baptized. Reached HYDE during the wakes. Held an open-air meeting with Thomas Sturges and James W. Walker, and then a Temperance tea meeting at Gee-cross.

14th.—Held another open-air meeting at HYDE, a Roman Catholic opposed. He asked how we could account for the change of the Sabbath from the seventh day of the week to the first, but by the tradition of the church? He asked me if I did not observe the Sabbath on the first day? I replied, that in the New Testament I did not read of any Jewish Sabbath being obligatory, and accordingly I observed the first day of the week, as the first Christians did. I denied that Christians are obliged to observe the Jewish Sabbath.

MOTTRAM.—In the evening, lectured on Primitive Christianity in a chapel where T. Sturges preaches. Afterwards, Thomas Sturges and I washed each other's feet, as Jesus Christ gave commandment. We had stood several hours, and walked several miles, the day was very hot, the cold water was most refreshing. We thought of the Saviour's example, and felt it pleasant to imitate him of whom it is written, that "He took a towel and girded himself, after that he poureth water into a bason, and began to wash the disciples' feet, and to wipe them with the towel wherewith he was girded." John xiii. 5.

15th.—To-day had some conversation with Joseph Barker, at John Clayton's. This was the first interview we have ever had. Heard him at night with great pleasure and profit. He first addressed sinners, and then saints, going over some of the neglected duties of the Lord's sermon on the mount, and also pointing out the answers which were given to the prayers of very holy men of old.

16th.—I lectured in the same chapel to a crowded congregation, on the Unity of the Church. The Lord was indeed with us. One Wesleyan Association preacher felt almost constrained to leave his shoemaking, to spread these great principles. About 75 members, all the society, with the chapel, have withdrawn from the Methodist New Connexion here; 55 at Newton with a chapel; 180 at Staleybridge; 65 at Hurst; 17 at Stockport; and several at Manchester. I was detained a day longer here than I intended to stay; perhaps I shall see the Providence of God, even in this.

17th.—Rose about 5 o'clock and walked to HYDE, took coach for MANCHESTER, then railway to LEEDS, where I met my father and my family. Slept all night at Spacey Houses. I do not like to sleep at these public houses.

19th.—While at GREWELTHORPE, YORKS, was refreshed in spirit by hearing from his own lips the confession of a believer, who preaches the Gospel, that he was awakened and found peace in Jesus Christ, by a sermon which I delivered about 17 years ago. May the Lord make him very useful in bringing many souls to know the truth.

Heard a very excellent sermon in a Wesleyan Chapel, after which I preached to only a few in the open air. At 2 o'clock attended a Primitive Methodist Lovefeast; lively speaking, but considering that some of them have been in the way to heaven many years, a deficiency of knowledge, which is very humbling. I spoke, and told them what I had found profitable to my soul, such as, being buried with Christ in Baptism, observing the Lord's Supper weekly, meeting simply in the Lord's name, where we have liberty of ministry, &c. Towards the close of the Lovefeast, a brother got up and spoke of the good which he had got by Total Abstinence. I made a few remarks in the same strain. When I sat down, Thomas Dawson, who led the Lovefeast, an old friend of mine, said the two last speakers had digressed, and in private he might take an opportunity of telling them so. It was remarked that this had damped the meeting. I fear this young man, from his appearance, will not be long in this world. I intimated an open-air sermon in the Love-feast, and the Primitive Methodists' gave their meeting house for the evening sermon. The place was much crowded.

20th.—Walked to WATLASS, where T. Dawson has a farm, he seemed quite warm against Total Abstinence, but moderate on other subjects. As I went, called at MASHAM, ascertained that Jane Pullen, of Knaresborough, whom I once thought of marrying, died 4 years and six months ago, in America, she was married for several years to John Cliffe, of Knaresborough.

21st.—Walked up to MIDDLEHAM to see my parents. In the evening held a meeting with a few disciples who meet in the Lord's name alone.

26th.—BRADFORD, YORKS.—Preached out of doors at 9 o'clock, at Bowling. At half-past ten heard a read sermon, where William Trotter usually preaches; it was very likely to injure the life of the church. At half past 2 preached in the same place as before, to a large congregation. In the evening, at 6, preached to a crowded congregation, where those meet who recently separated from the Methodist New Connexion. In this circuit all have left with the exception of about 20 members. Between three and four hundred throughout the circuit are now at liberty to learn and practice New Testament Christianity. The people seemed grateful for my services, and I trust, received the truths relating to Primitive Christianity, which the Lord enabled me to deliver.

27th.—Called on Ralph Waller, a New Connexion preacher still, but not greatly enamored of its proceedings. I should not wonder but he may yet leave them. In the evening, attended the annual meeting of the London Missionary Society, held at LEEDS, in John Ely's chapel, a new splendid place, with a very large organ; the chapel, it seems, cost about £12,000. What would the first Puritans have said to this? The Congregationalists in the large towns are manifestly carried away with pomp and worldliness. Of course, if they please the world, the world will follow them. One of the speakers told a good anecdote of Queen Elizabeth, the Earl of Essex, the Countess of Nottingham, and a ring of jewels. Had I been a speaker, and at liberty to utter my mind, I should have responded to their urgent solicitations for more money by pointing to the chapel, organ, &c., and three or four large seals on some gentlemen's watches.

28th.—Left Leeds, by coach to Selby, and by steam packet to HULL. Saw sister Wells, and was very kindly entertained by Mr. Thompson, a Baptist minister.

29th.—Sailed at half-past 4 p.m., by the *Erin* steamer for Dundee. Had a fine passage, and arrived on the 30*th*, about half-past 11. The dear brethren James Allan and James Grinstead (who has commenced business here), were waiting for us.

10*mo.* 3*rd.*—Two were baptized this morning, and after I preached at the West Port to a large congregation. We held a prayer meeting afterwards. At 11, broke bread in the Operatives' Hall. At half-past 2, preached in the same place, and at 6 o'clock in Lindsay Street chapel. The brethren Allan and Grinstead also spoke in the open-air. A few souls have been saved here lately. Both in Dundee and Arbroath, ministers, in and out of the Establishment, have been holding meetings for prayer, in which nearly all denominations join.

4th.—ARBROATH. Met a few friends, and expounded the Scriptures.

5th.—Should have proceeded to Aberdeen to-day, but was prevented by a storm. In the evening I held a conversational meeting, for disciples to teach and learn the whole religion of Jesus Christ; it was a very gracious season. It was stated in the meeting that one congregation, under Alexander Sorley's pastoral care, met to hear him on the 26th of last month, when he was suddenly taken ill, and the congregation dispersed without worship! they had neither singing, prayer reading the Scriptures, nor exhortation. How was this? It was not because they had no gifts in the congregation, but because they had no *ordained minister* to lead their devotions.

6th, 7th, 8th.—Still detained in Arbroath. This evening baptized George Menmuir and other two brethren. Have just read the following from the DUNDEE ADVERTISER, Oct. 8th, 1841. Superintendent Corsterphan will send his men for me no more. I shall meet him no more on earth before the Dundee Magistrates. God has taken the matter into his own hands, and called this active opposer of open-air preaching to give an account of his stewardship:—

"We have to mention the very sudden death of Mr. Corsterphan, Superintendent of Police here. He attended the court yesterday at 10 o'clock, and went through the usual business; after completing which, he went up to his parlour, lay down upon the sofa, and was reading a newspaper. His wife left the room to go down stairs, and on her return, a very short time afterwards, she found him in an alarming state, with a gurgling in his throat. She immediately called for assistance. When medical assistance arrived, an attempt was made to draw blood from his arm, but only a few drops came, and he never moved again. The cause of his death is not yet known." *

Sinners do not know what troubles they may have to meet with in their journey to the house appointed for all living. Trouble may seize their hearts, and they may die suddenly.

9th.—Took the *Bonnie Dundee*, for Aberdeen, and arrived soon after four o'clock. Visited several friends, and attended a prayer meeting in the evening. Was very full of thought, and much fatigued. I prayed without any satisfaction to myself.

10th.—In the forenoon read 1 Cor. xii., preached from xiii. 5. In the evening, endeavored to teach a little of the whole religion of Jesus Christ.

17th.—This morning eighteen were buried with Christ in baptism. At 11 o'clock was much refreshed while reading and expounding Rom. vi., and also while showing the propriety of a weeping spirit, and the success likely to attend it, from Psa. cxxvi. 5, 6. At half-past 2, from 1 John i. 6, 7. Rich season; it seemed peculiarly appropriate just before the Lord's Supper. In the evening one of the brethren intimated that he should have some Socialists present, and desired me to say something to them. I did so, from Matt. xvi. 26, but had little comfort in it.

20th.—Meeting of the church, to teach and learn the whole religion of Jesus Christ.

1st question. Is it right for Christians to go to war? The following passages were read against it, Matt. v. 38, 39, also 43—48; James

---

* Since the three days' trial in 1840, Baillie Johnson, became Provost (or mayor) It will be remembered that he was very active against me for preaching in the Greenmarket. I mention it as another remarkable event of Divine Providence, that, since then, his worldly affairs have become embarrassed, and he has been made bankrupt, and has had to resign all his civil honors. Surely such events as these will lead men to fear God. It is not the duty of Christians when reviled to revile again, nor when persecuted to threaten. They must commit their cause in quietness and peace to God. I preached there in the open-air frequently after these circumstances occurred without molestation. The authorities were as quiet as lambs. The opposers were either tired of their work, off the bench, or in their graves. GABRIEL MILLER, Clerk to the Magistrates, walked into the water, and was found drowned. We move in a world, under a government of rectitude, which will do right.

iv. 1, 2. If **wars** come from our own lusts, they are not from God.

When the religion of God prevails, the nations will learn war no more, but beat their swords into ploughshares and their spears into pruning hooks. Luke xxii. 35—38, was also considered. "They that take the sword shall perish with the sword." "My kingdom is not of this world, else would my servants fight." "The weapons of our warfare are not carnal, but spiritual."

2nd. question. Is it right for Christians to be in Clubs or Benefit Societies?

3rd. question. What can we do, more than we have done, as a church, to unite saints, and convert sinners?

On the second question, a beloved brother stated that he could not, from conscientious views. belong to the Guildry, or be a burgess, because they require so much before they will allow a man to trade, and if he do not pay it, they will fine him, and shut up his shop. We had a very trying conversation this afternoon with some professing Christians, some of them, I hope, real Christians, on not resisting evil; three of the company were for the peaceable and inoffensive commandments of Jesus Christ, delivered in his sermon on the mount, being understood and acted upon according to their literal meaning; the rest were against us. We asked this question. "Did Jesus Christ and his Apostles ever act contrary to the literal interpretation of the sermon on the mount?" We got no answer. If the Apostles obeyed, why not we?

21*st.*—This has been a day of sweet communion with the Great Spirit. I long to pray about everything. How sweet to go for everything I need to my heavenly Father! This evening, two souls were seeking mercy, after I had expounded Matt. iii. in a private house. One professed to give herself to God. She is the fourth in the same family, within these few months that we have preached here—two brothers and two sisters. Praise the the Lord for the freeness and richness of his grace!

To-day, I prayed the Lord to direct us to a suitable house. We sought in many parts of the town, to-day, and on former days, but found none to suit us. In the evening we heard that one which we saw last week, but which was engaged by another, had been given up, as his wife did not like it. Prayed to-day about a daily school.

24*th.*—Attended the 7 o'clock prayer meeting; a gracious season. The brethren pray too long; long prayers produce formality and hinder life. At 11 o'clock, read and expounded Matt. xviii. especially the 15th verse. At half-past 2, from Psa. cxvi. 7, "Return unto thy rest," &c. I contrasted the feelings of a child of God reviewing his Christian experience, with the feelings of an aged man reviewing life; also the feelings of the father and mother, with those of the church and God. It was a rich time. In the evening, delivered a second sermon on Matt. xvi. 26. A solemn time. Three or four seeking mercy. Two or three found peace.

25*th.*—Read and expounded Matt. xx. Three seeking mercy. Two sweeps; the wife of one was led to the Lord since I came hither at first. This man, indeed the whole family, were led to hear me by a little boy, who has been raised from being a sweep to learn a trade, by a sister in the Lord,

27*th*.—Interesting meeting to edify each other. Subject for next week, 1st. How the office bearers of the church were appointed. 2nd. Whether it is the duty of all Christians to unite and form one church, or to support sectarianism. Whether oaths of a judicial kind are scriptural.

28*th*.—Preached this evening, at 8 Park Lane, in a garret; very poor people. The place was well filled; several wept. I said I would shake hands with all who were willing to love Jesus Christ from this night. Several gave me their hands and promised to serve him.

30*th*.—Saturday. After conversing with candidates for membership, and attending the prayer meeting, I stepped aside, on my way home, into the Pavilion, where Feargus O'Connor, Esq., and Patrick Brewster, a minister of the Established Church, were discussing about the best means of carrying the Charter. The discussion consisted chiefly of personal abuse. It closed by a rejection of the moral force resolutions moved by P. Brewster, and the carrying of a resolution that Brewster was no Chartist, and unfit to represent any Chartist body. The meeting was exceedingly uproarious, and calculated to give a very humiliating view of human nature.

31*st*.—Attended the 7 o'clock prayer meeting, and was led to my forenoon's discourse, which was from John xvii. 15, by the prayer of a brother. Afternoon: had great difficulty to stay my mind on any text, but at last fixed on 1 Pet. iv. 17. The Lord gave me to weep over sinners, while pleading with them, for which I feel thankful to Him. Many sinners wept under the word. The Lord grant that their goodness may not be like the morning cloud and early dew, which soon pass away.

11*mo*. 1*st*.—We commenced a Day School, for all children to learn to read and write, whether their parents can pay for them or not; the school is to be conducted on Christian principles. In the evening lectured on Total Abstinence. One Christian came forward to join the cause, who said, she saw her hands were not clean, and she wished to wash her hands in innocency.

4*th*.—Was much blessed this day in visiting a sick woman. Jacquiline Jamieson proposed our going to Upper Canada with her in the spring. She offered to give me one half of her estate there, near Hamilton, of 200 acres, which cost £200, and 50 acres of it £200 clearing. She also proposed to pay the passage of the whole family out. I feel willing either to go or stay, as the Lord may direct. I desire to go to America that I may teach those truths there which the Lord has taught me; but I wait His will.

8*th*.—This morning was much refreshed. Attended the school, and conversed with the children about the things of God. As I was coming away, five boys were lingering outside. I asked them if they had come to the school? "Yes." "Why, then, do you not come in?" "We have na bawbees." I took them in; they all had fathers, who were chiefly weavers.

11*th*.—Commenced a Night School, for learning the young people who work in the mills, and cannot read, write, or use figures, and do not attend a day school. About twenty attended, among whom were some married people. Some were taught their letters; some could read imperfectly in the New Testament; one man could write well, but knew nothing of the use of figures.

13th.—Saturday; a precious prayer meeting. Peter M'Kay, a young man between sixteen and seventeen, applied for membership. He was, a few years ago, a sweep boy, and went to Jacquiline Jamieson's night school with his sooty face. She clothed him, and bound him an apprentice to a brassfounder. Since I came hither he got saved, by believing in the Lord Jesus Christ.

22nd.—Last night, after the evening lecture, seven were seeking the Lord. This evening preached, by desire, a sermon on "Justification by Faith." Four in one family have been led to Christ this year, and the father is much opposed to their coming to meet with us. He said he was afraid we were building on works. He said he would like to hear a sermon on justification by faith. I engaged to preach it. He was present.

28th.—Morning, prayer meeting. Afternoon, preached from Luke xvii. 10. Evening, lectured on church unity and prosperity, and addressed sinners afterwards. Two came forward to seek mercy, one a Roman Catholic.

Dec. 5th.—This morning we commenced observing the Lord's Supper in the forenoon service. It was a great weeping time while I was speaking on the love of Christ. One brother spoke. Two o'clock, preached from Eph. 8, 9. A very precious season. Evening, a large congregation, from, "The harvest is past, the summer is ended, and we are not saved." Jer. viii. 20. Four came forward to seek the Lord, two of them fine young men.

6th.—To-day I mentioned a few particulars in the Shorter Catechism opposed to the word of God. The hour from 7 to 8 was more than filled up with souls conversing to me about the things which relate to their eternal peace.

8th.—To-day, Gordon Gilchrist called on me, a very singular man, many years a Methodist class leader, he withdrew, on similar terms to the Wesleyan Association. He has attended our meetings several times. We thought of receiving him as a member, but his repeated instances of contention, and an unchristian spirit, induce us to desire him not to speak in any of our meetings. I have told him, in private, his sin, he seems to take very little offence. The last Lord's Day morning, after being told not to speak in our meetings, he took his seat among the brethren at the Lord's table, I desired him not to sit down, yet he remained. We passed him with the bread, yet he snatched a piece and ate it; and with the cup we passed him, he stretched out his hand and took it from a sister, on the form behind him. When we were retiring, he offered me his hand. I told him I could not regard him as a Christian brother, and declined his offer. To-day I warned him against the judgment of God, whose ordinance he had desecrated, and reminded him of the Corinthian, whom the church delivered over to Satan, for the destruction of the flesh, telling him, that should he repent, we should willingly forgive him, and if not, he would find it a fearful thing to meet God. If he do not repent, I should not wonder but the vengeance of God will overtake him. To-day he offered me his hand. I took it, and said, "I shake hands with you as a friend, not as a brother." This evening we had a rich meeting. I pointed out the various ways in which Christians may serve God, especially by economy in dress, furniture, and the dress of children.

13th.—Lectured on Rom. vii. 14. The church met. While I was engaged in the service, my only daughter arrived to tell me that Edward, who has been unwell some days, had taken a fit, and was thought for some time dead. He recovered sufficiently for me to return to the meeting.

15th.—I adduced the following passages in favor of pledges and vows. 1st. Laws are given to regulate vowing, in Num. xxx. 2nd. They are to be performed, Deut. xxiii. 21—23. 3rd. It is right to vow in trouble, Ps. lxvi. 13—14. 4th. It is a mark of a fool to vow and not pay, Ecc. v. 4. 5th. Jacob vowed in solitude, when difficulties were before him. 6th. The Rechabites vow, Jer. xxxv. 6. 7th. David, Ps. cxxxii. 1—5. Paul vowed not to eat or drink anything which would make his brother to offend. May we not vow to rise early, to reprove sin, or anything else?

It was proved that infants will be saved. 1st. As a matter of natural justice, because they have never sinned. "Sin is a transgression of the law," and they have not been capable of knowing or violating law. 2nd. It is granted that some infants will be saved in their infancy, why not all, since God is no respecter of persons. 3rd. Jesus Christ has said, "Suffer little children to come unto me," &c. The soul that sinneth it shall die. If a man poison a stream at the fountain, he may be guilty of murder, not those who are poisoned by drinking of the waters.

20th.—Lectured on Rom. viii. 1—18. A remarkable time of blessing.

21th.—Conversed with sinners seeking mercy. Three were seeking. I trust one got made happy in God.

22nd.—Fast Day. Morning prayer meeting at half-past 4. About 30 present. A very refreshing season. One brother acknowledged that we had been leagued confederates with the devil in overthrowing the kingdom of God, and deserved the burning gall of hell. At 9 o'clock, 11 present; still a blessed time. One brother, the same, prayed for our families, that the Lord might convert all, and that none of their places might be empty in heaven. I have had a blessed season in private meditation and prayer this day, have endeavored to remember the sins of my youth, and of my riper years, and feel astonished at the overflowing love of God.

31st.—This evening our Watch Night, or preaching and praying services, commenced. I opened them with prayer. Brothers Stewart, Crombie, M'Kay, and George Cornwall spoke. I gave a 15 minutes' address in the Temperance Hall.

It will be seen that I had no great reason to reverence the "Reverends" by whom I had been immediately surrounded. N. West, Hugh Hart, and last, but not least, Robert Aitken, had caused me intense mental agony. The Lord did not rend me away from them without difficulty. Never more do I desire union such as this, with hired ministers. As I had determined not to go to law with R. Aitken, after his return to the State Church, I called on his bishop, at Chester, to get a settlement, without going to law, but he referred me to the law courts. The law-church seems to know nothing, and care nothing, about settling differences between brethren by the Scriptures and the Church. She recommends and practises civil law.

It will be seen how I was set free in 1838, in 1839 and 1840 to promote Union among Christians, and to defend the faith in many places.

Infidelity in those years was rampant. New halls were erected in Liverpool, Manchester, Sheffield, and many other places. My discussions and lectures were blessed, and in a very few years, not one hall was left to them.

I was now fairly out of sectism and priestism. I had long quitted the former in name and spirit, but others made professions which they did not sustain. Any denomination, however liberal, would have confined my spirit, fettered my investigations, controlled my labors, and more or less hindered the outpouring of disagreeable, but necessary, truths. I exulted in my freedom, because the word of God was not bound. It requires to be told with tenderness, indeed, but also with unflinching boldness. Christ's servant should look to Him, not man, for approval and reward.

It is one of the enormous evils of the hired system, whether the payers of wages are many or few, that they expect to be consulted, pleased, and often to be at liberty to dismiss a servant who fails to give them satisfaction. He may please God, but if in acting thus, he should displease them, they know how to bring on the day of punishment by dismissal. It is not always so in State Churches, where the incumbency is either during life, or good behaviour; and if the latter is bad, few are disposed to proceed against an offender in his "cure of souls," or rather in his career of ruin to souls. Christ's servant, to be free, must not depend on the favor or remuneration of men. Satisfied with his Divine Master and his reward, he must not live on the smiles of many, or a few, rich patrons.

Two or three additional churches have been formed, viz., at Arbroath, Aberdeen, and a few have begun to meet at Woolton, and scores of souls have been led to the "Lamb of God, who taketh away the sin of the world." In our labors this year we have kept our eye on two objects—the gathering together of Christians into one Church, and the conversion of sinners. By the first we hope, under God, to promote *the Unity of the Church*. If Christians would only take the Bible as their sole rule of faith and practice, and consider the importance of going forth to the world as ONE BODY, appearing in the native dress of Christians, and not as many bodies, with the varied *party-colored robes* of their peculiar denominations—if they would obey the command which binds them to "do all in the name of Jesus Christ"—they would cease to act in the name of a sect or in the name of a mere man, and would be indeed "the light of the world." The importance of the *visible* oneness of Christians may be inferred from the Saviour's prayer, a short time before he suffered. Many Christians also, both in England and Scotland, are feeling the importance of unity.

It is in vain to expect that the church will be united while Christians remain "unequally yoked with unbelievers" in churches, societies, and associations. Christians must have more life from the Head, and more deadness, even a crucifixion, to the world; and then union will be sown in the spirituality of their nature. Then they will not aim at making the world right merely by the arts and sciences, human learning, political government, or worldly associations; but they will expect a change to result from the same means as the first Christians used—preaching and teaching the great truths of the gospel on a large scale, and practising the requirements of the gospel in their own lives, showing that meekness, gentleness, patience, temperance, longsuffering, zeal, peace, forgiveness of enemies, brotherly kindness, and the doing of good to all men, recommend religion more than the most eloquent defences in its favor. Written and spoken defences of the religion of Christ abound; we seek no more. What we now want are practical defences of Christianity, to undo the scandal which religion has long suffered from the inconsistencies of its professed friends. The great cause of the perpetuation of schism is the regarding of small, separate, isolated meetings, or churches, in towns and cities, as complete and scripturally constituted, while dozens of such churches exist in the same town. *The thousands of believers at Jerusalem formed but one Church.* The Apostle does not address "the churches" at Corinth or Thessalonica, but "the Church at Corinth," and "the Church of the Thessalonians;" indeed, those believers who have determined to content themselves with the *Christian profession*, having renounced everything sectarian, need caution lest they should regard themselves as complete, while hundreds of their brethren, still in the sects, meet not with them. If we are met according to Christ's revealed will, we shall regard every believer as a member of our Church, because he is a member of the one body, having life from the one Head, although, through ignorance or prejudice, he may not have found his way to our visible fellowship. We should only regard ourselves, while numbers of saints are not gathered to us, as a part of the spiritual house in our locality; and, therefore, we should teach, and persuade, and pray, and weep, till we bring all the living stones to form a holy temple in the Lord.

We also held weekly meetings to teach and learn the whole religion of Jesus Christ. In reading over the Acts of the Apostles, it is obvious that when the Apostles preached and taught, they permitted questions to be asked, and often "reasoned with the Jews;" hence we read that "Paul went into the synagogue, and spake boldly, for the space of three months, disputing and persuading the things concerning the kingdom of God," and after "the disciples were separated," he was found "disputing daily in the school of one Tyrannus, and this continued by the space of two years, so that all who dwelt in Asia heard the Word of the Lord Jesus, both Jews and Greeks."—Acts xviii. 19 and xix. 8—10. Why should we be afraid of being asked questions, or having our sentiments examined? We have no interest to serve but that of truth; if we be in error, any one that will point it out does us good service, and if we overthrow his, it is well. "He that doeth truth cometh to the light." These meetings have been exceedingly interesting, conducted in the spirit of love, without striving; and other churches might have them with great advantage. The subjects considered have been such as the following:—Baptism—The Lord's Supper—Who should be Ministers?—How appointed?—Should Christians fight, take oaths, pledge themselves, support the poor, join clubs and benefit societies? Interfere with politics? if so, how far?—Does it promote formality to teach unconverted children to sing and pray?—How should holy women adorn themselves according to Isaiah iii. 18—24; 1 Tim. ii. 2—9; 1

Peter iii. 3?—Ought Christians to fast?—In what way may Christian females serve God and be useful to society?—&c.

During the year, Joseph Barker, William Trotter, and Thomas Sturges, with several hundreds of Christian people, have been either expelled or suspended, or have withdrawn themselves, from the Methodist New Connexion, and seem aiming to have New Testament Christianity; and, if they do not split upon the rock of "Congregational Methodism," but hasten back to primitive Christianity, and if the new churches are not subject to *lordly* and *hireling ministers* (some of whom I hear are creeping in among them), and if they contend for the *whole* of primitive Christianity, its *doctrines* (not admitting Unitarians, as one of their ministers recommends; for if they admit them to membership, how can they hinder them from being ministers?), and its *ordinances*, not setting aside either Baptism or the Lord's Supper, for the first Christians were both baptized with or in the Holy Spirit, and also with or in water, (Acts xix. 4—6) they will be useful. Those who contend for the whole religion of Jesus Christ should not *set aside any part of it*. The new churches are, in many respects, more scriptural than the generality of Methodist churches.

Open-air Preaching has been attended by the Lord's blessing during the year. There is now preaching in the open-air, in Liverpool, by eight or ten preachers; also in Dundee by three; in Arbroath, by two or three, and the same in Aberdeen. Let us thank the Lord for sending out laborers into his harvest, and let those who preach study Christ's sermon on the Mount, and the Apostles' addresses in the Acts.

CHAPTER IX.

MACALLAN'S, AND OTHER LETTERS, ON CHRISTIANS MEDDLING WITH POLITICS.—PRAYING A WHOLE NIGHT.—HAPPY DEATH OF A CONVERTED INFIDEL.—DISCUSSION ON MORMONISM.—JOURNAL.—LETTERS.—DISCUSSIONS ON SOCIALISM WITH MR. ESDAILE—HIS AWFUL END—ALSO WITH MR. WATTS.—HEALTH OF BODY.—THOMAS HARDACRE'S SINGULAR CASE.—REMOVAL TO MANCHESTER.—1842, 1843, 1844.

Jan. 1st. 1842.—At 5 o'clock p.m., the church and others met to take tea, about 12 took "purity" with me. The speaking was very good and appropriate.

Went to the Temperance Hall after, and prayed.

2nd.—Lord's Day morning, 7 o'clock, prayer meeting. At 2 o'clock, preached, after which G. Cornwall delivered his reasons for uniting with us, most solemnly and impressively. His main reason was the great good that he has got by attending. Evening, preached from " This year thou shalt die."

3rd.—Conversed at 7 with candidates for membership. One woman stated, with tears flowing " When I went to hear other ministers, I thought that Jesus Christ died for the sins of the world, but when I came to hear you, I believed that Jesus Christ died for *me*, and this gave me greater comfort than I have derived from any other quarter." At 8 o'clock lectured on Rom. ix., many burst into tears, and sobbed aloud.

4th—This evening, had nine, either seeking mercy, or desiring to be members. One was blessed about a fortnight ago, but in consequence of not confessing Christ, she seemed to have lost the comforts of the Holy Spirit.

5th.— Two questions were considered. 1st. Which is the best method of praying ? 2nd. What is the thing signified by circumcision ? And we are to consider till the next week, 1st. If there is any perfection in this life, and if so, what it is and how far attainable. 2nd. In what the first ministers of the Gospel differed from those we have now ? These are to be considered on the 12th, when we spend a whole night in prayer to God; so Jesus did, Luke vi. 12; Neh. i. 6; Ps. lxxxviii. 1 ; Luke ii. 37 ; Luke xviii. 7, 8 ; Acts xxvi. 7 ; 1 Thess. iii. 10 ; 1 Tim. v. 5; 2 Tim. iv. 3 ; Rev. iv. 8 ; Rev. vii. 14, 18 ; Acts xii. 5, 12.

9th.—I preached about four miles from this place, in a parish where the minister has upwards of £800 per annum, for preaching. He has also two large farms the one about ten miles from the other. Some months ago, when several of his parishioners wished a new kirk, in a part of the parish some miles distant from the old, he appeared in the Presbytery to oppose it and said, " I beg to tell the Presbytery that we have religion enough in the parish." The people erected a school-room where all Christians, may meet, and they have commonly one sermon every Lord's Day. Perhaps the school-room may hold near 300 people. It is tolerably well filled.

12th.—Met this evening at 8 o'clock, and continued till 4, at the end of every two hours spent a little time in conversation, so that several went away at the end of the first two hours. We prayed, sung, exhorted, conversed, read the Scriptures, and confessed our sins to the Lord, and endeavored to devote ourselves to his service, in a renewed dedication.

20th.—To-day, visited STONEHAVEN, about 15 miles from Aberdeen, arrived before 8 in the morning; made one or two calls, but the inhabitants in general were in bed. Walked down to the shore for a time. About seven years ago I lectured in the Methodist Chapel, on the Unity of the Church. This chapel is now closed, owing to some dispute. I applied for the Temperance Hall; Robert Gleig, tin-smith, President of the Total Abstinence Society, was very kind. Wrote ten notices of two lectures, and sent the bellman round. Though an entire stranger, this friend invited me to breakfast, and I found his wife the daughter of a Baptist. The mother came and invited me to her house, though I knew not the family.

RELIEVING THE STRANGER.

About twice as many people attended as commonly attend week-night services. After the lecture, in which I inculcated benevolence of a larger kind than that which generally exists now, a well-dressed young man of good address desired to speak to me; after stating that I had brought several things before him that were quite new, he added that he was a stranger, without a situation, without friends here, being on a journey to seek a situation, and that he had not as much as would pay his lodgings, in fact, that he had not anything, and wished me to assist him. I told him if he could prove his case to be as he had represented, I would. His shoes, to which he pointed, showed that he had been travelling. He gave me his name, and wished me to keep it to myself. I gave him a little. He looked at me with a look of surprise and astonishment, which I shall never forget, and said, "Well I did not expect anything from you, you have taught me a lesson which shall not be lost upon me." He seemed to think that ministers only recommended benevolence in the pulpit, but would not practise it. I feel thankful that the Lord gave me the means of assisting him. On arriving at ——, I enquired for his mother in the street and at the number that he had specified, but could not find her. I concluded that he had deceived me. About twelve months elapsed,—I heard of a Christian widow who had a sceptical son. After hearing him described, I concluded that this was really the "stranger." I called on his mother and found it so. When I met with him at S——, he had been at home, but knowing that his widowed mother had nothing to give him, he had represented himself as still in a situation in Glasgow, though in reality without one; and his mother believed that when I met him he was without money, though it was unknown to her at the time. He went to London,—got into a situation,—is now in India, with a salary of about £500 per annum, and has settled about £100 per annum on his widowed mother. He once called upon me since, but I was from home.

Judge of my feelings when I received the the following letter from his mother:—

"———, 21st June.

My Dear Brother,—

I was sorry it was not in my power to see you before you left; but I have since heard from my son,—he is quite well, and has sent me a handsome remittance: and as he was disappointed of seeing you when he called on you with the purpose, no doubt, of returning the money you were kind enough to advance to him in his distress, I have always considered myself under obligation to pay you so soon as I should have it in my power. I therefore send you enclosed a post-office order for five shillings, in order that you may not be discouraged from assisting the unfortunate when they come in your way. I shall ever feel myself under deep obligation to you for the kindness shown to him. The family join me in respects to you.

Yours very sincerely," &c.

I have kept out the names of persons and places that the parties may not be known. The case appears calculated to stimulate others to be kind to strangers in distress: for even in this life there is a great amount of real happiness to be derived for making other people happy. Christians should not live a day without endeavoring to instruct the ignorant, reform the wicked, comfort the distressed, clothe the naked, or feed the hungry, and thus diminish the sorrows and increase the joys of mankind. What a vast amount of joy might be diffused among the sons and daughters of suffering, were selfishness destroyed, and if all that are called by the name of Him who "went about doing good," would live for God and the promotion of the best interests of society. While it must be admitted that sin is the greatest evil in the world, and the Saviour from sin the most precious,—the only Redeemer in the world; let us show our love to him by growing daily more like him, remembering that we can not only augment our own and other's bliss to an indefinite amount, by being filled with his mind, but we can even throw all heaven into rapture, by leading one sinner to repentance.

21st.—This morning took a walk on the South Road, on returning met with the young man just addressing himself to his journey. I was glad, as it afforded me an opportunity of showing him the plan of salvation, through the Lord Jesus Christ. He gave me the address of his mother in Aberdeen. To-day sister Graham, with whom I lodge, stated that she heard me in the Methodist Chapel, seven years ago, and that another woman now with God, was greatly blessed after the lecture; they walked together some time afterwards, talking of the things of God. When she expressed the following desire, "Oh! that all those who love the truth would meet together." I hope the Lord will soon answer this prayer.

January 21st, 1842.

Dear Friend,—

I cannot but admire the piety that is breathed through the letters of your friend, but I do not think they indicate great strength or comprehension of mind. Civil Government, as an ordinance of God for the good of society, must in itself be a good thing, though there may be much incidental evil connected with it. Now there can be no civil government without civil judgent, and if civil judgment be in itself right, it cannot be wrong in a Christian to administer it. The prohibition of Christians going to law with one another, instead of settling their disputes by the arbitration of their brethren, is quite another thing, as are also the prohibitions against censoriousness, and treating each other contemptuously. Trial by Jury is the best form of executing judgment ever devised, and if trial by jury is in itself good, it cannot be wrong in a Christian to take part in it. If a Christian were called upon to put a bad law into execution—a law that he believed to be inconsistent with the law of God, he must, of course, decline it, and abide the consequences. If he must, in the performance of his civil duties, do what he believes to be wrong, or relinquish his office, of course he must submit to the latter part of the alternative; but if no such sacrifice is required, it seems plainly to be his duty to take his share of public offices for the welfare of the society of which he is necessarily a member, whenever he is lawfully called to it. Although Jesus told his disciples, when they were persecuted in one city to flee into another, Paul appealed to Cæsar, and on several occasions stood up for his civil rights, when exposed to personal injury by the Jews; but Paul and Jesus could not have been opposed to each other, therefore your friend's interpretation of the words of Jesus must be erroneous. Indeed, were the principle of non-resistance of oppression and injustice carried out to the extent pleaded for by your friend, anarchy, violence, and bloodshed would soon take the place of social order, and social security. "Again," he says, "can I, in voting for legislators, really benefit mankind?—Can I by this means do the wicked any good?" etc. These are astonishing questions. What! Is it not for the good of the world that wise, and just, and humane rulers should guide the affairs of a nation, rather than fools, rogues and tyrants? Is it not manifestly for the good of religion itself, and favorable to its extension, that liberty of conscience should be guaranteed to the public. Can it be that your friend can suppose that it is of no consequence to mankind whether a Laud or a Wilberforce be at the helm of public affairs,—whether his friend Bowes should be permitted to preach to sinners when he pleases without molestation, or be lodged in jail whenever he opens his lips in the name of his Master? He goes on,—" Has legislation made the world really better?" &c. Yes, I say, much better. Had your friend lived in the days of the Charles's, he would doubtless have rejoiced in a transition to such principles of legislation as those under which we live, though there is still much that requires amendment. He forgets the double relation which the Christian sustains as a citizen of the world, as well as a citizen of heaven. It might just as well be said, "Can I, by giving food to the hungry, or clothing to the naked, 'do the wicked any good?'"—"Is the world any better now" for all the schools and benevolent institutions that exist for the temporal benefit of mankind, than it was five hundred years ago? The fallacy of your friend's argument lies in the assumption that a Christian ought to engage in nothing that does not immediately promote the *spiritual* interests of mankind, and savors much of monasticism. He proceeds,—The Christian is "a stranger here,—he is not of the world, though in it,—*are not politics of the world?*" &c. Yes, and so are buying and selling, eating and drinking, &c., &c., yet your friend will not say that the command to be "diligent in business" has become obsolete, or that to attend to the wants of the body is sinful. Again, "Would Jesus have sat in judgment," &c., There are many things lawful for us, nay, binding on us, that Jesus could not exemplify. It is lawful, for instance, for a Christian to marry, it is incumbent on him to provide for his family. So, if a king become a Christian, he is bound not to descend to the station of a subject, but "to rule in the fear of the Lord;" yet it was not expedient for Jesus to be an earthly king. Your friend asks, "Would Jesus have resisted evil by the civil power's assistance?" We are not here left to conjecture what Jesus *would have done;* we are plainly told, as I have already hinted, what Paul actually did, Acts xxv. 10, "Then said Paul, I stand at Cæsar's judgment seat, where I ought to be judged; to the Jews have I done no wrong, as thou well knowest. For if I be an offender, or have committed any thing worthy of death, I refuse not to die; but if there be none of these things whereof these accuse me, *no man may deliver me unto them,* I APPEAL UNTO CÆSAR.

I have thus, with great brevity, and in an easy, off-hand way, jotted down such answers, as occurred at the moment, to what I conceived to be objectionable in your friend's letter, and shall take in good part any animadversions that you may deem it necessary to make in reply. Meantime I am, dear friend, yours truly,

To J. Bowes.   DAVID MACALLAN.

In another long letter of several pages, from which I can only make brief extracts, dated 5 St. George's Crescent, Birmingham, January 26, 1842, Brother J. B. Thorne, my friend referred to in the above letter, writes:—

"I am a follower of him who said that his kingdom was not of this world, who had no home here; who was hated of the world, because he was not of the world; who was a stranger; who, when he was reviled and spoken evil of wrongfully, opened not his mouth, answered nothing; did not defend himself or his character even when an opportunity was given him by his judges; one who came to perform his Father's work and will, and who went about doing good, not seeking power, not seeking his own, not seeking an interest in the affairs of the nation, or town, or city, or councils of the great and honorable; he was occupied in doing good and reproving sin wherever he met with it; and he said, 'If any man will be my disciple, let him take up his cross and follow me;' 'Judge not;' 'Swear not;' 'He that will be greatest, let him be the least;' 'Humble yourselves;' 'Return not evil for evil;' 'Resist not evil;' 'Recompense to no man evil;' 'Vengeance is mine, saith the Lord;' 'Commit yourselves into the hands of God, who careth for you;' 'Take no thought for the morrow;' if ye love me, 'the world will hate you, even as it hated me;' 'Ye are not of the world, even as I am not of the world.' He did not say, 'Contend with Cæsar for the things that are yours,' but 'Render to Cæsar the things that are Cæsar's, and to God the things that are God's.' Christians belong to God, but, in seeking power on the earth, what are they doing? why, rendering themselves to Cæsar—rendering God's things to Cæsar, and placing themselves in the service of the prince of the power of this world. Satan reigns on earth, not God; if God reigned, 'then should his servants fight.' I cannot fight, because I have been born again, and am no longer a native of the soil of the world. . . . . Ah! my dear brother, you know better than I do that the world is not changed, but that Christians are changed; they are approaching as near to the world as they can, as they dare, so as just to get into heaven; while their conduct ought to be, to get as near to, and as much of, heaven as they can while in the world, so as to be as dissimilar to the world as their Lord and Master was. . . . . I know that I must fight the world as an enemy,—not hug it as my friend. The world will love her own; He is my friend whom the world hated. How is it that the world loves what is called in the present day Christianity? Is it not because Christians have submitted themselves to their greatest enemy—the god of this world? I will not seek persecution, but those that will live godly *must* suffer persecution—it is in the very nature of things."

JANUARY 30th, 1842.

DEAR FRIEND,—

. . . . You say, for instance, that it does not follow that because civil government is an ordinance of God, "a Christian, in any way, should become a willing partner of Nero's acts, or an executioner of his unjust decrees." Now in the very letter to which this is a reply, did I not say something to this effect (of course, as I did not keep a copy, I cannot furnish the words),—if a Christian in any civil office is required to do anything contrary to what he believes to be his duty, he must refuse, and abide by the consequences? Here, you see, we agree. I will go further, and say that, if any one is convinced that capital punishment is sinful, he ought on no account to become a juryman in trying a capital offence. I think it is quite a mistake to confound the civil administration of justice with the law of retaliation. You justly say, "The civil government of a Nero,"—you do not mean, of course, the particular acts of that government,—"is as much the ordinance of God as that of a Titus, or a Trajan." But there can be no government without laws, and what would be the use of laws without sanctions? If the civil law be disobeyed, punishment is the natural consequence;—" If thou do that which is evil (says Paul) be afraid; for he (the civil ruler) beareth not the sword in vain; for he is the minister of God; a revenger to execute wrath upon him that doeth evil." Surely it can never be supposed that the law of Christ against private revenge—"I say unto you, that ye resist not evil,"—can, in any respect, apply here. The two cases are essentially different, and to reason from the one to the other appears to me manifestly illogical. It is only on the principle here adverted to, that the 12th and 13th chapters of the epistle to the Romans can be fairly explained. The civil ruler who sends to prison the public offender, is not at liberty to touch a hair of his head from private revenge.

You say: "Whatever the fact of Paul's appealing to Cæsar may prove, it does not prove that he sought any earthly honors from the powers that then existed." I am sure I never adduced it to prove anything so very remote,—a thing that has no connection with it that I can perceive. But, "Besides (you remark), Paul did many things that you and I are not required to do." This is true; but here I cannot help remarking, that you and Mr. Thorne are on very delicate ground, and he especially, on very dangerous ground. Paul and Peter, it is true, were men of like passions with ourselves, but in their apostolical character, their example is as binding on us as their precepts. "Wherefore, I beseech you (says Paul) be ye followers of me," (1 Cor. iv. 16.) "Brethren be followers of me," (Phil. iii. 17) "Those things which ye have both learned, and received, and *seen* in me *do*, and the God of peace shall be with you." (iv. 9.) "For yourselves know how ye ought to follow us." (2 Thess. ii. 7.) "Be ye followers of me, even as I also am of Christ." (1 Cor. xi. 1.) These passages sufficiently indicate the authority of apostolic example ; but in the case of Paul's appeal to Cæsar, we have ample evidence of God's approval, for he was favored with repeated revelations on the way. On one of these occasions he says, " I exhort you, be of good cheer, for . . . . there stood by me this night the angel of God, whose I am and whom I serve, saying, Fear not, Paul, thou must be brought before Cæsar, and lo, God hath given thee all that sail with thee." There is nothing here like the language of reprehension, for appealing for justice to the civil power." See also Acts xxiii. 11,—" And the night following, the Lord stood by him, and said, Be of good cheer, Paul, for as thou hast testified of me in Jerusalem, so must thou bear witness at Rome." Instead of the " trouble " which Paul's appeal to Cæsar " brought him into " being a punishment, as Mr. Thorne seems to think, God said to Ananias concerning him (Acts ix. 15) " Go thy way, for he is a chosen vessel unto me, to bear my name before the Gentiles, AND KINGS, and the children of Israel, for I will show him how great things he must suffer for my name's sake ;"—not for his own sinful appeal to kingly protection. Again (xx. 22), " And now I go bound in the Spirit to Jerusalem, not knowing the things that shall befall me there, save that the Holy Ghost witnesseth in every city, saying, that bonds and affliction abide me ; but none of these things move me." "So shall the Jews at Jerusalem bind the man that owneth this girdle, and shall deliver him into the hands of the Gentiles. . . . . Then Paul answered, What mean ye to weep and to break my heart ; for I am ready not to be bound only, but also to die at Jerusalem for the name of the Lord Jesus." Moreover, when, in consequence of his appeal, he was brought before Cæsar, he says (1 Tim. iv. 16), " At my first answer, no man stood with me, ... notwithstanding," (as if in token of approbation) " the Lord stood with me and strengthened me." On the whole, I hold Paul's appeal to Cæsar, as not only a warrant, but an authoritative example for all Christians when placed in similar circumstances. I hold it unlawful for us to yield up our *liberty* to persecutors, when an appeal to the civil power can preserve them to us, and the resort of our friend to the dangerous supposition that the examples of Paul and Jesus were contradictory of each other, is a striking proof that his principle is untenable. Even in the case to which he refers, of Paul's reviling the high priest, I hold his example to be binding ; for as soon as he was told that it was the high priest, he apologised, and signified his submission to the Divine law ; but had it not been the high priest, there would have been no harm in the reproof that Paul administered.

But I must proceed. My reply respecting "committees, societies, &c.," as contrasted by Mr. Thorne with the religion of Jesus Christ, is that, in so far as their object is to do good—even present good to mankind, they are a part of that religion. Christ himself went about continually doing good to the bodies of men as well as their souls. I conceive Christianity ought to be carried into all the social relations of the present life, whether it be of parent or child, master and servant, magistrate and subject, friend and neighbor ; and that many duties will arise out of these relations, which a Christian is not authorised to desert, even though they should make considerable demands both on his time and his money. You ask, "Do you not think that it betrays a lamentable worldliness of disposition on the part of modern Christians when they obviously seek to be like the world in their habits, manners, companions, profits, honors," &c. I answer, most unquestionably. On the other hand, I think Christians ought to avoid all such singularity as would indicate that they were making too much of trifles, or as would produce the impression that they were exhibiting an affectation of humility. I do not believe that the Society of Friends furnish any example in their odd dress of Christian humility.

Mr. Thorne says, " It is evident that our friend (Macallan) is an expert advocate for power." Paul, on the other hand is justly mentioned "as not meddling with politics," &c. Joseph, again, he notices, " had influence, and place, and power in Egypt, but he sought it not, it was forced upon him (Query), and was a direct interposition of God for the good of His chosen ones,—it was power given him by God for His glory; but what is all the noise and clamor of the present day? Quite the opposite (Charity "thinketh no evil."). They are seeking after their own rights—for their own welfare." I will briefly notice these quotations in order.

1. As to my desire for power, our friend will perhaps be surprised to learn that, although I have held many offices both in civil and religious societies, I never, so far as I know, either directly or indirectly, made the least application for office in my life; and I think I must undergo a very great change indeed, if ever I shall do such a thing. When I am called to any lawful office, and feel myself competent to the performance of its duties, I must have new light before I refuse, if it do not interfere with more important duties; but, on the other hand, I sincerely pray that I may be ever preserved from hunting after power or worldly distinction or even occupying it, for its own sake, or for any other end than to promote the glory of God, and be useful to my fellow-creatures.

2. But Paul had no political office, how could he, and fulfil the duties of an Apostle? Neither did he marry, nor needlessly allow himself to be entangled with the world in any way, lest his Apostolic duties should be hindered; but it is not for that reason sinful to marry, nor to establish a business, nor to act as a ruler, or judge or juryman, &c. When the Roman deputy at Paphos "believed," Acts xiii. 12, we have no hint that he resigned his office; and, although, in New Testament times, not many nobles, not many mighty, were called into the fellowship of the Gospel, the Scriptures abound with instructions to men in power, to execute judgment and justice between man and man, to avoid oppression, &c., in such terms as to demonstrate that such duties are not only compatible with, but that they can only be rightly performed in "the fear of the Lord."

3. Mr. Thorne remarks, that the elevation of Joseph "was a direct interposition of God, for the good of his chosen ones," and that "power was given him by God, for God's glory." This is very true, but Mr. Thorne does not imagine, that God was so much at a loss for instruments to promote the good of the patriarch of his family, that he was under the necessity of thrusting his servant Joseph into a station that a godly man should not fill, in order to gain this end. If Joseph was invested with power for the public good, and the glory of God, may not other fearers of God be invested with power, by God, for the same purpose? I know that stations of worldly power are stations of great trial to the Christian, but the grace that sustained Joseph, and the "saints" who were even "in Cæsar's household," can sustain him there.—"My grace is sufficient for thee," involves all that is necessary to enable him, who confides in that grace, to fulfil the duties of any station, whether in the palace or the poor-house. It appears to me quite a misapprehension of the Christian calling, to suppose that it involves a relinquishment of civil duties of any kind,—just such a misapprehension as that which laid the foundation of monastries and nunneries in the dark ages of Popery.

Mr. Thorne says, "One thing is certain, that as a Christian, I have no power to contend for civil rights and religious liberty, &c." So different are my views, that I think there is nothing more certain than the contrary. Acts iv. 13,—"Now when they saw the boldness of Peter and John, . . . they marvelled, . . . And they called them, and commanded them not to speak, . . . But Peter and John answered, . . . we cannot but speak the things that we have seen and heard." Chap. v. 17,—"Then the High Priest rose, . . . and laid their hands on the Apostles, and put them in the common prison; but the Angel of the Lord by night opened the prison doors, and brought them forth, and said 'Go, stand and speak in the Temple, &c.'" Verse 27,—"And the High Priest asked them, saying, 'Did we not straightly command you that ye should not teach in this name?' Then Peter and the other Apostle said, 'We ought to obey God rather than man.'" Verse 41,—"And they departed from the presence of the council. . . . and daily, in the temple, and in every house, they ceased not to teach, &c." They contended for their religious liberty. Chap. xvi. 35,—"And when it was day, the magistrates sent the sergeants, saying, 'Let these men go . . . but Paul said unto them, 'they have beaten us openly, uncondemned, being Romans, and have cast us into prison, and now, do they thrust us out privily? Nay, verily, but let them come themselves and fetch us out.'" Paul contended for the rights of a Roman citizen. Chap. xxii. 24,—"The chief captain commanded him to be brought into the castle, and bade that he should be examined by scourging, and as they bound him with thongs, Paul said unto the centurion who stood by, 'Is it lawful for you to scourge a man that is a Roman, and uncondemned?'" He claimed his privileges. Chap. xxv. 9,—"But Festus, wishing to do the Jews a pleasure, answered Paul, 'Will thou go up to Jerusalem, and there be judged,' . . . Then Paul said, 'I stand at Cæsar's judgment seat, where I ought to be judged.'" He contended for the preservation of his freedom from the power of the Jews. Not to contend for civil and religious liberty, when there is any hope of obtaining it, would be to make ourselves parties to the perpetuation of injustice and oppression. Had the godly men of other days acted thus, we might still be groaning under the iron yoke of Popery, or the tyrannical laws of the Stuarts. God does not now deliver his people by miracles, but calls them to the use of means, and blesses them in their deeds. Mr. Thorne's statement, that he does not think that God used the Anti-slavery Society to effect the freedom of the slaves, appears one of the most extraordinary instances of the perverting influence of a false theory, that ever I met with. "But," says Mr. Thorne, "let me ask you one question in reference to—the Bible Society, Missionary Society, Tract Society, Anti-slavery Society, &c., do these combinations speak to the world, to sinners, and infidels, of God's power, or man's? do not people say, see what man can do by unity of purpose? do not Christians say, see what we have done, hence they emulate one another, and emulation is of the flesh."

I cannot but think that our friend is laboring under a morbid affection that gives a fallacious coloring to the conduct of his brethren whom he has left, and produces a temporary forgetfulness of the manner in which they speak of their successes. If there be any sentiment more familiar to my mind than another, in the Reports of the Societies to which he has referred, it is most decidedly this,—"What hath God wrought." . . . . .

I am, Dear Friend, Yours sincerely,

To J. Bowes. DAVID MACALLAN.

Feb. 24*th.*—EDINBURGH.—I have not been able to do much for the Lord on this journey. A soldier sat near me on the coach from Granton to Edinburgh, with whom I held a little conversation on the sinfulness of war. If Christians would speak to soldiers, and those who may be tempted to enlist, on the sinfulness of killing people, the evils of war would be better understood, and men would see that the command, "Love your enemies," does not mean kill them.

25*th.*—Took the railway train to Glasgow; it was only opened a few days ago. Called upon Elspet Cooper, she had just received a letter from her father, and another from her sister, informing her that I should call. She had also the tract, "New Testament Principles," before her. As a brother had been lost at sea lately, and three of her sisters had given themselves to the Lord and his church, her mind seemed open to divine truth. As the oldest of the sisters, I reminded her that she ought not to have been the last to give herself to God. I read a portion of Scripture and prayed with her. I called again in the evening, and did the same. She wept much and promised to be on the Lord's side. At 10 o'clock sailed by the *Princess Royal* for Liverpool, again I was very sick; it blew quite a gale at sea. We arrived about 9 o'clock; I expected some of the brethren to be waiting on the shore, but found none, they did not arrive till after I had gone. The following, in a letter to my dear wife, dated Liverpool, Feb. 28, 1842, may be worth preserving ;—

"I felt very well in body yesterday, indeed I thought my journey had done me good. I entirely forgot that I was in England last night, at Hill Street Room, crowded, and, as usual, when I forget, the English deep feeling carried me away, so that I was perhaps too much excited, the Lord only knows. It was a rich season."

March, 1*st.*—In the course of the discourse I made some more illusions to the danger of trusting in forms and outward observances, such as, baptismal regeneration, remission of sins in baptism, &c., instead of trusting in Christ. The leading men of the Mormonites were present, and asked privately for an opportunity to reply. This I could not grant. When the service was closed, they offered to grant me the Music Hall to lecture in, if I would grant Hill Street Room. The brethren informed them that the Room was not mine, that I was not pope there, and that they would not give it for a lecture on the errors of Mormonism. Still the Mormonites offered me the Music Hall; I told them I would consider of it and let them know.

We met on a subsequent evening to converse on their system, and I delivered a lecture to a crowded congregation in the Music Hall. They limited me to an hour, after which Parley P. Pratt, and G. J. Adams replied for about an hour, but refused me any rejoinder, in consequence of which several friends requested me to deliver two more lectures on the system.

During this visit to Liverpool the brethren were exceedingly kind and attentive, as the following extract from a letter to my wife will show.

"The friends continue kind. I have had meetings of the brethren at tea this week, at sister Dixon's, brother Curry's, brother Bedson's, and sister Hannah's. This evening I drink purity with Joseph Hasselwood, Monday with sister Philips, and Tuesday with brother Williams. They have generally a house full of the brethren and sisters to meet me. We spend the time in conversing about truth, singing, reading, and prayer. I have more invitations than I can attend. I lately took tea with Dr. Beaumont at Dr. Burrows'; did not feel at home, he was so full of levity. Took breakfast lately with Thomas Raffles, he continues as kind as ever. I have written him a letter on his expensive chapel.

15*th.*—I lectured in the Queen's Theatre, Christian Street, and gave the Mormonites an opportunity to reply, one of their elders did reply, though they published bills that they would not.

17*th.*—Lectured in the Music Hall, when they repeated a challenge which they had repeatedly given, to discuss the matter with me.

18*th.*—Met a number of Christians who worship in the Tabernacle, Great Charlotte Street, to converse about unity with the church. Having been Methodists, they still cling to some of the peculiarities of Methodism, however the meeting was well calculated to promote truth and good feeling, and the elders will sometimes preach in their place, and propose inviting their preachers to our place.

19*th.*—Met the Mormon Committee to arrange a discussion, and had great difficulty in coming to an understanding on the terms, at length all was amicably arranged.

HAPPY DEATH.

It was on the 18th that Evans died, who had once been a Socialist. On the 13th, after the labors of the Sabbath, I saw him. A young man of 29 years, worn to a skeleton by consumption, surrounded by an amiable wife and three little children, conscious of his situation, happy in God, and having no desire to recover. A sweet and heavenly smile pervaded his countenance. His voice was almost gone, and, when his cough permitted him to whisper his joy, he talked to us of the preciousness of Christ, and his desire to depart and be with him. He turned down his shirt sleeve, and grasped his poor skeleton arm, near the shoulder, with the other hand, and said, "The outward man grows weaker and weaker." I said, " but the inward man grows stronger and stronger day by day. As your affliction has continued some months, do you never feel tempted to be impatient?" "No," said he, "I would not change situations with the greatest prince." What a privilege, and how refreshing, to witness such composure and happiness in the prospect of death! Brother Burrows was with him when he died; he writes, "he took me by the hand as though it was for a final farewell. I asked if Jesus was precious; he said, 'yes; bless the Lord, bless the Lord!' He appeared to summon all his strength, and his whole frame was moved; he cried out, 'Glory, glory, glory, glory,' and thus departed."

MORMONISM.

22nd.—This evening the five nights' discussion commenced with Parley P. Pratt. Laurence Heyworth, Esq. was Moderator. It was carried on in a very orderly manner.

23rd.—This evening I called for miracles and new tongues, and as he did not give any, I called up J. Hassalwood, who uttered the same sort of jargon, having acquired it by hearing them, which they consider to be miraculous. P. P. Pratt endeavored to hinder this, but the Moderator decided in my favor. Pratt threatened to leave the meeting, and lost his temper for the first time. The Chairman had some difficulty in getting him to order. I had great pleasure in this night's work, as I got nearly half-an-hour devoted to the inculcation of non-resistance and universal peace. It is important not only to overthrow error, but to establish truth.

25th.—This evening we had the largest assembly by far that ever we have had. I took up New Testament Principles, as he said on the previous evening that he believed in them. This gave me an opportunity of establishing truth.

26th.—This evening the debate closed. The following things were proved, I believe to the satisfaction of the unprejudiced:—1st. That the Book of Mormon is not the word of God, but a fiction or forgery. 2nd. That the book of the Doctrines and Covenants, and their other pretended revelations, are unworthy of God. Take the following specimens:—"It is not right to persuade a woman to be baptized contrary to the will of her husband. To influence children to embrace any religious faith and be baptized, or leave their parents without their consent, is unlawful and unjust." "We do not believe it right to interfere with bond servants, neither preach the Gospel to, nor baptize them, contrary to the will and wish of their masters."—(Book of Doctrines and Covenants, pages 251, 254.) So that an infidel master, owning a hundred slaves, has power to keep them ignorant of the Gospel, and to hinder them from getting the remission of sin; for according to the Mormons, no one can obtain the Gospel or pardon, but by their priests and baptism. 3rd. That the twelve Apostles had no successors, that the Mormon apostles do not the works of apostles, and are therefore liars.—Rev. ii. 2. 4th. Several cases were mentioned in which they tried to cure the sick, but failed. We could not find one real cure. 5th That their speaking with tongues is a mockery, since they speak no language. One of our brethren gave the meeting a specimen of their tongues. 6th. That the whole scheme of Mormonism is intended to put money into the pockets of Joseph Smith, Jun., the founder of the sect, and his co-adjutors. Hence one revelation reads thus—"It is my will that my servant Joseph Smith should have a house built." It seems they boast near 200,000 followers—have an army—have fought in the state of Missouri, and been banished from it, and are now building a city of their own, in Illinois, called Nauvoo, and a splendid temple, and, after it is built, baptism for the dead is only to be acceptable to God when performed in the temple.

I received very satisfactory accounts of several who had either joined them, or intended to join them, who have resolved since the discussion commenced to have no fellowship with them, or their unfruitful works of darkness.

29th.—Preached at 7 o'clock, at Great Crosshall Street Room. Three or four souls were seeking mercy. Many of the saints accompanied me to the ship. It was about 11 o'clock when we left the Clarence Dock, and being almost worn out with lecturing, the discussion, preaching, writing, conversing, about 12 o'clock I went to bed and slept soundly till morning. I learned, when I awoke, that through the evening it had blown a terrible gale, but through mercy, I felt it not.

30th.—Visited friends. Called on E. Cooper, read the Scriptures and prayed with her. Her brother-in-law, who has lost his wife a few months ago, very kindly requested me to make his house my home in future visits. I trust, Elspit is accepted of the Lord. In the evening, attended a discussion on this question,—"Are the Brittish churches the bulwarks of intemperance?" held in a Hall in Ingram Street, where a Christian church assembles to carry out the principles of the New Testament. I endeavored to show that churches of Christ existed in various parts of the kingdom, who were bulwarks of temperance, and that it is the Lord's will that every believer should be added to the Church, whether he be a total abstainer or not. I referred to Acts ii. 37, "Repent," &c. Also to the Ethiopian Eunuch and the Philippian Jailor. After the first meeting was over, several friends wished me to remain, that they might hear my views on the Church of Christ generally. I continued to speak and answer questions till nearly half-past eleven o'clock.

31st.—EDINBURGH.—This evening heard the great revivalist, W. Burns, in Young Street Kirk. He seems a simple devout Christian. The Lord has made him a blessing to many souls in this kingdom. Afterwards I attended Richmond Place Chapel, and heard Henry Wight pray, and James Morrison, of Kilmarnock, preach. They are holding revival meetings all this week.

April, 1st.—Sailed at 6 a.m. for Aberdeen. Met with a vaunting, overbearing infidel, who was brow-beating the passengers with his views, and pouring out the bitterest invectives against the Bible. He talked so fast, and was so full of himself, that others could hardly be heard. He then engaged to disprove the Bible, and called upon me to defend it. I attempted to rebutt his objections, but his pride and impatience refused me a hearing. He then proposed a discussion with me. As I saw this was the only way to overturn his wicked insinuations, and silence him, I agreed. We elected a chairman, and were to speak ten minutes each, but he seldom occupied his ten minutes. This regular mode of speaking soon silenced him, and showed the passengers the weakness and hollowness of infidelity.

May 2nd.—This day James M'Kay died. When I came to Aberdeen, he wished to become a member, we declined him; he turned a bitter enemy, and wrote a letter against me and the principles which I hold, in the *Spectator*, without signing his name, through which one of the leading members left him, and then he gave over preaching some months after, not being able to get a congregation. Now he has gone the way of all flesh.

3rd.—To-day, accompanied by sister Roberts, I visited a sick man, John Imlay, so powerless that he cannot even stir a finger, and blind. He remarked "I never saw till I was blind." I asked him if he was afraid to die? "Death is a fearful thing, but Jesus Christ has taken away its sting, some," he said, "murmur, and this hurts me more than the stroke," (the stroke of palsy which he had.)

On the 8th of this month I received the following from Joseph Curry:—

"I am happy to be able to write unto you and inform you that Jesus is precious, for I know that my hope is centred in Him; this is my only plea, "for me the Saviour died." My present experience is, that my head is defended only when covered with the shadow of His wing. The world to me has no charms, "here I have no continuing city, but seek one to come." O that we may be made meet to be partakers of the inheritance of the saints in light. I think that much good has resulted from your lectures against "Mormonism," as the Mormonites are very quiet. That plant shall be plucked up. I had an interview with brothers Plunkett and Hargrove yesterday, they are Christ's disciples, they manifested much of a heavenly deportment. We shall break bread with them shortly. O for the time when the saints shall be one. Let us pray much for it, and cultivate a loving disposition towards all the dear people of God, then shall all men know us to be His.

"P.S.—My dear Jane's love to you all, she, with myself and all the dear brethren and sisters here, say, that we never felt so much attached to you as we did when you was last with us. O may our love yet more and more abound."

A NIGHT'S PRAYER.

We have spent one whole night's prayer in Aberdeen and another in Liverpool. We generally conducted them as follow:

I. THANKSGIVING.

1. Thank the Lord for all the blessing which has rested upon our labors, while we have sought to unite Christians and convert sinners.

2. Thank the Lord for the uninterrupted union and peace which He has granted His people ever since they were gathered together in His name.

3. Thank the Lord for the spirituality which He has given to some of the brethren, so that they have become crucified to the world, and the world unto them, and are led to bear one another's burdens.

4. Thank God, through Jesus Christ our Lord, for the light He has given us, to see many neglected truths, and to mourn over the present worldly state of the professing church.

II. CONFESSION.

1. Confess our individual sins solemnly before God, and ask Him to forgive them, for the sake of Jesus Christ our Lord.

2. Confess our remaining sinfulness as a church. (1.) Several of the members talk little of Jesus. (2.) Several seem to be inactive; either they are not seeing what they should do for the Lord, or they have no heart to work for Him. (3.) Few of us have been properly impressed with the state of the church and the world. We resemble too much

the formal professors of the age, and too little the first Christians. (4.) Our prayers have been too long, dry, and formal, and have not come sufficiently from the heart, and from the Spirit of God. (5.) The sermons have not had that unction in them, nor that success, which attended sermons in the first age. May the Lord lead us to see the defects of our sermons and prayers, and lead us to put them away. (6.) The brethren who can preach have not gone into the open-air, and neighboring parishes, to preach Christ as they might have done.

III. DEDICATION.

Seeing our sinfulness and the overwhelming greatness of Divine mercy, and the necessity of our souls being entirely devoted to God, that we surrender ourselves anew to God, that He may teach us whatever may render us holy and useful, and that he may use us entirely for His glory and the enlightening of the world; resolving by His grace not to shrink from publishing unpopular truths when they come from Him, nor hesitate to practice self-denying duties, whatever of worldly wealth, or ease, or fame, we may lose thereby. May He take us all—now—and employ us in His holy service for ever.

IV. PETITION.

1. That He may graciously forgive all our individual, family, and church sins, and cause the sunlight of his favor now to smile upon us, through Jesus Christ our Lord.

2. That He may lead us to keep separate from sinners, and save ourselves from the formality, party spirit, and doctrinal contentions of men of corrupt minds, and lead us to seek the fellowship of those humble and loving minds who hold fellowship with the Head.

3. That He may lead us to consider the loving life, death, and mediation of our precious Elder Brother,—that our hearts may be kindled into a permanent flame of brotherly love, so that we may never think, speak, or act unkindly towards each other, but continue to have a great increase of peace and love.

4. That He would lead us to consider the wants and necessities of our dear brethren, to aid them in business, or if destitute of employment, to feed and clothe them as we should wish them to do to us on a change of circumstances.

5. That the Lord would give us to watch over each other in love, so that, if any be absent or sick, we may visit them; or if in a backsliding state, we may admonish them, and thus provoke each other to good works.

6. That the Lord would pour out a spirit of prayer upon all the brethren and sisters of the church,—that we give Him no rest till He "make Jerusalem a praise in the earth."

7. That He would give teaching and ruling gifts to His church, that all his people may be taught and quickened, whenever we meet to edify each other,—that we may not speak in our own wisdom or might, but in the Lord, the Spirit of God himself speaking through us,—and that God would give unto each brother such a fear of Him, and such courage in His service, that he may not fail to teach at the times when the Spirit urges him to speak, and that he may utter all the counsel of God.

8. That He would give us a great and growing zeal for such a ministry as He has appointed; that we may testify fearlessly, but with much

tenderness, openly and fully, but with much wisdom and consideration, against the worldly, proud, sectarian, money-loving, and indolent ministry of this age.

9 That he would graciously hear our many prayers put up every day, and especially every Saturday, for the abolition of schism and the gathering together of his scattered saints into one church;—that he would send out laborers to make peace in his church, and gather together saints to be visibly one body.

10. That he would lead his people away from human traditions, to the laws and ordinances of his own gracious appointment, so that Baptism and the Lord's Supper may be observed by his people in His own way,—that thus we may derive all that blessing from them which they were designed to impart.

11. That he would lead his people to depend for the support of his cause upon him and his church, and not upon worldly kingdoms and worldly men.

12. That he would be graciously pleased to bless our families, and awaken and convert our unconverted children, wives, husbands, brothers and sisters, masters and servants, that we and our houses may serve the Lord.

13. That he would give us great concern for the salvation of our neighbors, whether rich or poor; that we may often pray for them, and invite them to hear the gospel, and teach them its truths privately ourselves, even every man his neighbor, and every man his brother.

14. That he would bless our Lord's Day and Day School, leading the teachers to travail in birth for souls, that Christ may be formed in them; that he would incline many young people to attend, and bless them when they come, that the rising generation may be a seed to serve him.

15. That he would bless the preaching of his word in the open-air, induce many to listen, repent, and believe the gospel.

16. That he would bless our Queen and her household, our lawmakers, judges, and magistrates, that all government may be based upon the equitable laws of the Holy Scriptures.

17. That he would abolish covetousness, intemperance, lasciviousness, formality, hypocrisy, lying, war, oaths, slavery, throughout the world, and bring all to know him.

18. That he would convert his ancient people the Jews, and make them preachers of the faith which they now endeavor to destroy; and that he would convert worldly people in great numbers. Amen.

We find that Jesus Christ spent a whole night in prayer (Luke vi. 12) and Jacob did this long before. The following Scriptures throw light on this practice:—Neh. i. 6, Psa. lxxxviii. 1, Luke ii. 37, xviii. 7, 8, Acts xii. 5—12, xxvi. 7, 1 Thess. iii. 10, 1 Tim. v. 5, 2 Tim. iv. 3, Rev. iv. 8, also vii. 14, 15.

Letter to John Ely, of Leeds.

22 North Broadford, ABERDEEN,
June 9, 1842.

DEAR FRIEND,—

In 1835, I and another minister called upon you, in Leeds, and requested the use of your chapel, for one service, to preach or lecture in, on the necessity of "Christian Union." You said that as we came as a deputation you could not receive us, but had I come as a minister you would have received me, and granted the use of your chapel. We, at that time, obtained the use of the Stone, Park, and South Parade Chapels. This week I saw you advertised with another minister, as "The Deputation from London." I attended the meeting at 12 o'clock, on the 7th curt., witnessed your appearance, and heard you speak as one of "The Deputation." This, of course, appeared to me very inconsistent with your avowed hostility to deputations, at Leeds, in 1835. During the last year I attended a missionary meeting, in your place of worship, at Leeds, and then I was strongly urged to mention to the meeting what follows:—I either read or heard, or both, that your chapel cost £12,000 building, and an organ, £500. I concluded that a chapel, equally as large and comfortable, with less of worldly ornament, might have been erected for £6,000, leaving £6,500 at liberty to be devoted either to the poor, or to the cause of missions. The interest of this sum, at 5 per cent., would be £325, so that the interest alone would support three Missionaries, to the end of the world, and who can tell how many immortal souls might have been led to Christ, in the course of ages, by three Missionaries? My dear friend, if souls be lost forever, through your sinful appropriation of wealth, at Leeds, it will be fearful for you and your wealthy friends to meet them. Now, it appears to me inconsistent with a deep concern for the salvation of souls, either at home or abroad, to urge the Lord's people, and sinners of the world to give their money to Missionary Societies, while professing Christians are wasting the Lord's money upon splendid chapels, organs, dress, and finely furnished houses, in which they reside themselves. Perhaps you and your Leeds friends may say, that more worldly people may come to hear at your chapel, when you please their taste, by giving them a fine chapel. And is this the way by which you hope to convert them from worldliness to spirituality, by, in the first instance, feeding their worldly taste? No; the church will never convert the world by going over to the world's fashions, and by bringing down the high standard of Christian morals, to the low level of a worldly taste. Jesus Christ has given us means in his powerful truth, His all-wise Spirit and the commanding influence of a holy life, by which we may bring the world over to us, without our going over to the world. Perhaps you may say you and your church had no control over the building, that wealthy men erected it for you, and that they would not have given the same amount of money for the cause of missions. But this plea is not admissible, because an "Independent church" is surely not so dependent on the world, that her members are not able to determine what kind of chapel they will have. Besides, my dear friend, if one Independent chapel costs £12,500, and another £13,000, in large towns, will not other places, all over the country, follow as closely as they can, the pernicious example set them by Leeds and Liverpool? Having felt more at liberty to testify against the pride and worldliness manifested in the objects first named, privately, in the first instance, than at any public meeting, I, am the friend of those who honour the meek and lowly, but heavenly Saviour, "the Man of sorrows who had not where to lay his head."

JOHN BOWES.

P.S.—With this I send a small tract, called "New Testament Principles of Church Order and Unity." J.B.

As I received no answer to the above, I now feel at liberty to publish it.

June 19th.—ABERDEEN.—It was twelve months yesterday, since a few brethren came together in the Lord's name here, to observe his ordinances and commands. In the course of the year 56 have been added from the world; 16 from the Kirk of Scotland; 7 from Zion Chapel; 7 from the Methodists; 5 from the Independents; 5 from the Baptists; 2 from the Episcopalians; 1 from the Secession; 1 from the Roman Catholics; 2 have come from a sister Church,—Total, 102. From 3 the church withdrew; 1 went out from us; and 1 removed to a distance.—5 altogether. 97 being now in fellowship.

29th.—Heard this morning, while bathing, that this is a Fast Day in the parish of New Hills. Went and heard a sermon at 11 o'clock, in the parish church at Woodside, John Longmuir preached. He endeavored to show that Christ really sweat blood in the Garden, but the text says, "as it were great drops of blood," &c. I preached out of doors at 1 o'clock, and again at half-past 4, and gave away many tracts against war. I trust some good was done. One old man said he had never heard his views so clearly expressed of what the Church of Christ ought to be. Evening, preached to a large congregation, and I hope, with good effect. At 8, in Castle Street.

30th.—This evening, and last week, the church commenced a subscription to cover the Hall rent and other incidental expenses, which was gone into heartily.

July 1st.—Went out this evening to Old Aberdeen. The Chartists had got the ground before me, though I had preached twice before, on the two previous Friday evenings. They made their proceedings a little shorter. I endeavored to show, that no government will answer for the community, if administered by selfish persons, and that therefore our great object should be to destroy selfishness, make men better, and then when they love their neighbors as themselves, they will make better citizens. On these principles Jesus Christ and his Apostles acted, they taught men truth, and showed them how to live, but left the governments of the world as they found them, yet they laid down principles which ultimately overturned the governments which opposed them. A Chartist named Henry replied, I replied again, and M'Pherson replied to me. I rejoice that they spoke against war and state-paid clergymen, and said many things useful, this furnished a fine opportunity of bringing New Testament principles before the people.

5th.—MONTROSE.—Came by steamer, was exceedingly sick one half of the way. Found that brother A. Stewart had preached here three times the last Lord's Day. Commenced preaching in the High Street, as the rain came on, adjourned, at the request of the congregation under the pillars. I intended to send round the drum, but the provost refused to allow the "Town's Officer to cry it." I called upon him; he did not state many objections against preaching in the High Street, but obviously preferred that I should take the Links.

6th.—This evening preached to a very large orderly congregation on the Links, after which I conversed with a few Baptists, who kindly offered me the Hall in which they worship, if I would labor a while in Montrose.

7th.—Called on an old friend by the way, but his views of me are changed, he thinks that I did not evince a Christian spirit towards the magistrates. 1st. I do not think, in preaching the Gospel we should obey magistrates, but God. 2nd. I do think we should refer to God's judgments when he is pleased to pour them out on persecutors. 3rd. We should wish them well. This I think I have always done. It is painful to differ from friends, but I must very often either displease even prejudiced friends or God. This gentleman was a magistrate, his political views might guide his opinion.

10th.—DUNDEE.—At 8 o'clock a.m., a very large congregation at the West Port. At 11 o'clock, a sweet time in breaking bread. The church requires to be a little more orderly. One o'clock, in the Green Market, in the very place where I was fined for preaching two years ago. Mr. Johnson, late Provost, came by while I was there, but he has lost all his power to injure, and the Superintendent is in his grave. God causes the wrath of man to praise him, and the remainder he restrains.

14th.—MONTROSE—On the Links. Brother A. Stewart has preached here the last two Lord's Days. After preaching, conversed with a few believers on the truths taught. A few of the admirers of A. Campbell contended for baptism as a test of membership, they admitted, however, that many unbaptized persons are believers, consequently, schism must be right, if it be right to keep them out of the church.

15th.—Took steamer for Aberdeen. A young man, a seaman, was intoxicated. He climbed the mast, the bowsprit, and hung over the vessel, keeping hold of a rope; he was quite unmanageable. The steamer's men bound him with ropes, but with great difficulty; he then used his feet and his teeth to kick or bite any one that came near him. In this state of madness, I went up to him boldly, kindly clapped him on the shoulder, and told him that it was better to be bound than be at the bottom of the sea. A momentary glance of kindness broke over his infuriated brow, and he thanked me for the interest I took in him, and admitted the truth of my observations. But I had scarcely left him before he was as outrageous as before. How terrible it was to see this tall, noble-looking man, all but destroyed by strong drink. He was put ashore at Stonehaven, though he ought to have come on to Aberdeen.

17th.—After the evening sermon, six souls, inquirers, came forward to be instructed in the plan of salvation.

18th.—Conversed with candidates for membership. One had been a deceiver and a hypocrite, though once a member of a dissenting body for twelve years. How awful to be deceived, or to be deceivers. If a servant be deceived with his master, if the master is more unreasonable than he expected, when his time of service expires, he may get another master. But if a man find out what sort of a master Satan is when it is too late to leave his service, he will be doomed to bear the result of his own sin for ever. If a man be deceived in a house or shop which he rents, if he find it unsuitable and injurious, he can give it up, leaving at the coming term, and engage another. But if he deceive himself by the forms of religion, and die without its power,

"With the fruits of what he sowed,
The sinner filled shall be,"

there is no change to follow. Should a person be deceived in marriage, death will cut the knot which was tied in ignorance and folly, and terminate the disappointment; but there is no termination to the sorrows arising from soul-deception. Eternity sets its indelible stamp on the suffering soul, and there is no hope of deliverance.

23rd. Preached to a large congregation in Castle Street. If we would convince men of their errors, we should show them the reasonableness of truth. I mean in future to act on this principle as to New Testament Christianity,—that is, to show men its reasonableness.

24th.—At half-past 6 this morning I baptized T. Hardacre, T. Brown, and sisters Addison and Young. The largest and most attentive congregation we have ever had. In the evening, after the sermon, five souls came forward to know the plan of salvation.

25th.—Conversed with candidates for membership, and was led to say, that when a soul is converted, every thing of a religious kind is seen in a new light. What a change!

31st.—After the evening sermon, three souls came forward as inquirers.

8mo. 4th—This evening, by request, I delivered a lecture on the "Present position of the Church of Scotland, and the further reforms required in her, and several other voluntary churches, in order to make them resemble New Testament Churches." The hall was tolerably filled. An opportunity was given for questions to be asked, and remarks to be made. A Churchman and a Mormonite made some remarks. The latter challenged me to discussion.

11th.—Hall crowded to hear the Mormonite and I. Mormonism was set before the people so that they understood it; but I was able to do very little for the Lord Jesus Christ, which I much regret.

12th.—This day James Grinstead should have prepared for returning home to Dundee to-morrow. He was hindered by several of the members wishing him to stop. Perhaps this is of the Lord.

13th.—Was requested to attend a meeting of the unemployed and speak. Wrote a letter giving my reasons for declining. Was much cheered by receiving a letter from my dear son in the gospel Samuel Askey, who lived to be the father of a numerous family, and a zealous preacher of the gospel. As it is short, I give it entire:—

LIVERPOOL, Aug. 12th, 1842,

DEAR FATHER IN CHRIST,—

Grace, mercy, and peace, from God our Father, and the Lord Jesus Christ, be with you and the church of God over which the Holy Ghost hath made you overseer, and the earnest prayer of your son is, that the church in Liverpool, with the church in Aberdeen and the overseer, may be preserved blameless until the coming of the Lord Jesus Christ. You, I have no doubt, think it very unkind of me not writing sooner, and I could feel ashamed myself, for it has the appearance of disrespect; but, dear brother, the memory of your name to me is sweet, and I have it in my heart to live and die with you. I often lift you up before the Lord, that the word of life through you may prove the savor of life to thousands. The Lord answer prayer. Amen. I understand you are soon coming to Liverpool. Praise the Lord! I long to see you, that you may impart some spiritual blessing to us. The Lord bring you, my brother, in the fulness of the blessings of the gospel. The brethren are all well, and I think the Lord is reviving spiritual life in the church. Praise His name! O may he revive my soul; for I feel a thirsting after the sanctifying power of the Spirit. My love to all the brethren, and Mrs. Bowes. I am, your affectionate son,

SAMUEL ASKEY.

14th.—This morning four were baptized. In the evening, James Grinstead delivered an exceedingly good address to the young.

19th.—ELLON. Preached in the open-air. Two young men conversed with me after. They intend to be baptized, and see most of the truths which God has taught me.

21st.—PETERHEAD. At 7 a.m. attended a prayer meeting in the Methodist Chapel, and was refreshed in soul. At half-past 9 preached in Keith's Mason Lodge; also at 2 and 8 o'clock. The last twice it was crowded to overflowing, and all the people could not get in. At 6, preached at the Cross to about 1000 people.

28th.—Have preached once each day in Peterhead since the 23rd. Held a prayer meeting this morning at 7, to pray for the union of Christians and the conversion of fishermen. In the evening at 6, I preached at the Cross to a deeply attentive and much affected congregation of probably 2000, as still as in a chapel. It was delightful to see about 1500 hats taken off at the time of prayer. While addressing the aged fishermen, I thought of old Jonas, the father of Peter and Andrew, and old Zebedee, the father of James and John. The Lord Jesus seems to have delighted in the society of fishermen. John, the beloved disciple that lay it his bosom, was a fisherman. Peter and John were indulged to be with him on the mount of transfiguration. Peter was made a successful fisher of men, as the events of the Pentecost day demonstrate. Oh! that some of my dear hearers, young fishermen, may become as loving and zealous preachers as John and Peter. Several persons have spoken to me under soul concern; a fisherman from Shetland kindly invited me to visit his native Isles. I was also invited to Cullen, Banffshire, and to Sellardyke, Fifeshire.

BODDAM, at 10 o'clock a.m., an attentive congregation. The fishermen here are very sober since they became Total Abstainers. To show with what interest and firmness they oppose any one who would seduce them, I may record a fact. One of them was paying an account in Peterhead, when he was repeatedly urged to drink, being assured that it would not hurt him; being teased and angry he took the glass and its contents, and dashed both on the ground, saying, "I have paid you many a pound, but as you have treated me in this way, I will never enter your shop again." At 7 this morning I bade farewell to the dear fishermen, and though the morning was misty and damp, there might be 400 present. Conversed with a few friends who are desirous to form a church on New Testament principles. A few baptists here are connected with an Independent Church. The minister and church were solicited to give the chapel, a few weeks ago, to a deputation from the Baptist Missionary Society. It was refused. The poor people have, however, declined communion since. They are not permitted to speak in church meetings and in many respects are bound down to abject slavery.

9mo. 6th.—Took steamer for LEITH; had to get into a small boat; three other small boats were driven back by the fury of the waves. This detained us some hours, and furnished me with an opportunity of speaking on shore with some friends about their souls, I hope profitably. Had an interesting conversation with a Christian from Frazerburgh; to whom I hope I was of some use.

7th.—Got to GLASGOW. Set off from Edinburgh by the early train. Was very thirsty, and bought a few pears from a man by the way. (This I fear prepared the way for a week of English Cholera.) Evening: preached on the Green, and afterwards attended a tea meeting at the Old Post Office Chapel; heard some very reviving speeches on unity and delivered one; I hope not in vain.

8th.—Preached on the Green at half-past 6, and delivered a lecture on the further changes which are necessary in the church in order to make modern churches like the primitive. Breakfasted with Robert Kettle. Spent most of this day with John Murray, Bowling Bay. His total abstinence and anti-war views have subjected him to considerable opposition; but it is blessed when we suffer for teaching what Christ taught, and for living as he lived. Evening, preached at half-past 6 on the Green; at 8, lectured in the chapel, Nelson Street, on the changes which are necessary in modern churches, in order to make them like the primitive churches.

9th.—Sailed by the *Princess Royal,* a noble vessel, for Liverpool. I was very ill with English Cholera, but slept tolerably through the night. Reached Liverpool from Greenock in 16½ hours.

11th.—LIVERPOOL. Attended Hill Street Room; so weak that I could scarcely be heard, but was refreshed in soul.

I never was more tempted to put any one into court for a debt than Joseph Peart. He knew I had given up all salary, and of course he was among us on the same principle; but when I sent in my bill of nearly £3, for publications, &c., he sent the following made-up bill to frighten me out of what he owed, and I suffered the loss of books and money. He did not prosper, but the reverse, and if any of my readers know his history, in life or death, since the above, I shall be obliged if they will forward it to me. He had been many years a Primitive Methodist minister, Sailors' Missionary, &c.

MR. JOHN BOWES,—TO JOSEPH PEART,—

To Twenty-one Weeks' Salary, at £2 per week, from March 17th to August 10th, 1840,		£42 0 0
By Cash, as per account adjusted at the Elders' Meeting, held in Hill-street Academy Room, August 10th, 1840,	£21 5 6	
By 400 Tracts, called "The Social Beasts," discount on sale deducted, and less by 81 tracts, to be returned when Mr. Bowes pays the balance, according to agreement,	£1 19 10½	
	£23 5 4½	£23 5 4½
Balance owing by Mr. Bowes,		£18 14 7½

SIR,—

Permit me to say, I can scarcely think it honorable on your part to have delayed the payment of the above balance of my salary, under the trying circumstances in which I have been placed, with an afflicted wife and expensive family. It is but a poor excuse for a Christian minister, to say you had not received my bill, after adjusting your account with me, and thus knowing what you owed me. I hereby demand you to pay me the above balance immediately.

Stanley Crescent, Liverpool,   JOSEPH PEART.
   Sept. 16th, 1842.

18th.—Forenoon and evening at Great Crosshall Street Room, and at 3 o'clock, preached out at the Prince's Dock. In the evening twelve souls came forward after sermon as inquirers, to be taught the way of life. Some, by trusting in Jesus, were blessed with peace and joy.

25th.—At Hill Street, at half-past 10; walked to Woolton, and preached in the open-air at 3 o'clock; at Gatacre at half-past 5, and in the preaching room afterwards. A dear brother and sister who reside here now, came lately from Liverpool, by Christian consistency and abiding firmly by their anti-sectarian principles, have been useful, and are likely to be more so. I hear very little of Mormonism lately.

10th. *2nd.*—BRADFORD. Preached out of doors at the Bowling-green at 9, and heard William Trotter deliver a sweet discourse on Matt. xviii. 7,—"It must needs be that offences come." "Offences," he proved, "arose, 1st, sometimes from the hypocrisy of those who profess religion. 2nd. From the backslidings of others. 3rd. From the faults of sincere souls, who are imperfectly instructed. 4th. In some cases from the want of Christian forbearance and love. However much Christians differ in opinion they should love each other." I said a few things after him, and regretted that the believers did not observe the Lord's Supper weekly. At 2 o'clock, Thomas Smith preached in the chapel, and afterwards accompanied me to the Bowling-green, where we had a considerable congregation. At 6 o'clock at PUDSEY, in Zion Chapel; a large congregation; one soul came forward to seek mercy.

VISIT TO A MORAVIAN SETTLEMENT.

3rd.—T. Smith and I visited the Moravian Settlement at Fulneck, in this neighborhood. It stands in a beautiful situation. We were conducted through several of the rooms, the chapel, (which contains an organ), and the grounds. The settlement does not appear to flourish as it once did. The property sustains only a small number in community; many of the society are not in it, and the poor members appear to be no better supported than the poor of other denominations. Connected with the establishment there is a bakehouse, grocery, drapery, and an inn, or public-house, not occupied by a member of the Society, but rented to a person who conducts it on the same plan as other inns. The people of Pudsey, who are disposed, come and get drunk at it; nearly all sorts of intoxicating liquors are sold in it. A drunken man was making an uproarious noise in it while we were passing. It seems humiliating to think that the proceeds of this inn, where drunkards are made, should go, in the shape of rent, to support the saints. Fulneck does not convince me that such establishments are scriptural. The few single brethren and single sisters, each sex residing in separate apartments, and the few married people there, may be more retired from the world than others not in the community, but this seems rather fleeing from the foe than giving him battle. In the evening, lectured to a large congregation at Pudsey, on the changes which are required in the church. We had one open-air service at mid-day.

4th.—This morning walked with T. Smith, and two other brethren, to visit the grave of William Bramwell, at the Wesleyan Chapel, Westgate Hill. It was affecting to stand over his earthly remains, and remember how many hundreds of souls he had led to the Saviour. We kneeled down on his tombstone, and prayed that, in so far as Bramwell's zeal for the conversion of sinners was scriptural, it might be kindled up in our souls. The following is

BRAMWELL'S EPITAPH.

"Here lies what was earthly of the venerable William Bramwell, a chosen, approved, and valiant minister of Christ, who died August 13, 1818. Aged 58. Stranger! when thou approachest this shrine, consecrated to his memory by an afflicted family, may his ashes still proclaim what he lived to publish, 'Prepare to meet thy God.'"

Perhaps both good and evil have resulted from attempts to imitate this celebrated revivalist and successful evangelist, in his piety and his work; in the language of a powerful writer, "Much which is good in another is good in him alone, belongs to his peculiar constitution, has been the growth of his peculiar experience, is harmonious and beautiful only in combination with his other attributes, would be unnatural, awkward, and forced in a servile imitator. The very strength of emotion which in one man is virtue, in another would be defect: for virtue depends upon the balance which exists between the various principles of the soul; and that intenseness of feeling which, when joined with force of thought and purpose, is healthful and invigorating, would prove a disease, or might approach insanity, in a weak and sensitive mind. No man should part with his individuality, and aim to become another. No process is so fatal as that which would cast all men into one mould (and in reference to revivals, perhaps none more tyrannical). Every human being is intended to have a character of his own, to be what no other is, and to do what no other can do. Our common nature is to be unfolded in unbounded diversities. It is rich enough for infinite manifestations; it is to wear innumerable forms of beauty and glory. Every human being has a work to carry on within, duties to perform abroad, influences to exert, which are peculiarly his, and which no conscience but his own can teach. Let him not, then, enslave his conscience to others, but act with the freedom, strength, and dignity of one whose highest law is in his own breast." For want of understanding these truths some Christians overrate ministers of their own peculiar taste, and depreciate others. But however much Paul may differ from Apollos, or Kephas from both, if they love and serve the Lord Jesus, "turn sinners from darkness to light," and "edify the church," instead of regretting, we should rejoice in their refreshing diversity of gifts.

Evening, lectured at BRADFORD on the present state of the church, desiring that questions might be proposed by hearers. Many from various speakers were asked and answered. This is a very instructive mode of arriving at truth. About 90 believers meet here. A note was sent up to intimate that they agreed, at a meeting held here last night, to commence, the next Lord's Day, breaking bread every first day of the week, and that there would be free ministration, every brother, gifted of God, would be at liberty to teach. My soul was truly thankful, and said aloud, "Blessed be God."

I have received information that I am advertised to Lecture against Socialism in Manchester, the next three evenings. The Lectures are under the auspices of the Manchester City Mission.

264 Great Colmore Street,
BIRMINGHAM, October 4, 1842.

DEAR BROTHER BOWES,—

I was happy to hear of your recovery and your ability to again raise your voice for Jesus, as also your success in the blessed work of leading souls to him. It is indeed blessed to know that our labor is not in vain in the Lord, for even if the testimony should be rejected, yet the judgment is with the Lord, who knows all the exercises of heart through which the soul has passed in its going out of desire after him, and he marks those who "sigh and cry over the abomination," without reference to the success of their labor or the effect of their sorrow upon others. I have been interested in the matter between you and the other dear brethren in Liverpool, and can say little more than commend you to Him in whose hands you are, and with whom you have to do. I would just put before you a few things not entirely irrelevant to the subject, though not bearing on it alone.

1st. The purity of the believers is of very great importance in the mind of God, and a large portion of his blessed word is allotted to the subject. It is urged by every motive, command, and example, and to this as individuals as well as churches it is our blessed privilege and duty to attend. The unity of believers is strongly conducive to this, as it encourages the soul to know in every conflict that the same afflictions are suffered by our brethren which are in the world. But though highly conducive, yet it is not essential for the holiness of the walk, for when we cannot take the ground of sympathy from brethren, we can take the higher ground of faithfulness in God. 1 Cor. x. 13. And I confess to you that I had rather see a man in Sectarian bondage, who did not see a bit beyond his own party, living in faithful, holy devotedness to God, than another who has "come out," as it is called, while his soul is withering into coldness, or his conscience is not clear on the step he has taken.

2nd. The Devil's object with a Christian is to get his mind entangled with some truth, some opinion or doctrine, and by it to displace the Lord Jesus from having the ascendency. I believe your acquaintance with your own heart will enable you readily to follow me here, as well as by your every-day experience and observation. How often do you find instead of your soul waiting quietly on God, your mind is running away after some great truth it may be, to the displacing of Jesus, both in your preaching and in your prayers and meditations. How often, also, do you find men—Christians—intrenched behind some darling doctrine, some hobby, if I may so speak, that to introduce the person of the Lord, in suffering, work, or glory, is like something strange and new. How do we see men entangled with baptism, with election, God's love to all men, with Church government, discipline, eldership, deacon's office, the Lord's Supper, &c., without end, many or all of which may be precious truths taught in the word, but displaced by the undue proportion of mind and attention they occupy. Hence we find men gathering around these things rather than around Jesus, in whom all the truths of God's word centre. Here we see that the most precious thing God has given becomes a canker worm in the soul, eating out the sweet intercourse Christians should have with one another, when meeting simply in the name of Jesus. "Sin by that which is good works death in me." I have heard men speaking on Dispensation, No War, Church Unity, and the like, till I felt cold and dry, because the object was not subjection to Jesus, but the urging of a favorite doctrine that had long had power over the mind. To me, Church Unity is as bad as church division, I hate them both, when the soul is not bathed in the love of Jesus.

3rd. It is not the way of God to take us beyond our light. This is what comes so blessedly out in the Scripture. One is a Chamberlain, another a Centurion. Christians are found in Cæsar's household. The Priests are obedient to the faith. The believing Jews are zealous for the law. Circumcision is nothing: herbs, days, meats nothing. All this is most precious—most practical; it shews me the full persuasion of my own mind—not another's measure of my duty—is the rule of my conduct. I may have the way pointed out to me most clearly—the reasons enforced—the results calculated, yet my light, which is my present measure of duty, does not lead me so far, nor so fast, well I must be faithful to conscience till it is enlightened by God. I may be severely judged in this, and ungraciously condemned, still Rom. xiv. and 1 Cor. viii. shew me my place and duty, and refer me to the Lord for judgment and that is enough. Thus one man may be a very faithful, sincere, consciencious churchman, another a dissenter. One comes out from Sectarianism, another sees no difference between those who come out and those who stop in. What am I to do in all this? Mourn over it, indeed, that we differ so much, and "speak" not "the same things," 1 Cor. i. 10, but rejoice in the love which glows in the heart of the Father and Son to all.

4th. I may expect that a great many things about me are wrong, though I see them not, that may hinder others from having communion with me. It is likely the great reason for the torn and divided state into which the church is now so fearfully mangled, are, in many instances, from the unexplainable, constitutional differences of men's habits and natures that may, or may not be pointed out by others, yet so inveterate in themselves, that till the man is made over again on the resurrection morn, or the circumstances altered, over which we have no control, we cannot make ourselves happy in his company. You know yourself how painful the company and conversation of some Christians are, their minds are so constituted that you can enjoy very little intercourse with them. This does not at all break off your love to them, you seem as if you could love them more from their seeming difference from you, yet outward communion with them you have none, or, at the most, but little. I know it ought not to be so; he ought to give up; I ought to give up. Our first place is the dust in the presence of God, dropping our differences behind us, and humbled to nothingness, confess our guilt, and seek to speak the "same things." I speak not now of duty, but of facts which have occured with myself.

5th. Now in reference to your case, dear brother, the first thing is, are we pure in our communion? Are we simple in our worship? Are our hearts open before the Lord? I put not these questions by way of suspicion, but to get to a point. Having come to this then, supposing that the brethren with whom you propose a union should find all that are with you Christians, yet feel in their souls that they would not, from certain other reasons either in you or in themselves, be happy in associating in your form of worship, what should you do? Assuredly not vaunt over their hypocrisy, but rather, I should say, mourn that any thing that seems to your sincere mind according to God, should appear not so to them. This, I believe, is the true position every child of God with you both should take. It is not by making proposals and settling every thing nicely, according to man's eye, that we are to set all to rights. Love has been lost, it has gone down between the joints of contending parties, and whoever will restore it must go down into the dust of self-abasement and bring it up. I should not rejoice to see your union till you were both brought down to see and feel the blame rested on your own shoulders. What is the consistency of a visible union unless the heart is broken to pieces in the power of real grace. Now I was not convinced of the downright out-breaking of love in the heart by either your letter, or that from the church, to Mr. H. I saw evidently a desire for a "visible union," that met me at once when I read the letters; of the spirit of love, breathed from the heart burdened with the thought of separation from those who are dear to Jesus, I was not so conscious. I don't say it was not there, nor it is not with you, yea, I have confidence in you, dear brother, that your heart lies in that love, but then, it is quite possible for this outward union to get hold of our minds, while the inward caring for the saints, whether they are outwardly one with us or not, is not at a high point with us, the very spirit of this is to "feed the flock of God." I was glad to see your heart so free in its desire for oneness, but O let us have it in spirit first, and that is not by calling each other hypocrites, but by carrying the whole burden before our gracious God, and mourning over it as our own sin. If I have learned any thing lately, it has been the gracious, loving, tender heart of our God, and when I go to him with my trouble, I generally find enough of reason to see why others will not join with me, and made rather to wonder how any one associates with me at all, for it only wants the hand of the Lord's preserving grace lifted off my poor wretched heart, to unfold to the world what an evil thing it is. Nevertheless I am not deterred from teaching and praying for the oneness of God's people, for I know that it is only by teaching them and praying Him that any can be brought to see its blessedness, and although I am but a babe, and know little, in the face of all my sins I can call him Father by the spirit through the blood, and desire to live in love with all who love our Lord Jesus in Spirit and truth.

My wife will be passing through Liverpool soon and may bring the book, should I let you know which day she comes, could you meet her at the shore? Call on Henry Herdsman, at Johnson's, Dyer, Ranelagh Street.

Have you heard of the meeting of fourteen of the church clergy at Swansea? The account of it is most blessed.

I believe, dear brother, if we are to be useful to the church of God, it will not be in any honor to the satisfying of the flesh. It is a thankless work, "The more abundantly I love you the less I be loved," will be our experience, if we are really seeking, in God's way, to benefit the saints, let us be willing to be unpopular in the world, aye, and in the church too, misunderstood and misrepresented, but if it is all for his body's sake, the Lord will honor that. "Ye did it unto me" will be the blessed word of comfort.

Yours in sincere love,

To J. Bowes.
P. ANDERSON.

5th.—MANCHESTER. Lectured on Socialism and Christianity, in the Manor Court Room, High Street, which was full to overflowing—hundreds could not get in. An opportunity was given for the Socialists to reply three times, fifteen minutes each, after I had lectured an hour. John Watts, Social Missionary, who seems to be popular among them as a lecturer, and draws large congregations to their Hall of Science, spoke three times, and challenged me to a public discussion with equal time. **My cloak, a very good blue cloth one, was stolen from my chair** back. [This is the only instance of the kind I have known in a long life.]

6th.—A Socialist, formerly a missionary, named Clarke, opposed. This evening again, my silver pencil-case and pen-holder was missing.

7th.—Finished the lectures. Two or three Socialists spoke in reply.

8th.—About forty Town Missionaries sent me an unanimous vote of thanks for the three lectures I have delivered in the Manor Court-room, and requested me either to re-deliver them in a still larger place, or accept of the challenge given by John Watts. I did the latter.

9th.—This morning broke bread with a few brethren who meet in the Lord's name in George's Street. It was to me a comfortable season.

11th.—LIVERPOOL. Met the brethren who meet in Hill Street and Great Crosshall Street rooms, at a Tea Meeting. Several things were said of great importance, and remarks were made on Benefit Societies. If a church is poor, and the members cannot both take their money to the club and spare something for the poor saints, it is plainly sinful to allow them to starve, and carry the money past them into worldly clubs. We are to "do good unto all men, but more especially unto them who are of the household of faith." Again; it brings down the honor of God's church, and publicly calls in question her love, when one of her own members goes over to a worldly association with his money, thereby particularly declaring that he has more confidence in a worldly association than in God's church. Again; this system surrounds the dying Christian with the agents of a worldly society, who minister to his necessities, instead of the church members pouring into his soul their offerings and instructions.

12th, 13th, 14th.—Public Discussion on Socialism and Christianity. A chairman was elected on each side, and an umpire to settle disputes. Mr. Poulter, a baptist minister, was mine, and Mr. Smith, a Socialist, Mr. Watts'; Joseph Hassalwood, was umpire. Upwards of 2000 people attended, and were in general orderly, except when my arguments were *deeply felt* by the Socialists, then several of them howled much more like *beasts* than men. On the first night of the discussion, a leading Socialist, a bookseller, named Johnson, declared my arguments unanswered and unanswerable, and the ground taken in my late lectures "impregnable."

16th.—Lectured in Bootle Street Room on "What Christianity is?" distinguished between Christianity taught in the New Testament and its corruptions. This is of great moment. If any one knew nothing of Christianity but what he could learn from corrupt communions, it would not be wonderful should he reject it. Indeed, it is rather a virtue than a sin to reject corruptions. Let Christians be careful to imitate Christ, and conform to his pure and righteous instructions, that infidels may be reclaimed by their good works. The congregation was large, and the time refreshing. At 3 o'clock, Brother Hassalwood and I preached out near the Birmingham Station, London Road. Met with some interruption from two drunken men; one said he was a Socialist. Several expected that the police would hinder us, owing to the late riots.

17th.—Came by the canal boat to LIVERPOOL. James Walker, preacher of the gospel, and his wife, were going to America. He says he believes it is the Lord's will that he should go, because it has been impressed on his mind. I asked him for a reason for that impression; he could give none.

19*th*.—The Christian Committee for conducting the discussion, having invited me to a Tea Meeting at MANCHESTER to-day, I was surprised beyond measure to find the following published through Manchester in a very large placard:—"CHRISTIANITY TRIUMPHANT! The public are respectfully informed that, as a token of respect to Mr. John Bowes (minister of the gospel) for the three instructive lectures which he delivered in the Old Manor Court Room, on the wicked, filthy, and demoralising doctrines propounded by Robert Owen, as laid down in the Book of the New Moral World, and in his lectures on the Marriage System, as recommended and approved by his followers, known by the name of Socialists, and also for the very able manner in which he, Mr. Bowes, met and refuted the arguments of his opponent, Mr. John Watts, social missionary, the unblushing advocate of the above-named abominations, in a discussion which took place in the Carpenter's Hall, on the evenings of the 12th, 13th, and 14th inst.,—a Tea Party will be held in the Old Manor Court Room, on the evening of Wednesday, Oct. 19, &c." When I entered the room, there met me in large letters, reading nearly across the room—"AFTER THE MANNER OF MEN, I HAVE FOUGHT WITH BEASTS." Several very interesting speeches were delivered, and I was formally thanked for my labors. In replying, I attributed any good which had been done to that merciful God whose aid I had sought before the commencement of the discussion. One speaker thought I was able to preserve good temper because I was naturally mild; I attributed it to the grace of God, which keeps my temper in these various trying discussions. Besides Johnson, other two or three have abandoned Socialism through these meetings. To God be all the glory.

In Liverpool, the Socialists have now no meetings, though they were once some hundreds strong, and built the Hall of Science. In most places, where they have been vigorously opposed by rational argumentation, and in a calm, candid spirit, they are either dying or dead. Infidelity, in this gross form, will never succeed; it attacks and shocks the very nature of man. Man needs a religion; and although, while he yields to his appetites, he may forget or spurn its restraints, his conscience and reason will remonstrate against indulgences which can only be obtained at the expense of tranquility of mind, the happiness of many of his race, and the hope of an eternity of joy.

Socialism cannot live; I entertain no fear of its success. It is too irrational for any but those who have determined to sacrifice reason and conscience to lust, and even they, in spite of themselves, must hear reason and conscience sometimes. The human mind has too great a sympathy with the Father-mind, the Eternal God, ever to be happy in any course upon which he frowns. It can only be happy as it receives supplies of light, and life, and love from Him. Communion with God is essential alike to our own happiness and usefulness. When did any one accomplish anything great or good for society, who made his boast, as Robert Owen does, of discarding his Creator? He who made us at first, made us for Himself: we are to know His character, to obey His laws, to follow His steps, and live to do good to our kind—to seek daily to remove ignorance, and crime, and misery from our race, and give over all our powers of mind and body, all our time, talents, property, and influence, without hesitation and without reserve, to subserve the highest interests of society. Then we cannot live in vain. We shall make the world feel that we live, and bring honor to our Creator and Redeemer. This, and nothing short of this, accords with man's rational and moral nature. He cannot part with his conscience and bar out his reason while he descends into the dungeon of a Socialist's paradise. He cannot there enjoy the delights of a rational being. He may descend, but his reason goes with him to remonstrate, and his conscience to infuse bitterness into his cup of pleasure, and lash him with the cutting stripes of its accusations.

20*th.*—LIVERPOOL. Attended a meeting of a few brethren who meet every Lord's Day to break bread, in Hope Street, and a number of those with whom I have been in the habit of meeting. The brethren meeting in Hill Street and Great Crosshall Street, had met and corresponded with these brethren some time before, and as both meetings profess that there ought only to be one church in a city or town, and yet they had not recognised each other as brethren, it seemed desirable that they should either unite, or cease to pray for union, and pretend concern for its accomplishment. It was proposed that a list of the names and residences should be furnished to each, and that the brethren should have an opportunity of being mutually satisfied with each other's piety. The brethren in Hope Street thought that as they were the first to meet in the Lord's name alone in Liverpool, we should go to them. As we did not know of their existence till after we had been sometime meeting as believers, and as this difficulty might be easily overcome, one brother remarked, that he thought those would show the most of a Christian spirit who should be the first to unite. Another meeting was appointed for next week.

21*st.*—Attended Hill Street, and addressed the brethren. Sailed at half-past 10 o'clock by the *Royal George* for Glasgow. I was disappointed of a bed, and had a very uncomfortable night. It was very stormy at sea; some of the waves struck the vessel with such force, and washed over her with such fury, as to create great alarm to several on board. I felt calm in the storm; Christ was my confidence, portion, and hope; I felt that the Lord's will would be the best, whether in a few moments I should meet a watery grave, or reach Glasgow in safety,

23*rd.*—Arrived in GLASGOW at 3 o'clock. What an evil and dangerous thing is sin. We had observed a young man who talked incoherently of some person having robbed a female of £2, and that he would give himself up to the police when he arrived in Greenock. We had entered the Clyde, when the cry was given, "A man overboard!" He was heard to cry two or three times in the waves. The vessel put round and round; the waves were high; but we could not see him, and we heard him no more. When we arrived at Greenock his aunt was waiting for him. His luggage was there, but he was gone! He was returning from Liverpool, where, after returning from a long voyage, he had spent about a fortnight in drunkenness. Thus he impaired his reason, and lost his life. Let the living avoid alcoholic drinks and drunkenness. At 11 o'clock I took my seat in the chapel, Nelson-street. I had sent the church word, through my friend John Murray, that I should be willing to preach once or twice, if they were agreeable and not better supplied. About this small matter they had met several times, without coming to any conclusion. As it was understood that some of those with whom I hold church fellowship are not total abstainers, Elder Anderson spoke to me on entering, and stated that I should not perhaps wish to say anything in the morning, as it was arranged for a number of the brethren to exhort; but the church was called together after the meeting, when Elder Anderson and Ronald Wright informed me, that some doubted whether I was consistent in maintaining that spirit-dealers are wholesale murderers, and refusing church communion with them, and yet holding fellowship with their customers. The week following, I had an opportunity of explaining this: That my observation applied to spirit-sellers as they now exist, who sell to all and sundry, making many drunkards, and thus slaying both bodies and souls. That I hold fellowship with Christians, not because they are total abstainers, but because they are Christ's,—that some sincere Christians take strong drinks, thinking that they do them good, and that if selling strong drinks were limited to the druggist, for useful purposes, or even if any spirit-seller could be found now carrying on his business with the view of doing good to society,—only selling strong drinks for medicines, and other purposes which he might deem useful, taking care never to make any one intoxicated, I should have no objection to acknowledge him as a Christian, and hold fellowship with him. A brother waited on me between the services, but I was not invited to preach. I preached out at 5 o'clock on the Green; it was intimated in the chapel. At 6, a young man read a sermon. Had the same sentiments been delivered without notes, I should have expected more good to result. More than a dozen of the brethren and sisters met me at my lodgings, and we spent an hour or two in Christian conversation and prayer. They were generally displeased at the conduct of the church, and felt that what was done to me was done to them. This was very brotherly.

24th.—Attended two Anti-Slavery meetings. That in the evening was addressed by George Thompson. There was very little spoken to honor the Lord in either of them.

25th.—Spent a great part of this day in retirement; found it very sweet and good. In the evening heard George Thompson deliver a spirit-stirring lecture. Afterwards took supper with Joseph Barker, in Wood's Temperance Hotel.

26th.—Lectured this evening at DUMBARTON, and walked afterwards to Bowling Bay.

27th.—Met a few of the brethren of Nelson Street Chapel at half-past 4, to converse about union. Joseph Barker was present. There is too strong a leaning on the part of some to the Total Abstinence question.

28th.—This day I spent in visiting various brethren and sisters in EDINBURGH and LEITH. These places seem to be ripening for a meeting of brethren.

29th.—Left Edinburgh at half-past 5; arrived, after a fine passage, at Aberdeen. One passenger, resembling a broken-down gentleman, drank largely, and amused the company by songs and jests. He had wasted three or four thousand pounds in drink in eight years. I recommended total abstinence and Christ. He received what I said with great attention. I gave him my address, and desired him to call on me. While I addressed him, I observed the silent tear stealing from his cheek.

THE "CHRISTIAN MAGAZINE."

It was no small delight to my own mind, when I found that the pent-up fires within, struggling for liberty, could go forth every month; but the child—The Christian Magazine—was nearly strangled at its birth, as the following correspondence will show. The printer was a brother, who endorsed my sentiments; but when he found that they would be unpopular with his Presbyterian employers, he would hazard nothing by even appending his name to the monthly. He printed the first without his name, and then I got another printer.

22 NORTH BROADFORD, ABERDEEN,
Nov. 15th, 1842.

MY DEAR BROTHER,—

When the Magazine was contemplated, I spoke to you as to the conditions. You informed me; I was satisfied, and sent you the manuscript. The first proof was sent with your name attached, as the printer. Last night, about nine o'clock, I received two copies with the printer's name *left out*. A few minutes after, you called. I asked, "Is it customary to print magazines without the printer's name?" "No, it is not." I said, "I understand it is contrary to law?" This you admitted, but said that many things were often printed without the printer's name. On considering the matter, and finding from our conversation that your name had been withdrawn intentionally, and that it was no mere oversight, I have to say —1st. I have never printed anything, according to the best of my recollection, without the printer's name. This is even the first proposal of the kind. 2ndly. I never intended the Magazine to be issued but in the ordinary way of all other publications and my own—with the printer's name. 3rdly. I see no reason why it should now be issued without it. If you will show, first, why you withdrew it, and, secondly, why I ought to issue the Magazine without it, my mind may change. My present conviction is, that I shall not break the law and deviate from my usual course by issuing anything without the printer's name, and consequently not the Magazine. I am, as ever, yours very affectionately,

To G. Cornwall.   JOHN BOWES.

P.S.—An early answer will oblige.

VICTORIA COURT, Tuesday, 10 a.m.

MY DEAR BROTHER,—

. . . . In replying to your note,—the simple reason of my having taken away my name from the Magazine was, because I did not wish to be identified with the sentiments which it contained, as well as, that I do not like the spirit in which they are conceived. I meant no offence to you however, and should be sorry to think that you had taken any. . . . . Yours ever,

To J. Bowes.   GEO. CORNWALL.

12*mo. 2nd.*—At twenty minutes before 11 p.m., Lawrence Heyworth Bowes was born, supposed by the doctors to be an eight-months child. He lived till half-past 3 o'clock on the 5th, and then expired. He was buried on the 6th at the Spittal. He was indeed a lovely babe. The Lord took him as a flower of His own.

YEW TREE, Dec. 31, 1842.

MY DEAR SIR,—

My time has been so much engaged, that I have not been able to acknowledge receipt, and pass my remarks, upon your pamphlets till now. To the first and last I have pleasure in expressing my approbation; but, my dear friend, I think you made a grave mistake in your interpretation of the Scriptures in regard to this world's possessions, which, so long as human bodies are to be sustained by the human means God himself has enjoined by the command "that man must earn his bread by the sweat of his brow," must not be despised, but received as God's blessing upon his creatures, when they obey his commands. For man lives not by bread alone; and however hungry, he must not expect it to be brought to him miraculously; for such word of promise has not proceeded out of the mouth of God, but to use the means appointed to obtain it, has. Great and many are the encouragements to industry and frugality contained in the word of God. Therefore our Saviour's animadversions on the possession of wealth, are intended to show, in strong contrast, the folly of immortal souls setting their affections upon it, and are utterly condemnatory of it, if not held entirely subordinate to his revealed will, and, of course, promotive to the greatest extent of bringing comforts to the industrious poor. To feed the hungry and clothe the naked is obligatory on every Christian, and he who knows the most effectual means of accomplishing this object, through the industrial channels of trade and commerce, and does it not, though he gave all his goods to feed the poor, in his own locality, might be obeying the word, but would not be obeying the spirit of our Saviour's precepts —and "the word killeth, but the Spirit maketh alive," which saying would be literally fulfilled, even in a temporal sense, if, in the case stated, the two modes were carried out practically. The first mode would create a flourishing community, enjoying God's bountiful goodness,—the latter would leave, with the exhausted wealth of the individual donor, a poor, helpless, indolent, and demoralised state of society.

I desire to condole with you in your bereavement, and hope you will excuse the haste in which I have put these sentiments before you, remaining yours sincerely,

To J. Bowes.   LAWRENCE HEYWORTH.

Jan. 1st., 1843—This morning addmitted to fellowship a young woman who had been under deep soul-concern for some days, when her neighbors got some elders and an Established minister, named Mitchell, to see her. Mitchel asked, "What is the matter with you?" as though he was entirely ignorant of the symptoms of a soul in distress.

30th.—This morning I received a note from Thomas Salmon, of 26, Shuttle-lane, by his son, a little boy. He stated that he and a wife and three children, the youngest at the breast, on this cold, frosty morning, were without food and fire, and desiring my aid. Not knowing whether he was a sober man or the reverse, I sent as much as would make a meal, and only a penny to get any little extra matter. A little after mid-day I called on the family; they had made a comfortable meal, seemed very thankful, and with one halfpenny's worth of coal had made a very small fire, around which they sat. He stated he was a Methodist, and that his wife washed for the minister that they had, previously to their present one. I called on his class-leader, found he was a sober man, I said that it was not enough to sing, and pray with, and teach poor starving people, but that as Christians we ought to supply them with food. This he admitted, but stated that they had many poor people in these hard times, and were not able to help all. I returned back to T. Salmon's, and saw one of the most heart-touching scenes of poverty that my eyes ever beheld. It was now dark. I knocked at the door, it was opened, but all was dark and dismal within, the small fire had gone out, they had no candle, no money, and no food. There were five human beings, one of them a young mother, with a child at her breast—sober people; the husband, a member of a church, in a literal state of starvation. I spoke kindly to them, for my heart was full, left them as much as would make them comfortable over the night and next day, and hastened away to explain the case to two or three Christians. One of them, a "Friend," not only gave a little, but when we found that a small sum would set him up in his wonted business, he contributed towards it. The Superintendent had visited Salmon and given him three half-pence at one time, and the boy had got some broth at another. Some circumstances connected with two preachers that visited him, and could have aided him, I omit, but if this should meet their eye, let them with great heart-searching consider that "we ought to lay down our lives for the brethren. But whoso hath this world's good, and seeth his brother have need, and shutteth up his bowels of compassion from him, how dwelleth the love of God in him?" (1 John iii. 17, 18.)—that is it does not dwell in him at all. Rich professors sometimes state that they are often afraid to give to strangers, lest they should encourage idleness and intemperance. Let them turn their attention to Christian churches, in which neither the idle nor the intemperate would be tolerated, and relieve the poor children of God, or if they cannot go themselves, give their money to those who visit them. And without the church, if they do not know of the honest and industrious poor, some of their christian friends may know; let them call in their co-operation, as the late Richard Reynolds of Bristol did. A main part of religion is neglected, if we neglect the suffering poor.

There was much to love and deplore in Geo. C. Had his principles been equal to his abilities he might have been of great use.

Victoria Court, ABERDEEN,
January 31, 1843.

DEAR SIR,—

As our intimacy is now broken up, and not likely to be renewed in this world, I embrace the present opportunity of expressing the deep regret I feel, on account of the unhappy circumstances which have combined to put an end to a friendship which, while it lasted, felt so sweet, and promised so much blessing. The plant was an exotic, and far too delicate for this atmosphere. It could not live under the uncongenial and blighting influence of unkindness. Look at it now—withered, alas, and all but dead. O I think I shall never again be so foolish as love any man half so much as I have loved you, for then the bitterness of disappointment when it comes, will not surely be so bitter as it has been in the present case. That I derived great benefit through your instrumentality, a year ago, I have ever been ready to acknowledge, and for this I loved you, and thought I ever should have loved you, more than any man alive. But thus saith the Prophet, "Cursed be man that trusteth in man, and maketh flesh his arm." I believe, however, that you have not disappointed me more than I have disappointed you. O let us both learn the very precarious tenure by which we hold our enjoyments in this world, and more than ever place our delights in God and in him alone. Farewell. With best wishes for your self and family.

I remain, Dear Sir, yours &c.

To J. Bowes.   GEO. CORNWALL.

I held a discussion on Socialism, at Aberdeen, with Mr. John Esdaile, and as matter of much importance was brought forward, I deem an "outline" of the discussion worthy of a place here.

FOUR NIGHTS' DISCUSSION ON SOCIALISM.

JANUARY 19th, 1843—FIRST NIGHT.

John Esdaile was to prove "That the character of man is formed for him, and that, in the common acceptation of the term, he is not a responsible being."

The Hall was so crowded that we proceeded with difficulty. J. Esdaile spoke the first, and employed more than one-half of his time in praising Robert Owen, and finding fault with J. B's lectures. He then said, the best possible character should be given to man; and character is, more or less, an emanation of the rational mind. Socialists aim at the perfection of humanity. How then can their sentiments be immoral? We seek to take man out of a polluted atmosphere, and to remove every thing of a quarrelling or immoral tendency. Every nation has a peculiar character of its own.

J. Bowes said: How would friend Esdaile account for peculiarities in families and nations. How was George Fox made a Quaker, or Robert Owen a Socialist, if circumstances form character?

Let us define the word "responsible." According to Walker, it is "answerable, accountable, capable of discharging an obligation." I shall prove that man is responsible by the following arguments:—

I. Man possesses the elements of responsibility.

(1) He acts independently. He feels that his actions are his own, not those of another—not the actions of circumstances.

(2) Intelligently—According to the knowledge he has acquired, he knows, or may know, what is right and wrong; and he is responsible to act according to the best of his knowledge.

(3) Freely, without coercion—He is neither coerced by his original constitution, nor by circumstances. Not by his original constitution, because some men, constitutionally prone to anger and other evil passions, become calm and regular in their tempers and habits, especially under the teaching and example of that heaven-sent prophet—the Lord Jesus Christ, not by circumstances, because, if he is actuated by external circumstances, it must either be by all or by some. Friend Esdaile will not say by all; and, if only by some, he makes his own selection.

(4) From sufficient motives, which if rightly considered, direct him into the path of rectitude.

(5) Man is capable of forming a moral judgment of what is right and wrong; and why does he possess these five elements of responsibility, if he is never to use them?

II. My second argument is drawn from the power of every man's conscience. Conscience sits in judgment upon our actions; pronounces sentence of condemnation when we act contrary to our convictions of duty; and punishes us by its painful accusations, when crime has been committed; or, if we act virtuously, conscience cheerfully approves, and rewards us by happiness and self-respect. But why should conscience blame us for doing wrong, or whisper its approval, when we do right, if all our actions are necessitated?

III. The marriage contract, however simply formed, whether before a clergyman or a Dissenters' meeting, implies responsibility. Husbands and wives feel that they are responsible to each other, as they are not to others. If there were no responsibility, the marriage contract would be a mere name. There can be no unfaithfulness where there is no obligation.

IV. Every family government, especially the relation of parent and child, proves responsibility. If it is right for the father to command, it is right for the child to obey. If the child injures his brother, or steals from his father, it is right for his father to disapprove and correct him.

V. Every commercial transaction confutes the sentiment which I oppose. You buy a coat or a watch, the merchant holds you responsible for the stipulated price. All the working-men in this assembly can understand this argument. After you have wrought for your master all the week, do you not hold him responsible to pay you your wages?

VI. Every well-regulated society, and every Christian church, holds its members responsible to obey the laws by which they have agreed to be governed; and holds them guilty when these laws are broken.

VII. Every human government in the world, whether monarchical, aristocratical, or democratical, proves the responsibility of its subjects and officers. It surely will not be pretended that, in those states in which the subjects make their own laws, that they are not responsible to the laws which they have enacted for their own government.

VIII. We go up from human government to the Divine, and affirm, that every enlightened and virtuous mind feels that it is responsible to the universal Parent; and that he who has created, supported, and redeemed us, and done all that boundless love could do to save, deserves our supreme regard. I beg to hand these four questions to J. Esdaile.

(1) If circumstances form character, and irrational or bad circumstances form an irrational or bad character; and if all the circumstances were irrational before Robert Owen arose, must he not be irrational? or, if he is rational, how did irrational circumstances happen to form him a rational being?

(2) Prove to this meeting, on Socialists' principles, that murder is a crime?

(3) Whether is the man who believes that he is responsible to love supremely his Creator, Redeemer, and Judge, and also to love every human being; and who accordingly endeavors every day that he lives to honour God, and to do some good, either to the bodies or souls of men; or the man who believes that he owes nothing, either to God or society, and who lives only to himself, likely to be the most happy man, and the most useful member of society?

(4) Ought an excellent father to look with equal approbation upon the honesty and dishonesty, the obedience and disobedience of his child?

J. Esdaile was only heard a few minutes after this. He said he did not stand before them as a sectarian or a declaimer, but as a philosopher. Man did not make his own organisation. Mental manifestation was connected with the brain and nervous system. Mr. Bowes had not touched the point of the formation of character. I am asked about murder. Christianity has given us plenty of murders. See how the poor Chinese have been murdered by Christians. The meeting was so crowded and restless, J. E. was obliged to stop. Order being restored, the chairman called on J. Bowes—who said: Every man that gave attention, and made a right use of his eyes, ears, and understanding, assisted in forming his own character. If man is a responsible being, he is responsible for the formation of his own character. Christianity neither teaches war nor murder. It condemns both, and says, "Love your enemies." Many professing Christians have gone to war; but they acted in opposition to Christian principles. Friend Esdaile has never tried to answer my arguments on responsibility. I shall proceed with them.

IX. The rules, laws, and proceedings of the Socialists disprove their own doctrine of non-responsibility. Their "constitution and laws," c 4, s. 6, is headed in Roman capitals—"RESPONSIBILITY OF OFFICERS." Yes, a servant is not to be responsible to his master; a child to his parent; nor a Christian to his God; but no sooner has the treasurer of the Socialists got their money into his pocket, than they hold him to be "responsible for all monies." Here is the rule:—"But every such officer shall be personally responsible for all monies, or other effects actually received by him;" and if he act unjustly, these men of no praise and no blame, no reward and no punishment, hand him over to the tender mercies of 10 Geo. 4, c. 50, s. 22. But let us come to John Esdaile himself. He shall disprove, in his own person, his own doctrine; and demonstrate that man is a responsible being. He comes hither to prove that man is not responsible, "not capable of discharging any obligation;" and yet he engages with me to discuss four propositions. He enters into an obligation to speak the first thirty minutes, and then fifteen minutes alternately with me. He rises and sits down at the appointed signals, thus proving that he is capable of discharging an obligation. He who disbelieves responsibility, holds himself responsible to this meeting. Did ever infatuation go beyond this?

SECOND NIGHT, JANUARY 26, 1843,—On the same question.

J. Esdaile—I am seeking truth, and truth is a gem above all price. All our evils arise from error, and from error alone. I entreat the audience to give a patient hearing to the propounder of a new system. All the old systems have failed. I wish man to be perfected as a practically religious being. The few have the means of acquiring property. The millions are the slaves of the capitalists. Circumstances form character. Every thing that we behold in the universe is a result. If we wish the bodily functions of man to be healthy, we place him in favorable circumstances. Man is like a plant in a bad soil, surrounded by adverse circumstances it withers. In a good soil, surrounded by favorable circumstances, it thrives.

J. Bowes.—Our friend exhorts us to "give a patient hearing;" that is something which we do ourselves. Now, if we can hear patiently, we can do something towards forming our own character. We are told, man is like a plant. Not exactly. If a man is planted in the midst of a storm, he can *walk away* to shelter. A plant cannot stir. A man has a *conscience*. A plant has none. By abstinence, a man may improve his own health. A plant has no power over itself. Thinking man is not, then, like a plant. All evil does not originate in our lack of knowledge. The slaveholder knows that slavery is wrong; but self-interest induces him to continue it. Every man's own conscience tells him that he has often acted contrary to his knowledge. Christianity has not failed. It has always made men happy when they have acted according to its requirements. We must learn to distinguish between Christianity and its corruptions. I shall now endeavor to prove that man's character is not formed entirely for him; but, partly for him, and partly by him. What is character? "A representation of any man, as to his personal qualities, on account of any thing, as good or bad; the person with his assemblage of qualities."—WALKER. Your dress is made for you, when you are not your own tailor ; that is, when another makes it ; but your character cannot be made *without* you, like your dress.

(1) Because, in the formation of character, *your own* aid is solicited. Socialists *ask you to read* their books. This you do by your own eyes. To *hear* their arguments and lectures. This you do by your own ears. They ask you to *judge*, to *decide*. This you do by your *own reason*.

(2) My next argument is derived from *industry*. An industrious man only can ever become a great character. Demosthenes might have had a good organisation; and surrounding circumstances might have conspired to make him a great orator; but he had great impediments to overcome, which industry only surmounted. Hence, he resorted to the sea-side, put pebbles in his mouth, and spoke to the waves, that he might accustom himself to the clamor of public assemblies. Sir Isaac Newton attributed his success, as a philosopher, to his industry. See Brewster's life of Sir Isaac, quoted in the published report of the discussion at Liverpool, between Lloyd Jones and myself, p. 15.

(3) All *courts of law* make a difference between the actions of a sane man, and those of a maniac,—between a man killed deliberately, and another killed by necessity. Were one of you on a ladder, above your own father, should a third person fall on you, and drive you against your father, so that he should fall to the ground, and you be a means of killing him by the fall, all mankind would acqnit you of murder; but should you take a pistol, and deliberately shoot your father, mankind would hold you guilty. Now, if all actions are equally necessitated, there can be no difference in the guilt of the two cases.

(4) The *difference* between *voluntary* and *involuntary* engagements shows that both are not equally forced. I will explain my meaning by an instructive fact. "The history of that good man, John Fletcher, (La Flechere) affords an example to our purpose. Fletcher had a brother De Gons; and a nephew, a profligate youth. This youth came one day to his uncle De Gons, and, holding up a pistol, declared he would instantly shoot him if he did not give him an order for five hundred crowns. De Gons, in terror, gave it; and the nephew then, under the same threat, required him solemnly to promise that he would not prosecute him; and De Gons made the promise accordingly. That is what is called an *extorted* promise, and an *extorted* gift. How, in similar circumstances, did Fletcher act? This youth afterwards went to him, told him of the 'present' which De Gons had made, and showed him the order. Fletcher suspected some fraud, and thinking it right to prevent its success, he put the order in his pocket. It was at the risk of his life. The young man instantly presented his pistol, declaring that he would fire if he did not deliver it up. Fletcher did not submit to the extortion. He told him that his life was secure, under the protection of God ; refused to deliver up the order ; and severely remonstrated with his nephew on his profligacy. The young man was restrained and softened; and before he left his uncle, gave him many assurances that he would amend his life. De Gons might have been perplexed with doubts, as to the obligation of his "extorted" promise; Fletcher could have no doubts to solve."—DYMOND'S ESSAYS, p. 56. Now, if the doctrine which I oppose be true, there is no difference be-

tween a promise or gift extorted, and one given freely. In Fletcher's case, we see the power of a man of principle; how different from a mere creature of circumstances!

(5) The *power* which a man may acquire over his own *constitutional anger*, even when placed in irritating circumstances, shows that man is not a mere creature of circumstances.

Should a man, in anger, kill his wife or child, he is not to blame, according to Socialism. Would you send your child to a school, where he should be taught that it is no crime for a child to kill his own father? Socialism is that school.

If a man would subdue his anger, let him watch against it, and look at the example of Jesus Christ,—" Learn of me," says Christ, " for I am meek and lowly in heart."

(6) From the feelings of *goodwill* and *gratitude*. A man denies himself, to give you £5, when you need bread. You find another £5 on the street. How is it that the goodwill of your friend affects you, and calls forth a gratitude for his £5 which you cannot feel for the other? In the one case, there was choice, and probably virtue, but not in the other. When a baker sends his man, horse, and cart, filled with bread, for poor people, according to Socialism, the poor man who receives his loaf might as well present his thanks to the cart which contained the bread, or to the horse that dragged the cart, as to the baker, since the actions of all were alike constrained by circumstances.

(7) I hold that man's actions are free, and that he is responsible for the formation of his own character, from *the power of will*. LOCKE defines volition, or will, to be " an act of the mind, knowingly exerting that dominion it takes itself to have over any part of the man, by employing it in, or withholding it from, any particular action." REID to the same effect, says: " The determination of our mind to do or not to do something which we conceive to be in our power." He adds: " Nothing in which the will is not concerned, can justly be accounted either virtuous or immoral. The practice of all criminal courts, and all enlightened nations, is founded upon it:" and that, if any "judicature, in any nation, should find a man guilty and the object of punishment for what they allow to be altogether involuntary, all the world would condemn them as men who knew nothing of the first and most fundamental rules of justice."

Imagine a man who forces the unwilling hand of his enemy's own son to kill his father by a dagger, is there no difference between the child and the man who forces him to destroy? No difference, says Socialism. The reason of the universe reclaims against it. If a wicked action should never be performed, it may be willed, and in that, its being willed, consists its guilt. In like manner, a benevolent action, which is never performed, may be willed, and in that consists its virtue. The vice and virtue of all actions originate in the will; but where coercion begins, deliberation ends; and where it ends, there is an end of all virtue and of all vice.

(8) The system which I support is the only one adapted to make *great* and *good* men. The school of Zeno, which held this doctrine, gave the greatest emperors and philosophers to Rome. Why? Because they believed that, by industry, they could be great or good; and, according to the light they had, they succeeded. And so it is now,

J. Bowes here read the four questions, and called upon J. Esdaile to answer them.

J. E.'s second speech, we fear, would not repay our readers. He was going on, when his chairman handed him the four questions. He thanked him for calling his attention to them, and promised to answer them; "But, before I do it," said he, "let me call your attention to responsibility." The audience laughed, but he sat down without answering the questions, and never more tried to answer them.

J. Bowes—You see our friend cannot answer these questions. I shall proceed with my arguments.

(9) The *supremacy of conscience.* While this power remains in man, Socialism cannot prove its doctrine. "No one can mistake the design of the artificer in putting a regulator into a watch. It was to make it go more regularly. And, as little should we mistake the design of the Creator in putting a conscience into a man's bosom. It was to make him walk conscientiously; even, although from some derangement in the machinery, the regulator had lost its power of control—yet, from its plan of control, the original purpose of it might still be abundantly manifest; and, in like manner, though from the enlargement of man's moral economy, conscience may have fallen from its actual sway, it still bespeaks itself to be a fallen sovereign; and that the place of sovereignty is that which natively and rightfully belongs to it."—CHALMERS' Works, vol. I., p. 326. Conscience sits as judge, and rewards or punishes. It gives a threefold reward, when we do right. First, we have the approbation of our own minds. Secondly, the pleasure of reflection. Thirdly, the hope of reward. Every man's conscience, according to the system which I oppose, is an unjust judge, because it praises and blames without reason.

(10) There is a manifest difference between a *mere creature of circumstances* and a man of *firm, unbending principle.* The former has no rule to guide him but his own selfishness. He will adopt any measure; break any agreement; sacrifice any friend; commit any cruelty; exercise any tyranny; abandon himself to any profanity; sell himself to any meanness; to please the wealthy, and secure his own interests. But look at the magnanimity of the latter—"The martyr to humanity, to freedom, to religion; the unshrinking adherent of despised and deserted truth, who alone, unsupported and scorned, with no crowd to infuse into him courage, no variety of objects to draw his thoughts from himself, no opportunity of efforts or resistance, to raise and nourish energy, still yields himself calmly, resolutely, with invincible philanthropy, to bear prolonged and exquisite suffering, which one retracting word might remove." Such a man is as superior to a mere creature of circumstances, as truth is to falsehood; as Howard and Thornton to Burke and Hare. Joseph, when tempted to act wrongly in the heat of youth, respected the friendship and honor of his master, and repelled the solicitations of his mistress, with this noble reply: "How then can I do this great wickedness and sin against God." In this spirit the martyrs acted, parting with their blood, rather than with their religious principles. They did not plead circumstances, as R. Owen did at Mexico; and abandon their principles, to avoid suffering.

(11) I adduce *the character of the Lord Jesus Christ* as perfectly unaccountable on the principle that circumstances alone form character.

There were no circumstances, either in his own, or any previous age, to account for his wonderful character. His own disciples were influenced by the prejudices of their countrymen. He rose above all prejudices; and, although trained up as a Jew, declared that he was "the light of the world;" that "men should come from the east, west, north, and south, and sit down in the kingdom of God;" and that the Jews should be cast out." He invited the world to come to him, saying: "Him that cometh to me, I will in no wise cast out." He was without spot. A perfect example of every virtue. Notwithstanding all the increase of science and philosophy since his time, the world has furnished no second to his character. The most advanced and elevated minds must still look up to him. Now, how will my friend account for this extraordinary, this glorious character, on his principles. It will not do to say that it was invented, for the difficulty remains, who could invent such a character when the universe furnished no model for imitation. The character of Jesus Christ is an unanswerable argument of the truth of his religion, and the falsehood of R. Owen's principles.

(12) *Praise* and *blame* imply that man can do something towards forming his own character. A gentleman is walking on the pier-head, with his only daughter. An enemy pushes her into the sea. Just when she is struggling with the waves, and about to rise do more, a young man, a stranger, dashes in after her, and, at the hazard of his own life, brings her in triumph to the shore. According to Socialism, her father is not to blame the enemy of his daughter, nor utter one word of praise to her deliverer. No! according to this cold-hearted, drivelling, unmanly system, he is not to utter one word of approbation. Human nature could not be restrained. Humanity rejects this contemptible system.

John Esdaile—Circumstances and organisation made bright characters; but the evil circumstances of society were not to be removed by praying and preaching. The murderer is insane, and ought to be treated as such. But why were so many poor persons in our jails? Because they were surrounded by bad circumstances. Mr. Bowes has delivered us an eloquent speech on the character of Jesus Christ. I wonder that Mr. Bowes should ask me to account for the character of Christ, when Mr. Bowes believes him to be the second person in the Trinity. He was omnipotent, and that is a sufficient circumstance to account for that. We do employ praise and blame; but we object to vindictive punishment.

J. Bowes—If friend Esdaile does hold praise and blame, reward and punishment, he abandons Socialism; and no doubt, we shall succeed, when we are both against Owen. What does he say—Book of the New Moral world, p. 10, "No man can have merit or demerit, or deserve reward or punishment." But though Robert Owen denies responsibility, in his discussion with A. Campbell, of America, he says (p. 50), "The responsibility which I have assumed in my continued earnest endeavors to subvert all the religions of the world." He assumes responsibility—that is, takes it to himself, puts it on, when it has no existence! Could you, sirs, put on your coats, if there were no coats in existence; just as easily as R. Owen can assume or put on responsibilty, if there be no responsibility. I would prove responsibility from the very cheers and hisses of the Socialists themselves. You cheer or praise your own advocate when you think he does well; and you hiss or blame me, when you think I do the reverse, albeit, I think your hisses no punishment when I am doing my duty.

J. Esdaile—Your religion was received from your ancestors. Had Mr. Bowes been born in China, he would have had six Mrs. Boweses, instead of one. The strongest motive in every case governs. Here J. E. entered into a long description of what Mr. B. would have been, had he been born in China; which, as it contained no argument, may be omitted.

J. Bowes—The strongest motive does not always govern. It only governs when considered. The drunkard has the strongest motive to be sober, in a starving wife and family; but it does not govern, because it is not considered. It has been considered by millions in America, Ireland, &c., and they have reformed. Friend Esdaile tells us that we receive our religion from our ancestors; but he has not told us where Robert Owen, once a professed Christian, got his present views; nor how George Fox was made a Quaker; nor how I am not now in the denomination in which I was educated. Can he prove that a good parent has never had a bad son; or wicked parents, a good son? No. Why are not all poor people in jails, if poverty, as a circumstance, invariably tends to crime? Many poor people are among the most virtuous in the land; and would rather beg than steal. Hence moral principle rises above circumstances. If riches always preserve from crime, no rich people would be vicious or go to jails.

I must congratulate the meeting on one important admission. The only way in which our friend could account for the wonderful character of Jesus Christ was, by admitting that he was omnipotent. Then, if Christ be omnipotent, let our friend serve him; for if he be omnipotent, he was a teacher sent from God, and his religion is true, and should be cordially received.

FEBRUARY 2nd, 1843—THIRD NIGHT.

Proposition.—"That the Religion of Socialism is true, and calculated to produce the greatest amount of good to mankind."

John Bowes.—I shall endeavor to show you that Socialism has no religion; but first, let us define what is meant by religion; according to Walker, it is, "Virtue, as founded upon reverence of God, and expectation of future rewards and punishments; a system of divine faith and worship, as opposite to others." According to this definition, Socialism has no religion, for it denies all worship, all future rewards and punishments; and, if we judge of it by the writings of Robert Owen, it denies the very existence of an intelligent God. The Socialists have committed themselves to the writings of Robert Owen. In the Report of the proceedings of Congress for 1839, p. 57, we find the delegates of Socialism from all parts of the kingdom voting him an address, in which they say that he has been enabled "to discover, and, in the spirit of kindness and charity, perseveringly to promulgate, truth without mystery, mixture of error, or fear of man." Thus they, who declaim against us for our faith, have more faith in Robert Owen than even very many Roman Catholics have in the Pope; for many of them attribute infallibility only to General Councils, but question its existence in any individual Pope. But the Socialists believe Robert Owen's writings to be "without mixture of error"—that is infallible. They have thus embraced his writings as a whole. Now, I mean to prove to you that Robert Owen is an Atheist. "Those," says Cudworth, "are Atheists who assert that there is no conscious intellectual nature presiding over the universe; or who assert that the first cause of all things (out of himself) is not an intelligent, conscious, active Being." In the Book of the New Moral World, p. 46, Robert Owen says, "The error respecting the law of human nature has led men to create a personal Deity, author of all good; and a personal Devil, author of all evil; to invent all the various forms of worship. There is not a single fact known to man, after all the experience of the past generations, that any such personalities exist, or ever did exist." In the same book (p. 91) he asserts; "that truth is nature, and nature God." So that his God is composed of the mountains, seas, earth, air, and, in fact, of unthinking matter; we have a part of his God in this table now before me. No wonder that he says, in his discussion with Campbell of America, p. 39, "Man is a being to whom no religion yet invented can apply; and accordingly he affirms, "that it is impossible to train men to become rational in their feelings, thoughts, and actions, until all such forms (of ' ceremonial worship ') shall cease."— *Social Bible*, p. 6. Those, then, are the Atheistical sentiments of Socialism, as propounded in the writings of its founder. Some Socialists may believe in a supreme, conscious God. Robert Owen does not, and, as we have seen, the Socialists, as a body, have committed themselves to his sentiments. I shall endeavor to show the unreasonableness of the Atheism of Socialism, and bring forward evidence to prove the existence of Deity. Before proceeding to direct arguments, I will bring before you the folly of Atheism, as expressed in the powerful language of Foster, in one of his Essays, " The wonder turns on the great process by which a man could grow to the immense intelligence to know there is no God. What ages and what lights are requisite to this attainment? This intelligence involves the very attributes of divinity, while a God is denied. For unless this man is omnipresent, unless he is at this moment in every place of the universe, the one that he does not know may prove God. If he is not himself the chief agent in the universe, and does not know what is so, that which is so may be God. If he is not in the absolute possession of all the propositions that constitute universal truth, the one which he wants may be that there is a God. If he cannot with certainty assign the cause of all that he perceives to exist, that cause may be a God. If he does not know every thing that has been done in the immeasureable ages that are past, some things may have been done by a God. Thus, unless he knows all things, that is, precludes another Deity, by being one himself, he cannot know that the being, whose existence he rejects, does not exist." The folly of denying the existence of a God is clearly set forth in these remarks. 1. My first argument in favor of the existence of an intelligent Deity, is derived from the marks of design and contrivance in creation. Were we to examine man alone, we should find evidence sufficient in his formation, to convince us that he was made by design. His head, his eye, his ear, his heart, his lungs, all furnish us with beautiful proofs of design. His 254 bones, all curiously united together; his 486 muscles, pervading his frame, and all contributing to one harmonious result, evince great skill and contrivance. Imagine a Socialist and a Christian passing a public-house, over which hangs the sign of the "Duke of Wellington." Should the Christian say, "That sign, those eyes, that countenance, that portrait, was made without a designing mind," would any Socialist believe him? No. Is a man, then, with his thinking mind, more easily made than his portrait? Is the unseeing eye more easily made than that which sees; the unhearing ear than that which hears; the lifeless picture than a man, with life and a soul with all its powers, its conscience, its understanding, and its will. Not only must every effect have a cause, but every effect must have an adequate cause; and is unthinking matter able to produce such a mind as that of reasoning Locke? We may well and triumphantly ask, in the forcible language of scripture, "He that made the eyes shall He not see; He that made the ears shall He not hear; and He that teaches knowledge shall He not know?" Look again at the vast field of creation; were the sun and moon made without design? I ask friend Esdaile if they were not made to give us light by day and night, what were they made for? Can you believe that this gas and these windows were not intended or designed to give light to this hall. Did no designing mind introduce the gas or put in the windows. Not one of you can believe that they came without design. Then how could the sun and moon be placed to illumine the world without design? Suppose you walk through the streets of Aberdeen, you will view the various buildings and reflect on man's work of contrivance and design, and so we ought to look on this vast world which gives us food and raiment, and see the vast munificence of a designing God.

2. My next argument is derived from Geology, which proves that man is but a recent inhabitant of the world. It is true that, for a long time, the Chinese chronology was alleged against the Mosaic account of the creation; and it was asserted by infidels that men had existed in China long before the period assigned by Moses for the peopling of the globe. It is remarkable that La Place, a man almost as much distinguished by science as any of whom infidelity can boast, should have been the first to disprove this theory, and to demonstrate that the Chinese chronology harmonises with the scriptural narrative. In like manner, Geology has been supposed to be hostile to the scriptures, but, properly understood, it confirms the scriptural history of man. The Bible is the only book that gives us a rational account of the creation, of what we are, and from whence we came. Can friend Esdaile name any other book that gives any thing like a credible account of the creation? That Geology confirms the Mosiac account of our origin may be learned from two of our most celebrated living Geologists. "We need not dwell on the proofs of the low antiquity of our species, for it is not controverted by any Geologist; indeed, the real difficulty which we experience consists in tracing back the signs of man's existence on the earth to that comparatively modern period, when species, now his contemporaries, began to predominate." It would not avail a hopeless cause to affirm that "man may have previously existed, for an unlimited period, but that some general destruction may have annihilated all traces of him." For, as Lyell remarks, "had these catastrophes been repeated through an indefinite lapse of ages, the high antiquity of man would have been inscribed in far more legible characters on the frame-work of the globe, than are the forms of the ancient vegetation which once covered the isles

of the northern ocean, or of those gigantic reptiles, which, at later periods, peopled the seas and rivers of the northern hemisphere." To this testimony we add that of Professor Sedgwick—"Geology tells us out of its own records, that man has been but a few years a dweller on the earth, for the traces of himself and of his works are confined to the last monument's of its history. Independently of every written history, we therefore believe that man, with all his powers and appertenancies, his marvellous structure and fitness for the world around him, was called into being within a few thousand years of the days in which we live."

It will be seen that no answer was ever attempted to this speech by J. Esdaile.

John Esdaile.—We are not here to discuss the evidence of a Divine Being, but the religion of Socialism. It will be its unceasing object to promote the happiness of every man, woman, and child, without regard to sect, party, country, or color. Mr. Bowes has gone a wool-gathering instead of discussing the question before us. It is left for me to do so. It is no enviable position which I occupy—to stand alone and unsupported, in opposition to those venerated doctrines which have been handed down for many ages to the present generation. We are met to contrast the religion of Socialism with the religion of Christendom, comparing the scope, the object, the spirit, and the instrumentality of both for effecting their purpose. Is there any danger attending religious inquiries? Where there is danger there are fears, and where there are fears there cannot be sober and dispassionate judgment; any danger that there is, must be in coming to wrong conclusions; but is there any penalty attached to religious error more than to any other kind of error? Christian divines tell us that a certain faith is a necessary condition of salvation, and that without this we must perish. It is a limitation of God's goodness if such is the case. The Koran tells us that God will cast all unbelievers into hell. The victim whom the Christian puts into hell is the outcast heathen, so the Mahometan puts the white man, who is damned, to hell, to keep company with dogs. The Christians take up this notion of faith in Jesus Christ from the Jews; they believed that he was the true Messiah, rose again, and would come to substitute a different order of beings—they believed that the second coming of Christ would take place in their own time, and spoke of it as an event that must shortly come to pass. And, as Paul expresses it, "The Lord shall come from heaven with a great shout, with the trump of God: then we who are alive and remain at his coming, shall be caught up to meet the Lord in the air, and so we shall be ever with the Lord." When, therefore, their anticipations met with disappointment, when they found that this second coming never occurred, their views took a different form, they came to acknowledge that it would be a long time before this event would occur, and that it would be to fix the general destiny of mankind, to rise to eternal punishment or reward; so they excluded all who did not believe in this system of faith, and there came to be different churches and different creeds. And not content with debarring mere heathens from salvation, they debar each other. Thus we see Catholics denouncing Protestants, and Protestants denouncing Catholics; Presbyterians denouncing Episcopacy, and Episcopalians, Presbytery; and so with every other sect. Mr. Bowes preaches one doctrine here, but go over the street there, and you have another—the one excludes and denounces the other, likewise with the unbeliever. Is it reasonable to think that the Bible comes from God, when its meaning is so obscure? The Bible contains many dangerous doctrines, such as, "He that believeth and is baptized shall be saved, and he that believeth not shall be damned." "He that believeth on the Son hath life everlasting, he that hath not the Son shall not see life, but the wrath of God abideth on him." "There is only one name given under heaven by which we can be saved." But there are passages in the Bible more liberal than these. Such as, "God is no respecter of persons." "He that walketh uprightly and worketh righteousness is accepted with him in every nation." "The heathen who have not the law are a law unto themselves." Scripture, you see, can be enlisted against scripture. Theologians have been warring this warfare for centuries, and I ask, Are they a bit nearer settling their disputes than at first? No: and no wonder, when we find the very authority to which Christians appeal so inconsistent with itself. Now, to refer the matter to common sense, and to common sense we are driven by the inconsistencies of religion, we ask, how it is consistent with a wise and good Deity to reveal that salvation depends on a certain faith, when a large portion of mankind are necessarily excluded from obtaining it? It is faith in a form which three-fourths of the inhabitants of our world have never heard of. It is faith in a volume which has not been translated into half the languages of the world; in a volume which nine-tenths of Christians have never read. How many possess their faith because they derived it from their forefathers? What merit is there here? How can they get merit from God, for nothing else than what makes the Turks Mahometans, and the Hindoos idolaters? What a prolific nursery for damned souls must the world have been for ages past, and must be for ages to come? How strange that God should send hundreds to hell for one he has reared for heaven?

J. Bowes—Our friend began by saying I was not at the question. I proved that Socialism is Atheism. Did he show that I was wrong, that Socialism was not Atheism? No. He never tried to refute my arguments. Atheism or Socialism is so far from doing good to mankind that it is the greatest evil to which mankind can be subject. If my friend do not show that Socialism is not Atheistical, it will go forth from this meeting, that Socialism is an Atheistical system. He told you that it was left to him to prove that Socialism is calculated to do the greasest amount of good to mankind, and I was waiting to hear what he would say about the religion of Socialism, and his proofs of its excellency; but he has never touched the question. He has gone to the Mahometans, the Jews, and the Christians, but to Socialism he will not look, perhaps he has discovered that it is not worth looking at.

We are not here to discuss the religions of Christendom, but the religion of Socialism, from which he has wandered, and I suppose I must follow him.

He says that Christians declare that all those who have never seen or heard of the Bible must go to hell. I tell him he has misrepresented our sentiments. The Christian Scriptures hold man accountable for his belief, when he has an opportunity of believing, but not when he has no opportunity. The passages which he has quoted, instead of contradicting, beautifully explain each other. Among those who hear the gospel, "He that believeth and is baptized shall be saved, and he that believeth not shall be damned;" but when a man has had no opportunity of knowing the gospel, he will not be judged by it, but by the light he has, for "God is no respecter of persons. But in every nation he that feareth God and worketh righteousness is accepted." But when a man has the Bible, it is his own fault if he be damned. Will God judge me by the opportunities of knowledge which the Chinese possess? No; but he will call me to an account for the opportunities which I possess. If I sin against much light, I shall be beaten with many stripes. If the Chinese sin against less light, they shall be beaten with few stripes. Is it not right to send men to hell who, in this country, refuse to believe the Scriptures? He has brought you to the bar of common sense. I will meet him there. He has appealed to the bar of reason, and to the bar of reason we will go. Is it not reasonable, when some firemen know that there is a fire in a certain house, that they should arouse the inmates, and tell them of their danger? And ought not the inmates to go and examine if there be any fire, and if there be, ought they not to extinguish it? Should the firemen give warning, and the inmates refuse to examine the danger, and be burned to death or killed, would it not be their own fault, would they not deserve to suffer? In like manner, it is not unreasonable that those should be condemned who, after the gospel has been preached to them, sin against light. God has commanded us to examine his word, and that word has sufficient evidence to support it, which, if a man examine, he will not be an infidel. My friend has not fairly represented the doctrines of the Bible. If he will carefully examine the evidences of Christianity he will become a Christian. And are we not responsible to examine evidence? I say we are. Again, he asks, "How are the Mahometans to blame?" I say, if they act not according to the light they have, they are to blame, but not for not believing the gospel, if it is never propounded to them; but if they have an opportunity of reading and hearing the gospel, and if they wilfully reject it, then they are to blame. He says the heathens and Mahometans believe they are favorites of heaven, as well as the Christians. Socialists say, "if there be a God, they are sure he will look favorably on them, because they are doing good to their fellow-men." In this they agree with Mahometans, &c. He said that the first Christians believed that there should be a resurrection of the righteous only; and when they saw that this failed and did not come to pass in their own days, their sentiments changed. He has appealed to reason and to Scripture. I do so too, and charge him with ignorance of the Scriptures. If he had known them, he could not have made this gross misrepresentation. Christ himself taught at the first, that there should be a resurrection of good and bad. Look at John v. 28. 29. "Marvel not at this, for the hour is coming, in the which all that are in the graves shall hear his voice, and shall come forth; they that have done good unto the resurrection of life, and they that have done evil unto the resurrection of damnation." Paul taught the same doctrine, see 1 Cor. xv. 22, "For as in Adam all die, so in Christ shall all be made alive." The first Christians never changed their views on the resurrection. My friend cannot have carefully read the Scriptures or he would not thus misrepresent them. He says Christians exclude all from salvation who come short of their particular creeds. This is another misrepresentation. Whatever some professors do, I and others do not; we believe that many true Christians will go to heaven, who think differently on some subjects from us. Let my friend now come to the point, and show Socialism to be a good system.

J. Esdaile—He has shown you that my remarks do not apply to his particular church. I was not aware that Mr. Bowes did not believe that all the heathen would be damned. There are so many opinions on religious subjects. God is said to have given us a book which contains the covenant of human salvation, and it is so mystified that those who believe in it are not agreed as to its meaning. Now surely we may presume that a book coming from God will be so plain that every man can understand it—that a book which contains the covenant of human redemption should be such as that all who run may read; if we are to expect clearness and precision in a human teacher, much more are we to expect it of a divine teacher. Here is a divine instructor, and none can know what are his essential doctrines. The Bible is so voluminous, and so various are its writings, by different hands in different ages, that it requires abilities and so much time as few have at their disposal. It has been found necessary to draw up short summaries of Bible doctrines—these do make it smooth and level to the capacities of men, but they are so numerous and various, that unlearned men are not able to judge. If God had given us a revelation it would have been such as all would read and understand at their ease. Let us bring this saving faith to a minute scrutiny. If faith be a belief in certain facts and statements, how absurd is it to punish a man who does not believe; would a reasonable person excite one's fears, to get the power of his understanding? What would you think of a man who would come and say to you, "Believe me, or I will knock you down!" Would not such a threat as this prove that he wishes to force an untruth on your understanding? and where is the difference of one, calling himself the messenger of heaven, saying, "If you believe not this you shall be damned." An appeal to one's fears always weakens the mind. Belief is also a sentiment of the heart as well as of the understanding, which makes it more inconsistent with the character of Deity. Faith represents a wrathful God appeased by the pleadings of his Son; it is a fond and grateful reverence for the Saviour, who intercedes with an angry God, and pleads the cause of man before him.

J. Bowes.—You are to believe that Socialism is an Atheistical system, for my friend has never yet denied it. He says he is coming to the point; a sure admission that he has been wandering from it. Faith arises from reading, hearing, or examining evidence; when a man has an opportunity of hearing or reading, and does not employ his time properly, he is to blame. His want of faith is the consequence.

We have heard a great deal of the different opinions of different sects, and that some believe that those who differ from them shall be damned. I should be ashamed to belong to a church holding such sentiments; in the church to which I belong every one can think and speak freely. I would not have the human mind fettered. I did not come hither to defend all the various opinions held by different parties, such as those held by Johanna Southcote, &c.

He says the Bible has only been translated into a few languages. It has been translated into one hundred and thirty-seven. He asks if God would have given us a book to teach us the way to heaven, and left the greatest part of even Christians ignorant of that book? I tell him that it is not essential to salvation that a man read this book; no Christian holds this sentiment. A man by hearing and believing may be saved who cannot read at all. He asks, if the Bible be a revelation, how so many are ignorant of it? I answer, when God has bestowed on us his good gifts he leaves us to manage them very much for ourselves. For instance, God gives us corn; the fields bring forth plentifully, but man holds it back. It is not, then, because God is not benevolent that men perish for want, it arises from the selfishness of men. God gives us light, but some men are confined in dark cellars, and by their drunkenness and other sins deny themselves the light of heaven. God has given us the bread of life—the Bible—but some monopolists will still confine it; yet a New Testament may be procured for sixpence in this country. Others, like my friend, deny the Bible; he will not eat of this bread. He will not be condemned because there is no mercy, neither will any one, but he is as much to blame if he will not receive it when it is offered, as the man who refuses to eat and perishes, when there is plenty of food. How unreasonable to blame God for the poverty, ignorance, and punishment of men, when he has given his gifts to all; the selfishness of men, not God, is the cause why many are poor, and why many have no Bible. J. E. says there are a hundred sent to perdition for one that gets to heaven. I tell him that such a doctrine is not in the Scriptures. No Christian holds it. You see he is always misrepresenting the doctrines of Christians, but never touching Socialism. Indeed, poor Socialism may stand or fall for him, for he will not look at it. He says there are contradictory opinions among Christians. Well, there are contradictory opinions among Socialists too. I know why there are conflicting opinions among Christians; it is because they do not follow out the spirit of their religion. The Bible is plain enough in all matters essential to salvation. Is there any mystery in the command, "Thou shalt love the Lord thy God with all thy heart, and all thy soul, and all thy mind, and all thy strength;" or in the command, "Thou shalt love thy neighbor as thyself." Obedience to these commands makes a Christian. A man that loves God and his neighbor will get to heaven, for if he truly loves God, he loves his Son and honors his Son. Did he not tell us last night that Christ was omnipotent. (No, no. Yes, yes.) I shall put this right. Some thought that he mentioned what I have said, that Christ was omnipotent; others thought that he said, that I believed Christ to be the second person in the Trinity, and that consequently he was omnipotent. What he did say was this, that I believed Christ to be the second person in the Trinity; then afterwards he said, he is omnipotent, and that is a sufficient circumstance to account for that. Take this meaning either way—if Christ was omnipotent, no doubt it was a sufficient circumstance to account for his character, but then my friend loses his doctrine; but if Christ had not omnipotence, my friend gives up his argument, that man's character is formed for him. I asked him how Christ's character was formed by circumstances? He says in effect—"Oh, I cannot answer it on my own principles, but on yours. I can tell how Christ's character was formed on your principles but not on mine." Take it either way and it is against him. If Christ was omnipotent he loses his doctrine; if he was not, he loses his argument. There is no need of quibbling here; if my friend is not stranded here there is not a shoal in the universe.

Again, he tells us that men have drawn up formularies of doctrine. I tell him that the Bible speaks more clearly than those formularies, and I advise all Christians to give up every creed but the Bible. My friend should show that the differences of Christians are to be attributed to the Bible. That there are differences is no wonder. Men differ about politics, slavery, and the corn laws. Why?—because it is not plain that slavery and the corn laws are wrong? It is plain enough, but self-interest hinders men from seeing what is plain. So of the Bible. Its principal parts are plain, but men's self-interest explain it away. Take the command "Thou shalt love thy neighbor as thyself." A hungry man asks bread from a miser, the miser says "Not a farthing will I give." What hinders him—want of plainness in the command? —no; covetousness, self-interest. Thus the slaveholder and the revengeful man violate this command. The selfish passions of men blind their minds so that they misinterpret the plainest precepts of the Bible, and this is the root of the differences among professing Christians.

John Esdaile.—It is the article of saving faith which has occasioned all the religious wars and religious persecutions among Christians. Mr. B. says the Christian loves God and loves his neighbor, but you don't do so. How is it that the great moral laws of Deity have never been written uncorrupted in any creed of any church? If it had been so, then there would not have been all this conflict and difference of opinion. Mr. Bowes has not replied to my argument that it is absurd to make man's salvation depend upon his faith. Faith is a reliance on the Saviour for salvation, who, it is said, has satisfied divine justice for sinners. They just represent religion as a charm; a compassionate Son interceding with a wrathful God. If men would exercise their understanding on religion, it would soon finish such forms and doctrines. The salvation which we all need is not a deliverance from a wrathful God, but what we want is deliverance from vicious habits, degrading practices, demoralising poverty. By the light of moral science men will see that natural evils are only to be removed by natural means. Now human guilt is not miraculous, and man is not accountable for it; there are natural causes for it, viz., human ignorance; there are natural remedies, we are to improve men, 1st, by infant training; 2nd, by habits which he receives from those among whom he is placed, not by speaking about the wrath of God. The Bible says nothing on education, and on the great principle that the character of man cannot be improved, until his condition in society be improved.

J. Bowes—As there is only one argument which our friend says I have not answered, viz., his argument on faith, I will take that up first. He says that man must believe when sufficient evidence is set before him. I will prove that man is not forced to believe when evidence is presented. Many remain in ignorance and unbelief because they do not take the time and trouble necessary for examining evidence. Suppose a gentleman of New York orders a thousand pounds' worth of cloth from an Aberdeen merchant. The Aberdeen merchant does not know that the New York merchant is responsible. He is ignorant of him.

What does he do? He writes about him, examines evidence, and if he is satisfied, he sends the goods. The slaveholder shuts his eyes against evidence, against every anti-slavery tract and lecture. Evidence is presented to him, but it does not produce faith, because it is not considered. So of faith in the Bible. It is not for want of evidence that men do not believe, but for want of considering evidence. But our friend says, a man is not likely to believe if you alarm his fears. I say, if I saw a man in danger I would alarm his fears. If I saw a man running into the fire, I should say, "Take care, sir, or you will be burned to death!" If I saw a blind man in danger of falling into the river or sea, or any man approaching a dangerous precipice of which he was not aware, I would immediately cry to him to run for his life. It would not be a time to go up and whisper to him or reason with him, before I could do that, the man would be killed. But my friend says, oh no, you must not alarm his fears, it is not likely he will believe if you do! Thus he would let the man perish for fear of alarming him. He says I cannot think of God but as a wrathful God. I say I can. I think of him as a kind and merciful Father. A drunken son has a kind and loving father. The father advises him and says, "Oh! beware, or you will be in an early grave!" He alarms his fears in love. So it is kind in God to warn his offspring of their danger, and it will be man's own blame if he go to hell; and when God warns men, he shows how they may come to Him. Our friend says that we hold that Christ intercedes with a wrathful God to make him merciful; we hold no such thing; we believe that God is love, and that he always loved man. "God so loved the world that he gave his only begotten Son, that whosoever believeth on him should not perish, but have everlasting life." We do not believe that Christ died to make a wrathful God merciful, but we believe that his coming into this world was the grand development of the love of God towards the world. Christ did not die to make an angry God merciful, but to open up a channel by which the mercy of God might reach the human race, and win all hearts to himself, and to each other. Religion, he says originated all the wars and bloodshed of Christendom. I say that Christianity is opposed to war, and the Quakers and others have written against it. Christians are commanded to love their enemies, not to kill them. Dymond, in his work on "Morality," p. 104, says, "The man who now pays £20 a-year in taxes, would probably have paid but two had there been no war during the last century. If he now gets £150 a year by his exertions, he is obliged to labor six weeks, out of the fifty-two, to pay the taxes which war has entailed. That is to say, he is compelled to work two hours every day longer than he himself wishes, or than is needful for his support. This is a material deduction from personal liberty, and a man would feel it as such if the coercion were directly applied, if an officer came to his house every afternoon at four o'clock, when he had finished his business, and obliged him, under penalty of a distraint, to work till six." Christianity disowns such practices—so opposed to its meek and mild spirit. He finds fault with the conduct of professing Christians, but here, in the New Testament, is the Christian's moral code; we do not require it to be divided into human formularies, but here it is, whole. Let my friend look at its contents, and he will find it the best morality; we will not yet part with it for Socialism. He says we are looking for miraculous means to improve men's character; I am looking for no such thing. I believe that God is doing every thing he can, consistently with his perfections, to make men happy beings, and if they would not trample on his authority, they would be happy. He says the Bible says nothing about education; I say it does. It says, "Train up a child in the way he should go, and when he is old he will not depart from it." The whole Bible is a system of education of the best kind, and would give the best education to all; it would give the best morality; we have an example in Christ of noble and dignified, yet kind and benevolent principles. If my friend can find any fault in his life, let him tell it. I have proved this night that Socialism has no religion at all, but Atheism; and if he believes in a supreme God, and cannot prove that Socialism is not Atheism, let him renounce it. Socialism pretends to do a great deal for man, but it does little or nothing for the poor. Friend Esdaile will give you plenty of speculation, but let him tell you what Socialism has done. I hope my friend will introduce no new matter in his last speech. He has spoken much against the faith of the gospel this night, but I wish he may live and die under its peaceful influence, it worketh by love, purifieth the heart, and overcometh the world.

John Esdaile.—We have had the Christian faith in the world for eighteen centuries, and I ask you when it has worked by love? The bishops and higher classes are living in luxury, regardless of the wants of the oppressed and starving millions. The differences of religion have prevented love from working in the world. Dr. Channing says, in his "Discourse upon the Church," "The primitive disciples were drawn to Christ by conviction. In that age, profession and practice, the form and the spirit, the reality and the outward signs of religion went together. But with the growth of the church its life declined; its great idea was obscured; the name remained, and sometimes little more than the name. It is a remarkable fact, that the very spirit to which Christianity is most hostile, the passion for power, dominion, pomp, and pre-eminence, struck its deepest roots in the church. The church became the very stronghold of the lusts and vices which Christianity most abhors. Accordingly, its history is one of the most melancholy records of past times. It is sad enough to read the blood-stained annals of worldly empires; but when we see the spiritual kingdom of Christ a prey for ages to usurping popes, prelates, or sectarian chiefs, inflamed with bigotry and theological hate, and the lust of rule, and driven by these fires of hell to grasp the temporal sword, to persecute, torture, imprison, and butcher their brethren, to mix with and embitter national wars, and to convulse the whole Christian world, we experience a deeper gloom, and are tempted to despair of our race. History has not a darker page than that which records the persecutions of the Albigenses, or the horrors of the Inquisition. And when we come to later times, the church wears anything rather than holiness inscribed on her front." Christ says, "By this shall all men know that ye are my disciples if ye love one another;" but theologians have never thus sought to vindicate their title to be considered his disciples; on the contrary, there has been little else than rivalry, hatred, and contention among them. In the present system of society we see the millions toiling hard and not able to live by their industry; their children dying almost as soon as born, for it is a fact that one-half of the infants die under two years of age, but they could not die so in community. You don't see the young of brutes dying that way. Knowledge, physiological, as well as moral, is indispensable to man's well-being.

The FOURTH NIGHT'S DEBATE was on "The Marriage System of Socialism." As similar ground was taken on both sides as in the Liverpool discussion, with Lloyd Jones, the reader is referred to that for information. The discussion of the marriage system of Socialism produced great excitement among the Socialists. They could hardly bear to hear its abominations exposed. It was to be expected that the meeting would be less orderly on this than on any other occasion, and so it was.

The FIFTH NIGHT'S DEBATE was on the Socialists' favorite theme—*Home Colonisation*. It is here that they expect to triumph, by holding out great promises to the poor. And it was on this occasion especially that the Socialists acknowledge their advocate failed, they say, by miscalculating his time. This takes one by surprise; Socialists seldom or never acknowledge a defeat. They always triumph. On this occasion, however, they say, "John Esdaile failed." Impartial hearers are the best judges; it matters little who triumphed if truth was victorious; and it certainly was. The following seven questions were put, but never answered. With these unanswered questions the debate must close in these pages.

1. As J. Esdaile, throughout this discussion, has assumed that all in community will have the best of every thing, at all times, will he tell us how good things, which are not the best, and inferior things, are to be disposed of?

2. There is to be equality, though there is no equality of intellect, of mental or even physical stature among men. Does he mean, then, that one man shall be all trades, and that men shall take their regular turn at all trades; say one day get coals, another write; one day make shoes, another hats; one day be a tailor, another a blacksmith; one day be a chimney-sweep, another be the governor or principal of the community? if he means this, is it not absurd and impracticable? Some trades which take months or years to learn, could never be learned by this process?

3. How does it happen that the late Governor claimed, and had conceded to him, nearly despotic power, and the present Governor of Titherly has claimed the same?

4. Have not many families lost their all by the failure of Orbiston, New Harmony, Pant Glass, and the present insolvency of Titherly? And are not these great losses increasing the evils of the poor, instead of removing them?

5. Show to us that any community any where, conducted on R. Owen's principles, has ever succeeded? Having denied a supreme, all-wise God and governor, all responsibility to either God or man; rejected Revelation, so that they have had no rule of *right*, with which to compare their actions; their lust being the only rule which they acknowledged, have they not all failed of course? With these principles show us how any can succeed?

6. You hold out the hope that by working less than four hours per day, you will be supplied with abundance of the necessaries of

life. Prove to us this assumption; 1st. By an appeal to facts. Has any nation of the world reached this state? Have the United States? Or have the Socialists themselves? If so, where? 2dly. Will you explain to this audience the principles by which a whole nation may obtain support by working less than four hours per day—taking care to provide for all infants, sick persons, and the aged, and to give all a proper education?

7. Is it not true that £50 must be paid into the community fund, either by the candidate or his friends, before he can be admitted, and that for some years £50 were required for each member of his family, so that every family of six persons had to raise £300? If there be any change, what is it? Does not the proposal tend to divide families, or to prove that Socialism is a mockery to the working classes, since not one in a thousand can obtain £300? And very few could afford to give one shilling per week; but if they could, would it not take 115 years before they could get into community? so that two or three generations would pass away before any benefit could be realised?

Feb. 1st.—Called on T. Salmon, he said that my friend had sent him a shilling, by the Preacher; I said, "But did the preacher give you nothing himself?" "No, but he said he would call again." He is well able to give, I understand. I desired the man not to starve, but to call on me when ever he wanted bread. I have just heard that the minister who gave Salmon the three half-pence, has given £50 for a pianoforte to his wife, I hope it is not true.

11th.—I have just extracted the following from the *Scotsman* of this date:—"Death of Gabriel Miller, Esq., of Dundee.—We regret to have to notice the melancholy death of this gentleman. His body was found at the Craig Harbour, on the morning of Wednesday, last week, after the tide had ebbed, under circumstances which left no room to doubt that his death had been occasioned by drowning. Mr. Miller was known to have left a house in that neighborhood on the previous evening, and the probability is that, having occasion to pass in the direction of the harbour, from the gale that was then blowing, he had accidently fallen in. Mr. Miller filled the office of Clerk to the Police Board."—*Dundee Warder.* Both he and the late Superintendent are now gone. Both signed the charge against me for open-air preaching in 1840 and 1841. Let us reflect on the providence of God, and reverence him.

Victoria Court, ABERDEEN,
February 21, 1843.

MY DEAR BROTHER,—

I intended to have called last night but was prevented, I had nothing to say particularly, but would have enjoyed a little conversation.

You are on the eve of undertaking a journey, and I do not think that you are so well equipped as the present stormy weather would make necessary, and I beg that you would therefore allow me to contribute to your comfort a little, by supplying an outside covering in the shape of a cloak. If you will accept of this as a small token of unabated affection from the unworthy scribbler, you will confer a great favor upon me. My mind is now at blessed peace again. I am delighted to think that there exists now no cause of offence or grievance with any brother or sister, that all is harmony and love. The Lord confirm and perpetuate this state of things! Farewell. The Lord bless you and keep you.

I remain, my Dear Brother, yours very affectionately,

GEO. CORNWALL.

P.S.—My neighbor, David Morrison, Clothier and Tailor, No. 2 Castle Street, if you will call on him, will attend to your instructions, and I beg that you may require him to furnish a garment every way to your mind. I have enclosed a note to him. I have a reason why I have not availed myself of the service of any of the brethren who are tailors, in the above matter.—G. C.

28th.—Sailed from Aberdeen to Leith. Snow was on the ground, and a heavy swell on. I was sick nearly all the way. Slept at Francis Sutherlands, Leith, he has had deep affliction, been bereaved of a dear wife, and gone to reside at Ipswich.

264 Great Colmore Street, BIRMINGHAM,
March 3, 1843

MY VERY MUCH LOVED BROTHER,—

. . . . I was favored since I wrote you with several interviews with that heavenly soul, W. Trotter, with whom I was much refreshed in the Lord. We had the honor—for honor it is—of sleeping him and Mons. Brettell at our house one night. He was a few nights at Pensnett when I met him first. The Pensnett friends, specially T. Fellows and H. Bennett, have kind remembrance to you, and tell me to assure you of a hearty welcome among them. Dear Fellows wished me to say that the report you heard of his violating his temperance principles was not true, for though he has got far above teetotalism both in principle and practice, as it respects his own standing and the reformation of the world, yet he has still to say with thankfulness that the lessons you taught him have not been lost on him. I see very little of that great conversion work here of which your soul seems full when you write. Yet it appears to me to be God's order that when his saints are edified, established and walking in love, that they become multiplied. Acts ii. 46, 47.—v. 13, 14.—ix 31.—xi. 20-25.—xvi. 5. Yet with all these standing in array against me, I have often to fall down in humbling confession before the Lord that we are doing so little here. I assure you that it is not for want of sinners that there are so few added to the church, nor do I think it unwillingness on the part of God to save them, but it lies on my heart that we are (and especially that I am) not faithful to the Lord as witnesses of the grace he has given. I desire to be much stirred up in this, and you know my sloven nature requires stirring up to do good.

Your unworthy brother,
P. ANDERSON.

Mar. 7th.—LIVERPOOL. In a letter to my dear wife, I say:—"The brethren are all very kind, and alive to God. We added nine to the church last Lord's Day."

12th.—Lord's Day. LIVERPOOL. Hill Street Room, at the breaking of bread. Read an extract from a tract called "Correspondence from the East." It tended much to honor the Saviour. We had a very melting season. Evening, at Great Crosshall Street Room, one soul was made happy by believing. Another sinner professed to receive blessing.

19th.—At 3 o'clock preached at the Prince's Pierhead. The brethren had been removed from the best preaching-place, where I used to preach. I took it and commenced reading the Sermon on the Mount, when a policeman came up and said something, I believe, about desisting. I made no reply. A large, attentive congregation. The brethren, Askey and Taylor, had also a large congregation at George's Dock. After I had done, a policeman very respectfully remonstrated against my preaching there, and we came quietly away. At 6 o'clock Hill Street, a large congregation, from Ez. xxxiii. 11. One or two souls were blessed.

20th.—Walked to WHISTON, eight miles, and preached to the colliers at 4 o'clock. Some were not at work, others came from their work and listened with deep attention. The tears did not make white streaks on their black faces, as when G. Whitfield preached at Kingswood, but tears stood in their eyes. It was most cheering to see their attention; but I was grieved to see an ale-house, close by, much frequented. The brethren visit this place, and Tarbock and Woolton, sometimes on the Lord's Day. A few brethren seem willing to put away sectarianism. Walked home; felt tired, but very happy. Praise the Lord for such opportunities of doing good.

On the 21st, I wrote home :—

"I hope you are well in body and soul, as I am now through mercy. Yesterday I walked 16 miles, and was well repaid by the attention of the colliers. I preached at 4 o'clock, as they were coming out of the pit. Many came with their black faces. My soul was refreshed and gladdened. . . . . We had the shock of an earthquake here last Friday morning. Did it reach Aberdeen? I go to Wales next week, but only for a few days."

THE VALUE OF VIRTUE.

By virtue, understand religion, obedience, Christianity, doing good, likeness to the Lord Jesus Christ. It is more valuable than human *learning* than *literature;* even here it sheds a brighter, purer lustre over the soul. One lesson from the prophet of Nazarth is worth more than all the teaching of the schools. It is more valuable than honor, than fame. Could the reader, without virtue, become a magistrate, a member of parliament, or the monarch of this empire, he would be less honorable than a virtuous peasant, possessing every Christian grace. It is more valuable than *worldly wealth*. With what attention you would read, could I inform you how to obtain £20,000; but I tell you, by reading, hearing, faith, prayer, watchfulness, you may obtain justification, meekness, truth, justice, gentleness, supreme love to God, intense benevolence to man, temperance, patience, courage, self-government; and these are far more valuable than all the gold of the universe. Virtue is more valuable than *earthly pleasures;* such as dancing, gaming, the stage, inebriety, sensuality, gay society, and, in one word, all the pleasures of sense. These are not worthy to be compared to the high pleasure of resisting sin; of having a mind firmly set on doing right, and a heart beating high with benevolence to our race. *Poverty* and *outward afflictions* are not our greatest evils. Man, under the power of *evil dispositions*, is more wretched than the holy Lazarus, who seeks the crumbs which fall from the rich man's table. The cruel and malignant man is more wretched than the sick; the drunkard, than the impoverished; the extortioner than the poor customer whom he fleeces; the profane than the bereaved. It is a great calamity to lose health, or property, or friends: it is a greater to lose decision of soul, cheerfulness of mind, self-respect, and to be doomed to perpetual murmuring and discontent. It is esteemed as a calamity to be born of poor, obscure parents, it should be viewed as a much greater, to be born of parents whose minds are poor and ignoble, whose minds soar not to the Saviour and the performance of his high commands. Food and raiment, about which worldly men concern themselves so much, are great blessings, and Christians should do their utmost that all may have them. But I had rather see my readers clothed with righteousness or virtue, than in the finest broad-cloth; and my female readers adorned with a meek and quiet spirit, than the richest silks and satins. Many of you can never reach the wealth of the rich and noble; but higher wealth is within the reach of you all. Many of the afflictions and losses of life you cannot shun, but you may all shun greater evils, bad dispositions and sins. You may all cease to do evil, and learn to do well.

25th.—Brother Joseph Hassalwood and I came to WALES. In the evening I lectured to a large congregation in WOODLANE CHAPEL, a very plain building, but paid for within a few pounds; its sittings all free; and, as no collections from the world are made in it, the gospel is presented to sinners without money and without price.

26th.—Broke bread with a number of brothers and sisters. The history of this is very interesting, a number of females met for mutual instruction and edification, and they wished to break bread; a number of brethren meet with them. They generally have wine, but this morning they could not get any unfermented, and they used water instead. At 9 'clock brother Hassalwood preached in the Lane, near Hawarden. At half-past 10 o'clock I lectured on Luke vi. 20, to a large assembly. At half-past 2 preached on Luke ii. 10, to a large congregation at Lane End, BUCKLEY; it was a time of weeping. At 6 o'clock Woodlane Chapel was filled to overflowing, some were standing at the windows outside. Preached from Acts ii. 21 and Rom. x. 3. After preaching invited all who wished further instruction to come forward; one young man came at once, and while weeping abundantly, sat down; three more came forward. We did one thing at a time; there is no need of confusion when souls get saved. At the close of the meeting I asked the young man if he was happy, and reconciled to God through the death of his Son. He replied, "Yes, glory be to God, he has forgiven me, and set my soul at liberty." This young man, and two others were awakened under the afternoon sermon, and got his mother and two sisters to pray with him between the services.

27th.—At a quarter-past 12 lectured at Hawarden. As William Trotter was hindered from preaching in this village by the Police, it was expected that I should be hindered, but it was not so. I made a few remarks on Puseyism and pleasing men. There are several clergymen in this neighborhood who are preaching Puseyite notions. The Christians of this village are much tempted to please the proprietor of the soil, and his brother, the Rector, who seem to be doing their best to put out, or keep out, of their property those Christians who have too much regard to the simplicity of New Testament religion to hear in the steeple house. When will those who profess the religion of love learn its kind and tender spirit? Evening, in Brother Bennion's barn, Moor; well filled. Three seeking mercy.

28th.—Woodlane Chapel crowded, as on the 26th. This evening and the last, I divided my lecture each night into two parts. One part I addressed to believers, and the other to unbelievers. Seven came forward as seekers of salvation. The greater part believed, and were made happy. I leave Wales with some degree of regret. Had I made arrangements for preaching for a week, I doubt not that souls might have been saved every night in considerable numbers. The meetings were deeply serious; some of them powerful and affecting. I trust the last day will show much fruit from this visit. Several of the brethren and sisters here have been buried with Christ by baptism; some still cleave to sprinkling, and some hold only the baptism of the Holy Spirit. Yet they all seem to live in love. Why not?

31st—HYDE, Cheshire. A few meet in the Lord's name. Preached in the Cross Street Chapel, but pure religion seems to be at a low ebb. The village is deluged with ale. Christian assemblies are less frequented than ale-houses. How should Christians discountenance drinking customs, when they see souls and bodies ruined forever by strong drink?

April, 2nd.—MANCHESTER. At half-past 10 discoursed in Bootle Street. The disciples who meet here have, during the last few months, renounced a sectarian name. On the evening of this day, after a brother had preached in this room, eight souls professed to obtain forgiveness through faith in Christ. At half-past 2 I preached on London Road to an interesting congregation. At 6, at Pendleton. Two souls professed to be blessed. One seemed a very clear case of conversion.

5th and 6th.—GLASGOW. Lectured in the Presbyterian Chapel, or Church, as it is called, near the Green, where Alexander Denovan and others preach without salary. The 6th was the Fast Day. Thousands were going on pleasure excursions by steam-boats, railways, &c. The Fast Days in Scotland, before the half-yearly or yearly communions, are mis-named; they are mere preaching-days. I never knew anybody fast on them, and being unauthorised by the Scriptures, as they are now held, they should be given up. Fasting is a Scriptural duty, but the Fast Days of Scotland are a mockery on Fasting. I preached on the Green at 4 o'clock to a large congregation, and answered some questions which were proposed, when I had done. When all the services were over, conversed for some time with a number of Christians, who wish to promote the unity of the church. I trust something will soon be done in this large city.

8th.—Sailed for ABERDEEN. I was looking over several numbers of "The Peace Advocate," a monthly, well-conducted paper, issued at one penny, from Newcastle. A gentleman desired to have one, then another, till they were all occupied. I read a few extracts from "A Kiss for a Blow." A soldier was reading the "Peace Advocate," as two or three soldiers did, and desired me to read an extract which he pointed out. I did so. It was severe against war; an interesting conversation resulted. This is a useful way of spreading Peace principles.

May 1st.—Had a most cheering church meeting. In some cases of discipline the church manifests greater soundness than formerly.

3rd.—OLD MELDRUM. Lectured and preached the Gospel in the Square to an attentive congregation, and was desired to hasten back again.

4th.—INVERURIE. Out of doors, an attentive congregation, one minister present. It seems a hard place.

5th.—Preached at Inverurie again, and brother William Keil, who was with me, went to KINTORE. He, being a stranger, inquired who was worthy—asked if there were any Christians in the village? He was answered in the affirmative. He took out his pencil and wished for their names; only one was given. He walked forward to another part of the village, made the same inquiry, and the same name was given. This scriptural plan led him to a Christian who treated him kindly, and assisted in getting up a good meeting.

10th.—Sailed for the south; did not know exactly what places to visit, but prayed for divine guidance; after taking a ticket for Arbroath, I did not see my way clear to land there, but arranged to go on to Elie. A friend of mine easily obtained the school-room in EARLSFERRY, in which the parish minister preaches every Lord's Day evening. We had many present, considering the short notice. One dear sister, my friend's wife, who used to receive me as one of the Lord's messengers, had passed into the skies. How uncertain is life! By parting with it the Christian loses nothing; "to die is gain." O that her children, and numerous grand-children, may embrace her Saviour, and follow her so far as she followed Christ.

11th.—ANSTRUTHER Independent Chapel. When I was here about eight years ago, the Independents and Baptists had been in one church and had divided, and since then neither party seems to enjoy much prosperity. Two ministers present at the lecture.

12th.—EARLSFERRY. When I was here some years ago, my friends had been the means of an agreement being come to, that any Christian minister of good character should have the chapel. Now one trustee agreed. The minister was seen; he had no objection, if I would not advocate baptism and church government. I and my brethren thought it better to be free from fetters, so I took the school-room again.

13th.—Rose before four o'clock and walked about six miles, through a very heavy rain to CELLAR DYKES, to preach to the dear fishermen. I was asked to two or three places to breakfast; told them all that I would breakfast with some of them, on the condition that no fisherman asked me. D. K., a fisherman, asked me, and I felt more honored at his table, than I should have done in sitting down with the Queen. When I sat down to the "loaves and fishes," I remembered that my Saviour used to partake of such provisions, and sat with such persons. May I resemble his moral qualities as well as parts of his outward condition. At half-past eight, A.M., should have preached on the Shore to the dear fishermen, but the rain drove us into a school-room, in which I preached with comfort, distributed tracts, and thanks to my heavenly Father, though I stood and preached in my wet clothes, and remained in them till I reached Dundee, after mid-day, I am not aware of taking the least cold. At half-past seven evening, preached to a very large congregation on the Shore of Dundee, without molestation. The authorities are quiet as lambs now as to open-air preaching. The opposers are either tired of their work, off the bench, or in their graves. Gabriel Miller, Clerk to the Magistrates, was found drowned near this place since I was here before. We move in a world, under a government of rectitude, which will do right.

14th.—At eight o'clock in the morning, open-air, West Port, an attentive congregation. Had four congregations to-day, all large and attentive; one soul, the child of many prayers, was smitten to the heart under the truth. She was made happy by embracing the gospel.

17th.—Another sister now believes. (Since the above was written they have both been added to the church).

ARBROATH.—At eight o'clock evening, open-air, very large congregation. As some Christians had desired me to lecture on Christianity, and against Socialism, as the the latter was spreading, I did so on the 18th and 19th, and gave the Socialists liberty to speak in opposition, after each lecture. At the last they challenged me to a regular discussion. I agreed, provided that the proceeds of the discussion, after paying expenses, should not be shared by either party, but given to the poor, or to some benevolent institution. The Socialists' Secretary said, that he was instructed by James Myles, the challenger, from Glasgow, to say that he would not discuss unless he should have half the expenses and the proceeds. I declined their terms, but accepted the challenge, on condition that neither party should reap any pecuniary benefit.

28th.—LEOCHEL-CUSHNIE. At half-past seven had a prayer meeting at the Mill of Eonentyre; at half-past nine preached in a barn at the Mill of Fowlis. The barn was tolerably filled. At three o'clock discoursed to a few old people, and at five, preached to a large and deeply affected congregation at the Mains of Corse.

30th.—Walked across the mountains to LUMPHANNON, amid snow and sleet; called on a Christian afflicted deeply, but very happy. Preached in the schoolroom.

31st.—Walked back to Mains of Corse. Lochnagar was covered with snow. A large congregation, and much liberty. Two young men proposed several questions, which I answered as clearly as I could. Circulated several tracts among them. The people in this neighborhood speak as though they were afraid of the Laird and the minister, though I could not see for what reason. Persons should never act contrary to their consciences merely to please man.

GREAT MEETING ON CHRISTIAN UNION.

On the 1st of June a great meeting was held in Exeter Hall to promote Christian Union. It was addressed by speakers of various denominations, from the Establishment, Presbyterians, Independents, Wesleyans, Baptists, &c. Why were not some of those brethren speakers, who have practically renounced sectarianism? About 5000 were assembled in the Hall, one congregation in the Lower Room, and another in Great Queen Street Chapel. Several of the speakers appeared to feel that something more was requisite to effect the unity of the church than meeting once a year in London. J. A. James, of Birmingham said, " There could no more two churches than two suns in the solar system, and however divided into sections, there was but one church, including within its limits the good of all, the bad of none." Then, if there is to be but one church, sects and parties must be abolished. Isaac Taylor urged the meeting to come to something tangible, and that they could not move forward consistently without church fellowship. Did he not know that there are brethren far in advance of this movement, in various parts of the kingdom, who meet together in the Lord's name, to learn and do all his will?

June 1st. Crossed over to ALFORD. In this parish lives William M'Combie.

27th.—A discussion in ARBROATH between myself and James Myles, of Glasgow, this evening. He was to prove that Socialism is true, and calculated to promote the benefit of mankind. I took the negative, and proposed a number of questions which he never answered.

28th.—This evening, James Myles and I continued the Discussion. I undertook to prove that Christianity is true, and calculated to benefit mankind. He took the negative. I seldom, perhaps never, heard such blasphemies uttered against the Bible. He dealt largely in assertion, without attempting proof. The second night has led me to question the propriety of subjecting a promiscuous audience to hear such blasphemies. The Lord give direction in all these matters.

July 2nd.—ABERDEEN this evening and the last two Lord's Day evenings. The Lord's work has been going on gloriously; five or six souls have been seeking mercy each evening, and always some have been made happy by believing the gospel. If the conversion of one sinner gives joy to angels, how much more the conversion of many sinners.

EVILS OF WAR.

11th.—Succeeded in obtaining Andrew Mackay's release from the army. Three young men, the sons or friends of Christians, have enlisted into the army. I have been led to ask,—Had I taught the parents, and had the parents taught their children, the evils of war, some years ago, could these painful events have transpired? Andrew Mackay, a fatherless and motherless young man, in Aberdeen, had enlisted while in a state of intoxication. He had been for several years sober, till within a short time before this. When he became sober again, he was alarmed at what he had done, but was without money and immediate friends. One pound was required in a few hours —four days from the time of his enlistment. This was called *paying the smart*. I collected a portion and borrowed the rest. If Christians were duly impressed with the sinfulness of war,—if they regarded it as a transgression of the commands of Christ and the Holy Spirit,—" Love your enemies. Do good to them that hate you. If thine enemy hunger, feed him, if he thirst give him drink," they would exert their influence to prevent young men from binding themselves to worse than slavery for *twenty-one years*. Then it seems there has been going forward a system of taking children from the workhouse into the army.

12th.—OLD MELDRUM. The last time that I was here, friends thought they could give the Temperence Hall. The Temperance Committee accordingly granted it. But they have let it to the Free Protesting Church, and have not the entire control; accordingly, the secretary gave a line to George Garoch, the minister, to say that they granted it for two meetings, and hoped he would throw no obstacle in the way. I waited on G.G., with one of the committee. A conversation ensued.

G.G.—"I know a little of you, but not so much as to induce me to grant the hall. What sect do you belong to?"

J.B.—"No sect at all. I am a Christian, and belong only to Christ's Church."

G.G.—"That is far too indefinite: we are all Christians."

J.B.—"The difference between us is this: I am a Christian ONLY, and wish to be nothing more, and to be called only by those names which I find in the New Testament."

G.G.—"But Christ has established a visible church on the earth, and we should make our Christianity visible. What church do you meet with?"

J.B.—"I also think the church should be visibly one. The brethren with whom I meet, assemble for worship in Flower-mill-lane, Aberdeen."

G.G.—"Do you belong to the Plymouth Brethren?"

J.B.—There are a number of believers meeting in the Lord's name in Manchester, and other places, called by the world 'Plymouth brethren,' but they deny the name; so do we. I am not aware that we are called 'Plymouth Brethren.' We do not wish any party name. We have no law-book but the Scriptures, and we wish to have none but scriptural names."

G.G.—"But Jesus Christ has established a government in his church—elders and office-bearers."

J.B.—"So we think, and because He is King, and has given laws to His church, neither Presbyteries, Synods, nor Assemblies, have any right to change or amend these laws any more than the Court of Session or Parliament."

G.G.—"But the elders have authority to expound those laws."

J.B.—"Yes, certainly, but not to amend them and make new ones: all that they have to do is to teach and practise the laws which Jesus Christ has given us."

G.G.—"You seem to be 'Independents,' as you seem to think that each church should manage its own affairs."

J.B.—"No, we are not 'Independents;' none but God is independent."

G.G.—"The Committee of the Free Church have the granting of the hall; I shall take no part in either granting it, or opposing its being granted. It rests with the Committee."

J.B.—"Are there many of them?"

G.G.—"About ten or twelve."

J.B.—"Could they be got together soon?"

G.G.—"I cannot say."

J.B.—"Perhaps you could give us some of their names, and we could call upon them?"

G.G.—"I do not think I shall give you any names: I will have nothing to do with it."

13*th.*—INVERURIE. Open-air congregation not large. Soon after I began, ———, Esq., in a gig with a spirited horse, which he whipped, drove up out of the road, through the congregation, at a rapid rate. One of the wheels of the gig hit the chair on which I stood, and brought me to the ground. I felt pain in my knee and right side, and somewhat sickly, but I immediately stood up, and proceeded with my discourse. Some wished us to apprehend him, but I told them that we ought to act upon the principle of non-resistance, taught by Jesus Christ, and "overcome evil with good." At the conclusion of the service, I was led to pray publicly for the poor man, who had acted thus towards us, and to thank God that no life had been forfeited by his unaccountable conduct. It seemed to be wonderful that no one was killed or seriously injured. We are in the hands of God, who says, "The very hairs of your head are all numbered." How soon are we made to see that we owe our lives to His care, who alone can secure them from danger!

15*th.*—William Maitland sent for me, and expressed his approbation of the truths which I had preached, and that he was much affected by the Christian manner in which I had treated Collehill.* Before I came away, he said, "I wish you to do for me what you did for Collehill." We kneeled down and I prayed with him; after which he desired me to remember him at a throne of grace. While on my way to the canal boat I saw the gentleman that drove his gig through us on the 13th. I accosted him, and asked him if he was aware of what he had done. He stated that he did not know; but was very sorry. I told him that I concluded that he was either a determined persecutor of the Lord's people, or intoxicated. He denied the former, but stated that he had been taking liquor, and was very sorry. I said that if he was intoxicated he should consider the consequence,—that he might easily have killed or wounded some one, and that in future he might either kill or injure himself if he continued to take strong drink. He was very sorry and kind. May the Lord make this a blessing to us all. I never witnessed anything so alarming in any part of these kingdoms.

30th.—FRASERBURGH. At half-past 9 a.m., in the open-air; the rain drove us off. The Free Church having no minister, wished the Congregational supply, Mr. Howison, in the forenoon. I had agreed and intimated last night that I should preach in the Independent chapel at 2 o'clock. They wished me to take the morning instead. I refused; but agreed either to preach for the Free Church, or take two services in the Independent Chapel. Had overflowing congregations at 11 and 2 o'clock. Heard Howison at 6; I think if he continues to preach he will not live long.

31st.—At 8 o'clock this morning had an attentive congregation of fishermen in the open-air. I do love to talk to these dear men. At 8 p.m., in the Independent Chapel. I begin to have some doubts whether it is well to lecture in these chapels against the sectarianism which the people support. The Lord direct me.

August, 1st.—Walked to STRICHEN, eight miles; preached in a place of worship open for all preachers; a small congregation, but a very refreshing season. One old man asked several questions, chiefly on baptism. As I could get no other place I slept at an inn, some drunken men made such a noise that I could not sleep till about midnight, when they broke up.

10th.—Fast Day, or preaching day. Spoke in the Square to a considerable number. Walked to NEW DEER. Small company, as they had little notice. Dr. Smith entertained me, he seemed anxious that I should return, or any other Evangelist, and he would aid us in our work.

11th.—At ELLON; large congregation. A drunken doctor rode into the congregation with his horse, and frightened a few. Set off to walk home at half-past four a.m.; a gig came up and took me near home, in this I saw the Lord's kindness. I think I have not walked so much in fourteen days these fourteen years.

16th.—This evening, after near two months' discipline, we were obliged to withdraw from George Cornwall, who once was expected to be a great blessing to the church.

---

* The name of the farm.

NEW DEER, August 20, 1843.

MY DEAR FRIEND,—

I have read most of your pamphlets with much pleasure, and I hope, with profit also. I long for another visit from you; I pray Divine wisdom may so direct your movements that you may have an opportunity of visiting New Deer again, and also, I trust that your efforts may be attended with success here, as they have been elsewhere. I agree with many of your sentiments, and only want strength from on high to enable me to act on them. With respect to baptism, I have for upwards of a year or more been of your mind on the subject, but alas, circumstances have been against my views, want of decision too, is a sad enemy. Self, in a word, is man's greatest enemy. Had such not been the case, Jesus would not have required us to deny ourselves, as the first step of grace. I much desire an interest in your prayers. Union among believers is a grand idea. New Testament principles must be adopted, as the grand means for effecting a union and a reformation of the church. Men are fond of novelties. New sects invent some imposing things or names, but as a wise man has it, there is nothing new under the sun, neither in matter or mind. The materials of the world are as old as the creation, only new combinations of old matter. Moral excellence is also coeval with its author. The plans of moral improvement may be new to us, but the plan of mercy was known to God from all eternity. The new commandment given by our Lord to love one another has been much overlooked by Christians. It is however the *sine qua non* of genuine Christianity, because every Christian must love the image of Christ, as he loves the original from whence the image is derived. I have often wondered much about the 2nd commandment, and thought really in presumption that the 1st almost comprehended the 2nd, and was partly led to think others were of the same mind seeing what is said about it by ministers and commentators; however, it now appears to me pretty clear that the propriety of such a command is necessary and indispensable, as man is liable to err. From the second commandment we may naturally infer that God wishes us to make no material representation of him, nor to bow down nor serve, &c., but he commands us to do what we can to make images of him and Christ in the human souls, and to love those which will be productive of the purest pleasure that we can enjoy from gratifying the social affections of the soul. To this love it is feared many even of God's people are too great strangers. Schism and denomination and party spirit have all done their work to destroy love among the brethren. Impure communion is a crying evil; no church can prosper while it is tolerated; no sanction is given for it in Scripture. Men are called on to make use of their judgment in reference to themselves and others,—Oh how kind to arouse the careless,—admit them once into communion with a reforming church, and it will act as a sedative to their feelings and merely keep them insensible, while the fatal disease, sin, is effecting its work of ruin on their souls. Now, much has to be done to clear away the mist from our eyes. Oh! for the divine unction of the eye-salve of the Spirit of truth.

Please send a few copies of the New Testament Principles which I wish to circulate. I would feel much obliged by your writing me a few lines. That it may be well with you in time, and that you may find mercy in that great day of dread, decision, and despair, is the wish of yours

In the bonds of love and Christian charity,

To John Bowes.   GEO. SMITH.

Dr. Smith, came to Dundee, united with us in Union Hall, left me one of his executors, and died in 1867.

DISCUSSION ON BAPTISM.

A friendly discussion or conversation on this subject took place between me and Alexander Monro, Independent Minister, Blackhills, in the Bellfield schoolroom, near Aberdeen, on August 22nd.

The meeting was crowded. Ere we went in to the congregation, Mr. Monro proposed, as the audience was English, that we should use no Greek. I rejoined, that as we were to discuss about a Greek word, we should give its meaning. He said there was no need, as he agreed with me that immersion was baptism. As I wished to instruct the people I had brought my Greek books, and used them. Mr. Monro said, "when the child was baptized there was a dipping in the case, as the minister's hand was dipped in the water." "Then," I said, "after this people retiring might say, on Mr. Monro's authority, "The minister's hand was baptized," not the child since it had only been sprinkled. This is one way that has seldom been tried of coming to a knowledge of the truth on this subject. Investigation must do good to well-disposed minds—these only are fitted to enjoy truth; minds ill-disposed get no blessing from even the gospel itself. Let us have the happiness of reporting many such friendly discussions among Christians as this. The friends of truth are always willing to hear both sides. If any one is unwilling to hear both sides, he is prejudiced, and not a sincere lover of God's glorious truth.

Sept. 3rd.—LIVERPOOL. In the morning at Hill Street; afternoon, broke bread at Great Crosshall Street; at six o'clock, preached at Hill Street.

The following communication will give some idea how we treated a a brother who pressed his own views on the brethren, the only case I remember of real difficulty.

"The church having learned that an erroneous impression has been made on brother Burrows' mind, in reference to a note sent him by brother Hassalwood, in the hurry of business, deems it right now to state its mind on this question.

"It deems it to be the duty of Christians 'to keep the unity of the Spirit in the bond of peace,' to follow the things which make for peace;' and it states 'that if any man be contentious, we have no such custom, neither the churches of God.' We fear that some of the late proceedings of our dear brother Burrows have tended to contradiction and contention, but we do not prohibit him from either teaching or preaching the truth in love, but we do prohibit him from teaching or preaching in the spirit of strife and contention, believing that the servant of the Lord should not strive, but be gentle, easy to be entreated, and full of love. We would now, therefore, request our dear brethren that teach and rule in the church, to reason with our dear brother, and we would beseech him in great love to listen to counsels of love, union, and peace, and be much in prayer with God, that he may guide him into all truth and wisdom.—*September 4th.*"

19th.—Tea meeting. Dr. Burrows gave us some views of sanctification which I should like to have inserted in the magazine. F. Drinkwater stated that he was brought to God about three years ago, by hearing me at Hyde. I was thankful to God, and led to say, "I expect to see many strange children in heaven that were converted by my preaching here, but without my knowledge." Glory be given to God.

20th.—This morning, learned from William Crossfield that two members were added to Great George's Street Independent Church, Thomas Raffles', a short time ago, who dated their conversion, William Crossfield believed, to their hearing me at the shore. I had heard of them before, they were led to Christ about two years ago. It was no momentary impression. Glory and praise to the author of the Gospel.

October 1st.—MANCHESTER. Preached the Sunday School sermons; I have not done anything like this for some years. The offering at the door, going out, was voluntary, only Christians were solicited to give. £13 11s. 9½d. collected.

12th.—MOSSLEY. Here labors Amos Dyson, formerly a minister in the New Connexion, author of a very useful work on "Primitive Christianity." He seems to be a zealous laborer. He and a few others purchased a large hand-bell to ring people together, when they wish to obtain hearers on short notice. This is better than singing through the streets to obtain a congregation. Several at Mossley have been baptized; a few break bread weekly, and upwards of 200 meet in the Lord's name alone. They seem a very loving, inquiring people. They have no seat-rents, but collections and instrumental music remain. They will not pretend that the New Testament sanctions either. The congregations here are very encouraging. If the rulers keep the church pure, and "hold fast the form of sound words" which they have received, and kindly forbear with each other, this church will be a great blessing.

HURST.—Amos Dyson and Thomas Grundy used the bell here with success; about sixty meet in the name of Christ only.

STALEY-BRIDGE.—About 130 meet here; but as I saw very few of them, I can bear no report. My lecture was miserably attended. I met privately with two or three vigorous minds and Christian hearts. John Russell, who seems to have been useful in Yorkshire, has come to labor among them.

LEES.—The Total Abstinence Society had announced a Temperance meeting, and the Christian brethren, in three separate places, had intimated my lecture in the same place; we divided the time. I have no hope of promoting temperance by downright levity. Men are not to be laughed out of their sins. Drunkenness is a serious evil, and should be treated seriously. About twenty or more Christians meet here.

OLDHAM.—Christians of various denominations attended the lecture. Several questions were asked, after, chiefly on baptism. Dear Baptist brethren, perhaps unintentionally, when they appear to contend for nothing so earnestly as baptism, seem to put it far above its place. Baptism is a part of the Christian religion, but it is not every part. No text says, "Faith, hope, baptism, these three, but the greatest of these is baptism." And yet there might have been some such text, were we to judge of Scripture by men's zeal for some parts. Every part of the written Word is important and beautiful in its own place; when taken out of it, it loses its attractions. Let us value "love" more than baptism. About fifty brethren meet here.

ROCHDALE.—About fifty or sixty meet here; and if they live in love, to the Lord and each other, they will be useful.

BIRMINGHAM.—Had a very sweet meeting with the brethren here—about twenty. Preached in the open-air, near the London Railway Station; a considerable number of attentive hearers. A local preacher of the Wesleyan Association got the open-air sermon intimated to his brethren in their own chapel; this was very kind and brotherly. In this large town our beloved brother Anderson preaches in the open-air, but his efforts are not sufficiently countenanced by his brethren.

TIPTON.—Canal Street Chapel. Some years ago, I was sent for to preach the anniversary sermons, and make collections in this Chapel. I was willing to preach, but not to make a collection. My services were, of course, declined, as the people wanted me chiefly for the sake of the collection, but they kindly offered me their chapel if I ever should come this way. This evening the promise was honorably redeemed. Several questions were asked after the lecture, chiefly relating to seat rents, chapel debts, and ministers' salaries. The Lord enabled me to speak faithfully, and I hope kindly.

PENSNETT.—Here a few very precious souls meet in the Lord's name alone. I was afraid, from a note which I had received from one brother, that their views on the Lord's pre-millennial advent, had made them so narrow as to border on sectarianism. When I visited them, my fears were removed. They were very kind and brotherly. It is possible, however, to put away sectarianism in name, while the thing itself is still retained. Let us carefully watch against this. I hope never to love a dear brother less, because he expects the Lord sooner than I do.

WEDNESBURY.—Here the early Methodists met with some of their fiercest persecutions. A dear brother circulated about 400 small bills, intimating "a lecture on the only true bond of union among Christians." As we had no church present, the lecture began and ended without singing or prayer. We never read of Jesus Christ and the early preachers either preaching or publicly discoursing to the world, in connexion with prayer and singing, these appear to be church ordinances.

BIRSTAL, YORKSHIRE.—Here lived and labored John Nelson. I felt no ordinary interest in the place. About sixteen have come together to learn and teach all the Lord's will. One of them, Daniel Hopkinson, was a Wesleyan local preacher, and was put off the plan for preaching John Wesley's views on the right use of money.

HECKMONDWIKE.—About seventy-five meet to break bread weekly. Congregation large.

BATLEY.—Very crowded congregations. An infant church very prosperous. They are commencing a new chapel: I hope they will not burden themselves with debt. I was informed by a minister of Christ that two highwaymen have been converted here, and are now found clothed and in their right minds. A mighty work is going forward; may the whole village feel it.

BERKENSHAW.—Between thirty and forty believers, they come chiefly from the Wesleyans, having chiefly come out since Jonathan Porritt, a local preacher, left them.

BRADFORD.—A sad falling off here since last year. The Chapel is in debt; seats are let to pay the interest. William Trotter and Thomas Smith have withdrawn from this place. The Lord draw together his own dear people. J—, who resided in this neighborhood some years ago, was seized with a rheumatic fever which confined him ten months. During all that time, though a local preacher in the Wesleyan Association, not one of the members visited him; had he been a rich man, would they have remained ten days without visiting him? After the ten months he went to Batley poorhouse, and remained there about three years. He used to go out and preach at surrounding Chapels on the first day of the week, and then return to the parish workhouse to eat and sleep. Surely there must be something wrong here. Christians should not forget the poor, especially if they labor in word and doctrine.

BRIGHOUSE.—About 130 meet here calling themselves after Christ, seat-rents and collections remain, and several New Testament usages have not been commenced. What a blessed thing it is to be willing to know, learn, and do all that God commands.

HUDDERSFIELD.—About seventy-five meet here. No seat-rents, no collections. One service for free ministration, for any brother to teach according to the ability which God giveth. About fourteen commenced the meeting two years ago; the increase has been very encouraging. They seem to be forward to remember the poor.

BERRY BROW.—There are a few dear souls meeting in much weakness. May the Lord strengthen them.

HOME-LANE-END.—By a singular chain of providential circumstances, I was led to this place. A brother from Bradford, through what appeared to be a mistake, had given out for me to visit this place on the same evening that I had arranged to go either to Baildon or Birstal. As it was intimated, I went; found about 30 brethren, having a comfortable place of meeting, about free from debt; but wishing some brother to reside among them as a teacher of the week-day school, and preacher. I recommended James Grinstead, who has since gone, with the prayers of the Aberdeen church, that he may make known the Saviour to the conversion of sinners, and the building up of believers.

GLASGOW.—A few brethren meet in the Lord's name alone here. Indeed, as in several other large towns or cities, there are two meetings. I got a few of the brethren of each to converse together, and I trust it will end in more brotherly union. The one meeting does not break bread weekly. I hope, while both are careful to add to their communion only the renewed and obedient believers, of whom the spiritual temple should be composed, that they will love as brethren.

Two young men at HAWARDEN, in Wales, one married, had wrought some years at the Iron Foundry, and after they were taught the sinfulness of war, they began to feel that it was wrong to make the instruments of death, guns and cannon. Accordingly, when required to make them, they respectfully declined. They were willing to take inferior work to oblige their employer, but this did not satisfy. They were dismissed, and were for some weeks without employment, but I believe are now in work in different and distant parts of the kingdom. If war is wrong, it is wrong to fire cannon; if wrong to fire it at our enemies, it is wrong to take it to the field of battle; and if wrong to take it, it must be wrong to make it.

At HUDDERSFIELD, I heard of two brethren, and conversed with one of them, employed in the cloth-finishing department. It was their business to write on the cloth its quality. It seems to be quite customary to write *Superfine* and *Saxony* on cloth which is not superfine, and not Saxony. They were required to do this at an establishment a few miles from Huddersfield. They refused to write what they knew was false. They were dismissed. They both have large families, and were a long time without employment, and must have endured great privation to keep a good conscience, and not to injure society. Clubs and Benefit Societies will support their members when turned off work for not taking lower wages than they allow, but not when turned off work for refusing to do what is morally wrong. Christian churches should be forward to aid and encourage such of their brethren as nobly act like those at Hawarden and Huddersfield.

Nov. 11th.—Sailed by the "Admiral" steamer for Scotland. Several sailors were fighting fiercely, gave each other black eyes, and wounded each other's faces to the spilling of blood. I saw one apparently about to throw himself overboard; another, the wildest of the whole, was again about to fight; I called him aside, and, in the language of kindness, remonstrated with him. He did not fight. Before we left the vessel, he was very thankful, and said, "You have acted like a father to me." How encouraging to meet gratitude in such a soil.

15th.—Sailed from Edinburgh (Granton) by the "Bonnie Dundee" for Aberdeen. An infidel, if not an Atheist, on board, tolerably well versed in the common-place objections which infidels generally bring against the Scriptures. He had not attended a place of worship for twenty years. He stated he was very miserable, and had long been so. He seemed to imagine that poor men were all miserable. I assured him that religion made many of them happy, and that I could find many men, as poor as he, whose Christianity had made them really happy. A passenger said to him, "It I believed as you do, I would rid myself of ALL my misery by committing suicide." I said, "You have made the candid acknowledgment that infidelity makes you miserable; leave it. I recommend Christianity to you; it makes me happy; I feel it is happiness to live. It will make you happy also, only embrace it.

Dec. 1st.—KINMUCK, Parish of Keith-hall. Lectured on the evils of schism, and on the love and union which ought to exist among Christians. Several written questions were given me to answer. This seemed to give information, which was needed. Temperance is a subject which gets exhausted in a few lectures; the minds of men require variety. It is the duty of Christian churches to furnish that variety; when they do not, it is pleasing to see divine truth promoted, either by individuals or associated Christians. "The Friends," who have only five meetings in Scotland, have a meeting here, the farthest north of any. They seem anxious to be useful to their rural neighbors. The truths taught seemed to be well received. Thanks be to God for all his mercies. Let Christians see to it, that the plan of salvation be clearly taught to their neighbors.

THE FREE PROTESTING CHURCH.

In May this year, the Free Church was formed; which I thus noticed in the *Christian Magazine,* Vol I. p. 119:—

"Upwards of 469 ministers, a large number of students, and tens of thousands of people, have withdrawn from the Scottish Establishment, and formed themselves into another denomination. What effect this large secession may have upon the promotion of love to God and man, time alone can fully show. There is much to hope and much to fear. To hope,—inasmuch as the ministers have nobly sacrificed earthly comfort and wealth to a sense of duty—such men, one would trust, if they only see their duty, will go farther. Some of them have already advocated greater purity of communion, than they had previously enjoyed, and have boldly attacked the impure communion of 'the Kirk.' They are exerting themselves zealously for promoting their own views. This is preferable to slumbering inactivity. In addition to this, they have shown a disposition to co-operate with Christians beyond the pale of their newly-formed society. They have also amongst them several men of considerable talent; and from their weight and influence, may hasten the separation between the now Moderate party in the church and the state. These, and more than these might be enumerated, are favorable symptoms. But, on the other hand, there is much to fear. Some of the ministers and churches have no knowledge of what a Christian church should be; they take all the old materials in a parish that choose to declare themselves Non-intrusionists—of course if they take those who do not even profess to be Christians, such societies do not deserve the name of Christian churches. They have also formed a *new sect* (as though we had not a sufficient number already) called the 'Free Protesting Church.' Perhaps they did not see the sinfulness of making a new sect, but they may yet come to see it, and to declare themselves Christians, and *Christians only*, willing to hold fellowship with all who hold it with the Head. They still adhere to the Confession of Faith and the Catechisms—to human creeds—and still they meet to make human laws, by their Assembly, for the governing of that church, which ought to obey no law but Christ's. Still they let seats; apply to wicked men for support; have a one-man ministry; hinder the teaching of the Holy Spirit through the members; call their ministers unscriptural names; have too much cheering in their religious meetings; neglect scriptural baptism; do not break bread on the first day of the week; and even hold the principle of an Establishment; and this, though many of them are still smarting for having contributed large sums of money to erect places of worship, now to be occupied, at the bidding of the state, with Moderate ministers, under whose ministrations (so much do they abhor them) they cannot sit. Let it be our prayer, that all these events may yet be overruled for the good of our race, and for the honor of Christ.

Jan. 15th. 1844.—ABERDEEN. I have now delivered a course of five lectures on the Errors of the Church of Rome, and of the followers of E. B. Pusey. These lectures were announced in consequence of a challenge received twelve months ago. Alexander M'Donald, who sent it, the Romish Priests, and Bishop Skinner, were all invited to defend their erroneous systems. One young man, an Episcopalian, opposed in a very mild manner. The lectures have excited considerable interest, and I trust have done good. I shall be happy to lecture against these dangerous errors wherever I go, if they prevail.

EDINBURGH.—Several of the Free Churches in this city have resolved to abolish seat rents, and are now going on without them. James Begg, one of their ministers, has just published "Reasons why no Seat Rents should be in the Free Church, with Practical Directions for getting on without them." There is also just published, at Dundee, an excellent pamphlet by an Elder of the United Secession, entitled, "The Renting of Church Seats Unscriptural and at Variance with the Voluntary Principle." These are hopeful indications that the churches are desirous to free the Gospel from some of its present fetters.

24th.—To-day I was in some doubt whether to go by sea to Dundee, or walk it. A sailing vessel would cost five shillings; I was a shilling or two short of this small sum. I concluded it was the Lord's will that I should walk it. Met with a Christian upon the road, with whom I had some sweet conversation about the Master. About five o'clock arrived at Stonehaven, intending to lecture on New Testament Principles of Church Order and Union, but was informed that the Socialists had challenged the ministers to discuss their system, and that having declined, they were triumphing over them. I lectured to a large congregation. Many questions were asked, after, such as, "Whether is a Socialist or a corrupt Christian the worst man, and most injurious to society?" I was told by the Socialists that they were not able to meet me, but they gave me a written challenge to meet Henry Jeffery of Edinburgh.

31*st*.—FAULKLAND. A considerable congregation. Hugh Smith, Congregational minister, informed me that his father visited an infidel at Irvine, in his condemned cell, who told him that he was one of thirteen infidels who met every Saturday evening to determine how they would spend the following day. "One," said he, "became a Christian, six were transported, four were hanged, in a room above me is one under sentence of transportation, and I am to be hanged to-morrow!" This was the end of the thirteen. "The wages of sin is death." Infidelity is produced by crime and leads to crime. Men disposed to sin hate the Scriptures because they condemn their vices; and when men have embraced infidelity, and banished the idea of an all-seeing God, and of future rewards and punishments, they feel at liberty to prey upon the feelings and property of mankind. If infidelity does not end thus in all cases, the remains of a Christian education, and the force of Christian principle in the community, may account for it.

Feb. 5th.—During the last seventeen days I visited STONEHAVEN, BERVIE, MONTROSE, ARBROATH, DUNDEE, STRATHMIGLO, FAULKLAND, and NEWBURGH. In about seven days I walked about seventy miles, and lectured and answered questions often two or three hours each night afterwards. In some of the places the seeds of peace and love have been sown by the Magazine, and some are longing and praying for the oneness of the church, and for the formation of churches on the plan laid down in the New Testament. My heart has been more encouraged than I can express. I would recommend Christians to meet together and try to ascertain by a calm but earnest investigation of the scriptures, what is the nature, order, and character of a Christian church. I found a few churches, without pastors, in the Congregational and Baptist denominations, so influenced by the old hierarchical notions, that they have given up the weekly observance of the Lord's Supper. The command, "This do in remembrance of me," although given from the lips of Christ the King, is weekly broken, and does not seem to oblige in the absence of a minister or priest. Is not this the Popery of Protestantism? Strict Baptists will not hold communion with those who cannot see baptism, because, it is said, they disobey a plain command; yet they themselves disobey the command, "This do in remembrance of me," for months and years together, if they have no ordained elder. So do the Congregationalists.

In several of the above places, the Socialists or Infidels were proceeding unchecked.

At STONEHAVEN, I was desired to lecture on their views. I complied; several questions were asked. They confessed they were not able to meet my arguments, and procured Henry Jeffery from Edinburgh. The debate occupied three hours each night, for three nights, viz.—February 6th, 7th, and 8th. The public papers indicated that my lecture had given them a death blow—they did not seem to think so. The first night, I asked, "Is not R. Owen an Atheist?" "Yes." "Are you an Atheist?" No reply. H. J. admitted the being of a God. The second night, I called on him honestly to avow his principles; he had indeed said "I believe in a God." The audience thought him no Atheist; but the second night he said, "I believe in a God, but I don't believe in an intelligent Deity." The third night he denied what he had affirmed the second night, but the chairman and every hearer were witnesses. This was a lamentable exhibition of the turnings of a man who denies responsibility and an intelligent God. I asked him to name what he believed his God to be? but no answer; this left me to conclude that Henry Jeffery is greater than his God, for he has intelligence, but his God has none.

The audience behaved well; at the conclusion, in presence of my respondent, it was proposed, and agreed to without dissent, to meet me and give me some token of approval for the manner in which I had conducted the arguments in favor of Christianity.—The 14th was fixed upon.

I hope something was done in this debate to honor the Lord Jesus Christ. As I was requested to give Henry Jeffery's Creed, I comply with the request of the hundreds who witnessed the debate.

THE UNBELIEVER'S CREED.

"I believe that there is no God, but that matter is God, and God is matter; and that it is no matter whether there is any God or no.

I believe that the world was not made; that the world made itself; and that it had no beginning; that it will last for ever, world without end.

I believe that man is a beast; that the soul is the body, and the body the soul; and that after death there is neither body nor soul.

I believe that there is no religion; that natural religion is the only religion, and that all religion is unnatural.

I believe not in Moses; I believe the first in philosophy; I believe not the Evangelists; I believe in Chubb, Collins, Toland, Tindal, Hobbes, Shaftesbury. I believe in Lord Bolinbroke, Hume, Voltaire, Diderot, Boulanger, Volney, and Thomas Paine. I used to believe in R. Owen, and 'received his writings,' like all other Socialists, as true, 'without mixture of error,' but I have found so many errors in them, that although he has written several hundreds of pages, I only believe in twelve pages of his writings, and if light continue to attend me, it is likely I shall soon disbelieve these twelve as I do all the rest.

I believe not Saint Paul; I believe not revelation; I believe in tradition; I believe in the Talmud; I believe in the Koran; I believe not the Bible; I believe in Socrates; I believe in Confucius; I believe in Sanchoniathan; I believe in Mahomet; I believe in Joseph Smith; I believe not in Christ.

Lastly, I believe in all unbelief."

14th.—Soiree. The following bill was circulated widely :—"TRIUMPH OF CHRISTIANITY! Testimonial to Mr. Bowes. The public are respecfully informed that, in honor of Mr. John Bowes, minister of the gospel, for the interesting and instructive information which he communicated in Stonehaven, on the evenings of the 6th, 7th, and 8th instant, in a discussion with Mr Henry Jeffery, of Edinburgh; in which Mr. Bowes, in the most able manner, established the *glorious truth* of Christianity, and triumphantly refuted the abominable, irrational, atheistical, and demoralising doctrine of Socialism, as propounded by Robert Owen, and adopted, and to a certain extent practised, by a class of men styling themselves Socialists, and pretending to be his followers. A Soiree will take place in the Temperance Hall, on Wednesday evening, 14th February, at seven o'clock, when a Testimonial, to be obtained by subscription, will be delivered to Mr. Bowes, in token of the estimation which the people of Stonehaven and its vicinity entertain of that victory, which, by the force of Immutable Truth, he has achieved over sophistry, blasphemy, atheism, and immorality,—the elements of the deplorable system of Socialism. Mr. Bowes will address the meeting. Subscription papers are in all the shops and public places in town." The tickets were all away early in the forenoon of the 12th. I received a purse of ten sovereigns, to which a minister sent 10s.6d. I was especially pleased to find that two out of the three members of H. Jeffery's committee subscribed to the testimonial; one of them publicly recanted Socialism. Fruits were handed round in the course of the evening. David Todd, U. P. minister, and I, addressed the meeting. He recommended the following measures for preventing infidelity. First, ministers should preach on it. Secondly, each person should at least have one treatise against it, such as Bogue's, Doddridge's, Paley's. Thirdly, Sunday school teachers should make the young acquainted with the evidences. I felt great liberty in stating many truths, which, I trust may do good many days hence.

29th.—Should have sailed this morning from Aberdeen to Leith, on my way to England. A brother who promised to assist me down with luggage, slept too long, and did not come. I was ten minutes behind the time. I trust that it will turn out for the honor and glory of God.

March 5th.—The Dundee steamer, having been damaged in the late gale, did not sail this morning.

6th.—The "Sovereign" was five hours behind her time. I received this morning £1 which I should not have received had the boat sailed at 6 o'clock, from a sister belonging to a Baptist church. We had some very wicked and drunken men on board.

7th.—Called at GLASGOW. Sailed in the "Admiral" for Liverpool. Learned that had I come last Saturday, I should have had a tremendous sea to encounter. Saw the Lord's hand in this and other matters in detaining me.

8th.—Arrived in LIVERPOOL, and was very happy to see a good congregation at Hill Street, which I addressed with great freedom and comfort from Phil. iii., on progressive knowledge, holiness, usefulness, and happiness. I trust my own soul is making progress.

On the 17*th* and 24*th*, I preached in the open-air at the Princes' Dock, in the usual place. A policeman came up, and said it was not allowed. Some of the brethren were a little timid. I told him my name and address, and that if the police wanted me, I would attend in court to-morrow. I finished comfortably without interruption, and heard no more about it. In the evening two souls believed; one the son of a person of some substance.

April 2nd.—ASHTON-UNDER-LYNE. Here a rich timber-merchant made a pernicious application of the wealth which he had acquired, chiefly by his own industry. By drunken and licentious practices he soon squandered tens of thousands of pounds. He produced great misery in several families by seduction, and after reducing himself to poverty and misery, he took a razor to cut himself in pieces; he cut one arm and his throat, of which he died. Not one of his relations or neighbors could be induced to follow him to the tomb; men were hired to put him into a dishonored grave. In one family he had seduced the mother and the daughter; the latter became a prostitute, and the former died about three months before he committed suicide. She had been drinking at a public-house with her husband, who, it appears, for the sake of money, connived at her conduct. After leaving the public-house, she went home alone, and was found dead behind her own door, standing upon her feet. Spontaneous combustion had burned her to death internally, while not a thread of her apparel was singed, but her throat, tongue, and mouth were burned. "The way of transgressors is hard."

7th.—MANCHESTER. Six souls seeking mercy after sermon. Some were made happy by believing the gospel.

8th—Attended the quarterly meeting of the church in Bootle Street. Much prayer was offered up that the differences of judgment might lead to no division. It was a calm, earnest meeting, and likely to do great good. I have for some time thought of removing my family further south. Manchester seems to be the place for the present; but I dare not fix anything definitely till I see the Lord's mind clearly.

12th.—Saw my father at LEEDS. Was deeply affected to learn that he had been severely attacked with spasms in the stomach, a few weeks ago, at Leeds, and narrowly escaped death. May the Lord fit him for His kingdom.

14th.—BIRSTAL. Here lived and labored the celebrated John Nelson, the mason. BATLEY at 6 o'clock, p.m. Four at least were seeking the way of peace: three found salvation in the precious blood of Christ. On the 7th, the brethren opened a new chapel, without a collection,— a new thing in this part of the country. On the day following, the church made a "Feast for the Poor," according to Luke xiv. 12,— "Then said Christ also to him that bade him, When thou makest a dinner or a supper, call not thy friends, nor thy brethren, neither thy kinsmen, nor thy rich neighbors, [the very persons that modern professors generally do call] lest they also bid thee again, and a recompense be made thee; but when thou makest a feast, call the poor, the maimed, the lame, the blind: and thou shalt be blessed; for they cannot recompense thee; for thou shalt be recompensed at the resurrection of the just." About a hundred of the poor, maimed, &c., were the guests at this New Testament feast, which commenced at half-past 4 o'clock, and closed about 9. John Russell and Thomas Smith addressed the assembly on the great truths of the gospel. What a lovely sight must this have been! I would go many miles to be present at such a meeting. I trust the command of Christ, and the example of Batley, will prevail over all the country. About 60 souls have been converted at Batley, some of them great offenders. Two highwaymen are now zealous Christians. Also, two young, but married men, in their wickedness, commenced holding *mock prayer meetings*, from house to house, in derision of the labors of the brethren. These men, and a companion, have embraced the gospel, and now pray in earnest. The Lord has done great things at Batley. Let all his people praise Him.

May 9th.—DUNDEE. I was again presented with a suit of new clothes, from head to foot, by my old Dundee relations in the Lord. Thanks be to the Lord for his goodness.

12th.—Received a letter from J. Grinstead, Holme-lane. He says: "I may just mention one circumstance in connection with your visit to Holme-lane. A person who heard your sermon, purchased your tract on Temperance, and since then has given up using intoxicating drinks, tea, and coffee."

16th.—Visited URY; once the residence of Robert Barclay; now the residence of his descendant, who delights in sporting. In the largest room, or hall, was hung up a painting of the present Robert Barclay, while he walked a thousand miles in London in so many successive hours; representatives of pugilists, cattle that he had fed, and hunting horses. The study of Robert Barclay is a small room close to the large hall. In one room we saw a portrait of a late member of the family who was member of parliament for this county. The "Friends" meeting house is still standing, but is now converted into the residences of servants. The burying ground is about a mile above the house in another part of this beautiful estate. The only excellency that was named to me of the present occupant of this mansion, which possibly may be inherited, is his being extensively kind to the poor.

17th.—John Longmuir, mariners' missionary, Free Church, Aberdeen, was brought up here. His father, who keeps the keys of Dunnoter Castle, and Margaret Duncan, accompanied me to see this romantic place. It is a huge rock, that stands out into the sea, and is almost surrounded by the sea, excepting a neck of land or rock that connects it with the main land. Here tradition says numbers of the Covenanters were imprisoned and tortured, and that some of them in endeavoring to escape, lost their lives by falling down the steep rocks.

20th.—NEWBURGH, near Ellon. As no place had been procured for the lecture, we obtained a barn, which the Free Church has taken for a place of worship. The elder, Mitchell, granted it freely. I was expounding Mark ii., when the proprietor came in and said aloud, "I must lock this door!" I thought the man was intoxicated, and proceeded: but he repeated the words, adding, "Who gave you authority to come here?" I stated our authority; however, as we were not allowed quietly to occupy it, we all quietly walked out, and the door was locked. Thomas Hardacre told the people that I should preach at a small cottage occupied by Elspet Bruce, an afflicted young woman who loves Jesus, but has been for several years confined to her bed. I walked away quite happy, wondering if the Lord intended a sermon for the sick woman, who seldom or never hears one. The cottage was crowded. A farmer, belonging to the Established Church, invited me to take a bed at his house, and when I came away, requested I would make his house my home, should I again come this way.

REMARKABLE CONVERSION.

The following remarkable conversion, from the pen of a Town Missionary, will yield joy to the Christian reader:—

"Albert Street, Dundee, May 23rd, 1844.—Dear Friend,—I received your letter to-day, saying that you would feel obliged if I would write you an early letter to let you know something more concerning the man who attempted three times to take his own life, and was greatly benefited by hearing you preach. I am glad that I can bear testimony to such a pleasing fact, and which must be interesting to all who love Christ and the salvation of their fellow sinners.

"I became acquainted with this man in 1837, his mind at that time appeared to be deeply impressed by the truth of God, and he was very anxious to obtain instruction concerning the way of salvation, and for this purpose he came to my house, sometimes twice a week, for a considerable time; he told me that for many years he had been a most notorious drinker of ardent spirits, that he was frequently in such a state that he did not know what he was doing for days, that his mind was in such a state that he had three times attempted to take his own life by suspending himself by the neck; the last time that he made the attempt he was taken down by some of my own neighbors for dead; a doctor of this town providentially past at the time,—a vein was opened, and the blood began to flow. In a few weeks he recovered, and became as hard a drinker as ever. He had a wife and a few starving children, the only food they got was by the industry of the mother; and not unfrequently would the unnatural father come into the house in the mother's absence, and take what suited him, and sell it for the murderous draught. While he was going on in this wretched course of wickedness to destruction, he happened to be passing the foot of Hawkhill Road, where he saw a crowd of people assembled listening to a person preaching,—he said it was Mr. Bowes—I think he said the text was Numbers, chapter xxiii. verse 10. 'Let me die the death of the righteous, and let my last end be like his.' He said his attention was arrested, and from that hour he had been led to see himself a rebel against God, and by sin exposed to the wrath to come. He went home with the prayer of the publican pouring from his heart, 'God be merciful to me a sinner.' He saw that the work of Christ was the foundation of acceptance with God. The grace of God produced a complete change in his whole character. He became very anxious about his wife and children, and frequently he would say, 'O that my dear wife, who is anxious for everything comfortable in the world, were as anxious about salvation.' This man became a member of a Christian church, and I have frequently seen him going to the house of God with a little boy in each hand, neat and clean, and as nicely dressed as the children of many public-house keepers, who are considered respectable; I have often looked after them with tears of joy. The man is still alive.

"As for my name, you may do with it as you please. I wish I could give information of this kind every day.

" Yours,

"GEORGE RAMSAY."

24th.—NEW DEER. Dr. Smith, convener of the Free Kirk Committee, had got the lecture intimated to be there. The Secession minister of Whitehills had intimated it to be in the Free Kirk. The minister called a few of the managers together, told them that the congregational minister at Stewartfield had seen me, was pleased with me in private conversation, but on hearing me, disapproved several new views which I entertained; so a place called a watch-house, erected close to the burying-ground, for relations to watch at, and prevent the bodies of their interred friends from being exhumed, was procured, and we had a select company of friendly attentive souls in it. I find I am becoming quite a thorn in the side of hired ministers. I declare, "Freely ye have received, freely give," that as we have got the Gospel for nothing, we should give it as we got it. They do not like this. As I give liberty after my lectures for questions and remarks, and am quite ready to discuss the matter with them, besides, my monthly magazine is open to them, why do they not refute my arguments if they can? I love all good men among hired priests or ministers, but hate the system under which they act.

25th.—Walked to-day 29 miles to ABERDEEN, and preached at Castle Street at night. Walked this week about 86 miles, I do not know that I ever walked so many in one week these twenty years.

26th.—Three were baptized in the Dee.

29th.—Understood that Mr. Burnett, proprietor of fifteen-sixteenths of the parish of Kimnay, was favorable to truth, found him from home. His son holds meetings and preaches in the parish; he treated me kindly, and I lectured at one of his meetings.

30th.—Walked to Pitcaple with Alexander Burnett, and met a man and two horses to convey me to Insch. Spent a part of the afternoon with Patrick Morrison, who assists his father to preach at Duncanston, also with the Congregational minister of Culsalmond, Rennie. A considerable congregation. We commenced the meeting soon after 7 o'clock, and it was near 11 before we closed. The two ministers asked several questions, and made several remarks in opposition to my views of a hired ministry and baptism. I offered to debate these matters with either of them, or any other minister they might think proper to name. We shook hands, but they gave no reply to this proposal. Peter Ferres, with whom I slept, is preaching and holding large meetings in various parts of the country, with considerable success. The Magazine seems to have produced a considerable impression in this neighborhood.

HEALTH OF BODY.

Though health of soul is the greatest of all blessings, yet, if the body be sick, it often retards the onward progress of the mind in the path of usefulness. If the sickness be sent of God, we may expect spiritual blessing; but if it be brought on through our own imprudence, unwatchfulness, or intemperance, it will injure rather than bless us. The following information, derived partly from investigation and partly from experience, may be useful.

1. *Good fresh air is essential to health.*—Windows or doors, especially in small rooms, should be open both by night and day, if there be no other way of ventilating them. A constant supply of fresh air is even more important than of food and drink. An individual may for a long time control the sensation of hunger, or even the more imperious one of thirst, but life will most certainly be destroyed if pure air be withheld from the lungs for a very short period. The air is rendered impure by being loaded with animal and vegetable exhalations, by its free circulation being prevented by a number of persons breathing it when confined in a close chamber, and by the process of fermentation and combustion.

2. *Insufficient Exercise.*—He who does not spend several hours every

day in some active exercise—as walking, riding on horseback, or in some amusement which calls nearly all the muscles into play—must inevitably suffer a diminution of bodily strength, defect of appetite, and imperfect digestion, and become, sooner or later, the subject of disease. Speaking much aloud in the open-air strengthens the lungs, and prevents consumption. The exercises of digging and walking give health to the husbandman and the traveller.

3. *Insufficient ablutions of the body.*—It is not enough for the preservation of health, that merely the hands, the feet, and the face be washed frequently, but that the whole surface of the body be repeatedly purified by immersion in a bath of appropriate temperature. To all, the frequent use of the bath is a frequent means of preserving health, but to none more so than to the laborer and mechanic; to such, the time and means for bathing should be afforded in every city, and in every extensive manufactory, wherever situated. The body may be washed all over with the common wash-hand basin; rub well till the skin be dry.

4. *Inattention to the cleanliness of Clothing and Dwellings.*—Independently of the injury which the health of the individual suffers from a neglect of strict personal and domestic cleanliness, the contamination of the air from the decomposition of filth, accumulated in and about a dwelling, has not unfrequently communicated disease to whole families and neighborhoods. Repeatedly whitewashing the walls of a house, and scrubbing the floors, is not merely, therefore, a source of tasteful comfort, but a direct means of preserving health.

5. *Food rendered pernicious by modern cookery.—Adulteration in foods and drinks, and abuse of appetite.*—While a moderate quality of plain, wholesome food—in other words, the food in ordinary use is essential to the maintenance of life,—all excess in its use, all complicated processes of cookery, and every artificial means—whetted by high seasoning, variety of dishes, or foreign savors,—of keeping up the appetite beyond the wants of the system, are decidedly injurious. Every species of adulteration, also, to which our food or drink is subjected, from whatever motive, detracts from its wholesomeness. Let it be recollected, too, that the health and the strength of the body are not supported by the quantity of food consumed, but only by so much as is capable of being converted, by the powers of the stomach, into pure chyle and blood. Old people require less food than the young, and persons who have not much manual labor require less than others, and it should be much lighter. Abstinence from food for a longer time than usual after sickness, and cold water, form the only medicine which some take.

6. *Defective and improper clothing.*—Injury to the health may be either by the clothes being inadequate to defend the wearer from the cold, or from sudden changes in the weather, by their impeding the free motion of the limbs, or by their compressing or binding too firmly some part of the body.

7. *Intense and protracted application of the mind.*—Alternate rest and activity, as well of the body as of the mind, are essential to the support of health. Long-continued mental application, whether in the study or the cares of business, wears out the system, and exhausts the powers of life even more rapidly than protracted manual labor.

8. *Giving way to the passions.*—Experience fully proves that nothing contributes more effectually to guard the system from disease and to

prolong life than a calm and contented state of mind. Individuals who give way on every slight occasion to the influence of passion, not only injure materially their health, but are often promptly destroyed. Violent anger and ambition, jealousy and fear, have produced the speedy death of thousands. In the cultivation of an amiable, peaceful, and virtuous disposition, therefore, a man not only insures his happiness, but promotes his health also. The graces of the Spirit of God not only give quiet and tranquility to the mind, but often health to the body.

9. *The unnecessary or imprudent use of medicine.*—Domestic quackery has ruined many constitutions. A dose of medicine taken with a view of preventing an attack of disease, not unfrequently invites one which otherwise would not have occurred. The absurd practise of loosing blood, or taking purgatives and other remedies in the Spring and Autumn, under the erroneous idea that by so doing the blood is rendered more pure, should be carefully avoided.(See Porter's Health Almanac, Philadelphia.)

10. *Particular attention should be given to the state of the stomach and bowels.*—It requires five or six hours to digest the food previously taken. If the stomach be overloaded, bile and sickness ensue. Some injure themselves by eating heavy food, such as animal food, two or three times daily. It is better to regulate the bowels by our daily provisions than by medicine. Almost every person may observe what effect his diet has upon his frame, and act according to the knowledge derived from experience.

11. *Avoiding cold immediately after heat.*—Many persons bring on sickness and death by leaving hot ball-rooms, and then rushing into the open-air; but, as I expect my readers never frequent such places, I need not call farther attention to them, but may caution others. Some by walking or running quickly to railway, or other coaches, and to boats, ships, &c., and by carrying luggage, perspire profusely, and afterwards take cold. After preaching for fifty years, I never recollect taking cold by preaching out of doors; but have frequently caught severe colds by large congregations and confined buildings. Let brethren see that windows are duly opened.

12. *Spending too much time in bed enfeebles and weakens the body.*—It is difficult to fix the amount of time required for all constitutions. Employments which are exceedingly exhausting and laborious call for more sleep than those which are easy and agreeable. It has been supposed that five or six hours in twenty-four are sufficient for men in general, but some require more, and seven, or seven and a half are needed by women.

13. *Retireing from business.*—I have seen so many men of active habits do violence to their nature when they have been able to live on the money which they have accumulated, and so many speedily die by doing nothing, that, if men capable of serving society do not wish to retire that they may die, they should continue in active life as long as they are able. All should labor for God and society as long as they can; and when their work is done, they may either glorify God by suffering or dying in the faith. No man should amass wealth: none should be idle; none should be without an object, or life will become a burden, and death alarming. The average lives of persons having nothing to do after retiring is about three years, the actively engaged live longer.

14. *Pleasures.*—The boundless love of God has supplied us with thousands of rational and innocent enjoyments, all of which conduce to our physical well being. But many pleasures may become excessive, unnatural, and injurious. The moderate indulgence in such pleasures as are lawful, is obviously accordant with our whole nature, and consequently healthful; but "she that liveth in pleasure is dead while she liveth."

15. *If we would enjoy health, we must reject the tyrant custom,* and resolve to take care of our own health, whether our mode of procedure shall please our friends or not. Firmness and decision are essential to the accomplishment of anything great or good in a world which surrounds us with so many adverse circumstances.

June 2nd.—ABERDEEN. Took farewell of the congregations. Deeply affected.

3rd.—Met the church. We sold off our furniture and some books. We start for Manchester, if the Lord will, going by Granton, Glasgow, and Liverpool, in the morning.

30th.—MANCHESTER. At the usual places. The total abstainers invited me to address a meeting on Stretford Road, at 8 o'clock. Very large congregation. I stated the truths of the gospel to them. To-day sixteen broke bread, and three were absent. This morning I answered this question, put by a Roman Catholic,—"Hear the church?" The Romanists were outrageous at the end of the lecture, and my friends were afraid that they would injure me. There seemed to be scores of them; some very furious. A policeman came to take me from among them, but I did not require his aid,—the Lord is my protection. They roared and made a great noise. The last Lord's Day, one proposed a question and I answered it to his satisfaction; not so to-day.

7th.—At the Cross, end of Oldham Street. The Roman Catholics were together when I arrived. I went up to them, and told them if they took the Cross to lecture on, I would take some other place. They said they did not want to lecture. I said I was a man of peace, and did not want any strife. After several words of explanation they seemed more peaceably disposed. One man asked, "Are you not paid for coming here?" I replied, "No; I never preach the gospel for pay."

21st.—At 9 o'clock a large congregation. An aged man stated, on walking with me after the discourse, that his minister, Mr. Taylor, a Wesleyan, on visiting him, advised him strongly to go to the poorhouse. He said, "I have lived with my wife about fifty years, and I should not like to be parted *now*. The children have always been about us, and I should not like to be separated from them" Thus when the ministers have collected the pence and shillings of the poor, and can obtain no more from them, instead of supporting them, they advise and allow them to go to the poorhouse.

27th.—Walked to STOCKPORT. The rain came on, and I could not preach. Returned home. We had now been in Manchester several weeks without any one asking us how we lived. We had not wanted. The book shop was not yielding expenses, as I would sell no books or papers but what I judged useful. Before retiring to rest, I asked my dear wife what she had left. She said sixpence, which with what she had in, would get the children breakfast next morning.

28th.—A MEMORABLE DAY. After the children had gone to school, there was no prospect for dinner. We could have borrowed, but that would have lowered our standard. We did not wish our brethren to think that we were leaning at all on them. I examined myself. "Am I doing all that I can for daily bread?" I did not see that I could do more just then with the shop I was preaching the gospel, and was cast on my great and only Master. He had often sent aid by the post, but the post man passed without calling. A brother from Salford had promised to call, but the rain descended in torrents. Here were we cast on the Lord. How would He look at dinner time. Before 11 a.m. the brother called. He stated that, as it was so wet, he did not intend to come, *but could not be easy*,—wondered how we lived—had never asked. I told him our dependence on the supplies of our Master, but not our great need. He said, "I make a deal of money, and should be glad if you would take that," handing me *ten shillings*. I do not remember that this brother gave anything since. Thus were we amply supplied, and, as the following letter will explain, the Lord was stirring up his people in various places to think about us. "Cast all your anxious thought upon him, because he is concerned about you."—1 Peter v. 7.

LIVERPOOL, July 29th, 1844.

MY VERY DEAR BROTHER,—
Jane and I have been thinking that perhaps you are in need of a little assistance, and we therefore send you by post office order the sum of 10s., which we beg you to accept as a small token of our love to you. We were saving a little money towards buying a winter coat for me, but we believe we shall have no more winter, and although we differ so widely upon these matters, [the Lord's Second Coming] still we love you, and pray that the blessing of God may rest upon you, and your family, and especially upon your labors in endeavoring to bring sinners to Jesus. We are all very comfortable at present, and the Room of late has been well attended. We have had also a few added to the church, such as will, we hope, be saved eternally. Give our love to Sister Bowes and family, and accept the same also, from your unworthy brother and sister,

JOSEPH & JANE CURRY.

P.S.—Brother Wright sends 4s also, and desires his love to you. He received 2s.8d from Woolton.
To J. Bowes.

AWFUL END OF JOHN ESDAILE.

In the course of the month I heard, and received information by letter, of the miserable end of John Esdaile, of Aberdeen, who had been at one time an Unitarian minister, afterwards a Socialist, and who challenged me to discussion in Aberdeen. He took poison. It seems about the time of his death, his wife gave birth to a child in the lunatic asylum. At the discussion she was on the platform with him; but the doctor at the asylum attributes her lunacy to her husband's having frequently mesmerised her. There is no hope of her recovery. Poor John Esdaile is said to have poisoned himself over a woman from Edinburgh, whom he met with at the Agricultural Cattle Show. She was to write to him. He said if a letter did not come by the next post, he would take poison. The letter did not come. He took prussic acid. The letter came the next post, but it was too late! What a lesson does his end furnish of the miserable consequences of a godless, licentious system!

ABERDEEN, 22nd of 7mo., 1844.

DEAR FRIEND JOHN BOWES,—
. . . . What thou hast heard respecting poor John Esdaile is too true

He destroyed himself by taking prussic acid. I do not know any particulars to be relied on. Rumor says the rash step was in consequence of a quarrel with a woman he had been keeping! How deplorable to die thus; but I think it probable he was partially insane. His poor wife is still an inmate in the Lunatic Asylum, and considered quite a hopeless case as regards restoration to a sound mind. Her head was, it is believed, greatly injured by her husband's experiments in mesmerising her, and the surgeon of the asylum believes this is the cause of her insanity.

I am pleased to hear thou art usefully employed in doing good to thy fellow beings, even amidst the dangers arising from the attacks of drunkards, infidels, and Roman Catholics, and it is a mercy they have not been permitted to harm thee. I cannot help thee at present with Peace Tracts, having just given a supply to a person to distribute at a lecture on the subject in the country; but there is, I believe, a Peace Society in Manchester, which thou mayst inquire about, and it is probable they will furnish thee with some. It affords us satisfaction to hear that thy wife and family are well. My wife joins me in kind remembrance.

I remain, thy sincere friend,

To J. Bowes. ANTHONY WIGHAM.

THOMAS HARDACRE'S CASE.

I give the following as one among the many instances of the power of the Gospel which I have witnessed. It is from Thomas Hardacre's own pen.

"DEAR BROTHER,—

"By your request I write the following abridged sketch of my life, which you will be at liberty to use as you think proper.

"My father was a native of Skipton, in Craven, England, he was twice married, and had a family of eighteen sons and three daughters; he had ten by his first wife, and eleven by my mother. My mother was a native of the town of Ayr, in Scotland, but spent her youthful days in Ireland.

"I was born in Aberdeen on New Year's day, 1821, and when old enough, I was sent to Bishop Skinner's school, where I learned to read and write a little; but I was soon taken away to go with my father, who earned his living as a travelling hawker. My early training was none of the best, for I had to spend my nights in low lodging houses, where I had to associate with the worst of characters, seeing sights and hearing words of the most corrupting kind. As a matter of course, I soon learned their slang language, and became one of themselves. Thus I spent twenty years of the best of my days, serving the Devil with all my might. When I was at home, I spent much of my time in low public-houses and singing clubs. My poor old father would sometimes go with me to these places, and take great delight in hearing me sing comic songs, for which I had some talent, and for which I received great praise from the world.

"About this time I took up with a woman of bad character, and left my father's house. He tried every means to separate us, but I was determined to have my own way. He even came one night and took the wheels off my cart, thinking by this to bring me back to dwell with him. But I went and told him I would never come back, and demanded my wheels, telling him, at the same time, that if he did not give them up, and let me to my work, I would come some night and take his off his cart, and keep them until I got my own. My father saw that I could do this, so he gave me back my wheels, and I never went to live with him after.

"I was now free from all restraint and spent all the money I earned in public-houses, and clubs, and theatres, and with the worst of company, going on from bad to worse, not knowing nor caring where my downward course would end. About this time the city of Aberdeen was visited by William C. Burns, and the Lord blessed his labors; some of my companions were converted to God, and came and entreated me to come and hear him, but I would not consent to go; they tried to induce me by saying, 'You like fun; come and you will get good sport, seeing all the factory lasses greeting.'* But I would not go, for I had a secret feeling within, that if I did go I might be brought to 'greet' also, for I knew that there was not a greater sinner out of hell than I was myself, so no one could persuade me to go to any place of worship. I believed that when I should die I should go to hell, so I determined to take my fill of sin as long as God permitted me to live. After this a minister from England (P. G. Anderson, of Birmingham,) visited Aberdeen, and as he was preaching in Castle Street in the open-air, I was passing on, when the young fair head of the preacher attracted my attention, and I stopped to hear what he had to say, and I then, for the first time heard God's great love proclaimed. The preacher told the people that God loved great sinners, in spite of their great sins, and the greater our sins the greater our need to be saved, and that Jesus delighted in saving great sinners, because it brought him great glory. 'O dear souls, Christ is willing, ready, and anxious now, at this moment, to save the greatest sinner within reach of my voice.' When 1 heard these words I said to myself, 'Then bad as I am, there may be a chance for me yet.' As it began to rain the preacher invited the people to follow him to Frederick Street Hall, where they would be more comfortable than in the rain; so a crowd followed, and I went amongst the rest, and that was the first time I had ever entered into a place of worship. And for the first time, that afternoon I was almost persuaded to be a Christian. Still I did not yield, but stifled God's Spirit that was striving within me by taking a deeper plunge into drunkenness and sin than before. Corrupted myself, I was only living to corrupt others, going to hell myself and taking all I could persuade along with me. I was like the London butchers' decoy sheep, which he has trained to lead the way to his slaughter house. When a flock of sheep is to be taken in, the decoy sheep is brought out and put in front of the flock, and where it leads the rest follow. Truly, I was the devil's trained decoy. Shortly after this I heard John Bowes preaching in the open-air, and as he was telling of God's great love I was reminded of what I had heard before from Mr. Anderson, and I began to feel uneasy about my eternal welfare. John Bowes generally preached in the open-air every night, and he always told the people before leaving them where he was to preach the following night. He was so zealous and self-denying that I often said of him, 'Truly he is a man of God.' I attended all the meetings I could get to, and I have more than once gone out of my way (when I saw him upon the street) to follow him, that I might get a look at his face, which I believed to be lighted up by the smile of heaven. One day I followed him as far as Old Aberdeen, saying as I went, 'O that I was like that good man. O that I had one spark of the joy which gladdens his soul. O, if he but knew of the poor miserable sinner who is now following hard at his heels, he might be induced to pray for me or speak to me; for it is impossible for me to speak to him.' Often, while he was preach-

---

*Weeping.

ing, have I imagined that his face was shining with angelic spendor, while the soul-saving truths of the gospel were flowing from his lips. I have great reason to thank God for open-air preaching; for if his servants had not gone out to the streets and lanes of the city, and proclaimed the gospel, I don't think I would have ever gone to hear it in their places of worship. But open-air preaching led me to inside preaching, and I did not attend the meetings (held in George Street Temperance Hall) long, before my awful state as a sinner, and the danger to which I was every moment exposed, was fully revealed to me. This compelled me to cry out, 'What must I do to be saved?' and when the preacher ended his discourse, it gave me not a little joy when he invited the anxious to stay, and he would speak to them. The front seat in the hall was cleared, and the anxious invited to come forward. I was the second to go; six of us went forward. I shall never forget the joyful look which brightened up the face of the man of God while he raised his eyes, heart, and hands toward heaven, and his soul swelled with gratitude, as he clasped his raised hands together, and exclaimed, 'Glory be to God, here are six souls seeking mercy.'

"This was the turning point in my life. It would baffle my tongue to utter, or my pen to describe, the agony of soul I was enduring at this time. I wondered why the earth did not open her mouth and swallow me up! John Bowes spoke to us. He told us of the love of Jesus, and how he came into the world to save sinners. But I went home that night to my lonely room without being able to trust to Him as my Saviour. I fell prostrate upon the floor and tried to pray, but could not, and I dared not go to sleep, for I was afraid of waking up in hell! Night after night was thus spent. Truly the terror of the Lord was upon me. When morning came, I longed for evening, that I might have an opportunity of seeing my best friend, John Bowes, who, when his discourse was over, did not fail to attend to me. Although I was dejected in appearance, and no one would have given a shilling for all the clothes I had on my back, yet the good man would have come direct to me, and, putting his arm into mine, would walk along the streets of the crowded city, conversing with me about Jesus and his wondrous love; while the enemies of religion would scoffingly call after us, and say to their companions as we were leaving, 'There's another poor fellow gulled.' Thus he conversed with me night after night, and on one occasion took me home with him to 22 North Broadford, where he conversed and prayed with me. But still I was without peace. I could neither take food nor sleep. I went home one night in such agony of soul, that I fell upon the floor and prayed to God either to save me or damn me at once! for I thought that even hell itself could not make me more miserable than I was. Upon the following Saturday I gathered together some old rags and sold them, and with the shilling I got for them I bought a New Testament. This was the first I ever had that I could call my own, and, as a matter of course, I was as ignorant of its contents as the ass which I drove; but felt thankful I was able to read it. Upon the Lord's Day, when I went to the meeting, John Bowes came to me and asked if I had yet found peace with God. I replied 'No.' He then said, 'Surely there is some sin you are not willing to give up?' I said, 'I am willing to give up all I know to be sin, and my life also, if the Lord shall require it.' I was then, by my consent, proposed to the church for fellowship. After enduring another week of misery, I was the next Lord's Day baptized in the river Dee, and added to the church.

"Some thousands of people went out of Aberdeen, a distance of about a mile and a half, to witness the baptism, among whom were hundreds of my acquaintances. After the baptism was over, as we were coming home, a brother in the church came up to me and said kindly, 'Now, brother, you will have to suffer persecution, so prepare yourself for it; but don't allow them to laugh you out of Christ.' I felt thankful, for his counsel was needed. I sat down that day for the first time to observe the Lord's Supper. Believing that I was unfit to be there, and that the presence of such a sinner as I had been was sufficient to pollute his holy table, and bring down instant judgment on my presumptuous soul, I expected nothing else but that the Lord would strike me down dead at his table, and send me direct to the hell I deserved. Then I said to myself, the Lord knows everything, and he knows that I am willing to serve him, and if he will not have me for his servant, I will perish at his feet. In the afternoon of that day John Bowes took his text from Luke iv. 18, 'He hath sent me to heal the broken hearted.' And the Spirit of the Lord put words into the mouth of his servant to meet my case. He showed me plainly that it was necessary that the sinner's heart should be broken; for if God did not break it, the sinner would believe sin to be a light thing, and be more apt to fall into it again: but if his heart is broken, he will flee from it as he would from a serpent;— also, that God loved to dwell with the man that is of a broken and contrite heart, and that 'a broken and a contrite heart the Lord will not despise;'—He has also sent Jesus to heal the broken-hearted; it was for this he came into the world; it was to accomplish this He endured the cross; therefore let all broken-hearted ones go at once to the Great Physician, and they shall receive His healing balm without money and without price. With reasonings such as these being placed before my mind, I at once saw that it was the hand of the Lord that was upon me, and that the troubles of mind which I had passed through were all necessary, and thanking God for all his dealings with me, I went home that afternoon filled with his love and rejoicing in him as my Saviour.

"My heart being now filled with the love of God, my first anxiety was to tell all my friends and acquaintances of the change the Lord had wrought upon me, but although they were my constant companions while I was living in sin, when I began to tell them about Jesus and his love, they would run away from me and shun me, and pass me on the other side of the street as if I had some terrible disease about me. But although this discouraged me at first, I was determined to persevere, for as I had been a ring-leader in the ranks of the Devil, I thought I might try now and do something to spread my Saviour's dear name and fame, so I commenced to hold cottage meetings. The first of these were held in Albion Street. I had William Melven for a companion, and while one of us spoke to the people the other would go out and invite in all he could persuade; thus our meetings were crowded, and often have I seen both old and young weeping on account of their sins, and seeking the Saviour, sorrowing. I now believe that these meetings which were held in old George Leslie's and other houses in Albion Street, were the beginning of that reformation which has changed the appearance of both the people and the place, so that where the Penny Theatre or Penny Rattler, as it was called at that time, stood, corrupting the morals of the people, there now stands a fine building, called the Albion Street Church, or ragged church, with schools, for the young, in which J. H. Wilson (now in London), labored with much earnestness and great success. We also at that time held meetings in different places through the city; the Lord blessing his word, although spoken in weakness, to the conversion of sinners.

"As William Melvin and I were going down Park Street to a meeting, we saw two sailors going away with two street women; we went up to them and told them that these women would lead them to hell, and we entreated them to come with us and not go with these women; they took our advice, left the women, and came to the prayer meeting, and I believe God blessed his word to them both, for they seemed much affected.

"I then went to Newburgh, a village 13 miles north of Aberdeen, but my father had been there before me, and told all the people that his son Tom had gone mad, so when I went among them many of them seemed to believe it, for they looked upon me with suspicion. At that time I was making my living by collecting rags and selling stoneware. And when I told the people I was to hold a prayer meeting in Elspet Bruce's house, and that I would be glad to see them there, they seemed astonished, and when the time came such a crowd came together to hear 'mad Tom Hardacre,' that I could not find any place about the village large enough to hold them. James Gowlick kindly gave me the use of his barn, and crowds of people came a great distance to hear the pig-man* preaching. There was an old blind woman lived in the village known as blind Maggie, she was at that time about 90 years of age, she had heard John Wesley preach in a park at Newburgh when she was a little girl, and when done with his discourse he came and put his hand upon her head, and as he stroked her hair, he prayed that God might bless her. And she believed that God did bless her at that time, and that the blessing never left her. She was one of the happiest old Christians I have ever met with; although stone-blind she could do all her house work and go to the well, or find her way to any house in any part of the village; she was also precentor in the Methodist Chapel; she had all the hymns upon her memory, and could set tunes to them all; she also had her mind stored with the word of God. O what joy it gave that poor old Christian when she heard that I was converted to God, and it would have delighted any real Christian, and put sluggards to shame to see her going from door to door inviting the people to the meetings, and pleading with them to come. I always used to spend about half-an-hour with Maggie before going to a meeting, and her rich displays of the love of God in Christ, and her prayers, would have fired my soul with such zeal for the cause of my God, that the fear of man was overcome, and I had boldness and courage to tell his great love to all I met with. One Lord's day I travelled from Aberdeen to Newburgh to hold meetings; I had William Melvin with me. When we arrived we called upon blind Maggie; she appeared to be dying, and it would be impossible to describe

---

* Or pot-man

the joyful smile which was spread over her face as her happy soul was under the prospect of soon departing to be with Christ. O how sweetly she sang of the land of pure delight, where saints immortal reign. We had some blessed meetings that day, and when we were coming home at night three anxious persons followed us as far as Foveran Church, and we conversed with them, (these women had followed us about two miles), and we knelt down by the road and prayed for them, and they went home rejoicing in the Lord. One of them was baptized and added to the church. Next Lord's Day I went out again with Frances Christie, and we called upon blind Maggie, she was sitting by the fire, singing 'Jesus lover of my soul.' I said, 'I am glad to see you so far recovered, Maggie.' ' O Thomas.' she said, 'if I had not been so impatient to get away, I would have been away long ago, but the Lord has taught me to wait with patience his own time for my removal.' She lived about four years after this."

"I got the use of a barn near Foveran Inn, at a farm called Bridgefoot, which was crowded to the door, to hear an address from me. The Lord enabled me to make some earnest appeals to sinners. I told them that they all knew what I had been, that none need despair of salvation since God had saved me. The next day a man came to me, and told me that I ought to be confined; that I was not only mad myself, but that I had made a whole country side of people mad. I said, 'would you be so good as give me some of the names of the mad people.' He gave me the names of some of their farms, so I wrote a letter to William Melvin, telling him to come out, and to try, if possible, and bring a brother with him; he came, and brought William Keill. I may here state that these brethren were both out of work at this time, William Melvin having got his leave from Mr. Heigg, manager of Haddan's Mill, for reading his Bible while at work, and William Keill, who was a moulder, got his leave because he would not tell a lie to screen his master's faults. These two brethren were very useful, and the Lord blessed their labors. Next day William Melvin and I went to see the 'mad' people, and William Keill went on to Colliston, a fishing village four miles farther north. After conversing with some of the 'mad' people, we were constrained to pray that the Lord might send more such madness, for not a few of them found peace and were brought to there right minds, by believing in Jesus. We had some precious meetings in James Gowlick's barn upon the Lord's Day following. William Melvin went home in the evening. Next day William Keill returned from Colliston, and we made preparation to start for Aberdeen. William Keill went into John Gowan's public house, and I was astonished to hear him say, 'I want a glass of whisky, mistress,' the landlady replied, 'You'll get that, sir.' Keill said, 'Gi'e me the worst you have in the house.' 'O,' she said, 'We hav'na twa kinds.' The whisky was brought and paid, and pulling off his boots he poured half a glass into each boot, remarking at the same time, ' You see, mistress, we dinna put nane o' that stuff in our bellies, but in our boots, to haud our feet cool when travelling on the road.' Upon the following Thursday there was a church meeting called, and the brethren who had been out laboring were called upon to state anything that might be interesting to the church. After brother Melvin and I had stated the facts above recorded, William Keill told us his adventures at Colliston: he said, on arriving he went to the church, and the minister gave out the text, 'The wicked are like the troubled sea, whose waters cannot rest but are continually casting up mire and dirt.' He read a discourse about the troubled sea, and the mire and the dirt, but there was not a word about the Saviour in the whole of his sermon. Besides, he used such uncommon words that the poor ignorant fishers did not understand one-half of what he said; how could they know the meaning of such phrases as the 'ineffable God?' He says, 'I sat and wept the whole time. The sermon being over there was an infant brought forward to be sprinkled: the minister addressed the man who held it up, 'My dear Christian brother,' I kept sight of the man for I intended to run after him when we got out to see if he really was what the minister had called him, and as I was about to set out after him my attention was arrested by another man upon the top of a grave-stone, crying out with a loud voice, a great sale of fenders and fire-irons and household furniture, which was to take place that week. After this I went into the town and found the fishers employed turning their fish and bleaching them upon the rocks. After some trouble I got an old school-house to hold a meeting in; I then went and invited the people, but when meeting time came I had only a few children: I told them to go and tell their fathers and mothers to come; they went but soon came back and told me that their fathers and mothers had no bawbees to put in the plate. I then told them to run and tell their fathers and mothers that I did not want their bawbees, and that I would not have them, to tell them and everybody they saw to come without any bawbees. The children went with this message, and the result was that we soon had a full meeting, and a number seeking the Saviour weeping.' After these things had been told to the church, a brother named John Low got up and said he did not think it right for the church to allow or encourage such young brethren to go out and hold meetings, as it required learning and experience to qualify men for such work, and without these qualifications we might do much harm, and assuredly we would do no good. I made reply, 'Brother Low has been longer a member of the church than any of us, but he has done nothing, he is doing nothing, nor is it likely that he will do anything, and his desire seems to be to bring down the active brethren to his own level, but as for my own part, I intend to use my tongue as the Lord may enable me, and recommend my Saviour to perishing sinners.' John Bowes then said, 'Go on brother Hardacre, and let not any of the active brethren be discouraged, and if brother Low, or any other brother, thinks you are liable to go wrong, let them go with you and put you right.

About this time I changed my way of living, for when the county police went on, I was not allowed to travel without a license, so I commenced carting coal in Aberdeen, although I had only a donkey to begin with. I also married a Christian girl, Jane Anderson, (May 24, 1845.) who proved a useful helpmate as long as she was spared with me. At this time I had meetings at the Printfield, which were continued twice a week for about three years. These meetings were always crowded, for the people came out of curiosity for miles to hear the coal carter preach, and in some instances got saved through the blood of the Lamb. One Lord's day evening, two men, infidels, came to the meeting for the purpose of giving annoyance; I did not know this, but the Lord led me to say something about the unhappy death of infidels, and one of them got up and went out of the meeting, the other fell down before all the people and cried out, 'What must I do to be saved.' He said he was an infidel and a drunkard, a wife beater and every thing that was bad, and that he had come into the meeting for the purpose of putting it down, for he hated all such gatherings. 'Oh! is it possible for mercy to be extended to such a sinner as me.' We told him he had not reached the uttermost yet, and if he had, Christ was able to save to the uttermost all who come unto God by him. The poor infidel found peace with God that night, and entreated us to accompany him to his house, about half a mile farther on, and speak the word of the Lord to his poor wife. As we went, he said he would invite in his neighbors, and we might hold a meeting; it was now half-past ten o'clock at night, and it certainly was wonderful to see the man who had been drunk and beating his wife the night before,—the man who was looked upon as a pest to the neighborhood, now inviting his neighbors to come into his house, at that late hour, to hear the word of the Lord. His poor wife thought he had lost his reason, the neighbors thought the same, but many of them came. Before twelve o'clock his wife found peace with God; they were afterwards both baptized and added to the church. The above is an account of the conversion of James Anderson and his wife, who afterwards opened their house for meetings, and the Lord blessed his own word to many who came to hear. But although we saw that the Lord was blessing our labors and that souls were being saved sometimes, yet we did not see the extent of good these meetings had done until about ten years afterwards, when a minister from Sheffield, J. Jefferson, came to Aberdeen, and when he went to preach at Cotton Chapel (Mr. Laing's) I went with him, and it gladdened my soul to see that most of the brethren and sisters who sat down at the Lord's Table in that church, had been gathered from the world by the meetings held at Printfield by Peter Beaton, William Melvin, and myself.

We also held meetings at Cove, a fishing village five miles south of Aberdeen; these were also well attended, and many sinners were awakened to see their guilt and danger, and some found peace. One Lord's day afternoon I went with William Troup, (now in America). We went into a large meeting gathered together to hear Mr. Henderson, a Mormon preacher. When he arrived with his friends, he saw us sitting in the meeting, and, addressing the people, he said, 'My dear friends, I perceive there is a certain party here who has come out of Aberdeen for the purpose of opposing the work of God, and unless you conspire with me to put these men out I cannot go on.' The fishers (who knew us) said they would put no one out unless they saw occasion. We replied that we would give them no annoyance unless they kept the meeting too long and wearied the people. Mr. Henderson replied, 'I intend to weary you, you are only a bit of a carter, you have got no right to speak at all.' William Troup said, 'It is true we are carters, and Mr. Henderson is a coach maker, all making our living at honest trades. It is no disgrace to be called a working man, but if there is any disgrace, he falls under the same condemnation, and when he can show his right to speak, we think we can show as good authority, but we will not put you to the trouble of putting us out by force, for we will walk out; and if any of you want to hear Mormonism exposed, if you will step out with us into the open-air, we will tell you something about that wicked and immoral system.' We then went out, and the whole meeting went out with us, and left Mr. Henderson to speak to the empty walls of the house. We told the people some of the evils of Mormonism, and also the plan of salvation through Jesus Christ. The people heard patiently, and the 'Latter-Day Saints' never attempted to go back.

"The brethren Beaton, Archie M'Donald, and myself, went out one Lord's Day afternoon to Rubslaw Quarries, and after some searching for a house to hold a meeting in, we got a large room from Mr Charles Fyffe, landlord of the public-house, 'Auld Lang Syne.' We invited the people and the room was filled. My two brethren stated the gospel with great earnestness, and I spoke from Acts xxiv. 25, Paul reasoning with Felix. While I was speaking on the word 'temperance,' I showed that it extended, in Paul's time, to everything: but it was now limited to 'abstinence from strong drink.' I said the drunkard was an idiot, and the man who got his living by making idiots of reasonable men and women, lives by a bad trade, and that I would sooner go through the streets of Aberdeen with a back-burden of besoms to sell, than make my living by such a trade. Praise the Lord for his goodness! He sent his word with power to the heart of the public-house keeper, who, at the conclusion of the meeting, came forward and shook my hand, and said, 'All you have said is true, and I will keep a public-house no longer; I will no longer make a living by destroying God's works, and making wise men into fools.' This man took down his signboard, and the house has not been a public-house since. I may also state, that William Leonard, an old man who lived next door to the public-house, got converted to God, was baptized, and added to the church.

"The above circumstance reminds me of an incident which happened at North Broadford. I was called into the shop of Mr. William Matthew, with a bag of coals, and while there, a poor woman came in clothed in rags, and called for half a gill of whisky. She got it, and drank it off at once, and went away. I knew that Mr. Matthew was an elder in Free John Knox's church, so I said, 'Do you not think that you are doing wrong in measuring out ruin to God's creatures, as you have done now to that poor woman.' He said, 'Well, Thomas, I do feel uneasy about it at times.' I told him that, as he held a high office in the church, he should be a pattern to others and show himself consistent. The next time I was round that way he called me in, and said he had taken my advice, at the same time showing me that his whisky barrels were turned with their crans next the wall. This man still has his shop, but will not sell drink. A word in season is often blessed by God.

"I had also some good meetings at the Bridge of Don. Frances Christie was a great help to me at these and other meetings. He did not say much himself, but, being well educated, he was able to mark down, and point out to me, all the blunders I made while speaking, and tell me how to correct them.

"On one occasion we were called upon to go and visit a dying woman. She seemed to be about 75 years of age, and dying without God and without hope. But as we told her of the Saviour, hope began to take the place of despair, and we left her trusting in Jesus. Next Lord's Day, when out at the Bridge of Don, we called to see her. She was still alive, and she told us she could now lay her happy head on the breast of Jesus, and say, 'Lord, thou knowest all things, thou knowest that I have affection for thee.' Soon after this she died, happy in the Saviour's love.

"I was called upon by two Christian brethren, who requested me to go to Upper Banchory, a village 18 miles up Deeside, and baptize a believing brother. James Robertson, and my wife and daughter, went with me. The brother to be baptized, Mr. James Coutts, had put up written notices of the coming event upon all the church doors and public places about the village. He thus showed that he was not ashamed to confess Christ before men. These notices brought together more than a thousand people. Numbers came in carriages and gigs from a distance, and I hope the blessed truths which were spoken were blessed in leading many of them to the Saviour. They were orderly, and listened to the word of God with great attention.

"FAITHFUL DEALING.

"One day I happened to be in the shop of James Moir, tea merchant, a useful Christian brother. The shop was full of people, and Mr. Gray, a wholesale merchant, happened to drop in, and the following dialogue took place:—

"MOIR.—'Well, how are you to-day, sir?'

"GRAY.—'Quite well, thank you.'

"M.—'I am very glad to hear you say so, sir; for you know you are a very faithful servant of the devil; you are one of his wholesale agents, sir, (referring to strong drink) and I have no doubt but you will get a wholesale reward.'

"Gray was silent. Moir was giving one of his customers a book to read, 'Alcohol; its place and power.'

"G.—'That is a book I should like to read.'

"M.—'I will give you it to read with the greatest of pleasure, sir.'

"G.—'Well, but I am reading some others at present, and I would like to get through with them before I take any more in hand.'

"M.—'I believe what you say to be true, sir, and I know you would leave this book to be last read,—it would grapple too hard with your conscience, sir.'

"James Moir and myself were happy to see that Mr. Gray not only gave up being an agent for the sale of strong drink, but he is often found at the corners of our streets, preaching Christ to perishing sinners. Instead of being a faithful servant of the devil, he is now a zealous servant of the Lord Jesus Christ."

Thomas Hardacre is now with us in Dundee.

THE PROPOSED DISCUSSION WITH JOSEPH BARKER.

In the early part of this year, as J. Barker was widely endeavoring to spread his semi-infidel sentiments, I was asked to meet him in discussion. On the 27th April, I sent the following letter, with my propositions for debate, to my friend G. Sands, for Joseph Barker's approval and acceptance.—

269 George Street, ABERDEEN,
April 27th, 1844.

MY DEAR GEORGE,—

I have just received yours of the 24th, and Joseph Barker's answer to your proposal, expressed in his brother William Barker's letter to you, in which W. Barker says, "I have received," &c. W. Barker further requests you as follows, "You had better," &c. Now I write to you first, because I do not exactly know the conditions expressed in your letter, as I took no copy; you can forward this, therefore, either to William Barker or Joseph, and forward me Joseph's reply. The first thing to be done is to fix in writing the conditions of debate, which I shall endeavor to promote by this letter. The second regards time and place. Since I saw you I have read with some concern J. Barker's views of the Bible, denying it as a rule of faith and practice, and unless we agree about a standard of appeal I do not see that we can settle anything. I should therefore propose that in the first place we discuss this question.

1. I undertake to prove that the teaching, laws, which proceed from Jesus Christ the Lord, and from his Apostles, as contained in the sacred Scriptures of the New Testament, are the proper standard by which to try what is true or false among Christians, not without the Old Testament, but along with it, as a great light which preceded, and gradually introduced the bright Gospel day, and this I maintain in opposition to the contradictory writings of J. Barker.

2. I engage to prove from the Scriptures the proper Divinity of the Lord Jesus Christ,—that he is truly and properly God, and that the Father, the Son, and the Holy Ghost are to be received as one God, though thus distinguished by three personal terms.

3. That the Lord Jesus Christ made himself, and was made by his Father (in the blood which he shed, and the sufferings which he endured in body, mind, &c.) an atonement for sin, a sin offering, a sacrifice for sin, so that God could be just in forgiving sin, without appearing to encourage men to commit it,—and this is in opposition to J. Barker's whole theory.

4. That the pardon or justification of every one that believes, is by faith; in opposition to J. Barker's views of justification or pardon, as given in his works, and that the works of believers, while they do not pardon them, justify them, or exempt them from blame, and prove their innocency in both time and eternity, and that the Scriptures use justification in the above two different acceptations.

5. That J. Barker's theory and practice have been for years deceptive to the souls of men. That on the above and other subjects, such as the fall and punishment of man, he has completely abandoned the truth, adopted semi-infidelity, commonly called Socinianism or Unitarianism, and, that while many of his practical writings have accorded with Scripture, his doctrinal sentiments are hostile to divine truth, and ruinous to the souls of men.

I do not know exactly what J. Barker means about "neither disputant being limited in point of time." If it is meant that we shall not speak fifteen or thirty minutes alternately, but more or less as we choose, I do not object, only the time should be equal, say, three hours to be occupied each day or night, and both speakers to have equal time during the whole debate. I would suggest that a Reporter should be obtained, and that the debate should be printed, under the inspection of the Debaters, and a Committee of three on each side,—that is, if this be agreeable to both sides, and can be arranged to our mutual satisfaction.

I shall endeavor, as far as possible, to make the time and place agreeable to J. Barker. Will he state whether he agrees with these conditions, and what would suit himself as to time and place? Hoping that He who gave us the sacred Scriptures will overrule all matters connected with this great controversy to the farther honor of Jesus Christ, and the instruction and salvation of souls.

I am yours in precious Christ,

To G. Sands.   JOHN BOWES.

P.S.—If I stated any other conditions than the above in Birstal, let me know, and I will abide by them, as they occurred in conversation, only I must have them sent to me as stated.—J.B.

To these conditions I added a sixth.—That while pretending that all opinions should be tolerated, he is himself one of the most intolerant and persecuting of modern professors to those who differ from him.

J. Barker has agreed to meet me, yet he declines making the requisite arrangements for the debate. It is now (7mo. 8th.) some time since my last letter should have been answered, and, after various delays, the matter rests with him still. His views may be collected from the following letter, which I give entire:—

"TO JOHN BOWES.

"I can hardly understand your letter to G. Sands. I understood you to charge me with being a semi-infidel, not a Christian, as teaching anti-christian errors about the plan of redemption, the way of salvation, the conditions of church fellowship, &c.; on these points it was I offered to meet you. The proper plan of proceeding would be, in my judgment, for you to take my sentiments on those subjects from my writings, and state your reasons for considering them anti-christian. You may state your views on one subject first, and allow me to reply, and then proceed to some other. It would be impossible to limit the time of the speakers, without doing injustice to truth, and turning the discussion into a battle for victory. Let each one occupy the time that he may think necessary for the full statement of his views, whether it take him one, two, or three hours, or only ten or fifteen minutes. As to a reporter, I leave the matter with yourself: I also leave to you the choice of a place, though I should prefer Leeds, Huddersfield, Manchester, or Liverpool. Yours in good will,

JOSEPH BARKER.

Newcastle-on-Tyne, June 6th, 1844.

This letter contains all the terms of the debate that I have received from J. Barker. Two items seem unreasonable. 1st.—that either speaker should speak "three hours." It would hardly be a discussion under such circumstances. 2nd.—that I should "read his writings," and he reply. He would thus speak twice for me once. I wish him to state what is unreasonable in my propositions, or to state propositions of his own; and let us discuss one point and then go on to the next. To this he has not yet agreed; I wait his answer. I wish no battle for victory; I wish to overthrow error, to be made rich in truth myself, and to teach it widely to others. He knows my sentiments; I speak out boldly, honestly, and everywhere as I have opportunity, the whole counsel of God. What I wish to defend and oppose I have defined in set propositions; let him do the same, and if I can agree to them I will say so. If it please the Lord, I should like the discussion to take place, and to be conducted mildly, meekly, and with boldness blended with love; and then, I doubt not, truth will spread. May the wisdom of God guide us, and may Christ in all things be honored even as the Father is honored. Amen.

He evaded this discussion. We did not meet for eleven years after.

Aug. 4th.—MANCHESTER. This morning, at the end of Oldham Street. One man, who seemed to be a Roman Catholic, was furious in his opposition, and swore he would murder me if he could meet with me. No one will do this without my heavenly Father's permission.

18*th*.—At Campfield in the evening. A soldier came up with two of his comrades; he was very unruly, and at last took off his belt to strike; he aimed a blow at me, but the dear brethren Stead and Montgomery stepped in; brother Stead received it. I was pushed down from the chair by the worldly young men, who would not stand to see me ill-treated, they had the soldiers out of the congregation in two or three minutes, and I saw them no more, but finished in peace. I heard after this that the same soldier was taken to the police-office for disorderly conduct.

21*st*.—To-day we were again reduced to the last meal. We had nothing for supper, when four brethren arrived from Liverpool; we expected them; my wife was concerned to know how we should procure a supper for them. "Should she borrow?" No; trust in the Lord. I called out brother Davies, who sells my magazines, and asked him if he had anything; he said he had ten shillings. We thus all had supper, and the Liverpool church sent nineteen shillings and threepence besides. Praise the Lord for his goodness, and wonderful works to us, his servants.

25th.—Baptized eight believers in Oak Street Chapel.

28th—John Jones, who had appointed a night to discuss a hired ministry with me, never came. The congregation was large and deeply interested.

29th.—My son John fell into an arm of the Bridgewater Canal, Pauling's works. An aged man, James Grundy, swam in after him; his own life was in danger, but he got John out. As the water was seven feet deep, if no one had been there, he would most likely have been drowned. It is the Lord's mercy that he is not taken away.

I have just been looking over a Methodist Magazine for the year 1808, and I find that then the ministers or preachers were called "Mr." but not "Reverend," and that the people were called "Methodists," not "Wesleyan Methodists," so that thirty-six years ago these two evils did not receive countenance from the Methodists. Now they do almost everything in the name of Wesley, instead of obeying the command, "Whatsoever ye do in word or deed, do all in the name of the Lord Jesus." Let men be honored less and Christ more. I do not remember in what year the ministers were dishonored with "Reverend," and the people with being called "Wesleyans," but it must have been since 1808.

Sept. 8th.—James Grinstead, Holme-lane, writes:—"A fortnight ago, I was summoned to attend as a juryman on an inquest to be held on the body of a man killed by the coal-waggons on a railway belonging to the Bowling Company. I went. The coroner proceeded to swear the jury. When he came to me, I told him I should not swear. He inquired, 'Why?' 'Because the Saviour and his Apostles forbid me,' I said. He said, 'What church do you belong?' 'The Christian.' 'Which of them, there are so many now a days?' I said, 'There is only one.' He put his question in several forms, but I returned the same answer. He said if I did not swear he would commit me to prison. I said he must use his own judgment and discretion about that, but I should not swear. Ultimately he dismissed me."

21st.—Saturday. Held a meeting in ABERDEEN. The hall was locked against the church by P. Crombie. We met in the small schoolroom. For some weeks there has been a division of opinion among the brethren respecting the admission of unbaptized persons into the church. This question was first started by James Strachan, formerly a Chartist speaker, who crept into the church unawares, and wished to preach in the church, contrary to the wish of some of the most pious of the brethren and one elder. He has endeavored to form a party. After the meeting I proposed to call the elders and deacons together. I called on deacon Monro, and found the party there assembled. I said, "So we have found the dividers of the church here!" Only two deacons and one elder present.

22nd.—John Mackie came at 11 o'clock a.m. I therfore went to the other elder's house. Peter Crombie had introduced William Thompson, who was preaching in the north as an evangelist, and endeavoring to spread A. Campbell's sentiments. I proposed, as one party wished me to preach, and another W. Thompson, that I would meet P. Crombie a quarter of an hour before the meeting of the church, that he, I, and Thompson might arrange. I waited in the school-room accordingly. Then Thompson, Crombie, and another opened the hall door, and without speaking to me, Thompson took the pulpit, and Crombie the precentor's desk. At the hour I went in and heard Thompson. When the service was over, as I thought, I desired the church to remain; I asked if they meant to have the Lord's Supper and whom they intended to preach, as a part had determined one should preach, and a part the other. Thompson stated that several of the brethren who had not heard him the last Lord's Day had left the church; this was denied. At last a majority determined that I should preach. However, to make all agreeable, I agreed to preach in the afternoon, and that we should both preach in the evening. I preached at two, and at Castle Street at four, but he took the pulpit at six and did not leave it till eight; however, I had much comfort in addressing the brethren at the after-meeting.

23rd and 24th.—Church meetings. After arguing over the matter of strict or open communion, the church came to an agreement to forbear with each other.

25th.—We met to arrange other matters. James Strachan had not conducted himself well and was afraid. Thompson saw he was not likely to make a party, and they therefore came to make a division. Crombie had presided over the church by force, not allowing any one else. He now left the desk, and declared that they, he and some others, did not intend to go with the church as it was, and declared the meeting dissolved. Another person was proposed to preside, and he, to prevent it, took the desk again. Union was now hopeless. All were baptized that were meeting. It seemed therefore folly and wickedness to divide the church about a question of theory. I besought them for Christ's sake, but all to no purpose. The division took place. As P. Crombie's party said they would keep the hall, if they could keep it; and although John Mackie and Alexander Cattanach's names were to the agreement (both with us) along with P. Crombie's, we determined to carry everything by reason and truth, and to use no other weapons, and if these failed to leave the matter with the Lord. The other party got possession of the keys and kept them. We took a place at Long Acre, at £11 a year.

26th.—I met those favorable to abide by the church, and had a comfortable meeting. About 22 or 23 remained.

29th.—Had a gracious day. Lectured twice on Campbellism; once to a large congregation in Castle Street, and to a crowded house in the school-room, Long Acre.

Oct. 1st.—DUNDEE. Saw the Queen and Prince Albert pass through. She was much more plainly attired than many of her subjects. In the evening a Mormonite commenced a debate after my hour's lecture.

4th.—I was able to bring forward much neglected truth during these two nights.

6th—Preached in the Nethergate Chapel to considerable congregations. ARBROATH, this morning at half-past seven, preached to about 2000 people. A Methodist local preacher, who has united with the brethren, was baptized. At ten o'clock took the mail train, and reached Dundee about eleven.

30th.—We had now held several meetings, both in Liverpool and Manchester, in order to promote union between the brethren with whom we fellowshipped, and others who also met in the Lord's name alone. Each meeting seemed to leave us more separated, and, as I was blamed by some on the other side with being the cause of this state of matters, I addressed the following letter to two of their chief brethren:—

58 NORTHUMBERLAND STREET,
LIVERPOOL, Oct. 30th, 1844.

To J. P———, and H. T———.

MY DEAR BRETHREN IN THE LORD,—

May the peace, wisdom, and favor of our Lord Jesus Christ be with you. As we all are aiming to honor the Lord, and draw together his saints, how lamentable it is that we cannot all meet together and co-operate visibly as Christians. To accomplish visible union, we have had conferences or conversations in both Liverpool and Manchester, which, I fear, have left us more disunited than we were before. Is it not strange that brethren cannot converse about union, and express different sentiments, and part without having less love and union than before? at least, so I infer from Brother T—'s letter to Brother P—, just put into my hands, which states that "the brethren meeting in George Street, Manchester, in several interviews with Brother Bowes, and the brethren with whom he was meeting in Camp Street, were very much annoyed by the frivolous objections of Brother Bowes, who was himself the originator of the conversations, and the chief hindrance to a union. We were also so much grieved with things, which the utmost efforts of charity could not construe into anything but misrepresentations, that several of our brethren felt constrained to speak to him in faithfulness before the Lord." Such statements, or stronger than this, had been made by "Brother B—," at Liverpool; so that when Brother C— invited me to go to a reading meeting at Hope Street, and I, to show love and union, passed by two other meetings to attend, I was told by Brother P—, that "Beatty's statements had made such an effect on their minds, that they would not wish to see me there." Accordingly, Brother P— called me out, and was unwilling that I should enter the meeting again, although I wished the brethren to hear both sides, and offered to give my views of the matter. Does Brother P— think this conduct—of refusing a brother liberty to attend a meeting—either Christian conduct, or likely to promote union? I would not have done so to *an unbeliever.* I would turn no man out of a meeting, or hinder him from being present; it is not courteous—it is not scriptural. "If there come in one that believeth not, or one unlearned, he is convinced of all, he is judged of all, and thus are the secrets of his heart made manifest; and so, falling down on his face, he will worship God, and report that God is in us of a truth." (1 Cor. xiv. 24, 25) I hope, Brother P—, you see that you did wrong, and that you are prepared to confess this fault. Does "Brother Beatty" think that reviling a brother in his absence is Christian conduct, and calculated to unite the church? Is it not rather "backbiting," which all saints should shun?

I wish now to state a few facts to prove that I have not hindered union, and that my "objections" against going over to the brethren in George Street, are weighty and scriptural, and not "frivolous," and that the "misrepresentation" is on the other side. I do not believe that it is wilful, however; but it is possible for Christians, when their prejudices and their party preferences are assailed, however gently, to be unduly excited. My objections, "frivolous" or not, are the following:—

1. The brethren in George Street will only receive Christians as individuals, and not as bodies. Hence they would not receive us at Camp Street as a body. But had we met in Salford, just across the *Irwell*, on the same principles as we now do, they could have received us, or recognised us as a body of believers, so as to break bread with us. We in Camp Street hold this to be sectarian, and that we are to receive those that God receives, whether they be individuals or bodies, and that not to do so is contrary to Rom. xiv. 1—3, and Matt. xviii. 1—6. We could

not ask a non-sectarian church in Manchester of 300 members to come either one by one or otherwise as individuals to us 20, but if satisfied that they were all Christians, we should just as much sit down with them in Manchester, as in Salford, or Bristol. If we found them impurely gathered, not all Christians, we should only receive the Christians. You yourselves act contrary to your own principles, when you visit other places. Should Brother T— come to Liverpool, he would not probably see all the Christians meeting in Hope Street. He would acknowledge them as saints on the testimony of two or three brethren, and sit down with them accordingly. Why did he not do so with us at Camp Street? Because he had the sectarian position to maintain. "We are the first gathering, you must come to us; we can receive individuals but not bodies." Why did brother T— and the brethren that are with him not examine us, when we offered to give a list of our names, if they would give a list of theirs? Why did they exact more than they were willing to concede?—than we conceded—in requiring us to reject any one found not to be a Christian among us—which we were willing to do—but declining, on their part, to say, that if we found one whom we regarded as not a Christian, that they would reject him?

2. The union did not take place, because we had no way left to unite with them but such as was open to us among the sects. (1.) "Come to us, but we will not come to you." So say all the sects; so said they, in substance, and so they acted, when we proposed to receive each other in the Lord. (2.) When we informed Brother T—, &c., that we would give them a list of names, if they would give us a list of theirs, that we might ultimately be satisfied of each other's Christianity, and unite. The brethren, we understand, were never convened, and no answer from them was given to our respectful and Christian proposal This conduct revived in my mind what I had seen in Exeter and Plymouth, and I do think soberly, that while "the brethren" profess to meet as such, and to reject the appointments, human or otherwise, of evangelists, elders, or deacons, that a few of them in each meeting, thinking themselves called of the Holy Spirit to rule and teach, in some cases rule like "lord's over God's heritage," being in reality *self-elected*— the worst kind of election. (3) We had no such names as "the Plymouth brethren," or "the brethren," and were unwilling to take any steps which might sanction these names to which too much countenance has been given by brethren in several places, if they are not a sect, and if they are, (which I incline to believe,) then the names may be correct enough for them, but not for us. We just longed for union with the Christians in George Street, as we longed for union with Christians among the Baptists, Methodists, &c. I believed that, so far as they met in the name of Christ alone, they met scripturally, and that so far as they received "Plymouth brethren" rather than others, and I understood them to acknowledge a preference, they were sectarian. For sectarianism I have no love; it is sin, just as drunkenness is sin, and I can give it no countenance. Brother T— may call this "frivolous;" it is not so to me. A brother asked, in a town hundreds of miles from Plymouth, "Where do the Plymouth Brethren meet here?" The brother replied in such a place; thus acknowledging that he was a Plymouth brother. I know the brethren in Manchester and Liverpool would not, generally, make any such profession, but in neither place are they sufficiently separated from "The Plymouth Brethren" for me to identify myself with them, and indeed I am growingly, but unwillingly, drawing on to the opinion that they cannot very consistently reject the name. (4) We do think that there ought to be deacons elected by the church to look after poor saints (See Acts vi.) There seems something strange to us in any brother taking the offering for poor saints of his own accord, or one brother taking it one time, and another at another, without election, or account being given to the body. We cannot believe, with "the brethren," that bishops and elders were required to teach and rule the church during the lives of the apostles, but that after their death, no more were to be set apart to the end of time! It is incredible that they should have been appointed when least needed, while the apostles lived, and that they were intended to cease, when most needed, after the apostles' death. (5) There was a narrowness of view taken by some of the brethren, as to teaching, which we did not like.

3. We did not see that they had proper scriptural discipline at George Street, nor do we see yet, and as it is on this head that I have been charged with "misrepresentation," I will state facts to the best of my recollection. Henry Turner and I had a conversation about the purity of the church, I said, an offender should be treated according to Matt. xviii., be first seen by one, and if he would not hear him, then by two or three, and if he would not hear them then it should

be told to the church; "But," said brother T—, "you have no church to tell it to." I thought we had, and that to falter at the last step, and not to expel the offender, would corrupt the church. Brother T—gave a case in George Street:—They were not satisfied with a person; two brethren spoke to the person; that person ceased to break bread from that conversation. I gathered that brother T's view was that offender's might be spoken to, but not expelled. He stated at the same time that he only gave his individual views. The effect of that conversation on my mind was as follows;—(1.) Though brother T— gives these as his views, he is an influential brother in the body and would of course hinder any expulsion if he could. (2.) He has stated a fact which relates to what the "gathering"—his brethren have done; this identifies them with his views. An offender has ceased to break bread, but is not "put away," and may therefore go and break bread, or call himself a brother or a member if he chooses. (3.) If a church will not "put away" an offender it must become corrupt. With these views, I gave up all idea of uniting with a system, which, looking at the whole case, I regarded as impure, for it seemed to me quite plain that a drunkard, a liar, or any other sort of a sinner who was not "put away," might call himself of the body, even if they did remonstrate with him, should they refuse to take the last step, mentioned in Matt. xviii. Now, brother T—, are not these things so? If they are, where is the misrepresentation? You may have spoken more guardedly since, as brethren, and more scripturally. It was necessary, not to prevent my "misrepresentation," but to prevent me from pointing out what was unscriptural and detrimental to the purity of the church. Will you state distinctly what the misrepresentation is? While you, brother T—, acknowledge me to be the "Lord's child," you say, "this desire to be something (which lurks in all of us) is the reason of brother Bowes' unfortunate conduct here, and I am not saying more than I have privately mentioned to him." And is this the love "which thinketh no evil?" How does brother T— know this "desire" of my heart? Is he a judge of my heart? I know, if I know anything of it, that this witness it not true. Will any of my brethren in Liverpool, Dundee, or anywhere else, who have met with me for years, affirm that I have manifested this pride,—for this is the name of what is insinuated among them? No, it is an unworthy calumny. Brother T—, Christian union can never be promoted by such means.

And now, my beloved brethren, I and my brethren are as fervent as ever in our desire for the union of saints,—we long for it. Both in Liverpool and Manchester we were willing to unite with you on scriptural terms, to receive each other in the Lord, and you declined. We were willing to make matters about which we differ in opinion, matters of forbearance. We think there ought to be church meetings, Evangelists, Bishops or Elders, and Deacons in the church, but we are willing to leave these matters for decision after being united.

Is it not a most lamentable thing, that in Liverpool and Manchester there are three or four meetings, all professing not to be sectarian, and to seek the union of Christians, and yet these Christians and meetings have no more union with them than the sects have with each other, nay, not so much? Consider this matter over. I beseech you, for Christ's sake, and for the honor of his Church, do not forget the union of the body, but seek to unite with all that are united with Jesus. With brotherly love in the Lord to you both, and to all saints, and trusting that you will make this known as widely as the evil report of Beatty,

I am, &c.,

JOHN BOWES.

P.S.—I shall be obliged to brother P—, if he will forward this to brother T—.

Nov. 3rd.—WOOLTON. When I was in Liverpool in the Spring, John Rushton, who has charge of his father's business, with about 20 men under him, found peace and joy through believing, united with a few lively brethren, and having taken a room, we opened it with great comfort. In the evening a very large congregation of Methodists, Episcopalians, &c.

4th.—LIVERPOOL. Preached in Soho Street Chapel; brother Jones baptized ten.

16th.—CARLISLE. Brother Daniels baptized three in the river Eden. One young man, a Christian, was persuaded only a few minutes before the time. I pressed upon him the command of Peter, Acts x., and commanded him to be baptized in the name of the Lord. He submitted.

17th.—Broke bread with about 80 brethren in Albert square. I set before the people the excellencies of the Lord Jesus Christ. At half-past two, preached Christ, repentance, faith, and baptism, as commanded—exemplified, and the promises made concerning them. At six, heard F. Daniel for a short time, to a large congregation out of doors. The room was filled at night.

18th.—Another was buried with Christ by baptism in the waters of the Eden. Baptism should no more be delayed than obedience to any other command. When a man believes, he should speedily be baptized. Thus, on hearing Peter's pentecostal discourse, "They that gladly received his word were baptized; and the same day there were added unto them about three thousand souls." Thus, also, we read of the jailor at Philippi, "And he took them the same hour of the night, and washed their stripes; and was baptized, he and all his, straightway."—Acts ii. 41—xvi. 33.

20th.—Brother F. Daniel mentioned to me the happy death of James M'Adam, a Christian, and a minister for many years. He visited the aged saint on his death-bed, and wishing to ascertain the state of his mind, though his wife thought him to be unconscious, and did not wish him to be disturbed, F. D. said, "It's hard work." The dying man answered strongly with a smile, "Pleasant labor!" These were his last words.

Dec. 5th.—DUNCANSTON, Scotland, near Insch. Here a few brethren and sisters have begun to meet in the Lord's name alone, as the following extract from a letter from a very dear brother shows:—

"Your visit to this part of the country has not been without effect. There are a number who see that a one-man hired ministry is unscriptural, and also the necessity of union among Christians." It states that a few believers have agreed to meet together on the Lord's Day "to exhort one another, and to observe whatsoever Christ has commanded us. We know that in so doing we are exposing ourselves to the reproach of those we have highly esteemed, but we also know that the approval of our own conscience and the blessing of our God are more than those that are against us. We are also in some measure convinced that we are responsible to our Master, and we are also convinced that in the day in which he will reckon with us, we will not be able to stand up and urge as a reason for neglecting some of his commands, that they were not popular, and that those whom we loved and esteemed would not join us in attending to them: and therefore we are resolved that whatever others do, we will serve the Lord in the way we believe he has commanded us."

"JAMES SHEARER."

"Croft end of Auchlyne, Dec. 5th, 1844."

The principle, self-denial, and decision of this letter, are worthy of imitation.

23rd.—To-day left Middleham. Before parting with my father he told me that he expected to be able to live on the interest of the money he had saved. I stated in my discourses, I hope faithfully, what the scriptures teach on this subject.

24th.—LEEDS. Called to see my uncle, Dawson Bowes. Found him upon a dying bed. He has been for some time lame, and dependent for support on others. When I called a few days ago, he seemed happy in the prospect of death and glory. He said, " I would not give the place to which I am going for a hundred such worlds as this." "John," said he, with tears and cheerful joy, "I have been a beggar all my life, but I shall be a King's son there." My aunt died last night. He only lived a few days after this. "To die is gain," when we live to Christ.

THE EVIL OF SECTS.

While the wicked and righteous remain in the world, we must have these two parties—we need no more. As the wicked are marshalled under the prince of darkness, and constitute but one army, so Christians, led on to victory by Christ the captain of their salvation, should constitute but one visible army. We have no warrant to divide those whom God has united. The true church, the body of Christ, is not bounded by the limits of the largest party; it is composed of believers, of the sons of God, scattered through every party. Present and powerful churches, rich in worldly wealth, and large in numbers, may have but few of the true church in them;—churches, poor in worldly wealth, may contain many members of the body of Christ. His body consists of many members, who should appear as one body. No sectarian appellation would properly describe a church thus united. "I groan over the divisions of the church—of all our evils, I think, the greatest—of Christ's church, I mean, that men should call themselves Roman Catholics, Church of England-men, Baptists, Quakers, all sorts of various appellations, forgetting only that glorious name of Christian, which is common to all, and a true bond of union. I begin now to think that things must be worse before they are better, and that nothing but some great pressure from without will make Christians cast away their idols of sectarianism—the worst and most mischievous by which Christ's church has ever been plagued."—*Arnold, of Rugby*. Dolby says,—"I have long felt an utter loathing of what bears the general denomination of '*the Church*,' with all its parties, contests, disgraces, or honors. My wish would be little less than the dissolution of all church institutions, of all orders, and shapes, that religion might be set free, as a grand spiritual moral element, no longer clogged, perverted, and prostituted by corporations and forms."

THE INFLUENCE OF WEALTH IN THE CHURCH.

The church is a spiritual community, in which all are the sons and daughters of the Lord Almighty—kings and priests unto God. When any one is received into the church, put into office, or honored because of his wealth, while his poorer brethren are overlooked and despised, the sin is committed mentioned by James ii,—"If ye have respect to persons, ye commit sin." No man deserves more respect than another because of his wealth. Such respect is not the love of the brethren, but the love of wealth. In the church no man should be honored because he is rich—no man should be despised because he is poor. The honor given to wealth in the world has been transferred to the church, to the great injury of its moral power. If a rich man has obtained his wealth by honorable means; if he distributes it in clothing the naked, in feeding the hungry, in entertaining strangers, in spreading scripturally the gospel, he deserves our respect, not because he is wealthy, but because he is *benevolent*,—not because his purse is long, but because his heart is large. He sows bountifully, and he will reap bountifully.

THE POWER OF THE TRUTH.

I fear many believers have underrated this power. They have expected their own sanctification to advance, and sinners to be saved in answer to prayer, without placing sufficient confidence in the truth. "Sanctify them through thy truth—thy word is truth," was the prayer and explanation of our divinely-appointed Saviour. If the truth as it is in Jesus is to sway and rule the soul, to penetrate and refine the inmost recesses of the man, and bring forth the rich fruits of holiness in the life, it must be *understood*—it must be more read, considered, and experienced. It is the great means appointed by our heavenly Father for subduing other rebels to his authority. We pray for revivals, and wonder why we see so few;—we ask for the conversion of our children and neighbors, and are disappointed that our prayers are not answered. Why are we unsuccessful? We have not made known the gospel. We have kept back the truth. We have prayed for the conversion of a sinner without at the same time telling him as much truth as would convert him, so that had he believed all we ever taught, he could not have been saved by it. We did not teach the gospel fully, plainly, and like men in earnest. If we wish our child or neighbor to be converted, let us take him aside and teach him the love of God to man. Men are ruined by hard thoughts of God. Let us proclaim his love, and prove it by the death of Christ for our sins, and by his burial and resurrection.

A BURNING AFFECTION FOR THE HUMAN RACE.

One of the first lessons which Jesus Christ gives his pupils is *self-denial*; one of the first examples he places before us is his own. He could set nothing more glorious before us. His was a life of untiring zeal, of arduous toil, of unquenchable love to mankind. The highest eulogium on his history is contained in these few words—"HE WENT ABOUT DOING GOOD." Let us drink into His spirit, and copy His example. The good we can do must necessarily be limited, but let us remember that it is an inspired injunction "to do good unto all men." Let us never ask whether they are rich men or poor men—English, Irish, or Scotch—it is enough for us that they are men—our fellow-creatures. Ignorant, let us instruct them; profligate, reform them; hungry, feed them; thirsty, if even our enemies, give them drink. Are they sorrowful, let us comfort them; in sickness, let us visit them. If we have wiped away the tears of a child, and sent him home with cheerful joy in his countenance, we have done something for suffering humanity. Let us address ourselves with firmness of purpose, with decision of soul, and, above all, with a large affection for man as man, to the work of doing good, and we cannot live and labor in vain. We shall diminish the burdens, lessen the sorrows, and wipe away the tears of many a suffering heart. We shall diminish the enemies, augment the friends, and add largely to the comforts and joys of our fellow-creatures. Oh, when will Christians hear more music, more charming melody in the songs of widows whose hearts they have made to sing for joy, than in the most costly organ. Christians talk of their doubts and fears while they are seeking comfort. Let them seek the comfort of others—employ themselves busily, earnestly, and constantly, for the benefit of society, and they will become happy in making other people happy, while they are so throng as scarcely to have time to think about personal comfort.

THE CHURCH IS THE GREAT REFORMER OF MAN.

But the church can only reform others as she teaches the truth herself, and sustains all her teaching by the weight of a consistent example. The church is indeed "the light of the world," just so far as she inculcates the truth, and walks according to its commands. She is "the salt of the earth," sending forth a penetrating, healthful influence far and wide, just as she is Christ-like; but if, on the contrary, the very salt loses its savor, it becomes an outcast thing, and instead of it being useful to men, they tread it under their feet. If we wish to make men right, to destroy their rebellion, and bring them over to Christ, we must first make the church right, by purging out the old leaven that we may be a new lump. The church that teaches humility must be humble—the church that teaches faith must show that she believes God for both temporal and spiritual bestowments. If I could not trust my body with God, I would not trust my soul with him. Shall he save from sin and hell, and leave us on earth without food and raiment? The church that teaches love to God and man must show it by actions. Her membership, ministry, institutions, all require searching reforms. My love for the church induces me to say this. He is his child's best friend who sets himself to correct what is amiss. He is my best friend who lovingly, but faithfully, points out my faults. "My love for any place, or person, or institution, is exactly the measure of my desire to reform them; a doctrine which seems to me as rational now as it seemed strange when I was a child, when I could not make out how, if my mother loved me more than strange children, she should find fault with me and not with them."—*Arnold's Life*, vol i. p. 415.

I fear that many Christians are overlooking the mighty influence which a true Christian church, such as she was in the beginning, had once on the world, and may have again. Without at all entering the arena of politics, I do venture to suggest to politicians of every school, that no government, of whatever kind, can be really good, only so far as it is composed of good men. Now, what is to make them good but the truth —the gospel which the church has to teach? And how can she teach it with effect, without walking according to it? I confess my utter ignorance of any other way by which men can be made good, Christlike men. Then, as bad men would govern badly, even under good laws, how can bad men make or keep good laws? Let us, then, first make men Christians by the truth—by the church—and then we shall find more agreement as to the modes or kinds of government. If there is any force in the adage, "whatever is best administered is best," we may rest assured that, as good men will make good laws, so they will administer them for the good of society. If Christian men, who, I grieve to say, spend much time and money in establishing their own favorite theory of government, would devote both to the great work of Christianizing the nation by the truth, they would act more in character, and do incalculably more good. Patriotism should prompt us to this. Whately said of Arnold, of Rugby, "He was attached to his family as if he had no friends—to his friends as if he had no family—and to his country as if he had no friends or relations."—*Arnold's Life, &c.*, vol. i. p. 237.

We can never be wrong, if we do not use wrong means, in attempting to make people Christians.

HOLDING CONFERENCES OF CHRISTIANS.

Christians have kept too much aloof from each other. If they would come together in the spirit of love and candor, and converse over their difficulties and plans of union and co-operation, truth would be elicited and diffused among many thoughtful and vigorous minds. Almost any kind of motion is better, more healthful, than a dead calm. If the church move at all in the way of scriptural investigation, and consequent action, she can hardly get into a worse position than she is in. With the scriptures as her text-book, she cannot go towards Rome. That is a journey which no man can take under biblical direction. The followers of Newman and Pusey first undervalue scriptural authority, and having got rid of its restraints, then, and not till then, they hasten towards Rome.

CHAPTER X.

GILLBENT CHURCH.—LETTER TO THE LIVERPOOL CHURCH.—MR. LEICESTER.—DEATH OF INFIDELS.—THE JEW.—ILLNESS.—RETURNING GOOD FOR EVIL.—STRANGE SCENE IN A WESLEYAN CHAPEL.—LETTER TO ROMAN CATHOLICS.—A CHRISTIAN GOVERNMENT.—PORTRAITS.—SPEECH AGAINST WAR.—BRYAN M'MAKEN AND HIS WIFE MADGE.—1845, 1846, 1847, 1848.

Jan., 1845.—GILLBENT. The second Lord's Day of this year, I spent at Grove Lane Chapel, Gillbent, Cheadle Mosely, Cheshire. A church has been gathered during the last four or five years, under the following circumstances.—WILLIAM FOWDEN, of Manchester, felt a concern for his native place—was anxious that it might have the gospel. He engaged a missionary to preach to the people, and visit them, who, after a few months, was called away into eternity. John Alcorn, who is now there acting as a missionary or evangelist, was engaged. About fifty believers meet in the Lord's name alone, having no bond of union but "love, which is the bond of perfectness." All who are united to Christ have access to their communion. Although all the members have now been immersed on a profession of their faith, baptism does not divide them from any of their Father's children. The talents of the church are at liberty to be exercised for the good of the whole. A chapel was erected for the people by the same brother that supports the evangelist, and when it became too small, he put a gallery into it. It seems capable of containing from three to four hundred, and the Lord's Day that I was with them, it was tolerably filled. While rich Christians should be careful to supply the wants of their poor brethren, they should also be anxious to spread the gospel all over the world. It is thought that had the first laborer not been removed by death, there might have been no church there yet. When God imparts the gifts of an evangelist to one of his followers, they cannot be employed in vain. If brother Alcorn has the work of an evangelist to do, while he endeavors to cultivate the gifts of the church, he should also preach Christ, as he has opportunity, in the neighboring towns and parishes. The church should not rest in the gifts of one or two brethren, but exhort one another—"edify one another." Depend more upon the Lord for bestowing gifts, and as good stewards occupy what they have to their Master's honor. As they have derived great blessing from the labors of an evangelist, they should unite to support evangelists, that the land may be filled with New Testament truth, and that it may be said of them, as of the church of the Thessalonians, "For from you sounded out the word of the Lord, not only in Macedonia and Achaia, but also in every place, your faith to God-ward is spread abroad."—1 Thess. i. 8. An active church, which spreads far and wide the truth by which it lives, resembles the onward progress of an overflowing, pure, wide-spread river. An indolent church resembles the thick waters of a stagnant lake, offensive to the eye, and injurious to the health.

LETTER.

TO THE CHURCH OF CHRIST ASSEMBLING AT HILL STREET, LIVERPOOL.

61 York Street, Hulme,
Manchester, Jan. 15th, 1845.

Dear Brethren in Christ,—

May the favor, mercy, and peace of God our Father, and the Lord Jesus Christ be with you all.

It has long been our conviction that Christians in order to be useful in this age, must not only come out from its peculiar evils, but endeavor to bring their fellow-Christians out of them, by exposing their unscriptural character and evil tendency. It is now some years since some of us tasted the bliss of meeting together as the disciples of Jesus—owning no human authority, that we might shew the greater deference to that which is divine. During the past year, impressed with the necessity of active labors in this populous district, I mentioned to several of the churches the necessity of co-operating to enable me to proclaim Divine truth amid its hundreds of thousands. About seven months ago I came, and although I have often been called off to other parts, my main labors have been in this district. Since I came, the opposition has been great, but the prospect was never so cheering as at this moment. The Manchester church is peaceful and happy, and contains about twenty-one precious saints. I have repeatedly preached and lectured at Stockport, where a great impression has been made, and a few brethren have resolved to meet in the Lord's name, and they are expecting great results. A Christian brother from Woodhouses, a few miles distant, was walking about, and came to hear me at Salford, on the first Lord's Day of the year. After preaching Christ, I showed how Christians should meet together. He said, "This is what I have long been seeking," and he and seven more have agreed to leave the Methodists, and to meet according to the revealed will of Christ. The last Lord's Day I spent at Gillbent, ten miles from Manchester, where about fifty brethren meet as we do. They have a congregation of about 300, and take 26 Magazines monthly. A brother built them a chapel, and supports an evangelist. The same brother has engaged an evangelist for Rusholme.

Hitherto, my mind has been tolerably free from care as to temporal support. Some of the churches, though few and poor, have abounded in kindness. I refer especially to Dundee and Arbroath, which have generally sent more or less every month since I came. Other churches have either sent nothing at all, or only once or twice. I suggested at the first, that where brethren are not rich, but willing to give a little once a week, or fortnight, that it would be better for one or two brethren to receive it thus, that either quarterly or yearly they may forward it in order to assist in carrying on the Lord's work. Individual brethren in Liverpool have assisted several times. It is possible that when the brethren look at my Yearly Report, they may think that I have received a considerable sum this last year; but when they remember that, in the course of the year, I have travelled about five or six thousand miles, beside removing my family from Aberdeen to Manchester, they will discover that I could not have done all the good I have without a considerable outlay. The shop, which I hoped might help us, has not cleared more than £2 in six months; so that we are as much dependent as ever upon the Lord and his people.

I would also suggest that the Scriptures require these labors of disciples. If we have given over seat-rents, and dependence on the world, it is not that we may do nothing ourselves, but that we may do more, while the world does nothing. The year opens with bright prospects. About 20 Magazines now circulate at Preston; 74 at Lancaster; and 50 at Carlisle, beside the Scotch circulation. I would have the brethren not only to think of supporting one evangelist, but as many as the Lord may send out. "Even so hath the Lord ordained, that they who preach the gospel, should live of the gospel." (1 Cor. ix. 1—14.) Paul said to the Philippians:—"Notwithstanding ye have well done, that ye did communicate with my affliction. Now, ye Philippians, know also, that in the beginning of the gospel, when I departed from Macedonia, no church communicated with me as concerning giving and receiving, but ye only. For even in Thessalonica ye sent once and again to my necessity. Not because I desire a gift; but I desire fruit, which may abound to your account. But I have all, and abound: I am full; having received of Epaphroditus the things which were sent from you, an odour of a sweet smell, a sacrifice acceptable, well-pleasing to God. But my God shall supply all your need, according to his riches in glory by Christ Jesus."

May the grace of our Lord Jesus Christ, and the love of God, and the communion of the Holy Spirit, be with you all. This will be sent to most of those churches which have been drawn together through my labors. Yours, &c.

JOHN BOWES.

Jan. 18th & 19th, 1845.—LEES. Delivered two lectures on Primitive Christianity. Several questions were asked. Saw a young man, drawn to the town in a cart, who had hanged himself. He had stated on the previous Lord's Day, that he would never enter the mill again. He kept his word. His wages were inadequate, considering his work and age. Had he resolved to live a little longer, he might have seen better days. How fearful to rush into the presence of God unprepared.

On the 24th of last month, J. H. of this place, an infidel, with a large weekly income, about fifty years of age, hung himself in the mill. He has left a wife and family. In the last year, about nine or ten months previously, F. C. father-in-law to J. H., cut his throat. He had been an infidel the greater part of his life.

A very few years ago, in this neighborhood lived a Socialist; he used to go to the Hall of Science, Oldham, and a young woman with him. She married a young man, and was found pregnant to the Socialist. A fortnight after her marriage she drowned herself. Some time after, her seducer, who was a married man with a family, was thrown out of work, and set off to America. He kept his bed on the passage, never rose again, and never landed. He died before the vessel reached America.

The Science taught in the Socialist's Hall, may be judged of by R. Owen's immoral writings, and by such cases as this. Sin is the only real source of misery; holiness the only real source of happiness.

Feb. 1st, 2nd, & 3rd.—WOOLTON. Several here, of late, have been brought to know the gospel, and to profess faith in it. The congregations were large and deeply attentive. I invited, by letter, the Clergyman, the Romish Priest, and the Wesleyan Methodists. The Priest wondered why I had not given him his title, "Rev." and would have come as a hearer, but he had a ball to attend! Blind leader of the blind. As the Clergyman has made some efforts to hinder us from doing good in the parish, and is circulating soul-destroying errors himself, I wrote him as follows.

WOOLTON, Feb. 1st, 1845.

DEAR SIR,—

Having been informed that very dangerous errors have been circulated in this parish through your efforts, and being persuaded that your whole religious system is contrary to the Holy Scriptures, I beg to call your attention to a Conference, which will be held, if the Lord will, in the School-room opposite Turner's Coffee House, at 7 o'clock, p.m., on the 3rd instant, as intimated by placards, which invite Christians of all denominations to attend. If I, and the few Christians who assemble in Christ's name alone be right, your views of the gospel, of the regeneration, or the being born again of unconscious infants, when a few drops of water are sprinkled on their faces, is a dangerous delusion, which you substitute for the being born of Spirit—being made children of God by faith, as John clearly asserts, (1 Epistle, v. 1.) "Whosoever believeth that Jesus is the Christ, is born of God." We believe that Christians should not remain in any society called a church, which takes no care to exclude the ungodly from communion; and that, if they sustain any such society, they perpetuate the corruptions of the apostasy. That you may see our objections to your sentiments and practices—objections based on the words of Christ and the apostles, I enclose a tract, which is being circulated by thousands, called "New Testament Principles of Church order and Unity." If we be wrong you will have a fine chance of setting us right, by an appeal to the Scriptures.

I am, your's in love and peace,
JOHN BOWES.

To Robert Leicester, Episcopalian minister.

4th.—LIVERPOOL, Hill Street Room. A singularly blessed season.

5th.—Welsh Baptist Chapel. The largest congregation I ever preached to, in it. Five were buried with Christ by baptism.

6th.—Independent Methodist Tabernacle. A lecture on Primitive Christianity. Christians of two or three churches present: all very loving. When shall these walls, which separate Christians be thrown down? Christians help, and they shall yet fall; for God is against them.

James Henderson, of New Leslie, near Insch, in a letter of Feb. 4th writes, "I was buried with Christ, by baptism, in the month of September last; and my wife in the month of October. I was a member of D. Morrison's congregation, at Duncanston, for several years; but as soon as he knew that I was baptized, he sent one of his congregation to inform me that I was put out of his church, and that I was not to be allowed to sit down with them at the Lord's Table. I heard the message, and I thought it a strange one." Well he might. The Congregationalists avow that they will admit all Christians to their fellowship; but instead of acting out this principle, the church at Duncanston either expels, or allows the minister to expel, a Christian for treading in the steps of his Master, who was baptized by John in the river Jordan. When J. Henderson desired the minister to allow him an opportunity of addressing the church, it was refused. Brother Henderson has united with the few Christians that meet in the Lord's name alone, at the Croft end of Auchline, one Lord's Day, and at New Leslie, parish of Leslie, Aberdeenshire, the other.

The church at Manchester has engaged the Temperance Meeting Room, Hardman Street, and proposes meeting there on the first day of the week, at half-past ten, half-past two, and six o'clock; and at eight on Tuesday evening.

James Strachan, the leader, and the chief cause of the late unhappy separation at Aberdeen, has been called away in mid-life to answer to God for rending his church. Let all who joined him in the schism, take warning. He died suddenly last month, the first of this year.

March 6th.—I have for some weeks visited Mr. B——. Ministers and others had visited and prayed with him. I commenced with the facts of the gospel, detailing the birth, life, miracles, death for our sins, resurrection, and ascension of the Lord Jesus Christ. His attention was fixed. He was astonished at the good tidings of pardon, as God's free gift, through faith. To-day he expressed his great gratitude for the truths taught him, and said to me, "I never knew, until you explained it to me, that Jesus Christ was ever upon the earth, and that he wrought miracles; though I had sung Christmas carols when I was a boy, it never occurred to me that he was born in a stable, and that he suffered for our sins." He seemed to be conscious that this ignorance was a shame to him, and spoke of it in that light to his nurse. He is nearly fifty years of age, is rated for the income tax, and has often heard sermons in a Methodist chapel! This is the most remarkable case I ever met with, and proves the importance of not taking it for granted that persons, whom we wish to believe, are acquainted with the facts of the gospel: we should treat them as though they had everything to learn.

30*th.*—PRESTON. I spent a few days here some years ago, and when I visited Lancaster last year, I called upon Brother Thomas Sinkinson, since which we have corresponded. I spent this, the Lord's day, and four following days here. Upwards of twenty brethren meet in the Lord's name alone, in Lawson Street Chapel, to observe the commandments and ordinances of Christ as they have been given to disciples. Several of them have been buried with Christ in the waters of the *Ribble*, and there seems to exist among them brotherly love.

I spent a few very happy days with them. I trust they will all seek zealously the conversion of souls. Let us never forget that two things are important, and should go hand in hand—scriptural order, and teaching the truth on a wide scale for the conversion of sinners. If the Christians that are now free from the sects would only seek more of the Spirit of Christ, like him they would "go about doing good." They would co-operate together to fill the land with scriptural churches and saving truth.

June 27*th.*—LIVERPOOL.—Preached to a large congregation in Williamson's Square. Deep attention seemed to be excited.

29*th.*—Great Crosshall Street Room, at half-past ten. Had a refreshing season at the Lord's Supper, as I generally have. How sweet to remember Jesus,—to remember that he died for our sins, while we were yet enemies, thus teaching us to cultivate a kindred spirit to each other, and to our worst foes. In this institution we are also animated to hope for our Master's return—" we show his death till he come." I had rather sit at the Lord's table than at the Queen's.

July 1*st.*—This morning a breakfast was given to Merle D'Aubigne, in the Music Hall, at 3s.6d. each. Such meetings reward the rich and punish the poor. I had neither money to spare—and if I had, I should not encourage such a course of proceeding—nor do I approve of such charges. Having a high regard for D'Aubigne, and a great desire to see him, I denied myself this pleasure, and sent him a copy of some of the most useful of my publications, with a letter containing my views of the breakfast. He sent the following note:—

"DEAR SIR,—I thank you for your books and letter. I believe there are many poor among the rich, and many rich among the poor. The Lord may give us to be poor in ourselves and rich in Him. Your brother,

"MERLE D'AUBIGNE."

1st July, 1845.

2*nd.*—Sailed for Scotland by the *Princess Royal,*—a fine passage. A Jew, rather intelligent, on board. He has been several years in England, and speaks English very well. States that the Jews are very kind to their poor, and still expect the Messiah. I endeavored to show him from their own prophets, that Jesus Christ was the despised and rejected one foretold by Isaiah, Daniel, &c., and read to him Zech. xii. 10, "And I will pour upon the house of David, and upon the inhabitants of Jerusalem, the spirit of grace and supplication; and they shall look upon me whom they have pierced, and they shall mourn for him as one mourneth for his only son, and shall be in bitterness for him as one that is in bitterness for his first-born." I asked him if any but Jehovah "could pour the spirit of grace and supplication?" He acknowledged that it applied to Jehovah. I then proved that the words "they shall look upon me whom they have pierced," could not apply to any one but to Jesus Christ, since God, as God, could not be pierced, and since God manifested in the flesh was pierced in the flesh by the soldier's spear: so that the person here spoken of must be both God and man, and that the text can apply to no one else but to the Lord Jesus Christ. To this he gave no satisfactory answer. His wife often wished him away, owing to the crowd of people that came around us, but he came back again, and was quite free to speak with me, but declined giving his reasons for not believing in Christ. I pointed him to the stupendous miracles wrought by the Saviour, and asked him if they did not prove that he was sent of God? He referred me to two Rabbis, one in Liverpool, and another in London, and told me they would give me satisfaction on the texts and miracles. He always referred me to them when he could not answer; exactly as the Roman Catholic refers to the priest. It appears that still the blind Jews, who reject the Messiah, are following their blind leaders. When will men break the yoke of priestly dictation, and freely search the scriptures for themselves? After this a Swedenborgian endeavored to deny a resurrection to come. I read and expounded the greater part of 1 Cor. xv.

3rd.—Met a few Christians in GLASGOW. They meet together weekly. Some of them are afraid of a church, others of them desire it. I do not expect them to do much good as a meeting while they are in their present loose state, but let them boldly and humbly imitate the first Christians, and they will do good in this great city.

4th.—Arrived in DUNDEE about twelve o'clock at night.

5th.—Preached on the shore, near the place where, a few years ago, I was fined £2 for preaching.

6th.—West Port.—Out of doors at eight in the morning. The rest of the day I spent happily with the church.

7th.—Preached again on the shore. The truth seemed to penetrate the hearts of the people. While discoursing on the love of God to us, and the love we should show to all the children of God and to all mankind, even to our greatest enemies, the power of love was mightily felt.

9th.—NEWBURGH. In the open-air; many listened to the truth. Held a conversation with two who have fallen into A. Campbell's errors on no forgiveness or remission but in baptism. One of them admitted that many had felt peace and joy on believing without being baptized. He said "It is like a man being satisfied with a piece of paper that he has put into his pocket, believing it to be a £5 note, because it was like one, and it gave him all the satisfaction of a real £5 note while he believed it to be one." This illustration turned against his theory with overwhelming effect, and he would feel it the more keenly as he has published this view. I proved that all that believe "do enter into rest,"—that Christ says, "Come unto me all ye that labor and are heavy laden and I will give you rest,"—that Christ promises "peace," "joy," "love," as well as "rest;" and then I asked, "Do you call all these no more than a blank piece of paper, or a forgery?" Out of the fulness of the heart men speak. When there is nothing but baptism in the heart, nothing else can be expected from the mouth; but when Christ is in the heart, he will be the theme of the mouth; when baptism is mentioned, it will be in its place, and hold a beautiful and lovely connexion with other parts of revealed truth.

11*th.*—FERRY-PORT-ON-CRAIG. In the Baptist meeting place. As there was a meeting of the Free Church the meeting was small. Two or three very kind families.

12*th.*—Crossed the Tay in a ferry-boat, engaged for the purpose, to reach Arbroath in time for the Steamer for ABERDEEN. Preached in Castle Street in the evening to a large congregation.

13*th.*—Spent the day in our meeting room, Long Acre, excepting that I preached out of doors at four o'clock. The room full at six.

16*th.*—Brother James Shearer met me at Pitcaple with a pony, to take me to his house at Croft end of Auchlyne, Clatt, where I discoursed in the evening.

17*th.*—Rode with brother Shearer to the GLEN OF FOUDLAND. A barn, fitted up with pulpit and seats, was the preaching place. The Established and Free church ministers preach occasionally in it. A large and deeply interested congregation. A cordial invitation from the farmer to return. May these sheep that pour down from the mountain sides ever feed in the richest pastures of divine truth. Remained all night at John Mackay's, on the mountain side. He is the chief teacher in a Baptist meeting, the members of which break bread sometimes with the brethren that meet at Clatt and Leslie parishes. This is as it should be. Why should little differences of judgment divide the children of God? Some are beginning to see that party names are evil.

18*th.*—INSCH. The hall was asked here from a professing Christian, and refused. Had I preached the doctrines of a sect the last time that I was here, the Hall would have been granted again. It is the same spirit that refuses sites to the Free Church. One of the brethren accommodated us nearly as well in his barn. The two ministers that asked questions the last time were not here. By the last visit good was done. Some began to meet in Christ's name alone.

20*th.*—CROFT END OF AUCHLYNE, CLATT. Ten of us sat down at the Lord's Table in the forenoon: had the Master's presence. As several more Christians were present, I should have liked every child of God to have taken his seat at his Father's Table.

Rode to AUCHLEVIN, parish of Premna, where Peter Ferres preaches every fortnight. More present than the hall would hold.

21*st.*—Rose about four, and set off for Banff and Macduff. Found, as the fishermen were out at the herring fishing, and as the night was cold and inclining to rain, that I should not likely get a congregation. Found a Christian brother, named Rettie, about returning to Cumminston. I rode in his cart about nine miles, and walked the rest to New Pitsligo, which I reached after eleven o'clock, having been travelling since five, a.m., and gone over about fifty miles of ground. The Christian family were gone to bed. I rested a few hours, took counsel with them, and set off before five o'clock on the 22nd, to get a coach for Aberdeen. After walking nine miles, met the coach.

23*rd.*—A large and deeply attentive congregation in Castle Street. Here I learned that Ellen Magee and her husband had been led to renounce Roman Catholicism through a discourse which I had delivered in Dundee some years ago. In the course of the series I dwelt upon the evil of withholding the cup from the laity, so that no living Roman Catholic, who is not a priest, has ever taken the Lord's Supper since he was born, and that for bread the communicant got a wafer. She went once after this, determined to see whether I had told the truth or not, and after the priest had put the wafer on her tongue, she contrived to take it off with her hand, unobserved, and to take it home and examine it. She found it to contain no body, soul, or Divinity of Jesus Christ, but to be a mere wafer. From that time she left the church of Rome, and on removing to Aberdeen, united with us. Through some imperfect instruction on her own part she left us, and some time after united with the Wesleyan Methodists. From all I can hear she is now united to Christ. Her husband has left Rome, but I fear does not yet know the Lord Jesus Christ as his Saviour. Since this occurred, I have conversed with John M'Guiness, who has left the church of Rome. He entered the Toxteth Hall, Liverpool, where one of our brethren was preaching. I asked him what in the preaching led him to renounce the church of Rome? He said, "The prodigal child." As the prodigal son was forgiven by his father without a priest, he thought God could thus forgive any sinner now. He said, "The priest makes himself God when he professes to forgive sins." I answered, "God only can forgive sins." He, his wife, and two daughters have left the church of Rome.

24th.—STONEHAVEN. A considerable congregation in the Temperance Hall. Several questions asked. I hope that several, who here approve of the truth, will act it out.

25th and *26th.*—Sailed for ARBROATH. Preached out of doors, foot of Bog Lane and Shambles Bridge.

28th.—Lord's Day, half-past seven, morning. Considerable congregation out of doors. Discoursed in the School-room at eleven, and Lord's Supper at two. Here is a very loving little church. They have been peaceful and loving since they began to meet. I never saw so many in the place of meeting as at six o'clock, when I endeavored to preach Christ to his enemies, and to teach his friends several important truths.

30th.—EDINBURGH. Got a chair from Prince's Street, and preached on the Mound to a large congregation. Had present a precious mother in Israel, who was led to know Jesus through a discourse which I preached here some years ago. Also, J. Jeffrey, who once aided me while I preached in a steam-boat, on the Tay, from Perth to Dundee.

PROGRESS OF THE TRUTH.

During the year churches have been organized according to the New Testament at Clatt and Leslie, in Scotland; Carlisle and Preston, in England. Two or three brethren have begun to meet in the Lord's name alone at Stockport. There are other four meetings in a state of transition from an unscriptural to a scriptural position.

During the year I have printed more publications than on any previous year.

1 of 24 pages—3,000 copies, making 81,000 pages.
.. 12 .. 24,500 .. .. 294,000 ..
.. 4 .. 28,000 .. .. 112,000 ..

Total copies, 55,5000   Total pages, 487,000

Aug. 12th.—I awoke this morning exceedingly ill, and remained so all day. Took my usual medicine, half an ounce of the best pulverized Rochelle salts. My dear wife wished me to send for the doctor, but I would not consent. I do not know that I have been so ill for twenty years. It seemed to me as though, from the pain in my head especially, I might be called into eternity in a few hours. How weak is the strongest, healthiest man, when God visits him by affliction!

14th.—I am recovering very fast. During my affliction I thought of death with calmness, without fear; and of life, only with desire if it should be the Lord's will. Sometimes I thought that the Almighty might see that I had done enough for one man's life, in this world; but on thinking what remains to be done, I see I have done nothing to what I might yet do, by divine grace, if spared a few years. Lord, help!

15th.—To-day, John Edge, a neighboring boy, the son of a widow, kicked my son Robert. It seems Robert threw a stone at him, and J. Edge struck him. This has been going on some time, J. Edge having used ill both of my boys. I complained to his mother some time last year, and told J. Edge to come and tell me if my boys did wrong; this he had not done. The mother said she had corrected him in vain; she now delivered him up to me to flog, if I liked. Instead of this, I gave Robert a New Testament to give him, with this inscription, "To John Edge, from his friend Robert Aitken Bowes." John Edge thanked him for it.

16th.—To-day John Edge gave Robert an egg!

17th.—This morning preached out at the New Cross. Was going on very quietly to a large congregation, when the Roman Catholics interfered, and offered to discuss their religious views with me. I named a committee; but I could not procure order. This evening was much comforted, under the persecution sustained at the New Cross, by the application made for church fellowship by a young man, who has been led to know the gospel through my preaching at this very place. Several others applied for church fellowship.

18th.—Visited a candidate for the church. She sees so much of her own imperfections, that she doubts whether God has saved her or not. If she saw no imperfections, would she not think herself entitled to pardon on account of her own goodness? How few are satisfied with what Christ has done for their sins, and willing to accept of salvation freely, as a gift from God's great grace.

9mc. 3rd.—STOCKPORT. After preaching, returned home by the railway. A gentleman observed me put up my umbrella to keep off the wind. He also came under it, remarking, "I like to be under the canopy of a friend." This was very frank in a stranger. I replied, "All mankind should be friends to each other, and if they were humanised and Christianised, would treat each other as friends and brothers."

18th.—SCRIPTURE-READING MEETING. Experienced joy in receiving Christ as my all-sufficient Saviour. Many, through excessive care, and lack of faith in him, distress themselves without any due cause. Their besetting sin has often overcome them; they fear that it will overcome them again. Their fear arises from having trusted in themselves in former contests with the enemy,—and having been often overcome, they doubt for the future. Their own arm has not given them the victory, and they fear that they may be vanquished again. They look too much to themselves, and too little to Jesus Christ. He saves us by *teaching*, and by his own power. The more we know of him, the greater will be our confidence in his love. Let us look to Christ, and attend to the divine commands—" Hear, and your soul shall live ;" " Be still, and know that I am God." We ought, indeed, to "watch and pray," and attend to all other Christian duties, and then leave ourselves, without fear, in the hands of the Saviour. He invites us to cast our burdens and all our care on Him that cares for us. Why should we distress ourselves as though we were our own Saviours. He keepeth Israel. He is able to save to the uttermost. His love can always be depended on. We may be distressed by *family cares*, as well as concerning our souls. We may not know the way out of difficulty, and not seeing the way through the cloud, may become anxious and distrustful; and if we look only to our own resources, and forget the promises of God, we may make to ourselves wearisome days and sleepless nights. The cares of the world, like noxious weeds, may thus prevent the growth of everything great and good. God is our Father: we love our children, but how much more does he love us! As little children run to their parents when they need food and raiment, ever expecting to be supplied, and are without care about to-morrow, let us trust God as simply as they trust us. Let us be industrious, economical, and believing, and we may rest assured that the Lord will either provide for us, or it will be for our good to suffer such privations as his wisdom may appoint. We may have unbelieving *church cares*. We may fear for Zion. Here, however, let us do what the Lord commands, and then we may very safely leave the rest to him.

21st.—Received a letter from Esther Grundy, Stafford, in which she states the following cheering circumstance :—" I have great occasion to bless the Lord that ever I heard Brother Bowes ; for he was the instrument in the hand of the Lord that turned me from darkness to light, and from the power of Satan to God. I would be glad of his advice under my present circumstances, but must leave with the Lord when I must return to Manchester."

61 YORK STREET, HULME,
MANCHESTER, Nov. 4th, 1845.

TO THE ROMAN CATHOLICS OF MANCHESTER.

Per care of Mr. Heane, Roman Catholic Priest, and Henry Turly.

DEAR FRIENDS,—

Yours of the 2nd current, signed by Henry Turly, in reply to mine, I now hasten to answer. Before doing this, I would state the reason why it was not delivered into your hands before the last Lord's Day of last month, although dated a month previously,—the reason was this : on the Lord's Day morning after its date, when I, at that time, commenced reading it to the Roman Catholics and others present, several of you struck a Protestant, and as you had thus commenced a physical force defence of your church, and my friends had more regard to moral force, we left the ground to you fighters, as Christ said " Resist not evil," " Love your enemies."

You want to know what church I "would defend?" My answer is,—That church with which I am connected, whose principles you have heard me expound. I send you by this a copy of "New Testament Principles of Church Order and Unity," that you may know more from my pen, also No. 3, Vol. ii., of the "Christian Magazine and Herald of Union." You may call us schismatics, say that we have no "bishop" or ordination, but these are matters which your advocate will have to demonstrate in the discussion. I hope to prove that you are the greatest of all schismatics,—that you have no scriptural bishop or ordination, though in Manchester you cry out with parrot sameness to those who preach the gospel—"Who sent you? Who sent you?" Now I shall prove that those Christians who meet and preach in Irwell Street, Manchester, Lawson Street Chapel, Preston, and Toxteth Hall, Liverpool, are churches of Christ, having scriptural officers. I deny that Titus was a bishop. The proof may be given in the coming discussion.

I understand the mater to stand thus:—I preached the gospel in Manchester; you frequently interrupted me. I and my friends never came to disturb your meetings. You declared that I was cowardly, and unwilling to allow you to assail my doctrines, which are not mine, but the doctrines of our Lord Jesus Christ. I told the Romanists that if they would bring forward any bishop, priest, or layman, as you call a person not a priest, appointed by your church, I would defend what I taught, and show that your doctrines and practices are inconsistent with the revealed will of God. The only way honorably open to you now, is to appoint your advocate, and fix upon the time and place of meeting.

I seek this discussion, not because I hate you, but because I love you; God knoweth. God loves us all; let us love one another, and expect that the time approaches when all the Christians in your church and Protestant churches will unite, not under the Pope, but under Christ. I wish your priests and bishop to see this letter, as well as the last. Yours in love and peace,

JOHN BOWES.

STRANGE SCENE IN A WESLEYAN CHAPEL.

Nov. 11th.—PRESTON. After our meeting was over, saw the following strange scene in a Wesleyan Chapel. As Edward Brookes, commonly called "Squire Brookes" had been preaching, I entered the chapel. Several were talking to each other, or to persons who were supposed to be anxious. He called out "Come this way; there is work here; do not give it up yet." Several seemed crying for mercy, but the praying people around them made the greatest noise. A person began to pray; he had not prayed long before a local preacher, or missionary, gave out the hymn "My God is reconciled," &c., and commenced to sing it. Several in the congregation joined, and thus by singing drowned the voice of the praying man, while in the very middle of his prayer! The singing being ended, another man began to pray, but he was only just audible, owing to the great noise about the pulpit, and at last could not be distinctly heard at all, only he seemed to go on in the midst of the confusion. At this stage a few commenced singing over again the same hymn; others were talking to the professedly anxious, who were kneeling about the pulpit. The local preacher, previously noticed, now ascended the pulpit, and stretching out his hand, cried, with a loud voice, "Stop! Silence!" The singing went on for some time; at length he succeeded in stopping it, and amidst a confused noise pronounced the benediction. Some few left the chapel, many remained, and the praying, clapping of hands, and discordant screams and noises went on about the front of the pulpit. Another person, at this stage, commenced praying aloud. He had not uttered many sentences before he was sung down by the leaders of the meeting before the pulpit. Talking, praying, and singing, seemed all going on together in singular discord. My attention during this indescribeable scene was attracted by a woman among the anxious, who lifted high her hands as if praising God, at the same time her bonnet gradually fell off backward upon her shoulders, and several came round her, smiled, and seemed to be praising God on her account. The local preacher now got up and said, "I have no hesitation in saying that this woman, who has come eight miles to get liberty, has got it through the blood of the Lord Jesus." "My God is reconciled" was now sung again. The meeting was then told "that if any would not go away, they might go into the vestry:" by this time the greater part of the lights were extinguished.

REMARKS.—The whole of this scene was anti-Christian. Christ and his apostles never sanctioned such irrational proceedings. They never set people to sing, pray, and talk to sinners in order to convert them. They never set a man to pray, and then silenced him by a song of praise. They preached the truth most earnestly—it affected the people—they asked questions. Christ and the apostles answered them—when the inquirers believed, the apostles or other disciples baptized them. This was the plain, rational way in which they proceeded. If this scene at Preston was not contrary to the command—" Let all things be done decently, and in order," I know not what is. It will not do to say the ignorant people like such proceedings, and that souls get converted by them.

1. Not ignorant people, but wise men should govern the church.
2. If persons are indeed converted at such meetings, it must be by the truths which they learn; and they would more speedily and easily learn them if not hindered by confusion.
3. They tend to harden worldlings and infidels, who look upon religion as only fit for the superstitious and fanatical, and they treat religious men as fools and madmen, who have neither religion nor common sense. There was nothing in the proceedings of Christ and the apostles to lead to such results. The Wesleyan preachers and leaders are responsible for such proceedings. The teaching of Christ was calm, dignified, and rational. Every thing irrational about Christianity is unworthy of it, and is not of it.

14*th*, 15*th*.—Have had a very sweet week in studying. Have written out three parables,—The son that went to India,—The self-willed wife, and—The stewards.*

Dec.—4*th.* Set off to RUNCORN. Lectured in a school-room. A few here are inquiring after the truth. A Methodist, who purchased the first volume of my Magazine some time ago for 2s. 6d., says he would not take £1 for it.

22*nd.*—LEES. Preached twice in a large room; excellent congregations. I chiefly preached the gospel. We had a bass viol. In the evening, after sermon, I was requested to state the principles on which the church met, and to invite the people to come again. I did so, and advised them to sell the bass viol, and give the proceeds to some poor widow, lest it should become an organ. Received 2s. 6d. from W. Burton, towards expenses.

25*th.*—What people call Christ-mass-day, because in the church of Rome mass is offered on this day in honor of Christ's birth. When will Protestants have done with Popery? Attended two tea meetings

---

* NOTE C., APPENDIX.

or love feasts, one by the Christians in Toxteth Hall, the other composed of members of several Baptist churches, in Hope Street Chapel, about 600 present, chiefly Welsh Baptists. The Stanhope Street church had intimated that I should address them in English. The aged pastor of Hope Street, who spoke in English before me, said "I am a Baptist—a particular Baptist. I hope you are the same, and that you will abide by your principles." He then detailed a calvinistic creed, and exhorted the people to abide by sound doctrine. After this speech, in which some good things were said of another kind, I thought, I am not a sectarian, and if I cannot speak as a Christian I will not speak at all. I was next called, the president remarking that I was not a particular Baptist, though a Baptist. I confirmed what the chairman said, that I was no particular Baptist, and corrected his mistake by denying I was a Baptist at all. I told them that "I had faith in the death, burial, and resurrection of Christ, and peace with God through these truths—that I love him and all his people—have been immersed and teach immersion, but take no name but that of Christ, my Master. 'The disciples were called Christians first at Antioch,' not Baptists. If you can receive me as a Christian, I am willing to address you, but I have no desire to deceive you by assuming false colors, and if you cannot receive me as a Christian I shall cheerfully retire." I was encouraged to go on, which I did, remarking, "before I finished, a previous speaker said, 'I do not love all Christians alike,' conveying the impression that he loved those most who had similar views to his own on several topics, which I understand were baptism and doctrine. I can say that I do not love all Christians alike, but, if I know anything of my own heart, I love those best, not who have been baptized, or who hold certain doctrines with me, but I love those best who love Christ best, and who love one another most, and thus show most obedience to Christ." These views seemed to be well received.

A CHRISTIAN GOVERNMENT.

This nation is generally spoken of as a Christian nation, and our government as a Christian government, but is the latter only Christian in profession, or in reality? That it is not in reality will appear by a consideration of what constitutes a Christian government.

1. A Christian government is composed of Christian men. It would be absurd and false to call a government of infidels and worldings Christian. They would not be actuated by the principles of Christ, but the reverse, and would therefore conduct their government on their own principles. A Christian government cannot be hereditary, because we cannot calculate with certainty upon the religion of sons and daughters being the same as that of their parents; and if not hereditary it must be elective, and the electors must be Christians, for they cannot be supposed to know whom to choose as rulers and magistrates unless they know the truth by experience. This would confine the power of election to Christians; for, if the government is to be Christian, it must be composed of Christians, and Christians only can be expected to elect Christians. An infidel could not be expected to elect a disciple of Christ to represent him in parliament, or to sit upon the throne. Then it is plain the English government is not Christian, because the Chief Magistrate is hereditary, the House of Lords is chiefly composed of

hereditary legislators, and the House of Commons is elected by a mixed constituency of Christians, infidels, and worldlings, the first class being a small minority. Some of the electors and members of parliament may be Christians, but many are not. Nor is the profession of Christianity any great recommendation to any constituency in the kingdom.

2. A Christian government is conducted according to the laws of Christ, otherwise, any government departing from these laws ceases to be Christian. Human government, in general, both in our country and others, is conducted according to laws made by the will of man. The Divine government any where, whether in the church or in heaven, is conducted according to laws emanating from the will of God. God's will is Christian law—men's will forms the laws of nations. Our own nation is no exception. Our legislators know well that they are not met together to expound, keep, and enforce Christ's laws, but to make new laws, according to their own wisdom, conceit, or folly, every year when they meet in parliament. Some laws made by our parliament may be in accordance with the will of God, but it is notorious to every person that the New Testament is not the guide and standard at St. Stephen's, much less is it the only law-book. Then, on what principle can ours be called a Christian government? The laws of Christ are very rarely referred to, and when they are, it is often as a matter of ridicule, or scorn, to the person who has dared a BREACH OF THE GOOD TASTE of the House by such an unusual introduction.

3. A Christian government would give no rewards or punishments contrary to Christian law, and adopt no measures for extending or defending its empire, but such as Christianity sanctions. As to rewards, if a government requires a president, a king, or queen, or head, if it requires officers of state, or magistrates, or ambassadors, it would pay them moderately, not giving them too little, so that they could not obtain the requisite supplies with their annual income, nor too much, to tempt them to indolence and extravagance, and thus lay greater burdens of taxes upon the people than they are able to bear with comfort. Then, again, a Christian government could not employ either soldiers or hangmen, for with it human life would be sacred, and it would not kill, but "love its enemies," not " rendering evil for evil," not resisting evil, but overcoming it with good. Viewed in this light, our government is most anti-Christian, and desperately wicked ; for it keeps in regular pay a number of soldiers to kill people either in France, China, or elsewhere, when it takes it into its head that it will destroy men's lives. The same principles may be discovered in the tremendous punishments of transports in Norfolk Island. Christianity should be taught to the vilest offenders, and although the injurers of society should be prevented from doing harm, they should be taught truth and trained in virtue.

4. A Christian government would aim at the glory of the great Creator and the universal good of mankind. Human legislation has generally aimed at the glory of the reigning monarch, or at the aggrandizement of a few rich favorites, while it has overlooked the good of the many. It has been carried on for the glory of the king, the prime minister, the clergy, or the army, while it has left the main body of the people to toil from early morn till late at night, not merely for bread and clothing—these could be won from the willing earth by fewer hours

of labor, but for war taxes, tithes, and great pensions to kings and statesmen. The result has been, that amid the toil of the body the education of the mind has been neglected, and an overwrought population, jaded and fatigued, have little inclination to learn or teach the doctrines and laws of heaven.

The conclusions to which we are conducted are the following:—

1. That ours is not a Christian, but an anti-Christian government and nation, and, consequently, that as a Christian should not be unequally yoked together with unbelievers, in setting up the will of man against the will of God, he can have nothing to do with co-operating with such a government. How can he be a magistrate in it if he believes that hanging is murder, when, as a magistrate, he may be called upon to commit a fellow-man, who may be ultimately executed? It will not do for him to say, "I am not a hangman—I am not the judge and the jury," while he concurs in sending the man to all these. Many a murderer, if taught Christianity, might be made as changed and holy as those who put to death the Lord Jesus, and afterwards repented.

2. We can see that a Christian government can never be set up but by first making the nation Christian. We cannot have a Christian government without a change in men's minds and morals produced by the knowledge, faith, and love of Jesus. Hence this should be the work of our lives to make known the truth, to embody it in our lives; for when the rebels who stand out against God submit to his authority, and are reconciled to him through the Lord Jesus, they will be the subjects of their new King—they will cease to do their own will, whether they be kings or subjects, and they will, with one accord, do the will of God, and thus set up a Divine government in the world.

3. It does not follow, if we had a Christian government, that every man in the nation or government would be a Christian. There might appear a Judas, but just as the church may be Christian notwithstanding a hypocrite creeping in unawares, so a government may be Christian notwithstanding the hypocrisy of a few; it would not be Christian, however, if it should be an "organized hypocrisy."

4. One difficulty presents itself here. It has been supposed by many, especially by Voluntaries, that religion has nothing to do with civil government, and hence they infer that every man is eligible to enter parliament, whether Christian or infidel, if he holds the right political views. This view has been lately contested in Southwark by the daring Miall. I cannot believe that religion has nothing to do with civil government. I believe the two have their respective spheres—that God has his rights and property, and Cæsar his; and that Christ has given Cæsar no law to establish the church of God, and take tithes and taxes forcibly for its establishment; and that when Cæsar does this he steps out of his own proper province, interferes between man and his Maker, and attempts to support Christianity by means which Christianity repudiates. But while I declare that Cæsar, as a civil ruler, has no place, office, or power in Christ's church, I dare not say that Cæsar may carry on his government without submitting to Christ's laws. I view Christ as King of kings and Lord of lords, and therefore all kings and lords ought to submit to his authority. A ruler, magistrate, or king, bound to do the will of Christ in his family, or, as a Christian, in the church, cannot lay aside his discipleship—his character as a child of God

—when he sits upon the bench, enters the senate, or ascends the throne. It is true he has new duties to perform, but he must discharge them all according to the laws of justice, truth, and benevolence established by Christ. Whatever he does must be done to the glory of God. While the Christian church obeys Christ, and disclaims all civil rule in the church, the civil ruler, if a Christian, cannot divorce Christianity, turn his back on Christ, and turn infidel when he takes the seat of civil rule. No; still he is a Christian, bound to rule according to Christ's law; and if he cannot rule according to his Master's law, through some other laws of the state, he is bound to one of two things—either to resign his civil rule and cleave to Christ, or retain his civil rule and deny Christ—he cannot serve both God and mammon. These are serious views of the present aspect of human government, but I believe they are correct views. Should any intelligent Christian think I am mistaken, my monthly pages are open to him.

PORTRAITS.

Many Christians see no evil in spending the Lord's money in costly portraits. The ministers of religion set them an example. The leading ministers in each denomination put their likenesses into their magazines, or works, and it is no wonder if they decorate their rooms with pictures of themselves, and of their wives and families, that the people should follow their pernicious example. Thus a vast amount of money is annually wasted which might be given to the poor. Children say that they wish to preserve the portraits of their parents, and parents wish to have the likenesses of their children. The best likeness which parents can leave to their children is, so to teach them, by precept and example, Divine truth, that they shall have the likeness, the moral likeness of the Lord Jesus Christ before their eyes, and in their hearts. This will survive the decays of nature—go on with their undying existence, and be as valuable in the next world as in this.

I have been often requested, chiefly by attached Christians, to sit for my portrait; various motives have been used to persuade me, such as —their wish to preserve my likeness—that other good men had no objection to it, and it would do good to the artist, and please the subscribers to the Magazine, to all of which I reply:—

1st.—I cannot spare the *time*. Time is precious, and I wish to spend it in either getting or doing good. To sit for my portrait would ensure neither end.

2nd.—Neither I nor my friends have any *money* to throw away on portraits. If we have any to spare, there are many living portraits of our Master that require food and clothing, which will really add to their substantial comfort. Let us "remember the poor."

3rd.—It is a proud, worldly expedient to *honor self*—to elevate man. See how the Wesleyans have honored John Wesley. Pictures of him may be found on canvass, on paper, in clay, and in almost all kinds of metals. Let us not lift up ourselves, lest God should throw us down; but let us humble ourselves that He may lift us up.

4th.—As to the plea that it does *good to the artist*. I deny it; that can only be for his real good which is beneficial to society. The vendor of intoxicating drinks may tell us that we should do him good by purchasing his poisonous liquids; but we tell him that that can never in the end be for his good which he derives from the vices of society, and which leads to quarrels, sickness, poverty, ruin of character, and death, and which does society no real good. So in the case before us, it would be better for the portrait painter, and better for society, if he would cease to minister to the pride and vanity of mankind, and employ himself in some honest, useful calling, which would answer the end for which he came into being.

Instead, then, of the followers of Christ following this fashion of the world, let them pull down the costly pictures from the walls of their houses, and spend their time in writing the truths of the gospel on the minds of their children and friends. Divine truth will do them more good than our likenesses. Let us be able to say to them, "Follow us, as we follow Christ."

[These are my sentiments now, in 1871, only in some cases it may be lawful, so that I have yielded to the importunity of friends so far as to give my portrait to this volume.]

Jan. 4th. 1846.—MANCHESTER. We held a fortnight's meetings here last year, with no appearance of fruit at the time. It is now appearing. To-day four souls, converted from the world, wished to unite with us.

During the first and early part of the second month, visited and preached or lectured at Middleham, Leyburn, Leeds, Birkenshaw, Birstal, Batley, and Heckmondwike. While at Birstal I went to see John Nelson's tomb, in the grave-yard. The following is inscribed on his tomb-stone :—"John Nelson, departed this life, July 18, 1774, aged 67 years. Martha, his wife, departed this life, September 11, 1774, aged 69 years.

> While we on earth had our abode,
> We both agreed to serve the Lord."

From this it would seem that Martha did not always persecute him, but at last got converted, though she once left her home because of his religion and his preaching. Since this visit, a few believers have commenced meeting weekly in the Lord's name alone at Gomersal.

After I gave up salary, various unfounded reports were circulated of which this kind letter is a specimen. I need only say there is not a word of truth in the report.

DUNDEE, Jan. 4th, 1846.

MY DEAR BROTHER,—

I write you these few lines in the hope that they will find you and family well. I hope you will excuse me for not writing before this. My reason for writing at this time is to inquire into your circumstances, as we have been informed that you are embarrassed, and feeling, as we do, for your welfare, we should be obliged by your letting us know if this report be true, and if all your effects have been taken from you and you left without a bed to lie upon, and if this be the case let us know by return of post, and at the same time state what might be done to relieve you out of your sad situation ; also, state if you received the post office order, for 18s., sent by the church. The statement came to us through a female from Aberdeen, to the Barrack Street Church. I will not enter, at the present time, upon the state of the church here, but will do so in my next. Please write by return of post, and relieve those of your friends here from the trouble of mind they are laboring under on your account. I will add no more, but remain, in the hope that you will write us immediately on receipt of this, with all particulars,

Yours in the hope of the coming Saviour.

To John Bowes.
JAMES ALLAN.

61 York Street, Hulme,
Manchester, 2mo. 7th, 1846.

My Dear Brother,—

May grace, mercy, and peace be with you, from God the Father and the Lord Jesus Christ. I received your letter with great regret, to hear of you having a party spirit among you. I had hoped, after the loving spirit and speeches at our meetings while I was over last, that you would henceforward live in love, as our common Master has commanded. If any brother sees "damnable heresies creeping in," he should know that that term is applied by an apostle only to those who "denied the Lord that bought them." I cannot think that dear Brother Askey has any charge against me, as he has never mentioned it to me, or anything like a charge; but if he has, tell him to send it to me. As to your elders' meeting next Thursday evening, I fear I cannot attend it, as we are going to have a week's meetings at Gillbent,—they commence on the 9th—but after them, I shall come down to Liverpool as soon as possible; not in strife, but in love to all the holy brethren. I do hope that you will all remember that it is written, "Let brotherly love continue,"—"Forbearing one another in love." As to my denying the Trinity, the complaint has no foundation in the world; I never held other views than what I do now on that subject. Who says that I deny it? As to praying for sinners, I pray for "all men" as commanded. I never said that believers were not to pray for more of the Holy Spirit, but "that they were not to pray for Him to be given to them when they had Him," as though they had him not. If faith will not save, then Paul did not teach the truth; for when the jailor said, "What must I do to be saved?" he answered, "Believe on the Lord Jesus Christ, and thou shalt be saved." But faith is never alone. Repentance and love always attend it, and many other excellencies. These are the most of the points noticed in your letter. Let me recommend you all to patience and long-suffering. Whether I may be able to be with you by next Lord's Day, I cannot yet say. I should think that some of the brethren have greatly misunderstood my sentiments. But do they not understand that Christian brethren, holding different opinions, are to love one another. The Elders have the charge of God's flock. Let them take heed to all the flock, and not allow any harm to overtake it; and may the Lord Jesus himself, the Great Shepherd of the sheep, preserve you all to eternal life. I only returned yesterday from Yorkshire, where the Lord is opening a door for his truth, and there are many adversaries. We have had several souls saved in Manchester, and 11 baptized since I saw you. Another local preacher has joined us. The church here is in a growing state. O, my soul is sorrowful about Liverpool. What care, and sorrow, and labor for your welfare I have had the last nine years, God knoweth; and if, after all, you having begun in the Spirit, shall end in the flesh —how sad! Any views of the Second Advent which lead to division, and bad feeling, cannot come from the God of love. The Saviour is all love, and whether he comes sooner or later, he will approve those the most who have been the most meek, loving, and forbearing. Never fear for the truth; it will yet grow. Cast all your care on Him that careth for you. Give this magazine to dear Hassalwood and Corf. Let me hear from you often, and the Lord knit your hearts together in love. Yours in the faith, hope, and love of Jesus,

To Thos. Wright.   JOHN BOWES.

Feb. 15th.—Closed a week's meetings at GILLBENT, large congregations, and they have gone on increasing to the last. John Alcorn, Ebenezer Syme, and I labored by day in visiting from house to house, conversing on the Gospel, leaving tracts, and informing the people of the meetings, and each evening we preached the Gospel. One address in the course of the week, showed what a Christian church ought to be.

SPEECH OF J. BOWES AGAINST WAR, IN THE FREE TRADE HALL, PETER STREET, FEBRUARY 17, 1846.

(Taken down by a Reporter, and given from his notes.)

John Bowes then came forward, to support the resolution, which having read to the meeting, he spoke as follows:—Now, sir, when I heard one of my friends, who preceded me, say that this was perhaps, one of the noblest meetings ever held by the friends of peace in Manchester, I began to think that possibly it was one of the noblest meetings that was ever held by the friends of peace in the world. I know not whether the friends of peace ever before had such a meeting as this, therefore, we ought to feel our responsibility, and it will, therefore, be my aim to lay a good foundation. The resolution says, "that war is opposed to the doctrine and precepts of Christianity." Now, sir, we ought to be dutiful subjects—subjects dutiful to the state—but when the state gives laws which are contrary to the higher laws of God, we say that the laws of God were made before states—were made for man before he existed in connexion with nations—are above the laws of nations, and will remain when states are annihilated.—(Cheers.) On the broad and everlasting principle of the law of God we therefore take our stand against the body and soul destroying system of war. (Hear and cheers.) Looking into that law we see that the laws of Jesus Christ are hostile to the laws of war—the laws of Jesus Christ are at issue with war, when we read as follows, "Resist not evil," "If a man smite thee on the one cheek turn to him the other also." The laws of war take a very different standing. Perhaps I cannot better express it than in the language of a modern professor at one of our colleges, who when repudiating the literal sense of this injunction, said to his students, "Here is a law which, if read literally, says, 'If a man smite thee on the one cheek turn to him the other also;' but I say unto you (said the professor) if a man smite you on the one cheek, knock him down if you can!" That, sir, is the principle upon which armies proceed—that is the principle upon which martial nations proceed. If a nation injures and insults you, and you have got the war-spirit strong within you, you are soon instructed what to do—to knock that nation down if you can. Therefore, I say, that that is contrary to the laws of Jesus Christ. The law of Christ says, "Love your enemies," and he would be a strange commentator who would write underneath, "This means kill them." Now, if "love your enemies" signifies kill them, what does hatred signify?

"Bless them that curse you?" "Pray for them that despitefully use you?" "Do good to them that hate you?" These are the laws of Christ, and if we act upon these laws we must be hostile to war "Recompense no man evil for evil"—"Avenge not yourselves"—"If thine enemy hunger, feed him; if he thirst, give him drink." What say the laws of war? If your enemy is in a besieged city, starve him out if possible. If the stream or rivulet which is supplying him with the means of quenching his thirst is in your way, cut off that stream, if possible, and let him be forced to capitulate for want of drink. Now, sir, nothing can be more contrary to the laws of Christ than the laws of war. Then, if we look again to the example of Christ and of his early followers, we find that it is said of him, that he is the Prince of Peace. I glory, sir, in fighting under such a banner. It is also said of him, and said by himself, "That the Son of man did not come to destroy men's lives but to save them." These are noble sentiments. Then his disciples, if they drink deeply into his spirit, should not go to China, France, or America, or any where else, wishing to destroy men's lives, but to save them. And it is this principle upon which we have met here, sir, to infuse into this large mass of human beings a spirit of kindness, mildness, and benignity to the human race, similar to that which our blessed Saviour breathed, when he said he did not come to destroy men's lives but to save them. (Loud cheers.) If, sir, we can have the happiness of saving the young man who is about to enlist—who is about to sacrifice himself at the sound of the drum—if we can have the happiness of infusing into you such a hostile spirit to war, that you will rather incur any loss, as the Friends have nobly done for the last two hundred years, in support of this principle—they have suffered all kinds of annoyances and confiscation of property, and even imprisonment, and thus they have wrought out a noble liberty to themselves by the passive principle of nonresistance. If we can save our young men, on that principle, from the army or the militia, we shall then be acting in the spirit of our Master, and on the side, and for the sake of humanity. The Prince of Peace does not extend his empire at the point of the bayonet, by the tramp of the war horse, or the roar of cannon. He extends his empire by the power of truth, and especially by the omnipotence of love. If, then, his empire is to be extended in this world, the means must be used, and our hearts be made to consider all mankind as friends and brothers to each other. (Hear, hear.) The primitive Christians, sir, as you have already heard, rather than submit to war, submitted to death, and if we have within us their spirit, and the spirit of Christ, we shall rather submit to die ourselves than to draw the blood of others. I will not detain you much longer, but I would like to give a few moments' consideration to one or two questions. I know that you are all expecting Joseph Sturge, and so am I, and therefore I will confine myself to a very few and brief observations; but I do wish to unburden my soul on this system in as brief a space of time as possible. (Cheers) Why, sir, standing armies in times of peace, are refinements upon ancient barbarism. In all the ancient nations, sir, and even among the most refined ones, as Greece and Rome, they had no notion of keeping up a regular trained army, a set of men to fight, in times of peace. They summoned their hosts in time of war, and disbanded them in time of peace; but we have arrived at the astonishing exhibition in our time, and within the last few centuries, in professing Christian Europe, of keeping up a large number of men to murder the people of any offending nation. And we do this in time of peace! (Hear, hear.) You, sir, very properly, told us something of the vast expenditure of war, and I will now continue that list, which has been the means of so frightfully increasing our national debt. About four hundred and fifty millions of money was levied from the British people from the year 1815 to 1841, chiefly for the support of such institutions as we are now calling in question! And this in time of peace!! Now, sir, it was a remark made by Dymond, whose work on "Morality" I will recommend to all here—(I repeat the name again, "*Dymond's Work on Morality*," it is worthy of your remembrance and perusal.) He calculates that every man in Great Britain, that is a producer, works upon an average two hours each day more than he would have needed to work had it not been for our war taxes and our war establishments. (Hear, hear, and cheers.) Now, sir, I ask if one of these red-coated soldiers, that is in our streets now, should come to the house of one of our producers in Manchester at four o'clock, when he had done his work for himself and family, and should insist that he should work two hours more to support the system of war, should we not regard the visit of that soldier as a badge of slavery and vassalism? Now, sir, I hold that these gentlemen around me, and this mighty number of producers before me, are as really slaves to the war system as though soldiers should compel them to work two hours a day more than they have any occasion to do; for we are obliged to support war whether we will or not, else this mighty meeting would say, "Let war be universally abolished." (Cheers.) Will any one in this meeting, think you, be so foolish as to hire himself out at thirteen pence halfpenny a day to be shot at? (Cheers and laughter.) Will any person in this mighty meeting be so foolish as to hire himself out at thirteen pence halfpenny a day to kill the human race? (Loud cries of "No.") We are not prepared for that: but if the meeting, with one great and unanimous resolve, shall determine not to fight, there is no power in the universe that can make us fight. (Hear, hear, and loud cheers.) But then it might be said by a Christian man, "Oh, sir, I would not fight myself, but as it regards the militia, I can afford to pay, and I have no objection against paying another man to fight for me." Strange Christianity that, sir. What should we think of a man, who has a great objection himself to steal, but is quite willing to hire another man to steal for him. I say that his crime is increased, because he not only does wrong in being a partner with another in doing wrong, but he hires another to do it, and there is a double wrong. (Hear, hear.) Now, sir, if the forty thousand who have to be enlisted into the militia only understood this, and if the nation understood this, our rulers would understand that it would be *necessary* to settle their national quarrels by arbitration, for the nation had resolved not to destroy men's lives, but to save them. (Cheers.) Now, sir, it may be said here, "But what will become of the Queen? and what will become of our constitution, and of our liberties? The Americans or the French might come, or the Hindoos might even come, and take away our liberties and lives, if we had not a standing army." And so we are to have a standing army to protect our liberties! And what *do* they protect now, sir, if not *abuses?* (Hear, hear.) I repeat it—what do they protect now but abuses? Our liberties, sir, would be far better protected by reason than by a standing army. (Hear, hear, and cheers.) Our liberties would be dearly wrought out at the point of the bayonet. We ought to be of all nations the most free, for we have had the greatest expenditure of property and blood. (Hear.) In this hall you have often met to obtain free trade, and now you have met here for the destruction of war. You are not free yet, but meetings like this will make you so by and bye. You, sir, referred to the success of the peace movement in Pennsylvania. I always refer to the history of that colony with delight, for we find that that wonderful man, William Penn, first bought the land from our government, and as he recognised the right of the Indians to sell their land, he bought it again from them, and paid them for it, and got arrangements agreed to that all disputes should be settled by arbitration. And, sir, what happened with these six nations of savages? Why this, that for 70 years, and during all the time that this policy lasted, and during the time it was recognised by the colony, frequently, in the morning when the Pennsylvanians arose, they saw their neighbors' houses on fire, and in other colonies and other states they saw their neighbors' corn and cattle frequently destroyed, but during all that time, so carefully did the six savage nations observe the treaty, that there was no loss of life or property, with the exception of three persons, who were shot either through mistake or from their desertion of principle. It is a noble fact of a colony, acting upon anti-war principles, settling every thing by arbitration for seventy years together, and that among savages this principle was respected. Now, sir, we are quite willing that all national quarrels should be settled in the same way. Let a number of persons be appointed in this country, and from America, and France, and other countries, to settle all disputes; and we are quite willing to pay delegates and arbitrators, but we are unwilling to pay soldiers. (Hear.) And why? Because soldiers settle the matter by might, and not by right. (Hear, hear.) It may be that a small state has right on its side, and might may be against it; and when the dispute is settled by the point of the bayonet, it is might against right; but in such a course of arbitration as we propose, right would be recognised, and right would prevail often against might. What is an ensanguined army likely to do for justice? Not a thousandth part so much good as a few proper men debating the questions, and settling them by their best judgment. Why, sir, this peace project is not such a foolish thing, after all, as men took it to be. Let us try for a hundred years without soldiers and cannon balls, and then, sir, if we cannot do without them, we will call them back again. (Cheers.) I have just another remark to make, and that is with regard to those who are anxious for fighting, and I will venture to give it in a Lancashire anecdote. During the French war there lived at Blackburn a half-witted man called "Silly Dick." A recruiting sergeant said to him, "Dick, will you enlist?" "Enlist," said Dick, "for what?" "To fight for the king," said the sergeant. "For 'th king," said Dick, "why, has 'th king faun oot wi somebody?" "Yes, with the French." "Why, then," said Dick, "let 'th king foight French his-sel, I'll foight noane." Now, sir, I say, if there are persons anxious for war, we'll do all we can to hinder them from going to war, but if we cannot prevail by reason, we'll say, "let them fight their enemies themselves, for we are determined to love them and be kind to them." I have just another remark. By boldness in speaking, firmness in action, and patience in suffering, I believe we shall work out the freedom of this great country. Though we are slaves in many respects, thanks to Divine providence, we have freedom of speech left, and the freedom of the press. Now, I believe, sir, that it is not merely this great hall, or the eloquent addresses which have been delivered in it, that have done so much for free trade; but the League has deluged the country with tracts and books. Now, sir, I lectured against war at Preston a short time ago, and proposed to the people there what I now propose to you—a great thing, and yet it can be done. What is that? It is to supply every family in the kingdom with a tract against war. These tracts can be obtained at one shilling per hundred. Well, Manchester contained a population, in 1841, of 359,390. Reckoning every family to consist of five persons, that would give 50,678 families; reckoning every family to have a tract, we could put into the hands of every family in Manchester a tract against war, for £35 7s., provided we could get gratuitous distributors; and I myself will engage to distribute 2,000 to reach 10,000 persons. Now, if we could do this, and had the funds, we could also do much from the platform, as well as through the press, to overthrow this gigantic abuse, and to give to all nations in the world universal peace. I am delighted to see the noble faces in the vast assemblage now before me. Let them attend to the instructions and impressions of this evening's meeting, and let them look after their comrades when near a recruiting army; but the best way is never to follow them—let them go into the streets by themselves, as they deserve, for no citizen should give them any countenance. As far as we can, let us live in peace and love with one another and with all the world, and we shall be the happiest in life, and the most joyful in death, and it will be the best preparation for that world of peace to which we aspire. (Protracted cheering.)

CONVERSION OF BRYAN M'MAKEN AND HIS WIFE MADGE.

The following interesting account of the conversion of Bryan M'Maken and his wife Madge, was communicated by Adam Clarke to James Everett, who gave me liberty to publish it, which I did, in the "Christian Magazine."

"Bryan M'Maken was a poor ignorant Roman Catholic, who acted as herd to a number of families near Newtown-Stewart, in the county of Tyrone, north of Ireland. The Methodist preachers visited the place to which he belonged, and Bryan, under the preaching of Joseph Armstrong, was so deeply convinced of his sinful state, that when he returned to his cabin after the sermon, he was unable to conceal his distress from his wife. On her inquiring into the cause, he said, 'I think God Almighty is looking at me every minute, and is angry with me.' She did her utmost to make him quiet, but to no purpose; and, as a last resource, she advised him to go to the priest on the following morning. He took this advice, and having told his case, the priest said to him, 'O, you have been hearing these Methodists; nothing better could come of it.' 'Oh!' said Bryan, 'it is they that have done it upon me; but, sir, what shall I do, for I cannot live this way?' After scolding him, the priest said, 'Well, I will tell you what to do, and you will be well enough. Go to the dance which is to be at John ——'s to-night, and when you return home, take a hearty glass of whisky, and get Madge (his wife) to sing you a song, and all will be well enough.' In obedience to his advice, Bryan and Madge went to the dance, but he had not been long there before he started up, saying to his wife, ' Madge come away, I am worse and worse.' On his return home, however, he took the rest of the advice—drank the whisky and heard the song—but to no purpose. In the morning, far from being relieved, his distress was greatly increased, and Madge advised him to go once more to the priest. He went next morning and told his reverence that he was no better, for God was 'still looking at him,' and was 'angrier and angrier.' He was then ordered to go to Lough-Derg, and heavy penances were prescribed —so many crossings, genuflections, stations, walking on his bare knees, &c. Having accomplished this task, he returned, and told the priest that he was no better. 'Then,' said the priest, 'You may go to the devil, for I can do no more for you; but mind, you must never go near the Methodists again.' 'O,' said Bryan, 'there is no danger of that, they have done enough upon me already.' Notwithstanding this resolution, being a short time after drawn by his employment to the meeting-house during divine service, he ventured to the door to listen to the singing, then heard the prayer, in which he thought there could be no harm, and lastly ventured in. The preacher, knowing nothing of the case of Bryan, was led to describe the state of awakened sinners, and the advice sometimes given to such, to relieve them from their distress. Bryan having, by this time, got near the pulpit, exclaimed, 'that is just what he said to me;' and there and then, before the congregation, he detailed the whole of what had passed between him and the priest. The preacher told him that he could never be happy till he was converted and obtained the forgiveness of his sins, adding, 'kneel down, and we will pray for you.' The whole congregation then fell upon their knees, calling upon God to have mercy upon the penitent. After some time he leaped up, clapping his hands, and said, 'I have got it!—I have got it! I know he is not angry with me now! O, sir, will you come and convert Madge?' The preacher replied that he would go and talk with her the next morning, but Bryan could with difficulty wait so long. As soon as he got home he exclaimed, 'O, Madge, sure I am converted; God is not angry with me now.' 'Bryan, dear,' said his wife, 'who converted you?' 'O,' said he, 'it was the preacher.' 'would he convert me?' said she, 'for I am as bad as you.' 'He would convert all the world,' said Bryan. The preacher visited Madge, and explained to her the plan of salvation by Jesus Christ, and she also was soon brought to enjoy the power and comfort of religion Bryan could not rest now without telling the priest. He was advised not to go, but go he would, and in the face of the congregation, in his own way, told the priest of the happiness of his soul. The priest ridiculed him, and threatened him with excommunication; to which Bryan replied, 'You may save yourself the trouble; you could do nothing for me in my distress, and I will never come near you more.' Bryan and Madge suffered much from their bigoted neighbors, but they held on their way, and are long since lodged in the paradise of God. They brought up their children also in the fear of the Lord, and one son became a respectable local preacher.'

27th.—I addressed the following letter to James Morrison, the leader of the Evangelical Union. I also give his curt reply.

April 27, 1846.

My Dear Sir,—

As I am writing a reply to your two letters on "Paid Pastors," I think of making some use of a circumstance which has come to my ears by two witnesses. It is this; that at a late annual assembly of your "Union," which you and your elders attended, you went in a first-class carriage, while your own elders went in a third class carriage. Now if this is true, as you are laboring by preaching to revive religion, does not this kind of distinction tend to revive pride and extravagance? I have, by letter, also, the following pleasing fact, if fact it be, concerning you, that not long since you lectured on Acts xx, or some similar passage, when you lifted up your hands and exclaimed, "Would that these hands had learned a trade." I write this hasty note to prevent any misunderstanding, thinking that, if there be any mistake in my information, you are the best able to correct it. If I hear nothing from you different from the above, I shall conclude it to be correct, but shall be glad to find, concerning the first particular, that I have been misinformed

Yours in love and peace,

To James Morrison, JOHN BOWES,

KILMARNOCK, May 2, 1846.

James Morrison presents his respects to Mr. Bowes, and begs to say that he does not choose to give Mr. Bowes any information on such subjects as he inquires about. J. M. was from home when Mr. Bowes' letter come, otherwise he would have written sooner.

4*mo.* 15*th.*—We have held meetings for eleven days at RUSHOLME. A few souls were led to believe the gospel, and a few were added to the church.

6*mo.* 16*th.*—Went to see a monument erected on a moss about two miles from Dalgig, in memory of the Covenanters. I give a verbatim copy :—" Here lies Joseph Wilson, John Jamison, and John Humphrey, who was shot on this place by a party of Highlanders. For their adherence to the word of God and their covenanted work of reformation. 1685." It seems this secluded spot, shut out from the world, surrounded by rising ground, and far from the dwelling of man, in a time of great persecution, was selected for worship, and while the covenanters were worshipping God they were shot. One feels sorry, that they were so far carried away by the martial spirit of the times as to carry arms, and sometimes fight the regular troops. This weakens their testimony. Christ, and the first of his followers who suffered martyrdom, suffered in meekness, and died praying for their enemies. But how much would the moral glory of their sufferings have been obscured, had they fallen while prepared with death-dealing weapons to oppose by force their enemies ? Several monuments, similar to the one I visited, are to be found in this county, and a few small congregations still abide by the sentiments of their forefathers.

18*th.*—KILMARNOCK. At 8 p.m., a very large congregation. A socialist opposed. The people very unadvisedly hissed him, which created such a noise as to bring the police. They removed him. Happily I had delivered my discourse before he began, and his remarks were not calculated to do much harm, though I should have wished to reply to some of them.

21*st.*—DARVEL. About fifty-five brethren are now meeting in the Lord's name alone here, being under no obligation to have any master but Christ, nor any laws but his in his church. The Darvel church has been connected with the Evangelical Union. After W. Landels saw baptism, and mentioned his views to a few, he was cut off by James Morrison, and two more of the Educational Committeee; but the main body of the church did not sanction this. During the 6th month, the yearly meeting of the Union was held at Greenock. A delegate from the church at Darvel attended. The church was charged with three sins, and cut off for them. " 1st. Because they received W. Landels as a preacher, after he was immersed. 2nd. They received Ebenezer Syme, who was supposed to be no friend of the Union. And because, 3rdly, they had intimated to receive J. Bowes, who was opposed to paid pastors, and was on a mission to Scotland to break up the Union !" Such were the sectarian reasons for not hearing this church in open court, and cutting them off; so that a church has less liberty and more power exercised over its proceedings in this new body than in any of the old Presbyterian churches, in which they can appeal from a Presbytery to a Synod, &c. To break up this union was no part of my plan. I visit Scotland yearly, at least. Many Congregational churches, holding the same doctrinal views, have no manner of connexion with this union. Several of the churches admit baptized believers, but not to all the privileges of members. A man's being at peace with God, being a Christian, is not enough to constitute him a member; he must be silent on baptism. Those who will bind themselves down to a regulation which obliges them to sell the truth, are not worthy to be called Christians. "Buy the truth, sell it not."

23rd.—Visited LARGUE, near INSCH, this year. A minister of the Free Church had been applied to for a school-room, but he sent word that it could not be expected that he should give the school-room this year, as Alexander Wilson, a Congregationalist, would not give his hall to us the last year. This year James Robertson, jun., again sent a kind note to Alexander Wilson, called him "brother, beloved," and asked it "from a Christian, for a Christian." Alexander Wilson says in reply, "I cannot comply with your request. I do not state my reasons at present, but I was not satisfied with him the last time that I gave him the hall." During the week the discourse had been intimated to be out of doors by written bills. On the 7th mo., 24th, I preached there. A few hours before preaching I was going along the street, when Alexander Wilson called after me, saying "that he had seen the bill, liked the subjects of the lecture, and that if I preached the Gospel, kept off controversy, not saying anything against any party, and not introducing anything sectarian, I might have the hall." I replied "that it was difficult to preach the Gospel without controversy, as almost all its truths had been controverted. That as to sectarianism I could cheerfully agree to that, as it was my object to destroy sectarianism; that all the churches I meet with are accessible to all the children of God,—being strictly non-sectarian. That as to saying nothing against any party, it was my practice to preach the Gospel, and then explain Christ's commands to his followers, and if people disobeyed them like the ancient pharisees, I took the liberty of pointing out their sin, as Christ did." This A. Wilson asserted was right. I said, "Let truth be free, and I shall be glad of the hall, if the evening should be wet or cold; if not, we shall be better in the open-air; but I cannot take it if truth is not to be free." He said there was some difference, and we parted in friendship. The evening was fine, the congregation much larger than we should have had in the hall, and the people greedily sought my publications. I took occasion to notice to a friend or two in private, that many people think A. Wilson a good man; but God is much better than he, for our good God allowed us to preach in the open-air without making any restrictive conditions—that he both sent us a fine evening, and left truth free—thus allowing us to declare truth without any let or hindrance. I do not say that all good men are fully instructed to act as God does, but I say if they do not it must be the remains of sectarian prejudice, or for want of more scriptural information. I like to have liberty to speak the truth, and never mean, by divine grace, to suppress it, to please man. I expect a great harvest from the truth sown in this neighborhood.

24th.—GLASGOW, near the Green. When I had delivered about three parts of my discourse, two policemen came with orders from their commander that I should remove to the Green. As we were not interrupting the thoroughfare, nor near it, I felt inclined to remain, believing that the police were going beyond their province; but while I was deliberating, a band of music connected with this "vanity fair" commenced playing in front of a kind of theatre behind me, which determined me to go to the Green, followed by a great crowd, for others now ran together to see what was the matter—hundreds of people following a man! In the day of accounts it may be found that even this interruption has done good to some poor wanderers.

7th mo., 12th.—ABERDEEN. Some time ago there was a division here, from various causes, chiefly because some adopted narrow views on several great questions. To-day I addressed both meetings; the one in the Guestrow in the forenoon, after which desires were expressed that we might have a conference to ascertain the possibility of re-union. I broke bread at half-past two o'clock with those who meet in Long Acre. Their principles are unchanged. At eight o'clock the conference commenced. I am sorry to find, after all these promising appearances, that there is no hope of union, in consequence of some of the members at Guestrow having fallen into the error that remission of sin can only be obtained in baptism, or, to use their own language, "that baptism is the scriptural way of remission." But a still greater error they have fallen into is baptizing and adding to their number two persons who hold similar sentiments to the Unitarians. While these two errors are held there can be no union. A man cannot be said to know the Gospel or believe it, who denies what "all the prophets witness, that through Christ's name whosoever believeth in him shall receive remission of sins." Thus I have found, among all who hold these errors, a lack of honest boldness in declaring what they really believe; or if they affirm they believe certain texts, when you ask their meaning they claim to believe them though they hold them in a new sense, which appears to be forced, unnatural, or contradictory. The Lord's spirit alone can guide us into all truth. What a wayward creature is man when left to the bent of his own headstrong will!

17th.—RHYNIE, several miles from Clatt. The discourse was intimated for the open-air. It rained while brother S. and I rode down in a cart. Enquired about the hall—found that the Free Church had taken it for a day school. Called on the minister—I was well acquainted with him while a student in Aberdeen. He seemed unwilling to give it. I asked, "What difference is their between your refusing me the hall and the proprietors of the soil connected with the Established church, refusing you sites on which to build." He said, "I have not refused you the hall." But as he talked as though he intended to refuse it, alluding to views on the ministry, I farther said, "Suppose you favor the Evangelical Alliance, at least many of your ministers do, how can its object of uniting the church be carried out if Christians refuse to give to each other any opportunity to spread the truth?" "O!" said he, "you may have the hall, but I will not charge you anything for it." We now sent a man to every house in the place to tell the people—probably 40 or 50 assembled. We left several publications among them. Reached home about midnight.

22nd.—Walked to the GLEN OF FOUDLAND, with James Wisely. Called at two farm houses. At the first, found them rather afraid and shy, but civil. Walked on to Mr Smith's, at Tommystone. The son, a middle-aged man, reads and approves the magazine. He invited us to stay dinner. We found there Mr. Smith, editor of the "Glasgow Examiner." After dinner, the father told the son he was wanted. We had talked with the son on divine truth alone. When the son departed, the father said to me: "We do not want you here; we have seven or eight ministers in this neighborhood, and there is no use for you." I replied, that I had many important truths to teach, and that the gospel ought to be preached to every creature. He said, "I have never heard you myself, but I see the effects of your teaching in unsettling the minds of the people, and drawing them off from their ministers, who are the servants of God." I told him I was anxious to love all the servants of God, and that I believed, instead of doing a great deal of harm, I was doing a great deal of good. His language, however, was so bitter and uncivil, that, after explaining to him our reason for remaining to dinner, we quietly retired. I said I hoped that we might yet so study the Christian religion as to profit by it, and that if we did not wish to see each other here, how should we feel if we saw each other in heaven? He said, "I hope I shall not see you there." It was after this we told him, that had it not been for his son's invitation, and indeed, had we known, we should not have taken dinner. We then spent several hours in the fields, studying, &c., till the preaching time drew on; then we entered the Glen of Foudland. John Craig, the farmer, treated us kindly, and at 7 o'clock we had a large congregation in his barn.

26*th*.—ABERDEEN. Preached myself, and heard G. McAllum preach. He delivered a very excellent discourse, but seems to have a tendency to obscure the simple gospel by his allusions to philosophy. The gospel itself is the greatest philosophy. In the course of his discourse he did what many preachers do, therefore I notice it. He said, "He that believeth shall be saved, but he that believeth not shall be damned,"—leaving out the words "and is baptized." What can be the meaning of this? Do preachers wish to blot out words which Christ gave to his apostles? Why should they? Let them remember that it is of great importance to quote Scripture honestly: as they quote Mark xvi. 15, there is not such a text in the Scriptures.

29*th*.—Fergus Ferguson, senior, was ordained to the pastoral charge of the church recently formed in St. Andrew Street Chapel. His son preached a good gospel sermon. The aged minister was addressed by W. Scott, of Glasgow, much his junior, and his inferior in success. But as the Scriptures say nothing of such addresses, I shall pass on, only remarking that in the address the church were called "your people," that is, F. Ferguson's people. John Kirk, whom I love much in the Lord, offered the ordination prayer. If F. Ferguson was duly pastor at Bellshill, why should he be ordained again at Aberdeen, not by the church, but by persons every way his juniors! Robert Morrison addressed the people, and told them "whether pleased or not with their ministers, their conduct was to be materially the same." This, to me, seemed unscriptural advice. He made some good remarks on worship. He attributes the decline of the revival spirit, to talking about it, and would not have new converts to talk of it themselves. He referred to a servant girl, if she got converted, he "would not have her to blab it." I could not but think of this text, "With the heart man believeth unto righteousness, and with the mouth confession is made unto salvation."—Rom. x. 10. It grated most harshly on my ears to have this confession designated by the word "blab." The discourse had little gospel in it. He confessed that he had preached thirty-five years, and only during seven had been converted by knowing the gospel, admitting that he is a child of God now, in his old age, and it would gratify Christians to see more of the spirit of a little child. How must that system be deprecated which educates an unconverted man for the ministry? These preachers seem, however, in general, very clear on the gospel of salvation by faith, but, both in their discourses and writings, careless of the "all things" which Christ commanded his servants to teach.

31st.—Sailed to PETERHEAD from Aberdeen in the "Samson" steamer. The fog was so dense that we were in great danger from the rocky shore. When we were about two-thirds of the way, we descried rocks. I believe I first saw them, and gave warning—they were just before the vessel. The captain cried, "Helm a port," and her engines were instantly stopped, just in time to save us. Thank God. Sometimes when I have been in danger by sea or land, I have derived great comfort from this text, "God so loved the world that he gave his only begotten Son, that whosoever believeth in him should not perish, but have everlasting life." Now, were I to be called in a moment to meet God, I could not depend on my past prayers, feelings, promises, labors, or successes. Nothing that I have done furnishes a ground of confidence before God. But he has been pleased to say, "whosoever believeth shall not perish." I believe; therefore, as God is true, I cannot perish. There is no hell for me. I do not fear it any more than as though it had no existence. God's promise saves me from it. Every word of God is true. How exceeding great his grace.

During this visit to Scotland, I heard one of the most remarkable testimonies from a Christian and a friend, in whose house I resided, concerning his excellent wife, that I ever remember to have heard. In the course of a friendly conversation, he said, "*I have been married twenty-seven years,* and IN ALL THAT TIME I HAVE NEVER HAD OCCASION TO FIND FAULT WITH HER, NOR DO I REMEMBER THAT SHE EVER ASKED ME FOR ANYTHING." I said, "I suppose you mean such as articles of dress, furniture, &c?" to which he assented. What a treasure is such a wife! Who can tell what grace can do? This is a Christian family.

9mo. 12th.—WHALEYBRIDGE. Had a comfortable meeting in a brother's house, where I preached.

13th.—KETTLESHULME. Large congregation. Some of the singers wished to bring their instrumental music. I directed the person that came to think of "singing with the Spirit and with the understanding also." The instruments were left behind. A number of brethren have met in Christ's name alone at Whaleybridge for some time. My introduction to Whaleybridge occured thus, as William Wild reports: A brother heard me at Stockport market-place, and when he returned to Whaleybridge, he said to W. Wild, "I heard a man on Stockport market-place that would suit you to a 'T.'" This led to a deputation, who came one Lord's day to Stockport, and invited me up to Derbyshire.

14th.—MANCHESTER. By appointment, met some of the committee of the Peace Society. They wished me to be the paid secretary of the Manchester society. I stated two objections; 1st., read pages 13 and

14 of my "Christian Magazine," Vol. I.;—2nd. The parent society has a money qualification. We had a very agreeable meeting, but my difficulties were not removed.

HIRED MINISTERS ALARMED.

11*mo* 1*st.*—The following letter will explain itself; it was addressed to John Flesher, editor of the "Primitive Methodist Magazine." Since my reply was written, four months have elapsed, and no notice has been taken of it. The readers will judge of the candor and honor of such conduct—inserting an attack and denying any opportunity of a defence. I ask the Editor, would you wish to be thus treated?

My Dear Sir,—

My attention has just been called to the following notice on the cover of your Magazine for April, 1846:—"J. Bowes, a wandering lecturer, must not be allowed the use of any of our chapels; and if he wish any of our friends to read any of his foolish tracts against a Hired Ministry, we advise them to wish him to see his ridiculousness exposed in the tract issued by the Rev. W. Cooke, Newcastle-on-Tyne." From this,—

1. It seems to be a crime to be a "wandering lecturer." If *wandering* means "going about doing good," as Christ and the apostles itinerated, I plead guilty to the charge; but surely it should be no disgrace in the eye of a Primitive Methodist preacher to *wander*. Wesley was a great "wanderer," and many of your preachers have large circuits. But I do not "wander" to collect money for chapels, hired ministers, and similar objects. I once did such things;—then you said nothing against me. Now I travel far and wide to preach Christ, and lecture on his blessed truth.

2. In the spirit of Roman Catholic sectarianism you command that I "must not be allowed the use of any of our chapels." And is this the spirit of Christian union, or the spirit of schism? The chief of schismatics—the Pope—could only speak thus. And will the obedient people succumb to this dictation of the Editor, or judge for themselves who should be admitted into their chapels? It is quite right to hinder those who do not hold the fundamental doctrines of the gospel, or who are not Christians, from preaching in their chapels, but it is the duty of all churches to receive those whom God has called to teach and preach. Neither you nor any other section of professors have ever charged me with being either corrupt in doctrine or practice.

3. The only reason which you give is a kind of prohibition issued against reading my publications. "If he wish any of our friends to read his foolish tracts against a hired ministry, we advise them, &c." It is not for me to pronounce my tracts to be otherwise than "foolish," however, persons who are not hired ministers have given a different opinion of them; and I can quite understand how you should think much "ridiculousness" connected with them, and especially if you love hire more than the truth. There is more danger of a person's being biased in those considerations which involve his own salary, than in those by which it is not affected.

Some of your preachers are not Evangelists, for they lack both the requisite faith and gifts; others of them have both, and they would loose nothing by becoming unhired, scriptural Evangelists. It must be very irksome and loathsome to the Christian and honorable minds among you to be spending a great deal of your time in obtaining money wherewith to pay yourselves. You have your quarterly collections to give out and make—the weekly pence to collect in some places, from the classes which you lead—the quarterly ticket money to collect; and if the leaders be supposed to be negligent in obtaining money, you have to admonish them to get more. This you do, both at leaders' meetings and quarterly meetings, and, after all, laboring as you do among a poor people, you often fall short of your small salaries, so that you have to devise very strange expedients to get them made up. In addition to this, you often collect for chapels, Sunday schools, &c., so that your time is very much taken up in obtaining your hire.

There is also a great inconsistency in your being hindered from going into trade, while you are all booksellers. It appears to me that there is no disgrace in the

Evangelist of our day working with his hands, as Paul did, if he has time, and preaching when he has done. We should be *all working classes*, and in some way or other contribute to the welfare of the human family. A scriptural evangelist ought to be supported by Christians. No hired Methodist preacher acts scripturally. He errs (1) in taking hire; (2) in making collections from wicked people; (3) in letting out seats to those who can pay; (4) in making charges at the door, or in sanctioning them while others make them.

The cry of "foolish" and "ridiculousness" will weigh nothing with intelligent minds, unless you point out what is "foolish" and "ridiculous" in my writings. Your opposition does not discourage me. I expect it. On the same principle that "Demetrius and the craftsmen" said, "this our craft is in danger," when Paul discoursed or lectured, so you know that if the people obtain correct views, they will not give hire, but leave you to say, "by this craft we have our wealth," and to concoct measures to sustain it. But would it not be better manfully to encounter my arguments, than to throw out insinuations which you cannot prove?

I know it is sometimes said, that the allowance to a Primitive Methodist preacher is so small, that no one would enter upon the office from improper motives. I have known men enter it to preserve them from want, and others who were either not willing or not able to work, and very incompetent to preach, have gone out for a time to enjoy an indolent life. Some, no doubt, have gone out from correct motives—from love to God and souls—and have labored hard, and will have their reward; but many of these, when they discovered what kind of men they were among, either opposed the evils among you and withdrew, or you expelled them because they disturbed your evil courses.

You call yourselves Primitive Methodist preachers! Do you not know that all the first Methodist preachers, for many years were unhired, and that all the Class Money was given to the poor?—(See Myles' Chronology of Methodism.)

W. Cooke's tract never mentions my "Hired Ministry Unscriptural," nor "exposes" the "ridiculousness" of a single thing in it; so that your assertion is plainly untrue. I am, however, replying to W. Cooke, and shall prove that his tract is neither consistent with Scripture nor with itself.

Now, instead of cautioning any of my brethren not to "allow" any of the godly and gifted men among your preachers "our chapels," I should say, receive them to preach Jesus, treat them lovingly, but do not give them hire, for it is contrary to Christ's word, "Freely ye have received, freely give."

I am so far from guarding them against reading any of your publications, that I hate such popery. The Church of Rome is afraid of certain valuable books because they expose her abominations. Is it thus with you? If your deeds were not evil, you would not be afraid of the light—if you had truth on your side, you would fearlessly say, "hear and read both sides." "Prove all things, hold fast that which is good."

If your readers have in them the spirit of men and Christians, they will not take the word of any priest or minister as a sufficient reason for not reading any proscribed work, but will read and judge for themselves.

I offer you space in my "Christian Magazine and Herald of Union" to show, if you can, that a hired ministry is scriptural. Give me the pages of your Magazine, if you wish to know the truth, and I will prove that a hired ministry is not scriptural. Your friend, and the friend of all men,

5mo. 23rd, 1846. JOHN BOWES.

P.S.—I trust to your fairness of what is honorable, after your attack, to insert this reply in your Magazine. J.B.

From this case we may see the consistency of the advocates of "The Evangelical Alliance." This same magazine advocates it, which also advocates the closing of chapels against me, because I hold different opinions from the Methodists. Any union of Christians which excludes other Christians and Christian ministers, on any pretence whatever, is adding another sect to the too numerous sects which already disgrace the church. Such is "The Evangelical Alliance," as this case proves.

11*th* mo. 1*st.*—LEES. Twice. Several of Joseph Barker's friends from a distance, came and wished to ask questions. Joseph Bowker sent a note, wishing to hold a public discussion with me. I sent him this message,—that at present I am resolved to hold a public discussion with neither great nor small, but only with Joseph Barker; and as he had offered to meet me, I am still ready to debate his views with himself, but see no good that can accrue from holding a public debate with any of his imitators. I wish to treat them kindly, to answer any of their questions, and help them to solve their difficulties; but I think they should stir up their leader to redeem his pledge, given before hundreds in Manchester.

2nd.—WILMSLOW. Temperance meeting in the Methodist Schoolroom. William Bolton in the chair. He introduced me to the meeting in a very kind and brotherly speech; over estimating, I fear, my poor services. A few friends of Temperance from Manchester, who reside here for a time, have set on foot this Total Abstinence Society.

8th.—WHALEY. At two o'clock had a very large congregation at Hatfield-fold; twenty disciples remembered the Lord Jesus as he gave commandment, by breaking bread. A crowded congregation in the evening at Stoneheads.

9th.—FURNESS. A crowded house. W. Wild spoke some time, as my voice could hardly be heard. It seemed to be affected ever since the 6th, when I preached in a cold, damp, empty house, at Chapel-en-le-Firth.

15th.—Commenced a week's meetings at PRESTON. Preached out of doors to a large congregation at three o'clock; also twice in Lawson Street Chapel.

ROMAN CATHOLICISM IN PRESTON.

After preaching in the morning, in Lawson Street Chapel, I and another brother entered a chapel, called by Roman Catholics, "St. Ignatius' Church." It was crowded to the door, being what is called "High Mass." A priest, covered with a muslin gown, cream-colored, was addressing the people in English, and exhorting them to give a collection for the band or choir.

There seemed to be three acting priests, dressed in robes of white or cream-color, lined with scarlet. First one priest and then another fell upon their knees. This disgusting appearance of kneeling down and almost as quickly rising up again, occured about twenty times in little more than an hour. At one time one was kneeling, another standing, and in a few minutes they were all seated together with little black caps on their heads. These were soon taken off again. Eight candles burned near the priests all the time we were present, and by and by six little boys, dressed in white, followed each other with six other candles burning in their hands; they held these a short time, and then walked away with them, from this curious scene. There seemed to be a small image of Christ, made either of gold or brass. A priest seemed to be crossing himself while he kneeled before this image. At times a censor, burning with incense, was thrown up by a priest at his fellow priests; some of the incense was thrown in the direction of the congregation, but we were too far off to catch any of the odor.

There was a large band of music above our heads, in a kind of orchestra. This band played such airs as are common in places of amusement, with instruments of varied kinds, accompanied with singing, in which the congregation took no part. The people were all mute. They seemed neither to join in singing nor in anything else. They kneeled down for a long time; one I observed with a prayer-book; he was reading it upon his knees. The priests conducted this part in Latin. All was Latin but what was said about the collection. This they wished the people to understand. What a pity the address about it was not in an unknown language also. I could not but think that the worst Protestant sect, holding the head, conveys more information to the mind than this church of forms and ceremonies. I am more than ever thankful for any church which teaches the people soul-saving truth. I stayed till I was tired and disgusted at the ignorance of my countrymen in this age. We withdrew. Brother S. seemed to know a man at the door, another came up to us, who seemed wishful to know our opinion. I asked what the fourteen candles meant burning at mid-day? He said "It is an ancient practice of the church." We remarked that the people could receive no instruction from what was spoken in Latin. He said it was universally understood! and that Jesus Christ instituted the Lord's Supper in Latin!! I told him that we had no evidence that ever Jesus Christ spoke in Latin at all.

As he grew angry, we left him. It is useless to talk to a man who wishes to strive.

Upon the whole the poor people are to be deeply pitied. For about an hour there was nothing that they could understand and receive instruction from. Pagan, unchristian rites were observed before them, rather calculated to lead into error than truth. The lamentable exhibition which we witnessed, was calculated rather to remind an attentive observer of the actors in a theatre, or the antics of pagan priests, than of anything taught by Christ and the Apostles. What can we do to reach the benighted people? Might not suitable tracts be given them as they enter their places of worship, as they retire, or at their own habitations? My heart's desire and prayer for them is that they may be saved, that some means may be found of conveying to their minds the good news of salvation, through faith in Jesus Christ our Lord.

22nd.—Preached at RUSHOLME. Two souls were led to Christ the first time I preached here; one a merchant, and the other a widow, the keeper of a Puseyite place of worship. She satisfied the church of her faith, and was buried with Christ in baptism. By living in a damp lodge, consumption commenced its work of death. On the 14th, she fell asleep in Jesus. I visited her, for the first time during her illness, on the 11th, and again on the 12th. When I entered she seemed dozing. I said, "Do you know me?" She mentioned my name, took my hand in her two poor dying hands, and expressed her thankfulness to God for what she had received of his truth at Rusholme; and, with a smile on her countenance, she said, "Many people say it is hard work to die; I find it is quite easy to die; I have nothing to do. JESUS HAS DONE ALL FOR ME." On the 13th I saw her again, for the last time in this world.

28th.—STOCKPORT. A young friend and a Mormonite had a discussion. Brother Holland and I went from Manchester. He took the chair on our side. I spoke twice; and we offered to show their errors in a regular debate; they declined it; they are much afraid of public debates. Now as, by the Lord's blessing, we who labored against

Socialism, succeeded in breaking it up entirely almost everywhere; might not a judicious and Christian opposition to the monstrous imposition of Mormonism result in a similar way? Reached home at half-past eleven o'clock. Next morning, the 29th, rose soon after five o'clock, and took the train for Woolton, where I spent a comfortable day.

12th mo. 7th.—John Bright, M.P., was addressing the electors of Hulme. He was questioned on many points of deep importance. His answers indicated his fitness to represent Manchester. His views were large, comprehensive, and liberal. I asked him a question about our military establishments, to which he gave a satisfactory answer. The answer inculcated the soundest principles of Christian peace.

13th.—WHALEY, at half-past nine. At two, at New Mills, in a large cold room; the day was the coldest I have witnessed; a considerable congregation for the first time. At half-past six, at Hatfield-fold. A few souls were saved here during the last visit.

1mo. 30th, 1847.—During the greatest part of this month, I was confined at home through the illness of my dear wife. She is now very weak, and slowly recovering.

2mo. 15th.—BIRMINGHAM. The brethren here seem loving and united. The room was tolerably filled while I stated the gospel in the evening.

16th.—Had to go to LONDON on some business for my father. Met with a very kind family from Liverpool, who invited me to stay with them. I called upon a few Christians, and visited several works of art.

THE TUNNEL under the Thames I went through. Foot passengers only can go through yet, though if the ends were open it is broad enough for carriages. Beneath the Thames people have shops or stalls, and sell different articles right under the river.

THE TOWER contains the arms and characters, or representations of the characters, of English kings, knights, &c., for many centuries. Here also may be seen weapons of war and bloodshed, by which our forefathers killed and tormented each other. When will the governors of the world learn to govern by wisdom, justice, and love, instead of coercion?

THE BRITISH MUSEUM.—This, unlike the rest, is open on certain days to the public free; and I would advise any reader visiting London, if possible, not to leave the city without seeing it. It contains works of nature and art from all parts of the world, and a skeleton, nearly complete, of the great Mastadon.

ST. PAUL'S AND WESTMINSTER ABBEY.— We had scarcely entered these splendid offerings to the glory of the priesthood before I was commanded to take off my hat, no doubt to remind me that I was now on *holy ground.* Not believing in the sanctity of earth and stone, as it was cold, I took no notice, till I was told I must either take off my hat or go out. I took off my hat, but soon left this continued deception of the priests.

THE HOUSE OF COMMONS, where the British parliament is held now, is a very plain building; and the members generally appear like plain country gentlemen, with a few exceptions. There was a tolerably full house while I was there, and the leading speakers on both sides spoke. The Secretary for Ireland seemed really wishful to do it good; but almost overwhelmed at the magnitude of the famine; I could not help sympathising with his good nature while defending the government. After staying some hours we left them sitting.

THE WORK AT BRISTOL.

22nd.—BRISTOL. Broke bread at Bethesda Chapel. George Muller presided; a large number present. I said a little on the benevolence of the gospel and its unity. In the afternoon said a little in the vestry of Bethesda.

23rd.—Preached, at the request of Henry Craik, at Salem, it was tolerably filled with an attentive congregation. This church, meeting in these two chapels, numbers about 700 disciples of Jesus ; contributes yearly £500 to the poor, besides paying for its chapels, supporting its schools, and helping to support preachers of the gospel at home and abroad; and all this without seat-rents, without ministers hired, and without asking the world for anything. While I was there they were sending between £20 and £30 per week to Ireland. G. Muller has purchased several acres of land for orphan houses and intends to erect them at an expense of about ££12,000. As he does not intend to begin the buildings till he has got the money, and as he speaks of commencing soon, it is inferred that he has either got the whole or a considerable portion of the sum required. He has long had upwards of 100 orphans under his care. While here 1 met with sister Murray, who has sojourned in France, and come over with her family to Bristol chiefly to be baptized. There are two interesting congregations in the Pyrenees, one at Orthez and another at Nay. The one numbering about sixty believers, the other near six hundred ; with the latter, a converted Roman Catholic priest, now married, and the father of a family, now officiates, and is supported, not hired, by the people. She, not seeing any way for any brethren going from any of the meetings to baptize the brethren in France, who are waiting for it, applied to the Baptist Society, who, I find, have sent the brethren Cox and Hinton, of London. As they are meeting now simply as Christians I hope they may never meet in any other name than that of Christ. The name of the converted priest is Camilou, he labors at Nay. The chief laborer at Orthez is Louis Barbey, both depend upon the Lord for support. It is gladdening to find that the Lord is calling the attention of his people to his truth in various parts of the world. May his work go on till they shall be all one. Since visiting Bristol, sister Murray, in a letter, states, "Three years ago I heard of a similar conversion to mine at Mulheim, a village not far from Heidelberg, in Germany. One of the bargemen on the river was seized with deep convictions of sin suddenly, and after some time trying to smother them, he spoke to another sailor about it ; he said he did'nt know what to advise him to do but to pray to God, and get a Testament. This the other did, and not only was he converted, but so well did he preach to others, that the demand for Testaments was so great as to excite astonishment ; and the authorities investigated the matter, and found that this man had been the means of making seven hundred Protestants in this village." In the same letter she continues, "There being no clergymen in the island of Cape Britton, in 1802, my father took upon himself the duties of one. He was aid-de-camp to the Governor, and a captain in the British army, and in his case truly were our Lord's words fulfilled, 'he that taketh the sword shall perish by the sword.' Each Lord's Day he read the Church of England service in his scarlet coat, but with a sincere desire to please his God; he buried the dead, he married and christened. One day a poor farmer came to him to say he wished to separate from his wife, for she was a bigoted Romanist, and her priest was eating him out of house and home; for when he came to their house, and it was frequently, the best the house contained was put before him, all his chickens were killed for the priest, and if he wanted an egg the freshest must be kept for the priest. My father told him he should be grieved to assist him in putting away his wife. He would advise him to try one plan first with his wife, and if it did not succeed, then he would speak further on the business. 'Go home,' he said, 'open the Bible, and leave it in some place where your wife will be sure to see it, curiosity will induce her to read, and she will there find something which will cause her to reverence her priests less, or I mistake her disposition.' My father heard no more of this matter until some months after, when he saw the farmer come into the church with his wife under his arm; after the service he spoke to him, and said, 'How did you bring this about?' 'Oh, your honor, I followed your advice, and the Bible did it; by the blessing of God my wife is now as staunch a Protestant as she was before a bigoted Papist.'" These are interesting facts—showing what God can do by his truth, even without the preaching of the gospel; and should encourage us to give the Scriptures to the Roman Catholics.

BRISTOL, May 11th, 1847.

MY DEAR BROTHER,—

I thank you for your affectionate letter. I have not the least wish to press the matter. I believe that you had no intention to hinder love. So far as I am concerned, I do most fully desire that brethren should have their liberty, and do not in the least wish to infringe upon yours. Your mind remains the same with regard to your thinking that you acted quite properly in writing about me what you did. I think, on the other hand, *still*, that there was a more excellent way,—that is, to have written *to me* about what you considered wrong in me, without exposing me publicly, except I had been fundamentally unsound, and the church of Christ needed to be warned against me. But let us have done with this matter, my dear brother. I do wish to continue to love you, and do desire from my heart to wish you God's blessing upon your labors. Brother Craik has been for about three weeks ill. Bodily weakness and great pressure of work *force* me to be brief.

Yours affectionately in the Lord,

To J. Bowes.   GEORGE MULLER.

I spoke or wrote freely on dear brother Muller's position. I could not see that I had any call to write privately to him, since what I called in question was published by him.

6mo. 7th.—Sent off the New Hymn Book to be considered by neighboring churches; finished the business I had to do as secretary of the Peace Society, packed up for Scotland, and at 8 o'clock preached to a vast congregation at the Preston Market-place; gave away a great number of tracts. Some had come nine miles to hear the truth.

8th.—At the same place, a large, deeply attentive assembly. Afterwards met the brethren. A few persons seemed to be present holding similar views to the Unitarians,—

First Speaker said,—" I wish to know whether your sentiment is still unchanged, or whether you are still unable to call any one a Christian who does not believe Jesus Christ to be the supreme God?" I answered,—" My views are unchanged. I would gladly receive all who believe in Christ: but then, if any one believes in Christ truly, he must believe Him to be the character which the Scriptures give him, and it is by this faith that men are forgiven and made sons of God. I would not tell any sinner any other way of salvation." After this, the other two spoke. Addressing myself to them all, I said, " What would you tell a sinner to do in order to find peace with God?"

Second Speaker.—" I would tell him to repent and do good works?" I replied, " And how long must he repent and do good works before he knows he is forgiven? The drunkard professes repentance after a debauch, and promises amendment, and he seems changed, till the next night, when he gets drunk again. Is that long enough? Is a day long enough for evincing that he has truly repented?" " No, he must repent and do good works till death." " What! before he knows himself to be a child of God? Then he can never have any comfort of religion in this life, for he can never know whether God has forgiven him or not. Miserable theology, that leaves a sinner all his life uncertain whether he is going to heaven or hell." I then stated the joy of the Gospel plan of salvation by faith.

Third Speaker.—" He can tell that he is accepted as soon as he begins to repent and do good works." " How can he tell? If he is to judge of the reality of his repentance by his good works, he must take some time to do them in. Now how many must he do before he can satisfy himself that he has done a sufficient number of good works to entitle him to a full pardon?" To this question I could get no answer; it was seen that should the man, doing good works to get pardon, fail in any thing, as men do constantly fail, his confidence would be shaken in himself, and consequently he would not know that he had done good works enow to get pardon. Though no sinner is in a condition to do good works at all till he receive the Christ. Good works spring from faith. They are the effects, not the cause. This was one of the most humiliating specimens of Unitarian views, and one of the most triumphant instances of the power of simple truth over error that I ever witnessed.

11*th.*—CARLISLE. Preached at the cross to a very large, attentive congregation. After I had preached the gospel and stated some of the commands of Christ, I stated that supported publicans and soldiers caused a famine, because they were not workers. A man cried out, " And what of preachers?" I said, I will come to them next, which I did, and stated the scriptural view of the subject.

17*th.*—Took coach for Scotland, and reached CUMNOCK in time to discourse on the truth as it is in Jesus. Saw Ivie Campbell here for the first time. Having heard that the church was more favorable than last year to receive none but the baptized, I informed them that I could not sit down in any church at the table, if any of the Lord's children should be shut out. The leading members satisfied me that they still met as Christians, and had never refused, and would never refuse, fellowship to any of the Lord's children.

22*nd.*—Cumnock. It was very cold, and I have not felt well since I came to Scotland; conversed with a hearer to-day who professes to believe the gospel; she stated to me that she looks upon immersion to be commanded by God. I said, "Will you do it?" she hesitated, I said, "I advise you to pray no more till you either get baptized or are willing."

23rd.—One of Ivie Campbell's men drove me to Mauchline, in the parish of which resided Robert Burns. To-day I was quite feverish, but managed to preach out of doors at night to a large congregation. One man professed to be a believer, and wished to be baptized; as there are a few brethren here I left him with them.

25th.—This morning I immersed, in the name of the Lord Jesus, James Little, a member of James Morrison's church, but it seems he was a member before he went into the water, but not when he came out, so easily may persons loose their membership in some churches. This church will not allow any baptized person to be a member, but he may be permitted or allowed to sit at their table without either voice or vote. That is if he will consent not to be a member of any church, to have his tongue tied, and his influence thrust out of the church; if he can submit to such degradation as this, and barter his Christian liberty, he may be a communicant! None who understand the liberty which we have in the Lord, could sanction a church for cutting off Christians for obeying Christ's commands and example. In the evening preached at KILMAURS; a considerable congregation.

27th.—Broke bread with a few brethren, who have increased since last year, in Clark Street. At one o'clock preached in the open-air; had such a sore mouth and tongue I fear several could not hear distinctly. At two o'clock, in the room, discoursed on several practical truths. At five o'clock preached out again, and at six held a conversational meeting in the schoolroom.

30th.—To-day I baptized James Bryce, of Darvel, and Alexander Brown, of New Milns, both teachers in the church at Darvel. As medicine had failed to remove what now seemed a serious complaint, I rested this evening. I slept at Graham's Temperance Hotel, in Glasgow, a kind friend being out of the city where I used to lodge: was charged for bed and boots cleaning 3s! Double what I was ever charged before anywhere.

7mo. 1st.—GLASGOW. To-day I baptized David Legatt and his household, but there was no infant in it; it consisted of himself, his believing wife, and their Christian servant. I have no doubt but the three households mentioned in Scripture were like this; especially when I read in Acts xvi. 34, of the jailor at Philippi, that, "He rejoiced, believing in God with all his house." After this we all walked out to RUTHERGLEN, where I preached to a considerable and attentive congregation in the open air. With very great difficulty I walked back to Glasgow. I was very earnestly requested to marry two disciples (which accords with Scottish law): I regretted that I had not time.

2nd.—Visited WISHAW, where truth is spreading, one hundred copies of "A Hired Ministry Unscriptural," having been ordered. Reached EDINBURGH too ill to preach; but as I was now near the German Ocean I bathed at Portobello.

3rd.—Arrived at DUNDEE, quite hoarse, and unable to preach out. Several were deeply affected at my altered appearance, having been ill several weeks.

4th.—Broke bread with the dear brethren at 11; could hardly be heard. At 2, I preached; my voice grew stronger, so that I ventured to announce an evening meeting at 6 o'clock. A blessed time we had.

5th & 6th.—Here I rested two days. Met my beloved brother Anderson, from Birmingham, and bathed again without effect. I consulted Dr. Nimmo, who gave me medicine.

7th.—Came by sea to STONEHAVEN. Was glad for the first time that I was sea-sick; it had little effect. Two discourses were expected in the Wesleyan Chapel. I begged off for one night. How unusual with me! For many years it has been—"Give me work!" not let me have less. How frail is man.

8th.—Feel a little better to-day. Preached to a very attentive congregation, with comfort to myself.

9th.—Was expected to preach in ABERDEEN; dared not—could not. Took medicine again.

10th.—Preached out to a large assembly. Felt now the good effects of the medicine; but weakness, a cough, and soreness of throat remained.

16th.—Wet morning. Set off for CLATT. Left my kind friends at Old Meldrum. Preached at CLATT.

17th.—Rested a night, which was most agreeable. As a horse has been kindly placed at my service for a few days, this helps me much in my weak state. Rode over to NEW LESLIE, to see my dear sister Henderson, far gone in consumption, but unspeakably happy in God. The last year, no sister in the church looked more healthy than she; about a month afterwards this disease commenced. For some time she had difficulty in giving up her husband, a dear brother in Christ, and her four young children. Now she seems with a clear mind, dead to all below. Speaking of her departure in the presence of her husband, she said, "He will have the worst of it; I shall have the best of it." Yes, dying and going to Jesus to her was better than life. O, 'tis worth our labor in preaching the blessed gospel, when such results are produced. The good news makes us happy both in life and in death.

18th.—Had a very comfortable meeting with the brethren at DUNCANSTON, and preached to a full place. One thing this evening astonished me,—though I had a very severe cough, preached an hour and a half without being troubled with it.

19th.—INSCH; out of doors. I now endeavor to get done before the darkness arrives.

21st.—LARGUE. For these few days have had a very severe cough, and spitting of blood, and threatening indications of consumption; indeed, I am directly thrown upon eternity, and if these symptoms continue, cannot be long here. Some advise me to cease preaching. What shall I do? If it be consumption, I shall soon have done preaching, and therefore I must work while it is day. In this view I must die; it therefore cannot hurt me much. I could not forbear telling some of my brethren, among whom I have gone for several years preaching the kingdom of God, "*If these symptoms continue, you will see my face no more.*" While here, I procured new flannels, having desisted from wearing flannels about three years ago.

22nd.—ABERDEEN. Did not dare to preach out. Rested again.

23rd.—Preached out, and bade farewell to Aberdeen for the present.

24th.—ARBROATH. Preached out a short time. Almost well, but very weak.

28th.—WISHAW. A very attentive congregation in a hall. This is my first discourse in this part of the country. Having written about a week ago to a Christian friend, the doctor in Liverpool who used to attend our family, stating my condition, &c., I received to-day the following reply:—" Your symptoms are serious and threatening; therefore cease to preach at present, as that will aggravate your pulmonary disease." How good is God. When I got this letter the cough was gone, the spitting of a saltish matter and blood had entirely ceased, and I am returning onwards home almost well: whereas, ten days ago, I expected to leave Scotland for the last time, and that I should see my dear brethren in Christ no more in the flesh. I ought to mention, that from the very day I put on the flannel the violent symptoms all abated, and in four days they had nearly all gone. If the Almighty be pleased to spare me to my family, yet unable to provide for themselves—though He no doubt could provide for them were I with him—and if he has anything more for me to do in the church and the world, His will be done. May I be more useful than ever.

8mo 1st.—Broke bread with about thirty believers. These have been chiefly led into their present position through a desire to have a New Testament ministry. Preached afternoon and evening also. I feel pleasure in recording that John Kirk's labors in the neighborhood have led many souls to God, over whom angels rejoice, and so do I.

5th.—Arrived in Manchester safe, and tolerably well, having come by sea to Liverpool.

My connection with the Peace Society brought me into correspondence and in contact with many estimable and public men. The following letter is from John Bright.

Rochdale, Sept. 13th, 1847.

Dear Sir,—

. . . . My opinion is, that very little good is done by sending petitions to Parliament on the Peace Question. What is really wanted is, that the public mind should be more awakened to a sense of the enormous folly and wickedness of war. There is one branch of the question which the Peace Societies have not much touched upon—I mean, that past wars have gained us little or nothing, and that the notion of our being called upon to interfere in every European squabble is false and pernicious. This is a great question you are agitating, and only by a slow process can it gain hold on the public sentiment. War can no more be put down by any sudden scheme of arbitration, than human nature can be, at once and by wholesale, regenerated. But labor, and perseverance, and faith will eventually do much. I am, respectfully yours,

To Mr. John Bowes, Manchester. JOHN BRIGHT.

11mo. 4th.—Sat as chairman in a discussion on Mormonism between George Barber and Richard Cooke, at OLDHAM. Crowded hall and very orderly congregation.

5th.—This evening George Barber introduced a book in evidence to which the Mormon chairman objected, because the Bible was the standard. I decided that evidence might be obtained from any quarter, while the Bible was the only standard, and that I was glad that the first attempt to suppress evidence came rather from the other side. The umpire, Mr. M'Farlane, was now appealed to, and decided with me.

8th.—This evening the Mormons refused to continue the discussion, though they were pledged to it. It was the largest congregation.

9th.—I lectured on Mormonism in the same hall. I offered them equal time, but none came forward.

10*th.*—The Peace Committee met and passed the following resolution,—"Min. 5th. A letter of resignation has been received from William Irwin, and the Committee, in taking it into consideration, having learned from those now present, that William Irwin had commenced law-proceedings against another member (after said member had proposed to settle the matter by arbitration) cannot receive this resignation without first recording its strong and unanimous conviction, that for one member of a Peace Committee to threaten law-proceedings against another member, is a direct violation of the principles on which the Peace Society is founded; and in so doing, would express its deep regret at being called on, in such a way, to vindicate the well-known principle of the society. Peter B. Alley is requested to make a copy of this minute and hand it to William Irwin."

"Min. 6th. That, in reference to the previous minute, James Thompson and John Goodier be requested to confer with John Bowes, and report to the next meeting."

Extract from the Minutes of the Manchester and Salford Peace Society, held 12mo. 6th, 1847.—"Min. 5th. John Goodier reports that James Thompson and himself have conferred with John Bowes respecting the subject of the 6th minute of last meeting. They found it needful to inquire into and investigate certain verbal statements detrimental to the character of John Bowes with reference to commercial transactions. After careful inquiry and a full investigation thereof, they find said statements cannot be substantiated; and they are united in the judgment, that the conduct of John Bowes has not in any wise been blameable in the transaction before alluded to, nor has his character at all suffered in their estimation thereby."

The case of William Irwin was this: He offered to reprint my "Hired Ministry Unscriptural," and I was to pay when convenient. He did print it, and soon after sent me bills to sign for the amount. I declined and kept him to his terms. He employed a lawyer; I employed none, and got well through it. I brought the case before "The Friends," in a letter which I wrote them, but they did not succeed in bringing about a settlement. Some months or years after, I met him full in the face in Mosley Street. He held out his hand and said, "John, let by-gones be by-gones." I gave him my hand, but was astonished at his unexpected address.

14*th.*—OLDHAM. The Working Man's Hall, a very large building, was taken for delivering discourses against Mormonism and in favor of Christianity. In the morning we might have 1000 people; afternoon and evening about 1500. Some fruit appeared. One young man believed the gospel. A Primitive Methodist determined to support sects and a hired ministry no longer.

UNFERMENTED WINE FOR THE LORD'S SUPPER.

A. C. Isaacs, a converted Jew, thus describes one mode of preparing this beverage:—"Raisins, or dried grapes, are steeped in water for two or three days previous to the passover, in a vessel placed near the fire. The juice is then strained and bottled off as 'the fruit of the vine.' Sometimes, if circumstances arise to prevent the raisins being regularly steeped, they are boiled in the afternoon of the day on which the passover is to be celebrated. When the saccharine matter is thought to be sufficiently dissolved, the decotion is boiled off and cooled. Such was our passover wine, so called, and not merely syrup or raisin water. These are the modes in which the wine was prepared by my own mother, during the whole period I was under the parental roof; and when, subsequent to my father's death, it fell to my lot, as the eldest son, to preside at the celebration of the passover, I administered the same kind; so, in short, did all my brethren in the neighborhood of Manchester use an unintoxicating wine. All the Jews with whom I have ever been acquainted use unintoxicating wine at the passover. If it ever should be fermented, it is certainly unknown to them, and against their express intention; but I never knew it to exhibit any of the symptoms."

It appears, from the testimony of Judge Noah, of New York, that the above mode of preparing the passover wine, and using it, is general in that State. Writing to a Christian friend, he says:—"I have your favor, requesting to know how the wine is prepared for the passover. If you wish to make a small quantity for the communion table, take a gallon demijohn (or stone jug), pick three or four pounds of bloom raisins, break off the stems, put the raisins into the demijohn, and fill it with water. Tie a rag over the mouth, and place the demijohn near the fire, or on the side of the fire-place, to keep it warm. In a week it will be fit for use; making a pure, pleasant, and sweet wine, free from alcohol. It is easy to make a small quantity for each time it is used. This is the wine we use on the nights of the passover, because it is free from fermentation, as we are strictly prohibited not only from eating leavened bread, but from drinking fermented (or 'leavened') liquors."

1 *mo.* 16*th*, 1848.—GOMERSAL, Yorkshire. At half-past ten o'clock, ten broke bread, and afterwards spent some time together in useful conversation; at half-past two, and six o'clock, discoursed at BIRKENSHAW. A considerable congregation in the afternoon; in the evening in the Temperance Room; well filled. Here also a few believers have commenced meeting weekly to remember the Lord Jesus in the breaking of bread. While here received the following letter from W. Trotter, arranging for me to go over to Otley.—

CROW LANE, OTLEY, Jan. 18th, 1848.

MY DEAR BROTHER,—

Your kind letter greeted me this evening on my return home, after an absence of several days. I do hope, please the Lord, to be at home next Sunday, and we shall be most glad to see you at the time you name. I need not tell you we shall rejoice to see you at the Lord's table. IT IS HIS TABLE, and our grief is, that so few of his people embrace the opportunity of sitting down at it. As to the other meetings you propose, the room in which we meet is at your service for gospel preaching on Lord's day evening, and the lecture on Monday evening. We hope by all means to see you here on Saturday, but Saturday evening would not answer for a meeting. I cannot promise you a large meeting, as prejudice is very strong here, and there is much opposition from the different denominations. Still, the Lord may incline the hearts of more to come than one would anticipate. I am not surprised at what you say of those called "Christian Brethren." I have not myself felt free to attend any of their meetings for several years. They seem as resolutely opposed to anything like an unsectarian position as any of the older denominations. Still, as in other sects, there are, doubtless, dear Christians among them. Praying that the Lord's blessing may richly attend your visit to this place,

I remain yours, dear brother, in the bonds of the gospel,

To J. Bowes. W. TROTTER.

He afterwards fell into the very errors which he here deprecates. How changed in a few years this beloved brother was, by the Darby schism, time will show. His letters prove he was non-sectarian when we corresponded and met.

17th.—BIRSTAL. In a school-room, a little south of the Wesleyan Chapel; as the snow descended rapidly, the congregation was small, though the town's bellman did his duty; as I entered the town, he told the people of the discourse, said that I should preach the gospel, and show what the Christian Church ought to be, and added, "It is my opinion, if all the people of this country knew what a Christian Church ought to be, it would be much better for them." I heard him above an hour after, when he added, "that if the people come, they will know how to provide food, and clothing, and coils (coals), this cold weather." Thus he went on, teaching the people in a very loud and clear voice. This was something new to me.

23rd.—OTLEY. Nine o'clock; W. Trotter discoursed in a house, after which I said a little. At half-past ten, broke bread with about twenty; several brethren not being well: spoke a little on the unity of the church. At half-past two o'clock, W. Trotter discoursed; at six, I preached to a considerable congregation; one man was there whom I had invited the previous night while he was in a state of intoxication.

25th.—This morning intended to set off for Pateley Bridge at eight o'clock, but was detained by conversation, till nine; then my walking-stick could not be found. This was sought for near an hour, and at last found, concealed in a singular place, by one of the dear children, beneath the table, where it might not have been found for a long time. I was easy, believing that there was some meaning in this. Brother Trotter set me on the way: I had not gone far before I was overtaken by a person with a pack on his back. I asked him the way: he was going to Blubberhouses; I asked him if he knew a person that used to take in the Primitive Methodist preachers. He said, "Are you a Primitive Methodist preacher?" I said, "I once was, and about twenty-three years ago used to preach there." "What do they call you, if you please?" "John Bowes is my name." He stretched out his hand and said, "Let me have a shake of your hand." I had slept and preached in his mother's house, and knew him and his wife well. We had some sweet conversation; he wished to have some of my publications, which I gave him. Had I found the stick in time I should not have met with this brother. In the evening, after walking thirteen miles through the snow, I discoursed at Pateley Bridge, where I had not been for about twenty-three years. I stood declaring the truth for nearly two hours; it seemed to be received, and I was desired to return and give them a discourse there on the same subject. I think it is likely that a few will begin to act according to the New Testament.

26th.—Walked to Grewelthorpe, and reached Middleham soon after dark; found my dear father very unwell.

30th.—SCRAFTON. At half-past ten o'clock, a house full of my old neighbors, and a generation of young people whom I know not.

MELMERBY, where I used to exhort when about seventeen years of age; walked through a very heavy rain.

CARLTON, in the evening, in Walls' long room, where I was first led to see God's great love for me and my own great sin, thirty years ago.

2mo. 5th and *6th.*—KEIGHLEY. Preached twice in the market-place. Heard two sermons, one in the Primitive Methodists' Chapel. They also have now an organ and a set of singers. They are holding revival meetings, but while the minister prayed with much earnestness, the singers were looking at their music books and talking with each other. It is of no use praying for a revival, and encouraging such mockery as unconverted singers manifest. They should sell the organ, and give the money to the poor. The Wesleyans have erected an immense chapel. The preacher had little gospel but much apparent sincerity in his sermon. He stated that there was something wrong in all denominations, since all agreed that there were fewer conversions than usual.

At seven o'clock, preached in a house. A few seem satisfied that a New Testament church is needed.

7th.—Preached in the same house as before, and visited a number of old friends, some of whom could not look on me so favorably as they would have done had I been in their sect. I do not value such love as can only reach me through a sect. I value highly that love which is truly Christian.

8th.—SILSDEN. In the Oddfellows' Hall; a large congregation, very attentive. Some friends were very active, one cried it through the town gratuitously.

9th.—Visited EAST MORTON. Saw some old friends, who would have introduced me into their chapel, but the following sectarian law stood in their way, which is published on their plans: "No person is allowed to preach amongst us whose name is not on the Plan, or approved of by the Circuit Committee." A man of God may arrive at such a place as East Morton, some miles from where the Circuit Committee reside, only an hour or two before the time, and thus be hindered through this wicked law, from preaching Christ's holy gospel, and leading sinners to the truth.

23rd.—THORNSET. A hired minister in this neighborhood has been opposing what he calls a cheap religion, he says, "If men pay for religion they will value it more."

The gift of the Saviour was cheap to us; cannot we value him till we buy him? His precious blood procured our pardon; it is cheap to us, though bought by him at a price beyond price. Cannot we value forgiveness till we pay for it? The gospel, the Holy Spirit, and all the blessings of grace are given, not sold, cannot we value them without paying for them? So far as giving the gospel to the world is concerned, we do advocate a cheap religion, and affirm that the gospel should be given without money and without price.

4mo. 16th.—HORWICH-END, at half-past ten. An old man here has recently commenced hearing because we have brought the gospel to his door; he had not been in any place of worship for twenty years. He had no faith in the Bible. Faith cometh by hearing, and when it comes it softens the heart. I saw him at his own house, with tears in his eyes; after we had spoken of the death of Jesus, he said, "If I should die to-night I believe I should go to heaven." Another precious soul came lately to hear the great, good news, concerning Jesus, and after many sorrowful days, was made so unspeakably happy by the truth that she could not sleep all night for very joy. When I was informed of it I said, "I am much better pleased that she could not sleep for joy, than as though it had been sorrow, for it shows it was the gospel, the good news that I had set before her."

5mo. 21st.—FURNESS. Twelve broke bread after preaching. It is only about a month since this meeting commenced.

HATFIELD-FOLD. Afternoon, in a barn, crowded, between two and three hundred people. As there is no place to be obtained suitable, they speak of getting a new chapel. Near fifty broke bread.

DISLEY. Half-past six o'clock. A full house; about fifteen or sixteen now profess to believe the gospel here, and break bread weekly. This commenced a few weeks ago. The brethren had preached here long without any apparent fruit; now it appears. This should encourage us to persevere.

23rd.—To-day I heard of a Methodist class-leader, at Fernilee, who did a great deal to keep the people from hearing us, and some things which were decidedly wrong. He was burned to death in a powder-mill a few days ago. Also conversed with a sister, who said, "Before I knew the truth, I was very much in the dark, troubled about my soul, and unhappy, because *I did not know what to trust to.* Now she can trust in the love of God, the death of Christ, and the promises of the gospel. Evening, preached at NEW MILLS. Moses Goodwin went through the place with a bell, to say "that I should show how individuals might be made happy; how to have happy families; happy churches; a happy nation, and a happy world." A great congregation, the largest I have seen in these parts.

6mo. 23rd.—Have just returned home from Bradford, where I last night finished a debate, held for nine nights, on Mormonism, with James Marsden. The ground of debate was entirely of his own choosing. I sent nine propositions, but they were all rejected, and I had no way left but to accept of his terms, or give up the discussion; and as the Mormons had declined to meet me at Manchester, Stockport, and Liverpool, I instructed my Committee to take them on their own terms.

25th.—MANCHESTER. Proposed three for fellowship. One has been made happy by the truth, through attending preaching in a brother's house in Salford. This should encourage us to preach from house to house.

30th.—While in the train for Scotland, several young men were speaking favorably of physical force. I handed them some Peace tracts, which they received and read. A lady, going to Moffat, wished a few; I supplied her, and she would deliver them there. Arrived at DOUGLASS, and met the few saints, with whom I spent a happy hour or two, pointing out to them what the Lord is doing in England, and the true grounds of Christian unity. The few Christians meeting here have been drawn together during the last few months.

8th.—WISHAW. Yesterday, brother Robert Dickie came over from Helensburgh, and assisted in visiting and worship. To-day, he and I visited the cottages where the colliers live. Thus, I have visited the whole of this town, leaving a tract in each house that I could find not locked; excepting three, whose inmates refused to take them. The first a Roman Catholic; the second the Free Church minister's family; the third an Old Light Burgher family. The whole three were very determined not to have a tract. The Free Church minister's sister stated that they had tracts enough. I asked, "Have you enough of the gospel?" These people are never likely to be anything beyond sectarians, if they will not read.

9*th*.—In Dalziel's Hall; large congregations all day. A very gracious season; at the Lord's Supper several united with us, who do not always meet with the brethren in Wishaw. At 2 o'clock, brother Dickie discoursed, before me, on the gospel, against dress, and smoking tobacco. At half-past 6, a very remarkable season; nearly the whole assembly was bathed in floods of tears, by the truth concerning God's love and the name of Jesus.

10*th*.—Lectured at HOLYTOWN against Mormonism, and introduced the gospel. The Mormons were allowed time to reply, but made little out. They gave me a challenge to discuss with a person from Edinburgh. A great part of the people sat as colliers and tailors sit—on the floor, from first to last.

19*th*.—Lectured in a Free Church, AIRDRIE, against Mormonism. About 1000 people present.

20*th*.—About the same number, or rather more. The Mormons published a bill, stating that I had declined to meet William Gibson in discussion, after engaging. The meeting carried an unanimous resolution, after hearing witnesses, that I had fulfilled all my engagements honorably. What a system of falsehoods is this!

22nd, 23*rd*.—HELENSBURGH. Here a few Baptists have met for several years; holding large views of God's love; but it is only about a year since the table was made the Lord's table, for all the true children, whether baptized or not.

24*th*.—A public debate on Mormonism, in a large church, AIRDRIE, about sixteen hundred people present; hundreds could not get in. I had to get in through a window. It was almost half-an hour before the excellent chairman could obtain order. William Gibson proved to be a very friendly, well-behaved man, a great recommendation in a Mormon, for I have repeatedly met infidels in debate, and they have behaved far better than the Mormons in the Bradford discussion. He lost his temper only once for a very few minutes. I believe great good will result from this discussion. I offered to meet him a second night to accept of his challenge to prove that the church with which I am connected is a church of Christ. He declined.

26*th* to the 31*st*, at HELENSBURGH. On the Lord's Day evening the chapel was crowded. During the meetings five have professed to believe the gospel.

8*mo*, 1*st*.—RUTHERGLEN. A large congregation to hear the gospel out of doors; after this I lectured to a considerable number in a hall, shewing what Christian churches ought to be. A few have been led to the Lord here lately.

10*th*.—GLASGOW. Was about to preach near the bridge and green, when I was told by two inspectors that they could not allow it. This comes of rioting. The authorities never prevented me here before, but since the riots, they now propose to hinder the preaching of the gospel. This is decidedly wrong. The gospel will make men peaceable, and at any rate, when God has said "preach the gospel to every creature," men have no right to prevent it. Two or three hundred people collected; I should probably have had thousands. It was now a question whether I should desist or proceed, and allow the police to take me away. Three reasons induced me to desist.—1st. I had labored hard lately and needed rest. 2nd. The late riots, and the present disposition of many riotous men, justify the authorities in caution. 3rd. I was only to stay one night, and had engagements in other places, so that I could not afford to be detained by the police. But after this, I mean to preach the gospel in Glasgow, or anywhere else, if the Lord will, in the open-air, and shall not desist because men make laws to break the law of God. The gospel must be preached to every creature.

16th.—DUNDEE. To-day, visited Alexander Boyack, he had united with the Mormons expecting to find piety and miracles among them, he was disappointed in each case. Evening, had a social meeting; three brethren spoke chiefly on the gospel and the duties of Christians. Had these brethren been under a one-man ministry, they could not have been expected to speak with so much edification as they did. The church here is improving considerably; a few have been added through the year, and there seems to be nothing in the body but love and union.

18th.—John Mackie and I sailed for STONEHAVEN, where we had a glorious meeting in the evening. A kind Baptist sister from Glasgow, had interested herself to procure the Wesleyan Chapel for me, which she had secured on condition that I would confine myself to the gospel, and say nothing about the errors of the church. I preferred the market-place, a large congregation, and liberty, to the chapel under these restrictions. Truth has nothing to fear from investigation. Deep attention sat upon every countenance. I never preached the gospel here to so many people. They were eager for the publications afterwards, and some wished a conversation. O that I could stay here a month, or that the Lord would send some one else to give them the blessed gospel. Many railway laborers attended and behaved well. This evening a great storm arose a few hours after I had left the steamer, by which about a hundred men along the coast, engaged in herring fishing, lost their lives.

19th.—The coast was surrounded and crowded with fisherwomen, and men seeking after their relations, or enquiring for the dead. Such a storm at sea has not been known, and so much loss of life, for many years.

20th.—Three meetings in Albion Court, ABERDEEN. Had a large congregation in Castle Street at four o'clock. An Independent from Fraserburgh, who professed to receive the truth from my lips many years ago, came into the hall after preaching, and regretted to see me in so small a place, when I might be preaching to hundreds. I told him to open the Independent chapels to me, and I would preach there, that I was following out my own convictions of duty, and believed that I never was doing more good than now.

MORMONISM AND SOCIALISM.

29th.—Just reached ABERDEEN in time to lecture on Mormonism, in "St. Andrew's Street Church." I do not much admire the calling of buildings, churches, but this practice is all but universal in Scotland. A discussion was opened with a Mormon after each lecture; John Henderson was the name of the defender of the system, but he did not reply to my arguments or evidence, but contented himself chiefly with personalities and untruths. These were not received in Aberdeen, where I resided near four years. Among the rest of the numerous untruths which he uttered, he stated that " I got my living by mending old shoes, and making shoes." As this honorable, because honest and useful calling I had never learned or practised, the people saw that the man would assert anything, for this was only a specimen of his powers of invention. Andrew Shearer was in the chair. The good resulting from these lectures is not the mere overthrow of Mormonism, but the establishing of important truths, such as Justification by Faith, in opposition to their remission only in baptism.

As I held a debate here on Socialism, which as a system is now extinct all over these kingdoms, I cannot reflect upon the part which I was led to take in its overthrow, without thankfulness to God. This is increased by a consideration of the recent events in Paris, (1848) where Socialism or Communism has deluged the streets with blood, even under a republican government; and had Socialism been as powerful in this country as it was some years ago, when it was regularly organized with thousands of members, our own country might have been now in a much worse state than France; but thanks be to Him who has blessed the labors of those who opposed the vile system in our country, it is entirely dead, or so abashed by its repeated exposures, as to blush to lift up its guilty head. The longer I live, the greater is my regard for human life, it should be sacred, and the more highly we value it, the more careful we should be to preserve it from the hand of every human assailant. Seeing as I do, that Mormonism is one of the most alarming impostures which has existed since the days of Mahomet, and that it already numbers its tens of thousands of men prepared for battle whenever their leaders shall call them into the field, every lover of order and of his fellow-men, should do what he can to extinguish it by truth and love.

31st.—After seeing W. K. Rose, and a few more Christians in EDINBURGH, I lectured in the Baptist Chapel, DUMFERMLINE, on Peace and Temperance. Friends and foes had been invited. A considerable number heard attentively; an opportunity was given for any present to question what was advanced, but none replied. A sister in Christ had fallen asleep in him only about a month before. The history of her marriage is somewhat singular. The husband, now a widower, used to attend a church where I used to preach occasionally, sixteen or seventeen years ago. On one occasion he took the liberty of stating to me that he was disposed to marry, but did not know any Christian whom he should wish to make his wife, and as he did not intend to select any but a Christian, he asked me if I could recommend him to any one,—I thought for some time, and then mentioned a sister at Dundee, a near neighbor of mine. On my return, I think I told her what I had done, he came over by her consent, they were pleased with each other, and in a few weeks married. I now enquired of her mourning husband, if he had found the marriage a happy one, after so many year's experience, and received a most satisfactory reply. Should he see this in print, I have no idea that he will be ashamed of the course which he took. He had confidence in me; I never regretted giving the advice which he sought, and now that she is gone, I have no doubt but it contributed much to her comfort while in this world of changes and cares.

VISIT TO BRUSSELS—THE PEACE CONGRESS.

9mo. 18th.—At 5 a.m., started for Stockport, and met other representatives from Manchester going to the Peace Congress at Brussels. Reached the Hall of Commerce, London, at half-past 7 o'clock, where the delegates were met; found them calling over names. A debate arose, about the propriety of holding a Peace Meeting on the Field of Waterloo. It was finally agreed to postpone it till we arrived in Brussels. At half-past 10 o'clock arrived at Blackwall, by railway, and took supper. About 150 persons present.

19*th.*—At 2 o'clock in the morning went on board. A great fog in the river hindered us from sailing, so that, although we tried to get down the Thames, we were obliged to cast anchor till half-past 9 o'clock, when the fog cleared away, and the *Giraffe* steamer made way down the Thames. As we passed Woolwich, we saw on the shore, the immense preparations of cannons and balls, made for destroying the human race. The day was very fine, and we held a peace meeting on board. Joseph Sturge, president. Several speakers addressed the meeting. We reached OSTEND about 12 o'clock, and were then informed what honors we had missed; the burgomaster, magistrates, and citizens, had intended to give us a hearty welcome to Belgium. Ostend contains about 14,000 inhabitants. We breakfasted at 5 a.m. in a spacious hall, and afterwards proceeded over a flat country eighty-five miles by a special train. We passed Bruges and Ghent. A great part of the country is highly cultivated, and the people seem cheerful and comfortable. The land seems in many more hands than in our country.

We met twice on the 20*th*, and the same on the 21*st.* About 130 members of Congress were present from England, a considerable number from Belgium, and some from France, Holland, and other parts of the Continent. The Congress was held in the Hall of the Societie de la Grande Harmonie; M. Visschers, was elected president. The speeches were chiefly in French. The chief speakers from England, able to speak French, were William Ewart, M.P., and J. S. Buckingham. The objects of the Congress were, (1st) to get governments to insert an arbitration clause in all international treaties; (2nd) to elect a High Court or Congress of Nations, to settle disputes without war; (3rd) to call the attention of governments to the advantage of a measure of general disarmament, as conducive to a friendly understanding among the nations, and tending directly to prepare the way for the formation of a Congress of Nations. Two persons only opposed these propositions, a Spaniard, and a Romish priest.

On the 22*nd*, the inhabitants gave us a *Soiree.* I was lodged at the Hotel Belle Vue, next to the King's palace. The city is splendid. The arrangements of the Committee were excellent, and the Belgians kind. The attention of Europe has been called to the Peace Question. Governors and people will be addressed, and when it is remembered, that Christ said "Blessed are the peace-makers, for they shall be called the children of God," I expect a blessing to rest on this work. I, however, am not so sanguine as some peace advocates as to the results. My conviction is, that although a man may, by reason of philosophy, see the evil of war, and resisting evil, that, as wars and fightings come from the lusts of men, that should such a man be insulted, without Christian principle he would resist evil, and what is true of a man, would be true of nations; therefore, the only *rational* way to abolish war, is to make men in all nations Christians. Peace Societies will do good just so far as they teach by precept and example what is scriptural on this subject, and call the attention of Christians to their duty. It is to be regretted that many Christians are taught to support war instead of peace.

A rather curious incident occured while here. I was quietly walking down one of the beautiful promenades, and took a rest on one of the public seats. Presently a female came up to me, and spoke something in French. I did not comprehend what she wanted, and she did not seem to know that I was English, and could not understand her. She got quite excited, which collected a crowd, and went for a *gendarmé*, or policeman. Untimately a person came up who understood how matters were, and explained to me that she was wanting two sous for the privilege of sitting on the seat! As it appeared the seat was hers, of course I paid the amount demanded.

I visited the large Cathedral in Brussels, and was much pained to see children at confession. Three or four priests were sitting each in a sort of sentry-box, with a little opening on each side. Each wore a white surplice, and was surrounded by from fifty to a hundred children, sitting on forms; they might be from ten to fourteen years old. One went up at a time, whispered outside the confessional, through the hole, into the priest's ear. Thus are children trained up from their earliest years to confide the interests of their souls to a priest, instead of committing them to the only Saviour. Many worshippers were surrounding a priest, who was drinking wine from a cup. Five or six widows were counting their beads, and when they came to a large one, they seemed to put up a prayer. I wish I could preach in French, how gladly would I preach the glorious gospel to these benighted people. Although I saw tens of thousands of both rich and poor, I saw no one drunk, and few so extremely poor as in our own country. The climate is admirable: the people generally look well fed and clothed, and cheerful. There is much promenading round the fine walks, and many sit with their coffee, wine, &c., out of doors. We visited the frog-market, where frogs are sold for eating, but we were too late, they were all sold. Only a very few of our party visited Waterloo, as it was thought wrong for men of peace to give way to a taste for visiting such places.

We left Brussels by special train at 12 o'clock at night, breakfasted at Ostend, and sailed about seven on the 23rd. Had an interesting Peace Meeting on board, and reached the Custom-house about nine o'clock, a.m. We were detained near an hour by our abominable custom-house laws,—all our carpet bags were opened and searched. These custom-houses and laws hinder trade and commerce, and should be all abolished,—government might save much by having direct instead of indirect taxation. Thus, through the great mercy of God, we all reached LONDON safe on Saturday evening.

24*th.*—Rose early and got into NORTHAMPTON, to a meeting of Christians, who had invited me over to visit them, but had no knowledge of my visit. Brother Pell was in the pulpit. I arranged for meetings, and preached the gospel with great freedom at 2 o'clock, in Zoar Meeting House, Castle-street; at 5, to a large assembly in the open-air, and to a crowded congregation at 6 o'clock in the room.

On Monday the brethren issued large bills for meetings during the week and the next Lord's Day. The meetings were well attended in general, some of them full to overflowing, especially on the Lord's Day evening, when many had to go away who could not get in. I never witnessed such a week of rain. MOULTON is about four miles from Northampton. The brethren, Dent and J. Rymill, and I were wet through, going. I got off my wet clothes, and preached to a housefull of people, after which we set off in a dark, wet night back again. The water covered the road, so that in one place for some distance we were up to the knees; I came out of a warm congregation, yet, through walking home quick, though again wet through, I took no cold. It is of great importance not to sit or stand in wet clothes.

At Northampton lived and labored Philip Doddridge; I walked through the chapel, was in the pulpit in which he preached, and the vestry in which he studied. There remains the chair in which he sat, and the table on which he wrote. The members are said to be about half as numerous as at his death. The chapel had no organ in his time, it was introduced a few years ago. The chapel may hold about 700 people. There are now other two Independent Congregations, and two or three Baptist churches.

6th.—WEDNESBURY. In the British School Room, about 150 present. A few believers have commenced meeting in this neighborhood, to remember the Lord weekly, as the first disciples did.

8th.—BIRMINGHAM. The room was full at the breaking of bread, and in the evening several were unable to get in. At three o'clock, preached near the new railway in Navigation Street, to a very attentive congregation. To-day, I dined with Samuel Lloyd, a brother upwards of eighty years of age, who has fifty children, grandchildren, and great grandchildren. After the day's labors I took the mail train for MANCHESTER, at twenty minutes past twelve, and arrived soon after four o'clock a.m.

24th.—Wednesday. Preached in the Welsh Baptist Chapel, LIVERPOOL; and brother Richard Taylor baptized nine, chiefly from the Portico, where I preached last Lord's day.

29th.—MANCHESTER. Broke bread as usual; and at three o'clock preached at Salford. While engaged, a Policeman came and wished me to give over, stating that he had orders not to allow it. I stated that I had considered the question, and was determined to preach the good news to the people, and should not desist unless compelled; that he might take me away if he pleased; and that I would sooner stand a trial than give over. He said he had done his duty, stood a while, and then walked away. I expected him to come with more of his class to take me away, but we were left to finish in peace. At six o'clock, an attentive congregation.

30th.—Monday. At Mackworth Street. One soul professed to receive the truth.

31st.—Tuesday. At F. Christie's, SALFORD. Another professes to see the truth here.

11mo. 1st.—At 57 Hargreaves Street. J. Naphthali, the Jew, preached. I said a little after him. Another in this neighborhood has recently believed the good news.

14th.—At HIGHLANE. Several have been led to the Lord here.

26th.—Never saw more in Manchester at the breaking of bread. At 3 o'clock, should have baptized in York-street Chapel, but the water had disappeared. Preached the gospel. In the evening, a considerable congregation. One wished to be baptized who was convinced this afternoon. Another applied for fellowship. At these two services, my only daughter, aged twenty, saw herself a sinner, and the Lord Jesus an all-sufficient Saviour. She has since been immersed.

12mo. 1st.—CARLISLE. This morning, about half-past 9 the post brought me a letter and bill, showing that I was advertised for this place last night; and that there was a large congregation disappointed. I was in Manchester. I publish the mode in which the mistake originated,—the only one of the kind that ever occured with me,—to prevent anything of the sort in future. The last week I wrote to the brethren here, stating that I could be here on the 30th, if they made arrangements for a week's meetings. A brother replied that they were to meet last Saturday and determine, and he would then write me. They met and determined, but did not write me; but published bills, concluding that I would know all about it without telling! When I got the letter this morning, I settled some little affairs in the town, took the train at eleven for Carlisle, and was here, 120 miles, by half-past 4. I came away without luggage or cloak, or bidding farewell to my family. The congregation was small, though the bell intimated my arrival; but the night was very wet.

3rd.—About fifty broke bread of various denominations as well as the saints who meet here; it was a most refreshing season. At two o'clock a considerable congregation. At six the chapel was full; several had to stand. There might be about four hundred present.

THE FALLS OF THE CLYDE.

13th.—Arrived at LANARK and visited the falls of the Clyde. About half way is New Lanark, once the scene of Robert Owen's operations. The mills are large, and built on the Clyde; its waters turn the vast machinery. The lecture room is spacious, and galleried on three sides, capable of containing, when crowded, about one thousand five hundred or two thousand people. Close to this is a large room which Robert Owen intended for a ball room; now both were used as schools. The latter had in it a beautiful representation of a large number of plants and flowers, on a canvass, turned on a roller, intended to teach the children botany. There is another large building resembling the lecture-room which was intended for Robert Owen's community. This is now an Independent congregation. A small church remains of old Scottish Independents, numbering about thirty members. The house in which resided Robert Owen stands in a beautifully picturesque situation, and is still occupied by the owner of the New Lanark mills. A female guide conducted us to the far-famed falls. As I had been for several days confined with visiting and preaching in Douglas, I enjoyed the walk and air much. The first fall is the Corra Linn; the water seems to fall about eighty feet; indeed there are two falls near together. The river was much swollen by recent rains, dashing down its mighty waters amid towering rocks on either hand; near this majestic fall is a flight of steps, by which we descended to the edge of the river's bed. We had to put up our umbrellas to prevent the spray from wetting us through: we saw it at some distance rising like smoke or steam from the white froth of the boiling torrent. It is difficult to form a conception of the height to which it rose over the immense rocks which enclose the rushing stream. Foot-paths are kept in good repair, and from the summit of these rocks it is awfully sublime to look below.

The next fall is Bonnington; it is close to what is called the Island, which we reach by a foot-bridge of iron; this divides two falls. It is a very small island, but commands a grand view of the mighty waters. Between the two falls is the lovers' leap, where the vast mass of waters rush to one side, so deep that at some seasons it is supposed possible to leap it; this has been done by persons alive. Nothing of the kind was practicable to-day. I could do little for Christ but carry out bills to New Lanark, see a brother and sister there with whom we had some useful conversation, and read a portion of scripture. Brother Anderson accompanied me to the falls, containing some of the finest scenery I have ever witnessed. The wonderful works of God are well worth seeing.

About three years ago, a marriage party visited these magnificent works of God. A young married lady pleaded that she was tired, and could not ascend to the top of the overhanging rocks; she would stay and rest herself. When the party returned she was nowhere to be found. She had either accidently or designedly gone over the rocks. Her body was found above the Corra Linn.

Preached at night for about two hours. A few have begun within the last few weeks to meet in the Lord's name alone here.

20th & 21st.—STONEHOUSE. Here a few Christians, once connected with the Congregational church at Strathaven, but who have not been sufficiently Presbyterian to join the Evangelical Union, seem anxious to form a New Testament church. The second evening we had about twice as many as the first.

THE RISE OF THE MEETING AT WISHAW.

Having agreed, at a meeting of the church that we should have a church record kept, for the double purpose of recording the most interesting events which might transpire amongst us, and for giving to succeeding generations an account of the circumstances which led us to meet upon simple New Testament principles, and to acknowledge no other name than that of our dear Lord and Saviour Jesus Christ, we narrate the following.

In the year 1843, our beloved brother, John Kirk, pastor of a Congregational church, Hamilton, anxious for the salvation of souls, held a series of revival meetings at Wishaw; principally through his instrumentality, under God's blessing, somewhere about sixty souls were converted to Jesus in Wishaw and vicinity, in something less than twelve months, when they were formed into a church upon Independent or Congregational principles.

At a weekly fellowship meeting, held at New Mains, for the reading of the Scriptures and mutual edification, we were brought in contact with the church of Christ as originally instituted. In considering it in this state, we were led to see many things in its order and government from which the church with which we were in fellowship widely differed. Our attention was at first more particularly taken up with the elders or pastors of the church as then instituted; we had little difficulty in seeing that there were always a plurality of them in every church. . . . . Although thus thoroughly convinced that, according to the law of God, the system we were supporting was wrong, yet we thought that by the law of expediency we were right in supporting it. In this state did we think to remain, but circumstances, in the providence of God, transpired which brought about what we now believe to be His will.

The preacher, John Hamilton, who had been with us for some time, intimated to the church about this period, that he thought the time had now arrived that he should be made pastor,—that is, ordained, for he had been pastor ever since he came amongst us,—to which, after considering the matter for a week, the church consented.

Previous to this, the church, at sundry times, had raised a small fund towards building a chapel, and at this time renewed efforts were made in order to augment the funds, so as to be able at once to get on with the building; calls were made upon us all for subscriptions. One of our brothers proffered his subscription, on the condition that the church would agree to send the pastor, at the rate of one Lord's day out of three, to preach the gospel in one or other of the surrounding towns or villages, where we believed it was not preached in its native simplicity, and that in his absence, the church should edify itself. This we all supported, thinking it was one step in the right direction. One chief objection we had to the system was, binding a preacher of the gospel up in the midst of a church able to edify itself, whilst unconverted souls were perishing for lack of knowledge in other parts.

This, however, the pastor strenuously opposed: lectured against our views almost every Lord's day after, and in these lectures advised us to leave the church; this, however, we were still unwilling to do, up to a meeting held on the evening of the 9th, 4mo., 1847, when, from the treatment we received from the pastor, we thought withdrawing from them the only course left us to pursue. This we one after another intimated, and after requesting them to join with us in prayer, the pastor leading the prayer, we quietly left the hall, bidding adieu to the church, evidently much to the pastor's satisfaction, though to the expressed grief of the majority of the members.

On leaving their meeting, we at once repaired to the house of brother James Smith, and, after prayer and consultation, agreed to commence meeting on simple New Testament principles every first day of the week; and, after joining again in prayer to our heavenly Father for his blessing and counsel, we separated for the time, in much love and apparent heartfelt sympathy. Accordingly, we met on the following Lord's day at New Mains, in brother Loudon's workshop. Brother Philips presiding at our first meeting. Here we continued to meet for some time, sixteen being in fellowship. . . . . We afterwards took James Watts' Hall, Wishaw. Shortly after this, at one of our meetings, a brother made a few remarks on the ordinance of baptism, purporting that it was an ordinance not thoroughly understood by us, which had the effect of causing brother James Philips to withdraw from our fellowship, alleging as his reason for so doing, that the water question would be introduced, which would split us up. . . . .

About this time, in the providence of God, we were made acquainted with our dear brother John Bowes, of Manchester, an evangelist in the Bible sense of the term, he being much in advance of us in the study of primitive Christianity, was of much use to us by his teaching and writings in helping us on. We had all along felt anxious about the spread of the gospel, and we felt that in that respect we were doing comparatively nothing; the world was prejudiced against us; with them, as well as many of our dear Christian brethren, *priestcraft* had rendered simple New Testament church order and government exceedingly unpopular, so that the gospel, however clearly and simply stated by any of our dear brethren, had but little effect; besides, this same prejudice hindered people from coming out to hear. In this we thought our Saviour's words verified, "A prophet is not without honor, save in his own country." These considerations led us to think of having evangelists sought out that might go up and down "the world and preach the gospel to every creature." Accordingly we opened a correspondence with the churches meeting on New Testament principles in the following places: Motherwell, Rutherglen, Paisley, Helensburgh, Kilmarnock, Darvel, and Cumnock. This resulted in a meeting of delegates from these churches, held in Paisley, in the month of October, 1847, to take into consideration the best means of obtaining and supporting evangelists. That meeting was unsuccessful in fixing on evangelists, but agreed that *example* in the New Testament taught that each church ought to minister to their necessities, and help them on their way as the Lord might give the means. We think this meeting was productive of good, inasmuch as it in some measure prepared the minds of the brethren in the different churches for supporting evangelists; and it so happened that, by the time the churches were ready, the Lord had evangelists ready, for immediately after that meeting two evangelists came amongst us, namely Frederick Daniel, from the church in Carlisle, and James Wisely, from the Duncanston church. They remained with us for a few days, and then went to Douglas, and there labored, brother Daniel for a few days, and brother Wisely for a fortnight. The result was a church formed there; which place some of our brethren still continue to visit, in order to water the young church, and assist to set in order some of the things the evangelists may have left undone, as well as to endeavor further to spread the gospel in that locality.

In searching the word of God, some of our number began to think that the system of sprinkling infants, which we had hitherto acknowledged, was not the baptism which Christ instituted. A little study of this subject convinced them they were right, and all of us being now in a position to do *whatever* we saw the Lord wanted done, about thirty of us were immersed, at different times, and by different brethren, eleven of these were immersed by brother Bowes, who was with us at the time, holding a series of revival meetings at Wishaw, fruit of which we have already seen, and trust more will be seen in eternity.

The above gives an outline of our history as a church of Christ up to the present date; and now would we seek to raise an Ebenezer in each of our hearts, and, like Samuel, say, "Hitherto hath the Lord helped us."

Wishaw, Oct. 12th, 1848.　　　　　　　　　　　　　　　JAMES SMITH.

The Hired One-Man Ministry church which these brethren left, has been broken up for several months; the New Testament church is going on well.

CHAPTER XI.

MY DAUGHTER'S CONVERSION.—PUBLIC MEETINGS ON HIRING MINISTERS.—BENEFIT SOCIETIES.—VISIT SOUTH OF ENGLAND.—A PEACE TRACT TO EVERY FAMILY IN MANCHESTER.—REMARKABLE CURE.—PUBLIC MEETING AT PRESTON.—BRADFORD AND NEWCASTLE DISCUSSIONS.—STONING AT STOCKPORT.—VISIT TO IRELAND.—COLLEGES FOR MINISTERS.—THE LITCHBOROUGH CHARITY.—THE DEVIL'S TRADE.—LETTERS TO LORD JOHN RUSSELL.—SECT MAKING AT YORK.—1849-50-51.

1*mo.* 1*st*, 1849.—Rose between five and six; took coach for GLASGOW. Here the cholera is very fatal. More than fifty or sixty deaths per day; and about one hundred or one hundred and twenty cases. It is taking off both rich and poor. By rail to Greenock; and steamer to Helensburgh,—arrived in time for the forenoon meeting. The brethren and sisters, after this, took breakfast together, or dinner, at two o'clock. At six preached in a crowded place. Feel very happy in God. Last year has been a year of abundant mercy. Praise the Lord, O my soul!

This year opened by the conversion of my only daughter. The first notice of serious reflection arose thus:—She was observed in the meeting not to sing any things which she could not sing truly. She would not sing such lines as—

"My God, the spring of all my joys,
The life of my delights,"

when it was not true. This was noticed in the meeting, as she was a good singer, people wondered why she ceased at sentiments which Christians only could sing. When interrogated, the substance of her answer was that she "would not tell lies to God." This serious thoughtfulness ended, as we hoped it would, in her conversion. A few lines from her own hand will tell the result:—"Moses Goodwin came from Rotherham last Friday morning; he had walked forty miles. He came to see you about lecturing there, on Mormonism, and he would like to know when you can go, for they want you as soon as possible. Dear father, I was received into the church last Sunday but one. I thought as there was not an opportunity at present to be baptized, that it was not right to wait. As I have been received in Christ's Church on earth, I hope and believe that I have been received into the family of heaven, through the precious blood of Christ. May the Lord keep me under his guidance and protection."

5*mo.*, 2*nd*, 3*rd*, & 4*th.*—I delivered three lectures at Preston, in the Temperance Hall, against Mormonism. The Hall was crowded each night. Elder Watts occupied the time each night, in three speeches, and complained of want of time. The following resolution was moved by Thomas Sinkinson, seconded by Mr. Fielding. "This meeting having heard J. Bowes' lectures for three evenings, and the speeches of G. D. Watts in favor of Mormonism, and J. Bowes' replies, concludes that the Mormon prophet, Joseph Smith, was a wicked deceiver; that his followers, the Mormon apostles and priests, are unfit for any Christian church or decent society; that the principles held by them have been proved to be most unscriptural and irrational, and the Book of Mormon, and the Book of Doctrines and Covenants, no revelations from God, and unworthy of any higher origin than that of ignorant and designing men. The Latter-Day Saints are therefore respectfully requested to yield to evidence, and abandon a community led on by artful men who live on their credulity." This resolution was carried all but unanimously. He gave me a public challenge to discuss Mormonism, with equal time. I accepted it. A committee on each side was appointed. After trying in vain to bind me in chains of their making, by putting forth new conditions, my committee received the following letter;—

Preston, May 10, 1849.

TO MR. BOWES' COMMITTEE,

Sir,—I am instructed to write the following :—That since Mr. Bowes will not attempt to disprove Mormonism from its principles alone, without having recourse to slanderous stories, we have agreed to have nothing more to do with the matter.

Signed, on behalf of the committee,

JOHN FOLEY.

13th.—MANCHESTER. We had a very gracious day; five were immersed into the name of the Father, Son, and Holy Ghost, nearly all led to the Lord from the world. Two more, after hearing and seeing the obedience of others, afterwards expressed themselves satisfied that it was their duty to follow the example of the Lord Jesus.

26th.—Set off this morning for Buckingham. Saw several hired ministers as the train stopped. Some I had not seen for several years; they spoke kindly. In the carriage gave tracts, chiefly on peace.

27th.—Preached twice out of doors. The congregations were very attentive, excepting some navvies, who talked at one meeting all the time. Broke bread with the church in W. D. Harris' house, and immersed two in the evening.

29th.—NORTHAMPTON. As the brethren here have opened a large room, more commodious every way than their former room, they had this evening a tea meeting—about 150 took tea. At the public meeting the room was near full. The first speaker, named Brightwell, connected with an Independent church, attacked our principles of Christian union, and the views which we promulgate on Christian ministry. I replied. J. Dyer, an Independent, delivered an address, nearly scriptural, in which he alluded to our views of ministry, attacking a hired one-man ministry. I should think; with his views, he will be compelled, by a due regard to conscience and consistency, no longer to support such a ministry, but to give all his influence towards a free ministry. Dear brother Anderson, from Birmingham, led our minds to purity and unity. I then addressed the unbelievers present on the great truths of the gospel. I was glad of brother Brightwell's opposition. He stated that there was a great deal more unity among the churches than we supposed. I offered to preach in the chapel which he attends if he could get it for me; he promised to use all his influence. We shall see whether they can admit a brother as we do. I shall be glad if they can.

30th.—AYLESBURY. Attended a public meeting of the Wesleyan Provident Institution. Driver, the superintendent minister, was in the chair. A deputation from Birmingham addressed the meeting; their names were, English, Lewis, and Hughes. They advocated the principle of laying by money for sickness, and assuring life to the amount of hundreds of pounds. They wished questions to be asked freely by the meeting; and as they receive members whether Wesleyans or not, I asked if they would allow me to ask a few questions, and make a few remarks? The chairman was afraid it might lead to a discussion if I made any remarks. So I proceeded to ask if their plan of hoarding money was according to Matt. vi. 19-23, 33? If a brother might not be out of work and unable to pay, and therefore starve his family? or if he might not have just 1s. 6d. to spare for either his club or a starving brother? And if it would not be wrong to allow his brother to starve? I also asked them if they had not misunderstood the text quoted in their report, in favor of laying by money for sickness and death, which reads, "If any provide not for his own, and especially for those of his own house, he has denied the faith, and is worse than an infidel?" 1 Tim. v. 8; and whether this did not refer entirely to widows already in want, connected with Christians by relationship? I stated this was my view of the passage, and that they had misapplied it. I told them the true benefit society was that established at Jerusalem. That their plan failed in two respects; it did not include the rich who had the means of supporting the poor, nor the very poor that could not pay; whereas they had most need of such a society, as had also a brother out of work. But of the church at Jerusalem it was said " that neither was there among them any that lacked." I told them that their society was neither scriptural nor Wesleyan; that John Wesley held right views on this subject; that while they would hoard wealth and hire ministers while they neglected the poor, they could not be right. Showed them, from Myles' Chronology of Methodism, that all their first class-monies were given to the poor. The chairman advised the deputation not to answer my questions. He then asked me " If I would give away every penny and leave nothing to myself?" After which, when I rose to answer he refused to hear it, until brother John Hamilton, Editor of the Aylesbury News, thought, as he had asked me a question, I ought to be allowed a reply, which was granted. I then answered in substance, that I would give away every penny which I did not need, and that not to do so, if my brethren were hungry or in need, would be to sin against Christ. And I told him what we do in Manchester, and other places, when a brother is out of work, we try to get him some employment, or raise money to set him to work. If he is ever able, we expect him to return it every penny, that we may do more good to others; if he is never able, we do not consider that he owes us anything.

As the deputation plainly were unable to answer my questions, J. Hamilton asked them if their institution had a scriptural basis? One of them thought he remembered a passage of scripture which bore on the point, but he failed to show any scriptural basis. Brother J. Hamilton proposed a vote of thanks to the chairman, which was generally carried.

6mo., 1st.—Another public meeting, showing that ministers should not be hired, and that the poor should be supported. Large meetings, —questions were asked.

2nd.—Out of doors in another open part. John Symonds, of Mursley, who nobly went to prison five weeks rather than pay a church rate of five shillings, addressed the meeting. Indeed several brethren have done this with me each night.

3rd.—Immersed four ; about twenty broke bread. The church here meets once for singing, prayer, breaking bread, &c., and twice for preaching the gospel, and have neither singing nor prayer. The chapel was full at half-past two and six, and at half-past seven I should think we had nearly 1000 people in the market-square. About a dozen inquirers.

4th.—Had a long conversation with a Roman Catholic priest. Told him that he had no church at all. Asked him whom I should tell a fault to if I should join them, as in Matt. xviii ? He said, "Tell it to me." I said, "Are you the church?" I was glad of an opportunity of bringing the glorious gospel before him in a long conversation, in which brother Hamilton joined.

7th.—POOLE. Preached near the Fish Market on the good news ; not a hundred people. Adjourned to the Bethel Room, where I discoursed on the duties of Christians. The meeting was interesting.

8th.—Two or three times as large a congregation as last night—the truth seemed to take hold. Held a meeting for teaching Christians, in the open-air, as the Bethel Room would not have contained more than one-half the congregation. Conversed with inquirers after, and with a few believers. One precious soul, awakened under the first discourse here, was so unhappy about her state, that when I conversed with her to-day, she said that one night she was afraid to fall asleep lest she should awake in hell. When I met her she was deeply concerned, but before our conversation ended she embraced the Lord Jesus, and trusted her soul on his finished work. It is worth all the trouble and expense of this long journey, if no more than this one sinner should be saved.

11th.—WEYMOUTH. Saw J. G. Deck, who wrote to Poole that he could receive me *as a brother*. Brother Jenkins wrote him to make arrangements ; but he had made none, because he could not receive me as *a teacher* without some intercourse. However, after some conversation, we sent the bellman round, and he opened the meeting. I proclaimed the gospel, after which, he also published the good news; but the congregation did not exceed a hundred; whereas, had it been published the previous day, we might have had several hundreds. If souls be lost through such proceeding the blame must rest somewhere.

12th.—While in the train for London, was near a barrister, lawyer, &c.; the former inquired, at one station, if any newspapers were to sell, remarking, "We must have food for the mind." After this, I had quietly taken out my Bible and read two chapters ; a passenger near me said aloud, "That is food for the mind," referring to my Bible; this opened up a very interesting conversation. Discoursed in Elstree-street chapel ; was not controversial, but desired to show the friends who meet here their error on baptism for the remission of sins, and excluding or keeping out the unimmersed from fellowship. I was asked some questions in reference to these subjects, which enabled me to speak fully my sentiments. The whole meeting lasted about two hours and a half.

17th.—BIRMINGHAM. Broke bread with about 50. The brethren here are much urged to act in the Newton controversy. A niece of B. Newton's broke bread to-day unknown to several. She was visited afterwards, and declared her faith in her uncle's errors; the brethren will not break bread with her again; but they are not prepared to exclude Robert Howard from Tottenham, who broke bread with us this evening, merely because he received brother Groves, who had been at Bethesda. The Tottenham gathering seems to take the right ground, as do many others, viz., to go on receiving all the Lord's children while they testify against B. Newton's errors. Preached out at 3 and 8 o'clock, and on the gospel in the room at 6 o'clock. A sweet season.

18th.—Preached in the same place again, after brother Anderson had done. While he was preaching, a very powerful drunken man made considerable noise. The people seemed angry with him, and this enraged him more. I went up to him, took him gently by the arm, spoke kindly to him, and desired him to walk away quietly with me. The lion became a lamb. "Let me take your arm," said he. I consented; and I should think the congregation would smile, to see a great angry man calmed, and walking quietly away by the force of kind words. O that kindness to man, in its greatest extent, were duly tried by the followers of Jesus! Having got the man along part of two streets, I returned, and preached in peace.

7mo. 2nd—SHEFFIELD. A large meeting at the Corn Exchange. On returning home found the Mormons out of doors. A clergyman, named Manners, opposed their errors, and so did I. The Mormon preacher, as soon as he had done, desired all the Mormons to go away. Several of them did, but others did not. This showed he was afraid of the truth.

8th.—Five broke bread in Bowden Street, after I had immersed two. At 6, held a conference; a few of Joseph Barker's followers, one a very kind man. What a pity that he cannot be set right on the person and work of Christ! At 8 o'clock, about a thousand people. A mighty influence attended the word; many hearts seemed melted, and many rejoiced, while I set forth Christ as the only foundation for sinners to trust to. We have been compelled to open a table at Sheffield around which all the Lord's dear children may gather without being expelled. The other meeting has taken up the Newton controversy, and is casting out the saints! I have written to the chief brethren, pointing out the sinfulness of their conduct, and stating reasons for our present line of proceedure.

11th.—MANCHESTER. A sweet church meeting. Dear W. Holland stated that he had prayed for me daily for several years—ever since we got acquainted. We have had agreement in judgment on nearly all subjects, except in one case; and I love him the more because he prayed for me daily during that trying case.

22nd.—CARLISLE. Immersed four in the Eden. Yesterday visited a sister, who, in the course of her conversation gave me an account of her conversion. For thirteen weeks of sickness, while no one knew her state, she said, "I had no companion but *my life!—my Bible!*" Yes, the Scriptures are indeed *our life*.

24th.—Started for Scotland at 5 o'clock; and at 8, preached to a large congregation at DOUGLAS. Visited John Barnes, who heard me the last time I was here, and saw the gospel. He was afterwards further blessed by the visits of brother Dickie. He has been for several months deeply afflicted, and yet happy. He said, "I have enjoyed more happiness on this bed, than in all the fifty-four years of my life before!"

Noble testimony to the power of truth to make happy. Met with a Christian who is beginning to see the necessity of the purity of the church, and I think cannot long remain where he is.

28*th*.—HAMILTON. A crowded hall though Saturday night. Twenty-eight have been immersed here since the year commenced; three of them elders in the United Presbyterian church; one of them a wholesale wine and spirit merchant, who now intends to give up the trade: on this understanding only are brethren satisfied to meet with him.

8*mo*. 1*st*.—Brother Dickie and I visited the prison at AIRDRIE. Twenty-four prisoners; 13 men and 11 women. One man, an Irishman, stated that he was in for taking a watch and breaking a window. He did it because he was starving, but would not do it again. Several were picking oakham. One was weaving. Two were breaking stones. One female, a prostitute, twenty-four years of age, had been in twenty-eight times, for being drunk and disorderly. She was Irish, and pleaded that she had nothing to do. One young woman, eighteen, was in for the murder of her child.

PUBLIC MEETINGS ON HIRING MINISTERS AND PROVIDING FOR THE POOR.

During my journey north, three large meetings were called by the inhabitants of Carlisle, Airdrie, and Hamilton, and in each case the hired ministers of each town or city were invited by letter to show scriptural authority for their position.

At CARLISLE the following letter was received from the pastor of the Baptist church:—

July 20, 1849.

"DEAR SIR,—In reply to your invitation to be present to hear the members of your denomination discuss the question 'whether ministers should be hired or free?' permit me to inform you that, for various reasons, I must decline such an invitation:—1st. Because I am not what you are pleased to designate a 'hired minister;' 2nd. Because I regard the question which your friends propose to discuss as a mere crotchet of their own brain, and one which they cannot discuss without most manifest degradation to themselves; 3rd. Because all the talk that I heard urged on the subject at the cross and elsewhere, constituted, in my judgment, the most pitiable twaddle, and involves the grossest abuse of powers which ought to be devoted to the physical, social, mental, and spiritual improvement and elevation of the working classes of this country.

"To aid you in any work characterised by utility,

"I am, dear sir, yours truly,

"J. J. OSBORN.

"Joseph Hodgson."

This letter is interesting, as it shows a disposition to put off the question without investigating it. This cannot be done. The church and the world will consider it, whether hired ministers will or not. Brother Joseph Hodgson, at the meeting, stated the case thus:—"Whatsoever tends to lessen and degrade the religion of Christ in the estimation of the world is a curse to society. That system which hires ministers to preach the gospel has always tended, and now tends, to lessen and degrade the religion of Christ in the estimation of the world, and is therefore a curse, and ought to be put away." Two hired missionaries employed to visit the city, spoke, but it appeared plainly that the great majority of the crowded meeting saw the truth. We invited Hugh Percy, Bishop of Carlisle, but he neither came to his flock nor sent,

At AIRDRIE, W. Walburn, Baptist minister, was present. I asked him afterwards why he did not speak. He said, "I could not, I trembled all over. I am so nervous, whenever I hear a powerful address, either on what I approve or disapprove, it unmans me." He immediately advertised a lecture on paid pastors, on Lord's Day. Very few beyond his own people attended. The following outline was furnished by one of our friends:—

"Mr. Walburn's discourse rested on the following propositions:— 1st. Preachers of the gospel and evangelists ought to be supported by the church. Proofs advanced, 1 Cor. ix. 11; Gal. vi. 6; 2 Tim. ii. 4. 2nd. Pastors, bishops, and elders, who labor in word and doctrine, ought to be supported by the church. Proofs, 1 Peter v. 1-3; 1 Tim. v. 17. He says that the word translated honor in the above instance ought to be rendered reward or support, and also in the preceding verse, where it is stated that the widows, being sixty years old, and having no children or nephews, were to be honored or supported by the church. Is it so? 3rd. The hirelings noticed in scripture are contemptuously spoken of, not because they received hire for their labor, but because they had no higher motive than that of hire. (John x. 13.)

It will be seen that on the first proposition our views are supported. To the second we should add, that bishops or elders should only be supported, like widows, when they need it, and at other times work with their hands, as Paul directed the elders of Ephesus (Acts xx. 34, 35). I cannot find that W. W. quoted this important text. In answer to the question on 1 Tim. v. 17, I say—No, it is not so. Honor just means honor, not support. The Greek word is *timee*, the proper word for honor. Let us, however, read it as W. W. suggests—"Let the elders that rule well be counted worthy of double support, especially they who labor in word and doctrine." Why should they have double the support of widows, or double the support of their brethren seniors who did not teach? They could not eat twice as much, and therefore should not have it. But on the view we take— the view of our own translation—the text and rendering is clear and consistent with other texts and with reason. Any one laboring in word and doctrine, would be doubly useful to the saints, and therefore ought to be doubly esteemed or honored. So taught Paul, "And we beseech you, brethren, to know them who labor among you, and are over you in the Lord, and admonish you; and to esteem them very highly in love for their work's sake."—1 Thess. v. 12. Now, cannot we esteem a man highly without paying him for his labor, and that, too, whether he needs it or not? The supporters of a hired ministry are driven from every refuge to which they betake themselves. The Lord's word is the weapon which puts to flight their helpless array of misrepresentation.

The last particular received a beautiful, though somewhat amusing illustration at the meeting. After brother James Smith and I had delivered what we regarded as the truth on the subject of ministry, and called for the hired ministers to respond, an ominous silence reigned over the large assembly, a brother stepped forward—a brother in a hired-ministry church—and said ironically, "The wolves have come in among the sheep, and where are the shepherds?" directing his question to us, and allowing that we had acted a proper part in allowing the shepherds to be invited. I replied, "He fleeth because he is an hireling, and careth not for the sheep."—John x. 13. Of course many of the shepherds regarded us as wolves, hundreds of the sheep were in our power, yet they did not come to rescue them! But, in truth, we were the true shepherds, caring for the flock, and the hirelings knew that they could not prove from the Scriptures their right to hire, therefore they declined to speak.

HAMILTON.—The hall was crowded. We invited the ministers by circular. No minister spoke but the Independent minister of Ardrossan, John Cross. Several things he approved, and to some he objected. We answered all his objections, until he had no more to offer. He spoke in a very kind Christian spirit, and I should think if he could see his way clear out of his present position, is almost ready to exchange it for one more scriptural. Some few real Christians are in the ministry; to them we should feel great regard, and try to get them into a better state.

I do not see any better plan of moving the kingdom than by holding a week's meetings—one night teaching the gospel, and teaching the church another; and at all our meetings, it appears to me, we should allow questions to be asked, as 1 have proved, in the article in *The Truth*, "Modern Preaching Wrong," was done in the early ages of Christianity. We have nothing in view but truth. We need fear no questions. We may sometimes receive important ideas from men in whose souls the well of knowledge has long been sealed up. I hope we shall never assume that we are infallible and have nothing to learn, but while we are in this world be always learning and teaching.

The first number of *The Truth* was issued in November, 1849, seven years after the *Christian Magazine*. It was intended to go out with the *Christian Magazine* for December. The following is from the *Christian Magazine*.

MR. BOWES AT NEWCASTLE-ON-TYNE.

NEWCASTLE.—On Tuesday, November 13th, Mr. Bowes arrived in Newcastle, and the evenings of Wednesday, Thursday, and Friday, were occupied with the subject of Mormonism. Mr. Palmer, minister of Providence chapel, in the chair on the two former evenings, and Mr. G. J. Grant on the Friday evening. Although these lectures did not excite that wide spread and enthusiastic interest which they have done in the south, yet there is reason to believe that good will be effected by them. The Mormon leaders (wise in their generation) declined attempting any answer to these lectures, but announced a reply in their own room, without, however, admitting discussion on the subject. On Lord's Day, Mr. Bowes discoursed in the Victoria Room, in the morning to a considerable, and in the evening to a large audience; and a large audience was addressed in St. Nicholas' Square. At half-past 5, about sixteen sat down to commemorate the death of their Lord. On the following Lord's Day, similar audiences were addressed in the same places, and two persons were immersed into the name of the Lord. During the following week a lecture was given on the evils of the nation and their remedies; and conference on hiring ministers and providing for the poor. The services concluded by a discourse in the lecture room. It would be premature were we to attempt to state, at the present time, the results of these labors. Being the first time that Mr. Bowes has been in Newcastle for fourteen years, and his first propositions coming into direct collision with wide-spread and deeply-rooted prejudices, it must be regarded as the time of *sowing*, and not of *fruit*,—as the spring, and not the harvest. Yet we can confidently say that a spirit of inquiry has been awakened, that light has been widely spread on most important subjects,—and a small band of believers, united in heart, have been gathered together to continue and extend the work. J. H.

12mo. 31st.—MANCHESTER. At 10 o'clock p.m., went into a Wesleyan Chapel in Radnor Street. Heard two solemn and affecting discourses from two preachers; after which the celebrated George Osborn got into the pulpit. Had some thoughts of coming out, not knowing whether to receive him as a friend or enemy to the Saviour. After hearing him, thought that he spoiled the meeting. I could see nothing of God in this "accuser of the brethren." He seems an unhappy man. Athough I expected not to be annoyed by collections at such a time, it was announced that the juvenile missionary society would meet. I find in several parts of the country young children, who, taught in the Sunday school, go about begging from door to door for the missionaries. The little children are thus employed to call upon all, whether saints or sinners, believers or infidels, or whether they themselves know God or not, to beg by house-row. The apostolic times knew nothing about such *priestly beggary* as this. If the ministers or priests cannot be made ashamed of their ungodly ways, the people and the little collectors should be taught better. All connected with the disgraceful business should be made to feel ashamed of it.

During this year the Peace Society delivered to every house in Manchester a Peace Tract. We had twelve different kinds, prepared by the Committee, of which I wrote a part, and reviewed all. About 70,000 were distributed, costing £37, or 10s. per 1000. Their titles were—War Anti-christian—War Immoral—Defensive War, and the Safety of the Peace principle—Horrors of War—Arbitration, not War—Free Trade a Bond of Peace—Statistics of War—War Prayers—Testimonies against War—An Address to Young Men on Peace and War—Peace Narratives—The Claims of Peace Societies.

REMARKABLE CURE OF RHEUMATISM.

James Gaskell's wife, at Furness, Cheshire, has been afflicted with rheumatism for about twelve years. Towards the latter end of 1848 she was immersed at Whaley. She was then so ill, her hands and joints so affected by this disease, that she could not dress and undress herself. She believed it to be her duty to be immersed in the name of the Lord Jesus, after which, in a few days, she was quite well; and when I saw her, a few weeks after her immersion, she had no pains nor remains of the disease. Had this occured to the Mormons, no doubt it would have been published as a notable miracle. I publish it as a fact, and leave my readers to reflect upon it. One thing, at least, it proves—it demolishes the objection drawn from the unsuitableness of cold water for weakly persons. In this country, at the present time, some weakly persons are bathing in cold water, winter and summer, nearly every morning the year round, in order to get strength, and they find from such ablutions the most beneficial effects. Then how can an institution of Christ, which is only to be observed once after teaching and faith, and that for the moment while the subject of immersion is under water, be supposed to hurt the health. I am satisfied that if any one is strong enough to go to the house of prayer to sing, pray, hear and observe the Lord's supper, that person is strong enough to follow the Lord Jesus Christ into the water. Persons have been alarmed at the idea of cold water, because they were ignorant of its useful and even healing properties.

1mo., 1st, 1850.—On reviewing the Lord's great goodness and my own ingratitude the last year, have much reason to glory in the former and be ashamed of the latter. May this be a year of love and activity in the service of Jesus. Was advertised for BINGLEY, and did not know till near noon—the letters were delayed. Was obliged to take the express,—just reached in time for preaching.

3rd.—All the hired ministers of Bingley were invited, by letter to attend a great meeting, to consider whether the poor should be supported or ministers hired.

6th.—Discoursed in the Temperance Room, KEIGHLEY, Sun Street, at half-past ten and two. The room full at two o'clock. At 6 at BINGLEY. A crowded congregation in the Odd Fellows' Hall, to whom I preached Christ and his great salvation. The truth took hold of the people. This hall is often devoted on the first day of the week to Chartist meetings. It gave me great joy to be able to preach the gospel to many who were present, who, I believe, never go to hear the gospel.

7th, 8th.—At the Mechanics' Institute, WILSDEN. Lectured on Mormonism. Agreed to give them equal time with myself if they wished it; but they were not prepared for a public discussion. On the last evening was invited to return and deliver a lecture on what Christian churches ought to be.

10th.—The hired ministers of KEIGHLEY having been invited by letter to meet in the Working Man's Hall, it was nearly full. One of the established ministers returned the letter to me by post unpaid. This showed a very bad spirit; not less so was the following act:—A shopkeeper put one of the bills with four tacks against his shop: a minister came and tore it down. Are these the only arguments which ye have, O ye hired ministers, with which to support your pay? If you have any better why do you not bring them forward?

12th.—This morning received a letter from home, containing the following sorrowful tidings: "The reason we did not write yesterday, we were waiting to see what turn Edward would take. Mother got medicine from Mr. T., but it did not do him any good; he kept getting worse. Mr. T. advised mother to call in some medical man, as he could not visit him; so she called Dr. R. John went for him at four o'clock on Tuesday morning. We thought he would have died; his breath kept leaving him. When the doctor came, he said the reason of that was, his heart was affected, and the spine also; that he had the rheumatic fever; but he is now getting on as well as can be expected. He has lost the use of his arms up to this time. Mother says that she could do with you at home now; for he is almost more than we can manage, night and day. Edward has just said that he wants you home again." I should have gone home at once, but six services were advertised for me at three different places. I committed the child to God, wishing his life to be spared, if it pleased God; and if not, that I may be able to say, "Thy will be done." I feel free to make no more engagements till I hear from home.

BIRKENSHAW.—A number of professed unbelievers asked a great many questions; some of which I answered, and some I postponed till to-morrow.

13th.—At half-past ten about 11 broke bread at GOMERSAL. At two answered the objection against the Evangelists' account of Christ's resurrection, as put in "The Infidels' Text Book," by asking either infidels or Christians to read aloud the account. Found that the book had put in "not" and "alone" to make a contradiction, and that there was none in the scriptures. At six, a larger congregation; urged upon the meeting our deep responsibility for what we teach and hear.

14th.—This morning my mind was set at rest by a letter from home, stating that my dear Edward is "very much better;" so that now I feel free to stay a little longer in Yorkshire, where the Lord is opening a door for his soul-saving truth. At half-past seven o'clock discoursed on the Christian church in the first three centuries; and how it became corrupted. Several more questions were asked.

15th.—Walked from Gomersal to WILSDEN, about ten or twelve miles through snow, in some parts deep under foot; it snowed nearly all the way. As I had not been very well, and had taken medicine, there was some little danger of taking cold; but I would not disappoint the people. As the day was very stormy, nobody seemed to expect me. I hope after this, that all my friends will understand that, as I never was, so I never intend to be, a mere fair-weather preacher. A considerable congregation was got together by the bellman. There would have been more, but the Committee of the Mechanics' Institution, who allowed us to examine Mormonism, would not allow their hall to examine other sects. Error is always afraid of the light. Truth is always fearless.

16th.—One soul saved at Bingley last night. DUDLEY HILL, in a large room. The people were attentive; but a great deal depends upon stability. The last year several seemed favorable to a New Testament church, but they have not been firm in their adherence to it. Only two or three seem unwavering in their love to all the laws of Christ, apart from any admixture of the commandments of men.

17th.—BRADFORD MOOR. Discoursed here for the first time. A congregation of serious people. Seven remained to form a New Testament church. After making a profession of their faith in Jesus, they agreed to meet next Lord's Day to remember the Lord. The greater part have been Wesleyans. Two sent in their resignation the last week, stating as a reason, that they can no longer submit to be governed by any other laws than those of Christ and his apostles. One soul, who heard me at Birkenshaw on 13th, has since found the gospel to be joy and forgiveness to his heart. There will be nine in all at this place to commence with.

SHEFFIELD.—I held meetings here for about a fortnight during the 2nd month. A few believed the gospel; five were immersed in the name of Jesus. The cases of conversion from the world were very interesting. The services were well attended on the Lord's Day.

SOUTHPORT.—During the 3rd month I delivered the lectures on what Christian churches ought to be, which I was requested to deliver. Mormonism is declining here. A few believers see that Christians should meet together in Christ's name, and I hope will have grace to carry out their convictions, and follow the Lord fully. I have since heard that a few have commenced meeting here in the Lord's name alone. The number is small, six or eight; but if they really love the Lord's truth, and obey all his will as soon as they ascertain it, they will soon increase.

24*th*.—BRADFORD. The Temperance Hall, engaged by the brethren. Preached in it twice, and learned afterwards that three souls were made glad by the gospel: one who had been a Wesleyan for several years. The lecture on Infidelity was the best attended, and elicited the most opposition. I was asked if I would meet G. J. Holyoake? I stated that I would defend the Bible against all opposers, to the best of my ability. A committee is now formed to arrange for a public discussion on the truth of the Scriptures, the folly of Infidelity and the free agency of man.

31*st*.—In the General Baptist Chapel, eight were buried with Christ by immersion. The congregations, morning and evening, were large, and the people uncommonly kind. I should think from the appearance of the chapel it will hold about a thousand people.

THE BRADFORD DISCUSSION.

The Discussion with Mr. Holyoake, at Bradford, for four nights, April 22nd, 23rd, 24th, 25th, proved that he was not prepared to refute my arguments for Christianity and Man's Responsibility. In a letter in *The Truth*, vol. i., page 134, the late James Grinstead gives Mr. Holyoake's remarks on the discussion. He (Mr. H.) says: "Those who have looked into the debate for a demolition of Mr. Bowes, have professed disappointment." J. Grinstead further says, "Let us hear what Mr. Holyoake says about the fourth night's debate,—'The last night, devoted to the formation of character question, was less satisfactory to me than the preceding. Next time I discuss this matter, I shall recast the whole technical mode of argument.'" His admission in his paper and lectures re-echoed the public sentiment. My arguments for the Truth of Christianity were unanswered. His, on the Formation of Character, being demolished, required reconstruction. In his lecture at Bingley, after the close of the discussion, he observed,—"Mr. Bowes has the hide of a rhinoceros; there is no penetrating it." This was considered a confession of his inability to cope with my arguments. Some years after I wrote him, wishing that he, as the leading teacher of his school, would engage in a discussion with me on the whole question between us, but he respectfully declined, or such a published discussion would have been useful.

SHEFFIELD.—The lectures here, in the 5th month, possessed a considerable amount of interest. The night devoted to Christianity and Infidelity, Mr. Nelson, an earnest man, opposed Christianity in such a way as led one to think that his opposition rather originated in the inconsistencies of professors, than in real unbelief in the Scriptures. It has seldom been my lot to spend a night so happily as this; for, though the discussion after the lecture did not embrace the ordinary objections of infidels, it comprehended many questions of great extent and value, of intense interest to the audience and to mankind. Richard Otley, who appeared to be smarting under the arguments which he found it so hard to grapple with at Rotherham, came forward, either by himself or his friends, every night but the last. During one night he read a written challenge. The day following I sent him four propositions, taking one of his own propositions one night, and one of mine another. He afterwards sent me a letter declining the discussion. So, after giving me a challenge, and blustering night after night, this bold pleader for Infidelity—to whom the sceptics of these parts look to as a leader—quietly retires from a contest which he himself sought.

The lecture on Roman Catholicism excited the adherents of that system amazingly; two or three got up to reply, but they seemed to have very little gift. I have repeatedly offered to discuss their doctrines with any of their priests, or others, who are competent, and would willingly go to any part of the kingdom to meet them; but the cowardice of the priests is astonishing, although they know that we accuse them of deceiving a confiding but ignorant people, they do not come forward to defend their deception.

MANCHESTER.—There are eight seeking immersion. One has been led to the Lord by reading *The Truth*, &c., and did not know of our meeting in Manchester before. This should encourage all those who meet in the large room, City Road, Hulme, to circulate *The Truth*; for we do not know where any particular seed may fall, nor what a rich harvest may be reaped from it, either in this or coming generations.

ROMAN CATHOLIC PERSECUTION—STONING AT STOCKPORT.

I have delivered more lectures lately on the errors of the Church of Rome than on any former occasion. They have brought out some features of that church which have surprised me. First: it appears that the people of the church are fond of discussion, for in almost every instance they have come forward to defend their church, and for an hour and a-half have disputed the positions of my lectures. This I was pleased with. I hope that if we make a right use of their love of discussion, and hear them kindly and patiently, good may result from it. Second: The other feature history might have prepared me for—the *persecuting character* of this church—but I was willing to believe that a milder, more humanising spirit had entered them, if not from their church, at least from the times and age in which they live. The following facts will show that I have had but too good reason to change my opinion:—

I lectured on the errors of the Church of Rome in a large room, Bamber's Brow, Stockport, on 6*mo.* 6*th.* There might be about four hundred present. Thomas Ward was called to the chair. In the course of my lecture I was repeatedly stopped by cries of "Time," and clamor; but by kindness, and the aid of one well-dressed Roman Catholic, who had considerable influence with the rest, I finished my lecture in peace, having been well heard. I had given liberty for a discussion on the subjects embraced in the lecture for an hour and a-half. Mr. Cleary from Manchester, now came forward, and was loudly cheered by the Roman Catholics. He said, "Mr. Bowes has treated us in a most gentlemanly manner; indeed, he is the only gentleman we have ever met." In the course of the evening's discussion he got very warm, and accused me of misrepresentation, from which I purged myself; but many Roman Catholics were very clamorous; and in the course of the evening, while I was sitting down, and while Mr. Cleary was asking, "What shall we do with him?" a man, close beside me, responded, loud enough to be heard by the whole meeting, "Damn him." Yet, when all was over, the meeting separated in peace, and the influential Roman Catholic on the platform again and again thanked me for my kind manner, stating that I had treated them like a gentleman. One of the brethren observed a man with a large bludgeon in his hand, who said, "I will give you this when we get out."

The congregation had all retired when I and two more brethren, Isaac Cookson and Thomas Ward, set off home. We observed that a few persons, who waited at the foot of the brow, followed us up the Hillgate, on the other side, and then came to our side. The two brethren started to run, and had not gone many yards before I was hit with a large stone on my back; it seemed to be as large as my hand, and a heavy stone; another hit me on the left arm, near the elbow, but it seemed much less. As the two brethren ran, I heard cries of "Police, police! Murder, murder!" One or two men came down the Hillgate from following them, and in a few minutes all was quiet; the brethren had disappeared and the persecutors were gone. It was very dark, and not a policeman or other person to be seen. A gentleman, half drunk, came up when I was half way home, but whether he was a spy or a friend I could not tell; however, I explained to him the cause of the cries he had heard, and he evidently was no friend to the Irish, which I was sorry to hear, for we should be friendly to all men, however they may treat us.

When I got within a few yards of T. Ward's house, a man was standing in the middle of the street, who never spoke. I said, "Who are you?" He replied, "A man." I said, "What are you doing here?" He said, "Which is the road to the Hillgate?" I told him, and left him. The same man had asked the same question at T. Ward's door about ten minutes before, and had fallen against the door as though he were drunk. It looked to me very suspicious, especially as he did not go towards the Hillgate when I told him. More than an hour after T. Ward got home, having come through fields and bye-ways. Both he and the other brother were unhurt. The reason of their running was, T. Ward saw a man close to him, with a bludgeon lifted up ready to strike him, and his opinion was that the persecutors sought to hurt him, not me; as he states, that while a churchman he often opposed them in a very unchristian spirit, which he now deplores.

I was not prepared for this manifestation of persecution. Although G. Achilli has, within this year, been confined in the prison of the Inquisition at Rome, I attributed his sufferings to the rage that always pursues a convert from the Church of Rome, and I did not expect persecution of this kind. I should have gone among Roman Catholics either by day or night, alone or accompanied by my brethren, fearless of all consequences, satisfied that as I have endeavored to do them good, and no harm, in the whole course of my life, that they had no just cause to injure me in person or property.

There was something about this attack very mean and dastardly. We had invited them to a friendly public discussion; they had come; yet they had retired to attack us in the dark! How like the midnight assassin!—how unlike the British character! The mobs of drunken, sottish persons who attacked John Wesley and his co-adjutors would have scorned to attack them in the dark. Bad as they were, they generally had something more manly about them than this. But while I point out the stupid conduct of these enemies of that cross which they profess to reverence, I wish to remember that it is written, "Love your enemies,"—"Bless them that curse you,"—"Bless and curse not." May the Lord indeed bless these benighted people, for they have got into a miserable condition. Talk of missions to the heathen!—we require missions to these ignorant and misguided people.

I do not regret the efforts which I have put forth for their enlightenment, nor shall I cease for their opposition—this, by the grace of God, shall lead me to pray more for them, to be more kind to them, and to hold more meetings for their benefit. Had they left me dead, instead of merely leaving me sore, and to say, "I bear in my body the marks of the Lord Jesus," it might have awakened the attention of others to their wretched condition. I have now, however, a reason of thankfulness to God, who delivered me out of their hands, which I hope not to overlook. I should like to know the names and residences of the persecutors, not that I might punish them, but to teach them a more humane religion than they know. It would have been better for them to have been left ignorant of all religion, than to be taught, by the curses and anathemas which their church pronounces upon heretics, to cherish ill feeling and vengeance against those who know Christ and his religion too well to be led astray by the ignorant and pagan rites of their system.

On Monday, the 12th, Mr. Cleary was to lecture on the "Infallibility of the Catholic Church," and called on me or my friends to meet him in the Lyceum. We did so. The Chairman was using very exciting language against me, such as, that "I told a lie when I affirmed that Roman Catholics said, 'Our Lord God the Pope.'" The following proof of what I said vindicates my affirmation, and confutes the chairman's uncharitable statement:—"Thus, by the Papal system, the kingly office of Him, who is head over all things to his church, was reduced to a mere sinecure or nominal trust; while to the Pope, as the actually reigning sovereign, all the prerogatives, honors, titles, and revenues were transferred. 'Universal Bishop,' 'Sovereign Pontiff,' 'Your Holiness,' 'Universal Father,' 'Christ's Vicar,' 'Representative of God,' 'God upon earth,' and 'Our Lord God the Pope,' are among the titles which he has either suffered or assumed."—Giles' Lectures in Edinburgh, page 42, March 28th, 1849; see authorities quoted in the *Protestant*, vol. i., pp. 34—38; also *Taylor's Popery, &c.*, pp. 199—201. "It is a mere quibble to deny the sanction of the Church to titles ascribed to the Pope by writers who published, when nothing could be published without the sanction of the Inquisition."—*Ibid*, p. 42. If Roman Catholics do not read or think for themselves, such instructors as Mr. Cleary's chairman will lead them into error, as well as uncharitable feelings towards their fellow-men. I therefore asked liberty to reply, but was refused. At length, a few of the more reasonable Roman Catholics prevailed on the chairman, and I engaged only to occupy five minutes in reference to the stoning, to which the chairman had alluded in terms not sufficiently, if at all, calculated to condemn such proceedings. Mr. Cleary said if I did speak, he would leave the room : which he did. Therefore, as Mr. Cleary's consent could not be obtained, and as the chairman had already excited the meeting, and as bad language was used in the meeting, I left it at once. I can meet their arguments, but having no disposition to fight them in the dark with stones, or, indeed, with carnal weapons of any kind, I and my friends quietly withdrew. Still I wish to let Roman Catholics see the truth, and therefore hereby engage to meet any Roman Catholic priest, in any part of the kingdom, to prove that the Church of Rome has departed from the doctrines and laws of Christ, and is a dangerous institution to the souls of men. My weapons are not carnal, but spiritual—not to be used in the dark to injure, but publicly to bless. I have done with all sorts of carnal weapons—a Christian should not fight. Roman Catholics and others will thus see, 1st; that I do not decline controversy with them—I seek it; 2nd; I did not stay in the meeting to hear Mr. Cleary, because I was not allowed to be heard, and when I told Mr. Cleary that I was stoned on the previous Thursday, he said, "I do not believe it." With a person of Mr. Cleary's character I shall only discuss when I cannot avoid it, although, with any Roman Catholic, in the confidence of his own church, whether priest or not, I shall be happy to talk over our differences, in a friendly manner, in the presence of hundreds.

From the "Protestant Witness."

Mr. John Bowes, of Manchester, the talented editor of "The Truth"—"The Christian Magazine," and other religious works, has been creating some excitement in the town of Stockport, by the delivery of a course of lectures on religious subjects, in the National Trades' Association Room, Bamber's-brow, Hillgate. The announcement of the lectures contained the notification that discussion would be permitted. The first lecture was delivered on Tuesday evening, the 4th instant, on "The Folly of Infidelity and the Truth of Christianity," to a numerous audience, who seemed deeply impressed with the important and soul-stirring truths uttered by the lecturer. On the following evening, the lecture was attended by many of the Latter-Day Saints of the town: the lecture involved the vital question, "Is Mormonism a wicked imposture?" The most important lecture, however, was delivered on Thursday evening, the 6th instant, when Mr. Bowes went into an examination of "The Errors of the Church of Rome." On this occasion, no doubt, attracted by the invitation for discussion, a numerous body of the Roman Catholics were in attendance, headed by a refractory leader, (invited for the occasion) a Mr. Cleary, of Manchester. These parties, however, found a redoubtable and staunch opponent in Mr. Bowes, who candidly and fearlessly reviewed the origin and practices of the Romish Church—their adoration of the Virgin Mary; their absolution after confession; their idolatry and superstition, credulity and ignorance. After the lecture, Mr. Cleary rose, and made some vague remarks in vindication of the Roman Catholic Church, endeavoring to raise its character and religious services in the estimation of the audience. He was, however, signally defeated, the meeting, on a show of hands, declaring in favor of Mr. Bowes, and in opposition to that religion which is the pest of society, and which is fast waning in public opinion, especially in its former stronghold—Ireland. So exasperated were the Roman Catholics at this victory of truth against error, that personal violence was used towards Mr. Bowes, bludgeons were brandished, and several blows inflicted upon that gentleman.

I sent a letter to the above paper, pointing out a few mistakes in this report. 1. The audience was not "numerous" on the 4th. 2. The most important error however is, that "on a show of hands, the meeting" declared "in favor of Mr. Bowes, and in opposition to that religion which is the pest of society," &c. No show of hands was asked or given, but a vote of thanks to the chairman, which even Mr. Cleary seconded.

VISIT TO IRELAND.

6*mo.* 27*th.*—Commenced my journey to Ireland, after seeing some friends in Liverpool. Tarried all night at Egremont.

28*th.*—Sailed by the *Athlone* steamer for Belfast, at half-past 1 o'clock. About forty passengers. A fine passage. We left the Isle of Man on our right hand, sailing between it and Ireland. I slept almost as well as if I had been at home. Reached BELFAST about 6 o'clock in the morning: as I knew no one, I made my way to the Temperance Hotel, Waring Street, and afterwards spent a few hours in looking over the town. Observed hundreds coming out of the Roman Catholic chapel, at 9 o'olock, Saturday morning. Saw a girl with black eyes; heard her swear by "the Holy Father;" she was not coming from the chapel.

29*th.*—Came by railway to BALLYMENA, a distance by the public road of 21 Irish miles; it is more by railroad. An Irish mile contains 320 perches, 7 yards to the perch, or 2240 yards. As the English mile is 1760 yards, the difference of 480 yards is more than one fourth. When I had talked with a few brethren, I found that they met as a Baptist Church at Tullymore.

30*th.*—TULLYMORE. Met with the church, but did not break bread with them for *two reasons*—first, they take in none *but Baptists*, and this to my mind makes the table much more the table of a sect than the table of the Lord; second, they have some *spirit-dealers* among them. The church, which is small, consisting of nearly twenty members, received me kindly to teach. I addressed them for about an hour on the precious truths of the Scriptures, telling them my reasons for not breaking bread with them, and proving that those reasons were scriptural. Here the church practices the "holy kiss." When the service commenced, each person rose and gave the salutation to the next one. In this neighborhood are several large Presbyterian congregations, which take the *regium donum*, or government pay. To the elders of one of these application was made that I might have their "meeting house" to preach in at 6 p.m. It was granted, and we gave it out; but when we returned to Ballymena, we found that a minister of another congregation, "Dr. Dobbin," had been consulted, and he had advised them not to give it; so when we came back, we found the evening wet, and no place to preach in. The Methodists have a small society and a chapel here, but as their minister was gone to Conference they could do nothing without him. So that it seems Ireland is just as much governed in this quarter by Protestant priests, as elsewhere by those of the Church of Rome. At 7 o'clock I discoursed in a large school-room to a considerable congregation, and several questions were asked, relating chiefly to Christ's dying for all.

7*mo.* 1*st.*—At CLINTEY FARM, in a barn; a serious and attentive congregation. Had much comfort in my own mind while proclaiming the gospel, and had some interesting conversation with the farmer after.

2nd—BALLYMENA. The rain prevented me from preaching in the market, so we got the school-room again, and had a congregation of Protestants, Arians, and Roman Catholics. No opposition was made publicly, though I again gave liberty for questions; but a Presbyterian minister, named Fleming, who has heard me twice, made a number of objections, in the presence of several, at the close of the meeting.

3rd.—BROUGHSHANE. In the open-air; a large and attentive congregation. I was published on a bill as the "Rev. John Bowes, Baptist minister." I began my discourse by correcting the mistake, showing that I was a Christian, and not a Baptist, minister. I then asked, "What is the gospel?" One man said, "Glad tidings." I showed that if a poor man, deeply in debt, heard news of a large sum of money being left, that it would be "glad tidings," but not the gospel. I then asked, "What is the gospel glad tidings about?" But after this they seemed afraid to venture any more answers. I then read Paul's definition of the gospel, 1 Cor. xv. 1-6, to which they paid great attention. I have not yet found a congregation that could tell me what the gospel is. The minister last night said that I confined it too much; "that we had the gospel of Matthew, Mark, Luke, and John." I said "Then we have four gospels! instead of one;" and I reminded him that the headings or titles of these books were of human, not divine, authority. When people do not search the Scriptures for themselves, when they never give their views of them or teach them, but leave all to hired ministers, they themselves remain in ignorance.

4th.—GALGORM PARK. A house tolerably full of very attentive people, who seemed to receive the word with readiness of mind. About a mile from this place is Grace Hill, a Moravian establishment.

5th.—To-day I walked to the top of a Rath, a round hill of considerable height, built up evidently by the hand of man; it is near BALLYMENA, not far from the small river which runs through the town; at the foot is a deep ditch, all round which must have been filled with water as a kind of moat. This ditch goes all round the hill. It is said, that, in some elevated situations, fifty Raths may be seen, and two or three, all over Ireland, may be found near each other. As they are so numerous, it is probable that they have been forts for protection in time of war; they are now often called forths or forts. Robert M'Master, whose word may be trusted, saw a canoe capable of holding two persons dug out of one of these ditches, a few miles from here, at the bottom of several feet of moss. No doubt these ditches will fill up gradually, and are now much less deep than they were some centuries ago. When bows and arrows were used, the breastwork at the top of the hill would protect the archers, while the circle of water at the foot would hinder the enemy from entering the fort.

In the evening preached out of doors to a considerable congregation, at Ballymena, and a good deal of interest has been excited.

6th.—To day had some conversation with a Friend. The "Friends" in Ireland do not swell the ranks of emigration; they are generally in comfortable and even wealthy circumstances; and while their morality commands the respect of all parties, their industrious and enterprising habits secure them competency and even affluence. It seems that while in England they are generally liberal in their political sentiments; here they are decidedly conservative. Have heard to-day of the death of a spirit-seller before he was thirty years of age. Many are destroying themselves by this trade. The police here carry guns and bayonets or swords, and, in fact, might be rather considered a sort of travelling soldier than police; so easily may the one system slide into the other.

7th.—To-day had a kind invitation from a Christian to visit Ballymony, a distance of several miles from here, where twelve Christians meet, and are prepared to receive all Christians.

9th.—BROUGHSHANE. A very attentive congregation out of doors. A few old foolish persons, apparently under the influence of drink, disturbed some of the rest by talking. A considerable degree of interest has been awakened in this large village by the truths preached and circulated. May the seed bring forth fruit speedily, and many days hence.

10th.—Was invited to-day to attend a *Soiree*, given that the proceeds might support a worthy Christian named H. Ross, whose age and piety the neighbors respect sufficiently to keep him from the workhouse. The party met in the Parade School, about two miles from Ballymena. As I was left perfectly free to tell them whatever would do them good, as I knew nothing that would do them more good than the gospel, I set it before them, and recommended temperance, Christian union, and benevolence. A Cameronian minister, Mr. Marcus, from Ballymony, some miles distant, spoke, and informed me that several of their ministers are total abstainers. In this country, where the whisky works much mischief, all Christians should abstain. I never saw such a patient people; I addressed them two or three times, and they seemed unwilling to part after eleven o'clock: it was near one before we got home. There were about thirty abstainers from strong drinks in the meeting. Two or three seem inquiring after truth here.

11th.—I and a brother visited ANTRIM. A friendly man at the Court House directed us to the hall of Lord Mazarine, whom we found walking in his beautiful garden. He, as a magistrate, granted the Court House immediately. We sent round the bell, and afterwards talked with an interesting Christian, who seems to have learned from the Scriptures nearly all that I teach. At present he meets with the Primitive Wesleyan Methodists, who originated about 1816; and while they have persons in society from nearly all churches, they form no church; they number about 11,000 members. We met with two of their hired preachers, who were on a visit to friends. We were very near *Lough Neagh*, the largest fresh water lake, I believe, in Europe; said to be nearly 30 miles long, and 12 broad. The river *Ban* runs through it. Had an interesting meeting at the Court House. Mr. Crossley, from Manchester, a city missionary, was present.

14th.—Met again with the church at TULLYMORE, but did not break bread. One of the members, who sells strong drinks, made a long address to show that the unbaptized should not break bread. I stated at length the grounds for breaking bread with all Christians, and showed that the course which he advocated really made baptism the bond of union, instead of faith and love; and that it was no longer faith in the precious blood of Christ. At half-past 6, the largest meeting I ever had yet at Ballymena, in the school-room.

15th.—BELFAST. Could get no crier, as no one is allowed to cry meetings. Got a quiet place at the end of Durham Street, near a meeting-house called "Christ's Church." A very attentive congregation. Met with William Lupton, Superintendent Wesleyan Preacher, and Chairman of the District; in Ireland, second only to Thomas Waugh. I had not seen him for twenty-three years. He did not know me at all. For about fifty years the Irish preachers have been confined to Ireland. He and another are the only English preachers out of 129. They number about 21,000 members. My old friend is a Tory Methodist, and glories in the name. His son, about eighteen years of age, he thinks of devoting to the law. The Baptists are few, and little known. I saw James Nelson, who seems to see farther than many. He is now acting as a town missionary.

16th.—Preached to a much larger company at the same place. Deeply attentive. One man, deeply interested, wishes to see a New Testament church here. After preaching accompanied brother Hartley, a Primitive Methodist Preacher, to a Total Abstinence meeting, in Frederick Street School, and addressed the meeting for a short time.

17th.—Sailed from Belfast to WHITEHAVEN. The captain was intoxicated all the way; the night was fine, and the vessel well managed by the subordinate hands, or I should have reported him in the proper quarter. The owners of steamers should never commit human lives, and a great amount of property, to a man that cannot take care of himself. As the evening was fine, I stayed on deck all night. It was very cold at sea about midnight. I got about an hour's sleep, but took no cold. I got a few hour's rest in Whitehaven, as we arrived at five o'clock in the morning. Called on a few Christians, to whom I had introductions. Preached on the 18th and 19th to large congregations.

20th.—Saturday. Preached out of doors at Caldewgate, CARLISLE. A female, who keeps a public-house, wished to drive the congregation away, because she had an idea we were injuring her trade in strong drinks; I hope she was correct. We removed a little from her house of ruin, and preached without further molestation.

21st.—Had two meetings within, and two very large ones at the cross. The people were deeply attentive. Some hired ministers heard.

28th.—MANCHESTER. Had two or three meetings in Salford and Manchester, out of doors. Brother Dickie assisted in the work. I took the last piece of flesh meat that I intend to take for several months, so as to give the Vegetarian principle a fair trial.

4th.—BRADFORD. Had two great meetings here, forenoon and afternoon: there could not be less, I think, than two thousand people. Other brethren assisted me. I wish to have help from brethren everywhere. One of the infidels who heard last night, gave a public testimony to the kind manner in which I had spoken of them last night. Let us treat all men kindly, and we shall find few so insensible as not to be moved by such conduct; but if, on the contrary, we use bitter words, what can we expect but that party will be embittered against party, and rendered unwilling and unfit to hear the truth calmly.

5th.—At six, evening, a large meeting at BINGLEY. Brother Wilson, formerly a preacher with the Irish Primitive Wesleyans, gave assistance. He has clear views of the gospel, expresses them clearly, and should never be idle while there is a hell-going world to teach. I think we had about 1,200 hearers.

6th.—At twelve o'clock, although wet, many came out to hear the good word; but still more in the evening. After I had preached out, about twenty met to see what the Scriptures teach on baptism. We commenced at Matthew iii., and took all the texts we could find. Many were astonished that the Scriptures say so much on the subject; some expressed a desire to be baptized. I believe this is the best plan, to take the Scriptures and see what they say on this subject.

6th.—KEIGHLEY. In the market-place. I should think 1,500 people heard the great good news; I trust the seed sown will bring forth fruit many days hence. This comes of discussions. People get to hear more about the preacher, and come in hundreds and thousands to hear the word of life. No settled minister, if he had three thousand hearers, would be likely to have such a sphere of usefulness as I have had of late. Let my old friends no longer wish that I should again become a settled pastor; in such a sphere I could not do a tithe of the good I am doing now.

THE NEWCASTLE DISCUSSION.

The Public Discussion, which has just been closed at Newcastle, occupied four nights, the 13th, 14th, 15th, and 16th, in the Lecture Room, which was crowded. The secretary of the "Young Men's Christian Association," had engaged to find a Defender of Christianity to meet Charles Southwell. He corresponded with me; and although in most circumstances I should have declined meeting Mr. Southwell, some peculiar circumstances existed at Newcastle which induced me to comply. The infidel party did not behave nearly so well as at Bradford, nevertheless I got a good hearing for truth. The first night on the being of a God, I pressed Mr. S. with the marks of design in man and in the universe. He admitted an Intelligent Author. I then considered the argument closed, and the being of a God established; but next night Mr. S. withdrew his admission. He acted in a similar manner two or three times; told the meeting repeatedly that I had used arguments which I never used, and then he valiantly refuted imaginary arguments really his own! As all is published, the reader will find Mr. S.'s speeches eccentric and quite amusing.

On the 22nd, I met a company of the "Young Men's Christian Association" at tea, in Bell's Temperance Coffee-house. They presented me with an imperial octavo Bible with references, containing the following,—"Presented to Mr. John Bowes, of Manchester, by the Committee of the Newcastle and Gateshead Young Men's Christian Association, in grateful acknowledgment of his services in the cause of Truth, during his four nights' discussion with Charles Southwell, in the Lecture Hall of this town. By order of the Committee. A. STRINGER, Secretary. Newcastle-on-Tyne, Aug. 22nd, 1850." They also accompanied this with a small donation, towards expenses, &c. I had an opportunity of hearing their sentiments, and of explaining my own, on a variety of topics. I recommended a course of lectures against the errors of the Church of Rome, with liberty of discussion. Such an association as this might attack prevalent errors with effect, if its members are really zealous for the spread of truth.

18th.—Three young men were immersed at NEWCASTLE. At half-past 10, I lectured at NORTH SHIELDS, and also at half-past 2 in the Temperance Hall. I have seldom had more comfort in delivering the Word. In the evening lectured on Infidelity. I asked any to stand up that had been made happy by it. None did so. I then asked any Christian to stand up. A seaman did so; and with great apparent sincerity and power detailed his conversion. He was a very wicked man; his shipmates the same; they encountered a gale, felt they were going to hell, resolved to change, got into port, and then were afraid to go ashore, lest they should break their vows. Looking about, they discovered a tract, which they all read, and this brought him to Christ. After that he ventured on shore. Two men, believers, spoke to the same effect. Nine broke bread here to-day, and steps were taken to continue a meeting in the Lord's name alone. The three meetings grew larger each time.

9mo. 5th, 6th.—GLASGOW. As the police interfere more here with open-air preaching than anywhere else, and I did not wish to loose a second night, I called at the superintendent's office, and told those in authority my intention, and that I had been hindered last year, and thought it unreasonable. I was first told to go far back on the green, where I was very unlikely to get a congregation. I asked why I could not preach where I had always done. At length they gave way, and I preached near the green, in my old place, to a large and deeply attentive people; several eagerly wishing to know whether I was not going to preach again. I have often thought of taking up my abode in this vast city, second only to London, and of trying to influence its hundreds and thousands. At present I do not see the way quite clear.

8th.—DUNDEE. Six services; three out of doors, and three in the chapel; all well attended. The brethren who preach, six of them, were ready to help me; so that they took half the work, or nearly so. The church is prospering, and the congregations good. The brethren are united to labor, and open-air preaching goes on. I have seldom spent so happy a day as here, and, although I engaged in six public services, did not feel unusually tired. The church met after all for an hour or two, which made a seventh service. How sweet it is to have fellow-laborers in the cause of Christ!

17th, 18th.—PETERHEAD. Got a singular letter from this place a day or two ago, which I suppose ought not to be published while the writer lives. He did not wish me to visit Peterhead; but I preached two nights with considerable comfort to myself. He became an unbeliever.

19th.—Started for OLD MELDRUM, across the country. Could only get a coach six miles, and walked twenty-five miles. After going half-way felt hungry, but found no place for refreshment. Begged a turnip, which seemed delicious. When within a few miles of my destination, called at a farm house, and asked for a little milk and bread, for money. Got what I asked with cheese, but the kind farmer's wife of Craig-dam would not take anything. At half-past 6 o'clock, preached for about an hour and a half in the market-place. More attentive than I ever saw them here before.

ANSWER TO A. DUNCANSON ON COLLEGES FOR MINISTERS.

CLATT, ABERDEENSHIRE, 9mo. 21st, 1850.

DEAR FRIEND,—

I only received your note yesterday. I had previously seen your circular, upon which I wish to offer a few observations. I see in it much to approve, and at least one particular to condemn.

1. An "Educational Academy" for "young men preparing for the ministry," will be a college for clergymen or ministers. Education in general is good. A college of this kind is to be deprecated, because it will *support the kingdom of the clergy*, already far too strong; and I do not expect Christ's kingdom to advance rapidly until the priesthood in all its forms be annihilated. The Romish priest, the Episcopalian prelate, the Presbyterian clergyman, and the Independent, Baptist, and Wesleyan ministers, hired to preach, and designated "Reverend," have all *distinct interests—class interests*, of their own; and while they continue, they wage war against both the interests of Christ, and those of his people. When men expend TIME and *money* to learn the preaching trade, they think themselves entitled to set up business wherever they can get customers to purchase the gospel, which they say they preach. Instead of encouraging this unholy traffic in God's free gospel, and in the souls of men, it is our duty to seek, by all possible means, its entire overthrow.

Jesus Christ and the Apostles founded no academy or college for the training of ministers. *If this is the best plan*, they obviously neglected the best interests of the church. This I cannot admit, and am therefore led to the conclusion that the best college is the church—the best professors, its most pious and judicious Elders or Evangelists: and as all Christians have access to this college, no exception can be made on account of poverty, want of time, or any other cause, while any one is a member of the church.

I have been informed, that one of your reasons for deciding to commence your institution *now*, was the case of *Findlay Wallace*, a brother from New Mills, who applied for admission into the Kilmarnock Academy, and was turned out within two days because he would not say that he agreed with the two professors on *paying pastors*. Was it not understood, when this academy was instituted, that it was to assist young men to preach the gospel? Now here was a young man, who had preached it with some success, excluded, not because he was not a Christian, or held wrong views on the gospel, but because he would not support the kingdom of the clergy. Had they allowed this young man, eager to acquire knowledge, to remain, what harm could have resulted? Were they afraid that one young man might teach his fellow-students, and subvert the whole college? Alas for consistency, when "expelled students" should themselves so soon support an institution which cannot tolerate freedom of opinion. It is to your honor that you have no sympathy with this priestly tyranny, and intend to take in the "expelled student."

You comprehend the needs of the churches when you say they want men, "whose chief aim is not to stand out as a distinct and worshipped class of the community, but who so feel the wants, and see the necessities of their fellow-men, as to be prepared to stand up and advocate and defend all that affects the happiness of man's body and the moral health of his imperishable soul."

Considering the excellent objects which your circular embraces, I cannot but regret that you do not *include all who may wish education, whether they intend to be ministers or not*. Who, before the streams of knowledge have entered his enquiring mind, can tell what he may one day become? Knowledge gives existence, as well as wings, to hope, because it gives fitness for office.

I have been accused of advocating an unlearned ministry; but am so far from being guilty, *that I wish all the community to be learned*. Why should ministers have more learning than others? Let all the people be well educated, and we cannot have an unlearned ministry; every one that opens his mouth in public will be a learned man. Once admit that ministers should have superior learning, and you form that "distinct class;" at least, if you act out the admission, which men hasten to "worship," and which you deplore. Lay the axe to the root, open your academy to all, and then you will do nothing to set up what you deprecate—a "distinct class." With the single exception I have pointed out, your Circular is good, and its views far in advance of those held by your contemporaries.

I should be glad to see you before I return, if we could arrange a meeting. Although I have never seen you, I have read your views as one of the "expelled students," and remarked that they contained more point and originality than are common with students, who too frequently are mere copyists.

I do not know of any of the "readers of the 'Christian Magazine'" likely to take an interest in your academy in its present form; but if I publish your Circular, it may call forth their sentiments. Wishing you success in preaching the glorious gospel of the grace of God,

I am, yours in truth and love,

To Alex. Duncanson.   JOHN BOWES.

23rd.—CLATT. Vegetarianism has been practised for ages in this neighborhood by the great body of the farmers and farm laborers. They seldom or never taste flesh meat. In the morning they have porridge and milk; at noon, milk porridge; and at night, supper, of either greens, potatoes, or something of the kind. They are fine, strong, able-bodied, healthy men and women, and seldom or never need a doctor. I visited a few persons on the way to Aberdeen. One sick, and near death, who was apparently well twelve months ago.

26th.—DUNDEE. Lectured in Bell Street Hall; last night on the "Truth of Christianity." To-night, a greatly increased assembly to hear my lecture on "The Primacy of the Pope and Transubstantiation." No Roman Catholic came forward for some time; but at last a very mild man occupied about an hour in discussion. He said the words of Christ to Peter, "Feed my sheep," meant "Feed my clergy!" If so, I advised all the clergy to go to Rome, as they were not shepherds to feed the flock, but sheep to be fed by the Pope! The meeting was deeply interesting.

29th.—Preached twice, to large congregations, in Bell Street Hall. In the evening the hall was crowded; several had to stand; there could not be less than nine hundred or a thousand people present. The brethren had taken the hall, and it was duly intimated by bills, &c.

30th.—A number of Christians took tea together in Lamb's Hall. There were some little differences of judgment; but after they were explained, there seemed to be a blessing in faithfulness. Human nature does not relish being told of its faults, yet it is a very important part of our duty. We had better displease our brethren than suffer sin upon them, and thus injure them by conniving at what is wrong.

10mo 1st.—Bell Street Hall crowded to overflowing, and many had to go away who could not get in, to hear a lecture against Mormonism. One of the Mormon priests had engaged to come forward to oppose. He came up at last evidently with great reluctance; his name is Murray.

As Infidel Lectures were announced, I was requested, before the whole meeting, to pledge myself to return, if the Christians of Dundee saw it necessary, to oppose in discussion the infidel's views. I wished to leave the matter, but it was of no use. My friends in several places, indeed, Christians of different denominations, seem to have constituted me, at least in their minds and acts, "The Defender of the Faith;" for they pass by all the ministers, and other gifted persons, and fix on me; so that I have abundance of employment of this kind. I afterwards learned that they had not found any infidel worthy of opposing, for I heard no more from them. I saw from the papers that R. Cooper was ill, and that an incompetent person took his place.

3rd.—GREENOCK. It must be about fifteen years since I once lectured here. I was then a hired minister. I had a very painful conversation at that time with a zealous Calvinistic minister of the secession church, on the doctrines of Calvin. He was then most rigid, unreasonable, and overbearing in maintaining his views and assailing mine. This evening I lectured in the Baptist Chapel. It was tolerably filled, and the people were deeply attentive. The church here has no hired pastor, but some of them contend for it; others are getting more light. To-day I received a letter from my daughter, in which she says, respecting my dear delicate boy, Edward,—"He is a great deal better, and able to walk about a little again; but he has a little cough which disturbs him a little. I asked him the questions you wished me—1st. Was he at peace with God? He replied that he was. 2nd. Does he know that Christ has taken away his sin? He answered that he did. 3rd. Would he be afraid to die? He said he would not. I then asked him if he thought he would go to heaven? He said, 'Yes.'"

4th, 5th, 6th, & 7th.—HELENSBURGH. The meeting on Lord's Day evening was thin. While here I saw Mr. Grant, the younger, of Grantoun. He seemed quite unable to receive any to the Lord's Table who do not agree with him on Calvinism. His father and he, however, seem to have been useful in the north of Scotland. I am thankful that I have done begging for chapels: it is a very unscriptural business, degrading to those employed in it, and often injurious to those for whom the subscriptions are made. I am not insensible to the fact that good and fine chapels increase the attendance of the world, but often too, they become the means of introducing worldliness into the church.

8th.—Lectured in the same Baptist chapel, Greenock; found several Christians very kind and affectionate. The meeting was quite as interesting as that held here the last week. I trust that the fruit of these two meetings will be gathered another day.

9th, and a part of the *10th*, I spent in making arrangements for a week's meetings in Glasgow.

12th.—CARLUKE. A small congregation; although a few Christians meet here weekly on a scriptutal basis.

13th.—WISHAW. We had a refreshing meeting at the Lord's Supper, and in the evening a crowded hall. Four or five of the brethren here have withdrawn, because one of the brethren has been appointed Inspector for the poor, and his office leads him sometimes to adopt legal measures to recover poor-rates. Although I do not see the least warrant in Scripture to go to law, I see distinctly that it is a sin to divide the church. Forbearance, therefore, must either be exercised with those who differ from us on oaths, going to law, &c., or the church may have endless divisions. I spent some time, after preaching, with these four brethren, and I shall be glad to learn that the church and they are reunited. At the breaking of bread the number seemed about as large as on former occasions.

14th.—LANARK. Found that the eight or nine brethren here, although meeting weekly, did not remember the Lord weekly. After discoursing in a cottage, met them, and they heartily agreed to break bread weekly.

15th.—DOUGLAS. The church here is improving both in numbers and gracious feeling. I saw the greater part of them either before or after the lecture, which was heard by several of their neighbors.

16th.—HAMILTON. Discoursed in Ebenezer Chapel, John Kirk's chapel before he removed to Edinburgh. I had a very attentive congregation. I did not shun to declare to them all the counsel of God. The New Testament church meets in a hall, about fifty in fellowship; double the number of hearers.

17th.—GLASGOW. Commenced a week's meetings here, in the Central Temperance Hall, Howard Street;—about three-fourths full. I felt the solemn responsibility of commencing in this great city—the largest in the kingdom out of London. I believe many are praying for us.

18th.—Lectured on Christianity and Infidelity, and allowed discussion after. Mr. Henrietta, as appointed by the Glasgow Anti-Theological Society, occupied the time. The hall was crowded—the people orderly.

19th.—Saturday. A gracious meeting, and well attended ; but I was very unwell.

20th.—The great City Hall, capable of holding 5000 people, was engaged for this day. Several hundreds in the morning—more in the afternoon. Felt weak. Met several Christians to converse about remembering the Lord together.

At the close of the afternoon service, nearly fifty, from several churches, met round the Lord's Table. In the evening it was thought we had 3000 people present. One or two clamorous professors, in asking questions, behaved unwisely, evidently intending to force their own views on the meeting, instead of obtaining information by questions. Was thankful to God that by the evening I was nearly well.

21st.—Cannon Street Church—three parts filled. The interest is increasing. I took some notice of the following bill :—

"Fast-Day Services: Congregational Chapel, Blackfriars Street, (Rev. F. Ferguson's.)—The four Churches under the pastoral care of the Rev. Messrs. SCOTT, FERGUSON, GALLOWAY, and GUTHRIE, will avail themselves of the half-yearly Fast-Day, on the 24th October current, as formerly, and assemble in the above chapel at the usual hours.—The forenoon services will be conducted by Mr. Galloway and Mr. Guthrie. Mr. Ferguson will preach in the afternoon ;—Subject : 'Why will unbelievers be condemned at the Last Day ?' A Religious Meeting will be held in the same place, in the evening, at half-past six. Tickets, price Sixpence, admitting two. Addresses will be delivered by the Rev. William Scott, on ' Man's responsibility for his belief;' the Rev. A. C. Rutherford, on 'Walking with God;' the Rev. John Kirk, on 'Christian Peace in times of Darkness.' A collection will be made at both forenoon and afternoon services ; and after defraying expenses, the remaining proceeds of the day will be applied to the liquidation of the Muslin Street Chapel debt, which still bears heavily upon the church."

There was neither tea nor fruit given, but the gospel was sold at sixpence a ticket for two! I am sorry that ministers will lend themselves to such a practice. Wherever the Christian church exists, the gospel of the grace of God should be given freely : so Christ commanded : "Freely ye have received, freely give." Persons should not build places in debt, and then sell the gospel to get out of it. One hired minister asked a question.

22nd.—In visiting to-day found the poor of several churches sadly neglected. In the evening, congregation increased. The best of all, God is with us.

23rd.—After this last meeting about one hundred remained, as friends to the formation of a Church of Christ on scriptural principles. They meet the next Lord's day in the Central Temperance Hall. I only found one young man who clearly saw the Gospel under these meetings, he believed the first night. The gospel was preached at each meeting, and the church was fed with scriptural truth. Many expressed themselves as greatly instructed and comforted.

The expenses of these meetings were all defrayed by the liberality of the churches at Wishaw and Hamilton. The meetings were all free, and no one was asked for a penny in any way. They were advertised in three Glasgow papers.

THE ATTACK OF "THE CHRISTIAN NEWS."

In 1849, having been repeatedly asked to forward my sentiments to *The Christian News*, and having repeatedly told my friends that it was of no use, as they would not be inserted, they have responded, "Have you ever tried?" and not being able so say I had, I forwarded a letter for insertion, at their request. In my letter I offered to bring before the readers of the paper the great questions of ministry—whether it should be hired or free, the unity of the church, the ordinances, and providing for poor saints. To this letter I received no reply, either through *The Christian News*, or in any other way, which confirmed my opinion of the paper,—that it was sectarian, and afraid of discussing anything that would be likely to damage the interests of the sect it was trying to establish. During the 10th month, (as will be seen by the preceding pages) I held a series of meetings in Glasgow, for preaching the gospel, and opening up before the public those questions which *The Christian News* refused to insert. In one of those meetings I commented on a bill, published by its chief supporters. The same week the attack appeared in their paper;—not an answer to the remarks on their proceedings, which I had made; but an *ill-natured* criticism on the Bradford discussion with Mr. Holyoake! They speak of Mr. H. in terms of mingled praise and blame, but for me they had not *one expression of approval*. I refer the reader to my reply (which also appeared in their paper) in *The Truth*, Vol. i. p. 108, and to two other letters which they did not insert, pp. 118, 124.

12*mo*. 3*rd*, 5*th*, 6*th*.—NORTHAMPTON. As this is the "see" of W. Wareing, one of the Pope's twelve new bishops, it was deemed the Lord's way to call public attention to the errors of the Church of Rome, in three lectures, with discussion after. The interest was great at first, and increased each night. Four Roman Catholics replied. One Mr. Lloyd said, that if the extracts which I read from St. Liguori were true, he would leave the church to-morrow, *hate* the Church of Rome, and go through the country preaching against her. To convince him I gave him the numbers of the pages quoted from, and told him where to find the extracts. We shall see whether he will leave the church.

On the 4*th* and 8*th*, I preached. At half-past 2, on the 7*th*, Dye Church Lane Chapel was far too small, as many could not get in. I set before the people the scriptural constitution of Christ's church. To-day I was invited to call on the family of John Philips, as his wife passed several years in convents abroad. She was able to give some interesting information. Many persons are put there by their parents, husbands, or guardians, and sometimes are married by their parents or guardians without having seen more of their future husbands than their portraits, which are commonly sent. Each nun has a bedroom and bed to herself, although occasionally they contrive to sleep two in one bed; yet this is done secretly and is contrary to law. The only male persons that have access to them are the priests, and they have keys, by which to obtain access to them either by day or night. The priests also are their doctors or physicians, and prescribe for their bodies as well as their souls.

This applies to Sicily, where, if the priest enters to converse with a man's wife, the husband must retire. My informants state, that considerable excesses exist among the priests. Hundreds of persons may sometimes be seen in the street bowing down before an image. Two brethren from Mount Zion Chapel, kindly offered their chapel for the evening; we took it. Before going into the chapel I met some of the leading brethren, who informed me that they intended to make a collection for the gas. I told them I never made any. It seems it was given out in the morning; but it had not been mentioned to me when I was kindly invited. I said I expected to be able to conduct the meeting in my own way, as I should have done at the other chapel. This was conceded, only it was hoped that, as we differed in some things, our differences might not be named. I stated that I could not pledge myself to anything, but to "the whole counsel of God," which I meant to declare, as far as time and wisdom might be granted. The conversation lasted several minutes, and I tried to blend kindness with firmness, until every point was yielded; so that I passed to the great congregation. I suppose 700 were crowded into the chapel, and some had to go away. I discoursed for nearly two hours. The minister of the place was present, and I understood, did not speak unfavorably of the meeting, although we had neither singing nor prayer in the ordinary way. We have both when we meet as a church. I rejoice that we had no collection; for as we have none from promiscuous congregations in any of our places of worship, had they made the collection it would have called me out, for consistency's sake, to declare I had nothing to do with it. When will Christian men be wise, and use the best means of doing good, free from the reproach which collections entail. Catholics, church people, infidels, and all sorts, heard the gospel freely for once. Sometimes, when friends take halls for lectures against Popery, Mormonism, &c., they charge a small sum to cover expenses; but we should charge nothing for the gospel of the grace of God anywhere, nor ask the wicked man for anything but his heart. When we profess to be concerned for his salvation, let us show no regard for his money.

9th.—MOULTON. A crowded meeting. The people had proposed to burn the Pope's effigy to-morrow night. I made some allusion to it. I hope the people will see that the best way to burn out Popery is not by an earthly fire, but by the burning flame of truth and love. A few souls meet here weekly to remember the Lord.

10th.—LITCHBOROUGH; nine miles from Northampton. Preached in a barn, which was filled to overflowing.

11th.—Again a large congregation in the same place. God's judgments are working with his word here. To-day a last night's auditor fell from his horse and dislocated his shoulder. He and his wife had intended to hear this evening, but were hindered. When preaching was first proposed in this barn, it did not please him; now he would come, but cannot. Let the Lord's word be precious to us, and then we shall hear it when we may. The brethren break bread here and at Grimscote alternately. Nearly twenty profess Jesus, and they hold meetings almost every night.

13th.—Visited the Bunyan Chapel, a new building capable of holding 1150 people, on the place where the old chapel stood, where John Bunyan used to preach. In the vestry is the chair in which he used to sit and study. It has an oak bottom, with round arms, and is very good, but beginning to decay. As I sat down in it, and remembered that near two hundred years ago, the great author of the Pilgrim's Progress sat and mused, and wrote his interesting thoughts in this very chair, I contrasted the durability of wood with the frailty of man, and remembered that it is written, " All flesh is grass." In the graveyard, against the chapel, stands a stone or monument, from which I copied the following:—" In Memory of Hannah Bunyan, who departed this life, 15th of February, 1770. Aged 76 years.—N.B. She was great granddaughter to the Rev. and justly celebrated Mr. John Bunyan, who died at London, 21st of August, 1688, aged 60 years, and was buried in Bunhill Fields, where there is a stone erected to his memory. He was minister of the gospel here 32 years, and during that time he suffered 12 years' imprisonment. 'The righteous shall be in everlasting rememberance.'—Ps. cxii. 6." This evening had an improved congregation at the chapel, and arranged to visit some villages next week. Brother Parkinson and I called on Mr. Jukes, minister at Bunyan Chapel. He has under his care some missionary students. Mr. Jukes retains the church-book and Bunyan's handwriting. There is an epistle, 1676, from the church at Bedford to a church at Braintree inserted. The handwriting in his will, which we saw, dated 1685, is similar to that in the epistle, which is signed by him, and contains seven other names in his handwriting.—There is another great granddaughter of John Bunyan, aged 88, living in London. Her name is Mrs. Sanigear; She is the only known descendant remaining. As John Bunyan died in 1688, his preaching hear must have commenced in 1656.

16th.—Walked to ELSTOW, to see the house in which John Bunyan lived. It is rather more than a mile from Bedford; has been rebuilt since his time; and all that remains of the house is an old beam which is seen in the new house. The cottage is very small, and has a little garden behind attached to it.

JOHN HOWARD.

From Elstow, once the residence of the celebrated author of the "Pilgrim's Progress," we walked to CARDINGTON, to see the abode of John Howard. Cardington is a retired village, about two and a half miles south of Bedford. The first objects which attracted our attention were several neat two-story cottages, with a circle on each front; some bearing date 1763, others 1764.

We then inquired for the house in which Howard lived. We were directed to Samuel Charles Whitbread's, M.P. The servants only were at home. The butler and gardener showed us through the house and gardens. The walks and trees still remain, arranged or planted, near one hundred years ago, by John and Henrietta Howard; some of them are now large, and some are decaying. The garden and house have both been enlarged. The former contains an observatory, and the latter has had several wings attached to the old house, which stands in the centre, and has not originally been large. We saw the best rooms of the old house which are low. An excellent likeness of Howard hangs among Mr. Whitbread's paintings. The countenance appears firm, manly, and generous. We sought out William Felt, 83 years of age, who entered the service of John Howard as gardener at 16, and remained till he was 23. He remembers him well, and stated that he used to worship at Bedford, at what is still called Howard chapel. The old man will soon go the way of all flesh. He has about ten shillings per week to live upon, as we were informed. We next sought out the sexton, who opened to us the large strong-built state church, on the east wall of which we found erected a marble tablet, containing the following, in the middle, and first inscribed :—" In hope of a resurrection to eternal life through the mercy of God by Jesus Christ, rests the mortal part of Henrietta Howard, wife of John Howard, daughter of Edward Leeds, Esq., of Croxton, Cambridgeshire, who died the 31st of March, 1765; aged 39. 'She openeth her mouth with *wisdom*, and in her tongue was the law of kindness.'—Prov. xxxi. 26. John Howard died at Cherson, in Russian Tartary, January 21, 1791; aged 64. 'Christ is my hope.'" The idea of unostentatious plainness may be seen in this tablet. John Howard, Esq., &c., would no doubt have been added had his name not been inscribed on the stone under his own eye, while living. On the top of the marble tablet we read—" John Howard, only son and heir of John and Henrietta Howard, died the 25th of April, 1799." Although we do not learn it from this stone, we do learn that he was dissipated, and lost his reason through taking medicine to expel the disease his vices had entailed. He spent the last years of his life in a lunatic asylum. Thus, instead of being a comfort to his father he was his grief, and he was lost to the world by his varied excesses. The rain came on rapidly as we returned to Bedford: but I was refreshed to find a considerable congregation gathered, notwithstanding the great rain, to hear the word of the Lord.

17th.—This morning received intelligence from home, that my son Edward died yesterday morning, at five minutes before one o'clock. The part of the letter which affected me most, was where I am told he said, "I shall never see my father again in this world." On arriving at home, I learned his mother added, "but you will see your brothers, and sisters, and father in heaven." He said, "Yes, I shall see you all there." And his sister said, "You expect to go to heaven, through Jesus who died for you and rose again?" He said, "Yes! yes!" The doctor who had prescribed for him arrived; but he went off suddenly.

19th.—We interred my dear son at Whaley, in the burying-ground near the chapel. Before we left home, brother Robinson read John xi., and prayed. At Whaley we sung the 430th hymn in "The Christian Hymn-Book." Brother Wild read the 103rd Psalm, and exhorted.— Edward has been long afflicted with a disease of the heart. His age was ten years and four months. I believe he died in the Lord, and I shall therefore meet him again at the resurrection of the just. I left all arrangements in the south for brethren to supply.

1*mo.9th*, 1851.—SOUTHPORT. The Independent minister, Mr. Melson, had publicly intimated a lecture on the Popery of Protestantism. It was, however, one on Transubstantiation, with a few concluding sentences which would have led any one to the conclusion, that any member of the church capable of preaching had as much right to preach as himself. His sentiments agreed with E. Miall's on the state of the British churches. So that, to be consistent, he must no longer be the only minister—the exclusive pastor of the church—but other brethren must have liberty to minister. What we teach in the pulpit we must practice.

10th, 11th.—Lectured in the Assembly Room, on the "Errors of the Church of Rome." Messrs Hargraves and Kay were appointed by the meeting to wait upon the priest, and invite him to defend his doctrines, but he declined.

15th, 16th, 17th.—ORMSKIRK. Having never opened my mouth for the Lord here before, I embraced the opportunity, by accepting an invitation to lecture in the Town Hall, on Popery. Mr. Stoner was in the chair. The hall was crowded the first night, but much more the second. The meeting almost unanimously requested me to lecture on the remains of Popery in Protestant denominations, on the 17th, which I did to a large assembly. Mr. Stoner filled the chair with great acceptance, but we had very little discussion. Two Roman Catholics came forward the first night, but they were ill prepared.

19th.—PRESTON. Twice in Meadow Street Chapel. In the evening, while in the chapel, a man was heard cursing us at the door, and while I was discoursing to a crowded congregation, two panes of glass were broken by a stone or brick being thrown at the window; happily it hit the wood-work, and no one was hurt. I have often preached in Preston before, and nothing of the kind has occured; but next week I lecture on the errors of the Church of Rome; and here, I take it, we have the great Roman Catholic argument for the truth of Catholicism—A STONE; it was thus at Stockport and Birkenhead.

24th.—Having now abstained from animal food for six months, I weighed myself, and found that whereas I weighed fourteen stones two pounds then, I now weigh fourteen stones nine pounds; so that instead of losing flesh, as I almost expected at first, I have gained. As I propose to take no more animal food for at least six months, I shall then be able, if the Lord will, to give an opinion concerning Vegetarianism. The last six months have increased my confidence in it.

THE LITCHBOROUGH CHARITY.

A considerable amount of money was left to this parish by a lady, from the Foxley and other property, to be distributed to the poor widows, &c., realising to each person not less than £10 annually. Also to put poor boys to learn trades, as apprentices, £10 each was left for a certain number. One great error was committed in the will, that is making the clergyman one of the trustees of the charity. The result is that the other trustees, the churchwardens, allow him to employ it for sectarian purposes. Take a case or two :—

Not long ago a Baptist had a new-born babe. The family were told that if they would allow the child to be " christened or baptized," that is sprinkled, they would get, not £2 which church people were getting, but 10s., and if not, they would get nothing! One of the parents yielded, the child was sprinkled, and the family got 10s. How disgraceful was this to all concerned! The clergyman sold his popish baptism, and the Baptist degraded himself by allowing his child to have it for money!

Another of the parishioners is a Christian. She sought the charity, but because she would not go to the church, she got nothing but insolent language,

Another had a certain amount of articles of dress given her. She was solicited to leave her church but refused—was told that if she did not, it would be the last time she would get anything! She was to get the articles at Towcester. Between giving them and her receiving them, she was sent for again by the clergyman. The noble woman would not sell her religion to please this unfaithful steward. The result was that 10s. worth of goods were struck off from the amount previously given; so that the gift was to act as a bribe, when it failed, the gift was partly recalled. By such mean methods as these does this clergyman administer the charity, and try to get people to church.

These are only a few of the examples which are furnished of the unfaithfulness connected with this trust. I heard such complaints that I procured a copy of the will. It did not say that church people only should have the charity—that Dissenters should be excluded—that poor boys should be only apprenticed to Churchmen, not to Dissenters. It is plain that the gifts or legacies bequeathed were for all the poor of the parish, without respect to their religious opinions: if, therefore, the trustees give it only to Church-goers, or such Dissenters as they can bribe, they are not faithful stewards—they make what was intended for the good of all a means of party jealousy, or even of hypocrisy; for when a needy person finds that church people only, or chiefly, receive the charity, he is taught to go to the church for the sake of the money.

LITCHBOROUGH, June 18th, 1851.

SIR,—

Presuming you are sincere in your wish to investigate "the truth," the whole truth, and nothing but the truth, I am induced to write to you to request you to inform me who is the author of an article inserted in a publication entitled "The Truth," and edited by you.

In justice to myself and Churchwardens, and to further the ends of truth, I feel myself called upon to make this application to you, as many of the statements are grossly misrepresented and perfectly untrue, and may tend to create a vast deal of discontent and uncharitable feeling, if allowed to be circulated without contradiction.

I am, Sir, your obedient servant,

To Mr. John Bowes.   WILLIAM A. TAYLOR.

MANCHESTER, June 20th, 1851.

DEAR SIR,—

I shall transmit a copy of yours of the 18th to the party from whom emanated the statements which you question, and if I get liberty to comply with your request, and we think it requisite, and for the good of all concerned, it shall be done, and in the meantime I can assure you that I am determined to do my utmost to treat all parties concerned, not only justly, but kindly, so that if you or the churchwardens wish to reply through "The Truth," your reply shall be inserted to the same extent, that it may be circulated as widely as the article in number 25. You will easily suppose, that living at this distance from Litchborough, and being entirely unacquainted with the parties noticed in the article, I can have no personal ill-feeling towards them. I do wish to cherish a kindly feeling towards all the poor, and to do them justice, but certainly without doing the least injustice to any other persons. Public charities being public property, are open to public criticism, but that should be in accordance with the facts.

Your friend and the friend of all men,

JOHN BOWES.

P.S.—I give no titles but such as are scriptural; I mention this lest you should think I mean you any disrespect, by not using the term "reverend." I have neither given nor taken it for many years.—J.B.

To W. A. Taylor.

I am glad to say I was not prosecuted, but some thought there was danger, and the poor of the parish did not complain after this.—1871.

THE DEVIL'S TRADE.

It is not far from forty years since Mr. Owen Clarke held a public meeting in Dundee, and afterwards invited the friends of Temperance to meet him in the vestry of the Congregational chapel, where he related the following interesting facts:—

"A Wesleyan local preacher, whose trade was that of a tailor—and this was no dishonor to him—had been importuned by a neighboring brewer to open a beer-shop in the village where he resided: to repeated solicitations he at length yielded, and the workmen were fitting up his house for a beer-shop, when it was publicly intimated that a Temperance meeting would be held in the Friends' Meeting House. While public notice was given to the people, by visitors going from house to house to invite all, the local preacher hoped that nothing might be said at the meeting against his new trade, but he resolved to go and hear for himself. He was just entering the meeting while a Quaker was addressing it. Quakers are often very quaint and significant in their expressions, and so it proved on this occasion. "Friends," said the speaker, "I have just been thinking, if the devil should come into this world and set up business, what sort of a trade he would be. He would not be *a tailor*, that would be too confining for him; he would not be *a joiner*, that would be too hard work for him;—What sort of a trade do you think he would be?" A female voice answered, "He'd open a BEER-SHOP, sir!" The local preacher had entered in time to hear this, and began to think, if selling strong drink was the devil's trade, how it would agree with his preaching. He waited during the meeting, and was convinced that it was what it had been called; joined the society, and was made a member of Committee the same night. He of course dismissed the joiners, refused to commence the devil's trade, and, a considerable time afterwards, expressed his thanks to God that he had never entered it; for he had seven daughters, and he very properly observed:—"However careful we might have been of them, they must have seen and heard many things which they ought not."

3mo. 22nd, 23rd, 24th.—GLASGOW. Good meetings; the last the largest, in the Mechanics' Institution, Cowcaddens, where those meet who have begun to gather around the Lord Jesus alone. Some very precious and happy believers have been gathered together here. About forty broke bread, but there might be ten or twelve more than usually meet. Very many hearers attended of all denominations and no denomination.

4mo. 7th.—SHEFFIELD. Had some very good meetings here, both in the hall where the Baptist Church meets, and in the market-place. J. Jefferson, late Congregational minister at Forres, formerly at Attercliffe, has taken a secular situation, and has followed the Lord in both immersion and the Lord's supper. When ministers have families, it no doubt requires faith and boldness to cast themselves on God and his church; but when it is seen that they take the requisite step, I have never known them to be deserted. God *cares* for his grateful ones. He knows their wants; and if in any instance he does try their faith for a few days, if Jesus passed through the world a despised, outcast one, why should not we deny self, and cheerfully suffer for his sake? He is worthy of being suffered for, and if we suffer with him we shall also reign with him.

5mo 5th.—Brother Lamb, late Congregational minister of Wakefield, has, from a conviction of its unscriptural character, given up hire. This evening he attended a cottage meeting with me, and preached the gospel of the grace of God very sweetly from John i. 11, 12—"He came unto his own, and his own received him not. But to as many as received him, to them gave he power (right or privilege) to become the sons of God, even to them that believe on his name." He observed, that receiving Christ is the same as believing in him. There is no difficulty in this: receiving this candle, or a cup of water, is just taking it; so receiving Christ is just taking him, and saying he is mine. Now this is blessedly true: every sinner under heaven may say, "He is mine," for Christ is God's gift to the world—to every man that believes the truth about him : takes home to his soul the precious treasure given of God, and has Christ in his heart the hope of glory, &c.

7th.—WEDNESBURY. Brother Anderson and I preached in the open-air. Sixteen meet on Lord's day here to remember the Lord. Three decided after our last meeting on this ground. I have just arranged for several meetings in Birmingham.

BRUTAL FIGHT AT BIRMINGHAM.

I was passing along Suffolk Street, Birmingham, on Monday, the 12th, with P. Anderson, when we observed a crowd in Navigation Street. On arriving, found there had been a fight. One man's hand was bleeding, another's face; and great anger was manifested by one part of the crowd against another. Presently, a stout, middle-sized man came out of a large public-house close by, walked about in considerable majesty, squared about in a fighting posture, throwing his arms in various directions, and calling "Fair play, fair play!" This was evidently a challenge for some one to fight. A less man, more cool and deliberate, prepared to encounter him. P. Anderson and I did something without using force to prevent the second fight, but in vain. The multitude, with a few exceptions, evidently wished it. They pressed on the human gladiators, and the fearful encounter commenced. Soon blood flowed on the strong man's face; the other seemed weakened. Again we tried to persuade the by-standers not to allow the fight, but in vain; either revenge or curiosity induced them to urge on the combatants. My soul melted within me. Some looked for the police, but none were near. I was agonized by conflicting sentiments:—ought I to throw myself in among them, and hazard blows to save them?—was it right for the police to interfere in such a case? The police were sent for, but none came. P. Anderson had business, and we left—we could do no good. I accompanied him with my heart bleeding for the poor ignorant fighters. When I had got far away from them, and had time to weigh my duty, I thought if we both had resolutely got round one man we might have prevented the fight. Should we not have done so for a brother? What grieved me most of all was the brutality of the people, in forwarding and delighting in such a scene of blood. For ought we know, by this time one or both may have died of abuse or be injured for life. God never made the human body to be bruised and wounded by a brother's hand. He never made the strong arm to be lifted up to strike injury and death to a brother's heart.

We speak of the brutal sports of cock-fighting, and some even speak of its being natural for them to fight, although no one pretends that they came into the world with steel spurs on. But what is this to the amazing folly and wickedness of men, employing their very reason to the injury or death of a brother man? We condemn the brutal conduct of the men who keep dogs to fight, and delight to see these useful animals tear each other for the pleasure of man;—but if it be brutal for animals to be trained to tear and bite each other, how much more brutal for men to train themselves to destroy their fellow men!

I am told that these scenes often occur in this great town,—

"And men like brutes
Each other tear."

No doubt, as in this case, one main cause is strong drink. These men had been in the slaughter-house—the public-house—drinking together; there one class of workmen thought that another class insulted them, and therefore to settle the matter they would fight—as though that could remove the insult!

13th.—WEDNESBURY. A very large congregation; it had been well published by bills. Zion Chapel, Birmingham. The Baptist minister of this place is Arthur O'Neil. I was shown a book with this inscription:—"Joseph Cappur, Tunstall, Staffordshire,—To my friend and fellow-prisoner, Arthur O'Neil, Stafford jail, August 7th, 1844." On looking at its title I found it was my own "Christian Union." When we sow the seeds of truth they may germinate even within the dark walls of a prison. A. O'Neil's conduct since his liberation has proved that his prison-readings were greatly blessed to him. The chapel was given for the Lectures on the Remains of Popery in the Protestant Churches. After one of them, I was importuned to lecture on Mormonism, by Mr. Ellis, of Hockley, whose daughter was pregnant, and he said the Latter-Day Saints had made her little better than a common prostitute. A Mormon priest had offered her bed and board if she would live with him. The father had threatened him, if he received her. This priest is a married man with a family. So they are practising the Spiritual Wife doctrine in England.

TO LORD JOHN RUSSELL, FIRST LORD OF THE TREASURY.

This letter, as the Editor of the enclosed paper, No. 24 of "The Truth, the only way to the freedom, elevation, and happiness of man," I send you for the public good, and hope that it may be read with your own eyes, or be heard with your own ears. For several years I have conducted this or a similar publication, and I cannot do the good which I wish for three reasons:—

1st. The duty on paper is a hindrance. I cannot give as much matter for a penny as the wants of the age require. My readers consist chiefly of the working or middle classes, and would be greatly benefited and increased in number by the abolition of the tax on paper.

2nd. If the duty on advertisements were taken off, I should be able to make my paper more interesting and useful. I know parties who wish to advertise for servants, for the sale of goods, &c.; I also know servants who often require places, but cannot afford to pay the present price of advertising.

3rd. If the stamp duty on all small papers sent by post were one farthing each, or whatever might pay the extra labor at the post-office, leaving me at liberty, as at present, to send others, without postage, by carrier, it would greatly aid in giving knowledge to the country. These three changes would take off the paper duty, the stamp duty on newspapers, and the duty or tax on advertisements.

I would urge you to adopt this course by the great consideration that ignorance produces crime, and consequently the present laws, tending as they do to keep the people ignorant, produce crime. Knowledge purifies the minds and morals of those who receive it. You would therefore confer an invaluable blessing on this great empire by abolishing all the taxes on knowledge.

If you say, "How am I to supply the deficiency which the remission of these taxes will produce?" I answer, from any landed or other property, only do not tax the food of minds.

If you make this proposal now, I have no doubt you will carry it to a speedy and successful issue, for who will stand up in Parliament to advocate for the ignorance and crime of the nation? You will thus confer a national benefit upon your country, and become entitled to the lasting gratitude of all who love knowledge and virtue. Your friend,

Manchester, 6mo. 5th, 1851.   JOHN BOWES.

DOWNING STREET, 6th June, 1851.

SIR,—I am desired by Lord John Russell to acknowledge the receipt of your letter of the 5th inst., and of the accompanying paper.

I am, Sir, your obedient servant,

Mr. J. Bowes.   ARTHUR RUSSELL.

6mo., 11th.—LIVERPOOL. Attended at the open area, St. James' Market, to preach. Soon after I arrived on the ground, a moveable pulpit was brought; it was for a town missionary; about fifteen minutes after he came. I told him it was my purpose to preach, but we could divide the time. This he declined, and alleged that the missionaries occupied the ground two nights in the week. I stated that as I was on the ground first, if he did not agree to divide the time, I must begin first. He said, "We are servants of a Committee, and must abide by our instructions." I thought seriously of this afterwards—What makes them the servants of a Committee? Is it not the pay? Would any number of well-informed men place themselves under a Committee, if that Committee did not pay them? Suppose them to be laboring at first without such a committee and without hire, would they implore another set of rich brethren, of different denominations, to take the oversight of them and rule them, and submit their journals to such a committee? I believe the world furnishes no such instance. Christ's preachers are his free men, and they should call no committee their masters.—At last the missionary preached, having agreed to divide the time. He gave a very meagre discourse of heads and divisions, but brought out little or no gospel. I had a very large congregation when he had done.

22nd.—WAKEFIELD. Had a sweet time in the morning in the Tabernacle, where a number meet, and Christ is preached without hire. Afternoon, broke bread with a number of brethren, perhaps fifty, who meet in Christ's name alone. Once, on the first day of the week, the church edifies itself. The other two services seem entirely in the hands of one brother, who pleads for this state of things. I endeavored —from Acts xx., Thess. iii.—to show them that Elders should feed the flock and work. Now if there were six, why not allow all to feed, and work? for if they keep one without working, they could not keep six without working, and there would be some danger that the one would silence the other five! How rarely do Christians keep close to the Scriptures in every thing! At half-past six o'clock I preached the gospel for a short time in the same room; and at half-past seven had a congregation at the head of West Street. A Wesleyan Local Preacher asked me publicly if I could stay two months in Wakefield. I answered I could not. But I engaged to stay another night.

30th.—STOCKPORT.—Market-place. I had not been long speaking before a Roman Catholic began to ask questions. His friends and he created a disturbance till I asked if Stockport was to be governed by a mob, and if their religion led them to peace or disturbance? when a large meeting closed in peace. I stayed lecturing, discussing, and answering questions till I was too late for the train, and set off to walk, but was overtaken by a spring cart whose owner knew me, so I rode to Manchester. Arrived at home between twelve and one o'clock, having to rise early to get off to Scotland. I would not have missed the meeting if I had been obliged to walk all the way from Stockport.

7mo., 2nd.—Sailed from FLEETWOOD at half-past ten o'clock. During the night the sea broke over the vessel fore and aft, and washed the decks. I expected to arrive at Troon, but found the steamer now sailed for Greenock. We arrived safe on the 3rd, about half-past one o'clock. After taking trains as fast as I could get them, I arrived at New Mills just in time to preach, on the steps of the Town House, to a considerable and attentive congregation.

A MERCIFUL DELIVERANCE.

6th.—DALGIG. Preached and broke bread. At seven, preached at Cumnock to a large assembly. On riding home, on a blood mare, I had a very merciful deliverance. Dalgig is about six miles from Cumnock; I rode down easily and comfortably to the meeting. On returning home I overtook one of the domestics of Dalgig, who seemed to be tired with a long walk from her father's. I offered to walk a mile or two and let her ride. She was not willing to ride alone, but expressed her wish to ride a short distance if the mare could carry two. She had no sooner got on than the mare began to kick, and she got off safely and well. I then rode on quickly for nearly a mile, when, crossing a brook, the mare drank. Fearing she might take too much, I drew her off before she was willing. She had not gone many paces before she commenced kicking fearfully, and as I sat still she showed some symptoms of rearing, although she did not rear but was very restive. I was on the road, amid some great stones just behind, and concluded, as she seemed determined, not to risk myself any longer. I therefore took my feet from the stirrups and threw myself from her on to the turnpike; escaping with a few slight bruises. She continued kicking while I was on the ground, and some time after, till she groaned loudly. I walked home, and thanked God. The mare was never known to do this before with a rider, therefore her temper must have been disturbed by the two things just mentioned.

8mo. 12th.—STRATHAVEN. Have just concluded a week's meetings here. To-day, while walking out, heard a little girl crying bitterly across a field. I called to her but got no answer, but the crying continued. I crossed the field, and found she had been gathering dung with a barrow, and the wheel had come off, and she was now trying, without hope, to mend it. I desired her to give over, and after a little trouble I mended it; as she never could, and as she wheeled it away happy, I felt thankful that I had done something to lessen the sorrows of the world, if it was only the drying up of the tears of a little girl. How many tears might we wipe away were we to set our hearts on doing good. Two have been immersed here, and others are thinking about it, so that it is likely a church will be formed here.

THE CONDUCT OF THE AIRDRIE POLICE.

9mo. 2nd.—AIRDRIE. Bills were published for me to preach in the open-air, Graham Street, at 7, and in the Baptist Chapel at 8. I had a considerable congregation, when the following conduct of the Police was manifested.—First, a police officer came up, and desired me to come away, he wished to speak to me. I told him as I had commenced I could not leave the meeting, and that he might say what he had to say there. He replied that I could not be allowed to preach there, as it was forbidden. I then said to him what in substance will be found in my reply to Superintendent Findlay, whom he now brought.

SUPERINTENDENT.—We cannot allow preaching here, and you must desist, or we must remove you.

J. BOWES.—About two years ago we held a week's meetings on this very place, and there was no interruption; why should there be any now?

S.—We have got a peculiar population here, and it becomes us to be careful. See what took place at Greenock. You can go to another place behind here.

J.B.—This is the best place for a congregation, and the people are all quiet. It was not the gospel which disturbed the people at Greenock, but something else. But why should we be disturbed now, and not two years ago? Were you superintendent here then?

S.—No, I was not; but I was at another place.

J.B.—The law allows us to address the inhabitants on public property when we do not interrupt the thoroughfare.

S.—This is not public property.

J.B.—Why, it appears not to be private; whose property is it?

S.—The property of the borough.

J.B.—Then of course it belongs to the inhabitants.

S.—You should not preach here; if you do not desist I must remove you.

SEVERAL VOICES (to J. Bowes)—O never mind, go to the other place.

J.B.—I should be quite willing to go to the other place, but it is not so good as this; and I have reason to know that the Police in other places endeavor to prevent open-air preaching through their hostility to the gospel.

S.—This is a breach of the peace already. You see what a crowd is collected.

J.B.—If there be any disturbance of the peace you have caused it. We were quiet enough until you came.

S.—I am ordered by the magistrates to prevent assemblies here, and I have no desire to get myself into difficulty with them or with you.

He now called up Henry Walker, baker, as a magistrate or member of the town council, who appeared to sanction his proceedings. I then said I would consult the people, and if they thought we should remove, I would do so. The majority were in favor of a removal.

S.—If you had any fitness for preaching the gospel you would remove, but your conduct does not become the gospel. (Here he began to lecture me on what became me; and then an omnibus drove up, and at the same time a drunken man in a gig, when he exclaimed,)—There is an interruption of the thoroughfare! Come down, or I will take you to the station!

J.B.—You see there is room enough for the omnibus to pass. It is my regard for the gospel which induces me to claim a right to preach here, not because of any hostility to the authorities. We must preach the gospel to every creature, whether the authorities forbid us or not. I was adducing the case of Peter and John, whom the magistrates commanded " not to speak at all nor teach in the name of Jesus; but Peter and John answered and said unto them, Whether it be right in the sight of God to hearken unto you rather than unto God, judge ye," (Acts iv. 18, 19) but in the midst of this, the superintendent, with his own hand, took the chair from under my feet, which was a piece of needless interference, as he was aware that I had declared a majority wished me to remove. He had several police-officers on the ground, and one warned me to " walk away quietly, or I should see what I should get myself to." I made no answer; the people followed quietly to an open space beyond Graham Street, to whom I preached with unruffled mind the glorious gospel of the grace of God. Several policemen stood all the time; but when a drunken or disorderly man disturbed the congregation, these men, who are to keep the peace, allowed him to proceed without interfering.

I could not understand this interruption until afterwards, when I learned that the races were on the 4th and 5th; that the magistrates subscribe 30 guineas for a cup; Mr. Baird, the member of Parliament, 50 guineas; that the stands for selling drink, sight-seeing, &c., have let for above £300; that the races have only existed here two years; and that the ministers of the town preached against them the last Lord's day, and they supposed I should be of the same stamp. My object was not indeed to preach against the races, but to teach a religion which would find better employment for the people.

6th.—Visited the coal mines, New Mains. The coal seam comes to the surface, so that for several hundred yards it has been wrought from the top like a stone quarry. We descended far into the mine. The coal in many places was about twelve feet deep. Here also are several blast furnaces, where the iron-stone is melted. We saw the iron run off in a stream into sand beds prepared for it—the refuse, rising to the top, ran off first. The engine which sends the blast through the furnaces is the largest I have ever seen. I am sorry to say that many of the men at these works feel no interest in the religion of Jesus. What can be done to awaken them? I have attended a few meetings in this neighborhood, but seldom had many of the workmen present.

16th, & 17th.—Brother R. Dickie and I, with our wives, visited Alexandria, and preached to large assemblies. We were sorry to find drunkenness, and its companion licentiousness, abounding. After the last meeting, about half-a-dozen met with us who had believed the gospel before our meetings, and agreed to meet again with the view of attending to Christ's commandments. One circumstance was deeply interesting :—A man from Glasgow came up while brother Dickie was speaking, and was arrested. He spoke to me afterwards, and wished a private conversation, apparently deeply moved. I appointed him to meet us half an hour afterwards, but he came much sooner, and was overwhelmed with feeling, and seemed thankful that he had come to the meeting, or he did not know what might have been the consequence. I inquired what this meant, and he stated he should have committed suicide. It seems he has a wife in Glasgow, had been turned off work for drinking, and his sins had made his life miserable. If in the day of accounts this brand is found plucked from the burning, my brother laborer and I shall rejoice that we have not labored in vain. This is one of the great advantages of open-air preaching; many attend who would go nowhere else.

VISIT TO THE GREAT EXHIBITION OF 1851.

29*th*.—Having some business to transact connected with my publications in Sheffield, Rotherham, and London, I took the advantage of a Temperance Trip to Sheffield. At 10 o'clock p.m., I took the train for London. I could not restrain those in my end of the carriage from smoking cigars. Two more joined them at Chesterfield. They got a candle and commenced playing at cards. I took out my pencil and a paper to write down their conversation, which was the most trifling. When they had proceeded some time, they noticed my writing, and I asked them what they would think if all their conversation should be published. They said little, but defended their amusement. They had spirits in bottles, and some of them were very unreasonable : so after I had warned them, I left the carriage and got into another. I did not like to report them in that state of drink to which they had brought themselves. I was with a quiet family in the next carriage, and had some sleep. We arrived in London about eight in the morning, and as I was too soon for business, I made my way to the Crystal Palace—it was just opening.

I was more struck than I expected with the vast extent to which the wonderful talents of gifted minds had been devoted to feed the pride of mankind. Tens of thousands of persons are evidently employed daily on beautiful, but useless vases, carving, sculpture, ornamented glass, embroidery, &c., &c. There were some splendid productions of nature, such as large blocks of rock-salt from Cheshire, and coal from Wales and Derbyshire. The Paisley shawls looked well, and the Sheffield cutlery appeared to great advantage. A model of brewing attracted great attention. I was examining some diving apparatus in the form of a man, when a countryman came up and said to me, " What is his name?" thinking that this was a real man! While examining the figure or skeleton of a human being in the French department, a countryman said, " See what a number of wanes (veins) he has on his face." Several other singular expressions were occasionally used. What interested me much, were several large newspapers, published in the United States at $\frac{1}{2}$d, 1d, and 1$\frac{1}{2}$d each. I am glad they were exhibited, as they will teach to all lookers-on, that it is important to take off all duty on knowledge. It was pleasing to see the good order manifested by the vast number of about 70,000 which visited it when I was there. It was also pleasing to see the different nations blending their industry and arts together, as one family in one building. The renowned jewel, and the Queen of Spain's jewels, although attractive, gave me little satisfaction. I fear many such things will promote the vanity of the females, who were looking on these jewels, and several displays of silks, lace, &c., with uncommon earnestness. There is much here to foster the vanity of poor, puny man and woman. I spent four and a-half hours in the Exhibition, did all my business in London, and arrived in Manchester on Wednesday, about mid-day, not having my clothes off since I left home, and lived chiefly on biscuits and apples, as I frequently do when travelling.

SECT-MAKING AT YORK, UNDER W. TROTTER, J. WILLANS AND OTHERS; INCLUDING MY VISIT TO YORK.

On the 19*th* of the 10*mo.*, a letter from William Darley, a brother beloved, who has recently gone to reside at York, contained the following:—"I have been visited by Wm. Trotter and Thomas Smith, but I fear they hinder the union of God's dear ones." I felt deeply when I learned this, and hoped that there might be some misunderstanding which a little friendly intercourse might remove. On arriving in York to see, if possible, all the parties, I called on Wm. Darley, and inquired for T. Smith, but found neither of them. I however found W. Trotter, and as the object of my visit was the union of all hereafter mentioned, and it failed, and as many, both in York, Newcastle, and other places, will be anxious to know the issue, I shall give from my own memory, and that of other brethren, as fully as I can, whatever tends to throw light on the subject.

Having explained to Wm. Trotter the occasion of my visit, and that I had the same faith and views as when I broke bread with him at Otley, a few years ago; he said he could say the same, only circumstances had arisen since which caused some change of conduct.

I said, that Darley and I would be glad to break bread with those whom he met to-morrow, if they would receive all Christians; and if not, we could not. He vindicated the right of the church to exclude Christians, if they were tainted with B. Newton's errors, or if they had not a holy walk. I said that neither I, nor any that I had fellowship with, held Newton's errors, or walked as he did: why should we be rejected? That on one occasion, when one of B. Newton's nieces broke bread, as she had done years before, when the brethren found that she held her uncle's views, and stoutly defended them, she was separated. But this would not satisfy W. Trotter, while we would receive Christians from Bethesda; and while I was at Otley, he and I had a difference of judgment on faith, while I might be a Christian and hold it, a teacher was different from a Christian! I wanted to know if my views of faith were any bar to fellowship? but got no definite answer. The chief point of difference was this—he claimed for himself and the brethren authority to separate from, or keep out, the children of God at Bethesda (Bristol), Manchester, Birmingham, and everywhere else, all but the ignorant, who have pronounced against Newton's errors. I claimed authority for receiving all the children of God everywhere on the ground of 1 John iv. 1, 2, 6, 15, 20, 21; also v. 1, 2. He referred to 2 Thess. iii. 6—14, to show that Christians were warranted to separate the children of God if they walked disorderly. I said the case was not in point; that the disorderly walking WAS NOT error in doctrine, but "working not at all," and being "busy bodies," and that it was a perversion of Scripture to apply such a text in this case. But he said, we get the principle that it is right to separate from a brother—"every brother"—because it is said, "Yet count him not as an enemy, but admonish him as a brother." I said this meant that we were to treat him "as a brother," that is, in a brotherly manner; not that he really was a child of God. How could an idle man who would not work, and was a busy body, be a child of God? since John says, "In this the children of God are manifest and the children of the devil: whosoever does not righteousness is not of God, neither he that loveth not his brother."—1 John iii. 10. And Ananias said, "Brother Saul," (Acts ix. 17) before Saul's sins were washed away. (Acts xxii. 16) This W. Trotter intimated he might say as a Jew, which I admitted; and therefore the Christians at Thessalonica might treat an offender "as a brother" man, though not as a brother *Christian*. But, said W. Trotter, was he to be treated "as a brother" when he was not one? As this question was answered before, the reader is requested to consider what is said above, and I also showed that the Greek word for *as* is often rendered LIKE, as in Matt. xxviii. 3—"His countenance was *like* lightning;" not that it was lightning, but it resembled it. So, the idle man was to be treated kindly, as we treat a brother, not that he was a brother; the same rendering may also be applied to many other passages of Scripture.

I further charged upon such as would divide the church, what is said in Jude 19—"These be they that separate themselves, sensual, having not the Spirit;" and that they were acting the part of "Diotrephes, who loveth to have the pre-eminence among them, receiveth us not. Wherefore, if I come, I will remember the deeds which he doeth, prating against us with malicious words; and not content therewith, neither doth he himself receive the brethren, and forbiddeth them that would, and casteth them out of the church." This was just the sin of the meeting in question, they "cut off the brethren,"—acknowledged brethren—and therefore Rom. xvi. 17 applied to such alarming conduct—"Now I beseech you, brethren, mark them which cause divisions and offences, contrary to the doctrine which ye have learned; and avoid them. For they that are such serve not our Lord Jesus Christ, but their own belly; and by good words and fair speeches deceive the hearts of the simple." To this W. Trotter replied that it was about doctrine—"contrary to the doctrine." I said, yes, and their conduct was contrary to the doctrine of LOVE—that the sin of schism was with them. I could receive him as a Christian to the table of the Lord any where, where all God's children could be received, but I could not go in to any table where the children of God were kept out.

About this time the brethren Darley, Stonehouse, and Beeby came to seek me, and were present during the rest of the evening.

J. BOWES.—Do you (at York) receive all the Lord's people?

W. TROTTER.—In the meetings to which we object there are three classes—the ignorant, the half-instructed, and the intelligent. The ignorant we would receive, the half-instructed we should deal with and teach.

J.B.—And if you failed to convince them that they were wrong, you would reject them with the intelligent?

W. T.—Of course; we could do nothing else.

J.B.—A brother from Inverness wishes to break bread at Newcastle; the brethren object. Why? Because he has broken bread at Inverness. Why, what has Inverness done? Some one has broken bread with the meeting at Hull? Why, what has Hull done? Received one from Manchester. What has Manchester done? Received a brother from Birmingham. What has Birmingham done? Received a brother from Bethesda? It is thus you cut off whole meetings for no offence.

W. T.—But you did not say what was at the end of it. (He here entered into a long explanation of the history of Newton's errors at Plymouth and Bethesda.)

I also explained a few things which W. Trotter had left out, or but slightly touched, and asked, could there be any way of seeing any more of the brethren in York?

W. TROTTER did not see any use for it—the brethren, as *advised* by him, would not meet upon the subject.

J. BOWES.—W. Darley had been several weeks in York, why was he not received?

W. TROTTER thought his case was settled, so far as his Christianity was concerned; but he could only have fellowship on the ground of all other Christians being received. He only applied conditionally.

J. BOWES.—And why should not a Christian be received from Manchester, Birmingham, or Bethesda, since you receive a Wesleyan or an Independent, if a Christian? You have done right to reject Newton's doctrines, and any whose practice is impure; but not in rejecting whole meetings, so far as I know, sound in faith and practice.

Before we retired, W. Darley stated that a few, not expecting union with the Christians in Little Stonegate, intended to commence the breaking of bread to-morrow.

10*mo.*, 9*th.*—Four of us arrived at the room, Little Stonegate, a little before half-past ten; and when a considerable part of the meeting had assembled, I said, "I would like to ask a simple question—whether the table spread here was the Lord's table, and free to all the Lord's children; or if it was a table only for a party? if the former, I should be glad to break bread with them. W. Darley had been hindered four or five weeks, two or three brethren had now come, and if we could not feel free to break bread here, had determined to obey the Lord's command—'This do in remembrance of me,' in another place. I only entered the city after dark. Sought brother Smith, but did not find him; found only Darley and Trotter. The views of W. Trotter were not satisfactory, and therefore this must be my apology for putting the question before the meeting.

J. WILLANS, of Leeds, whom I did not recognise, although I had once met him for a short time at Liverpool, rose, and declined to answer the question. We had come here for an object. You have come here for an object; and having gained it should rest satisfied. He made several remarks which at another time and place I should have answered, and then commenced to pray, without either saying that they received all Christians or denying it, and without giving an opportunity for another observation. But as we were men of peace, and entertain the view that when the children of God meet to remember Jesus nothing of controversy should disturb them, we sat quietly by while they ate bread and drank wine; but we were not invited, any more than as though we had been heathens or publicans. J. Willans did all the teaching, and applied the first Psalm to the Lord Jesus; I thought it applied to the saints. In the course of the morning, the prayers embraced the one church, the one body of Christ, and desired that "no fleshly narrowness might hinder communion with the Lord's children;" yet were these Christians resolutely keeping out us, and hundreds of others. When the meeting was quite closed, and they were about retiring, I only said—"We are now prevented from breaking bread with you; will you now appoint a meeting to talk these matters over?"

J. WILLANS asked if Mr. Bowes would state the meetings he was connected with? and added, that I ought to make an apology for interrupting the meeting.

J. BOWES.—When I go to any town, as I do in preaching Christ and seeking the union of the saints, I enquire if any meet in the Lord's name alone; if so, I break bread with them. I meet at Manchester at two meetings, City Road and Cookson Street; at Birmingham, Waterloo Street. I have broken bread once at Back Canning Street, Liverpool; at Newcastle, where these brethren come from; and several other places in England. But as to making an apology, none was needed, as I explained the extraordinary circumstances in which I was placed. I had no other way left. I caused no interruption, for I never spoke after your meeting commenced till it was closed.

W. TROTTER.—If you were going to Bristol would you break bread with the people meeting at Bethesda?

J. BOWES.—If I found they held Newton's errors and practices I would not; but I do not know one that holds his opinions, and therefore I should; and if any child of God come from Bethesda to Manchester we should receive him.

J. WILLANS.—This has been settled five years ago. Mr. Bowes must have known it, and been quite aware before he came here. It was not very courteous to brother Trotter to bring it before the brethren.

J. BOWES.—When I came here I was anxious to know if we could break bread here. Brother Trotter gave an adverse opinion; but he was only one. I do not acknowledge that one brother should speak for the whole gathering. He was only one, and I wished to know the sentiments of the brethren. I meant no offence. If the brethren where I meet had been asked such a question, it would not have been thought requisite to offer an apology. I had none to offer, but what they had heard. It is now plain, that if I and these brethren cannot obey Christ's command, "This do in remembrance of me," in this place, as we feel it is binding upon us, everywhere and under all circumstances, we must do it elsewhere. Before I sit down, I ask once more and finally, will you meet us this afternoon to see if we can adopt any means to prevent two tables being set up in York? For as we are willing to meet with you on the condition that you receive all Christians, if you refuse, the sin rests with you, not with us; as we seek union with all who love Christ, and it is our great grief that his children are so much divided, as it is offensive to Him ; for if you turn out any child of God, you turn out Christ, and if so, we go out with our Master ; and if you take in all Christians we come in with our Master.

W. TROTTER.—I leave it with the brethren.

One thought it was decided already.

Another.—It should be postponed.

W. DARLEY.—I cannot suffer it to lie over any longer, as two or three of us intend to remember the Lord to-day.

Several voices.—"May the Lord go with you !"

This ended the extraordinary scene. We came away satisfied, beyond a doubt, of the thorough sectarianism of the meeting, and accordingly five of us met in the afternoon to remember our gracious Lord, the table being the Lord's—not man's—for all the Lord's people. And in the evening we wrote down the chief part of these notes, at the request of a brother, which contain all the material points as far as we can remember.

10th.—As W. Trotter had requested me to call on him again, I did so. In the course of a long interview, many things came up beside this great question of communion, which need not be noticed. I charged the meeting with loathsome sectarianism, not only with rejecting the children of God, but refusing even to converse with them ; that if an infidel or two had solicited a friendly conversation with us, in Manchester, we should have granted it. He vindicated their narrowness by a reference to 1 Cor. v. 11. I said none of these were Christians. This was admitted. He next read 1 Cor. vi. 9: "Know ye not that the unrighteous shall not inherit the kingdom of God ? Be not deceived: neither fornicators, nor idolaters, nor adulterers, nor effeminate, nor abusers of themselves with mankind, nor thieves, nor covetous, nor drunkards, nor revilers, nor extortioners, shall inherit the kingdom of God." We both admitted that these were unsaved, and I pointed out to him the beauty of this harmony : all that are Christ's are in the kingdom—all that are unfit for the kingdom are unfit for the church. He read Gal. v. 19-21—" That they which do such things shall not inherit the kingdom of God." I reminded him that two words were against himself, "seditions" and "heresies," rendered elsewhere divisions and sects. This sense was acknowledged, and that those guilty of making "divisions" and "sects" could not inherit the kingdom of God. He asked, Did I mean to charge this upon him ? I said if *I* were guilty of keeping out God's children, and causing them to set up other meetings when they were willing to meet with me, that I should solemnly feel my deep guilt, and acknowledge that I should be no more fit for the kingdom of God than a drunkard ; but, I said, God only knows the heart, and I do not judge you. But this I say, that both J. Darby, Wigram, you, and Willans, ought to be brought under discipline for dividing the saints ; and you know it is written, an "Heretic," or sect maker, "after the first and second admonition reject."

I said, " you are more sectarian than the Baptist, for he can adduce a Divine command for baptism, but you cannot for your new creed." He said there was a great deal to be said on that subject of refusing communion to the unbaptized. I reminded him that believers were all of the one family—that we were made children of God by faith—that whatsoever made us children of God made us brethren, and consequently all believers should treat each other as brethren—that the church is one body, composed of all the saved—and whatever it may take to unite us to the Head it should take, and no more, to unite us to the members of the one body. To this there was no reply. He objected that we received Morrisonians—that my views of the Holy Spirit's work were not scriptural, and quoted from an article in "The Christian Magazine," vol. iv., p. 137, signed A. lnnes. I stated that I was not responsible for all that appeared, that we had articles for and against Election, and many other subjects. After expressing my own views on this subject, and referring to the Christian Magazine, the subject dropped.

I and another brother who had previously visited him, had proposed prayer, but he had declined in both cases, as prayer was a part of communion; but I waive this for a few concluding observations on the whole case.

1. Supposing B. Newton's errors and practices to be as bad as they are represented, let him and all that hold them be responsible for them. Neither I nor those with whom I meet hold them; then why should we be made responsible for others' errors?

2. Before the Lord and his Church I lift up my earnest protest against the new creed, which at York, Leeds, and other places is being set up; which is no longer faith in the Saviour alone, nor the gathering of a meeting in the name of Christ alone, for all Christians, and all saints; for in addition to faith in Christ, peace with God, and love to God and man, you must profess that "you renounce communion with Bethesda," and with all who go here, from all parts of the kingdom, or come from there, except the ignorant. This is a creed which I never adopted—shall never adopt—and which stamps with schism all its abettors.

3. Brethren used to be strong in advocating the unity of the body, and claim to meet in the name of Christ alone. Now it is not the name of Christ—nor the faith of Christ—nor love to Christ, which recommends to their fellowship. A child of God may have all these in an eminent degree—may walk closely with God, but they all go for nothing unless he can resolve to separate himself from hundreds of the saved at Bristol, and scores of other places.

4. If W. Trotter, J. Willans, and the rest, ever come to a better state of mind, for which I pray, I shall rejoice over them; but in the meantime, let all the children of God know that they are setting up an odious sect. They who profess to have left sectarianism, are more sectarian than the sects themselves; for no ordinary sect would refuse those whom they exclude; the Baptists, Presbyterians, Wesleyans, and Independents would not. Such meetings show themselves to be a part of the apostacy and mystery of iniquity. There is something good in them which deceives the simple, and makes way for what is schismatic. It therefore behoves all the children of God to flee from it, or if in it, to come out of it, and leave the dividing of saints to Satan; and join the Lord Jesus and the Holy Spirit in promoting union with all saints.

13th.—Heard Mr. Cumming, commonly designated "the Rev. Dr. Cumming," in "The Theatre" at Liverpool, on "Romanism as it is." The Young Men's Protestant Christian Association charged 6d. Gallery, 1s. Pit, 1s. 6d., and 2s. for the Boxes and Platform. These high charges do not look well. There was much in the lecture to approve. Christ was set before the people. But one sentiment was most pernicious. He compared the different sects—Episcopalians, Presbyterians, Independents, Baptists, and Methodists, to so many different parts in music, all making one harmony, as though there really existed unity and harmony among the sects. I wish the forms of the meeting would have allowed me to ask whether there existed harmony and scriptural unity between the Puseyites and the Evangelicals, Churchmen and Dissenters, when they never preach for each other? What union between the Established and Free Church of Scotland? What harmony between the Wesleyan Conference and the Reformers? Our divisions instead of being lauded as harmony should be denounced as sin. They do not form branches of Christ's Church, but branches of the great apostacy. Primitive Christianity cannot be practised in any of them.

12mo. 25th.—MANCHESTER. It was thought desirable to hold a meeting to consider the unity of the church. Accordingly, a Lovefeast or Tea Meeting was held at half-past 4 o'clock; brethren attended from both meetings in Manchester, from Reddish, Stockport, &c. W. Darley was present from York, J. Grinstead from Batley, R. Hunter from Birstal, and T. Grundy, Ashton. The meeting was addressed on various topics, calculated to promote love to the brethren, and zealous exertion in preaching Christ.

My views on the Lord's coming changed this year, chiefly through considering the Scriptures, at some scripture-readings in Manchester. A brother from Sheffield promulgated his views. I went chiefly to prevent any bad results to the brethren from these extraordinary meetings; but such passages as Danl. ii. and vii., with Luke xix., I could not answer; and, after prayerful investigation, I was led by the Scriptures to see the near personal return of the Lord, the rapture of his church, the fall of Antichrist, and the restoration of Israel, as a prelude to the conversion of the heathen nations.

CHAPTER XII.

THE HOLMFIRTH FLOOD.—"FREE TRADE IN RELIGION."—GREAT WORK AT CHELTENHAM.—ROMANISTS MOBBED AT STOCKPORT.—CONVERSION OF MY SON ROBERT.—REMOVAL TO CHELTENHAM.—SUDDEN DEATH OF MY DEAR FATHER.—REASON.—LETTER TO THE CZAR OF RUSSIA.—THE STOCK ORT DISCUSSION.—WM. TROUP OF AMERICA.—DISCUSSION AT NEW SWINDON WITH G. J. HOLYOAKE.—"THE HYPOCRITE."—LETTER TO C. H. SPURGEON.—1852—53—54—55—56.

PRESTON.—During the first month I visited several towns in the north. At Preston broke bread at Meadow Street Chapel, and preached in Corse Street Chapel, now occupied by the friends of an unhired ministry ; and I delivered five Lectures on the Truth of the Scriptures, &c. Some months before, George Jacob Holyoake had been asked here to meet me in discussion, and excused himself by making a personal attack upon me. At the request of my friends, I replied before the public congregation, in the Temperance Hall, and the audience carried a resolution unanimously that I had vindicated myself satisfactorily from his unfounded charges. It is always a mark of a bad cause when an opponent resorts to personal abuse instead of argument. I very seldom notice these petty personalities ; I thought G. J. Holyoake had been above them, but have been mistaken.

THE HOLMFIRTH FLOOD.

2mo. 17th, 1852.—This morning I walked from Dunford Bridge station to the scene of the Holmfirth Flood. The reservoir is situated between two high and rocky hills. It seemed to be about sixty or seventy feet in depth ; a large chasm was made in the middle of the front, the remains of which showed, 1st, that the materials had been too loose ; 2nd, it had settled down several yards in two or three places, and had evidently been leaking, and not repaired ; 3rd, the back wash, intended to let off the surplus water, was not workable on the morning of the 5th February, when it burst. A little below lives a young man and his sister, who stood with several more, and witnessed the awful flood ; indeed, all the people above Holme Bridge had left their houses on the fatal night. Had the other people of the valley been equally alarmed, many precious lives would have been spared. Over and Nether Bilberry Mills are not much damaged, but the Digley Works, valued at about £12,000, are all swept away but two chimneys. Mrs. Hurst, the proprietor, was prevailed upon with difficulty to remove. At Holme Bridge, the church-yard bears marks of ruin. Below this, at Hinchliffe Copper Mill, six houses were swept away, and thirty-eight individuals asleep in their beds. They would not survive long. One man escaped by getting hold of several planks, and by making a desperate effort. Nineteen persons were in a house. The flood subsided sufficiently to enable them to escape. Other houses had fallen close by, and soon after they were got out the only room left standing fell in, but they were safe. Holmfirth presents a dreadful scene of ruin. Houses swept away—shops closed—property and life destroyed—graves opened. There are seventy-one buried, and about fourteen bodies not yet discovered.

It reminds one of the coming of Christ—some will be taken and some left. He will come as unexpectedly as this flood. Some were waiting for it in the dark night, and some will be looking for Him; others will be sleeping, and carried away by the flood of wrath. The amount of property destroyed is estimated at more than £250,000. Subscriptions are being raised for the sufferers. Some large pieces of rock or stone had been carried many yards, each weighing seven or eight tons. What an immense effect must Noah's flood have had upon the surface of the globe, when eleven acres of water can produce such devastation? What must puny man be in God's hands, when he resolves to punish, when one of his agent's can destroy, in a few moments, so many mills, houses, and lives?

"FREE TRADE IN RELIGION."

Such was the heading of a bill, calling a public meeting by the Voluntaries of Manchester, held in the Corn Exchange, March, 1852. No doubt the meaning of it is that ministers and people are to be allowed to make the best bargain they can with each other—that ministers are to be at liberty to sell their services at the best market, to the highest bidder, and the people to make such purchases, as they best can, without being compelled to pay church-rates, or tithes, or anything which may be prescribed by the laws of the realm. Now, such a view appears to me to admit that religion is a trade—a money making system—and, like corn, should be sold in the market. In opposition to such a carnal sentiment, I would supply another motto—

"NO TRADE IN RELIGION"—

as it comes from heaven in the teaching of Jesus, in his sacrifice for sin and his love shed abroad in the hearts of all believers by the Holy Spirit imparted to them there ought to be no trade in it whatever. Its preachers should proclaim it, not because they are salaried, but because it fills their own hearts. All their labors should spring from love. The gospel should not be sold, but given, as Christ commanded its early proclaimers—"Freely ye have received, freely give." All trade in religion should be abolished. The two things are opposite in their very nature. Trade in religion lowers it, and reduces it to the management of men, whereas religion is from God. It shocks the mind and chills the heart, to think that a society, whose excellent aim is to free religion from the control of the state, should publish it to the world as a matter of "free trade,"—thus dishonoring religion, and free trade itself. One cannot but rejoice that the millions of this country may now enjoy the bread that perisheth at a reduced price, in consequence of free trade, but for "the bread of life," freely given of God, they have to give no price at all, but only to take it as the gift of God.

"THERE IS NOT AN HONEST MAN IN THE WORLD!"

Such was the declaration of a passenger of considerable intelligence who sat in the same carriage with me as I journeyed, 3mo. 27th, from Manchester to Wednesbury. His idea was sustained by another who sat next him. I intimated that I should like to have a better opinion of my fellow-men, and asked what he thought of the martyrs—whether a man was not honest when he gave his life for his opinions? This was generally granted, so that we found that a man would give all that he had in the world for his life, but these devoted men gave up their lives rather than pollute their consciences. I said to this friend that he put himself before us in a singular position,—either he meant to affirm that he was the only honest man in the world himself, or, if not, that he was really a dishonest man. He accepted the latter, and declared that he was not honest, nor was any other man. I did not tell the people to take care of their purses, but when any one avows himself dishonest, and consequently thinks himself so, he cannot blame other people for being of the same opinion. It shows, however, that there must be great dishonesty, widely prevalent in society, before intelligent men can adopt an opinion so detrimental to the comfort of him that holds it. I had rather be deceived a thousand times as think the whole human race dishonest. If I feel, as I do, that however I may fail in carrying out my purposes, that I intend well, that my aim is the good of all and the injury of none, I cannot convict myself of dishonesty, if I know that I would not knowingly rob any one of a penny in any way. Why may not other people have the same honest intentions?

GREAT WORK AT CHELTENHAM.

Towards the latter end of the 3rd month, a great and effectual door for the Word was opened at Cheltenham, and has been a most joyous circumstance. A series of five lectures were delivered by request in the British School Room. Four different ministers presided. The lectures were well attended, and the Lord's blessing rested on them. They were followed by two discourses in the Town Hall, and one in Cheltenham Chapel, the late Rowland Hill's. Large crowds attended, as they did one lecture on Mormonism, one on Popery, and one on what Christian Churches ought to be. After the last, about 1200 people were told that they could think over the lecture, which had occupied about two hours and a half in its delivery, until the following night, and then come to the Town Hall and deliver their sentiments, testing the lecture by the Scriptures. Many came, and a few of different denominations spoke.

The Town Hall was now taken for Lord's days; and the gospel was preached out of doors in various parts of the town, and in the surrounding villages during the week. I was occupied from morning to night in conversing with the anxious. The first young man, pierced by the word, came into the vestry with a broken heart, accompanied by his brother. He lived with his mother, a widow, whose heart was made glad beyond all expression by his conversion. After a few had believed and been baptized, it was a question what was to be done? There was a meeting of Christians in Albion Street: they were met twice, for some hours each time, to ascertain if they would receive all the children of God? It was found that they would not receive from Bethesda (Bristol), or Liverpool, Manchester, Birmingham, or anywhere else, if they received the children of God from Bethesda; and it was granted that there were many children of God there; consequently, as the newly converted could not go to Albion Street unless all the Lord's people were admissable, a table was spread at the Town Hall, to which in a short time several Christians belonging to different denominations, and a few from Albion Street, came. Thirty-six professed to obtain peace with God through faith in Jesus. But many more were anxious and enquiring. For several days one or more professed faith in the Lord Jesus daily. Employment was furnished from morning to night to converse with those saved, or seeking salvation. The congregations continued large. Many Christians profess to have received much blessing during this Revival of the Lord's work. One said, "I have no joy apart from the Lord Jesus;" and at another time, "I seek to be more and more dead to the world." Several hundreds have been reformed; and some who never used to attend any place of worship, now attend regularly. Miserable families have been made unspeakably happy, and great joy has been diffused through the assembly of the Lord's children. Several Mormons have left them at Cheltenham, and a few Infidels have abandoned their infidelity, and embraced the faith of the gospel.

Suffolk Villa, Cheltenham,
4mo. 6th, 1852.

Beloved Wife,—

You will be glad to hear that there is as great a movement here as in Dundee when I first went. God has directed me to serve Him here, and I cannot move hence for sometime. Hundreds are moved by the truth. The place will hold above 1000, and many cannot get in. We have ministers asking me to their chapels—the rich and the poor crowding to hear—and the former offering to pay all the expenses of the Town Hall. God is indeed blessing poor souls. I should be glad if you were here to enjoy it. The place contains about 40,000 inhabitants, —inland—full of fashion—as fine as Bath; yet God is using me among rich and poor; you might have seen them weeping together. One day last week I dined with a magistrate—his wife a dear Christian. I have taken baths there twice. My present purpose is to stay two more Lord's days here, and see what the Lord may do for His own glory. I expect much and am not worthy to be thus honored.

Your loving husband,

JOHN BOWES.

6*mo.*, 2*nd.*—BEDFORD. In the open-air; many listened attentively and then we adjourned to the room which the brethren recently opened. It seems that the trustees of the chapel built for the late pious and laborious Mr. Mathews, have let the chapel to Mr. Higgins, formerly a Primitive Methodist minister, and thus, in fact, sold over the people, Mr. H. endeavors, by seat rents, collections, tea-meeting, class-monies, &c., &c., to make as good a bargain of them as he can. But as preaching immersion and the Lord's return does not meet his views, some of the preachers he has silenced, and one or two he has promoted. It is really amazing that a Christian people can allow themselves to be sold in such a way as this! About twenty or thirty see something better, claim Christian liberty, and now meet weekly to remember the Lord, without being dragged through the mire of priestly arrangements. I cordially wish success to those who have freed themselves from the trammels of such an unscriptural system.

7*mo.*, 1*st.*—Passed through STOCKPORT, where some Roman Catholics and Protestants have been guilty of destroying property and life. The Roman Catholic Procession, which took place on the 27th, was regarded as illegal. Some altercation had taken place between the Protestants and the Romanists. The latter proceeded to break the windows of St. Peter's Schools of the Established Church. The Protestants now hastened to the Edgeley Roman Catholic Chapel—destroyed the windows, pews, organ, priest's furniture, library, as well as the interior of another chapel, and many Roman Catholics were driven from the town. One life was lost, and many were wounded. Roman Catholic houses were emptied of their furniture, and it was destroyed in the street; in short, the large Roman Catholic population were driven away, beaten, and their property destroyed—many of them had to take shelter in barns and neighboring villages. As many persons have given their judgment on the causes which led to these lamentable riots, being in a better position than several, I will give mine also. For several years past I have preached occasionally out of doors at Stockport, and within the last two or three years have found the Roman Catholics the most impudent and insulting of any in the country. Seldom would they allow either me or other brethren to preach Christ in the open-air without creating a disturbance. From all this evidence I conclude that the Roman Catholics had become insolent, that the other inhabitants, not under the mild forgiving spirit of the gospel, but in their own natural indignation, could stand it no longer, and thus, most unwarrantably took the law into their own hands to chastise the offenders with uncontrolled vengeance. I think all parties may learn a lesson from these proceedings. 1. Roman Catholics may learn that, if they would enjoy their own religion in peace, they must not insult other people while quietly proclaiming the gospel. There can be no question but if they could have had their own way, open-air preaching would have been banished from Stockport. 2. They tried stoning in the dark in my case, and about two years afterwards, when I was several miles distant from the town, and none of my friends there to avenge, they were, by the general inhabitants, stoned in the dark to their heart's content, so that they were glad to flee. Those who dig a pit for others often fall into it. "Vengeance is mine, and I will repay, saith the Lord." Punishment often treads on the heels of guilty persecutors in this world; how much more in that which is to come? 3. Protestants should be ashamed of attacking Romanists with carnal weapons. Let them use the Scriptures, if indeed they love them, but have nothing to do with persecution—that should be left to the enemies of God and man. It is too much to expect that unconverted Protestants will love and forgive their enemies, but true Christians will find their interest in treating kindly and meekly those that oppose themselves, if God peradventure will give them a change of mind, so that they will acknowledge the truth.

9*th*.—CUMNOCK. In the Market Square; a large, orderly, and deeply attentive congregation. On taking my fare to-day at Hurleford for Cumnock, I gave the station-master 1s.6d. and required 4d out, which he gave me, and 6d. more, insisting that I gave him 2s., instead of 1s.6d. I thought at first he might be right, although I remonstrated; but on going away, and taking time to reflect, I remembered that I had only sixpences, and not a single shilling in my pocket; then I knew he must be wrong, so I took him back the sixpence, telling him that he was wrong, and that I was right; at first he was hard to convince, but took it back. When one is satisfied that another has made a mistake in one's own favor, honesty demands that it should be promptly rectified; for if no one should know of the fraud but God and a man's own conscience, they would have power enough to make him unhappy, besides a lesson of stern adherence to what is just, when you seem to have an opportunity to act otherwise with impunity, will not be lost on the poor, selfish, money-loving world.

13th.—STRATHAVEN. A very attentive congregation out of doors. Several brethren from Hamilton accompanied me. A few wish to meet in the Lord's name alone here. I think it important to remark here, that John Graham, tailor and draper, who had several marks of consumption about him twelve months ago, which continued till about three months since, when he commenced bathing in cold running water every morning about a mile distant from his house; he now seems quite strong, has no cough, and has no mark of consumption about him. Few people know the real value of cold water bathing. [He is alive yet and well in 1871.]

23rd.—DUNDEE. Here my heart was sad by the removal to a better world, a few days ago, of Euphemia Cooper, who was led to the Lord while I was pastor here eighteen years ago, and has walked as a Christian of no common kind ever since. With many trials in her family, she trusted in the Lord, and had a large heart of benevolence to the poor and the cause of God;—her benevolence would have shamed many wealthy professors. Perhaps few Christians in Scotland loved me with a purer or more constant love. She prized the truth which saved her beyond all expression to her death. I scarcely expect to look upon her like again.

26th.—EDINBURGH. Out of doors in Adams' Square; an attentive congregation. While I was giving an earnest recommendation of Jesus as a Saviour, a Roman Catholic was offended because I did not take my hat off at the mention of His name. I gave him to understand that religion consisted in the substantial knowledge of Christ, of faith in His death, burial, and resurrection, and not in *taking off hats*. How lamentable that persons trained in forms of religion, should be prejudiced against its chief parts by these puerilities.

5th.—Attended a sale at NEWCASTLE, and bought a printing press, no worse than new. I hope, if the Lord raise up the means, in a few months to set it to work. It is now seven years since it was first talked about. As the object will be to spread more truth through the land for the Lord's glory, if it have his sanction and blessing it will not labor in vain.

THE LUTON DISCUSSION.

A few of the young men of Luton having espoused Infidelity, a Christian committee was formed to arrange for lectures or discussion on the subject. As the former seemed to prefer discussion, Robert Cooper of London was engaged 8mo., 16th and 17th. The subjects were, the being of a God and the truth of the Bible. I pressed R. Cooper to account for the existence of man as he argued for the eternity of matter. He said that "there was a progression in creation, until inferior races produced superior races, and thus men were formed." I asked for facts, but could get none. R. Cooper did not tell us whether men came gradually from lobsters, or turtles, or monkeys, or elephants, or some other animals, contrary to all the laws of existence. In all nature, like begets its like, and has done for thousands of years. One race never rises into another, or falls into races below itself, nor could Mr. Cooper show this from history. What a most unphilosophical thing is Atheism!

The second night, he did little but read his own printed objections, which were easily answered, so easily that my chairman, Mr. Jordan, Druggist, said publicly that he could have answered them himself.

Mr. Cooper had to go to London the third night, so I lectured, and allowed the infidels of Luton to reply, as one of them had been telling Mr. Cooper what he should have said, great things were expected from him, however, he broke down. Mr Willis, and Mr. Fuller, dissenting minister, spoke in a strain calculated to impress the minds of thoughtful men.

The Infidels seemed very angry when the audience, almost unanimously, thanked me for the defence which I had offered in favor of truth. I do not look for such things, but such a course tends to prevent opponents from misrepresenting discussions, which I have found them prone to do. The general expression of opinion seemed to be that Infidels had less to say against Christianity than was supposed. The argument from the life, miracles, and resurrection of Christ seems to be unanswered and unanswerable. Mr. Cooper did not even bring the witch story, which he detailed at Dewsbury against the argument.

On the 19th, I preached the glorious tidings of salvation to a large concourse of people, under the shade of a tree, on a fine green. The darkness of night set in before the discourse was finished. I am always glad of an opportunity of preaching Jesus after the discussions.

CONVERSION OF MY SON ROBERT.

The duty of Christian parents to command and insist on their children attending the public preaching of the gospel, so that they may be benefited thereby, was forcibly illustrated in my own conversion when a boy, and is so now by the conversion of my son, Robert. I was to preach in the open-air in Manchester, and had commanded him to be there. Sometime before the hour for the preaching, he had a heavy parcel to take to the station, and he hoped it might take him so long that he would be too late to attend the meeting, and thus have a truthful excuse to give me. However, he got through in time, and came to the meeting. During the discourse I had told the people that if I had a thousand souls I could trust them all with Jesus. This arrested his attention, and he thought—"Surely if father could trust a thousand souls with Jesus, I may may trust one." These serious impressions deepened, and as I immediately after went from home, he sent me the joyful news by letter. The following is my reply.—

BIRSTAL, 10mo. 19th, 1852.

"Praise the Lord, O my soul, and forget not all his benefits."

MY DEAR ROBERT,—
Your letter has given me more joy than I can describe. It is the first word I have had from either you or John referring to the Lord Jesus. You say that you can trust your soul with God, and that you have fled to the Lamb of God that taketh away the sin of the world. This is indeed good news—the best of news. If you take Jesus, it will be better to you and me than ten thousand pounds. Look to Him as performing miracles; satisfy yourself that he was truly God and man; read the Scriptures concerning Him; receive remission of sin through faith in His blood; feel that you love Him much, because you have had much forgiven. Trust in the exceeding great and precious promises of God. Let

your whole soul trust in the precious blood of Jesus. Read carefully Rom. v., Heb. xi., also x., and they will show you clearly that Christ is indeed to be rejoiced in as a crucified Saviour. Our sins have deserved wrath; but the precious blood of Christ cleanseth us from all sin, as you read in 1 John i. 6—8. When you receive Jesus you are made a son of God, as in John i. 11, 12. Then you will become a new creature in Christ Jesus, "old things will be passed away, and all things be made new." I shall be glad to talk further to you when I return home. May the Lord be with your spirit. Your loving father,

JOHN BOWES.

REMOVAL TO CHELTENHAM.

Through the Lord's goodness, I and the family arrived on the 29th of the tenth month. No. 23, vol. ii. of the "Truth Promoter" was the first printed by our own press. It is devoted to the cause of God, and as we mean to print nothing but what is for the public good, whether we have much or little work, we shall have the satisfaction of a good conscience. We have been asked whether we mean to print other works beside our own? The answer is that we shall be able to print anything for the public good from our friends in all parts of the country. I have two reasons for commencing this business, First, I hope when I have got the press at command to do more good by it, than I could without it :—Second, as two of my sons have spent nearly the whole of their time, since they left school, in printing offices, it seemed desirable that they should be able to print our own publications.

3mo. 22nd. 1853—CHELTENHAM. This morning my youngest son, 9 years of age, I had to call before me, for having used some improper words to the apprentice. In the course of our conversation he said "why do you not give me a flogging?" I said, because I do not wish to flog you; I want to make you sensible of your error without. I can chastise you without flogging. "What can you do?" I can send you upstairs by yourself or keep meat from you, or refuse to speak to you. "I don't care," was his constant reply. I then tried to convince him that he had done wrong in saying "I don't care," but he persisted he had not. I appealed to his mother, sister, and brothers, whether it was a proper way of speaking to his father. They all gave it against him, and he maintained that he was right against us all. I left him, telling him that I could not be friendly with him unless he confessed his fault. About an hour elapsed. He said nothing to any one, but came into my study, gently opening the door, as much as to say, " may I come in ?" I invited him in. He wept much, and said, " I did wrong in saying 'I don't care;' forgive me, for I am very sorry, and I will not do it again." I clasped him to my bosom, forgave him, and kissed him. He then went to his mother, without being prompted, and told her what he had done, and kissed her. Thus a great difficulty was blessedly overcome by moral force, without the power of the rod, which in his case I have never used. He has been often reproved, but never beaten by me, that I know of.

4mo., 18th 1853.—CHELTENHAM. It is twelve months this day since a few believers met to observe the Lord's Supper weekly here. Ninety-two have met during the year :—48 have been added from the world, 20 from kindred churches and gatherings, 3 from the English Church, 1 from Countess of Huntingdon's, 5 from the Methodists, 2 from the Mormons, 5 from the Congregationalists, 8 from the Baptists, total, 92,

20 have withdrawn, or been put away, or removed to other places, 72 being now in fellowship.

During the year 63 have believed the gospel to the joy and peace of their souls,—62 have been baptized, and several are still inquiring. For this great work let all the glory be given to the Lord.

7th.—LUTON, BEDS. Brother Gibbs writes, " I must tell you that your labors at Luton have not been spent in vain. Six brethren met on the 3rd of April to break bread, and remember the Lord in his name alone, and we intend to take the New Testament for our rule and guidance. We have taken a room to preach the gospel in, which will hold about 200 persons, &c." I am glad the brethren at Luton have at length acted according to what they have long seen to be right, and as they have two or three preachers, I hope from them will sound out the word of the Lord, to the surrounding neighborhood.

WALES.—G. Lawrence has gone to Wales, having sojourned some months in Cheltenham, and hopes to preach Christ at Monmouth and the neighborhood. He is spreading " The Truth Promoter," Tracts, &c., among the lovers of the truth.

DEATH OF JAMES GRINSTEAD.

On the 16*th* of 4*mo.*, James Grinstead fell asleep in Jesus, at Batley, Yorkshire. Dear brother Hunter preached his funeral sermon, from which I extract the following:—" He was a native of Stockport, and was born in the year 1814. While a young man he lived without God and without hope in the world; indulging in the various pleasures and vanities of this life, as if there had been no God, and no hereafter. When about 24 years of age he came within the sound of the 'good news' in Liverpool, and conviction seized upon his mind, and he felt and acknowledged that he was a rebel against God. I shall, however, give you the whole matter in the language of him who was instrumental in enlightening his mind, and bringing him to Christ, the sinner's best friend.—' Cheltenham, 4mo. 27th, 1853.—Beloved Brother—God, is good. May the Lord indeed be with the orphans. . . . . In the year 1838, in Liverpool, there was introduced to me, by one of our leaders, S. Kent, a young man with a fine, open, intellectual countenance, but weeping bitterly, and in deep anguish of soul, a prodigal, so he confessed himself to be. He was not long seeking before he found peace in believing. He united with the church at Liverpool, as did also his young wife, who soon after fled to Christ. This young man was James Grinstead. Since that time until his death, there existed an attachment and Christian friendship that was unsullied by a single cloud. He became a Christian in Liverpool, and the age failed to make him a sectarian. I believe he uniformly refused to be called by any other name than that of Jesus. . . . . Yours affectionately, with kind love to all,—JOHN BOWES.' Soon after his conversion, he began to preach the glad tidings which had made his own soul happy, and continued to do so as long as he was able."

SUDDEN DEATH OF MY DEAR FATHER.

5*mo.* 24*th.*—MIDDLEHAM. My beloved father died here on the 21st. Had he lived until the 28th of June, he would have been 74. He was born June 28th, 1779. He had been out working, talking, &c., the day before, went to bed in his usual health on the 20th, and in the morning was found with life extinct, having, as the doctor said, died in sleep,—possibly from either disease of the heart or apoplexy. This was the kind of death which he had so often desired, if it pleased the Lord; he had a great desire to avoid a tedious sickness, and the Lord gave him the desire of his heart. I saw him the last, in October, 1852, little thinking that it was for the last time. He set me about a mile on the way, and as I took the last look of him when returning, I discerned the feebleness of age stealing over him, more than I had done before. The sad intelligence reached me at Cheltenham, on the first day of the week, and as I was above 200 miles from him, I travelled nearly the whole day. Having a solemn, silent day, with the exception of reading a chapter in the railway carriage to the passengers; one of whom had just been interring a mother, another a father, only seven weeks before. I read 2 Cor. v., and was glad of the opportunity of preaching the gospel. Found my aged mother unwell, but as well as could be expected. She was married when 23, and thus they had lived together 51 years, for she was only about 20 weeks his senior. A few things are all which I have either time or heart to write at present. He was converted to God, according to a note in his family Bible, "August 19, 1810," consequently when I was about six years of age. At one time in his life, he had fallen into the wretched habit of profane swearing. I have heard him state this evil was cured thus: He had a sheep-dog, a most faithful, useful animal, when the dog sat down and looked at him, as though confounded by his passion and his oaths. He was more confounded at himself, and I think never swore afterwards. His conversion I have related in the beginning of these pages, and must refer the reader to them. What a mercy to me. I had a father that really loved the Lord. I heard his prayers and exhortations—his oaths never. His government was strict, perhaps rather too severe. How he was respected by all that knew him, the deep sorrow manifested at his death proved.

I said, after the funeral, in a public discourse, what I will record here, that had I known his value at eight years of age as I do now, if any one had proposed to me £10,000 per annum for life, on condition that I should be deprived of him, or if I refused that, I should have my father, and be poor for life, I should have rejected the £10,000 per annum, and have preferred *such a* father and poverty. He who teaches his son divine truth not less by his walk than his speech, confers upon him a blessing to which no amount of money can be compared. Great is the responsibility of Christian parents, and their children. If the Lord has used me in the conversion of many souls in various parts of the kingdom, the day of accounts only can tell how much of this was owing to the prayers, exhortations, and conduct of my late very dear father.

REASON.

Not long ago, I was conversing with a Christian, who said, "your views of the Scriptures, I grant, are far more reasonable than mine, but I do not look at that, if the Scriptures have revealed any thing, I am bound to receive what they teach." This objection, I fear, lies at the root of many horrid and dangerous views which men take of God and his word. I cannot receive it. He who gave us the Scriptures, gave us reason, that we might be capable of perceiving that they came from him; for without this highest endowment of man the Scriptures would be useless. I conclude then, that if we only understood the Scriptures, we should see them to be perfectly reasonable, and if I took a similar view of the unreasonable character of my opinions to that of the objector, it would be the strongest argument to me that my opinions were unscriptural. If however, such objectors will bow implicitly to the Scriptures, let them know that the Scriptures appeal to reason. The first twelve addressed the Christian Church thus, "It is not reason that we should leave the word of God and serve tables."—Acts vi. 2. "Paul, as his manner was," went into the synagogue of the Jews at Thessalonica, "and three Sabbath days reasoned with the people out of the Scriptures."—Acts xvii. 2. At Corinth " he reasoned in the synagogue every Sabbath, and persuaded the Jews and the Greeks." At Ephesus "he himself entered into the synagogue and reasoned with the Jews." Acts xviii. 4, 19. It was while he "reasoned of righteousness, temperance, and judgment to come" that "Felix trembled."—Acts xxiv. 25. Now, if reason had been such a dangerous instrument, why did all the apostles employ it, and appeal to it? They evidently regarded it very differently from those who speak of it as dangerous in matters of religion; it may be dangerous to their irrational and unscriptural theories, and if they wish them to succeed, it may be policy to abstract this witness from the court, lest his powerful voice should be given against them. Paul said to the Christians at Rome, "present your bodies a living sacrifice, holy, acceptable unto God, which is your reasonable service."—Rom. xii. 1. Why did he urge them to this important duty by the idea of its reasonableness, if we are to decry reason? The apostle wished brethren to pray for the early preachers, he says, "that we may be delivered from unreasonable and wicked men." —1 Thess. iii. 2. This is a prayer which I desire my brethren to offer up for me, and all who labor with me, for I expect nothing but evil from "unreasonable" men. I have always argued that the reason of man should submit to the higher reason of God. These views accord with those of Richard Cecil. "How does Paul labor to make the truth reasonably plain? How does he strain every nerve and ransack every corner of the heart, to make it reasonably palatable? We need not be instructed in his particular meaning when he says, ' I became all things to all men, if by any means I might save some.' His history is a comment on the declaration."

6 mo.—During this month I preached the gospel at NORWICH and at YARMOUTH on the sands. At the former place I was prepared, having read the " Quo Warranto?" to expect a people prepared for more enlightened measures than in some parts of the country, and I was not disappointed. Many earnest minded men who work with their hands, and go out every first day of the week to the villages to preach, are impressed with the idea, that all gifted brethren in a church should teach and preach. I had a little intercourse with some of the Christians who meet at the Bazaar, under the pastorate of Mr. R. Govett, formerly a clergyman in this city, but who came out of the Established Church, and now meets in the Bazaar; about 570 are in fellowship. They expect the second coming of the Lord, and are endeavoring to prepare

for it. Mr. Govett himself holds lofty views of his own prerogative; has taken a stand against the Norwich Conference, which surprises many, as he has made great sacrifices for truth, and, more than perhaps any other minister in Norwich, gives encouragement to the brethren to exercise their gifts, while however he remains the sole pastor and ruler. I found here that my discussion with G. J. Holyoake had been read at a meeting of the city missionaries. Those who have studied it, seem to think that the last night's discussion on "Man's responsibility for his belief and conduct," in opposition to the view of Mr. H. that he is only a creature of circumstances, entirely overturned the infidel arguments adduced, and established on a firm and lasting basis, the accountability of man.

10mo., 27th.—MANCHESTER. Having been away twelve months I was much refreshed by meeting the brethren in their meeting room, off Great Jackson Street, Hulme. Some attended from both meetings. I had a very narrow escape to-day, from what might have been a serious injury. The great rain had covered with water a part of the railway; as I crossed at Stockport, my feet slipped and I fell on the rails, cut my lip severely and expected I had broken my front teeth; but through mercy, although disfigured, I was not severely injured. No train was there. Thank the Lord for his Fatherly and preserving care.

12mo., 4th.—BIRMINGHAM. Not quite so many broke bread in Ann Street, at half-past ten, as I have seen, but some are unwell, and the morning was unfavorable. At half-past six, I have not had a more powerful sense of the greatness of divine truth and the nearness of God for many months. Aged persons wept like children. I trust angels saw some sinners repenting. Some seem anxious for a month's meetings here, which we can have if the Lord open the way.

TO THE CZAR OR EMPEROR OF RUSSIA.

SIRE,—I have been lately deeply affected with the immense responsibility which you have assumed in your warfare with the Sultan's armies. Much human blood has been shed which might have been spared. And who has originated this dark stream? Not the Government of the Sublime Porte; for it first conceded to Prince Menschikoff all his demands, and afterwards gave all the liberty to the professors of Christianity in the Greek Church which can be reasonably demanded. Finally, there was nothing to settle between Russia and Turkey but what might have been accomplished by persevering deplomacy. Consequently, the marching of your armies into the Danubian Principalities must be regarded as an act of aggression, and this fact makes you the real cause of the terrible war which has begun to rage.

When one sovereign has the supreme control of 60,000,000 of subjects, when he has only to command his hundreds of thousands of soldiers and they advance at his bidding to victory or to death, the lives of milions are in his keeping. How awful his responsibility! Already intelligence has reached us that many of your superior officers, and hundreds, if not thousands of your own men of war have been killed. I would remind you that God has made of "one blood all nations that dwell on the face of the earth," and that he wishes them to regard each other as brethren, and treat each other kindly. Had Turkey marched her armies into your dominions and slain your troops, you might have charged the murders you have committed upon the Sultan; but since you have been the aggressor, the blood of thousands is in your skirts. How terrible it must be for you to stand before God and give an account of this wholesale murder! If a man commits one murder, in this country, he is arrested, tried, and condemned to the gallows,—the last part of the sentence I disapprove of, for I think one might make a better use of him than this; but if society arrest and condemn the offender who takes one life, what ought to be done to him who takes thousands? Nay, unless you recall your men of war, who can tell where the evil may end. The greater part of the civilised world may yet rise up in horrible war with you, and tens of thousands of your fellow-men may perish through your rashness and recklessness of human life. Then mankind will regard you as the great author of all the misery that must accrue to your own subjects or to others.

I see you stimulate your subjects, or slaves, to war by the consideration that they are fighting for "*the orthodox faith.*" But surely it is not "faith" in Christ to which you refer, for he never taught his disciples to kill people; he said, "Love your enemies;" "Resist not evil;" "Overcome evil with good." "My kingdom is not of this world, if my kingdom were of this world then would my servants fight." If you had faith in Christ and love to him you would resemble him; you would "go about doing good;" but as it is, you go about doing all the evil you can, it would be difficult to find any human being doing more injury to society than yourself.

I suppose, were I in your empire the writing of this letter would cost me my life; but happily I am neither in your power, nor do I fear you. No one is responsible for this letter but myself. I write it because I wish you to repent of your deeds of darkness and cruelty, to become a new man, and act worthy of "the orthodox faith." If you have faith in Christ you know that "he loved us, and gave himself for us;"—that "he died the just for the unjust," that "we might be reconciled to God through the death of his Son." If you were at peace with God, and your conscience, you would not seek to disturb the peace of the world. We were placed here to serve, not to kill each other. If you did find enemies to Christ and to yourself, you would attack them by other weapons than swords and bayonets: you would say, like the great Apostle of the Gentiles, and what all Christians ought to say, (but you do not understand Christianity, and are no Christian except in name) "We do not war after the flesh: for the weapons of our warfare are not carnal, but mighty through God to the pulling down of strongholds, casting down imaginations and every thing that exalteth itself against the knowledge of God, and bringing into captivity every thought to the obedience of Christ." If you were a Christian those words would weigh with you. I quote them to show you how unlike a meek, gentle, follower of Christ your wars show you to be. I write this remonstrance that it may appear as the protest of one man against the gigantic wrong which you do; and although this warning is put forth in obscurity, truth is great; when sown, we know not where it will spring up. For the sake of bleeding humanity, and as you would escape eternal misery, cease your war, and if not, I at least feel clear, having uttered this warning, and pray that the God of love—the Omnipotent, may cause your wrath to praise him, and restrain the remainder.

I have no sympathy with Mahomedism, and if the Christians of Turkey are suffering, let them be told rather to suffer wrong patiently as Paul and Christ did, than kill people. I do not suppose, however, that your concern is so much for them as for the gratification of your own ambition in stealing your neighbor's territory. Ahab killed Naboth and then took possession of his property; you have taken possession first and killed afterwards.

Wishing you a better state of mind and heart, for the sake of suffering humanity,

I am, your sorrowful, and unknown friend,

JOHN BOWES.

5 Grosvenor St. CHELTENHAM. 12mo., 6th, 1853.

5mo. 2nd. 1854—LIVERPOOL. Intended to preach out of doors near St. James' Market, but found it too cold and windy; spent the evening in visiting. About ten o'clock began to think of looking about for a bed, but two or three friends were full, so I inquired for a Temperance Hotel, and found accommodation at Harrison's, Mill Street. I had not been in the commercial room many minutes, before the only gentleman present said, he thought I resembled a preacher that he remembered having heard at the Prince's Pierhead, some ten years ago, before his own departure for New Zealand. I said I was the preacher; for I had preached out of doors often in Liverpool for the last seventeen years. His joy seemed great that we had met. He had derived great spiritual profit from the open-air meetings; and we talked together of the things of God for some time, when it was arranged, as his brother had departed that day, that I should take a bed in the same room with himself. In the room I knelt down to pray, after I rose from my knees, he asked me to pray with him. I asked him to read a chapter, upon which I offered some remarks and prayed with him. We talked together until he talked me asleep. Who can doubt the providence of God? During seventeen years I have visited Liverpool, and never have needed to seek a bed before; yet this night I was directed to a place where my own soul was refreshed by good tidings of the result of seed sown ten years ago; and the joy of my friend was equally great at our meeting. How sweet it is to be guided by the Lord in the smallest matters!

18th.—Have just concluded four lectures in the Milton Hall, NORTHAMPTON, against Infidelity. We published large bills, and invited R. Cooper to defend his "Infidels' Text Book." In reply, the infidels issued a bill, intimating that I had behaved ungentlemanly to Mr. Cooper in the Dewsbury and Luton discussions. And that he would deem it inconsistent with his *self-respect* to meet me in debate; but he would be willing to meet any clergyman of Northampton! On this proceeding I make the following remarks:—1st. It is a mere pretence and not true, that I acted at Dewsbury and Luton as Robert Cooper affirms. The people who attended these discussions know that it is not true. I called him no names; I did not strike or abuse him. The head and front of my offending was, that I used strong arguments against Infidelity, with which Robert Cooper could not grapple, or he would have thrown aside his childish whining about my "unfairness," &c., and come forward at Northampton to defend his book. 2nd. Although two or three infidels occupied all the time after each of the four lectures, not one of them defended the "Infidel's Text Book," so that all now seem ashamed of it. 3rd. In regard to his preference to meet a "clergyman" of Northampton, it is evidently because they lay themselves open to the attack of the infidel in being hired, and many other errors, whereas I have nothing to defend but the pure Word of God.

I also spent two Lord's Days here, the 14th and 21st. Two precious souls found peace, and one has taught the gospel to his wife, who now also rejoices in the Lord. The work here was so great and so encouraging, that I wrote the brethren at Cheltenham, not to expect me home on the 21st.

NORTHAMPTON, 5mo., 20th, 1854.

BELOVED BRETHREN,—

It is because the Lord's work has opened out so greatly here, that I shall not be with you to-morrow. Nor will brother Anderson; you are therefore cast, where it is always sweet to cast ourselves, on the guidance of the Lord. I am his servant, and as such cannot do my own will. If you are taught of him you will not keep away from the meeting because I am not there: it will be your joy that Christ is with you. I have often thought that I should not feel any concern to be with those at all who would only meet with you because of my presence. It would not be worthy of our labor to have a meeting at all for such. If they meet on man's account, they may as well do that in the sects as with us. Not that we should give any countenance to the sects, for if we believe them to be Babylon, God's word to us is, "Come out of her my people, that ye be not partakers of her sins, and that ye receive not of her plagues." Rev. xviii. 4. The Lord give you all to see this. If we meet around the Lord, and not around any one man,—then we shall meet in the Lord's name alone, because the Lord himself is present wherever two or three are met in his name. This is your joy and mine.

I shall expect to give you an account of what the Lord is doing in several places where I have been, either on Tuesday or Thursday evening, when I hope to return, if the Lord will. One soul found peace and joy in believing, the last Lord's Day. John Leadbeater, the last year, while I was here. He is a "Friend" or Quaker, and since then his wife seems to have learned the Gospel from him. Indeed God is working by our tracts, "The Truth Promoter," and by lectures and discourses. I am encouraged when I think that so many brethren in different places are praying for me. May the Lord bless those who teach and preach with you; pray for them. If you cleave to the Lord and to one another, I cannot but think that your love and zeal will increase, and that the good Lord will make you a blessing to many in Cheltenham and the villages. Nine of us went to Harpocl last night, a village four miles off, where we had a glorious meeting, of which more when I see you. We expect hundreds to-morrow here. The Lord give grace in abundance that many may be turned to him.

From your loving brother, in the service and hope of the near coming of the expected King.

JOHN BOWES.

To the Christians assembling in the Town Hall.

6mo. 6th.—To-day my only daughter, Ann, was married to Samuel Lees, of Bolton. We spent the forenoon in reading the Scriptures which relate to the duties of the married state, in singing and prayer, and at 3½ o'clock they left us. May the Word of God be their guide, and the Lord Jesus their all in all.

12th—I am to-day fifty years of age, and have thus lived half a century, having preached Christ thirty-two years, seventeen of which I was hired, and fifteen I have been unhired; the last have been the happiest of my life. Left Cheltenham for STOCKPORT, where I arrived in time to preach in the market-place to a considerable congregation. One man asked a question, and then walked away, saying, "You are hired!" so that, although I receive only support not hire, as the great mass of those who preach statedly do, I must, with strangers, suffer this reproach.

25th.—LEEDS. In the Bazaar. About 30 broke bread. At half-past 2 at Vicar's Croft. The Town Missionaries gave me their moveable pulpit. The rain came on, so I finished in the Bazaar. At 6 the same place was decently filled, but an immense congregation at Vicar's Croft at 8. I should think two or three thousand. I spoke to them until my voice failed. A Romanist objected. I left Wm. Darley to reply, as my friends were afraid I should hurt myself. The Lord bless Leeds. Here are some of the blessed of the earth. While at Leeds, I was kindly invited to spend a few hours with the clergyman of St. James's, Mr. Jackson, who really seems to be an earnest Christian. Both in his church and the parish church, the Lord's Supper, and an offering for the poor, are weekly. I had an opportunity of hearing from him how my old colleague, Robert Aitken, A. M., now a clergyman in Cornwall, is going on. He had been preaching in Leeds eight days before. Should the correspondence between us be published, if I live to write my own life, the world will know what I think of this popular preacher, and if not, the roll of letters will fall into the hands of those who will do justice.

7mo., 26th.—GLASGOW. I started for Glasgow, the others for their destination; as I had no time to give notice, I borrowed a chair, and stood up among the shows on the Green, near the High Bridge. When I was about half through my discourse, a person came close to me and stood upon an erection, as an auctioneer, to exhibit wares. I consulted the people, who proposed that we should retire to the grass farther back—a kind friend took the chair—we were followed by hundreds, our congregation doubled, and a deeply solemn time we had, while I exhorted them earnestly to prepare for what is coming on the earth. The young man that carried the chair said he had been very wicked, until two of his children died, and as they were unbaptized, he wondered if they would be saved or lost! This singular idea led him to be thoughtful and sober. Why should any reasonable man think that a few drops of water falling on a child from the hands of a priest, would save it from hell and prepare it for heaven! When will such superstitious views of the God of love be banished from the human race? I rejoiced in this opportunity to preach Jesus to this anxious soul, and hundreds more.

29th.—Called and saw a brother or two at HAMILTON, and intended to visit WISHAW, but was hindered, not because the cholera has swept away about ninety in the district, some of whom I knew, but no train answered. I saw a few Christians at AIRDRIE, where the Baptist church now edifies itself, and thus all the gifted brethren have liberty of ministry. Mr. Waldbrun, the late pastor, who publicly called in question my views on the ministry, has gone to his long home. I fear some ministers shorten their days by immense mental toil, unbalanced by proper bodily exertion; if they would work an hour or two, at least, each day with the spade, as I do when at home, they would no doubt prolong their days. Left Glasgow for Greenock by the 4 p.m. train, which was so crowded with Glasgow merchants and people, now crowding down to bathe in the waters of the beautiful Clyde, that when we arrived about four miles from Greenock, one half of the train was left,

I was in the second part, and feared I might not get the steamer in time for evening preaching. Such a crowd surrounded the steamers, that I could hardly discern the Helensburgh boat, it seemed to have no name up; when I found it, it had just put off from the shore; I threw my carpet bag on board, and as I saw no other way, I hoped the Lord would preserve me while I leaped on board, which was done and all well. About twenty in fellowship at HELENSBURGH, who meet in Eastburn Chapel.

31*th*.—Had rather a remarkable party at Brother Dickie's at dinner; Mr. Lee, Baptist pastor, Glasgow; Mr. Anderson, Free Church minister, near Turriff, who has heard a few times; an officer in an Irvingite Church, Woolwich, who married an old servant of brother Dickie's; so that with our kind host and myself we were five preachers. The preacher from Woolwich seemed eager to teach us his views. How did his church get their twelve apostles? They say by revelation. But what proof have we that the man who said he had it from God, had it not from himself, or Satan the father of lies? They work no miracles—they have not seen the Lord—they will have no thrones; for these are to be filled by the first twelve. This is evidently a dangerous delusion; happy are they who treat these apostles as the church at Ephesus did—Rev. ii. 2. A very interesting incident was mentioned concerning the conversion of this servant. The Lord had used brother and sister Dickie in the conversion of a previous servant, who was acquainted with this young woman, when a very giddy, worldly girl; the former prayed for her, and desired that something might bring her under sister Dickie's care, that she might be converted. Little did she know that she was praying herself out of her place, but so it happened. Providence answered her prayers, brought the thoughtless young woman under the influence of her master and mistress, and ultimately she became not only a servant, but a converted servant, in which no doubt all parties had great joy. How often does the Lord gladden the hearts of his people, who seek prayerfully the conversion of sinners, by giving them the desire of their hearts; and often in a way which they do not anticipate. The giddy girl was now the staid matron at the table with us.

8*mo.* 13*th.*—NORWICH. Having understood that a few brethren meet here, I went to their meeting. I gave two or three of them to understand that if they received all Christians I should be happy to break bread with them, and if not I could not apply. This question was not settled to my satisfaction. Those who wish all Christians to be united and who live in Norwich, must decide for themselves whether the meeting is sectarian or not. I sought out Travers Madge, and found him. He was a student in the Unitarian college when I first met in with him. Then he doubted the system, now he has rejected it and has come as a poor lost sinner to the only Saviour. My spirit was refreshed with his. May the good and great Redeemer make him useful. I was also introduced to Mr. Crompton, whose sister Mr. G. Dawson, of Birmingham, married, he also is now away from the Unitarians. Yes, these men of boundless toleration! could not tolerate their own minister any longer, but expelled him from the chapel, because he preached to them too much of Jesus! He now confesses both the Godhead and manhood of Jesus, and preaches to a considerable number of different classes. I also learned while here that another celebrated Unitarian minister, Franklin

Howarth, of Bury, has abandoned that half-Jewish, half-Christian system.

18th.—Was delighted when I arrived at home to find my family well. Having travelled 1800 miles since the 24th of last month, and addressed in Scotland and Norfolk about 10,000 people, on the most momentous truths that can possibly occupy the attention of man. The Psalmist said, "O how I love thy law! it is my meditation all the day;" and surely those love the gospel law of love, who approve, admire, and obey it. If we love it as we ought we shall not violate but support it, and delight to do it, as the Psalmist of old said, "Thy law is my delight." To have great joy in the Lord's service we must be whole-hearted in it. I should think the true believer in Jesus who is like him, enjoys inexpressibly more happiness than the most indulgent worldling. "Whom having not seen ye love: in whom, though now ye see him not, yet believing ye rejoice with joy unspeakable and full of glory." No one can silence the song of the Christian. No poverty, or pain, or neglect. He blesses God for all; not only says, "thy will be done," but would not alter his lot; he most highly approves God's providential dealings as well as his written commandments, and blesses him for sickness, it purifies him; for poverty and disappointments, they wean him from earth; for he only can "count it all joy when he falls into divers temptations," or trials. He only can "rejoice evermore and in every thing give thanks." He only can "rejoice in hope," looking for that "blessed hope" the glorious appearing of the great God even our Saviour.

THE EFFECT OF CHRISTIAN BENEVOLENCE.

True Christian principle may be seen in the following case, which I regard with feelings of unmingled satisfaction. The brother who wrote the following letter has acted in such a manner as to encourage benevolence.

EVANSVILLE (Indiana), Nov. 12th, 1854.

DEAR BROTHER BOWES,—

A good many months have intervened since I have had the opportunity of hearing from you, and as I have delayed so long in writing, I have no doubt but you and the other Christian brethren to whom I stand so much indebted, will by this time think that it has become with me according to the old adage, "out of sight out of mind." But let me assure you that such is not the case, for I will ever consider myself under deep obligations to the various churches and Christians who contributed so willingly on your recommendation to aid me in moving my family to this country. I am glad to inform you that by the aid of Divine Providence, I am now prepared to return the amount received through you for the above object, and will feel obliged if you will return the same to the various sources from whence it came, with my heart-felt gratitude and earnest prayer that they may be enabled to do many such acts of kindness to others as they have done to me. The following are the names of those to whom I stand indebted, viz.: Helensburgh, near Glasgow, £1; Birstal, near Leeds, £1; Birmingham £1 10s.; Clatt, by Old Rain, £1; Dundee, £1; Manchester, £1; Aberdeen, £2. . . . . And to save trouble, I intend to send it altogether, with a few shillings over to defray the expenses of transmitting it to the various persons above mentioned. . . . . I am in the steady employment of a coal mining company, who are sinking a coal pit about two miles from our house, on the banks of the Ohio river, about a mile below Evansville. . . . I should be very glad if some Christian men would come to this place, who would not be backward to declare the counsel of God to a sinful and unbelieving people; if you know of any such, send them here. We feel very much the want of a few Christian friends to meet with on the

Lord's day. Any brother or sister coming from either England or Scotland, will find our house a home till they are employed, if they bring a recommendation from you or any of the Christian churches. . . . . Yours in love,

WILLIAM TROUP.

I wrote and received the money. Several of the meetings and brethren appropriated it to the tract and publication fund; a few took it for local purposes, as no other brother seemed ready to go. The above extracts will sufficiently explain themselves. It is cheering that our brother has shown such disinterestedness. He has not yet been away from us four years, and yet, with a large family of small children, by the blessing of God, he has now land of his own, and steady employment, with upwards of 6s. per day, and has been able to return £10 10s and send 10s. for publications. May the Lord give grace to our brother and sister to meet together till the Lord sends help.

THE STOCKPORT DISCUSSION.

This discussion took place according to the following bill: " Important Discussion in the Lyceum, Stockport. A Public Discussion will take place on the evenings of Wednesday, Thursday, and Friday, Jan. 17th, 18th, and 19th, 1855, between Mr. John Bowes, of Cheltenham, author of the "Truth Promoter," and Mr. Joseph Barker, of America. Question for Debate—'Are the Scriptures of the Old and New Testaments of Supernatural Origin and Divine Authority; and are the doctrines contained therein conducive to morality and virtue.' Mr. Bowes to take the Affirmative and Mr. Barker the Negative." Thomas Bailey, Esq., was chosen Moderator, and acted as Chairman, by the consent of Mr. John Humphries, chairman for J. Barker, and Mr. Jas. Hargreaves, for J. Bowes. The Moderator kept excellent order. The meeting was attentive and quiet each night. Mr. Barker crowded his speeches with objections—how they were replied to the Report, which is published, will tell, and due justice has been done to both sides. Cheering and hissing were avoided. The discussion is likely to do immense good, as well when read as heard.

I preached at STOCKPORT on the 21st, and had the pleasure of preaching the gospel to some who held with J. Barker, especially his committee.

SECULARISM AND CHRISTIANITY AT BLACKBURN.

I delivered three lectures here on the 7th, 8th, and 9th of 5mo., 1855, on the above subjects. The Chair was taken by three different ministers, and we had discussion after each lecture. W. Barker, Baptist minister, one of the chairmen, thus wrote of the meetings.—" The services were well attended, and the chair taken each evening by a minister of the gospel. The lecturer treated his subjects with a masterly hand, shewing from history, and from present facts, as well as the writings of modern infidels, that they have never fairly assailed the authenticity and divine origin of the Bible; nor proved by any real arguments the falsehood of Christianity. He proved that one routine of objections, from age to age, had been dished up, by infidel leaders, for their deluded followers, and that as often, the Christian advocate had successfully shewn the misery and death contained in them. The discussions which followed after each lecture, were of a far more satisfactory character than any previously held in Blackburn. Both the lecturer and his opponents seemed anxious to elicit the truth, and it is hoped the concessions made, on the last evening, by a gentleman, formerly an avowed sceptic, shew a disposition on his part to give to Christianity a fair hearing, and to study it for himself, apart from contending sectaries, and dogmatic creeds."

DISCUSSION AT NEW SWINDON WITH G. J. HOLYOAKE.

7mo. 18th.—At three o'clock, I received a letter from W. Ridley, Wesleyan Local Preacher, urging me to go to New Swindon to meet Mr. Holyoake. On reading his placard, and seeing his lectures were free, and being assured by my friend Ridley that Mr. Holyoake's friends would give me equal time, I took the Great Western train at 5.5. p.m., and arrived in due time. The Christian friends were not a little pleased to see me. Mr. Holyoake fell into the arrangements with a tolerably good grace. His first speech was an hour, mine the same; and then we had fifteen minutes each. The hall was crowded to overflowing. The second night Mr. Breeze, Baptist minister, kindly granted his chapel, and at the request of the meeting presided. This place also was crowded to overflowing, although it will contain double the number of the other hall. Mr. Holyoake's progress from Atheism to faith in a God, were expressed over and over again in such sentences as "Just in the sight of God,"—"accountable to God," &c. I reminded him that in our discussion at Bradford he was an Atheist, and congratulated him on the change, which he did not deny. The Chairman publicly expressed, that he believed the cause of truth and Christianity would be advanced by these meetings. Upon the whole, we feel ourselves, and Christians are feeling all over the country, that Infidel objections can be, and have been, satisfactorily answered, so that the Christian argument is in the ascendant. May G. J. Holyoake soon become a real Christian.

8mo., 14th.—I was walking from Muirkirk to Douglas, Scotland, when I was hailed by a man driving an empty cart, who had nice accommodation for me to ride, as he had been taking some passengers from Crawford-John to Muirkirk. I recommended Christ to him, and he seemed very kind before we parted, and I hope, benefitted. When I reached Douglas, I learned that the son of our brother and sister Haddow, who had kept the Temperance Coffee House, Trongate, Glasgow, whom I visited often in his long affliction, had departed in peace and hope, leaving behind a widow and a small family. This reminds me of another widow who has been bereaved this year in Scotland, and left with nine children, some of them adults; while mentioning the support which our heavenly Father had imparted, she remarked, that she regarded herself now as "having got another husband, only with a changed name, 'Thy Maker is thy husband, the Lord of hosts is his name'"! What a great name is this for a frail woman to trust in! There are no supports for the afflicted and bereaved equal to those furnished by the Scriptures. We had a large, attentive out-of-doors congregation. God, indeed, gave me a door of utterance to speak boldly and freely his word. Met a few of the Christians who convene here weekly to remember the Lord. They were most anxious for a week's labors, but I had arranged otherwise, but hope to keep this in mind for another occasion.

30th.—I had hoped to see at Newcastle-on-Tyne, Thomas Philips, who has been fourteen years in India, as a Baptist Missionary, and has just resigned his place and pay for Christ and a good conscience, with the good wishes of the London Committee. We had exchanged a few letters, but I learned he had gone to Bath. After visiting Sunderland, at four o'clock sailed by the "Daniel" screw steamer for Yarmouth, had a fine passage and arrived in NORWICH about nine o'clock.

31*st.*—As there did not appear to be any very pressing reason for remaining at Norwich, I started for London at 6. 15. a.m., and walked through the large cathedral at Ely. As I was approaching the door, I had put on my hat, when a clerical-looking gentleman asked me to take it off. "Why?" "What countryman are you?" "An Englishman." "You ought to be ashamed of yourself." "Why? my hat is no more unholy on my head than as though it were in my hand." He walked on and said no more. I was glad of this opportunity to show that I do not believe in the superstitious notions entertained concerning consecrated places. A Friend would not have taken off his hat at all; I did, while walking through that part where a few boys were assembling for their daily services, but just as I often put on my hat when going out of any place of worship, so here; but as I had not gone beyond the consecrated ground I gave great offence; it will be well if the offended consider the question.

10*mo.*, 7*th.*—Broke bread at MANCHESTER, after an absence from the table here of about three years. Found the brethren in as prosperous a state as I have ever known them. At three o'clock preached out of doors on Stretford Road, and at half-past six, Brother Robinson gave some particulars of the life and death of sisters Tipplestone and Heywood, both of whom fell asleep in Jesus the last month. After his address I made some remarks on the joy and comfort of the gospel. Some eight or ten years ago, we had preaching in a cottage in Salford, on a week-night, through which twelve or fourteen souls fled to Christ for refuge, these two sisters were of the number. This fact shows that continued labors to get our neighbors to hear, for a sister or two took great pains to get their neighbors to hear of Jesus, and telling the truth in private houses, are important methods of getting souls saved. Some four or five of this number have fallen asleep. We know not what an amount of blessing may arise from the labors of a sister; I instanced the following case:—"In 1788, or 1789," says Martin Boos, "I visited a sick person, who was respected for her deep humility and exemplary piety. I said to her, 'You will die very peacefully and happily.' 'Why so?' she asked, 'Because you have led,' I replied, 'such a pious and holy life.' The good woman smiled at my words, and said, 'If I leave the world relying on my own piety, I am sure I shall be lost. But relying on Jesus my Saviour, I can die in comfort. What a clergyman you are! What an admirable comforter! If I listened to you what would become of me? How could I stand before the divine tribunal, where every one must give an account even of her idle words? Which of our actions and virtues would not be found wanting if laid in the divine balances? No; if Christ had not died for me, if he had not made satisfaction for me, I should have been lost forever, notwithstanding all my good works and pious conduct. He is my hope, my salvation, and eternal happiness."—*Life, p.* 19. I also proved that Christianity gives the purest affection to wives as well as husbands, and instanced another case. John Smith, is a Manchester merchant who has preached Christ some years at Tipping Street Chapel. His wife died in 1850, the following interesting portion of a letter was read, which she had addressed to her husband while from home :—" I shall not forget you on the morrow (first day) ; though at a distance, we are one in spirit, bearing each other on our minds at a throne of grace, and drawing water from the wells of salvation. Remember me to all inquirers, and accept the best affection human nature can bestow." It is in such language as this that the virtuous love of a Christian woman only can vent itself. Christianity makes the best husbands and the most loving and devoted wives.

22nd.—SHEFFIELD. Monday evening a large assembly in Mount Tabor Chapel, built by the Wesleyan Reformers, Alderman Scholefield presided. The subject was, " Infidel Objections." An Infidel objected both yesterday in the open-air and this evening. I trust all his difficulties were satisfactorily solved.

23rd.—The Primitive Methodists kindly granted their large chapel, Coal-pit-lane. I contrasted " Infidel principles with the good news of the blessed gospel in their present and future tendencies." The influence was remarkable ; while proclaiming salvation by the gospel, a flame of love seemed to fill the chapel, the warm and devout Yorkshire Christians praised God with joyful lips. God filled the chapel with his own presence, and infidels seemed astonished and confounded, so that instead of objecting, as they did at two previous meetings, one person who disclaimed infidelity, made a few remarks more friendly than otherwise. Brother Henry Horner presided. I cannot pass over the Sheffield meetings without remarking, our brethren, especially Henry Horner, had zealously and wisely procured these large places ; that they were kindly granted in a Christian spirit by the owners, and that in both respects this example is worthy of imitation. Sometimes brethren are either discouraged by the schism around them from asking large chapels, or, they have neither faith nor courage for such services, and thus either burden themselves with the expense of halls, which have this great advantage, that truth is free in them, or the speaker is confined to a room that will only hold a few scores, when he might address hundreds on the most momentous truths. I thank our brethren at Sheffield for the Lord's sake, and for the sake of the many hundreds who heard his precious truth.

1mo. 23rd., 1856.—Spent a part of two days in LONDON, trying to prepare the way for future lectures, &c. While in a book shop, explaining the object to a brother, a stranger offered a room because the lectures were to be free ; he approved of giving truth without money and without price. Spent some time with my friend John Hamilton, at Dalston, editor of the *Empire*.

24th.—On returning home at night, via Worcester, a tall, good-looking Irishman commenced smoking a cigar in the carriage very near me. I warned him, he promised to desist, and did so, but only until we got past the station. I told him that I should be obliged to report him if he continued, as I judged the law was good. He continued smoking, used awful language, and said I deserved to be thrown out of the window. At the next station I told the guard, who asked *me* to go into another carriage ! I did not see that to be my duty—to remove the quiet passenger, and allow the offender to pass without a word. After this he was worse, but removed to the other end of the carriage, and two more joined him in smoking. He said, "If ever I find you, I will horse-whip you." Before leaving the train, I asked the guard to tell me his name. He gave it. I gave him an opportunity of confessing his fault; he declined. But as I did not like to complain to his employers before giving him another opportunity, I wrote him a very faithful letter, and got a satisfactory apology, and promise of future good conduct. Had I written or complained to his employers they might have ruined him at once, and this I did not desire. I exceedingly dislike smoking in the railway carriages, and approve of the rule which forbids it. In all my travels I never met with so much insult from a passenger, or such great neglect from a guard. Yet I feel pleased that I did nothing to injure the latter, but I hope the reverse.

It was thought, not without reason, that I was in danger of being prosecuted for a libel—"The Hypocrite"—which appeared in "The Truth Promoter," vol. iv. p. 209, to which I refer the reader. I suppose the article was invulnerable, or he would have prosecuted. Large numbers were circulated where he lived of whom I wrote.

CHURCH RATES IN CHELTENHAM.

2mo., 14th.—Attended the Cheltenham parish vestry in the Church. A friend requested me to watch this meeting. The roof of the building required repairing. A letter was read from Mr. Close, requesting the dissenters not to oppose the rate, as he wished peace. I remarked that the way to promote peace was to have no rate. It was carried to try voluntary subscriptions, and adjourned for a fortnight. The Chairman tried to hinder the free expression of opinion.

28th.—A much larger number attended. The same clergyman, Mr. Evans, was voted to the chair. He was again interrupting the speakers, when I told him that both sides ought to be fairly heard, and if he did not permit this, I should propose some one else to take the chair. After this he behaved so well, that at the end of the meeting I was able to propose a vote of thanks. The sum needed was about £220, but £10 had not been subscribed. The church-wardens proposed a rate of a penny per pound, which would realize about £400.

It was moved by Mr. Downing and seconded by Mr. Hollis, that subscriptions should be tried for six weeks and that the vestry should adjourn.

I supported the amendments on the following five grounds:—First. The Church Rate has a tendency to promote ill-feeling between the parishioners. Second. We are heavily enough taxed without having another; and if you do thus tax men they will speak of it, and in this way it will cause contention. Third. It is unnecessary. If the church can raise £222 to erect a church at Geneva, which is far distant, surely it could raise a similar sum to repair its own fabric here. Fourth. It is unjust. If other churches have to build and keep in repair their chapels, then, surely, a rich congregation like this ought to do it well when you have a place built for you. What would you think if we were to try to get a law passed in parliament for a chapel rate? It must have been a very cold asking for to have only got £10 subscribed. I venture to affirm had you asked for the subscriptions for the church at

Geneva in the same way, you would not have got them. Then repair your own fabric, and let charity begin at home. Again, it is unjust to assess poor Churchmen, Dissenters, and Infidels, some of whom never attend and do not believe in your religion. I could expose the injustice of a Church Rate in stronger language than I choose to use. If I do not pay the rate you can come and take my property: but if a man came and took away my property at mid-night, I should call him a robber, and if you send men to take it away at mid-day, if you have no authority from the law of God, the law of the land can never make that morally right which in itself is morally wrong, and I should therefore call it public robbery. Let every man support his own religion. Fifth. It is unchristian. In the Old Testament, if a temple was to be built, the people were appealed to, and they brought their free-will offerings. It is therefore doing violence to the whole principles of the Christian religion, to tell men they must be made to pay by law and the Church Rate tax-officers, or have their goods distrained. If you wish to promote love, union, and good-will, you will not resort to coercive exactions.

The amendment was carried by about ten to one. So we shall have no rate for six weeks. Nearly all the speaking, the arguments, and intelligence of the meeting were against the rate.

5mo. 1st.—Walked about 24 miles to-day without any inconvenience, to see my dear afflicted mother, and yet was set on the way from Swinton to East Witton by my friend Jonathan Bucktin, with his horse.

9th.—WEDNESBURY. Went down into a coal pit to preach Christ to the men, at their dinner hour; Mr. Bourne, the active missionary, being my guide. The men were all very kind, and shewed me the workings. We had singing, prayer, reading the Scriptures, and preaching. Mr. Bourne gave tracts to the men and boys, between thirty and forty, as he usually does. The descent into the shaft was very agreeable, but in the rapid winding up, the board on which we stood repeatedly went against the side. May the Lord of the harvest send many laborers into this densely populated district of coal and iron mines and furnaces.

13th.—Married Wm. Dash and Hannah Howell, at the Cheltenham Chapel, kindly granted for the occasion.

MEETINGS IN LONDON.

28th.—My two sons, John and Robert Aitken, having long desired to see London, availed themselves of my coming, and of a cheap train, to visit this great city of about three millions of inhabitants. Nothing very particular occurred excepting the Lord's kind direction, even at a late hour, to a quiet and comfortable home at No. 1, Bell Court, Doctors' Commons, near St. Paul's. My object in visiting London was threefold: 1st. Christians from various parts of England and Scotland, when visiting or residing in London, had consulted me about meetings to which they might go, of a similar kind to what they had been accustomed; and from the state of meetings in London, and my ignorance of their position and principles, I felt it difficult to answer their kind inquiries. This difficulty a short residence in London, I hoped, would remove. 2nd. I wished to deliver a series of lectures on the Lord's coming. 3rd. I hoped the Lord might make me useful to saints and unbelievers, especially the latter, in London as well as other places; but as the city was in a state of immense excitement through the Peace Rejoicings, I could do little for the Lord. In accompanying my sons to such places as they wished to visit, I was particularly struck while passing through the British Museum, with a human skeleton embedded in limestone, brought from Guadaloupe, by Admiral the Hon. Sir Alexander Cochrane, G.C.B. I had not seen anything like it before; I was aware that no such stratified remains had been discovered in the older rocks. Will any geologist say how long this limestone might take to form?

31*st.*—My sons returned home, and I addressed myself in earnest to my mission. I called on a few brethren in London and Tottenham.

6*mo.* 1*st.*—At 11 a.m., attended the Orchard Street Meeting, and found it profitable. Having besought the Lord to show *when* and *where* to preach, through a sister from Cheltenham I was directed to Paddington Green, where I found some Primitive Methodists met. I discoursed at 4 o'clock, and again in the evening to an increased congregation.

9*th.*—Attended a prayer meeting this morning at 7; about fourteen attended. On the 16*th*, a dear brother earnestly besought the Lord's blessing on my labors. The prayers of the Lord's people refresh me much; I believe they are answered remarkably.

10*th.*—The lecture in Hope Hall, on what Christian Churches ought to be was one of the best we have had in England. Many spoke wisely and in the Lord's fear, of what the church ought to be. My soul was abundantly refreshed and encouraged, as the Lord has so remarkably opened the way. Nearly all the Christians, City Missionaries, and others are remarkably kind; and there can be no doubt, if the Lord open a suitable place, much good would result from a meeting here to remember the Lord on the first day of the week, and then after that we must wait for other results.

My present thought is, that the Lord intends me to labor for a time in this great city. I desire the prayers of the Lord's people for it: not that He is unwilling to bless, but he will be enquired of. I desire the following things,—To keep, for days, and weeks, and months together, so united to the Lord, so full of hope as to Christ's glorious advent, that not a cloud may rest on the horizon. To walk with God is to walk in power. I further desire to be used in the conversion of many rebel sinners,—in comforting and directing many poor, or gifted brethren, and in calling attention to the grace which Christ will bring to us when he comes.

We have had lectures and the preaching of the gospel on Primrose Hill, Islington, and Paddington green. At Primrose Hill the congregation was always disorderly through scoffers. One evening when I had done, a well-dressed man blasphemed awfully against Christ. I expected the other mockers would unite with him; but they set upon him, and his life seemed in danger. I rushed in between him and his assailants and protected him. I hope he got safe off; but he was much alarmed. On another occasion, I was challenged to discuss with one or two Infidels. I agreed if they would bring one of their best men, naming three leaders. These all decline. Then, let all infidels in London know, that I would think my time thrown away, to leave the great work in which I am engaged, to debate with every one that thinks himself able to overthrow Christianity.

One night a Christian preacher, who is identified with the views of Messrs. Darby and Wigram, had been preaching; he closed as soon as I came to the green, as he said he would be always ready to do on my coming, as he was delighted with the gospel set forth. I stood upon a chair, our usual pulpit, and seeing the Infidels, said, that "it was neither manly nor rational to fasten themselves on a corner of our congregations at our lectures, had they not power to get congregations of their own? If they did, I promised not to act towards them as they did to us." Mr. Wynn said, "he had never disturbed any of my congregations, but one." This was when I put it to the congregation if they wished to hear him; and as all held up their hands against him, he was silent. To keep peace, we have been obliged to submit to the unreasonable questionings of an Antinomian in the same way.

Having had a favorable answer from Orchard Street, I broke bread there on the Lord's Day morning, as I did at Collier Street, the Lord's Day following. And in each case brethren attended the forenoon meeting at Bell Street.

My dear wife spent about ten days with me in London. I returned with her to Cheltenham, on Monday, 6mo. 30th. Had the usual weekly meeting on Tuesday, in King Street.

7*mo.* 20*th.*—LONDON. At 7 met for prayer. At half-past 7 baptized eleven in Shouldham Street Chapel, most graciously granted by the minister. One household was baptized, two preachers, one class leader, one youth from Armenia, and several who have received blessing at the meetings. At eleven, met in Newcastle Place Room, Edgeware Road, where between twenty and thirty obeyed the dying command of Jesus. This place has been kindly granted us when wet; we used it at half-past four o'clock; it is near Paddington green. Glory be to God for setting before us an open door, which no man can shut. May the great Shepherd watch over these lambs. Some from two other meetings seem to have a nice care of them. Several have been saved; many quickened. Two of my objects in visiting London are realized. There are seven meetings, to which I can recommend brethren from the country to go. God has given me some fruit.

21*st.*—BATH. In the old Moravian Chapel, now used by about one hundred and twenty Christians. The Lord made his own word a blessing. This meeting arose from sister B's visit to Cheltenham. How wonderful are the ways of God. It is sixteen and a half years since I preached in Bath before.

On the 3rd of the 7th month, I delivered, by request, two lectures in the Subscription Rooms, STROUD; at 3 o'clock on "Purgatory," (see the "Truth Promoter," vol. iv., pp. 273 and 286) and at 8, on "Transubstantiation." A large meeting of nearly all classes. Both these meetings would have been crowded, but a considerable charge was made, by those who got up the meetings, for admission. It would be easy to raise subscriptions to cover expenses, and thus make all free. There is a monastery, for about thirty or forty monks, near here. I saw a few of the idle fellows walking about the neighborhood.

23rd.—Crossed the *Severn* from Bristol to Chepstow. Had been unwell, which was caused by a large boil on the back of the head or neck, also general debility, since I left London. Walked by Bream from Lydney to COLEFORD. The day was hot. When I arrived at Coleford, about twenty minutes before the time, as no one asked me to sit down, I took my seat on the steps, wondering if I should be able to preach. A large congregation assembled, and I discoursed with more help than I expected; and through one or two kind friends, got lodgings in the town, which saved me a four miles' walk after preaching, for which I was quite unable. I was thankful for this mercy. Had a restless night.

24th.—Discoursed at BREAM, Forest of Dean, in still greater weakness, through the pain of the head and the fever of the body. As the ground was wet, I doubted, in my state of health, whether to preach or not; but as a considerable congregation gathered, I preached, but never, out of doors, with such weakness, and not long. May the Lord bless his own word.

25th.—CINDERFORD, Forest of Dean. Having rested a few hours on a sofa here, I preached out near the school to a very attentive people, and was surprised that I could preach at all.

26th.—Arrived at home, quite worn out with pain and labor. The boil has burst, but the whole frame is feverish.

27th.—Attended the chapel in much weakness.

30th.—Very little improved; restless nights; seldom in bed a whole night through pain. As it has been intimated for me to preach in Scotland next Sunday, after prayer, it seemed quite impossible for me to go. I felt at liberty to ask my son, Robert Aitken, to go in my stead. After some consideration he agreed, and started, this evening the 30th. This was plainly the Lord's way. Through the pain in my head, when I do sleep, my dreams are always expressive of difficulty or danger. The boil or the orifice, Dr. Turnbull says, now is two inches long, and three-fourths of an inch wide. It discharges largely.

8mo. 3rd.—Having heard much of a young preacher named Guinness, I went to hear him at 3 o'clock. He seems earnest and devoted; but while I stayed did not give much Scripture; I was too ill to stay all the time. The brethren had given him King Street chapel a few times.

20th.—My indisposition is passing away. It has now done three things. 1st. Sent my very dear son Robert to Scotland; may it improve his health of soul and body. 2nd. Kept me in Cheltenham, where some one is needed to teach and preach. 3rd. Brought me into intercourse with Mr. Guinness. I hope it may be blessed to us both.

I accompanied the writer of this to the monument which he so feelingly describes. Such instances of Roman Catholic hatred to truth and godly men, who oppose their errors, prove the blood-thirsty character of the church, and as she pretends to be always the same infallible church, how can we believe that she has changed, merely because she does not kill us now; it is because she has not the power. If she disclaims the disposition let her recant her murderous burnings of the godly, and declare officially that she does not approve them. Until she does this, we must believe that she is as persecuting as ever, and that she lacks the power rather than the will:—

"On the 11th September, 1856, being in the city of Gloucester, I paid a visit to the place of martyrdom of John Hooper. It is situated within the churchyard of 'St. Mary de Laud,' and close to the cathedral. The spot where the poor man was chained to the stake, and consumed to ashes, is marked by a square tomb-like monument, with sloping top, and resting upon a broad basement, the whole being about five feet in height, upon two sides of which are designs in alto relievo; one bearing the Episcopal Arms, the other and opposite, a lamb bound and being consumed by flames. Upon the one side of the monument above the pedestal is the following inscription:—'John Hooper, D. D., Bishop of Gloucester and Worcester was burnt on this spot, on Saturday, February IX., MDLV., for his steady adherence to the Protestant religion.' On the opposite side is the following inscription:—'This Monument was erected by James Clealan, Esq., Rath Gaed House, Bangor, Ireland, 1826.' Where was the Protestant spirit of England, to suffer a spot so consecrated, to remain unmarked so many years? I, for one, thank the benevolent donor of the memento which tells of the sainted hero's murder, and covers the place where rest the calcined remains of one of the victims of the proud 'Harlot of Babylon,' whose dreadful but just doom slumbers not. O Rome! Rome! thou who hast made thyself drunken with the blood of the saints and with the blood of the martyrs of Jesus, prepare thyself, for the day of thy visitation and doom is at hand, when thou shalt be rewarded as thou hast rewarded others, and when thou shalt drink of the wine of the fierceness of his wrath whose followers thou hast slain, and who are now crying beneath the altar 'How long, O Lord, holy and true, dost thou not judge and avenge our blood on them that dwell upon the earth.' Farewell, John Hooper, thou noble confessor, a while farewell; thou has obtained the claim to a martyr's crown, and if thy murderers should suffer the 'vengeance of eternal fire,' thou shalt shine illustriously with all thy compeers in the everlasting kingdom of our Lord and Saviour Jesus Christ, and help to swell the never-dying anthem, 'Worthy is the lamb that was slain to receive, power, and riches, and wisdom, and strength, and honor, and glory, and blessing. Amen.' "J.C."

10mo. 21st—LONDON. Seven o'clock; between twenty and thirty present at a prayer meeting. At eleven o'clock, had a refreshing season at the breaking of bread; about twenty present. 1 was asked to consider whether the Lord had not opened the way in London, and whether I ought not to continue. I expressed my readiness to continue, if I saw it to be the Lord's mind. A few have been added, and a few seeking baptism.

12mo. 2nd.—CHELTENHAM. This evening six were baptized. A large congregation. One from the Sunday School was baptized.

4th.—To-day received a letter from my son Robert Aitken. He states that five were baptized at Dundee on the 2nd, and that more are inquiring.

In 1856 we had meetings at Cheltenham for reading the Scriptures in the original Greek. They arose thus. At the desire of Miss. S. Countess we met weekly, and the meeting consisted of Dr. Turnbull, my son, R. A. Bowes, and the late Miss Bruen. Miss Countess took notes, which I reviewed and published in "The Truth Promoter," vol. v. pp. 63, 70; vol. vi. p. 70.

CHAPTER XIII.

GOD'S WONDERFUL PROVIDENCE.—THE SWEDENBORGIAN DISCUSSION.—REVIVALS IN HELENSBURGH AND DUNDEE.—REMOVAL TO DUNDEE.—LECTURES IN DUNDEE.—USEFULNESS OF TRACTS.—VISIT TO THE GREAT EXHIBITION.—JOURNAL.—1857.—58.—59.—60.—61.—62.

3*mo.* 12*th*, 1857.—I and my dear wife sailed for Scotland. She was very sick. I did not wholly escape, as it was stormy part of the way. Arrived at Greenock at half-past six a.m., got to NEILSTON at eleven o'clock. At eight o'clock a tea-meeting, called here a soiree. About 130 present, to whom brother T. J. Hitchcock, W. Fulton, and I declared the truth. It was a very happy, well conducted meeting, altogether a superior meeting to that of last year.

14*th.*—The steamer could not land at Helensburgh, so that we were taken to the Row, up the loch. The Lord provided us a conveyance.

15*th.*—HELENSBURGH. A very stormy day without, but happy within. Two professed to be made happy by the gospel. A boy was there whom a brother has got to a trade. He first met with him at the door begging. He affirmed at first that he had no father, but at length one was found. The boy is now clothed and fed, taught a trade, and above all, the way of life, which I trust he has embraced, or will soon embrace. What a happiness it must be to save a neglected child from ruin. It seems he has a father in Glasgow, married again, and that the stepmother has driven the children away by her severe treatment. Fathers should not forget their duties to their children because an unfeeling step-mother may pay no regard to their interests. Those who take in the stranger and feed and clothe him, if they can also lead him to the knowledge of Christ, will have a double reward. The highest good is that which is done to souls for eternity.

28*th.*—Left Helensburgh, where we have held meetings for two weeks, only one night we had a discourse at C— Farm. The most of the meetings were in Eastburn Chapel, excepting on the 21st, Sunday evening, the Congregational Chapel, which was well attended, was kindly granted for a lecture on "The Coming King," as was the United Presbyterian Church on the 27th, for a lecture on Temperance. I have heard of one tobaccco smoker who gave up his pipe from that night. In the course of the meetings several seemed anxious, and a few professed to believe the truths taught, and (including two on the 29th,) four were baptized. Some of the discourses were on Election and Imputed righteousness. Upon the whole I trust the seed sown will be found after many days. There are now above twenty in fellowship.

29*th.*—Commenced a series of Revival Meetings at NEILSTON, with brother T. J. Hitchcock, these continued every night until 4*mo.* 13th, when they closed. During this time, I discoursed to about 30 hearers in the Poorhouse, at the regular weekly meeting, which is generally addressed every Tuesday by some minister. God blessed the word. Several after this attended the evening meeting, and two were added to the church. At the different meetings we conversed with about fifteen anxious, eight or ten professed to believe the gospel.

On the 12th four were baptized. The visiting and going from house to house with tracts was attended with blessing. Nearly one half of the population seemed to be composed of Irish Roman Catholics. One woman told us plainly, " I want nothing to do wid ye." Several refused to take our tracts. One denounced the Bible as "a bad book" which she had not, and spoke of "the blessed mother of God." I quietly told her that God, as God, had no mother, but was from eternity. One family through visiting and preaching, should the case end as well as it has begun, will more than amply repay all parties that have been engaged in these meetings.

4mo. 2th.—DUNDEE. About 50 in fellowship. At 6 o'clock, the Baptist Chapel, Meadowside, always kindly granted for preaching, was full to overflowing. Some supposed it might have been filled two or three times over.

28th.—On Puseyism and Irvingism. The Thistle Hall crowded. One of the advocates of the latter explained, that it was not *one man* that appointed the twelve. I told the congregation a secret which is not commonly known, that the Irvingite twelve apostles originated thus: One of the party foretold, as though he were inspired by God, that they ought to have twelve apostles, and it was done. Now if this suggestion was not from God, but from Satan, or what is the same thing, from himself, then the Irvingite governors originated in a deception. Their sympathy with Roman Catholics and Puseyites was demonstrated by their adherents having been recommended in Aberdeen to unite with the late bishop Skinner, and the Roman Catholics having received the chapel of Mr. Drummond, M.P., one of their apostles, whose agreement with Rome has been publicly expressed.

29th.—To-day, my dear wife commenced her journey to England; family matters requiring her attention. My son-in-law informs us that on the 25th my daughter gave birth to a son, whom he has been pleased to name after me.

5mo. 2nd.—PERTH. Guided by two kind friends, from the Hill of Kinnoul I had one of the most sublime and splendid views that I ever witnessed. Far in the west and north-west were seen the Highlands, like a vast panorama; below, from the tower, the awful rocks perpendicular for many hundred feet high, create a feeling of awe as one looks below to the rich Carse of Gowrie, the beautiful river Tay, spreading out its waters for more than twenty miles to the German Ocean. Tradition says that when the Romans looked down on this splendid river, they exclaimed, "The Tiber! The Tiber!!" I am to hold meetings in Perth for a week.

6mo 11th.—BOLTON. The brethren have had Hope Chapel for a month. We held a meeting to-night to consider whether we should continue it another month. Several spoke of having received good in the chapel and out of doors, and some new friends promised their support, so that we were encouraged to take it another month.

15th.—For more than a week there has always been one or two large penny theatres in the Market-place, making a great noise with music, drums, &c., but they never drove us quite off.

29th.—Reached CHELTENHAM, having been from home four months. Many things in the church, &c., require instant attention. My son Robert starts on the 1st of next month for Bolton to continue the meetings.

7mo. 25th.—Three were immersed, and one more was hindered, being a servant. Three were also immersed the last month; altogether 23 in ten months.

29th.—BOLTON. My son Robert had expected me to preach, but the train did not arrive until he had finished. On the 30th he sailed for Scotland. His labors have been much blessed here this month.

8mo. 2nd.—At 6 o'clock, conversed for half an hour with seven men. The greater part have obtained peace through believing since the meetings commenced. Some were blessed before I left for Cheltenham, some since Robert came. My son John preached Christ this evening at the market-place.

4th.—SOUTHPORT. To-day visited Mrs. T., who heard me last night. How my heart rejoices at God's goodness. Saw her sister, Mrs. J. They were both led to Christ while I preached in Hope Street Chapel, Liverpool, about twenty years ago, and I never heard the good news until to-day, when it came from their own lips. They reside at Southport. It is cheering to those who sow the "incorruptible seed" of the word, to know, that while it often springs up under our own eyes, it often remains undiscovered by the sower, because the hearer goes away from his sight, and he only knows of it after many days, or perhaps never at all in this world.

16th.—BOLTON. To-day preached and baptized eight in the Baptist Chapel, Moor Lane, kindly granted for the occasion. Many heard the word. At a quarter to six held a Bible class. A large number present. At half-past six o'clock preached on "The Rock," Matt. xvi., proving it to be Christ, not Peter. By far the largest congregation I have seen in the Chapel. The whole of those baptized broke bread but one. The greater part have been led to Christ lately.

17th to 20th.—CHESTER. Bowling Green, out of doors. Our congregations on the 19th and 20th greatly improved. I showed local preachers and others the plan of getting hold of the masses. Several questions were asked, and a great excitement seemed to be produced by the discourse. The last night a clergyman asked my name, and publicly expressed his approbation. I asked him his name and abode. He said —Craig, Coventry, and that he preached out of doors at home. He thought we should forget our differences and labor for the public good.

9mo. 23rd to 26th.—Commenced a series of meetings on Paddington Green, &c., LONDON. Although it was dark considerable congregations listened. One evening I asked the congregation if they could tell me a greater name in history than that of the Lord Jesus Christ? "Yes," said a Mr. O'Neil, "Napoleon and Bacon were greater names." I read an extract from my Eight Lectures proving that Napoleon himself regarded Christ as a far greater name. As he complained of a want of time, I gave him an hour the night following, when he quite gave up Napoleon and never mentioned him. We had four speeches of fifteen minutes each before my lecture began. The discussion turned on Lord Bacon, whom I showed to be, as Pope describes him, the

"Greatest, wisest, meanest of mankind."

Great in talents but publicly convicted of bribery, so that in his hands

" Justice was sold."

and he was rendered incapable of sitting in Parliament. A flatterer at court he resigned Essex to his fate, and at that time retained court favor. He was so prodigal as to die more than £20,000 in debt, although he had an income of some thousands annually. And as to greatness many of the people knew little or nothing of him. As to his philosophy of inductive evidence, it was good. Mr. O'Neil said it was evidence against faith, in our controversy, whereas I showed that all true faith was built on evidence. Mr. O'Neil in his second speech gave up Bacon.

10mo. 22nd.—ASHTON-UNDER-LYNE. A Room, connected with the New Hall, Stamford Street, well filled to hear my lecture on the Grand Proposal. A few were ready to act upon it. To-day, as my wife and I returned from Derbyshire, at the New Mills Station, a plain working man got in, who might be about forty years of age. As he seated himself at the other end of the carriage, he said softly, but loud enough to be heard, " Praise God—Praise God." Taken by surprise, I made no remark, but longed to speak to him. When the train stopped at Disley he repeated the words. I said, " That is a blessed employment." This led him out, and he preached Christ to the people, telling them to come all that were weary and heavy laden, and they should find rest. I asked his name. He said, " Do you want to know what they call me now or before I was converted, for I have been a great sinner ?" I told him he might answer as he pleased. " They used to call me ' Dick the devil,' because I was the greatest sinner in the whole neighborhood ; but now they call me ' Praying Dick,' or Richard Challoner. I come from Hazel Grove, where we have great numbers converted every night, and our meetings continue until twelve o'clock." He seemed full of love and praise. A Wesleyan minister sat next me who seemed deeply affected. Here was a plain man, only converted six years, who opened his mouth for Jesus while we both sat silent ; at least until his burning zeal opened the way. Surely if our hearts were more full of love, we should oftener speak to our fellow-travellers of the Saviour.

11mo. 8th.—BOLTON. Baptized six in the Moor Lane Chapel, kindly granted for the occasion. Seventeen have now been baptized here since Hope Chapel and the Temperance hall were taken.

GOD'S WONDERFUL PROVIDENCE.

Considerably more than forty years have passed since, at a lovefeast at Wintringham, on the Yorkshire wolds, the person whom it concerns, related, in substance, the following particulars. The late John Storry, who was present, formerly over a congregation at Thirsk (where I frepreached when nineteen years of age), afterwards a Wesleyan minister, detailed them to A. E. Farrer, another minister of the same body. He was a venerable man, gravely dressed, but stone blind, and said:—" So many years since (naming the time), I was a farmer in this village, and a malignant persecutor. I was blessed with a wife of decided piety, whom I hated because she was a Methodist. Fruitlessly did I labor to withdraw her from this way; and at length my opposition became so infuriate, that I determined to burn her to death. For this purpose, one Sunday morning, when she was at her class-meeting, I heated the oven, and as I saw her returning up the village street I hastened to seize her, to accomplish my infernal design, when God seized me, I fell on the threshold, horrified with myself, trembling beneath the eye of God, and weeks passed over me of sorrow and fear, of tears and prayers. I obtained mercy. That was a season of indescribable blessedness! I was surrounded with a family of five children; my wife had become greatly endeared to me, and Providence smiled upon our pursuits. But my heart proved treacherous, I trifled,—and a disease got among my cattle. One died, then another, until I was obliged to sell the rest to pay my debts, and retire into a cottage as a day-laborer. He who sent, sanctified the visitation. My children and my wife were spared; and God restored me to friendship with himself. Again, however, I became lukewarm. He saw fit to bereave me of my children; one was smitten, then a second, until the last was removed. My wife, however, was spared; and God became gracious. But—she was taken! The world was now a desolation; and I was tempted to murmur at the Disposer of my lot. I was now employed in breaking stones upon the road; and one day it occurred, and the temptation was too readily indulged, ' Well, God has done his worst : He has taken my property, my children, my wife—He can do no more!' when, in an instant, I was struck blind! Overwhelmed—bewildered—I fled to Him : and, as though a voice had uttered it, I heard, ' I will never leave thee; I will never forsake thee.' The promise has been accomplished. Years have passed, but God is still with me. Yes, friends, God is with me: and I shout to call the Saviour mine!"

In "The Truth Promoter," vol. v., p, 147, I wrote a paper to prove that "thou" and "thee" are more in accordance with grammar and Scripture than "you," when a second person is addressed. I tried to get into the way, but old customs prevailed over my judgment; so after a short trial I gave it up. But I am still of the same opinion.

I addressed a letter, Jan. 29th, 1858, which appeared both in "The Truth Promoter," vol. v., p. 281, and in the "Alliance News," to Her Majesty's ministers, on "The Murder and Treason of the Liquor Traffic." I would have given it, and many more things, but I must curtail.

1mo. 31st.—WEDNESBURY. A very happy day with the brethren, and the New Chapel, or room, decently filled in the evening. A few anxious.

2mo. 1st. 1858—Not so many this evening. One young man said, "Last night, while you said, the prodigal son said, ' I will arise, and go to my father, and will say unto him, Father, I have sinned against heaven and before thee,' I felt I could say this, and I did say it for the first time in my life." I trust he fled to Christ.

14th.—BOLTON. Lectured in Fold Street Room, on "Swedenborgianism." A good meeting; discussion being allowed. Mr. W. Woodman, minister, of Farnworth, opposed, and challenged me to Discussion, which I accepted.

The following is the intimation bill which was published, with the subjects for discussion each night:—

"Public Discussion, between the Rev. W. Woodman and Mr. John Bowes, of Cheltenham, Editor of 'The Truth Promoter,' in the Temperance Hall, Bolton. First Night, Thursday, March 4th, 1858.—That Swedenborg's views concerning the next world, and Heaven and Hell, so far as they teach the existence of an intermediate state, the relationship and general state of the Angels, and of the miserable in Hell, are not Scriptural. Second Night, Friday, March 5th.—The personality of the Father, the Son, and the Holy Spirit. Third Night, Monday, March 8th.—That the New Church view of Justification and Regeneration is not Scriptural. Fourth Night, Thursday, March 11th.—That the doctrines of the New Church on the Resurrection are not Scriptural; that they make the Resurrection to take place at death, whereas it will be at the coming of the Lord.—Affirmed by Mr. Bowes.—Negatived by Mr. Woodman. The Chair to be taken at a quarter before Eight o'clock, by Mr. Raper. Admission:—Side Seats, 1d.; Gallery, 2d.; Middle Seats, 3d. The surplus, if any, after defraying expenses, to be equally divided between the Dispensary and the Mechanics' Institution."

The Discussion upon the whole was orderly. Each speaker occupied about 1 hour and 15 minutes, or $2\frac{1}{2}$ hours together. The average attendance might be about one thousand; the last night some hundreds more. The people have made some remarks, and occupied their time in speaking of it at their mills and workshops. Swedenborg's 'world of spirits' or intermediate state, which Mr. Woodman had to defend, they call "the finishing off room," in reference to a room in which the cotton is finished off. One of the speakers was said to be "working by the piece," the other "day-work;" because the one had too little time for his matter, and the other appeared to have some difficulty in filling it up. The reporter of the "Bolton Chronicle" was engaged, and both sides have agreed to the printing of the report. It is arranged that each speaker shall revise his own speeches. More than four hours were occupied with Mr. Woodman before he could be induced to agree to any ground of debate. Our readers will see that it is not every thing that could be desired. Mr. Woodman wished to close every night. This was deemed objectionable; and therefore each speaker opened and closed alternately, Mr. W. only stipulated for the last speech, which he got, and never speaker took a more unfair advantage, by the introduction of new arguments on subjects settled on previous evenings, and new topics never before mooted. The meeting might have been upset by calling him to order, which he deserved; for the sake of peace he was allowed to finish in his own way, which will always tell against his candor. But our conviction is firmly settled that after a four nights' debate it matters little who has the last speech; for if the work be not well done before, it is too late to begin; and if it is well done, the last speech can add little to the success.

GOOD EFFECTED BY THE TRACTS.

St. George, near Bristol,
March 22nd, 1858.

Dear Brother,—
I am happy to inform you that the tracts are read by some hundreds of persons with delight; and they of themselves, and also my feeble endeavors, are

honored and blessed by the great and loving Head of the church, to the conviction and conversion of both men and women, young and old. Others, who were the subjects of doubts and fears, are now (to use your own words) no longer subject to dark days, bad days, &c., but they have all good days now they have become acquainted with God, according to the true scriptural meaning of the word; or, in other words, they now know God as a GOD OF LOVE, and that Christ has borne all their sins away, and that they have nought to do but believe it, in order to be justified and accepted in and through God's well beloved Son. And one dear sister in particular, who is very unwell, on my asking her how she was, replied, "I feel very low this evening." I rejoined, "I hope your faith is not low." She said, "Oh! no; I have no occasion to fear, since Christ has died for my sins—its enough, and I believe it." I am yours in the gospel,

To Brother J. Bowes, Senr.   H. MILLS.

3mo. 31st.—NEW MAINS. Discoursed on the Second Advent, by desire. My friend and brother, John Wardrop, occupied three quarters of an hour in reply, to which, at the request of the meeting, I replied. We walked home happily together; I slept at his house, as I usually do when in this locality, and, so far as I remember, although we talked freely on all other subjects, we never mentioned that which had produced our controversy. Why should not brethren hold and express different views, and yet live in brotherly love?

4mo. 17th.—I have now been at Helensburgh altogether about three weeks, with meetings nearly every night. The chapel was never so crowded as on two Sunday nights. At the week night meetings never more attended. Three have been immersed; about nine profess to have peace in believing, and ten or eleven more see scriptural baptism. There was a nice spirit among the people. A tea meeting was held in Eastburn Chapel, and it was very harmonious. If preachers would only expect conversions every time they preach, speak privately and publicly to the anxious, and if Christians in general would labor to bring others under the sound of the word, as well as address them directly on their salvation, no doubt more would be saved. The salvation of sinners is an object of such vast moment that nothing should be allowed to hinder us from incessantly seeking it.

FROM THE BRETHREN AT HELENSBURGH, AND THEIR FRIENDS, TO MR. JOHN BOWES, AT PARTING.

Servant of Christ, ere from us thou dost part,
  For all thy labors here we would express
Our thanks from the deep fountain of our hearts;
  And pray that Heav'n may all thy labors bless.
The peace of God be thine where'er thou art;
  His righteousness thy theme; and may'st thou win
  To Christ the souls of many sunk in sin,
By the high teaching of His holy word.
Oh! it is passing lovely to record,
  Amidst a world enslav'd with sordid thrall,
And Churches fill'd with hireling Wolves abhor'd,
  A single-minded Preacher, like Saint Paul,
Obedient only to his heav'nly Lord,
  Dependent upon none, yet doing good to all.

HELENSBURGH, April 13th, 1858.   S. A.

5mo. 14th to 17th.—HELENSBURGH. The chapel enlarged within, and a new baptistry since I was here last month. About nine more profess faith in Christ: about the same number baptized, and six or seven more see it. Excellent congregations out of doors, and also within, and the brethren very loving, as usual. The brethren would be glad if the Lord would raise up a suitable brother to evangelize in this district.

6mo. 16th.—BOLTON. Preached in the Baptist Chapel, Moor Lane, and baptized thirteen, all, or nearly all, lately won from the world. It was a very joyful evening. Five in one family—a father, mother, and three daughters. The believers rejoice over so many, but they are few compared with the thousands that have heard the word; yet, let us thank God and take courage.

18th.—HALSHAW MOOR. A vast congregation; there must have been 1000 people. An unbeliever asked, "Do you believe in Jesus?"—"Yes, I do." "Then what do you make of John xiv. 12?" I replied by reading the context, and showing that it was true to those that were addressed by our Lord. I said, "I will now ask you a question, Do you believe in Jesus?" After a little fencing to get rid of the question, he said, "No, I do not." "Then what became of the dead body of Jesus, if he did not rise from the dead?" He answered, "This book says he went to heaven." "Then if he went to heaven, he was raised from the dead as an evidence that he was a true prophet, and that God had accepted of his sacrifice; therefore your last answer reproves yourself for not believing in him." The man was now called upon by the meeting to sit down, and he meekly obeyed! Mr. Hurst now asked a question, having been noisy for some time, and it is answered. I then asked him the same question about the body of Jesus, which he put off, but I continued to wait for an answer. He then said, "If his body was in the grave, it was stolen away." "But how could that be when a Roman guard was sent to watch it?" No answer. Before parting it was put to the meeting, whether all questions had been answered. All but one hand voted that they were. As Mr. Hurst was very noisy and unruly, the meeting would have used him severely, had I not besought them to treat him kindly. It is very humiliating when a great advocate for liberty and "fair play" will allow no one else to speak but himself. This is like advocating liberty for the purpose of oppression.

8mo. 6th.—To-day I buried with Christ by immersion, at PILLAWELL, two believers, and then started through the forest for Cinderford. My wife, two sisters, and I, sung in the lonely forest the 131st hymn. An aged laborer came up. We never spoke to him but continued our hymn. Attracted by its sweetness, he kneeled down beside us until it was finished, after which we said a little to him about the Lord. A large attentive assembly at Cinderford.

12th.—LONDON. Accompanied a few Christians to Epping Forest, in which we read Matt. xii.; had sweet communion over it. It is a solitary place. A school party was also there. Several gipsies wished to tell us our fortune. I was walking with the rest, when I stopped suddenly and said, "I will tell you *your fortune*." and I quoted to her John iii. 16, and in a few words recommended her to the Lord. These poor people should not be encouraged in this evil and deceptive practice.

8mo. 22nd.—NORTHAMPTON. Market Place, at three o'clock, about 1500 or 2000. At half-past six, in the Cow Meadow, about 4000 or 5000 heard with serious attention. Heard of the following affecting instance, and saw the person. Her leader said to her, "I have got two shillings poor money for you." She was struggling hard to keep herself from the workhouse, and was glad. "But," added the leader, "you owe one shilling and a penny for your class, and sixpence for your ticket, that will leave you fivepence. The poor woman did not take it up. She had formerly contributed liberally to all the funds. A few shillings would have been a great relief to her. Had her leader given them, if she had said afterwards, " I owe thirteen pence for my class and sixpence for ticket, take this out," it would have been very different. She was told that her leader could get her two shillings quarterly, if she would agree to this. But she did not, to her honor be it said. I saw this woman myself. It appears, then, that almost every collection finds its way into the pockets of the preachers! I was informed of another case here of a similar kind. An aged man had occupied a pew in a chapel forty years, and given liberally to all the funds, but his prosperity began to wane, and in his old age he could not pay his pew-rent. Connected with the chapel was the chief constable: this man of authority was employed to remove him from his pew. When another Christian heard how his brother had been treated he wept like a child, and from that time to the death of his aged friend, to his honor be it recorded, he paid his pew rent for him. "The tender mercies" of some great professors "are cruel." It is such conduct as this that brings religion into contempt. Those that support such a system are answerable to God and man for supporting evil.

10*mo.* 16*th.*—HELENSBURGH. Closed a fortnight's meetings here last night. The brethren, as usual, very kind. During this visit, four of them here and two from a sister church, New Mains, presented me with a costly suit of new clothes, including over-coat, adapted for a northern winter. I thought my old one might have served me this year, however, they, and He who put it into their hearts, thought otherwise. While I am quite willing to appear in well worn clothes in the Lord's service, and this cannot damage one's ministry or influence in churches, and congregations where one is known, yet among strangers, who judge by " the outward appearance," it is different. No one should feel himself inferior to others merely because of inferior clothing, or superior, because of superior clothing.

"A gentleman and a gentlewoman, may be, and, indeed are, confounded, in our current dialect, with a genteel man and a genteel woman, but these are the mere creatures of the tailor, or mantua maker, the barber, or the milliner, professing the fashionable diction of a Bostonian, a Londoner, or a Parisian."—*A. Campbell.*

It is well, however, to feel, that our real wants are but few, and soon met.

> "Man needs but little here below,
> Nor needs that little long."

While I minister to others spiritual things, and deem it a privilege, it is theirs to minister carnal things and feel it a privilege as well as a duty.

11*mo.* 22*nd.*—DUNDEE. Visited W. W. My son Robert gave him a tract, and spoke to him about eternal realities, since which he professes to be a new man. His wife says he has been changed since. Also called on S ; is not in church fellowship, but avows his faith in the gospel, and states that his first good was received many years ago, while I preached on the shore.

12mo. 12th.—New Corn Exchange Hall, Bank Street, Reform Street. About 1000 forenoon, near 2000 afternoon; in the evening many could not get in. The doorkeepers say some hundreds went away; there might be from 2500 to 2700 in the hall, though the evening was very wet; quite a row of cabs at the door. I suppose it was the largest congregation ever held within walls, to hear God's truth, in Dundee.

An attack of George Herod, Primitive Methodist Preacher, having appeared, against my leaving them, I replied to it in the T. P. vol. vi. p. 89. I intended to insert both here but want of space only prevents.

In 1858 and other years, Mr. Hanson, a Wesleyan Reform Preacher, agreed to defend a Hired Ministry, in a regular Discussion, but neither I nor others could get him to fulfill his engagement. See Truth Promoter vol. vi. p. 95.

1mo. 20th, 1859.—Ann Bowes, my dear mother, died at Middleham, Yorks, I have just heard at half-past eight a.m., on the 19th, and am hastening from Scotland to her interment. All that attended her say they have no doubt of her salvation. Her end was peace.

21st.—After travelling nearly all the night arrived at Middleham about ten a.m.,—found that our old neighbor and friend, John Watson, who has attended to my late dear mother with little less than the care of a son, had made all due arrangements for the funeral. To-day, was gladdened by the account all gave of my mother's happy death. She was laid beside my dear father's remains. The age on the coffin was 80. May we be a family in heaven when the Lord comes.

23rd.—At six o'clock preached to a chapel full of people in the Primitive Methodist Chapel, kindly granted. The congregation as well as the preacher deeply moved. The Primitive Methodist Minister, of his own accord, kindly offered the chapel for Tuesday evening.

25th.—The sale of mother's furniture. At seven p.m., preached with much pleasure in the Primitive Methodist Chapel; quite crowded.

26th.—Saw the other Wesleyan Minister, who gave a cheering account of dear mother's departure. Got all affairs comfortably settled, and reached Newcastle at thirty-five minutes past ten p.m. I only determined to return to Dundee after leaving Middleham. Was much affected while looking over the graves of my dear parents.

29th.—DUNDEE. Removed to a very airy, commodious house, Ash Bank, Magdalene Green. To-day Mr. I. called to give a curious history of himself and one of my books on "Union," published in 1835. He said I made him a present of it, when I was his tenant, (that would be when it was issued) and it saved him from an asylum. He had read it carefully, when his wife, since deceased, and those who aided her, succeeded in getting him into confinement for a space of six weeks, but when his sanity was tested by the Commissioners, he was asked what he thought of the disruption? He gave a distinct answer against sectarianism of all sorts, as he remembered the sentiments of the book, he believes they delivered him—he was set at liberty. He called up to present me with four times the value of the volume, and as he was able would take no denial.

3mo. 2nd.—DUNDEE. The Lord is indeed saving souls here. As I cannot stay longer at present, the church desired me to write for my son Robert. He arrived to-day, having left yesterday the marriage party at Leeds, where his elder brother, John, was married to E. A. Archer; may they both be like Christ in all respects, and they cannot fail to be happy.

3rd.—Commenced a series of meetings at HELENSBURGH, which were very happy; all held in Eastburn Chapel, excepting one on the *6th*, Sunday evening, when the United Presbyterian Church was kindly granted. It was well filled; the minister said there would be 600 people. This church rings its bell or bells to worship, and as I was going it occurred to me,—it is not often that church bells are rung for *me* to preach.

21st, 22nd.—NORTHAMPTON. Discussion, two nights, with " Iconoclast," Mr. Charles Bradlaugh, London. The theatre was the only place which the committee could secure. Two more nights are agreed upon when the theatre can be obtained. (See T.P., vol. vi., p. 256.)

29th, 30th, 31st.—DUNDEE. Discussion with T. H. Milner, on Baptism, Justification, and the Second Coming of Christ, &c., held in the Thistle Hall. The subject of salvation by faith, or by faith and baptism, I trust is settled. The last night's discussion on the Lord's coming only ventilated the question; it would require three or four nights to discuss it fully. The discussion is published, and I must refer the reader to it.

4mo. 15th.—A terrible catastrophe in Dundee! by the bursting of a boiler at Messrs Edwards' mill, a building of three stories, walls and roof included, was thrown to the ground, and about 30 people were buried in the ruins. The number killed amounts to 19.

17th.—Improved the solemn event by a discourse, chiefly based on Luke xiii. Some incidents deeply touching. One woman, who had a grown up family, was killed, who could not be hindered from going to work there this week. The overlooker had just stepped out of the building, looked back, and it was gone! A young woman "slept in," stayed away, and was saved, One entered from Aberdeen the day before, and was killed. There were four boilers; it was the outer one that burst. Had it been the one close to the great mill, the evil might have been far more deplorable. Boilers should never be under, but always outside of the buildings.

5mo. 29th.—Opened the St. George's Hall, High Street, CHELTENHAM. A decent congregation in the forenoon, and a precious time at the Lord's Supper. As it was wet in the afternoon our congregation was small, sheltered by the trees, At half-past six in the hall, and a very large assembly on the Promenade at half-past eight; read and preached with much liberty from 2 Cor. v. chapter. I trust the love of Christ was felt in many a heart.

6mo. 5th.—More observed the Lord's Supper than I have seen since my return. Two have found joy and peace in believing. Spent the week chiefly in preaching, aided by two brethren, out of doors, to improved congregations.

12th.—This being my birthday, age 55, I took a review of my life, especially the 42 years I have been in connexion with the Church, at half-past six o'clock to a considerable congregation. Several deeply interested. Preached out twice, as well as the three meetings in the hall.

13th.—LONDON. Train an hour behind time. Dear brother Jones occupied the time till he was hoarse. It was nearly twenty minutes past nine when I reached Paddington Green; I preached till about ten. This dear brother has been turned out of the London City Mission for writing a letter which displeased a Puseyite clergyman, and the Bishop of London. The Committee wished him to confess. He refused, and was dismissed. He goes on working, having cast himself, wife, and family on the Lord, who sustains him. Let the Lord be always trusted, and men will find that he is as good as men are cold.

19th.—NORTHAMPTON. At half-past ten o'clock had a sweet meeting at the breaking of bread, in a room off the Corn Exchange, where the brethren meet. At three o'clock about 1500 or 1800 in the Market Place, and about 6000 in Cow Meadow, at half-past six o'clock. Those outside would hear well. Both meetings deeply attentive. Who can tell the everlasting results of such meetings. May the Lord greatly fit his servants to fill such spheres of usefulness as his Providence opens.

22nd.—Market Place, about 2000. When I had nearly done, Mr. Shipman, an avowed unbeliever, cried out "humbug" twice. I wanted to know the meaning, and asked him to come up and explain. The people seconded my call, and he came up. He said the reason why he called out "humbug" was because he, Mr. B., had affirmed that he had answered all Iconoclast's arguments whereas he had not answered all. When requested to state any not answered, he replied what was said about Christ being three days and three nights in the grave, and evidence that Christ was born in the reign of Herod the Great. I said, is that all, or have you any more reasons? He answered, No. Now it so happened that I had answered both these points very distinctly and repeated the answers to the great assembly, and requested all that were satisfied that I had answered in the debate to hold up their hands. On the contrary, that I was a "humbug" for not answering. Not one, not even Mr. Shipman's. The people then told him he was the humbug, and he got quietly down. A more triumphant ending of a discussion could hardly be imagined. Iconoclast repeated over and over again the same things. This had impressed Mr. Shipman, who, as I was content with answering once or twice, had not remembered the answers.

REVIVAL IN DUNDEE.

Not to speak of many awakened who have not been conversed with, between thirty and forty have embraced the joyous gospel, and been added to the church, whose numbers have been doubled this year. Thirty have been baptized, and six more are waiting. During August, souls have professed peace with God weekly; sometimes five in one week, and one day three. There has been deep feeling; many tears shed; but no prostrations. Anxious people are conversed with after every meeting. One deeply interesting young man, a Roman Catholic, deeply anxious, followed me nearly a mile, until he got me alone, and then opened his heart. He has a Protestant Bible, which he reads; and has attended several of the meetings. A Christian young woman has been useful to three of her fellow servants; all have found peace lately, and one or two more in the same house are anxious. A Christian brother was for a few weeks an assistant in a shop. Such was the weight of his character, that three in the same shop are concerned, deeply, and two of whom have believed the gospel to their unspeakable joy. Drunkards have confessed their former error publicly. It will be seen in this great work, that the laborers in it WORK for what they pray, and pray for what they toil.

REVIVAL AT HELENSBURGH.

9mo. 22nd.—I have often preached three times a day for days together. Many clear cases of conversion, and doubly the number anxious. Eastburn Chapel too small, overflowing almost every night, and scores if not hundreds unable to get in. One young man was in liquor on Friday forenoon, came to the meeting, was arrested. I have seldom seen a more wretched sinner imploring "What must I do?" The next night he found peace, and in two days confessed it before the congregation. A father of an up-grown family, devoted to the world and strong drink, was awakened under the following circumstances:—A beloved sister, a mother in Israel, had "the Barracks" laid on her heart. It is not the abode of soldiers, but of Roman Catholics and Protestants carried away by strong drink and other sins. The first day that I went, a Roman Catholic ordered me out, or he would drive me. I spoke on firmly the word of God, and he fled to the end of the building. A young man, not a Catholic, remonstrated, he struck him; they fought terribly; the women parted them. I said a few words and left them. It increased our congregations for three days consecutively. At a quarter past two I preached Christ for about half an-hour to a deeply attentive audience numbering about 100. A man attended, was arrested, prays in his family; has found the Lord and confessed him before hundreds. On the 21st the Ragged School was crowded; it holds 500. Many children sobbed aloud at the prayer meeting, perhaps with sympathy. Several of those converted within these few days, have spoken with great power, as have others led to the Lord at different times. Those who have aided me in preaching have been the brethren Dickie and Steadman, and others here, and God has greatly blessed the new testimonies of the new converts. Christians of other churches help us in prayer. I had hoped to be off to other places, but have been detained here by this blessed work. The people are flocking to the Gospel like doves to their windows.

25th. About 30 saved; scores, if not hundreds, anxious. Free Church at half-past six: about 1500 hearers; several ministers present.

26th.—The Union Prayer Meeting, which we joined. The Free Church nearly full, ministers of two churches present.

30th.—Congregational Chapel, overflowing. At the close of the prayer meeting, addressed the assembly each night, but few in the meetings took hold of the work, but few of the anxious came forward to converse, yet each day furnished some anxious and some conversions.

10mo. 2nd.—This morning brother Dickie baptized nine believers. At eleven, preached in the Ragged School, which was full. Eastburn Chapel full at two, and the Ragged School at half-past eight p.m.

3rd.—CARDROSS. National School, full. Major Gills got up the meeting; two or three anxious. At twelve o'clock, attended a prayer meeting in the Congregational Chapel. Mr. Heather, a minister from the Old Church, or Primitive Methodists of Ireland, addressed the meeting in a gracious, useful speech. Mentioned a case at Manor Hamilton, County Connaught, which he had visited. The people were looking to the north for a Revival. He told them to look to God. This day a letter informed him that last week, on Sunday, thirty were converted, Monday, sixty. All were gladdened by this good news.

4th.—GARELOCH HEAD. The largest week-night meeting ever held, where the Free Church minister preaches weekly. Major Mylius, with whom I was kindly lodged, never spent so happy a night in this world. One of his servants found peace during the night.

5th.—HELENSBURGH. My last night. Ragged School-room crowded, nine conversions were reported. Six or eight anxious. Some think the total amount of conversions during this visit about 150 ; double the number anxious, indeed the whole town seems to be moved. At this meeting, through the Provost, (in England, the Mayor) who attended several of the meetings, and sometimes either spoke or prayed, said in a very feeling speech, that he had been requested by several young friends, to present me with a purse of gold. It contained £14 6s. As I had been detained here from visiting England, &c., where I expected supplies for "The Truth Promoter" and Tract Funds, this was a Providential donation from those who had received "spiritual things." In a long experience I have ever found, if we only attend to the will of God and do his work, he will attend to the rest. We need have no concern about supplies.

6th—Left Helensburgh with the good wishes and prayers of many that did not pray at all a month ago.

1*mo.* 16*th*, 1860.—DUNDEE. Seven were buried with Christ in baptism in Lamb's Hall, Dundee. A very attentive congregation. One Christian said he was convinced, and was ready to be baptized the next time.

21st.—Reached BOLTON, where death by scarletina, has swept away two grand-children, to eternal rest. Was glad that their parents had wisdom not to dress in black. Their sorrow was deep, but their joy should be greater.

24th and *25th.*—CHELTENHAM. Busy preparing to remove all to Dundee.

2*mo.* 21*st.*—I lectured in Bell Street Hall, to a large assembly, on "The Rifle Corps, War, Panics, &c." My old and tried friend and brother, James Webster, was called to the Chair. He had some difficulty in preserving order, as several of the Riflemen behaved ill, yet my lecture was tolerably well heard. It occupied seventy-five minutes in delivery, and then discussion followed. I was glad to teach love and peace to so many. Mr. Kidd occupied the chief part of the time allowed for discussion in advocating the Rifle Corps, War, &c., when required for self-defence. He quoted Scripture to prove that God commanded his people to take Ai, &c. This was conceded also, they were to defend their country by divine command. This was my strong point; the Jews were commanded by God, then since no one can plead a divine command now to fight the French, fighters should wait for the command, and not go in the face of a command to the contrary, which says, "Love your enemies." Mr. Kidd stated that my principles were a hundred years before the age ; they were too pure and refined for this age. I asked if the principles were right whether they should be the guide of the age, and the age be brought up to them, or should they be trampled under foot by the age? The landlord of the Royal Hotel wished to say a little when the meeting was over, which was granted.

RIFLE CORPS AND CHRISTIANS IN THEM.

3mo. 20th and *21st.*—HELENSBURGH. Meetings continued. On the 21st, a convert who found peace on the 13th confessed it; he had been sober and prayerful before. God blessed to him an address by one of the converts. So good is our Lord that he gave us this soul, a married man, a mason, on the first evening of the series of meetings. We have now several drawbacks which we had not in the great work of last year. Our beloved brother and sister Dickie are growing infirm, and cannot help much except by their prayers,—the weather prevents open-air preaching. The Rifle Corps and the Volunteers for the Artillery are so taken up with their dangerous playthings, that they have little or no time to attend God's word; from this folly the publicans reap a harvest. One day two converts met. The one was a volunteer, the other reasoned against it. The former pleaded that he must defend his country. The other said " This is not your country at all! your country is above !" pointing upwards. What a cogent reason! Are we Christians? This is is not our rest, our affections and country are above. Here we are strangers and pilgrims. Napoleon will never molest our country. " Our citizenship is in heaven." The French will never invade it. But some one says, " I arm to defend my life." " Your life is hid with Christ in God," and needs no defence from the rifle. But amid all the cold influence of the world a few are anxious, and the Comforter gladdens his flock.

"WOULD YOU MOTHER?"

4mo. 9th.—KIPPEN. About ten miles west of Stirling, in the Free Church School. The minister opened the meeting with praise and prayer. My visit to this place was most deeply interesting from the following memorable incidents:—The young man that invited me was over at Helensburgh during the Revival of last year. I spoke to him about the Lord while in the house where I have been hospitably entertained for many years. He remained a few days only at the meetings, found the Lord, and confessed his faith in the Messiah. About a dozen met me, after preaching, at his uncle's, where I was cordially welcomed. His mother rose with tearful eyes, her cheeks bathed in sorrow and joy, and said, "Some months ago this son had expressed how happy he should be, if the Lord should return soon, to see him, adding, '*Would you, mother?*' I felt I would not, for I was not prepared; but now I would be happy to see the Lord." Uncles, aunts, and cousins were present, nearly all now happy through faith in the good news. It was a place of joyful weeping; nearly every eye indicated the deep feeling within. Here I learned that John Vitters, another convert from the Helensburgh meetings of last year, had been holding two meetings in the Free Church school, and that he is likely to be useful. Who can tell when a few souls are saved what the end will be! When a child is born for eternal day, well may the angels rejoice. They know better than we the greatness of the occasion,—a man is born for an eternal crown.

2mo. 21st., 1861.—Four lectures against Infidelity just concluded, in opposition to Joseph Barker's four lectures in the public hall below Bell Street Church. The managers granted the church to counterwork Mr. Barker's influence, as his friends had obtained the hall from the managers under pretence that it was for *literary* lectures. I did not intend to lecture at this time, but to issue a public notice, showing that Mr. Barker was afraid of discussion in Dundee. I felt, before God willing either to do *anything* or *nothing* in the matter, as might be most for the public good and the Divine glory. Never was I less concerned about anything, when a Committee, formed to oppose Mr. Barker's views had secured Mr. Borwick's large U.P. Church, and he, its minister to aid. I could delay no longer, but cheerfully addressed myself to the important work cut out for me—for the Committee wished me to take up the same subjects as Mr. Barker. The congregations were large and deeply interesting all the four nights, while Mr. Barker lectured to almost empty benches. George Gilfillan, in alluding to these lectures at Mr. Cooke's soiree, said—"There is blasphemy below, and *cant* above." Is not this calling religion by a bad name? What is cant?" It is "*a whining pretension* to goodness." Now we made no pretensions to anything but defending the faith. Therefore this term is inapplicable. Can it be possible that a professed minister of Christ dislikes earnest religion, and calls it cant! Just as he derided revivals as the work of Satan! For myself, I hate cant—mere whining—mere form—but when an avowed Christian minister calls opposition to infidelity cant, I do ask,—Who is it that pronounces this opinion? Is he remarkable for his own consistency? Does he walk as a true Christian? Does he aid the Total Abstainers in his congregation against the Spirit Dealers, or patronise them and oppose the Total Abstainers? Is he renowned more for favoring the liquor traffic, than for his attempts to reform drunkards? And when he speaks of Revelation, does he play into the hands of infidels, so that they quote his writings in favor of their own unbelief? Ought not such a minister either to renounce his office, or be consistent? Can a revival of religion be of Satan, or the defence of the Bible be cant? Does not the man who thinks so "cant" when he goes into the pulpit to preach, and has pledged himself to preach, a religion in which he does not believe? Such preachers make more infidels than Robert Owen. Rigid observance of religious ceremonies is often combined with ignorance of religion itself, and with an utter destitution of its spirit. We see, both north and south of the Tweed, men taking the pay and eating the bread of the church, while they are the greatest enemies of its best interests.

3mo. 12th.—DUNDEE. Baptized seven. The largest assembly we ever had at an immersion. I took up the chapter on Baptism in the Confession of Faith, and its proof-texts, and commented on them. We are now about 140 in fellowship in Dundee.

27th.—For some weeks we have held Revival meetings every week, and almost every night excepting Saturday. We have had the assistance of Robert Craig, from London, who is very useful. Several have believed the gospel during the meetings. Generally half a dozen speak each evening, some of them new converts. This week we are carrying on Revival meetings, generally each night, both at Dundee and Lochee—the attendance is good at both places.

To-day my youngest son believed the gospel. His companion found peace on Sunday evening.

4mo. 4th.—Immersed 12 in Lamb's Hall, Dundee. Among the rest my youngest son, now about 17½ years. His conversion has yielded me much joy, for I was deeply concerned about his state for some time before.

6mo. 28th.—We have added to the church, in seven months, 102, and 90 have been baptized in that time, chiefly from the world. Conversions take place weekly. The church now numbers 201, while several more are anxious or believing the glad news. God is with us in the use of means.

MY PHRENOLOGICAL DELINEATION.

GIVEN BY FOWLER AND WELLS, SEPTEMBER 26, 1861.—SPECIALLY REPORTED.

"Here is a very prompt man, off-hand. He is not accustomed to hard work, yet is not wanting in effort. Only works when he cannot avoid it; but has an active mind, and would be better pleased when he could get his living by the exercise of his brain. He is not often found at very hard physical exertion, but would labor early and late when he works with his mind. I should not be at all surprised to hear that he was hard-working and laborious in his younger days. He is not a credulous man. He will believe nothing unless he has sufficient evidence. He will sift truth from error; he throws away the shell but saves the kernel. You will not find his mind stuffed with creeds or opinions. He is a practical, common-sense man. He is easy, good-natured, joyous, but a very spirited man and quite ambitious. He has order, method, system; but he is not 'more nice than wise.' He is easy in conversation, and can express himself; he has not more words than ideas. If he writes, my impression is he uses italics very much in his writing, to give point and emphasis to what he writes. He would be careful as a manager. He can make money easier than he can keep it. He would like to have enough to serve his purposes, but the balance he would devote to some useful object. He has conscientiousness large. I have no doubt he has met with much opposition to his views and principles; but he maintains these views at all hazards. He has the martyr-spirit. He has a good memory of persons and places, and would be very fond of travelling. He has taken his knowledge chiefly from observation, more than from books. He expresses himself freely and openly. He has a very executive and mechanical mind. He is fond of his children, and has a strong social nature that he knows more about than you do. When he writes he has a good deal of point, pith, and spirit. He likes to take life easily. Lives a real life, not a theoretical one. He has a combative disposition, but would not merely fight for his home, but for principles. He would not live long alone if it were possible to avoid it. He is very original; forms his principles and opinions for himself, and is just like himself—like nobody else. He can write and talk, but would rather talk. He can labor; but had rather talk than do anything else, and would be useful to all."

The faithfulness of the portraiture is most striking, as I understand that Messrs. Fowler and Wells had no previous knowledge of my character. A committee having been appointed to obtain the consent of gentlemen to be examined, I was asked by it and consented to the examination before a vast assembly.

1mo.19th,1862—Some zealous laborers and friends during the last few years have fallen asleep; amongst these I have now to number James Webster, saddler, Dundee, who fell asleep in Jesus yesterday, aged 47. He was led to the Lord in early youth, joined the church at Dundee, and remained growingly attached to Christ and to his servant, from whom he received the gospel, for nearly thirty-two years.

VISIT TO THE GREAT EXHIBITION OF 1862.

8mo 4th.—As I had to visit England, took an excursion ticket from Dundee to London. Our train left Dundee at 3.3. p.m. When the passengers were seated at Perth, there came into our carriage a well-dressed drunken man. A railway guard put him in, into whose hand we saw him put silver; from this incident we concluded the guard should take care of him, and then asked him to get a quiet place for him. He at once removed his *protogee* into the next compartment, which turned out to contain some of our most sober neighbors. Before the end of the journey he was sober. One asked, "If God had intended man to be an idiot, would he not have been born so?" "Yes." "Well, as he has not been born so, has he any right to destroy the reason that God has given him, and make himself an idiot, which, for the time, the drunkard is?" We arrived in London at 2.45 next day. On the 6th, having secured the company of a dear friend in London, who had visited the exhibition several times, we made our way on a shilling day. We were early in the Picture Gallery. There we could have spent hours with delight. The Foreign pictures seem more splendid than the British. There were about sixty thousand people in when we were there. It was pleasing to see all nations and all classes there, generally well dressed, sober, and orderly. Indeed we were often drawn from the pictures on the walls to those looking at them, taking quite as much interest in the flesh and blood exhibitions as in those without life, furnished by the painters. Articles of interest are furnished from coal pits; large blocks of coal, iron, copper, and gold, may be seen either from Great Britain or other parts of the world. In one department, not far from the agricultural, we could have remained long, considering the adulterations, which one exhibitor takes care to explain, that prevail in our provisions, luxuries, &c. I had long believed that lozenges were adulterated, and he states they are, with very dangerous material, as was demonstrated in the Bradford poisonings. For the first time we saw the printing of a portrait from an engraving on steel. Each is well inked on the steel, then carefully rubbed over with several cloths of a net-like form, dry and wet, much of the ink rubbed off, and when all is completed, put on the press, which rolls the paper as it prints it over a cylinder. The number of improvements in machinery—the great and the minute, attract attention and command admiration; and if from the great variety and numerous kinds of wood and minerals exhibited, not to speak of seeds, you admire the wisdom, goodness, and power of the Great Creator—you are astonished at the skill and enterprise of man in forming them to every kind of use. Here you find sledges from Russia, and garments from Siberia, and the richest carriages from nearly all parts of the world. You have armor of varied ages and nations, as well as their costume, from the peasant to the king. Pumps throw up rivers of water and steam, and the telegraphs perform their peculiar wonders. Rooms of refreshment are provided for your accommodation; seats for your rest; and the great palace will accommodate and delight you for nine hours, if your walking and examinations do not exhaust you before evening. No close observer, can fail to make large acquisitions to his stock of knowledge. Those who go to London for amusement and information, should spend several hours daily in this grand manifestation of art and human progress. Nations once at war are here seen in all the glory and wealth of peace and concord. One cannot look over it without longing for the time when war shall be for ever banished from this fair and beauteous creation.

9*mo.* 1*st*—Brother and Sister Curry from Liverpool, with us, whom I have known since 1837. He preached twice; this lessened labor. The usual out-of-door services.

5*th*—Three of my family accompanied them to the *Reekie Linn*, a Fall on the river Isla, about 3 miles from Alyth, to which we took the train. The rocks rise in majestic grandeur a long way beyond the Fall, which is only inferior to those of the Clyde.

10*th*—To-day, in company with Brother Fife, Brother and sister C. and I visited the splendid scenery which appears from the hill of *Kinnoul*, near Perth. It was awful to look down the perpendicular rocks, into the beautiful Carse of Gowrie, now white with the golden harvest crowning the beautiful banks of the Tay. At 7, Brother C. preached an hour in the open-air, at the end of South Street; I about an hour after him. It was inspiring to see a large number of people stand with wrapt attention, immoveable, for about two hours in the dark, to hear the word of truth. About ten meet in Perth to remember the Lord on the first day of the week.

27*th*.—Messrs William and James Scott gave tea and supper to their work-people. It was a very happy meeting. William Scott presided, and the meeting was usefully addressed by Messrs David Scott, Moncur, Swinton, teacher in the day-school, and others. I spoke nearly an hour on whatever was likely to do them good. Such meetings must unite the employers and the employed. The chairman invited the people, if they had any complaints, to mention them freely, either by letter, (not anonymous) or by a personal statement. Surely this is a step also in the right direction. I was much pleased with his decided inculcation of God's truth. Besides, here are schools for young and old, so that all may learn to read and write, and also the way to a better life.

In 1862, for 24 numbers, my sons printed a weekly paper, named "The Peoples' Guardian," which I edited. The following appeared in it, which I wrote:—

GREAT EVENTS FROM TRIFLES.

More than thirty years ago, we heard the following narrative adduced by the late Mr John Campbell of Bonnington, as a proof of the folly of married persons quarrelling about trifles, and the Irish "three year olds" and "four year olds" brought it vividly to our recollection. Not many miles from Edinburgh, on the banks of the Forth, a newly married couple were taking breakfast together, when a mouse crossed the floor. The husband said it came from under the door, the wife, from under the drawers. Husband—"I saw it come from the door." Wife—"I saw it come from under the drawers." Thus the strife began—neither could change the other's opinion. The contest waxed stronger, their feelings became soured, their hearts alienated, and they separated, through a mouse, for seven years. At the end of that time their asperities had cooled down, and they agreed to live together again. They were sitting together at breakfast, seven years after their difference, when they remarked to each other that it was a curious circumstance, that they should be sitting together again in the very same house as seven years before, and that so slight a cause should have parted them so long; and as they had never talked it over before, might they not now quietly settle the controversy? The husband saw the mouse come from the door, and the wife, from under the drawers. Both were positive—neither could be mistaken. Again the quarrel waxed hot, both were sure, and this time they quarrelled, and parted for life, and never more united. Now, whether this is a parable or a fact, our friend gave it as the latter, it exhibits the folly and evil of a trivial matter being allowed to separate intimate relations and friends. That a similar trifle in Ireland should produce disastrous results over many families, parishes, and for generations, is most deplorable. We do not wonder to hear of Roman Catholics and Protestants being enemies, although it is foolish and wicked, but for persons all of the same church to fight and kill one another, all because their fathers or grandfathers could not agree whether a certain bull were a "three year old" or a "four year old," is surely the climax of human folly and sin; and it is time to put such men under better tuition.

This year, the Dumbarton Discussion with Mr. Mitchell, on "Universalism," was much blessed in opposing this error.

CHAPTER XIV.

JAMES MURRAY'S REMARKABLE CASE.—ISABELLA ARMSTRONG.—ASCENT OF BEN LOMOND.—LOSS OF STEAMERS.—SICKNESS.—PRESENTATION OF A BIBLE.—THE AMERICAN JOURNAL.—CANADA AND THE UNITED STATES.—LETTER TO "THE ALLIANCE NEWS."—EDWARD ASTON.—BAXTER.—KIDDERMINSTER.—NEW TRANSLATION.—W. WILD WRIGHT.—MR. CAMERON AND TWO LETTERS ON DISCUSSION ON BAPTISM.—A MINISTER IN LANARKSHIRE.—OLDHAM.—HOLLINWOOD.—A GUINEA PLATE.—JOURNAL.—PERSECUTION AT BRECHIN.—ANECDOTES.—FROM 1863 TO 1872.

2mo. 24th, 1863.—GLASGOW. Visited a little in Glasgow on our way to Dumbarton. There is a meeting so little Christian and so thoroughly sectarian in this city, that two believers have been hindered from entering it, because they believed in God's love to all men. I have never been there; and as matters now stand, since believers are drilled into the doctrine of Calvin, instead of being received when they carry with them epistles of recommendation, I should decline to give any countenance to any Calvinistic sect; and what else is in any meeting that refuses fellowship to saints who reject the opinions of Calvin? Such persons are guilty of the sin of Diotrephes—(3 John 7—11)—and should be reproved and left, when they persist in it, to the consequences of their own bigotry. We should gladly welcome saints, whether Calvinistic or not, and treat with great tenderness those who differ from us. It is not honest to profess to receive all Christians, and then to refuse some.

3mo. 22nd.—Nothing very memorable occurred since my last, excepting after preaching at WOOLTON on the 17th. I was in the waiting room, Exchange Station, Liverpool, when a tall young man came in, three of us present, and seized my travelling bag, and without a word was walking out with it. I said, "That is mine." He laid it down, and seized a paper parcel of mine, which I claimed. He said, "An uncle of mine sent me for a parcel," and then walked quite out of the station. I reported the matter to the porters, and found that several robberies had taken place there. I was thankful I was there, as the bag contained a mortgage deed for £400, which as trustee of property belonging to another, I was responsible for. A few days after it passed safely into other hands. The same thing of running away with my travelling bag occurred at the Preston station, when a man dressed as a sailor was going away with it, when I observed him. I have no doubt but both were dishonest persons.

24th.—I have had some communications, pro and con, on the meeting in Glasgow. When the matter ends, well or ill, for the Lord's Table to be open to all Christians or not, we hope to report; and in the meantime we ask for facts only.

4mo. 22nd.—GLASGOW. It is arranged for three meetings here on the Green at seven, and three in the Lyceum Room, Nelson Street, City, at eight p.m. On the first evening, while brother Langton and I addressed the people on the Green, a woman covered her face, and wept all the time. She followed us to the room, and confessed that she was on her way to throw herself into the Clyde, when she saw us and was arrested. She seemed sober at the time, but confessed to a fortnight's drunkenness. This meeting will be memorable to her forever, if, instead of suicide and a watery grave, she finds Christ and salvation. Was glad to meet here a brother, who has not yet been converted two years. He resided at Woolwich, where he could earn 10s. or 12s. per day, making Armstrong guns; but he began to see that if it was wrong to take "sweet life," it was wrong for a child of God to be employed on guns to be so appropriated. It is refreshing to find that he has thrown up this lucrative employment for conscience' sake, and is now working as a mechanic, and preaching Christ.

23rd.—Good meetings, both on the Green, at seven and in the Room. One man professed that he had been a great hypocrite, but now believed the gospel. He said, when he had come home intoxicated, and found his wife on her knees praying in a corner, it terrified him more than as though he had seen Satan himself.

24th.—At half-past two, preached to the workmen of Barclay, Curle, & Co., shipbuilders, &c. There might be seventy or eighty men present. These meetings are held for thirty minutes, at this hour, three days out of the six. Thus any man, whether he goes to the church or not, may hear of Christ, if he will, without even washing his face and hands. This evening was wet, yet W. Langton preached Christ in Nelson Street, after which I lectured on the Lord's Second Coming, in the Lyceum Room.

9mo. 7th.—Preached at Mid Wynd. Sailed for NEWCASTLE by the "Dalhousie," which we reached in twelve and a half hours. I had no sickness to impair the delightful voyage, although the wind was alarming before we sailed. A decently dressed man and his little girl were in danger of falling into the dock, as the vessel had put off, while he grasped her side with one hand and his daughter with the other. By the morning he came to me before I had risen, and kindly offered me some brandy from his bottle! I said, "No, thank you; I never take poison." This opened up a conversation on the evil of drink, which he quite admitted. Several had spoken to him of his danger of the previous night. Before we parted on the Tyne, he said he would never forget this conversation, and promised amendment.

16th.— LONGTON, Staffordshire Potteries. Had never been here before. Our publications had been sowing seed for years. Reuben Woolley, who had never seen me, although we had often corresponded, met me at the station. A large congregation in the large covered Market. Many questions asked after. Several candidates for Baptism, the Lord's Supper, and a New Testament Church.

23rd—LONGTON. On my way distributed a good many tracts on the London down train. Baptized two in the Stoke Baths; seven came to be baptized, but five were too late. On the 20th, seven broke bread at Dresden, near Longton, mostly from the latter place. This is the first church, in all the Potteries, as far as we know, drawn together in Christ's name alone, to observe the Lord's Supper weekly simply as Christians. Some have read our publications long, and we expect, by keeping near the Lord, and being zealous for his truth, they may be burning and shining lights in the Potteries. My discourse here last week has produced good results. Some oppose truth and some receive it.

11*mo.* 14*th.*—GLASGOW. Baptized fourteen in Blackfriars' Street Chapel. Brother Ritchie opened the meeting. Arthur Massie gave his reasons for being baptized, and I preached. An elder and member in fellowship with Brother Ritchie were of the number baptized. We have now baptized sixty in Glasgow within the last four months, and have fifty-seven in fellowship. I could not forbear praying, as brother Massie ascended from the water, that he might lead hundreds and thousands to Christ and baptism. He goes to Helensburgh, with many prayers for success. Some unwell, or working, or we should have baptized twenty at once.

22*nd.*—Baptized ten more; making seventy that I have buried with Christ by baptism, in Blackfriars' Street Chapel, within the last six months. We are now about this number in fellowship.

1*mo.* 16*th,* 1864.—Erigmore, BIRNAM, near Dunkeld,—the residence of Mrs. Napier Campbell. She reads and expounds the Scriptures to her servants and neighbors.

17*th.*—BIRNAM. Nine broke break, being five more than last Lord's Day, when the meeting commenced. In the evening preached again at Erigmore, and baptized five; the footman and his wife of the number. It is marvellous how truth spreads. A lady from India goes among her neighbors here, recommends Jesus, finds a stray volume of "The Truth Promoter," which has found its way through a brother at Dundee; orders the whole volumes, sees other Christians from Dundee, invites the Editor to preach, and baptize some who, through her labors, have been led to Jesus. May great grace rest upon the little flock.

27*th.*—GLASGOW. This morning at half-past one, I awoke with blood running down my throat. I rose, when it poured from my nose and mouth. Tried to get a light, but failed; rang six times and got one. I had discharged a good deal of blood. It was almost like sudden death for a few minutes. Two or three days ago my nose began to bleed suddenly, as though some blood vessel had burst; possibly this is a return of the same thing with greater force; it may be to ward off apoplexy, or to be always ready. I hardly expected to see my friends again in this world.

A month has now elapsed without any return of former symptoms.

5*mo.* 21*st.*—W. D. Thomas called in question my views on Baptism; I asked him for texts; a discussion is appointed for the 30th. He is to prove Infant Sprinkling from the Scriptures!

30*th.*—The Discussion with Mr. Thomas, U. P. student and city missionary, on "Whether the Scriptures sanction Infant Sprinkling?" Mr. E. J. Scott presided, by consent of both speakers. As Mr. Thomas spent a good deal of time on the opinions of the Fathers, and on *eis* and *apo*, the time, and his three speeches, had about gone when he began to look at the question of the infants.

JAMES MURRAY'S REMARKABLE CASE.

6*mo.* 14*th.*—James Murray, window-cleaner, Glasgow, and Leonard Waterson, accompanied me to PAISLEY. We got a lorry, set two chairs on it, and had hundreds round us for nearly two hours, although it rained most of the time. James Murray's is a remarkable case.—He was born in the Old Wynd, Glasgow, Aug. 12th, 1833. His parents died when he was two years old. He was put into the poorhouse, but given out to nurse. When ten years and a half old, he was apprenticed to a weaver at Kirkintilloch, and remained there three or four years. He ran away from his master, and came to live in Glasgow with a brother and sister-in-law; both drunkards. "They stripped me," he says, "of my clothes, and sent me to beg. So I had to leave them through frost and snow, with my bare feet. I was brought back by my master at Kirkintilloch, and severely punished. Again I ran away, and began to steal and plunder gardens, until I was put in jail. At length Mrs. S. put me out, and told me I might go and sleep with the pigs. I went away next morning. When about fourteen, I began to work in the coal pit at Airdrie. I got only my provisions and one suit of clothes for two years. While here, I used often to be engaged in fights. One day, while working in an iron-stone pit, the men cursing and blaspheming, an accident of powder explosion left me wounded and blind for some weeks, and blind of one eye for life. I was insensible for about ten days. I came to Glasgow in the year 1849, and again had to beg; but learned to clean windows. The money I earned thus, I drank, and many's the night I have spent in the police office." His time passed in fighting, lying, and stealing, to fill the bottle. "I have laid below a cart for a week at a time, till the publican with whom I spent my money drove me out by pouring water on me and the straw." When he was married, he often turned his wife and family to the street, and often mocked open-air preachers as he was passing along the street. The wife's mother expressed her fear, when any murder was cried, that it would be James Murray for her daughter's death. He came to hear me last October, having been for about 18 years drenched in drink, so that he had to borrow a shirt to come to the meeting in. After one of the meetings in the hall, I was called to talk to him, and such a scene of flesh and bones I never remember to have encountered. He seemed a sot without a spiritual idea, and my labor appeared useless. I left him to talk with some one that had some ideas about religion; for it seemed to me the least among us could instruct him, at the same time I expected to see him no more. But, contrary to my expectation, he came again the next night, and on the 15th of October, while the words were quoted, "He that cometh to me I will in no wise cast out," he believed. To use his own words: "The publicans had cast me out; my friends had cast me out; I now took God at his word, and believed he would not cast me out." He at once gave up that agent of hell that had hurried him to the brink of the pit—alcohol, and, a few months after, tobacco. This is the most singular case I ever met with. For eighteen long years, and he is now only 31, he was sunk in darkness; he could not be called an infidel and atheist in the common acceptation of these words, for he did not oppose God, revelation, and eternal rewards and punishments. He had no thoughts of such things —he had no belief in God, or Christ, or heaven, or hell. He says, "My bible was the newspaper—my god, the publican." He thought there might be some Power above us in creation, but he knew and cared nothing about it. In what a state of degradation,—in what a prison of flesh, sense, and sin, is such a mind shut up! For three or four months he has opened his mouth to recommend the Saviour. As he knows the depths of wickedness, may he rescue many.

(He has induced hundreds to become total abstainers, and has led a few souls to Christ. I found him, 11mo. 5th, 1871, addressing about 1000 in the Jail Square, Glasgow, from a pulpit.)

ISABELLA ARMSTRONG.

I saw her first soon after she came from Ireland to Helensburgh, about 1859, a poor young girl, as most Irish girls come to this country, yet preaching. Some years afterwards, she was recommended by a brother at Wishaw, and labored with us in 1864, in Glasgow and Dundee, to which I introduced her, where the brethren took for her the Corn Exchange Hall, and thus gave her all our congregations. I was then preaching in Glasgow, and as my family resided in Dundee, I proposed to visit the church, and wrote her accordingly that I should be glad to join her in preaching, to which she replied:—June 1st, 1864. "I am, God willing, to preach on Thursday in the Watt Hall, and on Sabbath, at a quarter past two, in the Exchange, and also on Wednesday, and Sabbath evening, 12th June, and at Newport, on Friday the 10th. I do intend, God helping me, to take all these services alone." I remonstrated with her by letter and personally; asked her, "Suppose I had gathered a congregation at Edinburgh, and left my son Robert to preach there, and informed him that I intended to come and preach along with him, and he had written me, 'I intend to take all these services alone,' should I not think his conduct presumptious and impertinent? As she persisted, I took another with me; he wept over her, but in vain. The next morning I told it to the church, having decided that if she did not preach with me on Sunday, she should not on Monday. For the time some in the church were carried away with her, and in the end left us, and formed a separate meeting, to which she went, and broke bread with them. The meeting did not last long; some came back; others went into the world; one leading man in the division died. But they soon had to take similar steps with her to what I have narrated, and their union with her was dissolved. On the whole nothing does the church more harm than these divisive courses. There was some uneasiness about my being so much away; also some forward young men wishing to preach, without the scriptural qualifications, and were kept back, joined her movement, and got the liberty they sought in the schism, until they differed with her, with one another, and thus broke up. There was not the least appearance of a division until her conduct blew the embers into a flame. I have not conversed with her on the subject since, except at Wishaw in 1870, when I hoped years and the grace of God might have produced a change, but I am sorry to say I found none for the better. This is not written to condemn female preaching, but the selfish usurpation and divisive conduct manifested at Dundee.

ASCENT OF BEN LOMOND.

8mo. 17th.—Having preached and slept in Dumbarton, on the following morning, as the weather was fine, brother and sister Currie, A. Monro, and I, took train for Balloch Pier, and a return ticket on the Loch Lomond steamer for Rowardenan, at the foot of the huge mountain. As a pony or donkey may be procured for invalids, we concluded that a road made by them and by pedestrians would sufficiently guide us, or we could have procured a guide for three shillings, but the path is so plain no guide is needed. We had not proceeded far, before we discovered that the donkey path diverged to the right, while that of pedestrians kept to the left; this we followed. The heat of the day, which however was moderated by a growing breeze and covering clouds, impelled us, when we had ascended about a mile, to leave our coats concealed behind some bushes, a little distance from our path. When we had reached what might be half way, we rested for five minutes, while our eyes were astonished and delighted with the splendid scene of the "Queen of Scottish Lochs," and the "many islands" now spread out before us in enchanting beauty, such as no king's park could parallel, and as we could not have seen them except from this elevation. Eager not to miss the boat and disappoint our evening congregation, we hastened up the steep sides of the mountain. When we were within a few hundred feet of the top, my companion, fearing we might yet lose the boat, advised a retreat, which met with no response from his fellow-traveller, so in about two hours and ten minutes we had traversed the five miles from Rowardenan where the steamer left us. We found ourselves on the summit, soaring 3192 feet above the level of the sea, and 3160 feet above the surface of the Loch. The sight was sublime. I had never seen anything to compare with it. Eighty miles in the distance, far down the waters of the serpentine Clyde, stood Ailsa Craig. Around us for miles upon miles in the west and north peered the mountains of the highlands. Rugged rocks and hills in countless numbers and variety, enriched the exciting panorama. The north east side of the mountain presents a precipice of about 2000 feet of awful majesty. Just as we reached the lonely peak, five other travellers met us who had ascended without a guide from Inversnaid. It had taken them more than three hours; and what with coats and knapsacks, and the terrible acclivity without any path which they could discover, one of them having been in some danger, they arrived much more exhausted than we were. Three of them were not to retrace their steps, but take our path. On the sides of the mountain, all the way up, we found stones and rocks of white marble, of which I procured a specimen for home. The mountain is barren; very few, if any, birds to be seen in the higher parts, but sheep graze amid the short heather and scant herbage. Leaving our companions behind, we hastened down the declivity faster than we came up, so that our descent cost little more than an hour and fifteen minutes. We had some minutes to wait for the boat. Going up, we met only one solitary traveller out of the path, which we did not care to keep closely either going or coming. Found our coats safe, and were glad that we had accomplished our purpose. I said to my brother, "You have been nearer heaven than ever you were in your life; not the heaven where saints are, for you are no nearer that by ascending the highest mountain, but nearer the heaven of the stars." Nearness to the paradise of God arises from the holy state of the soul, rather than from any elevation on the earth's surface.

Ben Lomond has the appearance of a volcanic origin. Some of the white or marble rock is joined to grey stones as though they had been fused together by the action of fire. Possibly some of the mountains around may have taken their position by earthquakes. It is almost impossible to conceive that these oval and irregular mountains, in vast masses, covering scores of miles, could have taken their present shape merely by the cooling down of our once liquid and burning planet.

11*mo. 25th.*— DUNDEE. This morning the "Dalhousie" screw steamer, of Dundee, from Newcastle, and all passengers and hands perished at the entrance of the river Tay, not leaving a living soul to tell the tale of woe. Thirty-four persons, including the crew and passengers, drowned. The same night, the "Stanley," sailing from Aberdeen to London, was wrecked at the mouth of the Tyne, a few saved, but about fifty lost. Among the lost were two noble fellows in the lifeboat, who risked their own lives to save those struggling in the waves; but they did not belong to St. Andrews, where those concerned take care of the life-boat, and keep it and their own lives safe, whatever may become of the poor seamen.

This year, in March and April, we held two Conferences of the Churches, the one in Manchester and the other in Glasgow. The proceedings were of a deeply interesting nature. Any difference of judgment on any point being expressed and received in the spirit of kindness and union. Means of increasing our usefulness and holiness were suggested, and meetings were held, and addresses on various topics delivered each evening.

PRESENTATION OF A BIBLE.

2*mo. 7th.*, 1865.—About 200 Christians, of various churches, spent the evening happily together in Union Hall; tea, fruit, &c., being also provided. Niel Steel, Esq., in the chair. The circumstances under which the meeting met were as follow:—Some short time ago, a number of the brethren thought fit to separate from the meeting in Union Hall, and along with them took the large pulpit bible, which had been subscribed for by members of the church for my use and the church's use. This conduct coming to the ears of several Christians connected with other churches in the town, particularly Mr. James Scrymgeour, in order to show their entire disapproval of such conduct, apart from any consideration of whether they were right or wrong in leaving, proposed to subscribe for a new one in lieu of the one taken away. Such was the strong feeling in this matter, that, in two hours, Mr. Scrymgeour got subscriptions sufficient to procure a large, handsome bible. The Bible was presented to-night, by the subscribers, and contains the following inscription:—"Presented to Mr. John Bowes, preacher of the gospel, by members of various denominations, as a token of respect for his Christian character, and untiring exertions in the cause of truth. Given at a public meeting held in the Union Hall, Dundee, 7th of February, 1865. Niel Steel, Chairman; James Scrymgeour, Secretary."

Had space permitted, I should have been glad to have given the whole of the speeches and proceedings, but must refer the reader to a full report in "The Truth Promoter," vol. ix. pp. 192—195.

2*mo. 21st*, 1865.—On coming from preaching on the 21st, we saw a meteor of splendid appearance flash across the sky, from north to south, illumining surrounding objects with its dazzling blue and red lights for several seconds. It first assumed the form of a magnificent firework having a long fiery train, but steadily increased in brilliancy until it suddenly disappeared. While attentively occupied with this startling phenomenon, it flashed across the mind in a moment, "Is this the Lord coming like lightning?" but after the luminous and grand appearance all was over. It is thus suddenly that the Lord Jesus Christ shall make his august appearance. One gentleman states, that "he was startled by a glare of light almost as bright as the sun at noonday—only the color was of a yellowish green. The light seemed to be arrested, and was extinguished before it reached the earth, bursting into several distinct waves of light before it finally disappeared. Independent of the bright nucleus, there was a kind of luminous haze about it that was quite visible to the eye. The meteor must have been at a great distance from the earth, as all who saw it thought that it was immediately above where they themselves stood."

3mo. 5th.—I replied to the "Rev. James Gall's Dipping not Baptism," in the Union Hall, Dundee. To quiet his own people, he tells them that "baptizo," baptize, means, according to classical authority, "to drown" by putting under water. And without a single scriptural warrant he assumes that among Jews and Christians it means to sprinkle or pour. I wrote Mr. Gall, and desired him to defend his treatise against my objections in a public discussion in Edinburgh or Dundee or both, but this he politely declined; so I felt free to consider it for the good of the public.

7mo. 5th.—DUNDEE. To-day, sixteen of our family met at Westfield House, the first time that all have met together; grandfather and mother, our three sons, two wives, one daughter and her husband, three grandsons and four grand-daughters. We had one friend, Mr. Beswick of Bolton, with us. We sung the 269th hymn, read the Scriptures and made a few remarks, and three prayed. Possibly we may never all meet again in one company until the day of the Lord.

8mo. 28th.—DUNDEE. For nearly a month I have been unwell; having only preached once in the open-air since the attack. It began with the stomach and head, and when these mended, rheumatic or similar pains confined me to the house one whole Lord's day. I was the Lord's prisoner. It is many years since any such incident occurred in my history. For some days it was doubtful how it would end, in death or life. For a long time I have had no fear of death, nor had I when it seemed near. There were some reasons for life—chiefly that I might win more souls to Christ. To all appearance I shall survive this attack. I was able to be at two services yesterday, but had to be taken, as well as returned, by a cab. Will my beloved brethren pray that, if spared, I may be more useful than ever. Sin only can prevent our happiness and usefulness. Jesus can save us from all sin.

During this year I issued a Prospectus for this work. My illness has reminded me of the uncertainty of this life, and has been greatly blessed, so that I have sung—

"I'll praise Him for all that is past,
And trust him for all that's to come."

I have been able to say of all the forty-eight years—now nearly forty-nine—that I have served Him, that I can praise him for sickness and health, friends and foes, prosperity and adversity, the deepest trials as well as the greatest joys; and it is easy to rely on Him for the unseen future when such are the lessons of the past, so that, should I be permitted to see the end of 1866, I have no idea that it shall be an exception to all the other years, and that I shall have no reason to praise him for this. Full of hope we sail over the ocean of life again,—another voyage when so many voyages have been crowned with success, nothing can come wrong to us. Every hour is big with mercy, and however threatening and dark the clouds on the horizon they contain no evil for me, or any that love the Lord.

The next considerable matter which will interest many of our friends is the proposed visit to America.

I am not proposing to go because of any lack of support here, for the Lord sends me as much or more than I can need, although I have not saved one penny for the American Mission, but no doubt many brethren who cannot go, will help in this good work as they do in others.

3mo. 13th, 1866.—On my way to Liverpool had a merciful deliverance. At the Beatock Station I was getting out, the train not quite stopped, when my legs seemed useless, and I fell my whole length on to the stone platform; I rose without being much hurt. Whether it was the stiffness of my limbs caused by the long ride, or the train's motion being greater than I expected, the lesson remains—never get out of a train while in motion. My glove was cut through, but the skin remained whole. I was comforted by this promise: "For he shall give his angels charge over thee, to keep thee in all thy ways. They shall bear thee up in their hands, lest thou dash thy foot against a stone."—Psa. xci., 11, 12. Preached in the evening to an attentive congregation in Hill Street Room.

18th.—At half-past 10, broke bread with the brethren at Tomlinson Street, MANCHESTER. One aged brother came to meet me, perhaps for the last time, contrary to his doctor's orders. At half-past 2, preached out to an excellent and attentive congregation on the Chorlton Road. A preacher preceded me on the ground, to whom I listened with pain, while he preached "the old prophet, and Jeroboam, and Rehoboam," and hardly mentioned Christ; I privately urged him in future to preach Christ. At half-past 6, preached in the hall, Lloyd Street, Hulme, where God is blessing Mr. Birch's labors; a crowded audience of about 1200, the largest audience I have preached the gospel to in Manchester. An orphan house connected with it.

25th.—BIRMINGHAM. Refreshing meeting at the Lord's Supper. Twenty missionaries are going out to China; the brethren are supporting them; their passage out is provided for. My proposed mission to America was also spoken of, and both were prayed for. Thus, far East and far West does the Lord send out laborers. At 3 p.m. in the Bull Ring, where I and P. G. Anderson again spoke. We were mobbed here twenty-eight years ago at the time we preached in Batty's Circus, and some of the actors were converted. At half-past 6, discoursed to a large congregation of serious attentive people. Some engaged to meet me in heaven that were not before preparing. Praise the Lord for this happy day.

THE MISSION TO AMERICA.

The great event of the year 1866 was the proposed visit to America. I was accompanied by John Sommerville, who had been useful at Glasgow and Cambuslang. We sailed on the 2nd of May, and on the 2nd of October arrived back in Liverpool. In those five months, tens of thousands heard the Gospel, the necessity of Christian Union, and the

Lord's Second Coming, in both Canada and the United States. Our persecution by the Irish Roman Catholics of Canada is detailed in the journal which follows, and the Lord's fatherly care over us during the Fenian Raid.

We found all the pulpits we wished more open to us in the States than we expected, so that the Methodist Episcopalian Church, Primitive Methodist Churches, Baptists, Presbyterians, and Second Adventists, gave us a hearty co-operation. There is less bigotry and sectarian narrowness than in Great Britain. Every pulpit we wished was open. I attended two Camp Meetings, and believe them, for that country, adapted to do much good. I preached several times to colored congregations; no people in the States were more deeply serious and attentive. The intercourse I had at London with a Mohawk Chief, as he was a preacher, may sow the good seed by our tracts, among the tens of thousands of Indians on the Grand River.

The Education of the United States far surpasses our own. Property is taxed that schools may be free. Rich and poor, Roman Catholics and Protestants, mingle in these schools, and receive an education for nothing. Books only have to be purchased. The Teachers are of a superior class, and we should do well to educate the whole of our own people at home.

My visit to the Baptist Theological College at Newton Central, Mass., where I lectured to the students, was a most providential and important opening in this journey.

The Temperance question commands public attention, and among the ministers, of all churches, is zealously supported, with rare exceptions. The Maine Law has been carried in several States, and when it is honestly carried out pauperism and crime have been almost annihilated; so that, when the vexed question of President Johnson's policy is settled, Temperance Reformers will be free to push on their legislative conquests. But our readers will form their own impressions from the following journal.—

5mo. 2nd.—Brother Sommerville and I reached the "St. Patrick" steamer by eleven o'clock a.m. Several brethren from Strathaven, Rutherglen, and East Kilbride, and Glasgow came and saw us off. We looked out long, but in vain, for brother Stone, but as he had a sale of cattle yesterday, we concluded he could not come. Our berths, "intermediate," are pretty comfortable, far better than in the steerage, where about ten persons lie as close together as may be only separated by a thin piece of board; so that, excepting that each knows his own little space, their arms must often meet each other. She started from her moorings about one p.m., dropping slowly down the river. Brother Watson, farmer, once near Helensburgh, his wife, his daughter, and her husband, all going out to Canada, are also in the "intermediate," so that we know four out of the ten in our room. An American mate, from Maine, draws up to us, and seems to have respect for religion. several on board drunk; a fight between two of the crew; two or three of them drunk. An officer states we have, or are to have, 350 on board. We hope to deliver tracts, of which we have some hundreds, and exchange them often, and recommend our Master yet to all that will hear us. At four p.m. the steamer let go her anchor at the Tail of the Bank, off Greenock, near the middle of the river. I asked the captain when she would leave, and if we go ashore when we should return. They think if we return by nine or ten a.m. we shall be in time, but give no authority, and throw all on our own responsibility. Brother Somerville inclines to stay by the ship, when lo! a passenger in a little boat hails us; it is dear James Stone, who finding himself too late in Glasgow, hastens by train and hires out a little boat for half an hour's sail. This decides brother Sommerville, and we both, and the American mate, in another half hour, land at Greenock pier; see brother Stone off by train, and then call on a few Christians, one of whom invited me to spend a night with him before sailing. Brother Sommerville, in a voice well fitted for open-air work, commenced, and perhaps two hundred round him, when he was stopped by an officious looking gentleman, who ordered us off. I told him if brother Sommerville desisted I should go on, as we were in an open square and in no thoroughfare. I told him that if they removed me they would have to take me to the police office. I asked him if he was the superintendent of the police; he said no, but he represented him. I had said before we began, "I will thank any of you for a chair to sit down on." I was sitting when the interruption occurred, and now stood upon the chair; we continued till after nine p.m.; many hundreds, perhaps five hundred at once heard us. At the close I asked the gentleman's name; he said it was serjeant Sim; so, if the people of Greenock will suffer it, the police will close the best place for open-air preaching, but if they will stand up for the Gospel, the police must yield to law and liberty. Brother Sommerville closed, after which we had gracious intercourse with a dear brother, B., known before to brother Sommerville, and at half-past ten reached the hospitable home of brother R., where we tarried for the night. I had only one sleep, better than on board, rose refreshed, and had a shower bath. Brother Sommerville says he would not again stop preaching, but would rather go to the police office. We were both thankful for the great opportunity of preaching Christ; neither regretted that we came off.

3rd.—Left Greenock by a little steamer for the "St. Patrick" at mid-day, with the inspector and directors. While waiting on shore had some profitable conversation with Captain Brotchie, the Sailor's Missionary here. I was pleased to find that in asking sinners to believe, he is careful to show them what to believe, and thus avoids an error into which many fall. Steamer sailed down the Clyde. A substantial dinner of soup, beef, and potatoes.

Four o'clock. Asked the captain to grant liberty to hold religious services on board, and told him we intended to deliver tracts. He was very gracious, and granted all I asked, and said on Lord's Days we might have religious services in the saloon. Sorted tracts assisted by brother Watson. Three of us delivered a gospel tract to all on board we could meet with; a few only refused them, chiefly card players and Romanists. Thus far the Lord hath opened the way, and prepared us and the people for our work.

At 6 p.m., tea. At 7, Brother S. opened our preaching on deck by singing a hymn and prayer; I preached and then he; we then sung the 40th Psalm, in which several joined; a large company listened; all seemed impressed.

4th.—Friday. Reached *Loch Foyle*, about 21 miles from London-derry, about 4¼ a.m. I have slept well all night; sickness on board, but not in our room of ten berths. All are friendly, so that by making a screen with my plaid, I got a little room to myself and washed all over. This loch is nine miles across here, separating County Donegal from County Derry. We shall return to the main ocean when we have received 170 more passengers. We carry 400, and shall then be quite full. I like the ship, she is steady, and all are very respectful to us. This is the last place we touch at in Europe, and hope to leave at mid-day or soon after.

12th.—I have not been able to write for above a week. After leaving the west coast of Ireland the weather became changed and the sea boisterous. I was slightly sick a few hours; brother Sommerville very sick. When 800 miles on our course, in a less sea-worthy vessel, danger might have been apprehended, but ours is like a life-boat, sinking down to the level of the waves, then mounting over them in splendid style, while the foam of the waves covered the ocean, and the billows rose like mountains. I stood on deck admiring the greatness of God, and the skill of man in constructing such a vessel. One day we only got over 60 miles, another 160. A head wind all along has prevented our progress. A young lady was sitting with several more of us at the after part of the vessel, when she said with the simplicity of a child, " Which part of this ship is going to America ?" As though the one part could go without the other ! Last night we had preaching on board. We sang the hundredth Psalm ; Brother S. prayed and I preached. He thought he should be unable to preach, but when I had done he spoke forcibly for some time. He has been a long time unwell, but is recovering. While I was preaching a great cry got up at the fore end of the vessel. It seemed to be some Roman Catholics who had discovered a fleet of porpoises. This disturbed us a little ; but we sang again, and Brother Watson says it doubled our congregation. Several Christians have made themselves known to us. Last night I fell asleep about 10 o'clock, and awoke at 5 a.m., much refreshed. Wind favorable now, and nearly all sails set; the sea calm. While I walked on deck, our hundreds of passengers all quiet, probably most of them asleep. Thus in the midst of the great Atlantic we are quiet and happy; " God is with us," and this is the best of all. After dinner to-day, the Captain said we had sailed 1130 miles, and we had yet 1700 to go. A curious incident occurred to-day. A woman desired to see me.—

WOMAN.—" Do you marry people ?"

J. BOWES.—" Sometimes."

W.—" There is a young man and I wish to be married."

J.B.—" I advise you to wait till you get to Quebec."

W.—" I cannot wait that long ; if I am not married now, I will not marry him at all."

J. B.—" But your love cannot be great to him if you cannot wait so short a time. The great matter with you is to be married to Jesus Christ. Do you love him ? (Here I quoted texts, and preached Christ to her.)

W.—" Yes, I love Christ ; have done from a child ; but I love the young man far better."

J.B.—" That is wrong ; you should love Christ above all."

W.—"I heard you last night, and felt something warm about my heart, and especially to the young man. Then you will not marry me?"

Here the mate came up, and said, "I will marry you." She followed him a few steps, and then sat down. She was Irish.

13th.—Lord's Day. At 11, 3, and 7 o'clock, had preaching on board three times. Some Roman Catholics were trifling, but soon either became quiet, or retired. Distributed seven Testaments, many tracts, and between the forenoon and afternoon services was asked to visit a sick lady in the female part opposite ours. All were very respectful while I read, prayed, and expounded. Brother Sommerville helped me blessedly in the open-air work. Here on board we have a parish of nearly 500 souls. The Captain attended one discourse, and several officers and the doctor attend occasionally. This day has been most blessed; many opportunities of doing good have occurred; the tracts are eagerly read. We have twice given them to nearly all the passengers, and exchanged them at each meeting. The last 24 hours we have run 139 miles. We are now more than half-way.

14th.—It was cold and blowing, so that few attended the meeting on deck. Brother Sommerville unable to take part or bear the cold.

15th.—Noon. We have steamed 189 miles the last 24 hours, and are about 100 miles from what are called the banks of Newfoundland. As they are fishing banks, I do not expect to see them. Have just conversed with a young man converted on board. The reading to him of the New Testament has been blessed to this grand end, as well as the other means. At 3 o'clock, read and expounded Luke xix. Understood that an unbeliever was sowing his errors in the steerage. I met him on deck, accosted him kindly, and a discussion followed. He fell into the same error as Mr. Holyoake on Rom. xii., the "coals of fire" meant persecution. He said he might have come from a monkey! I said he was welcome to such a father, but I claimed a higher parentage. He ran off into abuse of wars and persecutions of professors, which I showed the Scriptures condemned. I offered him my tract in reply to Holyoake, but he refused to read; others asked for it, for a congregation had gathered round us.

17th.—A concert was held in the saloon. I was offered a ticket, and urgently invited, but I remembered this command, "Is any merry, let him sing psalms." Gave away a Testament and a few tracts, but was not able to say much through the seamen's labors on deck. We are now about 130 miles from Cape Race. The "St. Andrews" passed us about mid-day on her way home. Brother Sommerville told me to-day that, while we labored in Hutchesons' Street, a young man, about two years ago, understood that one of us was taken up by the police, (likely J. Mackenzie or W. Langton) and *he came up to fight for us*, if needed, when he got awakened and converted. What various motives bring men under the sound of the gospel! He said, "I came down the stair a poor lamb."

19th,—Had we been in the steerage with the Irish emigrants, we should have been most uncomfortable. We shall be several days beyond the fourteen, owing to head winds and stormy weather at first. A boy had stowed himself away, about 14 years of age; he was set to work. Land appeared, after two weeks of sea, partly covered with snow. It is called Cape Ray; we had passed Cape Race in the fog;

weather cold and wet. At dinner one of our number was grossly insulted. I had retired for the evening, when four, chiefly of our room, commenced playing at draughts. As I could not sleep, I remonstrated, as one half of our room were in bed. They gave over at once.

20th.—Two whales in sight; their blowing, seen at a distance, was like a sail or vessel. They were of the real Davis' Strait kind. Hitherto, at all our meals either Brother S. or I had given thanks. I explained that we had mistaken in so acting, as we thought all would be agreeable; finding it was not so, we should confine ourselves to private thanks. Not a remark was made. The offender, if he can feel anything, will feel this keenly. Ship in full sail. The island of Anticosta in the distance. Lower Canada in sight. Hills covered with snow. I counted twelve vessels at sea. Preached three times; many very attentive, but some more observant of the villages that adorn the margin of this great river,—for we are now in the St. Lawrence.

21st. –On deck at 7 a.m. St. Ann's mountains deeply covered with snow; none on the shore. Cottages and farmhouses all along the shore of this great river. The people live by fishing and farming. At 9 a.m. we are 250 miles from Quebec. I stood, meditating on the happiness of the heirs of salvation. The ship's doctor came up and said, "It is nice to see them all enjoying themselves." I said, "The child of God is happy because he is prepared to die." He replied, "If the sailors were always looking at death they would be uncomfortable." This is the great error of the world. He said that he had seen so much injury by the revival work in Glasgow, it had perfectly disgusted him. I said I had seen so much good from it, that it had fascinated me to Christ and his cause. He said, "I was called on to visit a young woman that was very ill, and he put her attendants all out of the room, and asked her about her disease. She said she had been hearing a minister and she was all bad since. I pointed to the Psalms, and she got consolation. She is now married, and seems happy." I asked what he would think if, on the great day, she rose against him, and accused him of being guilty of her blood. I should have pointed her to the redeeming blood of Calvary. He then said he would talk with me to-morrow.

21st.—FATHER POINT. Pilot came on board; stormy.

22nd.—About 30 miles yet to sail. The doctor came on board; all passed before him, 471 souls. Had been nearly put four days in quarantine through a soldier's sick child. The firmness of our doctor and captain saved us. Before reaching our destination the St. Lawrence divides into two branches, separated by the island of Orleans, about eighteen miles in circumference, and about nine miles below Quebec. We observed the falls of the Montgomery river. They are large and splendid, inferior only to those of the Niagara. At half-past three landed at Point Levi; took to six o'clock before we got our luggage passed; it was all driven for us into the Emigration Office. Ours passed without opening, and at half-past six crossed to QUEBEC in another steamer. Left brother Sommerville by the luggage, while I sought out Mr. Salmond, Seamen's Missionary. The Lord directed us to a Christian family. It seems we have had no death on board but a child two months old, overlaid in a stormy night. But we had fire in the galley, put out by the water pipes; the crew only knew of it till it was extinguished. Thus mercifully has the Lord preserved us.

23*rd*.—No open-air preaching here in this fine city, with beautiful villages and a thickly populated country round about. We were told there could be no open air preaching until the consent of the Roman Catholic Mayor should be granted. We waited on him, but while he was kind, he would neither hinder nor forward our work. The people are expecting a review of the soldiers under his command on the plains of Abraham; however snow is falling, and the weather unfit for open-air work. About twenty meet here in fellowship with John Darby; had a genial conversation with a chief brother. The ship sent on her passengers last night by train to all places in Canada and the United States. She goes up to Montreal without passengers.

24*th*.—Walked out to the plains, and saw a plain monument where General Wolfe fell, on which was inscribed, "Here died Wolfe, victorious, Sep. 13, 1759." This is about a mile from the City. We walked on to the heights where his men climbed up but could not come near. It is on the farm of John Gilmore. At three o'clock we preached on the platform; were told that two thirds of our congregation were Roman Catholics; they heard quietly, and I trust the good effected may be seen after many days. We had three Roman Catholic priests, three friars, three ministers, fourteen lawyers, and one city missionary, who reported this to us; about 200 or 250 heard. The day was fine. Praise the Lord for this meeting. After the sea voyage my health is improved in all respects, and brother Sommerville is quite recovered from his sea illness. Quebec is the most warlike place I have seen. It abounds with French Roman Catholics; the Protestants are in a very humble minority. Lower Canada has few English in it, but all are quite loyal to the Crown. The horses here are small, lively animals, quite different from those of Liverpool and Manchester; they are more like ponies than cart horses. Snow is yet on the distant hills, but it melts as it falls here. In winter the St. Lawrence is frozen over some miles below this.

25*th*.—We have decided to remain here a few days. We then go on to Montreal in one night by rail. We should rejoice much should the Lord use us among the Canadian or French Roman Catholics. We meet to-day at tea, Mr. Marsh, Baptist minister, and Mr. Normandeau, a converted priest of the Roman Catholic Church, who had been engaged as professor in the Seminary at Quebec for five years. I have seen his wife. He is connected with the Grande Ligne Home Mission, which is well spoken of as useful to the conversion of nearly 2000 Roman Catholics. They apply to almost any person for subscriptions; in this and a few other things I do not agree with them, but they are doing real work for God, but I shall see and hear more of them. We have evidently been led here of the Lord at every step, and expect great blessing from him in the future. General Neal Dow sailed for Scotland on the 19th.

26*th*.—Dined on board Captain Howe's ship "William Yeo," with our kind friend John Salmon, seamen's missionary. Walked beneath the Rock; half way up, in large letters, is written, "Here Montgomery fell." In the evening we were told the police would require us to desist our open-air preaching, and if we refused and remonstrated, take us off to prison. So as we left our room, we remarked that, instead of spending the night in our comfortable bed, it might be among the prisoners of the city. Brother Sommerville opened the meeting; I was preaching on God's love to a great audience, and nearly twenty lawyers present, when two policemen pressed through the crowd to attract my attention, but I would not notice them. At last one of them desired me to stop; I said, "Wait till I have finished my sentence," it was on God's love in Christ; when I had finished the sentence, I paused to know what they wanted. They said we were to desist; it was contrary to law. Several influential voices said, "It is not contrary to law." I said, "I will give you my name and address, and answer before any court of law for what we are doing." The policeman, trembling, took out his note book, and said they were ordered by the chief. We finished in peace, excepting that a number of boys hooted and followed us through the street.

We have had much conversation with one servant who had been six months servant in a nunnery. She said to me, "What are you? are you not a Protestant?" "No, nor a Roman Catholic; I take no name but that of Christian." I was able to set much truth before her, and urged her not to become a nun, as she intends. Have seen Mr Normandeau, the converted priest, several times. Many priests evidently remain with Rome for the living or money.

28*th*.—At 7 p.m. crossed the St. Lawrence, 5 cents each, and took the cars at Point Levi for

MONTREAL.

Montreal is 180 miles up the St. Lawrence; three dols. first class, and one dol. second class; we took the second. Smoking is allowed, and nearly every one smoked. We stayed nearly an hour at Richmond, when we were put into a first class; we reached Montreal at 6.45 next morning. I slept a little. Brother Sommerville had a serious fall on the platform at Richmond; I hope he is not much worse.

29*th*.—Can have a room and bed with Mr. Guthrie, a Scotchman, the husband of Jane Dippie, the daughter of parents passed into the better country. She had not seen me for more than twenty-two years, she burst into tears, and for some time was nearly overwhelmed with emotion. Preached to from 400 to 500 at the Wharf. The editor of the "Montreal Witness" had prepared our way and announced our meeting. Several Christians who had heard us in Scotland present; one a preacher who wishes more intercourse with us. Here also, in a city of about 120,000, the Romanists number about 80,000, or two thirds. We crossed the Great Victoria Bridge, 7000 feet long, supported on stone pillars.

30*th*.—We preached in the same place; much disorder. The superintendent of the River Police objected that the foot path was obstructed; we asked the police to open it, but the Roman Catholics crowded it the more.

31*st*.—Haymarket. Great congregation; when I had half done, a rush to throw me down, noise, and confusion; one gentleman stepped towards me and said, "The first man that makes a disturbance, I will hand him over to the police." After this, we had quiet for a while; then, when I had nearly finished, a rush upon me. Twice I was obliged to leave the stand; fighting commenced; a doctor knocked down one after another, five or six, who attacked him. One young man named Fraser was sadly hurt, and had to remain at the doctor's all night. A friend took me by the arm and led me away. Brother Sommerville got another way. Many were afraid that I was killed, whereas we were neither of us struck or hurt. Many counselled that we should give up open-air labor here.

6mo. 1st.—We waited on the superintendent of Police and asked him if we could calculate on the protection of British subjects. He said he had only a few police, 100, for the city—that the Haymarket was a bad place, but if we would preach before the office, on a green, he would send a man or two; he would not engage that no blow would be struck. We published this in the "Witness." We preached in Jacque Carier Sq.; night came on: we knew not but we might be killed or wounded, but felt it right to go. The police were not required to act, but they were ready. A large congregation. The M'Gill College students came down in a body to protect us, and offered to escort us home, but we declined, as the meeting had gone off peaceably and the students had each a formidable staff about him, I told a leader of them to take the Bible only as a weapon. The public are afraid of our lives. Several, even Roman Catholics of the more respectable kind, are determined we shall have a hearing. The Temperance hall is taken for us, so we shall expect to be useful.

2nd.—Disorderly meeting; many of the Romanists so drunk they did not know what we said. We were obliged to desist.

During the week have had intercourse with several who meet (in all about 120) under the auspices of John Darby. They will do nothing to displease him, and hence exclude thousands because they will not denounce those brethren who receive all Christians. I said I never met a man holding Newton's errors as doctrine. As we found them to be so exclusive, we gave our testimony to several courteous and kind brethren, who use the knife to cut off living members as gently as may be. Here we learned that Mr. Darby is against the immersion of believers.

3rd.—At 9 a.m. addressed a meeting of reclaimed girls, taken from the street, in a reformatory; about 12 present; several deeply in tears.

11th.—Temperance Hall. On "What Christian churches ought to be." At two, brother Sommerville preached at the Square. I was only opening my address when the clamor became loud and general. I was forcibly pushed off the step by a young man, bold in his manner; we could have arrested him. He retired a little when a volunteer came up and requested me to desist. Ten policemen could hardly have kept sufficient order.

It is a great day for the Roman Catholics; processions and singing in the streets. At three discoursed again on the Saviour and his Church. At six very few present outside, as the city was moved to see a review of the volunteers: I said a few words to the few people about me. One man pushed violently between brother Sommerville and me. At seven, a nice congregation; I, brothers Sommerville and Gray spoke. It was a blessed season. We have received much hospitality from several Christians here, and could one remain, I doubt not, much union and blessing would result. The Lord of the harvest send laborers to this great fashionable city. I thank God that the Romanists are not our governors. The lowest are more like savage beasts than men; they are insensible to kindness, and more set against the Gospel than Pagans. The latter love their idols; the former are trained to oppose the Scriptures and the Gospel. Many priests never read, or study, or preach from the Scriptures. The little preaching they give the people is from the prayer books. Here I met Dr. Hutcheson, once a Wesleyan minister, but for many years a preacher of the Gospel and the Lord's Second Coming, in Canada and the United States. He resides fifty miles off. One of the blessings of our visit will be the good which may result to the inquiring and gifted minds around us.

4th.—This evening at 9 p.m., we start by the cars for Toronto, and travel all night. The whole country is excited. The Fenians have landed, and taken Fort Erie, killed several volunteers, and beat them back, but were repulsed when the regular soldiers got up. Five hundred of them were taken prisoners; the rest fled to the Niagara river, but are not permitted to land in the United States. It is believed this morning that there is not a Fenian soldier on British soil, but hundreds of them are hovering about. The weather is now as hot as it is usually in Scotland in the heat of summer.

TORONTO.

At 9 p.m. started for Toronto. We were detained on the road 3½ hours, as the Fenians were near us. Arrived, after travelling all night, at 4 p.m. The streets thronged with people, owing to the funeral of five volunteers of the *Queen's Own* that had fallen in battle. The streets were hung with black and other emblems of mourning. We walked out to the house of James Leslie, Esq., who married Mrs. Jacqueline Jamieson, of Aberdeen, at whose retired mansion we spent the evening happily. He drove us in next morning to Mr. Galbraith's, who had married some years before one of the daughters of Mrs. Wright, of Neilston. They, like many others with large families, find, by attention to business, prosperity attends their footsteps. After calling on a few Christians, we determined not to remain in Toronto, as even the Bible Society meeting is put off owing to the excitement of the war. For the same reason, and as we despaired of doing very much in Canada together, and thought of only going to such places as had some claims on us through our brethren, Brother Sommerville took a through ticket to New York, I to St. Catharines, where the brethren Thomas Simpson and Richard Taylor were glad to see me. At St. Catharines Brother Sommerville and I parted, with mutual prayers for blessings to attend our footsteps. We never intended both of us to take the long journeys in the United States.

8th.—St. Catharines. Brother Simpson furnished horse and buggy, a four-wheeled carriage, and I started for the farm of Thomas Archibald, formerly of Strathaven. I found him about a mile beyond Thorald, on the Welland Canal, on which sail large ships from Lake Erie to Lake Ontario, connecting the two. As he was only about seven miles from the Falls of Niagara, we started off.

THE FALLS OF NIAGARA.

These mighty Falls can sometimes be heard ten or twelve miles off, and the rising spray may be seen many miles away. The quantity of water in this mighty river, as it rushes down amid high rocks on each side, is surprising. The Niagara River is 36 miles in length; its waters are supplied by the great lakes Superior, Michigan, Huron, and Erie, which pour their floods from Erie into Lake Ontario through this channel, called the Niagara River; it is part of the boundary between Canada and the State of New York. Twenty-two miles above the famous Falls, is Lake Erie. We first came to the American Falls, 900 feet wide, by 164 feet high. These are divided from the Horse Shoe or Canadian Fall, which is 2000 feet wide and 158 feet high, by Iris or Goat Island. It is indeed a "Thunder of Waters," as its name signifies. Over this magnificent precipice the vast river rushes at the rate of 100 million tons of water every hour. "It is computed that the precipice is worn away by the friction of the ever-flowing flood at the rate of about one foot a-year, and it is believed that the Falls have gradually receded from Queenston, seven miles below, to their present position." The river above the Falls is studded with islands of various sizes, 37 in number. The width of the stream varies from several hundred yards to three miles. At the Falls it is about three quarters of a mile wide. The total descent from Lake Erie to Lake Ontario is 334 feet. These famed Falls were first seen by a white man only about 188 years ago. Father Hennessin, a French Jesuit missionary, first saw them while on an expedition of discovery in the year 1678. We walked on to Table Rock, which is not the extensive platform it once was; large portions of it having fallen from time to time. It overhangs the boiling caldron close to the Horse Shoe Fall, and the view which we took is indeed sublime. In 1818 a mass of 160 feet long and 40 feet wide broke off and fell into the terrible flood; and in 1828 three immense masses fell with a shock like an earthquake, and thus it has often fallen. Just below the falls the river narrows abruptly, and flows rapidly through a deep gorge, varying from 200 to 400 yards wide and 300 feet deep. This gorge extends downwards seven miles. Guides provide you with dresses for a dollar or one half, and you can go for a short distance covered with spray between the rocks and the descending flood; we descended as far as we could without the protecting dresses, and stood gazing with admiration on a river which has poured its waters down from lake to lake probably since the time of Noah, or even that of Adam.

> "From age to age—in winter's frost or summer's sultry beam,
> By day, by night, without a pause—thy waves with loud acclaim,
> In ceaseless sounds, have still proclaimed the Great Eternal's name."

We drove down the river past the museum and hotels (one of vast extent) to a wonder of art—

THE NIAGARA SUSPENSION BRIDGE.

The height of the towers on the American side is 88 feet, and on this side 78 feet; the bridge is 800 feet long, 24 feet wide, and 250 feet in height above the river. It is suspended from tower to tower by four enormous wire cables of about ten inches diameter, which contain 4000 miles of wire; the bearing capacity of the four cables is about 12,400 tons. The total weight of the bridge is 800 tons. From Canada the Great Western and New York Central Railroads send their cars across the bridge without the slightest vibration. The road for carriages, horses, &c., is suspended 28 feet below the railway line.

The Rapids, above the Falls, extend a mile. During this short distance the river falls 60 feet, and it is fearful to see the tumultuous rolling and foaming of the mighty waters ere they dash below. Should any unfortunate boat or canoe get into these rapids it is generally dashed to pieces, with its human freight, when carried over the Falls; thus many lives have been lost. The Rapids remind one of the dangerous eddies of sin: if you once get among these, it is difficult, not to say impossible, to escape destruction, excepting by the Almighty Saviour.

9th.—ST. CATHARINES. Preached at the Square, near the Post Office, to an attentive assembly of about 200. I trust everlasting good was done. At eleven, nine observed the Lord's Supper. As they receive brethren here from Toronto, where about 100 meet, and Hamilton, where about 20 meet, and these meetings are among the denouncers of Bethesda, I told the brethren distinctly I could only regard the Table as the Lord's if they received all known to them to be Christians. As they conceded that all disciples, brethren, saints, members of the one body, should be received, I was most happy to go in; brother Archibald also comes for the first time, for although he only resides a few miles off, he could not find out the meeting. At half-past two preached to a small company in the Nephalist Hall. At half-past five to more out of doors. At half-past six in the Hall, to a thoughtful people; much interest in my subject—the Lord's early return.

I am now engaged for four different places this week and next, brother Archibald having procured chapels or churches for four different discourses,—two next Lord's Day in the Wesleyan church. The weather is now very hot, and I am warned not to labor so much as in the old country. Here are no poor laws, and very few poor people, as work is plentiful and wages good. The number of vehicles, light waggons, &c., employed, in which people drive about, is quite surprising. But it is so hot in summer they cannot walk far, and winter produce is carried to the market. Wood is fetched for the fire by sleighs. Here, wood, in large supplies, cut to from one or two yards in length, to supply the place of coal, is spread out in large quantities at all the stations.

12th.—Visited, with Mr. Robinson, the hospital of the wounded, who have been shot in the late battle. Spoke of Jesus by each couch, then to all; I was requested to pray by a fine looking fellow who has been five years a Christian; gave tracts; was coming away when I was told of two Fenian prisoners; visited them; one, a strong, powerful man, likely to be a match for two or three men. I quoted the words, "Him that cometh to me, I will in no wise cast out." "What is that," said he. I paused. "Repeat it again." I did. He seemed astonished, and exclaimed, "Is not that beautiful." Both were Roman Catholics, one from the States, the other a Canadian. Afternoon; met brother Archibald at Allanburgh Station and walked on to FONTHILL; preached in the Second Advent Chapel on the King's return.

13th.—Chapel again; more crowded than last night. Spoke on the Gospel and the Church. Mr. Walker, of Aberdeen, now Baptist minister, present. My visit was much needed. I was hospitably entertained in the family of Mr. M'Clellan. The chapel is erected on his farm; he set me in his buggy. The climate is good, and the farms around Fonthill are well cultivated, and all are in very comfortable circumstances that choose to be so. Cultivated land and buildings may be purchased at from 60 dols. to 100 dols. per acre. Some families have 100, some 25, and some 10 acres. All afford a good living, if the land is the farmer's own.

6mo 14th.—PORT DALHOUSIE, on Lake Ontario, the termination of the Great Welland Canal, on which ships of two and three masts are drawn by four or six horses each; several locks raise the vessel gradually over the mountain; ships come from Chicago to Liverpool. Mr. Doig heard me to-night, a native of Dundee, who has been above 20 years in the army. He heard me once, at his mother's recommendation, in the Nethergate Chapel, Dundee, more than thirty years ago. He has been led to Christ only twelve months.

20th.—THORALD. I have now spent a week here and in the district, and have had some good meetings and some blessed opportunities of speaking truth.

21st.—Started for LONDON, 108 miles. It is the great thoroughfare from New York to the Western States.

22nd.—Attended the mid-day prayer meeting with my kind brother and host Marcus Holmes. Arranged to preach twice in the Congregational Church; the minister, Mr. Dickson, a Scotchman. Visited with Mr. Holmes many cottages. To some of the cottagers he has told the glad tidings with saving effect.

24th.—The Congregational Church at 11 and half-past 6. Well attended both services. The minister was present, also several officers in the evening who are interested in the Second Coming of Christ.

26th.—The largest congregation that we have had in the Market Square. The Bishop of Huron was present. How important are these open-air labors. London contains about 15,000 people, and has its Thames, Blackfriars, and Westminster bridges. I was driven out in the morning by Mr. Mitchell, and in the afternoon by Mr. Holmes.

28th.—Preached to the soldiers between the barracks; as many civilians as soldiers; a good congregation. Several of the soldiers seemed deeply interested. I had an opportunity of speaking about Christ to several of the officers in private, also on such texts as "Love your enemies," "Do good to them that hate you," &c. I have learned that the colonel and the bishop were present when I spoke on what Christian churches ought to be. The bishop would have been better pleased had I kept to the gospel, no doubt.

29th.—Peter Hill, a Mohawk Indian, from Tuscorow, called on me to-day. He owns 50 acres of land; preaches Christ, and meets to observe the Lord's Supper weekly. He has not been baptized, but I hope will be; I gave him my 24 paged tract on baptism; about 16 meet with him. A brother, Grant, had immersed his infant child of two years. (Heard to-day of a believer who got sprinkled! How Christ's institutions are perverted.) He says the Mohawks number about thirty or thirty-six thousand on the Grand River in Canada. Some are yet pagans, some Episcopalians, and others are Methodists. I gave him a dozen of our tracts for himself and his tribe. Evening: had a meeting, chiefly of Christians, in Mr. Holmes's large room. A few meet weekly here to remember the Lord; possibly more may meet after this.

30th.—Took a second class ticket from London to Milwaukie, 4 dols.

50 cents, first class being 8 dols. 50 cents; rode first class to Sarnia; had to wait there until 1.30 p.m., July first, about ten hours. Found second class a deck passage, without seats, no place fit for a pig; I offered to pay first class fare from London, which was refused, so I paid one dollar extra over first class, as my hope of usefulness would have been cut off. This was the most unreasonable demand ever exacted from me.

7mo. 1st.—From London to Sarnia, on the St. Clair river, is 90 miles, and from Sarnia, by the lakes, to Milwaukie, is about 500 miles. We sailed all this day along Lake Huron, until mid-night, when we reached the Straits of Mackinac, and so passed into Lake Michigan. At one view we counted forty-five vessels in full sail on Lake Huron. These lakes are great inland seas; sometimes we lost sight of land. At dinner, the captain having consented, I announced preaching in the saloon at three o'clock. A kind friend told the second class passengers, chiefly Germans. I have also delivered a large number of tracts. The captain and some officers present; found I could only get one service. Our boat, the "Antilope," sails well, about ten miles an hour: her saloon is 100 feet long. We take our meals thus:—breakfast at 7, dinner at 12. and supper at 6. We have also every thing that the heart can wish for.

3rd.—All night on Lake Michigan. Landed at MILWAUKIE, which now contains 56,000 or 60,000 inhabitants. Here I took the "Prairie du Chin" (Dog of the Prairie) cars to Boseobel, travelling all night, as I have done since Saturday.

4th.—Took stage for LANCASTER, 25 miles, the county town of Grant Co., Wisconsin; arrived at 11. This, the 4th of July, is a great day in the States, being the Anniversary of the National Independence. While standing to write the perspiration dropped from my forehead. Here I tarried two nights with my affectionate niece and her kind husband, Samuel Moore; he is the Treasurer of the County. The people are so carried away with national exultation, and the weather so hot, that preaching seemed out of the question.

6th.—PLATTVILLE. A beautifully situated town. Made satisfactory arrangements for preaching. As a funeral procession passed my sister's door, I followed it to the chapel, where a church of the late Alexander Campbell's views meets; it was filled with a decent audience. The body of the hearse was made of glass, and the coffin was visible. The address, from a working man, was very scriptural, and perhaps better than would have been delivered by a clerical speaker.

8th.—A class met at nine a.m. in sister Snowden's. I had not seen her for 39 years, before which I received her into the church or society. She spoke very feelingly; the meeting was very refreshing; I declined to lead the class, having a great day's work before me, however I found an opportunity of speaking to Christ's honor. The question proposed by the leader was an improvement on some that I have learned, it was —"Brother (or sister) is it well with you?" and the answers tended much to the Lord's honor. At half-past ten preached in the Methodist Episcopalian Chapel, where Mr. James Lawson, who was born a few miles from where I was, ministers. At two, preached in the Primitive Church on the Gospel and Church Union; crowded place. At a quarter-past seven a great congregation in the Methodist Episcopal Church. Mr. L. has assisted in the services all the day. The last continued two hours; I discoursed on the Second Coming of Christ with much comfort, as I judged the people needed this truth. All the pulpits I have been in are open, capable of holding four or six speakers, indeed they are not pulpits but platforms. The people are more open and willing to hear both sides than in Europe. The Primitive Methodists have no seat-rents, and very few collections.

9th.—BLOCKHOUSE. Three miles from Plattville. Primitive Methodist Church nearly filled, with an attentive congregation. I have now had much conversation with Joseph Robinson, P. M. Local preacher, who married one of the three daughters of my wife's sister, Snowden. He has now about 280 acres of land, cleared. It seems land of this kind here is worth about £9 per acre with buildings on. My brother-in-law, the late Henry Snowden, lived some years in such circumstances that he could either work or not, and he has also left all his family in comfort. All farmers, that work, get rich here, and obtain a competency by mid-life. Few do well who begin farming here without knowing anything about it. Miners of the old country have success here in their own calling, and can often earn 2 dols. per day. The farm laborer is worth £40 per annum, with board and lodgings.

12th.—LINDEN. By the labor of Thomas Mellor, with whom I lodge, and the activity of Joseph Mellor and others, we had an excellent meeting in the Public School, given freely for all such discourses. The weather is exceedingly hot; persons wisely come to worship here very lightly clothed.

13th.—Thomas Mellor, now a local preacher among the Primitives, drove me beyond Wingfield, about 15 miles, to see James Heathcote and his wife, both in fellowship once at Whaley Bridge. We went over many miles of rich unbroken prairie land, and other parts cultivated and adorned with rich crops. Everybody here rides. Lands can be had, with buildings, in this State, at 14 dols. per acre, and in other places not cleared at 5 dols. per acre.

15th.—Lord's Day. As there did not seem a door open for usefulness here, where James Heathcote resides, he yoked "a span" of horses, and in his waggon took me to

A DAY'S MEETINGS IN A GROVE AT NEW PROVIDENCE,

to which I had been invited. The Primitive Methodists and others came in waggons, buggys, &c. There might be 300 people assembled. I addressed the meeting before dinner, and was announced to preach after dinner, but Mr. Haw informed the meeting that infant baptism would be observed immediately. I publicly asked him to give his scriptural reasons, which he said it was not customary to do. Neither is it customary to sprinkle children at such open-air meetings. Great excitement was produced by my question, but after dinner allayed when I opened the meeting with prayer. Three sermons in the afternoon. I took up a good deal of time, as was expected, on needful truths. The people very attentive. Many shook hands with great affection, and one middle-aged female regarded my discourses as forming one of the most memorable days of her life. The grove of trees protected us from the sun, as well as the numerous horses tied to them. Mr. Patfield took me to MIFFLIN in his waggon, and as they desired a sermon on the

16th.—I gave them a discourse with my coat off, it was so hot, and the people had set me the example! The Primitive Methodist Church filled to overflowing, and I have no doubt good resulted. I desired the people to make an appointment to meet me at the right hand of Christ at his coming. Many said they would "try."

19th.—Took the stage for Dunleith. Six miles below Galena, we crossed the *Mississippi* (the "Father of Waters" is its meaning) in a boat, here near a mile across ; the Fever River joins it. The ferry boat was rowed across the river by machinery. Two large horses set and kept in motion the wheels which ran under them; their fore feet higher than the hinder, and as they set down their feet the wheels ran down on each side. Here I sleep and write in an hotel close to the great river, 2,800 miles long ; the Missouri, to its junction with this river, is 2,900; to the sea 4,100 miles long, which is the longest river in the world. I had intended to proceed on to Chicago, but a letter received at the Post Office, inviting me to Annawan, determined me to take this course, and go over and help them, if the Lord will. I observed, both in Illinois and Iowa, oats and barley ripe and cut down. I have now travelled over twenty or thirty miles of its fine prairie land, on one side often covered with the finest crops, and on the other its native grass growing in a virgin unbroken soil.

20th.—Have just observed a large float of timber passing down the river, on which two dozen men are employed, with temporary wooden huts upon it. They press their oars to the bottom of the stream, and so move it along. At 9 a.m. took steamer on the Mississippi to Rock Island, and from thence by the cars to Annawan.

22nd.—ANNAWAN. Once the name of an Indian Chief; now a town. It has a Baptist Chapel, in which I preached this forenoon at eleven, and Methodist Episcopalian Church, in which I heard a Congregational minister at three p.m. He occupies it statedly at this hour. He read nearly every word. At five I preached to a large congregation in the same place. They did not seem very much interested in my discourse on the Lord's return until I had got nearly half through, then they seemed deeply interested. The Baptist minister, at present not settled here, who has been a chaplain in the army, prayed after my morning discourse. He also and the Congregational minister heard in the evening. As several wished me to continue longer, and put it to the congregation, those who wished future meetings were requested to lift up the right hand, and as several did and none were against them, we announced two more meetings The reasons for this were—the custom of the place, and it is harvest time.

23rd.—Mr. Heagle, the Baptist minister, opened the services in the Methodist Episcopalian Church very nicely at 8 p.m.; large congregation. It was proposed to hold the meeting in the same place to-morrow evening.

24th.—Sick and unable to preach; so that the bell tolled for the church, and two ministers in town, but did not hold a meeting as I was unable to attend. I suppose the diet, heat, and not being yet acclimated, had to do with this sickness. I was urged by all to send for a doctor ; but I doctored myself and asked the Lord's blessing on my simple means. I said, any doctor here not knowing my constitution might kill me.

25th.—Elder M'Derment, went out to the prairie and shot some prairie chickens. As I could not dine with him he sent me one, which I was able to eat, and sup with him at 6.

26th.—Nearly well; but instead of going to Chicago. as I purposed, I hasten some hundreds of miles to Evansville, Indiana.

27th.—Arrived at EVANSVILLE at 10 p.m. Found my friend Troup with difficulty. He and sister Troup overjoyed to see me after more than fifteen years. Evansville is on the banks of the Ohio, which divides Indiana from Kentucky. River a mile wide here.

31st.—In the Methodist Episcopal Church Lecture Room; a good attendance. Mr. Pentecost enters heartily into the Lord's Second Coming, and prayed earnestly after I had done. Mr. Sims, of the Methodist Episcopal Church, told me to-day that all the ministers of this church are temperance men. This must have a mighty influence for good in the denomination and in the world. This nice letter of introduction was given me from Mr. Pentecost to Mr. Sims:—

July 28th, 1866.

BROTHER SIMS,—

I have the pleasure of introducing Brother Bowes, of Scotland, who is now in this country, earnestly laboring in the cause of Christ, presenting three especial points:—1st. The simple Gospel as received by all evangelical Christians. 2nd. The great subject of "Christian Union." 3rd. "The Second Advent of Christ." He comes well recommended, and I think his cause is a good one. I have offered him, very cordially, my pulpit for the morning; I bespeak for him yours in the evening, especially as you preach in the afternoon. He is also an earnest out-of-door preacher. He will, however, speak for himself. I introduce him at his own request.

I am, &c.

GEORGE F. PENTECOST.

8mo. 5th.—Addressed the colored children in the Baptist Chapel; they are as well behaved and intelligent as white children. At half-past 10, preached in the Methodist Episcopal Church, Ingle Street; a large attentive assembly. At 8, preached to a crowded audience of colored people in the Baptist Chapel. Above a dozen came forward to seek the Lord. I trust some found him.

10th.—Left the hospitable home of my friends, amid some tears, and started for

YORK, PA.

which I reached at 10 a.m., on the *12th*. Found the brothers Watt at church, where I heard Elder Slaysman preach; my brethren introduced me to him.

20th.—Have had large congregations every night for near a week in the Covered Market.

21st.—Started 27 miles for a Camp Meeting, held near Pinetown; brother O'Neale and his wife took Andrew Watt and me in a covered waggon. We arrived as the people of the Camp were breaking up for the dinner. Saw several elders; heard one preach, and then I took the stand. There was much joy in the Camp; two or three thousand there on Lord's Day. Several hundreds heard me, and I wish I could remain longer among these earnest people. Hastened 12 miles to a Bush Meeting. These are called United Brethren, and have sometimes as many as 500 for some hours even at night when their work is done.

22nd.—Baptist Chapel. Many longing for my longer stay, but bade these loving people farewell.

23rd.—Elder Slaysman accompanied me to PHILADELPHIA. I called to see Charles Campbell, formerly a Baptist pastor; his wife reported him in Canada; so I bade my friend and dear brother Slaysman adieu, perhaps a lasting one for time. This is a vast city of regular dimensions, and as large as Glasgow.

NEW YORK.

24th.—Reached New York. I shall reside with William Holmes, a member of the Baptist Church, corner of Bedford Street, Elder or Dr. Dowling, pastor. I was requested to address their prayer-meeting in the Lecture hall; which I did with comfort, and several expressed a desire to hear me again. My friend Holmes took me with his horse and buggy through a large part of this great city. The Fifth Avenue and surrounding streets contain many mansions of merchant princes; a wealthy citizen is building one of marble; two vast hotels are built of marble. The Central Park is about two miles long and three quarters broad in some places, with lakes, walks, and carriage drives. Found Brother Sommerville well. Called on Pastor Dowling with my friend Holmes, who wished me to see his pastor. He offered me his pulpit for Tuesday and Lord's Day, but hoped I would say nothing but what they were accustomed to hear! He did not like the Second Advent. I said wherever I went I must be free, therefore I declined on these grounds. This is the first time that an attempt has been made to suppress free thoughts and words since I reached the United States. New York contains about a million of souls, and in some streets seems as busy as London. Trees grow in many of the streets to keep off the sun.

26th.—At 2 p.m., Brother Sommerville and I crossed the East River to BROOKLYN. Held a meeting on Fort Greene; a large attendance. An Irishman, surrounded by a few more, cried out, "Give us some Fenianism!" I said, "I will," and gave them my visit to the Fenian prisoners at St. Catharines. This kept all quiet, and I was enabled to preach Christ to them. At 4, a Union Tent Meeting was held of the Young Men's Association; so we closed our meeting for it. The tent or awning was capable of holding several hundreds. A young man preached a gospel sermon. I was called upon to speak, and cheerfully responded.

29th.—To-day, President Johnson, General Grant, Secretary Seward, and Admiral Farragut visited New York. I saw the Grand Procession from a shop in Broadway. The President and Government were very well received. A. Glass and his wife called on me in the forenoon. As they had travelled far to see me I said, "Are you not going to see the President?" They said "No, we have now seen you, and that is all we came for." I replied, "I am highly honored indeed when you prefer to see me to the President." I trust I was made a blessing to them more than thirty years ago, which may be more lasting than this presidency—for ever.

30th.—Attended the Fulton Street prayer meeting. In front of the congregation, behind the President's desk, was printed in large characters, "Prayers and exhortations not to exceed five minutes, in order to give all an opportunity. Not more than two consecutive prayers or exhortations. No controverted points discussed. Brethren are earnestly requested to adhere to the five minutes' rule." Some had been at a Camp Meeting, and had got converted; among the rest a judge, who spoke in tears on the evil of strong drink, and the power of pious parents. Many friends received well what I said, and requested me to come again, and a minister, to visit him at Long Island; this was Mr. Anderson, of Newton, Reformed Dutch Church.

31st.—Again attended the Fulton Street prayer meeting. Spoke on the Lord's Second Coming, after which I was asked, " Will the brother from Dundee lead us in prayer?" I felt happy to pray.

9mo. 1st.—Started by cars for LOWELL. Arrived at 6.35. p.m. We crossed over Connecticut; the river of that name divides this State from Massachusetts. Lowell used to contain 46,000 inhabitants; it has now 42,000. The workers, girls, average each $1\frac{1}{4}$ dols. a-day; they board for $2\frac{1}{4}$ dols., or 9s. of our money, consequently they may save £1 or more per week. The Corporation pays 75 cents additional to the boarding house keeper. A young woman in five years may save £250, as much as would buy her a farm, and make her, married or single, independent for life. Some foolishly spend their earnings in dress. A mechanic can make 2 dols. or rather more, daily; but laboring men should go west. The public works run $11\frac{1}{2}$ hours per day.

4th.—This evening the student with whom I preached on Lord's day left his address, and an invitation that I should address the students at the Theological Seminary, Newton Central, before leaving Massachusetts.

5th.—Sought out Joel Kellett, a brother from Glossop, at LAURENCE CITY, which may contain 20,000 people, after I preached on a platform specially erected for public meetings on the common. We erected a lamp, and several sat round the platform; many sat on seats or stood around before it. I asked them whether they had rather be rich in faith or rich in dollars? Many voices cried, " Dollars! dollars!! dollars!!!" I said, " I believe you, you prefer these to Christ." The meeting was generally orderly, but a few noisy mockers showed their spirit. These were, as usual, chiefly from that land of restless spirits—Ireland.

6th.—The congregation about double last night, but at times noisy. A number, all from England, gathered after at my lodgings, we had a "good time," as they say here.

BOSTON.—SHARON CAMP MEETING.

7th.—Entered Boston. Found that Dr. Litch was not at home. I started for Sharon Camp Meeting and reached there at six o'clock, and spoke at the Lovefeast, which was refreshing.

8th.—It rained tremendously last night, so that the ministers' tent in which I slept had more rain in it than any other; it was boarded round: I got very little rain, however. Preached at half-past seven p.m., and enjoyed the services of the day.

9th.—Slept as well as in my own bed. Rose refreshed at eight o'clock. A Lovefeast; probably 60 or 80 spoke, of both sexes, often no more than a text, at times several verses, chiefly on " the blessed hope of the Lord's early return." One brother said we had the best hope of any people in the world. This led me to say that we ought therefore to be the best people in the world, and the happiest and most useful, and that we could well afford the persecution of the world. There must have been near 4000 present in the middle of the day. Seventeen have been baptized; five to-day. One aged farmer was much interested who never attends any place of worship; before parting he affectionately kissed my hand, wished my address, and says I shall hear from him. Thus such meetings effect good. The preachers missed the mark to-day, and dwelt more on Israel, &c., than on Christ, so that the best part of the day was nearly lost to the unconverted. I spoke a little before the close of the forenoon service, and preached in the evening on the Gospel, its holiness and hopes; a very blessed time, and am requested to visit distant places. I will overtake what I can before sailing, but that will not be one-half of those kindly asking me to visit them. At nine o'clock the camp services closed with great joy.

10th.—I arose early and washed in the lake. Having now camped out three nights, I am able to speak of camp life. It is healthful to both body and mind. Christians agree to come together in a grove, near water, in some retired part of the country. This was near Sharon, about twenty miles from Boston, and two miles from the station. Those intending to stay a week or more, for the Camp meetings last a week or ten days, take their tents with them, each of which will accommodate pretty large families. During the great rains the canvass tents were generally dry and warm. At 7 a.m., the bell rings for breakfast, after which, at 9 a.m., a prayer meeting or lovefeast begins. The time all occupied until half-past ten, when a sermon is preached; service closes at twelve; dinner at one; preaching at two, which closes about four; then tea or supper at five or six; after which prayer, conversation, and singing in the tents; then at half-past seven preaching until nine, when services chiefly of a family kind are resumed in the tents. Before the public stand, erected for the preachers, are about 700 seats, when these are filled the people stand or sit down on the grass. I was received among them most cordially.

"THE CAMP MEETING

closed triumphantly on Sunday evening. A better meeting as it respects harmony, spirituality, and interest for the cause of Christ, we never attended. It was a perfect success, and all went to their homes full of joy and gladness. We were favored for the last two days with the presence, labors, and counsels of a brother beloved from Scotland, Elder John Bowes, whose communications gave unmixed pleasure and great profit. He is to preach at Newbury Port on Tuesday and Wednesday evenings, in Boston, at Hudson Street, Thursday and Friday evenings; and at Providence, on next Sabbath."—*Advent Herald*.

Having been invited to visit Newton Central Theological Seminary, Mass., by J. V. Osterhout, to lecture to the students, I reached it about 4 p.m. of the 10th. No notice of the service could be given, as I had only this day to spare before sailing, all the rest of my time being preengaged. We called on President Hovey, who gave his consent; I met the students at tea at six, where it was intimated I would lecture in their new hall, a large building inaugurated only to-day at ten a.m., by a large assembly. I was glad that the first service held in it was a lecture on the "Union of Saints and Christ's Second Coming." My discourse lasted an hour and a half. How wonderful are God's providential plans! Had I not gone to the First Baptist Church at Lowell, on the 2nd, I should not have seen the student, nor have preached to the students, in which I greatly joy, for, as many of them are preachers, and all hope to be, they will carry the truth to many congregations in different parts of this great country. Newton Central Seminary stands upon a lofty and healthful hill.

NEWBURY PORT—WHITFIELD'S BURIAL-PLACE.

11*th*.—At half-past seven discoursed at Newburgh Port, 36 miles from Boston. Mr. Campbell Presbyterian minister who kindly drove me round the city in his buggy, the Baptist pastor, and other preachers, present. The wet evening prevented a large assembly.

12*th*.—To-day, my kind host, John Pearson, Junr., conducted me to the Old South Church, Federal Street, which contains the following lines, inscribed on Whitfield's monument, here erected by an ardent friend:—"This cenotaph is erected with affectionate veneration to the memory of the Rev. George Whitfield, born at Gloucester, England, December, 1714; educated at Oxford University; ordained 1736. In a ministry of 34 years, he had crossed the Atlantic 13 times, and preached 18,000 sermons. As a soldier of the cross, humble, devout, ardent, he put on the whole armor of God, preferring the honor of Christ to his own interest, repose, reputation, or life; as a Christian orator, his deep piety, disinterested zeal, and vivid imagination gave unexampled energy to his look, action, and utterance; bold, fervent, pungent, and popular in his eloquence, no other uninspired man ever preached to so large assemblies, or enforced the simple truths of the Gospel by motives so persuasive and awful, and with an influence so powerful on the hearts of his hearers. He died of asthma, September 30, 1770, suddenly exchanging his life of unparalleled labors for his eternal rest." Before the pulpit stands this inscription:—"Under this pulpit are deposited the remains," &c. It was here I saw the remains of the great preacher, consisting of bones and a fine head, the reasoning powers largely developed. What a lesson to visit his tomb! Two other ministers are interred there, one of them a man of color. The vault is carefully locked. Here is the church in which he preached, a large wooden erection which has withstood 110 winters, having been erected in 1756. From the 17th to the 20th September, 1770, he preached every day at Boston, and on the 20th at Newton. Before he came to Newbury Port, where he had engaged to preach next morning, he was importuned to preach by the way at Exeter. At the last he preached in the open-air to accommodate the multitudes that came to hear him, no house being able to contain them. He preached nearly two hours by which he was greatly fatigued; notwithstanding which, he came to this place, where he arrived in the evening, and soon retired to rest, being Saturday night, fully intent on preaching the next day. His rest was much broken; he awoke many times in the night, and complained very much of an oppression in his lungs; breathing with difficulty, and at length about six o'clock on the Lord's Day morning, he parted this life in a fit of the asthma, aged 56 years. He said before his death, "I had rather wear out than rust out," and his desire was granted. The day before, Mr. Clarkson, observing him more uneasy than usual, said, "Sir, you are more fit to go to bed than to preach:" to which this great laborer answered, " True, sir," and turning aside he clasped his hands together, and looking up, said, " Lord Jesus, I am weary in thy work but not of thy work. If I have not yet finished my course, let me go and speak for thee once more in the fields, seal thy truth, and come home to die." This prayer was answered. His last sermon was from 2 Cor. xiii. 5. We visited also the house in which he died, at least we saw it outside but did not enter.

16th.—PAWTUCKET. In a large hall at half-past 10: excellent congregations. This is four miles from PROVIDENCE, Rhode Island, where I preached in the Second Advent Church, crowded. Mr. Osler intimated that he was going to take up a collection for me, which called me up to stop it, as I had not allowed such a thing for twenty-seven years, that I was unhired, and never asked the world for money, only their hearts, therefore it was not for me, I could not accept it. Mr. Osler said it would be made and put into his hand. At 7, the congregation was still larger. Vast numbers promised, as they said farewell, to meet me in heaven at Christ's right hand. Several said—" Your faith is ours." I trust in the day of accounts it will be found that the multitudes that have heard to day have accepted precious truth.

18th.—NEW YORK. Brother Sommerville and I have taken berths in the *Hecla*, for Liverpool, which sails to-morrow.

We had some very severe weather crossing. On one occasion I was going on deck to look at the gale, when a great sea rolled over the deck and nearly washed me off the ladder; I clung to the rail, however, and only hurt my shin, but I was wet all over. Mr. H——, a passenger, opened his distressed mind to me. He had left his wife in Richmond; had differed with her through drink, but would give the world now to tell her where he was. He has resolved to taste it no more, and to write to his wife. We had one conversion on board, that of a man from Cornwall, who had been seeking Christ ten years. We landed at Liverpool on the 2nd of October, exactly five months from our sailing from Glasgow. We were $12\frac{1}{2}$ days on the passage home.

Now that the voyage is over, we both see the Lord's guidance at every step. We have been preserved from danger by sea and land, guided in our movements, and have added largely to our friends, and fellow-laborers in the Lord's service.

I give entire, from the *Alliance News*, a letter which I wrote to the editor while at Evansville, Indiana. It was also printed as a tract.

METHODISM AND TEMPERANCE IN THE UNITED STATES.

EVANSVILLE, Banks of the Ohio,
Indiana, August 7th, 1866.

DEAR SIR,—

Having been informed that many of the Christian ministers in the United States were total abstainers, I have made inquiry, and find that it is true. The Methodist Episcopal Church, one of the largest and most influential denominations in the United States, requires all her ministers, as a part of their calling, to promote temperance. This I had from the lips of Mr. Sims, one of the influential ministers of Evansville, a city of about 25,000 inhabitants. In a work, published by authority, called the " Centenary of American Methodism," by Dr. Stevens, 1866, it is stated that they have " 60 conferences, 928,320 members north, and 10,105 churches;" and if we add the southern members, who became separated some years ago through slavery, and will probably be reunited soon, since the idol of the south has fallen, and also count the other branches of Methodism, there must now be in the United States, 1,950,000 members, and 12,000 travelling preachers, although they do not travel so much as formerly, each minister often having no more than one church, like the Congregationalists. In this whole western hemisphere, including the West Indies and British North America, there are at least 2,100,000 Methodists. They reckon each member here to influence three more, which would give 8,400,000, or about one-fifth part of the people, more or less, under Temperance influence. It may give you some idea of public opinion, should I report a conversation of some on-lookers at Plattville, Wisconsin, where I spent one Lord's Day, preaching in two of the churches referred to in what follows:—"What do you think of ——— church?" Answer: "It is the aristocratic church." "And of the ——— church?" "It is the fashionable church." "And of the third church?" "It is the drunken church." And why did it receive this unenviable title? Because several of its leading members were known to take intoxicating drink. It has been repeated to them nearly as I have given it, and I hope will be a warning to avoid what stings them with reproach.

Dr. C. R. Agnew, of Boston, a prominent member of the Sanitary Commission, recently delivered a lecture on "Health, and how to keep it." This was reported in a religious journal. He related an incident in the experience of an English sea captain, who made voyage to South America, and always compelled his crew to wear flannel next the skin, never allowed them to sleep in damp places, changed the diet according to the latitude from flesh to vegetable food, and *vice versa*, and prohibited the use of alcohol on board; and while in the port of Valparaiso, during the hottest summer, there was not so much as one man on the sick list, while in five other ships lying beside him, the deaths were from thirty to fifty per day. There is no nutriment whatever in alcohol, yet thirty-five millions, out of the ninety million gallons manufactured annually in this country, are consumed by the people of the United States. This, at 2 dollars a gallon, makes seventy million dollars. Six million barrels of beer are also consumed by us annually.

The following is deeply interesting:—Some years ago a Methodist minister, Mr. Axley, of eccentric but pious memory, had preached to one of the congregations in his circuit, and after the sermon, according to the custom of Methodist ministers, the preacher had a class meeting. He had questioned each brother and sister on the subject of their experience, practice, and enjoyment in the divine life, giving to each a word of encouragement, comfort, and advice, as the case seemed to require, filling up the intervals by singing a suitable verse with life and spirit, until all the members had been questioned. But a certain very prominent member of the church owned a distillery, and by some means the preacher found out the fact; and, after the most serious conversations with the others, the following examination took place:—

PREACHER.—"Well, Brother Jerry, how do you come on making whisky?"
THE BROTHER (somewhat startled)—"O, I don't know, tolerably well."
P.—"Well, brother, tell us how much money you give for a bushel of corn?"
B.—"Twenty-five cents a bushel."
P.—"Twenty-five cents! Very cheap that, I should say. But another question, brother,—how much whisky do you suppose one bushel of corn will make?"
B.—"Can't say. I suppose about three gallons." (seeming very confused.)
P.—"So, three gallons! Why, that's a considerable turn out, I should judge. But, brother, what do you get for a gallon of whisky?"
B.—(Looking rather wild)—"Seventy-five cents."
P.—"Seventy-five cents! two hundred per cent! and that too, I reckon, by the barrel; you get more, I suppose, by the jugful. But, brother, tell your brethren, isn't the slops very good to fatten hogs on?"
B.—"Yes; pretty good."
P.—"And won't the hogs you fatten for nothing on the slops come nigh paying for the corn?"
B.—"Well, very nigh it."
P.—"But, to come to the question, brother, do you make a real good article? Will it bear a bead?"

But by this time the brother was so perfectly confused by the old preacher's interrogations, that he began to wish he had never seen the preacher or the distillery either. The class could scarcely maintain their gravity during the dialogue, and we need not add that the poor fellow was so tormented every time he met a neighbor, by the salutation, "Well, brother, how do you come on making whisky?" and "Do you make a real good article—will it bear a bead?" that he actually broke up his distillery and became a consistent Methodist.—*Religious Denomination (Belcher), p.* 58.

Preachers such as Mr. Axley are much needed on both sides of the Atlantic. There is no calculating the effect of a well-directed attack on the fortresses of evil, it will be felt and seen long after its immediate effects disappear. So many ministers of this influential denomination spread over all parts of the States, from Maine to California, with their rigid temperance example and influence in thousands of congregations, must, and do, make themselves felt both in the church and the politics of their country.

Our friend General Dow sailed from Quebec to Europe the Saturday before I and my colleague landed there. As I shall be yet some weeks in the Eastern States, should anything of importance occur, I shall not fail to write to you again.

Trusting the Wesleyan ministers of Great Britain may be induced to follow the noble example of their brethren of America, I am, yours very truly,

—*Alliance News, care of Mr. Barker.*   JOHN BOWES.

2mo. 4th and 5th, 1867.—FALKIRK. Discussion with Mr. Mitchell, Universalist, in the Corn Exchange; about 700 present each night. As I went by train from Larbert, one of Mr. M.'s disciples left his wife and joined us. He entered freely into conversation, and said, "The Prodigal Son said 'I perish.'" J.B.—"That was his body with hunger; he could not get the husks." Mr. G.—"His perishing was spiritual, by false opinions—they were the husks." J.B.—"Whatever it was, had he fed on the husks, they would have saved him. You could not feed swine on false opinions, at least, if you could, I should promise you plenty of employment, and you would make a fortune among the farmers by feeding their hogs on opinions instead of either oatmeal or husks." This silenced him, and provoked mirth among the passengers. When men get into error, they adopt the most foolish conceits.

There is a gracious work going on in this district, and hundreds are being converted, at Falkirk, Bainsford, Stenhouse Muir, Denny, Kilsyth, and several other places. The brethren Geddes, Holt, Sommerville, and Henderson, have also been greatly used of God in this work.

EDWARD ASTON.

5mo. 19th.—BIRMINGHAM. Temperance Hall; about 70 at the Lord's Supper; about 120 in fellowship; a happy season. At half-past 6 I preached in Holder's Concert Hall, which holds about 2000 people, but it was not full. As I was coming from dinner to preach at the Bull Ring this afternoon, I observed a man walking down the street rapidly, talking to himself. I hardly thought he could be in drink, but I feared lunacy. I stepped up to him and gave him a small bill of the evening service. "John Bowes," said he, reading, "do you know John Bowes?" "Yes." "Are you John Bowes?" "Yes." He stopped, gave me a warm shake of the hand, and said, "I am Edward Aston," of Liverpool. I knew him at once. "I have been twelve years in the asylum, and am going to see my wife." Had I been five minutes sooner or later I should have missed him. He talked rationally on all subjects but one. When a young man he met in a Wesleyan class. Was out of town, and accosted by another member of the class —"How is it, Edward, we have not seen you at the class lately?" "I am not going back until you go and fetch Jesus Christ from the workhouse." "What do you mean, Edward?" "When I was with you, a number of us gave our threepence or sixpence per week to keep that blind brother from the work-house. I understand since I left you, you have let him go, and the Lord takes what is done to the least of his members as done to himself, therefore go and fetch Jesus Christ from the work-house."

24th.—Sturge's monument, five ways; on one side is the figure of a colored woman, emblem of Charity, nursing a child and giving drink to one in chains; another female form, Peace, with a dove in her hand and a lamb at her feet, emblem of peace; on the pedestal also Temperance is inscribed. Thus Birmingham celebrates the virtues of one of her citizens. Visited Edward Aston in the asylum, and J. H. almost recovered, with brother Anderson. Saw E. A.'s wife and family. God, whom she serves, has provided for herself and family. At eight, Temperance Hall crowded; addressed them for near three quarters of an hour.

RICHARD BAXTER.

7th.—KIDDERMINSTER, where, more than two hundred years ago, Richard Baxter preached. His house stands in the middle of the street; it bears an inscription telling that Richard Baxter resided there in 1641. His church is now the Established church, in which the vicar, just elevated to be the Bishop of Rochester, preached. He is a very different man from Richard Baxter, and has kept Dissenters at arms-length, so that when he visited a mother whose daughter was not of the church, knowing his distaste for Dissenters, she said, " Shall I go out into the next room, sir ?" His answer was, " Out of the house, if you please !" And this high churchman is now a bishop ! The church contains the oak chair in which the great Baxter wrote, on which is carved, " Rev. Richard Baxter, born in Shrewsbury, in 1615, and died in London in 1691, Chaplain to King Charles II." So that amid all his ailments he lived to the age of 76. I discoursed on the Lord's Second Coming, in the Temperance Hall, to a full congregation; a gracious influence attended the Word. My kind friend and brother, John Lyall, of Birmingham, accompanied me.

THE NEW TRANSLATION.

Having studied the Greek language, and especially the Greek Testament, more than forty years, I was anxious to give to society any advantage which my knowledge enabled me to impart before going hence. Towards the end of 1869 it seemed doubtful whether I should live to see it printed, but the mercy of my good Father has provided. When I commenced printing I was dependent on him for supplies. The paper was all bought and paid for so as to secure the discount on cash and the printers have been all duly paid. I note this peculiarity in the supplies, that none of those brethren have helped at all that I might have expected, and that all needed aid has come from unexpected quarters. A few donations, most unexpected, have come in, and the loans will be discharged from the subscribers, who now number 536. While I have consulted all possible MSS. and authorities, I only am responsible for the Translation. I mention this, because some have asked whether I have any assistants? and one of our translators, himself largely assisted by others, has given it as his opinion, " that the work is too great for any one man." I freely acknowledge the work has been at once most laborious and most pleasant. New views of texts have constantly opened up to patient investigation, and have often solved considerable difficulties. The denominations may and do feel the need of a New Translation, but they do not yet seem at liberty to proceed. I have had one undeniable advantage, in being free from the control of any party. I trust that it may be made a great blessing to those who love the pure Scriptures "more than gold, yea much fine gold," and find them " sweeter than honey or the honeycomb."

The price of the New Translation :—to subscribers 2/6, to others 3/6.

WILLIAM WILD WRIGHT'S CASE.

For want of space, I have been compelled to abbreviate much this interesting case, but will give a few extracts from his own pen. He resided many years ago at Stockport, now in Manchester. His case has only recently come to my knowledge.

"I continued meeting with the Friends regularly for about ten years, and what I went through neither tongue nor pen can describe or express. However, as I grew in knowledge and experience, and a desire to keep close to the Holy Scriptures, I discovered I was still in the wrong place; for with all my reading and praying, weeping and study, I could get no true and lasting peace ; neither could I reconcile the Friends' doctrine with the word of God. "Silent waiting," is very good in its place, and to some extent proper and necessary, but certainly not to the extent that Friends practise it ; for I have been at scores of meetings where I have not heard a single word, and at a time too when I have been 'hungering and thirsting after righteousness,' and perishing for lack of knowledge. When believers are met together to worship God, to instruct the ignorant, and build up each other in their most holy faith, it is certainly not the time to sit an hour or more in total silence. I often looked around me at the various sects in the town, but could see none that I could join; they were so mixed up with the 'traditions of men.' I may here state, that what led me into such a train of thought and research, was hearing Brother Bowes preach in the Market-place, Stockport, as I returned home from work at night,—showing the difference between modern and primitive Christianity. I saw at once the necessity of proving all things in order to hold fast that which is good. This was about the year 1844, and I saw little or nothing of him afterwards till 1855, when I heard him in discussion with Joseph Barker. I attended two nights out of the three, and was deeply interested. On the following Lord's Day, I went to a small meeting of believers where he was, and was much edified and instructed, but most blessed, humbled, and affected by the singing, having been away from that exercise so long, the power of truth in song had a wonderful effect upon me. I went no more amongst the Friends, except on one or two special occasions. Brother Bowes did not see the seed as it dropt by the wayside into my heart and brought forth fruit, for many years afterwards ; and none but myself can know the preciousness of that fruit to me. 'For thou knowest not which shall prosper.'"

He then goes on to describe his conversion and adoption of believers' immersion. It is thus the open-air preacher is often cheered by seeing fruit; possibly much he never sees.

4mo. 22nd, 1869.—DERBY. At 8 a.m., addressed, for nearly half-an hour, about 150 mechanics, employed at the Midland Station, while at breakfast. The men sang two verses with much interest. I prayed briefly, and all started for work. Many with happy faces shook hands.

This address, by some one, is regular. Of course all sorts of professors would be there. This visit to Derby arose from letters which I received from Benj. Carter, formerly in our printing office, and a member in the assembly at Cheltenham. He reminded me that I had immersed both himself and his wife. I was glad to hear that we had been of use to him. My visit was looked to as one of the most joyous events in their history; their hearts and house were open to welcome me.

THE LANARKSHIRE MINISTER.

5mo. 18th.—AUCHINHEATH. A great work, in hearts and homes, has gone on here since my last visit. Attentive meetings outside, and large in the school room. Sinners continue to believe and live. I had the following from the brother himself. He had joined a church unconverted, got awakened and anxious, called on the minister for light, who said, "Read Burns' Poems, and Shakespeare, and take care of the quacks." By attending on the gospel, the seeker found peace, and is now recommending Christ to others. As many were anxious, he was afraid the minister might give similar advice to others, he therefore called upon him to warn him. The minister, highly offended that he should presume to teach him!—"Are you a member of a church, sir?" "Yes." "What denomination do you belong to, sir?" "I do not believe in denominations." Without giving him time further to explain, he took him by the collar and walked him out! Now, who was the quack? Evidently the minister, and not those gospel preachers whom he reviled, and, thank the Lord, here and at Lesmahagow there are about a dozen of them, who can show the way of salvation. A "quack" is "a boastful pretender to arts which he does not understand." We have now many blind leaders of the blind, but seldom has any one evinced more blindness than this. The real quack is he who pretends to teach the way of salvation and is ignorant of it. May the Lord deliver the people from such blind guides.

OLDHAM AND HOLLINWOOD.

3mo. 20th, 1870—Oldham Town Hall, three times. Happy to see my friend Chadwick, from Manchester, who also addressed the evening meeting. The Hall crowded. Here there is a good work and even a number break bread weekly, but I did not join them, chiefly because at Hall services they send the collecting box round to saint and sinner at most of the services. This is worse than the sects who do allow an unbeliever or worldling to go sometimes without having the box presented to him by a man going round with it, begging of every one. But I supposed they had heard of my opposition to the system of asking the world for money, and merely stood outside the door with boxes placed within sight of the retiring assemblies, so I made no public remark. The Lord teach his people all his will, and may they willingly do it.

21st & 22nd.—HOLLINWOOD, four miles from Manchester. In the Primitive Methodist Large School, holds six or seven hundred. Mr. Hands, minister of the Free Church, presided the first night; Mr. Platt, the second. Crowded audiences. Discussion allowed. Mr. Henshall took up all the time. Mr. Woodman had been asked to a regular discussion. The letter and his reply were read at the meeting. As no regular discussion could be secured I was invited to give these lectures, from which I expect great blessing. Having been invited to preach in the Congregational Chapel here on the Lord's Day, and having previously engaged for Oldham, I delivered a lecture in it on the Lord's Coming, to a considerable and attentive audience. Several from Oldham present. The Swedenborgians call Emmanuel Swedenborg, "Master." He admits the resurrection of Jesus, but denies that of all others. 1 Cor. xv. was found effective as well as many other texts; v. 20, "But now is Christ risen out of the dead, a first fruit of those fallen asleep;" v. 23, "But each one in his own rank; a first fruit, Christ, afterwards those that are Christ's in his presence." The Scriptures abound with similar testimony, but if the first fruit is of the same nature as the following harvest, and as they concede a literal resurrection in the first fruit, I claimed the same for the whole harvest. The New Jerusalem Church affirms that Christ and the general judgment came in 1757. Whoever understands the New Jerusalem of Rev. xxi. can overthrow this conceit. They also hold the Godhead of Jesus, unlike the Unitarians; but again, like them, they deny that there is any more than one person in the Godhead. Against this I cited many texts; none seemed more convincing than such as, "Seek the things above, where Christ is, sitting on the right hand of God." Col. iii. 1. If God and Christ are only one person, then Paul represents Christ sitting at his own right hand! I had not been at Hollinwood before. My publications, however, had preceded me. I was cordially entertained, and grand opportunities were afforded to establish truth, as well as overturn error.

9mo. 4th.—BIRMINGHAM. A considerable number at the Lord's Supper. Met with the school teachers at 5 o'clock, who have a monthly tea. At 6, out of doors; a large banner unfurled with several texts on, on which I commented; at half-past 6, on "Christ's First and Second Coming." During the week's meetings, had several times the attendance of a beloved brother, once a resident in Dundee, yet a Wesleyan, and a member at Aston Village Chapel. He was recently visited by one in office, who told him they were going to have a collection at the farewell sermon of one of their ministers, and he was asked if he would take

A GUINEA PLATE!!

The collectors below were all to be furnished thus; each collector was expected to put a sovereign and a shilling on his plate, no doubt as an example to the people from whom he was to collect. Each collector in the gallery was to have a half-guinea plate. Brother L— was indignant, refused, and gave his reasons, which seemed to satisfy his interrogator. The Wesleyans seem to out-run the other sects in their eagerness to convert the world's money to their own purposes. While here I resided with a brother who gave me the following account. He had preached at Daventry, and related a circumstance of a wife, a scold, who was changed into kindness by a preacher's singing—

"In heaven above where all is love,
I'll never be cross again."

He related and sung this, and a sinner was changed by it. But if we would enter heaven, we must be heavenly minded, and not *cross* even now upon earth.

A WONDERFUL PROVIDENCE

brought me on 7*mo.* 21*st*, 1871, to PETERHEAD. I had written to be at Aberdeen, when I received a post-card saying that it would be more convenient for next week. I at once wrote to Peterhead to be there three days; but, to my surprise, on passing through Aberdeen to-day, saw a bill posted for me to be in that city next Lord's day. Some blamed the brother that wrote, expecting that one place would be missed. I said, "Wait; good will come out of it." Now mark, dear reader, how the Lord ruled, and made everything to answer his purposes. When I reached Peterhead, it rained much and was misty, so that the fishermen could not go out, and those who started returned. By 7 o'clock, a brother sent round the bellman to announce my preaching at the Cross. A policeman stopped him, and said I should not be allowed to preach. The brother asked the bellman, "Who employed you?" "You did." "Well, then, go and do your work." Then he asked the Lord to help. At 8 o'clock it was fair, and I preached to from 2000 to 3000 people, chiefly fishermen and women, from various parts of the coast, for about two hours. Some had not heard me for thirty years; one aged man in Frazerburgh thirty-six years ago. Converted souls sang sweetly. heard with glad faces, and not a few looking through their tears. My own soul was delighted with the open door to proclaim the Gospel and to address Christians. See now, how the Lord ruled all: had I not got the Aberdeen card about the holiday, I should not have been here. No one knew but the Lord that the thousands of fishermen gathered here could not get out. Had the night been fine all would have been at sea; had it been wet I could not have preached. Had the brethren in Peterhead arranged before they saw me, I should have refused to go to Aberdeen.

8*mo.* 17*th.*—BRECHIN. The following appeared in the *Dundee Courier and Argus*, a few words I correct :—

"APPREHENSION OF MR. JOHN BOWES FOR STREET PREACHING.

". . . . Mr. Bowes was ultimately delivered from 'durance vile,' when he proceeded to St. Ninians Square, and addressed a large assemblage there, relating a few of his adventures such as had been gone through that evening, remarking, that as he preached for nothing, he would as soon lie in jail as pay any of their fines for preaching. It is greatly to be wondered at, how that, on a former occasion, Mr. Bowes was not checked for preaching at the Cross, and that they should only object to it being done now. Also, that they will allow all kinds of 'quacks,' vendors of medicine, and such like, to attract a crowd of persons round the Cross, and they will not allow a person to speak who is likely to do more good than either of those parties quoted. It were well that this were looked into."

It is possible as Bailie Duncan sells strong drink in the same street, that my congregation, a few weeks ago, hindered its sale, and that his policy was to keep me an hour in the Police Office, while his shop was open to sell whisky, and my congregation free to go in.

I wrote to Bailie Smith and got an approving letter, also, to the Provost, who showed this letter to the Bailie, who expected him to reply.

10 Market Street, Montrose, 8mo. 18th, 1871.

Sir,—

It was intimated by the newspapers, and by your city bellman, that I should preach at the Cross, High Street, Brechin, on the 17th, at eight o'clock. I had opened by singing the 100th Psalm, in the midst of which I was seized by two policemen, P. C. Grant, No. 3, and P. C. M'Ewan, and forced off the chair into the Police Office, where I was forcibly kept for thirty minutes. I asked by whose authority I was thus imprisoned, without a charge, trial, or hearing? The answer was, "By the authority of Bailie Duncan and the Superintendent." I requested them to give me a charge, let me go, and I would answer to-morrow. But they proposed to keep me an hour! Two men in the office began to smoke their pipes in my presence, and only gave over, or went out, when I protested against it. At last the Superintendent came. He said, "I am sorry to see you here." I said "It is not my fault;" which he admitted. He said it was that of the Crier, and asked him to give me back what I had paid him. This I declined to receive as he had done his work. Rather than further contest this particular place, where all sorts of congregations have often assembled, I agreed to go near the Railway Station, but then it was almost nine o'clock before I began my discourse. Besides, this is a private place compared to the High Street. I measured the ground this morning, and found the street 63 ft. across from where I stood, exclusive of the side walks. The law sanctions preaching anywhere, if we do not obstruct the thoroughfare. And I had preached there before, a few weeks ago, without hindrance. Having preached the glorious gospel of the blessed God 50 years, I take the most public places. By this means many wandering sinners have been led to Christ. Do not attempt to hinder such conversions by banishing the gospel from the most suitable places. I never have been detained a prisoner for half-an-hour before. The authorities of the hour have immortalised their names in Brechin by this tyrannical conduct. I was sorry to see this morning that the Bailie who interdicted the gospel sells strong drink, which produces four-fifths of the crime of the land. I trust that you will be able to give me such satisfaction, as well as my hearers, as may hinder a recurrence of the serious grievance of my being kept half-an-hour a prisoner, when I ought to have been proclaiming to listening hundreds the blessed gospel. I ought to add that, after the Superintendent did come, his conduct was very courteous,—just as that of the men was the reverse,

Yours very truly, JOHN BOWES.

Did my time allow I doubt not but by persevering to preach, I could secure liberty for the gospel at the Cross of Brechin as everywhere else.

PROPOSED DISCUSSION ON BAPTISM.

The following correspondence will explain itself :—

Free Gaelic Manse, Renton, Oct. 14, 1868.

Dear Sir,—

You wrote me sometime ago challenging me to a public discussion on the subject of baptism. I was from home when you wrote, and, therefore, I did not receive your letter for some time after it was written. When I did receive it, I felt, on several grounds, considerable doubt as to the propriety of accepting your challenge.

1. I could not see what right you had to challenge me to a public discussion in regard to a lecture delivered to my own people, and afterwards, at Mr. Williamson's (Dumbarton) request, to his meeting, but avowedly, not for a controversial purpose. I was therefore inclined then, as I am still, to regard your challenge as a piece of impertence.

2. You stated in your letter that you had learned that I had assailed Believers' Immersion, "and defended Infant Sprinkling as Christian Baptism." I had then neither done the one nor the other. Your information, therefore, must have been erroneous. At that time, indeed, I had not discussed the *mode* of Baptism at all. I therefore thought then, and think still, that you ought to have made sure of the accuracy of your information before writing me, and that, when you neglected to do so, I was not bound, even in courtesy, to acknowledge your letter.

3. I have good reason to believe that your views and mine in regard to the nature and constitution of the covenant of grace differ widely, and, on that account, I am afraid that little good will result from our discussing one of the signs and seals of that covenant, for any one can readily perceive that parties are not likely to discuss satisfactorily the signs of the covenant when they do not agree in

the main, in regard to the covenant itself. My views in regard to the covenant of grace agree entirely with the views of such distinguished Baptists as Mr. Spurgeon, and the late Messrs Haldane—men by whom the views which I understand you hold and teach are emphatically condemned.

4. Nothing would give me greater pleasure than to discuss, in a friendly way, the subject of Baptism with any Baptist clergyman holding orthodox views in regard to the covenant of grace. When agreeing in regard to what the sign signifies, I would be very hopeful that a calm and unprejudiced consideration of the whole subject might lead us to see eye to eye in regard to the sign itself. But even were your views in regard to the covenant of grace in exact accordance with mine, I could not have discussed the subject of Baptism with you at any time since you wrote me, in consequence of other and pressing work. This alone would have prevented me writing you sooner.

My doubt as to the propriety of accepting your challenge still remains, for the reasons which I have now stated; but as you seem eager to discuss the subject of Baptism, and as I expect to have a little more leisure now, I shall give you the benefit of that doubt, and accordingly I accept your challenge. I believe that the challenged party has the privilege of choosing his weapons! Of that privilege I avail myself, and choose the pen as my weapon. This I do because—

1. I do not approve of public debates on religious subjects. I never take part in such debates, nor even attend them.

2. A written discussion is more suitable for such a subject as Baptism, and is far more likely to lead to the ascertaining of the truth, than an exciting debate.

3. A written discussion, by being afterwards published, would give such persons as might feel an interest in the subject an opportunity of studying both sides of the argument, calmly and deliberately, at their own homes, and thus they would be better able to arrive at a right decision in the matter than they could be from being present at an excited public debate.

As this mode of discussion would give me no advantage whatever which would not equally give you, and as you are yourself the party challenging, I cannot doubt but you will readily agree to it; and, therefore, I may state that I have no objection to the order in which you lay down the subjects for discussion. . . . It will, however, simplify the discussion considerably to tell you at once that I have not "assailed Believers' Immersion," for I hold that believers are proper *subjects* of Baptism, and that Immersion is a proper *mode*. . . .

I shall now be glad to receive at your convenience, your argument "disproving Infant Sprinkling as Christian Baptism," which implies—1. that Infants are not proper *subjects* of Baptism; and 2. that the putting of the baptizing *element upon the subjects*, instead of putting the subjects in the baptizing element, is not a proper *mode* of Baptism. I am, yours faithfully,

Mr. John Bowes, Dundee.   ALEXANDER CAMERON.

WESTFIELD HOUSE, DUNDEE, 10mo., 23rd, 1868.

DEAR SIR,—

Yours of the 14th did not arrive until the 16th, I had given up all expectation of a response to my brief note. Your reasons for allowing months to pass without a reply are not satisfactory. You regard, you say, my "challenge as a piece of impertence."* As there is no such word in English, I suppose you mean "impertinence." My answer is, your lectures were public, and therefore open to public investigation, one of them indeed delivered, as you say, in true priestly style, "to my own people," as though they were yours, not Christ's. His people belong to no mere man.

I pass over your reasons for no discussion, since you have agreed to one by "the pen." I accept your offer, and proceed at once to the theme which you propose. I am pleased that you honor the great names that you mention, and trust that like them you have the faith, love, and hope of the gospel. All that love Jesus are brethren, however widely their opinions may diverge. To trust in his death for the remission of our sins, his burial, resurrection, and second coming, gives peace with God and joy in the mind, effected by the Holy Spirit. Whatever may be our mistakes in theology, Christ within enables preachers to honor the Christ of Calvary. I am gratified that you "hold that believers are proper subjects of baptism, and that immersion is a proper mode." Thus we are sure that we are right when we immerse believers, and that you are wrong when you sprinkle water on babies and call it baptism, while it is no baptism at all, because it is not immersion. As you will "be glad to receive my argument disproving Infant

*Mr. C. called to prove that this was a slip of his pen.

Sprinkling as Christian Baptism," I herewith send it, "Baptism; Scripturally, Critically, and Historically Considered in its Nature and Subjects," 24 pages. As this has reached a second edition, and a hundred copies have been circulated in your locality, should you be able to refute any of its arguments, your pen will do something to the purpose.

Waiting your reply when you have had time to consider my arguments, and hoping that nothing will occur in this correspondence of which we shall be ashamed when the Lord comes, I am yours in love and truth,

To Alexander Cameron. JOHN BOWES.

I note that now more than three years have elapsed without a reply, so that whether Mr. Sawyers, or Cameron, engages to hold a discussion, the first by speaking, the second by writing, both fail. It now appears that they wilfully go on with an unscriptural practice which they neither can nor dare defend.

JAMES SILK BUCKINGHAM.

Being at Glasgow once when a large Soiree was given in honor of James Silk Buckingham, late M.P. for Sheffield, after a vote of thanks had been given him, I proposed one in consequence of the presence of Mrs. Buckingham. He returned thanks for her, and said,—" I always take my wife with me to such places as this; for if there be anything to be suffered, I am sufficiently selfish to wish her to have half of it; and if there be anything to be enjoyed, I wish her also to have her share." This had a fine effect on the large assembly. If husbands, who seek pleasure for themselves, but are careless about the happiness of their wives, would adopt Mr. Buckingham's plan, there would be more domestic felicity than very many families realise.

THE MILKMAN AND THE BEER-SHOP.

During one of my visits to Northampton, I heard that an old member had taken a beer-shop; he used at one time to sell milk, during which I knew him, his wife, and daughter. I was sorry for them, and therefore started off at mid-day to find out and enter the beer-shop, hoping, as I was known to be a total abstainer, that no one would see me. I found C— at home, and said, " Whatever has brought you into this den ?"

C.—" A man must live."

J.B.—"I do not see any particular need for you to live, when you live only to do evil to the bodies and minds of men, you would be as well away, and then you would do no harm."

C.—"You are very plain."

J.B.—"I design to be plain. When you sold milk, you were employed in what did good to society; but now it is the reverse. Whatever made you bring your wife and daughter into this place, where they must see and hear many things which they ought not ?"

C.—" Why, this trade is as honest as that at any rate."

I never knew before that he put water into his milk ! but this was a plain confession. So that one evil leads to another. He appeared to get on prosperously in his wicked traffic some years, when he committed some mistake in law, on account of which the whole of his property was swept away, and he became a very poor man. I believe he is still living : may it be to do good and not evil, and may he become wiser. Society owes no man a living who lives only to do harm to its members,

APPENDIX.

Note A., Page 209.

The large chapel, in Lindsay Street, now occupied by the Museum and the Episcopalians, intended to hold 1400 people, was projected for me, before I got the invitation to go to Liverpool, to which, however, I went with the sanction of a large majority of the congregation, after I had told them that if they deemed my presence necessary I would remain in Dundee some time. After my departure five of the Trustees got afraid and resigned. The church, however, after hearing several candidates, unanimously elected G. C. Reid, of Preston, and every thing prospered, until he determined not to go to the new chapel, and divided the congregation. This brought them into difficulties. The Trustees and what remained of the congregation, about half, gave me an invitation to return, and become their pastor, in the new building, but by this time, my engagements for usefulness were such in Liverpool and other places, that I could not return to Dundee. The chapel, however, was erected, and Mr. Kelly became their pastor, and again divided them, but the Trustees having signed a bill which they could not meet, some of them suffered imprisonment, after which, my enemies, and I had enemies among the publicans, and others whose errors I had often openly assailed, referred to this circumstance to my prejudice, while all who knew the facts knew that I could not be held responsible for the conduct of my two successors, nor for the conduct of the Trustees in signing a bill when they had not the means of meeting it. These are facts which can be verified by letters and evidence in my possession. Though often implored to reside in Dundee after this, I never saw it to be the Lord's way for twenty-one years, but at last he opened the way and I returned A printed circular, sent me by James Allan, a Trustee, in a letter, Feb. 19, 1839 in which he signs himself, "Your ever affectionate son in the gospel,"—the circular itself signed by "P. Stratton," another Trustee, and "J. Kelly," as pastor, —states that they had raised £600, nearly one-half of which I had collected for them. This, with union and prudent management, could have given them the needed bond on the property. I have their letters to prove that they did not blame me for their difficulties. I have only space for a few brief extracts. W. Menmuir, a Trustee, who kept up friendship with me as long as he lived, thus writes as to my difficulties in England, June 12, 1839.—"My confidence in your integrity is such that you will support your consistency with prudence." James Allan, June 13, 1839,—"I often meet you at a throne of grace, and the Lord grant that we may see each other in heaven," and again, April 4, 1838,—"However, I am at the same time convinced that you believed it to be for the glory of God that you should go to Liverpool, yours most affectionately, in the Lord, James Allan." In Dec. 18, 1838, Peter Stratton writes, "The United Christian Church is now disunited, Mr. Reid and his party in the old chapel, the Trustees and their friends in the new. . . . Expecting the same support and interest you have hitherto granted us, we wait with confidence and patience for your answer, I am, dear sir, yours most affectionately, Peter Stratton." I now got two letters, one a regular call from the church in the new chapel, intimating that it was unanimous. Now, would the Trustees all have joined in this had they been, as the misinformed say, brought to suffering through me? James Allan, one of the Trustees, thus writes, Dec. 24, 1838.—"Last Sabbath we held a church meeting; the church gave you a unanimous call to be their future pastor."

I left Dundee more than eighteen months before this. The Trustees were not imprisoned for about five years after this, and that entirely through the fault of others, not mine. Surely my opponents find it difficult to coin slanders when they make me responsible for this. Had the Trustees not signed the bill they would not have suffered. Nearly ten years after my removal from Dundee, Jan. 20, 1847, James Allan again writes in answer to my letter, "You ask me if I have lost all brotherly confidence in you, that I did not even hint the matter (his temporary withdrawal from the church) to you. I answer, no, my brother, my confidence in you remains the same. . . . . I do not feel that I have deserted you; I am, as ever, your brother, nay, you are to me more than a brother

I have a right to call you father, for I was begotten by you through the gospel; I shall never desert you till you desert my Lord." This is not a tithe of the evidence I have that the Trustees and congregation had every confidence in me years after I left Dundee.

NOTE B., page 232.

CLERICAL HAUGHTINESS.—The nature of my letter to Mr. Ould may be judged by his reply, and my letter to Mr. Dumbville. This correspondence proves the haughtiness of the clergy. Mr. Ould was considered evangelical.

29 West Derby Street, July 6th, 1838.

SIR,—In reply to your note which has just reached me, I beg to say that the expressions to which you allude are substantially, though not verbally, correct.

Mrs. Stirrup's daughter has been for several weeks past under my care, and has been frequently visited by myself and my curate. I understood her to say that she did not wish for your visits, from which she alleged she had received *more harm than good*. It was on hearing this, that I intimated to Mrs. Stirrup the propriety of not allowing her daughter's mind to be disturbed by the visits of teachers for whom she had no desire, and that if she acted otherwise, I would feel it my duty to decline any further attendance. To this determination I intend to adhere.

I remain, Sir, your obedient servant,

To Mr. J. Bowes. F. OULD.

---

11 Vine Street, July 6th, 1838.

MY DEAR BRO.,—I send you the two enclosed letters, that you may ascertain from Mr. and Mrs. Stirrup, members of your class, whether their afflicted daughter said, before the Rev. F. Ould expressed his determination as mentioned in my letter, that "she did not wish for my visits," and that she "had received more harm than good." Perhaps, my dear brother, you can ascertain this from the parents, without troubling the young woman about the matter. I deeply feel for her, and the more so, as the first time that I went to pray with her, I was informed that her husband, a Roman Catholic, had requested a priest to visit her, who had greatly agitated her by one or two interviews, in consequence of which he was prevented from seeing her any more. Now what will her Roman Catholic husband think of Protestantism, when he sees that our religion leads us, not only to decline the services of his priest, but also leads an Established minister to say, "I will not follow any Dissenting minister?"

When I first saw this interesting young woman, she did not profess to enjoy that "precious faith" which brings pardon, peace, and love to God and love to man—disarms death of its alarming sting, and eternity of its confounding horrors. But on my last interview with her, I learned, with gratitude to God, from her own lips, that through you and other members attending her, she had been led to seek and find the pearl of great price. You will see that Mr. Ould allows that Mrs. Stirrup's statement is "substantially correct." In that statement he is represented as saying, that "If I attended her he would not, for he would not follow any Dissenting minister." Now, if she had first expressed a wish not to see me, he did not require to say that "if I attended her he would not;" for that implies a threat to induce her to dispense with my attendance, and no wonder, when it is Mr. Ould's avowed principle "not to follow any Dissenting minister!" How lamentable is the bigotry, undisguised, comprehended in this sentiment! Here is a minister of Christ, who professes to devote his life to the great work of "winning souls," who will sooner allow the dying to leave the world in ignorance and sin, and consequently to perish for ever, than afford saving instruction by following a "Dissenting minister." If a Dissenting minister teach the Gospel, and be a man of God, why will not Mr. Ould not follow him as cheerfully as a minister of the Established Church? And if an ungodly Dissenting minister attend a dying man and teach error, there is the greater necessity that Mr. Ould should not abandon him to everlasting ruin.

When Mrs. S. informed me of Mr. Ould's decision, I said, "So far as I am concerned, I am ready to visit any one that wishes my aid, no matter whether a Catholic Priest, an Established clergyman, or a Dissenting minister has preceded me, and if I am informed that my services are no longer needed, I cheerfully withdraw." Mrs. S. wept, and hoped that I would not think any worse of her and her husband through what had happened. I assured her I would not.

I am, my dear Sir, yours very affectionately,

To Mr. J. Dumbville, Liverpool. JOHN BOWES.

Note C. Page 414.

This I have used in a discourse:—A young woman had been educated in her father's family, where her mother's will was law. She commanded, the husband and father submitted. Her daughter became acquainted with a young man, whom she ultimately married, who had been educated very differently. His father was the head of the house, and he kept his place, while his mother as cheerfully yielded submission. The two young people had not been long married before the wife attempted to assume the reins of government, as she had been educated at home ; the husband not only refused, but mildly and kindly claimed to rule in his own house, as his own right, after the example of his worthy father. The wife was unhappy and often in tears ; she complained she was like no other wife, and could not have her own way in any thing. Her husband kindly asked, " Do I not provide for you all that you require? do you lack either food or clothing or indeed any comfort?" " No, you are a good husband in all but government, and I never saw such conduct as yours at home." Time wore on, two children were born, and her discontent reached its climax. If she could not have more of her own way she threatened that she would return home. At last she did, many miles to her father's house. Her brothers and sisters and parents were kind, but she was unhappy, for she was obliged to give her husband a first-rate character, with the exception of his government, which some thought excellent. Months elapsed, she heard nothing of her husband, beyond kind messages at intervals to return, but months had now elapsed without any intelligence. She could bear this silence no longer, but returned to the old farm house to find it closed, the window shutters closed, and green grass covering the walk before the door. "Was he dead?—that could not be." She sought information; from his friend, a neighboring shopkeeper, she ascertained that he had sailed, some months before, for America. She was overwhelmed with grief; she had lost a good husband by her self-will. "If," she said to his friend, "I had only his address, and the means of going, I would yet go after him for he was an excellent husband." Her friend replied, "I have money left with me and his address ; I was to give you both should you ever be willing to return." She hastened her departure. When they met she took all the blame to herself, and exonerated her husband He as speedily forgave all, and she became a contented and happy wife. Thus it is that self-will and a bad education often spoil domestic bliss. Had she been differently educated she would have made a happy home at first, as it became at last.

The same cause hinders self-willed man from bowing to Christ, the head of the Church. Yet nothing but misery can be expected in such a contest, and nothing but happiness in submission to the claims of the divine head. Self-will and selfishness are sin and misery. The most obedient and benevolent are the most happy. Look at the peevish, ill-natured lady, who has no work ; her very countenance looks discontentment, and is a faithful index to her heart. Her servant has a miserable life, and she is blamed for almost every thing,—the fire is too large or too small. Her friends, also, distress her by too many calls, or neglect her by too few. Now, the secret of all this misery is self-will and selfishness ; she lives only to herself. But let her know the gospel; let its benevolent truths be diffused through her heart, expelling self-will and selfishness, and she will be unspeakably happy ; they teach her to be holy, and active in instructing the ignorant ; yielding to their influence, she now makes garments for the poor like Dorcas. What pleasure in buying the material, in making it up, in presenting the finished dresses, in seeing them worn, in receiving the grateful acknowledgments of those blessed by her labors, and, above all, in the blessed change which grace has effected in her own mind. Such are the blessed effects of giving up self-will to God's will, and selfishness for the happy toils of benevolence.

WORKS BY JOHN BOWES.

1.—The NEW TESTAMENT, translated from the PUREST GREEK, Price 3/6. to subscribers, 2/6.

2.—CHRISTIAN UNION, 310 pages, Price 5/

3.—Published Monthly, or oftener, since 1842, THE CHRISTIAN MAGAZINE, in 4 vols. about 300 pages each, Price 2/6, or all. 7/6.

4.—Also 10 vols. of THE TRUTH PROMOTER up to 1870, about 300 pages each, *now* issued monthly, Price 3/6 each, or all, £1 10/.

5.—Six Lectures on THE ERRORS OF THE CHURCH OF ROME, 72 pages, Price 6d.

6.—MORMONISM EXPOSED, (Second Edition) 84 pages, Price 6d.

7—Eight Lectures on THE SECOND COMING OF CHRIST, 140 pages Price 1/, by post 1/1.

8.—PUBLISHED DISCUSSIONS yet in Print, with L. JONES, on SOCIALISM, Liverpool 1840, 108 pages, Price 1/.

9—With G. J. HOLYOAKE, "On the Truth of Christianity and the Folly of Infidelity," Bradford 1850, four nights, 157 pages, Price 1/6

10.—With JOSEPH BARKER, on "Are the Scriptures of Divine Authority and Conducive to Morality, &c;" three nights, Stockport 1855, 106 pages, Price 1/.

11.—With WOODVILLE WOODMAN, Minister of the New Jerusalem Church, on "Swedenborg's Views," four nights, Bolton-le-moors, 1858, 176 pages, Price 1/.

12—With the late T. H. MILNER, on "Baptism for Remission of Sins—Justification—and the Lord's Coming," Dundee and Edinburgh, three nights, 1859, 115 pages, 1/

The Discussions were generally taken down by competent Reporters, and revised by each speaker. The Newcastle-on-Tyne Discussion with the late C. SOUTHWELL, on "Atheism and Christianity," is out of print. Some account of other discussions with Unbelievers, Universalists, Unitarians, &c., may be found in the monthly volumes.

13.—A CHRISTIAN HYMN BOOK, 564 Hymns. Price 1/, calf 1/6

14.—MEMOIR OF MRS. JESSIE DICKIE, 70 pages, Price 6d.

15.—Republished, SWEDENBORGIANISM depicted in its true colors, by the late J. G. Pike, of Derby, 66 pages, Price 6d.

16.—WORKS ON MINISTRY,—BAPTISM, 24 pages each, Price 1½d & 1d.

17.—220 Gospel and other Tracts to instruct Christians, 4, 8, and 12 pages—1/4 and 1/2 per 100. The whole works, £4; direct from the office, £3.

All to be had from the Publisher, J. BOWES, Westfield House, Dundee.

www.ingramcontent.com/pod-product-compliance
Lightning Source LLC
Chambersburg PA
CBHW080417230426
43662CB00015B/2130